SOVIET PARTISANS IN WORLD WAR II

SOVIET PARTISANS I

MADISON 1

WORLD WAR II

EDITED BY JOHN A. ARMSTRONG

WITH A FOREWORD

BY PHILIP E. MOSELY

IE UNIVERSITY OF WISCONSIN PRESS

Published by
The University of Wisconsin Press
430 Sterling Court
Madison 6, Wisconsin

Printed in the United States of America
by the George Banta Company, Inc.
Menasha, Wisconsin

Library of Congress
Catalog Card Number 64-12729

Foreword

Soviet Partisans in World War II is a summation and an extension—both carried out with great talent by Professor John A. Armstrong of the University of Wisconsin—of a postwar program of research into the origins, doctrine, operations, and effectiveness of Soviet irregular warfare. The volume can be read as an original and important contribution to the history of World War II and to the study of the Soviet political system operating under extreme stress. Today, when Soviet policy lays strong emphasis on "wars of national (or people's) liberation" and on Soviet backing for them, these studies likewise provide a fresh examination of the most recent and intensive Soviet experience in the waging of unconventional warfare.

Extreme claims have been made, as Professor Armstrong points out in his Introduction, about the character and military value of the partisan movement in World War II, and official Soviet appraisals have varied widely in the relative importance they ascribe to "spontaneous" and patriotic reactions of the population, to the courage and organizing skill of local Communist Party officials, and to the control and direction exercised from above by the central Party and military authorities. This volume represents the first attempt to clarify these questions through a systematic investigation of a vast amount of first-hand documentation, partly Soviet, mainly German, which was captured at the close of World War II.

After the German invasion of June 1941, which brought a large part of the Soviet population under Hitler's control, had been halted in the heroic defense of Moscow, Leningrad, and Stalingrad (now Volgograd), a long road of suffering and sacrifice stretched out before the invaders could be expelled from Soviet territory. How far did the partisan forces, operating in the rear of Hitler's armies, weaken the German military effort and thus lighten the burden of the Red Army? These studies suggest new and significant answers to this question and also to the question of how the people in occupied areas reacted to the German presence and to the prospective restoration of Soviet rule. It thus presents, as Professor Armstrong points out, a study of "shadow" rule at a distance, in which the partisans served as a reminder of the impending or eventual return of the Soviet system.

Finally, the partisan experience in World War II constitutes the largest single body of Soviet experience in irregular warfare. That experience is embedded in the minds of many Soviet leaders, of high rank and low; many of them, now active in Soviet policy or administration, were closely concerned with the organization and direction of that arm of military and political action. Soviet policy is actively concerned today with the prospect of new wars of "national liberation" which, the leadership asserts, can bring important accretions of strength to the Communist bloc while still holding the risks of general or nuclear war to an acceptable level. The expectations of Soviet policy-makers about actual or prospective partisan wars, as one possible stage in any struggle for "national liberation," are doubtless influenced by past Soviet experiences as well as by current analyses of local factors that may favor or inhibit new revolutionary initiatives in various continents. The factor of doctrinal and psychological continuity therefore makes it useful for students of present-day Soviet policy to examine the experience of the Soviet partisan movement in World War II, even though no firm conclusions can be drawn from it with respect to future Soviet actions.

The studies that form the major part of *Soviet Partisans in World War II* were originally prepared as part of Project Alexander, a research task which was undertaken by the War Documentation Project (A.F. Contract 18[600]-1), under contract with the United States Air Force. The research program was monitored by the Human Resources Research Institute of the Psychological Warfare Division, particularly by Dr. Raymond V. Bowers, Dr. F. W. Williams, and Dr. Charles E. Hutchinson. Special thanks go to these officials and likewise to Major General James McCormack, Jr., USAF (ret), who was then Director of Research and Development in the Office of the Deputy Chief of Staff, Development.

Without the farsighted decision of officers and advisers of the United States Air Force to devote a small fraction of its defense research funds to a systematic investigation of this problem, and to open up the vast body of captured documents for investigation, the study could never have been started, much less brought to successful completion. Great credit is also due to the Chief and staff of the Departmental Records Branch, Advocate General's Office, Department of the Army, who generously provided full cooperation and many facilities indispensable to the work of the project. The work of the project benefited greatly from the advice and support of the

Human Resources Research Institute and from the suggestions of an inter-departmental committee consisting of representatives of interested government agencies.

Project Alexander proceeded through several distinct research phases. In a first period of planning and survey, the major research purposes were defined and a voluminous mass of source materials was screened and sifted; a large part of the relevant materials was catalogued in an extensive punch-card filing system. As the investigation proceeded, it drew more and more on the records of corps, divisions, and even regiments, and therefore the process of identifying the contents and research significance of additional bodies of records was continued on a reduced scale throughout the remainder of the three and one-half years of the project.

In the first research phase the documentary raw material was tested by carrying out studies of several major topics within defined chronological and geographical limits. In the second research phase the inquiry widened its focus to embrace a full range of functional subjects, but was held to manageable proportions by limiting the studies to selected geographic areas or individual partisan organizations. Special attention was given to the "classic" partisan areas in western Russia, Belorussia, and northern Ukraine. In the selection of regions for study, the main purpose was to make sure that the case studies would represent a wide diversity of geographic and natural conditions, ethnic composition, social and economic situations, and methods of partisan operations. As a safeguard against excessive concentration on the "classic" areas, two additional studies were made of partisan movements in the central Ukraine and the north Caucasus. In a third research phase the findings of geographical studies were collated and compared to produce a series of functional studies; among them were the role of airpower in partisan warfare, organization and control of the partisan movement, composition and morale of the movement, and partisan psychological warfare among the German-occupied population.

Credit for this difficult and comprehensive research effort belongs first of all to the talented and devoted scholars who constituted the staff of Project Alexander: John A. Armstrong, Alexander Dallin, Kurt DeWitt, Ralph Mavrogordato, Wilhelm Moll, Eric Waldman, Gerhard L. Weinberg, Earl Ziemke. Each of them brought long experience, fresh insights, and great devotion to this task, and it was these qualities that made the effort possible and fruitful.

Fritz T. Epstein served in the first stage as Director of Research; after he was called to other duties, Hans J. Epstein became Director of the Project, and Alexander Dallin served with great talent as Director of Research. Philip E. Mosely, then Director of the Russian Institute, Columbia University, served part-time as senior consultant on research and Chairman of the Standing Committee of the War Documentation Project. The contract was administered through the Bureau of Applied Social Research, Columbia University, and Dr. Charles Y. Glock, then Director of the Bureau, and his staff did a great deal to facilitate the smooth operation of the project.

From the beginning the scholars engaged in the project and the officers and officials who sought and found modest support for it believed that its findings should eventually be made available to the public, and I take pleasure in expressing, on their behalf, our deep appreciation to the Department of Defense for making this possible. Professor John A. Armstrong, who had been author or co-author of several of the most important studies, then undertook, at a considerable sacrifice to his other research interests, to prepare this volume for publication. Because of the overlapping of the successive research stages, as outlined above, it was necessary to combine and condense the individual studies, in order to eliminate repetition and bring out those findings that are of central significance. Since a good deal of new Soviet information has become available in recent years, it would have been desirable, ideally, to rework all the studies. However, a sampling of the new materials, derived from Soviet official histories and memoirs, made it clear that the new data, in turn, would have to be checked against the original records, at great cost in time and with only slight scholarly gain for the final product. Only minor corrections, apart from condensation, have therefore been made in the studies as completed in 1953 and 1954.

Instead, Professor Armstrong has prepared, in his Introduction, a comprehensive review of the partisan movement, based on a wide range of new Soviet materials, on the Alexander studies, and on his own continuing researches into these problems, parts of which have been published in his *Ukrainian Nationalism* (second edition, 1963), *The Soviet Bureaucratic Elite* (1959), and *The Politics of Totalitarianism* (1961). The Introduction serves a dual function: it sums up with masterly sweep and clarity Professor Armstrong's many years of research into the partisan movement and its role in Soviet political strategy; it also sets the background for the more specific studies of the experience and significance of the Soviet partisan movement in World War II and for the selection of original documents in translation. Through his double contribution, as author and editor, to making possible the publication of these studies, John Armstrong has again placed the scholarly community under great debt.

PHILIP E. MOSELY

Editorial Preface

This book is based primarily on a group of studies prepared by the War Documentation Project for the United States Air Force. Since the total length of the studies was far too great for a single printed volume, it was necessary to leave out much of the original material. Three analytic studies of social and political aspects of the Soviet partisan movement in World War II were retained substantially intact as Chapters II, III, and IV. Two analytic studies which dealt with intelligence and air power aspects of partisan warfare now constitute Chapters V and VI. These studies were somewhat condensed to eliminate material of a technical nature which now has only historical interest. Five case studies of special geographical areas of partisan activity are now Chapters VII through XI. All of these studies were considerably shortened to eliminate material which has been summarized in substance in the analytic chapters. In the Appendix of Selected Soviet Sources, 69 of the 125 documents originally translated have been retained; five additional documents formerly appended to individual studies have been added. The documents which were omitted for the most part contain material of a technical nature or material which is essentially similar to that in documents which have been retained. Two special War Documentation Project studies on the partisans have been omitted altogether. The "History of the First Belorussian Partisan Brigade" appeared to have rather limited interest. "The Soviet Partisan Movement in World War II: Summary and Conclusions" has been omitted also, but much of the data presented in this study has been incorporated in Chapter I. Wherever feasible the original source references for specific data of major importance derived from the "Summary and Conclusions" have been indicated in Chapter I. The Selected Bibliography contains a considerable amount of material appearing in the original, but has been thoroughly revised to eliminate several relatively insignificant items and to incorporate many new items. The Glossary is substantially the same as the original.

In the ten years that have elapsed since the War Documentation Project studies were prepared, many important publications on the partisans have appeared in the Soviet Union. Ideally, one might have preferred to incorporate information from these works in each of the relevant chapters of this book. However, many of the Soviet works—especially those relating to particular geographical areas of partisan activity—are not available outside the USSR. Furthermore, complete revision of the studies included in this book would have been wholly unsatisfactory unless one could have compared the new material to the original German documentary sources; but the great bulk of these are still under security classification. Consequently, a page-by-page revision of the original studies did not appear to be feasible. Instead, the studies (apart from the deletions described above) have been presented very nearly as they were written. The only substantial changes are in such items as personal names, population data, and specific organizational features which have proved to be inaccurate. On the other hand, a great deal of new information from Soviet sources has been incorporated in Chapter I, which was written specifically for the present book. The Soviet material is interesting not only because of the new light it throws on the partisan movement, but because it indicates how a careful reading of published Soviet descriptions tends to corroborate most of the findings derived from the wartime German and Soviet documents.

The arrangement of the materials in this book is designed to facilitate an analytical understanding of the partisan movement rather than to present a chronological history. Consequently, Chapter I presents an interpretation and a summary which, it is hoped, will provide the reader with a general understanding of the subject. Chapters II–VI contain more detailed analyses of specific aspects of the partisan movement, while the case studies in Chapters VII-XI (which constituted the basis for many of the generalizations presented in the earlier chapters) are intensive examinations of all aspects of specific groups of partisans. The Appendix of documents enables the reader to catch at first hand some of the flavor of the partisan movement and, to some extent, to make his own evaluations.

The principal credit for this work, as Philip E. Mosely points out in his Foreword, should go to the devoted research team of the War Documentation Project, and to the many persons in Government agencies and elsewhere who assisted it. I want to add that Dr. Mosely himself played an indispensable part in initiating the Project, supervising its research, and, more recently, in making this book possible. I am especially grateful to him, to Alexander Dallin, and to Gerhard L. Weinberg, for advice on aspects of

the editing. At the same time, I want to make clear that 1 am wholly responsible for the entire contents of Chapter I, and for the deletions and
minor substantive revisions in the rest of the volume. I only hope that my
changes and additions have not seriously distorted the work of the original
authors. Finally, I wish to express my thanks to the National Security
Studies Group of the University of Wisconsin, and its director, Bernard C.
Cohen, for financial support for the expensive process of revision.

J.A.A.

August, 1963

Contents

List of Figures

SOVIET PARTISANS IN WORLD WAR II

CHAPTER I

Introduction

John A. Armstrong

---

§I. The Significance of the Soviet Partisan Experience

Viewed from the perspective of the 1960's, partisan activities in the USSR during World War II appear as part of a series of guerrilla movements which have constituted a most significant aspect of twentieth-century warfare. There are indeed important resemblances between Soviet partisan activity and other contemporary guerrilla operations. In several respects, however, the Soviet experience is highly unusual, though not entirely unique. One way to approach an understanding of this experience is to analyze the peculiar objectives of the antagonists which shaped the conflict in the German-occupied territory of the Soviet Union.

A. THE OBJECTIVES OF THE ANTAGONISTS

1. The Soviet Objective

Historically, guerrilla forces have been the weapon of the side which is militarily weaker. When they first arise, guerrillas are a substitute for an adequate conventional force, though they may become the auxiliaries of an offensive army if the military balance shifts in the course of the war. From a strategical standpoint, the Soviet partisans clearly played these traditional roles. When the Soviet regime began developing partisan forces, its conventional armed forces were apparently greatly inferior in strength, though not in over-all size, to those which Nazi Germany could employ on the eastern front. At least until December 1941 the very existence of the Soviet system was in doubt; the margin by which the Red Army succeeded in stopping the German advance was an extremely narrow one. Under these circumstances, even a very small increment of help from irregular forces could have been decisive; consequently, it seems clear the prime immediate objective in developing the partisan forces was military. No human costs, in individual or social terms, were regarded as too high, so long as the partisan activity contributed to the overriding goal of preserving the Soviet system.

In this respect, there was little distinction between the sacrifices exacted from Soviet citizens affected by partisan activity and the sacrifices exacted from those involved in other aspects of the war effort, as exemplified by the starving population of besieged Leningrad, the millions dispatched to industrial relocation sites with wholly inadequate living conditions, or the Red Army soldiers. The principle that no opportunity to impede the enemy should be renounced because of "humanitarian" considerations was emphatically stated by the Soviet regime from the moment it became involved in the war and has been reiterated consistently since then. Even major allies such as the United States were criticized for weakness in surrendering positions to avoid loss of life. This accusation of pusillanimity has been a constant theme in Soviet attacks on the non-Communist European resistance movements which sought to preserve their forces by avoiding action until the general military balance became more favorable.[1]

As the threat to the existence of the Soviet system gradually diminished, political objectives for the partisan forces became more significant; indeed (as will be discussed in Sect. III below) one may infer that they became dominant. But the position of the Soviet regime in this regard was peculiar. Ordinarily, a government which employs guerrilla forces to help it *regain* its territory is interested in maintaining the social system of the country *and* restoring the authority of the government. Certainly the Soviet regime was interested in restoring Soviet government in the occupied territories. Moreover, the objective was clearly the restoration of the embracing Communist totalitarian system, of which the government was only a subsystem. But, before 1941, Communist totalitarianism was a goal rather than the status quo even within the USSR. The Communist prescription calls not only for the imposition of a new set of institutions upon a pre-existing society, but for a complete reshaping of society and even of individual psychology.

It is true that in those parts of the USSR which had been under Soviet control since the end of the Civil War the process of reshaping society had by 1941 made considerable headway. Especially after the agricultural collectivization and forced industrialization of the 1930's, much of the old social fabric had been disrupted. From the formal standpoint Soviet society had been reconstituted on a new basis. However, one-fourth of the population in the territory occupied by the Germans had lived under Soviet rule for such a short time (since 1939 or 1940) that the process of reconstructing society had hardly begun. In those areas, therefore, the existing social structure was fundamentally objectionable to the regime. Even in the "old" Soviet areas many traits of the pre-Soviet society survived. The bulk of the population (particularly, as will appear later, in areas where partisan activity was feasible) consisted of peasants. Although formally grouped in collective

---

[1] John A. Armstrong, *The Politics of Totalitarianism: The Communist Party of the Soviet Union from 1934 to the Present* (New York: Random House, 1961), p. 166.

farms (which were officially regarded as only a step in the direction of "socialization"), the peasants retained many of their traditional communal and familial ties. Under normal circumstances the regime hesitated to disrupt these ties violently. The political and economic costs to the peacetime Soviet system of the resistance which such disruption might provoke would be high. Moreover, the traditional ties served certain short-run purposes of the regime, such as maintenance of a high rural birth rate and suppression of juvenile delinquency. These considerations, however, ceased to have much if any force once the population passed under enemy control. On the other hand, if the objectionable social features dissolved in general chaos, the ultimate construction of Communist society in the postwar era might even be facilitated.

There is no direct evidence that the Soviet leaders pursued the calculation presented above, nor is it likely that any will be forthcoming. It is quite possible, indeed, that no one in authority ever consciously reasoned along these lines. However, it is evident, at least, that the Soviet leaders had far less reason to be concerned with preserving the traditional substructure of society than would normally be the case with a regime seeking to restore its authority. The Soviet regime's position in this respect was, of course, entirely consistent with its insistence on all-out attack against the enemy, regardless of human cost:

I knew, of course, that the Hitlerites might send a punitive expedition to the village, accuse its citizens of contacts with the partisans and cruelly avenge themselves on the peaceful population. But I also knew that the population, which was driven to repair the enemy's roads, whether voluntarily or involuntarily, delayed the hour of victory by some time. But who can determine what a minute of military activity costs?[2]

One is forced to conclude, therefore, that, while on the surface the Soviet partisan movement appears to resemble that of a guerrilla force seeking to restore the authority of an invaded state, in many respects it was really closer to the guerrilla movements in countries where Communists are trying to build a new system on the wreckage of the traditional administrative and social structure. As Franz Borkenau has pointed out,[3] Communist partisans in Europe during World War II had an incalculable advantage over the non-Communist resistance movements, for the former, having a vested interest in social disruption, were prepared to face drastic reprisals, while the latter were constantly restrained in their tactics both by moral considerations and by the desire to avoid extreme civilian losses. The paradox of the Soviet situation lies in the fact that a guerrilla movement enjoying the support of the established government of the country could be used for ruthless, unlimited action.

[2] G. M. Linkov, *Voina v tylu vraga* (Moscow: Gosudarstvennoye Izdatelstvo Khoduzhestvennoye Literatury, 1959), pp. 93–94.

[3] Franz Borkenau, *European Communism* (New York: Harper Brothers, 1953), pp. 319, 358.

2. The German Objective

In its way, the German position in regard to the partisans was just as unusual as the Soviet. Most contemporary antiguerrilla forces have been seeking to re-establish legitimate authority. Their task is usually enormously more difficult than the guerrillas' because the latter have only to smash an intricate and delicate web of economic installations and social relations while the defenders must not only defeat the guerrillas but do so in such a way as to preserve the system which is under attack. Failure to realize this basic difference between objectives, or lack of the patience and resources required to complete the more difficult defensive task, have been major causes for failure in antiguerrilla operations. Occasionally commentators on the Germans' antipartisan activities attribute the same shortcomings to them. In fact, however, the German objectives were so basically different from those of "defensive" antiguerrillas that the comparison has little meaning.

The overriding German objective at all times was to knock the Soviet Union out of the war. This objective was, of course, essentially Adolf Hitler's personal goal, for he realized that only complete victory would preserve his own position. Once Hitler had taken the foolhardy step of attacking the USSR, his only real prospect of eventual victory over the "Grand Coalition" of his enemies lay in eliminating Soviet military strength before Great Britain and the United States could bring the full weight of their resources to bear on Germany. At most, Hitler had only one or two years in which to achieve this goal. All longer-range considerations in Eastern Europe were subordinated to the military defeat of the Soviet Union. Though his premises are abhorrent, and his specific measures were often absurd by any standard, there was logic in the way in which Hitler tenaciously pursued this objective.[4]

Hitler's overriding objective of destroying Soviet military power within a very short time meant that the German command regarded the partisans as crucially important only insofar as they impeded the German war effort. Whatever success the partisans might achieve in controlling territory or influencing the population was insignificant, as long as it did not reduce German capacity to strike at the basic Soviet military position. The vast stretches of occupied Europe between Germany itself and the German armies at the front were important only as a necessary avenue of communication and a source of materials (including slave labor) for pursuing the war. As a result, the German authorities did not feel that they were faced with many of the problems which usually confront an antiguerrilla force. Secure control of territory, allegiance of the population, maintenance of institutional patterns or the traditional social system did not per se interest

---

[4] Hitler's intervention in the strategic conduct of the war on the eastern front was notorious for its blunders; in addition, Hitler's racial prejudices led him to divert important resources from the war effort, as in his ruthless extermination of the Jews.

the German authorities. Of course, the Nazi regime intended to dominate and exploit the occupied areas of Eastern Europe for centuries. Nazi ideology, however, regarded the inhabitants of the area (or at least the Slavic majority) as inferiors who were to be exploited ruthlessly and slowly reduced in numbers if not exterminated. If the course of military operations produced chaos which reduced the numbers and social viability of the Slavs, so much the better.

Consequently, no considerations of the welfare of the people in the area of partisan activity were in principle to act as impediments to ruthless conduct of antiguerrilla warfare. The Nazi leadership itself sometimes recognized the desirability of securing the cooperation of the local population for the sake of the war effort. The limits which Hitler placed on this cooperation, however, suggest the limits to the "rationality" of Hitler's conduct of the war. Until the war was almost certainly lost, he refused to allow former Soviet citizens (with minor exceptions) to bear arms even to fight the Soviet regime. To be sure, it seems very likely that even an early and massive attempt to enlist military manpower in the occupied territories would not have been decisive, for the crucial battles were lost by the Germans long before (given shortages of matériel and other factors) the Slavic anti-Communist armies could have become really effective forces.

3. The Resultant of the German and Soviet Objectives

The combination of Soviet and German objectives produced a situation in which measures of almost unparalleled ruthlessness became the norm of guerrilla and antiguerrilla warfare alike. Nazi doctrine glorified the use of violence and looked with distrust upon anyone who exhibited inclinations toward showing mercy. For the German antiguerrillas, ruthlessness became not only a practical norm, but a rule. While some antiguerrilla leaders, particularly among the middle and lower army officer corps, did try to exercise moderation, for reasons both of expediency and of humanity, among others sadistic tendencies toward wanton brutality and destructiveness led to excesses even beyond those encouraged by the official policy.[5] Apart from individual instances of sadism, Soviet partisan activity was guided not by *desire* to inflict suffering, but by *disregard* of suffering, which was viewed as "necessary" for war purposes. Frequently the practical distinction between the two types of motivations was not very evident, however.

B. THE RELEVANCE OF THE SOVIET PARTISAN EXPERIENCE

The peculiar objectives of the antagonists constitute a major reason for the special nature of partisan warfare in the occupied USSR. In addition—

[5] On German policy, see especially the comprehensive discussion by Alexander Dallin in *German Rule in Russia, 1941–1945* (London: Macmillan, 1957, New York: St. Martin's, 1957).

as will appear in the following sections of this chapter—many other special factors, such as the nature of the terrain, the role of economic activities, and the availability of military forces, contributed to make the Soviet partisan experience unique. It is understandable, therefore, that some writers have tended to depreciate the importance of the Soviet experience for understanding more recent guerrilla operations.[6] One is certainly inclined to agree that the differences between the Soviet partisans and nationalist or even Communist guerrillas in tropical underdeveloped areas is so great as to render it impossible to make many generalizations applying to both. In many instances, however, the sheer extent of contrasts may make a comparison useful. Moreover, it is by no means certain that future guerrilla movements will operate in the conditions which have characterized the "national liberation" guerrillas of the 1950's. The latter have been, at the outset at least, far less well provided with modern instruments of war than the counterguerrillas. As will be shown, however, Soviet partisans were often better equipped in light weapons than their adversaries, and had a considerable measure of air support. There are several contingencies in which such "technical parity" between guerrilla and counterguerrilla forces might arise in the future.

One contingency—probably remote—is "broken-back" warfare following major nuclear strikes. If such warfare can be envisaged at all, it might include relatively well-equipped guerrillas battling an "occupying" force which had scarcely better weapons. A considerably more likely situation would be an artificially limited war. One can certainly conceive of circumstances in which the opponents would agree tacitly to restrict air operations to a limited area, for such, in effect, was the nature of the Korean conflict of 1950–53. If the side supporting the guerrillas were able to obtain air parity or superiority in the limited area, the equipment and techniques of the guerrillas might resemble the Soviet situation in many important respects. In situations such as the Greek Communist revolt of 1946–49 and the Vietminh advance in 1954, Communist extension of air support to the guerrillas was no doubt inhibited by Western technical superiority in the air and by the possibility of nuclear retaliation. These factors certainly cannot be assumed for all future situations.

However useful an examination of the Soviet partisan experience may be for understanding unconventional warfare, it is, in this writer's opinion, far more useful for the insights it provides into the nature of the Soviet system. Since the nature of these insights will be presented at some length in Section III of this chapter, here one need only stress their importance. Between 1918 and the early 1930's, the Soviet system was relatively open to outside observation. Western visitors could travel about the country with

[6] E.g., Raymond L. Garthoff, "Unconventional Warfare in Communist Strategy," *Foreign Affairs,* XL (1962), 570.

considerable freedom. Restrictions upon contacts between individual Soviet citizens and foreigners were limited. The regime published a great deal of information (for example, the voluminous 1926 census data). Evidence of controversy within official circles was abundant, sometimes even taking the form of published debates in Communist Party meetings. Major dissident leaders like Leon Trotsky revealed much of the real nature of Soviet politics. Taken together, these sources of information provided a basis, though by no means a wholly satisfactory one, for the objective analysis of the Soviet system. Since Stalin's death in 1953 there has been a tendency for similar sources of information to become available, although so far, at least, the sources are greatly inferior to those of the early decades.

It is the intervening twenty years which really constitute the "dark ages" of our knowledge of the Soviet system. Yet these were the years in which the system, still embryonic in the early thirties, became the mature Communist totalitarianism which we know today. Any evidence which relates to that period is, therefore, of enormous importance.

Recently two monumental scholarly studies based upon unique bodies of evidence relating to the period before Soviet entry into World War II have appeared. Merle Fainsod's *Smolensk Under Soviet Rule*[7] is a comprehensive analysis of the voluminous records of a single provincial Party organization. The work lays bare the dynamics of institutional interactions, and provides irrefutable documentation for a wide range of practices employed by the Soviet regime. *The Soviet Citizen* by Alex Inkeles and Raymond Bauer[8] is based upon interviews with over two thousand former Soviet citizens, the vast majority of whom left Soviet control in the early stages of World War II. While Fainsod's book views the Soviet system primarily from the "insider's" vantage point, Inkeles and Bauer look at it from below, as it affects the ordinary citizen. Together these works complement each other admirably to provide a kind of base line against which later developments in the Soviet system can be measured.

It is hoped that the present volume can make a contribution toward further definition of this base line. Our work lacks the quantity and variety of Soviet political documentation which characterizes Fainsod's work, and does not rest upon the wealth of sociological information which Inkeles and Bauer accumulated. The present study has, however, some special advantages. It deals with a crisis situation of extreme intensity. It is undoubtedly true that the Soviet system—at least until fairly recently—has been one of constant crisis. But the problems posed in the effort to assert Soviet authority in areas nominally controlled by the enemy implied a crisis of the system far exceeding any other it has faced. This crisis related predominantly to a rural environment, for which our other sources of informa-

[7] Cambridge, Mass.: Harvard University Press, 1958.
[8] Cambridge, Mass.: Harvard University Press, 1959.

tion are unusually meager. While our information on the partisan episode is partially based on contemporary Soviet documents, we have the advantage of being able to check the documents against two other kinds of information: subsequent Soviet accounts, which are unusually numerous and detailed; and the voluminous reports of the German occupation officials. While no one of these types of sources is satisfactory by itself, taken together they provide about as much information as the student of social and political processes can ordinarily expect to obtain.

In the following sections the two themes which have been outlined above —the partisan movement as irregular warfare and the relation of the partisans to the Soviet system—will be discussed in somewhat more detail. One should not gain the impression, however, that these two facets of the partisan experience are separable except for purposes of analysis. Even more important, one should not make the facile identification of the partisans' relation to irregular warfare with the "military aspect" of the subject, for irregular warfare is by its very nature political and social as well as military. The meaning of irregular warfare in the occupied USSR cannot be grasped without constant attention to the political circumstances in which it arose and the social and political conditions under which it developed.

§II. Soviet Partisan Operations as Unconventional Warfare

A. THE ORIGIN AND TASKS OF THE PARTISANS

1. Precedents

In the preceding section it was suggested that there is a kind of natural affinity between Communism and guerrilla warfare, for the special objectives of Communist movements enable them to employ guerrilla tactics with unusual effectiveness. It is scarcely surprising, therefore, that even prior to 1941 there was a long tradition of Communist guerrillas, or, as Soviet writers preferred to call them, partisans. In 1906, Lenin himself wrote on the subject, although his discussion of terrorist tactics which might be employed by the Bolsheviks against the Tsarist authorities has had little practical relevance to more recent partisan operations.[9] During the Russian Civil War of 1918–20 the Bolsheviks employed partisan units very extensively. The "regular" armies of the Reds and their various opponents

[9] Trans. in Franklin M. Osanka, ed., *Modern Guerrilla Warfare: Fighting Communist Guerrilla Movements, 1941–1961* (Glencoe, Ill.: The Free Press, 1962), pp. 65–79.

were in a state of reorganization; the armies' training was inadequate and their arms were far below the standard of Western European military forces of the period. In addition, the rapidly fluctuating fronts and the enormous extent of the theaters of military operations placed a premium on swift, stealthy maneuvers. Under these circumstances, irregular forces were very useful militarily. A considerable number of partisan commanders like Nikolai Shchors gained places (albeit minor ones) in the pantheon of heroes of the Revolution and Civil War. On the other hand, the Bolshevik drive for centralized control and iron discipline was opposed to the individualistic and anarchic tendencies of the irregulars. "Ataman" leaders like Nestor Makhno and G. Grigoryev, who had built up their own guerrilla followings before joining the Bolsheviks, fiercely resisted attempts to reduce all guerrilla leaders to complete subordination. Even loyal Communists who had been assigned to direct partisan activities sometimes developed tendencies toward independence. It is unfortunate that no detailed study has been made of the voluminous Soviet publications during the interwar period on the Civil War partisan experience, for such an examination might throw considerable light on the early evolution of the partisans in World War II. In the absence of such a study, all one can profitably say is that the regime learned the lesson that partisans were promising as an auxiliary weapon but apt to prove two-edged if not kept under strict control.

The evidence on Soviet evaluation of foreign Communist guerrilla activities is slighter but better known. At least as far as this writer has been able to discover, Soviet writers have never given any attention to such feats as Luis Prestes' march through the hinterlands of Brazil in 1924–27, although soon after this episode Prestes became a Communist. The Soviet Communists, on the other hand, were deeply involved in the use of guerrilla tactics during the Spanish Civil War. A high Soviet NKVD official, Eitingon, was in charge of organizing Republican guerrilla activities. Since during World War II Eitingon became second-in-command of the Fourth Administration of the NKVD, the division concerned with partisan activities, it is very probable that the Spanish experience was utilized.[10] Spanish refugees in the USSR were especially trained for technical assignments with the partisans such as demolition work.[11] The first commander of the partisan movement in the Crimea had been one of the small group of high-level Soviet military advisors in Spain.[12] On the other hand, Soviet writers who have discussed the Spanish Civil War have tended to depreciate the im-

---

[10] Armstrong, *The Politics of Totalitarianism,* p. 163.

[11] See Chap. II, Sect. III, E; and M. Makedonskii, *Plamya nad Krymon* (Simferopol: Krymizdat, 1960), p. 154.

[12] Cf. the accounts, virtually identical from the factual standpoint, in the reports of the German Eleventh Army (GMDS, AOK 11, 35774/16) and Yekaterina N. Shapko, *Partizanskoye Dvizheniye v Krymu v 1941–1944 gg.* (Simferopol: Krymizdat, 1959), pp. 155–56.

portance of guerrilla activities there. One writer of an unpublished dissertation denies that the Spanish Republican partisans were comparable to those in the USSR during World War II, because the former did not represent a "mass movement" holding a broad stretch of territory, but were basically "diversionist" groups sent into enemy territory for a limited time to perform specific tasks.[13] While the Soviet regime employed such "diversionist" units (analogous to the American Rangers) itself, it always considered them to be less significant than the partisans.

Whether or not the Soviet evaluation of the Spanish Republican partisans is wholly accurate, there is no doubt that the latter were far less important militarily and politically than the Communist guerrillas operating in China at the same time. Every serious student of Chinese Communist guerrilla warfare has concluded that Mao developed his partisan movement without much reliance upon Soviet models. In his "Problems in the Guerrilla War of Resistance against Japan" (1939), Mao refers respectfully to the Soviet Civil War experience, pointing out that it demonstrated that guerrillas were only secondary as compared to the regular forces.[14] But Mao devotes no more attention to Soviet precedents than to many non-Communist guerrilla episodes, and nowhere suggests that the Soviet experiences should form a detailed guide for the Chinese.

Indeed, there is considerably more reason to think that the Soviet concept of guerrilla warfare was influenced by the Chinese experience than the reverse, though here, again, lack of detailed investigations limits the degree to which one can generalize. As noted below, the early Soviet scheme for partisan warfare appeared to embody some of Mao's principles, applied, however, in a mechanical fashion. The most striking parallel was between the original Soviet scheme for a partisan company in each rayon and in Mao's prescription for a detachment of platoon or company strength in each small administrative unit (hsien, roughly equivalent to the Soviet rayon).[15] At least one Soviet commentator paid close attention to this scheme of organization, but appears to have underestimated the importance of the fact that this territorially based detachment was only the lower link of a chain which included progressively larger and more mobile units.[16] In general, Soviet observers seem to have misunderstood many aspects of the Chinese experience; there is, conversely, some evidence that the Chinese Com-

[13] Marklen T. Meshcheryakov, "Kommunisticheskaya Partiya Ispanii v borbe za demokraticheskiye svobody i natsionalnuyu nezavisimost Ispanii (1936–1939 gg.)," unpublished dissertation, Lenin Pedagogical Institute, Moscow, 1953, pp. 207–208.

[14] "Problems in the Guerrilla War of Resistance against Japan" (1939), trans. in Gene Z. Hanrahan, *Chinese Communist Guerilla Tactics: A Source Book* (n.p.: mimeographed, July 1952), p. 14.

[15] *Ibid.,* p. 22.

[16] A. Kolan, "Partizanskaya voina v okkupirovannykh rayonakh Kitaya," *Kommunisticheskii Internatsional,* No. 6, 1940, pp. 60–72.

munists regarded Soviet World War II efforts to develop a distinctive partisan doctrine with contempt.[17]

2. Planning

Even taken by itself, Soviet concern with earlier examples of partisan warfare would suggest that the regime devoted some attention to the possibility of employing guerrillas in the event of a future invasion of the USSR. Nevertheless, the evidence that a concrete contingency plan for using partisans had been developed before June 1941 is not wholly conclusive. Two reasons for this are fairly obvious. In the first place, no regime can afford to make the defeatist admission to the general population or even to large circles of its officials that it expects to lose much of its territory. If the Soviet authorities had widely disseminated instructions for partisan warfare it would have been an admission not only that Stalin's boasted policy of keeping the USSR out of the war through the Nazi-Soviet pact was a failure, but that the failure would entail tragic losses for the country. Secondly, the top officials of the regime almost surely did not expect that the enemy would occupy very large areas of the USSR, even if war did occur. In this connection it is interesting to note that Mao (writing before the Nazi-Soviet pact) predicted that even if an invader of the USSR were not repulsed for some time, the territory he occupied would not be extensive.[18]

In the circumstances just described, one may hypothesize that a contingency plan for partisan activity would be a carefully guarded secret confined to the inner circle of the regime and a few trusted specialists, preferably in the security-conscious police agencies. Because it would not be safe to consult lower officials familiar with local variations, the plan would tend to be highly schematic and rigid. Because there would be insufficient time to select and train personnel, the tendency would be to rely on especially committed members of the Party and state apparatus, especially the police. In fact, the initial scheme of partisan organization (see below, and Chap. II, Sect. II) very closely approximated the hypothetical model just sketched. This coincidence provides a certain measure of indirect evidence that prewar planning had taken place.

There is some direct evidence. The German counterguerrilla staffs concluded that plans were made before the war, though the credibility of the Germans' statements is diminished by the fact that they quite obviously grossly exaggerate the extent of preparation. If the Germans possessed in-

---

[17] Charles P. Fitzgerald, *Revolution in China* (New York: F. A. Praeger, 1952), p. 96, quotes a story, current after World War II in Peking, that one of Mao's generals said, on reading a book which Stalin had sent Mao on the Soviet partisan experience during the war, "If we had had this as our textbook we should have been annihilated ten years ago." Cf. Edward L. Katzenbach, Jr., and Gene Z. Hanrahan, "The Revolutionary Strategy of Mao Tse-Tung," *Political Science Quarterly*, LXX (1955), 321–340.

[18] Translated in Hanrahan, p. 22.

formation from secret Soviet documents or from interrogations of high-level Soviet officials, they do not cite it. In fact, one of the better-informed NKVD officials interrogated denied that the NKVD took any steps to prepare for partisan activity before June 25, 1941.[19] (See Chap. II, Sect. II, A.) But postwar Soviet publications are considerably more revealing. It is true that most of them do not provide any information on the very early stage of partisan planning. However, Aleksei Fyodorov, in one of the earliest and most important partisan memoirs, states that the Ukrainian Communist Party Central Committee "had already mapped out the entire organizational scheme of an underground movement" by July 4.[20] The first official directive (kept strictly secret when issued) which postwar Soviet sources quote, is a paragraph in a letter of June 29 from the Central Committee of the All-Union Communist Party.[21] A very recent Soviet memoir, however, indicates that Nikita Khrushchev (then head of the Ukrainian Communist Party) gave fairly detailed instructions on partisan organization to a provincial Party secretary as early as June 27—five days after the beginning of the war.[22] That same day, Moisei S. Spivak, Ukrainian secretary for cadres, began organizing partisans in Kamenets-Podolsk oblast (province).[23] It is, of course, possible that the Soviet sources wish to overemphasize the role of the regime, and especially of the current leadership, in initiating partisan activities. On the whole, however, the Soviet statements made in so many different forms over a period of fifteen years, seem plausible. If instructions could be issued within a week after war started, it is almost certain that some contingency planning had taken place before hostilities began.

3. Tasks

As indicated in Section I of this chapter, the initial, overriding objective of the Soviet regime in forming the partisan movement was to contribute to the military defense of the system against the invader. While political objectives were very probably considered from the beginning, they were distinctly secondary until a considerably later stage, and need not be considered here. Even the important military objective of intelligence-gathering was secondary in the initial scheme for partisan activity. Underground

[19] AOK 16, Ic, Interrogation of GPU Lieutenant Alexandr Zhigunov, 18 November 1941 (U.S. trans.), EAP-3a-11/2.

[20] Aleksei Fvodorov, *The Underground Committee Carries On* (Moscow: Foreign Languages Publishing House, 1952), p. 16. This version is translated from the 1947 Russian edition.

[21] Quoted in *Partizanskaya borba s nemetsko-fashistskimi okkupantami na territorii Smolenshchiny, 1941–1943 gg.: Dokumenty i materialy* (Smolensk: Smolenskoye Knizhskoye Izdatelstvo, 1962), p. 18.

[22] Vasilii Begma and Luka Kyzya, *Shlyakhy neskorenykh* (Kiev: Radyanskyi Pysmennyk, 1962), p. 26.

[23] *Sovetskiye partizany: Iz istorii partizanskogo dvizheniya v gody velikoi otechestvennoi voiny* (Moscow: Gospolitizdat, 1960), p. 441.

intelligence networks altogether apart from the partisan organization were set up; agents of these networks were ordered not to contact partisans. (See Chap. V, Sect. I.) The partisans' initial scheme of activity would in any case have left them poorly equipped for intelligence operations, for they were meagerly supplied with radio transmitters and air liaison. Instead, the principal activity of the partisans was to be direct, though small-scale, attack upon the German forces. Partisan tactics were to emphasize attacks on isolated or unguarded German installations and units, disruption of communications, and sabotage of military facilities. (See Appendix, Documents 1 and 2.) In other words, the partisans were to carry on a "little war" in the strictest sense of the term, by chipping away at the enemy military machine. Though their effect would necessarily be limited, it would be directed to the most crucial immediate objective, the avoidance of a complete Soviet military catastrophe.

B. THE ENVIRONMENT OF PARTISAN OPERATIONS

This, as nearly as one can infer, was the original Soviet concept of partisan activity in 1941. In practice, as will be shown below, the partisan movement developed along quite different lines. This development was very largely shaped by the peculiar environment in which the partisans operated.

1. The Natural Environment

One occasionally encounters the view that the worse the terrain is for ordinary economic and military purposes, the better it is for guerrilla operations. This is rather less than a half-truth. If partisans are to be effective militarily, they must be within easy striking range of military objectives; if they are to operate politically, they must be in contact with a significant population. For partisans to withdraw into impenetrable terrain means that they voluntarily end their effectiveness as instruments of irregular warfare. Since such terrain nearly always cannot provide enough food to support a significant number of partisans, they often end their lives as well. The partisans can operate effectively only in areas which are relatively impenetrable to regular military forces equipped with heavy weapons, yet which can be fairly easily traversed by lightly armed guerrillas moving on foot or horseback. These areas must be fairly close to important settled districts and channels of communications; very commonly the most suitable areas are in zones of transition between easy terrain and unproductive wastes.

Mountainous areas so frequently provide the appropriate environment for guerrillas that one can almost consider the typical guerrilla as a "mountaineer." In the occupied USSR, however, mountainous areas were few. There were only the northwestern portion of the Caucasus and its foothills, the small Yaila range in the Crimea, and the Carpathians in the extreme west of the Ukraine. Soviet partisans tried to utilize all of these mountain areas, but with very little success. The basic reason was the highly unsympathetic attitude of the local populations. Some of the most likely Caucasus areas were inhabited by Moslem groups which rebelled against the Soviet regime even before the German armies drew near. Outside the rebellious areas there remained enough suitable terrain in the Caucasian foothills for a small-scale Soviet partisan operation. However, the partisans attracted practically no local support, and as outsiders they were evidently unable to take advantage of the terrain. It is rather striking to note that the most successful "North Caucasus" partisans actually operated in the swamps of the Kuban River delta rather than in the mountains. (See Chap. X.)

The Crimean partisans—whom we cannot treat in detail in this volume —were much more numerous (their strength ranged between two and ten thousand), but they probably underwent more hardships for the sake of fewer accomplishments than any group of partisans of comparable size. Early Soviet accounts freely admit that a very large part of the difficulties of the Crimean partisans arose from the fact that the inhabitants of the Yaila were Tatars violently opposed to the Soviet system. The post-Stalin accounts are more guarded, but recognize the crucial role that Tatar anti-guerrillas, familiar with the mountain terrain, played in helping the Germans track down the partisans.[24]

The great distance of the Carpathians from the Soviet lines prior to late 1943 would have made it difficult, at best, to establish a partisan force there. In the summer of 1943, however, the "roving band" under Sidor Kovpak tried to establish a footing on the north Carpathian slope. The bitterly anti-Soviet West Ukrainian population gave him no support or information; under these circumstances his unit was nearly destroyed. Later this region became the seat of the strongest *anti*-Soviet guerrilla force which has ever developed.[25] As will be shown later (Sect. III, D), Communist partisans operating in other Carpathian areas where the population was at least not uniformly hostile achieved significantly greater results.

The above analysis suggests that even the most favorable terrain is more than offset by a strongly hostile local population. Throughout most of the nonmountainous portions of the occupied USSR, the population was never uniformly hostile to the partisans and became increasingly favorably disposed toward them. (See Sect. II below, and Chap. IV.) However, over half of the territory occupied by the Germans consisted of steppe, flat and treeless except for small swamp and forest areas along the watercourses. The original plan of partisan operations made little distinction between the

---

[24] Ivan Kozlov, *V krymskom podpolye: Vospominaniya* (Moscow: Sovetskii Pisatel, 1947), pp. 69–70; Makedonskii, p. 189; Shapko, p. 18.

[25] John A. Armstrong, *Ukrainian Nationalism* (2nd ed.; New York: Columbia University Press, 1963), pp. 296 ff.

steppe and less open regions. Each district in the steppe, as elsewhere, was to have its partisan detachment. It is interesting to note that a Chinese Communist commentator (1938) on guerrilla tactics had argued that partisans could operate in the plains by taking advantage of small areas of forest and other impassable terrain.[26] With certain exceptions noted below, the steppe proved in fact to be quite untenable for the Soviet partisans. The detachments which were formed tried to maintain themselves in isolated forests or swamps, but, unable to evade attack in these restricted areas, they were quickly destroyed by the Germans. (See Chap. XI.)

The northern third of the occupied area was far more suitable for partisan activity. While flat, it was forested and intersected by numerous swamps, lakes, and sluggish watercourses. This region alone became the seat of a vigorous and extensive partisan movement. It should be emphasized, however, that the partisans did not operate extensively in the Pripet marshes, historically one of the least accessible regions of Europe. The depths of the Pripet marshes provided neither food for large numbers of partisans nor attractive targets for partisan attack. Instead, the partisans were based in better-drained forest areas such as Bryansk, in the innumerable small swamp regions, and on the settled fringes of the Pripet.

Even in the northern portions of the occupied area, the partisans suffered under certain handicaps in comparison to many of the postwar guerrilla groups. Whereas the latter have typically operated in regions of tropical or at least mildly temperate climate, the Soviet partisans faced winters of extreme severity. Nearly all partisan accounts stress the fact that the famous Russian winter was no friend of theirs. In the tropical jungle, guerrillas are sheltered by a perpetual screen of dense foliage, which counterguerrillas have sought, with limited success, to eliminate chemically. Winter naturally defoliated most of the trees and underbrush in the occupied areas of the USSR. At the same time, the snow covering prevented the partisans from concealing their tracks. The frozen swamps and lakes were easily traversed by counterguerrillas. (See Chap. VIII, Sect. III, B, 3.) Equally important was the fact that sheer survival in the rigorous climate required the Soviet partisans to devote much of their energies to accumulating food supplies and building shelter. Early directives to the partisans stressed the crucial importance of preparing such quarters; evidently part of the suffering of the Crimean partisans (an inordinately large proportion of whom were of urban background) was due to the fact that they constructed aboveground shelters resembling teepees.[27] In most areas the dugout became at an early stage the standard form of shelter. While uncomfortable, it was liveable; but it greatly restricted the partisans' mobility, and almost forced them to organize in sizable groups capable of beating

[26] Chu Te, "On Guerrilla Warfare," trans. in Hanrahan, p. 73.
[27] See the photograph in Shapko, p. 40.

off all except large-scale attacks. (See especially Chap. III, Sect. II, E.) The type of guerrilla who operates in very small groups, moving constantly, living in the open much of the time, and even able to obtain a portion of his food from the forest, was simply unviable during the Soviet winter.

2. The Military Environment

The effect of climate and terrain was to restrict the area of operation of the partisans and to force them to combine in large groups. If the anti-guerrilla forces had been numerous, well trained, and well equipped, the result might have been elimination of the partisan movement. In fact, however, there has probably never been a guerrilla movement which enjoyed such a fortunate technical position vis-à-vis its opponents as did the Soviet. When the Germans invaded the USSR, they were inferior both in manpower and in quantity of military equipment. The sweeping initial victories were due to a combination of surprise, superior strategy and training (in part the result of the Germans' years of experience in fighting), greater individual initiative, and (to a less marked degree) qualitatively superior equipment. Between approximately July and October 1941 the Germans because of their victories enjoyed a quantitative ascendancy in certain classes of weapons, particularly the air arm. By the beginning of 1942, however, Soviet production, Western aid, and German diversion of forces to other theaters had redressed the balance. By the middle of 1942 the Soviet air force was superior, except over the southern portions of the front; even there the Germans were inferior by 1943. (See Chap. VI, Introd.) The Germans were so short on tanks and other mechanized equipment that these instruments could rarely be used in quantity against the partisans. Even in small arms, the partisans were often better equipped than the Germans. (See Chap. III, Sect. II, D.)

From the negative point of view, the technical parity between guerrilla and antiguerrilla meant that the Germans could not employ some of the tactics which have proved most effective against guerrillas. From the positive standpoint, it meant that the partisans could use modern techniques of communication and supply on a scale never before or since attained by large guerrilla forces. The basic technological devices employed were the radio and the airplane. Evidently the initial Soviet plan for partisan warfare did not fully envisage the possibilities of either of these instruments. Radio receivers and transmitters were provided, but evidently frequently did not work.[28] Part of the difficulty no doubt arose from the Soviet expectation that only limited areas would be occupied. Many months after the war had started the available radio equipment was so limited in range that a partisan leader setting off for the western portion

---

[28] For an example see *Partizanskiye byli* (Moscow: Voennoye Izdatelstvo Ministerstva Oborony SSSR, 1958), p. 128.

of the occupied area was warned that he would lose radio contact with his headquarters.[29] Another difficulty—which, of course, affected other types of equipment as well—was that the catastrophic decline in Soviet industrial capacity in 1941 made it simply impossible to turn out sufficient equipment for the partisans.[30] As late as midsummer 1942 the Central Staff of the Partisan Movement (the principal headquarters) was in radio contact with only 10 per cent of the partisan groups. By mid-November of that year, however, it had got in touch with 20 per cent, and many more were in radio contact with lower-level control centers.[31] By the first of the year there were 424 radio transmitters in partisan groups, connecting the Central Staff with 1,131 detachments.[32] Even at that date, however, there were numerous partisan units in the western occupied regions which were still not in regular contact with any control center.

The positive effect on partisan morale of being in contact with the unoccupied parts of the country was enormous. Possession of a radio was a major factor in enabling certain partisan commanders to assume control over neighboring partisan groups. It also convinced the local population that the partisan commander represented authority, and enabled him to carry on effective propaganda activities based on Moscow reports. (See Chap. IV, Sect. I, B, 5.)

A partisan staff which had a radio station was, in the eyes of the population, an official organ of Soviet power, and a detachment commander with whom Moscow dealt was an official representative of the Soviet state for both partisans and population, its plenipotentiary in the occupied territory. Personally, I consider that the very greatest service of the Ukrainian Staff of the Partisan Movement during that time [late 1942–early 1943] was the organization of widely ramified radio connections between Moscow and the population of the temporarily occupied regions.[33]

It is hard to distinguish the importance of radio as an isolated factor, because in practice its use was almost inseparable from another typically

---

[29] Linkov, p. 306.

[30] Institut Marksizma-Leninizma, *Istoriya velikoi otechestvennoi voiny Sovetskogo Soyuza, 1941–1945,* ed. P. N. Pospelov *et al.* (Moscow: Voennoye Izdatelstvo Ministerstva Oborony SSSR) [hereafter cited as *Istoriya velikoi otechestvennoi voiny*] III (1961), 357, states that in *1943* the growth of war production made it possible to supply the partisans with munitions and supplies such as means of communication. An officer of the Belorussian Staff of the Partisan Movement writes that in August 1942 K. Ye. Voroshilov (then nominal head of the entire partisan movement) told him that, unfortunately, the regime could not supply the partisans adequately; the officer comments that the supplies which the staff could send (including, specifically, means of communication) were quite insufficient. Akademii Nauk Belorusskoi SSR, Institut Istorii, *Iz istorii partizanskogo dvizheniya v Belorussii (1941–1944 gody): Sbornik vospominanii* (Minsk: Gosudarstvennoye Izdatelstvo BSSR, 1961) [hereafter cited as *Iz istorii partizanskogo dvizheniya v Belorussii*], p. 113.

[31] *Istoriya velikoi otechestvennoi voiny,* II (1961), 487.

[32] *Istoriya velikoi otechestvennoi voiny,* IV (1962), 468.

[33] M. I. Naumov, *Khinelskiye pokhody* (Kiev: Derzhavne Vydavnytstvo Khudozhnoï Literatury, 1960), p. 373.

modern military device—the airplane. Together the two devices enabled the partisan command to reinvigorate the partisan movement and to weld it into a centrally directed instrument of Soviet military and political strategy. The quantitative importance of air contact is somewhat difficult to assess because the nature of the front lines made it possible to establish surface contact between the unoccupied territory and the partisans to a far greater extent than is usual in guerrilla operations. The "Vitebsk corridor" which led through the German lines into northern Belorussia from the end of 1941 until 1943; the "Kirov corridor" opening into the northern Bryansk area during a considerably shorter period; and the "Ovruch corridor" into the northwestern Ukraine during the winter of 1943–44 were the most important of these gaps. For all partisan groups during certain periods, and for most of them at all times, however, air was the only available physical contact with the "Great Land," as they called the unoccupied USSR. As is pointed out in Chapter VI (Sect. II, A, 3, a), where the problems of air support are discussed in detail, the proportion of the partisans' arms which had been supplied by air actually increased as the war went on, from perhaps one-fourth in early 1942 to half in the summer of 1944. If radio could transmit information and orders to the partisan commanders, only air could supply them with especially trained personnel— and bring in the inspectors and "trouble shooters" of the central command who made sure that the individual partisan commanders remained fully responsive to the regime's demands. The visible evidence of higher concern for the partisans which air contact provided was probably even more important to partisan morale than was radio contact. (See Chap. III, Sect. II, C.) While provision of supplies, other than weapons, explosives, and technical devices such as radios, was not a quantitatively important aspect of air support, the possibility of supplying food to the partisans in emergencies gave the latter a margin of staying power which occasionally meant the difference between survival and near annihilation. What complete absence of air supply could mean was demonstrated in the Crimea when German air superiority combined with excessive distances from Soviet airfields (after the surrender of the fortress of Sevastopol the nearest bases were in the Caucasus) completely severed air contact for four months in the winter and spring of 1942–43.[34] The partisans were admittedly reduced to eating the meat of horses dead since autumn, and, according to German reports, to cannibalism.[35] It is true that air support had some negative effects on the partisans; mobility was sometimes reduced by the need to build and guard airfields and to wait for planes. Apparently a delay resulting from the desire to keep a rendezvous with planes was a major factor in the near destruction of M. I. Naumov's group, one of the most

[34] Makedonskii, p. 82.
[35] *Ibid.*, p. 64; AOK 11, Ic, Report No. 40 (GMDS, AOK 11, 35774/15).

important.[36] On the whole, however, these liabilities were minor. Perhaps the most striking evidence of Soviet recognition of the importance of air and radio contact with the partisans is the fact that the principal "Republic" partisan headquarters were located near Moscow, rather than closer to the groups they directed, in order to utilize the superior radio transmission and air base facilities of the Moscow area.[37]

C. THE PARTISAN RESPONSE

Much of the misunderstanding of the Soviet partisan movement which has often been evident in works otherwise characterized by profound scholarship and keen judgment has arisen from the paucity of information about this aspect of the war in the USSR and from the peculiar objectives and environment which affected the partisans. Even more confusing, probably, has been the fact that the Soviet partisan movement did not develop uniformly. Instead, there were three distinct stages of partisan activity; the first stage was so different from succeeding stages that one can almost characterize it as a separate episode in the history of guerrilla warfare.

1. The First Stage: June–December 1941

The first stage of partisan activity was based on the plan referred to in subsection A above. It is unnecessary to describe the highly schematic organization which the plan envisaged, since this topic is treated in detail in Chapter II (Sect. I, B). One need only note that essentially it provided for the uniform distribution of small partisan units throughout the administrative subdivisions of the occupied territory. The apparent disregard for the importance of terrain features may have been due in part to a misreading of the Chinese experience. It was also based on the erroneous assumption that partisan activity would be restricted to a relatively small area of enemy occupation during a comparatively brief period of time. Given the rapidity of the German advance and the preoccupation of the Soviet leadership with other problems, it is scarcely surprising that the original plan could not be fundamentally altered during 1941. Moreover, it had certain politically attractive features (see Chap. II, Sect. IV) which evidently led the regime to retain this form of organization wherever feasible. The most serious erroneous assumption, however, was that the territorial partisan detachment could rely on intimate clandestine contacts with the local population. The core of the partisans was to be "full-time"— they were to live together in the forest rather than concealing themselves as individuals in the villages after operations. However, the partisans were

[36] Pavlo P. Vershigora, *Reid na San i Vislu* (Moscow: Voennoye Izdatelstvo Ministerstva Oborony SSSR, 1960), p. 226.
[37] *Sovetskiye partizany,* p. 331.

to have important clandestine auxiliaries among peasants enlisted for brief raids. Furthermore, some partisan groups, at least, anticipated that they could dispose of their wounded by leaving them in the care of the villagers.[38] Obviously, had these assumptions been accurate the partisan detachments could have remained small, flexible, and (within their limited areas of assignment) highly mobile. But these assumptions in turn presupposed a degree of unanimous support among the local population which the Soviet partisans rarely ever obtained, and were very far from securing in 1941. Probably the single most important development affecting the partisans in that year was the profound lack of popular support for the Soviet system following the massive German victories. The bulk of the population of the occupied regions was convinced that the Soviet system had proved weak, and would not be re-established. One need not stop here to estimate the extent to which the population welcomed this development; clearly a majority were willing to acquiesce in it. Even in this majority some helped the partisans because they, too, were "Russian men" (frequently, just "men," "our men," or, rarely, "Ukrainian men"). The partisans never lacked enough supporters to provide good intelligence on enemy activities. But the Germans were also able to secure volunteer informants on a large scale, both from sincere opponents of the Soviet system and from opportunists. While their success was highest in 1941, even later in most rural areas counterguerrillas continued to get a great deal of information. For example, one partisan recounts how he was forced to transport his dying comrade twelve miles because, although there were no German troops in the numerous villages along the way, he knew that if he stayed in one for more than a few hours he would be reported to the occupation authorities.[39] Under these circumstances, while partisans could get some assistance from friendly villagers, the units had to be practically self-sufficient.

The isolation of the 1941 partisans was enhanced by the fact that most of them were "shareholders" of the Soviet system rather than average citizens. A very high proportion consisted of city men or men who had held managerial or clerical jobs in the countryside; few were peasants. The Party and NKVD affiliations of the leaders and many of the rank and file did not endear them to the typical rural citizen. (See Chap. II, Sect. II, A, and Chap. III, Sect. I, A, 5.) While these circumstances made it more difficult for the early partisan movement to attain popular support, they did endow it with a fairly high degree of group cohesion and loyalty to the regime. Moreover, the German policy of shooting known Communists left these "shareholders" with little choice. But, in spite of the effort to enlist "Old Bolsheviks" with conspiratorial experience, the apparatus men lacked

[38] S. Gnyedash, *Volya k zhizni* (Moscow: Voennoye Izdatelstvo Ministerstva Oborony SSSR, 1960), p. 49.

[39] *Partizanskaya borba ... na territorii Smolenshchiny*, p. 274.

adequate training as well as familiarity with the local terrain. Perhaps even more important, they lacked something which only time can give a new guerrilla movement—the benefit of the process of "natural selection" by which those who are psychologically unfitted for guerrilla life are eliminated or at least removed from command positions.

The result of these deficiencies can be stated succinctly. The original partisan units suffered enormous losses; in many areas, especially the hostile West Ukraine, they vanished without a trace. Practically nothing of military significance was accomplished. The remnants of the groups hid in the forests or villages, or escaped to the Red Army lines. In Stalino (now Donetsk) oblast, for example, an unpublished Soviet source admits that many underground and partisan members deserted or even went over to the Germans. Others evacuated to the Soviet side of the front without permission; in a single rayon such evacuees comprised twenty-seven of thirty-three assigned to underground work. After the war some of these men invented stories of fictitious partisan detachments to justify their behavior. In May 1942 it was necessary to create an entirely new "parallel underground obkom."[40] A recent Soviet memoir sums up the situation fairly bluntly when it states that the extensive but short-lived partisan activity (in Kiev oblast) in the late summer of 1941 was a "prologue to the organization and carrying out of partisan war in the Ukraine."[41]

2. The Second Stage: December 1941—Autumn 1942

The opening of the second stage, which was characterized by the development of what almost amounted to a new partisan movement, was signalled by the repulse of the German attack on Moscow. This was not merely a check, but a defeat of great magnitude. Although the German forces were able by a narrow margin to avert a catastrophic rout, the ability of the Red Army to fight again on at least equal terms was evident. The majority of the population in the occupied territories was no longer sure that the Soviet system was finished. The average man no longer had to think in terms of permanent accommodation to German rule, however harsh it might be; and he might find it very unsafe to make that accommodation if the Soviet power returned.

It is ironic that the earlier German victories themselves had been partly responsible for a situation in which this drastic shift of public opinion

---

[40] A. D. Kholodenin, "Kommunisticheskaya partiya—vdokhnovitel i organizator borby trudyashchikhsya stalinskoi oblasti protiv nemetsko-fashistskikh zakhvatchikov (oktyabr 1941—sentyabr 1943 g.)," unpublished dissertation, Kiev State University, 1956, pp. 42–48. While reticent about the reasons, a recent Soviet publication also admits that it was necessary to form a "parallel underground" organization in Stalino oblast. Yu. P. Petrov, "Kommunisticheskaya partiya—organizator i rukovoditel partizanskogo dvizheniya v gody velikoi otechestvennoi voiny," *Voprosy Istorii*, 1958, No. 5, p. 27.

[41] Begma and Kyzya, p. 49.

could provide the basis for a revived partisan movement. Millions of Soviet soldiers had been cut off behind the enemy lines during the summer and early autumn. Most were rounded up by the Germans. While many (mostly of Ukrainian origin) were then released, hundreds of thousands were callously left to starve in barbed-wire enclosures. As rumors of this treatment spread, soldiers remaining at large tried desperately to avoid capture. Countless thousands settled down in the villages and tried to sink out of sight. Those who could not do this hid in the forests and swamps. There they formed bands for self-protection and mutual support in obtaining food. The presence of these spontaneously formed bands is the grain of truth behind the myth, widely disseminated in postwar *émigré* circles, that the partisan movement was really a spontaneous Russian national uprising against the German occupation. In fact, the "spontaneous" bands were concerned almost wholly with survival. What attacks they carried out were against local German auxiliaries in the villages, and were designed to secure food.

In any event, most of the drifting groups of Red Army men soon came under control of representatives of the regime. Like the apparatus "shareholders," political workers of the Red Army (commissars and politruks) were proscribed by the Germans; consequently, they had no choice but to remain loyal to the Soviet regime. Many Red Army officers also felt bound to the system. As long as the outlook for the Soviet regime seemed hopeless, these men could do little to activate the bands of soldiers for concerted action against the Germans. Indeed, many of the officers and commissars themselves sank into apathy. The prospects of eventual Soviet victory raised by the German defeats of December 1941 galvanized the hard-core supporters of the system into activity; at times even minor Red Army successes (see Chap. VII, Sect. I, A) had this effect. Usually the hard-core elements were able to gain ascendancy over the lower or less resolute elements of the cut-off Red Army men. Very often the Red Army officers were assisted by remnants of the territorial partisan organizations.

The process just described was restricted to the northern forest and swamp region: Belorussia, the Bryansk forest, and the more northerly parts of the occupied Russian Republic (RSFSR). At this point there were practically no partisans in the Ukraine or the RSFSR steppe provinces, for the Germans had rapidly swept up cut-off Red Army elements there. From the immediate military standpoint, however, the embryonic partisans were very well placed, for they were astride the German communications to the principal battlefields. Consequently, despite its other preoccupations, the regime (operating largely through Red Army commands and the attached political sections) devoted enormous efforts to organizing, supplying, and bringing under central control the scattered and loosely structured soldier-partisans. Here radio and air contact were utilized to the greatest extent possible. Teams sent in by parachute or through the "corridors" contacted the partisans, superseded unreliable commanders, and brought about the subordination of others to Moscow.

The partisan detachments which, by the summer of 1942, were the result of the process just described were far larger than the units of under two hundred which the territorial scheme had envisaged. In general, the partisan group (which we may refer to generically as a "brigade") ranged in size from 350 to 2,000 men. (See Chap. II, Sect. III, B, for the factors which determined this size.) In contrast to the territorial detachment, the brigade was not necessarily restricted to a single administrative subdivision, and in fact many partisan groups moved from time to time. In general however, their movements were infrequent, the result of necessity rather than plan. If the unit happened to be favorably located in relation to German communications, its operations could be fairly effective. Even in these circumstances, however, only a small proportion of the available manpower was effectively employed at a given time. (See Chap. III, Sect. II, C.) There was a general tendency to avoid very risky or strenuous operations, for the partisans, after a period of extreme hardship, had by this time attained a status of relative security and well-being. Since they were mostly former soldiers recruited over large areas of the USSR, few had permanent local attachments; but many formed liaisons with local women. These ties further reduced the partisans' inclination to bring down German vengeance upon "their" areas. Consequently, the revived partisan movement, while impressive in numbers and in extent of territory controlled or influenced, represented a heavy investment of manpower in proportion to military accomplishments. At the same time, since the partisans were restricted to areas of favorable terrain, their only effect on most of the occupied area was to demonstrate that Soviet power could not be permanently excluded.

3. The Third Stage: Autumn 1942—Summer 1944

It is obvious that the state of affairs just described was not fully satisfactory to the Soviet regime. It had devoted considerable effort toward reviving the partisan movement and had invested scarce trained manpower and matériel. In return it had obtained a powerful political instrument (discussed in Sect. III) and a measure of disruption of German communications. More was desired, particularly since the numerical strength of the partisan movement constantly grew.

The measures taken by the Soviet regime were of two kinds. First, wherever possible partisan detachments were forced to intensify their attacks on German communications. The resulting German counterattacks stirred up the partisans, and forced them to abandon their sedentary life. The "family attachments" were disrupted. The result, in the Belorussian and northern RSFSR regions, was a certain intensification of partisan activity, but the amount of armed conflict remained limited in comparison to the very large number of men involved. In the south, a somewhat different course was taken. The partisans in the Bryansk forest region were in an exceptionally strategic location, close to major German military positions. By the end of 1942, with the Soviet victory at Stalingrad, German withdrawal was evidently only a matter of time. The location of the partisans would then cease to be strategic in relation to the German army. On the other hand, the Bryansk forest also occupied an especially strategic position in regard to the occupied Ukraine. It was close to the northern limit of the east Ukrainian steppe (there being a transitional zone, or forest-steppe, in between). In addition, a route sheltered by scattered forests led all the way from Bryansk to the Dnepr River. Beyond the river lay the great forests of the northwest Ukraine, which up to then had been practically undisturbed by partisans. The Bryansk forest was envisaged, therefore, as a gigantic base, or *place d'armes,* from which to extend partisan activities to new regions.[42] The plan of activity of the Ukrainian partisans (practically all of whom were then located in the southern fringes of the Bryansk forest) called for their transfer to the west and southwest during 1943.

Implementation of this most important assignment involved serious difficulties, especially in areas which had few forests or were steppe; and these constituted the larger part of the territory of the Ukraine. They could be overcome by sending strong, well-armed unifications, provided with all necessary supplies, from the northern, forested areas of the Ukraine to the right bank of the Dnepr and farther to the south and southwest in the areas where the most important communications of the enemy army were located. Just this assignment was given by the Party leaders in the Kremlin on 2 September 1942 to the commanders of the two strongest Ukrainian partisan unifications—S. A. Kovpak and A. N. Saburov. Their unifications were to open the route to the west, the Right-Bank Ukraine, for the movement of other powerful partisan unifications.[43]

These "roving bands" were a distinctive feature of the last phase of partisan warfare. Taking advantage of the German disorganization and extreme scarcity of troops and equipment after the defeat at Stalingrad, they moved as units for hundreds of miles. Usually the "roving bands" kept to the forest. The partisan headquarters exerted considerable efforts to get the "roving bands" to penetrate the steppe, but even these partisan "shock troops" hesitated as a rule to move into the open country south of the Kiev-Rovno railroad.[44] A major exception was M. I. Naumov's mounted brigade, but its experience was not altogether encouraging. The brigade left the Bryansk area in February 1943, swung south to the Dnepr (which

[42] *Partizanskiye byli,* p. 253.
[43] *Sovetskiye partizany,* p. 475.
[44] Vershigora, *Reid,* pp. 106–108.

it crossed on the ice near Cherkassy), and traversed much of the south-western Ukrainian steppe before being nearly wiped out in a wood west of Kiev. Of 1,400 men who started the raid, barely 300 escaped to the deep forest on the northern fringe of the Ukraine some miles west of the Dnepr. There Naumov and his cadre of survivors played a part in developing the partisan movement in the forested northwest Ukraine.

More important in this transplanting of the partisan movement to almost virgin territory were the brigades under S. A. Kovpak and A. N. Saburov, which went from Bryansk directly across the middle reaches of the Dnepr where it flows from Belorussia into the Ukraine. These partisan groups were followed by others until by the summer of 1943 the whole north-western Ukrainian forest, east of Volhynia, was a new partisan stronghold. On the whole, the military accomplishments of these incursions were limited; but they had enormous political influence, as will appear later. Moreover, in 1944, the roving bands constituted a ready instrument for extending the Soviet partisan movement into neighboring countries.

D. ANTIGUERRILLA WARFARE

1. Infiltrators

Postwar experience, particularly in Malaya and the Philippines, has shown that one of the most effective antiguerrilla techniques is the use of small units of highly trained men who infiltrate the forests where guerrillas are established. The counterguerrillas have the support of all the technical instruments of modern warfare, but they move in a random pattern in order to avoid breaches of security which might warn the guerrillas of their approach. Their attacks have a disruptive and demoralizing effect on all the guerrillas in the area of operation; but the prime targets are the leadership cadres of the guerrilla movement.

Occasionally the Germans employed this type of tactic with great success. The "Graukopf" unit, composed almost entirely of Russians, combined deception with infiltration. It played a significant part in disrupting the large partisan concentration in the Yelnya-Dorogobuzh area although the latter was eventually destroyed by other methods. (See Chap. VII, Sect. V, A, 2.) There were a few similar instances. To some extent, Bronislaw Kaminsky's collaborator organization in the southern Bryansk region employed infiltration tactics. Small units of Crimean Tatars, supported by German and Axis troops, harried the Soviet partisans in the Yaila Mountains. The Ukrainian nationalist partisans (generally without German support), fought a truly bilateral guerrilla war against Soviet partisans in the northwestern Ukrainian forests.

It is notable that in all these instances the burden of the counterguerrilla operations was borne by indigenous units, with the Germans playing at most a directing and supporting role. Recent experiences have demonstrated that counterguerrilla infiltrators need not be local men; but obviously strangers require a longer period of training and familiarization with the terrain. The Germans lacked the time and resources to become good infiltrators themselves. They were never willing permanently to divert even moderate numbers of first-rate troops to antiguerrilla warfare. In view of the terrible manpower shortage at the front, the German position is understandable. Yet only very vigorous, adaptable young men can stand the rigors of the infiltration type of counterguerrilla fighting. Older men, who predominated in the German security troops, were not only physically limited but had an inordinate dread of the dark forests. If the Germans had been willing to recruit Soviet citizens early in the war, they might have developed many effective units like those described in the preceding paragraph. But by the time Hitler's injunction against giving arms to the "inferior" Slavs was somewhat relaxed or evaded, there was too little time for the careful preparation which successful infiltration requires. The partisans were too well entrenched; and the loss of morale among the anti-Soviet elements in the population of the occupied regions made it difficult to secure the high quality recruits required. Moreover, the special nature of Soviet partisan warfare would have made the infiltration technique somewhat dubious as the major tactic of the counterguerrillas. The large partisan brigades could have been harried, but they could not have been wiped out by small infiltration units. In addition, lacking air support or superior weapons the infiltrators' advantage over partisan units of equal size would have been much reduced.

2. Strongpoints, Encirclement, and Combing

The principal antiguerrilla tactics actually employed by the Germans were a combination consisting of maintenance of strongpoints to guard vital roads and railroads plus periodical large-scale efforts to reduce the partisan forces by encircling and combing their forest strongholds. The first tactic was purely defensive, but it went a considerable way toward attaining the Germans' prime objective of keeping the partisans from seriously affecting the German war effort against the main Soviet military forces. In the northern, economically unproductive regions the Germans did not greatly care what happened in the areas away from the towns, highways, and railroads, so long as the latter remained secure. The towns were garrisoned by security troops, who set up posts at intervals along the roads. Small mobile units periodically patrolled the roads, or went to the assistance of strongpoints under attack. Ordinarily these defensive measures, combined with a very efficient system of repair, were adequate to keep open the lines of communication. The measures could not prevent isolated breaks in the highway and railroad system, nor could they (in

1943 and 1944) avert sudden concerted traffic interference over a wide area, but they could prevent protracted interdiction of movement.

The Germans were, of course, concerned with the potential of the partisans for disrupting traffic at a crucial moment of a campaign. Consequently, the German command recognized the need for some offensive action to restrict the development of the partisans' strength. The tactic of encirclement and combing constituted the principal German response to this need. Large numbers of military units surrounded a forested area where partisans were based. When all the assigned units were in place, they began moving concentrically toward a point within the area, destroying all partisans whom they encountered. Theoretically, if the circle was kept intact and the area was carefully searched, there would be no partisans left when the operation was over. Where the surrounding troops were very numerous, the area to be covered small, and the partisans weak or inexperienced, the tactic occasionally worked. (See Chap. XI.) It also worked in one instance (the Yelnya-Dorogobuzh area) where the partisans were numerous and strong. There an important factor seemed to be the conventional military qualities of the partisan organization, which had been reinforced by large numbers of regular Red Army troops. The Yelnya-Dorogobuzh partisans were so successful, well equipped, and trained in standard military operations that they played the Germans' game by standing and fighting. The partisans inflicted heavy losses on the Germans, but were wiped out themselves. It is notable that the partisan movement was never substantially revived in this area. (See Chap. VII.) Occasionally in later years the Germans caught considerable partisan groups like Naumov's and Kovpak's in open or inhospitable areas where they could be destroyed or almost destroyed by encirclement tactics. In the deep forests and swamps of the main partisan areas of operation, however, it was almost always possible for at least the hard core of encircled partisans to break through a weak point in the necessarily thin line of encirclement and to escape to nearby forest areas.

The German tactic, therefore, rarely eliminated many partisan units or leaders, and the rank and file could always be replaced. This does not necessarily mean, however, that the tactic was ill-chosen. It disrupted the partisans' build-up and planning; drastically weakened their morale, especially when it deprived them of their winter shelter, food reserves, and air contacts; and temporarily reduced the threat to the communication lines. The tactic took advantage of the weaknesses inherent in the partisans' reliance on fixed camps and airfields; it also utilized certain strengths in the German position. While the Germans were unwilling to assign more than a restricted number of second-rate security troops to permanent antiguerrilla warfare, they could at times afford to detach sizable numbers of front-line troops for brief operations. The Yelnya operation, which was exceptionally large and protracted, utilized two army corps for about two months. In the late spring of 1943 a force of about the same size was used for some weeks in the northern Bryansk area. Since the troops employed received no special training, the net loss of time was not much greater than the period of the operation itself. Similarly, enough airplanes for observation purposes could be obtained for relatively brief operations at times when front demands were not high.

3. Anticivilian Operations

Given the objective of security of communications rather than pacification of the country, the combination of tactics the Germans employed was not in itself a bad means of reducing partisan damage with minimum resources. The German tactics meant, however, practically abandoning the population of the partisan-held areas and the "twilight" zones adjoining them. Assuming that the Germans were willing to pay this price, they would probably have been wiser, even from a strictly military point of view, to have disturbed the helpless civilian population as little as possible during the course of antiguerrilla operations. In the remarkably successful Yelnya operation, civilians were in fact treated with consideration. Most of the time, however, the German counterguerrillas took the position that the civilians, since they had supplied the partisans with food and information, ought to be punished. The Germans also imagined that by destroying agricultural production they would starve the partisans. Consequently, horrible atrocities were committed against the civilian population, including the elderly, women, and children. Village-burning was the main feature of most of the combing operations. In addition, the Germans rounded up all able-bodied younger men and women for the Ostarbeiter program of labor in Germany. The combined effect of these measures was to turn neutral elements of the population toward the partisans, and particularly to send them a constant flow of new recruits seeking to escape the Ostarbeiter program. Theoretically, the Germans might have succeeded in isolating the partisans by complete evacuation of the areas where they could operate; but the size of the areas and populations involved, the difficulty of the terrain, and the strength of the partisans themselves made such a "solution" impossible. The inhumane half-measures completed the alienation of the population from the Germans, and considerably eased the Soviet problem of regaining popular support.

4. Local Defense

An antiguerrilla tactic of some effectiveness is the arming of the local population for self-defense against the demands of the bands. Given the objectives of the Germans, this could have been at best only a secondary tactic. Where strongly anti-Soviet elements collaborated with the Germans, as in Kaminsky's Lokot district of Bryansk or in the Yaila Mountains, village self-defense was combined with antiguerrilla infiltration at a fairly early stage. Slightly later, the Germans began to arm auxiliary native police *(Ordnungsdienst)* in the villages. These played a significant part in the continued maintenance of order in the Yelnya-Dorogobuzh areas. (See Chap. VII, Sect. V, C, 2.) Generally the police units were too poorly armed and too low in morale to be effective, but the "Wehrdoerfer" (fortified villages) introduced in some areas in 1944 were occasionally successful in beating off partisan attacks.

E. EVALUATION: THE EFFECTIVENESS
OF THE PARTISAN MOVEMENT
AS AN INSTRUMENT OF UNCONVENTIONAL WARFARE

Once again it is essential to emphasize that it is impossible to separate the political from the military aspects of any guerrilla operation. The preceding pages make it abundantly clear that there was a constant interaction between the military and the political environment in which the partisans operated; and that both their and the Germans' military operations inevitably had political repercussions. It is possible for analytic purposes, however, to distinguish the effect of partisan operations, both military and political, upon the outcome of the war from the longer-range effect of these operations upon the Soviet system. In the following subsection we shall try to determine what effect the partisans had upon the relative strength of the belligerents.

1. Disruption of Communications

The principal initial task which the Soviet regime set for the partisans was to disrupt German communications with the front, and (as the quotation in subsection A, 3, above indicates) this objective was emphasized throughout the war. As indicated in the preceding paragraphs, German countermeasures prevented complete severance of any vital roads. From the summer of 1942 on, partisan attacks, while they did not imperil the German front, slowed down supply and troop movements, created a tight margin in supplies, and acted as a drain on rolling stock. Occasionally (as at Drissa, northwest of Polotsk), the partisan attacks put a major bridge out of action. Special campaigns of widespread disruption of communications were coordinated with Red Army operations. One of these was directed in the spring of 1943 at the main railway to Bryansk when the Germans were building up their forces for their last major offensive ("Citadel"). The ensuing postponement of the offensive may have played some part in its complete failure. Similarly, the partisans aided the Red Army counteroffensive which immediately followed the German repulse by a concerted attack on the railways during the night of 3–4 August

1943. The great Belorussian offensive of the Red Army the following summer was preceded by a concerted partisan attack which resulted in nine thousand attempted demolitions. The resulting temporary paralysis of rail communications greatly impeded German mobility.[45] While it is unlikely that any of these demolition campaigns fundamentally altered the strategic balance, they were certainly factors of some significance. Given the fact that the Soviet forces could never attain the degree of air supremacy necessary to interdict German movement, the partisan operations were a valuable supplement, and occasionally were employed deliberately as a substitute for air strikes.

2. Combat Support of the Red Army

Like all irregular forces, the Soviet partisans were designed for harassing operations rather than full-scale combat with regular troops. Apparently realizing this, the Soviet command did not often order the partisans to engage in direct attacks on the rear areas of German troops in front-line positions. Such attacks would have had the maximum short-range military impact; but they would have been one-time affairs, for the partisans taking part in them would almost inevitably have been destroyed. Under special circumstances, however, partisan units were employed as battle auxiliaries for the Red Army. During the German counteroffensive at Zhitomir in November 1943 several large partisan units acted as a shield for the withdrawal of the regular Soviet forces by covering their right flank in the forests and swamps of the southern Pripet region.[46] Direct partisan participation in Red Army offensives was apparently less successful. The strong concentration of partisans and Red Army troops in the Yelnya-Dorogobuzh area was partly the result of a Soviet attempt to cut off a major portion of the German Army Group Center in front of Moscow. The attempt failed, and the partisans were eventually destroyed. Partisans did help hold some of the salients (at Kirov and Vitebsk) driven into the German lines during the winter of 1941–42, and later occasionally assisted the Red Army in river crossings. But the over-all results of direct partisan participation in battle were meager.

3. Intelligence

The role of the partisans in obtaining information of military importance was undoubtedly greater, but hard to assess. As was pointed out earlier, the original plan did not call for the partisans to play a significant role in intelligence-gathering. Throughout the war the Soviet regime maintained a number of clandestine networks of informants in the occupied regions. Some of these doubtless remained completely independent of the

[45] Hermann Teske, *Die silbernen Spiegel: Generalstabsdienst unter der Lupe* (Heidelberg: Vowinckel, 1952), pp. 210–225.
[46] *Sovetskiye partizany*, p. 491.

partisans. Many clandestine agents, however, came to use the partisan base as a refuge when they were in danger of being arrested by the Germans, or perhaps just for temporary respite from the constant strain to which the hunted spy is subject. Even where the clandestine agent did not actually go to the partisans, the knowledge that there was an emergency refuge much closer than the Soviet front must have improved his morale. Besides, the partisans provided the more tangible advantage of a direct radio link with Soviet headquarters through which intelligence could be transmitted and instructions received. Probably the desire to provide for rapid transmission of intelligence data was an important reason for the stress (see B, 2, above) placed on equipping partisan units with radio. The partisans contributed more directly to the intelligence service by building up their own network of informants, often designed primarily to keep the guerrillas aware of enemy plans concerning themselves, but useful for general intelligence purposes. In the late stages of the war, partisans were even able to tap German telephone lines. All of these intelligence services were undoubtedly highly useful to the Soviet war effort, especially since the Red Army does not appear to have been as skilled at using radio monitoring to detect enemy concentrations and battle plans as were the Germans.

4. Economic Disruption

The Germans relied heavily upon the economic output of the occupied territories, especially for the support of their armies in the field. If the partisans had substantially diminished production, they would have inflicted serious injury on the war effort. In fact, however, the areas in which the partisans operated were the least significant from the economic standpoint. The partisans prevented the Germans from collecting foodstuffs in Belorussia and the adjoining Great Russian provinces throughout much of the war; from 1943 on, they disturbed food collection in the northern Ukraine. These regions, however, were traditionally food-deficit areas; their poor, leached soils could not even support the indigenous population. Even if they had been completely undisturbed the Germans could have wrung from this impoverished land only a small portion of the grain, meat, and dairy products which they planned to extort from the occupied territory. The really important food surpluses were in the southern and central Ukraine and the occupied black-earth provinces of the RSFSR (most of which, apart from Kursk and the Crimea, were held by the Germans for only a short time). The partisans could do little to disrupt food procurement in these steppe regions. Available statistics on German food collection suggest that at least until 1943 the grain delivery quotas were largely fulfilled, mostly from Ukrainian production. Quotas for meat and dairy products were not fully met; partisan activity played some part in causing these deficiencies, but peasant subterfuge, direct (unaccounted) requisitioning by German troop units, and such material short-ages as insufficient fodder were probably more important.[47]

The mining and metallurgical industries were also almost entirely con-centrated in the southern steppe, in the Donbas and Dnepropetrovsk cen-ters. If the partisans could have disrupted the procurement of manganese, in particular, they might have dealt a serious blow to German industry; but (as described in Chap. XI) the partisan detachments in the vicinity of the manganese mines were easily and quickly eliminated. In the ex-treme western Ukraine, Kovpak's roving band attempted to destroy the important Galician oil field, but without notable success. Industry, too, was largely concentrated in the steppe cities. Even the secondary manu-facturing centers in the cities of Belorussia and the Bryansk area were sufficiently well garrisoned to be secure from partisan attack. Fanatical Nazi crimes like the brutal kidnapping of labor for German plants, the systematic starvation of urban populations by prevention of food deliveries, and the murder of hundreds of thousands of skilled Jewish craftsmen were far larger factors in disrupting manufacturing than anything the partisans did.

Apparently the most serious effect of partisan activities on nonagricul-tural production was interference with lumber production. Obviously, the sources of timber were also the areas of intense partisan activity. The partisans destroyed or captured many of the small sawmills in the Pripet and Bryansk areas, and interrupted the floating of logs on the Pripet, Berezina, Dnepr, and Sosh Rivers. By August 1943 the Germans were deprived of about 80 per cent of the logs and sawed timber they needed in the Ukraine, while half of the Belorussian sawmills were destroyed and 44 per cent of the timber quota remained uncut. Over-all in 1943 the partisans reduced logging operations by about 35 per cent and sawing by 42 per cent. The interference with timber cutting had an important in-direct effect on coal production, for the Donbas mines could not be worked properly without an adequate supply of pit props.[48]

5. Matériel and Manpower Investment

Thus far, the evaluation of partisan accomplishments indicates that the material damage they inflicted upon the German war effort and the ma-terial assistance that they rendered to the Soviet war effort were signifi-

---

[47] Wirtschaftsstab Ost, Chefgruppe Landwirtschaft, "Geschichte des Wirtschafts-stabes" July–October 1944 (GMDS, Wi/ID 2.1345), particularly tables Ia, II, and IV; GMDS files Wi/ID 2.1375 and H3/510; these data diverge from the less reliable but stimulating discussion in Karl Brandt, ed., *Management of Agriculture and Food in the German-Occupied and Other Areas of Fortress Europe* (Stanford: Stanford Uni-versity Press, 1953), pp. 128–133.

[48] Statement by Paul Pleiger, Delegate for Coal in the Occupied Areas (Rosenberg to Hitler, 9 April 1943, Centre de Documentation Juive Internationale, Paris, CXLIV–442).

cant but far from spectacular. Before completing the balance sheet of material accomplishments, however, one must consider the costs to the Soviet system of these accomplishments, and the drain upon German resources resulting from the antiguerrilla measures required to limit partisan achievements.

The German diversion of matériel to antiguerrilla operations was inconsiderable. The Germans simply did not use any considerable number of armored vehicles or other very scarce weapons. Even the German security troops were poorly armed; and the locally recruited auxiliary units usually were given captured weapons which could not have been effectively used by the German front-line troops. The small number of aircraft assigned to antipartisan missions could nearly always be withdrawn for other uses in an emergency. Soviet matériel investment in the partisans was somewhat more significant. Major partisan headquarters like the Ukrainian Staff of the Partisan Movement had small fleets of planes and the Red Army assigned many others for partisan support missions on a temporary basis. (See Chap. VI.) However, these uses of aircraft did not constitute a major drain upon Soviet air power, especially since the Soviet forces were rarely in positions (after the summer of 1942) when air transport was a crucial military requirement. Since there are many indications that the Soviet regime was unable to assign the partisans enough munitions and equipment until late 1942, it is evident that the quantities which were assigned prior to that time constituted some drain on the very limited Soviet resources. As the war went on, the increasing quantities of munitions supplied the partisans were probably relatively less important as drains on Soviet stocks, for Soviet production and the receipt of aid from the Western allies rapidly relieved the initial strain.

The balance of manpower investment is much more significant. By combining German reports and postwar Soviet accounts, it is possible to make fairly adequate estimates of the numerical strength of the Soviet partisans. At the beginning of 1942 there were perhaps as few as 30,000 active partisans in the entire occupied territory. (See Chap. III, Sect. II, A.) By summer of that year, however, the number had grown enormously. Of about 150,000, the bulk was certainly in Belorussia and adjoining regions. A Soviet claim that there were 33,000 in the Ukraine in June 1942 is exaggerated, even if one includes the considerable number of partisans from the Ukraine who had taken refuge on the southern edge of the Bryansk forest.[49] Other Soviet sources, however, are much more modest in their estimates. One states that there were 58,000 partisans in Belorussia at the beginning of 1943 and 40,000 in the RSFSR, with a total of 120,000 in all of the occupied territory.[50] Another Soviet work indicates

[49] M. Suprunenko, *Ukraina v velikoi otechestvennoi voine Sovetskogo Soyuza, 1941–1945 gg.* (Kiev: Gosudarstvennoye Izdatelstvo Politicheskoi Literatury, 1956), p. 200.

[50] *Istoriya velikoi otechestvennoi voiny,* III, 446.

that there were 75,000 "armed" partisans in Belorussia in May 1943 and 20,000 in the Ukraine.[51] If anything, the latter figures would suggest a lower total than that based on German reports, which indicated a total of 200,000 partisans in mid-1943. It is probable that the German estimate that the total number declined to about 175,000 as partisan-infested territory was recovered by the Red Army during the following year is accurate. (See Chap. III, Sect. II, A.) German estimates and Soviet accounts tend to agree on the over-all numbers of men ever involved in partisan activity, however. The Soviet figure is 360,000 armed partisans in Belorussia, 220,000 in the Ukraine; allowing for those in the RSFSR and other areas, a grand total of 700,000 is indicated.[52] Considering the many factors which necessarily render all estimates of partisan numbers imprecise, the Soviet figure is not seriously at odds with the estimate of 400,000 to 500,000 derived from German reports. Obviously the partisan attrition rate was high; but one cannot tell how much of it was due to actual casualties, and how much to authorized departures or desertions from the partisan units.

The total of perhaps half a million represents a very considerable manpower investment, especially in view of the enormous Soviet military losses and the resulting shortage of military recruits and labor. It is obvious, however, that it is meaningless to use this figure as a basis for appraising the cost of the partisan movement to the Soviet war effort unless the Soviet regime had practical alternative uses for the men engaged in partisan activity. Clearly it was preferable to have men enrolled in the partisans, even if they accomplished nothing, rather than to have them at the disposal of the Germans in the occupied territories. The available evidence suggests that there usually were alternative uses for the partisan manpower. Several Soviet memoirs tell how reliable commanders and political officers dissuaded cut-off groups of Red Army men from trying to make their way back to the Soviet front, insisting that the regime demanded that they carry on the struggle against the enemy as partisans. In the winter of 1941–42 the "corridors" through the front made it relatively easy for men from the main partisan concentrations to go back to the Soviet lines if the regime so desired. As a matter of fact, partisan units in northern Belorussia did recruit and dispatch to the Red Army some 25,000 men.[53] There appears to be no reason why the great majority of the Belorussian partisans could not have been dispatched to regular military service in the same fashion. Even after the gaps in the front lines were closed, the numerous air missions to the partisans could have been used to bring back men. There is no indication that this was done, however,

[51] Petrov, p. 37.
[52] Ibid., p. 42.
[53] Iz istorii partizanskogo dvizheniya v Belorussii, p. 460.

except in the case of seriously wounded partisans. On the contrary, flights to the partisans were utilized to send in a constant, though numerically small stream of highly trained technicians and officers. Consequently, one must conclude that for the most part the Soviet employment of men as partisans was the result of deliberate choice, and therefore can be properly characterized as an investment in unconventional warfare. The great majority of partisans were of military age, and consequently represented a net loss of men available for Red Army service. At the end of the war the total strength of the Soviet military forces was about 10 million. A total of perhaps 15 million to 20 million men were enrolled in the Soviet armed forces at one time or another after the beginning of 1942 (the enormous numbers lost in 1941 have no relevance for our calculation, since there were no options in the use of partisan manpower before the end of that year). Consequently, one may estimate that the partisans absorbed between 2 and 4 per cent of the total available military manpower.

To the extent to which the Soviet manpower in the partisans tied down equivalent German manpower, the investment was clearly justified, regardless of other partisan accomplishments. We can dismiss fantastic Soviet claims of losses inflicted by the partisans on the Germans, although these are still reprinted. For example, it is claimed that the Orel partisans killed 147,835 Germans.[54] Actually, total casualties inflicted by partisans in all areas probably did not exceed 35,000; and no more than half of these were German soldiers. A loss of 224 German soldiers in an attack on a troop train stands out in the German reports as an unusually heavy loss. (See Chap. VIII, Sect. III, A, 4.) It is true, on the other hand, that the number of security troops employed in the occupied territories (an average of 200,000 to 250,000 in 1943 and 1944) closely approximates the number of partisans active at the same time. About half of these men were Germans. Superficially, one might conclude that the drain on German-controlled manpower available for the front roughly equalled the drain on Soviet manpower. This was far from the case, however. Any army with long lines of communication in a conquered country must detail a considerable number of troops for security purposes, for, even in the absence of evident armed resistance, it must protect vital connections with its home bases against acts of sabotage or sudden popular uprisings. The Germans were, in fact, exceedingly sparing in assigning units to the lines of communication; in 1941 a single security division protected 250 miles of the main railroad across Belorussia. Undoubtedly the partisan attacks compelled the Germans to increase their security forces to some extent. On the other hand, the Germans could in case of dire need send some of their security troops to the front. At other times (as noted in subsection D

[54] *Orlovskaya oblast v gody velikoi otechestvennoi voiny (1941–1945 gg.): Sbornik dokumentov i materialov* (Orel: Orlovskoye Knizhnoye Izdatelstvo, 1960), p. 259.

above), regular troops could be temporarily withdrawn from the front to reinforce the security troops for special antiguerrilla operations. The Soviet command, on the other hand, had very little flexibility in the short run in the use of partisans to reinforce its front troops or even to reinforce one another. Ordinarily during an antiguerrilla campaign each partisan area constituted an island which the Germans could deal with in isolation.

A second, even more important factor in considering the extent to which counterguerrilla forces constituted a drain on German manpower was the quality of the security troops. Generally the men in these units were too old or physically limited to serve at the front. Twenty to 25 per cent of the security units were detachments stationed in the occupied territories so as to be available for guard duties while completing their ordinary military training. While the use of such units as counterguerrillas may have impeded the training program to some extent, these troops would not generally have been available for front duty in any case.

The Germans also employed considerable numbers of satellite (mainly Slovak, Hungarian, and Rumanian) troops for antipartisan warfare. The training, morale, and equipment of these units were generally so poor that they would have been a liability at the front. Similarly, the large numbers of auxiliary security police recruited from among citizens of the occupied territories would have been of very limited use at the front except for the unlikely possibility (discussed in Sect. II above) that a real anti-Soviet army of citizens of the occupied territories could have been developed early in the war. As it was, if the police had not been needed, its members would simply have formed another contingent of Ostarbeiter, of little significance in the total manpower pool in Germany.

6. The Balance Sheet

On the whole, one must conclude that the resources diverted to antiguerrilla warfare, while tangible, were considerably lower than those which the Soviet regime devoted to the partisans. Since the material accomplishments of the partisans were also very limited, one may question whether the partisan effort was worth the investment from the standpoint of winning the war. When one is dealing with so many incommensurate factors, one cannot, of course, answer this kind of question with finality. There were certain highly intangible ways in which the partisans may have contributed enough to the war effort to make up for their lack of material accomplishments. Their unpredictable attacks lowered German morale, though there is no evidence that the German will to fight was ever seriously impaired. The great accomplishment of the partisans in the psychological field was their major contribution in turning the population of the occupied territories against the Germans. However (as was shown in Sect. I) the Germans did not really seek to gain the loyalty of the population; and if they had it is difficult to see how this loyalty could have affected the course of the war to a decisive extent. One is therefore inclined to conclude that from the narrow standpoint of winning the war the whole partisan effort was dubious. But, as will be shown in the next section, the partisans made a much longer-range political and psychological contribution to the Soviet system.

§III. The Partisans and the Totalitarian System

A. MAINTAINING THE SOVIET PRESENCE

Whatever else the partisans accomplished, they performed one service of incalculable importance for the Soviet system: they maintained the Soviet presence in the occupied territories. Probably even more than other forms of political organization, totalitarian dictatorship requires the maintenance of inflexible habits of compliance to its demands. The totalitarian system may owe its original success to the use of force; but the habit of conformity, insofar as it is conscious, rests upon belief in the omnipotence of the regime far more than upon overt use of violence. Along with the myth of omnipotence goes the myth of the omnipresence of the regime's instruments of control. When, however, the illusion of omnipotence and omnipresence is shattered by military defeat, a totalitarian regime is in greater danger than one which rests upon a higher degree of voluntary consensus. The habits of obedience are shattered. The effect is especially serious if the regime's instrumentalities of control are removed for a considerable length of time, and are replaced for several years by an alien power. Even if the latter is eventually ejected, it takes a long time to rebuild the myth of the omnipotence and omnipresence of the restored totalitarian regime.

The theoretical picture just presented resembles what might have happened to the image of Soviet authority in the territories occupied by Germany for periods ranging from two to three years. Some of the effects described were in fact apparent after the war. The extreme measures taken by Stalin's regime to screen the occupied population and to restore rigid control reflect concern with reinforcing the shaken myths by overt use of violence. There is no doubt, however, that the task of re-establishing Soviet authority was much facilitated by the fact that *this authority never completely vanished from most of the German-occupied territory*. To a considerable extent the remarkable degree to which Soviet authority was preserved was due, directly or indirectly, to the partisans.

At first sight this assertion appears to be incompatible with the conclusion presented in Section II that the partisans were unable to operate in most of the occupied territory. The entire population of the territory occupied for considerable periods by the Germans (leaving out such areas as portions of Moscow oblast and the North Caucasus which were occupied for only a few weeks or months) was about 70 million—approximately two-fifths of the entire prewar Soviet population. Only about 1 per cent of the population in the occupied USSR lived in "partisan territory"; i.e., areas which were under firm partisan control except during major antiguerrilla campaigns. Almost all of the latter population lived in isolated areas of Belorussia, the extreme northern edge of the Ukraine, or the northern parts of the occupied RSFSR. A far larger number of persons in the same regions—between 15 million and 20 million—lived in a "twilight" zone subject to physical pressure from both partisans and Germans. In some portions of the twilight zone the Germans succeeded in maintaining a precarious framework of administration. Local men were appointed as starostas (elders) in each village. When volunteers were no longer available, the office was assigned arbitrarily; frequently it was passed around among the heads of households. Sometimes the starosta was assisted by a small native police unit. He was held responsible for the conduct of the village: he was obliged to report all signs of anti-German activity; to see that German proclamations were read; to keep the roads clear of mud and snow; and to bring in the quotas of food and manpower demanded by the Germans. If the starosta was really anti-Soviet, he found that these onerous duties made the population regard him as a German tool. The partisans, who were generally very well informed on the attitudes of village officials, made the anti-Soviet starosta their special target. Hundreds of starostas were killed; when the starosta could not be reached personally the partisans might massacre his family. (See Chap. III, Sect. III, D.) If, on the other hand, the starosta had been compelled to assume his position, the partisans in turn forced him to become their secret collaborator. Not being as well informed as the partisans, the Germans often did not know of this situation; if they did, the starosta's punishment was summary. And even the starosta who was loyal to the Germans often fell victim to the collective punishment measures meted out during antiguerrilla campaigns.

The terrible dilemma of the starosta was typical of that faced by anyone who held a position of responsibility under the Germans in the northern rural areas where the partisan "long arm" of the Soviet regime could reach. From 1942 on, the partisans devoted a major effort to making it impossible for any kind of organized administrative or economic life to continue under German authority. The justification advanced by Soviet writers is simple: any collaboration was treason. There are occasional indications that Soviet spokesmen saw the campaign against collaboration precisely as a reaffirmation of the omnipresence of Soviet power. A partisan leader is said to have told a starosta: "There's nowhere to go to get away from us. There is no salvation anywhere on Soviet soil for a traitor, and never will be."[55]

The threat was exaggerated, but not vain. Countless collaborator officials fled to the German-garrisoned towns or to the southern steppe regions. There, as described earlier, the partisans could not apply physical pressure. But nearly every city had an active underground of agents of the regime. In Soviet theory the underground was distinct from the partisans, except that the underground Communist Party committees had a certain amount of authority over the partisan units. As was suggested in connection with intelligence operations, this distinction became blurred when the underground needed partisan support. In September 1942 a political section was established in the Central Staff of the Partisan Movement to direct underground propaganda.[56] For propaganda and psychological pressure partisans and underground became complementary members of a team. The underground agents distributed pro-Soviet propaganda in areas where the partisans could not go. Often the underground conveyed warnings to individual collaborators. Sometimes threats were followed by assassination, but even if most persons in the occupied areas untouched by partisans did not encounter violence from a Soviet agent, they knew that the regime's secret representatives were in their midst. If, for the moment, the regime could not maintain its aura of omnipotence, the average citizen of the steppe or the city could not doubt its omniscience. Nor was he unaware of the strength and ubiquity of the partisans in the northern areas, for rumor, whether or not stimulated by Soviet agents, spread and exaggerated the story of partisan activities. Even in the areas most remote from their bases, the partisans helped to maintain the myth of Soviet omnipotence.

The influence of the partisans, direct or indirect, was by no means confined to demonstrating that there could be no alternative to Soviet rule. In every way possible, the partisans sought to re-establish in a positive sense some form of Soviet authority. Their effort was enormously aided by shrewd selectivity in the treatment of the population. The partisans rarely collectively punished a community. (Treatment of very anti-Soviet, non-Russian ethnic groups like the Crimean Tatars may have been an exception, but even there it is not certain that the *partisans* were indiscriminate in their reprisals.) The hard core of anti-Soviet elements was liquidated, opportunistic or apathetic collaborators were humiliated, forced to perform dangerous tasks, but usually given some hope of redemption; ordinary citizens were sternly held to their obligations to the Soviet system,

[55] G. Artozeyev, *Partizanskaya byl* (Moscow: Voennoye Izdatelstvo Ministerstva Oborony SSSR, 1956), p. 223.
[56] Petrov, p. 29.

but otherwise were well treated. The partisans did not hesitate to subject the civilian population to terrible risks and hardships when these were thought necessary to further the interests of the regime, but they did not inflict purposeless suffering.

The partisan commander himself was a prime representative of Soviet authority (see the quotation in Sect. II, B, 2, above). His connection with "Moscow" was the sign of continuity in Soviet power; it is worth remarking that many of the parachute team commanders were native Muscovites who so identified themselves among the population. (See Chap. II, Sect. III, E.) The commissar (except for a few experimental situations in 1944 the partisans, unlike the Red Army, always retained the commissar system)[57] had charge of propaganda among the population. As soon as possible in areas of secure partisan control, however, the local Party structure was reintroduced. (See Chap. IV, Sect. V, C.) Where feasible, men of military age were drafted for the Red Army. Other aspects of the Soviet system, including the collective farms, were handled in accordance with circumstances and current propaganda requirements. (This subject is discussed in detail in Chap. IV, Sect. VI.) The model approach, however, was complete reintroduction of Soviet institutions.[58]

B. PRESSURE ON THE PEASANT

In considering the influence of the partisans on the occupied population, one must constantly bear in mind that the direct impact was almost entirely upon rural people. In 1941 the population of the USSR was two-thirds rural; that of Belorussia was nearly four-fifths rural. The peasant was still the dominant element in the Soviet population. The small rural "intelligentsia," composed of petty bureaucrats and semiprofessional men and women was much more likely than the peasant to have evacuated with the Soviet forces. Consequently, the peasants (apart from Red Army stragglers, most of whom had peasant backgrounds) constituted nearly the entire population of the partisan-influenced areas.

The overwhelming majority of the peasants in the areas where the partisans operated were Great Russian or Belorussian. The latter showed few signs of separate national consciousness. The small group of Ukrainian peasants in the extreme northeastern Ukraine and along the southern fringes of the Pripet marshes also exhibited little national consciousness. The nationality situation was, as noted earlier, entirely different in Volhynia and Galicia, as well as among the Tatar peasants of the Yaila Mountains. Leaving the latter groups aside, however, one can say that the peasants affected by the partisans formed a nationally homogeneous Russian

[57] Vershigora, *Reid*, p. 64.
[58] See, for example, the Orel *obkom* directive for rebuilding Soviet institutions in *Orlovskaya oblast v gody velikoi otechestvennoi voiny*, pp. 220–222.

mass. They also were homogeneous in social and economic status. The poor lands they inhabited were for the most part adequate only for mixed subsistence farming. As a result, the economic impact of the establishment of kolkhozes (collective farms) was less extreme in these areas than in the rich black-earth districts to the south and southeast. The proportion of peasants classed as "kulaks" (a flexible term ultimately used to cover all who resisted collectivization) was smaller, and the average peasant had less property to lose when the kolkhoz was established. Nevertheless, the peasants were strongly opposed to the collective farm. While the "kulaks" numbered no more than about 5 per cent, they were disproportionately important in economic life of the area, and apparently exerted a strong influence on the other peasants. When the kulaks' property was expropriated and many kulaks deported, the disruptive effect, economic and psychological, was very great.[59] Still, there was no mass famine such as decimated the Ukraine, and the proportion of uprooted peasants was smaller than in the south.

By 1933 the main collectivization drive was completed; a measure of agricultural stability had been achieved. But the German invasion eight years later revealed that the peasants were by no means reconciled to the collective system. The mass of detailed evidence on this point (treated at length in Chap. IV) can only be summarized here. Wherever possible, the peasants distributed the land and property of the kolkhozes among the individual households. There was great disappointment when the German occupation authorities insisted on retaining the kolkhoz as a convenient device for food procurement. The Soviet regime was forced to recognize the strength of the peasants' opposition to the collective farm system. There is some evidence that partisans were directed to tolerate division of the land among the peasants, and even to spread rumors that the Soviet system of collectivized agriculture would be abandoned after the war. Even published Soviet sources indicate that during the first period of the war the regime at least avoided directly informing the peasantry that the collective system would be reimposed. The traditional term "peasant" *(krestyanin)* was used in place of the Soviet term "collective farm worker" *(kolkhoznik)*. In the spring of 1942, at a time when the Smolensk partisans were under great pressure, the oblast Party organizations continued to refer among themselves to "kolkhozniks"; but simultaneously the Soviet authorities formed a "Lenin Peasant Antifascist Union."[60] Apparently the terms "peasant" and "antifascist" were designed to appeal to the peasants'

---

[59] By far the best picture of collectivization in these areas is presented in Fainsod, *Smolensk under Soviet Rule,* Chapter 12. The Smolensk oblast (which during collectivization included a much greater extent of the RSFSR than it did in 1941) was very typical of the northern occupied territories.

[60] *Partizanskaya borba . . . na territorii Smolenshchiny,* pp. 122–123, 513.

patriotism; propaganda emphasized German mistreatment of the peasants rather than the virtues of the Soviet system. After the emergency was over, however, the "Union" was quietly dropped, and the positive symbols of the Soviet order, "Communist" and "kolkhoznik," predominated. Up to the end of the war, however, the partisans tolerated (and sometimes encouraged) the peasant inclination to active attendance at Orthodox religious services. Even today Soviet sources admit that the toleration of religion was necessary to avoid offending the peasants.

The position of the partisans among the peasants was ambiguous. In some respects the peasants identified the partisans as "ours." The ethnic background and speech of the partisans were probably the most powerful factors inducing this identification in Belorussia and the RSFSR. Probably four-fifths of all the partisans were Belorussian or Great Russian by nationality. (See Chap. III, Sect. I, C.) A Soviet source (using admittedly incomplete data) indicates that 70 per cent of the Orel oblast partisans were Russian, 15 per cent Ukrainian, and 10 per cent Belorussian.[61] Given the fact that this partisan concentration was in a Great Russian area near the borders of the Ukraine and Belorussia, the nationality distribution would seem to have been well balanced from the standpoint of securing local identification with the partisans. The situation was rather different in the Ukraine. A Soviet source indicates that there were 23,097 Russians and 5,747 Belorussians in "the largest partisan detachments of the Ukraine."[62] The total strength of these detachments is not given, but one can infer from the relatively small number of partisans active in the Ukraine before mid-1943 that these non-Ukrainians must have constituted a considerable portion of the earlier partisans operating in the Ukraine. One Soviet source (criticizing an earlier work by the present writer) maintains that the fact that V. A. Begma's brigade had 73.5 per cent Ukrainians and Belorussians in August 1943 and 82 per cent Ukrainians, Poles, and Belorussians in February 1944 shows that the partisan movement in the Ukraine was predominantly indigenous.[63] In fact, these data would appear to show that the partisans *tended* to become Ukrainian as the war went on and larger numbers of local peasants were recruited, rather than that the initial partisan movement and the cadres were Ukrainian. On the whole, the evidence suggests that in the Ukraine, in contrast to the more northerly areas, the partisans represented an ethnically as well as a socially alien element.

The partisans were basically a socially alien element everywhere. As was shown above, the first-stage partisans were predominantly members of the Party, police, and state apparatus; urban in background; and rela-

[61] *Sovetskiye partizany,* p. 237.

[62] *Ibid.,* p. 504.

[63] Colonel S. Doroshenko, "O falsifikatsii istorii partisanskogo dvizheniya v burzhauznoi pechati," *Voenno-Istoricheskii Zhurnal,* No. 7 (1960), p. 103.

tively well educated. So were the hard core of Red Army officers and commissars and the members of the special organizing teams who combined
to revive the partisan movement in the winter of 1941–42. While the rank
and file of the cut-off army men were predominantly peasant in background, many were former industrial workers. As late as 1943 these elements predominated in a partisan force whose composition differed sharply
from the peasantry among which it operated. The incomplete Soviet data
cited above indicates that 38.8 per cent of the Orel partisans were industrial workers; 30.2 per cent white-collar workers; and only 31 per cent
peasants.[64] In contrast to the overwhelmingly low level of peasant education, 74 per cent of the partisans had at least some secondary education.
Up until the latter part of 1943, therefore, the partisans were an educated,
urban group. As such, they resembled the forces which for generations
had sallied forth from the towns to impose the demands of central authority upon the reluctant peasant mass.

In 1943 and 1944 the composition of the partisans changed sharply.
The Red Army contingent declined absolutely as the German antiguerrilla
operations took their toll. On the other hand, the partisans absorbed tens
of thousands of peasant youths. Some of these were fugitives from the
Ostarbeiter program, or, more commonly, men whom the partisan officers
drafted to prevent the Germans from filling their labor pools as well as to
replenish the partisans' own ranks. A smaller number of police deserters
and other persons of rural background who sought to prove their loyalty
to the Soviet regime were enlisted. Even voluntary recruits were regarded
scornfully as "partisans of 1943," i.e., those who wanted to get on the
winning Soviet bandwagon. Frequently such men were segregated from the
hardened partisans of Red Army background and given inferior supplies
and equipment. This treatment was not wholly a matter of rewarding the
tried supporter of the system and punishing the lukewarm. The partisan
command knew that the peasant recruits, in contrast to the army men,
were apt to pay attention to German propaganda, and even to desert if
they had a chance. Moreover, the peasants were most reluctant to accept
the regime's prescription for movement of units away from their home
bases. (See Sect. II, C, 3, above; Chap. III, Sect. II, C, and Sect. III, C,
1.) There was a definite status-order among partisans apart from (although
often coinciding with) their official ranks: (1) volunteers of 1941 (usually
apparatus members); (2) cut-off Red Army men; (3) peasants drafted or
voluntarily joining after 1942; (4) police deserters. The Red Army men
were never fully trusted by the officers because the latter recognized that
if German treatment of prisoners had been milder and if the Soviet regime
had not exerted pressure upon the stragglers, they might never have been
brought into an organized partisan movement. Nevertheless, the army men

[64] *Sovetskiye partizany,* p. 237.

were invaluable because (in spite of some local ties which they acquired) they were relatively easy to persuade to move. Without the continuing strong numerical position (about 40 per cent) of the Red Army men in the partisan movement, it is doubtful whether it could have become as flexible an instrument as it did. Consequently, although the peasants by 1944 probably constituted a majority of the partisans, they were not first-class citizens of their units. This was another reason why the peasants continued to regard the partisan movement as an essentially alien force imposed from outside.

There seems to be no doubt that the peasantry resented the partisans, viewing them at best as the lesser evil. Yet it is worth noting that no spontaneous peasant organization, no popular peasant hero, arose to express rural grievances. In a very few instances the Soviet regime sought to portray one of its partisan leaders as a representative of the peasantry. The outstanding example was Sidor Kovpak, who was acclaimed as a simple, fatherly man, a descendant of the Zaporozhian Cossacks. Whatever his earlier background, Kovpak actually held a minor government post when the war began. Generally, however, the regime did not stress the peasant affiliations of its partisan commanders. On the other side, none of the anti-Soviet leaders who came forward during the occupation arose from the peasant masses. Of those whose bases of support were most thoroughly rural, Kaminsky was Polish in ethnic background and had held white-collar jobs; the Ukrainian nationalist partisan leader Taras Borovets had operated a small quarry before the war. Although the Germans would have made a real *Jacquerie* impossible, there were few signs of even incipient rebellion by the peasants against their tormentors, whether partisan or occupation forces. This does not mean that the peasantry was passive, or that it did not know what it wanted. The spontaneous partition of the kolkhozes is sufficient evidence to the contrary. But when they were confronted with force the peasants adopted a cautious, waiting attitude. This is scarcely surprising in the light of the peasants' unhappy history during the preceding quarter of a century.

C. THE PARTISANS AND THE SOVIET CONTROL APPARATUS

In 1941 the Soviet totalitarian system had only begun the difficult process of digesting the peasant mass. The leadership cadres of the partisans, on the other hand, were as close as any element of the Soviet population to being the "new men" who were the goal of the "socialist" transformation. Nearly all of the officers had been brought up and educated under the Soviet system, and had been through protracted courses of Communist indoctrination. In the 1941 partisan movement (in Moscow oblast) 63 per cent of the partisans were Communists, 15 per cent Communist Youth

League members (Komsomols).[65] By the end of the war, however, Party members were scarcely more numerous in the partisans than in a cross section of the Soviet male population of military age. Only 7 per cent of all the Ukrainian partisans were Communists, and less than 12 per cent of the remainder were Komsomols. The proportions were somewhat higher in Belorussia and, probably, in the partisan movement as a whole.[66] (See Chap. III, Sect. I, A, 5.) But throughout the war practically all of the officers were Party members. Most had been Party members before the war, but if a nonmember distinguished himself as a "natural leader," he was soon enrolled in the Party ranks.

The leadership cadres just discussed constituted a small portion of the apparatus officials (numbering several hundred thousand) whom we have called the "shareholders" of the Soviet system. These men had far greater status and far heavier responsibilities than the average Party member, to say nothing of the average citizen. They were also the material from which the "elite" was chosen. The elite itself, however, may be defined as the middle level of the apparatus: officials who occupied positions of great executive power, although without direct influence on policy making. This elite (a few thousand men) included Party officials of proconsular power, such as the *obkom* first secretaries; directors of important departments in the central and Republic offices of the Party, NKVD, and more crucial state administrative agencies; and high political and military officers in the Red Army. The inner circle of officials (whom we have called "the regime") consisted of the few dozen men who had fairly frequent access to Stalin. Stalin's power was absolute in those matters which received his attention, but he was compelled by circumstances to delegate broad areas of responsibility to members of the Politburo, the State Defense Committee, his personal secretariat, and the more important People's Commissars. Members of "the regime" were not, of course, engaged in commanding partisan units. Several members (such as Khrushchev and Zhdanov) played an important part in directing partisans, but this activity was never more than a minor part of their duties. It is possible that a few top officials engaged in full-time partisan direction, such as Strokach, were on the fringe of those enjoying access to Stalin, however. (See Appendix, Document 6.)

There is considerable indirect evidence that the regime did not ordinarily assign even its middle-rank officials to the hazardous business of commanding partisan or underground organizations behind the enemy lines.

[65] Institut Istorii Partii Moskovskogo Oblastnogo Komiteta i Moskovskogo Gorodskogo Komiteta KPSS, *Narodnye mstiteli* (Moscow: Moskovskii Rabochii, 1961) [hereafter cited as *Narodnye mstiteli*], p. 115.

[66] Cf. John A. Armstrong, *The Soviet Bureaucratic Elite: A Case Study of the Ukrainian Apparatus* (New York: F. A. Praeger, 1959), pp. 131, 139–140; and Armstrong, *The Politics of Totalitarianism*, p. 163.

The highest official known to have received such an appointment was A. F. Fyodorov, a Party *obkom* first secretary.[67] Other oblast officials assigned to partisan and underground work had nearly always held lower ranks. One official apparently was suffering from tuberculosis when assigned to underground work.[68]

There is reason to suspect that some officials assigned to command partisans were "expendable" in another sense. A possible example was S. A. Oleksenko, who acted as head of the Kamenets-Podolsk underground *obkom* and partisan detachments from the spring of 1943 until the arrival of the Red Army. Oleksenko had been first secretary of the Kamenets-Podolsk *obkom* in November 1937, but thereafter had not been mentioned in the Soviet press. One is inclined to suspect that he fell into disfavor or worse during that year of Stalin's Great Purge and was given the underground assignment as a chance to rehabilitate himself. The circumstances of Oleksenko's appointment are not unique. S. V. Rudnev, who, until his death in action in 1943, appears to have been the guiding force in Kovpak's roving band, is described as a professional Red Army officer with wide experience. It is hard to understand why he was rusticating in a minor post in Sumy oblast when the war broke out, unless he had felt the effects of the purge. The veteran advisor of the Spanish Civil War, Mokrousov (see Sect. II, A, above) held the insignificant post of director of a game preserve until war brought him back to a key position. Since Old Bolsheviks who had served in Spain were special targets for the purge, one would suspect that he, too, required rehabilitation. There is only one instance, but a very significant one, in which we can be certain that rehabilitation occurred through partisan service. D. M. Medvedev has recently been the subject of a full-scale biography written by one of his partisan lieutenants. The biographer recounts how Medvedev, an old Chekist (political police officer) became involved in difficulties after he criticized the methods of the higher police officials under N. I. Yezhov and L. P. Beria. Shortly before the war broke out Medvedev, though relatively young, retired because of "poor health." A few days after the German invasion began, however, Medvedev went to the People's Commissariat of State Security (NKGB) with a plan for forming a partisan parachute detachment.[69] Eventually he commanded an important partisan group in Volhynia.

1. The Revival of Conspiracy

A major reason for bringing Old Bolsheviks and Old Chekists back into service was that these men, unlike the majority of the "men of 1938"

---

[67] See Fyodorov, *The Underground Committee*, especially pp. 16–18, 21, 39–40, 42–44.

[68] Suprunenko, pp. 82–83.

[69] A. Tsessarskii, *Chekist: Povest* (Moscow: Voennoye Izdatelstvo Ministerstva Oborony SSSR, 1960), pp. 309 ff.

whom Stalin had promoted after the Great Purge, were experienced in the conspiratorial tactics which underground and partisan organization required. In effect, the regime had to revive the tradition of fanatic individual initiative which had prevailed in Lenin's day. The frame of mind which this tradition fostered had become increasingly repugnant to Stalin and his lieutenants. It conflicted with the rigidly centralized control which marked the establishment of Stalin's complete dictatorship in the 1930's. Individual initiative, or even too much enthusiasm, seems to have aroused Stalin's suspicions. Moreover, he increasingly sought a measure of institutional stability which was hardly compatible with a reversion to primitive Bolshevik fanaticism. It is clear that the emergency of war forced Stalin to reconsider his policies in these as in other respects. Nevertheless, the regime was obviously nervous about the inevitable relaxation of organizational rigidity among the partisans. Any dictatorial regime faces problems when it arms large bodies of ordinary citizens. The Soviet regime had worked out an elaborate system of controls to maintain the loyalty of the citizen-in-arms in the Red Army, but these controls could not be fully applied to partisan conditions. The very essence of the partisan movement was defiance of authority. Even though Soviet propaganda constantly described the German occupation officials as "bandits" and usurpers, the psychological step from tricking and resisting them to adopting the same tactics toward Soviet authority might not be a long one. Younger partisans were likely to develop irregular habits of work, family relations, and personal behavior which would make them misfits in postwar Soviet society. "Illegalism"—the habit of using lies, deceit, stealth, and violence against occupying power—might leave a residue of behavior patterns which would present problems for any ordinary government. In part (as was suggested in Sect. I) these liabilities were offset by the benefits which the Soviet regime might derive from the break-up of traditional patterns which had impeded the full imposition of totalitarianism. Purges of the partisans after the Germans were ejected removed the most suspect individuals. After the war the carefully domesticated myth of partisan glory tended to turn the memories of partisan experience into channels beneficial to the system. Nevertheless, it was very important to the regime to act immediately to control the potentially dangerous aspects of the partisan movement.

2. Means of Ensuring Control

The first and basic step was the insistence on strict discipline. Officers were to be obeyed without question. "Unnecessary democracy," such as the practice of consulting rank-and-file partisans before making decisions was sharply condemned.[70] Strict subordination was also demanded of de-

---

[70] Anton P. Brinskii, *Po etu storonu fronta: Vospominaniya partizana* (Moscow: Voennoye Izdatelstvo Ministerstva Oborony SSSR, 1958), pp. 254, 349–350.

tachment commanders, although they were allowed more leeway to express their opinions. An especially severe controversy arose in 1942 over the combination of smaller detachments into big brigades. Aside from the military reasons for this reorganization, the regime probably considered that it was desirable as a means of increasing control. Many of the detachment commanders had attained their positions more or less through accident. Even though they were sufficiently capable and loyal to be left in subordinate posts, the regime could control them more surely if it placed them under carefully selected brigade commanders.

It is interesting to note that one of the brigade commanders who was most effective in overcoming the detachment commanders' resistance was A. N. Saburov, a former minor NKVD official. The general reliance of the regime upon NKVD influence in the partisan movement is striking. Much of the evidence for this influence is presented in Chapters II and III; there is no need to recapitulate it here. However, a careful reading of Soviet sources indicates that police influence (the NKVD and the NKGB may be regarded as interchangeable for our purposes) was perhaps even greater than the German reporters realized. An extraordinary number of partisan officers, high and low, are casually identified in Soviet works as men with police backgrounds. Occasionally there is even a suggestion of group solidarity among these men. For example, M. I. Naumov, who had been a police frontier guard officer, remarked in reference to a partisan of similar background that once a man had been a frontier guard one could trust him.[71]

From the organizational standpoint, the NKVD was closely involved with the partisans at all times. The "special sections" ("OO") which eventually were placed in all units were important checks on partisan loyalty. Before the establishment in mid-1942 of the Central Staff of the Partisan Movement and the regional staffs, the NKVD shared directly (along with the Party and the Red Army) in partisan control. In 1941, for example, partisans in Moscow oblast were selected jointly by the Party *obkom* and the oblast NKVD administration, and the detachments communicated with headquarters through dual radio networks, one operated by the *obkom,* the other by the oblast NKVD.[72] For unexplained reasons, the Central Staff was disbanded on 13 January 1944.[73] It appears very unlikely that it had no successor as central control agency. Quite possibly the Fourth Administration of the NKVD, which was the police agency directly concerned with partisan operations, assumed this function.[74] The Fourth Ad-

[71] Vershigora, *Reid,* p. 234.
[72] *Narodnye mstiteli,* pp. 112, 115.
[73] *Istoriya velikoi otechestvennoi voiny,* IV, 469.
[74] Armstrong, *The Politics of Totalitarianism,* p. 162; cf. Suprunenko, p. 200, who notes that his information on the numerical strength of the partisans was obtained from the Fourth Administration of the MVD of the Ukraine.

ministration director was P. A. Sudoplatov (assisted by Eitingon), but it is possible that the mysterious "Sergiyenko" had some connection with this agency. (See Chap. II, Sect. III, C.) Much of the authority of the Central Staff passed to the Ukrainian Staff of the Partisan Movement, which was headed by T. A. Strokach, former deputy People's Commissar of the Interior of the Ukraine. Many of the Party leaders who were intimately associated with the origins and development of the partisans were from branches of the Party apparatus, particularly the cadres sections, which had had especially intimate contact with the police. In this category were M. A. Burmistenko, M. S. Spivak, V. A. Begma in the Ukraine; L. Z. Mekhlis, the head of the Red Army Political Administration in 1941; and P. K. Ponomarenko, who was chief of staff of the Central Staff of the Partisan Movement itself.

It should be stressed, however, that the NKVD never controlled the partisans as a "private empire" in the way that the SS controlled certain aspects of the German war effort. In the first place, the NKVD was divided against itself—probably at Stalin's instigation. The Fourth Administration directorate was composed of secret police officers who were evidently (if postwar alignments can be projected backward) closely associated with Beria. Most of the prominent police officials in the Republic partisan headquarters and in the field whose backgrounds can be identified were, on the other hand, from the frontier guards. There has evidently been a long history of friction between the latter and the secret police around Beria. The most prominent of the frontier guard officers, Strokach, became a particularly bitter opponent of the Beria group in later years. (See subsection E below.) In addition, major Party officials not especially beholden to the police played a very important part in directing the partisans. N. S. Khrushchev's role may have been exaggerated in recent years, but there is no doubt that it was significant. A. A. Zhdanov is credited with having established the "prototype" of the partisan directing staff in his Leningrad oblast command.[75] Finally, all the most important questions (such as plans for Ukrainian partisan activity in 1943) were reviewed by the Politburo of the Soviet Communist Party headed by Stalin himself.[76]

3. Operational Characteristics of the Partisan Elite

Even when there was no question of rebellion against the regime's orders—and except in very minor instances such rebellion did not occur— the partisan leadership exhibited many characteristics which were dysfunctional from the standpoint of the regime. Most of these characteristics do not seem to have been peculiar to the partisan movement, but reflected certain general traits of the Soviet leadership strata. The peculiar conditions

[75] S. M. Klyatskin, "Iz istorii leningradskogo partizanskogo kraya (avgust 1941— sentyabr 1942 g.), *Voprosy Istorii*, 1958, No. 7, p. 27.
[76] *Istoriya velikoi otechestvennoi voiny*, III, 464.

of partisan life tended to bring these traits to the surface. Furthermore, the great amount of information which is available concerning the partisan leaders enables us to scrutinize these traits more carefully than we can in most other segments of Soviet officialdom. The same is true, generally, of the positive characteristics (again, viewed from the standpoint of the regime) of the officials who were engaged in directing the partisans.

The partisan experience provides ample evidence—if more is required—that Soviet officials are not selflessly devoted to serving their system. While the possibility of accumulating property is eliminated, the opportunity for personal gratification is not. It is evident, of course, that "gratification" is a relative term, for nearly all partisans underwent severe deprivations and physical suffering. In a sense the extent of deprivations and risks made the opportunities for gratification more attractive. These opportunities were available in accordance with rank. Officers received symbolic rewards such as medals, new uniforms, and Nagan pistols. At times they received better rations. Frequently they had more comfortable, private living quarters. One memoirist comments that the commander's living in a separate dugout could lead to abuses, but that sometimes the practice was justified.[77] Perhaps the grossest privilege of the officers—closely related to their separate living quarters—was their enjoyment of sexual "rights" to the small number of women partisans. Although there is abundant evidence that this practice was common (see especially Chap. III, Sect. I, A, 7), it is so obviously contrary to the puritanical code publicly proclaimed in the USSR that Soviet memoirists rarely refer to the partisan officers' sexual behavior. One writer does describe an instance in which a supply officer brought a girl from a civilian refugee camp to live in his quarters. He even let her interfere with his duties: "Who was to be given weapons first, who second, was decided not by him but by his forest wife."[78]

Probably more significant than the evidence of personal selfishness is the indication of trends toward group autarchy. Much of the effectiveness of any fighting unit depends on the development of group solidarity and *esprit de corps*. In regular military formations, negative aspects of this development are curbed by constant subordination to higher authority. Since the partisan units necessarily operated in a more isolated fashion, group solidarity frequently turned into looking out for unit interests at the expense of other partisan detachments. The success of the commander depended to a very large extent upon the prestige he enjoyed among his own men; consequently he tended to look after their interests to the exclusion of others. Some commanders insisted on their "sovereignty"; they tried to avoid subordination to any authority except the distant Central Staff.[79]

[77] Brinskii, p. 382.   [78] Makedonskii, p. 179.   [79] Linkov, p. 399.

This tendency was closely related to the opposition which some detachment commanders showed in 1942 toward the formation of brigades. But apparently Saburov, who insisted on forming one of the most important brigades, was just as adamant in refusing to take the next step of subordinating *his* enlarged unit to a higher group command within the Bryansk region. Saburov succeeded in maintaining his group's "independence." This was due partly to the fact that the regime did not wish to form too large partisan units. However (if a captured partisan staff officer's account is reliable) Saburov's privileged position was due also to the fact that he had used his control of a radio transmitter to inflate his reputation so greatly that the Soviet headquarters feared the impact on morale if he were to be downgraded.[80] Months later other partisan brigade commanders found that Saburov's men were unscrupulous in grabbing air-dropped supplies which had been intended for other units. The despoiled partisans retaliated in kind.[81] Any student of Soviet industrial management will find striking parallels between these "autarchical" traits and the practices of plant managers and regional economic directors.

Often "autarchy" went hand in hand with an effort to escape control in order to be able to avoid dangerous and difficult tasks. Sometimes, on the other hand, partisan commanders evidently desired independence because they feared that the dead hand of bureaucracy in higher headquarters would cripple their efforts to operate effectively. A major characteristic of the Soviet bureaucratic apparatus is a reluctance to reach decisions. This reluctance, which ordinarily may lead only to inefficiency, can be fatal in partisan affairs. In a striking passage, one of the partisan leaders who was most insistent upon subordination of individual detachments to partisan field headquarters criticizes his Moscow headquarters:

I requested a decision from my superiors. But Moscow did not answer. Every day radiograms dealing with various matters came in, but they did not even contain a hint about the question we had raised. This is the way I understood it: our proposal still had not been placed before higher authorities, and the immediate directors did not want to take on themselves the full responsibility for such an important decision.

But we couldn't evade the responsibility of fighting. I reflected: if the assignment is fulfilled, nothing will come of it except the thanks we shall have earned; if, on the other hand, we die, there will also be somebody to remember us with kind words.[82]

The approved personality for a partisan leader was one which emphasized decisiveness, willingness to take risks, and contempt for routine. One

[80] Alexander Ruzanov, "Pravda o partizanskom dvizhenii," *Frontovoi Listok,* 28, 30 October 1943.
[81] Aleksei F. Fyodorov, *Podpolnyi obkom deistvuet* (Moscow: Gosudarstvennoye Izdatelstvo Khudozhestvennoi Literatury, 1957), pp. 475, 506.
[82] Linkov, p. 269.

major brigade commander relates how he, as a Party secretary before beginning his partisan duties, dealt with a "legalist" in the state banking system. The official refused to pay out money without the specific authorization from Moscow which the rules required, even though the Germans were at the gates of the city. After some argument, the Party secretary curtly told the bank official that his money was "mobilized" for the war.[83] The recounting of this incident at the beginning of the memoir seems to strike a keynote for the book. It indicates that the demand for placing effectiveness above bureaucratic compliance with rules is not confined to paramilitary operations, but is the expected response of the efficient Soviet official to any of the numerous emergencies which have beset the Soviet system. General orders are to be treated no more inflexibly than standing regulations. Anyone who takes refuge in literal conformity to the rules is a "legalist," anyone who relies on inflexible obedience to orders or conformity to doctrine is a "dogmatist." Rejecting the plea that maintenance of small detachments was necessary in 1942 to comply with *obkom* orders issued in 1941, a major partisan commander said: "However, it is just there that the great strength of our Party lies, that it nowhere and never fell into dead dogma, never and nowhere lived by a routine worked out once and for all. Every time the Party made a decision corresponding to the circumstances. At present the circumstances have fundamentally changed."[84]

The partisan officer was no more permitted to rely on obedience to a single superior than he was allowed to take refuge in standing orders or fixed regulations, As described in Chapter II (especially Sect. III, I) the Soviet regime never relied upon a single chain of command to control the partisans. All our efforts to reduce the complex control system to a precise and all-embracing table of organization have been fruitless; and the more evidence one obtains, the more difficult it becomes to work out precise delineations of authority. It is possible that we still do not have enough information, or have analyzed what we have improperly. It appears far more likely, however, that the regime deliberately maintained areas of ambiguity in its command structure. By maintaining multiple, overlapping chains of command it avoided giving the individual officer a secure spot in a hierarchy. As a result, he could not be sure who would inspect his work or give him orders. He could not, therefore, cultivate a comfortable relationship with a single superior who could be trusted to protect him in all circumstances. The tendency toward "family relations" up and down the levels of authority was diminished, if not eliminated altogether. Left naked,

---

[83] Begma and Kyzya, p. 13.
[84] A. N. Saburov, *Za linieyu frontu (partizanski zapysy): Kniga persha, Partizanskyi krai* (Lvov: Knyshkovo-Zhurnalne Vydavnytstvo, 1953), p. 181.

in a sense, before the demands of unknown superiors, the partisan commander remained in a state of uneasiness which induced him to use his initiative to anticipate demands.

One is compelled to admire the ingenuity by which the Soviet regime, deliberately or not, established control mechanisms which tended to squeeze the maximum effort from its lieutenants. It would appear that flexibility and ambiguity in the chain of command have been common attributes of Soviet control systems. Another general characteristic reflected in the partisans was the tendency of the regime to create a new organizational system whenever a major new problem arose. When the original scheme of partisan organization proved unviable, there was a long period (autumn 1941—spring 1942) of improvisation. Part of the territorial system of organization was salvaged; NKVD agencies continued in directing roles; Red Army front commands were used as organizational centers; and in September 1941 a "staff of the partisan movement" was formed in Leningrad. In May 1942 the Leningrad "solution" became the model for the Central Staff, and, in following months, for a number of regional staffs. The new organizations had the advantage of identifying the partisans with the Party rather than with the Red Army. As a result, in future years, the partisan movement could be hailed as a distinctive Party contribution to the great victory. At the same time, the staff arrangement brought together regular military personnel, Party officials, and the ubiquitous police officers in a body which constituted a formal recognition of the institutional interests in the partisan enterprise.

The formation of the staffs did not mean, however, that the system of partisan control became frozen. The increased responsibilities of the Ukrainian Staff after the Central Staff was abolished at the beginning of 1944 were clearly related to the need to extend partisan activity to politically unassimilated territories in the West Ukraine and to the prospective East European satellites of the USSR. The Ukrainian Staff functioned (although Strokach was replaced as chief of staff by a partisan brigade commander, V. Andreyev) at least until June 1945, after the war in Europe had ended.[85] There was nothing sacrosanct about the jurisdiction of the Ukrainian Staff, however. For example, in the summer of 1943 the Staff formed a special operating group at the Red Army Voronezh Front headquarters in order to coordinate partisan operations with the rapid advance of the regular forces.[86] Altogether, the ability of the Soviet regime to improvise new solutions to changing situations is strikingly demonstrated by the history of partisan control arrangements.

[85] See the signature on the letter published in "Soviet-Czechoslovak Relations during the Great Patriotic War," *International Affairs* (Moscow), 1960, No. 8, pp. 119–121.
[86] *Istoriya velikoi otechestvennoi voiny*, III, 307.

D. THE EXTENSION OF THE COMMUNIST SYSTEM

1. The Western Territories Claimed by the USSR

So far our discussion has dealt primarily with the partisans' relation to the Soviet system in the "old" territories where Soviet power had prevailed for over two decades before the German invasion. As noted in Section I above, the situation in the areas which had been incorporated in the USSR in 1939 and 1940 was quite different. There, in June 1941, Soviet power still had a provisional look. The former governments were supplanted, but Soviet authority was still largely alien, dependent upon tens of thousands of imported officials. While the shape of the coming social transformation was apparent, traditional patterns of life (except among repressed elements and their families) were not fundamentally altered. Some of the basic institutions of the Soviet system, such as the collective farm, had not been introduced on a large scale. When the Germans arrived, the elements of the Soviet system which had been introduced vanished almost at once. To the Soviet regime, this situation meant that nearly all of the work of incorporating the new territories into the Soviet system would have to begin anew when they were reconquered. In the meantime, it was just as important in these territories, though far more difficult than in the "old" Soviet Union, to demonstrate that Soviet authority, though temporarily eclipsed, was inescapable. The sheer size of the areas affected made this a major Soviet objective. Some twenty million persons, over one-fourth of the population of the occupied territories, lived in the newly annexed lands.

The partisans constituted one of the few available instruments for reaching these territories before the Red Army could fight its way back from the gates of Moscow and Stalingrad. Unfortunately, the scope of the research into German documents upon which most of this book is based precluded detailed studies of the western areas. Nevertheless, enough information has come to light from various sources to permit one to present a fairly clear picture of partisan activity there. One is immediately struck by the wide variation in local conditions which the Soviet attempt to extend partisan activity encountered.

In Belorussia, the transition from "old" to "new" areas was a gradual one. Except for the lack of habituation to the Soviet system, the half of the Belorussian population which had been acquired from Poland in 1939 did not differ fundamentally from the older Soviet Belorussian population. For centuries both had consisted overwhelmingly of poor peasants of Orthodox faith. What national consciousness the western Belorussian possessed was directed primarily against the Poles. In extending partisan activity to western Belorussia, the Soviet authorities were careful to de-emphasize the specifically Communist features of their system somewhat more than among the peasants farther east. As there were no kolkhozes to revive, the rights of individual peasants could be stressed unambiguously, though deceptively. In place of the Party, "antifascist committees" were publicized. Undoubtedly the partisans obtained less positive support in these areas than in eastern Belorussia. However, the enormous partisan concentration in eastern Belorussia simply spilled over into the western part of the Republic, becoming diluted the farther west it went, but not altering fundamentally in character. (See Chap. IX, Sect. I, D.) The only special obstacle encountered—aside from distance and the presence of fewer pro-Soviet elements—was the Polish national "Home Army." The Soviet partisans began the ruthless liquidation of the underground and guerrilla groups loyal to the exile government in London long before the Red Army arrived to destroy independence in the central Polish lands.[87]

The situation was entirely different in the Baltic Republics. Though Latvia, Lithuania, and Estonia had been sovereign for little more than twenty years, they had developed firm traditions of independence. In addition, their populations differed fundamentally from that of any part of the old USSR in terms of religion and ethnic background. In 1939–40 the Soviet regime confronted these small nations with overwhelming force. When this force was withdrawn there was scarcely a vestige of support for Soviet authority. There was no viable partisan organization in 1941. But later penetration of the Baltic countries should have been greatly facilitated by the fact that they bordered on the Leningrad and Belorussian areas where the partisans were exceptionally numerous and vigorous. Nevertheless, even Soviet sources are compelled to admit that the partisans achieved nothing in the Baltic lands. In the summer of 1942 a "Latvian partisan regiment" started out from the Leningrad area, but got only as far as the Latvian frontier. In December 1942 the remnants of this unit, organized as a detachment numbering only one hundred, succeeded in getting into Latvia; but a year later the total number of Latvian partisans claimed by Soviet sources was only 854. The final total, in September 1944, was under three thousand.[88] Soviet writers blame these meager results on the lack of extensive forests in Latvia; in fact, the terrain there is nearly as favorable as in the adjoining Russian and Belorussian districts. There is scarcely any doubt that the fundamental reason for the partisans' failure was the uniformly hostile human environment. Results of partisan activity in Estonia and Lithuania appear to have been no more significant.

The effort to use partisans to maintain Soviet presence and reinstall Soviet authority was equally a failure in the Moldavian Republic, although the reasons may have been different. The Moldavian Republic was almost

---

[87] See especially L. F. Tsanava, *Vsenarodnaya partizanskaya voina v Belorussii protiv fashistskikh zakhvatchikov*, II (Minsk: Gosudarstvennoye Izdatelstvo BSSR, 1951).

[88] *Sovetskiye partizany*, p. 610; *Istoriya velikoi otechestvennoi voiny*, IV, 337.

identical with the province of Bessarabia, governed by Rumania despite Soviet protests until 1940. Most of the population consisted of relatively poor peasants, Orthodox in religion, with a long history of incorporation in the Russian Empire, but Rumanian in language. There are few indications that this population displayed the sharp antipathy toward Soviet rule that characterized the Baltic nations. On the other hand, there is no evidence of positive support for Soviet authority. In an effort to implant partisan activity in Moldavia, two "Moldavian" brigades were formed fairly early in the war. It appears that their personnel was predominantly Russian and Ukrainian, and they were subordinate to the Ukrainian Staff of the Partisan Movement. In any event, these brigades admittedly stayed in the Ukrainian forest 300 to 500 miles from Moldavian territory until the Red Army had reached "their" republic.[89]

The situation in the annexed West Ukrainian territories was far more complex. Since the present writer has described it in detail elsewhere, it can be summarized briefly here.[90] The Soviet regime devoted enormously greater efforts to installing the partisans in the West Ukraine than it did in the Baltic republics or Moldavia. Great sacrifices were made in 1942 to develop an underground network, supported by small partisan detachments, in the northern part of the region.[91] The West Ukraine was also a major objective of the roving bands. Kovpak's brigade arrived on the fringes of the area in early 1943; at a very high cost, the brigade traversed the heart of the West Ukraine during the following summer. Many of the other large roving bands operated in the West Ukraine, although usually with closer support from the Red Army. There seem to have been four principal reasons for this concentration of Soviet effort in the West Ukraine: (1) The region was the natural gateway to East European regions which the Communists wished to penetrate. (2) The West Ukraine had constituted a tranquil economic base for the Germans. (3) The Soviet regime hoped that a show of force would attract real support from certain West Ukrainian elements. (4) The Soviet partisans could play an important role in undermining the Ukrainian nationalist partisan movement, which presented a serious long-range threat to the installation of the Soviet system.

The Soviet effort succeeded to a limited extent only. Soviet partisans were able to use the West Ukraine as a highway to other areas, but only after the Red Army was close enough to provide substantial support. What injury was done to German economic resources (apart from the days immediately preceding the arrival of the Red Army) was due mainly to the nationalist reaction to the Soviet incursions rather than to direct accom-

---

[89] Vershigora, *Reid, p. 107; Istoriya velikoi otechestvennoi voiny*, IV, 470.
[90] Armstrong, *Ukrainian Nationalism*, especially Chapter VI.
[91] Dmitrii N. Medvedev, *Silnye dukhom* (Moscow: Voennoye Izdatelstvo Voennogo Ministerstva SSSR, 1951).

plishments of Soviet partisans. The effect on the population was more complex. The Galician Ukrainians were nearly unanimous in refusing support to the partisans; if anything, the latter exacerbated anti-Soviet national feeling in Galicia. A considerable number of Volhynians (who, unlike the Galicians, were Orthodox in religion and had a long history of incorporation in the Russian Empire) did at least accept the partisans as representatives of an authority which would inevitably be reimposed. In Volhynia, as in western Belorussia, the partisans set up "antifascist committees" and encouraged religious services; these devices were recognized as necessary because the national, social, and religious differences in Volhynia were so great.[92]

The partisans did not succeed in attracting a great deal of popular support even in Volhynia. It is possible, however, that their efforts contributed to eventual Soviet success (after the military reoccupation of the area) in establishing an informer network which hampered the activities of the Ukrainian nationalist partisans. Probably the greatest service which the Soviet partisans made toward eventually reducing the threat which the nationalist partisans posed for the Soviet system was to induce the nationalists to abandon covert activity in favor of a full-scale guerrilla movement. The nationalists formed permanent guerrilla detachments both to fight the Communists and to prevent the Soviet partisans from drawing in all who wished to fight the Germans. This "deconspiration" certainly made it easier for the Soviet authorities to deal with the nationalists in Volhynia. Even in Galicia, where the population was nearly unanimous in supporting the nationalists, their efforts at partisan warfare may ultimately have played into the Soviet hands.[93] The Soviet partisans had little to do with the physical crushing of the nationalist guerrillas, however; Soviet sources admit that in the summer of 1944 the Red Army found it necessary to detail one cavalry and two motorcyclist regiments to assist an undisclosed number of NKVD troops combatting the nationalist partisans.[94] Other evidence suggests that the number of regular Soviet troops required in subsequent years, at least until 1947, was even larger.

2. The Satellites-to-Be

Soviet partisans writing since the war admit that they encountered special problems in the territories annexed in 1939 and 1940, although they take it for granted that the partisan campaign there was part of a single effort to drive the invader from Soviet soil and to reassert the authority of the legitimate government. The partisans were not to stop, however, when they reached the "new" Soviet frontier. If a postwar account is to be

[92] Brinskii, p. 366.
[93] Armstrong, *Ukrainian Nationalism*, p. 165.
[94] *Istoriya velikoi otechestvennoi voiny*, IV, 224.

credited, a partisan commander was given a sealed order from the Ukrainian Staff to be opened when he reached the frontier. The cryptic order read: "On arrival at the frontier of our country remember the liberating mission of the Soviet Union. . . . Act independently according to existing conditions and the conscience of a Soviet citizen."[95] The commander, relying on his "socialist" conscience, interpreted his "liberating mission" to mean that

There, beyond the rickety frontier marker, lives and struggles a fraternal Slavic people. It was pouring forth its blood. Thirty-two parties had brought it to war and defeat. . . . And only the single, workers' party, together with us, could lead Poland on the road to national liberation. . . .[96]

The "workers' party" was, of course, the Polish Workers' Party, which was in fact the Communist Party under a new name.

If the roving bands had been a prime instrument for "transplanting" the partisan movement from the Bryansk forests to the northwestern Ukraine in 1943, in 1944 they became a major device for grafting the highly developed Soviet partisan organization on the weak Communist-led guerrilla forces of the USSR's neighbors. Just as the Soviet partisans attacked and destroyed the guerrillas of the Home Army representing the London Polish government, they aided and equipped the guerrillas of the much smaller "National Guard" formed by the Polish Communists. In the spring of 1944 regular radio communication between Soviet headquarters and the National Guard was established, and the Polish Communist partisans were supplied by air. About the same time, a Polish Staff of the Partisan Movement was organized.[97]

Many months before this, Soviet partisans throughout the occupied territories had emphasized recruitment of East Europeans. Some of these (especially Poles) came from long-established colonies in the USSR, or escaped from German labor camps.[98] Most of the Slovaks, Hungarians, and Rumanians were deserters from German satellite occupation units, or were captured by the partisans. Very probably at an early stage of the war the Soviet regime began to think in terms of using such men as cadres for building up Communist resistance forces in their home countries. In February 1944 a large number of the Poles serving in three of the big roving bands were screened out and reassigned to a Polish partisan brigade. In April selected partisans of Polish and Czechoslovak nationality were withdrawn for special training. They were instructed in a camp in Volhynia by experienced Soviet partisan officers, radio operators, and demolition experts.[99] At the beginning of the summer this intensive partisan training pro-

---

[95] Vershigora, *Reid,* p. 256 (ellipses in the original Russian text).
[96] *Ibid.,* p. 258 (ellipses in the original).
[97] *Sovetskiye partizany,* p. 798; *Istoriya velikoi otechestvennoi voiny,* IV, 489.
[98] *Sovetskiye partizany,* p. 797.
[99] *Partizanskiye byli,* pp. 542–544.

gram was expanded, supposedly on the request of Communist leaders from Czechoslovakia, Poland, and Rumania. According to Soviet sources, the plea was addressed to Khrushchev as head of the Ukrainian Communist Party. He turned the matter over to the Ukrainian Staff of the Partisan Movement, which became the directing center for training, supporting, and controlling the partisans in all of these countries.[100]

It is probable that the net accomplishments of the Soviet roving bands and the Soviet-sponsored Communist partisans in Poland were slight. Occasionally they may have incited the nationalist Home Army to rash actions motivated by the desire either to protect Poles from the Communists or to demonstrate that the nationalists were more effective as a resistance force than the Communists. Considering, however, the overwhelming power which the Red Army ruthlessly employed to suppress the nationalist underground, any effect produced by the Communist partisans was at most ancillary.

The situation along the southwestern edge of the Ukraine was considerably more favorable to partisan activity. Here, in reality, there was no frontier. Legally—even in Soviet eyes—the Ukrainian SSR ended at the crest of the Carpathians. Beyond lay Carpatho-Ruthenia or Carpatho-Ukraine, ethnically almost identical with the Soviet Ukrainian Republic. The Carpatho-Ukraine was formally claimed by the *émigré* Czechoslovak government, which had been despoiled of the territory by Hungary in 1939. Most of the Ukrainian population, which had been more or less passive under Czechoslovak administration, sharply opposed the harsher Hungarian rule. The largest native faction supported Ukrainian nationalism, but Communist elements were much stronger in the Carpatho-Ukraine than in Galicia. Some Communist-led partisan groups were formed, although they were not very active until just before the arrival of the Red Army in the early autumn of 1944. In the meantime, Eduard Beneš, head of the Czechoslovak government in exile, had apparently reached an understanding with Moscow to transfer the Carpatho-Ukraine to the USSR after the war. As a result, the Communist partisans evidently were permitted to act as though they were already operating on Soviet soil; they set up "national committees" which later served as nuclei for the Soviet transitional administration.[101]

For the Soviet regime much of the value of a strongly entrenched position in the Carpatho-Ukraine lay in its strategic position. Not only did the region contain many of the important Carpathian passes, but it made the Soviet Union directly contiguous to Slovakia and Hungary. In mid-1944 these were prime targets for the extension of partisan activity. Soviet efforts to implant partisans in the third neighbor of the Carpatho-Ukraine,

[100] *Istoriya velikoi otechestvennoi voiny*, IV, 490; *Sovetskiye partizany*, p. 804.
[101] See Armstrong, *The Soviet Bureaucratic Elite*, pp. 108–110, and the sources cited for this account.

Rumania, were almost total failures. Soviet sources refer in passing to minor partisan groups active in various parts of Rumania, but it is obvious that these were unimportant.[102] Apparently the strongly anti-Russian feeling of the Rumanian peasantry prevented Communist partisans from taking root. From the practical standpoint, partisan activities in Hungary were scarcely more significant. One Soviet source admits that the small units (totalling something in the neighborhood of two thousand men) sent with the assistance of the Ukrainian Staff into Hungary rendered no direct military services to the advancing Soviet forces. The Soviet source claims only that the existence of the Hungarian partisans had a high morale effect.[103]

The situation in Slovakia was entirely different; there, and there alone, was the Soviet regime able successfully to transplant a partisan movement beyond its frontiers. In 1939, Slovakia had been set up as a nominally "independent" country; in fact it was completely under German tutelage. Whether or not the majority of the Slovaks welcomed the dissolution of the Czechoslovak state, they unquestionably resented the burdens placed upon them by Hitler's war effort—especially the dispatch of Slovak troops to the USSR. Slovak units were used almost entirely as security troops; they acted reluctantly, and there were numerous desertions to the partisans. As the war turned against the Axis, the Slovak army at home also became restive, and more inclined to recognize allegiance to the exile Czechoslovak government in London. But the army leaders wished to carry out a revolution which would take the country out of the Axis with most of its institutions intact and with as little risk of drastic German repressions as was possible. Since the war Czechoslovak Communist and Soviet sources have complained that even the Slovak Communist leadership inside the country fell under the influence of the "London conception": i.e., it wished to delay the uprising until the Red Army was near; to carry out a coup d'état rather than a "revolutionary struggle"; and to preserve the "bourgeois" structure of the country.[104]

This plan did not, of course, suit the Soviet book. It appears very probable that the Soviet regime in conjunction with Klement Gottwald, Rudolf Slansky, and other Czechoslovak Communist leaders in the USSR, determined to force the hand of the anti-Axis leadership inside Slovakia, Communist and non-Communist alike, by instigating large-scale partisan activities. In 1943, while on his Carpathian raid, Kovpak had sent some of his partisans of Slovak origin on to Slovakia to organize native partisan units. The rapid defeat of Kovpak's roving band soon severed this contact, however.[105] As a result, the partisan detachments trained and organized by the

[102] *Istoriya velikoi otechestvennoi voiny,* IV, 257.
[103] *Ibid.,* p. 378.
[104] *Ibid.,* p. 317.
[105] Vershigora, *Reid,* p. 29.

Ukrainian Staff constituted the essential instrument for carrying out the plan for stimulating guerrilla war in Slovakia. Mixed detachments composed of 220 of the especially trained Czechoslovaks and 450 Soviet partisans were sent into Slovakia by parachute beginning in June 1944. By the end of August, thirty such detachments, averaging a score of men each, had arrived. They served as a stiffening and organizing element for the local partisan forces which the underground Communists in Slovakia were organizing. At the same time, large roving bands of Soviet partisans were able to penetrate the extreme eastern portion of Slovakia.[106]

By the latter part of August a partisan movement totalling 8,000 had created turmoil in a large part of the country. On the formal request of the Slovak puppet government, German troops began to occupy the country. Confronted with this situation, leaders of the regular Slovak army felt that they must begin their uprising or forfeit all chance for taking Slovakia out of the Axis. The regular army revolt began on 30 August 1944. The Ukrainian Staff of the Partisan Movement sent in many more partisan detachments (ultimately 3,000 Soviet partisans were in Slovakia) and large quantities of munitions.[107] But there was little coordination with the Slovak National Council (directing the army rebellion), and no significant Soviet aid was sent to it. Rejecting the "Slovak Main Staff of the Partisan Movement" formed in mid-September by the National Council as "ineffective," the Communist leadership asked the Ukrainian Staff to send in an organizing group. At the end of September this group, headed by a Soviet colonel, arrived.[108] By that time the isolated Slovak nationalist forces were in desperate straits; a month later they were obliged to surrender to the Germans. The Communist-led partisans continued to fight a guerrilla war. It had little serious effect on the German occupation; but it turned Slovakia, which had had a traditional peasant society, into chaos.[109] Undoubtedly this breakdown of established institutions made it easier for Communists to gain ground in Czechoslovakia after the arrival of the Red Army. Simultaneously, the Communist leadership acquired a patriotic aura because of its apparent heroic effort to prevent German occupation. The effect of these developments upon the eventual Communist seizure of power in Czechoslovakia cannot be assessed precisely. It is significant, however, that from being the most conservative portion of the prewar Czechoslovak Republic, Slovakia by 1946 had become a Communist stronghold.

[106] "Soviet-Czechoslovak Relations during the Great Patriotic War," pp. 119–121; I. A. Peters, "Dopomoha radyanskykh partyzaniv slovatskomu narodnomum povstannyu v 1944 r.," Akademiya Nauk Ukraïnskoi RSR, Institut Istorii, *Naukovi Zapysky,* VII (1956), p. 90; *Sovetskiye partizany,* p. 804.

[107] *Istoriya velikoi otechestvennoi voiny,* IV, 333.

[108] *Ibid.,* p. 327.

[109] See Armstrong, *The Politics of Totalitarianism,* pp. 167–168, and the sources cited for this discussion.

On the whole, the Soviet essay in transplanting partisan activity to its neighbors was not spectacularly successful, especially when it is compared to the achievements of the Yugoslav partisans in aiding Communist guerrillas in adjoining countries. The Soviet effort is sufficient, however, to indicate how important the Soviet regime considered guerrilla tactics to be in spreading Communism. Ultimately Red Army occupation was the means by which Communist governments were fastened on most of the East European countries bordering on the USSR. But military intervention could never achieve the appearance of mass popular support which a cleverly managed partisan movement could attain. Forcible interference with established institutional patterns which constituted barriers to Communism was much more apt to create resentment than was the "automatic chaos" created by partisan activity. Guerrilla activity also strengthened the self-confidence of the local Communists, even if Soviet partisans provided the essential stiffening. Partisan training in the USSR and partisan activity in the field also provided an excellent opportunity for screening native Communist leadership elements. For a relatively small investment, the Soviet regime not only provided a minor auxiliary force for the Red Army but in the few areas where partisans were successful obtained enormous political dividends.

The whole episode of the partisan advance into East Europe shows how fluid national boundaries are in Soviet thinking. From the old Soviet territory to the newly annexed regions to the secretly promised Carpatho-Ukraine to the territory of the USSR's formal allies—all these were moves on a chessboard of political expediency. Soviet planners carefully assessed the differing social and political circumstances in each area and adjusted the superficial aspects of their policies accordingly. Considerations of legal obligation or popular self-determination were never given serious weight, however. Throughout, the objective was the establishment of Communist regimes, concealed under the euphemisms of aid to "workers' parties," "development of the revolutionary struggle," and "elimination of the bourgeois structure." The key roles in these plans ascribed to Khrushchev and his NKVD minion Strokach are extremely interesting. In a way, the quick, intuitive response of Soviet partisan commanders (or, at least, their present claims to have made such a response) to the vague orders they received is equally interesting. It suggests that there is a depth of indoctrination in the expansionist aims of Communism which permits the regime to count on its lieutenants' exercising initiative in furthering a dynamic policy beyond the Soviet borders.

E. THE PARTISANS IN THE POSTWAR USSR

In subsection B above it was suggested that the Soviet regime probably regarded the conspiratorial attitude and irregular habits fostered by partisan life as potentially disruptive in postwar Soviet society. As far as the rank-and-file partisans were concerned, the "treatment" of this problem was begun soon after the Red Army reoccupied the areas of partisan activity. Except for the large roving bands and other detachments which could profitably be dispatched for continued activity farther to the west, the partisan units in the reconquered areas were scheduled for rapid disbandment. Frequently the partisans were permitted a victory parade through the towns on whose outskirts they had skirmished. Sometimes they were then allowed a few days or weeks of leave. In the meantime, according to rumors which are hard to substantiate definitely, suspect or recalcitrant elements were screened out and sent to concentration camps. Most of the rank-and-file partisans appear, however, to have been sent very quickly to the Red Army. One Soviet source indicates that of 3,149 partisans in the Vinnitsa area, 2,345 went to the army.[110] There—if they survived the war —the partisans acquired a salutary dose of stringent discipline, while their particular partisan experience became submerged in the general experience of war-time military service common to Soviet men of their age group.

Treatment of the partisan leadership cadres was rather different. Undoubtedly there was some screening of unreliable elements in this group, too. Generally speaking, however, the screening of the officer corps had proceeded throughout the years of partisan activity. In one area, at least, the Red Army was forbidden to induct commanders and commissars of detachments or higher partisan echelons without approval of the Party *obkom* secretary.[111] One of the great, though unplanned, side benefits to the Soviet regime of the partisan episode was its value as a testing ground for new leadership personnel. If under the trying conditions of partisan activity an official displayed the positive qualities outlined in subsection C, while at least avoiding flagrant display of the negative qualities, he clearly was a valuable asset for the future. In particular, a man who displayed initiative while maintaining complete loyalty and self-discipline even when he could not be immediately checked by his superiors possessed a combination of qualities which could be put to excellent use in the peacetime totalitarian system. The regime appears to have recognized this potential during the war by taking special steps to evacuate partisan commanders like Kovpak when their units were in danger of annihilation. Since the war, men with partisan leadership backgrounds have often had brilliant careers.

It would require a special monograph to trace the postwar careers of former partisan officers in detail. Some trends stand out, however. Former NKVD officers generally returned to police service, but at higher levels. Thus Naumov and Saburov, who had held minor police posts before the war, became heads of the police administrations in important frontier ob-

---

[110] *Istoriya velikoi otechestvennoi voiny,* IV, 472.
[111] H.Gr. Mitte, Ic, 2 August 1944 (GMDS, 113/1175).

lasts. S. S. Belchenko, chief of staff of the partisan movement at the Kalinin Front, had risen by 1957 to the high post of Deputy Chairman of the Committee on State Security. Party officials tended to return to the Party apparatus in positions resembling those they had held in the partisans. Usually they also remained within the same Union Republics. V. N. Malin, the head of the political section of the Central Staff, was by 1958 a section chief in the Soviet Communist Party central Secretariat. Aleksei Bondarenko, a minor official in a rayon in the Bryansk area before the war, became first secretary of the Bryansk *obkom* after his brilliant partisan achievements. Moisei S. Spivak, prewar secretary for cadres in the Ukraine, who played a major role in the initial organization of the partisan movement there and later was prominent in the Ukrainian Staff, enjoyed a few years of prominence after the war. After some published criticism, he disappeared shortly before Stalin died; possibly he was a victim of the secret purge of Jews. Other members of the central Ukrainian partisan apparatus who were prominent in the Ukrainian Staff, such as A. N. Zlenko, continued to hold important posts throughout the Stalin period and after. A very high proportion of the lower officials assigned as secretaries of the underground Party committees were killed during the occupation. This was the fate of the *obkom* secretaries in Dnepropetrovsk, Kharkov, Kirovograd, and Poltava, as well as many in lower posts. On the other hand, several (usually those sent in as replacements after the initial debacle) who survived were rewarded with high posts in the Ukrainian provinces after the war. S. A. Oleksenko, after his successful direction of the Kamenets-Podolsk underground, regained the status of regular *obkom* first secretary (in Drogobych) which he had apparently lost during the Great Purge. P. Kh. Kumanok, who directed the Sumy underground, held secondary secretarial posts in *obkoms* after the war. The prewar Vinnitsa *obkom* secretary for cadres, D. T. Burchenko, was promoted after his direction of the Vinnitsa underground to head the state apparatus in that oblast. M. A. Rudich became secretary of a Party district committee in Lvov after heading the underground in Lvov oblast.[112]

Apart from its value as a testing ground for officials of the Soviet apparatus, the partisan movement had enormous potential for use by the regime as an inspirational legend. That the regime has recognized this potential is indicated by the enormous outpouring of books about the partisans. It is evident that the publication of documents, memoirs, and histories on partisan activity has been closely related to shifts in the "general line" of Communist propaganda and to power rivalries in the Soviet regime. A detailed investigation of these relationships would require close examination,

---

[112] For additional details on the postwar careers of underground and partisan leaders in the Ukraine, see Armstrong, *The Soviet Bureaucratic Elite*, pp. 131–132.

employing the tools of content analysis, of the themes treated in books appearing at various times. Such an investigation would also include careful comparisons of the textual variations, small but often significant, in successive editions of the same book. In the absence of such a detailed investigation, the observations presented in the following paragraphs are necessarily somewhat impressionistic; but they at least suggest the main lines of development in the partisan literature.

During the war and for a short time thereafter works on the partisans tended to picture the movement as a popular, patriotic uprising against the Germans. While the partisan movement was never described as spontaneous, the elements of Party and NKVD direction were played down. This treatment seems to have been in close accord with the general Soviet propaganda line, which stressed an all-embracing patriotism as long as it was necessary to use all means to rally the Soviet peoples against the Germans. By 1946 the regime apparently felt that the time had come to re-emphasize the pre-eminence of Party controls and ideology. During the following two years (in what has been known as the "Zhdanovshchina") several of the earlier works were criticized for not emphasizing the decisive role of the Party in organizing and guiding the partisans. The emphasis on the close association between partisans and Party was closely related to the prestige of A. A. Zhdanov, whose Leningrad partisan operation had been especially successful. Toward the beginning of 1948, however, Zhdanov appeared to be losing his influence; in August he died. There are even some indications that Zhdanov's patronage of ex-partisans may have been involved in his decline.[113]

In the Soviet East European satellites a background of partisan activity tended, between 1948 and 1953, to make a Communist leader suspect of "bourgeois nationalism" and "Titoism." No doubt the primary reason for this suspicion was the strident Yugoslav emphasis on partisan warfare as the best way for Communist parties to come to power.[114] It is notable, however, that the Slovak ex-partisans, who had been entirely under Soviet rather than Yugoslav guidance during the war, were prominent among the purge victims of this period. Within the Soviet Union, ex-partisans had to tread warily. The most striking instance of the danger inherent in glorifying partisan and underground exploits is, significantly, connected with D. M. Medvedev, whose partisan career had originally been a path to rehabilitation after his disputes with higher-echelon NKVD officers. In 1952 (in a Ukrainian magazine) Medvedev published an account of the Vinnitsa under-

[113] Armstrong, *The Politics of Totalitarianism*, p. 177.
[114] See especially Eugenio Reale, *Avec Jacques Duclos au Banc des Accusés à la Réunion Constitutive du Cominform à Szklarska Poreba* (22–27 Septembre 1947) (Paris: Librairie Phon, n. d.), especially pp. 110 ff., 134 ff.

ground called "On the Banks of the Southern Bug." The series of articles was sharply criticized in a Vinnitsa newspaper for glorifying men who were poseurs rather than real underground heroes. In February 1953, just before Stalin died, the criticism was picked up by the influential central periodical *Literaturnaya Gazeta*.[115] After Stalin died Medvedev's account, apparently unchanged, was published in book form with a circulation of hundreds of thousands. An editorial note to one edition commented that the work had "required not only great labor, but also civil courage; when Medvedev went to work on the book, there was much which was unclear in the history of the Vinnitsa underground and several of its participants were subjected to unjustified accusations."[116] But Medvedev himself had died in 1954 at the age of fifty-six.

Immediately after Stalin died, some of the more prominent police officials who had participated in partisan direction became deeply involved in the conflict over Beria's position. Strokach played a key role in the events which ultimately led to Beria's downfall. One reason, probably, was that Strokach (if his wartime adjutant is to be believed) was bitterly anti-Semitic—he had once even accused Khrushchev of favoring Jews—while Beria was bringing back Jewish police officers whom Stalin had purged. Apparently the main reason, however, was Strokach's unwillingness to join in Beria's scheme to discredit the Ukrainian Party apparatus. Very likely this reluctance was partly due to the close ties with the Party which Strokach (and some of his subordinates with frontier-guard backgrounds) had developed while directing the partisans.[117] At any rate, while Strokach was retired as head of the Ukrainian ministry of the interior in 1956, accounts of the partisan movement have continued to acclaim his role. On the other hand some—though by no means all—of the high police officials involved in central and Belorussian partisan direction were purged as followers of Beria. Sudoplatov and Eitingon, who had worked behind the scenes in the Fourth Administration of the NKVD, disappeared just as obscurely. L. F. Tsanava, head of the Belorussian police apparatus and author of the most detailed history which has been published on any phase of the partisan movement, was purged in 1956—and his book disappeared with him.

For most of the former partisan leaders, however, Khrushchev's rise to supreme power must have been highly gratifying. He is said to have ordered the compilation of manuscripts of partisan accounts as early as 1944.[118]

[115] The article is translated in *Current Digest of the Soviet Press*, V, No. 7, pp. 38–39.

[116] Dmitrii N. Medvedev, *Na beregakh yuzhnogo Buga* (Kiev: Radyanskyi Pysmennyk, 1962), introductory note, p. 2.

[117] Armstrong, *The Politics of Totalitarianism*, pp. 242, 406n48.

[118] Naumov, p. 402.

In 1949, Khrushchev conspicuously praised the partisans in spite of Stalin's tendency to suspect them. After Khrushchev secured control of the Soviet Communist Party, Soviet works emphasized the "fraternal aid" rendered to partisans in the East European Communist states, and a background of partisan activity again became a sign of distinction there. In the USSR the flood of partisan memoirs and documentary collections rose. For some unknown reason, however, Khrushchev has frowned upon systematic historical investigation of the partisan movement. In March 1962 he scornfully compared a dissertation on "Partisan Operations in the Belorussian Forests during the Patriotic War" to one on "The Ecology and Economic Importance of the European White Stork, the Black Stork and the Common Gray Heron in Belorussia." Both, he said, were "ludicrous" wastes of Soviet money. If there were to be treatments of the partisans and other phases of the war, let them be memoirs, articles, and literary works.[119]

In view of Khrushchev's frequent changes of course, it would be unwise to conclude that no detailed histories of partisan operations can be expected in the near future. There may be, however, a certain long-range significance in his remarks. As indicated above, the story of the partisan movement has provided the regime with a highly useful legend. The partisan legend forms part of the larger epic of "The Great Patriotic War," which is the heroic age of the generation now in power in the USSR. The partisan legend, however, has the advantage that it dramatizes the role of the Communist Party and its present leaders, while emphasis on regular military operations tends to enhance the prestige of the army. Several recent memoirs assert (with dubious historical validity) that service in the partisans was harder and more dangerous, and (by implication) more commendable than in the Red Army.[120]

In addition, the story of the partisans is particularly adaptable to indoctrination of youth. The theme of a daring band of dedicated young men living robustly in the open air, fighting against terrible odds, and wreaking vengeance on the blackest of villains has attracted young people from the days of Robin Hood to the Wild West. Add to this recipe the ingredients of a detective thriller, and an ideal vehicle for indoctrination is at hand. It is scarcely surprising that, even in the last years of Stalin's life, the output of partisan stories continued. The great majority of these are based on fact, but the literary editors (and occasional skilled writers from among the partisans, like Pavlo P. Vershigora) have recast the recollections of real partisans in dramatic form. Though unsophisticated,

---

[119] Speech to Central Committee Plenum, March 9, 1962, as translated in *Current Digest of the Soviet Press*, XIV, No. 12, p. 11.

[120] Begma and Kyzya, p. 487; Makedonskii, p. 105.

these stories provide a welcome contrast to the drab, obviously didactic tone of most officially favored Soviet writing. At the same time, the "literary" reworking of the partisan memoirs provides ample opportunity for the skilled propagandist to stress the positive elements of the partisans' characters and to warn indirectly against those characteristics which the regime regards as negative. In this way the partisan genre of literature is made to play a significant and probably effective part in the machinery of Soviet indoctrination. Its role is unlikely to diminish for many years to come.

PART I

Analytic Studies

CHAPTER II

Organization and Control of the Partisan Movement

John A. Armstrong and Kurt DeWitt

§I. Introduction

Questions of organization and control were fundamental in the Soviet partisan movement during the Second World War. Their importance is clearly shown by experience in other incidents of modern guerrilla warfare. Decentralized organization is a necessary feature of all guerrilla warfare, for the complex structure of modern armies cannot be fully duplicated by irregular military forces compelled to maintain themselves in areas where the principal technical facilities are in the hands of the enemy. The guerrilla forces behind the enemy lines do not have a regular system of logistics. They must avoid large concentrations which would permit the potentially superior forces of the enemy to engage them in regular warfare, in which they are necessarily inferior. Aside from being essential for the preservation of the guerrilla units, simplicity of organization has certain subsidiary advantages. It requires a very small "overhead" of staff, communications, and technical services. Most guerrilla officers and noncoms need not be so specialized nor so highly trained in a military sense as those of regular units of the same size. As a result, elements of widely varying background and experience can be used in the command structure of guerrilla bands. Like all groups which have a comparatively primitive type of organization, guerrilla units are hard to destroy, for the apparently shattered group tends to re-form quickly.

However, the advantages inherent in simplicity and decentralization have been offset for most of the modern guerrilla movements by serious disadvantages. Although a guerrilla group can recover quickly from physical dispersion by the enemy, it may disintegrate if certain key leaders are eliminated, because, unlike a regular military force, it frequently has no alternative organization to which the survivors are bound to attach themselves. Since even the unimpaired guerrilla band is not a part of a permanent institutionalized body, serious problems of morale and discipline may arise. [See Chap. III.] Although these problems are outside the purview of this study, the role of the guerrilla unit within the general strategy of war is of real pertinence. Guerrilla operations against the enemy are of comparatively little value to the over-all war effort unless they can be coordinated from the center and directed against important objectives. This is especially true because guerrilla units, particularly when they operate near the homes of their members, tend to shun activity which would result in strong enemy reprisals. As a rule, actions which the enemy counters energetically are, of course, precisely those which would be of most value to the over-all war effort of the country to which the guerrillas belong. For the Soviet regime the importance of controls was even greater, since, unlike countries where the guerrillas have arisen in a spontaneous reaction to foreign invasion, the occupied Soviet zone tended at first to accept the German occupation passively.

Aside from the military value, however, an important advantage of centralized direction lies in the political field. In a guerrilla movement where centralized control is not effective, individual commanders tend to become a law unto themselves. At first the leader of a band passively evades the control exerted by the central authorities, then openly sets up an opposition center. Experiences of this sort were frequent in civil wars in countries like Mexico and China in the second and third decades of this century and during the civil war in Russia and the Ukraine. The Soviet rulers vividly remembered their experiences with guerrilla leaders like Nestor Makhno in the Ukraine, who declared their allegiance to the Soviet regime when it seemed expedient to do so, but eventually had to be forcibly suppressed when they refused to conform to Soviet decrees. They were determined to prevent the reappearance of such centrifugal tendencies in the event of another protracted war in the Soviet Union. The emergence of independent leaders from among its own citizens is to a totalitarian regime almost as distasteful as the complete control of these citizens by a foreign invader.

In order to preserve the advantages of guerrilla activities and, at the same time to avoid their traditional pitfalls, the Soviet leadership during the Second World War employed two types of control which had been little used in earlier guerrilla warfare. Because it was the Soviet Union, a major industrial power, which was supporting the bands, modern technical devices like the airplane and the radio were available. Of equal or greater importance where the techniques of political and social control peculiar to the regime. The central subject of this chapter is the manner in which the organizational and control structure of the Soviet partisan movement evolved. One aspect concerns the application of established Soviet methods of control to the partisan movement; another is the manner in which the special circumstances of partisan warfare resulted in improvising new methods, or in modifying established ones. Taken in this way, the study of partisan warfare provides important insight into the functioning of the Soviet system under conditions of stress.

§II. The First Efforts
of Partisan Organization

A. THE PREWAR SOVIET CONCEPT
OF PARTISAN WARFARE

Partisan warfare occupied a fairly prominent place in several areas of Soviet thought during the interwar period. Military textbooks and courses in Red Army academies analyzed partisan operations of the Civil War period and occasionally referred to partisan activity in other periods or countries, such as the guerrilla war conducted against Napoleon in both Russia and Spain. Historical and political journals, especially those concerned with the history of the Communist Party, printed lengthy articles on the Red partisans of the Civil War. These articles analyzed the social and political background of the Civil War partisans and stressed political as well as military aspects of the movement.[1] Partisan leaders were extolled as models of "militancy" and devotion to communism. While many of the Civil War partisan leaders sank into obscurity soon after the Soviet regime was firmly established or were purged during Stalin's efforts to consolidate his dictatorship, several prominent Soviet leaders, such as Marshal Klimentii Voroshilov, continued to be acclaimed as heroes of the partisan movement.

Partisan warfare therefore was not an entirely new concept for the generation of Soviet citizens, or at least the Communist Party members among them, which experienced the German invasion of 1941. Nevertheless, this generation was not psychologically prepared to carry on underground resistance against an occupying power. As the first secretary of the

[1] See Raymond L. Garthoff, *Soviet Military Doctrine* (Glencoe, Ill.: Free Press, 1953), pp. 391–94.

Chernigov Oblast Committee of the Communist Party, Aleksei Fyodorov, puts it in his memoirs, the very term "underground" seemed archaic and "bookish" to Party members who had lost all feeling for conspiratorial work during their twenty years of undisputed power.[2] In part this may be explained by the fact that the regional Party officials apparently were unaware that higher Party authorities had drawn up plans for a clandestine organization to take over in the event of enemy occupation. When Fyodorov went to Kiev shortly after the outbreak of war to consult with Nikita Khrushchev, then first secretary of the Ukrainian Communist Party, he was amazed to learn that such plans had indeed been made very much earlier at the all-union and union republic level of the Party.[3] Evidently, prewar planning was confined to generalized schemes worked out by the central Party authorities. The lack of detailed preparation at the regional and local level may seem to indicate an incredible lack of foresight, but it more probably was an inevitable corollary of the prevailing Soviet doctrine which envisaged a future war as an offensive campaign.

The overt signal for partisan organization was given in Stalin's radio speech of 3 July 1941. This lengthy address, dealing with many aspects of the war, contained one paragraph on partisan warfare:

In areas occupied by the enemy, guerrilla units, mounted and on foot, must be formed; diversionist groups must be organized to combat the enemy troops, to foment guerrilla warfare everywhere, to blow up bridges and roads, damage telephone and telegraph lines, set fire to forests, stores, transports. In the occupied regions conditions must be made unbearable for the enemy and all his accomplices. They must be hounded and annihilated at every step and all their measures frustrated.[4]

At about the same time, several agencies of the Soviet Government began feverish preparation for partisan activity. In all probability there was no formal coordinating body, although it is likely that the principal Party, Red Army, and NKVD officials concerned conferred from time to time on the roles that their respective departments should play. Such coordination is suggested by the fact that, in spite of certain ambiguities, the basic orders issued for the formation of the partisan movement indicate some general delineation of areas of responsibility.

[2] Aleksei Fyodorov, *Podpolnyi obkom deistvuyet* (Moscow: Voennoye Izdatelstvo Ministerstva Vooruzhyonnykh Sil Soyuza SSR, 1947), I, 15; see also Ivan Kozlov, *V krymskom podpolye: vospominaniya* (Moscow: Sovetskii Pisatel, 1947, pp. 10, 17–18.
[3] *Ibid.*, pp. 12–13. Some German reports refer to extensive Soviet prewar planning for partisan activity. However, these reports are either couched in vague terms, without specific evidence to support them, or are based on interrogations of low-ranking and obviously poorly informed members of partisan bands.
[4] J. V. Stalin, *The Great Patriotic War of the Soviet Union* (New York: International Publishers, 1945), p. 15.

B. THE TERRITORIAL ORGANIZATION

1. The Role of the Party

One of the major agencies involved in partisan organization during 1941 was the Communist Party itself. The Central Committee of the All-Union Party directed the formation of partisan units which were to parallel the existing territorial structure of the Party. Probably certain officials of the All-Union Party occupied themselves with this task from early July on, but there is no precise information on this point. Much more concrete evidence is available with respect to the organization of the partisan movement at the level of oblasts in the RSFSR and at the union republic level elsewhere.[5]

In the Ukraine, the secretaries of the Central Committee, Nikita Khrushchev, M. A. Burmistenko, and D. S. Korotchenko, directed the preparations, apparently without the assistance of an apparatus especially created for this purpose. For a time, as indicated above, their work was carried on in Kiev, which was not captured by the Germans until September 1941. Here Khrushchev and his assistants formed special organizations to direct the creation of partisan units in the oblasts of the Ukrainian SSR. In each oblast which was to have a partisan movement, a secretary of the oblast

[5] Since there was no separate Party organization for the RSFSR, its oblasts, krais, and autonomous republics constituted the level immediately below the All-Union Party, nominally on a par with the Party organizations of the union republics. During 1941 partisan activity in the Karelo-Finnish, Moldavian, and the three Baltic republics was small, and little information is available concerning it. In the Belorussian republic, available material suggests that the oblast Party organization, which was much smaller and less important than the Ukrainian oblast organization, played a comparatively minor role during the first months of the war.

The discussion in this section is centered on the territorial organization of the Party, consisting of the levels described above. More important cities had their own Party organizations, which in most respects were equivalent to the rayon, and in some cases even to the oblast territorial organizations. The larger cities were divided into urban rayons, or wards. The city Party organizations formed underground centers; and in some cities destruction battalions, which later furnished most of the manpower for partisan units, were formed either for the city as a whole, or in each ward. The major level at which partisan organization was carried out in most larger cities (both those which were occupied, and those like Leningrad which remained in Soviet hands) was the primary Party organization in individual enterprises. This was quite logical since the average factory, commercial enterprise, or transportation facility usually had as many Party members as an entire rural rayon. Apparently destruction battalions were not formed in the enterprises, but very similar home defense units known as "civil air defense" or "home guards" were formed, and provided many of the recruits for the partisan detachments.

The Party organizations of certain major enterprises, such as sections of the railroad network, which extend across several rayons and connect various cities, were not subordinate to the usual territorial Party organization below the oblast level. In the development of the partisan movement, such Party organizations appear to have acted in a fashion similar to that of the urban enterprises, but under the direction of the oblast Party committee rather than the city Party committee.

committee (*obkom*) was assigned this task.[6] At the same time, another official was secretly appointed to the post of "underground secretary," and was ordered to remain behind to direct Party activities, including partisan organization, after the Germans arrived.[7] In many instances, it seems, this appointee was not one of the prominent Party officials, although there is one significant case in which the man so designated was the first secretary of the oblast. The person in question was Fyodorov, the Chernigov Oblast official mentioned above.[8] Fyodorov maintains that he was given this appointment after urgently requesting it from Khrushchev; his record as a trouble shooter in the Communist organization of the Ukraine suggests, however, that there may have been other reasons. Several bits of evidence support the assumption that persons like Fyodorov, who had been in close contact with the NKVD while performing certain disciplinary tasks within the Party, were considered particularly well suited for the job of organizing the partisans.[9]

2. The Role of the NKVD

Several features of the Party underground organization made it especially necessary that those in charge be capable of working in harmony with the NKVD. One major component of the underground was a network of diversionist groups. This network, which was to cover the entire occupied territory, but was especially important in urban areas, was organized by the territorial NKVD, usually from NKVD informants or agents. It remained under direct control of NKVD officials who stayed behind in the occupied regions. Apparently its connection with the Party underground was maintained only at the oblast level.[10] The network consisted of groups

[6] Fyodorov, p. 13. A list of the oblasts in which partisan secretaries were chosen may be found in a German intelligence report which is based on extensive partisan interrogations. (GFP Gr. 725, "Partisanen-Erfahrungsbericht," 22 January 1942, GMDS, HGeb 30910/37.) In practice, not all of the secretaries chosen could fulfill their assigned tasks; in the Ukraine west of the Dnepr and in most of Belorussia no oblast-wide organization could be formed during 1941.

[7] In addition to the partisans and the NKVD diversionist network described below, a considerable underground organization of Party agents existed in some areas. They were under the direction of the underground secretary and apparently carried on sabotage and forays, in addition to propaganda activities.

[8] Fyodorov, p. 13.

[9] According to his own account Fyodorov had fought in the Red Army during the Civil War, but had not entered the Party until 1927, after which he gradually rose in the trade union apparatus. He later became a member of the control commission in Chernigov Oblast, then second secretary of the oblast Party committee, and in 1938 —shortly after the major purges—first secretary. During the war he and his band were sent to re-establish Soviet authority in the Rovno and Volhynia Oblasts, an especially difficult assignment in view of the hostility of the population to the Soviet system. After the war he acted as first secretary in several oblasts. As noted below, the director of the underground in the Crimean ASSR (where organizational arrangements were somewhat different) had been chief of the cadre section of the Party, i.e., in charge of personnel problems which involved disciplinary matters.

[10] See Kozlov, p. 17; see also this book, Chap. V, Sect. I.

of three to seven persons each (including many women). It was designed primarily for sabotage and other disruptive tasks ordered by the Soviet authorities. The members continued their usual occupations as covers for their clandestine activities. For further protection, each group member was permitted to know only the leader of his group, who, in turn, knew only his group members and his chief at the next higher level.

There was no organizational connection between the diversionist network and the partisan movement, because the former was specifically required to avoid risking discovery by contact with elements overtly hostile to the Germans, such as the partisans. In practice, however, many diversionist group members did find it necessary to depend on the partisan bands for assistance and refuge. [See Chap. V, Sect. I.]

A second activity of the NKVD did have a direct bearing on the partisan movement. On 26 June 1941, Lavrentii Beria, People's Commissar of Internal Affairs (NKVD), ordered the NKVD rayon organizations to form home defense units known as "Destruction Battalions" (*Istrebitelnye Bataliony*). [See Chap. VII, Sect. I, B.] According to this order, the destruction battalions were to be of company size (100–200 men), and the rank and file largely comprised men too old, too young, or otherwise unfit for duty with the Red Army. At the same time, the officers and a large part of the enlisted men were NKVD officials or trusted Party members. The direction remained in the hands of the rayon or inter-rayon NKVD organization, though the Red Army cooperated by providing arms and possibly by furnishing training staffs in some instances.

It is probable that the destruction battalions had been planned considerably before the outbreak of war, at a time when the extent and rapidity of the German penetration of Soviet territory could not be foreseen. They were primarily defensive units, charged with guarding important installations to prevent sabotage or attacks by German parachutists. However, at least as early as July 1941, NKVD orders provided that the destruction battalions in areas near the front should be transformed into partisan detachments. In this transformation, the NKVD officials were to cooperate with the territorial Party organization, which, as indicated above, was formally assigned control over the partisan movement. Nevertheless, the NKVD was given the extremely important task of screening persons considered for membership in the partisan units. [See Chap. VIII, Sect. II, B, 2, c.] In practice, a rayon Party secretary was selected by the oblast Party committee to direct the organization of the partisan movement in his rayon. He was confirmed by the union republic central committee of the Party.[11] To assist in the work of organization and possibly to carry on other semi-military work, a "military section" of the rayon Party apparatus, which had been organized down to the rayon level before the war, was available. Throughout the period of partisan organization and development, how-

[11] For the RSFSR the confirming agency was the All-Union Central Committee.

ever, it is readily apparent that the NKVD played a most significant role.

The officers of the otryads,[12] as the newly formed partisan units were called, were, like those of the destruction battalions from which they were largely drawn, trusted adherents of the Soviet system. While a majority appear to have been Party or Government officials, about one-third were NKVD officers. The rank and file of the otryads were also reliable men; the less useful elements of the destruction battalions, including those either unwilling to face the dangers of partisan life or physically unfit for rigorous living conditions, were dismissed. A high proportion of the remaining partisans consisted of Komsomol members too young for military service.

3. The Otryad in Operation

Not all partisan otryads were formed from destruction battalions; in some instances the territorial Party organization formed otryads by direct recruitment of men considered desirable, without drawing on the home defense formations of the NKVD. In a number of the larger cities no destruction battalions were formed; instead similar home defense units served as the basis for partisan recruitment. [See n. 5.] A number of special methods were also employed in forming partisan otryads, corresponding usually to exceptional branches of the Party structure. During the first months of the war, however, the destruction battalions were apparently the major source of manpower for partisan detachments in the nonurban rayons throughout the occupied Soviet Union.

Once formed, the otryad withdrew to an inaccessible spot and established a concealed and fortified camp. Apparently the original plans envisaged the operation of one or more such otryads in each rayon, or at least the concentration of a few otryads from neighboring rayons in one well-protected hide-out.[13] In one case, a special "oblast otryad" was formed to act as a nucleus for the partisan movement and as a guard for its oblast headquarters.[14] It appears, however, that the initial plan provided for general direction of the partisan movement in oblasts not immediately adjacent to the army fronts by the underground Party secretary and his staff. This staff was not to join an otryad but was to remain in hiding.

Presumably the rayon otryad commander was to direct specific harassing operations, while the underground secretary was to receive and pass on general directives from the union republic committee on the Soviet side of the front. This is only speculation, however, for the general system of control over the territorial partisan movement never really operated. A

---

[12] "Otryad" can mean either "detachment" in a general sense, or (as for example in the Red Army) specifically, "company."

[13] Fyodorov, pp. 18, 19, 68; see also Sidor Artemovich Kovpak, *Ot Putivlya do Karpat* (Moscow: Gosudarstvennoye Izdatelstvo Detskoi Literatury Narkomprosa RSFSR, 1945), pp. 5, 9.

[14] Fyodorov, p. 22.

considerable number of rayon otryads withdrew as planned to their hide-outs and began operations against the German forces. In one case, at least, the underground oblast secretary visited the partisans in his region and issued directives, but he soon disappeared. In other cases, the contact with the designated underground secretary was never established, for the secretary was captured immediately by the Germans, or was swept out of his oblast in the general confused retreat of the Red Army. A lack of adequate radio equipment prevented most rayon otryads from establishing direct contact with the unoccupied areas of the Soviet Union. As a result, most otryads in areas distant from the battle fronts were unable to coordinate their operations with any over-all plan.

If the territorial system of organization had succeeded, the Germans would have been confronted with a network of small partisan detachments in every administrative subdivision of the occupied Soviet Union. Such bands, operating on their home territory, would have been extremely important not only because of the material damage they could have inflicted, but also because they were foci for political resistance to the occupier. The potential political importance of such a system undoubtedly helps explain the major roles accorded the Party and the NKVD in efforts to develop it. In practice, however, such a pervasive network of partisan bands could not be established. It is necessary, therefore, in order to assess the real value of the initial movement, to examine the ways in which the territorial formations were adapted to a different basis of partisan organization.

C. THE PARTISAN MOVEMENT
AND THE RED ARMY

It is clear from NKVD and Party directives that the territorial partisan organization was intended to operate in cooperation with the Red Army; such orders emphasized repeatedly that special attention should be given to the organization of partisans in areas near the fronts. At the same time, the Army authorities were ready to adapt the partisan bands organized by the Party territorial apparatus to their own military needs. The military council (soviet) of the Northwest Front[15] issued an order envisaging the formation of partisan units on a territorial basis: "It is desired that each administrative rayon should contain at least one partisan combat unit." At the same time, the order placed great emphasis on the military utilization of the partisans. It tended to regard the territorial system merely as a framework for the formation of units to be employed as army auxiliaries:

First and foremost, partisan detachments and diversionist groups must be established in the main operating areas, that is, the areas of greatest concen-

[15] One of three Soviet Fronts (army groups) operating in the first weeks of the war. Probably the others issued similar directives.

tration of the enemy. . . . The operations must be carried out in areas in which forests furnish cover for the units. Such an area can consist of up to two or three administrative rayons; operations are to be carried out only against the main lines of communication of the enemy. . . .—*Appendix, Document 2.*

For a brief time in June and July 1941, the task of utilizing the partisan movement for military purposes was assigned to the NKVD "OO" section of the Red Army, but after mid-July the job was assumed by the Political Administration sections of the army staffs.[16] In practice, the Political Administrations of different armies appear to have employed varying methods in utilizing the territorially formed partisan units. In one army on the West Front, a battalion commissar was assigned the task of liaison with partisan units in his area of military operations. The commissar admits in his memoirs that he had previously known nothing about partisan warfare, and that he was told by the chairman of the military council of the West Front that until shortly before his assignment no one in the Front command had taken partisan activity seriously. Now, however, the Army authorities felt that the partisans could assist militarily and were therefore prepared to furnish arms, advice, and cadres. The commissar held conferences with the rayon Party committee in the area in which his army was operating, presenting the army position to the Party secretary, the commander of the rayon military section, the representatives of the village soviets, and the plenipotentiary of the NKVD.[17] The army commissar was not impressed by the ability of his new associates, however, and practical cooperation appears to have been minimal. Even if the basis for joint action had been more promising, it is probable that the rapid retreat of the armies from this area would have rendered extensive cooperation with the territorial partisans impossible.

Farther to the north and to the south, however, the territorial units were utilized to a greater extent by the Red Army. The Political Administrations of army formations on the Northwest Front actively cooperated with the rayon Party apparatuses, and even sent officers to assist in organizing partisan detachments. Probably some of these detachments remained in the rayons in which they were formed, but others, after they had been recruited by the Party committees, were transferred to the Red Army for training and equipment. After completing their training, the

[16] The Political Administration was charged with propaganda and indoctrination within the Red Army. The existence of a brief period of NKVD control is asserted by Zhigunov, NKVD officer with an army staff (interrogation of 24 April 1942). Zhigunov also reported the transfer to Political Administration supervision, a change which is confirmed by the fact that as early as 13 July 1941 the Administration of Political Propaganda of the Northwest Front submitted a report on the organization of partisan units to General Lev Mekhlis, head of the Main Administration of Political Propaganda of the Red Army. [See Appendix, Document 4.]

[17] V. Andreyev, *Narodnaya voina (zapiski partizana)* (Moscow: Gosudarstvennoye Izdatelstvo Khudozhestvennoi Literatury, 1952), p. 49.

units were placed under the operational control of the staff of the North-west Front, which used them for scouting in the rear of the Germans.

A similar pattern evolved in the northern section of the West Front—but with some interesting variations. In Smolensk Oblast, the "Western Railways Administration" joined the oblast Party committee in the formation of a partisan detachment from among the railroad workers. [See n. 5, concerning the status of party organization in such transportation enterprises.] Apparently the "OO" (NKVD) section of the railways administration was actually assigned the organizational task. After it was formed, the otryad was trained, presumably under army direction, and was turned over to the military command for operational purposes. As the commissar of the unit, a man chosen by the NKVD and the Party organization, stated shortly after the otryad had completed its training, an "army commissar and a high staff officer" gave the following instructions:

1. The detachment is to operate in the general direction of Gusin.
2. The tasks of the detachment are destruction and sabotage in the rear of the German forces.
3. Liaison is to be with the staff of the central [part of the ?] West Front.
   a. The liaison point is to be in the village of Kovshi.
   b. Contact is to take place on the 25th of each month.
   c. The password is "Haven't you seen any horses here?"; the countersign is "The horses have left Kovshi."

This detachment was undoubtedly considered to be of special value to the Red Army in attacking German communications, since it was composed of technically experienced men. Its importance and the close control exercised by the army command are indicated by the fact that a Red Army officer was detailed to guide the unit through the front lines and that it was then placed under the supervision of an army commissar assigned to direct disruptive activities in the enemy occupied area. In a similar fashion, the South Front employed territorially formed partisan units to establish a center for disruptive activities in the Nikopol area.

The partisan units just described, while trained and directed by the Red Army, were used in the administrative divisions from which they were recruited. A somewhat different system was followed in Leningrad, which was besieged, but never occupied. There units of up to regimental size were formed by the Party organizations in the factories and were provided with Party officials as commissars and with men of military background as leaders. They were turned over to the Northwest Front command for training, and when they were sufficiently prepared were sent through the enemy lines by the Front command. Once in occupied territory, the large formations were broken up into battalions of 100–200 men each (apparently this size, corresponding to that of the rayon otryad, was considered most efficient for operational purposes), and carried on activities under the control of the Front command.[18] There were also a number of partisan detachments led by officers who had been selected by the Party organizations in large unoccupied urban centers such as Moscow; they were trained by the Red Army and were then used to carry out partisan-type missions of strategic significance. Party cadres from the unoccupied regions played a more important role in organizing local units in German-occupied territory; they will be discussed below.

Not all the men sent across the lines by the Red Army were ordered to act as partisans. Many parachutists were hastily recruited and trained, then dropped in an indiscriminate fashion, evidently with the hope that some would succeed in sabotaging German installations. Other parachute and infiltration units were composed of regular Red Army personnel, including many staff officers, and were sent on specific commando missions such as the destruction of enemy communications and the collection of information. These elements were of some importance in the partisan movement since they frequently found it necessary to join partisan bands when they could not make their way back to the Soviet lines. During 1941, however, they were of little significance.

D. THE FATE OF THE TERRITORIAL PARTISAN ORGANIZATION

During 1941 the territorial detachments were of minor importance everywhere even when, as noted above, they could be used by the Red Army for specific military missions. As the Germans established firm control over their newly won sections of the huge areas of the USSR, a large number of rayon bands vanished. Many seem to have dissolved of their own accord to escape the threat of physical destruction. Consequently, during the first four months of the war, the number of territorially organized partisans seems to have declined steadily. Later, more favorable conditions probably enabled a number of the remaining rayon Party organizers to re-form their partisan groups and allowed the existing groups to recruit new members. By that time, however, the territorial detachments in most areas were far outdistanced by detachments formed through the efforts of outside organizers, as described below. Before turning to this phase of partisan organization, however, it is necessary to consider the important regional differences in the outcome of the territorial system.

1. The Northern Regions

While there were some rayon detachments in the northern regions—corresponding roughly to the area north of the Brest-Chernigov-Kursk line—they were of little relative importance after 1941 because of the

[18] A very interesting personal account of the way in which a member of the Leningrad Factory Air Defense organization (apparently similar to the destruction battalion) was recruited for a partisan unit is contained in OKH/GenStdH/GenQu/Abt. K., Verw., "Tagebuch eines Partisanen," 31 October 1941 (GMDS, H 17/218).

enormous influx of other elements into the partisan movement. Territorial detachments which continued to operate in their own rayons were most important in areas of Belorussia remote from the front. In other sections the rayon otryads frequently survived but operated in areas other than those in which they had been formed.

In most areas some vestige of the territorial system survived. In the northern Ukraine the names of the rayons were kept as detachment designations even after the original personnel had largely been replaced. In most areas, the surviving members of the territorial bands were important in providing a nucleus of trusted Party and NKVD functionaries in the expanded partisan movement. These men played a significant part in maintaining the allegiance of the partisans to the Communist system and could also be used to assist in re-establishing Party control over the civilian population in the areas where the partisans operated. This was the case in Chernigov Oblast, where Aleksei Fyodorov headed territorial partisan bands which became the nucleus for a major partisan group. For a time Fyodorov and his lieutenants from the oblast apparatus directed underground Party activity among the civilian population in addition to acting as partisan officers. However, the partisans were unable to remain within the oblast, where the terrain is not favorable enough to permit protracted evasion of superior forces. By early 1943 the top Soviet authorities were also anxious to transfer most of the large Ukrainian partisan bands to the area west of the Dnepr. Consequently, in the spring of 1943, Fyodorov's group was transferred to the western oblasts of the Ukraine; there he was able to play an important part in the political as well as the military restoration of Soviet authority in this area, which, since it had not come under Soviet rule until 1939, was a difficult yet important region to bring under Communist influence.

In many areas, however, the territorial Party officials did not become leaders of partisan bands. Especially in areas where Red Army influence was great, the Party territorial apparatus relinquished control of the operations of the partisan units and confined itself to political indoctrination, stimulation of morale, and cooperation in disciplinary measures. Its functions were similar to those performed by the territorial Party organizations for Red Army units within their areas, although in most cases the rudimentary development of political control and indoctrination in the partisan bands gave the territorial Party organization a somewhat wider scope.

2. The Steppe

The territorial partisan detachments in the occupied regions of the south were less fortunate than those in the northern regions. Since by far the larger part of the south consists of open steppes, the system of rayon otryads operating in close proximity to their home districts soon proved impractical. The otryad had to seek any available shelter, even though it might be scores or hundreds of miles away from its original rayon. At the same time, the unfavorable terrain, which hindered the implementation of the territorial organization plan, prevented the development of a mass partisan movement. On the open plains isolated Red Army soldiers, who in the north could have hidden in the woods or swamps until they could join partisan bands, were quickly rounded up by the Germans. Disgruntled peasants had little incentive to flee their villages, for no secure shelter was available. As a result, the territorial detachments remained relatively more important in this area even though in absolute numbers they remained insignificant.

Even in the first weeks of the war little partisan activity was apparent in the Ukrainian steppes west of the Dnepr. The advancing German forces encountered some bands in the woods and marshes along the rivers. Apparently these were similar to the band at Nikopol [see Chap. XI], but were much smaller and possibly were under Party rather than Army direction. Only scant information is available on the principal center of partisan operations west of the Dnepr, in the "Black Forest" near Cherkassy. This wood was evidently a gathering point for partisans from a considerable area of the central Ukraine; apparently the band was liquidated by early 1942, but nothing is known of its organization. Smaller bands east of the Dnepr in the scattered forest of Kiev and Poltava Oblasts were evidently under the control of the underground Party and NKVD structures. [See Appendix, Document 5.] They also vanished by early 1942, with the members possibly seeking refuge in the deeper woods to the north. Small groups in the forests of Kharkov Oblast were liquidated by Ukrainian auxiliaries of the Germans in late 1942. A succession of small bands appeared in the Donbas, but they were apparently sent in by the Red Army.

Although the territorial partisan organization in the steppes of the Ukraine appears to have been completely destroyed by early 1942, disruptive activities continued to be carried out by underground groups, especially in the cities. The underground Party committee in Kiev was apparently even able to direct the activities of one partisan band in the forested northern edge of the oblast. The underground groups carried out sabotage, and probably served as auxiliaries to spies sent in from the unoccupied USSR. Their most important function, however, was to impress the population with the omnipresent shadow of Soviet control. Although these activities lie outside the scope of this study, it is worth noting that by performing them the undergrounds filled part of the role played by the partisans farther north.

3. The Crimea

Probably utilizing the experience of their counterparts farther north, the Party and NKVD apparatuses of the Crimea were able to retain the territorial framework for recruitment and organization of otryads, yet to adapt it to the special geographic conditions of the peninsula. In order to utilize the most favorable terrain, the otryads were transferred sometimes over very considerable distances; the practice of maintaining the otryad for operations in or near the district where it was formed was abandoned at the outset. Moreover, a carefully planned system of command, the Staff of the Crimean Partisan Movement, combining over-all direction with flexibility of operation, was present from the start; the unworkable attempt at control by an underground oblast committee physically separate from the partisan forces was abandoned entirely. In addition, the system of organization by "rayons" (a special term referring to a partisan command superior to the otryad but subordinate to the staff) maintained some vestige of connection with the territorial administrative divisions, while permitting sufficient flexibility to enable the incorporation of large numbers of former military and naval personnel in both officer and rank-and-file positions.

The Crimean partisan movement remained an effective force in spite of severe handicaps until 1944. In the last months of its existence, possibly as part of a standardization effort, the territorial organization appears to have been altered somewhat to conform more closely to the quasi-military forms prevalent elsewhere. That the territorial form was able to persist so long and that it apparently enjoyed the sanction of higher authorities indicates that this type of organization cannot be dismissed either as universally unviable or as definitely rejected by the Soviet regime. As will be shown, the introduction of this form of organization in a new area of occupation as late as the summer of 1942 furnishes additional support for the belief that the Soviet authorities were reluctant to abandon it.

4. The North Caucasus

The German armies first entered the North Caucasus region in the summer of 1942, at a time when the territorial partisan organization in most occupied areas of the Soviet Union had been reduced to a subsidiary branch of the total movement. Consequently it is of interest that the partisan organization in the Caucasus region followed the familiar territorial pattern. Destruction battalions were organized by the NKVD in many of the rayons of Rostov Oblast, Krasnodar and Stavropol Krais, and the Kabardino-Balkhar SSR, and were transformed into partisan units under the direction of the Party and NKVD apparatuses. Unlike most of the earlier rayon partisan otryads, however, most of these groups made no effort to operate in the immediate vicinity of their home territory, but evacuated at once to the favorable terrain of the Caucasus Mountains and their foothills. Each otryad retained its identity and usually established a separate camp, but several otryads were placed under the command of a "kust."[19] There was no partisan operative headquarters above the kust. Operational directives were apparently given by the army headquarters in whose general area the kust worked, while over-all control remained in the hands of either the krai or oblast Party organization, or the partisan staffs for the territorial divisions. Apparently there was also some remote subordination to the staff of the "Partisan Movement of the South."

In numbers and effectiveness the Caucasus partisans formed a very insignificant part of the entire partisan movement. Most of the bands disappeared after the German retreat to the Kuban bridgehead in the winter of 1942–43, but a few remained operative in that region until the Germans evacuated in the autumn of 1943. Apparently the chain of command of these small groups remained predominantly in the hands of the Party; an intermediary kust between the otryad and the Party committee existed for a time. Later the staff of the "Partisan Movement of the South" sent in a single otryad to reorganize the depleted partisan force in this area.

The persistence of the territorial framework of partisan organization in the Crimea and its extension to the Caucasus some time after major changes had been made in the partisan structure farther north suggest that the Soviet authorities considered this system desirable. The most likely reason was apparently its usefulness in integrating the partisan movement into the Party and NKVD political control mechanism. Quite probably the increasing control over the partisan movement exerted by the Red Army, which assumed direction of many of the surviving territorial detachments during the winter 1941–42, caused some misgivings among Soviet leaders, who possibly feared an overextension of the Army's prestige and power. In this respect the later developments of the territorial partisan movement form only one part of the broader picture of the transformation of the partisan movement and the changes introduced to reinforce Party influence.

[19] A headquarters corresponding apparently to the brigade or "unification" in the north, and the "rayon" in the Crimea. In the Caucasus, too, the term "unification" was occasionally used to describe the headquarters.

§III. Expansion and Reorganization of the Partisan Movement, 1942–44

A. THE REVIVAL OF THE PARTISAN MOVEMENT, EARLY 1942

It has already been noted that the original Soviet intention to develop a network of resistance groups which would deny the Germans control of the areas evacuated by the Red Army was not realized. Nevertheless, a combination of circumstances, most of them unanticipated by the Soviet regime, made possible a revival of the partisan movement during the winter of 1941–42, though on lines considerably different from those originally planned.

One of these circumstances was the scale of the Soviet defeats. The Soviet authorities had not, of course, anticipated the great encirclement battles, or *Kesselschlachten,* which resulted in cutting off several million soldiers from the body of the Red Army forces. Over two million of these men were soon rounded up by the Germans and consigned to prisoner-of-war camps. Such was the fate of the vast majority of the troops trapped in the Uman pocket on the Ukrainian steppe west of the Dnepr and of most of those cut off in the Poltava steppe east of Kiev. In the forest and swamp area of German Army Groups Center and North, however, many eluded capture. This was true of numerous isolated survivors of the two pockets near Bryansk and of the other five encirclement battles on the road to Moscow—Grodno, Minsk, Smolensk, Roslavl, and Vyazma. Some of the soldiers who escaped from the battlefields were members of small units which had become separated from their higher commands but still remained under the control of their own officers. In other cases, Red Army or NKVD officers who escaped alone or with a few followers rallied stragglers, whom they induced to become part of an *ad hoc* military formation—either through their authority as representatives of the Soviet regime or through force of personality. These two types of groups frequently endeavored to make their way to the main battle front in order to rejoin the Red Army, but they were often unsuccessful because of the rapid retreat of the Soviet forces. Many then disintegrated although others remained intact in remote areas, generally inactive and primarily concerned with their own preservation, yet unready to submit to German rule. There were also hundreds of thousands of Red Army men and officers who had lost contact with any sort of regular authority and frequently made their way about in small groups for self-protection. In addition, thousands of Red Army men who had been cut off behind the German lines made their way home, where they attempted to merge with the civilian population, or simply lingered in an out-of-the-way village, sheltered perhaps by lonely peasant women.

Several hundred thousand ex-soldiers living illegally and without supervision in the occupied areas would have made it difficult for an occupier to maintain order under any circumstances, and the policies pursued by the Germans greatly increased the danger. [For details of German treatment of population and partisans, see Chap. III, Sect. I, A, 1–4.] For this potential danger to become a real threat to the Germans it was necessary that the masses of men available for partisan activities be organized by leaders determined to conduct systematic attacks against the occupation forces. One source of leadership was the surviving territorial otryad, which was able to take advantage of this situation by swelling its ranks with former Red Army men; at the same time numerous small underground groups of Party officials who until this time had been unable to organize real partisan bands could now form detachments from the ex-soldiers. More important, probably, were the line officers, commissars, and NKVD officers to be found among the isolated troops. The latter two groups, at least, knew that German policy called for their execution upon capture; consequently they had no choice but continued evasion or resistance. As noted above, officers had formed bands of cut-off Red Army men from the beginning, but there often was a tendency among such groups merely to stay alive when they could not cross the front to rejoin the main Soviet forces. At first many of the rank and file tended to melt away, but, when it became clear that surrender to the Germans or endeavors at individual evasion involved even greater risks than partisan activity, they more readily submitted to the authority of the officers.

In the long run the isolated Red Army and NKVD officers were to become a key element in the revival of the partisan movement. In spite of the fact, however, that the former Red Army rank and file rapidly developed a willingness to participate in anti-German activities, the operations which could be initiated and directed by individuals or small groups of officers who had for months been out of contact with the Soviet authorities were limited. In order for them to become part of an effective partisan force it was necessary to have organizers provided with definite instructions for the pursuance of resistance activities and equipped with means for maintaining contact with the unoccupied areas of the Soviet Union. At the same time, the presence of such organizers, determined to form a partisan movement regardless of the cost to the population of the occupied areas and endowed with the prestige of being direct representatives of the Soviet regime, was essential in many areas in order to induce the former Red Army personnel to fight the Germans, even after a generally negative attitude toward the latter had developed.

There is little doubt that the higher levels of the Soviet regime became aware of the situation in the occupied areas by the fall of 1941 and that they made plans to take advantage of it. In numerous areas of the unoccupied USSR, special training camps for partisans who were to be sent into the occupied areas by parachute had been set up as early as August 1941. Personnel assigned to these camps fell into several categories. At first most of those intended as officers or partisan organizers were apparently selected by Party organizations from among trusted members, including a number of fairly high officials. Party apparatuses in large urban centers of the RSFSR, especially the huge organization in Moscow, were particularly useful for recruiting.[20] Later in the fall, the large mass of Party and NKVD functionaries who had fled or had been evacuated from the occupied regions furnished an additional important source of recruits. Evidently these men were assigned to partisan warfare in part because of contacts in their former areas of activity, and in part to expiate their "sin" of flight before the enemy. Similarly, in the fall a large number of the subordinate partisan trainees were chosen from among Red Army soldiers who had become separated from their units but who were still on the Soviet side of the front, while during the summer most of the rank and file were evidently drawn from men already inducted into the Red Army. [See Chap. VII, Sect. II and Sect. IV, B; Chap. VIII, Sect. II, B, 1 and 2; Chap. IX, Sect. III.]

While it may be presumed that the selected Party personnel were given intensive briefing by Party officials on the political and military implications of their new assignment, the technical training was conducted by the Red Army and the NKVD. It lasted about two weeks only and consisted of very limited instruction in parachuting and the use of demolition materials. However, special effort appears to have been made to recruit radio operators and other enlisted men familiar with special techniques needed by the groups, so that extensive training was not imperative in all fields.[21]

After training, the recruits were divided into small groups of less than platoon size led by a commander, a commissar, possibly other officers, and including at least one radio operator and other specialists. The officers were assigned ordinary Red Army ranks. From the training camps the groups so formed were sent to a Red Army headquarters—apparently a Front headquarters—were given specific instructions, and were assigned an area of operation into which they were dropped by parachute.[22]

Upon reaching these areas, the small parachutist groups first endeavored to contact persons loyal to the Soviet system whose names had been fur-

[20] L. Tsanava, *Vsenarodnaya partizanskaya voina v belorussii protiv fashistskikh zakhvatchikov* (Minsk: Gosizdat BSSR, 1949, Vol. I; 1951, Vol. II), II., 30; G. Linkov, *Voina v tylu vraga* (Moscow: Gosudarstvennoye Izdatelstvo Khudozhestvennoi Literatury, 1951), pp. 14–17.

[21] Linkov, p. 11.

[22] *Ibid.*, pp. 19, 30, 74.

nished by the Soviet authorities before the group's flight into occupied territory. Often these persons were members of the Party underground, and, of course, many of them had disappeared during the weeks following the Soviet evacuation from their districts. Even more often, apparently, they were minor Soviet officials or Party members who had exhibited no great desire to run the risks of resistance activity, but could be persuaded nonetheless to cooperate with the parachute teams. To secure such cooperation, the teams were given authority over all Soviet and Party organizations, including whatever partisans might exist, in their area of operations.[23] They also bore the prestige of direct representatives of the central authorities, especially of the Red Army command. Equally important, probably, they were usually in direct contact with the latter by radio.[24]

The parachute teams set about reorganizing the Soviet sympathizers into a network of agents and using others as recruiters or cadres for partisan detachments. Most of the partisans, however, were drawn from the cutoff Red Army personnel, to whom the authority of the parachutists as Red Army officers representing a high headquarters was especially important. For several months, however, until the beginning of winter, the parachutist teams were concerned primarily with contacting local supporters and groups of Red Army men and officers in the woods, rather than with developing a large-scale partisan movement. During December the severe German reverses before Moscow produced a profound effect on the opinion of the great majority of the population of the occupied territories. [See Chap. IV, Sect. VII, A.]

Almost simultaneously, the tactical conditions for large-scale partisan operations improved greatly. The Germans denuded the rear areas of troops in order to bolster their collapsing front. This left their lines of communication vulnerable at the very time when the uninterrupted flow of supplies to the front was most vital. At the same time, the partisans could be reinforced by the Red Army on a large scale through gaps which developed in the German lines. One principal gap east of Vitebsk—the so-called Vitebsk Corridor—served as the gateway for thousands of partisans, many of whom were recruited from among evacuees of that area. The Kirov gap farther south furnished large numbers of partisans for the region between Bryansk and Vyazma. By using these gaps, it was possible to send in not only organizers and technicians but also whole units of partisans who could reinforce those recruited within the occupied territory.[25] In addition, supplies and reinforcements were sent through the front in places where difficult terrain and troop shortages made it impossible for the Germans to maintain a continuous line.

[23] *Ibid.*, pp. 31, 69, 109.
[24] *Ibid.*, p. 73.
[25] Tsanava II, p. 28; see also this book, Chap. VIII, Sect. II, A, 2.

Aided by the increased Soviet prestige after the winter victories, the various groups of organizers were able to transform a considerable proportion of the former Red Army men plus recruits, especially adolescents who had never been in the Army, into a partisan movement of substantial size. At the same time, it must be stressed that a very large proportion of men falling into these categories never joined the partisans and many actively collaborated with the Germans. The patterns followed in various areas differed considerably, however. In Leningrad Oblast numerous Party-organized partisan detachments were sent through the front line from early autumn on [see Sect. II, above]; no major encirclements had taken place in this area, and apparently most of the other recruits for the partisan movement in the winter of 1941–42 came from local village inhabitants. As indicated, partisan organizers and detachments sent through the gaps in the front lines were especially important in the part of Orel Oblast north of Bryansk, in Smolensk Oblast, and in Vitebsk Oblast. In the southern part of Orel Oblast and the adjoining districts of the Ukraine, on the other hand, surviving territorial Party officials and Red Army and NKVD officers cut off in the encirclements played the major role in organizing the partisan movement. [See subsection F, below.] The parachute teams were relatively most important in the south-central areas of Belorussia, inaccessible to the Soviet side by land, where the territorial partisan organization had been severely crippled.

While in area this region comprised only a small part of the occupied territories, its central location and favorable terrain made it a major factor in the later development of partisan activity. Consequently it is reasonable to assume that the use of parachute teams in this region exerted an influence out of proportion to the number of men included in them, or the area to which they were assigned. [See subsections E and H, 2, below.]

B. THE DEVELOPMENT OF THE PARTISAN BAND

Before discussing the repercussions of the rapid growth of the partisan movement during the winter of 1941–42 on the higher levels of control, it is necessary to describe the development of the basic unit of partisan warfare; its organization exerted great influence on the future conduct of partisan operations. Necessary as such a generalized picture is, however, it is likely to be misleading unless one remembers that from the beginning to the end of this period (1942–44) hundreds of bands existed and that no two were exactly alike. Hence it must be stressed that variety, not uniformity, was the characteristic of the partisan movement, and the broad tendencies of size, organization, and command described in this section do not represent a uniform pattern but offer merely generalizations derived from the study of numerous examples.[26]

[26] The generalized description of the growth of the partisan band is based on a

The various ways in which partisan detachments originated have been outlined above. By the winter of 1941–42, when they were actually ready to begin operating as a partisan band, however, most detachments, whatever their origin, were of somewhat similar size (20-200 men) and organization.[27] The key personalities were the commander and the commissar. While the commander, who more frequently than not had been chosen because of his special military training or prestige in the area where the group was organized, was nominally the supreme authority, sometimes the commissar was the real director of the unit. [For an example, see Chap. VIII, Sect. II, B, 1.] The background of these men and of whatever other officers were included in the group varied according to the band's origin. They could be territorial Party or NKVD officials, Red Army line or staff officers, Red Army commissars, officers of NKVD sections of the Army, and in a very few cases persons from minor positions such as managers of small industrial establishments or kolkhoz officials. Whatever their origin, their importance can scarcely be exaggerated. It was they who made the decision to organize resistance to the Germans at a time when the rapid Soviet retreat made such activity extremely dubious. These former members of the Soviet hierarchy based their decision either on loyalty to the Soviet regime or on fear of falling into German hands. If they were not parachutists, frequently they had been hidden by sympathizers or had lived in small fugitive groups in the woods for months before they could organize their bands. The parachutist leaders achieved quicker results, but were exposed to equal perils in areas with which they often were not familiar. As much through force of personality as through rank, the partisan leaders whipped their units together and controlled them with great firmness, and when necessary with violent methods.[28]

---

large number of sources, including in particular the memoirs by Tsanava, Andreyev, Linkov, Fyodorov, Kovpak; as well as Dmitrii Medvedev, *Silnye dukhom* (Moscow: Voennoye Izdatelstvo Voennogo Ministerstva Soyuza SSR, 1951); Anatolii Shyyan, *Partyzanskyi krai* (Kiev: Ukrainske Derzhavne Vydavnystvo, 1946); and P. Vershigora, *Lyudi s chistoi sovestyu* (Moscow: Sovetskii Pisatel, 1951). These discuss the growth and formation of numerous individual bands. For additional descriptions of the development of such bands, see Chap. VIII, Sect. II, A, I; Chap. IX, Sect. III.

[27] This statement as well as the following description of the typical development of the partisan band applies to most of the groups in the major areas of partisan concentration throughout the greater part of Belorussia and the Bryansk forest, and to many bands in Smolensk, Kalinin, and Leningrad Oblasts. Conditions differed considerably in areas where the territorial framework of Party organization was dominant from the beginning (Crimea and North Caucasus; see this chapter, Sect. II, D) and in areas where military control and organization were especially significant (the areas east of Smolensk and parts of the northern Bryansk forest; see this chapter, Sect. III, F).

[28] Postwar Soviet partisan accounts sometimes assert that the surviving territorial Party organizations controlled the partisan bands during this period, either as underground directing centers or as staffs actually present with the bands. Available contemporary evidence and close analysis of the Soviet memoirs themselves, however,

The subordinate partisan commanders had origins similar to those of commander and commissar, though they were drawn as a rule from somewhat lower levels of the Soviet hierarchy and included, for example, a large number of Komsomol officials, kolkhoz chairmen, and minor Party and Soviet officials. Frequently they lacked the determination as well as the organizing ability and technical qualifications of the top leaders of the bands. Many were either weeded out as the partisan movement grew or remained in comparatively insignificant posts, although a few showed unusual capacity for the special activities of partisan warfare and advanced rapidly. During the early stage these men in many cases exerted considerable personal influence over the members of their units, who frequently were drawn from one small community or had developed feelings of comradeship while they were hiding out in the woods before entering the partisan band.

In the next stage of development, during the winter and early spring of 1942, the average band increased enormously. It was natural that the bands which were led by the most successful, capable, and forceful officers, or by officers who had been given special authority by the Soviet regime, tended to expand most rapidly. In some cases—especially after the spring of 1942—such units sprang from insignificance into formations of 1,000 or more men within a few weeks. In such cases, the new, enormously expanded otryad was soon redesignated a "brigade" and was divided into a number of subordinate otryads. Like the brigades described below, which developed in a more complicated manner, usually one of these otryads was considerably larger than the others and more closely associated with the brigade commander. Some partisan commanders not only increased the size of their own otryads, however, but frequently brought other otryads under their leadership. The resulting new formation was designated in various ways. In its early stage, it was frequently called a *soyedineniye*, i.e., a "unification" or "complex," but for the sake of convenience it may be referred to here as a brigade. The brigade did not always act as a unit. Many operations continued to be carried out by individual otryads which

----

indicate that at least during the winter of 1941–42 the few surviving underground Party committees led too precarious an existence to act as effective directors of the partisan movement. On the other hand, in cases where the committees permanently joined partisan bands, they were usually, if not invariably, subject to the control of the commander and the commissar in all operational matters, although they (like the *ad hoc* Party organizations soon formed in most other partisan bands) were given such functions as political indoctrination and assistance in maintaining morale and discipline. While the territorial Party organization as such declined in influence, in a number of cases individual members held positions of extreme importance in the partisan bands; several were even commanders or commissars. Consequently, it would be incorrect to minimize the importance of the territorial Party organization as an element contributing to the development of the partisan movement. (See Fyodorov, pp. 192, 194, 319; Tsanava I, 109; II, 331; Andreyev, pp. 181, 208; Linkov, pp. 305, 378.)

received only general direction from the brigade commander. On the other hand, in defense against German attacks, except in hopeless situations when the band broke up into very small groups and sought safety in unorganized flight, its parts tended to operate together. It also generally operated as a unit in carrying out attacks on railroads. Some of these attacks required only a few men for the actual demolition, although sizable forces were needed to hold off the German forces guarding the road. A more important reason for maintaining bands of considerable size was to have enough men available under one command for rotating groups to carry out sustained attacks on considerable sections of a railroad. Such operations became increasingly important as time went on.

By late summer 1942 there were very few areas in which bands of less than 350 men predominated. A few such bands, for the most part engaged in carrying out specialized tasks, were generally present in most areas. Other bands in the process of being formed or after being mauled by German forces frequently fell below 350 men, although the depleted brigade usually regained at least this number after a short time. If it failed to reach its old strength, it usually disappeared or joined a larger unit.

On the other hand, very few bands exceeded 2,000 men for any length of time. The upper limit occurred partly because, in the summer of 1942 when most bands had reached the level of 350–2,000 men, heavy German attacks against the partisans caused the over-all strength to stabilize, and as a result it became increasingly difficult for individual bands to expand. About the same time the institution of higher control centers for the partisan movement on the German side of the lines tended to freeze the bands at the size already reached.

In a unit much above 2,000 men it would have been impossible for the commander and his associates to be personally familiar with the capacities of each subunit, and to be well acquainted with each of their subordinate officers. Such personal knowledge and contact were essential to the flexibility of command necessary under partisan warfare conditions, and were especially important because the rudimentary military training of the partisans ill prepared them for carrying out elaborate, long-range directives. Personal contact was also of great value in maintaining morale and discipline. The Soviet regime was protected against the potential danger of insurrection arising from overly strong allegiance to a band leader because no single band was strong enough to carry out a dangerous revolt. At the same time, a group of over 350 men was likely to contain sufficiently heterogeneous elements for the development of a cliquish spirit of passive resistance to Soviet orders to be met by opposition, or at least to be reported to higher authorities.

A most important reason for limiting the number of bands, and thus keeping the individual bands fairly large, was the scarcity of capable commanders and commissars. It was possible to find such leaders for several hundred brigades averaging 800 men each, but it would have been difficult to locate enough to lead thousands of bands averaging 100 men each. From the prestige viewpoint, too, the larger band was more effective. Whether it was more efficient operationally is much more difficult to decide. As we have noted above, some operations required groups of brigade size, but these were comparatively rare. Defensively, the additional strength was useful, although it was probably more difficut for individual partisans to escape from a defeat which involved an entire brigade than to melt away from an encounter involving only a few score men. In general, the principal advantage of the brigade level of 350–2,000 men seems to have been the fact that it represented the maximum number of partisans who could be controlled effectively by one command.

Not only was the size of the bands important, but also their mobility. At first most of them operated within very small areas. This was of course especially true of the territorial otryad, which had been formed in a single rayon and was intended to operate close to it, but it was also true to a limited extent of many of the bands composed of ex-Red Army men, who for months stayed in a limited region. It has already been noted that the limitation of the partisan band to a small area was evidently a major feature of the original plan of partisan organization. Within the framework of that plan, it was not illogical. However, when the territorial system as a whole disintegrated in the greater part of the occupied section, it was no longer desirable for the few remaining territorial otryads and the new otryads being formed on other bases to remain within their original area. In many regions it was impossible, since open terrain could be combed by the German security forces without great difficulty. Even when a band was able to maintain itself in one locality, however, this soon proved undesirable. The Communist leadership evidently thought that the familiarity of the territorial partisans with their areas would be a great advantage; in practice even some of the specially selected Party and NKVD men in these groups were inclined to maintain themselves in comfortable and relatively permanent hide-outs without attracting German attention. Many leaders of the partisan movement thus found that it was desirable to keep their bands moving about frequently, though often within a small district, in order to avoid vegetation through inactivity. A second factor was equally important in persuading the officers to transfer the bands out of their home areas. While the Party and NKVD officers often had no strong personal attachments in the areas where they had served, the rank-and-file members frequently had families there who would suffer at the hands of the Germans, either as special victims of retaliation or as objects of the general repressive measures carried out by the Germans in areas where partisans operated. Consequently, most partisan bands were moved to regions at least a number of miles from their point of origin.

As the partisan band increased in numbers and moved from its territorial base, its organization tended to become more military. The individual otryads were subdivided into platoons of roughly equal strength. More important, a regular headquarters detachment was set up, including intelligence, "OO" (NKVD), and quartermaster sections. Many otryads had had "chiefs of staff" from the beginning, but in the brigade this post was much more important. Frequently the brigade chief of staff was a regular Red Army officer, who had joined the partisans after being cut off from the Soviet force, or had been sent in from Soviet-held territory to assume the function of military specialist. In addition to planning military operations, the chief of staff evidently often had considerable influence on the organization of the band, which he tended to mold along army lines. As will be described below, these changes were closely connected with the establishment within the occupied territory of a permanent higher echelon of command over the partisan bands in various regions.

While these changes, which began as early as the spring, but became general only in the summer or autumn of 1942 after the bands had reached their full strength, tended to transform the partisan unit into something resembling a regular military formation, there were many extremely important ways in which the bands' irregular origin and development revealed themselves. The brigades differed widely in size, equipment, and internal organization, as did their component units, the otryads. While a headquarters detachment and a regular staff were established, the commander continued in many cases to direct not only the brigade as such, but also the otryad within it which had originated as his personal band. Moreover, this otryad was usually far larger than any other in the brigade (frequently as large as all the others put together), and often possessed better equipment. It is obvious that this superiority arose from the intimate connection of the commander and the commissar with the larger otryad, and, conversely, that its allegiance to them as individuals tended to strengthen their position within the brigade as a whole.

The highly generalized plan of organization of a partisan band at the end of 1942 [Fig. 1] may illustrate some of the factors described above, though it is essential to recognize that no such standardized pattern was ever developed for any large proportion of partisan units.

C. THE CENTRAL STAFF

The rapid growth and increasing activity of the partisan bands during the winter of 1941–42 not only led to a reorganization of the individual band, but to a far-reaching transformation of the superior command structure. On 30 May 1942 a central agency for the over-all direction of the partisan bands was created in Moscow in the form of the "Central

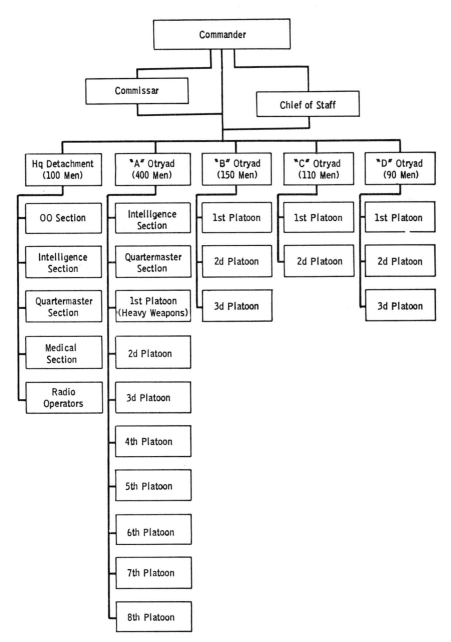

Figure 1.—Generalized structure of the partisan brigade.

Staff of the Partisan Movement."[29] Shortly afterwards, similar staffs were set up on the union republic or Army Front level to serve as focal points of Soviet control over the bands in a large area of operations. [For a discussion of the union republic and Front Staffs, see below, Sect. III, D.] Before proceeding to an examination of the functions and organization of these staffs it is necessary to discuss briefly the agencies which had directed the partisans during the winter of 1941–42, and the problems of control which prompted the introduction of an entirely new top command structure.

By the beginning of 1942 the framework of control by territorial Party organizations had disintegrated, and the influence of the Red Army had increased greatly. As noted above, the various Red Army commands took over a large proportion of the territorially formed partisan otryads. At the same time, the teams of parachutists, while frequently led by men recruited by the Party, had been turned over to the Red Army for assignment and operational employment as partisan organizers. The influence of the leaders of such teams arose in considerable measure from their newly acquired status as Red Army officers. Moreover, the increasing numbers of isolated Red Army officers who assumed command positions in the bands tended to identify themselves with the Red Army in the partisan movement. Even among bands which had no special reason to be bound to the Red Army, strong factors induced a feeling of dependence. The Party and the NKVD lost rapidly in prestige during the final months of 1941 as a result of the precipitate retreat and confused evacuation, which indicated lack of preparation and in many cases poor morale in the political branches of the regime. Whatever share the Red Army had in this loss of status was regained by its impressive victories during the winter months. Moreover, there was an important practical factor which induced the partisan band, whatever its origin, to seek attachment to the Red Army. Especially after the German advance came to a halt, the Red Army sent out long-range scouting teams composed of regular military personnel and usually including radio operators. Encounters with these teams were often the first contact the bands were able to establish with the Soviet side of the front. Not only was such contact important for information and morale, but it frequently led to material assistance from the various Red Army commands, primarily through the air force units which they had at their disposal. [For a detailed discussion of air support to partisans, see Chap. VI, Sect. I.]

The combination of factors described above gave the Red Army considerable influence on the partisan bands operating in early 1942. In addition, military control was exercised more formally. The Red Army commands at various levels—Fronts, armies, corps, and divisions—issued orders directly to the partisans. When a partisan band was able to main-

[29] Vershigora, p. 390; Fyodorov, p. 436.

tain contact by air, radio, or courier with an army unit, it depended on the army unit for information on the tactical situation as well as for supplies, and in return it was required to execute tasks which the army outfit thought desirable. Since such contact was difficult to maintain, and the number of tasks of military value which a partisan band could perform at this time was limited, the control exercised was in the great majority of cases irregular and sporadic. For bands operating in close proximity to an irregular front across which communication could take place relatively easily, control was of some importance; for distant bands, even those created by Red Army emissaries, control was practically ineffective, or at best extremely difficult. For example, in the late spring of 1942, G. Linkov, one of the major parachutist officers, was cautioned against moving his headquarters to western Belorussia, as distance would then make radio communication impossible with higher headquarters on the Soviet side of the front.[30]

The German reports and postwar Soviet memoirs provide only scant information on the institutional mechanism used for controlling the partisans during this period of late 1941 and 1942. Apparently the arrangements were of an *ad hoc* nature. The political administrations at various levels of the Red Army command structure continued to exercise some measure of control, but the partisan movement apparently became too large and too complex to be supervised by these organs. The NKVD "OO" sections in the Red Army commands also played an important part, but it was apparently primarily an indirect one. A major role, at least in formulating the most important decisions, appears to have been played by the military councils, especially at the Front level. The importance assumed by these organs arose in part, it appears, from the fact that, as bodies which included representatives of the political as well as the strictly military sections of the Red Army, they assembled leaders interested in many facets of partisan activity. Very significant in this connection was the fact that the military soviets of the Fronts included several top Party officials who had played leading roles in territories in which the partisans were now operating. For example, A. A. Zhdanov, the first secretary of the important Leningrad *obkom,* was a member of the military council of the Northwest Front, and of the Volkhov and Leningrad Fronts, when these were formed; Khrushchev, first secretary of the Ukrainian Party, was a member of the military council of the South Front, and later of the Voronezh Front; Peter A. Kalinin, a secretary of the Belorussian Party, was a member of the military council of the West Front. Little is known concerning the activities of these Party leaders at the Fronts, but that their membership in the military councils was not merely formal is suggested by the fact that for a considerable time they were physically present at the Front headquarters.

[30] Linkov, pp. 257 ff.

Since very little information on the actual operation of the control structure is available for the period under discussion, it is difficult to explain why it was superseded after a few months. A few hypotheses may be advanced, however. We have just noted that the arrangements for control by various Red Army organizations were of an *ad hoc,* makeshift nature. Possibly no element of the Red Army was fully prepared to handle all the complex problems arising in the large-scale partisan movement which was developing during the later winter of 1941–42. Quite possibly—though there is virtually no evidence on this point—friction arose between the ordinary military staffs, the political administrations, and the "OO" sections. It is likely that an increasing number of questions had to be referred to the military councils, which included high representatives of these groups, but which were scarcely able to devote a major share of their time to the partisan movement. As a result, it probably became increasingly obvious that a new institutional framework was needed—one which would combine the various viewpoints essential in dealing with the partisan movement, contain a number of specialists who could devote full time to supervising the partisans, and at the same time continue to bring together Party and Army officials of sufficient stature to make major decisions. The creation of such a new institution was, moreover, a standard Soviet practice when the system was confronted with a new set of problems.

Aside from the purely functional considerations just outlined, there were probably political motivations as well, although these are even more difficult to demonstrate in the absence of direct evidence. As will be indicated below, one motive behind creating and publicizing the distinct partisan command structure was to give the impression that the partisan movement was a more widespread force than was actually the case. A second political motive is harder to establish. It seems probable, however, that many of the top Soviet authorities, especially in the Party, were becoming somewhat alarmed at the Red Army's rapid increase in power and influence after its impressive winter victories. Very likely they feared concentrating too much of the war effort in the hands of the Red Army command, and were apprehensive about the increased Red Army prestige resulting from successes against the enemy. The separation of the partisan movement from the Red Army by creating a distinct command structure served in some degree to remove this increasingly important element from the army command, and to establish another center which shared the prestige obtained by armed attack on the invader.

Though the Soviet regime may have intended to lessen Red Army influence by establishing the Central Staff of the Partisan Movement, no open break with the previous system of control through the Red Army was made. The Central Staff was formally attached to Army supreme headquarters; Marshal Klimentii Voroshilov was appointed commander in chief of the partisan movement. At the same time, however, Panteleimon Pono-

marenko, first secretary of the Belorussian Party, who for some time had
been one of the inner circle of the regime, was appointed Chief of Staff of
the partisan movement.[31] Ponomarenko was in fact the real director of the
Central Staff: its orders were issued over his signature, he appointed and
removed major partisan officers, and the partisan leaders apparently regarded him as their direct superior.[32] [For the text of an operational order
issued over Ponomarenko's signature, see Appendix, Document 8.] The
renewed influence of the Party was enhanced by attaching the Central Staff
to the Central Committee of the All-Union Communist Party, although
this link was not so frequently stressed in orders and propaganda pronouncements as was the attachment to Army supreme headquarters.

Little is known about the internal organization of the Central Staff. Apparently it was always physically located in Moscow, in close contact with
the highest authorities.[33] Undoubtedly the Central Staff had considerable
personnel at its direct disposal, and a complex organization. One German
report, which is possibly overdetailed in view of the available evidence,
lists the following eleven sections of the Staff:

1. Operations	7. Code
2. Intelligence	8. Cartographical
3. Communications	9. Finance
4. Personnel	10. Transport
5. Administration and Quartermaster	11. Propaganda and Press[34]
6. OO	

D. THE FRONT STAFFS

Although from the spring of 1942 on, when the Central Staff was the
central coordinating command of the partisan movement in close contact
with the highest Army and Party authorities, the principal operational con-

[31] Tsanava II, 30; Vershigora, pp. 74, 396.

[32] This is best brought out in the account of the big meeting of partisan commanders in Moscow in August 1942, which is given in Soviet postwar memoirs. (Vershigora, p. 42; Tsanava II, 30; Linkov, p. 518.)

[33] According to some reports the deputy chief of staff of the Central Staff was one
Sergiyenko, who, it is said, had been People's Commissar of the Interior of the
Ukrainian SSR, and after the outbreak of the war L. P. Beria's deputy. (Alexander
Ruzanov, "Pravda o partizanskom dvizhenii," *Frontovoi Listok,* 28, 30 October 1943.)
Actually, the Ukrainian Commissar of the Interior had been I. A. Serov. It is hard
to see how Ruzanov, who had been a special aide of T. A. Strokach, chief of staff
of the Ukrainian Staff of the Partisan Movement [see Appendix, Document 6], could
have confused the name of so well-known an official as Serov. The article cited above
is based on Ruzanov's interrogation, after his capture, by a German officer. In the
article Ruzanov also states that he worked for A. S. Shcherbakov in the Central Staff,
but there is no confirmation of Shcherbakov's being in that organization. A much
later German document confirms Sergiyenko's being a high figure in the Central Staff,
however, even stating that in 1944 he succeeded P. K. Ponomarenko as Chief of
Staff. Possibly Sergiyenko—whoever he really was—headed a more secret agency for
central control of the partisans after the Central Staff was officially abolished on 13
January 1944.

[34] OKH/GenStdH/FHO, Nachrichten ueber den Bandenkrieg, Nr. 3, 28 July 1943,
Anlage 10 (GMDS, H 3/738).

trol of most of the partisans continued to be exercised from command centers distant from the capital, the circumstances under which the partisan movement was developing led to an important division in the control of bands in different parts of the occupied area. As was previously described, the territorial partisan organization, where it was effective at all, tended to come under the control of the Army field commands in areas near the front lines. The greatly increased partisan activity during the early months of 1942 also took place, for the most part, in areas near the fronts, although there was a growing tendency to reinforce or revive the partisan movement in more distant areas through the use of parachute teams. It was with the areas near the front that the military councils and the other organs of the Red Army had naturally been most concerned, and it was in these areas that arrangements for control of the partisan movement were most advanced when the Central Staff was formed, although even there the control system was makeshift.

Within a period of four or five months after the formation of the Central Staff, Front Staffs of the Partisan Movement (referred to hereafter as "Front Staffs") were formed at most of the Red Army Front headquarters. Basically, these new organizations appear to have been developed from the military council control system. Like the Front military council, the Front Staff contained representatives of the major Soviet agencies concerned with the conduct of the war in the area of the Front concerned. Unlike the members of the Front military council, however, these representatives as a rule were permanently assigned to the task of directing the partisan movement. While the members of the military council were confronted with multitudinous duties, both military and political, the Front Staff members were or became specialists in partisan warfare. At the same time, they were persons of lower rank than the military council members. While the chief political official at a Front military council was usually a Politburo member who was a regional first secretary, such as Khrushchev or Zhdanov, the corresponding position in the Front Staff was as a rule held by a second or third secretary or a first secretary of a smaller territorial division. From one point of view, the Front Staff acted as a technical committee of the military soviet; in some documents the Front Staff is referred to as being "at the Military Council of the Front." Undoubtedly the Front Staff received orders from the military council, and probably major policy questions were referred to the latter body. At the same time, however, the Front Staff received military operational orders directly from the Red Army Front commander, or from the appropriate sections of his headquarters, such as the intelligence section. [For an example of an order of Front headquarters intelligence section to the Front Partisan Staff, see Appendix, Document 15.]

The preceding paragraph indicates the strong ties of the Front Staff to the Front headquarters. However, the Front Staff was not a mere tool of the previously existing structure for control of the partisan movement by the Front command. It was also both formally and actually a subordinate command of the Central Staff of the Partisan Movement and an integral part of the newly formed system of partisan control. While, because of scarcity of evidence, it is difficult to assess the degree of subordination of the Front Staff to the Central Staff as compared with the Front headquarters, apparently major directives on a wide variety of topics were given to the Front Staff by the Central Staff. Moreover, one member of each Front Staff was formally designated a representative of the Central Staff; in one case, apparently, this member was also the Chief of the Front Staff.[35] The *de facto* control of the Central Staff over the Front Staff was enhanced by the fact that it conducted training courses for partisan officers under Front Staff jurisdiction, and probably it also appointed and removed the more important partisan officers.[36]

The Front Staff was provided with a fairly large technical staff, including sections for radio and cryptography, administration and intelligence. In some cases special squadrons of planes were placed at its disposal for communication with the partisans under its command, and the Front Staff frequently kept at its headquarters special groups of partisans or scouts who were used only on temporary missions in the occupied areas. In addition, there were liaison and inspection officers detailed to maintain contact with and control over the partisan bands.

By early 1943 staffs of the partisan movement were apparently established at most Red Army Front commands. Since the sections controlled by each front remained fairly stable from early 1942 until late 1943, a brief discussion of these areas and the peculiarities of the development and organization of the Front Staff in each area may be worthwhile. At the extreme northern end of the line was the Karelian Front, which included the long section from Lake Onega to the Barents Sea. Although there was a well-organized partisan staff at this front, its activities are of restricted importance, and little is known of its origin. Farther south, Leningrad

[35] S. S. Belchenko, who became People's Commissar of the Interior of Belorussia after the war, was chief of the Kalinin Front Staff; in some cases, apparently, a territorial staff also had a representative at a Front Staff.

[36] Little exact information on this subject is available. It seems likely that the Central Staff did not itself appoint members of the Front Staff. These very important officers were probably selected by the Party directly, or by the Party, Red Army, Central Staff, and possibly the NKVD acting together. On the other hand, the Central Staff probably played a major role in selecting the principal officers of headquarters under the Front Staff, such as the operative center in the rear of the enemy, as well as the commanders and commissars of some of the more important bands. E.g., Yemlyutin and other partisan commanders in the Bryansk area were either appointed or confirmed by the Central Staff at the Moscow meeting in August 1942. (Vershigora, p. 42.) For an example of training courses directed by the Central Staff, see Appendix, Document 9.

Oblast was divided among three fronts, the Leningrad Front, the Volkhov Front, and the Northwest Front. Each had its partisan command center, but, unlike those at other Fronts, they were not semi-independent headquarters, subject only to the Front Command and the Central Staff, but were dependent upon an intermediate command. This command, the Leningrad Staff of the Partisan Movement, was located in the city of Leningrad, and was directed by M. N. Nikitin, a secretary of the Leningrad *obkom* and, therefore, a lieutenant of one of the major Soviet leaders, Zhdanov. Nikitin directed the Leningrad Staff personally, issuing major operational orders and instructions concerning personnel to partisans throughout the oblast, either directly or through subordinate partisan commands with the Northwest Front and Volkhov Fronts. These partisan commands were called "operative groups."[37] Apparently this arrangement, which was unique in the partisan movement, arose from the fact that the territory of Leningrad Oblast had originally been included entirely in the zone of a single Front, the Northwest Front. It appears that the Leningrad Oblast Party apparatus, which was very active in the formation of partisan groups, controlled the whole area, in conjunction with the Front command in 1941. When the Northwest Front was divided, it was evidently felt most desirable to retain this unity of control; possibly Zhdanov's great influence played a part in maintaining a more centralized partisan command structure in his oblast.

South of Leningrad Oblast, the Kalinin Front, after the winter battles of 1941–42, stretched across almost the entire width of Kalinin Oblast and the northern half of Smolensk Oblast, as well as extending to Vitebsk Oblast, in Belorussia. In this case the unity of military command prevailed over the unity of the administrative territories, and all three oblasts were assigned to Kalinin Front Staff. The same arrangement existed at the next front to the south, where the West Front staff controlled the partisans in the southern half of Smolensk Oblast and the northern and western parts of Orel Oblast. [See Chap. VIII, Sect. II, B, 2.]

The southern half of Orel Oblast (or more properly, the southwestern corner, since the greater part was under the West Front) for many months formed an exception to the general scheme of organization by Fronts. Instead of being subject to the Bryansk Front, which was the closest military command, it was placed under a partisan command based on the administrative territorial division, and was known as the Orel Staff of the Partisan Movement. This staff apparently continued to exist until early 1943. Based at Yelets, the seat of the Front Command, it operated in close conjunction with it. In 1943 it was replaced, apparently without great changes of or-

[37] P. Sheverdalkin, ed., *Listovki partizanskoi voiny v Leningradskoi oblasti, 1941-1944* (Leningrad: Leningradskoi Gazetno-Zhurnalnoye i Knizhnoye Izdatelstvo, 1945), pp. 3, 7.

ganization, by the Bryansk Front Staff of the Partisan Movement, and later by the Central Front Staff, when the Central Front took over the area of Bryansk Front. [See Chap. VIII, Sect. I, B and Sect. II, A and B.]

The great stretch of open steppe to the south was divided among several fronts, the designations of which changed from time to time during the period under discussion. Some of the control relationships of the partisan movement in this area have been described above. In certain areas, and at certain times, the Front military commands (which apparently had special operating groups of the territorial staffs attached to them) here exercised control over partisans close enough to the front line to make such arrangements practicable, but for the most part the number of partisans was not sufficient to make a regular institutional control system necessary, and apparently no "Front Staffs" were formally established.[38]

Below the Front Staff, when it happened that individual Soviet armies were in close contact with partisan bands on the German side of the lines, "operative groups"[39] were set up at the army headquarters to coordinate the partisans' operations with the activities of the Army. Organizationally these groups were miniature Front Staffs, including in some cases even Party officials from the territorial administrative division covered by the army command. The rank of the partisan operative group commanders, was, however, lower than it was for the Front Staffs, and the technical apparatus was smaller and less complex. Apparently there was no effort to establish operative groups at each army command; instead they were organized only in those areas where they were especially needed. The operative group played an important role in directing the activities of the partisans, and sometimes arranged for their supply, but did not as a rule concern itself with major political activities, or appoint and remove command personnel.

The discussion on the foregoing pages can be made a little clearer by examining one Front Staff and its subordinate commands. Perhaps the most complicated of all the Front Staff organizations was the Kalinin Front Staff, since it included sections of two separate oblasts of the RSFSR, as well as an oblast of the Belorussian SSR. The staff was physically located near Toropets, in Kalinin Oblast. It was headed by Colonel S. S. Belchenko, described as a secretary of the Central Committee of the Communist Party of Belorussia, and after the war People's Commissar of the Interior of Belorussia. It is fairly clear that, as Chief of the Kalinin Front Staff, he also was formally given the posts of member of the military

---

[38] None was established by October 1942, at least at the Voronezh Front, where the military council continued to direct the few partisan detachments.

[39] The term "operative group" was used by the Soviet partisans to designate several types of intermediate commands. The operative group with the army headquarters is not to be confused with the operative group in the rear of the enemy described elsewhere.

council of that front, and representative of the Central Staff of the Partisan Movement. It is also very probable that his staff included a delegation, or advance section, of the Staff of the Belorussian Partisan Movement (see below). Staff sections included the following: operations, intelligence, communications, personnel, general, quartermaster, records, and code. Twenty-five aircraft were assigned to the staff.

The partisan bands in the area under the Kalinin Front Staff were directly controlled from three headquarters. A number of the bands were immediately subject to the directions of the Front Staff. Others were controlled by two operative groups subordinate to the Kalinin Front Staff. One of these operative groups was located at the headquarters of the Third Assault Army, and was under the command of Senior Battalion Commissar Sokolov. Most of its bands operated in Kalinin Oblast, but there was no apparent connection between the administration or Party organization in this territorial division and the operative group. The second operative group, with the Fourth Assault Army, however, controlled most of the Vitebsk Oblast partisans, and was apparently closely associated with the Vitebsk Party *obkom*. As will be described a little later, both the Front Staff and its subordinate operative groups issued orders in some cases directly to individual bands, and in others passed them on through partisan operative groups in the occupied areas.

E. THE TERRITORIAL STAFFS

The control exercised by the Central Staff over the Fronts Staffs was real, especially in matters concerning appointment and dismissal of personnel and in the conduct of operations of a broad political or strategical nature. Conditions of military operations in the areas close to the front demanded that a dual responsibility be set for the Front Staffs, however, and in practice many of their operational orders emanated from the military front commands. The introduction of the partisan staff system at the Front level seems chiefly to have served the purpose of institutionalizing joint control of Party and Army authorities over the partisans near the fronts, and of enhancing the prestige of the Party and of the partisan movement as such.

The relationship of the Central Staff to the territorial partisan staffs was much more intimate. Apparently the Staff of the Partisan Movement of the South was not very significant; except in the Crimea, where direct Army control was most important, it had only a few scattered bands under its administration.[40] The Belorussian Staff of the Partisan Movement (formed

---

[40] In addition to the Staff of the Partisan Movement of the South, and the staffs of the two major union republics (Ukrainian and Belorussian), eventually territorial staffs were set up in most of the other occupied union republics. There was a Latvian Staff which operated a number of bands composed in part of Latvians, in part of Russians; the relative unimportance of this staff is indicated by the fact that even in 1944 it had

9 September 1942) played a greater role. Earlier in this section it was noted that the parachutist organizing teams were relatively most important in the southern, central, and western Belorussian areas, i.e., in those parts of the republic most distant from the front. As these teams progressed in their organization of the partisan bands, the territorial Party organization was also able to regain much of its strength. By early 1943 Party oblast committees had been reintroduced or revived in all or most of the Belorussian oblasts, and they played a major part in aiding the partisans and in strengthening resistance to the Germans. About the same time oblast partisan staffs were set up. It is impossible from the meager information available to delineate with any exactitude the lines of responsibility exercised by these two types of centers, but it appears that the Party committees played a considerably greater role in selecting partisan personnel, controlling the civilian population, and perhaps even in selecting operational objectives than they did elsewhere.[41]

One might assume that the revival of the Party organization as a major element of the partisan movement would have been hindered by the presence of the parachutist teams, which had received their early training and instruction from the Red Army. As noted earlier, however, most of the team members, or at least their officers, were especially selected by the Party organizations. Some had been chosen by non-Belorussian Party groups, especially the Moscow city apparatus, and there is evidence that a certain amount of friction arose between these "foreigners" and the native party organizations.[42] The solution seems to have been, in some cases at least, to use the "Muscovite" parachutists as shock forces, sending them farther to the west and south where conditions were more difficult and the local organization more disrupted, while turning over command of the partisans to local staffs in oblasts like Minsk and Bobruisk.[43] In this connection, it is also important to note that certainly not all the parachutists were non-Belorussians; many, perhaps a majority, of those sent in early in 1942 were men who had fled from Belorussia before the German advance. Frequently they included Party officials who were being sent back to reconstitute the Party organizations in the areas from which they had

---

only three small brigades; the Lithuanian Staff also controlled a considerable number of partisans. A Moldavian Staff was set up originally as a subsection of the Ukrainian Staff, but in February 1944 it was made at least nominally independent, at a time when bands from outside first reached the territory of the Moldavian Republic. On the other hand, while there is some evidence that an Estonian Staff existed, it never played an important role. Apparently partisans in the Karelo-Finnish SSR were under control of the Karelian Front Staff.

[41] *Obkoms* were frequently located with the operative groups on the German side of the front. Apparently they received orders from the Belorussian Staff in Moscow. (Wi/ID 2.375)

[42] Linkov, pp. 378, 392–93.

[43] *Ibid.*, pp. 305, 324, 374.

escaped. These men formed an important section of the territorial partisan staffs which developed later in the year.

The Ukrainian Staff of the Partisan Movement was first formed as the Ukrainian Partisan Staff in the military council of the Southwest Direction (a major military command). Apparently this staff was first formed in Voroshilovgrad, although shortly afterwards it was forced to retreat along with the Red Army to Stalingrad. Since Khrushchev, the first secretary of the Ukrainian Party, was in both these cities because of his duties with the Red Army, it seems likely that postwar Soviet claims that he played a major role in directing the Ukrainian partisan movement are correct, at least for this early period. It is also clear, however, that Khrushchev exercised only general supervision over the Ukrainian Staff; the post of Chief of the Ukrainian Staff was given to Timofei Strokach, who was deputy People's Commissar of Internal Affairs for the Ukraine. Moreover, on 29 June 1942 the Ukrainian Staff was detached from the military command (the Southwest Direction having been dissolved). Sometime in the middle of 1942 Strokach and the Staff were moved to Moscow. Khrushchev was also in Moscow for a time, apparently engaging in some of the high-level planning for the partisan movement, but he later returned to the armies in the south. Nevertheless, Soviet accounts give Khrushchev major credit for Ukrainian partisan operations.[44]

At the time of its organization, the Ukrainian Staff, unlike the Belorussian and the Front Staffs, had no major partisan bands under its control. As has already been noted, the original territorial partisan organization west of the Dnepr had scarcely begun before the German occupation, while, except in the extreme northern area, those bands which began operating east of the Dnepr were wiped out either before or during the winter of 1941–42. The exceptions were the Chernigov Oblast otryads, which during the winter were gradually brought together under the command of the *obkom* secretary, Fyodorov, and a number of rayon otryads in adjoining Sumy Oblast. Strong German antipartisan drives in the winter of 1941–42 compelled even these bands to retreat to the deeper forests of Orel Oblast in the RSFSR. Consequently, except for brief raids, the Ukraine was practically devoid of partisans during the spring and summer of 1942.

In spite of, or more correctly, because of the situation just described, the higher Soviet authorities seem to have devoted more attention to the Ukrainian Staff than to any other level of partisan command below the

[44] The account given in this paragraph was originally based primarily on German sources; the Soviet version is in the official Soviet war history: Institut Marksizma-Leninizma, *Istoriya velikoi otechestvennoi voiny Sovetskogo Soyuza*, ed. P. N. Pospelov *et al.* (Moscow: Voennoye Izdatelstvo Ministerstva Oborony SSSR), II (1961), 476–78. In general, the Soviet version (from which most of the dates of staff formations and dissolutions are taken) confirms our earlier reconstructions.

Central Staff itself. When the Central Staff was dissolved on 13 January 1944, the overt role of the Ukrainian Staff increased still more. Undoubtedly the major reason for this emphasis was the importance of the Ukraine among the occupied territories. It contained one-half of the Soviet population under German rule and far more than one-half of the economic resources of the occupied regions. Moreover, the people of the East Ukraine had suffered especially from collectivization, and might have been expected to be more susceptible to anti-Soviet propaganda. The presence of large collaborationist elements and a vigorous, though small group of anti-Soviet nationalists, reinforced by nationalist propagandists from the Western Ukraine, increased this danger. If a strong Soviet partisan movement could have been developed in the Ukraine it would have hindered German exploitation of the region's material and human resources, and at the same time would have weakened and terrorized anti-Soviet elements.

Some indication of the importance attached to the Ukrainian Staff is furnished by an examination of its internal structure with attention to the relatively high positions of the officials assigned to it. [See Fig. 2.] In addition to the highly organized staff in Moscow, a special forward command section (at first in Starobelsk, later in Voroshilovgrad) under the command of a Colonel Metyelev was established, with a complex organization largely duplicating that of the parent staff. Moreover, thirty-eight of the scarce Douglas airplanes were assigned for the use of the Ukrainian Staff. [See Chap. VI, Sect. IV.] Perhaps more important as an indication of the influence of the Ukrainian Staff during 1942 and early 1943 is the number of articles, poems, and books which have been published concerning the Ukrainian partisans, several of them signed by Strokach himself (although without indication of his positions as NKVD officer and chief of staff of the Ukrainian partisan movement).[45]

As we have seen, the task of the Ukrainian Staff of the Partisan Movement, unlike that of the other major partisan staffs, was not to control and coordinate existing partisan formations, but to create a new partisan movement. Three fairly distinct methods were employed. The earliest is not clearly connected with the Ukrainian Staff as such, and may well have developed independently. It consisted of using parachutist teams to penetrate the Ukraine west of the Dnepr and to attempt the formation of partisan centers which would gradually develop into nuclei for major bands. Evidently a considerable effort was expended; in the spring of 1942 experienced partisan leaders from the Bryansk area were selected for this task and were assigned a large number of specially trained Spanish officers who had lived as refugees in the USSR since the Spanish Civil War. Nevertheless, when these teams were sent in late in the spring of 1942, they were

---

[45] See for example, *Komunist,* 24 December 1943, p. 3; and Strokach's book, *Partyzany Ukraïny* (Moscow: Ukrvydav TsKP(b)V, 1943).

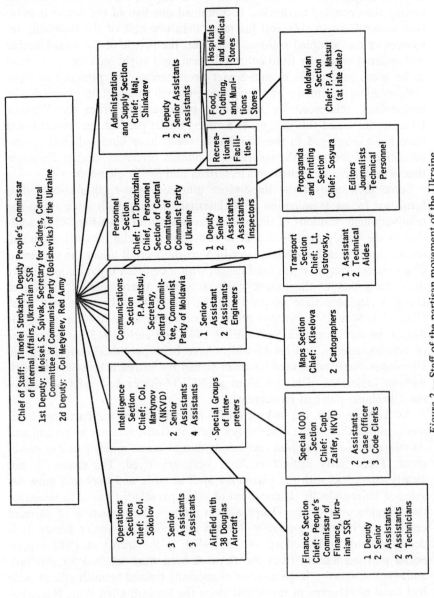

Figure 2.—Staff of the partisan movement of the Ukraine.

unable to maintain a foothold in the Ukraine itself, but were forced to establish their headquarters in Mozyr Oblast in Belorussia. Only gradually were they able to extend their activities to the extreme north of the Ukraine during the following summer and autumn. Somewhat later, "Muscovite" parachutist organizers moving south from the western oblasts of Belorussia were able to extend their activities to the extreme northwestern corner of the Ukrainian SSR.

A second type of operation was probably conducted under the direction of the Ukrainian Staff although direct evidence is lacking. It consisted of frequent incursions by small partisan groups (of 100 men or less) into areas of the southeast Ukraine in the vicinity of the Red Army lines. Since several of these groups are known to have been formed in Voroshilovgrad at a time when Strokach, as head of an NKVD school, was active there and Khrushchev was in the vicinity with the South Front military council, it seems likely that the directors of the Ukrainian partisan headquarters at least assisted in the formation of these bands. Their principal field of activity was the industrial region of the Donbas; here the groups as a rule were very small and were designed for espionage and contact with underground networks, rather than for the usual type of partisan warfare. However, one group, concerning which somewhat more detailed information is available, was a more ordinary type of partisan unit. It was formed in Voroshilovgrad in April 1942, under officers who were experienced partisan leaders. In late May with a strength of 100 men it crossed the front lines about forty miles south of Kharkov, then pursued a northwesterly march route across the extreme western part of Kharkov Oblast. Its tasks, revealed by several captured members to German interrogators, were: "Terrorization of the population which was willing to work [for the Germans], especially the Ukrainian auxiliary police and the newly appointed mayors; disturbance of German troops; destruction of railroads and important military objectives; liberation of prisoners of war; and assembling of scattered partisans and parachutists."[46] What the band was supposed to do after it had carried out these sweeping assignments is unclear; some interrogations suggest that it was to remain in the wooded areas northeast of Poltava; others state that it was to turn northeast and regain the Soviet lines in Kursk Oblast; still others suggest vaguely that the band try to reach the main partisan areas in Bryansk and Smolensk. As it turned out, the group was unable either to accomplish any significant number of its assigned tasks or to find a safe refuge, for, after having traversed about seventy miles of occupied territory, it was caught and destroyed by German security forces about midway between Kharkov and Poltava.

The efforts described in the two preceding paragraphs were extremely

---

[46] Korueck 585, Abt Ia, "Bericht ueber die Bekaempfung einer Partisanengruppe vom 1.–18.6.42" (GMDS, Korueck 24430/4).

marginal and scarcely affected any sizable proportion of the Ukrainian population. In the meantime, during the summer and autumn of 1942, considerable efforts were being devoted to propaganda designed to create the illusion of a powerful Ukrainian partisan movement before such a force actually existed. Fyodorov, under the pseudonym of "Orlenko," and S. A. Kovpak were built up as popular heroes, and great emphasis was placed on the Ukrainian origin of their bands, although their actual operations during this period barely touched Ukrainian soil. At the same time, however, the Ukrainian Staff was preparing to transform these exaggerated claims into reality. The instrument it employed was the "roving band." Sometime in the early summer of 1942 the Soviet authorities conceived the plan of using the Bryansk forest as a base, or *place d'armes,* for the development and strengthening of partisan groups of Ukrainian origin, which would then sally forth to carry the partisan movement into the hitherto neglected areas of the Ukraine.

The first of the roving bands to be sent to the west was under the command of Kovpak. To his own "complex" was joined the "complex" under Alexander Saburov, a Kiev NKVD official who had formed his group from among isolated Red Army men, but who could claim at least some connection with the Ukraine. The Kovpak-Saburov bands entered the region west of the Dnepr in November 1942. In February 1943 the bands made a brief raid through the northern rayons of Rovno and Zhitomir Oblasts, but for almost the entire winter remained in the Pripet swamps of Belorussia. In spite of the fact that Kovpak was now under control of the Ukrainian Staff, his own authority temporarily extended to all the partisan groups in the Belorussian areas in which he operated, apparently embracing the entire Pripet Valley. Moreover, the "Moscow" parachutist teams which represented the major organizing force in the extreme southwestern areas of Belorussia were also placed under his control. In effect, therefore, Kovpak represented a special type of command, which superseded local partisan control centers regardless of the administrative division in which he operated.[47]

In the spring Kovpak was able to move south into Rovno and Zhitomir Oblasts proper, although his group had to keep on the move almost constantly. As a representative of the central command of the Ukrainian partisan movement, Kovpak was the supreme partisan authority in the Ukraine west of the Dnepr. The importance which the central authorities, both on the Ukrainian Staff of the Partisan Movement and in the Ukrainian Party, attached to their "plenipotentiary" in the northwest Ukraine is indicated by a number of factors.[48] Kovpak was regularly supplied by air, in spite

---

[47] Linkov, pp. 378, 384; cf. Kovpak, p. 105; Shyyan, p. 130.

[48] Some postwar Soviet memoirs imply that Kovpak and Saburov were under the control of the Central Staff, ignoring or barely mentioning the Ukrainian Staff. On

of his considerable distance from Soviet airports and the customary difficulties of Soviet planes in making night flights of over a hundred miles. The same planes which brought his supplies (whose distribution enabled him to influence his subordinate bands) brought major officials to stimulate the morale of the partisans, to check on their activities, and to issue orders. Strokach himself was among the high officers who visited Kovpak's camp at this time. In addition, Korotchenko, third secretary of the Ukrainian Party, stayed for some time, as did Mykola Kuznetsov, first secretary of the Central Committee of the Ukrainian Komsomols. In addition, a representative of the Central Staff or the Ukrainian Staff, a Captain Shevardin, was permanently assigned to Kovpak's staff.

In the wake of Kovpak's band there appeared a number of groups whose spheres of activity were more permanently set by territorial limitations. During the remainder of 1943 these groups established throughout most of the wooded area of the Ukraine a general network of partisan groups which resembled in strength and density the network established a year earlier in the northern areas. One such group was under Begma, the former first secretary of the Rovno *obkom*. Another was Fyodorov's complex. In the winter of 1942–43 the Fyodorov partisans had been able to re-establish themselves throughout the northern part of Chernigov Oblast, and from then on, this section of the Ukraine east of the Dnepr (like the northern section of Sumy Oblast) may be regarded as partisan-infiltrated to about the the same extent as the northern regions. In the spring Fyodorov followed Kovpak to the west, and at about the same time was appointed first secretary of the Rovno *obkom*. His complex established its major base of operations in the northern areas of Rovno and Lutsk Oblasts and continued to operate in this area until the Red Army arrived.

By the middle of 1943 the technique of sending in strong, well-organized, and self-contained roving bands had converted the northwestern forest region of the Ukraine from an area almost devoid of partisans into one of the major centers of Soviet partisan activity. Only in the central areas of Rovno and Lutsk Oblasts, where nationalist sympathizers were strong, were the Soviet partisans unable to achieve significant results. The Ukrainian Staff was apparently dissatisfied with these achievements, however, for neither the enormous steppe regions of the Ukraine, most im-

the other hand, the best contemporary source (the various materials in the German documents based on the interrogation of Ruzanov) makes it clear that these units were under the Ukrainian Staff. As explained elsewhere, the postwar Soviet memoirs are unreliable on such points, because of their authors' desires to enhance the prestige of various elements and personages in the Soviet system. It is likely, however, that a very close coordination between the Ukrainian Staff and the Central Staff existed in matters concerning the roving bands, which frequently operated in parts of two or more Soviet republics; it is also quite possible that representatives of the Central Staff were present with the Ukrainian roving bands. Recent Soviet memoirs and histories clearly indicate that Kovpak and Saburov were subordinate to the Ukrainian Staff.

portant economically, nor the most disaffected West Ukrainian area, Galicia, was affected by them. As a result, two spectacular operations were conducted by the Kovpak band and another major roving band under M. I. Naumov during the spring and summer of 1943.

Both Kovpak's and Naumov's bands were almost wiped out in carrying out these raids, but the two commanders escaped and immediately began to reconstitute their bands. By the winter of 1943–44, when the Soviet armies advanced west of the Dnepr, these bands together with Fyodorov's, Saburov's, and a number of newly organized bands of similar size (i.e., about 2,000 men) constituted the major striking force of the partisan movement in the northwest Ukraine. Apparently, however, control of these bands was transferred from the Ukrainian Staff to the Red Army (First Ukrainian Front). Under this new direction, their activities were extended even beyond the borders of the post-1939 Soviet Union, several penetrating eastern Poland and Naumov's going as far as Slovakia.

The significance of the Ukrainian Staff of the Partisan Movement lies in the scale of its individual operations and in the fact that it directed a movement which had to be started from scratch. The use of the large, comparatively tightly organized, highly mobile roving bands was essential to its special purpose. In effect, the bands under its control were built up and organized in the Bryansk "hothouse," then were transplanted to the Ukraine, thus enabling them to flourish on soil which had hitherto produced no lasting growth of partisans. Materially, at least in the early stages, the efforts devoted to this process may have been out of proportion to the results achieved, but for psychological reasons they were essential.

F. THE INTERMEDIATE PARTISAN COMMAND STRUCTURE

As has been indicated, the principal control agencies of the partisan movement for over-all planning of operations, for liaison with the Party, Red Army, and other organs of the Soviet regime, and for general supervision of partisan activties, were the Central Staff of the Partisan Movement and the Front Staffs and territorial staffs directly subordinate to it— in all about ten staffs. The immediate, day-to-day conduct of partisan activities and the control of the lower levels of partisan personnel were concentrated in the hands of the brigades or similar units. It is evident, however, that the small number of high-level partisan staffs could not effectively direct the operation of perhaps 200 to 300 brigades without using some intermediate command level. In part this intermediate command was provided by the operative groups at the army or division level. Such control agencies were established at only a limited number of Red Army commands, however, and the supervision they exercised over bands in proximity to the front line was confined primarily to military operational questions. In order to coordinate effectively the activities of the brigades, an intermediate command echelon *within* the German-occupied regions was essential.

As a matter of fact, such partisan command centers in the occupied territories were formed even before the creation of the Central Staff and its subordinate staffs. Possibly the first major centers of this sort were set up by the Red Army in the late winter of 1941–42. One major region in which the Red Army took direct command of the partisan movement was the Yelnya-Dorogobuzh district of Smolensk Oblast. This area was the scene of a major Red Army effort to isolate the German troops stalled before Moscow by sending in large units of regular ground and airborne troops. These troops failed to achieve their objectives, however, and as a result were themselves cut off from the main Soviet armies. They were not immediately destroyed by the Germans and for several months maintained a pocket of resistance. In command was Major General Belov, who had been commander of the First Cavalry Corps, and was now put in charge of all units in the pocket. Belov stimulated a number of local partisan groups to develop rapidly into units of considerable size. The resulting partisan forces, which were called "regiments," averaged over 1,000 men and were consequently much stronger than most other partisan bands of this early period. While there were considerable variations in the internal organization of the regiments, apparently as a result of the superimposition of military organization upon groups of very diverse origins, they more closely resembled regular military formations than did other partisan bands, even at a much later period. Each regiment had a staff detachment of considerable size and was divided into a number of battalions ranging from 300 to 800 men each. These in turn were divided into companies, the companies into platoons, and the platoons into squads. At the regimental and battalion levels, at least, the major officers were the commander, the commissar, and the chief of staff; politruks were assigned to the companies. The regiments and the battalions had supply, reconnaissance, and "OO" sections.

Altogether there were about ten partisan regiments in the Yelnya area by April 1942. Apparently by this time Belov and his staff were finding their task of directly controlling the activities of these regiments, in addition, of course, to commanding the regular Red Army units, to be burdensome. As a result, an intermediate command echelon was instituted, and, in accordance with the general tendency of Army commanders to adopt regular military organization and nomenclature for the partisan movement, was called a "division." There were two divisions, one controlling five regiments, the other three, while one or more regiments remained directly subject to Red Army corps headquarters. Little is known concerning the actual functioning or internal organization of these divisions. One at least was commanded by a regular army colonel from Belov's staff. Apparently they acted in a manner analogous to that of army divisional headquarters, although certainly exercising less continuous supervision over their regiments. [For details of the partisan organization in this area, see Chap. VII, Sect. I, B and C.]

The Yelnya type of military command structure was destroyed, along with most of the partisans in the area, late in the spring of 1942. It was not altogether unique in the partisan movement, however. Farther south, although also under the direction of the West Front, the Red Army played an equally active role in organizing and reinforcing the partisan groups, which for a time were in direct contact with the Soviet forces through the large Kirov gap. Here, too, "regiments" were set up, frequently under the command of regular Red Army officers, and similar in size (1,000 to 1,500 men) and internal organization (battalions) to those in the Yelnya area. [See Chap. VIII, Sect. II, A.] It is uncertain, however, whether an intermediate command structure corresponding to the Yelnya "division" was set up, although some German reports for early 1943 state that the brigades in the area were later combined into partisan divisions. In mid-1942, however, when army control was closest, the regiments which formed the basic partisan organization apparently operated directly under command of a nearby Red Army division. [See Chap. VIII, Sect. II, B.]

More typical was the intermediate command structure which developed in the southern part of the Bryansk forest. This center remained one of the most important intermediate commands, and in a general way it was similar to those operating farther north. Some time during the late winter of 1941–42 a group of partisan officers, headed by D. V. Yemlyutin, a high NKVD official of Orel Oblast, and A. D. Bondarenko, a Party secretary of one of the occupied Orel rayons, formed a headquarters in Smelizh, near the edge of Orel Oblast. These leaders probably had some authorization from the Soviet regime, although contact with the Soviet side of the front was intermittent until late spring. Within a few months Yemlyutin (who became commander of the new center, while Bondarenko became commissar) was directing 10,000 partisans, divided into about thirty bands, of which perhaps ten were of brigade size. In August, Yemlyutin, Bondarenko, and the major band commanders were flown to Moscow. After a conference with leading officials of the Party and the partisan movement, Yemlyutin was officially confirmed as director of the partisan center in the forests of southwestern Orel Oblast. His headquarters was designated as the "United Partisan Detachments of the Western Rayons of Orel Oblast," but was usually known as an "operative group."[49]

Little is known about the internal organization and activities of the Yemlyutin operative group. [For a German version of the organization of

<hr/>

[49] Andreyev, p. 316; see also this book, Chap. VIII, Sect. II, A.

a typical operative group, see Fig. 3.] By 1943 there was a staff of specialists of some size, including in particular a considerable force to service the airfield, which formed the principal base for receiving supplies from the Soviet forces; communications personnel, who maintained regular radio contact with the Soviet authorities; and generally a partisan force of almost brigade size to provide close-in protection for the headquarters. The operative group, as previously noted, was for a long time under the direction of the Orel Staff of the Partisan Movement and did not come under the direct

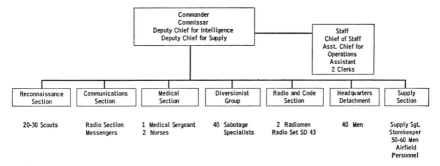

Figure 3.—Operative group in the rear of the enemy. *Source:* OKH/GenStdH/FHO, *Nachrichten ueber den Bandenkrieg Nr. 3,* 28 July 1943, Anlage 9 (GMDS, H 3/738), with minor alterations.

control of a Front Staff (the Bryansk Front Staff), an arrangement that was customary until early 1943 for partisan forces so close to the front lines. Under ordinary circumstances, the following were apparently the chief duties of Yemlyutin and his staff:

1. Passing on major operational orders to the subordinate bands. In particular these included orders for coordinated attacks on the German railroads, which were of crucial importance in the Bryansk area.
2. Receiving and dispatching to the bands men and supplies, as well as messages and information, which could best be received by the powerful radio station and well-established airfield of the headquarters.
3. Exercising general supervision over the bands, making sure that they were active against the enemy, and guarding against any tendency to thwart the wishes of the regime. It is not certain whether the operative group was authorized to appoint or dismiss band officers.

In addition to these ordinary duties, the operative group appears to have assumed many more operational command functions in times of crisis when major German offensives were under way against the partisans. The southern Bryansk forest formed in effect a huge armed camp, impenetrable by any ordinary German force, from which the partisan bands sallied forth for raids and to which they could normally retire in complete security. However, when a major action against the forest base was under way, most of the bands retreated to prepared defensive positions within a fairly restricted radius. Under these circumstances, it became necessary and feasible for the Yemlyutin operative group to assume active direction of the entire force.

In many respects the Yemlyutin operative group was similar to other intermediate control centers which, unlike the Yelnya and Kirov groups, were not directly formed by the military commands. Such nonmilitary partisan centers were active principally in Belorussia, Kalinin Oblast, and Leningrad Oblast. In Belorussia there was an intermediate command known as an "operative center," which roughly corresponded to an oblast (it is to be remembered that the oblasts in Belorussia were much smaller than those in the Ukraine or the RSFSR). These commands evidently operated in a fashion roughly similar to Yemlyutin's, but differed in two important respects. Most of them—especially those in Minsk and Mogilev Oblasts—appear to have worked in very close conjunction with the underground Party committees, with the personnel of the operative center and the committee frequently overlapping.[50] The role of the Party in directing these operative centers was doubtless enhanced by the fact that they were directed by the Belorussian Staff, a territorial partisan echelon, while the Orel Staff, although in a sense a territorial organization, worked in close conjunction with a Front command. In addition to its high degree of Party control, the Belorussian intermediate command organization was distinguished by a two-step structure. Between the band and the operative centers were operative groups, which controlled comparatively small areas, one or a few rayons. The operative groups also worked in close conjunction with the Party organizations, in their case the rayon committees. Apparently the high concentration of partisans in Belorussia (in 1943 probably well over half of all the partisans in the occupied USSR, and far more than half in 1944) and the influence of the Party organization were the key factors in the erection of the two-step system.

The intermediate partisan command structure in Kalinin and Smolensk Oblasts does not seem to have been outstandingly different from that in Belorussia. In Leningrad Oblast, on the other hand, a distinguishing characteristic was the confusing use of the term "brigade" to designate the operative group, while individual bands of ordinary brigade size were called "regiments." There were about ten brigades of this type, and no other intermediate command level on the German side of the lines existed. Since each of the three Soviet Fronts in the Leningrad areas corresponded in size to an army, the partisan commands at these Fronts were similar to operative groups at other army headquarters. [See subsection D, above.]

---

[50] Though Yemlyutin and Bondarenko were officials of Orel Oblast, the fact that they were available to direct the southern Bryansk partisans was partly accidental; in central Belorussia the relationship of Party to partisan was evidently part of an over-all plan.

As a result, each operative group at the three Fronts controlled only a relatively small number of bands. It is not surprising, therefore, that a one-step intermediate command structure on the German side of the lines was adequate.

Numerous variations and peculiarities in the intermediate command structures could be listed. As in the brigades and other organizational forms of the partisan movement, diversity rather than uniformity was characteristic. Nevertheless, in all the major areas of partisan activity, such an intermediate level of control was developed shortly after the partisan movement became significant. It is apparent, therefore, that such a center filled a real need in the partisan organization. It served to coordinate the activities of brigades too numerous to be commanded directly by the Front or territorial staff. Especially through its superior technical facilities—radios and airfields—it directed and supported the brigades in a fashion which could not have been achieved by a headquarters located outside the occupied territory. In view of the rapid development of these centers and the manifest advantages which they possessed, it seems likely that the high command of the partisan movement ordered their establishment in areas where they had not sprung up spontaneously, although there is no direct evidence to support this supposition.

G. DISTRIBUTION OF COMMAND FUNCTIONS

The preceding pages have presented a detailed, although far from exhaustive, summary of the complicated organization of the partisan movement at its period of greatest development. In describing the levels of command contained in this organization, frequent reference has been made to the types of orders issued by each level. These references have been based on many sources—interrogations of captured partisans, statements of postwar partisan memoirs and writers, and undocumented analyses by competent German officials. To some extent, too, they have been based on the direct evidence provided by captured Soviet orders or intercepted Soviet radio messages. However, passing references to orders issued by widely varying types of commands do not adequately cover the questions of division of command responsibility; moreover, the disparate sources necessitate a certain amount of vagueness in describing the authority of many command levels. Consequently, it seems worthwhile to present a generalized schema of command functions based on captured or intercepted orders of unquestionable authenticity.

In order to do this, it is necessary to confine discussion to five command levels, since authentic information on other types is extremely scanty. These levels are the Central Staff of the Partisan Movement; the Front Staff, as illustrated by the Leningrad Staff, the Kalinin Staff, and the Bryansk Staff; the army operative group, as represented by the Valdai

Front operative group under the Leningrad Staff, and the two operative groups under the Kalinin Staff; the operative center in the occupied territories, as represented by the 113th Leningrad "Brigade" (Leningrad Oblast) and the Yemlyutin operative group; and finally the principal partisan unit, e.g., the brigade.

1. The Central Staff

The ordinary procedure of the Central Staff was to issue orders to the next lower echelon of command, the Front Staffs and the territorial staffs, but this procedure was altered so frequently that it can scarcely be called a rule. Instances exist in which the Central Staff issued orders addressed in a general way to all brigades as well as to the higher echelons; one signed by Ponomarenko, for example, reads, "From the commander of the Military Staff[51] of the Partisan Movement at the Headquarters of the High Command; to all Commanders of Staffs of the Partisan Movement at the Front Headquarters (Front Military Councils), Commanders of the Operative Groups at Army Headquarters (Military Councils of the Army), to all Partisans, Commanders, and Commissars of Partisan Groups." [For full text of this order, see Appendix, Document 8.] At other times, the Central Staff issued orders directly to operative groups in the occupied territory and even to individual partisan bands. Some of these orders were detailed, providing for the execution of specific operations and even prescribing tactics to be employed. Others, of a more general nature, were exhortations to increase activity. It is hard to understand why such irregular channels were used by the Central Staff, although the fact that several of the specific orders dealt with attacks on railroads leads one to suspect that, when it was extremely important for military reasons to put the German communications out of action, these extraordinary channels were used to avoid delay. Moreover, an order which carried the prestige of the supreme partisan command was probably more likely to command unwavering obedience.

As indicated above, most orders of the Central Staff were probably sent through the Front Staffs. These included the general directives for attacks on railroads, and it is evident that the Front Staffs were especially zealous in seeing that these important commands were carried out. Orders of a more routine nature were transmitted through the same channel. For example, the operative group with the Fourth Assault Army passed on to one band the Central Staff order that outstanding partisans should be sent to a school. [See Appendix, Document 9.]

2. The Front Staff

In addition to passing on commands from the Central Staff and making sure that they were properly executed, the Front Staff issued a wide va-

[51] Obviously referring to the Central Staff of the Partisan Movement.

riety of commands on its own. Some of these were sent directly to brigades, either those which (as frequently happened) were subject to no intermediate command, or for special reasons, to those directly under operative groups or similar headquarters. Other orders were sent to the operative groups in occupied territory, and still others to operative groups
or subordinate staffs with military commands on the Soviet side of the
lines.

The Front Staff had the power to appoint and remove commanders
and other principal officers of both the operative groups in occupied territory and the brigades, though in several especially important cases this
function was exercised directly by the Central Staff. The Front Staff was
also greatly concerned with collecting reliable intelligence information on
such subjects as the location of German divisions and German preparations for gas warfare. [See Appendix, Document 13.] It demanded detailed
reports on the activities of individual bands, although these were usually
submitted through the channel of the operative group and/or the subordinate staff. The reports were to include information on the location of
nearby partisan bands; accounts of recruiting activities of the reporting
band; and information obtained from captured Germans. [See Appendix,
Document 15.] In addition, the Front Staff sometimes ordered an individual band to undertake a mission of special importance; for example,
some time after Lieutenant General Andrei Vlasov began propaganda
efforts for the Germans, the Leningrad Staff ordered the 1st Partisan Regiment through the Northwest Front Staff to find him and liquidate him.

3. The Subordinate Command Center on
the Soviet Side of the Lines

Information on this type of command level is more scanty than on most
others and relates primarily to the Northwest Front Staff, a subordinate
command on the Leningrad Staff but roughly analogous to the army operative group. The Northwest Front Staff had the power of confirming
all appointments of commanders and commissars of otryads and of de-
moting officers from these positions. Possibly other operative groups had
similar duties, since the operative group with the Fourth Assault Army,
for instance, demanded efficiency reports from bands under its command,
but this cannot be ascertained definitely. [See Appendix, Document 10.]
The Northwest Front Staff also ordered general types of operations (destruction of unspecified bridges and enemy transportation facilities, liberation of prisoners of war, etc.) and demanded reports on the activities of
the bands and any information which they might have on neighboring
bands. Most important, perhaps, was its apparent responsibility for furnishing supplies by air to the partisans; it received the requisitions and
discussed arrangements with the bands and with the operative group, or
"brigade," for sending in planes with these supplies.

4. The Command Center in Occupied Territory

The command headquarters in enemy territory (which for convenience may be called here "operative group") served as a major center for relaying orders from high partisan commands, but in addition issued many of its own directives to individual bands. These orders may be grouped under three headings:

a. *Intelligence reports*. There was a constant need for information on the location and activity of the reporting bands and of other bands with which they had contact. In addition, of course, information on the Germans was essential. Some of the orders for such information came from the operative group itself, others came directly from the *razvedotdel* (intelligence section).

b. *Supply*. Many of the operative group's communications with the brigades concerned supply matters. The brigades requested supplies, sometimes in a most urgent manner; and the operative group required reports on the existence of food depots.

c. *Operations*. The operative group issued three types of orders about operations. Some were of a general nature, requiring, for example, that the brigade conduct demolitions on railroad tracks. Others were detailed directives on special types of activities such as the use of magnetic mines, or methods to be followed in destroying water pumps at railroad watering points. The third type of order consisted of detailed instructions for particular operations; these sometimes went so far as to prescribe the number of men and the types of armament to be employed.

5. The Brigade

The range and diversity of control of the brigade (or corresponding type of individual band) over its subordinate units was so great that no generalized picture can convey its real nature. To complete the schema of command functions, however, orders issued by the 1st Regiment of the 3d Brigade of Leningrad Oblast to its subordinate units may be briefly analyzed.

a. *Personnel*. Although, as noted above in the orders of the Northwest Front Staff, all promotions or removals from otryad command posts were confirmed by the Staff, the regiment issued the initial or temporary orders. Moreover, it provided for punishments consisting of reprimands, fines, and in one case (a sentry found sleeping on duty), death. In addition, individual partisans were cited for bravery.

b. *Supply*. Orders were issued for gathering food supplies, and for strict accounting for munitions.

c. *Organization*. The internal organization of the otryads was prescribed.

d. *Morale*. "Socialist competition" between units was ordered.

e. *Operations*. The area of operation of each otryad was prescribed. Specific otryads, platoons, and regimental staff members were designated to carry out certain assignments, and temporary commanders of special task forces were appointed.

In the survey of command functions in the partisan movement, two features stand out. One is the lack of any clear delineation of command functions between the various levels of the control structure. Established channels of command were often by-passed, and not infrequently the very top command issued orders directly to units near the bottom, disregarding several intermediate echelons. As noted above, the basic reason for this procedure was probably a need for speed and certainty of execution of the most important commands. Possibly the complicated and somewhat makeshift partisan command structure could not be trusted to transmit such important orders quickly; nevertheless, the frequent by-passing must have contributed to insecurity among officers in intermediate positions, and to a diffused sense of responsibility. Such a state of affairs is not unknown in other parts of the Soviet system, and the ill effects which it might engender are at least somewhat offset by the use of special control mechanisms.

A second feature of the command structure is closely related to the first; namely, the tendency to issue specific and sometimes minutely detailed orders on aspects of operations which in other systems might be left to officers on the spot, who presumably are more familiar with local conditions. Even the Central Staff, confined as it was to Moscow, did not hesitate to issue highly specific orders to individual bands. What effect this practice had upon the operations of the bands cannot be determined. Again, it appears to be a reflection of the usual Soviet practice of closely circumscribing the area of responsibility allowed its subordinates.[52]

H. IMPLEMENTATION OF CONTROL IN THE PARTISAN MOVEMENT

The discussion so far has centered in the organizational system and the chain of command within the partisan movement. Control of the partisans could not be maintained, however, merely by establishing a pattern of organization and outlining a hierarchy of command. This is true of all social bodies, but it was especially true of the partisan movement because of its irregular origins and extreme diversity of organization. Moreover, as we have seen, irregular channels were used frequently in issuing orders, even when the partisan movement had reached its full force. Consequently, it is extremely important to examine in detail the ways in which the Soviet regime ensured the execution of its will.

1. Technical Means

In the introduction to this chapter, it was stated that in the Second World War the existence of new technical devices, the airplane and the

---

[52] For a discussion of command responsibility in the Red Army, see Garthoff, p. 211.

radio, made it possible for the first time in history to convert the traditionally unregulated activity of guerrillas into a means of warfare consciously planned and directed by central authorities. The role of airpower has been frequently alluded to in the preceding pages and is discussed in Chapter VI. The radio has also been mentioned; and it was unquestionably a key element in the partisans' success. In the early days of the territorial partisan movement, the activities and morale of many bands seem to have been severely impaired by their inability to establish regular radio contact with the Soviet side of the front. Prominent partisan leaders like Fyodorov and Kovpak recount the joy they experienced in first receiving radio broadcasts from the unoccupied area, and they imply that lack of receiving sets was one of the major handicaps of their bands in the early stages.[53] Even when bands possessed receiving sets, however, they were often crippled by their inability to reach higher authorities to obtain new instructions or to ask for air support. The ability to request such instructions by radio transmitters seems to have saved a part of a band at Nikopol in September 1941, since Moscow replied with an authorization to disperse in order to escape enemy attack. Lack of an adequate transmitter, in spite of possession of a receiving set, possibly resulted in the complete destruction of another Ukrainian group at Novomoskovsk. [See Chap. XI, Sect. II.] Possession of adequate radio equipment was undoubtedly a major reason for the survival of the Crimean partisans. Although some of the first partisans were not provided with radios, their crucial role was certainly recognized at an early date by the Soviet officials, as indicated by the widespread use of parachutist teams provided with radio equipment—the example par excellence of the combination of new technical devices. From the winter of 1941–42 on, one can say that the partisan system of organization depended almost completely on radio. Those bands, like the roving bands, which could be provided with powerful sending and receiving sets were more or less independent and could even bring numerous other partisan bands under their jurisdiction. Smaller units, which perhaps had only feeble or unreliable sets, were subordinated to operative centers, one of whose major tasks was to maintain a powerful and constantly functioning radio station.

2. Special Means of Control

In addition to the extensive use of technical devices, the partisan command employed several special control methods. One of these methods was to make rather numerous changes in the chain of command itself. The relative frequency of such reshuffling has already been noted, and it is likely that, in addition to reasons of convenience, there was also on occasion a desire to replace a command echelon which had become inefficient

[53] Fyodorov, pp. 194, 309, 336; Kovpak, pp. 15, 59.

or untrustworthy. Such was certainly the case when the "Moscow" parachutists were used as reorganizers of the oblast partisan organization in Western Belorussia in mid-1942. [See subsections A and E, above.] One probable purpose in giving Kovpak complete control in the Pripet region was the desire to supersede the ineffective command system there.[54] In addition to reshuffling the chain of command as such, there was the reassignment of necessary individual officers which had the same result— the replacement of inefficient direction by more vigorous and capable leadership or the removal of sources of insubordination. Though it is impossible to estimate statistically the turnover of officers in key positions, it seems clear that such officers were changed more frequently than losses or need of rest would require. While comparatively few cases are known in which major officers were dismissed from command or were executed, a much larger number of such men disappeared for no apparent reason. The power of the regime to relieve a partisan officer of his command was rarely, if ever, challenged. Even when defiance was physically possible, such an officer in many cases would have been reluctant to resort to it because his family was "safely" in Soviet territory.

The power of the central partisan authorities was further enhanced by the physical dispatch of staff officers to the partisan bands. Generally these either were liaison officers who remained more or less permanently with a single band or operative group, or were inspectors or special emissaries who periodically and briefly visited most of the bands and operative groups under a particular staff. At times, the function of such officers appears to have been to make an unexpected check on the morale and efficiency of the band, at others to convey a special order of the staff, or to secure essential, on-the-spot information needed by the staff.[55] Obviously the frequent dispatch of such special emissaries was possible only by using air transport. Taken together, the specially assigned officers and the regular liaison men were the eyes and ears of the staffs in the occupied regions, and acted as a constant reminder of the omnipresent central control. Ordinarily, however, these officers seem not to have played an important role in directing operations. In a somewhat different class, but equally important for impressing the partisans with the reality of Soviet power, were visits from high-ranking officials of the partisan movement and the Party; these seem to have been timed to help reassert control at decisive moments in the course of partisan operations.

One other type of special control should be described. Frequently individual partisan leaders were flown back to Soviet-held areas for con-

[54] Cf. Linkov, p. 378, for a report on the violent objections made by some of the band commanders in this area to being placed under Kovpak's command.

[55] The best example of such an officer is Captain Ruzanov, Strokach's adjutant, who claimed to have visited at one time or another most of the bands in the Bryansk forest.

sultation with their superiors. Occasionally a major conference of partisan leaders was held. The most important meeting of this sort took place in Moscow in August 1942; the list of assembled partisan leaders, including Yemlyutin, Kovpak, Saburov, and Shmyrev (a leading Belorussian commander), reads like a *Who's Who* of the partisan movement. Postwar Soviet accounts place enormous emphasis on this meeting, perhaps in an ex post facto effort to enhance the role of Stalin, Khrushchev, and other high Party leaders who attended. At the same time, it is certain that the meeting occurred at a crucial period in the development of the partisan movement and that major decisions were imparted to the band leaders gathered there. Probably a major purpose was to bolster the morale of the partisan commanders by impressing them with their own collective strength and with the interest the Soviet regime took in their activities—at the same time, however, reminding them that they were only instruments of the regime.

Similar meetings were held on a smaller scale within the occupied regions. For example, in the late spring of 1942, Yemlyutin assembled the commanders of the major bands in the Bryansk region for a conference. The following year most of the commanders in the northwest Ukraine were called together at Kovpak's headquarters for a meeting with Korotchenko and other high officials who had flown in.[56] It is probably safe to say that the lower the level of the presiding officers at such a meeting, the more important was the role of planning and decision-making; while the higher the level of the presiding officers, the more important were morale and discipline.

3. The Party

In the partisan movement, as throughout the Soviet system, the Communist Party exercised an all-pervasive influence. Precisely for this reason, it is very difficult to define briefly its role as a control agency. From one point of view, the Soviet system is the Communist Party; all else is subordinate to, and an instrument of, this group, which was officially acknowledged as the exerciser of the dictatorship. Nevertheless, other organizations exist, other hierarchies are established, and every student of the system can point to cases in which a representative of the Party has been worsted in the struggle for decision-making by some one who nominally is lower than he in the Party scale. Consequently, such simple generalizations as "nothing exists but the Party," or "the Party (if any concrete manifestation of it is meant) is always right" are not acceptable.

The very creation of the Central Staff and other organs of the partisan

---

[56] One of the major decisions handed down by the Soviet authorities to the partisans at this meeting concerned Kovpak's raid into the northwestern Ukraine (see Kovpak, p. 89 and Shyyan, p. 62). It also seems likely that orders were given for the bands to concentrate on the increasingly important job of destroying German rail communications.

command structure indicates that, to some limited extent at least, a hierarchy of authority not directly identifiable with the Party existed. As was indicated above, the creation of these organs represented to a certain degree a compromise between Red Army and Party interests. At the very top, of course, Party officials—Stalin, Zhdanov, Malenkov, Voroshilov, Khrushchev, Ponomarenko, and Beria—remained supreme. At this level, however, it is almost impossible to speak of Party interests per se, for these men represented individually or collectively all of the power elements in the Soviet system. As soon as one looks down the ladder, it becomes apparent that there was a divergency of interests and power affiliations among the partisan leadership. The second echelon partisan leaders, like all Communists, were nominally subject to the discipline of their cells, or primary Party organizations. In practice, this evidently meant little when one could appeal to powerful persons outside the cell. Certainly major officials, and even individual band leaders who possessed the confidence of high authorities, had little to fear from the action of these primary organizations, although they were certainly bound to observe the forms of procedure established for such bodies. Moreover, in some areas at least, the *obkoms* sent out special inspectors to partisan bands, who were empowered to call their officers to account for delinquencies and to recommend disciplinary measures. Apparently, actual removal and appointment of partisan officers was reserved for higher elements of the partisan command structure. [See Appendix, Documents 22 and 23.]

The foregoing account, vague as it is, is all that can profitably be said in the limited context of this chapter on the role of the Party in the control of top echelons of the partisan movement. At a lower level, however, the Party's control function was less ambiguous, although even here it was characterized by many variations and shadings. As we have just noted, the ordinary partisan—even a subordinate officer—was subject to his primary Party organization in matters of discipline and morale. The Party organization interpreted this authority broadly, not only calling its members to account for personal derelictions or political wavering, but also demanding an accounting of their record as partisan fighters.[57] As in other "operational" phases of the Soviet system, the partisan officer who was willing to go counter to Party "suggestions," and succeeded in his mission, was usually safe, while the man who failed after rejecting the Party's advice was ruined.

The Party organization within the partisan band was especially important for conducting political activities among the population in areas where the territorial Party did not exist or was too weak to undertake these tasks. In some instances the commissar of the partisan band was charged with general supervision of political activities among the population, in par-

---

[57] Fyodorov, pp. 319, 325; Andreyev, pp. 181, 279.

ticular with propaganda work. Even where a vestige of the territorial Party organization existed, the partisan band seems to have carried on many of the physical tasks connected with propaganda work. It received material from the Soviet side of the front, reproduced articles, and distributed propaganda leaflets, although the territorial Party officials may have had a decisive role in determining the content of the propaganda and were usually listed as the issuers. [See Chap. IV, Sect. I, B.]

Within this general picture there were many variations. The Party organizations of some of the bands, such as those composed primarily of isolated Red Army men or those under the domination of a strong personality like the famous leaders, S. A. Kovpak or S. V. Grishin, were probably rather secondary affairs. In areas where the territorial Party organization worked in close conjunction with the partisans or where powerful Party officials led the bands, the Party organizations were much stronger. In any case, the influence of the Party unit within the band was much stronger on the rank-and-file partisan members of the Party than on major officers. [See Chap. III, Sect. III, B.]

Of special importance in this connection was the "junior" Party, the Komsomol, which undoubtedly played a major role in controlling young partisans, who were much more frequently Komsomol members than the older ones were Party members. It is doubtful whether the Komsomol organization significantly affected the direction of the partisan organization, however, except in the few bands whose nuclei consisted of Komsomols.[58]

One special feature of the partisan-Party relationship deserves mention. While the partisan movement was in a sense a tool of the Party, the Party organizations in the occupied area were frequently dependent upon the partisan bands for their effectiveness and indeed for their existence. This was true of many territorial Party organizations, which could maintain themselves only by physically joining a band. Numerous Party *raikomy,* especially in the areas annexed from Poland in 1939, were actually reintroduced into their areas by the partisan bands. As has been previously noted, one method used to reintroduce the *obkom* in the West Ukrainian oblasts was to send in the *obkom* secretary as the commander of an important band.

4. The NKVD

We have already noted that the NKVD was the co-sponsor of the initial territorial partisan organization. In the over-all picture, its influence in the partisan movement was almost certainly less after the fall of 1941. Nevertheless, the prominent role of such men as Sergiyenko, People's Commissar of Internal Affairs of the Ukraine, and apparently number two man in the real direction of the partisan movement, and Strokach,

---

[58] For mention of such bands, see Tsanava, II, 206, 919, 953.

his lieutenant in the Ukrainian NKVD who took charge of the Ukrainian Staff, suggests that NKVD influence remained strong at the highest level of authority. At other levels, it varied. It appears to have been strongest in the southern Bryansk area, where the Chief of the Orel Staff of the Partisan Movement, Matveyev, was an *obkom* secretary described as an "old Chekist,"[59] while the commander of the operative group on the German side of the lines, Yemlyutin, was a chief official in the oblast NKVD. In this area, too, the important Kiev NKVD official, Saburov, was one of the major band leaders at an early date and continued to play an important role in the Ukrainian partisan movement. It is not entirely clear what influence the NKVD exerted in Belorussia. The Chief of the Kalinin Front Staff, Belchenko, who was very important in one section of Belorussia, was an NKVD officer. [See subsection D above; also n. 35.] The fact that L. Tsanava, who at one time was a high NKVD official in Belorussia, was chosen to write a history of the partisan movement in that area also suggests an intimate connection.

At a lower level, the control exercised by the NKVD was less pervasive, but more tangible. Every staff, every operative group, every band (at least under normal circumstances) had its "OO" section, which represented the NKVD. Available evidence indicates that the "OO" sections were the most tightly organized of all elements in the partisan structure. "OO" sections at the Front Staffs were parts of the "OO" NKVD machinery of the Red Army Front Command. "OO" sections in bands and operative groups under the territorial staffs, on the other hand, were directly controlled by the People's Commissariat of Internal Affairs in their respective union republic.

Control by the higher NKVD authorities was probably equally tight in both cases, but more is known about control by the union republic NKVD's during the later stages of the war. A quotation from a German summary of interrogation, in August 1944, of the member of a band brings out clearly the basic functions of the "OO" section:

> The tasks of the "OO" are to maintain a watch on its own troops and also on any persons outside the unit who could impede its activity. In addition, the "OO" is charged with defense against spies. The "OO" is under a "commandant" of the [band] headquarters. He commands a "commandant" platoon of twenty-five to thirty men. Such a "commandant" platoon exists also in the battalions [of the band].
>
> The gathering of intelligence for the [partisan] unit and battalions is directed by the "OO." In the area of operations agents are recruited from among the civilian population.[60]

From this and other material it is clear that the "OO" section performed

---

[59] The Cheka was an early predecessor of the NKVD.
[60] FHO (IIb), "Auszug aus Kgf.-Vernehmungen (IIb-Nr. 3821)," 5 August 1944 (GMDS, H 3/476).

two fairly distinct functions. One was the gathering of information, and need not concern us here. The other was the maintenance of security and political control within the band. In this respect the "OO" section functioned as a covert control apparatus within the overt control system. Under normal conditions, it probably did not interfere with the control of operations and personnel exercised by the commander, the commissar, and other officers,[61] but it was constantly spying on them and other members of the partisan band, and was ready to intervene in case any tendency toward insubordination or laxity in carrying out the orders of the regime became evident. The NKVD personnel was able to perform this function effectively because it represented an in-group, in a sense a special elite, independently organized and in the last analysis subject in crucial matters to different authorities from those immediately commanding the partisans in general.[62]

5. The Red Army

The major role of the Red Army in the control of the partisan movement has already been discussed. In comparison to the Party, which played a pervasive but ill-defined part in controlling the partisans, and the NKVD, whose role was very significant but covert, the authority of the Red Army was precise and direct. It could order the partisans in its zone of operations to carry out tasks of a military nature and could insist on the execution of these orders. As a rule, the Red Army formations appear to have adhered to the chain of command established by the creation of the Front Staffs and their subordinate partisan headquarters, but, as noted previously, in the early stages of the partisan movement many important bands were controlled directly by Red Army commands. Even at later stages of the war this sometimes occurred when a Red Army unit

---

[61] Sometimes, it appears, the "OO" section chief was also one of the major officers of the band, but this was probably unusual.

[62] One case outlined by the Germans on the basis of interrogation of a captured NKVD officer is particularly illuminating in this respect:

In mid-1944 a special NKVD task force under the command of a first lieutenant was parachuted into Vileika Oblast in Belorussia. It was sent by the People's Commissariat of State Security (for our purposes identical with the NKVD) to carry out the following functions, in relation to the brigades under Machulsky, a representative of the Staff of the Belorussian Partisan Movement, and commander of an operative group: (a) to train the "OO" [of the brigades] in espionage and counterespionage, (b) to supervise the activity of the "OO's," (c) to organize a unified network of agents, (d) to act as a surveillance and executive organ for Machulsky in relation to the bands.

At any rate, it is clear that the "OO" sections were essentially dependent on an NKVD chain of command which intersected that of the partisan movement only at a fairly high level, and that, far from being subordinate to the band commander, the "OO" section at times at least was his master. In this way, every partisan band contained a control force which might be of only secondary importance under normal circumstances, but in time of crisis could be depended on to execute the will of the Soviet regime.

came in close proximity to a partisan band. [For examples, see Chap. VIII, Sect. II, B, 2.] Apparently the prestige and authority enjoyed by the Red Army were sufficient in most cases to induce band commanders to follow its orders without hesitation. In the final stages of the German withdrawal from Soviet territory, especially in the West Ukraine, such instances of direct subordination of partisan units to Red Army commands increased; sometimes the partisan bands cooperated directly in important Red Army tactical operations, such as the crossing of rivers. Cases are also known in which bands were directly incorporated, at least temporarily, into Red Army formations.

In addition to these more general types of authority, the Red Army at many times possessed a special means of checking and controlling the partisan bands. From the very beginning of the war Red Army commands frequently dispatched into the rear of the enemy special commando-type units which occasionally ranged hundreds of miles into the occupied area. The role of such units in re-forming the partisan movement in the winter of 1941–42 has already been described. In later years, their importance was less, but they continued to carry out special tasks such as obtaining information and destroying important installations. These tasks brought them into direct contact with the partisans and sometimes into competition with them, since such a force might be assigned to carry out a mission in which the partisans had failed. They acted as a source of information for the Red Army on the real activities of the partisan movement and at the same time reduced the dependence of the military on the partisans.

I. SUMMARY

In one way the preceding description of means of control helps to clarify the manner in which the partisan movement was directed. We have seen that the Soviet regime was not dependent on any single system of control, but had at its disposal numerous alternative chains of command and methods for impressing the partisans with its authority. If one method or channel proved ineffective, an alternative one was available. At the same time, however, the existence of these diverse methods, and especially of the several chains of command, reinforces the impression gained in the examination of types of orders: namely, that here was no clear-cut allocation of responsibility.

Apparently the average partisan band commander was never certain from whom his decisive orders would come. Nominally he was subordinate to a specific intermediate command level of the partisan structure. However, a higher level of this structure might at any time issue superseding orders directly to the band commander. Moreover, under certain circumstances, he might receive orders directly from the Red Army. The existence of this multiple command channel was only the beginning of his perplexity. He was also subject to the advice of the Party organization, which on certain occasions might affect operational matters. It was undoubtedly risky to disregard this advice, unless he was very sure of his own Party status. Moreover, the ubiquitous "OO" section, with its considerable independence of the partisan chain of command, exercised a constant surveillance over the band commander, and could scarcely fail to influence his actions. In some cases, he was permanently assigned the liaison officer of the partisan staff to which he was subject—a person whose observations could not be wholly ignored. And his band might at any time be visited by an inspection officer from this staff, or a high partisan or Party official. Finally, the band commander might himself be called suddenly to Soviet territory to report to the highest officials of the Party and the partisan movement.

In the scope of this chapter one can only indicate the complicated nature of this control system and the resulting perplexity of its objects, and perhaps hint at the reasons behind it. To a considerable extent, this system was a more or less accidental growth, resulting from the complex and diverse origins of the partisan movement. To some extent, the varied functions of the partisans—military, political, propaganda—required that they be directed by different agencies. Moreover, like all totalitarian systems, the Soviet regime required numerous competing elements, each checking and reporting on the other. One may suggest, however, that another related factor was present. By failing to delineate clear-cut areas of responsibility, by depriving the individual partisan officer of the security attendant upon the occupancy of a definite niche in a recognized hierarchy, the system denied him the feeling that he was secure so long as he acted in accordance with definite orders from a designated superior. As a result he was thrown on his own and became a more pliable and helpless instrument in the hands of the regime.

Many band commanders, of course, were not directly subject to all of the pressures listed above. As a rule, orders from headquarters other than the partisan operative group and the Red Army unit which was concerned with the band were infrequent enough not to form a major preoccupation of the commander. In most cases it was possible, rather than actual, interference by conflicting authorities which made for insecurity among command personnel. As previously noted, if the commander was a man of bold and decisive character, he could disregard the advice of the Party organization and the NKVD officer in his band, and if successful would not be called to account. Probably "family arrangements" such as those frequent in other phases of Soviet organization were sometimes made between representatives of the various chains of command in one band. Such arrangements might more or less tacitly have provided that the "OO" section chief, the commander, the commissar, and the Party would settle all disagreements among themselves, without reporting to their respective headquarters outside the band. All of these circumstances tended to mitigate in practice the ambiguity of command responsibility; however, at crucial times lack of definite patterns of responsibility must have made the partisan commander's position unenviable.

§IV. Conclusion

The foregoing discussion on means of control presented a review of many major aspects of the partisan organization and command. The broader political implications of the partisan movement have been treated in a wider context in the introductory chapter. Therefore, instead of summarizing such aspects of the movement here, it seems best to present a brief analysis of the rationale which lay behind the systems of organization used in the partisan movement, and the implications which these systems may have for the future.

There were two basically different systems of partisan organization. The territorial, described above in Section II, provided for relatively small partisan detachments (fifty to one hundred men) in each administrative subdivision of the occupied USSR. This system was to have been erected on the framework of the Party and NKVD territorial administrations, and all their command personnel as well as many of the rank and file would have been drawn from among their trusted members. The units would occasionally have conducted hit-and-run attacks against small enemy forces and would have terrorized collaborators, but would have rigorously avoided major engagements. Permanent camps, primarily supply depots, would have been maintained in isolated districts but the partisans would not have attempted to control any definite area. The emphasis would have been on stealth and surprise. In some cases, it was apparently hoped that partisan members could resume their normal occupations of ostensibly peaceful workers after the completion of each operation. The points of command above the bands were to have been underground Party committees, which would usually have been located in cities. Their members would have perhaps hidden in concealed quarters or perhaps have acted under the cover of normal occupations.

The way in which this scheme collapsed has already been described, and there is no need to review it here. It should be emphasized, however, that its success depended on several factors which were absent during the first months of German occupation in the USSR.

1. *Preparation.* Such a system needed a great deal of planning and preparation before the arrival of the enemy. Camps and supply depots had to be carefully constructed and completely camouflaged. Precise and accurately defined systems, including alternative methods, of communication had to be established between the bands and the underground centers. In particular, powerful hidden radio transmitters and secret landing fields were necessary. The personnel of the detachments had to be selected and trained with extreme care. This was necessary not only to ensure the partisans' loyalty and technical proficiency in disruptive tactics, but to acquaint them with the purposes of their activity and to make certain that they would continue to mount vigorous attacks even if the result was the decimation of their units. In fact all of these prerequisites were lacking, or at least very scarce. Planning at a high level had taken place before the war, but the persons who were to carry out the plans had never even been informed of the possibility of partisan warfare. A brief period of feverish and haphazard training and preparation took place after the war began, but the attention of responsible authorities was too divided and the time too short to achieve major results. Finally, the unexpected rapidity of the Red Army retreat produced a wave of panic which swept up many of the partisan cadres, while the chaos of the retreat disrupted physical preparations.

2. *Support of the population.* This territorial plan of partisan warfare, relying on concealment and stealth, presupposes the active support of a large majority of the population in the occupied area. The bulk of the population remaining in most of the territories occupied by the Germans was by no means strongly pro-Soviet. From the Soviet standpoint, it was at best passive, unwilling to cooperate with either old or new master until the victory of one was apparent; at worst, important elements of the population revealed the composition and hide-outs of the partisan bands to the Germans and cooperated in wiping them out by force.

In those areas where the territorial partisan movement enjoyed a measure of success, i.e., the North Caucasus and especially the Crimea, such success was due to the time available for preparation, the ability to profit from previous experience, and probably the presence of a greater proportion of Party and NKVD officials. Even in these areas, however, the territorial system survived only by abandoning several of its prescribed features, in particular the plan for a network of small groups in each district and the reliance on stealth. Indeed, changes were absolutely essential in these areas, partly because the contrast between favorable and unfavorable partisan terrain is sharpest there, and partly because a large element of the population consisted of Moslems bitterly hostile to the Soviet regime. That the Soviet authorities continued to use the territorial system at a late date under these adverse conditions indicates, however, that they favored it. Where feasible, the system was extremely useful to the regime, for it retained firm control of the partisan movement in the hands of the elements which were most reliable and most capable of maintaining the subordination and loyalty of the remaining population of the occupied areas. Under ideal circumstances it could accomplish more with less expenditure of resources than any other type of partisan movement, for it required no large additional increment of cadres to ensure loyalty. Moreover, since they avoided large-scale engagements, partisan detachments needed no extensive supply of arms and munitions.

The almost universal failure of the territorial system meant that another type of organization had to be relied on. The system, if it can be so called, described in Section III was as much the product of circumstances as the result of conscious planning. To be sure, the later partisan movement was not, as some authors have claimed, a "spontaneous popular uprising." It was rather the result of the efforts of thousands of supporters of the Soviet regime who, through the fortunes of war, found themselves in occupied territory, or who were sent in purposely to organize resistance to the occupier. Only gradually did the higher authorities of the Soviet regime introduce order into the haphazard growth of this type of organization. The control system superimposed on the partisan bands did indeed succeed in maintaining an extremely high degree of overt loyalty to the regime. It also guaranteed that the bands endeavored to execute missions of military or political importance. It did not, however, introduce a sufficient degree of uniformity and efficiency to transform the partisan bands into units capable of conducting military operations comparable to those executed by Red Army formations of similar size. Moreover, the resulting partisan organization could operate effectively only under certain favorable conditions, and not throughout the occupied territory during the entire period of occupation.

In order to understand why the partisan movement took the organizational form it did after the winter of 1941–42, it is necessary to examine very briefly the nature of the war on the eastern front. In a sense, the German attack on the USSR was a tour de force of astonishing magnitude. Considering how incredibly brutal and stupid the German policies in the occupied area were, it is amazing that for two-and-one-half years after the defeats during the winter of 1941–42, the Wehrmacht continued to occupy substantial portions of the Soviet Union. From early 1942 on, the Soviet forces were considered to have superiority in the air; they had a large and increasingly superior artillery force; and from the very beginning of the war, they possessed a wide numerical margin in manpower. Nevertheless, the better organization, leadership, discipline, and military qualities of the lower ranks of the Wehrmacht enabled the Germans to hold out until 1944. Rarely, if ever, has an invading force maintained itself on enemy territory for so long a period of time, when it was so enormously inferior in manpower and military equipment. Occupation under such circumstances involves very severe risks and disadvantages. It was the business of the Soviet partisans to maximize these risks and enhance these disadvantages.

German inferiority in technical equipment gave the partisan bands enormous advantages. There was little to fear from German airpower since it was too scarce to be assigned to antipartisan operations frequently; on the other hand, the bands received matériel and personnel of incalculable value through almost unimpeded air transport. Lack of armor and fire power on the part of German and auxiliary outfits made it possible for the partisan unit of brigade size, even though of dubious military quality, to fight at least a delaying action by supplying a screen of fire from its numerous automatic weapons. Since the Germans lacked equipment and air support, only large, carefully prepared offensives could overcome the major partisan concentrations. These offensives were necessarily infrequent; as a result the partisans could completely control large areas for months at a time. Lack of manpower restricted the Germans to major towns and roads in those regions where the partisans were really active, and left the countryside almost at the mercy of the Red forces.

These conditions made feasible the creation of large brigades. Under favorable conditions, such units could fight German forces of considerable strength, were generally well able to dispose of collaborator outfits, and could present an imposing appearance to the population. Such forces, multiplied many times, and coordinated by headquarters both within and outside the occupied territories, were gradually able to transform most of the northern part of these territories into a sort of twilight zone, which was neither German domain nor fully regained by the Soviets. As the Germans weakened, the area of partisan control was extended, and more and more of the population in the "occupied" areas were made to feel that they were already reincorporated in the Soviet system.

Large bands of this type, relying on the possession of fairly definite base areas and subsisting on food supplies drawn from a population controlled by force, had definite limitations. Since the Germans lacked airpower and armor, the partisans could from time to time conduct sweeping raids into open country, such as the famous raids of Kovpak and Naumov in the Ukraine. They could not engage in continuous activity in such open regions, however, for, as long as the Germans had the strength to react forcefully, they could send in sufficient regular troops to wipe out the poorly trained and undisciplined partisans who were then caught far from the shelter of marsh and forest. Since the large band was the only generally successful form evolved by the Soviets during the Second World War, the richer half of the occupied territories, the Ukrainian plain, remained relatively free of partisans until almost the end of the occupation.

CHAPTER III

Composition and Morale of the Partisan Movement

Earl Ziemke

§I. Composition of the Soviet Partisan Movement

A. DISTINCTIVE COMPONENT GROUPS

1. The Peasants

The peasants in the occupied territory were united in one overwhelming desire—to have the collective farm system abolished. Few peasants were convinced Communists, and the political system and form of government were matters of considerable indifference to them.[1] They were practical-minded opportunists, willing to tolerate the German regime if they could extract economic advantage from it. German occupation policy frustrated most of their hopes.

Although they were disappointed in the Germans, the peasants never identified themselves with the partisans. While they may not have been entirely indifferent to the major issues in the war, they wanted economic stability above everything else. They disliked turning their produce over to the Germans, but they liked even less turning it over to both the Germans and the partisans. Their concentration on economic self-interest made them reluctant to join the partisan movement, since, from their point of view, it was disruptive and economically a waste of time.

Paradoxical as it may seem, however, the peasantry probably furnished between 40 and 60 per cent of the total partisan recruits; virtually all of the peasant recruits were drafted into the movement. Since the partisans were able to move freely through most of the rural districts, it was a relatively simple matter for recruiting agents to enter the villages, select men,

[1] Prop.Abt.W.beim Befh.d.rueckw.H.Geb.Mitte, "Taetigkeitsbericht," 31 March 1942 (GMDS, OKW/749). *Ibid.,* "Stimmungsbericht," 15 November 1941 (GMDS, OKW/634).

and march them off as partisans. The Germans liked to picture the process as kidnapping; in fact, however, this type of recruiting was carried on so widely that it assumed the appearance of a regular administrative procedure.

Within the partisan movement the peasants remained a distinctive group. They comprised nearly nine-tenths of the so-called "forced recruits." The draftees were a distinctive though not a cohesive group. They were held in the partisan movement less by force, as the Germans claimed, than by the hopelessness of their situation. The partisans claimed a legal right to their services and, in view of the progressive disintegration of German control, the peasants could not help but recognize this right. They wanted to be neutral, clearly an impossibility; consequently, without surrendering any of their basic attitudes, they allowed themselves to be drawn into the partisan movement where they formed a passive, unenthusiastic group.

2. The Urban Contingent

The working population of the cities was more strongly influenced by communism than the peasants. The Soviet program of industrialization had impressed the workers.[2] Though the standard of living was abysmally low, German investigators reported that the city people were pleased with the advances which had been made: greater opportunities for education, low admission prices at the theater and cinema, and new factories and public buildings.[3] Nevertheless, at the outset, many of them hoped to benefit from the German occupation. However, the occupation, if anything, soon increased their support for the Soviet system. They believed that progress had been made under the Stalin government. By contrast, the war brought widespread destruction and the collapse of economic activity in the cities; the urban residents, who had believed themselves the most advanced element in the population, experienced a rapid economic decline to a level below that of the peasantry

The position of the city laborer was hopeless. Market prices bore no relationship to pay scales, and a week's pay was not enough to live on even at a subsistence level. While the worker was sometimes fed on the job, his family literally starved. The result was a loss of desire to work and, finally, a refusal to work. Such conditions forced many of the workers, particularly young, unmarried ones, into the ranks of the partisans.[4]

It is impossible to estimate how many left the urban areas to join the partisans. Probably their numbers were small in relation to those of the peasants and former Red Army soldiers. By and large, they were motivated

[2] *Ibid.*, "Taetigkeitsbericht," 31 March 1942 (GMDS, OKW/749).
[3] *Ibid.*
[4] HFPCh im OKH/GenStdH/GenQu, "Entwicklung der Partisanebewegung in der Zeit vom 1.1—30.6.1942." 31 July 1942, p. 2 (GMDS, HGr Nord 75131/113).

less by ideological considerations than by economic pressures, but in comparison with the peasants, for instance, they were a dedicated group.

3. The Intelligentsia

The term "intelligentsia" is used here less with reference to the upper intelligentsia—professors, writers, editors, etc., most of whom were evacuated and who in any case were few in numbers—than to the broad, lower reaches of the class—local doctors, teachers, and administrators of various kinds—and the subprofessional people—clerks, bookkeepers, and others. These men, because they thought in terms of their careers, were likely to believe that they had to choose one side or the other. Furthermore, they did not possess the personal anonymity of the peasantry, for instance, and it therefore behooved them to give serious consideration to their attitudes. From the partisan point of view, they were people well worth recruiting in order to deprive the enemy of the benefit of their skills and because they were persons whose attitudes generally influenced others.

In the main, the members of the intelligentsia had fared better under the Soviet regime than they did under the Germans. Many of them were men who had been in line for advancement; under the Germans their careers were placed in jeopardy. Even those who had been dissatisfied with the Soviet system soon learned that they would gain nothing from the German occupation. Of the 5,000 teachers in Vitebsk Oblast, to cite one instance, the great majority were unemployed most of the time between 1941 and 1944. As a result a large number made contact with the partisans as early as May 1942.[5]

The intelligentsia formed a sizable group in the 1941 partisan units, comprising most of the officer contingent and a segment of the rank and file as well. As the movement grew, the intelligentsia declined in numerical importance, although it remained an important element in the success of the partisan movement.

4. Red Army Stragglers and Prisoners of War

The German Army took over 3,000,000 prisoners in the first six months of the war. Several hundred thousand prisoners were taken in each of the great battles of encirclement—Bialystok, Minsk, Smolensk, Kiev, and so forth. It is certainly true that not all of the Soviet soldiers trapped behind the lines surrendered. If, as can probably be safely estimated, one in ten avoided capture, the total would have come to more than 300,000. Then, too, in the first flush of success, the Germans released some thousands more, chiefly Ukrainians and others who were considered anti-Soviet. Wretched conditions in the prisoner-of-war camps forced more thousands to try to save their lives by escaping. By January 1942 the former Soviet soldiers

[5] 201. Sich. Div., Ia, "Monatsbericht," 6 May 1942, p. 18 (GMDS, 201 ID 29196/2).

at large in the occupied territory probably totaled between 300,000 and 400,000.

These men formed a new social group with a very sharply defined reaction pattern. They had no legal status; if they came into contact with the Germans, the best they could expect was to be sent to a prisoner-of-war camp, which was tantamount to a death sentence. With the front moving rapidly eastward, most of them found it impossible to return to the Soviet side; moreover, many had had enough of war and were not eager to return to the Red Army. A few were assimilated by the local population, but most remained involved in the war regardless of their personal desires. As soldiers they had a clear and potentially enforceable commitment to the Soviet Government, in whose eyes they were already all but guilty of treason. Therefore they were constantly under pressure to rehabilitate their reputations, and this pressure became irresistible once the tide of the war turned in favor of the Soviet Union.

German policy added other pressures. In July 1942, the chief of the German secret field police described the problem as follows:

The partisan movement received its greatest increment of strength from the stragglers of the great battles of last year and the escaped prisoners of war who at first had settled down in the villages. Some of them had even married local women in order to pass as natives of the village. In the reorganization of the system of agriculture, these people were not given consideration, and when they reported for duty with the local militia or applied for work in Germany, most of them were turned down because they possessed no credentials. Besides that, as has already been explained, at the beginning of the drive to recruit workers for Germany, the wildest rumors were spread concerning the fate of the recruits. Finally, when it became known that former Soviet soldiers were to be interned in German prisoner-of-war camps, they left their places of employment in droves and went into the forests where they joined partisan bands.[6]

The massive upswing of the partisan movement which followed the successful Soviet winter offensive of 1941–42 brought thousands of former army men into the movement, until, by the summer of 1942, they formed the largest single increment. In July 1942 the Germans estimated that the stragglers and escaped prisoners of war made up 60 per cent of the total partisan strength.[7] In 1943 and 1944, the partisan units consistently averaged about 40 per cent former Soviet Army men. In many ways these men became the backbone of the partisan movement: they had military training and experience; for the most part, they had neither family nor property ties in the occupied territory; they had definite legal and moral obligations to the Soviet Union; and their previous experiences led them to prefer partisan activity to life under the German occupation.

[6] HFPCh im OKH/GenStdH/GenQu, "Entwicklung der Partisanenbewegung in der Zeit vom 1.1.—30.6.1942," 31 July 1942 (GMDS, HGr Nord 75131/113).
[7] Ibid.

5. Communist Party Members

Some bands organized in July and August 1941 evidently consisted of up to 80 per cent Party members.[8] Such units, however, were not typical even in this initial period; still, the earliest bands had a relatively high concentration of Party members—between 25 and 40 per cent. After the spring of 1942, when recruitment was begun on a mass basis, the Party contingent declined sharply in relative numbers. The captured Party records of two partisan companies operating in the spring of 1942 show that one company had 6 (4 per cent) Party members out of a total strength of some 150 men;[9] the other, with a total of 142 men, had 7 (5 per cent) Party members, 3 (2 per cent) Party candidates, 24 (16 per cent) Komsomols, and 108 (77 per cent) men with no Party affiliation.[10] In September 1943 a brigade with a total strength of 1,113 men had 40 (3.5 per cent) Party members, 87 (7.8 per cent) Party candidates, 334 (30 per cent) Komsomols, and 652 (58.7 per cent) men with no Party affiliation.[11] It appears that Party men, including candidates, rarely made up more than 10 per cent of the strength of individual units. The percentages of Komsomol members ran higher, between 15 and 30 per cent, probably because the requirements for admission to the Komsomol were less stringent than for the Party and also because a large proportion of the partisans fell in the younger age groups. In addition, the ranks of the Komsomol were not so severely thinned by Soviet evacuations and German police action as those of the Party membership.

The Party men remained an elite group in the partisan movement throughout the war; no other group ever achieved significant influence. At the same time, the Party segment was important chiefly as an instrument through which Soviet control was strengthened; there is no indication that the Party members acted as a spontaneous, creative guiding force.

6. Collaborators

The taint of collaboration fell on a great many people in the occupied areas. By definition, anyone who did not actively fight the Germans was culpable. Soviet propaganda constantly reiterated the questions: "How did

[8] HFPCh im OKH/GenStdH/GenQu/Abt.K.Verw., "Erfahrungen ueber Aufbau, Aufgaben, Auftreten und Bekaempfung der Partisanenabteilungen," 15 January 1942 (GMDS, Wi/ID 2.217).

[9] 707 Inf.Div., Ic, "Feindnachrichtenblatt fuer die Truppe Nr. 16," 10 November 1942 (GMDS, 707 ID 27797/4).

[10] Gen.Kdo. XXXXVI. Pz.K., Ic, "Partisanenregiment Shabo," 2 June 1942 (GMDS, 23 ID 24182/16).

[11] PzAOK 3, Ic/AO, "Nr. 5394/43 geh.," 19 September 1943 (GMDS, PzAOK 3 40252/7, Anlage 30–33). Cf. the estimates in John A. Armstrong, *The Politics of Totalitarianism* (New York: Randon House, 1961), p. 163; though the latter are based entirely on Soviet statements, they correspond very closely to the estimates given in the present text.

I fight the Fascists? How did I defend my native land? Where was I when the entire Soviet people were engaged in a heroic fight against the enemy?" Those who could not produce satisfactory answers were promised short shrift at the hands of the returning Red Army. To nearly everyone, then, participation in the partisan movement was valuable chiefly as an alibi, a means of avoiding prosecution as a collaborator. One consequence of this situation was that in the later years of the war the Red Army apparently was inclined to regard all partisans as a crew of former collaborators trying to save their skins by hiding in the woods and putting up a feeble show of resistance.

The most significant collaborator group was the so-called "military collaborators"—the policemen, army auxiliaries, and members of German-organized indigenous military units. These men acted as the main German antipartisan force. Estimates on their number range from 800,000 to 2,000,000.[12] If all the types—police, regular military formations, and army auxiliaries—are included, the total can be safely set at over 1,000,000 (more men than served in the partisan movement).

Once it became clear that the Soviet Union would win the war, the situation of the military collaborators became desperate. The partisans tried to complete their demoralization by promising an amnesty to those who deserted and enrolled in partisan detachments. The appeal was successful. Occasionally entire collaborator units went over to the partisans. In the summer of 1943, in Belorussia, an SS detachment composed of 2,000 former prisoners of war was taken over to the partisans by its commander, a former Soviet Army colonel. Several months earlier, in the same area, 700 Tatars from another German unit had deserted to the partisans.[13] The mass defections were more dramatic but less important than the constant trickle of individual deserters who made their way to the partisan brigades. The small groups of local police, scattered throughout the countryside, were particularly affected; every German withdrawal occasioned a wave of desertions from their ranks.

In general, the promised amnesty was honored by the partisan units. The collaborators made useful recruits, for many of them had had military training; moreover, their prospects of surviving a desertion back to the Germans were extremely poor. In contrast to the Germans, the partisans were usually careful to avoid giving the lie to their own propaganda. On the other hand, in terms of additional strength for the partisan movement, the collaborators were not important. By mid-1943, when the collaborators were prepared to desert in significant numbers, manpower was no longer a prob-

[12] George Fischer, *Soviet Opposition to Stalin* (Cambridge, Mass: Harvard University Press, 1952), p. 45.

[13] PzAOK 3, Ic, "Entwicklung der Bandenlage im Bereich der 3. Pz.AOK," 1 February 1944 (GMDS, PzAOK 3, 62587/12).

lem for the partisans. In the last year of the war the collaborators may have composed between 10 and 20 per cent of the strength of the movement.

7. Women

To the Germans, who summed up their conception of the role of women in society with the slogan *Kirche, Kueche, Kinder* (church, kitchen, and children), the enlistment of women for combat duty was an outright abomination. The Soviet Government, on its part, publicized the participation of its women in partisan activity as evidence of superior dedication and resolution.

In the detachments women were used chiefly as scouts and intelligence agents. Soviet intelligence tended to rely heavily on women agents, particularly in partisan-infested territory where women made the best agents, since men of military age were liable to arrest on sight. Some of the women had training as radio operators and nurses, and a large proportion of the doctors assigned to the partisan units were women. The trained nurses and doctors had officer status. Sometimes the women were assigned to combat missions along with the men, but it appears that, aside from intelligence missions, they were more often used as medical personnel, cooks, and washerwomen.

Few women were drafted. For the most part, they were volunteers, motivated by political convictions, a desire for adventure, or the wish to achieve distinction. Some who were trained on the Soviet side of the front were not volunteers in the strictest sense, since their assignment was often not a matter of choice; however, even they were usually Komsomol members and were otherwise politically reliable.

Almost every partisan detachment had some women members, although they usually numbered no more than 2 or 3 per cent of the total unit strength and hardly ever more than 5 per cent. This was roughly the number of women that could be utilized effectively in a given partisan unit. Women added little to the combat strength of their detachments. Their value as scouts and intelligence agents has already been mentioned. Aside from these jobs, they served mainly as noncombatant personnel, and because of the limited food and equipment of the partisans, such noncombatant personnel detracted from the combat potential of the units.

A principal reason, if not the principal reason, for including some women in nearly every partisan detachment was that a woman to share his quarters became one of the perquisites of the partisan officer, along with a Nagan pistol and, when he could manage it, a leather windbreaker. Customarily, the officers from the brigade commander down to the battalion commanders "married" the women enlisted in the unit. The rank and file had to content themselves with less convenient arrangements. The result was a cynical attitude toward the participation of women in partisan activity. With a few women cast into an exclusively male society, the sexual element became dominant. The lower-ranking partisans were kept from intimate association with the women for reasons of morale and discipline; and the women became the property of the officers, which by implication gave them officer status, with such attendant privileges as quarters with the brigade staffs, relief from combat assignments, and so forth. The women, in turn, were often willing to content themselves with their contribution as officers' "wives." More serious still, as the following excerpt from a partisan diary reveals, they sometimes came to believe that their association with the officers elevated them to command status:

. . . Everyone who married while serving with the unit will not be regarded as married and must live in separate quarters [from his wife] in the companies to which he belongs. The women of the staff are being assigned to the individual companies and their immediate transfer to these companies is demanded. This caused a great uproar which I consider justified. This order was necessary because the wife of the chief of staff of the brigade, Malvina, considered herself rather than her husband as the chief and continuously interfered in military matters. Furthermore, there are many women in the unit who literally do nothing and consider themselves only as wives of the staff members. Such conditions could not be tolerated any longer. However, it was not necessary that the dance [sic] should start this way. The most important [way] to begin would have been to ask the officers [not to permit] their wives to interfere in official business any longer. The way [in which it actually was done] makes the entire business smell like an enforced separation from a legitimate wife. [The writer, a battalion politruk, may have had a wife himself.]—Appendix, Document 74.

One indirect result of this sort of situation was that captured women partisans often were exceptionally well informed and could give valuable information.

B. SHIFTS IN COMPOSITION

The Soviet partisan movement was by no means a static institution. Virtually no generalized statement can be made about it without qualification as to place and time. The partisan movement of 1943, for instance, was so different as to be more of a successor than a lineal descendant of the 1941 movement. This state of constant flux was evidence of both strength and weakness. It demonstrated the ability of the Soviet command to exploit new situations as they arose. It also indicated that, had the occupying power been able to take advantage of new trends by reversing them or preventing their development, the partisan movement might have been crippled at any one of the several stages in its development.

In 1941 the partisan movement bore something of the character of a volunteer organization. It depended heavily on Party members and others who, if the word is used loosely, could be considered volunteers. The number of men impelled by eagerness to throw themselves into partisan activity was probably small. Most were brought into the movement by fairly conventional motivations—a sense of duty, acquiescence to established authority, a desire for recognition, and so on. With the exception of three or four detachments in the Ukraine and a few more in the Crimea and near Leningrad, the units formed were small, seldom as many as 100 men. They were expected to remain in their home localities, drawing on local men for reinforcements and replacements. There are indications that if the military situation of the summer and fall of 1941 had been prolonged until well into 1942, these detachments would have disintegrated or, at best, stagnated. They displayed few signs of genuine vitality. With the shift which came in the spring of 1942, they were rapidly engulfed in the masses of new partisans, although a large number of officers from these early units managed to retain and augment their commands.

The most decisive and clearly discernible shift followed the victories of the Soviet Army in December 1941 and January 1942. The partisan movement came to life with a rush, stimulated by the Red Army and Soviet policy. The victories created a new atmosphere, charged with a nice mixture of fear and optimism, which facilitated a mass recruitment drive in the occupied areas. The most important contingent of recruits came from the Red Army stragglers left from the 1941 battles. The group characteristics of these men: their hopeless position vis-à-vis the Germans, the necessity to rehabilitate themselves in the eyes of the Soviet regime, their vulnerability to reprisals, and so on, have already been described. They were better material than most of the men taken in later. In a limited sense, they were volunteers; they had been turning to partisan warfare in small groups since as early as July and August 1941. After the winter battles they joined (or were drafted) in large numbers until, by the summer of 1942, they amounted to nearly 60 per cent of a total partisan strength of 150,000 men.

At the same time, in the spring of 1942, the partisans began drafting men on a wide scale. Many former Red Army men were so inducted, although most of the draftees came from the indigenous civilian population. The draft was supported by official Soviet and partisan policy, which made all men between the ages of fifteen and sixty liable for service. It served two purposes: it increased the numerical strength of the partisan detachments, and it tied up manpower which might otherwise have been exploited by the Germans. The drafted men were far from being ideal partisan material; they were almost exclusively peasants, whose general characteristics were described above, and they had exhibited a remarkable lack of enthusiasm for participation from the outbreak of the war. The draft gained momentum in 1942 and continued until 1944. By the end of 1942, however, it reached a ceiling imposed by food and equipment supplies. Thereafter, the drafted men remained the major source of replacements, the result being that losses and attrition in the other groups were compensated for by drafted peasants, who by late 1943 composed about half the total partisan strength.

In 1943, there was a new wave of volunteers. Many of these people were of doubtful antecedents, military and political collaborators or managers and professional people who had tried to carry on their peacetime occupations under the German administration. Others either decided "to get on the bandwagon" or joined because they found life between partisans and Germans intolerable. How many such people were taken into the partisan movement cannot be estimated; it is likely that in the Ukraine, in particular, they became a significant element. They were important for two reasons: they signalized and, in part, hastened the disintegration of German authority in the occupied areas; and they lent credence to the opinion which undoubtedly prevailed in some Soviet quarters that the partisan movement was chiefly notable as a refuge for slackers and collaborators.

C. NATIONALITIES

The nationality problem was of minor significance in the Soviet partisan movement. Four-fifths of the total partisan strength was concentrated in Belorussia and the Russian SFSR. The remaining major area which came under the German occupation, the Ukraine, was not partisan territory until after the summer of 1943. The absence of intensive partisan activity there might, with some justification, be credited to national attitudes, but on closer examination the nationality factor declines in significance. It is true that the Ukrainians reacted more sympathetically to the German occupation than either the Russians or Belorussians; on the other hand, popular opposition to the occupation was not decisive in the growth of the partisan movement, even in the northern regions. A variety of other elements—distance from the front, unsuitable terrain, less social and economic dislocation, absence of large numbers of Red Army men cut off by the German advance—take precedence over nationality in accounting for the weak Ukrainian partisan movement.

The majority of the partisans, again four-fifths of the total, were either Belorussians or Russians. By accident, an admixture of other nationalities appeared everywhere. Since remnants of Red Army units and escaped prisoners of war formed a large segment of the partisan movement, Ukrainians, Tatars, Cossacks, and members of the Caucasian and Asiatic nationalities turned up in nearly all detachments. As the war progressed, deserters from German collaborator units composed of Tatars and Cossacks appeared in increasing numbers in predominantly Russian or Belorussian units.

D. AGE GROUPS

By Soviet decree all males in the occupied territories who had reached the age of seventeen were required to report for duty either in the partisan movement or in the Soviet Army. The minimum and maximum age limits were fifteen and sixty, but the bulk of the partisans fell within the seventeen to thirty-five age group. The presence of large numbers of Red Army stragglers made this very satisfactory age distribution possible. Men over forty were recruited, but apparently in limited numbers; in view of the tight supply situation there was constant pressure to reduce the overhead of inefficient personnel. A noteworthy, though small, group among the older men consisted of veteran partisans from the Civil War years. Although most were in their fifties and sixties, they were valuable because they helped create romantic associations with the Civil War partisans. They also had experience; some, like Shmyrev who commanded the First Belorussian Partisan Brigade, became successful unit commanders.

§II. Conditions of Partisan Life

A. THE SIZE OF THE MOVEMENT

The exact total strength of the Soviet partisan movement will probably never be known. The best evidence indicates that it reached a total of 30,000 men by 1 January 1942, rose to 150,000 by the summer of 1942, to 200,000 by the summer of 1943, and then declined slightly to 150,000–175,000 by June 1944 as partisan territory was retaken by Soviet forces.[14] The personnel turnover resulting from casualties, sickness, and desertions over a three-year period, brought the total of men who at one time or another participated in the partisan movement to about 400,000 or 500,000. These figures represent the number of partisans enrolled in regular, permanently organized combat units. In addition there was a host of agents, saboteurs, demolition teams, and others, who sometimes operated independently and at other times were in contact with the partisan detachments.

More significant for this study is the size of the combat detachments. These tended to be large; the brigades ranged from 300 to 2,000 men or over, with the standard unit strength averaging between 800 and 1,400 men. The trend toward concentration of partisan forces in brigades and, further, in operative groups and centers was an extremely significant feature of the Soviet partisan movement. From the point of view of the Soviet command it had great prestige value; it also facilitated supply operations. The large units tended to become entities in themselves, impersonal and readily

[14] The official Soviet war history, put out by the Institut Marksizma-Leninizma, *Istoriya velikoi otechestvennoi voiny Sovetskogo Soyuza,* ed. P. N. Pospelov *et al.* (Moscow: Voennoye Izadtelstvo Ministerstva Oborony SSSR), IV (1962), 468, states that there were 120,000 partisans in touch with the Central Staff in January 1943; 250,000 in January 1944. In view of the fact that many units were not in regular contact with Soviet headquarters at the earlier date, these figures correspond fairly closely to the estimates given in the present text.

amenable to Soviet control. It had effects within the movement as well. The size and apparent permanence of the brigades gave their members a valuable sense of security. The feeling of being isolated, impotent, and hopelessly outnumbered in small detachments which nobody knew or cared about had impaired the efficiency of all the 1941 detachments and had led many to collapse altogether. The brigades, on the other hand, were part of an established force, in close contact with the Soviet command, and carried out recognized and even heroic missions. The individual partisan counted for less in the mass organization; at the same time, he achieved a greater sense of personal importance since he could claim membership in one of the well-known brigades and thereby reassure himself that his services would not go completely unnoticed. The large units also made possible the recruitment of doubtful elements. A 1,000-man brigade could carry 40 to 50 per cent drafted men. Within operative groups whole brigades, with the exception of their officer complements, could be organized, utilizing only drafted men or former collaborators.

B. RECRUITMENT

The partisan movement was not a volunteer organization. There was a constant trickle of volunteers, but the majority of members in the non-officer group were drafted. According to one German source, most of the volunteers in 1942 were young men from towns and cities where they could not find employment.[15] In the countryside the draft was proclaimed publicly, generally in terms similar to the following:

Members of the [Soviet] Armed Forces, Citizens in the
Area Temporarily Occupied by the Bandits!

All members of the armed forces who escaped from the pocket [Operation "Seidlitz," which cut off a Soviet army in June 1942] and are at home, also all men in the class of 1925 [those born in 1925], report to your regular units or join the partisan units! Those who remain in hiding and continue to sit at home in order to save their skins, and those who do not join in the patriotic war to help destroy the German robbers, also those who desert to the Fascist army and help the latter carry on a robber war against the Soviet people, are traitors to the homeland and will be liquidated by us sooner or later. Death to the German occupiers! We are fighting for a just cause! In 1942 the enemy will be totally destroyed.

2 August 1942[16]

With the German hold on the occupied territory greatly weakened by the winter battles of 1941–42, the partisans were able to regularize their draft procedures. In a district south of Bryansk the detachments were or-

[15] Prop.Abt.W.beim Befh.d.rueckw.H.Geb.Mitte, "Stimmungsbericht fuer den Monat August 1942," 4 September 1942 (GMDS, OKW/733).
[16] XXIII A.K., Ic, "Uebersetzung, Tagebuch der Kampfhandlungen der Partisanenabteilung des Oblt. Morogoff," September 1942 (GMDS, XXIII AK 76156, Anlage 12).

dered to draft all men between the ages of seventeen and fifty and also childless women fit for military service. Three-man examining commissions, each including a medical officer and a representative of the special section of the NKVD ("OO"), were created. The detachment commanders were required to draw up lists of men eligible for service, submitting the following information about each person: first and last names and patronymic, place of birth, date of birth, Party membership, nationality, education, occupation, military service status, active service in the Red Army, rank, membership in partisan or self-defense units and reasons for leaving, and names and residences of relatives.[17] In May 1942 a Soviet Army battalion appeared near Bryansk and, according to its orders, carried out recruitment for the partisan movement in the following manner:

1. Drafted all Red Army men who had remained in the area as survivors of the encirclement battles or as discharged prisoners of war.

2. Mobilized the men born in the years from 1923 to 1925.

3. Organized partisan units. (The Red Army men were to be used, first, to bring the strength of the battalion up to 300 men and, after that, to reinforce the partisan units.)[18]

From time to time, local officials of the German administration reported on the recruiting procedures. A member of the *Ordnungsdienst* (the indigenous police) described conscription in his district, where all the men between the ages of sixteen and forty-five from five villages had been summoned to appear for examination and induction at a central collecting point. There, he said,

> They were given physical examinations by a military mustering commission and were either taken along by the partisans or sent home if they were unfit for service. The partisans were led by Russian officers in black uniforms with regular insignia of rank. Those found to be fit were told that they had been drafted into the Red Army and now had to render service as soldiers.
> . . . All of them were immediately armed with rifles and assigned to companies and platoons.[19]

On another occasion a village mayor reported that he and three other men from the village had been taken from their homes at night by armed partisans. They were marched to a collecting point where, in the course of the night, sixteen men were assembled. They were registered and assigned to squads of six men to be sent to various units. The mayor stated that in the course of the registration one of the partisans, probably a politruk, addressed the recruits as follows:

[17] Korueck 532, Ic, "Auszug aus dem Befehl fuer die Partisanen-Abteilungen im Rayon Wygonitschi," 19 October 1942 (GMDS, PzAOK 2, 30233/66).

[18] 339. Inf.Div., Ic, "Interrogation of Sidor Kletschko," 5 July 1942, p. 1 (GMDS, DW 55 B).

[19] GFP Gr. 729, Aussenkdo. 5, "Bandenbewegung im Gebiet noerdlich des Iput," 3 October 1942, (GMDS, 221 36509/11, Anlage 1).

"You have now joined the partisans." To the reply that we had been brought by force, he answered, "That is not important. Those who do not want to go along can say so." No one answered, since all believed they could count on being shot if they protested. He [the politruk] continued, "You are not to regard yourselves as drafted men, but as voluntary members of a partisan unit which has set itself the task of defending the fatherland."[20]

The method of processing men after they had been assigned to detachments is described in the German documents.

Each recruit goes through a probationary period and, as a rule, is not given a weapon until he has been with the unit at least four weeks. He is first detailed to tend the cattle and horses and perform other menial duties. Later, he may stand guard without a weapon, accompanied by an armed partisan. During the probationary period he is constantly under close surveillance. If a recruit manages to desert in spite of all this, all the members of his family are sought out and killed. When the unit changes camps all the recruits who have not yet demonstrated their reliability are shot. During the probationary period, the recruit's name is submitted to the Soviet authorities by radio for a background check. If the recruit comes through the trial period successfully, he is given a rifle and told that from that moment on he is a dead man if he falls into the hands of the Germans. The procedure is effective. It makes infiltration by our agents difficult, gives sufficient time for screening out undesirables, and places the remaining men in the position of believing themselves too deeply involved in partisan activity to risk reprisals from both sides by desertion.[21]

This statement must, of course, be regarded more as a composite of practices which appeared frequently in many partisan units than as a description of standardized procedures.

Periodically, particularly in the spring and summer of 1942, the partisans were able to conscript more men than they could use. The surplus recruits, wherever possible, were sent across the front to Soviet territory. A German summary report, written in the summer of 1942, contains this account:

In addition to forced recruitment among the male population, which has been observed to bring up to strength or bolster the partisan units, regular draft notices are distributed in the villages according to which the male population are enjoined to assemble in the center of the village. The draft notices state that anybody who does not appear will be classified as a deserter and will be punished according to the laws of war. All men are taken through the front to the Red Army. . . . The population were warned for the last time that in case they did not appear at the proper time, their property would be confiscated and their houses burned down.[22]

[20] Chef Sipo u. SD, Teilkdo. Surash, "Partisanenmeldung fuer die Zeit v. 19–21.5.42," 21 May 1942, p. 1 (GMDS, 205 ID 24746/5).
[21] Kav.Regt. Mitte, "Erfahrungsbericht ueber die Kampftaktik der Partisanen und Moeglichkeiten unsererseits die Banditengefahr zu beschraenken," 23 June 1943 (GMDS, HGr Mitte 65002/22).
[22] Chef Sipo u. SD, Einsatzgr. B, "Taetigkeits- und Lagebericht der Einsatzgruppe B fuer die Zeit vom 16.8–31.8.1942," 1 September 1942, p. 4 (GMDS, EAP 173–g–12–10/2).

The commander of the First Belorussian Partisan Brigade, whose men held the Vitebsk Corridor, one of the major points of contact between the partisans and the Red Army, claimed that 25,000 recruits had been sent through the front from his operating area by August 1942.[23] That this traffic, involving thousands of men, was carried on regularly during 1942 and 1943 is substantiated by German observations. Occasionally the men were armed, trained, and returned to the occupied territory as partisan replacements.[24]

C. TRAINING

Within the individual partisan detachments the levels of training varied widely. After the summer of 1942 a well-organized brigade might have had 1–5 officers and a similar number of noncommissioned officers on detached duty from the Red Army; 10–20 other officers, usually former Party or civilian officials; 20–30 specialists trained in Soviet territory, most of them demolitions men; 150–200 former Red Army men, either stragglers or escaped prisoners of war; 50–100 men who had some training in Soviet territory before being committed as partisan reinforcements; 100–200 men with no formal military training but with several months' experience as partisans; 200–400 raw recruits, chiefly peasants with neither training nor experience; 1–10 women, some with no training; 1 or 2, perhaps, trained behind the Soviet lines as nurses or radio operators. Such a brigade would, in fact, have ranked above average. Not infrequently, brigades which suffered heavy losses carried as many as 75–80 per cent inexperienced recruits.

This large number of raw recruits was less of a handicap than it might seem at first glance. The Soviet authorities were willing to sacrifice quality for a mass movement, since the missions demanding skilled specialists could, in any event, be carried out by small trained detachments sent in for the purpose. While the wholesale drafting of untrained men may have decreased the over-all efficiency of the units, it served a purpose by sequestering manpower which was potentially useful to the enemy and it strengthened the Soviet hold on the people of the occupied territory.

Training was one of the major functions of the partisan units. The brigades regularly scheduled military and political lectures, inspections, and weapons drills. There was ample time for such activities. One partisan stated that: "There were days, especially in the spring when the snow started to melt and the partisans, who were badly shod, could hardly move, when only the most important operations were carried out, i.e., procuring food or performing some sort of urgent job. Usually for a few weeks

[23] P. Vershigora, *Lyudi s Chistoi Sovestyu* (Moscow: Sovetskii Pisatel, 1951), p. 393.
[24] Gen. Kdo. II.A.K., Ia, "Bandentaetigkeit im Maerz 1943," 29 March 1943 (NMT, NOKW 2369).

in the spring we sat in the camp and took military training, just as in the army."[25]

Most of the brigades were sedentary and operated from fixed bases, from which they sent out details to perform specific missions. The combat activity of a brigade was generally low in relation to its numerical strength. From the point of view of targets, opportunities, and equipment, the brigades were very often overmanned. In the larger partisan centers, where between 12,000 and 20,000 men were sometimes concentrated in a small area, it was possible for entire brigades to go for periods of several months without any noteworthy combat assignments. Under such circumstances, recruits were given training in handling weapons, employed in building fortifications, or sent on foraging details.

The training programs of the brigades were hampered by two major difficulties: one was lack of *esprit de corps;* the other was the quality of instruction. Partisan warfare requires a certain amount of individual initiative even in the lowest ranks. In combat, for instance, mass maneuvers are of no importance; the individual must be able and willing to make his own decisions. Personal dedication to the cause is also necessary; one defector could, conceivably, bring about the destruction of an entire brigade. Generally speaking, while the brigades gave their drafted recruits a basic knowledge of tactics and some training in the handling of weapons, they failed to stimulate genuine *esprit de corps.* The peasant draftees remained, at best, indifferent. The most debilitating effects of the situation were kept in check by close surveillance of the men and by brutal reprisals against the families of deserters. Furthermore, the course of the war after 1941 made it clear to even the most reluctant recruits that their future did not lie with the Germans.

To achieve and maintain a reasonable standard of quality in the training of partisans remained a problem throughout the war. With a large contingent of inexperienced officers and a high percentage of low-caliber recruits there was constant danger of the partisan movement sinking into various kinds of erratic behavior, losing its military usefulness, and, possibly, becoming a political liability. The situation was dealt with in part by the development of rigorous external control and in part by the infusion into the partisan detachments of regular army officers and noncommissioned officers and of personnel trained on the Soviet side of the front. By late 1942 every brigade had some Soviet-trained partisan officers or regular army officers to supervise training and discipline.

Early in the war an extensive partisan training program was launched on the Soviet side of the front. It proved particularly valuable in the crucial 1941–42 period. By mid-1942 there were fifteen training centers lo-

[25] Harvard University, Russian Research Center, Project on the Soviet Social System, interview protocol series B 7, # 3, p. 31.

cated in the vicinity of Voronezh alone. Others were established at Voroshilovgrad and Rostov, and those at Moscow, Leningrad, and Stalingrad were among the largest. These schools trained partisans and diversionists who were to carry out special sabotage and espionage missions, provide the nuclei for new partisan units, or take over the leadership of existing detachments. For this type of training Communists and Komsomols were preferred, but Party affiliation, except in courses for leaders, was not mandatory.

In one of the centers near Voronezh the course of instruction lasted six weeks, and the classes numbered between 170 and 250 men. A school at Moscow turned out classes of 450 men. At the Sport Institute in Leningrad, training was given to Estonians who had been evacuated by the Red Army. Schools near Rostov turned out specialists in espionage, railroad demolitions, disruption of communications, and aircraft signal work. The NKVD operated additional centers of its own. Thus, one NKVD school at Moscow trained officers. At Voronezh, classes of 400 to 500 men and women, selected for their special skills as telegraphers, railroad workers, pickpockets, and so on were trained in sabotage and espionage techniques.[26]

A typical training course covered the following:

1. Training in demolition of rail lines, bridges, airplanes, and airports and use of various kinds of explosives.

2. Instruction in how to act in the German rear area; how to seek out local Communists; how to secure German identification papers; how to recognize German rank insignia.

3. Instruction in map reading and use of the compass, and knowledge of terrain.

4. Instruction concerning methods of carrying out missions for the Soviet intelligence service.[27]

At the conclusion of the training period the classes were divided into groups of eighteen to twenty persons, each under the command of an officer and a commissar. Dressed in civilian clothes, or occasionally in uniform, the units were parachuted behind the enemy lines. Some groups were assigned several women or children to act as scouts and agents. Standard armament consisted of one light machine gun, several submachine guns, four rifles, four hand grenades, and five kilograms of explosives.[28]

In the spring of 1942 the Germans observed that partisans trained behind the Soviet lines were being sent into the occupied territory in large

[26] HFPCh im OKH/GenStdH/GenQu/GFP, "Entwicklung der Partisanenbewegung in der Zeit vom. 1.1.—30.6.1942," 31 July 1942 (GMDS, HGr Nord 65131/113).
[27] *Ibid.*
[28] *Ibid.*

numbers. For example, it was known that, within a period of two to three weeks early in 1942, 450 parachutists were landed in a small area west of Mogilev in Belorussia.[29] Very often these people merged with locally organized detachments, where they assumed command, instituted strict discipline, and organized militarily useful operations.

Not all the partisans sent in from Soviet territory were highly trained, however; many training courses were superficial. Often units were hastily formed, armed, given some vague instructions concerning what was expected of them, and dropped by parachute, or else they infiltrated through the German lines.

D. EQUIPMENT AND FOOD SUPPLY

Although captured enemy weapons and ammunition were used extensively by the Soviet partisans, viable combat units could not be maintained solely on the basis of a hit-or-miss collection of enemy equipment. After 1941 the partisans relied increasingly on weapons, ammunition, and explosives of Soviet manufacture brought in by air. The logistics of this supply operation and its contribution to military effectiveness are not of primary concern to this study; however, its possible effect on the individual partisans is worth mentioning. By the very nature of his position, the partisan is an underdog, fighting an enemy vastly superior in numbers and equipment; consequently, anything which reduces his feeling of fighting against hopeless odds is likely to boost his morale and increase his military effectiveness. The Soviet partisan undoubtedly derived a sense of confidence from carrying a new Soviet-made submachine gun or rifle. Indeed, by 1943 and 1944 he was frequently better armed than the second- and third-rate German troops sent against him.

The Soviet Air Force was not able to transport food in addition to weapons and ammunition to the partisans; moreover, it was sound strategy to make the partisan movement a drain on the agricultural resources of the occupied territory. Thus the partisans had to live off the land. Foraging became a major activity, almost the exclusive occupation of some units. A captured partisan gave this description of the food situation in his brigade:

We brought ten horses along to the camp and, in the course of the month, slaughtered and consumed eight of them. It was possible to secure enough potatoes by uncovernig the storage bins of the burned-out villages in the neighborhood. In the same fashion, we secured some rye. In a village eleven kilometers from the camp, we found a larger supply of unthreshed rye which we threshed and milled, using millstones found in the village. At the beginning there was no salt at all. We never had canned goods although the officers may have had some.[30]

[29] Ibid.
[30] 218. Inf.Div., Ic, "Aussagen einer Banditin, Krankenschwester," 10 June 1943 (GMDS, 12 ID 35220/17).

Irregularity characterized the partisan food supply. A given unit might eat well for several weeks or months and then be reduced to sheer starvation for a similar period. There was a chronic shortage of salt, which was sometimes brought in from Soviet territory.[31] Horsemeat, potatoes, and unmilled grain were the staple items of the diet.

Some of the large brigade complexes gained virtual control of extensive districts, where they were able to regulate the food supply to some extent by establishing storage centers, gathering herds of cattle, requisitioning from the peasants, and controlling the rations of their subordinate units. The complexes, however, had the nearly fatal tendency to overstrain the resources of their zones of operation. At best they managed to achieve a delicate balance between consumption and supply. If a German counter-operation intervened to upset that balance the recovery of the entire complex was often seriously delayed or rendered impossible.

E. THE CAMP

The permanent camp was a distinguishing characteristic of the Soviet partisan movement. The climate made substantial housing a necessity throughout the greater part of the year. In the main regions of partisan activity the terrain afforded cover for fairly extensive installations and Soviet preference for large units of 1,000 or more men led to reliance on a relatively secure permanent base rather than on mobility of the unit. The permanent camp was a characteristic of the first detachments organized early in 1941. Prior to the occupation, some of the most elaborate installations of the entire war were constructed in the Ukraine. One of these was described in a German report of 1942:

. . . construction of the reinforced dugouts was ordered. Taking tactical considerations into account, the dugouts were arranged to form a triangle [three dugouts facing each other so that each could be covered by small arms fire from the other two]. Each dugout had space for fifteen to thirty men. The average size was eighteen by twenty feet, with small passages leading off from the sides for protection against shell fragments in case of attack. The depth at the entrance was about four feet, and the floor slanted toward the rear to a depth of nine feet. The doorway was slightly more than a yard high. Beside the door there was a glassed-in window which offered observation into the forest [and could serve as a fire port]. The dugouts were blended into the forest cover. Trees of various sizes were planted on the roofs of the dugouts, and the excess earth from the excavations had been hauled away. A yard-wide passage ran down the center of each dugout. Wooden platforms built on either side of the passage served as bunks. The walls were faced with small logs, partly covered with boards. A stove for heating and cooking was built in one corner. Most of the cooking, however, was done in a separately constructed kitchen dugout. The chimneys ran up through the roofs, usually into a tall tree, so

[31] References to the salt shortage appear repeatedly in the documents pertaining to the food situation and partisan morale. The shortage also affected the civilian population. The Germans frequently used salt as a premium for extra work.

that the smoke would be dispersed among the leaves and branches. Each dugout also had a table and benches.

At the time the work on the dugouts was begun, large stocks of food—salt pork, beef, flour, and so forth—were brought into the forest and buried in sealed containers. The food caches were scattered over an extensive area and carefully concealed. Ammunition and explosives were stored in well-built underground storerooms, likewise well camouflaged.[32]

The dugout (*zemlyanka*) described above was constructed according to specifications issued by the Soviet central authorities after it was learned that, left to themselves, the partisans were likely to solve their housing problems in various fanciful but impractical ways.[33]

The dugout became standard in all partisan areas, and the Germans were often moved to something approaching admiration for the simple utility and painstaking camouflage of the structures. A German lieutenant submitted the following report on an attempt to locate and destroy a partisan camp:

With a patrol composed of one officer, two NCO's, nine men, and thirteen OD men [indigenous police] I left Kletnya at 1230 to clean out this partisan nest. The patrol was guided by a captured partisan under guard. At the beginning we marched along fairly good sled trails. . . . Scattered blood stains on the snow indicated that we were on the right trail. [That same day, in a skirmish, German troops had captured two partisans and wounded several others.] After one hour we reached the end of the sled tracks.

From there on faint footprints were observed which followed winding forest paths. Here and there more blood stains appeared. Frequently, secondary tracks led off into the forest, obviously made to confuse pursuers. Zigzagging back and forth in the forest I lost my sense of direction, but I think we went in a generally northwesterly direction. At 1400 . . . we came to a clearing. . . . According to the prisoner we were still about two miles from the camp. Knee-high snow made movement difficult. . . .

After another twenty minutes' march [we came to another small clearing where one track branched off to the left]. We had all gone on past, when an OD man who had followed that track called our attention to a man standing in a fir thicket sixty to seventy yards away. He had already opened fire on us. Splinters of birch twigs fell around me. We returned the fire as the man turned and ran. I sent several men [to cut him off].

With the OD men and three or four of our men, I formed a skirmish line and moved forward through the forest. The fleeing man, of whom we caught occasional glimpses through the trees, fired on us several more times. After we had moved on another 500 yards or so, I suddenly found myself in a clump of scattered fir trees. Catching sight of horses' hooves hanging out of the trees [carcasses hung there for storage], I thought I had come upon the dugout we were looking for. As I circled the spot, I was fired upon from nearby. I took cover and noticed for the first time an excellently camouflaged bunker-like structure about thirty yards away. I ordered hand grenades thrown into the bunker. . . . It was empty. . . .

[32] GFP Gr. 725, "Partisanen-Erfahrungsbericht," 22 January 1942 (GMDS, HGeb 30910/37.
[33] *Ibid.*

The bunker was solidly built. The walls were made of five to six inch logs, extending only about a foot above the level of the ground. The dugout was covered with earth, with only the entrance and window left uncovered. The roof was supported by two log beams and covered with a foot of ground. . . . The bunker on the inside measured about twenty-six feet in length, sixteen feet in width, and six feet in height. Nearby we found a supply of firewood, a kitchen dugout, and a well. The small stock of food was worthy of note.[34]

The camps varied in size. Ordinarily, however, the brigades and other larger units did not establish a single contiguous camp but set up separate sites for each otryad or even for each company. A brigade might be dispersed over ten or twenty square miles. Groups of brigades occasionally occupied areas of several hundred square miles. In the larger concentrations the partisans proceeded as well to the construction of machine gun and mortar emplacements, earthwork fortifications, and roadblocks.

In the final analysis, the camp provided barely tolerable living quarters. In the spring and the fall, if the bunkers did not fill up with water, they were certain, at least, to be damp and muddy. In the winter they could be heated but only at a risk of revealing their location. In the daytime they were never heated; and at night, as long as snow was on the ground, fires were lighted only for cooking, in order to avoid smoke stains on the snow which could be detected from the air.

F. TERRAIN AND CLIMATE

The forests and swamps were the best allies of the partisans, for they provided cover and some protection. At the same time, however, they made for a rather strenuous existence. Under pursuit, two or three days of steady marching could bring whole units to the verge of collapse. Accounts similar to the following appear frequently in the partisan diaries:

We are crossing the Lebyashka swamp. The villages round about are in flames. In the distance the thunder of cannon can be heard. Every five to six hundred yards we have to rest. We sit right down in the water, and, after ten minutes, move on. Everyone is weak. The swamp sucks us down. We sink in often, sometimes up to the hips. There is no end; the forest seems to be moving away from us. Finally the order is given to rest until dawn. During the march it is hot, but when one stands still for a few minutes he begins to shake with cold. Everyone lies down to sleep. Camp fires are forbidden; the swampland is flat; and the Germans are all around. We lie pressed against each other for warmth. One wakes often because his wet side is freezing.[35]

The author of the diary was killed on 17 September 1942. From 7 to 17 September the unit had wandered in the swamps, using up its food supply; finally, it requested permission by radio to change its operating

[34] Kdo Baran, "An die 2. Kompanie Cholopenitschi," 24 February 1942 (GMDS, 286 ID 9970/2).

[35] Korueck 584, "Ein Tagebuch, das von der Gruppe Findeisen 21.9, gefunden wurde," 21 September 1942 (GMDS, Korueck 38998/2).

area. By 17 September, however, the unit had broken up as groups became separated or lost in the almost impassable terrain.[36]

The climate added to the rigors of the partisans' life. Summer brought hordes of mosquitoes and flies. In July 1943 a German antipartisan expedition reported, "After two days our horses are already showing signs of strain, mostly because the clouds of mosquitoes prevent them from grazing."[37] The captured documents of one partisan unit which operated near Bryansk reveal that in the summer of 1942 the unit, unable to endure the mosquitoes, abandoned its camp in the forest and moved into villages where it was exposed to destruction by the Germans.[38] Winter imposed other hardships. After the war a partisan commander wrote, "The cold, incidentally, is no ally of the partisans. Maybe it did hold the Germans back from an offensive, but we suffered from it to a much greater degree."[39] In the winter the forests provided less cover, and the chances of detection by air or ground observers were greatly increased.

G. MEDICAL SERVICES

In one unusual case, a unit of 500 men, organized in 1941 in the Ukraine, had seven doctors, one for each company and two with the staff.[40] At the end of the same year, the German secret field police reported: "It has been repeatedly determined that, in the larger partisan camps, there are also doctors available who care for the health of the partisans. In December 1941, in Tatin-Bor, a partisan hospital was reported, and later captured, which was headed by a Russian doctor."[41]

In the north, somewhat later, probably not before the late summer of 1942, nearly every brigade had at least one doctor and several nurses, some of whom had medical training. The trend toward large, sedentary partisan detachments facilitated the establishment of relatively adequate medical service. Some of the doctors were flown in to the units, but because of their potential usefulness both to the Germans and the partisans, it was preferred to recruit as many as possible in the occupied territory—by force if necessary. The brigades and brigade complexes usually set up

[36] Korueck 584, "Gefechtsbericht ueber die Bandenbekaempfung in Abschnitt des Kdt. rueckw. A. Geb.," 3 October 1942 (GMDS, Korueck 38998/2).

[37] Abwehrtrupp 210 bei PzAOK 3, Ic, "Unternehmen 'Winter,'" 29 July 1943 (GMDS, OKW/209, Anlage 6/4).

[38] GFP Gr. 639 b. PzAOK 2, "Dem Panzerarmeeoberkommando 2 Ic/A.O.," 20 July 1942 (GMDS, PzAOK 2, 30233/66).

[39] A. Fyodorov, *The Underground Committee Carries On* (Moscow: Foreign Languages Publishing House, 1952), p. 416.

[40] Ltd. Feldpolizeidirektor bei der 444. Sich. Div. "Monatsbericht," 5 November 1941 (NMT, NOKW 1519).

[41] HFPCh im OKH/GenStdH/GenQu/Abt.K.-Verw., "Erfahrungen ueber Aufbau, Aufgaben, Auftreten und Bekaempfung der Partisanen-Abteilungen," 15 January 1942, p. 27 (GMDS, Wi/ID 2.717).

some sort of permanent hospital facilities. In January 1944 a deserter from the partisans of the Mogilev center in Belorussia gave this information:

The hospitals of the partisans are located in the same forest as their camps. [There were four regiments of between 1,500 and 2,000 men each.] They [the hospital structures] are dugout bunkers with windows, and they are well-furnished. The Osmanov Regiment has at its disposal five hospital bunkers plus two bunkers for contagious diseases. There is plenty of trained, capable medical personnel. The over-all direction of the hospitals is in the hands of a doctor brought in from Moscow.[42]

Partisan hospitals are mentioned frequently in German reports. During an operation against the partisans north of Borisov (June 1943) SS troops captured a complete dental station. Generally, the facilities in the occupied territory were designed to handle only emergencies or minor wounds and illnesses. Serious cases were evacuated by air to Soviet territory. [See Chap. VI.] A partisan woman doctor, captured in September 1942, described this procedure:

The recent [August 1942] German attack brought the number of wounded cases to eighty, more than half of them serious. All but five of the seriously wounded were evacuated by air at night prior to 8 September. During that time [31 August to 8 September] about six aircraft, always three to a flight, made three trips per night between Valdai [on the Soviet side of the front] and Suselnitsa. They were small planes which could carry only one seriously wounded man at a time. Since 8 September the nearness of German troops has made it impossible to continue the air traffic.[43]

In the larger partisan centers it was often possible to land two-engined planes (C-47's and similar types) and evacuate fifteen to twenty men on each flight.[44]

Hospitals, air evacuation, and the presence of medical personnel greatly stimulated partisan morale and made the men more willing to take risks. At the same time the medical service suffered from one outstanding weakness: during a German counteroperation, when the greatest number of casualties were likely to be suffered, air evacuation was generally disrupted and the ground facilities were often in such a state of hopeless confusion that all too frequently, at this time of greatest need, medical service was not available.

The quality of the medical service was impaired by chronic supply

[42] H.Gr.Mitte Ia, "Ein Ueberlaeufer aus der Gegend nordostw. Klitschew berichtete ueber die Organisation der Banden in diesem Raum," 5 January 1944 (GMDS, HGr Mitte 65002/69).

[43] Lw.Div. Meindl/Ic, "Vernehmung Nr. 74," 22 September 1942 (GMDS, AK X 44431/78).

[44] 404. Inf.Div., Ic, "Vernehmungsbericht Nr. 22P," 5 June 1943 (GMDS, 4 PzD 34335/16).

shortage. The Grishin Regiment, one of the best detachments, raided hospitals in the occupied territory for its medical supplies.[45] A former nurse, interrogated after the war, declared that sometimes her unit had plenty of supplies, and at other times it had nothing at all. She reported that most of the medical supplies came from a doctor employed by the Germans, with very little being sent from the Soviet Union. Generally bandages were washed and reused. Narcotics were always scarce and were used sparingly. There was a shortage of soap, and vodka was used as a surgical disinfectant.[46] A doctor, who deserted in June 1943, stated that her unit had received a small quantity of serum for immunization against typhus and a supply of special soap for delousing. She also stated that orders "from Moscow" forbade the use of medicine in the treatment of venereal diseases.[47] In another detachment ten men and two women who had contracted syphilis were executed on the grounds that it was impossible to cure them under the circumstances.[48] (This was undoubtedly a disciplinary as well as a medical measure.)

The general health level in the partisan movement is difficult to assess. The Germans did not learn of any serious incidence of epidemic diseases. Typhus broke out regularly, but it was endemic in the Soviet Union. A former partisan commander wrote that the most frequent ailments in the partisan units were rheumatism, scurvy, pellagra, boils, and toothaches.[49] According to the statement of a former partisan nurse, stomach and intestinal disorders were the most common complaints.[50] Probably the major health hazards were contaminated water, poor and insufficient food, and, to a lesser extent, exposure to cold and dampness. Both observers agree that health problems were less serious than might have been expected. On the other hand, captured tables of strength of the Grishin Regiment indicate that in 1942 the unit lost 261 men through sickness, which meant a loss of 38 per cent of its total strength of 737 men. In the same period only 52 men were lost in combat and 20 deserted. The loss through sickness of 27 men in August 1942, 192 in September, and 29 in November suggests that some type of epidemic disease was responsible.[51] No other instances of this sort have been discovered.

[45] OKH/GenStdH/Abt. FHO, "Nachrichten ueber Bandenkrieg Nr. 7," 8 December 1943 (GMDS, H3/738).

[46] Harvard University Refugee Interview Project, B Schedule Interview No. 41, p. 17.

[47] 404. Inf.Div., Ic. "Vernehmungsbericht Nr. 22 P," 5 June 1943 (GMDS, 4 PzD 34335/16).

[48] 707. Inf.Div., Ic, "Feindlage im Hauptbandengebiet Kamenez-Mamajewka," 22 December 1942, p. 2 (GMDS, 707 ID 27797/4, Anlage 239).

[49] Fyodorov, p. 422.

[50] Harvard University Refugee Interview Project, B Schedule Interview No. 41, p. 17.

[51] OKH/GenStdH/Abt. FHO, "Nachrichten ueber Bandenkrieg Nr. 8," 8 December 1943 (GMDS, H3/738).

§III. Group Characteristics

A. INFLUENCE OF THE OFFICERS

The brigade commander was probably the most important individual in the partisan movement. On the German side of the front there was no permanently assigned superior troop commander. Of necessity, the orders he received from superior authorities were usually general rather than specific, with the exact method of execution left to his discretion. The brigade itself was often the commander's creation. With no regular supply or recruitment services, the size and operating efficiency of the brigade frequently depended on the commander's ability to organize stocks of weapons and food. His energy and ability in finding recruits and integrating them into the brigade were undoubtedly important. To a certain extent, the reputation of the commander, based on his demonstrated ability to keep his men fed and armed, and his skill as a tactical leader (one who achieved success without excessive casualties) served to attract recruits and contributed to the spirit of the brigade. The commander's reputation probably also influenced the amount of support that the brigade received from the Soviet side. Above all, the operating efficiency of the entire partisan movement depended almost entirely on the individual brigade commanders. The brigade was the focal point for the control of partisan operations. Orders from higher echelons could be put into effect only by the brigade commanders. Since each brigade operated as a self-contained unit, the execution of orders depended directly on the energy, intelligence, and daring of the individual commander to a far greater extent than in any comparable regular military unit.

The decisions of the brigade commander were determined by his response to two conflicting pressures: one from the Soviet authorities, in the form of demands for bold, militarily useful operations and the other, amorphous but extremely persistent, pressure from the mass of the partisans, in the form of passive insistence on provisions for personal security and reduction of risks. Almost invariably the commanders responded to the pressure from below by reinterpreting orders from the Soviet side, by falsifying reports, and by selecting relatively safe missions and avoiding more important but dangerous assignments. There are numerous instances of brigade commanders who allowed their brigades to sink into passivity but no demonstrable cases of commanders who hewed precisely to the line of Soviet requirements. The best commanders managed to find a middle course, keeping their units active militarily and simultaneously controlling the drift toward passivity by recognizing and abetting it within reasonable limits.

With the partisan brigades operating independently, no clearly defined standards of officer conduct and performance were established. The Soviet authorities sponsored the development of a partisan officer group modeled on that of the Red Army. Regular army officers were installed at all levels in the brigades. The nonprofessionals in the movement—the Party men and others—were given assimilated army ranks. In some brigades the officers wore Red Army uniforms and insignia of rank. One of the most remarkable, and in some respects incongruous, results of the introduction of formal military procedures was the appearance of bureaucratic tendencies in the partisan movement. The brigade staffs sometimes were inclined to keep aloof from their subordinate units, avoiding personal contact, and relying instead on written communications, with the result that the partisan movement developed into what the Germans sometimes called a "forest bureaucracy." The units accumulated substantial files of orders, directives, and reports, and, in some cases at least, became absorbed in the proliferation of paper work because it was fashionable.

Despite these tendencies, however, and the effort to introduce formal military procedures, the partisan officer contingent developed some distinctive characteristics. In partisan warfare it was impossible for the Soviet Union to control men purely by the force of delegated authority and the trappings of rank. In his postwar memoirs, a partisan commander wrote: "But restraining people only by the force of an order or a Party decision, that is, relying exclusively on the discipline inspired by the authority of the command and the Party leadership, could not be done for long in underground work."[52] Because of the relative isolation of each partisan brigade, there was no chance for a sharply defined class of partisan officers to develop. The officers were inclined to identify themselves more closely with the interests of the rank and file in their own brigades than with the officer groups of the other brigades or of the movement as a whole. Moreover, there were strong leveling processes at work in the brigades. The officers enjoyed some privileges, primarily of a minor nature. Generally speaking, the officers faced the same hardships and dangers as the men. The result was that the officers tended to rely on personal authority rather than on formal military authority. While this may have been regarded with grave misgivings by the Soviet regime, undoubtedly it contributed greatly to the cohesiveness of the partisan units. The men and officers developed a community of interest which centered on their own brigade. Many who could not generate much enthusiasm for the Soviet cause itself sometimes developed strong feelings of loyalty to their own detachment or to their commanders. At the same time, the process led to a weakening of Soviet control, since the officers and men tacitly joined forces to evade or interpret in their own favor the directives imposed from above.

Much of what has been said about the partisan officers can be said

[52] Fyodorov, p. 353.

about the commissars and "OO" officers as well. In the long run, they, too, were likely to identify themselves with the group interests of the brigades and to modify their conceptions of their own roles as Party or NKVD representatives. The commissars and officers were less sharply distinctive groups in the Red Army. Many of the brigade commanders had at one time been commissars, and many others were as much Party men as the commissars who served with them. At the lower levels, the political officials were often not career men but *ad hoc* appointees. Less is known about the NKVD "OO" officers, but it appears that many of them were not professionals, and the "OO" in the partisan movement was not the thoroughly integrated organization that it was in the Red Army.

While the trend in the partisan movement was toward informal officer-man relationships, the authority of the officers was not sacrificed. On the contrary, the conditions of partisan warfare brought the determined, resourceful, and even brutal officer to the fore. Punishments were harsh and swift; summary executions were commonplace. Instances of abuse of authority were far from rare. Still, even deserters usually believed that such harsh measures were necessary. They seemed to think that the standards of justice were attuned to the conditions of partisan warfare. [See below, Sect. III, D. 3.]

The Germans frequently claimed, with some justification, that the majority of the partisans were held in the detachments only through fear of the officers and commissars. For the drafted men, former collaborators, and other allegedly undependable elements, who did indeed form a numerical majority in the partisan movement most of the time, fear of the officers was a primary motivation. It was their misfortune to be treated as a class in which each man at any time might be subjected to indiscriminate and ruthless intimidation. On the other hand, the men against whom there was no presupposition of unreliability could work out some sort of personal *modus vivendi* and needed to fear punitive action by the officers only for specific offenses.

B. THE INFLUENCE OF THE COMMUNIST PARTY

Party influence in the partisan detachments centered in the commissar system. Generally speaking, the commissar had two functions: as the equal and associate of the commander he shared responsibility for military command decisions [for a discussion of the function of the commissar system in relation to the military command structure, see Chap. II], and as the political officer he had direct responsibility for political affairs within the unit. As is customary in Soviet practice, of course, everything had its political aspect. In the partisan detachments, cut off as they were from direct contact with Soviet society, it was the primary function of the commissar system to maintain the all-embracing, pervasive political atmosphere which was the dominant feature of life under the Soviet regime.[53]

The formulas of Soviet socialism, plans, norms, Socialist competition, self-criticism, agitation, and so forth, were transferred and adapted to partisan warfare. To the outsider the "Socialist" approach to partisan warfare often appears ludicrous. For instance, quantitative norms were established to govern the awarding of decorations. According to a document found among captured papers of the Kovpak band, the Order of Lenin could be awarded to a partisan commander whose units had accomplished one of the following:

The destruction of a large railroad center with the result that it is put out of use for not less than 20 days; the demolition of 2 railroad bridges not less than 100 meters long with the result that they are out of use for not less than 20 days; rendering a railroad station unusable for a period of not less than 30 days, including the destruction of the water tower, the track and crossings, the depot and shops, and other installations; the capture of not less than 10 railroad trains involving the liberation of not less than 10,000 persons being shipped from the USSR to Germany as forced labor; the liberation of not less than 5,000 men from a prisoner-of-war camp; the destruction of not less than than 10 railroad trains loaded with military equipment, supplies, men, fuel, food, and material of general military usefulness; the capture of an enemy supply point containing military equipment, motor fuel, food, or not less than 300 vehicles; the capture of not less than 500 horses belonging to the German-Fascist army; the destruction of an armored train of the enemy; the destruction of 10 enemy tanks; the capture for use in the unit of 1,000 rifles, or 150 machine guns and submachine guns, or 15 heavy machine guns, or 20 company and battalion (sized) mortars, or 9 heavy mortars, or artillery of different calibers.

Within the detachments strong efforts were exerted to have life proceed in accordance with accepted Soviet forms, with trumped-up competitions, indoctrination sessions, and demands for special efforts in celebration of various Soviet holidays. A Komsomol official reported:

The Komsomol members of the Kirov Detachment addressed themselves to all the Komsomol members of the brigade concerning the activation of the struggle [and] the establishment of Komsomol demolition details [demolitions being somewhat unpopular because of frequent premature explosions resulting from makeshift equipment] consisting 100 per cent of Komsomol members.

The appeal of the Komsomol members of the Kirov Detachment was joyfully received by the Komsomol members of the other detachments.[54]

All of this served at least the one purpose of keeping the partisans in the routine patterns laid down for Soviet society.

Intensive political indoctrination of its own personnel was a major activity in every partisan unit. This "educational" work was directed by

[53] The commissar system was never abolished in the partisan movement as it was in October 1942 in the Red Army.

[54] PzAOK 3, Ic/AO, "Nr. 5394/43 geh.," 19 September 1943 (GMDS, PzAOK 3, 40252/7, Anlage 30–33).

the commissar, who, in the larger units, had at his disposal a sizable staff of battalion, company, and platoon politruks, agitators, and Party or Komsomol members. The scope and methods of indoctrination are illustrated in the following excerpt from the work log of a company politruk:

(a) Explain to the company what partisans and partisan warfare are.
(b) 18 June: 1000–1400 hours, publication of a wall newspaper; editorial conference.
(c) 19 June: 1000 hours, preparation of a discussion in the company on the subject: What does hatred of the enemy mean?
(d) 20 June: Discussion in the company regarding use of common sense and security by partisans. Note: I must give instructions for all operations before departure and must also personally participate in the operations.
(e) 21 June: 1400 hours, preparation of a lecture on the anniversary of the outbreak of the war.
(f) 22 June: 1600 hours, conduct meeting of all company members on the anniversary of outbreak of war.
(g) 23 June: 1600 hours, political information to the soldiers.
(h) 24 June: Publication of a front newspaper (editorial conference).
(i) 25 June: Relate to the soldiers how the Hitlerites bomb the peaceful population.
(j) 26 June: 1800 hours, conference with the members of the editorial staff of the wall newspaper, *The Red Partisan.*
(k) 27 June: Talk with the Communist Party members and candidates (six men) in the company.
(l) 28 June: 1600 hours, preparation for a meeting of Komsomol members.
(m) 29 June: Meeting of Komsomol members and organization of a primary Party organization.
(n) 30 June: 1900 hours, publication of the second issue of the wall paper, *The Red Partisan.*[55]

The program of indoctrination did not dwell exclusively on the glorification of the Communist Party and the Soviet regime. In fact, after the debacle of the 1941 partisan movement there was a noticeable tendency to play down the Party and the Soviet form of government and to appeal instead to broader national patriotism. The partisans were frequently called "Soldiers of the Red Army in the Rear of the Enemy." The partisan oath, for instance, contained no references to Stalin or communism and began instead with the formulation, "I [name], a citizen of the USSR, true son of the heroic Russian [Ukrainian, etc.] people swear . . ." [See Appendix, Document 3.] A German intelligence report of July 1942 stated, "The politruks give lectures on the meaning of partisan warfare. They emphasize the idea of a national war of liberation of the Russian people."[56] On the whole, however, the appeals to nationalism and the soft-pedaling

[55] 707. Inf.Div., Ic, "Feindnachrichten fuer die Truppe Nr. 16," 10 November 1942, p. 1 (GMDS, 707 ID 27797/4).
[56] 707. Inf.Div., Ic, "Feindnachrichten fuer die Truppe Nr. 1," 23 July 1942 (GMDS, 707 ID 27797/3 Anlage 100).

of the standard themes of loyalty to Stalin and the Soviet system were directed more at the civilians on occupied territory than at the partisans themselves. Within the units the function of indoctrination was exercised exclusively by dependable Party men, and the lip service given to some of the unorthodox propaganda themes approved by the regime for reasons of expediency counted for less than the propagation in the partisan detachments of the standard attitudes and behavior patterns fostered by the Soviet system.

The force of political authority and the techniques of indoctrination were brought to bear on all individual and group activities within the detachments. Discipline, care of weapons, and individual and group accomplishments all fell within the province of the commissar. He concerned himself in particular with the new men, the draftees, and the unreliable elements. As a part of his "educative" work he instituted measures against desertion, weeded out the cowards, "instigators of panic," and other undesirables, and accompanied details on combat missions, where it was frequently claimed, the partisans often fought desperately out of fear of the commissars. The commissar controlled the source of news and general information of the detachment. He worked constantly to counteract German propaganda, stressing especially the brutal German treatment of prisoners and deserters. The rank-and-file partisans were isolated as far as possible from outside contacts. This process was greatly facilitated by the blatant hypocrisy of German propaganda and by the inflexible ruthlessness which the Germans displayed in their approach to antipartisan warfare. Partisan counterpropagandists never had to create baseless fears, but instead needed only to heighten those already inspired by the Germans themselves. A partisan commander captured early in 1943 said, "At present the situation is this: we in the forest believe that communism (which 70–80 per cent of us hate) will at least let us live, but the Germans, with their National Socialism, will either shoot us or starve us to death."[57]

The political officers had at their disposal the Party and Komsomol contingents of their detachments. For the rank-and-file partisan, Party membership was not an unmixed blessing. He enjoyed a slightly superior status and was not quite so subject to surveillance and coercion as the non-Party men; but the demands on him were heavy. He was expected to be an exemplary fighter and, in addition, was required to take an active hand in the supervision and indoctrination of the non-Party elements. Because of the small percentage of Party members in most units, the Party contingent was expected to perform conspicuously. The Komsomols, in turn, were urged to assume the role of partisan shock troops.

Each brigade or independent detachment had its Party organization

[57] Amt Ausland Abwehr/Befehlsstab Walli/Abw. III, "Auswertung von Angaben sowjetischer Agenten und Kriegsgefangenen," 23 February 1943 (GMDS, OKW 639).

(Party collective), which included all Party members. The Komsomol members were similarly organized. The Party collective operated under the direction of the political officers. Usually the commissar or one of the politruks was the secretary. He reported separately to the Soviet authorities on the state of Party activity within the unit. Committees were delegated to edit wall newspapers and front newspapers and to prepare propaganda. Agitators and speakers were selected to work among the non-Party personnel. The meetings invariably revolved around the theme of "intensification of the work" or "activation of the struggle," which meant hearing and accepting new demands from the political officers for sharper discipline, greater military accomplishments, special achievements to celebrate holidays, and so on.

One meeting of a Komsomol group, according to a captured protocol, went approximately as follows:

Agenda

    (1) Discipline of Komsomol members during fighting and in quarters.
    (2) Confirmation of the work plan.
    (3) Elections.
    (4) Miscellaneous.

It was said:

    (1) Comrade Filipov spoke on the first item of the agenda. He said, "Discipline among the Komsomol members is far from satisfactory. The main reason for lack of discipline is the use of filthy [*netsenzurnykh*] words; this cursing among Komsomol members results not only in insulting each other but sometimes [is directed against] those who do not belong to the Komsomol.

    "The behavior of the majority of the Komsomol members in battle is good, but there are also some (for example, Yegorov) who do not show the necessary courage."

    Party Member Solovyov: "The question of discipline concerns the entire partisan unit but especially the Komsomol members. There are Komsomol members with us who should be imprisoned. One can observe cases in which Komsomol members seriously quarrel with each other and incite non-Party members to do the same."

    Unit Commander Vasiliyev: "if we want to act like Komsomol members, then we must not only be an example, but we must carry the others along. This is our principal task."

    (2) Confirmation of the work plan of the bureau of the Komsomol organization. The plan was accepted as a whole.

    (3) Election to the bureau. Rybakov, 3; Bukatin, 15. Bukatin was selected by a majority.—*Appendix, Document 20.*

Under the fourth point of the agenda (miscellaneous) the meeting returned to the topic of discipline, hearing complaints made by the officers against two of the members and voting them public reprimands in addition to the punishments they had already received from the officers. [See below, Sect. III, D, 3.]

The assembly technique was also applied to the personnel at large. It is illustrated in the captured bimonthly political report of a brigade commissar.

1. [Here are listed names of members who performed acts of heroism or were "models of discipline."]

2. The entire personnel of the unit took the oath as Red Partisans. After taking the oath, the men and officers show even better and closer unity.

3. [Communist] Party and Komsomol organizations were established within the unit (Communist Party members and candidates total five men; there are fourteen Komsomol members). They did great work in the unit and also among the population. Five conferences of Party and Komsomol members took place within the unit, and the following topics were discussed: (a) discipline, (b) care of weapons, (c) condemnation of actions of individual fighters, Communists, and Komsomol members. There were about ten general meetings concerning the questions: (a) discipline within the unit, (b) care of weapons, (c) condemnation of actions of unstable comrades.

4. Orders No. 55 and 130 of the People's Commissariat of Defense were thoroughly gone over with the men and officers and were understood in their entire depth. Molotov's note, the patriotic war of the Soviet people, the morale of the German armed forces, the conduct of Comrade Litvinov at the Conference of the [Great] Powers, the proclamation of the partisans of the Kalinin Front, to which 55 men from our unit added their signatures, [were] also [discussed].—*Appendix, Document 17.*

At other times the meetings discussed (1) "the bandit-like behavior of the former officer Ivanov," (2) "comprehensive discussion of the Order of the Commissariat for National Defense No. 130 and the proclamation of the partisans of the Kalinin Front," (3) "formulation of sentences for the criminals, the former partisans D. I. Piskunov and G. A. Kozlov," and (4) "field inspection of equipment"—all under the supervision of the political officers of the brigade.

Soviet authorities have claimed, both during and after the war, that the partisan movement demonstrated the ability of the Communist Party to rally its own members and the "masses" in defense of the Soviet system at a time of crisis. The evidence does not substantiate such a claim. In 1941, admittedly under adverse circumstances, the Party failed to bring an effective partisan movement into being. The movement as it emerged in the later years must be credited largely to the ability of the Soviet regime to extend its direct authority into the occupied areas, aided by a favorable turn in the war and by German political errors. The Party influence in the movement was only a product of that extension of direct Soviet authority. It was used to keep the movement operating exclusively in the Soviet interest and to forestall the possibility of unorthodox political developments. As a result, the Party, in this connection, must be characterized as an instrument of Soviet control rather than as a motivating force.

C. MORALE IN GENERAL

The details of partisan morale almost defy analysis. The German reports based on interrogations of captured partisans and deserters use the terms "good" and "bad" so indiscriminately that they lose their significance. More important are the reports which, like the following, recognize that low morale did not always impair the operations of the units:

1. The food situation among the bands is poor. . . . There is a complete lack of salt. Morale is low and, during the last days . . . things are hopeless; but, because of fear of the leaders, and also because of punitive measures by the [German] troops, nobody deserts.[58]

2. Communists and members of the troops [Red Army personnel] stand together and have a relatively high combat potential. Morale among peasant boys who were impressed is poor. However, there are hardly any deserters. Often [partisans] commit suicide rather than be taken prisoner.[59]

3. The enemy unit, although without doubt composed of a large proportion of draftees, fought tenaciously and desperately under pressure from the commissars.[60]

4. For the most part, the morale of the partisans is to be described as "not good. . . ." The combat strength does not suffer as a result of the low morale since there is close surveillance. Furthermore, the commanders and commissars are able to develop intensive political propaganda, which is not difficult for them since we can only appeal to the dissident elements with vague promises for the future.[61]

These observations are borne out by the statistics regarding desertions from the partisan units. Table I lists the numbers of partisans who deserted to the Germans in the zone of Third Panzer Army in the period from May 1943 to May 1944. The total number of partisans in the army area was estimated at 27,000. For comparison, the numbers of killed and captured partisans are included. During most months, the number of deserters was very small when compared either with the total number of partisans who operated within the zone of the Third Panzer Army or with the numbers of killed and captured partisans. The statistics from the other armies indicate that the low rate of desertions prevailed throughout the zone of Army Group Center, which embraced the region of most intensive partisan activity. In the months from September 1943 to April 1944, for instance, desertions in the area of Third Panzer Army averaged only five per month.

[58] 318. Inf.Div., Ic, "Vernehmungsbericht Nr. 4," 22 May 1943, p. 2 (GMDS, 18 PzD 32207/12, Anlage 412).
[59] Korueck 532, Ic, "Feindlage im Korueck-Gebiet (Stand 26.1.1943)," 30 January 1943, p. 3 (GMDS, Korueck 44404/3).
[60] 221. Sich.Div., Ia, "Bericht ueber Unternehmen Osterhase," 2 May 1943, p. 5 (GMDS, 221 ID 36509/13, "Osterhase" Anlage 41).
[61] Okdo. H.Gr.Mitte Ic, "Erfahrungsbericht," 23 June 1943 (GMDS, AOK 16, 44185/70).

TABLE 1

Partisans who deserted to the Germans in the zone
of Third Panzer Army, May 1943 to May 1944

	1943							
	May	June	July	Aug.	Sept.	Oct.	Nov.	Dec.
Killed	1,227	658	126	275	166	289	546	762
Captured	372	271	136	158	144	79	115	97
Deserted	227	247	121	44*	13	2	6	5†

	1944					
	Jan.	Feb.	March	April	May	Of the May totals one large-scale antipartisan operation, "Fruehlingfest," accounted for:
Killed	699	194	342	969	6,667	6,425
Captured	177	23	43	167	8,133	7,023
Deserted	2	2	3	8	374	358‡

* PzAOK 3, Ic/AO, "Entwicklung der Bandenlage im Bereich der 3. Panzer-Armee," Anlage 3, 4 July 1943; Anlage 1, 1 August 1943; Anlage 1, 1 September 1943 (GMDS, PzAOK 3, 40252/7).

† Ibid., Anlage 1, 1 December 1943; Anlage 1, 1 January 1944 (GMDS, PzAOK 3, 49113/37).

‡ Ibid., Anlage 1, 2 April 1944; Anlage 1, 27 May 1944 (GMDS, PzAOK 3, 62587/12).

It is worth noting that in the months from May to August 1943, and again in May 1944, the rate of desertion far exceeded the level of the other months. Both times the immediate cause was a large-scale German antipartisan operation. While the number of killed and captured rose as well, the increase in desertions was disproportionate. This revealed more than the fact that partisans were willing to desert when faced with over-whelming enemy forces. The German reports indicate that most of the desertions occurred after the operations had been concluded, when the brigades were disorganized and individuals found it safe to desert from small, straggler groups. Desertion from a partisan detachment was no simple matter. Individuals were always under close surveillance by military and political officers and NKVD representatives. Poor morale and general dissatisfaction with life in a partisan unit were not sufficient to move men to take the risks of desertion. Generally, a catalyst was required to free the individual or produce a crisis which forced a decision. Therefore, the largest numbers of desertions occurred after extensive antipartisan operations when the heat of combat had subsided and the bands were sufficiently disorganized for the individual to make his break. In at least one instance the Germans noted another kind of crisis-producing motivation. In June 1943, after Operation "Maigewitter," some of the partisan brigades began to move out of the Vitebsk area to take up new zones of operation south of the Dvina River. At that time large numbers of locally recruited personnel deserted. As long as the bands operated near their native villages the draftees remained as partisans, but they would not move with the brigades to distant areas. From the deserters of one such partisan unit a German local commandant actually recruited a 150-man antipartisan police force.[62]

German policy was a deterrent rather than an encouragement to desertion. The potential deserter who was prepared to run the risks imposed by the partisans was by no means assured of reasonably good treatment when he reached the Germans. Moreover, German failure to institute a satisfactory economic or political program made the deserter's long-range prospects far from encouraging. Many deserters, probably far more than the number who reported to the German authorities, tried to avoid contact with either side. Even their numbers were limited, however, since they exposed themselves to reprisals from both Germans and partisans.

Partisan morale and desertions cannot be considered in isolation but must be judged in the light of the possible alternatives for the individual. The Second World War placed almost every Soviet citizen on both sides of the front in exceptionally desperate circumstances. Morale in the conventional sense was probably abysmally low most of the time—among the civilian population, in the Red Army, and in the partisan movement. As far as the effects of partisan morale are concerned, one need not look so much at psychological motivations as at the logic of events. For the average partisan, service in the bands was not a matter of choice, but of necessity. After the summer of 1942 it became increasingly clear that those who went over to the Germans were joining the losing side, while service in the partisan movement was prima facie evidence, if not of loyalty to the Soviet Union, at least of noncollaboration. Dissociation from both the partisans and the Germans was no solution. Life in the partisan brigades was hard, but life as a civilian under the German occupation was no easier. In the brigades a man was usually fed; under the Germans he was likely to starve or be deported to Germany for labor service. In the partisan movement he had made his choice; outside he was at the mercy of both the partisans and the Germans.

Given the helplessness of the individual in the face of catastrophic conditions of life, the partisan movement under certain conditions offered him limited material advantages. For the average partisan, life was difficult but not much, if any, more difficult than life as a soldier in the Soviet Army. For the partisans, some of the time at least, both the rations and living accommodations were fairly satisfactory, since the partisans lived

[62] 8. Pz.Div., Ic, "Lage im bisherigen Einsatzraum der Brigade Sakmarkin," 9 June 1943 (GMDS, 8 PzD 44131/28).

by their own requisitioning efforts, which at times were quite successful. Furthermore, the partisans did not, as one might suppose, live in constant danger. For long periods, sometimes remarkably long periods, the bands were relatively secure. The individual was not confronted constantly with the inexorable statistics of losses that weighed upon the front soldier of the Red Army; there was the appearance, at least, of better chances for his survival. The aim of the partisan unit was to avoid rather than seek out pitched battles, and the record shows that the partisans were successful in this endeavor. They were aided by the inability of the enemy to launch a thoroughgoing antipartisan campaign.

This discussion so far may have given the impression that the partisans formed a homogeneous group which reacted uniformly to all stimuli. Such an impression would be misleading. Some sharp internal differentiations must be noted. There was a hard core, not small in absolute numbers, though a relatively small proportion of the total movement, that was distinguished by high rather than low morale. It was composed of Party members and officials, regular army officers and men, some stragglers, and some convinced Soviet patriots. These men were likely to maintain their enthusiasm under the most adverse circumstances. They were important because they formed the leadership contingent; moreover, their attitudes certainly influenced to some extent the thinking of the remaining groups. Without this group, the partisan movement would probably have collapsed. Nevertheless, the most significant distinction in terms of morale within the partisan movement was between the local, drafted recruits and the Red Army stragglers. With some variations in time and place these two groups made up about 90 per cent of the total partisan strength. Under interrogation concerning partisan attitudes and morale, captured partisans and deserters almost invariably drew sharp distinctions between the two. The following excerpts show how these were expressed:

1. Morale is not very good. Only the Red Army stragglers still go along, while those recruited by force are all waiting for an opportunity to escape (*zuverschwinden*).[63]

2. The morale of the drafted local inhabitants is bad. . . . The morale of the former Red Army men is good. They expect the return of the Red Army any day.[64]

3. The morale of the partisans in Shcherbino is not good. The partisans who come from that area are waiting only for an opportunity to escape. Even the former Red Army men say that as soon as it gets dry [at the end of the spring thaw] they will be smashed. That they do not desert is partly connected with the fact that they do not have a chance to go to their home villages and partly

[63] 221. Sich.Div., Ic, "Vernehmung von 2 Ueberlaeufern aus Kamenka," 15 April 1942 (GMDS, 221 ID 22639/6, Anlage 18).
[64] 221. Sich.Div., Ic, "Ueberlaeufer im Jelnya Abschnitt," 23 June 1942 (GMDS, 221 ID 22639/6, Anlage 54).

with their fear of being badly treated or shot by the Germans in spite of the [German] propaganda.[65]

The former Red Army men were not much more enthusiastic as partisans than the drafted peasants. But they were, in a sense, volunteers, which gave them the advantage of somewhat higher status in the partisan movement and at the same time made it more dangerous for them to fall into German hands. The Red Army men had no strong ties outside their detachments; the drafted men, on the other hand, often had families and property which were endangered as long as they remained in the detachments. Significantly, the dissatisfaction of the drafted men most often did not lead to thoughts of outright defection, but rather toward a state of indecisive despondency.

Some specific external factors influenced the morale of all partisans. Of these, medical services, food supplies, rewards, and the concentration of partisans in relatively secure areas are discussed at length in other sections of this study. The most important single, sustaining factor in partisan morale was the establishment of close contact with unoccupied Soviet territory by air. The ease, relative safety, and regularity of air contact influenced partisan activity in all its aspects. [See Chap. VI.] On the material side, it made possible an adequate supply of arms, ammunition, and equipment, evacuation of the wounded, some medical supplies, and mail. Psychologically it reduced the feeling of isolation and technological inferiority. The general failure of the Germans to interdict partisan air operations at times actually engendered a sense of superiority. Air ties with the Soviet Union became so close that units hundreds of miles behind the enemy lines felt nearly as secure as if they had been on Soviet territory. Furthermore, with arms and ammunition of the latest Soviet make, the partisans were often armed as well as, if not better than the German troops sent against them.

Partisan morale was further bolstered by the inability of the Germans to commit significant airpower against them. When the Germans were able to use aircraft in operations against the partisans startling effects were sometimes noted. A group of deserters reported, "The partisans are especially afraid of the German Air Force. In case of future raids many of the local inhabitants [among the partisans] would run away and use the opportunity to desert."[66] On another occasion, three collaborators who had been captured by the partisans escaped during a panic caused by a German bombing raid.[67] A German soldier who had been held in

[65] 221. Sich.Div., Ic, "[Meldung] an Befehlshaber Heeres-Gebiet Mitte," 28 April 1942 (GMDS, 221 ID 22639/6, Anlage 122).

[66] H.Gr.Mitte, Ic/AO, "Partisanenueberlaeufer aus dem Kraftzentrum Cholm-Schtscherbino," 20 April 1942 (GMDS, Korueck 29236/3).

[67] 221. Sich.Div., Ic, "Vernehmungen," 31 March 1942, p. 3 (GMDS, 221 ID 22639/6, Anlage 7).

the jail at Dorogobuzh while the partisans occupied that town reported that the guards locked the jail and ran for cover whenever there was an air raid.[68] In another instance the effects of a bombing raid were described as follows: "Formerly the staff [of a partisan regiment] was located in Syutsova; since the bombing of 30 March 1942 it is in Solaveka. The air attack caused no losses among the partisans. The houses are also all still standing. Bombs dropped behind the village. Nevertheless, there was a great tumult and an immediate evacuation."[69]

I. Classes of Partisans

As a result of its diverse elements the Soviet partisan movement developed a mass of sharp, internal tensions. The situation thereby produced perhaps can best be understood if it is viewed for a moment from the point of view of the theoretically ideal Soviet partisan type: a patriot, very likely a Party member, who had volunteered for partisan service early in the war and was unreservedly dedicated to the Soviet cause. In his brigade there might be another 100 or so men similarly motivated. In the same brigade, however, there would be 100–200 former Red Army men, stragglers and ex-prisoners of war. Many of them had been the victims of circumstances and made excellent and dedicated partisans; others had surrendered without a fight or had deserted in the face of the enemy. All of them, had they made their way back to regular Soviet forces, would, at best, have been handled as material for the punishment battalions. Another 200 or 300 would be drafted men, not always too bad as fighters, but an unenthusiastic crew who worried more about what was happening to their cows than about the outcome of the war. Finally, in addition to the stragglers and drafted men, any one of whom might also have at some time or other collaborated with the enemy, there might be another 50 or 100 men tainted with treason—former policemen and mayors under the German occupation, deserters from the German indigenous administration, kolkhoz directors, factory managers, teachers, and others who had worked for the Germans before they realized that they were on the losing side. Neither the Soviet command—though it did adopt an anomalous attitude for the time being—nor the partisan with a demonstrably clear record was prepared to grant these doubtful or tainted groups a blanket absolution. The antecedents of each partisan were remembered, and class attitudes arose within the partisan movement which were clearly defined and, in some of their manifestations, ugly.

The intensity of the class tensions is occasionally reflected in the surviving evidence. In the Grishin Regiment the "old partisans," i.e., those who

---

[68] 221. Sich.Div., Ic, "Aussagen des aus russischer Kriegsgefangenschaftentflohnen Schuetzen August Moj," 27 May 1942, p. 2 (GMDS, 221 ID 22639/6, Anlage 62).
[69] Sich.Div., Ic, "Ueberlaeferaussegen," 7 April 1942, p. 4 (GMDS, 221 ID 22639/6, Anlage 8).

had joined the unit during the period of its founding (January 1942), considered themselves an elite group and kept aloof from the later recruits.[70] In another instance 700 Tatars who deserted from a German unit were assigned in small groups to various brigades so that they could be kept under close watch. A deserter from another unit related that: "The commissars and politruks have their own moonshine vodka and often get drunk. It then sometimes happens that they ask individual men who have been drafted into the partisan movement why they did not join the partisan movement earlier. If they do not find a good answer immediately, they are shot."[71] The writer of one partisan diary noted that vodka and tobacco had been delivered by air "for the regular partisans."[72]

The Germans occasionally picked up reports of impending purges within the partisan units, which were expected to be aimed principally against the former police and military collaborators.[73] The class attitudes are often most clearly delineated in statements written by the partisans themselves. Former military collaborators, for instance, were generally treated with outright contempt. A partisan commander writing after the war stated: "Repentant *polizei* began to come to us, too. We ourselves invited them through leaflets. If they didn't leave the police force, we wrote, we would shoot them down like dogs. When they came to the detachment, they were held under special observation for a long time. The men kept a watchful eye on them."[74] A unit politruk noted in his diary that: "Eighteen hundred Cossack deserters have reported to the Dyatshkov brigade. One hundred and eighty Cossacks have gone over to the Grishin Regiment, taking along all their equipment. These deserters are not to be trusted. They were untrustworthy as fighters." He goes on to say, "If so much as a strong wind blows out of the East, these miserable traitors get so excited that they do not know what to do."[75]

The army stragglers, although they were a recognized mainstay of the movement, also remained under lingering suspicion. Fyodorov, an old-line Communist and volunteer partisan, has this to say about them:

But there were all kinds of men among the escaped prisoners of war. Some had voluntarily surrendered to the Germans. Later, when they had been eaten up by lice in the camps and had become sick and tired of being punched in the jaw, they repented and escaped to join the partisans. Not all of them by any means told us the whole truth. And, of course, very few of them admitted they had surrendered of their own free will.

[70] VI. A.K. Ic, "Feindnachrichtenblatt." 29 May 1942 (GMDS, VI AK 44653/14).
[71] 221. Sich. Div., Ic, "Ueberlaeufer aus dem Suedabschnitt," 10 May 1942, p. 2 (GMDS, 221 ID 223639/6, Anlage 37).
[72] VI. A.K., "Tagebuch des politischen Leiters der Aufklaerer-Kompanie der Partisanen-Abteilung 'Morjak,'" May 1943 (GMDS, VI AK 44653/15).
[73] PzAOK 3, Ic, "Entwicklung der Bandenlage im Bereich der 3. Pz.AOK," 1 February 1944 (GMDS, PzAOK 3, 62587/12).
[74] Fyodorov, p. 425.
[75] VI. A.K., Ic. "Tagebuch ... 'Morjak.'"

These men joined the partisans only because there was nothing else for them to do. They didn't want to go back to the Germans but, on the other hand, they didn't fight them any too energetically either.

Some of the formerly encircled men who joined us had been "hubbies" [a reference to the stragglers who tried to lose themselves among the civilian population by settling in the villages and "marrying" local girls]. These were soldiers who for one reason or another had fallen behind the army. . . . Among the "hubbies" there were specimens who would have been glad to sit out the war behind a woman's skirt, but the Hitlerites would either drive them off to work in Germany or else make them join the police. After turning this over in his mind such a guy would come to the conclusion that, after all, joining the partisans was more advantageous.[76]

The drafted peasants formed the most distinct class in the partisan movement. In the detachments they were often regarded as mere ballast. An ex-partisan, interviewed after the war, said:

In our detachment there were three brigades [battalions ?]. The first two were fighting brigades . . . excellent and very aggressive. These were composed of ex-war prisoners. The third brigade was no good at all. [It] was recruited from the local peasantry according to an order from Moscow which instructed us to get all the local peasants and [take] them into partisan detachments before the Germans could recruit them, as they were doing for their labor force in Germany.[77]

Captured partisans and deserters, when questioned about the composition or morale of their detachments, invariably spoke of the drafted men as a separate class with uniformly low morale.

It is significant that the majority of the partisans had second-class status in the movement and, more serious still, that many of them knew that the fact that they were partisans would very likely not gain them redemption in the eyes of the Soviet Union but would only postpone the day of reckoning. Despite the personal and group tensions thereby produced there was no serious threat of mutiny or even widespread defection. In the atmosphere of hopelessness which the German and Soviet authorities produced between them, day-to-day survival itself became an objective worth fighting for.

2. Rewards

Superficially, at least, partisan activity was not unrewarding. Almost everybody could remember the days when the partisans of the Civil War era occupied a privileged position in Soviet society. Soviet propaganda tacitly promised similar recognition for World War II partisans. Newspapers, radio, and other media of information and propaganda were unstinting in their praise for the partisans. The partisans became the glamorous heroes of the war.

[76] Fyodorov, p. 424.
[77] H. S. Dinerstein, "Rand Partisan Interview No. 3," 19 May 1952.

Soviet officials encouraged the partisans to take an inflated view of their own importance; units were not relegated to the anonymity of numerical designations but were given distinctive names with patriotic associations, such as, "For the Homeland," "The People's Avengers," "Chapayev," "Stalin," "Suvorov," "Alexander Nevsky," and so on through the list of national heroes. Decorations were awarded freely. Nearly every important brigade commander was a Hero of the Soviet Union. Commanders were instructed to nominate their good fighters for decorations, and medals were flown in to be awarded on the spot. Relatively minor achievements of the partisan units were given wide publicity.

These efforts caused the partisans themselves to think highly of their own activities. Twenty or more diaries kept by partisans survive in the German records. That so many fell into German hands indicates that keeping a diary became something of a fad in the partisan movement. The diarists were usually motivated by a strong sense of the importance of their activities. They believed their experiences were worth recording on the spot. The more modest believed they were compiling valuable records for their families; others expressed the intention to publish their reminiscences after the war.

The partisans were encouraged to extol their own achievements and sacrifices in letters to the unoccupied territory, as the following excerpts show:

1. Recently we have engaged in heavy fighting. Both we and the Germans have had losses, but the Germans had the heavier losses. Life is difficult, since everything around us has been burned down; but we do not lose our courage. Part of our people fight the Germans, and the others occupy themselves with farming and work in the forest. We have built a mill where we mill our grain. We have also built an oven in which we bake bread. Naturally, everything is done secretly and with caution. Our forest is surrounded by the Germans, but one needs to live in order to fight. The Stalin Order No. 130 will be fulfilled. Everything he demands of us will be accomplished. We dedicate our lives to the victory.[78]

2. Dear Comrades! [The letter is written to former fellow workers in a factory which was evacuated to Soviet territory.]

Last winter I called on you to enter into competition. We agreed that each was to improve his work in his own sphere of competition. Now, after three months I am ready to settle accounts. What have we done in enemy territory? I won't bore you with details. I will say only that our commitment has been met. My commissar and I have received the Order of the Red Flag. Other partisans have received decorations as well. Now we must improve our methods of fighting the enemy. I call on you, my comrades, for better work. In the future may I hear only good of you.[79]

[78] Gr. GFP 639 b. Panzerarmeeoberkommando 2, "An dem Panzerarmeeoberkommando 2," 20 July 1942 (GMDS, PzAOK 2, 30233/66).
[79] *Ibid.*

Such letters were undoubtedly propagandistic in intent and did not necessarily reflect the personal attitudes of the writers; still, they probably stimulated a conviction among the partisans themselves that their achievements
were heroic and would be recognized and remembered.

In the matter of material rewards the attitude of the Soviet authorities
was ambiguous, though, on the surface at least, still generous. Technically,
membership in a partisan unit was the equivalent of service in the Red
Army, with equal rank, pay, and privileges. Brigade commanders were
often given the rank of army colonel; otherwise, comparatively few commissions were granted purely on the basis of service in the partisan movement. The whole question of pay was postponed until after the termination
of hostilities. Leaves and rest periods behind the Soviet lines were the
partisans' due in theory but were almost never granted.

On the whole, the rewards were intended only to stimulate expectations
for the future. For most individuals the final result was a profound disappointment. During the period of the great Soviet advance in 1944, German agents reported that partisan units overtaken by the Red Army, instead of receiving the preferential treatment they expected, were granted
short leaves and then thrown into front line units.[80]

Given the intensely suspicious nature of the Soviet regime and the heterogeneous composition of the partisan units, it is likely that even the dedicated partisans, after their return to Soviet territory, counted themselves
lucky if they avoided being remanded to an army punishment battalion.
Probably only the trusted Party men in command positions benefited materially from partisan service. Those fortunate partisans who managed to
survive political screenings and enmity of the regular troops, which followed immediately upon their return to Soviet territory, probably at best
managed to bask modestly in the glory of the continued favorable publicity
given the partisan movement as a whole in Soviet newspapers, magazines,
and published memoirs of the more prominent commanders.

3. Inertia

In contrast to a regular army, a partisan force is not expected to win a
war but only to contribute to the victory. The question of what constitutes
an adequate contribution is difficult to resolve even in a tightly controlled
movement such as that in the Soviet Union. The average partisan does not
engage in a single-minded pursuit of a heroic demise, but is rather more
inclined toward preoccupation with his personal survival. Finding himself
in a service which is by definition dangerous, he engages in a constant
effort to reduce his risks. The same is true of the whole partisan move-

---

[80] Abwehrkommando 304, Meldekopf Renate, "Abwehrmaessige Ueberpruefung der
V-Leute," 24 May 1944 (GMDS, HGr. Nord 75131/31). XX AK/Ic, "Jenseits der
HKL," 28 May 1944 (GMDS, XX AK 54486/2).

ment. As an institution it becomes dedicated to its own preservation—not to its self-destruction. These attitudes are persistent and irresistible. At best, they limit the theoretical military potential of the partisan and, at worst, they reduce the movement to impotence.

The corrosive action of these forces was a major factor in the failure of the 1941 partisan organization. In many of the original partisan detachments the men simply decided that resistance was impossible, and the units dissolved. Those that survived did so by a series of rationalizations which resulted in the setting up of personal and group security as their primary objectives. In his memoirs, written after the war, an oblast Party secretary who had been intimately associated with the 1941 partisan movement describes one partisan unit as "a haven for a group of people who were defending only themselves against the enemy."[81] "Another band," he writes, "was split into two factions: those who wanted to prepare forever and those who wanted action for the sake of adventure." The commanders, he says, had no definite objectives, but favored a middle course which leaned toward passivity.[82] The situations he described were representative of a phenomenon which was almost universal. Those units which survived the first shock of finding themselves in enemy territory and, looking around, discovered that they were probably not in imminent danger of annihilation, began to redefine their objectives in terms more comforting to themselves. In the process they convinced themselves that merely remaining in existence constituted a heroic achievement; and therefore they should lie low and prepare for a big attack on the enemy some time in the vague future, or husband their resources in preparation for the return of the Soviet forces.

In the spring of 1942 the Soviet command intervened to pump new life into the partisan movement by sending in regular officers and cadres and by bringing the partisan detachments under tight control. That process continued until the early summer of 1944. One of the most striking features of the 1942–44 period, however, was the tendency toward concentration of partisan forces. The units grew to strengths of 1,000 to 2,000 men or more. Moreover, they did not range freely throughout the occupied territory; instead, they drew together to form centers of partisan concentration. This process reached its fullest development in Belorussia, where a dozen or more centers appeared, one totaling 15,000 men, in and around Rossono Rayon, north of Polotsk; another totaling 12,000 men, along the Ushach River between Polotsk and Lepel; another in the swamps along the Berezina River between Lepel and Borisov; more, of 8,000, 9,000, and 14,000 men, near Minsk, Senno, and Vitebsk. By 1943 at least three-fourths of the total strength of the partisan movement was concentrated in centers like these.

[81] Fyodorov, p. 196.
[82] *Ibid.*, p. 176.

Such centers were created largely in response to tactical considerations and the dictates of terrain; but it seems worthwhile to consider that they might also have represented a stagnation of the partisan movement resulting from the pervasive individual and group desires for security. Militarily, the large centers were not worth the expenditure of men, effort, and equipment required to create and maintain them. Ostensibly they denied the enemy access to vast stretches of territory; actually most of them grew in areas which had been by-passed by German troops and were never brought under military occupation. The centers served as fixed bases from which small detachments could be dispatched for attacks on the German lines of communication, but the process meant a very low efficiency in the utilization of personnel. Of 10,000 to 15,000 men only about 10 per cent could be used effectively at any one time. Superficially, the centers formed concentrations of strength; but they were islands (a comparison with the Japanese situation in the Pacific may be apt). Lacking mobility, they did not constitute striking forces, nor could one center muster its forces to aid another under attack. Faced with a determined enemy assault, a center could avoid annihilation only by disbanding and permitting its forces to disperse piecemeal.

The greatest single advantage of the centers seems to have been the security they offered the partisans themselves. In swampy or wooded terrain, loosely held by the Germans, partisan units could develop undisturbed. Having reached a strength of 5,000 to 10,000 or more men they became immune to small enemy counteractions, and, since the Germans could rarely spare enough troops for large-scale antipartisan operations, centers could function relatively undisturbed for months, or even years. While it was certainly not the nature of the Soviet regime to permit its partisans to idle away their time in relatively secure strongholds, something of the sort apparently could not be prevented. The centers produced good morale and discipline, although at the expense of miltiary efficiency and effectiveness. This situation is reflected in the following German report on the partisans of the Ushachi center:

Most of the brigades are reinforced with Red Army men and are led by officers of the Red Army. Discipline and battle morale are good. At the same time, the majority of the partisans have not yet been engaged in combat with German units. As a result of the so far undisturbed development of the Ushachi area the morale of both the population and the partisans is good.[83]

The function of the centers as a response to the forces tending towards inertia in the partisan movement is illustrated in the following excerpts from letters to the Soviet hinterland captured near the Rossono center in 1943:

[83] HSSPF Russland Mitte und Weissruthenien, Ic, "Feindlage im Raum Lepel-Ulla-Polozk-Doksohyze," 11 April 1944, p. 2 (GMDS, Waffen SS, Dirlewanger 78028/15).

1. Rossono Rayon has become a closed region of the partisan movement; the whole population has risen and taken arms against fascism.

2. Our rayon is completely cleared of Germans and the population lives more quietly and happily with us partisans. On 19 September we celebrated the anniversary of the liberation from the 'Fritzes'; a whole year has passed since they were tramping around in their iron boots in Rossono Rayon.

3. I live passably and remember the times gone by which will certainly not return in the former fashion. You well know how our partisan life is—not as it was earlier. When we came here from the Soviet hinterland, the Germans were everywhere and it was not very pleasant. There were many police and other riffraff who fought side by side with the Germans. The population was also against us. This last year has brought about perceptible changes. Our partisan area has become large. Now you see no Germans in the rayon center. This work had to be carried out under difficult conditions; now, however, it has become easier; the population of the whole area stands behind us.[84]

Concerning living conditions, several individuals wrote:

1. In our partisan region the harvest was brought in without damage and without a fight.

2. We live well; food, clothing, and footwear are at hand. One needs no more. We harvest the German grain so that we can well provide bread for ourselves.

3. My life passes quite tolerably at present. Food, footwear, and vodka are at hand in sufficient quantity.[85]

The claim of having cleared the Rossono region of the enemy is far from accurate; the Germans never had more than token military forces there. If rhetoric is disregarded, the dominant theme which emerges from these letters is one of relief at dwelling in a relatively secure spot. This is coupled with a sense of achievement derived from living dangerously but not *too* dangerously.

D. DISCIPLINE IN GENERAL

The existing documents indicate that, with the development of large units, the trend in the partisan movement was toward organizational and disciplinary measures closely approximating those of the Soviet Army. In the summer of 1943 a German unit reported:

While Third Panzer Army succeeded in diminishing partisan activity in the zone near the front, the Rossono area had been reinforced to some extent by the erection of fortifications and by improvements in the partisan organization. In Rossono the appearance of regular Red Army troops with complete military equipment, the existence of a "tight" organization, and the distribution of numerous active Red Army officers throughout the command apparatus indicate that the enemy is trying to build a center of strength in this area which

[84] PzAOK 3, Ic/AO, "Entwicklung der Bandenlage im Bereich der 3. Pz. Armee im September 1943 (abgeschlossen 30.9.43)," 2 October 1943, Anlage 3 (GMDS, PzAOK 3, 40252/7).
[85] *Ibid.*

should not be underestimated in its importance to the conduct of operations at the front.[86]

Earlier the same source had reported that the partisans were enhancing their effectiveness by instituting a unified command, importing Red Army officers, and introducing insignia of rank. One captured partisan stated that as early as May 1943 the commander and deputy commander of the brigade in which he had served were wearing Red Army officers' uniforms complete with insignia of rank.[87] It appears that the Red Army officers wore their uniforms wherever possible. By 1943 most of the higher officers within the brigades had acquired assimilated army ranks ranging from lieutenant to major general.

The introduction of titles and rank insignia served three purposes: it strengthened the authority of the officers; it gave the officers consciousness of rank, which probably had been lacking in some of the nonprofessionals; and it established reasonably clear lines of command. On the side of discipline, it resulted in the introduction of formal military procedures as far as was feasible under the circumstances. All of this never quite overcame the persistent trend toward informality which developed in the bands themselves. With the brigades operating independently, disciplinary procedures to some extent were always suited to the occasion, and discipline did not become the compelling abstract force that it is in regular military organizations.

Because of the precarious situations in which most of the partisan detachments found themselves, the problems of discipline centered almost exclusively upon the more serious offenses: negligence on guard and in connection with concealment and camouflage, disobedience of orders, cowardice, and desertion. Enough instances of such offenses occurred in every unit to require the constant vigilance of the officers. The politruk of one detachment operating near Bryansk noted this in his diary:

Ryasanyev, the leader of the 1st Platoon, performed very poorly in battle; the leadership rightly deprived him of his command and demoted him to the rank of private. This, however, only after he vowed never to be a coward again. Private Sapozhnikov (Jew): He not only refused to shoot, but even threw away his gun. For this, he was arrested by the detachment commander. Group Leader Mariyev, machine gunner, is a coward. He deserted the scene of battle, leaving his machine gun behind. At this time, he is under arrest.[88]

Another politruk made the following entry in his diary:

14 April 1943: We made a list of all those who had deserted from our detachment since it was organized [date not known]. Unfortunately, the number of deserters is really impressive. On the basis of not very accurate records, we

[86] Okdo. H.Gr.Mitte, Ia, "Monatliche Meldung ueber Bandenlage," 4 July 1943, p. 2 (GMDS, HGr. Mitte 65002/22).

[87] 8. Pz.Div., Ic, "Vernehmung," 18 May 1943 (GMDS, 8 PzDiv 44131/28).

[88] 707. Inf.Div., Ic, "Feindnachrichten Nr. 14," 26 October 1942, p. 2 (GMDS, 707 ID 27797/4, Anlage 201).

estimated a total of sixty-nine desertions. These fools actually took along with them one machine gun, three submachine guns, thirty rifles, and a substantial quantity of ammunition. . . . According to informants, these deserters are already in the German police, and, if the occasion arises, will shoot at us with our own weapons.[89]

The partisan officers had to keep a close watch on most of their men. The regular agencies for surveillance, the commissars and the NKVD special sections, performed the same functions as they did in the Soviet Army. In the partisan detachments, however, surveillance became the keystone of the organization, militarily as well as politically. Accounts similar to the following appear frequently in the documents:

Vetitiyev [a drafted partisan who had deserted] declared that escape from the partisans is difficult, since guardposts are set up everywhere. If a deserter is captured, he is first tortured and then shot. As a result of the "many" desertions, the partisan officers have become so mistrustful of the partisans who are local men that they have scattered the local men in among the former Red Army soldiers. Consequently, the drafted partisans cannot communicate with each other without being observed. Vetitiyev believes that if the number of desertions increases all the partisans who were drafted locally will be shot.[90]

In April 1943 a unit politruk issued the following order:

As a consequence of the serious food situation there have been some desertions from the detachment. To prevent such occurrences I order (1) all of the men are to be checked for dependability, and a list of undependables is to be submitted to the staff; (2) the guards are to detain all men who appear near the posts without passes, disarm them, and turn them over to the staff; (3) whoever absents himself from the detachment without leave or remains absent after a mission for longer than the permitted time—without a good reason— will be regarded as a deserter.[91]

A German intelligence agency which examined the captured records of the Grishin Regiment listed as the most frequently mentioned offenses: failure to carry out combat assignments, sleeping and smoking on guard, plundering, drunkenness, and "lack of restraint in relations with women." A captured partisan, questioned concerning discipline in his detachment, stated: "Orders were carried out well by some, by others negligently. Those who did not carry out orders satisfactorily were given corporal punishment [*pruegelstraffe*]. Often there were quarrels among the men (e.g., because of tardy relief [while on guard] since there were too few to man the posts). For example, a young, untrained partisan was shot because he fired a round accidentally."[92] A captured nurse stated that the men in her brigade

[89] VI. A.K., "Tagebuch des politischen Leiters der Aufklaerer-Kompanie der Partisanen-Abteilung 'Morjak,'" May 1944 (GMDS, VI AK 44653/14).

[90] 221. Inf.Div., Ic, "An Befh. d. H. Gr. Mitte," 28 April 1942 (GMDS, 221 ID 22639/6).

[91] VI. A.K., Ic, "Tagebuch . . . 'Morjak.'"

[92] 221. Sich.Div., Ic, "Vernehmung der in den Kaempfen am 8.4.1942 Gefangenen," 9 April 1942, p. 2 (GMDS, 221 ID 22639/6, Anlage 12).

were forbidden to associate with the women. On one occasion the commander of the Grishin Regiment issued the following order: "My persistent requests to maintain order and discipline are disregarded again and again. Lack of restraint in relations with women has been noted at different times. In seven cases this has resulted in pregnancy. These women reduce the combat readiness of their men and are a burden to the regiment in combat." [See Appendix, Document 58.] Drunkenness among both the officers and men is frequently mentioned, but generally the scarcity of alcohol seems to have served to keep that problem under control.

1. Special Disciplinary Measures

The partisan commanders made a constant effort—undoubtedly on orders from the Soviet command—to curb looting and unregulated requisitioning by their men. Because the partisan detachments lived off the land this problem assumed great importance. Regarding themselves as legal, political, and military representatives of the Soviet Union, the partisans claimed a right to requisition supplies from the population and to confiscate the property of collaborators. For psychological reasons, it was desired to mitigate as far as possible the adverse effects that the requisitioning was bound to have on public opinion. This did not mean that the population benefited materially. One brigade, for instance, forbade the requisitioning of bread and ordered that "the collection is to be so organized that the people do it themselves."[93] There were good reasons for restraining individual inclinations toward looting. Each detachment depended to a large extent on the good will of the population in its operating area. Furthermore, with forced requisitioning necessary and officially sanctioned there was a constant danger of the detachments' descending to outright banditry. With a major segment of the partisan personnel motivated by desperation rather than by political or moral objectives, there was the additional danger that the detachments would take the line of least resistance and devote themselves exclusively to bullying the noncombatants.

A partisan officer entered the following comments on this problem in his diary:

Today the detachment was visited by the brigade commander, who conversed for an extended period of time with the enlisted personnel as a fellow-soldier and [spoke] especially about the question of relations with the peaceful population; the reputation which the brigade had in its old combat area must be kept up. This conversation was prompted by the whole series of complaints which have reached the brigade commander about unjust actions of our partisans and illegal confiscation of property.

An order: In the detachment, cases of an unfriendly attitude toward the peaceful population have recently been noted. I order that the strictest measures

[93] GFP Gr. 714, ["Captured Orders of the First Regiment of the Third Leningrad Partisan Brigade,"] 3 June 1943 (GMDS, 281 ID 45072).

be taken against the guilty persons upon complaints of the peaceful population concerning unjust actions of the fighters and commanders (abuses, rudeness, threats, use of arms, unlawful confiscation of property belonging to the peaceful population).—*Appendix, Document 74.*

Another brigade issued orders banning looting by individuals and regularizing requisitions from the population:

Recently instances of thefts of cattle, horses, and other goods from the population have been noted. Individual partisans obtain supplies during the night. All these activities, on the part of elements hostile to us, terrorize the population and incite them against the partisans. Such activities are nothing but banditry. Because of this, I order all commanders and commissars of the detachments in my command as follows:

1. The members of the platoons may not collect supplies at night outside of designated villages.

2. If night raids are noted, the persons concerned are to be disarmed and arrested, regardless of their detachments or brigades, and are to be sent to the detachment or brigade staff.

3. Supplies are to be collected during the day only and through the village elders. A receipt must be given for food and cattle received, and a copy of the receipt is to be sent to the detachment.

4. Any partisan caught red-handed stealing cattle, horses, or other goods is to be shot as a looter.

5. The commanders and commissars are responsible for the execution of this order.

6. This order is to be brought to the attention of all personnel in the detachments under my jurisdiction.[94]

2. Combat Discipline

German reports on antipartisan operations contain frequent references to the "desperate" and "tenacious" resistance offered by the partisans. Nevertheless, disciplinary action against partisans accused of such offenses as willful desertion of a post in combat, abandoning weapons in combat, and failure to carry out orders were common in the partisan units. On the whole, it appears that in small-group engagements, where they were under the close observation and control of their officers, the partisans fought well. Very often, even in such instances, however, their resistance could better be described as desperate than as determined or skillful. In decisive engagements involving a whole brigade or several brigades, the partisans, again, often resisted desperately; but their performance was likely to be uneven, revealing wide variations in the combat effectiveness of the units.

Early in 1942 the establishment of a large partisan center was begun in Ushachi Rayon, south of Polotsk. Free from major German countermeasures it grew, by January 1944, to a strength of 12,000 men or more

[94] PzAOK 3, Ic/AO, "Entwicklung der Bandenlage im Bereich der 3. Pz. Armee im Dezember 1943 (abgeschlossen: 31.12.43)," 2 January 1944, Anlage 3 (GMDS PzAOK 3, 49113/37 Anlage 43).

until it controlled most of the forty-mile stretch of swamps and lakes between Polotsk and Lepel. It was expected to serve as a gigantic roadblock,
forcing the enemy to detour to the north and south as the Soviet front
advanced westward. Before the Soviet summer offensive of 1944 got underway, however, the Germans launched Operation "Fruehlingsfest," and in
about three weeks destroyed the center and most of its brigades. Some of
the problems which the commander of the Ushachi center faced are described in the following excerpts from German and partisan documents.
After the first assault, a German unit reported: "The behavior of the
partisans was uneven. While the partisans of the Lenin Brigade fled from
their positions northwest of Ulla as soon as the Germans attacked, our
troops observed that the partisans of the Smolensk Regiment in the area
south of Fainovo followed their orders to the letter and some even held
out in their bunkers to the death."[95] The German estimate was substantiated in orders issued by the partisan commander.

During the battle there were instances of panic. During the retreat, the
civilians hiding in the forest were not evacuated even though it was possible
to do so. Cattle and food supplies were abandoned. The leadership of the
Chapayev Brigade displayed a lack of initiative. The leadership also failed to
attempt to master the panic. The Central Committee of the Belorussian Communist Party Brigade and the Lenin Brigade commanded by Fursov offered
no resistance to the first pressure of the enemy. The brigades did not take the
necessary defensive measures to prevent the enemy's crossing of the Berezina
River and his breakthrough in the forward defense perimeter. In individual
instances it was observed that partisans created panic among the civilians in
order to rob them of their goods and possessions.[96]

In another order he stated:

The following shortcomings have become apparent:
1. Insufficient reconnaissance of the enemy territory, with the result that in
some cases he surprised us.
2. Lack of determination on the part of commanders and commissars resulting in an unorganized retreat. Insufficient defense in spite of good positions. No
action was taken against those who created panic or against cowards.
3. Bunkers are badly constructed and poorly camouflaged.
4. Main line of resistance, including deployment [not properly prepared].
5. Command posts poorly prepared.
6. Lack of precision in giving commands.[97]

In the same document he ordered:

Courageous partisans and commanders are to be rewarded and promoted
by all available means. Cowards and those who create panics are to be punished

---

[95] PzAOK 3, Ic/AO, "Entwicklung der Bandenlage im Bereich der 3. Panzer-Armee,"
1 April 1944, p. 4 (GMDS, PzAOK 3, 62587/12).
[96] PzAOK 3, Ic/AO, "Entwicklung der Bandenlage im Bereich der 3. Panzer-Armee,"
28 April 1944, Anlage 62 (GMDS, PzAOK 3, 62587/12).
[97] Kampfgr. Gottberg, Ic, "Auswertung von Beutepapieren," 4 March 1944 (GMDS,
Waffen SS, Dirlewanger 78028/15).

in the most severe manner. Commanders failing to prosecute such elements will be punished. Discipline must be improved through the application of the most stringent methods.

Mutual assistance of detachments is to be promoted.[98]

3. Punishments

The death penalty was the foundation of partisan discipline. Under partisan warfare conditions, which greatly reduced the effectiveness of all less drastic measures, it was not surprising that even relatively minor offenses, such as drunkenness and contraction of venereal diseases, should have been potentially, at least, punishable by death. Usually executions were carried out on the order of the brigade commander, although each officer had the authority to order summary executions at his own discretion. In practice, while the threat of shooting was frequently invoked, executions, except in cases of desertion, were used chiefly to set examples. They were ordered as often as was deemed necessary to achieve the desired purpose—intimidation; there was no determined effort to achieve a uniform standard of justice. In that respect, too, it is likely that the status of the individual went far toward determining his liability to punishment. A drafted peasant, a former collaborator, or a partisan under suspicion for political reasons might stand in constant danger of being singled out and sentenced to death for almost any minor offense, while a partisan who was politically and otherwise in good standing might receive nothing more serious than a reprimand for an aggravated offense.

The better-organized brigades evolved graduated scales of punishment —reprimands, confinement to quarters on short rations, demotions, or expulsion from the Party. A favorite measure against cowardice took the form of a public admission of guilt by the accused followed by his pledge not to repeat the offense. In the light of the heterogeneous composition, tensions, and devious forces at work in every partisan unit, it is not likely that even the sentences formally announced always grew entirely out of the charges stated. The average partisan probably stood in about as much danger of losing his life as a result of the general atmosphere of suspicion which prevailed in most units as he did of being formally cited and sentenced for a specific offense. It was a simple matter to dispose of a man by assigning him to exceptionally dangerous missions. Captured partisans and deserters stated repeatedly that men were often marked for execution without their being informed either of the charges or of the sentence and were simply shot while on patrol or during a minor skirmish with the enemy.

In the execution of punitive disciplinary and political measures the special sections of the NKVD played an important part. The brigades, almost without exception, had an NKVD officer attached to their staffs. In some

[98] *Ibid.*

cases he had a squad of ten to twenty men for such special "administrative" measures as executions of civilians, partisans, and collaborators. The special sections also, apparently, kept track of persons slated for deferred punishment, civilian collaborators, partisans who had collaborated, political unreliables, and Red Army stragglers suspected of dereliction of duty in the 1941 battles. The NKVD officer organized his own agents within the partisan unit and ran an intelligence network which extended throughout the unit's zone of operations; however, the special sections seem not to have achieved the ruthless efficiency of their counterparts in the regular Army. Many of the special section officers were not professionals; moreover, isolation in the brigades probably inspired a certain amount of circumspection in the performance of their work.

Various trial procedures evolved in the partisan movement. Summary executions were common. Generally, however, charges were brought before the brigade commander, who, usually on his own authority but sometimes with the commissar and the chief of staff, issued an order for the execution of the sentence. As far as can be determined, once a charge had been brought, guilt was presumed. The trial procedure involved only an evaluation of the seriousness of the offense and a determination of the severity of the punishment. While the special sections also had the authority to pass and execute sentences, the hand of the NKVD can seldom be detected in the captured partisan records—most likely because the NKVD measures were carried out covertly. Occasionally the Party collective of the detachment was called upon to participate in a trial. Then the charges were brought either by the commander or the commissar, and the participation of the assembly at large was limited to the "formulation" of the sentence.

Among the partisan records captured by the Germans are numerous orders relating to sentences passed against individuals. They illustrate, incidentally, the high degree of bureaucratization which prevailed in the partisan movement. While they represent a certain adherence to formal legal procedure, they are almost always more didactic than judicial in form and content; the charge is stated in general terms and then carefully related to a broad disciplinary problem. The main purpose always is to present an object lesson which reinforces a standing order. The following example is typical:

Order No. 12
To the First Partisan Regiment of the Second Partisan Brigade
of the Northwest Front
26 April 1943

Under the conditions of partisan warfare in the enemy rear areas, guard duty is of tremendous importance for the protection of the garrisons against unexpected attacks by the enemy. Still, some partisans do not have the necessary sense of responsibility. Instances of gross contravention of the regulations pertaining to guard duty have been observed.

On 24 April 1943 the partisan of Detachment No. 13, Boikov, while he was charged with the responsible mission of guarding a sector assigned to him, criminally and traitorously neglected his duty by sleeping on guard. Comrade Boikov knew that sleeping on guard is treason and disloyalty to the fatherland.

I order:

1. For criminal behavior while on guard duty and for sleeping while on guard, which is treason against the fatherland, the partisan of Detachment No. 13, Boikov, is to be shot.

2. I warn the personnel of the regiment that in the future I will punish mercilessly all offenses against the regulations pertaining to guard duty.

The order is to be brought to the attention of the personnel.[99]

Desertion invariably brought the death penalty. In addition the names of close relatives of each partisan were kept on record; if he deserted, his family was exterminated in reprisal. The sentences against captured deserters were given wide publicity in the units.

On the basis of the decision of the Commander of the Special Section attached to the Shabo Regiment, we have executed the Red Army straggler Ivan Yakovlevich Khokhlov (born 1920, not a member of the Party, from the village Lokhovo, Zhnamenka Rayon, Smolensk Oblast).

Facts of the case: The Red Army straggler Khokhlov deserted on 12 March 1942 when the 1st Company was being transferred from Velikopolye to Belyugino and stayed in hiding in the attic of his house at Lokhovo until his arrest on 11 April.

There is no place for deserters in the Red Army! Khokhlov has been shot in front of the assembled detachment. The consequences of desertion have thus been called to the attention of each soldier.

[Signatures]	
Commander of the 1st Company	Sverev
Commander of the 1st Platoon	Belov
Assistant to the commander of the 2d Platoon	Kramskoi
Red Army man	Imayev

12 April 1942[100]

In keeping with traditional Soviet practice, the individual was not only liable to disciplinary action by his superiors, but was subjected as well to the allegedly spontaneous criticism of his fellows. Every brigade, often every company or platoon, had its own wall newspaper (a typed or handwritten bulletin devoted to news supposedly of immediate interest to the unit). Theoretically a product of the men in the unit, the wall newspaper was actually controlled by the officers. As a major feature it carried comments on the accomplishments and deficiencies of the unit members. The partisan who found himself cited by name in the wall newspaper as a coward or "instigator of panic" might justifiably have become seriously concerned for his future. Similarly, the offenses of partisans were aired

[99] GFP Gr. 714, "[Captured Orders of the First Regiment of the Third Leningrad Partisan Brigade]" 3 June 1943 (GMDS, 281 ID 45072).

[100] XXXXVI. Pz.K., Ic, "Partisanenherrschaft im Smolensker Gebiet," 18 June 1942, pp. 3–4 (GMDS, 23 ID 24182/16).

publicly at Party and Komsomol meetings. The excerpt below, taken from the protocol of a Komsomol meeting, illustrates the procedure.

The conduct of Komsomol Member Shulga.

Platoon Leader Brylkin: "Although Comrade Shulga is good in battle, he often likes to talk too much. He always has objections, a habit which is incompatible with his conduct as a Komsomol member. I want to cite the following example: I gave the order to bring a saddle. Shulga replied that no one had received a saddle. For this answer he was put in jail for twenty-four hours. For all this, for the remark and for the nonexecution of the order, I propose a reprimand for Comrade Shulga."

Unit Leader: "Every Komsomol member must set an example. He must always support the leader; Shulga, however, does the opposite. I second the motion of the platoon leader."

Decision: Komsomol member Shulga is to be punished with a reprimand to be entered in his record because of his remark and the nonexecution of the order of the platoon leader, which amount to undermining the authority of his superior.—*Appendix, Document 20.*

This procedure made the group accountable for the offenses of its single members, and it increased the vulnerability of the individual by narrowing his sphere of personal freedom from disciplinary interference.

§IV. Conclusion

The manpower of the Soviet partisan movement was drawn predominantly from the peasantry and the Red Army stragglers. In the years 1943 and 1944 these two groups accounted for about 80 per cent of the total strength of the movement. The peasants, for the most part, were drafted into the movement. As partisans they were characterized by a fatalistic indifference. Their immediate interests led them to regard partisan warfare primarily as an additional element contributing to economic disruption and reducing the profits from agriculture. At longer range, they viewed the Soviet and German systems as identical cvils, the only difference being that the Soviet Union seemed more likely to win the war. To a minor degree, since the German system offered no compensatory attractions, they were also influenced by a sense of obligation to the Soviet regime as the legal and indigenous political authority. The Red Army stragglers, on the other hand, were somewhat more positively motivated. The "business as usual" desires of the peasantry meant nothing to the soldiers, and their espousal of the Soviet cause represented a choice of the lesser of two evils. As soldiers they had clear legal obligations to the Soviet state, and as stragglers they were already, in the Soviet view, guilty of desertion. Partisan activity offered them the opportunity to honor their obligations and, possibly, to restore themselves to the good graces of the Soviet regime. German policy enhanced the advantages of partisan activity as far as the stragglers were concerned. Outside the partisan movement they had three choices: to live illegally, subject to arrest at any time and cut off from legitimate employment; to surrender and endure the hardships of the German prison camps; or to add treason to the charges already against them by joining collaborator police and military units. Even though faced with these conditions, the majority of the stragglers dissociated themselves from further active participation in the war as long as possible, joining the partisan movement sometime after early 1942 largely out of fear of retribution aroused by the advance of the Red Army.

After 1941 the percentage of Communist Party members in the partisan movement declined rapidly. In 1941 Party members comprised as much as 80 per cent of individual units, and units averaging between 25 and 40 per cent Party members were not unusual. In the later years the Party contingent rarely accounted for more than 10 per cent of the total strength. This shift was significant because it reflected a basic change in the Soviet concept of partisan warfare—from the idea of a relatively limited, elite movement which would depend heavily on loyal Party members to a mass movement utilizing all available sources of manpower and substituting for political loyalty as the motivating force, the ability of the Soviet regime to extend its authority into the occupied territories. From 1942 on, the Party contingent in the partisan movement was important only as one of the instruments of Soviet control.

The contingents of urban workers, so-called intellectuals, and women were all small percentage-wise but, for various reasons, were important nevertheless. Women (children were also used) were valuable as agents and scouts. Their usefulness, however, was apparently limited, since they were not drafted and there was no attempt to enroll them in the movement in large numbers. The intellectuals—doctors, teachers, administrators of various kinds, and others—were important in the 1941 partisan movement, for which they frequently provided the leadership. Throughout the war, the partisan movement aimed at attracting these people as a means of depriving the enemy of their services, if nothing else. They were a highly unstable element in the population of the occupied territories. Subject to constant Soviet and partisan pressure and often suffering economically from the occupation, many went over to the partisans; or, still worse from the German point of view since their limited numbers could not add significantly to the numerical strength of the movement, they became agents for the partisans. As such, they were often very effective, since they had somewhat superior social status and often, as in the case of doctors and administrators, had access to medicine and other supplies. In the main partisan areas, the urban workers were a minority, under normal conditions (i.e., before the invasion and occupation) less than 25 per cent of the total population. Furthermore, the partisan detachments operated outside the cities. Under those circumstances, the urban population could not furnish recruits to the partisan movement on a wide scale; nevertheless, the Germans reported strong pro-partisan sentiment in the cities. The urban population, in general, tended to accept and support Soviet communism. Such attitudes were, if anything, enhanced by the economic dislocation of the war, which was felt most severely in the cities. Numbers of men and youths left the cities to volunteer for duty with the partisans, and, as the war progressed, underground organizations affiliated with the partisans were created in most of the major cities.[101]

The morale of the partisan movement is difficult to gauge. It is certain that there were very clear-cut class distinctions, resulting from the conditions under which the various component groups came into the movement. The relatively small number of volunteers and Party men formed the only group which could be assumed to have been entirely acceptable to the Soviet regime. Nearly all the others were tainted in some way— the stragglers with desertion, the drafted peasants with general unreliability, the former collaborators with treason. The majority of the men in every detachment were, often not without reason, considered basically unreliable. This situation was reflected in morale, particularly of the drafted men who lived under the constant suspicion of their commanders and who themselves were generally apathetic. Desertion was a persistent problem, although it did not reach catastrophic proportions largely because German and partisan policy and the course of the war combined to make desertion a poor alternative even for the most desperate men.

In the final analysis, it can probably be said that the partisan movement was the product of a Soviet effort to create an active resistance movement by drawing on sources of manpower which, in the main, can be characterized as unresponsive and apathetic, and which, therefore, acted as a constant drag on the effectiveness of the movement. To create such a movement, the Soviet regime instituted close control and strict military and political supervision. It was able to rely to a high degree on the force of its authority to offset the absence of a voluntary response, and it was further aided by the disastrous shortcomings of German policy.

---

[101] The Germans discovered at least one such underground group in each of the following: Vitebsk, Minsk, Bryansk, Lepel, Borisov, Bobruisk, and Novozybkov.

CHAPTER IV

Partisan Psychological Warfare and Popular Attitudes

Alexander Dallin, Ralph Mavrogordato, and
Wilhelm Moll

§I. Organization and Technical Aspects of Partisan Psychological Warfare

A. ORGANIZATION OF PARTISAN PSYWAR

1. Central Direction

The difficulties involved in the organization and control of partisan psychological warfare at the highest levels were due in part to the general diversity and fluidity of partisan organizational patterns. They were compounded by the specific demands of propaganda work and by the "legitimate" interest that various agencies—Party, Komsomol, Army, NKVD, and Central Staff—had or staked out in these endeavors.

The evidence on the central direction of the propaganda effort is scanty and contradictory. It is clear that, in the early stage of partisan activities, relatively little attention was paid either by Moscow or the partisans themselves to the streamlining and coordination of propaganda efforts. To the partisans, propaganda was something of a luxury at a time when they were not only hard pressed to justify their existence but also when they were often cut off from Soviet news sources and had neither the technical means nor the leisure required to produce printed materials. At this time their efforts were restricted to word-of-mouth appeals and, wherever practicable, to printed media produced on the Soviet side of the front.[1]

After the creation of the Central Staff of the Partisan Movement, on 30 May 1942,[2] institutional channels were further developed and through

[1] As early as January 1942, however, the Germans noted that, occasionally at least, drop-areas for Soviet leaflets were selected so as to concentrate drops in locations where partisans on the ground could assure their distribution. (Befh. H. Geb. Nord, Ic/AO, "Taetigkeitsbericht fuer die Zeit vom 1. bis 31.1.1942," p. 2, GMDS, HGeb 18320/6.)

[2] S. Golikov, *Vydayushchiesya pobedy sovetskoi armii v velikoi otechestvennoi voine* (Moscow: Gosudarstvennoye Izdatelstvo Politicheskoi Literatury, 1954).

them substantive psychological warfare operations were coordinated on the German side of the front. Evidence of more centralized control is further supplied by (a) the existence of a training school for partisan propagandists in Moscow, presumably operating under the Central Staff; (b) the available text of a broadcast containing directives to be followed in partisan propaganda; and (c) the fact that propaganda materials, including newspapers and leaflets printed in Moscow, were regularly brought in to the partisans for guidance and distribution. Moreover, the themes employed in partisan propaganda showed striking parallels (along with significant differences) when compared with Soviet propaganda.[3]

Toward the end of 1942 and the beginning of 1943, German reports recorded a more systematic organization of partisan psychological warfare. This development may have been the result of two Stalin orders. The first, dated 5 September 1942, called for the organized distribution of newspapers, leaflets, and other printed materials on occupied territory.[4] The text of the second is unfortunately not available, but its existence is confirmed by numerous German reports fixing its date as December 1942. It reportedly called for tighter control and intensification of partisan press and propaganda activities. It specifically provided for the establishment in Moscow of one-month courses for editors, proofreaders, correspondents, and printers, who after graduation were to be assigned to the partisans. Information for inclusion in partisan media was to be sent regularly by radio, and special propaganda and press sections were to be activated at various partisan levels of command.[5] Many of the above measures had already been implemented well before the order was issued; the remaining ones were complied with in varying degrees.

By mid-1943 the Central Staff and the territorial (Belorussian and Ukrainian) partisan staffs each had a propaganda and press section directing the work of editors, journalists, and technical personnel.[6] The Political

---

[3] Other evidence of a centralized direction of partisan propaganda is implicit in the requests for information on all aspects of life under German occupation, including the German-sponsored press—information which could in turn be put to good use in propaganda material prepared on the Soviet side.

[4] AOK 9, Ic/AO, "Auszug aus dem Befehl des Volkskommissars der SSSR, Nr. 0189," 19 August 1943, p. 3 (GMDS, H 14/14).

[5] OKH/GenStdH/FHO, *Nachrichten ueber den Bandenkrieg,* Nr. 4, 10 September 1943 (GMDS, H 3/738) [hereafter cited as *Nachrichten*], p. 4.

[6] The Ukrainian Staff's section was reportedly headed by the prominent Ukrainian poet, Sosyura. (*Nachrichten,* Nr. 3, 28 July 1943, Anlagen 6 and 10.) According to a questionable report by a former partisan, in Belorussia "a Central Propaganda Section was established at the Central Committee of the KP(b)B. . . . Its staff included a representative of the Political Administration of the Red Army, who acted as a liaison man to the partisan propaganda staff." (Harvard University, Russian Research Center, Project on the Soviet Social System [hereafter cited as Russian Research Center], interview protocol series B 7, #140, p. 86.)

Administration of the Red Army Fronts and the Political Sections of the Armies were charged with propaganda to the civilian population in the rear of the enemy and with supplying propaganda materials to the partisans. Operative groups on the Soviet side of the lines apparently did not have separate propaganda and press sections.

The precise interrelation of Central Staff Propaganda, Party, and Army psychological warfare sections remains unclear. It may be asserted, however, that coordination did take place at least on the most important issues and themes. A high-ranking partisan officer told the Germans after his capture that the question of how to treat the Vlasov movement in Soviet and partisan propaganda had been discussed jointly with the *agitprop* section of the Party's Central Committee and the Main Political Administration of the Red Army. Likewise, the time lag repeatedly observed before partisan propaganda responded to the most crucial and controversial German measures, notably the German agrarian reform of February 1942, suggests that coordinated directives had to be obtained at the highest levels before psychological warfare operations could begin. At the same time, the organizational structure remained sufficiently flexible to permit the lower echelons at all times to exploit local conditions and specific themes within the general framework and context of approved propaganda lines.

2. The Communist Party in Partisan Propaganda Activities

The point of departure for the integration of the Communist Party and its adjunct Komsomol network into psychological warfare activities in the German-occupied areas of the USSR was the great role played by the Party organs in peacetime "agitation and propaganda." In the initial stages of the war the Party had sought to leave behind an underground apparatus in each city, rayon, and oblast of the occupied areas. [See Chaps. II and III.] Among other things, the underground Party was to be responsible for the creation and control of the partisan movement on a territorial basis. Some measures for the movement's propaganda work were adopted even before the German arrival. An order of the Party's Central Committee of 18 July 1941, for instance, provided for the direction of partisan groups by small underground Party units, specifying that arrangements were to be made to send leaflets and posters to the partisans or to prepare for printing such materials on the spot. In Chernigov Oblast, the underground Party committee, which also constituted the original staff of the partisan movement, institutionalized propaganda activities as early as the end of July 1941, when a Secretary for Agitation and Propaganda was appointed and charged with "selecting literature, setting up a print shop, collecting and packing newsprint." Similar preparations were made in the Crimea, Krasnodar, and Stalingrad regions. In the last two areas the Party secretaries of the rayon and city committees were made responsible for the preparation of propaganda work.

Where bands actually engaged in propaganda activities, the interrelationship of Party and partisan work was so close that any distinction between them would not correspond to the realities of the situation. One German intelligence report, discussing underground Party-directed propaganda in the summer of 1943, found that "systematic construction of an illegal network of Party and partisan propaganda" was taking place "throughout the entire Eastern occupied territories under central direction from Moscow." The outstanding feature was "the close coordination of partisan propaganda with Party propaganda"—a conclusion fully borne out by other available data. Another report stated that special propaganda groups set up by partisan brigades were administered jointly by the partisan staffs and the underground Party committees. In some instances the underground Party committees were actually set up by partisans; in others the Party committee was physically attached to or even identical with the staff of a large stationary brigade. Party secretaries, especially at the rayon level, often were partisan officers at the same time.

The difficulties in distinguishing between Party and partisan-sponsored propaganda activities are compounded by the frequency with which German reports fail to distinguish between Party organizers and partisan groups; they often assumed that the entire partisan movement was under direct, or even exclusive, Party control, and Soviet postwar accounts generally tend to exaggerate the role played by the Party as the "organizer of victory," either by conveniently ignoring the unpopular activities of the NKVD apparatus, or by seeking to inflate the part played by Communist organs, compared with the politically more neutral and less articulate Army. It must be concluded that the role played by Party and Komsomol in partisan psychological warfare was greater than that of any other institution, especially since the work of the Red Army in this field was handled through the Main Political Administration, which at the same time was the Military Section of the Central Committee of the Communist Party of the USSR.

a. Party Control over Partisan Propaganda

Partly because of the chaotic retreat and general disorganization, partly because of the unfavorable conditions in which the small staffs were compelled to operate during the initial stage of the occupation, in many rayons the Party nuclei left behind in effect dissolved and disappeared. The scattered evidence suggests that, during the first phase of the partisan movement, the revival of the Party organization above the local level was crucially handicapped by the same factors that rendered difficult the survival and extension of the partisan movement itself.

In line with general endeavors to intensify anti-German activities and organization behind the lines, the Communist Party in the unoccupied areas began dispatching its representatives back to German-held soil in order to reorganize Party and partisan units and spread propaganda among the population. Such a development took place, for instance, in Leningrad Oblast when the Oblast Committee sent underground Party groups to German-held territory to engage in Party-political work.[7] There is every indication that a similar process took place in other oblasts.

The Party Oblast Committees, for the most part located on the Soviet side of the front, supplied the underground press with the necessary materials, printing equipment and paper, and supervised the publication and distribution of propaganda materials.[8] The Central Committees of the Belorussian and Ukrainian Communist Parties (located on the Soviet side) published their own materials and provided the partisans and the civilian population with copies of their papers, mostly by air.[9]

The Leningrad Oblast Committee played a somewhat unusual role in the partisan control structure, since the *obkom* secretary, Nikitin, also commanded the partisan staffs attached to the Northwest and Volkhov Fronts. When supplies were shipped to the partisans, the propaganda sections of the partisan staffs at the Volkhov and Northwest Fronts sent along considerable quantities of leaflets.[10]

The material at hand permits few generalizations about the changes in Party direction of partisan propaganda. Only in the spring of 1943 did the Germans find a set of directives ostensibly issued by the Central Committee of the VKP(b) with a "Work Plan" for Party organs behind

[7] P. Sheverdalkin, ed., *Listovki partizanskoi voiny v leningradskoi oblasti 1941–44* (Leningrad: Leningradskoye Gazetno-Zhurnalnoye i Knizhnoye Izdatelstvo, 1945), p.7.

[8] L. Tsanava, *Vsenarodnaya partizanskaya voina v Belorussii protiv fashistskikh zakhvatchikov* (Minsk: Gosudarstvennoye Izdatelstvo BSSR, Vol. I, 1949; Vol. II, 1951), II, 930.

[9] A Soviet postwar source credits the Central Committee of the Belorussian Communist Party and the Belorussian Staff of the Partisan Movement with instituting a regular newspaper supply service. This source alleges that, on the average, the rather impressive number of 350,000 papers was sent in daily, in addition to 30,000 copies of *Sovetskaya Belarus,* the official organ of the Central Committee of the Belorussian CP. Other newspapers included issues of *Pravda, Izvestiya, Komsomolskaya Pravda,* and *Krasnoye Znamya.* Despite the seemingly exaggerated number, the source admits that material sent in from the Soviet side proved to be insufficient and needed to be supplemented by material printed in the German-held areas (Tsanava, II, 68).

[10] Sheverdalkin, p. 7. These Party-operated sections should not be confused with the Political Administrations of each Front, which also sent psychological-warfare supplies to the partisans.

In some areas inter-rayon committees were established, covering several or parts of several rayons. These Party committees, generally created where it was not feasible to set up rayon committees, are credited by a Soviet source with having played "a tremendous role in the development of the partisan press" in Leningrad Oblast.

the German lines. The excerpts given in the available document fail to indicate that the plan was aimed specifically at the partisans, though in all probability it was. Among the various points, the directives stressed: "The Party member is obliged ... to explain the war situation on the anti-Fascist fronts of the war to the non-Party masses and to restore and strengthen among them the belief in the final victory of Soviet power over fascism." The extensive point-by-point program attached to them included drafting civilians for work with the underground, increasing inducements to collaborators to desert, infiltrating German and indigenous collaborator agencies, and preventing German requisitions and recruitment of forced labor.

Certainly the *obkomy* remained the key bodies in the formulation and transmission of propaganda policies to the partisan units, subject to broader directives at a higher level. The rayon committees of the Party were at first constrained to operate independently and without extensive underground means; more often than not, the German occupation had deprived them of cadres, means of supply, and for some time of liaison with higher echelons. As the Party committees were revived on a territorial basis behind the German lines, each *obkom* and *raikom* was instructed to publish its own newspaper and leaflets. While the themes employed show enough general similarities to suggest rather specific directives from above, often rayon workers had to fend for themselves both in amassing technical equipment and in drafting specific appeals adapted to local conditions. By 1944, in most areas behind the German lines, each *raikom* was publishing newspapers and leaflets, though many of these were technically inferior, small in circulation, and irregular in appearance and distribution. [See also below, subsection B, 2.]

While many such Party committees were, in operation, at least formally separate from partisan groups, a corresponding Party network permeated the partisan structure itself. [For further details, see Chap. II, Sect. III, H, 3.] As the partisan movement grew and its institutional framework expanded, so did the Party organizations and the Propaganda and Agitation Sections within them. While the major task of such sections was customarily indoctrination within the unit, at least in some instances the Party cell also functioned as a nucleus for the reinstallation of the Party apparatus among the civilian population as well. In some cases, the Party units within the partisan bands were closely tied in with the territorial Party organizations for the area in which they operated;[11] in others, they

---

[11] This was particularly true in instances where the underground Party was also the organizer of the partisans and where Party secretaries were simultaneously partisan officers. In Kalinin Oblast, 48 *raikom* secretaries; in Smolensk Oblast, 85 *raikom* secretaries worked as organizers of partisans units. In Belorussia [at the peak] 9 *obkomy*, 174 *gorkomy* [city committees] and *raikomy* were operating under the Germans. (Golikov, p. 100.)

were directly responsible to higher Party echelons on the Soviet side of the front.[12] In addition to conducting political propaganda among the population, they were responsible for the collection of political intelligence.

As the partisan movement expanded, there was a growing tendency to transfer partisans who were Party members from combat and administrative duties to political and propaganda work, either within the Party cell or at the propaganda section of the partisan unit. In one way or another, the Party continued to play a decisive role in the psychological warfare work of the detachments. It provided special propaganda troops and individual lecturers and agitators, who were filtered through the lines or flown into the occupied areas, and who occasionally brought propaganda directives and printed material with them for distribution behind the German lines. In other cases, high-ranking officers were temporarily sent in by the Party to give advice to partisan units and at the same time to deliver lectures and reports to partisans and neighboring civilians.

b. The Underground Komosomol in Psychological Warfare

As an adjunct of the Party, the Komsomol possessed an equally extensive network throughout the Soviet Union. With the advent of the German occupation, its apparatus on occupied soil also disintegrated, although its membership did not fully disperse. Though gravely weakened by mobilizations and evacuations, a probably larger percentage of Komsomol cadres than of their Party counterparts remained on occupied soil. It is likely that defeatism was less widespread among the Soviet-trained younger men and women than among skeptical older persons aware of alternatives to the Soviet regime and hardened by a generation of life in the USSR. It was thus an obvious measure for the Soviet regime to attempt a revival of the Komsomol apparatus, which was particularly well suited for employment in psychological warfare: Komsomol members were likely to be more literate, physically more hard and resilient, and at the same time more reliable from the Soviet point of view.

The revival of a Komsomol organization is described in various Soviet memoirs and postwar belles-lettres. The Chernigov and Krasnodar "Young Guards" are of particular interest since they operated in conjunction with partisan units.[13] Led by a "political education inspector," the Kholmy

---

[12] This procedure paralleled the Red Army policy of keeping the Party and Komsomol organs within the military establishment exempt from the territorial network of the Party and making them directly responsible to the Central Committee of the VKP(b) through the Main Political Administration of The Red Army. See Zbigniew Brzezinski, "Party Control in the Soviet Army," *Journal of Politics* (Gainesville, Florida), November 1952.

[13] See also the Stalin Prize-winning novel by Konstantin Fadeyev, *Molodaya Gvardiya* [Young Guard].

Young Guard gradually became a substantial center of propaganda work. According to a Soviet account, "they printed leaflets containing the Soviet Information Bureau bulletins [a general practice of virtually all propaganda units] and news of district life with the regularity of a newspaper and faithfully delivered them to specific addresses. There, more copies were made by hand and passed on. In the course of [a few months] they had printed and distributed thousands of such leaflets."[14] Other Komsomol groups engaged in propaganda activities in Minsk and Baranoviche Oblasts; they published their own newspapers and leaflets. Komsomol members also formed the nucleus of an *agitkollektiv,* whose main work consisted in the distribution of printed material under Party supervision.[15]

In general, as a Soviet pamphlet stated frankly early in the war, the Komsomol was enrolled to win over the fence-sitters, especially the youth, in occupied territory. It was felt that such people frequently "needed merely a push, and it was this push that the Komsomol partisans were to provide."[16] Though the degree to which Komsomol units were revitalized varied greatly (in rural areas, generally in direct proportion to the prevalence of partisans), the oblast and rayon Komosomol committees were restored to a considerable extent and played a notable role in the field of propaganda.[17]

c. Propaganda Organization within the Partisan Movement.

During the early stage of the partisan movement, the propaganda apparatus was both primitive and haphazard. In some units which had no facilities to print propaganda material—and in 1941 this included most of the bands—the commissar would dictate prepared texts of leaflets to a few partisans who would copy them; in smaller units the politruk assumed responsibility for drafting leaflets, and the commissar remained in over-all charge of political affairs.

In 1942–43, in accordance with orders from higher headquarters referred to above, separate Propaganda and Agitation Sections were established in operative groups, brigades, and independent otryads on the German side of the front. The institutionalization of psychological warfare efforts reflected the increased strength of the units, more time, and additional technical equipment and personnel for propaganda work.[18]

---

[14] A. Fyodorov, *Podpolnyi obkom deistvuyet* (Moscow: Voennoye Izdatelstvo Ministerstva Vooruzhennykh Sil Soyuza SSR, 1947), pp. 373–74.

[15] See also Tsanava I, 217–18; II, 912, 921.

[16] N. Mikhailov, *Komsomoltsy v tylu u vraga* (Moscow, 1942).

[17] Tsanava (II, 64 ff.) claims that over 2,500 Komsomol agitators operated in Minsk Oblast in 1943. Regular meetings of underground Komsomol agitators allegedly were held in Minsk in October 1942 and February 1943.

[18] Fyodorov, a leading partisan commander, claims that the size of partisan units was determined in part so as to enable them to engage in propaganda and political activities (Fyodorov, p. 355).

Separate Propaganda and Agitation Sections were reported in operative centers in Belorussia, in Mogilev and Bryansk Oblasts. One Belorussian operative center apparently had such a section as early as May 1942; it was allegedly headed by a former political commissar of the Red Army with an assimilated rank of major general.

Such sections were also formed on the operative group and brigade level from the spring of 1942 on.[19] Though this effort clearly accorded with the general streamlining of the partisan structure, some brigades established them much later; or they never had such sections. The Grishin Regiment, one of a handful of important "roving bands," created a section for propaganda and agitation in July 1943. The order setting up this section sheds some light on the tasks which it was expected to perform:

A Section for Agitation and Propaganda is to be created in order to increase agitation and propaganda activities in the regiment and among the civilian population. A section chief, two instructors, and an editor for the newspaper will be appointed. The assignments of the section for August are the following:
1. Increase of agitation in the regiment.
2. Discussions with officers and men in which the international situation, the situation at the front, and the tasks of the Red Army and the partisans in the struggle against the enemy, as well as the relations with the civilian population are to be explained.
3. Publication of leaflets for the civilian population.
4. Publication of the newspaper, *Death to Our Enemies* (one issue every five days).
5. Recreation activities for the troops.
At the same time intensive propaganda directed at the enemy is to be carried on. This type of propaganda has had considerable success among the indigenous units during the last few months.—*Appendix, Document 61*

A few days after the activation of this section, leaflets specifically requested for work among the indigenous units were distributed among two companies of collaborator troops.

By 1943 another roving band, under Sidor Kovpak, also had its separate propaganda section, which distributed printed matter among the population.[20]

In addition to publishing leaflets and newspapers, the partisans also engaged in considerable oral agitation among the civilian population. Generally such activities were carried out by the partisan propagandists who manned the *agitprop* sections. In some units, however, special agitation otryads were set up, consisting of artists, musicians, and singers, as well as experienced agitators. One such unit, during six months of its life in Vileika Oblast in 1943, performed sixty-five times before civilian audiences

[19] According to a German intelligence summary, the standard table of organization for a brigade included a political and propaganda section, consisting of a commissar and thirty-five to seventy men (*Nachrichten*, Nr. 1, 3 May 1943, p. 8).
[20] HSSPF Ost, "Bericht ueber die Bekaempfung der Kolpak-Bande ...," August 1943, p. 4 (GMDS, EAP 170a-10/5).

and fifty-five times among the partisans. A seventy-man agitator collective was reportedly organized by the First Bobruisk Partisan Brigade; it engaged primarily in lecturing among the rural population. Such activities were exceptional and were apparently organized by particularly zealous Party or partisan leaders.

3. The Red Army in Partisan Psychological Warfare

The obvious interest shown by the Red Army in the psychological warfare efforts of the partisans can be documented first for the period in August 1941 when the Political Administration of the various army groups intervened directly in the organization of partisan detachments. In a "Program for the Training of Commissars and Political Officers" of the Red Army, Lev Mekhlis, chief of the Main Political Administration of the Red Army, stated that:

Commissars and political officers are obligated to contribute with all available means to the furtherance of the partisan movement in the enemy's rear, to maintain relations with the partisans and to direct them. Special attention is to be paid to printed propaganda among the population of the occupied territories, especially to the exposing of Fascist lies and misinformation. The population of the occupied areas is systematically to be supplied with Soviet newspapers and special leaflets.[21]

It was along these lines that Army support to partisan psychological warfare was actually given; in addition, the Army dropped by air substantial quantities of printed material directly among the civilian population behind the German lines. The key organ in this effort was the Main Political Administration of the Red Army (GPUKA) and its Political Administrations of the several Fronts.[22]

For the purposes of this study, it will be sufficient to mention some practical aspects of Army propaganda material produced for use and dissemination by the partisans. Though the Red Army, through the GPUKA, presumably received the same over-all directives about themes and slogans as the Party and partisan units did through their staffs on the Soviet side, the former produced leaflets without any apparent reference to or coordination with media issued by the latter.[23]

The actual influence of the Red Army in partisan propaganda was

[21] AOK 16, Ic, "Auszugsweise Uebersetzung: 'Program fuer die Schulung der Kommissare und Politarbeiter,' " 27 October 1941 (GMDS, DW 65).

[22] Each of these had a special section for propaganda addressed to the enemy and to the civilian population in the enemy rear area. German sources reported in the later part of the war that the Soviet Army was dispatching special propaganda teams behind the German lines. These were not identical with the groups of Party propagandists assigned to the partisans. However, according to a former partisan interviewed after the war, these special groups were dispatched primarily for subversion and intelligence work and had "very little interest in propaganda." (Russian Research Center, B 7, #140.)

[23] Among the material produced by the Army for the occupied areas, one may distinguish: (a) material of the Main Political Administration, including reprints of news-

probably greater than the available evidence indicates. A postwar source claims that, in general, the control which the GPUKA exercised over the wartime press increased considerably. It also asserts that, in early 1942, when the Red Army was playing a major role in revitalizing the partisan movement, the Main Political Administration dispatched propagandists to the German-held areas to work with the partisans; such assignments were presumably independent of parallel Party efforts.[24] Moreover, the controlling partisan staffs attached to Red Army Fronts, armies, and even divisions received all logistical support through Army channels. Such support included considerable quantities of printed material. The Army also presumably had a major voice in the treatment of military collaborators— a subject which, as is shown below, was of considerable importance in partisan psychological warfare.

In 1941, when the partisans were left to operate largely on their own initiative, the Army sought to intervene in partisan propaganda, perhaps contrary to the original conception. The role of the military in psychological warfare can be assumed to have increased, at least temporarily, after the failure of the initial territorial partisan organizations. Various aspects of partisan work, ranging from recruiting men for the Red Army to co-ordinating demolition activities with the Red Army and using material disseminated by the Army Political Administrations, required close co-ordination between military and partisan staffs.

The apparent conflict of interest created by the participation of both the Army and the civilian Party apparatus in partisan psychological warfare becomes less significant if one remembers that the Main Political Administration of the Red Army, though distinct from the territorial Party organization, was also an organ of the VKP(b). Because of its long experience in political propaganda, the Party naturally was anxious to supervise all efforts in the psychological warfare field, yet its extreme concern also reveals the high importance attached to all such efforts by the Soviet leadership.

B. TECHNICAL ASPECTS OF PARTISAN PRINTED PROPAGANDA

1. 1941

Preparations made before the arrival of the Germans were inadequate for most partisan units, though by 1942 they were equipped for the publication of printed materials. The speed of the German advance, disorgan-

---

paper editorials, the daily series of *News from the Soviet Fatherland,* and other leaflets; (b) material printed at the Front level, including various leaflets without special markings but identifiable by signature, such as "Political Administration of the West Front"; (c) material produced for the Army at other printing shops, e.g., the Lithographic Plant, and Gosplan publishing house in Moscow.

[24] Arkady Gayev, "Sovetskaya pechat na voine," *Vestnik instituta po izucheniyu istorii i kultury SSSR* (Munich), No. 8 (1954).

ization during the Soviet retreat, in some instances lack of planning and foresight, and above all, the fact that many partisan detachments which emerged were not the product of specific Soviet planning before the occupation, all contributed to the paucity and in most cases absence of printing facilities.

This fact, as well as the difficult straits in which the inchoate partisan movement found itself during its first months of existence, contributed to the drastic restriction of printing activities. In general, partisan psychological warfare at that time consisted principally of word-of-mouth exhortations and rumors; Soviet-side propaganda to the population on occupied soil, restricted as it was, was quantitatively and qualitatively far more significant than that of the partisans. Moreover, the partisans were handicapped in the selection of themes that were both permissible in terms of Soviet myths and slogans and effective in persuading the indigenous population. Acting as small bodies, isolated from most of the people and from the Soviet command, the partisans concentrated much of their verbal propaganda on their *own* members rather than on neutral or hostile civilians.

If such was the over-all picture, there were nonetheless significant exceptions even during the early months of the occupation. Admitting that in 1941 most partisan groups had no printing facilities, Soviet sources reproduced the text of miscellaneous appeals put out by partisans in small numbers of handwritten copies—the prevalent medium during this first stage. The first "newspapers" were issued in this fashion as one-page handwritten sheets in perhaps eight or ten copies. Crude both in appearance and content and usually limited to a few simple slogans and exhortations to steadfastness, they were surreptitiously left in neighboring villages or with friendly individuals. Their effective range was exceedingly limited.[25] Yet they served the purpose of making the existence and, at least nominal, resistance of the partisans known to a few outsiders, and gave the partisans themselves the illusion of being engaged in essential, dangerous, patriotic work.

A few units possessed typewriters, often decrepit, on which leaflets were also reproduced. How propaganda work was then conducted is described in two Soviet sources:

Polygraphic means [a partisan propaganda officer wrote] were quite limited. We had one typewriter. I had learned to type, and I had to spend whole nights at the typewriter copying the dispatches of the Soviet Information Bureau [received by radio]. We wrote leaflets by hand. We had very little paper; we wrote on cardboard, on thin wooden boards, on glass, and we typed even on cloth and birch rind [sic]. In the morning our boys would distribute the leaflets in the villages, railroad stations, and even in Bryansk.[26]

[25] Tsanava, I, 222–23, II, 924; M. Abramov, ed., *Bolshevistskiye gazety v tylu vraga* (Leningrad: Leningradskoye Gazelno-Zhurnalnoye Izdatelstvo, 1946), p. 5; Sheverdalkin, p. 4.

[26] V. Andreyev, *Narodnaya voina (zapiski partizana)* (Moscow, Gosudarstvennoye Izdatelstvo Khudozhestvennoi Literatury, 1952), p. 212. See also Tsanava, II, 924.

Though perhaps overdramatized, another account reports in a similar vein: "Usually in breaks between combat operations the otryad commissar would gather five to ten partisans who had a good hand, and would dictate to them the prepared text of a leaflet. In this manner the text would be reproduced in the desired number of copies."[27]

Only rarely was more satisfactory equipment available. A few units had brought along a "shapirograph," a Soviet model of a rudimentary hectograph machine capable of producing a few dozen copies of a prepared text. Where it was available, it served as the "printing press"; even as late as December 1942 the publication of partisan "newspapers" was begun on such machines. More exceptional was the availability of a regular printing press. Here and there a rayon committee's staff had disassembled a small press and taken parts of it with them into the woods or had hidden them with local residents. Where the partisans were particularly adventurous and possessed the requisite contacts, equipment was stolen from German-controlled printing shops. In the city of Minsk, the Communist underground workers (exposed and executed by the Germans early in 1942) used type stolen from the German operated "Proryv" printing presses. The "Iskra" detachment filched type and some equipment from an abandoned Soviet printing shop in Lida (in northwestern Belorussia). Later it found in the woods type from a Red Army divisional printing press abandoned during one of the encirclements early in the war and hidden by stragglers. In the same manner, the first *tipografiya* of the Fyodorov unit was established with type stolen from the German-held district center.

The primitive nature of the material thus produced, as well as the loyal unanimity of partisan *agitprop* officers, is mirrored in the fact that the most frequent single texts employed were Stalin's famous wartime speech of 3 July 1941 and, later, his address of 7 November 1941. Both German and Soviet materials confirm that copies were surreptitiously circulated to demonstrate to the unbelieving peasants that "Soviet power" and "Party and Government" were still in existence and fighting. Some versions were copied by the partisans from issues of *Pravda* dropped by Soviet planes; others were produced from newspapers obtained before the occupation; still others were copies of copies, with all the errors in spelling and at times in contents that this process entailed.

However devoted the efforts of a few determined men, in 1941 the technical appearance, frequency of issue, distribution, and effectiveness of partisan printed media were negligible.

2. Equipment

As the war continued, the partisans' printing equipment improved. Though handwritten appeals and leaflets reproduced by shapirograph and

---

[27] Tsanava, I, 223.

typewriter continued to appear, regular printed materials increased in number and importance.

There were three major types of presses employed by the partisans. The first was the improvised press, which might consist of parts stolen, found, or dropped from the Soviet side. At times, it required considerable resourcefulness to get such a press into working condition. After hiding one press during a German attack, a partisan unit near Polisto Lake found that all the parts could not be reassembled, and ink had to be applied with a shoe brush for lack of other tools. One of the Leningrad brigades attached a hammer to its press when the crank handle broke off. From 1942 on the situation improved; as in other forms of partisan activity, the decisive help came from the Soviet side. With the increased membership in partisan units, the establishment of radio and air contact with the Red Army command or higher partisan headquarters, and the general formalization of partisan institutions and controls, greater importance was attached to propaganda work. The inadequacy of equipment was amply apparent and was promptly reported to higher staffs. By mid-1942 Soviet industry had started producing a special portable printing press for partisan use. This so-called "Liliput" press, weighing between sixteen and twenty kilograms, had a supply of type sufficient to set one-sixteenth of the Soviet printer's *list* (i.e., one small sheet up to 20 by 30 centimeters in size) and a press of equal dimensions; the whole set could be strapped to a partisan's back and carried along.[28]

In time, thanks to the number of sets flown in by the Soviet Air Force or transported across the lines, the Liliput became the standard model in most units. Another type of press, in existence in the Red Army at the outbreak of war and known by the name of "Boston," also made its appearance. Much heavier in weight, it was also more sturdy, produced more copies, and printed leaflets and newspapers of larger size (up to 30 by 40 centimeters).[29] In some cases, larger partisan brigades were apparently supplied with Bostons through the Soviet Air Force, which in general was instrumental in enabling the partisans to engage in larger-scale printing.[30]

In theory, at least, every partisan brigade was to have at least one Liliput press; so was each underground Party *raikom* (often identical with the press of a brigade). Party *obkomy* and some of the larger partisan

[28] Abramov, p. 7. A detailed description is contained in *Nachrichten*, Nr. 4, 10 September 1943, pp. 5, 11–14.
[29] Andreyev, p. 56. According to Abramov, the 2d Leningrad Brigade started printing its paper, *Narodnyi Mstitel* [People's Avenger], in February 1942 on a Boston press after a few cases of type had been dropped from the Soviet side. While the Liliput printed about 250–500 copies, the Boston could easily produce 2,500 copies.
[30] According to the official Soviet version, Stalin in "his immeasurable love for the population on occupied soil, thirsting as it was for reliable news," ordered the production and delivery of printing sets in considerable numbers. (Tsanava, II, 925.)

complexes were to have Bostons. By late 1943 most of the regular partisan brigades had at least a Liliput at their disposal. Indeed, the Germans concluded, probably correctly, that from about August 1943 on, propaganda conducted by partisans gained in importance as compared with printed materials disseminated from the Soviet side of the front. Likewise, many partisan units and Party underground committees, especially on the rayon level, began systematically to publish their own papers only in the late summer or fall of 1943. Even then, however, many appeared irregularly.

At the same time, the output from the Soviet side, apparently produced for the most part at the Front level, continued to be of primary importance. The newspapers of the Orel *obkom, Partizanskaya Pravda,* and of the Smolensk *obkom, Rabochii Put,* were both technically superior to most partisan papers, contained considerable information on life behind the Soviet lines and on international affairs, and used illustrations and various mats and fonts. The imprint (on the Orel paper, NA 031) suggests strongly that the copies were produced at a Soviet-side printing plant. Even more important in quantity were the leaflets dropped by Soviet planes on occupied soil; the absence of statistical data makes quantitative evaluation impossible.

Special mention should be made of the comparatively strong multiplication and scattering of publishing units.[31] The resulting disadvantages of small circulation and inferior quality, often also of poor liaison with Soviet-side propaganda units and difficulty of control, were at least partially offset by three advantages:

1. Proximity to the target, resulting in less waste of printed media through their being lost or remaining unread; at the same time, greater ease of distribution because of familiarity with local conditions and personnel, and a better chance of overcoming German restrictions on movement.

2. A more equitable distribution of the technical burden among various units; also great self-glorification for the editors in being spokesmen for the Soviet authorities.

3. Most important, an adaptation of contents to local conditions. This latter point is repeatedly stressed in German and Soviet accounts. While some of its aspects will be treated below [e.g. Sect. IV, A, 1, a, and Sect.

[31] The actual spread of partisan printing facilities, as well as the occasional clandestine use of urban printing plants nominally under German control, must not be confused with the device employed by the partisans in listing, as places of publication, locations thoroughly held by the Germans. Thus one partisan leaflet, for instance, appeared with the imprint of a Novozybkov printing shop, while it was actually produced on a portable press in the woods nearby. Other leaflets made use of Slynka and Klimov in similar fashion, just as newspapers produced on the Soviet side of the front and dropped on occupied soil at times carried the names of German-held towns as places of origin.

V, A, B], it deserves stress at this point because it was a recognized reason for the widespread scattering of partisan propaganda centers. "The editors of the underground papers organized their work," an official Soviet account asserts, not without reason, "so as to take into account local conditions."[32] The Germans, on the other hand, were constrained to admit that the rigid central direction of their own psychological warfare occasioned a perpetual lag in the utilization of current events and new themes, something the partisans could successfully overcome while still complying with broad Soviet propaganda directives.[33] As a result, German atrocities were promptly reported; partisan propaganda gained in effectiveness by giving local names and places, by appealing to specific individuals to help prevent food and cattle deliveries to the Germans, and by eulogizing the accomplishments of individuals known to local residents.

3. Supply Difficulties

The partisans had frequent difficulties in obtaining essential printing supplies. The typical editor during the period before the delivery of Liliputs by the Soviets "would have a bag full of type, sometimes collected letter by letter, and a primitive printing press." According to a Soviet admission, "to issue a paper or leaflet, the editor had to adjust his notes and articles to the number of letters he had on hand, and to write so that there would be enough *a*'s and *o*'s to last through the article."[34] Another editor stated that he had to set one column at a time and then break up the type for the next column. Printing took place, in this instance, in a small hut.[35] In other instances, special mud-huts or bunkers were built to accommodate the press. During German attacks, the printing equipment, if it could not be easily carried along, would be concealed in holes dug in the ground or in the swamps.

Printer's ink was in short supply much of the time. Some quantities were flown in from the Soviet side; others were stolen from German-managed plants. In the winter, ink had to be heated before it could be used. But the greatest problem was the paper shortage. All partisans were ordered to get whatever paper they could and to requisition it along with food, whether it be wrapping paper, notebooks, or other sorts. The partisans would pay huge sums to agents who stole paper from German stocks. The bulk of the newsprint for those units which had regular contact with the Soviet side came by air. "But it was impossible to carry five to six poods[36] when the otryad was on the move," a Soviet analyst comments. "Thus the

[32] Tsanava, II, 80.
[33] OKH/GenStdH/FHO (IIb/Prop), "Prop.-Unterlagen, Truppenmeldungen vom 1.–31.12.43, IV 'Propaganda in die Zivilbevoelkerung," n.d., p. 5 (GMDS H 3/474).
[34] Sheverdalkin, p. 8.
[35] Andreyev, p. 331.
[36] One pood is about thirty-six pounds.

paper had to be collected among the population," a difficult and most un-satisfactory undertaking. The paper shortage contributed to the reduction in size, to the frequently far from impressive appearance, and to the poor legibility of the leaflets and newspapers produced by the partisans. It would appear that the transport of newsprint, while occurring systematically, did not have top priority in Soviet air supply to the partisans.

4. Personnel

Various sources indicate that the editors of partisan papers and leaflets could be regular Party members, commissars or deputy commissars, former journalists, and minor officials, but frequently also men who had had no previous experience in psychological warfare, particularly not in under-ground printing. There were only a few Civil War veterans with such ex-perience (and perhaps men who had engaged in underground work abroad); on the technical level especially nonprofessional personnel was employed; for instance, a tank officer worked as a printer.

The standard staff of a partisan (or underground Party) printing unit consisted of the following: (1) Boston type press: 1 editor, 1 proofreader, 2 staff writers, 6 printers (who also wrote articles and features and dis-tributed the paper); (2) Liliput type press: 1 man, who did all printing, setting, and writing, under the direction of a *raikom* secretary or partisan unit commissar.[37]

Often the same personnel was used for other political and propaganda purposes, although a good deal of nonprinted psychological warfare (such as lectures, "agitation" meetings, etc.) was conducted by partisans assigned to these tasks exclusively. The greatest demand on personnel without special skills was to distribute the papers. Here everybody would be en-rolled—local women, children, partisans on raids, lecturers, and others.

5. Sources of Information

Partisan leaflets, and particularly newspapers, drew on a variety of sources for their information. These may be broadly divided into Soviet sources and local sources.

The regular Soviet radio broadcasts were frequently monitored by par-tisans, and their dispatches were reproduced (particularly those slowly dictated after midnight). It was primarily in this manner that the partisans learned the latest war communiqués and world news. Other overt sources included Soviet newspapers, which, as indicated, were brought into oc-cupied territory in considerable numbers and with striking regularity from mid-1942 on. Finally, partisans also copied the texts and themes from

[37] *Nachrichten,* Nr. 4, September 10, 1943, p. 5. In a unit in the Bryansk forest, the editor of the two-page *Partizanskaya Pravda,* Korotkov, had two assistants as staff writers, and two girl partisans as typesetters. (Andreyev, p. 330.)

Soviet propaganda material which they received either for distribution or reproduction on occupied soil, or which they happened to find.

In addition, however, there were Soviet *agitprop* directives of a classified nature. Instructions were occasionally dropped from planes or brought in by individuals flown into partisan-held areas, though during the first year or so of partisan activity there is no evidence of any systematic flow of instructions. Radio messages aimed specifically at the partisans (whether in code or clear cannot be determined) also periodically contained instructions on psychological warfare. Since only one German summary of such propaganda directives by radio is available, it is quoted here to indicate the tenor and scope:

Agitation

Agitation among the population in the occupied areas, if correctly conducted, is extremely valuable. Communist posters, such as the well-known "Let Us Crush the Fascist Monster," leave a particularly deep impression in the occupied territory. They give evidence of the strength of Soviet power. Also, the illegal newspapers in Belorussia, *Sovetskaya Belarus* and *Partizanskoye Slovo*, are effective. The importance of the printed word in the occupied area should not be underestimated.

One partisan division in Belorussia has made available 23 agitators for propaganda among the population. In spite of the strictest surveillance by the occupiers they have held indoctrination assemblies and have made speeches in 15 Belorussian communities occupied by the Fascists. The theme was "The Defeat of the Germans Before Moscow in December 1941." The impending change in the course of the war through the establishment of a second front in Europe constitutes an appropriate theme for mass indoctrination (*Massenaufklaerung*).

Reconstruction of the Party Organization

Each city, each district must have its illegal Party organization and Young Communist League.

Elements Friendly to the Germans

In some areas of Belorussia the partisan leaders have succeeded in winning the confidence of the Germans and in getting their people placed as policemen, mayors, and kolkhoz administrators. Under certain circumstances, those trusted men render good service.[38]

Likewise, the so-called Stalin directive of December 1942 [see Sect. IV, A, and n. 64] falls into the rubric of basic Soviet instructions for partisan propagandists.

The partisans used their own ideas and experiences for psychological warfare. Editors, commissars, and politruks, heads of political sections, secretaries of underground Party and Komsomol units, as well as commanders of partisan otryads contributed themes, slogans, and texts. News

---

[38] PzAOK 3, Ic/AO (Abw. I und III), "Awehrnachrichtenblatt Nr. 8; Sendung eines russ. Senders fuer Partisanen," 1 August 1942 (GMDS, PzAOK 3, 25784/43).

items to be exploited in verbal propaganda could be suggested by any band member or civilian informant. In addition, the partisans used captured German and collaborator material.[39]

Except for the small number of "staff writers," there seem to have been no institutionalized sources of information in partisan printed media. It appears that the unit's intelligence section periodically provided the propagandists with information. In some instances, efforts were made to organize a more regular (and at least apparently, more formidable) network of indigenous correspondents along the lines of the widespread and well-established peacetime system of *rabkory* and *selkory;*[40] likewise, partisan commanders and staff officers periodically wrote up the accomplishments of their units and reported on agitation rallies held in the units or villages.[41]

Though persuasive bits of local news received considerable attention, special emphasis was given to statements and writings of men whose names were presumably surrounded with an aura of prestige or fear. In addition to the pronouncements of Stalin, those of other Soviet leaders, such as Ponomarenko or Kalinin; dispatches concerning partisan leaders, even in distant bands, such as Kovpak or Fyodorov; and writings by popular poets and journalists—the Belorussians, Yanka Kupala and Yakub Kolas, or the Ukrainian, Volodymyr Sosyura—were communicated from the Soviet side to the partisan staffs, to be specially featured.

§II. Partisan Psychological Warfare Directed at German Personnel

A. THE PROBLEM

"Propaganda and agitation" traditionally occupied a primary place in Soviet thinking and indoctrination. However, the application of propaganda methods to partisan warfare against the Germans presented specific problems for which the partisan leadership was ill prepared.

The orthodox Soviet approach concentrated on articulate and recognizable "propaganda" in the narrow and direct sense, though indirect nonverbal techniques were frequently and successfully practiced by Communist

---

[39] One report suggests the existence of something approximating a partisan news service, disseminating the same items to a variety of units, presumably by radio. Other captured materials, used also in front-line propaganda, were the Reichenau order of 1941 described in Sect. V, D, and the Keitel order on the branding of prisoners of war.

[40] Workers' correspondents and village correspondents—amateur journalists who would occasionally contribute items of local or technical interest.

[41] For a discussion of this system, see Tsanava, II, 73 ff.

groups. Yet there appeared to be virtually no body of theory to prepare the partisan commander or political officer for systematic use of psychological warfare against enemy forces. Because of the nature of partisan-German relations and because of the ratio of their forces, the partisans could not realistically aspire to the wholesale conversion of German troops and civilian officials. Positive appeals could be made to non-Germans fighting against them, both to ex-Soviet citizens collaborating with the Germans and to non-German Axis troops. Psychological warfare aimed at the Germans themselves was largely restricted to general discouragement, since the partisans seemed to assume that inducements to surrender would be futile and probably none too desirable for practical reasons of guarding, feeding, and control.

The partisan approach to the Germans thus overwhelmingly utilized the "stick" rather than the "carrot" technique. Verbal efforts—be they leaflets, posters, newspapers, or broadcasts—were minimized. In part, this resulted from the belief that positive appeals were futile; in part, it reflected the shortage of printing facilities and supplies, which were restricted largely to appeals aimed at other elements more likely to respond, notably the indigenous population; in part, it was due to the lack of German-speaking partisans and of effective means of transmitting prepared materials.

Furthermore, a considerable number of measures intended to undermine German morale and discipline were aimed simultaneously at the civilian population on occupied soil. Frequently one gathers that the efforts were really aimed at the latter group, in an attempt to establish close identification of purposes and interests against the Germans.

Finally, partisan preoccupation with psychological warfare directed at the Germans was proportionate to the units' strength and relative security. During the early months of the occupation, the handicaps under which the small detachments labored led them to concentrate on more vital problems. Conscious psychological warfare operations on their part appear to have begun only in 1942, when the expansion and consolidation of the units took place and a change in popular temper occurred.

B. DIRECT AND VERBAL PROPAGANDA

Virtually no partisan leaflets directed specifically at German personnel have been found. Not even in the later stages of the war, when the partisans were sometimes employed by the Soviet command to distribute propaganda material on occupied territory, did they act as middlemen for the dissemination of appeals such as these that the Red Army launched in the name of the Free Germany Committee and other groups of German prisoners in the USSR.[42]

[42] There are some (unconfirmed) indications that in a few instances they might have engaged in such work where they were located near the front lines and could distribute material to German combat forces.

From time to time, however, the partisans did distribute German-language leaflets dropped from Soviet planes and did engage in almost prankish small-scale operations. Many of these seem to have been carried out by members of urban underground groups rather than by combat partisan detachments, largely because German personnel were located in urban areas. According to the postwar memoirs of a Soviet political officer in the Bryansk area, a rather harmless operation consisted of placing a handwritten note in the napkin of the Trubchevsk Field Police chief, which read: "You are celebrating the victory of Fascist arms too early, you dog. Hitler will be *kaputt*. The partisans." Similar notes, the same source avers, were placed in the pockets of German soldiers and collaborators while they were attending a movie.[43] In another instance, leaflets were placed on the seats of a local movie theater prior to the beginning of a show for the Germans; in a third case, German-language leaflets were smuggled into German billets in Novozybkov. Both the latter reports appear to speak of leaflets dropped from Soviet planes and distributed by individual "agitators."

Only in the very first and last months of the war were there direct appeals to German soldiers involving the partisans. In the early weeks of the war, before Soviet psychological warfare had outgrown some of its early doctrinal limitations and when Red Army leaflets still contained appeals to "workers and toiling peasants" in the German ranks, there appeared a leaflet, evidently produced and distributed by the Soviet Army, hopefully "explaining" the nature of the partisan movement to the German troops.

WHO ARE THE PARTISANS? [it began]
German soldiers! You are told that partisan warfare waged by the Russians is dishonest and the partisans shoot at you from behind. The German courts want to treat them as bandits.

It proceeded to explain that the partisans were patriots in the same tradition as the German and Austrian heroes of resistance under Schill, Luetzow, and Andreas Hofer in the days of Napoleon. "The partisans are the people itself, seeking to defend their home and homeland against Hitler the tyrant. The Russian partisans are not the enemies of the German workers and peasants." The Russian toiler, the leaflet continued, had not freed himself from tsarism and capitalism to succumb to German *Junkers* and plutocrats. Therefore, it concluded with a *non sequitur,* "German soldier, come over to the side of the Red Army."[44]

It did not take long for Moscow to realize the futility of such efforts. There is no evidence that leaflets of this sort were used after October 1941. Only in the last victorious stages of the struggle, with the Germans in retreat and the partisans increasingly operating a quasi-military

---

[43] Andreyev, p. 257.
[44] "Wer sind die Partisanen" (Red Army leaflet) n.d. (GMDS, 217 ID, 17415/26).

auxiliary force coordinated with the regular Red Army, were there partisan leaflets again specifically calling for the surrender of German soldiers.[45]

Occasionally partisans would post or distribute letters addressed ostensibly to German officials. Written in Russian, their purpose was largely to impress the indigenous population by ridiculing the enemy and stressing his cowardice or brutality.[46] Small-scale and sporadic though they were, such operations undoubtedly had some effect on the Germans, even though their primary target was the indigenous population.

Even less use was made of oral communications. Word-of-mouth propaganda and the spreading of rumors, so feasible in partisan relations with the population, were virtually impossible with the Germans; however, some rumors spread among the civilian population did indirectly reach German personnel as well. Nor is there any evidence of the use of loudspeakers by partisans in combat operations against the Germans.[47]

C. NONVERBAL PSYCHOLOGICAL WARFARE

The "creation of impossible conditions for the enemy" was a prime object of partisan activity from the outset. This included harassing civilian and military personnel and engendering panic and terror among the Germans. Most partisan psychological warfare efforts against the Germans fell into this rubric, but there is little indication of any articulate plan or theoretical basis on which this campaign was waged.

Its first, and in many respects most effective, asset was the very existence and activity of the partisans, who were living proof that the rear areas had not been subdued and that the war continued hundreds of miles behind the front. The partisans could strike suddenly, now here, now there, blowing up trains and trucks, attacking individual German officers and men, cutting communications and supply lines. Among the scant German forces responsible for the security of the vast alien areas, partisan activity, regardless of its military significance or failure, was bound to promote a state of nervousness and insecurity. This indeed was one of the primary purposes of partisan warfare, and it was in this, more than in other ways, that it was strikingly successful.

[45] In December 1943, when the Germans had partly evacuated the town, partisans distributed such appeals in Mogilev.

[46] Thus one Russian-language poster in the Bryansk area was ostensibly addressed to a local German official: "Do you still remember, Mr. Heinroth, when, during the fighting at Pervomaisk, you threw away your field glasses, maps, and plans, and cried: 'My legs! My legs! Save my head from the partisan bullets!'?" [See Appendix, Document 36.]

[47] One Soviet account mentions, more in the nature of a practical joke than as a serious PsyWar operation, the tapping of German telephone lines by a subordinate of Sidor Kovpak, a partisan commander. The partisan called the local "Gestapo" office to threaten an attack on its post. Kovpak was apparently displeased with this and reprimanded the partisan for disclosing the proximity of his men. [P. Vershigora, *Lyudi s chistoi sovestyu* (Moscow: Sovetskii Pisatel, 1951), p. 145.]

The initial impact was greatest on the lower German ranks who came into physical contact with the partisans and the effects of their operations. Higher echelons, and especially German staff officers, were at first all but oblivious to the potential threat that the partisans repreesnted. Gradually, however, a feeling of imminent danger and even panic penetrated higher command levels as well as the civilian and economic administrations.[48] This insecurity was heightened by the shortage and inferior quality of German rear area personnel and supplies. Finally, psychological unpreparedness for operations of this nature contributed to the failure of German antipartisan warfare.

Results of these conditions were frequent German overestimation of partisan strength and potential, as well as widespread physical fear among personnel assigned to partisan-threatened areas. The partisan-controlled territory expanded rapidly, and, in addition to depriving the Germans of sources of food and manpower in 1943–44, it contributed to the enemy's realization that the war was being lost. Increasing defection of "neutral" and collaborating elements to the partisans only emphasized this trend. In the latter part of the war, German soldiers would not stray from the main arteries of communication or walk singly even in the most strongly garrisoned towns. The feeling of isolation and danger was particularly pronounced among the thinly manned outposts and strongpoints which dotted the countryside.[49]

To some extent, the Germans' own attitude contributed to this frame of mind. By first ignoring the problem and then proscribing the partisans as "bandits" and "marauders," the German High Command encouraged the feeling that the opponents were not orderly, "respectable," military adversaries but men whose activities were unpredictable and characterized by "deceit." Partisan warfare was certainly unorthodox. Raids from ambush, while employed primarily for tactical reasons, tended to produce terror among the Germans. As early as 20 July 1941 an order of the Political Administration of the Northwest Front of the Red Army, speaking of "sudden short raids from ambush on live targets," advised: "Such raids engender panic in his [the enemy's] ranks, induce him to flight, and create confusion among his units and subdivisions, whereby his further movement is held up and serious losses are inflicted on personnel and matériel." [See Appendix, Document 2.]

[48] The atmosphere was typified by the ditty popular among rear area security units in 1942:

"Vorne Russen,	[Russians ahead,
Hinten Russen,	Russians behind,
Und dazwischen	And in between
Wird geschussen."	Shooting.]

(E. E. Dwinger, *Wiedersehen mit Sowjetrussland*, Jena, 1942.)

[49] For two fictional but psychologically sound accounts of the climate in which such German units operated, see Theodor Plivier, *Moskau* (Munich: Desch, 1952), and Gerhard Kramer, *Wir werden weiter marschieren* (Berlin: Blanvalet, 1952).

Another 1941 Soviet order authorized partisans to wear German uniforms because "this permits the group to approach its target undetected and to exploit rumors regarding the activity of partisans in German uniforms, to arouse mistrust among individual [German] soldiers, and to undermine their morale."[50] In both instances, the psychological impact, aimed at terrorizing and demoralizing the Germans, was a by-product of military action; yet the Soviet command was unmistakably aware of its effectiveness. For evidence that operations of this nature were conducted specifically for psychological warfare purposes, there are only scattered Soviet assertions. Thus in January 1942 a group of partisans in Western Belorussia raided the town of Slutsk ostensibly "to spread panic among the Hitlerite garrison." That other aims were included in this operation is indicated by the remark that during their raid the partisans seized the city bank and absconded with all of its valuables.[51]

Partisan use of assassination, especially of German (and collaborating) officials and civilians, was in part also calculated to spread fear and panic. Indeed, the effect on other Germans and collaborators as well as on the indigenous population was probably more important than the sheer desire to eliminate a despised (and at times even an unknown) German. While the partisans' call for "vengeance" helped fortify their own morale and provided a potent stimulus to the enrollment of the population, it was also meant to—and did—serve the cause of terrorizing the Germans.

Unfortunately most of the available German reports focus on tactical and technical aspects of partisan raids, and Soviet accounts generally fail to give details of assassinations and terror raids staged by the partisans. Nevertheless, the general impression of the psychological effect which such attacks produced on the Germans is confirmed by postwar statements of German officers and Soviet refugees.[52] The assassination of specific individuals, such as German district commissars, police officials, or agricultural supervisors, was often left to urban underground and partisan teams, many of which acted in conjunction with partisan field combat staffs; these generally sought to avoid direct contact with the Germans.[53] In addition to the casualties that the occupation administration suffered in this manner, the climate of fear and suspicion was intensified by the pub-

[50] "Denkschrift ueber die Kampftaetigkeit von Partisanengruppen und -abteilungen im Ruecken des Feindes" (GMDS, 112 ID 19643/24).

[51] Tsanava, I, 125.

[52] For instance, a refugee respondent gives examples of militarily useless partisan attacks, which "made the Germans tremendously nervous." (Russian Research Center, B 7, #192, pp. 45–46, 66.)

[53] Other attempts on Germans and collaborators were carried out by special diversionist teams and individuals either sent in or left behind by the NKVD or the Red Army.

licity, both German and partisan, attending the death of the victims of such attacks.[54]

The peak of "terror attacks" (as the Germans were anxious to call them) was reached in the late summer and fall of 1943. Its most spectacular example, widely exploited in partisan and Soviet propaganda, was the assassination of Wilhelm Kube, General Commissar for Belorussia, in September 1943. Other officials were threatened with a similar fate; sometimes there may have been false rumors, but frequently such threats, even if not carried out, were sufficient to induce panic. The widespread attacks on collaborators likewise had a damaging effect on German morale. In addition to depriving the occupying authorities of their "grass roots" contacts, these attacks once more emphasized the ubiquitous presence of the partisans.

Related to these partisan efforts to increase German insecurity was infiltration of German and collaborator organizations. Agents who achieved this could and did spread rumors in addition to pursuing their basic tasks of gathering intelligence or sabotaging German endeavors. Paradoxically but obviously, it was often the German *discovery* of such agents, sometimes in positions of considerable trust, that made the occupation personnel jittery and aware of being surrounded, watched, and exposed to constant dangers. The feeling of insecurity and nervousness that was created among the German occupation personnel probably had a far-reaching psychological impact on the individual German. It is a common phenomenon that individuals with a pronounced inferiority complex will go to considerable lengths to disguise their feeling of insecurity by an outward show of superiority and aggressiveness. It is likely that the partisan movement caused many a German to react in a similar manner. The individual German soldier, SS man, or official may well have compensated for his fear by an open show of contempt for the "inferior" Slav. Thus the partisan movement helped increase the Germans' tendency to alienate the indigenous population through psychologically unsound treatment.

D. PROVOCATION

In the conduct of their operations, the partisans periodically impersonated German officers. In some instances, the purpose was primarily to deceive the German administration (a difficult task) and the local collaborators (a more likely possibility). In other cases, however, such deceptive maneuvers were apparently intended to widen the gulf between Germans and inhabitants. A refugee source speaks of the leader of a small partisan detachment in the Vinnitsa area who posed as a German on visits

[54] Obituaries and eulogies appeared regularly in the newspapers and magazines published by and for the Germans in the occupied territories.

to small and isolated villages. If he encountered Germans there, "he would get close enough to be able to shoot before they realized what was happening. Actually he did very little military damage but the spectacular nature of his activities aroused a lot of public sympathy and admiration [and] he frightened the Germans."

Another hypothesis, which cannot be supported by clear-cut evidence, has been advanced most frequently by Soviet refugees who lived in partisan-threatened areas: the inevitable result of partisan attacks on German personnel was ruthless German retaliation—not so much against partisans, on whom they generally could not lay their hands, as against innocent civilians. The result of this process was a chain reaction in which the interests of the Germans and those of the bulk of the indigenous population drew further and further apart. German eradication of entire communities in retribution for partisan raids could only rally neighboring residents to the partisans' side.

To what extent the touching off of this chain reaction was a conscious purpose of their attacks cannot be ascertained. At any rate, partisan technique strengthened the hand of the most uncompromising elements in the German Army, SS, and bureaucracy, and provoked the extremes in anti-partisan warfare which came to characterize most German operations. In turn the provocation of the Germans won for the partisans the support of the indigenous population, as it were by ricochet. Even those who initially had little or no enthusiasm for the Soviet cause, and particularly for the partisans, usually were constrained to regard the partisans as their only effective protectors against German retribution. Though other factors contributed to the extremes of antipartisan warfare, the partisans' own efforts mightily accelerated the trend.

E. TREATMENT OF PRISONERS OF WAR

The partisans focused their efforts on subversion rather than conversion because they had realistically appraised the situation. By its very nature, however, their approach limited the scope of psychological warfare possibilities. Furthermore, German conviction that "ruthlessness" and "deceit" characterized the activities of the partisans (a conviction that they generally made no effort to dispel) eliminated any possibilities of attracting Germans to the partisan side.

However, in one area (the treatment of German captives), partisan behavior was likely to influence German reactions directly. German reports, probably exaggerating, frequently stressed that the partisans killed captured troops; others spoke of instances in which prisoners were tortured and the bodies of soldiers killed in battle were mutilated.

Undoubtedly, killing and mistreatment of German soldiers occurred, partly because of the spontaneous quest for revenge and because of general lack of discipline. This was especially true of the early stage of partisan warfare, when controls were lax, directives few and unenforced, and the partisan bands often had no permanent headquarters where prisoners could be kept or guarded, and no opportunity (as there was later) to transfer captives across the front or by air to the Soviet side. General Red Army policy, on the other hand, apparently discouraged indiscriminate shooting of prisoners, even by partisans.

As the partisan movement expanded and assumed the characteristics of a regular military organization, treatment of captives reportedly improved, apparently so that the partisans could obtain intelligence and win the active support of those Germans who had fallen into their hands.[55] In the later stages of the war, instances multiplied of German prisoners being employed by the partisans not only for menial tasks (as was at times the case in 1942) but for military and intelligence work. Nevertheless it would seem correct to conclude that fear of the partisans remained a serious deterrent to German defection until the very end—an inevitable result of the partisans' emphasis on terror methods in their dealings with the Germans.

F. CONCLUSION

Because the partisans were preoccupied with demolition and military pursuits, and with attempts at influencing indigenous personnel, they restricted distinctive psychological operations aimed at the Germans to a few sporadic efforts. At the same time, the psychological impact of *other* partisan activities on the Germans, economic or propagandistic, was impressive.

One difficulty involved in conducting psychological warfare against the Germans was the lack of direct contact between partisans and Germans. The partisans preferred not to risk their lives in distributing leaflets or posters among the Germans. They seemed to realize that the impact of sporadic verbal propaganda upon the occupying forces would be small and that any effect obtained would stem more from the over-all climate of insecurity and the terror policy than from individual and narrowly propagandistic operations. If they had the choice, they would rather kill a German official than place a leaflet on his desk.

No evidence has been found to indicate whether or not the relative neglect of verbal propaganda addressed to the Germans was in line with

---

[55] A report of the German Ninth Army in November 1943 stated that prisoners were well treated and well fed. They were offered cigarettes as an inducement to furnish information and were assured that letters to their relatives would be surreptitiously delivered to German Army Post Offices. Moreover, in July 1943, the 3d Leningrad Partisan Brigade was ordered not to shoot its prisoners, but to bring all of them, including the wounded, through the lines to the Red Army rear area. Contrary to previous practice, deserters from the German Army, whether Russian military collaborators or Germans, who volunteered to fight with the partisans, were to be accepted as members of partisan units.

Soviet directives. It appears likely that it was. This is partly borne out by the fact that the Red Army Political Administration, which ordered the partisans to distribute all sorts of printed matter, never seems to have used them for the dissemination of delicate and sensitive material employed in persuading German, as distinct from Axis, troops to defect. The Communist Party does not appear to have been at all concerned with the conversion of the Germans. One may suggest that such a restriction reflected a decision of higher Soviet propaganda agencies, which preferred to have the partisans concentrate on operations for which they were uniquely fitted. In addition, they were not entrusted with tasks requiring close coordination with and attunement to general Soviet psychological warfare as well as a linguistic skill that the average partisan political officer failed to possess.

There were additional objective factors that hindered partisan appeals to the Germans. Their target was limited to rear area security troops and civilians, rather than combat forces, and even there the range of effective action was narrowly circumscribed: in partisan-controlled areas, there were no Germans; in thoroughly German-held areas there were no partisans to speak of. Efforts were hence limited to the twilight zones between German and partisan control, and to urban areas where occasional forays could be conducted with the aid of resident anti-German elements.

The impact of the partisans on German morale and discipline was striking, but its success stemmed largely from the wide range of partisan activities, as well as from their reputation as savage avengers and assassins, rather than from distinct and purposeful psychological warfare operations conducted by the partisans themselves.

§III. Partisan Psychological Warfare
Directed at Axis Troops

In the course of the war on the Eastern front, the German armed forces were supplemented by contingents of non-German Axis troops.[56] Many of these—notably the Rumanian and Italian divisions—operated in the south, where there were few partisans.[57] Other sizable units—primarily Hungarian

[56] The terms Axis and allied troops, as used in this section, refer to armed units stationed in occupied Soviet territory and consisting of nationals of countries allied with the Reich (but neither German, nor indigenous to the Soviet areas).

[57] These forces encountered some partisans in the Crimea and the North Caucasus. Moreover, urban Communist undergrounds existed in various Italian-controlled communities in the Don Basin and in Rumanian-held Odessa. However, there is little evidence of partisan appeals to the occupation forces and military government there. This is due in part, it seems, to the fact that the population and partisans here looked

and Slovak but also some French and Croatian—were assigned to rear areas in which the partisans were active.

In their attitude toward such Axis troops, the partisans appear to have taken several factors into account. Notably, the non-German troops were much inferior to German forces in training, leadership, and morale. Once the tide of war had turned, it was therefore easier to capture them and to induce them to join the partisans. In addition, these forces represented nationalities which, in the Soviet outlook, had been victimized by the Germans and whose "most progressive elements" were fighting on the Soviet side against the Axis. These factors became the basis for a substantive and important distinction that arose between the partisan approaches to Axis and to German troops. The German forces were largely written off as enemies, but appeals could be made to Axis soldiers along lines similar to those used in persuading Soviet collaborators, the major theme being the community of interest of all nationalities oppressed and enslaved by the Nazis, and hence a unity of purpose between partisans and Axis forces against the Germans.

The available material is particularly poor on this aspect of partisan psychological warfare.[58] The following must therefore be regarded merely as suggestive of the partisans' approach; moreover, part of the material stems from Soviet postwar accounts and is therefore open to some doubt.

The evidence indicates that generally Axis troops were neither killed nor maltreated after their capture by the partisans. When five Hungarian soldiers were seized by partisans in the Bryansk area in July 1942, the partisans (as one of the Hungarians reported to the Germans after his subsequent escape) "believed [they had] found in us good fellow-fighters against the German forces. We were therefore relatively well treated." According to a Soviet account, the partisans in this area had a Hungarian Communist with them who wrote leaflets in conjunction with the editorial staff of the partisan newspaper:

Partizanskaya Pravda and Paul [Feldes, the interpreter] distributed hundreds of leaflets among the Hungarian soldiers and the troops of the Hungarian Labor battalions, appealing to them to revolt and take over. The soldiers replied, 'You are deceiving us.' We had neither the task nor the time to engage in diplomatic negotiations with them. It proved far easier to convince the soldiers of the sincerity of our intentions by other partisan means.[59]

---

upon them as the occupiers and not, as farther north, as semiconscripted mercenaries likely to desert the German cause.

[58] Though it cannot be discussed within the framework of this section, we must record the overwhelming impression that, by and large, the indigenous population viewed the allied troops, notably Rumanian and Hungarian, with greater hostility than it felt for the German. (See Russian Research Center, series B 6, #81); for a contrary view, at least so far as Italian relations with the Ukrainian population are concerned, see Giovanni Messe, *Der Krieg im Osten* (Zurich: Thomas-Verlag, 1947), and Aldo Valori, *La Campagna di Russia*, 2 vols. (Rome: Grafica Nazionale, 1950–51).

[59] Andreyev, pp. 331–36.

This statement contains an implicit confession of the failure of partisan verbal propaganda to convince men before they captured. When larger groups of Hungarian troops were seized by the partisans in October 1942, they were well treated. Though at first refusing to help the partisans, later a good many of the Hungarians joined them. One was assigned to the unit's political section, and three were flown to Moscow for "political work" there. On the whole, the partisans followed a simple policy, "As soldiers, you must be ruthless avengers; as captors, you must teach the prisoners the truth."[60]

A French legionnaire who fell into partisan hands near Khotimsk (Eastern Belorussia) in November 1942 recounted a similar tale: he and another French soldier were well treated and encouraged to join the partisans. There is little doubt that the bulk of Axis forces and their allies knew, even though they may have had doubts, that after capture they would be accorded more favorable treatment than German prisoners—a fact that was bound to affect their steadfastness in combat.[61]

Frequently partisan units took the initiative in encouraging defection among Axis troops. According to a Soviet account, the partisan leader, Sidor Kovpak, attempted to induce a Slovak lieutenant colonel to desert with his men. After initial contact was established and the colonel refused to come over in spite of his strong anti-German feelings, a secret deal was arranged by which partisans and Slovaks agreed not to fight each other. Another Soviet account records the efforts of the Saburov band to induce the surrender of the Slovak garrison at Buinovichi, an operation which, through the use of personal letters to Slovak officers and of girl messengers, eventually proved successful.

There are various reports that in 1943 and 1944 Axis deserters and captives were fighting with the partisans, though it is hard to determine to what extent partisan propaganda had influenced them. In the latter part of the war many defections were caused, largely by a realization that the Germans were losing the war and mistreating their allies. The above quotation concerning the Bryansk forest operation against the Hungarians suggests that leaflet propaganda was far from successful unless it was supplemented by persuasion in action. The role of verbal psychological warfare is difficult to assess because of the circumstances in which the Axis forces operated. To be successful, preparations for defection had to be kept secret from

[60] *Ibid.*

[61] Another example of partisan behavior to prisoners and deserters among Axis troops is furnished in a German report on Rumanian units in the Crimea in 1943. According to the report the Rumanians were treated "correctly and well." The partisans explained to the Rumanians that only the Germans were their enemies. The captives were allegedly given the choice of returning to their former units or of remaining with the bands if they so desired. However, in this instance no additional desertions to the partisans ensued.

the Germans; therefore, no public appeals or arrangements could be made. Hence little German documentation is available on the clandestine negotiations and appeals that at times led to defections of German allies to the partisans.

There is no adequate sample of leaflets to permit a meaningful analysis of propaganda themes. What little there is suggests persistent use of anti-German patriotic themes and, at least in the case of the Slovaks, resort to the pan-Slavic slogans introduced in Soviet propaganda early in the war. A girl emissary from the Kovpak band, in delivering a message to the Slovak commander, was reported to have appealed to him: "If your fatherland is dear to you, if you want to see a free Slovakia, act as Colonel Svoboda[62] did." The Saburov band likewise made reference to the All-Slav meetings in Moscow in its correspondence with a Slovak garrison it was trying to win over.

While the sum total of partisan psychological warfare measures undoubtedly had some effect on the Axis troops, the question remains to what extent specific propaganda operations can be credited with the defections. It appears likely that such operations contributed to a situation in which German military setbacks, material and moral frustration among the Axis troops, and anti-German resentment back home were probably more decisive.

§IV. Partisan Psychological Warfare Directed at Collaborators

A. MILITARY

The war in the East produced two striking phenomena: (1) large-scale collaboration of former Red Army men with the Germans, and (2) the return of a considerable number of these military collaborators to the Soviet fold.

The initial stage of the campaign followed the plans formulated by Hitler and most of the top Nazi hierarchy calling for unequivocal opposition to the arming of Soviet nationals. The rigid opposition in German government circles fitted in neatly with Nazi ideas about Soviet Russia and the war. The conviction that the German armies would be victorious after a short and decisive campaign, the concept of the Russian as an *Untermensch* (subhuman), and the goal of exploiting Russia's economic resources without regard to the fate of her people were based on ideas which left no room for any political incentives that might be offered to potential Russian col-

---

[62] A prominent Czech refugee and former Minister of War, then in the Soviet Union.

laborators. German realization that Soviet strength had been greatly under-estimated, combined with the rise of the partisan movement, which the in-adequate German security troops were unable to bring under control, brought about some changes in policy. The recruitment of former Soviet soldiers into small military collaborator units, undertaken experimentally in the fall of 1941, was gradually extended, reaching its peak in 1943. In fact, by the spring of 1943 military collaborator units, most of battalion strength, made up a large percentage of the German security forces en-gaged in antipartisan warfare.[63] Yet, in spite of such action, there always remained strong Nazi opposition to a full use of military collaborators.

In the official Soviet view military collaboration with the German forces naturally constituted treason. Nevertheless the Soviet Army made the col-laborators one of the primary targets of its psychological warfare cam-paign, expending considerable effort to regain physical control over them and to prevent the Germans from exploiting this source of manpower. For obvious reasons the partisans played an important role in these efforts. The very existence of collaborator units was a military challenge to the partisans, since most of these units were engaged in antipartisan warfare. It would have been impossible for the partisans, whose organization was not designed for offensive warfare, to eliminate their opponents by military force. Moreover, given the tensions within collaborator units, a psychologi-cal approach appeared more promising; it was even planned that at a later stage it would supplant military operations. In addition to the military danger, the collaborators represented an even more serious psychological threat. They demonstrated the lack of cohesion and homogeneity in Soviet society once Soviet controls were removed and emphasized the limitations of twenty years of Soviet indoctrination and training. At the same time they tended to neutralize the psychological impact of the partisans on the population, to whom they offered an alternative "indigenous" channel of action. Finally, and most important, they seemingly belied Soviet prop-aganda, which insisted on the solidarity of the Russian people, while the apparent willingness of the Germans to "ally" themselves with Rus-sians contradicted (however spuriously) the Soviet claim that the Germans considered the Slavic people as inferiors.

One group of military collaborators needs special mention. This was the indigenous police (Ordnungsdienst, or OD), originally organized on a local basis, with limited functions. As the partisan movement gained momentum and German security forces no longer could adequately deal with it, the OD received better weapons and was largely committed against the par-tisans. The OD men were locally recruited and were therefore more ex-

[63] For discussions of military collaboration, see also George Fischer, *Soviet Opposi-tion to Stalin* (Cambridge: Harvard University Press, 1952); Peter Kleist, *Zwischen Hitler und Stalin* (Bonn: Athenaeum-Verlag, 1950); Alexander Dallin, *The Kaminsky Brigade* (Maxwell Air Force Base, Ala.: HRRI, 1951) [hereafter cited as *Kaminsky*].

posed to partisan propaganda and more vulnerable to partisan reprisals than the better-armed and more cohesive units of regular collaborators. Moreover, their families were often exposed to partisan retaliation. On the other hand, the OD men were well acquainted with local conditions, knew the terrain, were able to inform the Germans about local contacts with the partisans, and wherever they enjoyed some prestige were able to counteract partisan propaganda.

The military collaborators, almost from the beginning of their existence as units, became vulnerable to Soviet psychological warfare. Particularly sensitive spots were their motives for collaborating and their reaction to experiences with the Germans. One may distinguish between those who, without strong political convictions, had joined collaborator units primarily to regain freedom and to escape suffering in prisoner-of-war camps; those who, initially convinced of German victory, sought affiliation with the winning side in the hope of improving their own status and material condition; and finally those who became collaborators out of sincere anti-Soviet convictions and a belief that German victory would produce a better Russia. All three groups, whose motives frequently intertwined, were soon disillusioned, and, as the result of personal experiences with the Germans, substantial numbers in each group became easy targets for Soviet psychological warfare. Those who had joined the units to escape from prisoner camps had accomplished their purpose and were bound to their new masters by no deep loyalty. The opportunists often lost their enthusiasm as they realized the limited openings for advancement and prestige on the German side and the increasing military reversals suffered by the Germans. The anti-Communist patriot frequently came to the painful conclusion that continued indigenous rule, even Soviet, was the lesser evil when compared with the abuses of the invaders.

Soviet and partisan propaganda sought to appeal to all three groups of collaborators. The partisans provided the conditions that made it relatively easy to desert from the Germans, while their propaganda acted as a catalyst that speeded up the mental and emotional processes of the collaborators before they took the difficult step of changing allegiance a second time. The major prerequisite for partisan propaganda effectively to encourage the defection of collaborators was assurance that they would not be punished for disloyalty. The cardinal obstacle was fear of retribution for treason. In what appears to be full awareness of this problem, an important Soviet policy decision was made some time in 1942, giving the military collaborators an opportunity to "expiate their mistakes" and redeem themselves by joining the partisans.

In the first months of the war, the question of military collaboration was secondary; the few Cossack and Ukrainian units established largely on a local basis by German field commanders were not significant enough to

230 / IV. PARTISAN PSYCHOLOGICAL WARFARE

warrant extensive Soviet countermeasures. There is no evidence that a distinction was made in 1941 and early 1942 between collaborating civilians and former Red Army men; whenever possible Soviet and partisan forces treated them as traitors and killed them. Whatever propaganda efforts the partisans made at this time aimed at the prevention of collaboration rather than at the defection of collaborators.

A change in tactics occurred in 1942 when the problem of collaboration became a real challenge to the Soviet regime. A number of partisans interrogated by the Germans indicated that there was a specific Stalin order providing for the "redemption" of collaborators by having them join the anti-German forces; unfortunately this order has not been found.[64] It is virtually certain that such a policy decision must have been made at the highest political level. Thereafter, it formed the cornerstone of partisan propaganda directed at the collaborators: to present convincing arguments to bring about defection and to alleviate fear of punishment.

1. Methods and Content

a. Verbal Propaganda

The propaganda media directed at military collaborators did not differ greatly from those used for other targets. Leaflets were employed extensively: many were produced on the Soviet side and distributed by partisans; others were printed by the partisans themselves.[65]

The basic theme was that collaboration, though treasonable and despicable, could be atoned for if, and only if, the collaborator voluntarily became a partisan to prove his worth and loyalty in the "Patriotic War." Soviet propaganda appeals were designed to produce a hope-and-fear reaction among the collaborators: hope that by joining the partisans they would redeem themselves as members of Soviet Society, and fear that failure to defect would mean certain death, either immediately at the hands of the partisans or after the "inevitable" victory of the Red Army. A typical leaflet ran, "The homeland will forgive your disloyalty to the Russian people; it will forgive all those . . . who voluntarily come over to our side. . . . Do not hesitate—soon it will be too late." At the same time, the fate of those who failed to heed such advice was outlined clearly: "A ter-

[64] It is possible that after some months of trial and error, this order was formalized in the general directive of December 1942 dealing with various aspects of partisan psychological warfare. However, leaflets printed as early as the fall of 1942 contained appeals to collaborators promising them immunity from prosecution if they joined.

[65] It is often impossible to determine whether a specific appeal originated on the Soviet or partisan side, was dropped by plane, or was distributed by agents or partisans. For the purpose of this section it will be assumed that any leaflet addressed to the collaborators was, if not produced by the partisans, at least distributed by them. Most leaflets in this category contained appeals to join the partisans; in a few, desertion to the Red Army was urged.

rible day of vengeance awaits all those who continue to collaborate with the Germans." The leaflets went to considerable length to alleviate fear. Besides emphasizing that "everybody who comes over to us voluntarily will be allowed to live and will be accepted in our ranks as a true son of the fatherland," many appeals contained ready-made excuses for the collaborators: "Everybody will forgive you, since it is known that many of you were prisoners of war [and suffered accordingly], while others were forced to help the Germans. Many of you were deceived and misled in various ways by the German cannibals."

The knowledge that the partisans would accept a man without branding him permanently as a traitor made his decision to defect easier. The implication of the ready-made formula given above was that the collaborator need not be ashamed of his past gullibility and change of heart, itself a curious admission, however inarticulate, of the potential effectiveness of German anti-Soviet themes. Leaflets almost acknowledged that some collaborators fought for the destruction of bolshevism, and even they were the objects of appeals. Significantly, wartime tactics did not call for attempts to convince them of the righteousness of communism but rather for a demonstration that the destruction of bolshevism was not the real goal behind the German invasion. "The Germans occupied France, Poland, Norway, Czechoslovakia, Belgium, Holland, Denmark, and Yugoslavia—and why? Because Bolsheviks were ruling there and the kolkhoz system was introduced?" In the same vein one partisan leaflet addressed to Ukrainian collaborators implied that a "true patriot" may actually have been a collaborator: "In appealing to you we hope that you too, as *true patriots,* will cease serving the Fascists." Partisan propaganda then attempted to show that not by collaborating but by joining the partisans could a Russian express his patriotism, even if he was anti-Soviet in his attitude.

We partisans took up arms consciously to defend the honor, freedom, and independence of our native country—the Soviet Union. We are defending our people from destruction and slavery; we are defending our blood-soaked soil and the descendants of our fathers and our children. But what are you defending? You are defending the life of the German henchmen who mishandled your families . . . you are defending the interests of the German landowners.

A special effort was made to fan anti-German feelings among the collaborators by such statements as: "The German officers despise you in their hearts. They regard you as traitors to the fatherland, who hold German money dearer than the blood of your brothers, fathers, wives, and children." Another approach sought to stress the German purposes in recruiting collaborators: "The Fascist robber army has lost 6,400,000 officers and men, killed and captured. Don't you see that the Hitlerites want to use you only as cannon fodder for their own purposes?" Finally, the inevitable defeat of Nazi Germany was emphasized. With all the arguments presented, the same question was posed: "Do you really wish to shed your blood and sacrifice yourselves as mercenaries of fascism in the fight against the Soviet people?"

The emphasis on German atrocities was not peculiar to leaflets directed at collaborators; however, in such appeals, stress was laid on the fact that, by their collaboration, the indigenous troops became accomplices in the German crimes. "Soviet soldiers, is it not against your honor that you are helping to continue this criminal war? Don't you understand that you are helping the Fascists destroy innocent brothers, sisters, wives, and children of your own people?" Another series of slogans pertained to such German long-range aims as economic exploitation, enslavement of the Russian people, and the prospects of colonizing vast stretches of Soviet territory— aims which, it was asserted, the collaborators were unwittingly supporting.

Some account was also taken of the nationality question. German re- cruitment of collaborators favored, especially until 1943, non-Russian nationalities or those groups that the Germans considered more likely to oppose the Soviet regime. Thus Ukrainians, Cossacks, Baltic and Caucasian nationals were preferred. Soviet psychological warfare did not ignore the non-Russian nationalities, although there is no evidence that great stress was laid on national peculiarities or themes. It seems that an attempt was made to show the hypocrisy of German claims that specially favorable treatment was given to non-Russians. Thus one leaflet emphasized that Germany attacked the Soviet Union in order to grab the raw materials of the Ukraine, the Caucasus, and Belorussia. Others showed by implication that the ultimate German war aim of dominating Europe precluded favor- able treatment. "The Fascists need you, your lives, your blood, in order to fulfill their idiotic plans of bringing the peoples of Europe and of the Soviet Union into slavery." There were occasional pan-Slav overtones in appeals to Ukrainians and other collaborators.

Appeals to Lithuanian, Latvian, or Estonian collaborators were similar to other appeals; German atrocities, Soviet victories, and German war aims were stressed. However, there was a tendency in some leaflets to identify the Soviet cause with the true national interests of the formerly independent states. One leaflet addressed to Lithuanian soldiers described how the Ger- mans suppressed Lithuanian nationalist students, and how the partisans came to their rescue. Without making any real concessions to Lithuanian nationalism, leaflets portrayed the partisans as the champions of the Lithu- anian cause. Leaflets addressed to Estonian collaborators also sought to show that the Soviets were the champions of Estonian national existence, while the Germans were using them only as cannon fodder. The fact that many Estonians were killed at Stalingrad in the winter of 1942–43 was cited as proof. Another leaflet claimed that Estonian soldiers were being sent to Africa to fight for German imperialism rather than Estonian independence.

Particular nationalities seem to have been taken into account mainly in local appeals, though those distributed by the partisans were often addressed to "Russian, Ukrainian, and Belorussian soldiers" or to the "Lithuanian Soldiers," and in some cases to specific units such as the "Ukrainian Regiment commanded by Major Weise." Leaflets composed by the partisans themselves were frequently addressed to specific target groups. They had the advantage of adding local color to the more general themes and of showing a collaborator the specific way in which to go about deserting. After the customary appeals one partisan leaflet concluded with the following:

We, the partisans of the Markov . . . Brigade, make the following proposals to you:

1. Kill your leaders who are serving the Germans faithfully.
2. Take your weapons and ammunition.
3. Proceed in the direction of the village [name], Myadelsk [?] Rayon, where we shall expect you. Your arrival time should be the first opportunity which presents itself. We will agree then and there on other conditions [of accepting you in our ranks].

Greetings from the Soviet partisans.

The staff of the Voroshilov Partisan Brigade.

At times the partisans employed letters addressed to individual collaborators as a means of encouraging defection. In one instance, a member of an Ostbataillon corresponded with a partisan group and received assurances of specific concessions for his battalion if its members deserted en masse. Another letter, addressed to the chief of an indigenous antipartisan unit in the Bryansk area, requested certain intelligence information and threatened to turn over to the German police incriminating evidence against him if he refused to cooperate.

Soviet psychological warfare directed at collaborators also relied on oral propaganda spread either by men who worked through civilians in touch with the collaborators, or by agents who had infiltrated collaborator units. In many cases it would be difficult to show that these agents were partisans; in all instances, however, it was necessary for them to establish contact with the partisans, since one major purpose of infiltration was to promote desertions to the partisan units operating in the vicinity. Such agents spread rumors and sowed distrust in an effort to drive a wedge between the collaborators and the Germans. Though rumors were widespread, their point of origin is naturally impossible to trace. It appears likely that the Germans often attributed them to Soviet agents when in fact they were the natural expression of discontent and distrust by a frustrated population. It remains true, nonetheless, that partisans and their agents did spread propaganda, and that everybody—including the civilians, the collaborators, and probably the Germans themselves—contributed to its dissemination.

b. Nonverbal Psychological Warfare

(1) TREATMENT OF CAPTIVES.—The treatment of captured collaborators by the partisans scarcely figured in the direct propaganda campaign aimed at collaborator units. Its importance was nonetheless considerable. Since in the eyes of the Soviet government the troops fighting on the German side were *ipso facto* traitors, it could not appeal to them, as one customarily appeals to enemy forces to induce desertion, with promises of good treatment, safe conduct, and a speedy return home after the war. However, as has been shown, the collaborators had a chance to redeem themselves by voluntarily joining the Soviet side. If they were captured by force, they had failed to avail themselves of this opportunity and could not expect treatment as bona fide prisoners. Moreover, the partisans could not capture or keep them in large numbers, for the same reasons that the Germans could not keep masses of prisoners. As in many forms of partisan warfare, there were only two extreme alternatives: Either a prisoner was killed or he became a partisan himself. *Tertium non datur.* Instances of captured collaborators being kept alive and being flown to Moscow for interrogation are reported only at moments when the Soviet authorities were eager to increase their knowledge of the German approach to the problem of military collaboration.[66]

The fate of the captured collaborators depended primarily on the attitude of the individual partisan commander. In a large stationary brigade the chances of a rank-and-file collaborator being kept alive were somewhat better, especially where the partisans controlled the surrounding area. Not so the officers. The following observation by an officer of the Kovpak Brigade, a leading roving band, is probably typical for such units: "If the rank-and-file [collaborator] could hope for generosity from the partisans, the traitor chieftains [and] officers had little cheerful to look forward to if they fell into our hands."[67]

Those collaborators who voluntarily heeded the appeal of the partisans to desert the Germans were usually incorporated into the partisan units. At times they were accepted as equals, and no stigma was attached to them.

[66] Such was the case in 1942 when, for the first time, recruitment of collaborators was carried out on a large scale; and again in the spring of 1943, when the Germans initiated the so-called Vlasov propaganda operation.

[67] Vershigora, p. 193. Those who were accepted into the partisan organization were sometimes grouped together in special "punitive" units; presumably, this was the case where the partisans were relatively secure. [G. Linkov, *Voina v tylu vraga* (Moscow: Gosudarstvennoye Izdatelstvo Khudozhestvennoi Literatury, 1951), pp. 486–88; see also Chap. III of this book.]

Former collaborators were frequently credited by the Germans as fighting with particular stubbornness; they knew that certain death awaited them if they fell into German hands. Individual former collaborators even received medals and decorations from the Soviet government for their subsequent performance as partisans; some of them, however, may have been Soviet agents all along. In at least one known instance, several hundred Cossack collaborators, who deserted to the partisans in Belorussia, were divided into smaller groups and distributed among several brigades, to avoid a dangerous concentration of unreliable elements.

It is significant that in almost all treatment of collaborators the partisans kept the letter but often violated the spirit of their propaganda promises. There is evidence that former collaborators were usually not accepted as equals but were treated as second-class fighters. They were assigned to less desirable or less dignified tasks, or to missions unlikely to endanger the safety of the main partisan units. Former collaborators seeking to escape from the partisans were of course shot without question.

Ex-collaborators were frequently used as bait to induce others to join the partisans; they signed leaflets, for instance, appealing to their former associates to follow their example. These leaflets would point out how well they were received and how glad they were to be fighting with the partisans. One such leaflet read:

To all so-called "Ukrainian Soldiers," "Cossacks," and "Policemen," from former soldiers (captured Red Army men) of the 221st German Division, 230th Battalion, Ukrainian Company, now "Red Partisans" [13 names follow].

Comrades! Follow our example. . . . On 23 September 1942, we . . . went over to the Red partisans. The partisans were very friendly in receiving us. After a friendly conversation we were told that from now on we were partisans and citizens of the USSR with full rights. . . . We felt suddenly as if a different blood ran through our arteries, the clear and hot blood of a citizen of the USSR.— *Appendix, Document 30.*

In one case a group of ex-collaborators was reported to have been fitted out with new weapons and equipment and paraded through the villages of the Bobruisk area; word of their treatment undoubtedly got back to those members of their unit who were still with the Germans.

The following example, referred to earlier, shows what concessions the partisans were willing to make to individual collaborator units. The Germans captured correspondence between a partisan brigade and an Ostbataillon in which the partisans were attempting to persuade the battalion to desert en masse to them. The following proposals were made:

1. The whole battalion with its weapons and equipment was to come over to the partisans.

2. The entire personnel of the unit were to be given a guarantee that their lives would be safe, that they would keep their freedom, and that they would receive a definite assignment within the partisan unit.

3. Members of the battalion would be given every assistance in finding their wives, children, and parents.

4. The battalion would maintain its unity as a partisan group, directly subordinate to the Central Staff of the Partisan Movement.[68]

It is not known whether the battalion did in fact desert. A similar case occurred, also in Belorussia, when the 2,000-man SS collaborator unit, the so-called Druzhina, deserted to the partisans. It afterwards operated as an independent partisan brigade and was commanded by the officer who had led the group under the Germans. There is some reason to suspect that several of the leaders of this unit, including the commanding officer, may have been Soviet agents.

(2) INFILTRATION.—The large-scale recruitment of former Red Army men into collaborator units offered the Soviets ample opportunity to infiltrate these units. Not all the prisoners of war who volunteered to fight with the Germans were eager to carry out their pledge, and some were susceptible to recruitment as Soviet agents. While exact figures cannot be given, a liberal sprinkling of pro-Soviet elements in collaborator units can be assumed to have existed, although their distribution among the units was largely a matter of chance. In addition, there were agents specifically assigned to subvert individual groups of collaborators.[69] Other persons were ordered to undermine the morale of collaborators from without, through civilians or other agents.

In many instances whole units infiltrated by agents deserted to the partisans after first killing the German personnel and then taking their arms and equipment. Such operations required the presence of liaison men who negotiated with the partisans in advance. The pattern seems to have required a Soviet (or partisan) attempt to win over some of the most important members of the units, some noncommissioned officers, and those holding machine guns or artillery, for instance. Often the rank-and-file collaborators had no advance knowledge of the desertion plans; at a favorable moment, usually in a place prearranged with the partisans, the switch took place. Those considered hopelessly hostile or those resisting the defection were shot, while the remainder had little choice but to obey in order to avoid being killed by the partisans or the ex-collaborators controlling the heavy weapons.

It was thus to the advantage of the partisans that the Germans for

---

[68] The last concession would indicate that the unit was to function as an independent partisan brigade and that the correspondence was carried out with an operative group in Belorussia. The German report relating to this incident referred to captured documents from which this information was gained; the documents themselves have not been found among the German records, but there seems to be no reason to doubt the German account.

[69] In April 1943 the Germans discovered that several Soviet political officers had infiltrated a collaborator unit and concluded that they had instructions to volunteer for such units if captured.

"ideological reasons" kept their collaborator units small, usually not exceeding battalion strength. It was much easier to arrange the desertion of a few hundred men than to induce a whole division to change sides. While the desertion of whole units was more spectacular, the steady trickle of individual defectors was equally important, and here the role of Soviet agents is more difficult to demonstrate.

In some instances, agents organized "conspiratorial" groups with ambitious goals. One such group, unearthed in the Kaminsky Brigade, had the mission of killing the unit commander, together with his closest associates, and of arranging for the transfer of the entire brigade, consisting of 7,000 men, to the partisans.[70] Another unsuccessful attempt against Kaminsky was made when the *Za Rodinu* Partisan Brigade received instructions from the Central Staff of the Partisan Movement and allegedly from the NKVD to organize a secret group, which (according to an order intercepted by the Germans) was assigned to "terror attacks against Kaminsky and his following, against quarters of the troops, staff headquarters, etc. [Special noiseless arms and magnetic mines were to be supplied for this purpose.] Preparation of an insurrection among the Kaminsky troops." The preparations had already begun, and the insurrection was to be staged simultaneously with a frontal attack of the Red Army at the Bryansk front.[71]

The effectiveness of Soviet infiltration techniques is borne out by many instances of desertion, to which agents contributed but for which they were by no means solely responsible. By the spring of 1943 the number of deserting collaborators was so great that the partisans set up special recruitment offices to receive, screen, and assign them.[72]

2. Conclusion

The Soviet approach to the problem of military collaborators with the Germans, as revealed through the partisan "middlemen," revealed a striking measure of tactical flexibility. On the one hand, partisan psychological warfare appealed to non-Communists as well as Communists, and it did so in non-Communist terms.[73] On the other hand, it appealed to traitors,

---

[70] This was in the Lepel area of Belorussia, to which the Kaminsky Brigade was transferred in mid-1943. From the German point of view, it was one of the most successful experiments in antipartisan warfare. (See *Kaminsky.*)

[71] The order was intercepted in March 1943 while the brigade was still in the Lokot area. Gruppe Ruebsam, Ic, "Bericht ueber die im Maerz aufgedeckte Verschwoerergruppe in Lokot," 24 March 1943 (GMDS, XLVII AK 37241/9).

[72] This was in the area just north of Belorussia. Another recruitment office in the Bobruisk area appealed to collaborators as early as the fall of 1942. Agents sent there by the Red Army to establish recruitment centers also conducted propaganda activities; they succeeded in forming a cell within a collaborator battalion stationed at Bobruisk and through it accomplished the defection of several groups of men.

[73] Significantly, in some instances German propaganda, e.g., on the Vlasov issue and on the agrarian reform, forced the Soviets to counter German appeals through par-

and in substance promised them immunity. It is worth noting that, while the former device had its slightly milder counterpart in the Soviet-side press, the permissive policy toward collaborators was not mentioned at all in overt Soviet propaganda, which depicted the collaborators as despicable traitors.

There can be little doubt that the partisans and Soviet policy-makers correctly gauged the situation calling for such tactics. Suffice it to cite the example of a Red Army major who, after his capture by the Germans, volunteered for service with a collaborator unit as a noncommissioned officer. In October 1942 a German observer described him as an idealist who genuinely hated the Soviet regime and had been willing to fight with Germany "for a free Russia against bolshevism." Unwilling to fight for the oppression of his homeland and having become acquainted with German aims and methods, the major deserted with sixty of his men. Such individuals could be reached by precisely the tactics the partisans adopted.

The longer the war continued, the more unreliable the collaborator units became. In October 1943, therefore, the German leaders ordered the transfer of all "Eastern battalions" out of Soviet territory to the West. While it is impossible to estimate to what extent partisan propaganda was responsible for the disintegration, it may safely be assumed that the process of alienation from the German side, perhaps inevitable under the circumstances, was measurably speeded up by the partisans. Their major contributions in this field lay probably not so much in the specific slogans they used but (1) in providing a "purgatory" through which the collaborator could pass to redeem himself in the eyes of "his" country; (2) in acting as a catalytic agent speeding the decision to break with the Germans; and (3) simply by being present and thus making defection possible and relatively easy.

B. CIVILIAN

The civilian collaborators constituted a separate target group for partisan propaganda, quite distinct from the military collaborators. As defined by the partisans and their Soviet superiors, a collaborator was anyone who assisted in the German war effort or the administration and exploitation of the occupied territories, i.e., virtually everyone not helping the Soviet or partisan cause. The attention of the partisans, however, was concentrated largely on those who served the Germans in some administrative or semipolitical capacity, such as mayors, village elders, newspaper editors, and members of municipalities. These officials were considered traitors in a more definitive and irrevocable sense than were the military collaborators. While the latter usually were anonymous individuals who represented a challenge not as individuals but because they belonged to a

---

tisan propaganda. This counterpropaganda was the weakest and least convincing part of Soviet psychological warfare. See Sect. V, D, 2.

specific group, the civilian administrators exercised much greater influence because of their position and standing in the community. It was this difference that accounted primarily for variations in partisan psychological warfare directed at civilian, as contrasted with military, collaborators.

In the early months of the German occupation, partisan propaganda appealed principally to those who had not yet committed themselves to the German side, warning them of the disastrous consequences such commitment would provoke. The embryonic nature of the movement as well as the rudimentary quality of this early propaganda severely limited its effectiveness. When the partisans had sufficient strength, their most common approach to the problem was to kill as many civilian collaborators as possible.

Beginning with the spring of 1942, as the strength, organization, and facilities of the partisans increased, a more systematic attempt was initiated to discourage collaboration and, in addition, to appeal directly to collaborators. The themes used in printed propaganda were similar to those employed in leaflets addressed to the military: German atrocities, Soviet victories, partisan heroism, Soviet patriotism, crimes of collaborators, threats of annihilation, and promises of forgiveness should the collaborator abandon his treacherous work. Printed appeals were usually aimed at the population at large, instead of at those who more specifically took an active part in the struggle.

Here, unlike the approach in appeals to military collaborators, threats decidedly prevailed over promises, and partisan leaflets were not nearly so likely to provide excuses for collaboration. The difference, however, was largely one of degree and emphasis, not of kind, since the idea that the civilian collaborators were deceived and threatened by the Germans into accepting their posts was also expounded. A further reason for a difference in emphasis was that the civilian target group was more exposed to partisan reprisals than the military. Unless accidentally captured or killed by the partisans, an individual military collaborator was immune from partisan wrath; not so the civilian collaborators, for, especially in twilight zones which neither Germans nor partisans controlled thoroughly, the partisans could almost always stage raids on small towns and kill or abduct German-appointed officials. Threats against collaborators' families were also used extensively—and carried out. This, too, was a technique reserved for the civilian collaborators, since unlike the military they generally lived in the area, with their families nearby.

The obvious effect of such terror methods was the increased difficulty the Germans had in finding administrators who were both willing to take jobs and possessed some prestige in their community. Mayors would visit "their" towns or villages only in daylight or accompanied by German escorts, or they would transfer residence to the nearest safe town. In some communities, no one was willing to accept the position of village elder, and it became necessary to rotate the office among the eligible males. Undoubtedly partisan terror thus seriously impaired the usefulness of the indigenous administration to the Germans and, indirectly, the economic benefits the Germans derived from the occupation.

There is some evidence that, as the war continued into 1943, the emphasis on terror became less pronounced. Captured collaborators were reported to have been released in the Bryansk area, largely for propaganda purposes, and a greater effort was made by the partisans to win over other collaborators before taking drastic action against them.[74]

A letter [See Appendix, Document 34] from the partisans to an individual civilian collaborator—in this case, the head of a local labor office —illustrates another partisan technique. The man and his family were threatened with death if he failed to comply with the demand of the partisan commander who wrote the letter. It pointed out that, to be accepted in the good graces of the Soviet authorities, the collaborator would have to engage in specific intelligence missions, including the compilation of rosters of other known collaborators. The man was also asked to sign a note pledging to carry out the assigned tasks for the partisans. The partisans could threaten to turn such a note over to the German police. A similar technique was employed in another instance when a collaborator was warned that, if he failed to cooperate, his correspondence with the partisans would be delivered to the Germans.

By such methods, and assisted by the variegated system of Soviet infiltration into indigenous organizations, the partisans succeeded in placing their men in strategic spots.[75] By direct terror they eliminated some and deterred others from working with the Germans and by threats and promises they won over to their side a considerable number of collaborators. The total impact of this two-pronged program was considerable. It must

[74] This change of tactics was probably directed from higher Soviet quarters. As early as the summer of 1942, a high-ranking Soviet official and (then) member of the Politburo, Andrei Andreyev, was quoted as having indicated his displeasure at partisan terror methods:

It is completely wrong [for the partisans] to kill or manhandle representatives of the [German-controlled] indigenous administration, Russian policemen, starostas, etc. Quite the opposite: a very friendly relationship is to be established with Russian officials who serve the German forces, and they are to be told that their activities with the Germans will not be held against them ... if they covertly collaborate with the partisans now.... The Russians [in German service] shall under no circumstances be embittered against the partisans.

If this report is trustworthy, Andreyev's attitude cannot be considered the official Soviet view. For some speculation on his special position in this connection, see Sect. IV, C, 2 and Sect. VI, M.

[75] The existence of such agents in the German administration was occasionally uncovered by the occupying forces. They included not only clerks and interpreters but even high-ranking officials in such towns as Polotsk, Bobruisk, Vitebsk, Minsk, Kiev, Kharkov, and others. In some instances, they were in close touch with the partisans; in others, they operated independently.

be borne in mind, however, that, while it seriously hindered German control, it also antagonized wide strata of the civilian population who, though disillusioned with the Germans, did not take kindly to partisan terror.

C. VLASOV AND THE PARTISANS

In the spring of 1943 the Germans launched an extensive propaganda campaign designed to regain the allegiance of the Russian population on occupied territory, to recruit ex-Soviet nationals for military service, and to encourage desertion among the Red Army soldiers. Extensive use was made of the name of Andrei Vlasov, a captured Soviet general who had become well known for, among other things, his role in the defense of Moscow in late 1941. General Vlasov was made the leader of a Russian anti-Soviet movement promoted in large part by the propaganda section (WPr) of the OKW and the intelligence branch *(Fremde Heere Ost)* of the OKH. At the same time, the numerous small units of collaborators on the German side were given the collective name of "ROA" (*Russkaya Osvoboditelnaya Armiya,* or Russian Liberation Army). Though neither the character of these units nor their subordination to the German command was in any sense altered, the creation even of a mythical Army appears to have given some of the collaborators a feeling of belonging and was susceptible to propaganda exploitation.

The Vlasov propaganda exemplified the belated German espousal of what was called "political warfare," i.e., the use of political themes and a political program, ostensibly *by* Russians addressed *to* Russians, and intended to serve as incentives for political collaboration with, and desertion to, the German side. The political program, prepared by German officers working with General Vlasov, as embodied in the so-called "Smolensk Manifesto," contained rather general promises regarding the abolition of the collective farm system and forced labor, freedom of religion, national self-determination, and future cooperation with Germany.[76] After the first use of "Vlasov leaflets" in late 1942 and early 1943, Vlasov was permitted to visit the German-occupied areas in the spring of 1943 to deliver speeches and attempt to persuade the population to join his movement (and thereby support the Germans).

The new German approach to the question of military collaboration presented a challenge to Soviet and partisan propaganda, which had insisted on the mercenary character of the collaborators. Moreover, the Soviet authorities were clearly afraid that the change in propaganda was the harbinger of a genuine shift in German policy. The struggle behind the German scene which prevented such a reversal of policy from being

[76] Though issued over the name of Vlasov and some of his Russian associates, the "thirteen points" were actually drafted by officers in the Wehrmacht Propaganda staff. They were never approved as a political program by Hitler or other leading Nazi officials. On the Vlasov movement, see Fischer.

instituted was not at all, or only imperfectly, known to the Soviet government. According to his aide, the Chief of Staff of the Ukrainian Partisan Movement (subsequently Minister of the Interior of the Ukraine), Timofei Strokach, realized that it had been primarily the stupidity and cruelty of German occupation policy which enabled the partisan movement to succeed. The Vlasov movement caused considerable consternation among high-ranking Soviet officials. Thus Alexander Shcherbakov, head of the Moscow Party organization and a member of the Politburo, is quoted as having characterized the pre-Vlasov era as the golden opportunity for the partisans: "We have to be thankful to the Germans that their policy enabled us to fan the flame of the partisan movement in the Ukraine." The Soviet leadership evidently feared that the Vlasov movement necessitated a substantial change in their own tactics. The Smolensk Manifesto, for instance, was characterized by Moisei Spivak, a secretary of the Central Committee of the Communist Party of the Ukraine, as capable of exciting the masses against the Soviet regime; and allegedly Stalin himself declared that the Vlasov movement constituted "at least a great obstacle on the road to victory over the German Fascists."[77]

The new German propaganda line should not have come as a complete surprise to the Soviet command. General Vlasov was captured in July 1942; in early September the first German leaflets appeared over his signature, blaming Stalin for all the sufferings of the Russian people. In December 1942 and January 1943, the Smolensk Manifesto appeared; and from early 1943 on the use of Vlasov's name and the ROA in German propaganda was steadily increased, at first experimentally on occupied soil, and later in the spring on a large scale, also directed at the Red Army. It is clear that the Soviet authorities at first sought to remain silent about Vlasov and only decided to act when he became a sufficiently important challenge to disturb Soviet loyalty. Initially, Moscow pretended to believe that Vlasov was being used by the Germans against his will and that the whole movement was but a clever trick initiated by Goebbels' Propaganda Ministry.[78] Since the Germans had previously abstained from political warfare themes employing the Russians against Russians, and since Vlasov received little publicity from the Germans in 1942, Soviet political propaganda seemed content to discount the "Vlasov movement" as at most a potential danger.

While publicly refraining from mentioning Vlasov after his defection— i.e., resorting to what German propaganda called *totschweigen,* killing by silence—behind the scenes the Soviet leaders reacted promptly to Vlasov's

[77] RFSS, Pers. St., "Betr. Kapitaen Boris Russanow," 19 October 1943 (GMDS, EAP 161-b-12/94).

[78] If this reflected the genuine view of Moscow, it is an indication of the poor intelligence available to the Soviet leadership, since the Propaganda Ministry played a negligible role in starting the Vlasov campaign.

disappearance. When his assault army was annihilated on the Volkhov Front in June 1942, Nikitin, the ranking partisan commander of the Leningrad area, ordered partisan units operating in the vicinity to find Vlasov and assist him in reaching safety on the Soviet side.[79] There are no indications that this mission was motivated by any awareness of Vlasov's potential defection; it was rather an attempt to prevent a high-ranking Soviet general from falling into German hands. When this effort failed, silence fell. His capture was in no way mentioned by the Soviet press and propaganda machines.

Early in 1943 a high-level decision on the matter must have been made, apparently with the joint approval of the Main Political Administration of the Red Army and the *Agitprop* Section of the Party's Central Committee. The subsequent actions taken by Soviet and partisan psychological warfare organs suggest that the following was agreed upon:

(1) The civilian population on the Soviet side would presumably learn least about the Vlasov movement from German sources; hence the need here for counterpropaganda was slight. It was therefore decided to ignore the Vlasov question in the Soviet-side civilian press.

(2) The Red Army press, on the other hand, had to attempt to neutralize the effect of German "Vlasov propaganda." There was a certain lag between the onset of the German psychological warfare campaign and the Soviet reaction, but by late spring 1943 front area newspapers began "explaining" the movement to Red Army troops. The very fact that the Soviets reacted openly to the Vlasov movement only after the Germans forced the issue indicated Soviet perception of their own vulnerability and showed a reluctance to fight the Vlasov program on ideological grounds. A typical sample of Soviet counterpropaganda argued that (a) Vlasov had been forced by the Germans to give his signature to the appeals issued over his name; (b) the ROA was merely a German propaganda device; (c) German treatment of the prisoners was barbarous; (d) the German shift in propaganda themes was only a reflection of German weakness after the defeat of Stalingrad; (e) hostile collaborators were traitors.[80]

(3) On the German side of the front, the Vlasov movement became known so widely and so rapidly that a positive Soviet response to it was deemed necessary several months before the one initiated on the Soviet side of the front, lest silence be interpreted as indicating that there were no effective counterarguments. Countermeasures included overt media, such as leaflets published or distributed by partisans, newspaper articles in the underground Party and partisan press, rumors spread by partisans and special agents about the "real" nature of the ROA; and covert measures, such as infiltration and

[79] X.A.K., Ic, "Taetigkeitsbericht," 1 November 1942 (GMDS, X AK 44431/39).
[80] AOK 20, Ic, "Nr. 214/43," 26 June 1943 (GMDS, AOK 20, 36560/15).

subversion of collaborator units from within and without, and special assignments both to partisans and other Soviet agents to assassinate Vlasov and
high-ranking officers of his movement.[81]

1. Overt Propaganda

Printed propaganda intended to neutralize the effect of the Vlasov
movement emphasized themes (1) to discredit Vlasov personally, (2) to
discredit the ROA, and (3) to debunk its political program.

(1) Before July 1943 the attempts to discredit Vlasov personally were
sporadic and haphazard. Until then partisan propaganda had employed
such uncomplimentary epithets as "Vlasov the traitor," or "the spy of
1936." In particular, he was accused of having sold out the Second
Assault Army, which he commanded on the Volkhov Front. Other partisan leaflets and newspaper articles ridiculed Vlasov's claim to the role of
"savior of Moscow" in the winter of 1941. The most serious and probably most telling accusation, however, was leveled not against his own behavior but against his alliance with the Germans, which made him an ac-
complice of their atrocities. Finally, he was rebuked for having in cowardly fashion failed to take the opportunity to be rescued when he found
himself encircled by the Germans.

In July 1943 the propaganda line changed. Several Red Army front
newspapers made outspoken, though infrequent, reference to Vlasov in a
version which also received wide dissemination in at least the northern
German-held areas. The manner in which Vlasov was discredited is
strongly reminiscent of the standard treatment preferred in such Soviet
purges as those of Tukhachevsky and Beria. They "proved" that Vlasov
was not only a spy and traitor but had been a capitalist agent for the
better part of his career. The Main Political Administration of the Red
Army officially accused him of involvement and participation in the
"Trotskyite" conspiracy, along with Tukhachevsky. It was alleged that
he was "unmasked" only when the danger of the conspiracy had been
eliminated and that therefore he had been given another chance. The
accusations further charged him with conspiring with the Germans and

---

[81] Thus the same Nikitin who, a year earlier, had ordered the partisans to search for
Vlasov after his disappearance, in May 1943 charged other partisans with the mission
to capture or assassinate Vlasov when he toured the Pskov-Gatchina area of the occupied USSR under German auspices. Radio communications from Nikitin's staff to
a Leningrad Partisan Brigade, the text of which fell into German hands, contained the
following instructions: "Nikitin has ordered that you should be alert to Vlasov's arrival in your rayon. Report immediately what steps you will be able to take to receive him." A few days later another communication stated: "The traitor Vlasov
will speak on 10 May at Dedovichi [and] Porkhov. . . . Take all measures to capture
or kill Vlasov no matter what the cost, otherwise we will be too late." (Amt.Ausl./
Abw. III, "Auftraege d. sowj. Agentendienstes gegen Vlasov," 6 July 1943, GMDS,
H3/853.) Later in the war, other Soviet agents were sent to Berlin to assassinate
Vlasov.

Japanese during his tour of duty as military attaché with Chiang Kai-shek in 1937–38 and with having "sold" the Far Eastern Maritime Province to Japan, and the Ukraine and Belorussia to the Germans. He was allegedly tried by a Soviet court and pardoned on the condition of redeeming himself by service in the Red Army.

At the beginning of the German attack in 1941, it was claimed, he had been captured by the Germans when encircled near Kiev and had rejoined the Soviet Army as a German agent. To explain his stand before Moscow, the official version pointed out that he became fearful and therefore did not carry out the assignment the Germans had given him. In the summer of 1942, however, he reverted to his role as German agent and "sold out" his army at the Volkhov Front.[82]

Needless to say, there is not the slightest evidence that these allegations were based on fact, and there are numerous indications of their falsehood. It is worth recalling that it took the Soviet Government a whole year after Vlasov's capture to make them public. While perhaps some Soviet soldiers believed these "revelations," it is unlikely that they impressed any sizable group of collaborators or civilians on the German side. It is interesting therefore that these charges, though officially released by the Army, were not widely used by the partisans. Partisan propaganda concentrated on Vlasov's activities *after* his capture by the Germans and particularly on his participation in German "crimes."

(2) Leaflet propaganda aimed at members of the ROA and miscellaneous *Osttruppen* did not differ materially from general appeals to collaborators, which would seem to indicate that in this area the Soviet leadership drew no sharp distinction between Vlasov's followers and "ordinary" collaborators. Indeed, no such differentiation was possible since the ROA was what has been called a "phantom army," i.e., an organization existing on paper but not in reality, of battalions spread widely over the area, under German command and without central and effective indigenous direction. Perhaps without realizing how close they came to the truth, the authors of a leaflet attacking Vlasov's claim that the ROA was fighting for the liberation of Russia, argued that the ROA was not Russian but German-led, that the Germans had created it not to liberate but to enslave Russia, and that it was not an army but an assemblage of prisoners amassed through force and deceit. Even this leaflet, however, reflected Soviet fear that a change in German policy was about to give substance to the Vlasov claims.

(3) Some leaflets distributed by the partisans took issue with specific points of the Smolensk Manifesto. The promise to abolish forced labor was countered by a reference to the "right to work" as an inalienable privilege of Soviet citizens, whereas it was the Germans who instituted

---

[82] FHO (IIId), "Sowjetpropaganda zur Wlassow-Aktion," 18 July 1943 (GMDS, H3/853).

forced labor—a fact supported by reference to a captured directive by General Zeitzler.[83] To those collaborators who knew of the existence of forced labor camps in the Soviet Union, such an argument could scarcely be convincing, except that it stressed the use of compulsory labor by the Germans, too.

Equally weak were Soviet attempts to ridicule Vlasov's agrarian program. While rumor propaganda insisted that the Soviet Government could abolish the collective farms [See Sect. V, E, 2], printed Soviet and partisan appeals emphasized that the Soviet regime had given the land to the peasantry in perpetuity and that the kolkhoz members had the use of the fruits of their labor. At the same time, such leaflets insisted that Germany aimed at re-establishing large estates, owned and operated by "barons" and German landlords. [See Appendix, Document 46.] The question of popular hostility to the kolkhoz system was ignored.

Soviet and partisan propaganda went to some lengths to disprove Vlasov's claim that he was a patriot working in the interests of his people. His committee was ridiculed as consisting of German puppets; its slogan of "neither bolshevism nor capitalism" was countered by the assertion that Vlasov's Fascist masters were in fact the worst capitalists and exploiters. As for Vlasov's appeal to Russian nationalism, the partisan leaflets replied that actually he was inciting the people to civil war from which only Germany could gain. Perhaps more persuasive than all these arguments was the partisans' insistence that the Reich showed its basic insincerity by failing to establish the ROA in 1941, and by doing so only in 1943, when it was losing the war and needed cannon fodder.[84]

2. Covert Propaganda

There was a pronounced difference between the "official" anti-Vlasov line, as evidenced in articles and leaflets, and the equally official but clandestine rumor propaganda spread by partisans and agents (sometimes without the knowledge of rank-and-file partisans). While the former adopted themes similar to those used against regular military collaborators, the latter utilized themes never formally admitted in the USSR. They were specifically directed at those elements which were known to be anti-Soviet but were considered patriotic. It is likely that only trusted and high-ranking partisan officials participated in this more subtle form of psychological warfare.

The substance of such themes was revealed by a Soviet agent, Semyon Nikolayevich Kapustin, after his capture by the Germans. Kapustin was a Soviet major who was apparently recruited by the NKVD to execute

[83] AOK 18, Ic/AO, "Uebersetzung eines sowj. Flugblattes," 1 June 1943 (GMDS, H3/853).

[84] Heereswesen-Abt. (Abw.) beim Gen.zbV b.OKH, "Propaganda gegen Wlassow [translation of Soviet leaflets], "20 June 1943 (GMDS, H3/853).

a mission against the Vlasov movement after he had been convicted on the Soviet side of a criminal offense and sentenced to serve a prison term of several years. By accepting this mission, he was told, he could redeem himself and, at the same time, achieve positions of great honor. Kapustin "deserted" to the German side on 24 May 1943 with the mission of "joining" the Vlasov movement, contacting Vlasov as well as others in his entourage, setting up cells to subvert the movement from within, and killing Vlasov. In order to win followers he was authorized by Moscow to use the following themes:

1. Germany wants to enslave, not liberate, the Russian people.
2. The ROA is a German, not a Russian idea, and results from a lack of German manpower.
3. Russian troop concentrations before the German attack had no offensive purposes against Germany or any other country but were intended to forestall German expansion into Turkey and to protect the Dardanelles.

While the first two themes contained nothing novel, the third reflected an awareness of the effectiveness of the German propaganda that dwelt on Soviet offensive intentions, and a perception of the strongly nationalist flavor of the ROA, to whose members such a traditional, imperialist goal as the Straits was presumed to appeal.

4. Soviet Russia has already satisfied many demands of the people by reopening churches, abolishing the Comintern, and discontinuing the commissar system in the Red Army.

Such concessions were made during the war, but they were not presented in overt Soviet propaganda as concessions, because of an understandable reluctance to admit that the Soviet state had found it necessary to barter for the support of her subjects.

5. The war has proved the instability of the Soviet system of an international union of republics. The burden rests entirely on the Great Russian people, all others having failed us. For this reason the republics will be abolished after the war and become merged in one undivided Soviet Russia.

This theme was obviously meant to appeal to the Great Russian nationalist element within the Vlasov movement. It illustrated Soviet willingness to appear as the champion of the non-Russian nationalities or of Great-Russian nationalism as the situation demanded.

6. The political system of the USSR is to undergo important changes after the war.
   a. The union republic system will be dissolved.
   b. The Communist Party will be reorganized into a people's party, with special emphasis on education and propaganda.
   c. Stalin will be replaced as head of state by Andrei Andreyev.

d. Kolkhozes will be dissolved after the war; such a step is not feasible during the war.

The choice of Andreyev as the head of a mythical, reformed Soviet State is particularly interesting; he had the reputation of being a rather less doctrinaire member of the Politburo who placed greater emphasis on individual responsibility within the kolkhoz system and allegedly even maintained that it was not the task of the partisans to restore the kolkhozes. After 1948 Andreyev rapidly lost out in a struggle with Khrushchev over agricultural policy, and he no longer occupies a position of real power in the Soviet Union.[85]

7. Collaborators serving in the Vlasov movement who return voluntarily to the Soviet fold will be well treated, decorated, and given new clothing and a furlough.

This last offer was in line with regular partisan propaganda, except that leave was rarely promised.

8. Russians will correct their own mistakes and do not need the assistance of the Germans.

This, of course, was an admission that there were mistakes to correct, though it was also an appeal to the patriotic spirit of the Russian people not to let foreigners interfere in what the Russians should and could correct by themselves.[86]

These apt themes were to be spread by Kapustin among Vlasov's men; in addition, he was to recruit other agents within the ROA. To ease his infiltration he had been instructed to write an anti-Soviet article in the German-controlled Russian-language papers, *Zarya* and *Dobrovolets,* using such phrases as the "Jewish-Communist" Soviet state and such devices as attacks on Stalin and the NKVD—all revealing indications of the way Moscow construed German-sponsored propaganda and indigenous areas of vulnerability. Should he accomplish part or all of his mission, he was to return to the Soviet side by October 1943 with the aid of the partisans; after his return he was promised the decoration of Hero of the Soviet Union and promotion to colonel and political officer in the Red Army.

The strange mixture of truth and fiction which Kapustin and others like him were to spread would probably have constituted a fairly effective series of themes. The truth of some of the themes dealing with existing situations was well known, while the promises for the future were safe because they were unverifiable.

Similar rumors were circulated in other areas to combat the Vlasov movement. According to one Vlasovite officer, a former Soviet colonel,

[85] See Sect. VI, L. But even after Khrushchev's rise to supreme power, Andreyev has retained honorific posts in the Central Committee and the Supreme Soviet.

[86] OKH/GenStdH/FHO (IIIf), "Uebersetzung: Gesamtergebnis der Vernehmung des Spions Ssemjon Nikolajewitsch Kapustin," 22 July 1943 (GMDS, H3/853).

Soviet agents and/or partisans around Pskov were spreading the clandestine theme that "the weapons are now in the hands of the people. The people will dethrone Stalin after the war. One should not forget, however, that the Germans are the most treacherous enemy and must therefore be beaten first. In order not to weaken the fight against the Germans, for the time being we must continue to fight under Stalin's leadership." Such a notion might well have arisen spontaneously. Its exploitation by Soviet agents grew increasingly effective as the populace became disillusioned with the Germans.

Partisan and Soviet propaganda was most convincing when it emphasized German "mistakes" and "crimes" and German military defeats. With such themes as assistance, the partisans could argue that it was not the collaborators, but rather the Red Army and partisans, who were fighting to help the people. When the Soviet forces were again in the ascendant, mention of the Bolshevik Party reappeared, "The Communists [a leaflet now declared] are the friends of the people—unlike the Germans who kill your wife, burn your village. . . . The Communists are concerned about the welfare of the people and want the best for you."

In the last analysis, neither partisan propaganda nor German defeats bore the major responsibility for the failure of the Vlasov movement to grow in strength. Rather, the unwillingness of the Nazi leadership to design a palatable political program, implement it, and utilize it to the utmost in political warfare forced the "Vlasov operation" to grind to a halt. Vlasov himself was shelved, and the use of his name and program was reduced to a minimum after mid-1943. Only after the Germans had, for all practical purposes, lost the war was the Vlasov movement revived in November 1944. By then it was too late even to test its propaganda appeal.

§V. Partisan Propaganda Aimed at the Local Population

A. INTRODUCTION

An analysis of partisan propaganda encounters several basic difficulties. One is the incompleteness of available source material. In view of the paucity of partisan newspaper files and the specific difficulties involved in analyzing the word-of-mouth propaganda reported by German observers and informants, the following discussion restricts itself primarily to leaflet propaganda. The major unknown is the extent to which the leaflets were produced by Soviet Army Groups (Front) Political Administration staffs or by partisan propaganda sections. Wherever possible, a distinction between these various origins has been made.

Another difficulty is that the leaflets gathered by the Germans represent an accidental selection. Quite possibly many Soviet leaflets never became known to them; moreover, most of the leaflets were collected in urban areas, and none was from an area firmly held by the partisans. Naturally the various repeated stages of selection, from the German seizure of leaflets down to the choice of material for this present analysis, prevent any quantitative study, such as line or frequency count, from being meaningfully attempted. However, the recurrence of themes in partisan propaganda is sufficiently striking and uniform to permit some inferences about their content.

B. TARGETS

A large part of partisan propaganda was apparently aimed at no specific segment of the population in the occupied areas. Sometimes no direct address was used in leaflets, especially in short slogans. More frequently, however, appeals opened with such general salutations as "To the Population of the Areas Temporarily Occupied by the German Fascists," or "Brothers and Sisters in the Areas Temporarily Seized by the Enemy!" Units operating more or less permanently in a given area would appeal to the population of that rayon or oblast, often signing in conjunction with the underground Party committee.

At times Bolshevik stereotypes appeared in leaflet addresses, in such formulas as "To the Toiling Population" or "Toilers in Smolensk Oblast!" In the text, there are likewise occasional references to the "toiling intelligentsia." No special significance need be attached to such formulas, except as they indicate the lingering effect of the traditional Soviet outlook, distinguishing the productive elements (workers, peasants, intellectuals) from the "parasites" and, under the occupation, collaborators.

If the area in which the partisans operated was suitable for such work, leaflets were at times addressed to members of a given nationality. In particular, those to Latvians, Lithuanians, and Estonians were always so designated and were composed in the native language. In the Caucasus, no examples of specific appeals to national groups have been found, except for occasional references to local patriotism, such as Kuban pride and Cossack tradition. In the Ukraine and Belorussia, some leaflets appeared in the local language, some in Russian; it seems that leaflets produced by Army straggler units and Komsomol teams tended more frequently to be in Russian, while those of other partisan units and Party *obkomy* and *raikomy* were both in Russian and in the native tongue. Often such leaflets would begin with salutations like "Belorussians!" or "Sons of the Ukraine!" in a slight attempt to play on national emotions. It was only natural that leaflets in Belorussian or Ukrainian, though otherwise similar to those of Russian printed media, avoided references to specifically Great-Russian national themes and slogans; on the other hand, "all-union" patriotism was in evidence in these leaflets, too.

A number of leaflets, though decidedly a minority, were designed to appeal to specific social and economic groups of the population. In such cases, the contents were adjusted to suit the target, especially if the leaflets could be distributed to a specific group, such as workers in a factory or on a collective farm. Railroad workers, for instance, would receive special exhortations to wreck tracks; workers generally were persuaded that their lot had been far better under the Soviet regime than under German servitude. Most frequent among such group appeals were leaflets to peasants, a logical target, considering the composition of the population in partisan-threatened areas. While the salutation, "Kolkhoz workers," recurs from beginning to end, during the period of appeasement of the population (late 1941—late 1943) leaflets frequently appealed to "peasants," a term generally avoided in Soviet parlance after the early thirties.[87] In contents, appeals to the peasantry differed little from other leaflets, except for their frequent emphasis on agrarian problems, a subject sometimes avoided in leaflets aimed primarily at the urban population.

Only a few leaflets aimed specifically at the intelligentsia. Where such appeals occurred they illustrated better than any others the ability of the particular authors to adapt style and content to the target group. For instance, a leaflet dated October 1942 and addressed "to the intelligentsia of the temporarily occupied rayons of Leningrad Oblast" showed considerable sophistication. Quoting one of Rauschning's books as well as *Mein Kampf,* it stressed the "unique upsurge in science, arts, and literature" under the Soviet regime, with which it contrasted the German destruction of objects of art, museums, and academies. By contrast with German plunder, "Soviet man has obtained unique opportunities for deploying his creative forces. The right to work, the right to leisure, and the right to education, the right to old-age assistance and help for invalids have become inalienable rights of every Soviet man." The purpose of the leaflet was thus to create a feeling of nostalgia among the insecure and largely unemployed intelligentsia in the German-held areas.

Some partisan leaflets appealed specifically to "women," or "Mothers, Wives, and Sisters," playing on their equality in Soviet society, or on the fate of their male kin. Most frequently, leaflets addressed to women contained specific instructions rather than ideological themes, e.g., "Hide all the food from the Germans" or "Don't wash the Germans' laundry!" Numerically, a considerable number of appeals went to "youth." This happened, in part, because of the great need of both partisans and Ger-

---

[87] It is possible that at least some such instances reflected a more deep-seated readjustment, since a definite correlation exists between the use of the terms "peasant" and "Russian," and between "kolkhoznik" and "Soviet."

mans for young men as replacement forces and as laborers; in part, because of the special zeal exhibited by Komsomol groups in propagandizing the population. Moreover, a distinct feeling pervades some leaflets that the younger people were considered more "pure" and less likely to be contaminated by non-Soviet views.

Other target groups in 1941 included Red Army stragglers, who were exhorted to join the partisans; and in 1943–44 civilian evacuees, who were encouraged to defect, being promised that their sufferings would soon be over, and being forewarned of the cruel fate awaiting them in Germany if they followed the retreating troops.

Most partisan leaflets showed little content variation arising from their being addressed to different target groups. However, in a few instances (e.g., the appeal to the intelligentsia cited above, and a few of the leaflets to Ukrainian groups) they exhibited unusual flexibility and sophistication, perhaps thanks to the individual officers responsible for their production.

C. MEDIA

By means of oral and written propaganda and agitation, by publishing underground newspapers and numerous leaflets, by conducting thousands of meetings and lectures among the population, the Party and Komsomol organizations drew everyone capable of bearing arms into the sacred struggle with the usurpers.[88]

This is how the official Soviet version summarized the various media used in the partisan psychological warfare campaign. The emphasis on both the written and spoken word corresponds to the broad Soviet concept of "agitation." Sometimes, media were selected according to particular purposes; at other times, the choice of media was determined by the availability of one or the shortage of another. Finally, while the written media could be considered "official" Soviet propaganda, rumors were often utilized to disseminate unorthodox themes.

1. Oral

During the initial stage of the partisan movement, oral communication was virtually the only medium of appeal available to the guerrillas. In many cases, "propaganda" was restricted to individual conversations of pro-Communists with local residents, intended to recruit members or deter collaboration. This rudimentary propaganda was soon succeeded by a more highly developed form of "agitation" that included incitement to active sabotage, calls to disobey German orders, and denunciations of the occupation regime. Furthermore, persuasion occupied a major place in early psychological warfare efforts, particularly in drawing Red Army stragglers and displaced civilians into the partisan movement.

[88] Tsanava, II, 589.

At an early date, as the partisan bands coalesced, individual "talks" were superseded by meetings and "mass agitation." The Shmyrev band, for instance, which operated east of Vitebsk, was reported to have conducted twelve political meetings in July and August 1941. Other groups, moving from village to village in search of food, manpower, and shelter, organized discussions with local residents, communicating to them the "latest news" on the military situation (as they knew it or wished to pass it on), appealing for support, and where possible issuing orders. The "mass meeting" continued to be the outstanding oral form of partisan psychological warfare to the end of the occupation. It might have taken the form of any one of the following:

a. Lectures

Probably the most highly developed form of partisan agitation was the political rally held under the leadership of trained speakers. To this end, the larger bands provided "agitators" or "propagandists" who organized meetings in areas under partisan control. In 1942, for instance, one partisan brigade sent out twenty-three agitators who made speeches in fifteen communities on the topic: "The Defeat of the German Forces Before Moscow." Komsomol members of partisan units or local territorial organizations also specialized in this type of activity. The topics discussed at such meetings generally ranged from military developments (which were presented to cast a favorable light on Red Army or partisan activities) to German "atrocities" and "barbarism." The primary purpose of the lectures was, in addition to informing the local population about current events, to "encourage tenacity, discipline, and stamina" and to instill "a will to win."

The importance assigned to lectures or speeches within the context of partisan verbal propaganda may be judged by the fact that individual partisans who had mastered the art of public speaking were often detailed from regular combat duty to presenting lectures and conducting meetings. Nevertheless, the number of trained or effective speakers remained small, a handicap that limited the usefulness of this type of oral agitation.

b. Discussions

Closely related to lecture-rallies were the fairly formal "discussions" held with groups of local residents. Such meetings often served to spark definite action on one specific issue. In 1943, for instance, a partisan unit held meetings with peasants to discuss "Order No. 130 of the People's Commissariat for Defense"; other discussions centered on such problems as reaping the harvest. Often at the end of such discussions, resolutions were passed, presumably to formalize decisions and bind the participants to carry them out. Thus the discussions may be regarded as, among other things, apparent democratic processes used to disguise the transmission of specific partisan orders.[89]

c. Readings

Because of the shortage of trained lecturers or discussion-group speakers, meetings at which official pronouncements and news bulletins were read aloud by a partisan "reader" played an important part in oral psychological warfare. The partisan equivalent of the old town crier ranked below the "specialist-agitators" and lecturers. The material largely consisted of Soviet war communiqués and such texts as Stalin's wartime speeches. Two further reasons for the widespread use of the "reading" system apparently were the shortages of copies of news bulletins, and the partisan belief that public readings were more desirable than the distribution of printed appeals, because joining together in a group and watching, rather than reading, produced a greater emotional effect on the peasants.

d. Special Events

In addition to the gatherings outlined above, the partisans staged a variety of other meetings. The formal gatherings included celebrations of national holidays. Speeches, music, and sometimes parades marked May Day celebrations in partisan-held areas. Occasionally, nonverbal devices were used; for instance, forty-five red flags were hoisted on the First of May 1942, with mines attached to them to blow up any Germans or collaborators trying to pull them down. Informal gatherings included village dancing, group singing, amateur shows, and plays. All of these served to glorify the partisan movement and evoke patriotic emotions. Legends of old partisan leaders were a favorite theme of partisan music. Another medium of partisan expression and propaganda was the traditional Russian ditty (*chastushki*), widely used to ridicule the Germans but also to poke fun at partisan life itself.[90]

The total of these various forms of verbal psychological warfare was impressive. Even if Soviet figures are exaggerated, they give some indication of the magnitude of partisan activities in this field. According to one source the partisans in one rayon had, in 1943, "4 propagandists [includ-

---

[89] A postwar memoir describes "group participation" in a meeting. Upon opening the discussion, the commander of a partisan unit thanked the peasants for their support and proceeded to describe recent victories of the Red Army and the partisans. Some of the peasants thereupon spoke out against the German robbers (the Soviet account relates) and expressed the people's gratitude for the help the partisans had given during harvesting. At the end of the meeting, a resolution was passed expressing confidence in the Red Army's ability to win under Stalin's leadership. As a result of the meeting, the Soviet author concludes, 20.5 tons of grain were delivered by peasants of four villages to the partisans.

[90] See, for instance, the examples in Andreyev, p. 214; Tsanava, I, 221–22; and the strange example in Document 16 of the Appendix to this book.

ing trained writers], 18 agitators [lecturers, speakers, discussion leaders], and 25 readers." According to another postwar account, Komsomol agitators in Vitebsk Oblast serviced 1,700 inhabited points and delivered a total of 14,000 lectures and readings during the occupation. The Kalinin Brigade is said to have conducted a total of 866 lectures; the Kotovsky Brigade, 500 meetings and some 1,000 readings, reaching a total of 10,000 people.

The obvious limitation of such oral propaganda was that it could be conducted only in areas that the partisans controlled. In German-held areas, other media had to be adopted, although on occasion the partisans used agents for the dissemination of rumors and slogans even there. [On rumors, see subsection E, below.] On the whole, however, oral communication in German-held areas was more widely employed by the urban undergrounds than by combat partisan bands, which rarely ventured into German-held areas except on combat or intelligence missions.

2. "Action Propaganda"

Mention should be made of what German antipartisan warfare called partisan *Tatpropaganda,* or propaganda by action or "living" evidence. The sum total of partisan behavior inevitably colored the response of the local residents to them. Occasionally it appears that specific modes of behavior were ordered by the partisan command in order to elicit a favorable popular reaction. Thus, according to German reports, some bands were said to have helped the peasants to dissolve the collective farms; in doing so, the partisans declared, "Kolkhozes may not exist after the war, but the Soviet power remains." This type of "action propaganda" was definitely aimed at winning popular support.

In a less spectacular manner, partisan psychological warfare "actions" included helping the peasants with sowing and harvesting; distributing to the population food or supplies captured from the Germans; and repairing churches and shrines, reopening Belorussian schools, and establishing soccer fields—these facts being reported toward the end of the occupation—in an area south of the Baranoviche-Bobruisk highway.

The impact of such "action propaganda" appears to have been considerable. While it was often offset by other, less pleasant, contacts with the partisans, nevertheless it had a good effect, in part because of the contrast with German behavior; news (and often exaggerated rumors) of such partisan actions spread quickly and served to embarrass the German propaganda machine.

3. Printed Media

The production and dissemination of printed media entailed considerable technical difficulties for the partisans [see also above, Sect. I, B] and required a number of trained specialists and technicians. The written word, more than the oral appeal, needed to be carefully chosen as a permanent and more official record of Soviet policy, and hence required greater policy guidance from the Soviet side.

The leaflet was the most widespread and the most important medium of partisan written propaganda. In addition, "straight" news reports, such as war communiqués and speeches, were often disseminated in leaflet form. Distribution took place inside and outside partisan-held areas; in German-controlled towns and villages, leaflets could be left in public places, such as markets or inns, as well as in private homes. Others were left with Germans and collaborators, or even carried to their billets and strongpoints.

Handwritten and printed posters were also employed; these generally contained brief slogans, orders, warnings (such as threats to prospective *Ostarbeiter*), orders not to deliver grain to the Germans, partisan "induction" notices, and appeals to hold out until victory. Other posters were used to intimidate collaborators; thus, German reports speak of posters bearing the names of collaborators working for the Germans, and other posters enumerating collaborators liquidated by the partisans.

Another partisan medium designed specifically for collaborators was the personal, handwritten letter. Generally dispatched through messengers (or occasionally sent through regular postal channels), such letters were addressed to mayors, OD men, and other employees of the Germans, and contained threats of retribution, offers to defect, or orders for sabotage or intelligence assignments.

Compared with leaflet propaganda, partisan newspapers played a secondary role. However, the number of organs was considerable, in part because of a belief in the symbolic value of a rayon newspaper as a token of the re-establishment of Soviet control and orderly conditions. The newspapers were well suited to combine "factual" news of local and international interest (the latter when the editors had access to radio or Soviet news dispatches) with propaganda appeals, editorials, lists of newly decorated partisans and local residents, and articles of a more basic political nature. Moreover, the newspapers, though generally limited to two pages (one sheet), provided a medium for the dissemination of pictorial matter, caricatures, cartoons, and maps. The effectiveness of partisan humor, expressed in cartoons and songs, is frequently mentioned in Soviet postwar accounts. Other illustrative matter, especially in newsprint produced in the latter part of the war and brought in from the Soviet side to the partisans, included pictures of Lenin and Stalin, and occasionally photographs of targets blown up by the partisans, groups of German prisoners captured by the Red Army, or a town recaptured by the Soviet forces.

This account has not considered all the written media employed by the partisans. However, most other material—such as picture postcards, pamphlets, and books—was brought into the occupied area from the Soviet side of the front. As examples, one might point to the collection of Stalin's wartime speeches; a pamphlet of Molotov's diplomatic notes on German atrocities; and the volume, *Truth About Religion in Russia,* which was symbolic of the change of Soviet tactics toward the Orthodox Church during the war.

4. Theaters and Movies

Amateur theatrical performances were occasionally staged by partisan bands, both for their own entertainment and for the "enlightenment" of the local population. In the latter part of the war, when air contact with the Soviet side was regularized, movies were also used as a psychological warfare medium. There are reports from different sectors behind the Central front in 1943–44 which indicate the use of small movie projectors by the partisans; only one film, "The Fall of Stalingrad" is mentioned by name. By its very nature the use of cinematographic equipment was so difficult in partisan situations as to make the role of movies very minor.

5. Black and Gray Propaganda

The German documentation repeatedly refers to the use of Soviet "black" and "gray" propaganda behind the front. Actually, none of the available examples warrants the conclusion that it was disseminated by the partisans rather than by the Red Army or special agents. Moreover, no actual specimens have been located. There is evidence that the partisans used special devices to make the discovery of their propaganda more difficult. Thus an appeal to the Minsk population in the spring of 1944 appeared on a usual German-produced poster containing a German text and its Belorussian translation. While the German reproduced an authentic Nazi text, the Belorussian "translation" contained a partisan appeal. In this manner, it was intended that the Germans should not discover the real message of the poster until they were tipped off by some collaborator. At the same time, one may assume that the ingenuity of the technique appealed to the readers.

6. Effectiveness of Media

Both written and oral media had their limitations in partisan warfare; oral media could not be used extensively outside partisan-held areas, and printed materials were difficult to produce. Not unnaturally, printed material supplied from the outside (i.e., from the Soviet side) played a considerable role, especially in the second stage of the movement, when the partisans were still insecure and mobile but already had regular contact with the Army fronts.

Evidence on the relative effectiveness of different media is spotty and contradictory. There is some indication that the peasants were generally distrustful of print; it is reported that rumors and oral agitation were more readily believed. On the other hand, German propagandists reported consistently that oral claims and promises were by themselves inadequate to produce any marked effect on the population. The technique of supplementing oral media with printed materials, widespread in partisan propaganda during 1943 to 1944, may have arisen because the partisans realized that the combination was most effective. The written media, though less flexible than the oral, offered proof that partisans were active in the vicinity, and oral agitation reinforced or "explained" and supplemented printed information and slogans.

At the same time, the great hunger for news of any sort made the population comparatively receptive to any type of information, including unconfirmed rumors—a receptivity due in part to German failure to fill the vacuum left when the peacetime Soviet propaganda machine was destroyed. Consequently, within limits, all media may be judged as successful in furthering partisan psychological warfare aims.

D. PARTISAN LEAFLETS: CONTENTS

1. The Initial Period

In the first weeks of war, Soviet propaganda witnessed a survival of traditional Bolshevik and "Marxist" themes, concentrating on appeals to German "workers and peasants" and attempts to stimulate "anti-Hitlerite" revolts in the ranks of the Wehrmacht. This first brief stage, preceding the suppression of militant Communist slogans, was barely felt in partisan propaganda, both because it antedated the formation of most partisan units and because the units existing in June–July 1941 were absorbed in tasks other than the dissemination of Marxist orthodoxy. Nevertheless, leaflet propaganda spread by the Red Army to the population on occupied territory in July 1941 still bore the motto, "Proletarians of the World, Unite" —a slogan soon supplanted by the more universally appealing, "Death to the German Invaders!" which adorned virtually all partisan propaganda from December 1941 on.[91]

The partisans' own first appeals, rudimentary in technique and highly limited in distribution, concentrated on simple and brief statements—either declamatory (such as "The Red Army is Fighting for the Freedom of the People") or hortatory (such as "Rally for the Patriotic War!" or "Death to the German Robbers!"). From mid-July 1941 on, however, first Soviet-side and later partisan propaganda turned out a variety of new slogans em-

[91] Mekhlis, the Chief of the Main Political Administration of the Red Army, ordered this change to be made in all Red Army printed propaganda material, with the exception of certain appeals to the enemy. (AOK 17, Ic/AO, "Anweisung des Chefs der obersten politischen Verwaltung der R.A.," 10 December 1941, GMDS, AOK 17, 16719/18.)

bodying most of the themes that Soviet psychological warfare attempted to exploit.

The themes generally foreshadowed those used later in the war and are discussed at greater length below. There were strong efforts to identify people and regime in the popular mind, to arouse patriotism and willingness to fight. On the one hand, the appeal was made to Soviet citizens as "brothers and sisters"; on the other, German plans and intentions (real or fictitious) were widely cited to show that "the Fritzes want to make a colony of our country" or "the Prussian and Bavarian landlords are coming." As early as July 1941 such attempts were supplemented with specific references to German practice and examples of Nazi atrocities.[92] This approach was typified by the following excerpt from a leaflet of a small partisan otryad operating in Minsk Oblast in the late summer of 1941:

For the Belorussian people, 'the new order' means hunger and poverty, jail and gallows, thousands of our youths at forced labor. We have not forgotten how our brothers, prisoners of war, were burned and shot. We witnessed the death of Soviet captives in Minsk, Bobruisk, Slutsk, Baranoviche, and other towns. Before the eyes of the residents of Minsk 3,000 prisoners were cruelly killed in a single night. More than 5,000 prisoners were burned at Logoisky camp in Minsk because a few of them had contracted typhoid fever.[93]

The combination of slogans,

> The Germans intend to enslave you.
> They have begun to implement their program.
> The Red Army is fighting the Germans.
> The Fatherland and you are in danger.

dictated the conclusion offered by partisan leaflets:

> Hate the Germans and avenge their victims!
> Join the partisans!
> Help the partisans!
> Sabotage German efforts!

[92] So far as can be determined, many instances reported in partisan leaflets were correct, if not in detail at least in general tenor, though both the number of victims and some forms of cruelties (such as burning children alive) were apparently exaggerated for psychological warfare purposes. German violations of promises of decent treatment, and abuse and maltreatment of prisoners of war, received considerable attention. Partisan leaflets and newspapers also gave numerous examples of German requisitioning, looting, and confiscation.

[93] Tsanava, II, 223. In October 1941 when the Red Army captured a copy of the famous order of Field Marshal von Reichenau (commander of Sixth Army) which, with Hitler's approval, provided for ruthless annihilation of all actual or potential enemies, the destruction of objects of art and historical monuments whenever "necessary," and in effect sanctioned the starvation of the population, Soviet propaganda disseminated the text (in facsimile with a Russian translation) in the German-held areas. Likewise, echoing propaganda on the Soviet side of the front, the Molotov note of 25 November 1941 to all accredited diplomatic missions concerning German abuse of prisoners of war was distributed in leaflet form on German-held territory.

The themes of revenge, retribution, and hate, widely publicized on the Soviet side of the front, appeared in partisan propaganda as early as July 1941. Sometimes to the accompaniment of strongly worded exhortations, the partisans predicted the doom of the Germans.

> Let the ravens eat the eyes of the German scoundrels!
> There is only one answer: Death to the cannibals!
> They are sowing death, and they shall reap death!
> Instead of bread, give them bullets!

The methods to be used were suggested in simple fashion: "The only way out is to unite in partisan otryads and to help the partisans in every possible way. Everyone's duty is to defend, with arms in hand, the grain, the soil, and the independence of our fatherland." It was particularly this change from anti-German attitudes to anti-German actions that received emphasis and reiteration in partisan leaflets. One device was to establish in the reader's mind an identification of partisan and popular interests, and to depict the partisans (or, better yet, individuals among them) as glorious, unselfish heroes. At the same time, an identification of partisans and Red Army foreshadowed future victory, presumably because the palpable weakness of the partisans induced the civilian population to doubt their effectiveness. In these first months of the war, commands to withhold grain or other goods from the Germans, while present in Soviet appeals, were still subordinate to more general exhortations to oppose the Germans and join the partisans.[94]

[94] This amalgam is well shown in the following leaflet (whose text, although available only from a Soviet postwar source, tallies closely with themes and clusters of slogans found in records captured by the Germans):

The savage hordes of Fascist robbers have temporarily seized parts of our territories, are looting our goods, killing our fathers and sons, raping our wives, sisters, and daughters, destroying our houses.

The war has been on for almost seven weeks. On all fronts the glorious Red Army is offering the Fascist robbers increasing resistance.... The best German divisions have been crushed bodily. The Hitlerite plan of lightning warfare has failed.

The bulk of forces of the Red Army rises to destroy the German Fascists.

The mighty Soviet people has risen to defend the fatherland, to fight the Great Fatherland War.

The many thousands of heroic partisans have risen in the enemy's rear areas to help the Red Army. Their glory is spreading all over the country.

The partisans are the doom of the German usurpers. The *bogatyri* [knights of Russian antiquity] of the Soviet soil are giving the enemy no respite by day or night....

For their courage and heroism in fighting the German Fascists, Comrades Bumazhkov and Pavlovsky have been awarded the highest decoration of the country, the title of Heroes of the Soviet Union.

Dear comrades, workers, peasants, toiling intellectuals of Belorussia! At the call of the leader and friend of the Belorussian people, the Great Stalin, arise, like one man, for the holy Fatherland war against the German usurpers, robbers, and murderers! Arise to fight for your dear homeland, for your honor and for freedom! Sons and daughters of Belorussia, organize partisan otryads and groups everywhere

Several facets of this early propaganda campaign deserve notice. In addition to the frequent, intensive use of emotion-laden expletives, Soviet leaflets abounded in phrases which by reiteration acquired the characteristics of axioms—or so Soviet propaganda intended. Another facet is the reference to high authority; thus the Stalin speeches of 3 July and 7 November 1941 were disseminated perhaps more widely than any other single Soviet document of the war years; and special efforts were made to have nonpolitical individuals who were respected among the population contribute their all to the propaganda effort. In the Ukraine, the national poet Sosyura became head of the propaganda section of the partisan staff; in Belorussia, the well-known poet Yanka Kupala wrote short poems and prose appeals which were distributed by the partisans in leaflet and poster form. These efforts reflected the characteristic emphasis on the national past, traditions, and heroes, which were joined with specifically Soviet themes.

The curious combination, unusual in prewar Soviet domestic propaganda, of references to Stalin and the Soviet leadership along with non-Communists of name and prestige produced an ambiguity which Soviet propaganda was deliberately unwilling to resolve. At a moment of crisis, an appeal was to be made to nationalist as well as to pro-Soviet elements; patriotic Russian, Ukrainian, and Belorussian emotions were to be enlisted, even while the sense of an all-Soviet community—political, cultural, and multinational—was exploited to arouse a feeling of strength and devotion. This resort to national themes, apparent early in the war, was perhaps the most striking single new element in partisan propaganda; it corresponded fully to the introduction of the same element in propaganda addressed to the Red Army and the Soviet population.

Another aspect of early partisan propaganda also made some concession to popular feelings, and at the same time, strengthened the theme of prospective Soviet victory. This was the greater emphasis on the West. As early as July and August 1941, Soviet leaflets aimed at the occupied areas reproduced statements made in the United States press expressing the belief that eventually the Red Army would win.[95] Early in November 1941 a

---

behind the enemy lines; seize the enemy's arms and supplies; give no quarter in destroying the Fascist reptiles by day and night, in open combat or from 'round a corner! . . .

Avenge the tears and blood of our dear ones, the desecration of our soil, the outrage to our honor! Take revenge on the enemy, every day and every hour! Starve him, burn him, shoot him, kill him with a hammer! . . . Leave him no goods, not one kilogram of bread, nor one liter of fuel!

Comrades, the hour of reckoning has struck. [Muster] all the forces for the struggle with the enemy and his liquidation! Blood for blood, and death for death! . . . Forward to the utter defeat and destruction of the Fascist robbers! [Tsanava, I, 219–20.]

[95] See, for instance, a report on the Walter Duranty article in *The New York Times,* in *Vesti s sovetskoi rodiny,* 28 August 1941.

partisan lecturer told a group of peasants that the effects of British and American help would "soon" be felt at the Eastern front. Early in 1942 the Main Political Administration of the Red Army widely disseminated to the population in German-held territory a leaflet form of a speech delivered by Averell Harriman after his return from Moscow. Pursuing the same end of attracting the elements not fully wedded to the Bolshevik cause, the leaflet reproduced a statement by Harriman containing an unmistakable implication for the population in the occupied areas: "We Americans don't want communism in our country—[but] I think that most Americans now clearly see that help to Russia in her struggle against the Nazi invasion does not in any respect change our attitude toward communism."[96]

This was the essence of Soviet propaganda: to persuade those elements who had doubts about the Communist cause. As a partisan leaflet frankly put it later in the war, the only alternatives were to fight on the Soviet side or to fight against it: "There is no third way."[97] In line with the old Leninist dictum, "He who is not with us, is against us," the partisans' major effort was to polarize public opinion, to arouse the masses from inertia and tacit acceptance of German rule, and to demonstrate that there was no other course than to fight actively either with or against the Germans. The futility of any third course, hinted at in the leaflets, was even more clearly discernible in word-of-mouth propaganda.

Early partisan and Soviet propaganda addressed to the population behind the German lines thus closely corresponded to Red Army and Soviet-side propaganda. No significant thematic distinctions can be drawn at this time between Soviet-to-population and partisan-to-population psychological warfare, except with regard to agriculture (discussed below) and with regard to the citing of local events such as German atrocities, a device which appears to have aided the effectiveness of partisan propaganda. As yet there were few appeals to collaborators to desert to the partisans, largely because of partisan weakness and the difficulty of reaching military collaborators, who were themselves still few in numbers. Though threats were used to deter the people from collaborating, this technique was still decidedly subordinate to others, except in those areas where the partisans had gained a solid foothold. At this stage, the Soviet political machine was apparently aware of partisan weakness and felt that threats were likely either to push the civilian population into the enemy camp or to remain empty words because Soviet and partisan organs were unable to enforce them.

Strikingly enough, virtually all themes later employed in partisan propa-

[96] *K sovetskomu naseleniyu okkupirovanykh nemtsami oblastei,* n.d. (GMDS, PzAOK 4, 22457/61, Anlage 40).
[97] Sheverdalkin, p. 244.

ganda were apparent in the first six months of the war. After a brief period of uncertainty, a firm line on all major issues was evidently established and kept. As will be shown, only certain German measures, as in agriculture, religion, and military collaboration, wrought some confusion and awkwardness in Soviet counterpropaganda. Thus the factors that distinguish the later stages of partisan propaganda from the early months amount largely to: (1) technical superiority of propaganda media; (2) some greater subtlety in contents, though this is not striking; (3) greater use of persuasive examples and factual details on German and partisan activities; (4) better coverage and more thorough penetration of the occupied area with propaganda.

In the first months of the war partisan propaganda played a distinctly secondary role. If it became a more impressive tool later on, this change was due largely to technical improvements and factors unrelated to partisan psychological warfare. Indeed, probably the change in popular attitudes, above all, created a climate of opinion that made the citizen more receptive to partisan appeals later on. German "errors," both intentional (such as forced labor, liquidations, and failure to satisfy the peasantry) and unintentional (such as the day-to-day behavior of German personnel), contributed mightily to the change of political atmosphere that distinguishes the later part of the campaign from the first months.

In this respect, partisan propaganda was successful in a manner which could not have been predicted by the Soviet regime. As is perhaps true of psychological warfare generally, it failed when the partisans were weakest and succeeded when the population was, for other reasons, inclined to proffer its support. Effectiveness was determined in large measure by factors over which neither partisans nor the Soviet regime had control, i.e., German policy and behavior.

Curiously enough, however, partisan themes even in the summer of 1941 anticipated many of the German "errors." What was then propaganda later became reality. Thus partisan psychological warfare scored its successes in considerable measure because German behavior, obligingly but unwittingly, complied with the clichés which the Soviet propaganda machine had posited in advance. From 1942 on, the line between "propaganda" and "facts" was so blurred that the wildest claims could be regarded as within the realm of the possible.

2. 1942–44

a. Identification Propaganda

(1) TRADITIONAL.—Certain appeals and information striving to make the Soviet population identify itself with its government and armed forces, and aiming at their glorification, amounted in essence to a more intense utilization of themes and devices employed in prewar days. Briefly, these included emphasis on the community of Soviet peoples; a *sui generis* Soviet

patriotism (as distinguished from Russian or other nationalism); pride in the accomplishments of the Soviet era, ranging from "liberation from the exploitation of man by man" to industrialization and cultural progress; glorification of the wisdom and infallibility of the Soviet leadership; efforts to have the Communist Party recognized as the vanguard of society. All these elements were also to be found in wartime propaganda.

The striking phenomenon, however, is the slurring over of themes specifically Soviet (in the political sense) and Communist in content. "Soviet" is used overwhelmingly as a collective term to identify the regime and people, not as a term laden with values or emotions. Thus "Soviet soil" or "Soviet government" appear in neutral connotations. Likewise, the use of such adjectives as "Red" appears to have been devoid of urgently political content; the hoisting of a red flag by the partisans, naming an otryad "Red Star," or labeling its newspaper "The Red Partisan" were scarcely means of asserting communism, but were rather making use of terms which had become fully ingrained in Soviet everyday life. Only slightly more significant in terms of Party content was the emphasis on Soviet holidays. The anniversary of Lenin's death (January 21); May Day; International Women's Day; and the anniversary of the October Revolution usually provided occasions for lectures, operations, the issue or reprinting of slogans, and at times for demonstrations and parades, but these were occasions of national rather than political celebration.

Even though references to Stalin continued, they dealt largely with his position as head of the government or of the armed forces, not as the symbol of bolshevism. His picture appeared in various partisan newspapers; his speeches were widely circulated; and his orders were reproduced. Within limits, the same was true of other Soviet leaders such as Molotov and Zhdanov.

Only from the end of 1943 on, when the Soviet command was aware of the new tide of popular support and military predominance, did "Party" and "Bolshevik leader" themes begin to reappear. Thus, in January 1944, partisan leaflets again spoke of the glorious life charted by the great Lenin and "the GREAT GENIUS of mankind, STALIN"; the Soviet theme once again prevailed over the narrower national one, and Komsomol and Communist Party received greater attention.

However, at no time was there any indication in *printed* propaganda of abandoning communism. Partisan units and publications continued to bear the names of Soviet and Communist leaders; the slogan, "Under the banner of Lenin and Stalin," while decidedly secondary to the ubiquitous "Death to the German Occupiers!" never entirely disappeared.

One may well assume that the measure of ambiguity which partisan (like Soviet) propaganda maintained in this field reflected a conscious effort to appeal to non-Bolshevik elements of the population without antagonizing devoted Communists and Komsomol members or admitting former mistakes or failures. This ambiguity was most apparent in the use of the terms "Fatherland," "Patriotism," and "People" (in the sense of nation). The frequent use of slogans like "For the Fatherland *(Za rodinu)*" and "the holy Fatherland War" strongly suggest a digression from the traditional approach, but by implication only. On the surface they continued the trend, already apparent from the late nineteen-thirties, of sanctioning and even playing up "Soviet patriotism."

(2) New Concessions

(a) Nationalism.—Much more pronounced than the traditional references to Soviet patriotism, communism, and Bolshevik leadership was the new, and in its impact crucial, resort to themes of Russian nationalism. Abandoning the ambiguity of Soviet-patriotic vs. Russian-national themes, the policy-makers permitted the dichotomy suddenly to widen, and (judging from virtually all partisan, German, and refugee reports) it was the national theme that proved to have the greatest appeal.[98] At a moment when large segments of the Soviet population were found to be wanting in determination and will to fight to the finish, and when considerable numbers were collaborating with or surrendering to the enemy, the previously diffuse "Soviet patriotism" was extended and crystallized to include "love for the Fatherland," "Mother Russia," "national liberation," and similar concepts. The subsequent effectiveness of these slogans throws an interesting light on the failure of the Soviets to "forge a new man" and of the Germans to pose as the defenders of Russian national interests. Often the distinction between Soviet and Russian (or Ukrainian or Belorussian) patriotism was not clearly drawn—intentionally, one may assume, so as to leave an impression of their identity in the reader's mind.

In the new hierarchy of themes, as they appeared in the occupied areas, the political-ideological elements were usually subordinate to the traditional-national. A typical order of slogans was "For Fatherland, for honor, for freedom, and for Stalin!" Introduced early in the war, the appeal to Russian national emotions and traditions flourished especially in 1942–43. "You are soiling the honor and dignity of the Russian [not

---

[98] In this context it is irrelevant to estimate the extent to which the reintroduction of national themes reflected a genuine evolution in the Soviet regime. The clear-cut changes in propaganda themes indicate that, whatever the motivation and rationales of the leaders themselves, the use of national appeals could be turned on and off at will. The effectiveness of the slogans was of course in no sense restricted to the occupied areas and the Red Army. Even in the West the belief that "Stalin has abandoned communism" and "Russia is again conducting a national policy" was widespread. See Nicholas S. Timasheff, *The Great Retreat* (New York: Dutton, 1946). For a stimulating discussion of the Russian national element, see Frederick C. Barghoorn, "Stalin and the Russian Cultural Heritage," *Review of Politics,* XIV, 4 (April 1952), 178–203.

Soviet] people!" a partisan leaflet accused collaborators. "Our Russian people were never traitors and will never betray their Fatherland," proclaimed another. Special leaflets and pamphlets glorified the accomplishments of national heroes, from Suvorov to the partisans of 1812 who, like Denis Davydov, fought against the foreign invader. Commenting on German destruction of cultural centers and objects of art, a partisan leaflet proclaimed:

But you cannot destroy the culture or the people who gave humanity such men as Pushkin, Tolstoy, Gorky, Pavlov, Mechnikov, Michurin, and Tsiolkovsky. Seven hundred years ago Alexander Nevsky crushed the ancestors of the Hitlerite bands; a hundred and eighty-two years ago Russian troops entered Berlin, crushing the equally "invincible" armies of Frederick II. The Russian people destroyed the army of Napoleon, who dreamt of putting down Russia. In 1918 the young Red Army crushed the Germans at Narva and Pskov. The defeat of the Hitlerites is inescapable now that the Soviet people in their righteous wrath have risen.[99]

In a possible overstatement, German summaries noted as late as October 1943 that partisan propaganda to the population "stressed the struggle for the Fatherland out of national idealism; not a word any more about the Soviet system." The German propaganda machine admitted that it had little with which to counteract Soviet appeals to Russian nationalism. "This nationalist propaganda," another German summary concluded, "is probably the most dangerous weapon we have encountered, for it aims at uniting the Russians without regard to political persuasion, and at kindling the fires of popular revolt."

Unspecified in terms of social groups or ideology, nationalism was the greatest common denominator and perhaps the most effective theme adopted by partisan propaganda during the war.

(b) Non-Russian Nationalism.—Special reference must be made to nationalism in non-Russian areas. While the term "Russia" was widely (and apparently not unsuccessfully) employed even outside Great Russia, Belorussia and the Ukraine called for somewhat different tactics, to counteract German propaganda catering to separatist, "anti-Muscovite" sentiments of the indigenous ethnic groups, and to win over these groups to a new consciousness of Russian nationalism. In substance, these efforts were far less straightforward and more awkward. The difficulty consisted in arousing nationalism without fostering anti-Russian, anti-Soviet, or separatist tendencies. The result was (1) silence on the national question in most partisan appeals, even outside the RSFSR; (2) denunciation of German goals as plans for colonizing and enslaving the Ukraine and Belorussia—from which only partisan warfare in alliance with the Red Army could bring salvation; (3) denunciation of anti-Soviet nationalist partisan groups in the Ukraine as German stooges, provocateurs, and criminal terrorists.

[99] Sheverdalkin, p. 36.

At the same time, Soviet partisan psychological warfare could safely eulogize Ukrainian heroes such as Bohdan Khmelnitsky and Taras Shchevchenko, or invoke the prestige of contemporary Belorussian figures such as Kolas or Kupala. Leaflets appealed to "Belorussians, brothers and sisters!" and insisted above all that only under Soviet rule had the non-Russian nationalities obtained "independence" (as union republics) and an opportunity freely and fully to develop their cultural and linguistic distinctiveness. Occasionally this catering to nationalist sentiments went so far as to declare that "only through partisan warfare against the German-Fascist conquerors [can] a free and independent Belorussia [be won]."

Appeals to national groups made more concessions to them than had been usual in prewar propaganda. In this national field, too, partisan slogans generally paralleled Soviet-side developments in propaganda, though it is important to remember that the partisans operated primarily in areas where non-Russian nationalist sentiments were weak.[100] At the same time, there were obvious limits to the Soviet "concessions" policy; there could be no compromise with the nationalist bands (regardless of their popularity or unpopularity). Soviet denunciations of them were intense; and positive exploitation of assumed nationalist sentiments was limited to such techniques as transmitting appeals from prominent Soviet Ukrainians evacuated to Moscow and Ufa, using historical precedents involving prominent Ukrainian and Belorussian anti-German or pro-Russian "fighters for liberation," and stressing the ethnic background of some of the prominent present-day partisan leaders.[101]

The Baltic States presented a special case, where no appeal to common traditions with Russia or the Soviet Union could be effective. The Soviet occupation had been too brief, its effect too negative, and communism too unpopular to be used widely in propaganda. Since here nationalist and anti-Russian feelings predominated, as they did not in the Ukraine and Belorussia, Soviet propaganda refrained from attacking them; on the contrary, it sought to outdo them by insisting that only the Red Army could bring the Baltic nationalities genuine freedom. In substance, it sought to revive a tactic which Comintern and Soviet foreign policy had repeatedly adopted in the past: at a moment of weakness, to strive for a coalition with the weaker middle groups against the major foe. All the "bourgeois" and "nationalist" elements, except those actually collaborating with the

[100] This is true, of course, of the areas of the RSFSR which saw any partisan warfare and of most of Belorussia. In the Ukraine, nationalist sentiments were at their strongest in many areas where there were no Soviet partisans. (See John A. Armstrong, *Urkrainian Nationalism* [New York: Columbia University Press, 1963]. For an exception, see this book, Chap. X, Sect. III.)

[101] A special case obtained in the Baltic States (to be discussed in the following paragraphs) and in the newly annexed areas of Belorussia and, to some extent, the Western Ukraine, where "anti-Fascist committees" were established. See Sect. VI, F.

Germans, were eligible for this sort of popular front. Thus the Presidium of the Latvian Supreme Soviet and the Central Committee of the Latvian Communist Party appealed in a leaflet:

Fight for Latvia's soil, which for centuries has been stained by the sweat and blood of the Latvian people and which time and again German landowners have sought to steal. The Latvian soil belongs, and will belong, to the Latvian people and the Latvian peasants alone. Fight for the preservation of the people's property and struggle for our Latvian culture! . . .

. . . To all citizens of Latvia! The portentous moment has come when all the forces of the people must be pooled. Join the ranks of the active fighters against the German invaders, without distinction of rank or income![102]

In Estonia, Communist partisans and Soviet propaganda resorted to similar appeals. While mentioning the "Estonian Communist Party" and stressing its active role in the "struggle for liberation," leaflets played up Estonia's century-old struggle against the Germans and Teutons. As for the future (a German report summarized the leaflets), "Estonia's return to the Soviet Union would amount to the restitution of 'popular sovereignty' in the form of a Union Republic, whereas the Germans would attempt to Germanize the country."

The effectiveness of such tactics in the Baltic area and the Ukraine cannot be adequately assessed. Elsewhere, the Russian national theme along with the all-Russian (or all-Soviet) one was, however, a clear success; it made converts and antagonized none of the possible supporters of the partisan movement. Equally significant was the fact that no obvious hiatus developed between partisan themes and Soviet-side themes on the national question, nor between propaganda and practice. All reports on "national" reforms in Russia, such as the symbolic reinstitution of officers' epaulettes, the dissolution of the Comintern, and the use of names such as Kutuzov and Suvorov as military symbols, tended to lend credence to partisan claims in this field, an asset which German propaganda could not match.

Some slight use was made of pan-Slav themes in partisan propaganda. They appeared more prominently in media produced on the Soviet side— perhaps an indication that this approach was not a natural one to the partisans. Soviet-side exploitation of them, as shown in leaflets to the occupied areas as early as August 1941, dovetailed with political efforts initiated promptly after the German attack. They were used by the partisans particularly to appeal to Slavic troops fighting on the German side; and in Soviet-produced leaflets in two other connections: the pro-Soviet declarations of Czech and Yugoslav prisoners of war in the Soviet Union, disseminated by the Main Political Administration of the Red Army among the population in the German-held areas; and the frequent refer-

[102] Leaflet, no title, undated (GMDS, EAP 99/54).

ences to the rise of partisan warfare among fellow-Slavs, particularly in Serbia. Pan-Slav themes likewise recur in the official Soviet slogans on the occasion of such holidays as the Twenty-fifth Anniversary of the October Revolution; these slogans were distributed in the German-held areas, too. The result of such efforts appears to have been largely to create a feeling of wider community and support, stressing that the Soviet people did not stand alone but had friends and admirers abroad. Mention should be made of the use of this theme in counterpropaganda against the Germans, when the partisans made effective use of the German concept of "Slavic subhumans" to forge a counterconcept of the community of Slavic peoples struggling against the invaders.

(c) Religion.—A more significant and substantial government concession to popular aspirations—and in part, an effort to neutralize German tolerance in this field as well as an acknowledgement of American hints on the desirability of relaxing antireligious activities—was the change in Soviet attitude toward the Orthodox Church. Largely a matter of psychological warfare in the broadest sense, the concessions in this domain were a logical, albeit surprising, reversal of earlier tactics. They were sufficiently important, too, in terms of the response elicited from the population in the German-held "East," to cause the Germans concern and to induce them to sponsor various (abortive) countermeasures.

The partisan cadres, generally Communist and younger than the rank and file of the population, were themselves apparently not particularly susceptible to religious influences. At the same time, their actions reflected an awareness of the faith which existed among a sizeable segment of the population, largely consisting of older persons and women.

The first partisan written efforts in this field appeared in the spring of 1942. By then Soviet leaflets dropped over the occupied areas were disseminating information indicating the "mobilization" of the Orthodox Church in rallying the population of the Soviet Union, including pastoral letters and appeals by high church dignitaries. Most of the partisan propaganda consisted of references to religious activities in the unoccupied areas. Such references occur repeatedly in the latter half of 1942, but even more frequently in connection with the elevation of the Metropolitan of Moscow to the Patriarchate in the summer of 1943. As for the occupied areas, the partisans hardly mentioned the church problem there, except to counter German propaganda. In particular, they sought to give examples of desecration of churches and German abuse of the clergy. The theme here (as exemplified in a partisan leaflet in November 1943) was: "The German scoundrels yell at every street corner that they are the defenders of faith and religion. Nice defenders who destroy churches and abuse the priests! No, robbers will be robbers!"

Such awkward and somewhat negative propaganda was made even more

difficult because a considerable number of the clergy collaborated with
the Germans. Hence there were instances where the partisans, too, treated
the clergy as "traitors," to the point of killing them and burning their
homes. A broadcast to the partisans intercepted by the Germans included
the following directive in July 1942: "Traitors are to be watched and if
possible liquidated. Death to the traitors! This includes the priests who
have made a pact with the new heathens serving the Germans—the same
Germans who killed clergy in Lvov with bayonets, who suppress freedom
of conscience, and who have destroyed and desecrated the churches of
Belorussia!"

Partisan "prochurch" psychological warfare, in line with Soviet efforts,
was concentrated largely on nonverbal operations: "action propaganda"
rather than leaflets. In numerous instances, the Germans reported that
the partisans, regardless of their personal religious convictions (which
were usually lukewarm at best), sanctioned or even encouraged the opening of churches in areas under their control, in a transparent but nonetheless successful effort at ingratiating themselves with the local peasantry.
In some instances they themselves attended church services. Interesting
and typical in this connection are the following excerpts from a report by
Exarch Sergius, the Soviet-appointed Metropolitan of the Baltic States,
who retained his position under the Germans until his assassination in the
spring of 1944. After a tour of the adjacent old-Soviet areas and on the
basis of various reports from his subordinates, he wrote in March 1943:

> The partisans are conducting clever propaganda to win the sympathy of the
> population. This propaganda appears to be centrally directed. It assumes that
> the people are religious and takes this as a fact to which one must adjust.
> Therefore it avoids everything that may insult religious feelings. Priests and
> churches are not being attacked; services are not molested, though this would
> be easy for the partisans to do. . . . The partisans seek to persuade the peasants
> that Soviet church policy has changed radically; the struggle against the church,
> it is claimed, was an error pregnant with consequences, and this is now being
> admitted by the Soviet Government. [In one case] the partisans simply or-
> dered the peasants to attend church; the priest was told that the partisans had
> addressed the peasants more or less in this manner: "Why don't you go to
> church? The priest has come on your account to conduct the services. . . . Re-
> ligion is now free in Russia. The war has changed many things for the better.
> We [partisans] now have no time for churchgoing; we have urgent things to do.
> But all of you, young and old, go to church, and do not forget to pray for
> Russia."[103]

It is indicative of both the flexibility of partisan propaganda and its subordination to Soviet themes that its Communist leaders readily switched
their traditional outlook on the church. At the same time, the awkwardness of some partisan propaganda and the preference of dealing with this

[103] Orthodoxe Kirche, Metropolit von Litauen [etc.], "Verhalten der Partisanen
gegenueber der Kirche," 19 March 1943 (GMDS, EAP 99/54).

matter in other than printed media reflected the novelty of the problem and the extent to which the partisans viewed it as somewhat unorthodox.

(d) Agriculture.—In the fields of nationalism and religion, partisan psychological warfare roughly paralleled efforts aimed at the Soviet population east of the front lines; in agriculture, however, a distinct difference between partisan and Soviet-side themes is apparent. [See also below, Sect. VI, L.]

From the first period of partisan activity to the institution of the German agrarian reform, i.e., from about October 1941 to February 1942, partisan propaganda dealing with agriculture was limited largely to word-of-mouth media. To capitalize on German behavior and procrastination, the partisans in some areas pretended to share popular aspirations to terminate the collective farm system and reproached the Germans for their failure to implement a reform. Their themes in this period may be summarized as follows: (1) The Germans do not intend to give the Soviet peasantry land and freedom. (2) The Germans are bringing back the despised landlords and kulaks. (3) The Germans want our land for themselves. (4) The Germans are not keeping their promises to give the peasants land. (5) There are no free peasants in Germany, either. (6) The Soviet government and the partisans are not fighting for the preservation of the collective farm system; on the contrary, collectives are already being dissolved (or will be dissolved) with the consent of the Soviet regime.

While some of the themes, especially (2), (3), and (5), occasionally appeared in leaflet form, reports of changes under the Soviet appeared only in the form of rumors or occasional oral addresses. [See the discussion of partisan rumors in subsection E, below.]

The German agrarian reform of February 1942 momentarily stunned Soviet psychological warfare. German reports for February and March note a complete absence of partisan reactions to it, and no partisan or Soviet counterleaflets have been found for the two months following its announcement. It may therefore be assumed that the subject was considered to be so important that a policy decision in Moscow was required. Given the limited nature of the reform, however, and the delays in implementing even the small substantive changes in the kolkhoz system pledged in the German decree, the partisans by May 1942 had a good opening for effective counterpropaganda. Indeed, there is every indication that German failure to satisfy popular aspirations in this area contributed substantially to the psychological divorce between conqueror and peasant.[104]

---

[104] For a discussion of the agrarian reform, probably exaggerating its significance and scope, see Karl Brandt, *Management of Agriculture and Food in the German-Occupied and Other Areas of Fortress Europe* (Stanford: Stanford University Press, 1953), pp. 3–152.

Soviet and particularly partisan propaganda faced a dilemma, nevertheless, in countering German propaganda. It could either (1) defend the collective farm system as a major accomplishment, contrasting it with the deterioration of conditions under the Germans as the only alternative; or (2) blame the Germans for maintaining the collectives against the peasants' will, and thus identify the partisans with the aspirations of the rank and file. In substance, Soviet propaganda attempted both, naturally concentrating on the former in printed appeals but also using the latter in verbal media and, to some limited extent, in actual practice in areas under partisan control. Some themes could successfully be employed for both purposes: (1) The Germans are out to restore large landed estates. (2) The Germans are in effect re-establishing serfdom. (3) The peasant is worse off under the Germans than ever before.

Propaganda could likewise insist that German concessions, meaningless as they were, were not at all a measure of German long-range intentions but rather the reflection of Soviet victories at the front and a sign of German weakness. Citing captured German records, Soviet leaflets insisted that, later on, the Germans would tighten the vise even further. Finally, they could argue that from the summer of 1942 on, the Germans were not even carrying out the reform they themselves had promised; thus, regardless of one's estimation of the reform, action showed that German promises and pledges were empty and were broken at will.

Partisan leaflets on agriculture were almost exclusively devoted to countering the effect of German measures. From mid-1942 on, they appeared sporadically, though their numerical dearth in the over-all total of leaflets may indicate that the subject matter offered greater difficulty and the approach was less rewarding than others, to which more attention was paid. Bearing in mind the difference between Soviet oral pronouncements and their actual efforts, we can trace in the following extracts from partisan leaflets the line "officially" adopted—and pursued with some vigor only in the middle of 1942, but dropped almost entirely from 1943 on:

Why have the Fascists introduced this regulation? To make it easier for them to rob you. As soon as the harvest is in, it will be immediately taken away from you and sent to Germany. . . . The Fascists will act according to the following principle: "The work is yours, the product ours." . . . The German robbers want to distribute the land of your kolkhozes not among you, but among the German landowners and holders of large estates.—*Appendix, Document 46.*

The official policy was evidently promulgated in a small brochure published by the Soviet or partisan command in May 1942; its authorship cannot be established, but it must have originated on the Soviet side of the front, though the text was reprinted and the same formulations were later employed by the partisans themselves. Under the title, "The Latest Provocation of the Fascist Robbers: Why the Hitlerites are Conducting a Land Reform," it declared: "The Germans are afraid overtly and forcibly to chase the Russian peasants from their land. They dare not openly tell of their goals: this would anger and arouse the people." The Germans, the pamphlet asserted, wished to abolish the collectives so that the peasantry, now welded into a community, would fall apart and become easy prey for the invader. The brochure was somewhat hard pressed to show why a commune was in principle worse than a collective, except that the tsars had always maintained the commune, and the result was abomination. It went to great lengths to dismiss German promises of private plots as a fake, thus tacitly admitting the effectiveness of the German appeal: "In reality, the Germans have no intention of dividing the land among the Russian peasants." Retracing in detail the reasons why collective sowing, tillage, and feeding under the Soviet system had the advantages of orderliness, mechanization, and rational use, the appeal concluded: "Peasants, don't fall for this ruse; sabotage the German land reform!"

Another leaflet, also in the summer of 1942, sought to combine peasant attachment to the land with patriotism and devotion to Soviet ideals, producing an amalgam of which the following excerpts are typical:

The soil! The word has survived thousands of years. The peasant remembers the feuds over the repartition of strips; he remembers the difficult days of serfdom when the landlords seized the best land. Those were hard years. But even then the land was the dearest thing to the peasant; he always called it the mother-provider. Never was the land so dear and close to the peasantry as after the Great October Revolution. The Soviet power turned over to the peasants 150 million hectares of land. The fields and meadows were given forever to the free use of the kolkhoz peasantry. The happy peasant would go out of the village and scan the yellow fields and say: "All this is mine; all this is ours." . . . Now the Germans have taken the land from the peasants. Like hungry insects they raid our dear fields. All sorts of scoundrels, specially trained in Fascist brothels, have appeared. . . . In order to cover up their pillage, the Hitlerite clique has worked out a so-called new agrarian order. What noise they have made over it! The Fascist propagandists say at every corner, "The land to the peasants!" This is a brazen lie. . . . Peasants, the land will not be yours until the Germans are chased from our fatherland.

Certainly these themes dealt fairly cleverly with the difficulties inherent in Soviet methods of solving the agrarian problem. They sought, in substance, to submerge it in the larger issues of German intentions and practices; to erase the distinction between private and collective land ownership ("All this is mine, all this is ours") in the peasant's mind; and to exploit peasant attachment to the soil, without acknowledging the unpopularity of past Soviet practices. Whatever concessions of a more substantial nature were promised by the partisans were restricted to oral media.

(3) SOVIET STRENGTH.—With relatively little sophistication, a number of partisan leaflets glowingly described various manifestations of Soviet strength in an obvious effort to instill fear in the recalcitrant, give hope to the loyal but suppressed, and provide a stimulus for action to those desiring to be on the side of the victors. The following brief summary of the major themes is no index to the attention the partisan command paid to the subject, the importance of which can scarcely be overstressed.

(a) *Soviet victories.*—Though, at a moment of severe setbacks at the front, the theme was launched, "The Fatherland is in danger—defend the Fatherland!" the call to steadfastness in the face of adversity and defeat was rapidly abandoned. From about October 1941 on, the theme of Soviet victories and German defeats never disappeared from partisan reports.[105] It recurred with greater frequency than any other single "factual" theme, perhaps even more often in Soviet-produced than in partisan leaflets. In addition to broad generalities about Soviet advances, much of this propaganda centered on individual victories. The battle for Moscow in December 1941, for instance, provided a subject for extensive exploitation; Soviet directives specifically ordered discussion of this event in partisan propaganda, and numerous leaflets were geared to it. Likewise, the victory at Stalingrad a year later was widely heralded in partisan leaflets and newspapers. Finally, in the summer of 1943 and again in the summer of 1944 Soviet advances were given detailed attention.

Frequently the accompanying reports gave "statistical" information on the number of enemy soldiers killed, wounded, or captured; the number of tanks, trucks, or planes destroyed; the number of villages or rayons liberated. German casualties were exaggerated without particular scruples (for instance, it was alleged that 6,000 German planes had been destroyed by mid-August 1941), but such exaggeration seems to have become less prominent in the latter part of the war. It seems to have been calculated to (1) destroy the myth of German invincibility, (2) instill hope

---

[105] There was no real exception to this rule, even when, in July 1942, after a series of Soviet reverses in the south, Stalin issued an order impressing on his troops the fact that the recent German successes represented a grave danger to the Soviet Union and that further loss of territory must be prevented at all costs. This order (No. 227) was widely used in the political indoctrination of all combat troops and led to the formation of so-called blocking units to prevent further withdrawals—by force if necessary. At the same time the order contradicted prevailing partisan propaganda, which from the winter of 1941 to 1942 and thereafter insisted that the Red Army was about to reoccupy the territories "temporarily lost to the enemy." So far as is known Order No. 227 was never brought to the attention of the rank-and-file partisans —not only because they could not have retreated anyway, but also because of the impression it might have made on the civilian population and the collaborators. That a real danger of a German victory still existed in 1942 would have been a rash admission for the Soviet authorities to make, when they were still trying to keep or regain the loyalty of the population in the occupied areas.

of "liberation" in those elements who preferred Soviet rule, and (3) arouse fear of Soviet retribution among those who chose to side with the Germans. In substance, it provided a rational basis for partisan activity, which in the initial "shock treatment" about German successes had appeared as perhaps heroic but hardly destined to succeed. Much more reliable were the indications in printed media of the geographic progress of the Red Army, though oral partisan propaganda was frequently inclined to place Soviet troops much farther west than they actually were.

(b) War Communiqués and "Objective" News.—A special category of reports consisted of "factual" and unannotated reproductions of the war communiqués by the Sovinformburo, either printed as leaflets by the Red Army, or printed and distributed by the partisans on the basis of Soviet broadcasts. In particular, the daily *News from the Soviet Fatherland (Vesti s sovetskoi rodiny),* distributed to the population in the German-occupied areas, contained extensive excerpts from these bulletins. The dailies likewise carried other "factual" news, in particular about life in the unoccupied USSR, occasionally about international events, and other items—all selected to raise the morale of pro-Soviet elements, produce an impression of Soviet and Allied strength, and forecast German defeat.

Given the general thirst for information in the occupied territories and the interest in events at and behind the front, these formally "objective" statements, presented without appeals to action, were unquestionably received with avidity by the rank and file.

(c) Partisan successes.—A lesser but still significant number of leaflets sought to play up the achievements of the partisan movement in the eyes of the civilian population. Their themes were, in substance: The partisans are good; the partisans are winning; the partisans are fighting for you. This glorification underwent some changes. In the early period, perhaps until the late spring or summer of 1942, emphasis was placed on individual heroism and martyrdom; the glorification, for instance, of a young Komsomol girl, Zoya Kosmodemyanskaya, whose death at the hands of the Germans was exploited to the hilt by partisan and Soviet propaganda. On the other hand, when organized partisan action became more successful and provided a factual basis for propaganda reporting, individual accomplishments were subordinated to collective action—the increasing *élan* of the movement and the systematic influx of manpower. At the same time, individual partisan operations were described in detail: "punishing" Germans, "avenging" their cruelties, "rewarding" Soviet patriots and innocent victims, "helping" the peasantry by distributing grain and other supplies. Finally, in the last stages of the war, stress was laid on the theme, "The partisans are smoothing the path for the returning Red Army."

A few specific themes were added to the series of partisan victory reports; these included: (1) Not only the civilian population but also collaborators and Axis troops, such as Slovaks and Hungarians, are joining the partisans. (2) The partisans are constantly among the population, watching the people's behavior. (3) The Soviet Government and people fully appreciate the sacrifices and accomplishments of the partisans and are rewarding them with decorations, honors, and pledges to be redeemed after the war.

(d) Allied successes.—Both to strengthen the image of German defeat and to produce the impression of a wide, popular, international coalition fighting against the Nazis, a good deal of attention was devoted to events outside the USSR—less than would have been normal in other countries but considerably more than one might have expected from the Soviet authorities. At a time when the Red Army was still hard pressed, shipments of supplies (lend-lease, etc.), friendly pronouncements by Western leaders and journalists, victories on other fronts, and the conclusion of treaties of alliance with the Soviet regime provided a welcome source of relief and comfort for partisan propaganda. Later on, descriptions of Allied bombings of the Reich, landings in North Africa and Sicily, the defection of Italy from the Axis camp, and the prospect of an early opening of an Allied second front in Europe, all helped clarify the image of imminent German doom and underline the fact that the anti-Fascist coalition was not limited to Communists. There is some suggestion that references to Britain and the United States were more prominent in 1941–42 than in 1944, although no conclusive quantitative analysis can be made. If this is true, it would reinforce the impression that, within limits, emphasis on the Western powers was in the nature of a "concession."

Finally, some use was made of information on partisan movements and anti-German revolts in other parts of "Fortress Europe." The Soviet partisans thus became a part of an international community of underdogs, an important element acting in concert with the masses revolting in other countries, all engaged in the same purpose of ousting and downing the foreign invaders.

The basic aims of this campaign stressing the successes of the anti-German forces were (1) to restore the myth of Soviet invincibility or, inversely, shatter the myth of German invincibility; (2) to guide the behavior of the population by predicting the imminent return of the Red Army; (3) to reinforce the conceptual image of the partisans as an integral part of the Soviet armed forces successfully defeating the Germans; (4) to ridicule the Germans even while exposing their cruelties.

There is little doubt that this stage of partisan psychological warfare was at least partially successful in determining popular action.

b. *Counterpropaganda*

Directly or indirectly, much partisan propaganda was intended to neutralize, or belie, the claims of German propaganda. The partisans endeavored to depict the Germans as liars, deceivers, and breakers of promises, and to dispel German-fostered misconceptions which might have gained credence among some of the population. Within limits, the themes selected for counterpropaganda may be considered as an index to the way in which the partisan propagandists gauged the effectiveness of German themes.

Leaving aside the problem of agriculture, which was recognized as an area of particular Soviet vulnerability, the following were among the major German subjects which evoked partisan counterefforts: (1) Russia is beaten. (2) The Soviet regime is the enemy of the people. (3) Come out of the woods and return to your villages. (4) Join and help the collaborators. (5) The Soviet regime will punish you if you fall into its hands. (6) Germany, not the Soviet regime, is really national and socialist.

These themes were not used with equal insistence by the Germans. Some, such as (1) and (5), could not be used at the same time: the first prevailed in the early months of the war; the fifth was widespread at the end. All, however, seem to have caused the partisan propaganda machines some concern.

At times, partisan counterefforts limited themselves to such general appeals as "Don't believe the Germans!" or statements contrasting German "lies" with Soviet "truth": "Do not believe the gibberish of the German dogs. Read the truth about the Red Army and life in the Soviet fatherland." At other times, partisan leaflets contrasted German promises and reports with German practices, seeking to show that reality belied German propaganda.[106] In a broader effort to "expose anti-Soviet slander," such exhortations as the following appeared: "Sometimes the German scoundrels, posing as benefactors, spread sweet words. They need this dirty trick to deceive the toilers. First they conduct propaganda rallies, then they hang the people."[107]

The theme, "Russia is beaten," was difficult to counter during the first months of the war, but thereafter the partisans had little trouble in persuading the population that the war was continuing. Indeed, the Germans themselves soon abandoned this theme.

Far more difficult for the partisans was the neutralizing of German national "socialism" slogans. Used rather infrequently by the Germans, they were nonetheless a sufficient nuisance (if not more) to stimulate repeated efforts by the partisans to demonstrate that only the Soviet Union

[106] See Tsanava, II, 52 ff.
[107] *Bolshevistskoye Znamya,* no. 9 (21 December 1941). See also Tsanava, I, 53 ff.

was genuinely socialist, that Hitler was "a dog of the German capitalists" and that the Krupps were growing rich on the war.[108] No apparent effort was made to discount German propaganda emphasizing that Stalin had allied himself with the "plutocrats and imperialists" of the West.

Partisan propaganda generally made no attempt to counteract German themes of anticommunism; it trod lightly among the problems of appeals to national minorities; and it ignored German slogans on the Soviet labor camps, the activities of the NKVD, the dictatorship of Stalin, and the victims of Soviet policy.

Apparently counterpropaganda was one of the least successful facets of partisan psychological warfare, in part because of its rigidity in reacting to German charges, in part because of the impossibility of disproving certain German allegations without either stating palpable untruths or compromising the Soviet regime.

c. Fission Propaganda

If the common purpose of all themes discussed so far was to establish a bond of identification between Soviet regime, partisans, and civilians, or to re-establish it by rejecting German attempts to disintegrate it, the complement to it consisted of an effort to drive a wedge between the Germans and the indigenous population. In substance, this fission propaganda consisted of two elements: an exposition of German goals and intentions, and detailed accounts of German practices in the occupied territories. Such themes served a number of purposes. Accounts of atrocities and abuses were designed to produce hatred of the enemy and to encourage "revenge," while discussions of long-range German goals served to arouse suspicion and apprehension, to counter German propaganda claims, and to re-emphasize the fact that there was no "third way." The choice lay between accepting and helping the Soviet regime or becoming German slaves, exposed indefinitely to brutal and selfish Nazi policies. The propaganda that utilized German atrocities and revealed German goals and policies created the image of the enemy as a cruel, selfish, power-hungry monster, contrasted with the image of the partisan as the righteous avenger and heroic protector of the Russian people.

Such themes apparently resulted from high-level Soviet directives. Thus the Stalingrad Oblast Committee of the Communist Party issued instructions in August 1942 that the population must be stimulated to hate the Germans through a recitation of German atrocities. Earlier, in the spring of 1942, a partisan newspaper agitated that the enemy must be "exposed" in order to make the masses rebellious and to breed hatred.

The technique usually employed in partisan leaflets contrasted Soviet

[108] See, for instance, Sheverdalkin, pp. 203–6.

achievements and heroic partisan deeds with German destructiveness and specific German atrocities or oppressive policies. The German plans most frequently outlined in partisan propaganda were: (1) colonization of the USSR and the enslavement of its peoples; (2) exploitation of the natural resources of the USSR; (3) laying waste those regions not slated for colonization; (4) elimination of educational institutions, so as to prepare the Russians for their future role as "German slaves"; (5) assignment of the land to German estate owners and barons.

As proof of these goals, one leaflet issued by a high partisan command on the Soviet side quoted a statement attributed to Hitler: "In order to dominate the Great German Reich and the whole world we [the Germans] must first destroy all Slavic peoples—[Great] Russians, Poles, Czechs, Slovaks, Ukrainians, Belorussians. To reach this goal it is necessary to lie, betray, and kill."[109] The same leaflet quoted an order of a German military command which made it mandatory to shoot even at women and children if they were found outside their villages. Another leaflet addressed to the Belorussian population read:

Workers of Belorussia—you must know that it is Hitler's aim to transform Belorussia into a wasteland and to "liberate" the Eastern regions for the German colonizers. . . . In Vitebsk Oblast alone more than 40,000 women, old people, and children were shot . . . the partisan fight is the fight of the entire Russian population.

Yet another leaflet, issued in 1942, explained German atrocities as the result of German frustrations at the front: "Not being successful at the front, the German bandits are giving vent to their rage by taking revenge on the peaceful civilian population." "In the village of Kholmy, in Smolensk Oblast, Hitlerites seized six girls, 15–17 years of age. These girls were raped, their breasts cut off, their eyes pierced."

Specific incidents of atrocities allegedly perpetrated by the Germans were frequently used as pegs for partisan appeals. Such examples, even if they had a factual basis, apparently were presented in an exaggerated form while others were clearly invented.

One atrocity theme which, significantly, the partisans and Soviets did not stress in their psychological warfare was German treatment of the Jews. The hypothesis that the Soviet authorities did not realize the sufferings of the Jews under the German occupation must be dismissed in view of their excellent intelligence network and occasional references to the problem. It is possible that the theme of anti-Semitism was omitted from propaganda to avoid singling out any one national or religious group as having suffered more than others (and thus perhaps making it feel entitled

---

[109] This quotation amounted to a garbled and slightly "expanded" version of a statement contained in *Mein Kampf,* changed to increase its effectiveness as a partisan theme.

to future privileges). Moreover, given the Soviet effort to portray life under the occupation as hell, it was scarcely good tactics to reveal differences and gradations in the measure of suffering sustained by the population, and to suggest that non-Jews were not quite so badly off. Another possible explanation lies in the growth of anti-Semitism in the German-occupied areas (and perhaps also on the Soviet side) and in a desire to avoid identifying the Jewish with the Soviet cause, which could lend support to German slogans concerning the Jewishness of the Bolshevik regime.[110]

Another topical theme used frequently in partisan propaganda from 1942 on was the extensive German use of forced labor for work in the Reich—the so-called *Ostarbeiter* program. This labor force provided manpower for German industry, freeing more manpower for military service. At the same time, the program deprived the partisans of a major source of recruits; quite logically, the people taken for *Ostarbeiter* service were those most likely to be physically fit to serve as partisans. On the other hand, the program resulted in a heavy influx into the partisan movement of previously uncommitted or even pro-German elements, who joined to avoid being seized as forced laborers.

Partisan psychological warfare "exposing" the *Ostarbeiter* program was designed primarily to produce fear: fear of their fate for those who might go to Germany, fear for their families who remained behind, and fear for their personal safety should they survive and be returned to Soviet jurisdiction after the war. The future that awaited them was described in gruesome detail: they would be starved, beaten, or killed by the Germans, by epidemics, or by British-American bombs in air raids. "Whoever Goes to Germany Will Perish," is the title of one leaflet addressed to the population of Gomel Oblast; it expounded the theme, "Do not go to Germany, for death awaits you there. Hide in the woods . . . go to the partisans. Help the partisans . . . Block the plans of the Hitler bandits to send people to Germany."

Once *Ostarbeiter* were recruited in a systematic fashion, they were forced to wear a special emblem during their term of duty in the Reich. This was widely, and correctly, regarded as a German attempt to brand the Russian as a second-class being, and caused widespread resentment. The partisans were thus provided with an additional theme and opportunity to exploit another German "blunder."

The methods of compulsion used by the Germans were a measure of the people's unwillingness to volunteer for work in Germany. The treatment they received was well known in the occupied territories through a variety of channels. Thousands of men and women jumped off the trains taking them to Germany and found their way to the partisans. Those few

---

[110] See also Solomon M. Schwarz, "The Soviet Partisans and the Jews," *Modern Review* (New York), January 1949, pp. 387–400.

who preferred work in the Reich to joining the bands were confronted with partisan threats; handwritten leaflets would proclaim "Death to the families whose sons and daughters have let themselves be recruited for Germany's labor!" In the Bryansk area, the "treacherous" nature of forced labor was emphasized by the partisans' slogan, "Whoever goes to work in Germany raises his hand against his own people."

The forced labor issue was also utilized to sharpen the image of the partisan as the avenger of those who had been wronged and the protector of those who were in danger. Thus, in August 1942 partisan-spread rumors claimed that the heavy rail demolitions carried out during the month in the Mogilev area were to prevent the Germans from transporting to Germany eighteen-year-olds, drafted for forced labor—a most questionable assertion.

The importance that the Soviet authorities attached to the *Ostarbeiter* problem is apparent from the number of leaflets devoted to it. At moments of particularly intensive German roundups, as in the summer of 1943, the question received more emphasis in partisan propaganda than did the most popular theme of Soviet victories and German defeats.

A special effort was made to counter German attempts, during the later stages of the war, to round up the civilian population for evacuation westward. Judging from the intensity of Soviet propaganda dealing with this subject, the Soviet and partisan authorities apparently feared to find the reoccupied areas stripped of their population. Soviet efforts in this field followed the customary pattern of fear vs. hope: fear that those evacuated would meet a horrible fate at German hands and that by consenting to evacuation they would in fact become traitors to the Soviet cause, with the implication of severe punishment; and hope that, by avoiding voluntary or forcible evacuation, they would earn a better life under Soviet rule.

The element of fear played on such emotions as these:

Everyone who flees with the Germans awaits an inevitable doom. Some will starve to death, others will die of Fascist torture, and others by the bullet. Already thousands of Soviet people who were forcibly driven to Germany have perished of hunger and torture in Fascist slavery. . . . The German cause is hopelessly lost.

This contrasted with the prospect offered to those who remained (and was intended to offset German efforts to depict a return to Soviet rule as dangerous for those who had lived in the German-occupied areas):

Stay where you are! You must not be afraid. . . . Nobody thinks of punishing you because you have remained in the areas that were occupied by the Germans. We know that you had no opportunity to retreat with the Red Army. . . . *The Red Army* [and the partisans] *will bring you a happy and free life in your own homeland.*[111]

[111] ERR, Hauptarbeitsgr. Mitte, 27 July 1943 (GMDS, EAP 99/54).

Apparently this leaflet received wide distribution. It was found near Minsk, far behind the front lines, and bore Ponomarenko's signature.

At times other promises were added to induce resistance:

The Germans are spreading rumors that the Soviet Government organs upon their return shoot or recruit as forced labor all people who stayed under the German occupation. This is a German lie. They do this to win the people to their side. The Red Army consists of workers and peasants; they are your husbands and fathers and sons. The Soviet regime is our own regime, and the people's interests are uppermost. Millions of people already freed from the Fascist yoke have received material aid in bread, seeds, cattle, money, and wood. Kolkhozes on liberated soil receive tax exemptions and privileges in delivery quotas.

A German report on partisan propaganda asserted that in October 1943, at the time of the first Soviet offensive on Vitebsk, the partisans even revived the rumor that kolkhozes would be divided in the Soviet Union after the war, in order to prevent peasants from retreating with the Germans.

The alternative to being evacuated was depicted as hiding in the woods or joining the partisans: "The population of villages near the enemy garrisons [a partisan leaflet proclaimed] saves itself from being sent to Germany by living in tents and mudhuts in the forest. . . . We know that it is hard for you to live in the forest, but it is better to suffer privations for a month or two than to face permanent serfdom in Germany."

To judge from German reports, popular resistance to evacuation measures was considerable. However, it would be exceedingly difficult to attribute this to the effectiveness of propaganda-generated promises and fears. Germany was rapidly losing the war, and there was little that could have made the rank-and-file Soviet rural resident desirous of abandoning everything to go to the Reich at that time. In addition, evacuation was in many cases a hazardous undertaking, far from certain to succeed.

The effectiveness of partisan psychological warfare stressing German goals, atrocities, and abuses depended on the ability to make the image of the enemy vivid and meaningful. German policy and behavior in the occupied areas insured the success of such propaganda, even though the specific charges made in partisan leaflets were often invented or at least exaggerated. A peasant whose village had been burned down was not reluctant to believe an account that thousands of other villages had met the same fate. In essence, German behavior conformed to the stereotypes which the partisans spread.

d. Propaganda to Induce Action

The two basic axioms of Soviet propaganda, as examined below, were "We are good; the Germans are bad." The corollary was the appeal, "Therefore, help (or join) us."

It will suffice to list some of the slogans used by the partisans on this subject. They amounted to two main exhortations; first, stop collaboration with the Germans, and second, induce active work against them. The appeal to patriotism and self-interest was coupled with a vague reference to future status. "Where was I when the Soviet people fought?" the fence-sitter was requested to ask himself after the war. The fear of guilt in the eyes of either public opinion or the state was strong enough, the propagandists hoped, to spur the timid and cowardly to action on their side.

Some slogans remained generalized and diffuse. These may be summarized as:

> Arise!
> Hate!
> Avenge!
> Kill!
> Oust!

and they were supplemented by the customary "Eye for an Eye, Tooth for a Tooth" in numerous variations. Others called for specific action. There were "don'ts" and "do's"—the former to deter collaboration, the latter to produce active support. Among the "don'ts" were:

> Don't help the Germans!
> No food deliveries to the Germans!
> Don't give them a single gram of bread!
> No milk for the invaders!
> Hide the grain!
> Don't pay taxes!

Later on, to these were added specific orders not to respond to the *Ostarbeiter* program. Threats were likewise used to keep the Belorussian population from responding to the so-called mobilization decrees of the collaborating Belorussian Central Council in the spring of 1944. [On threats and inducements to military collaborators, see above, Sect. IV, A.] Finally, action demonstrating the reality of partisan threats—the destruction of collaborators' houses and their physical extermination—can be considered a form of psychological warfare aimed at deterring the population from collaborating.

The "do's" among partisan slogans ranged from the vague, "Use any means at your disposal to harm the invaders!" and the generalized "Sabotage their efforts!" to the more specific, "Attack troops!" and "Destroy German supply and fuel dumps!" In the early stages of the campaign, when the number of stragglers was considerable, leaflets called on soldiers to "Do your duty and fight!" In line with the major partisan activity, a number of leaflets called on the population to "Destroy railroad tracks and cars!" Finally, and importantly, numerous leaflets included such direct references as:

> Join the partisans!
> Help the partisans!
> Join the Red Army!
> Help the Red Army!

At times, these slogans were used in combination. At other times, they appeared singly; not unnaturally there was a preponderance of references to the Red Army in the material dropped from the Soviet side, while the partisans most frequently appealed for help to themselves. This distinction, however, was by no means ironclad, since the partisans frequently sought to depict themselves as a branch of the Soviet armed forces.

e. Clusters of Themes

While the combination of different themes varied, a few typical constellations apparently recurred with considerable regularity. The following two indicate the general pattern of such clusters:

(A) 1. Soviet patriotism.
  2. German atrocities.
  3. Revenge!
  4. Soviet Army advances.
  5. Join and help the partisans!
(B) 1. Soviet accomplishments.
  2. German aims and practices.
  3. The partisans are fighting the Germans.
  4. Help beat the Germans!

In general, the leaflets were not distinguished by particular brevity (with the exception of some one-sentence leaflets dating from early 1942 and apparently dropped by the Red Army), and did not hesitate to use several slogans, resorting to frequent repetitions and numerous examples.

E. PARTISAN RUMORS

On the border between the fields of partisan-steered psychological warfare efforts and the autonomous transmission of word-of-mouth communications among the population at large, lies the amorphous area of rumors. Considering the long popular distrust of official news, dating back to the Soviet and even pre-Soviet years, the striking paucity of legitimate news media under the German occupation, and the crisis situation which made the rank-and-file population ready to listen to and transmit news from any source, word-of-mouth reports played a considerable role in the German-occupied areas. Their importance was perhaps further enhanced by the intense Soviet practice of oral "agitation," a practice fully adopted by the partisan movement.[112]

---

[112] On partisan "agitation," see Sect. V, C, 1. German reports frequently stressed the population's hunger for news and receptiveness to rumors. Soviet memoirs likewise recognize their importance.

German statements on partisan propaganda distinguished between word-of-mouth and whisper propaganda (*Mundpropaganda* and *Fluesterpropaganda*), the former being the verbal effort, corresponding to the Soviet "agitation," and the latter implying *sub rosa* communication. Unfortunately not all German reporting officers observed these definitions or distinctions.

The Soviet command and the partisans understood the role that rumors could play. One of the earliest partisan directives permitted the wearing of German uniforms because this would enable the group "to exploit rumors regarding the activity of partisans." Otherwise, no specific directives on partisan rumor-spreading have been located. Soviet memoirs, however, readily acknowledge the use of rumors to inflate the prestige and size of the bands in the popular mind.[113]

Partisan rumormongering among the civilian population appears to have followed two major lines: (1) of acting as a substitute for, or complement to, other forms of propaganda; (2) of injecting themes and "news" which the Soviet and partisan authorities could not overtly sponsor or publicly acknowledge. A major difficulty in assessing techniques and effectiveness, however, is inherent in the very nature of rumor propaganda. At no time can it be ascertained whether a given rumor picked up by the Germans was actually spread by partisans or merely reflected the repetition, frequently with considerable distortions, of "news" heard or read by other civilians. Even where a clear partisan source can be assumed, it is impossible to judge whether a specific rumor was the result of a conscious effort on the part of the partisan command to spread it among the civilians or (as was often the case) was merely a by-product (not unwelcome to the partisans, to be sure) of the casual conversation of a partisan with a local middleman, a chance contact in a village, or an inquiry by a stranger about the latest war news, details of German atrocities, or other matters of interest. A very substantial part of partisan rumor propaganda must be considered the product of a general, and evidently widespread, desire of the partisans to spread their word anywhere, in any place, among anyone willing (or even unwilling) to listen; another substantial part was the repetition, with natural distortions, of statements made by partisan officers at public meetings and lectures arranged by the partisans for the population.

Especially during the early stages of the movement, when facilities for printed media were inadequate, rumors constituted an easy and convenient means of propaganda. In the words of a partisan leader, "Leaflets are a difficult business, and especially on the move it was difficult to produce them, while oral agitation, personal contact, and talking to people was always possible for us. And what could be more effective than the living word!"[114]

The evidence suggests that rumors were not merely an outlet for popular attitudes and drives but also a deliberate weapon of psychological warfare employed by the Soviet authorities and, in particular, by the partisans. One obvious advantage of rumors was facility and speed in their

[113] See, for instance, Fyodorov, English ed., p. 297.
[114] Dmitrii Medvedev, *Silnye dukhom* (Moscow: Voennoye Izdatelstvo Voennogo Ministerstva Soyuza SSR, 1951), p. 32.

production and distribution. Unlike leaflets, they could penetrate areas where no partisans operated; their dissemination was less dangerous than that of leaflets; and their effect was at times greater.

Rumor dissemination was partly in the hands of rank-and-file partisans, partly entrusted to special agitators, often in conjunction with more institutionalized media of psychological warfare.[115] In addition, the urban underground, whether in contact with partisans or not, was active in rumor-spreading.[116] Finally, special agents sent into the occupied areas at various times had among their tasks the spreading of what the Germans called "tendentious" news reports. The most striking difference between rumor dissemination and other media, however, lies in the fact that non-Soviet elements, even those hostile to the partisans, were unwitting carriers of their propaganda.

One may distinguish between those rumors which, so far as can be determined, were disseminated by the partisans, along lines paralleling printed partisan propaganda, and those which made use of concepts and "news" that were not permitted in printed media.

1. Orthodox Rumors

Among the first, the most widespread were those prognosticating the early defeat of the Germans and the return of the Red Army, and exaggerating the victories and growth of the partisan movement. As has been shown, Soviet propaganda made extensive use of these themes on both sides of the front. In addition, appearing especially at times of crisis at the front, rumors about the ostensible recapture by the Red Army of towns far behind the front were calculated to create confusion and panic among Germans and collaborators.

A major concentration of such rumors, quite naturally, occurred at the time of German defeats before Moscow in December 1941 to January 1942. By early 1942 such rumors, speaking of heavy German casualties and withdrawals, even claiming the Soviet reoccupation of large cities—Smolensk, Kharkov, Kiev, or Odessa—were reported from virtually all parts of the German-held areas.[117]

Thereafter, the theme, "The Red Army Returns," never disappeared

---

[115] The complementary nature of leaflet and rumor propaganda is illustrated by the simultaneous occurrence of rumors calculated to deter peasants from harvesting for fear of partisan reprisals, and Soviet leaflets instructing the partisans to destroy the crops. In other instances, rumors and printed media were distributed on the same subject; at times, one preceded the other.

[116] For instance, a secret Party unit uncovered by the Germans in Kiev in November 1941 had, among other things, engaged in rumor propaganda inciting the population against the occupying forces.

[117] At times these reports would give specific details that were calculated to make the "news" more credible, e.g., that only trains evacuating wounded German soldiers were moving on to the Pskov-Krasnogvardeisk railroad.

from partisan rumors, much to the concern of the Germans, who repeatedly commented that such rumors intimidated the people so much that they were now, as they were not in the summer of 1941, inclined to help the partisans with food and to abstain from reporting them to the Germans. In some instances, collaborators hearing such rumors were reported to be actually packing their bags to escape apprehension by the Soviet forces.[118] The theme, somewhat less emphasized in the spring and summer of 1942, naturally recurred with greater frequency when the Red Army did indeed win. In early 1944 a partisan source insisted, with some justification, that the "daily growing partisan groups" had effectively established a second front, which sealed in the Germans between the Red Army and the partisans. These partisan-spread rumors were, like other propaganda efforts, most effective when they were based on favorable facts which could be inflated or exaggerated, but not at times of Soviet setbacks.

Special mention should be made of rumors about the alleged landing of British troops near Leningrad to help the Red Army and the considerable aid being furnished to the Soviet forces by the Western Allies. Another category of rumors dovetailed with printed propaganda in discrediting German war aims and stressing the treatment of the civilian population as "white Negroes." From 1942 on, a particular effort was made to depict in the darkest hues the fate awaiting those who responded to the German forced labor drive, which was at times compared with banishment to Siberia under the tsars (and by implication, perhaps, under the Soviet regime); in other instances, rumors claimed that the Germans would use the *Ostarbeiter* as cannon fodder. By contrast, the partisans' own demolition of German transportation facilities was held up as a model effort to save people from being forcibly shipped off to the Reich.

Finally, partisan-spread rumors were at times calculated to deter specific segments of the population from collaborating with the Germans. In the Borisov area, for instance, a rumor in February 1942 stated that the Germans were about to kill all young men. When the Germans began to round up former prisoners of war who had settled among the rural population, another rumor had it that, if apprehended, the prisoners would either be shot or shipped off to Africa. Another rumor spoke of the impending extermination of all invalids, while a third predicted the extermination of all former Communist Party members—in part, to foster defection of collaborators who had admitted Party membership. One may assume that, in all the above instances, the way in which the rumors were presented played on actual information or experiences of the population

---

[118] For instance, in Minsk in June 1942. Such reports of lightning Soviet advances in the first half of 1942 were based on actual sallies made deep behind the front, by individual Soviet teams and vehicles, through the existing wide gaps, especially in the north-central sector of the front.

and tried to use genuine occurrences or rumors of occurrences (such as the killing of Jews, politruks, and others) as starting points for partisan psychological warfare efforts.

There was no obvious limit to the range of rumors spread by the partisans. They sought to utilize local conditions, specific grievances or problems, and to stress the same themes that appeared in printed media, though at times they went further in allegations either of German abuses or Soviet successes and generous acts than written pronouncements dared to do. They sought to arouse hope or fear, or to induce confusion—in substance, the same purposes that printed and more institutionalized word-of-mouth propaganda sought to achieve.

2. Unorthodox Themes

Certain categories of rumors, unlike those discussed above, represented a more substantial deviation from the official line. Inasmuch as they were not duplicated in written propaganda, these themes are of particular interest; precisely because they were not otherwise spread, they appear to have been absorbed and repeated with striking speed and frequency. In all instances for which documentation exists, these rumors were intended to stimulate the identification of Soviet regime and population, to promote the notion that the Soviet government was being reformed to satisfy popular aspirations, and that therefore a return to the Soviet fold would be far less evil than life under the Germans. While the attitude of "let bygones be bygones" was also mirrored in some written partisan appeals (for instance, to military collaborators), and while the basic approach in these rumors constituted merely an extension of the catering operation implicit in the entire "Patriotic War," "people's front," and "nationalist revival" propaganda, rumors could spell out or promise what printed media dared not do.

Some of them dealt with the national character of the war effort and the change of Soviet intentions. Greatly varying from area to area, but recurring, partly because they corresponded to the wishful thinking of at least a large segment of the population, the most powerful statements asserted that "the Soviet regime has changed" or that "a better life" awaited everyone after the war. Perhaps the most striking report, verbalizing many of the notions implicit in other and less specific rumors, was spread in the Bryansk area in January 1943: "The Soviet constitution has been abolished, because riots have occurred. The Soviet Government no longer exists in its previous form. Russian soldiers don't fight any more for the Soviets but for the fatherland and for private property. The Church has been reinstated with its former rights."[119]

The partisans went even further—sometimes, one may assume, in ac-

[119] 221. Sich.Div., Ic, "Einzelnachrichten des Ic-Dienstes Ost," 28 October 1942, p.l. (GMDS, 221 ID 29380/3 Anlage 184).

cordance with directives from higher up; sometimes, in a sincere expression of their own views and hopes—for they themselves were not only mechanical media for the dissemination of propaganda but also subjects for Soviet indoctrination. The avidity with which such rumors, true or false, were seized upon and repeated testifies to the potency of the themes. In print, however, no such hints were allowed. In a sense, such rumors amounted to an admission that the orthodox Soviet and Communist approach had failed to win over those people who had other aspirations, and in part at least the rumors were calculated to anticipate German changes, particularly with regard to private property and religion.[120]

Most frequent, perhaps, was the idea spread in conversations of partisans with the peasantry that the partisans were not fighting for the restoration of the Soviet regime, as it existed before the war, but for a new order—a theme that recurs with infinite variations.

Many such rumors were clearly an attempt to win the support of non-Communist elements of the population. In practice, some of these partisan rumors must be considered a reflection of the conviction of the individual partisan who had come to believe that things would really change after the war. In conversations with the peasantry he might occasionally go well beyond the measure of sanctioned concessions to the popular view, at times so far as to discount Stalin, at others depicting him as a victim of circumstances who "did not know that the population was suffering so." [Cf. in this connection the word-of-mouth efforts of the agent infiltrated into the Vlasov movement's leadership to produce belief in the existence of a non-Stalinist faction attuned to the wishes of the rank and file, as described in Section IV, C, 2.] Acknowledging that mistakes had been made in the past, such rumors insisted that the Soviet regime would no longer either wish or be able to make them after the war. The unstated implication was that the victorious people-in-arms had, by its victory, won the right to make its voice heard.

---

[120] While "proreligious" attitudes and rumors cannot be considered strictly an unorthodox psychological warfare device, in view of the genuine relaxation of antireligious activities on the Soviet side of the front during the war and in view of the partisans' overt behavior in this domain, the population largely perceived it as unorthodox—a natural attitude when they contrasted it with the latest Soviet themes they recalled before the German occupation. Such rumors stressed that "freedom of religion" had been fully re-established in the Soviet Union. According to an Orthodox priest who traveled in the Pskov area in March 1943,

> the partisans talk the peasants into believing that Soviet church policy has completely changed; freedom of religious conscience must under all circumstances be recognized; antireligious propaganda has been a grievous mistake, and the Soviet Government now publicly regrets and acknowledges it as such before the nation and before God.

Occasionally the partisans would encourage church attendance by the civilians, promising that it would not be held against them when the Red Army returned; some were reported to have participated in services to pray for the liberation of Russia.

Beginning in October 1941, German reports frequently mentioned rumors, attributed to partisans or their underground counterparts in cities, about alleged changes in the Soviet economic system. By far the vast majority of such rumors dealt with the collective farm economy. While some asserted bluntly that the kolkhozes had actually been dissolved in the unoccupied part of the USSR, other rumors merely included promises that private property would be restored, that land would be distributed (without specifically referring to the kolkhozes), that the kolkhozes would be dissolved only after the Germans had been expelled from Soviet territory, or that the peasants would no longer be forced to work the land collectively (implying that, after the war, the peasants might be permitted to withdraw from the kolkhozes). Occasionally other aspects of Soviet economic life were mentioned together with themes on the abolition of kolkhozes, such as promises about the introduction of private trade and the suspension of labor discipline.

There can be no doubt that themes stressing the actual and intended change of the kolkhoz economy had an important effect on peasants in rural areas. Changes in attitudes on account of such rumors were noted as early as October 1941 in the Smolensk area. At that time, the Germans stubbornly refused to make any meaningful concessions, even in their propaganda. Partisan rumors, therefore, fell on fertile soil. After the announcement of the Agrarian Reform in February 1942 partisan propaganda along these lines abated somewhat but quickly resumed in the summer of that year. During this period partisan promises on the agricultural issue were frequently coupled with themes designed to discredit the German reform. As early as December 1941 partisans in the Army Group Center Rear Area stated that the Fascists were merely making empty promises while the Moscow government would actually distribute land. In February 1942, in the same area, a rumor claimed that Stalin was dissolving the kolkhozes in the unoccupied part of the USSR, while private landholdings did not exist in Germany where the peasants had been dispossessed. German peasants, the rumor went, had merely been granted long term (thirty-three-year) leases. Another slogan reported in February 1942 from the Bryansk area, and disseminated concurrently with the promise that the Bolsheviks would distribute land, ran: "It is better to work with a spade or with bare hands on one's own soil, than with tractors on foreign soil." According to the German reporter, that rumor was designed to further the prevailing desire for land ownership among peasants. During 1942 other rumors aiming to discredit German propaganda efforts alleged that the Germans were abolishing the kolkhozes merely because of their difficulties in the occupied area, which, in turn, led them to appease the peasants. In reality, kolkhoz land would later be distributed among German settlers and landholders. Another rumor asserted that the new German agrarian policy did not conflict with Stalin's views on the subject, because in the unoccupied USSR similar reforms had been introduced.

The frequent combination of partisan agricultural themes with arguments against the German agrarian reform indicates that partisan rumors about actual or intended changes in the kolkhoz economy in the USSR were motivated largely by the desire to combat German propaganda. This assumption is also supported by the fact that, as soon as a majority of peasants realized that German promises were not meant to be carried out on a large scale, partisan rumor propaganda in this field subsided. Nevertheless, the "dissolution of the kolkhozes" should be viewed as part of a larger propaganda effort aimed to mislead the rural population (which was more hostile toward the Soviet regime and therefore more accessible to German propaganda than some other segments of the population) into believing that profound changes in the economic system had been carried out in the unoccupied USSR or would be instituted after the victorious conclusion of the war.

"Unorthodox" themes appeared in partisan-spread rumors as early as October 1941 and extended almost to the end of 1943. Thus they covered precisely the period which has been elsewhere characterized as that of relative Soviet weakness, the months when the regime was prepared to make concessions so as to attract wavering elements by actual or token promises or relaxations of unpopular laws. These rumors, strong in late 1941, subsided somewhat about February 1942, after Soviet victories and after the German agrarian reform, which required some readjustment of partisan themes; but they reappeared with renewed intensity during the late summer and fall of that year. After the victory at Stalingrad was exploited, unorthodox themes declined in frequency. By 1944, with the Red Army, partisans, and concomitant Soviet institutions again in the ascendant, there was little need for such propaganda. At the end of the war, it was abandoned for more direct emphasis on Soviet victory, glory, and promise of rich production, contrasted with German failure, ignominy, and depredation.

3. Effectiveness

It is nearly impossible to assess the influence of partisan-spread rumors on popular attitudes and behavior. Moreover, it is usually futile to attempt to trace the origin and extent of a rumor or to evaluate its effectiveness. Other psychological warfare media, and objective developments, provoked reactions without help from partisan rumors. The analyst is nonetheless struck by the frequently expressed and uniform opinion in German reports that partisan rumors were an exceptionally effective tool of psychological warfare. Likewise, the considerable number of instances in which "rumor-

mongers" were severely punished, even hanged, by the Germans bears indirect witness to the effectiveness of rumors.[121]

Even the Germans themselves occasionally became victims of partisan
rumors. In January 1942, for instance, German agencies arguing for a
more extensive agrarian reform referred to an alleged Stalin speech promising the abolition of the kolkhoz system, a speech that repeatedly crops up
in rumors but was never actually delivered. In the summer of 1943 German reports, seeking to explain the negative effect of the proclamation of
private land holding of 3 June 1943, attributed its failure to rumors of
prior land distribution by the partisans, in terms vastly exaggerating actual
partisan practices but corresponding to allegations contained in the rumors.

Their effectiveness was subject to variation and fluctuation. The available
material contains no conclusive data on the vulnerability of different social
strata to rumor propaganda.[122] Nor can definitive statements be made about
the geographic variation in rumor effectiveness. Most clearly, a rumor
did not necessarily become more effective as more people heard it and
passed it on, or as other rumors were added to it. A single rumor was at
times sufficient to produce panic, fear, or hope, if other conditions were
favorable. Rumors appear to have been launched with the greatest measure
of success when objective conditions made them believable, and when they
were used in actual crisis situations.

Rumors of Soviet successes do not seem to have been widely believed
in 1941 until the Red Army actually stopped the Germans near the end
of the year. At a moment when the myth of German invincibility was still
generally treated as fact, partisan rumors usually fell on deaf ears. Rumors
of Red Army advances caused panic in Nevel and Polotsk, forcing the Germans to take summary measures to stop a mass exodus, and producing
friction between rulers and ruled. Rumors of the impending evacuation
of the Crimea in September 1943 caused collaborators to pack their bags,
a development which was in turn exploited by further rumors. In both
cases, an actual crisis situation existed to make the partisan rumors believable.

The effectiveness of partisan-spread rumors was also enhanced by German policy. Not only did German abuses and atrocities in general create
an atmosphere in which otherwise fantastic rumors were readily accepted
as facts, but German failure to engage in systematic and subtle counterpropaganda virtually allowed partisan rumors free rein. The Germans de-

[121] It should be borne in mind, however, that a significant number of rumors attributed to the partisans—perhaps the majority—were probably unrelated to them. For
purposes of German reporting, it was convenient to claim continued mass support
and write off hostile manifestations to "bandits."

[122] For some hypotheses applicable, within limits, to the occupation situation, see
Raymond A. Bauer and David B. Gleicher, *Word-of-Mouth Communication in the
Soviet Union* (Maxwell AFB, Alabama: HRRI, 1953).

cided not to respond directly to partisan rumors about "Stalin's promise" (fictitious though it was) to dissolve collective farms in the future, because, according to the reasoning of the Wehrmacht Propaganda office, recognizing it officially would help to disseminate it more widely, in particular among the Red Army. In another case, the suggestion of a German security division that some residents be taken from Bobruisk to Smolensk, to demonstrate the baselessness of partisan rumors claiming that the Soviets had recaptured Smolensk, was not carried out.

A vital asset of partisan rumors was the speed with which they could react to local situations. Their greatest effect lay perhaps in helping to crystallize popular hopes for a better life after the war. While exaggerated reports of Red Army advances became less believable after having been proved wrong time after time, the actual "appeasement policy" of the Soviet government toward its own population seemed to support the Soviet and partisan themes of more far-reaching changes—present or future—in the USSR. By appealing to such hopes the partisans gauged popular sentiments far more correctly than the Germans did.

F. PARTISAN PSYCHOLOGICAL WARFARE:
CONCLUSIONS

From the very start, the Soviet partisan movement was expected to achieve political and psychological warfare purposes. According to the general outlook and early practice of the Soviet leaders, such activity would be considered a natural function of any organization. On the one hand, propaganda was to be an additional tool in the struggle against the Germans; on the other, and far more important in terms of political goals, it would assist in the maintenance or recapture of popular allegiance behind the German lines, a primary task of the partisan movement and the political apparatus of Party and Komsomol cells operating generally in conjunction with it. While it is futile to assess the relative importance of the political and propaganda tasks in comparison with the paramilitary and economic functions of the partisans, there can be no doubt that the former remained significant to the very end.

Considering the complex and effective Soviet control mechanism over the partisan movement, it is scarcely surprising that the choice and use of psychological warfare techniques, media, and themes, once contact with Soviet organs was established or re-established, took place in strict accordance with official Soviet rules. Though there may have been examples of individual partisans or officers engaging in propaganda on their own initiative, in an informal manner, along lines not officially sanctioned, the institutionalized psychological warfare operations of the partisans hardly ever deviated from the framework imposed from the Soviet side. In this sense, Soviet controls imposed some rigidity on propaganda activities. In general, the range of variations in official partisan propaganda was relatively small, and there was almost no spontaneity in introducing new and otherwise "unorthodox" themes.

It would appear, however, that these tendencies toward rigidity were all but counteracted by a remarkable flexibility in the official adaptation of proaganda slogans and themes to the specific wartime conditions in which the partisans operated. This is most strikingly exemplified in the "concessions" policy introduced after the first weeks of war (during which the traditional prewar pattern was maintained). From the late summer of 1941 on to nearly the end of the occupation—with obvious and not inconsiderable variations—partisan propaganda passed over Communist, ideological, and class themes in favor of strong emphasis on patriotism and popular-front slogans. To this extent, partisan and Soviet-side propaganda were fully in step during the war. The significant differences between the two may be summarized as follows:

(1) Partisan psychological warfare, operating in a more critical environment than Soviet-side propaganda, was likely to go further, at least in promises, in meeting popular aspirations in such crucial areas as agriculture.

(2) In the face of German propaganda operations, it could not combat certain enemy moves by ignoring them; in particular, although Soviet propaganda to the civilian population never responded to the German army's widespread publicity for the Vlasov movement, partisan propaganda was constrained to take issue.

(3) At the same time, the limits of the "concessions" tactics were clearly defined. Not even for propaganda purposes were themes or slogans permitted that specified Soviet errors in the past or suggested a criticism of the Soviet leadership. Only in oral propaganda, never in printed media, were statements made (at times with official sanction, often undoubtedly without it) about the fact that the Soviet regime constituted the lesser of two evils; that the German attack demanded a *Burgfrieden,* or temporary composition of internal differences in the face of the greater external foe; and that the Moscow government would in the future mend its ways.

Thus both the concessions policy itself and its limits were defined by the Soviet understanding of vulnerability in rank-and-file loyalty at times of stress—a vulnerability that had become amply apparent during the initial stage of the German-Soviet war. In fact, the Soviet response to certain German propaganda themes was a measure of Moscow's estimate of this vulnerability, particularly in such areas as agriculture, religion, and national non-Bolshevik political activity; obversely, the failure of the Soviet regime to adopt or tolerate other German-inspired themes on their own side, such as anti-Semitism, indicates either a feeling that German use of this theme did not constitute a kinetic propaganda threat, or else that its use on the Soviet (and partisan) side would itself expose an area of vulnerability.

Another reflection of the Soviet and partisan command's own perception of possible disloyalty was the rapid abandonment of the propaganda line initially adopted in 1941 and stressing the extreme danger to the Fatherland. The line was promptly replaced in partisan propaganda by the (highly premature and exaggerated) argument, "we are the stronger and therefore we shall win."

With some variations, this theme, nicely balanced with the "concession" policy, remained essentially static until 1943–44. Only in the last months of the German occupation, as Soviet strength objectively increased and was subjectively recognized as superior to the German, were certain elements of "concession" abandoned, while others (such as patriotism and religious tolerance) survived, even into the postwar period.

The other major line in Soviet propaganda was the "exposure" of German aims and practices. At first more stress was laid on Nazi colonial ambitions; later, as the population's practical experience of actual German behavior grew, the partisans were supplied with plentiful examples of atrocities and abuse to be thoroughly exploited in partisan propaganda. Perhaps paradoxically, it was this potent line that the partisans had least influence in starting; although German atrocities were a vital cause in the change of popular allegiances and fell into a pattern predicted by Soviet and partisan propaganda, the depth of their cruelty and their ubiquitous occurrence constituted, as it were, a windfall unforeseeable by the partisan propaganda officers themselves.

Indeed, in assessing the effectiveness of partisan propaganda, these German practices must be considered decisive. During the first months, there was a good deal of conscious untruth in partisan leaflets, particularly in exaggerating German casualties and even atrocities. While, later on, the same lack of scruples permitted Soviet propaganda to distort or lie whenever convenient or expedient, the objective need for lies decreased as German practices provided the partisans with genuine source material. Thus, in the popular conception, other criteria for choosing between, or being influenced by, the two competing systems became less important than this significant difference between them: the gap between propaganda and reality was far smaller on the partisan side than on the German; where it was large, it was least susceptible to verification by the population, since it occurred either in promises of future benefit, or in statements about events outside the occupied territories.

At the same time the partisans, unlike the Germans, were able to emphasize the accuracy of their statements and predictions by enforcing their threats. Fear of the partisans (as of the Germans) was most effective in compelling merely overt compliance and assistance without necessarily producing deeper loyalties; nevertheless, the image of partisan strength was certainly intensified by terror measures. Of those used by the two regimes, partisan terror perhaps had a somewhat less devastating effect on general popular judgment because the partisan commands were more selective in their use of it. For them it remained not an end in itself but a means. Its use, though extreme in its violence, did not blind the partisan leaders to the realization—not shared by the Germans—that the only basis for success was widespread popular support, to be won by the most effective combination of strength and concessions backed up by action.

After threats, more positive inducements were needed to maintain popular allegiance when the partisans had, for instance, departed from a village they had "visited" (or raided). So partisan, as well as Soviet, propaganda generally coupled threats with promises. The carrot-and-stick combination, however, seems not only to have been used less subtly by the partisans but also, in comparison with the technique in Soviet-side leaflets, to have concentrated more often on threats and the use of force than on "temptations"—an attitude probably induced by the very nature of partisan existence and activity. At the same time, the partisans' appeals to military collaborators with the German army, though naturally reflecting a decision made at a high level on the Soviet side of the front, showed the partisans' ability to employ systematic and far-reaching "temptation" themes and devices when they were deemed essential.

Given the situation in which, during the early months of the war, a large part of the population in the German-occupied areas was not firmly wedded either to the Soviet or to the German cause, the task of the partisans may be summarized as (1) to deter people from collaboration and (2) to win the mass of neutrals, fence-sitters, and seekers of a third way to their own side. Everything else being equal, the stronger side tended to command more popular support; so that as soon as the partisans represented a real force and when they almost continuously gained in influence, the odds were in their favor. Moreover, they had obvious advantages over the Germans in that they were indigenous people speaking the native language, and sometimes were even personally known to the local inhabitants. Finally, the experience of the occupation period was fresher and deeper in impact than the more diffuse and remote recollection of prewar Soviet frustrations; the effect of German behavior and treatment overshadowed, to some extent, the anti-Soviet proclivities latent in 1941, especially since these lessened under the influence of Soviet and partisan "concession" propaganda.

To evaluate the effect of partisan psychological warfare is difficult and hazardous. There can be little doubt that, even in the absence of the partisans, strong anti-German feelings developed—for instance, in large parts of the Ukraine. If anything, the growing acceptance of the partisans by the population was a consequence, rather than a cause, of anti-German sentiments. Likewise, where pro-Soviet feeling was least strengthened by German measures (as in the Caucasus), the partisans won decidedly less popular support. Yet, undeniably, in their areas of operation, partisan psychological warfare played a significant part in determining the allegiance and behavior of the civilian population. Above all, the very presence and activity of the partisans undermined German attempts at "pacification" and weakened faith in German victory; it emphasized the continued presence of "Big Brother's watchful eye"; and, quite apart from military operations, it unnerved Germans and collaborators alike and helped align the rural population on the partisans' side. Soviet awareness of this fact is shown in the assignments given to the various raiding bands in 1942–43, in which the psychological impact on the indigenous peasantry was unquestionably significant.

In the areas where the partisans remained, their presence was substantially important in offering those who had turned against the Germans an opportunity to translate their hate or sense of duty or revenge into action. If, in the sum total of factors explaining the alienation of the population (or at least overwhelming segments of it) from the German side, partisan activities played only a minor role, their existence helped to crystallize choice and channel action for those who had made the decision. In this light, the generalized psychological effect of the partisan movement as a whole on the population in the occupied areas must be viewed as far more important than the specific propaganda techniques, devices, and themes employed by particular partisans. These merely helped by giving rationales, basic ideas, and easy and effective slogans for converting anti-German resentment into patriotism, and righteous wrath into a holy war. However, from constant exposure to indoctrination, the Soviet population was so deeply inured to propaganda, so skeptical of and relatively insensitive to the printed word, that verbal media in partisan propaganda had considerably less influence on the course of the war than did the general psychological warfare effects of the continued existence of the partisans, and of their ability to follow up and translate into action many of their verbal statements. These efforts, though surely not decisive, were significant and lasting, for, with crucial though unwitting German assistance, they re-established the loyalty to the Soviet cause of a latently disaffected population.

§VI. The Partisans as the Long Arm
of the Soviet Regime

A. INTRODUCTION

As has been suggested earlier, the Soviet government viewed the partisan movement as its "long arm," which would fulfill a variety of functions—military, economic, intelligence, political—that were at least theoretically in accordance with the purposes and tactics of the regime. This section attempts to summarize one part of such functions that was the natural corollary of the techniques and efforts previously discussed: the reimposition of Soviet institutions and policies in areas controlled by the partisans. [The question of the extent to which the partisans operated as a military adjunct of the Soviet authorities is not considered here. The intelligence aspects of partisan activities are discussed in Chapter V.]

The difficulty in analyzing partisan policy is largely created by the fragmentary nature of the available material. It was inevitable that the Germans were least informed about areas thoroughly controlled by the partisans, and Soviet accounts are generally reticent about all but the most orthodox partisan administrative and policy measures. Moreover, the variation of administrative practices appears to have been great. Finally, both organically and subjectively, Germans and partisans at times had difficulty in distinguishing between narrowly utilitarian measures adopted in areas temporarily controlled by the partisans, and policies intended to revive a more permanent institutional framework. In villages temporarily "liberated" from German rule, partisan administration was likely to be adapted to psychological warfare considerations and to the partisans' immediate needs. Often the first decrees would include, in addition to the securing of peace and order, such dramatic steps as the convocation of a political rally, the arrest or liquidation of prominent collaborators, the return of property seized by collaborators, and, on the other hand, the requisition of billets, the commandeering of vehicles and horses, the seizure of food, the selection of informants, and the recruitment of men for the bands. Thus two aims were generally pursued: to impress the population with the strength and good will of the partisans, an impression presumably intended to linger after the visitors departed; and to obtain such goods and services as the partisans could find.

The situation was substantially different in areas that the partisans held for a protracted period of time[123] Here the goals, in addition to the control

[123] Occasionally such an area was clearly distinguishable from neighboring villages

of resources and manpower, included the re-establishment of Soviet authority and institutions, not only as a psychological warfare measure intended to impress on everyone the existence of Soviet power, but also as an administrative technique in dealing with the objective problems of directing the activities of local authority and population.

Some institutions and functions ubiquitous in the Soviet Union—for instance, the activities of the *Gosplan* and other economic agencies—were unsuitable or unnecessary in the partisan areas. Others, such as the draft of manpower, were adapted and improvised to suit local needs. Still others, like the local soviets, were revived as phantom tokens of rigid Soviet controls.

B. LOCAL GOVERNMENT

Though varying considerably, organs of local government appear to have conformed to four distinct patterns. All of these were in small and predominantly rural areas.[124]

(1) In some instances, the partisans did not establish local government. In its place the commander or commissar of a unit gave orders directly to the population and posted such announcements as the partisan unit desired to make. This appears to have been the arrangement when there was no initial assurance that the partisans would remain in the area; though at times this pattern was transformed into one of the types discussed below.

(2) In other cases, the partisan commander or commissar would appoint one of his officers as a commandant (or assume the position himself) of a given village or group of villages. The commandant, himself a partisan, was directly under the staff of the partisan unit and subject to its orders. His "rights and duties" are described in detail in a partisan order whose date and place of origin are unfortunately not identifiable. They included the accounting of cattle, grain, foodstuffs, and means of transportation; police functions such as surveillance of movements of nonresidents, organization of local guards, and prevention of plundering; secret police activities ("to know the attitude of everyone"), and the transmission of "all information brought to his attention" to both the partisan unit's

---

as a result of partisan orders forbidding the residents to leave, and establishing a network of guards around it—or even burning down villages around its fringes.

[124] The partisans rarely controlled urban areas. An exception, the town of Dorogobuzh, was under partisan rule from 15 February to 7 June 1942. A system of municipal government was re-established; so were the NKVD, a rayon military commissariat, a rayon militia, and a rayon Party committee. (See Chap. VII, Sect. IV, A.) The situation here may have been exceptional, however, in that military control and direction rested to a great extent with regular Army units under General Belov rather than with the usual type of partisan units. The more complete administrative and political network reintroduced here may, therefore, have reflected not only the urban but also the military-governmental character of the situation.

staff and its Special Section; the billeting of partisans, and the distribution of food and fodder to the unit. In short, his were the typical functions of a Soviet military government officer concerned primarily with the assurance of material supplies and services to the partisans and with the preservation of law and order.[125] It appears that this type of administration prevailed in areas where temporary partisan control was envisioned.

(3) There are instances of the appointment of civil officials to form a new local government. After ousting the German-appointed local officials the partisans would select a new mayor, starosta (the German reports speak of "village elders"—one to a village—though perhaps they were chairmen of collective farms), or other local administrators, whose functions were similar to those described above. Examples of such appointments come from widely different areas and dates. It would seem that in all instances, however, villages so administered were those where partisans were not permanently billeted and where they perhaps made only periodic calls. So far as the partisans were concerned, one of the most important tasks of their civilian appointees was supervision of agricultural activities and collection of grain for the partisans.

(4) A peculiar three-man board, or troika, was occasionally established as an organ of government. The fragmentary evidence suggests that these troikas constituted an executive nucleus combining partisan sponsorship with Party, State, and NKVD functions. They were in existence in several areas of Leningrad Oblast before the end of 1941, where they continued (unless the Germans were able to uproot them) until 1944; a few German reports also speak of troikas in other parts of occupied territory.[126]

Evidently some confusion existed about the formal character of the troikas. It seems most correct to describe them as being established by the partisans as the smallest unit representing the various branches of Soviet and Party power. An order issued to a local official by a troika during a raid near Novaya Russa in December 1941 was signed: "By decision of the Rayon Troika: Chairman of the Rayon Troika, N. Alexeyev, Secre-

[125] See Linkov, p. 373; also this book, Chap. VII, Sect. IV, A; and Appendix, Document 44.

[126] There is no indication that the troikas were used anywhere else as systematically as in the Leningrad area, where the organization of partisans and underground differed from that in remaining areas in several significant respects. It is also possible that troikas used elsewhere had less sweeping functions than had those in the north. Thus the first Order of the Day issued by Fyodorov on 30 October 1941 provided for the "confirmation of an Extraordinary Commission of Three, consisting of [x, y, z] for the prosecution and punishment of traitors to the Motherland." (Fyodorov, English ed., p. 161.) In Cherven Rayon the partisans appealed in mid-1943 to the population to elect a "three-man commission in every locality" to supervise the changes in agricultural relations necessitated by the war. In such cases, one suspects, the three-man team was a convenient device for supervision and control, rather than an organ of government.

tary of the Molvotitsy Rayon Executive Committee of the Communist Party (of Bolsheviks)."[127]

The most detailed information is contained in a unique ten-page report sent by the troika which operated in Dedovichi Rayon (south of Dno, in Leningrad Oblast) for the period from November 1941 (when the troika was established) to July 1942.[128] The report states that, after the first months of the occupation, during which the population was evidently willing to collaborate with the Germans, by October (of 1941) "the situation had changed so much in our favor that the formation of a troika and the re-establishment of Soviet authority could be considered." In early November, the troika was formed "by order of the [partisan] Brigade." It consisted of a former official of the "civil administration of Dedovichi" (perhaps an inexact German translation) as chairman; a woman (who had worked in the Party *raikom*) as delegate for Party affairs; and a former police official from Dedovichi as delegate for "special tasks" (in substance the equivalent of NKVD work). Thus each represented one branch—State, Party, and NKVD. In addition, the troika had individuals assigned to such special subjects as agriculture, food, propaganda; a secretary of the troika; and the commander of a special partisan detachment assigned to the troika, presumably as a guard.

The same report outlines the tasks of the troika:

1. . . . A broad propaganda program of mass indoctrination and recruitment among civilians;
2. The re-establishment of all Soviet organs of government;
3. The re-establishment of all kolkhoz institutions dissolved by the Germans;
4. Abolition of all German measures;
5. Organized help of every kind by the population for the partisans;
6. Death to all traitors.

The team promptly set out to accomplish these tasks, although German antipartisan operations impeded their fulfillment. Allowing for considerable exaggerations in its report to higher Soviet-side headquarters, it is clear that the partisan government was successful in commanding the obedience of a large part of the rayon's residents and, except near highways, strongpoints, and state farms where Germans were stationed, in carrying out the sowing of grain, the removal of collaborators, and the

[127] Sdf. von Minden [no title], 27 December 1941 (GMDS, II AK 33947/7). The rayon "executive committee" was either (1) a confusion of terms, or (2) a smaller body than the *raikom,* left behind as an underground organ; or (3) the executive committee of the soviet, rather than the Party. There are no peacetime Party *raiispolkomy*. The accompanying German documents state that Alexeyev had been second secretary of the Party in this area.

[128] A German translation appears in Korueck 584, "Uebersetzung. Rechenschaftsbericht der Troika, aufgefunden bei der Kampfgruppe Nord," 28 September 1942 (GMDS, X AK 44431/48).

propagandizing of the population that had been among its basic assignments.

By the summer of 1942 at least three other rayons in the neighborhood also had troikas, whose tasks were presumably similar; some of their activity was retributive (liquidation of collaborators), some economic. According to Soviet postwar accounts, troikas existed in the same vicinity in December 1943 to January 1944, when the partisans controlled more sizable territory. The account—in this instance, an article published in the partisan newspaper of the Dno *raikom*—contains an appeal of the Dno Party *raikom* and "its" Organizational Troika.[129] The text suggests that the troika was intended to be an organ distinct from the Party committee, presumably occupied largely with administrative and economic functions, but that, in name at least, its activities were either subject to or closely coordinated with Party directives. On 30 December 1943, according to the newspaper of the Fifth Leningrad Partisan Brigade, a conference was held of "representatives of the people's power." One of the speakers began, "As plenipotentiary of the troika of N village, I have been responsible for the organization of forest camps for the people . . . a bakery, a public bath." Thus the troikas operated not only on a rayon basis but also within individual villages. More generally, however, the troikas sought to re-establish organs of local government in each locality under their control.

The above material confirms the impression that there were often no clear-cut distinctions between civil and military partisan activities, nor between partisan, Party, and State roles in the re-establishment of local administration in partisan-held areas. It is unlikely that a clear-cut division between civilian and military authority existed in the partisan-controlled areas, for the simultaneous control of the partisan brigades by both political and military authorities would have made a complete separation of their political and military functions impossible.

C. PARTY AND KOMSOMOL

The role of the Party in actual administration remains obscure. On the one hand, German reports as well as Soviet postwar accounts often tended to exaggerate the part played by Communist organizations; on the other hand, a network of Party cells was supposed to exist in the underground, often in close conjunction with the partisan movement. Frequently the Party committees existed merely on paper until a partisan unit arose in the area and permitted their activation. In the absence of other evidence, one must conclude that the revival of local government in partisan areas involved the transformation of the phantom network of Party com-

[129] *Dnovets*, New Series, no. 1, 10 January 1944.

mittees into an overt and effective body. The putative prestige of the Party and its local representatives was intended to facilitate the fulfillment of partisan orders; while, in reverse, the physical force of the partisans made it possible to restore Party organs in a political no man's land.[130] Orders to the local population were often issued over the joint signatures of partisan and Party commanders.

In virtually all instances, the re-establishment of Party and State organs resulted in a series of *local* bodies, the highest at the rayon level. In fact, and quite naturally so in view of the limited size of the partisan-controlled areas, no actual administrative bodies on a higher echelon seem to have re-emerged, though in name (and in the underground) oblast committees of Party and Komsomol existed, and occasionally appeals were distributed in the name of a mythical (or evacuated) USSR or BSSR soviet.[131]

D. SOVIETS

Though the phantom Party bodies were restored in fact, the local soviets remained largely fictitious even in partisan-held areas. Mention of them—sometimes merely of Executive Committees of rayon soviets— in partisan leaflets, newspapers, and orders must be considered an attempt to provide a cloak of legitimacy for the new State (as distinguished from Party) organs and to "demonstrate" the presence of these bodies, which in Soviet mythology had become an inalienable part of the Communist order.

In many cases, a "chairman of the village soviet" was reappointed, in addition to the kolkhoz chairman. Both carried out partisan orders on the delivery of grain and other goods and services. In another case, an order on local curfew and guard regulations was issued jointly by the commander and commissar of a partisan unit in Kalinin Oblast and the "chairman of the Executive Committee" of the rayon soviet.[132]

References to rayon soviets appear most frequently on the masthead of partisan newspapers, always following the reference to the Party *raikom*. Likewise, an order of 8 April 1942, providing for the establishment of

---

[130] The territorial Party structure must not be confused with the Party cells functioning within the partisan units themselves. In addition to the Party, the Komsomol was likewise reactivated. It appears that Komsomol members were widely used for political propaganda activities under Party direction.

[131] Evidently inter-rayon committees (generally troikas) were instituted in areas where it was physically impossible to organize separate *raikomy* in each of several adjacent rayons.

[132] The confusion is heightened by the fact that their order, evidently in an attempt at "legitimacy," was based on a decree of the Supreme Soviet of the USSR and was addressed to the "Rayon Soviet of Workers' and Red Army Deputies of Nevel"—an institution of Civil War days that had long been defunct. This was either a characteristic improvisation of a local partisan and Party official, or else simply an error in terminology. See Appendix, Document 40.

home guard units in Klichev Rayon, one of the more thoroughly partisan-controlled districts in Mogilev Oblast, was signed by the Party *raikom* and the "Rayon Soviet of Toilers' Deputies."[133]

E. JUDICIARY AND EXECUTIVE

There is no evidence of a systematic restoration of judicial organs. Considering the nature of partisan activity and the conditions under which areas were seized and held, it is scarcely surprising that no "civil courts" were established. The only pertinent data reveal the creation of a "Revolutionary-Military Tribunal" (once more the revival of a Civil War term) in the Dedushka Partisan Regiment. According to a newspaper account, this was established in October 1941 as a three-man board.[134] A German report stated that, in the spring of 1942, partisans "officially restoring Soviet authority" in a group of villages in Baranoviche Oblast, in addition to hoisting a red flag, began by proclaiming their assumption of judicial authority, probably for the conviction of collaborators and perhaps marauders. Other partisan units established various revolutionary tribunals, special three-man boards reminiscent of NKVD troikas, and courts-martial, to deal with discipline and treason cases within the unit and to "handle" collaborators.

The report of the Dedovichi troika discusses at some length the liquidation of collaborators in the partisan-held area; this more orderly extermination must be distinguished from individual attacks and assassinations of collaborators in German-held territory. As the report states, "The special task of the troika was the struggle against traitors and other counterrevolutionaries . . . to destroy these elements and to establish, in the enemy rear area, a basis of unhindered work in the spirit of the Soviet regime." During its first nine months, the troika and sixty "traitors" shot, including twenty-two alleged kulaks.

F. ANTI-FASCIST COMMITTEES

A peculiar form of organization that arose during the war was the Anti-Fascist Committee, which was intended largely as a political and propaganda organ, not as a unit of administration. In essence, these committees paralleled the network of Communist Party rayon and oblast committees in the areas annexed to the USSR in 1939–40: Western Belorus-

---

[133] Tsanava, I, 163. In the comment, the author speaks merely of the *raikom* and "rayon executive committee," rather than a full soviet. The appeal itself, curiously enough, in speaking of "Soviet organs," asks the population to help "military [i.e., partisan] and local organs" alike, listing the two as separate categories. On the home guard, see Sect. VI, H.

[134] *Fokinskii Rabochii* (organ of Dyatkovo Rayon Party Committee and Rayon Soviet), no. 55 (25 April 1942). According to this account, the board was "elected" and evidently tried collaborators apprehended by the partisans.

sia, the Western Ukraine, and the Baltic States.[135] In some respects they resembled the anti-Fascist Jewish and Women's committees established in the USSR and abroad during the war, as well as the "Fatherland Fronts" and "United Fronts" created in some of the subsequent satellite states. Their basic purpose was to enlist personnel *outside* the ranks of the Communist Party in areas where the Party, in numbers and popularity, was assumed to be too weak to provide sufficient cadres and pulling power for political and propaganda work.

The plan to establish such bodies appears to have originated early in the war. If Soviet accounts are to be believed, the Belorussian Party sent organizers into Brest Oblast in August 1941. By early 1942 they had succeeded in establishing an indigenous organization and in April formed the "Oblast Anti-Fascist Committee for Struggle Against the German Occupiers," whose central office consisted of a Secretariat, a Special Section, an Agitation and Propaganda Section, and a Training Section; a typical counterpart to an underground Party or Komsomol *obkom*. It had assembled several typewriters, a ramshackle printing press and supplies, and began publishing daily news bulletins as well as leaflets. Its range of activity is suggested by the fact that it published leaflets in German and in Polish as well as in Russian.[136]

Likewise, in Vileika, Baranoviche, and Bialystok Oblasts, Anti-Fascist committees arose in 1942–44.[137] In the latter two and in Brest, the oblast Anti-Fascist Committees published their own newspapers in addition to those issued by the Party. They also issued their own leaflets and helped with the distribution of others. In Vileika, a Soviet account states, their organization was speeded up by order of the Party *obkom* from August 1942 on; by November 1943, 100 such cells, including youth groups, are alleged to have existed there, some probably being temporary units.[138] In all instances, the sponsorship and direction of the Anti-Fascist Committees were in Party and regular partisan hands. In Brest, Party organizers established them; in Vileika they were created "from the *aktiv* connected with the partisan movement." Unmistakably "front" organizations, the committees also carried out specific operations in conjunction with the underground and the partisans. An Anti-Fascist Committee is alleged to have seized and delivered alive to the partisans the first deputy mayor of Baranoviche, a certain Ruzak; others carried out demolition tasks. By

---

[135] In addition, one reference has been found to "anti-Fascist cells" which were to be established in the Bryansk area in conjunction with the formation of local indigenous assistance groups. It is likely that this refers to the groups described below as home guards. See Sect. VI, H.

[136] Tsanava, I, 197, 226.

[137] There are suggestions that they also existed in Lithuania and Volhynia. No evidence has been found to show their existence in Galicia.

[138] Tsanava, II, 954.

April 1944, when the partisans were ready to strike all-out blows in co-operation with the advancing Red Army, at least some of the Anti-Fascist Committees were transformed into regular partisan detachments.

Whether the special device of establishing Anti-Fascist Committees on a broader basis than Party cells was successful cannot be judged from the available material.[139] Their very creation, however, is indicative of the flexibility of the Soviet authorities in recognizing that the "new" areas called for a more subtle approach than was required in the "sovietized" regions, and that popular support had to be sought by means that constituted a typical, though by no means unique, concession and temporary deviation from standard procedures.

G. ADMINISTRATIVE MEASURES

Standard measures of the partisan administration included the establishment of law and order, albeit of a peculiar sort. The removal of local officials appointed by the Germans was one of the first steps; at times, the "disposal" of irregular bands, marauders, and criminals was undertaken. Posting guards, proclaiming police regulations, registering residents and livestock, and establishing a pass system for entering or leaving the locality usually followed. In addition, the return of state and communal property distributed by the Germans, or of private property "reassigned" or plundered under the occupation, frequently took place. The general pattern, though fluid and often informal, aimed at the restoration of the *status quo ante bellum* in fact as well as in form, with such alterations as the military situation demanded.

In parts of the Northern Ukraine, Belorussia, and Leningrad Oblast where, during the last months of the occupation, the Germans made attempts to evacuate the entire population westward—either as a punitive measure occasioned by partisan activity, or in an attempt to rescue manpower—the partisan administration sought to establish special "forest camps" to which the population could flee from the villages and escape German seizure. Conditions in such camps, especially during the severe winter of 1943–44, appear to have been horrifying.[140] German records are virtually devoid of information on them, but even accounts in partisan newspapers and leaflets suggest that there was considerable dissatisfaction among the civilians. The administrative side of the camp organization is best revealed by a report on a conference of local soviet, Party, kolkhoz chairmen, and police representatives held near Plyussa (southwest of Luga) on 30 December 1943. The partisan administrative functions discussed covered:

[139] No effort has been made to investigate their activity in the Baltic States.

[140] The earliest such camps were reported in January 1943 in Belorussia. See also Sect. V, D, 2.

Organization of material aid to the partisans;
Defense of the Revolutionary Order;
Saving the peaceful inhabitants and their property from the German robbers;
Public works [i.e., mud-huts] in the evacuee forest camps;
Preparations for spring sowing.[141]

Here as elsewhere, the formula for partisan administration was: "The people's power in the German rear rests on the armed force of the partisans, who in turn lean on the constant help of the popular masses."

H. HOME GUARD

A standard function of local organization in partisan-held areas was the establishment of an auxiliary force composed of indigenous personnel. This force—variously referred to in both German and Soviet sources, probably in accordance with actual variations on the spot—amounted to a combination of militia and service agencies. There is no indication that such home guards existed before the spring of 1942, but between March and May 1942 they were organized in a number of partisan-held areas. It is possible that their creation followed a special order from Moscow.[142] In Kalinin Oblast, a partisan unit and the rayon soviet revived by it ordered such a "guard unit" to be organized from among the residents. By early April 1942 the Klichev partisans, in the name of the rayon soviet and Party *raikom,* ordered: "For the purpose of guarding inhabited localities from Fascist occupiers, Red partisan otryads of self-defense are to be organized in each locality.[143] Soviet memoirs likewise indicate the formation of such units in the first half of 1942. In the Bryansk forest, they were established nominally by the underground Party *raikom* and had a squad of partisans attached to them. They acted as a police force to keep local law and order, distributed leaflets, and later engaged in regular military operations with the partisans. There are also indications that some disagreement arose within the partisan command on the question of forming such "assistance groups." As was explained in one of the Soviet memoirs, some partisans, even before the official organization, had used local

[141] *Partizanskaya Mest* (organ of the Fifth Leningrad Brigade), no. 36 (3 January 1944). One of the speakers discussed the construction of a public bath, a bakery, and an enclosure for the cattle driven from the German-held villages. "We have already figured out," he added, "that when the Red Army returns we must sow no less than eighty hectares."

[142] According to the record of the Morogov Detachment, operating in Smolensk Oblast in May 1942, meetings were held in four villages at which the commander and commissar of the unit staged a "comprehensive discussion of Order No. 130/1942 of the People's Commissariat for Defense [concerning] the tasks of the kolkhoz peasants in the rear of the enemy. . . . According to the resolution of the kolkhoz peasants, self-protection groups will be organized from among the local inhabitants in the villages." [See Appendix, Document 19.] The Stalin Order No. 130/1942 is his First-of-May appeal and contains merely a brief general exhortation to the partisans.

[143] Tsanava, I, 163.

personnel to help guard villages and gather uniforms and food. "What remained was to organize these groups properly, to direct them, and to protect them from surprise attacks." But opposition arose from two sides: security-conscious partisan leaders who feared that mixing "old women and invalids" with the partisan movement (something of an exaggeration) would increase the chances of infiltration by German agents; and the most stalwart Communists who insisted that the partisan movement and Communist Party had to remain a small "vanguard" and should not be "diluted" among the non-Party mass. With Stalin's order supporting their stand, those arguing for the extension of the home guard system prevailed.[144]

By August 1942 home guards existed in Kalinin and Smolensk Oblasts, near Bobruisk, Bryansk, and Navlya. In some instances, women and boys fourteen years or over were drawn into the units. In all verifiable cases, they were either under the command of a partisan attached to the home guard or were headed by "experienced Comrades" (as one Soviet writer puts it).

It appears that home guard units were established only in areas where the partisans were comparatively strong and expected to maintain their control. Civil administrators, such as mayors, could be put in office even if their control were to be transitory, but the establishment of the home guard presupposed continued contact. Its main tasks, as they evolved from 1942 on, included the prevention of local unrest and marauding; the maintenance of some defense in case of raids by German and collaborator forces; the alerting of regular partisan units in emergencies; limited assistance to the indigenous population in agriculture, construction, and other tasks desired by the partisans; and, especially in 1944, outright participation in partisan operations, in some instances as regular partisan units.

There is evidence that at least in one instance, in April 1943, a "Red Home Guard," headed by the old militia chief, took control of an area in Kharkov Oblast when the Germans abandoned it and before the Red Army could take over in strength. The home guard was organized ostensibly by local partisans largely for police purposes.[145]

In substance, the home guards were a partisan counterpart to the German-sponsored *Ordnungsdienst* and *Wehrdoerfer,* "armed villages," established for self-defense against partisan raids. On the German as on the partisan side, one major reason for such organizations was the shortage of trained military personnel. In each instance, some disagreement arose over the usefulness of drawing the more indifferent mass of rank-and-file

---

[144] Andreyev, pp. 193–97, 206–7.

[145] GFP Gr. 647, Aussendienststelle IV, "Schlussbericht," 27 April 1943 (GMDS, XXXXVIII AK 40773/22, Anlage 177). There had been virtually no partisan activity here before the German retreat.

inhabitants into the movement; in each instance the process was found to be necessary. In the general polarization of attitudes in the occupied territory the local police, both under partisans and Germans, was gradually transformed into a fighting force. At the same time, the partisan home guard does not appear to have played a leading part in paramilitary operations; it remained in large measure a defensive organization.

I. RECRUITMENT

An important part of the reimposition of Soviet controls was the recruitment of personnel from the occupied territories for the partisan movement and the Red Army. This process marked the transition between direct partisan action, often involving threats or compulsion, and the reimposition of regular mobilization procedures. It is only the latter that falls within the purview of this section. [For discussions of recruitment, see also Chap. III, Sect. II, B.]

Once the somewhat haphazard seizure of men was superseded by a more orderly draft, the partisans and the partisan-imposed local government proceeded to decree mobilization on the basis of Soviet laws. Usually draft notices were posted publicly in partisan-controlled villages; in some instances such notices were even sent to individuals residing in German-held towns (for instance, in Bobruisk and Latvia). The peak of formal recruitment activities apparently was reached during the second half of 1942, i.e., the period when partisan strength was sufficient to command obedience, but when there were still available stragglers and local inhabitants of draft age. Thus, a poster in a partisan-occupied village in the summer of 1942 ordered:

All members of the [Soviet] Armed Forces who escaped from encirclement and are at home, also all men born in 1925, report to your regular units or join the partisan units! Those who remain in hiding and continue to sit home in order to save their skins and those . . . who do not help destroy the German robbers . . . are traitors to the fatherland and will be liquidated by us sooner or later.[149]

In other instances, the call to arms was far more specific, stipulating date and place to which prospective recruits were to report. In the more highly organized partisan brigades, a regular examination procedure was established, in which the secret police organs (i.e., normally the "OO") assumed responsibility for screening. [See Chap. V, Sect. I.] Ordinarily, the partisans themselves would carry out the mobilization; at times, local mayors and village chairmen were employed to help induct draftees; and occasionally the partisans revived a sort of draft board resembling normal Soviet procedure *(voyenkomat)*, i.e., a special agency (on a territorial

---

[146] XXIII A.K. Ic, "Übersetzung, Tagebuch der Kampfhandlungen der Partisanenabteilung des Oblt. Morogoff," September 1942 (GMDS, 339 ID 29087/4).

basis) which selected recruits according to rosters of the indigenous population and mobilization classifications previously assigned.

A special situation obtained in the Yelnya-Dorogobuzh area, where the role of the Soviet Army, along with that of the partisans, was greater than elsewhere. [For a detailed analysis, see Chap. VII, Sect. II, B.] Here Army officers were brought in from the outside to muster recruits; regular medical examinations were conducted by Army officers; a substantial number of men were exempted from military service, and those accepted were sent either to the Red Army or to the partisan units operating in the area. Elsewhere, the procedures seem to have been less formal. However, in almost all partisan-held areas, the mobilization of men, gradually extended in age groups, remained a key activity, carried out by resorting both to Soviet "legality" and physical force.

J. REQUISITIONS

To an even greater extent than recruitment, partisan requisition activities fall into the border zone between haphazard seizure and organized collection of compulsory deliveries. Only the latter type, amounting to institutionalized taxation in kind, can be considered a governmental activity by the partisans; the rest was a form of looting, primarily for purposes of immediate use.

Formal requisition notices, demanding the surrender of specified quantities of grain or other products, were posted by partisans even in localities where they had established no indigenous administrative apparatus. Frequently the orders contained specific quotas; in other cases, the partisans announced the quantities to be surrendered at public meetings held in the village to celebrate the "liberation." Generally receipts were given for foodstuffs procured in this fashion. Later on, some of the partisan units adopted special forms and seals for their receipts, in part to give the transactions a stamp of legality.[147] Moreover, such orderly procedures were aimed at reducing looting by undisciplined partisans. [See Chap. III, Sect. III, D.]

Where the partisans had established a modicum of local government, usually requisition requests were transmitted through the mayors, kolkhoz chairmen, or other newly appointed officials; at times the local "auxiliary committees" (forerunners of the home guard) did the collecting. There are numerous partisan directives addressed to rayon soviet chairmen, mayors, or managers of individual farms.

The intensity of the requisitioning, and the extent to which compulsion

---

[147] Generally receipts were given in lieu of payment. In at least one instance, however, the partisans paid in German-issued currency at higher rates than the Germans paid—largely for psychological reasons, one may assume. In another case, a band offered premiums for superior deliveries, in the form of increased land assignments.

was used in extracting food and other products from the population, varied from area to area. While some regions were stripped of virtually all produce and sometimes were constrained by considerable intimidation and summary punishment, in other areas the peasantry was left decidedly better off than it had been under German rule. Though details are lacking on organizational changes reflecting varying local conditions, it is clear that the partisans were content wherever possible to restrict themselves to stating quotas and quantities they wished to obtain and to leave the implementation of their orders to their indigenous appointees.

On some occasions the partisans issued, rather than collected, food among the local population; in particular, scarce commodities such as salt, tobacco, and textiles were at times distributed either free or at low prices. Such efforts cannot properly be considered as administrative tasks; usually they were psychological warfare measures carried out shortly after the partisans' arrival, aimed at impressing the inhabitants; or they were emergency steps to satisfy the local population or enable it to work for them; or they were rewards for "good behavior" after a successful operation in which such supplies were procured.[148]

K. CASH AND STATE LOAN COLLECTIONS

In well-controlled partisan areas, a special effort was made to collect funds for Soviet armament and to underwrite Soviet state loans. Such efforts, it is true, were a far more customary means of milking the inhabitants in the USSR than might appear at first. Nevertheless, their relative success (if one may believe Soviet sources) does indeed testify to the considerable measure of control and compulsion exercised by the partisans. At all times an effort was made to depict the contributions as spontaneous, voluntary moves by the population. They were widely acclaimed at partisan rallies as an achievement to be emulated elsewhere; the Soviet press on both sides of the front made considerable use of them, and, at times, direct messages of gratitude were transmitted in token demonstrations of the solidarity of Soviet and partisan-held territories. In substance, the political and propaganda purposes of the operation clearly outweighed the financial and monetary benefits derived from it. Not the least of the former was the closer bond of identification that the operation established between the civilians (and partisans) and the Soviet regime.

As early as the spring of 1942 some villages in Leningrad Oblast were reported to have sent 3,000 poods (108,300 pounds) of food to the starving population of Leningrad—a widely hailed move that was acclaimed in

[148] There are some indications that, everything else being equal, the partisans preferred to be more severe toward people in marginal areas (who were also more exposed to heavy German levies) than toward the residents of the partisan-held areas. from whom further quotas could be exacted at future times.

312 / iv. partisan psychological warfare

a *Pravda* editorial in March. A few weeks later, both in this area and in the Bryansk forest, a collection of money for the "State Defense Fund" was begun. According to V. Andreyev, the author of a volume of memoirs on the Bryansk partisans, a sum of 2,500,000 rubles was collected by Party, Komsomol, and partisan units for the "purchase" of an armored column, which was then ordered and delivered to the Red Army on behalf of the partisan area. During the same period, a group of village soviets in the area in which the Morogov detachment conducted systematic and intensive propaganda also "received the assistance of ten men to explain the announced state loan." As a result, contributions were made to purchase state bonds.

L. AGRICULTURE

By far the most crucial and controversial problem was the fate of the collective farms.[149] Given the close identification of the kolkhoz system with the very essence of the Soviet regime—a link carefully nurtured by official propaganda over a number of years—and the evidence of wide-spread popular hostility to the maintenance of collective farms, the Soviet policy-makers faced a difficult dilemma. Theoretically, the reimposition of Soviet institutions and controls in partisan-held areas called for the re-establishment of collective farming as one of the first measures. On the other hand, the process of wartime accommodation to popular senti-ments in a variety of fields, ranging from Russian patriotism to religious sentiments, involved a temporary retreat from prewar Soviet practices and slogans in an effort to rally popular support for the regime. On the Soviet side of the front, the collective farms were maintained; their abolition in wartime was both impossible politically and impracticable economically. Though in practice Soviet controls loosened to such an extent that a stringent tautening was required after the war, officially Moscow could not and presumably did not seriously envision a genuine change in agrarian relations.

At the same time the potency of the antikolkhoz theme was not lost on Soviet propaganda. The few German propaganda efforts made in this direction, feeble and halfhearted though they were, appear to have had a considerable measure of success during the first months of the war; reports on spontaneous action by kolkhoz farmers immediately following

[149] Scattered efforts were made in partisan-held areas to stimulate the activity of artisans and small-scale industries. Given the areas and conditions involved, such en-deavors were bound to be meagre and sporadic. They amounted to the reopening of a carpenter shop, a leather factory producing shoes, and a workshop building barrels. Most frequently such "production" was geared to partisan needs, especially in wear-ing apparel or equipment. No complex or rigid organization was needed to control it. In addition, instances are reported in which partisans drafted the population (and occasionally prisoners captured by them) as compulsory labor.

the withdrawal of the Red Army speak of a general effort to abolish the collective farms and reintroduce private ownership of garden plots, cattle, equipment and inventory, and in some instances, land holdings. Soviet psychological warfare exploited the antikolkhoz sentiment in the Red Army by systematically spreading rumors about the prospect of an alleged dissolution of collective farms by the Soviet government after the war. Such rumors were too ubiquitous to be considered either spontaneous or accidental.

The partisans faced substantially the same dilemma. During the first months after the German invasion no particular changes in partisan attitudes toward collective farms were apparent: the partisans were too weak to control kolkhoz areas and were usually cut off from Soviet commands; apparently it also took a certain time for Soviet directives to be readjusted. Again, during the latter part of the war, from about the fall of 1943 to the end, there is no evidence of deviation among the partisans from orthodox Soviet attitudes toward collective farms; at that time, the partisans were strong enough to control the areas and to make headway without resorting to exceptional and, in the minds of the Soviet leaders, highly dangerous tactics. Thus the crucial period was from October 1941 to the spring or summer of 1943.

In Chernigov Oblast, the Party *obkom* which organized the partisan movement sanctioned a transfer of garden plots and peasants huts to the private ownership of their users. The memoirs of the oblast partisan leader, Fyodorov, confirm the fact that the rayon soviet (directed by the *obkom*) "instruct[ed] the kolkhozes to divide the property among the peasants without delay," though the instructions referred, apparently, only to movable property.[150] In this instance, one purpose may have been to prevent the farm implements from falling into German hands. That such a decision could not be taken without at least tacit assent from higher Soviet organs is suggested by Fyodorov's reference to the *obkom* decision, his discussion of it after the war, and the fact that another German report from an adjacent area likewise asserted that, by December 1941, partisans acting on orders from higher Soviet authorities divided farm tools and cattle among the peasantry.[151]

The tactical element was no longer in evidence at the end of 1941. In December of that year Army Group Center reported that the partisans "by instructions from Moscow had distributed kolkhoz land to the peasants." There is virtually no documentary proof that a full-fledged dissolution of collective farms was undertaken by the partisans; most

---

[150] Chef Sipo u. SD, "Ereignismeldung UdSSR, Nr. 107," 8 October 1941, p. 4 (GMDS, SD-29); Fyodorov, p. 104.

[151] Befh.d.rueckw.H.Geb.Mitte, Prop.-Abt.W, "Stimmungsbericht zum Propaganda-lage- und Taetigkeitsbericht vom 1.–15.12.1941," n.d. (GMDS, OKW/479).

German reports discussing it were based on hearsay or interrogation. Yet the frequency and geographic distribution of German statements suggest that the reports were not fabricated by individual officers or indigenous informants. In March 1942 the Second Panzer Army reported that north of Bryansk peasants in partisan areas "received land and a share of the harvest as their property." Farther west, in Glusk Rayon, the Germans claimed that "the partisans had divided the agricultural enterprises fully among the rural population." Other reports for July and November 1942 likewise spoke of the partition of kolkhoz land in partisan-held areas, as well as the institution of premiums in the form of enlarged land grants to those who exceeded grain delivery quotas.

Only one official Soviet publication, as far as can be determined, admits that collectives were not re-established in all areas captured by the partisans. Viktor Liventsev, in an account of the Bobruisk area partisan movement, describes the election of a new *raikom* in Klichev Rayon in April 1942, following the disintegration of the original underground Party organization left behind in 1941. This new *raikom* settled the question of spring sowing in 1942 by a decree that stated: "Spring sowing and use of the land in 1942 is to be carried out either collectively or individually, according to the wishes of the kolkhoz members."[152]

Whether the technical-economic or the political considerations weighed heavier in permitting the peasants to choose between collective and individual farm work in this instance, of course, cannot be established.

Nevertheless, there is substantial evidence that the myth of the kolkhoz system was fully maintained in official Soviet and partisan (printed) propaganda; the names of partisan newspapers continued to include the word "kolkhoz" in their titles (though in fewer instances than in 1941 and 1943–44); and while Soviet psychological warfare in general addressed its target more frequently as "peasants" than as "kolkhozniks," there was not the least suggestion of disparaging the concept of the kolkhoz. Quite the contrary; propaganda, whenever it belabored the agrarian theme, displayed pride and insistence on the maintenance of collective farming. Thus the prevalent phenomenon in 1942 appears to have been the re-establishment of the institution and form of the kolkhoz in most partisan-held areas, while introducing substantial changes in actual practice. This device permitted the partisans loyally to maintain Soviet slogans

[152] Viktor Liventsev, *Partisanskii krai* (Leningrad: Molodaya Gvardiya, 1951), p. 173. The decree also authorized the peasants to use draft animals "jointly or individually" subject to the approval of either the village soviet or the kolkhoz chairman (where there were collectives).

A former partisan states that the Voroshilov Brigade, operating in Belyi Rayon, was popular with the inhabitants because it "permitted the peasants who had dissolved their kolkhozes to continue in the same manner." (Russian Research Center, B 7, #140, pp. 47–48.)

and façades while capitalizing on popular satisfaction with changes in practice.

The major changes, within the looser frame of kolkhoz organization, concerned private ownership of livestock, agricultural implements, dwellings, and in some instances land. Their extent varied from area to area. In September 1942 the partisans northeast of Minsk were reported to have "in some instances introduced a new agrarian order on the basis of collectives, which, while maintaining the old delivery quotas, grants the peasantry greater land plots." The authors of Chapter IX of this book conclude that, in the Polotsk area, the partisans, in order to assure the cooperation of the peasants, went "so far as to institute an agrarian reform which, as a German observer points out, was superior to a similar German reform." This, "carried out on orders from Moscow," provided for an increase in individual peasant garden plots, while retaining the kolkhoz system. One German summary report even claimed to know that the new agrarian order on the distribution of land and the revision of delivery quotas in partisan areas was based on a Stalin order. "In some of the thoroughly partisan-held areas an entirely new delivery system is being introduced by order of Stalin. The peasants in these areas must turn in only half the amounts demanded in the areas controlled by us [i.e., the Germans]. In addition, there are cases in which peasants have been given their own land, and usually in larger allotments than by us."[153]

An order of the Klichev Rayon partisans and Party committee on the distribution of the 1942 harvest points in the same direction, without making explicit the extent to which the directives deviated from Soviet peacetime standards. In this instance, there is no evidence that land or cattle were made private property, but the harvest distribution went further than had been previously allowed; special privileges were accorded to wives and widows of partisans and Red Army soldiers.[154]

In some areas, however, there is no indication that partisans permitted a relaxation of the kolkhoz system. This was particularly true in Smolensk and Leningrad Oblasts. In the Smolensk area, collective farms were promptly restored in the territory seized by the partisans who operated under the over-all direction of General Belov. A letter, ostensibly signed by 15,000 partisans and civilians and sent to Stalin, stated: "In the villages and towns liberated from the German occupiers we have re-established the organs of Soviet administration. On the collective farms we have begun the spring sowing." [See Chap. VII, Sect. IV, A; Appendix, Document 19.]

[153] PzAOK 2, "Anlage zu Pz. AOK 2, Ic/AO Nr. 960/42 geh. vom 3.12.42" (GMDS, PzAOK 2, 37075/159). See also *Nachrichten,* Nr. 3, p. 8.

[154] Tsanava, II, 87–88. It is interesting that Tsanava, in discussing the Klichev Rayon in 1942, does not cite the Liventsev order quoted above.

Likewise, southwest of Leningrad the administrative troikas were charged with re-establishing the kolkhozes. Slogans and titles in partisan printed propaganda in this region abounded with references to collective farms. A letter sent by partisans and civilians from the territory held by the 2d Brigade to Andrei Zhdanov, secretary of the Leningrad Party *obkom,* declared that "in our area we live in Soviet fashion. . . . In the collective farms, general meetings are taking place, agitators are at work, the harvest is being gathered."[155] The report of the Dedovichi troika, quoted earlier in this section, specifically describes how: "Since the kolkhozes had been dissolved in most of the selsoviets and the harvest had already been divided equally among the peasants according to the [total] number of persons, a very difficult situation presented itself to the troika. The kolkhoz cattle had been distributed among a few kolkhozniks and often the edinolichniks [those who had not belonged to the kolkhoz] too had received cattle." To implement the reinstitution of the kolkhoz, "All German-appointed starostas were fired and the former kolkhoz officials were called back again. The whole inventory of the kolkhoz and the herds of cattle were collected together again. The harvest was redivided, not according to the number of persons but according to working days performed. The elements hostile in attitude to the kolkhoz were liquidated."

By the spring of 1942, the Dedovichi troika averred, all sixty collectives in its area (along with eight sovkhozes) were well prepared to proceed with the spring sowing. Nowhere in Leningrad Oblast does a division of kolkhoz property seem to have occurred with the sanction of partisans or underground Party.

The above examples suffice to illustrate five possible hypotheses about the agrarian policy pursued by the partisans.

(1) Did the Germans attribute a reformist policy to the partisans when in reality spontaneous acts by the peasantry itself were all that had happened? Though this may have occurred, the consistent references to Party and Soviet directives, as well as implicit statements in Soviet sources, permit the rejection of the hypothesis. Likewise, some German descriptions of partisan land reforms may be ascribed to efforts of German advocates of agrarian reform to impress their own superiors; however, this does not adequately explain all the evidence on partisan-conducted reforms.

(2) Did the partisans spontaneously institute the partition of property and land without sanction from Moscow? Though such action may indeed have taken place, especially during the winter of 1941–42, many of the examples cited above refer to units and time periods when the partisans were under fairly rigid control from the Soviet side. This hypothesis must likewise be rejected as, at best, only a partial explanation.

[155] *Narodnyi Mstitel,* no. 11 (31 August 1942).

(3) Did the partisans promote agrarian reforms in areas on the fringes of their territory and beyond, but seek to maintain the collective farms in areas they held firmly? The evidence does not suffice to form a positive answer. There are some hints that the partisans encouraged outright abolition of collective farms in German-held areas, in an obvious attempt to undermine German efforts and, after the limited German reform of February 1942, to outbid the Germans in catering to peasant demands. It is also clear that in centers of strength, especially in 1943–44, the partisans nowhere considered, let alone implemented, a breakdown of such Soviet institutions as the collective farm. Nevertheless, some of the material adduced above pertains to areas firmly and rather permanently held by the partisans, and these still witnessed a substantial agrarian reform.

(4) Thus one is tempted to conclude that the *de facto* loosening of the kolkhoz structure, while maintaining its *de jure* status, was a widely applied partisan policy, which had official Soviet sanction as an important stage in wartime "concession" tactics, designed to win the fuller support of the population. The policy was not introduced until after the relatively widespread defection of the peasantry had become apparent; it stemmed from weakness, not strength; and it was revoked as soon as Soviet and partisan power had become sufficient to permit once again a greater disregard for popular aspirations.

One can only speculate about the reasons for the geographic variations in agrarian policy, which appear to have been more than random. The scant available information suggests that the Soviet government consciously reserved the "final" reimposition of Soviet controls and institutions, as well as the conduct of purges, for the Red Army (and the NKVD operating in conjunction with it), even in areas where partisans had ruled previously. This would explain the kolkhoz policy adopted in Smolensk Oblast in 1942, where the partisans were under more thorough Army control than elsewhere.[156]

It would seem that the exception found in Leningrad Oblast reflected

---

[156] The skepticism exhibited by the Red Army toward the partisans in 1943–45 is reported by several former partisans and soldiers. See also V. Gromov, "Stalinskaya nagrada partizanam," *Na rubezhe* (Paris), no. 3–4 (July–August 1952), pp. 43–44. The substitution of Army for partisan controls is well illustrated in the following German report:

In Khomutovka Rayon the partisans had ruled by themselves for several weeks. . . . They had not established a regular administration. . . . The regular Soviet troops who succeeded them promptly established a complete administrative apparatus with NKVD, Party organs, etc. It included the former institutions, i.e., also rayon and village soviets. At the same time, a court was installed which thoroughly screened all former employees and workers of the German agencies. . . . Initially there were partisans among the judges; however, since they were not without prejudice, persons from among the civilian population were co-opted [in their place]. (Wi Kdo Kursk, "Lagebericht fuer die Zeit vom 16.5.—15.6.1943," 17 June 1943, GMDS, Wi/ID 2.773, Anlage 35.)

a policy disagreement at a higher Soviet level. The Leningrad partisans, whose organization was marked by a variety of divergences from
other patterns, were under the general direction of Andrei Zhdanov and
his staff, which was filled with what may be considered the left wing of
the Bolshevik Party—a trend that is assumed to have contributed substantially to the Zhdanov-Malenkov feud in the postwar years. It thus
appears likely that the Leningrad *obkom* stood pat on the maintenance
of the collective farms, while other Soviet leaders advocated a "temporary
retreat."[157] Andrei Andreyev, another member of the Politburo, seems to
have represented the opposite extreme. Andreyev, who after the war was
dropped from the Soviet hierarchy primarily because of agrarian policy
differences, was at times depicted, even by Soviet wartime agents, as a
"moderate." In the summer of 1942, during the conferences of top partisans in the Kremlin, he reportedly discussed the problem with Bondarenko,
commissar of the Southern Bryansk Operative Group. According to a German interrogation, "The partisan leaders reported [in Moscow] that they
had reintroduced the Soviet system in 170 populated points. Andreyev
countered that the partisans must change their tactics. It was not their
task to re-establish the Soviet system; this was the task of the Red
Army. . . . Andreyev advised against reintroducing the kolkhoz system."[158]

---

[157] Some support for this thesis can be derived from a reference to the re-establishment of collective farm regulations in partisan-held areas "on orders from Comrade
Zhdanov," in the troika report already cited. See Appendix, Document 16.

[158] PzAOK 2, Ic/AO, "Meldung," 6 December 1942 (GMDS, PzAOK 2, 30233/
64). On the Moscow conference of the partisan leaders, see also this book, Chap. II,
Sect. III, H, 2.

Andreyev's role in Soviet agriculture bears special investigation. He was the only
member of the Politburo tainted by past association with Bukharin, though he quickly
managed to get on the "Stalin bandwagon" in the twenties. By 1939 he favored an
extension of the *zveno* system (small groups of about a dozen men working the land,
in contrast with the larger brigades), since "the more work on the collective farm is
individualized . . . the more efficient it will be." After the war, Andreyev headed a
special Council on Kolkhoz Affairs and in this capacity extended the use of the *zveno*.
After 1947 his position became progressively weaker; in 1950 he was attacked in
Pravda for his agricultural policies and was replaced by Khrushchev as chief of
agrarian problems in the Soviet hierarchy. A qualified analyst suggests that the Soviet leadership was apprehensive lest "the small *zveno* unit eventually supplant not
only the brigade but also the kolkhoz itself." [Lazar Volin, *A Survey of Soviet Russian
Agriculture,* U.S. Dept. of Agriculture, Agriculture Monograph 5, p. 30; Merle
Fainsod, *How Russia is Ruled* (rev. ed.; Cambridge: Harvard University Press, 1963),
p. 538.] It is possible that Khrushchev, in charge of the partisan movement in the
Ukraine, tried to follow there a policy similar to Zhdanov's in Leningrad, aiming at
a prompt revival of strict kolkhoz orthodoxy. However, the evidence does not suffice
to prove or disprove this hypothesis.

Andreyev's attitude toward the collectives in partisan-held territory during the war
assumes special importance in this context. It is also curious that the mission entrusted
to a Soviet agent to subvert the Vlasov movement included the theme that the
kolkhoz would be abolished after the war and that Andreyev, of all people, would
then become head of state. See Sect. IV, C, 2.

M. SUMMARY

Almost everywhere in their areas, the partisans attempted to establish a form of administration responsive to their demands. Some of their moves were aimed primarily at satisfying their own needs; requisitions, to some extent recruitment, the security functions of military commandants, and the home guard fell into this category. Other tasks, such as the liquidation or arrest of collaborators and some military functions were conditioned by the specific environment in which the partisans operated. And yet in some significant respects the essence of partisan administrative policy was the reinstitution of the Soviet system, with all its associations of fear and authority, power and prestige.[159] The very terminology current among the partisans—references to the Soviet side as the "Great Land" and to their own areas as the "Little Land" (*Malaya Zemlya*)—indicates the psychological warfare effort implicit in this attempt. The actual administrative work carried out was of little significance beyond immediate partisan demands. On the other hand, the symbolic nature of the partisan areas, the much heralded "re-establishment of Soviet power" in widely scattered areas behind the German lines, and the references to the partisans as a "second front" clearly had an impact on the morale of partisans and Germans alike, and on the attitudes of civilians on both sides of the front.

Many facets of partisan administration remain little known; NKVD activities and the "purges" conducted in areas seized by them need further examination. Yet such moves as the creation of phantom soviets, rayon committees, and other typically Soviet institutions indicate the long-range goals of partisan policy. Inevitably, perhaps, of all branches of the Soviet edifice, State institutions were most tenuous and least "essential" for the reassertion of the regime's authority; military, police, and Party machines proved far more substantial.

At the same time, partisan administration and policy showed considerable awareness of the necessity of "flexibility" and adjustment, albeit momentary, to the particular demands of the population. Distribution of food, variations in agrarian and religious policy, as well as the general manipulation of propaganda themes, all tend to support this conclusion. Thus the Soviet formula, as reflected here, amounted to rigidity in institu-

---

[159] In this connection, the sporadic psychological warfare efforts of the partisans are of interest in so far as they sought to impress the population that they were still *bona fide* Soviet citizens, and that they were vicariously "participating" in Soviet political life. This even reached the point where a Soviet leaflet, distributed in the occupied areas, over the signature of Mikhail Kalinin, chairman of the Presidium of the Supreme Soviet of the USSR, informed the people on 9 December 1942 that elections to the Supreme Soviet had been postponed for one year. (FK 550, "Lage- und Taetigkeitsbericht fuer die Zeit vom 24.11. bis 22.12.42," 23 December 1942, GMDS, 203 ID 32104.)

tions and long-range aspirations but considerable fluidity in short-term tactics.

§VII. The Population Between
Germans and Partisans

A. FIRST PHASE OF THE OCCUPATION

As the events of the war revealed, the Soviet population showed both loyalty and disloyalty to the regime. Certain elements of society, particularly those who because of their personal status had a vested interest in the preservation of the regime, were firmly committed on the Soviet side. It seems that among the younger elements and in part among the urban population, especially industrial workers, pro-Soviet sentiments were relatively stronger than among older people and rural elements; among the latter, the kolkhoz farmers constituted a particular source of latent disaffection. At the same time, at least a part of the intelligentsia was not so firmly attached to the Soviet regime that it could be indifferent to disaffection propaganda.

Among the population remaining behind the retreating armies during the early weeks of the 1941 campaign, potential defection from the Soviet cause was heightened by: (1) the evacuation eastward of the most stalwart Communists, including a large part of the bureaucratic and managerial elite; (2) the absence from their places of residence of a sizable number of presumably loyal elements who were serving in the armed forces; (3) the general disruption and disorganization caused by the German onslaught and the Soviet retreat, which tended to weaken the affective and institutional channels of command and loyalty. Thus it may be assumed that a foreign power gaining control of a large part of the Soviet Union had the opportunity to exploit the grievances of the population against its regime and to seek to win its allegiance. These grievances arose from the frustrations sustained under Soviet rule; varying in intensity and impact, they included the general drive for higher standards of living; friction generated by the kolkhoz system; the manifold ramification and menaces of a police state; forms of compulsion and forced speed-up in production, and labor discipline; and, for some elements, there were also religious and national frustrations.

Initial Soviet wartime measures revealed some awareness of these areas of potential disaffection. On the one hand, harsh forms of reprisal and repression were used against individuals suspected of harboring anti-Soviet designs. On the other hand, an intensive propaganda campaign was begun in two major directions: the "exposing" of German and Fascist aims and practices; and the institution, in word and partly in deed, of tactical concessions to popular aspirations, in an effort to marshal all emotional, physical, and psychic resources of the Soviet people for the war. During the first months of the war, however, much of this Soviet psychological warfare campaign toward its own population was neutralized or canceled by factors partly of its own creation, partly beyond its control. These included the legend of German invincibility, strengthened by initial victories and rapid advances; Soviet scorched-earth measures, which caused resentment among the population; a strong popular quest for tranquillity and "being left alone"; and the impact of war and all its disruptions.

By and large, therefore, the population that found itself under German rule seemed at first prepared to throw in its lot with either side. It was up to the two contending parties to win the allegiance of the rank and file, which was neither sufficiently disaffected to accept any alternative unquestioningly, nor sufficiently attached to the Soviet cause to remain blind to other opportunities.

Germany utterly failed to take advantage of the chance thus offered for winning over the Soviet population. It received, just as the Soviet regime did, overwhelming overt obedience to its rule; but surface adjustment—especially when a generation is inured to mimicry—cannot be taken as a guide to its comparative judgment of the two regimes or to its innermost loyalties. German failure was largely inherent in the very approach of the Nazi leadership to the Soviet problem and the aims which it had set itself in the East. In terms of long-range goals, it utterly disregarded popular aspirations; in terms of immediate demands, it assumed that the war's victorious conclusion within a matter of weeks or months allowed the occupiers to ignore the problem of popular allegiance.

Within a brief span of time, a combination of German moves brought about the first stirrings of disillusionment among those (probably an overwhelming majority) of the population who had adopted a wait-and-see attitude, hopeful but watchful. This early gap between occupier and occupied was to deepen as time proceeded and was never to be closed. Among its early stimuli, the most important was German behavior—the physical and personal experiences of the rank-and-file citizens with the German soldier. The effect was at times positive (because of the evidence of "Western culture," hygienic and cultural standards, and other indications of the "good life" in peacetime Germany) but more often negative (because of German stereotypes about the "Eastern *Untermenschen*," or the sense of insecurity of the German soldier operating in occupied Russia). Extensive requisitions and increasing physical abuse, at times militarily unnecessary and even senseless, contributed to this negative effect. More-over, rapidly spreading reports of German maltreatment and neglect of the masses of Soviet prisoners of war in the occupied areas, as well as the activities and atrocities of the SD *Einsatzgruppen,* increased popular disillusionment with the Germans. So did the deterioration of material conditions, bordering on outright famine in many towns and cities, es-pecially as winter approached. Finally, German failure to satisfy popular aspirations in such crucial areas as the dissolution of collective farms alienated the peasantry from their new masters.

By the end of 1941 the early willingness of the Soviet population in the occupied areas to be shown that the Germans were bringing them a better order was vanishing. Disillusionment turned into hostility when, during the winter of 1941–42, the German advance not only came to a standstill but also the Red Army momentarily regained the initiative and returned to the attack. The protraction of the war and the Soviet counter-attack brought about a severe deterioration in German matériel and morale and, indirectly, increased the amount of goods and services commandeered from the indigenous population. All of these facts undermined the myth of German invincibility in the minds of the population which, both in overt behavior and often subconsciously, too, sought to join the stronger of the two contending powers. German victory was no longer sure; pre-vious experiences of Soviet rule suggested that there might be retribution for collaborating with the invaders; the German behavior was worsening; for all these reasons the population began to change its attitude.

By early 1942 the many elements who had sought to escape a choice by simply standing pat were gradually forced to take sides. Though the initial disillusionment was unconnected with it, the emergence of the partisan movement in some degree intensified the spiral of increased terror and counterterror in whose midst the population (particularly in the rural areas) was soon caught up. Only from early 1942 on, after the initial two traumatic experiences—the shock of Soviet displacement and defeat, leading to the substitution of German authority; and the shock of experience with the Germans, the failure to win, and the German failure to satisfy popular grievances—was partisan activity significant.

B. EARLY STAGE OF THE PARTISAN MOVEMENT

In its first months of existence the partisan movement, rapidly estab-lished or improvised before the Soviet retreat, lacked popular support—a fact of which not only the German but even the Soviet authorities were well aware. The partisans were commonly looked upon by the population as desperadoes fighting for a lost cause, or as professional Communists having a stake in the regime. On the other hand, here and there rank-

and-file peasants would help partisans hiding in neighboring woods with food, clothes, or information, sometimes because they were "our people," speaking the same language and sharing the same background, as distinguished from the foreigners who had come to Russian soil. More often such assistance sprang not out of admiration or sympathy for the partisans' activities and goals but simply from the fact that they were Russian human beings and in need of help, the same sort of help extended to stragglers from the Red Army.

Soon the sparsity of German troops permitted groups of partisans, even if they were small and none too well armed, to raid individual villages far from German garrisons. At first, they would perhaps infiltrate singly and establish contacts with remaining agents and sympathizers; later, they might come in force. Usually, the rural population would look upon these sallies as unwelcome nuisances; sometimes, they would take active measures to protect themselves; only rarely would they wholeheartedly join the budding partisan groups. At other times, individual would-be partisans abandoned their groups and returned to live in the villages as civilians, just as the Army stragglers sought to submerge themselves among the remaining indigenous population.

Initial hostility toward the partisans in the village arose for several reasons. The bands represented an unwelcomed intrusion in a situation where the peasantry strove hard for a return to normalcy and for freedom from interference by any and all authorities. So the partisans were resented as much as the Soviet authorities, the Germans, or any other form of power. Also, the partisans sought to exact help in goods and services from the population, thereby doing violence to the acquisitiveness of the rural residents, which had grown after the change of regimes. Finally, the partisans by their existence and activity produced a sense of insecurity which made the civilians realize (1) the Germans' inability to extend effective protection to them, and (2) the continued vigilance of the Soviet authorities or their lieutenants on the spot, in whose eyes all those who complied with German orders were collaborators with the enemy and *ipso facto* traitors.

The Germans were generally in no position to take action against partisan groups in the first period of the war. Not only were there too few security troops, but also many of the indigenous reports reaching them about partisan activities were dismissed as alarmist and fictitious; indeed, more often than not, when the Germans attempted to ferret out the partisans, they would refuse to give battle, retire to concealed positions, and leave the Germans and the population resentful and distrustful of each other. The population tended to become depressed because of their inability to get away from the partisans (as representatives of Soviet authority), especially when the signs multiplied that the focus of Soviet power, east of the battle line, was failing to dissolve under the German onslaught. At the same time, the partisans were still so few in 1941 that (many civilians reasoned) they could be eliminated; neither militarily nor politically were they yet so formidable a contingent as to be a menace. German failure to take prompt action permitted their growth; German failure to discriminate between partisans and civilians brought costly reprisals upon the heads of the civilians and exposed them to attacks and retributions from both sides; and German inability to satisfy the people's basic aspirations while inciting hatred of the partisans enabled the partisans to recruit members and agents among men and women who initially refused to support them.

By the spring of 1942 the bands in many areas had grown sufficiently strong to represent a permanent force, thanks to a combination of circumstances that included Soviet support, recruitment of local stragglers, change in the tenor of popular attitudes, and German setbacks.

From then on, popular attitudes developed along two distinct lines. On the one hand, the desire of the peasant to be left out of the struggle was enhanced by the double jeopardy to which he was subjected by partisan raids and German reprisals. Regardless of all politics, and often utterly rejecting all but the most obvious physical and material considerations (his own survival, and securing his property and stocks of produce and cattle), the civilian came to feel equally cold toward both sides. On the basis of the individual's own past experience, particularly in so far as the kolkhoz members were concerned, he rejected both Soviet treatment and policy and German attitudes and behavior as failing to satisfy his basic aspirations, be they for the welfare of his country, security, a high standard of living, peace of mind, cultural opportunities, or acquisition of property and symbols of prestige. Logically there could have been a third choice— neither Soviet nor German—but in practice this was not possible. However unreal this outlook, it was significant in that it was thus shaped by both political and apolitical factors, all of which increased the gulf between the individual (or the indigenous community) and the authorities, past and present.

Yet the very crystallization of feelings and behavior that contributed to neutralism also prevented increasingly wide circles of the population from practising it. Neutralism was the luxury that the occupation did not permit, at least not in those areas where partisan and antipartisan activities took place. Sooner or later everyone was exposed to the impact of external forces and had to take his stand on one side or the other. The motives that determined a person's choice varied from case to case, from area to area, but more often than not they arose from several major considerations: (1) his experiences with the Soviet regime—frustrations or satisfactions, all tending to be dimmed by the passage of time; (2) his experience with the Germans—the behavior of individual soldiers and officials, requisitioning, forced labor, the fate of prisoners and of his own relatives; (3) his experience in the community during the occupation—the emergence of new administrative cadres, attempts to partition the collective farm, a new and strange order that perhaps brought some welcome relaxations but also abuse and new restrictions; (4) his experience with partisan and anti-partisan activities—raids, political rallies, requisitions, even pitched battles; burned-down houses and barns; sabotage of German facilities; assassination of collaborators; and public hanging of partisans and innocents; (5) his own desires, such as his quest for survival, his drive for advancement, his frustrated search for prestige and recognition, his inertia, his unwillingness to abandon the homestead; his desire for self-enrichment and his adventurousness.

The result of weighing these considerations seems usually to have been a greater alienation from the Germans than from the Russians, so that the population tended to throw in its lot with the partisans whenever there was a reasonably free choice.[160] The partisans were the lesser evil. This

---

[160] The attitude of the peasantry is reflected in the following report by a Russian rayon chief and collaborator, which, it is true, presents the situation from the occupiers' point of view but shows considerable insight:

In the struggle that the German Wehrmacht is waging against the partisans, the population cannot remain neutral, for, as the experiences of recent times show, a neutral attitude of the population leads to repressive measures from both sides and, in the end, to a destruction of the civilians by this or that side.

There can be no doubt that the overwhelming majority of the population is unequivocally hostile to the partisans and would be prepared to fight against them. This is quite natural, for the partisans rob, burn, murder, and prevent the development of a normal life. In addition, they declare themselves to be the representatives of the despised Bolshevik system. The population unanimously declares, "If there were no partisans, we could already live well, even while the war continues.' However, the peasantry is unfortunately placed in circumstances which compel it either to join the partisans directly or at any rate to give aid and comfort to them. . . .

When the peasant faces the problem whether to go with the partisans or with the German troops, unfortunately he must frequently observe that it is impossible to refuse help to the partisans. Indeed, he sees the partisans almost daily, and the Germans very seldom. Even if he wished to fight the partisans wholeheartedly, how should he do this? To throw himself into a direct struggle with them, unarmed as he is, is nonsense. Joining the OD means to deprive his land of the only manpower there is to work it and to expose his family to annihilation by the partisans. When the peasant follows the activity of the partisans and reports about it to the kommandantura, this fact rapidly becomes known, as almost nothing remains secret in the village, and retribution ensues swiftly. Moreover, the population has convinced itself that its reports [to the Germans] in the overwhelming majority of cases lead to no action whatever. The kommandanturas receive, day after day, reports about the partisans from all parts of the rayon but can react to them in only few instances, because they lack forces.

The above state of affairs is extremely dangerous, as it leads to the growth of the partisan movement and hence entails a complete disintegration of the [German] administrative and economic system.

(FK[V]181, Abt. VII, "Auszugsweise Abschrift aus Lagebericht fuer die Zeit vom 1.–30. IX. 1942," 25 September 1942, GMDS, 201 ID 29196/4.)

choice was reinforced by Soviet and partisan psychological warfare, seeking to depict both the regime and its new assistants as patriotic, reformed, revitalized, and, by implication only, non-Communist.

It was also reinforced by stubborn German failure to appeal effectively to the population by offering a concrete political program and promises for the future. At the same time, the amalgam of elements determining the choice varied sufficiently to lead a smaller number of men to side definitely with the Germans (and the indigenous collaborators) against Soviet forces and partisans. A civil war was thus superimposed on a partisan war, and both raged in the shadow of the battle of the titans.

C. EFFECTS OF CHANGES IN GERMAN TACTICS

In the occupied areas, many of the same factors that fostered the growth of the partisan movement—notably the prolongation of the war, increased Soviet resistance, and German failure to win the civilian population to its side—also brought about, in the course of 1942, certain significant changes in German tactics, though not of goals or basic outlook. Their effect, paradoxically, tended in two opposite directions: some measures were aimed largely at enlisting popular support; others strove to help the German war economy and military operations regardless of the indigenous reaction. Several of these were most painful to the population caught between the German hammer and the partisan anvil.

One of the strongest sentiments among the peasantry in the occupied area was overwhelming rejection of the kolkhoz system, or at least of the compulsion and expropriation that characterized it. To people who felt like this, it was clearly disillusioning to find that the Germans sought to perpetuate, in one form or another, a system that seemed to be strikingly similar to that of the collective farms. It is true that, precisely where the partisans were strong (i.e., in the North and Center, rather than the South) the Germans, particularly in the areas of military government, were more inclined to acquiesce in the partition of kolkhoz property among its members. At times they even sought to exploit antikolkhoz sentiments for German ends. By the turn of the year (1942), pressure by partisans had become sufficiently substantial to endanger both peace and productivity; at the same time, as a means of reviving German prestige and stimulating indigenous initiative for the impending spring sowing, plans were drafted, discussed at length, and finally adopted for an agrarian reform. Enacted in February 1942, it was unevenly applied and in substance indicated only a nominal German movement away from the collective farm. The alternatives that the reform outlined were either purely theoretical or else resembled the earlier system so strongly as to reduce the actual effect considerably. Nevertheless, the reform itself, especially in the areas outside of the Ukraine, tended to improve the morale of the peasants and at times also their attitudes toward the Germans.

The help given by the agrarian reform to German popularity was more than offset by the large-scale forced labor program instituted in the summer of 1942. The compulsory transfer of millions of men to work in German industry, mining, and agriculture was accompanied by ugly instances of terror and abuse and left an indelible imprint on the population. It showed the Germans at their worst and associated them in the popular mind with the breaking up of families and the institution of slavery; everyone liable to be conscripted became more violently incensed than ever against the Germans, the collaborating police, and the civil administration that carried out their orders; the partisans were provided with considerable reinforcements, because many preferred joining the partisans to being deported to Germany; both the partisans and Soviet propagandists were supplied with another tangible object lesson to use effectively, and local agriculture, industry, and defense forces were deprived of some of their best actual or potential manpower. In many ways, this program had the most direct and telling impact of all German measures, more striking than that of the occupation itself.

A third German change of tactics consisted in recruiting indigenous collaborators not merely for police but for antipartisan and paramilitary duties. This was to some extent a response to the increase in partisan strength, coupled with German realization that (1) the Germans themselves were unable to provide the necessary forces to inflict a fatal blow on the partisans, and (2) it was also politically wise to provide the indigenous population with a channel and institution for the expression of active antipartisan sentiments. There was little difficulty in recruiting the necessary personnel; however, their moral and intellectual caliber was frequently low. The net effect of the formation of indigenous collaborator units is difficult to assess. On the one hand, it tended to establish a closer bond of identification between the population and the Germans; on the other, frequent abuses by the collaborators, and the not inappropriate label of mercenaries that was often attached to them, alienated them from the civilian masses. However, the very establishment of indigenous units, even under German command and with severe limitations, involved in some measure a new departure from the original *Untermensch* outlook. In some individual instances, German army commanders experimentally granted collaborating chieftains even more far-reaching autonomy than before, as long as they followed the general precepts and military directives of the occupying forces. Though such a German tactical retreat from colonization may have been militarily important, and may have tended to increase popular good will, its psychological effect may be judged to have been less significant than the sum total of negative experiences.

The military aspect of antipartisan warfare constituted the fourth important innovation in German tactics. Beginning in the spring and summer of 1942, the first larger antipartisan operations were conducted, in the

Yelnya and Bryansk areas, for instance. Their military effect was frequently to weaken, but only rarely to destroy, a given partisan concentration. Since the German and indigenous forces fighting the partisans could not remain in the areas being combed, the partisans could soon return to their former areas and resume their work, though often crippled in matériel and reduced in manpower. The operations, however, often involved wholesale evacuations of civilians by the Germans, and wholesale reprisals for alleged concealment of, and assistance to, the partisans. It seems that among the victims of these operations there were more innocent civilians than actual partisans or even partisan-helpers. The effect of the antipartisan operations was once again twofold: it strengthened the pro-German and decidedly anti-German elements, but, especially in the areas directly affected, drove most of the neutral population into the hands of the partisans. They seemed more discriminating in their terror tactics against innocent civilians; they spoke the same language (literally and at times figuratively) as the population; and more and more they appeared to the people as supporters of the victorious side.[161]

Thus the total effect of German measures adopted in the crucial year of 1942 was to further the cleavage of the population into hostile camps, with a minority rallying decisively around the Germans and the collaborators and a greater number turning against the Germans. In this polarization, the partisans played an important part.

D. SUMMER 1942—FALL 1943

The year from the late summer of 1942—when the partisan movement had become consolidated as a force to be reckoned with and had organizationally realized its full potential—to the summer and fall of 1943 saw the remaining civilians on occupied soil caught between two fronts. Their attitudes and behavior were determined by several new and important considerations.

Military developments unrelated to the partisan movement played a role. German victories in the latter half of 1942 were largely in the south, precisely the area where the partisans were weakest or nonexistent. In the north and center of the Eastern front, the situation remained substantially unchanged, thus deflating German hopes and promises that, say, Moscow and Leningrad would soon fall. In the area where the partisans were active, the German victories were of little consequence, while the ensuing debacle at Stalingrad and its impact on the entire German structure in the East was considerable. It unnerved the Germans, weakened them physically, and strengthened and encouraged the partisans. Even though

---

[161] Another subsidiary factor was the behavior of the Axis troops fighting with the Germans. While less given to wholesale extermination, they aroused widespread hostility by their wanton looting, theft, and abuse.

some elements, especially collaborators, continued to believe that Stalin was bound to lose the war—a sort of rationalization and wishful thinking for which the Germans were largely responsible because of their biased reporting—the prevalent feeling was that the tide had turned.

In this period one can divide the territory behind the German front into three fairly distinct areas: of effective German control, of partisan domination, and of shifting control. The tremendous expansion of the partisan movement in early 1942 had taken place in those areas where crucial support was available: Soviet help in supplies, manpower, radio contact, air support, and intelligence; stragglers from the Red Army; and finally— an essential for partisan survival—some measure of support from the indigenous civilians. By early spring 1942 whole areas were nominally under partisan control; in the Bryansk area even small towns, such as Dyatkovo and Trubchevsk, fell into their hands, though generally the partisan-held areas were restricted to rural and especially forest districts. Initially, the civilians who found themselves in these areas had little choice. They were generally obliged to adjust to partisan rule and make the best of it, for only individual residents either wanted to or could abandon their homes and escape to German-held areas.

With the passage of time, the civilians in the partisan districts came to identify themselves more closely with their new masters. The survival of the partisans became a prerequisite of their own survival, since their fate was certain should the Germans reoccupy the area. In this manner, German tactics contributed to the closer relationship between partisans and people. It was not so much the product of great affection or admiration, though such sentiments may have developed at times; rather, it could be characterized as "an involuntary marriage, with no chance of divorce except by suicide." Moreover, direct and daily contact with the partisans enabled the peasants to establish personal relations with them. They were exposed to intensive Soviet propaganda which consequently strove to convince the civilians that things had changed, or at least would change after the war, and to satisfy some of their more obvious patriotic, agrarian, and religious aspirations. With German influence uprooted, with collaborators exterminated, and Soviet institutions and procedures revived, there is little doubt that the surviving civilians in the areas more or less permanently held by the partisans did, willy-nilly, again come to consider themselves subject to the regularly established authority of Moscow, represented by the partisans and the partisan-sponsored administration. There is no evidence of any major civilian revolts or outbreaks against partisan rule, even though resentment against requisitions, recruitment, and reinstitution of Soviet practices can be assumed to have been widespread.

Such areas of thorough partisan control, however, while increasing in size and strength, covered only a fraction of the territory behind the German front. It may be a fair estimate to say that no more than one million civilians, and probably fewer, lived in all of them combined. The areas gradually spread but were limited chiefly to the Bryansk forests, the Polotsk-Lepel district, around Bobruisk, and the southwestern part of Leningrad Oblast.

A far greater number of people lived in what may be called the twilight zones where neither Germans nor partisans held permanent sway. In some instances, German garrisons would have nominal control, but partisans would be able effectively to raid and take reprisals by night; in others, neither side had sufficient forces to command constant popular obedience. Generally, the Germans would only occasionally send in troops and civilian officials to recruit forced labor, round up food, or simply conduct reconnaissance. Though life under either German or partisan rule was fairly unpleasant, it was generally secure; to live in the twilight zone exposed a resident to requisitioning by both Germans and partisans, and to reprisals from either (or both) for collaborating with the other; even refusal to work with one granted no immunity from punishment by the other. Collaborators of the Germans were able to carry on only under great difficulty, often escaping to the nearest rayon centers or hiding at night in the fields to avoid partisan retribution; partisan helpers were generally more secure because they remained unknown to the Germans. German terror tactics were frequently indiscriminate, while partisans sought to attract those elements to their side who could be expected to desert the German cause.

The net result was that the civilian population in these border areas was worst off, being caught, sometimes literally, between two fires. With the passage of time, and the greater ability of the partisans to "get away" with their activities, popular attitudes swung, if not in their favor, in the direction of accepting them as the stronger and somewhat more predictable of the two authorities.

The German-held areas tended to be limited, more and more, to the towns and cities, garrisoned points, and villages along the major arteries of communication. Here, by and large, the population was secure from partisan activities, except for occasional raids, but was aware of their existence as well as of the work of the Soviet underground; in addition, Soviet and partisan agents engaged in extensive infiltration, provocation, and sabotage even in areas where there were no combat partisans. The civilian population was again subjected to double pressure. German requisitioning, forced labor programs, and other abuses were frequent and drove civilians into active opposition. On the other hand, to those people who lived quietly and "normally," the partisans loomed as the outsiders seeking to disrupt a fairly stable, albeit imperfect, order. Thus fear of the partisans pervaded some of these areas, fear heightened by the fact that they were most ruthless in dealing with the population outside the localities they controlled. It is curious that one of the more perspicacious Soviet women-agents, whose reports are available, noted some time in 1942 that:

in those areas where the partisans are not active, the people are against them. In the imagination of the population the partisans are like bandits and robbers. There were instances where small groups of partisans (five to seven men) raided villages. In these cases the people, especially the men, fled from the villages in panic. Even where there were only false rumors that partisans were coming, the men ran from the villages.[162]

While the areas immune from partisans decreased in 1942–43 in the entire forest zone—roughly the entire occupied territory south to the northern Ukraine—the central and southern Ukraine and the adjacent areas to the East (i.e., in late 1942, the plains extending as far as the Stalingrad and Kuban area, and parts of the North Caucasus) were relatively free of partisans. This suggests an important consideration: In the Ukraine, the extremes of the policy pursued by the Germans antagonized the population there as much as, or even more than, anywhere else; this hostility (which, in some of the western sections of the republic, found expression in the formation of nationalist Ukrainian bands) developed without reference to, or support from, the Soviet partisans. Thus the presence of the partisans was not a prerequisite for the crystallization of popular hostility toward the Germans. At the same time, in the North Caucasus, where an attempt was made to establish a partisan movement in a propitious terrain, it failed to flourish; though various reasons (including the lack of time and the lack of stragglers) were responsible for this failure, one significant factor was the distinctively more lenient policy adopted by the Germans. One may conclude that the success or failure of the partisan movement in terms of attracting rank-and-file popular support was importantly influenced by the policy pursued by the antipartisan forces.[163]

In general, the period of 1942–43 witnessed a further and conclusive decline in pro-German attitudes, even where the partisans were weak or nonexistent. By the middle of 1943, one may assume, the hostility had become so strong and widespread as to be ineluctable, whatever the Germans did. With only minor variations between different social and nationality groups, the change of attitude that had taken place between the fall of 1941 and the early months of 1943 is attributable in large measure to German conduct—sins of commission (*Ostarbeiter,* antipartisan terror) and sins of omission (agrarian reform, famine); it was also affected by the gradual rise of Soviet strength and prestige, to which the partisans contributed, as did the Soviet victories and the successful exploitation of national-patriotic sentiments in Soviet and partisan propaganda.

[162] 299. Inf.Div., Ic, "Uebersetzung der Eintragungen im Notizbuch einer Partisanin und Agentin, die . . . am Morgen des 13.10. auf der Flucht erschossen wurde," 14 October 1942 (GMDS, 299 ID 28102/10, Anlage 53). It is evident from the text that the woman was an agent and not a partisan.

[163] On the Ukraine, see Armstrong; see also this book, Chap. X, Sect. II.

These conditions were exploited and accentuated by the partisans in the areas over which they ruled or for which they vied. German inability to protect civilians in fringe areas increased the myth of partisan strength; so did the militarily nonsensical but psychologically effective operations of the raiding bands that crisscrossed the Ukraine in early 1943.

At the same time, the promises and threats made by the partisans to the civilians, and especially collaborators, in the twilight areas—and the partisans' ability to carry them out—tended to set them above the Germans in the awe (and/or fear) in which they were held by the population.

E. 1943–44

At this late date, German occupation policy underwent some further changes intended largely to mollify popular sentiments and to anchor the allegiance of those who were still pro-German. A decree in June 1943 provided for the recognition of private peasant ownership of land; greater tolerance in educational, cultural, and religious matters prevailed; some attempts were made to cater to national sentiments; for propaganda purposes, the so-called first Vlasov operation was initiated, making use of the names and prestige of Soviet defector generals; special privileges were pledged to Red Army and partisan personnel who voluntarily deserted to the Germans. At the same time, somewhat more realistic appraisals of the partisans and somewhat more effective techniques of antipartisan warfare began to be employed. All of these, however, may be considered to have been too little and too late. The basic outlook and practices of the occupation forces did not change.

It remains a matter of speculation whether at that stage a dramatic and radical departure from past dogma and practice could have produced a significant change in popular attitudes in the so-called "occupied Eastern territories." Whether or not it might have, no such fundamental change was permitted by the top Nazi leadership.

The German offensive in the summer of 1943 boomeranged into a large-scale retreat; first the Soviet troops advanced to Stalino, Bryansk, Smolensk and other eastern outposts; then a new offensive placed them at the Dnepr along a front extending approximately over Kiev, Gomel, and Vitebsk. These victories shattered the remaining prestige of German military might and valor in the eyes of the population. At the same time, the Axis position was wrecked by the fall of Mussolini, Western landings in Italy, and intensified bombing of the Reich. All these events were widely exploited in Soviet propaganda. While it continued its "national" line by such measures as the dissolution of the Comintern, the re-establishment of officers' shoulder insignia, and the revival of the Moscow Patriarchate, it confirmed what was presented as a democratic alliance by such outward demonstrations as the Teheran Conference. The same elements that seemed to impress

Western public opinion also seemed to influence the civilian population under German rule.

From late 1943 to the end of the occupation, one can scarcely speak of systematic German policy. In its place, there was a somewhat frantic and at times hysterical attempt to evacuate manpower and equipment, to use all available civilians to dig ditches, clear roads, build fortifications, and before abandoning them to clear entire stretches of territory of men and matériel. The wind sowed by the Soviets in their scorched-earth policy of 1941 was reaping a German whirlwind. If anything, these extreme measures, adopted when everything seemed to be lost, tended further to antagonize the civilian population. The partisans were now fully conscious that Soviet victory was around the corner. Feeling their strength, they could afford to make all sorts of promises in order to induce collaborators to defect.

At the same time, by attacking trains and retreating columns on a large scale, and seeking to prevent the evacuation of civilians, they interfered with German retrograde movements. The easternmost partisans were swept up by the advancing Red Army; other partisan groups moved westward where they achieved a greater density; finally, the Germans were compelled to withdraw their remaining garrisons from all but the most important centers and highways.

Popular attitudes were fairly well set by this time. There was a core of collaborators who either had decided—out of fear, hate, or other motives—that, come what might, they would not return to the Soviet side, or had found neither opportunity nor courage to join the partisans. There were those who had resigned themselves to the return of Soviet rule and looked upon the partisans as its precursors. And there were those who acclaimed the partisans and the Red Army as the liberators. That the partisans, to the bitter end, continued to evoke mixed sentiments and even hostility was borne out by the last-minute German attempt to establish "self-defense villages" in which the peasants, at last permitted to carry arms and organize, would seek by their own power to ward off partisan raids. Even in the spring of 1944 this measure served to boost popular morale in various parts of Belorussia by instilling in the civilian population a sense of self-rule and strength, a feeling that it was able to protect its material goods and command the respect of any and all outsiders.

More characteristic for this last stage, however, were large-scale defections from collaborator units to the partisans (which led to the transfer of all paramilitary formations westward in late 1943) and mass breakouts from the German-sponsored treks of evacuees.[164] Equally typical was the attempt of many civilians, foreseeing an early Soviet return, to procure

[164] It must be stressed, however, that the number of collaborators remained considerable to the very end. Thus, there were at least 40,000 men in the OD (auxiliary police) in the area of Army Group Center alone; in addition, there were sizable contingents of military units, army auxiliaries, and the entire gamut of civilian collaborators and officials.

themselves an alibi or record of active anti-German activity by conducting sabotage, killing German officials, or joining the partisans. The situation was entirely oriented on the coming Soviet victory. By the middle of 1944 this prospect had become reality throughout the old Soviet territories.

F. DEMOGRAPHIC CHANGES UNDER THE OCCUPATION

When the Red Army returned, it found villages that had often changed not only in appearance but also in the kinds of people that now inhabited them. During the course of the occupation a typical village, if it was located in an area of partisan activity, might have undergone the following changes in demographic composition. A large percentage of the able-bodied males was mobilized into the Red Army; a far smaller number, including officials and technicians, were evacuated eastward before the Soviet withdrawal. This loss of manpower was only partly made up by the influx of three elements during the first stage of the occupation: refugees from other parts of the occupied areas, stragglers from Red Army units cut off or destroyed by the Germans, and urban residents seeking sustenance and safety in the countryside. During the subsequent period the excess of mortality over births, as well as deaths from starvation and epidemics, further reduced the population figure. Statistically more significant were the departures from the village; a small number of men who went to work as collaborators of the Germans elsewhere, perhaps a larger number of stragglers who were apprehended by the Germans, a few persons who voluntarily joined the partisans, and, largest of all, those people who were conscripted for forced labor in Germany. Finally, partisan recruitment was stepped up, especially in the latter part of the occupation. When the Germans retreated, a number of villagers were evacuated with them, notably collaborating officials, local auxiliary police, kulaks, and some rank-and-file ex-kolkholz members. Thus, when the Red Army returned two or three years later, the population may have been only one fourth of the 1941 figure, the preponderance being old persons, women, and small children. Naturally there were different statistical changes in parts of the occupied areas where partisans were weak or where the occupation did not last long, as there were in areas firmly held by the partisans.

G. MOTIVES BEHIND POPULAR ATTITUDES

Even more difficult to summarize simply than shifts in demographic composition are the motives behind all the complex and varying manifestations of pro- and antipartisan activity. Many of these motives have been alluded to earlier. Some of the population's help for the bands was voluntary, some forced. Some acceptance was tacit and passive, some explicit and active. Obviously, perhaps, where the partisans were strongest (or the Germans absent) and where local experience of the German occupation was most horrible, the partisans were most successful in gaining popular support; they were perhaps particularly fortunate where a sizable indigenous element existed in the local partisan force. Though until the end the partisans were often regarded unfavorably as the long arm of Moscow, they appeared less like "Communist die-hards" and "bandits" as the composition of the movement changed and as experience with the Germans strengthened the belief that the partisans were preferable.

Popular acceptance of the partisans varied to some extent with the social, national, and age groups involved. Those social elements most likely to accept the partisans were absent; most Soviet officials, administrators, and Communist enthusiasts were evacuated to the East, or drafted into the Army, or were themselves partisans. By and large the stragglers were initially anxious to merge with the indigenous population and be left in peace; though some had been cut off and isolated much against their will and were prepared to continue the fight if and when an opportunity arose (as they did with the partisan movement in the winter of 1941–42), most tended to consider the war as lost, themselves as delinquent in Soviet (though not in their own) eyes, and the whole occupation as a situation in which they preferred to be as inconspicuous as possible. The kulaks and the clergy, who, after a decade of repression, reappeared on the scene, and the criminal elements for whom the German occupation brought a heyday, were of course hostile to the partisans.

The urban population, partly because of its closer, earlier identification with the Soviet regime, partly because of the more miserable conditions of life and work in the towns under the Germans, was inclined to turn against the occupying authorities sooner and more decisively than the rural population (though there were many exceptions); yet, paradoxically, the partisan movement was largely a rural phenomenon, and urban dissidents either remained isolated or joined Communist underground groups in the towns. Only in relatively few instances did they escape to join the partisans. In the countryside, the peasants were originally reluctant to side with the partisans; as described above, when they later turned increasingly against the Germans, they wasted little love on the partisans though generally supporting them when they had to make a choice.

Nationality played virtually no role in the Russian and Belorussian areas. Only in the Crimea and the North Caucasus did it influence the composition of the partisan movement itself or the relations of partisans to civilians. In the Baltic States, to be sure, it was of considerable importance; this area, however, was not studied in the context of this chapter. In the Ukraine, a paradoxical situation arose in which (1) there were few Soviet partisans, largely because of the terrain, though the Communist urban underground was active in a number of towns and cities; (2) anti-German sentiment was considerable; (3) there was, especially in certain parts of the republic, a measure of nationalism that contributed not only to anti-German but also to anti-Great Russian (and anti-Polish) sentiment; but (4) most nationalism was strong in circles of the intelligentsia rather than among the peasantry, who usually provided the cadres for the partisan movement. Unquestionably, some people disliked the partisans because they seemed to be emissaries and agents of Moscow; on the other hand, except perhaps in Volhynia, Galicia, and other scattered parts of the Ukraine, national sentiments were not so profound as to influence decisions more than did other and more basic motives, such as sheer survival, improvement in standards of living, the experience of relatives with the Germans, and dissatisfaction with German policy toward the collective farm.

In the last analysis, the decision to side with Germans or partisans seems commonly to have been determined by the individual's wartime experience —not by abstract considerations and evaluations of the merits and demerits of the two regimes, nor even necessarily by likes and dislikes or experiences under the Soviet regime before the occupation—and also by the accident of which regime was the stronger and happened to control a given area. At the same time, nonmaterial and nonpersonal factors also had some influence. The existence of the *Wehrdoerfer* (armed villages), some local self-government, the Kaminsky Brigade, and the separatist bands suggests that the Germans had an opportunity to exploit desires and political aspirations broader than the customary grievances within the peasants' sphere of life. Yet they never produced an articulate or distinctive political program for the peasantry. The Soviet authorities, for their part, and the partisans with them, managed successfully to evoke and play upon wider and deeper emotions, like patriotism and anticolonialism. Though neither side offered an appreciably improved standard of living, in the way of expectation of future security and present satisfaction with the value of one's role as a participant in current events the partisans had more to offer than did the Germans.

H. CONCLUSIONS

Thus the partisans contributed to the crystallization of public opinion, and especially of public action, in the occupied areas. As in the Ukraine, they were not always the cause but often the effect of anti-German sentiments. At the same time, they influenced popular attitudes and eventually decisions by (a) physically controlling the lives and destinies of a small group of civilians; (b) constantly reminding the population of the continual presence and watchful eye of the Soviet regime; (c) playing the part of avengers and thus blocking collaboration with the Germans; (d) provoking German terror and retaliation, so that many civilians were induced to look upon the occupation forces as the greater of the two evils; and (e) both acting as a catalyst and providing a real opportunity for effective action, in giving those who wished to fight or to escape the Germans a stimulus and a chance to do so with relative ease.

The partisan organization constituted a model example of an involuntary resistance movement. It did not begin as a popular mass revolt; it could not have developed without Soviet help and direction. Nor could it have succeeded without sooner or later winning considerable numbers of the population to its side. That it did so is explained in some measure by its own tactics and behavior, but to a much greater degree by circumstances beyond its control.

CHAPTER V

The Partisans in Soviet Intelligence

Kurt DeWitt

§I. Relations Between the Partisans and Soviet Intelligence

Although partisan warfare on the Eastern front during the Second World War has been recognized as a factor which contributed to the German defeat in Russia, one feature of the Soviet partisan movement which has received little attention was its integration with the Soviet Intelligence system. The purpose of this chapter, a by-product of an intensive investigation of the partisan movement in the Belorussian-Great Russian area, is to describe the intelligence activities of the Soviet partisans. These activities will be discussed both as a special aspect of partisan warfare and in terms of their contribution to the operations of Soviet Intelligence. The methods employed by the partisans in gathering intelligence for their own purposes are naturally of interest, but what is far more significant is that the partisans supplied Soviet Intelligence with a vast reservoir of agents and informants behind the German lines.

During the early phase of the war apparently little or no formal cooperation existed between the partisans and Soviet Intelligence as far as intelligence operations were concerned. This, at least, was the opinion of *Fremde Heere Ost,* which in 1943 began to study partisan warfare and to publish a series of reports on the partisan situation in the entire Eastern theater entitled *Bulletins on Partisan Warfare (Nachrichten ueber den Bandenkrieg).* In No. 1 of this series we find a rather categorical statement to the effect that early in the war partisan and Soviet agents were strictly separated:

> During the first period of the war no relations existed between partisans and Soviet Intelligence, and [Soviet] intelligence scouts and agents were not even

permitted to establish contact with the bands; now [1943], however, it is possible to observe in increasing measure a cooperation between them which takes the form of assigning to the bands the task of gathering information in areas dominated by them. . . .[1]

This statement is supported by information found in some of the German field reports, like the 339th Infantry Division report which deals with the capture of several Soviet parachute agents in October 1941: "The group in question is one of four parachutist groups which had orders to engage in espionage behind the German front without contacting partisans or other elements and to report regularly by radio on troop movements and weather conditions. Their wireless set was of American origin. . . ."[2] In July 1942 three other Soviet agents were arrested who had also been dropped by plane and had been instructed not to work for or with the partisans. They were told of the presence of a large partisan band located in their drop area but, "in case of encounter with this band, they were allowed to established contact, but they were strictly forbidden to work with or for the band. . . ."[3]

Nevertheless, in the form cited above, the statement of *Fremde Heere Ost* appears to be an oversimplification. There is some evidence that Soviet agents cooperated with the partisans even before 1943, as is indicated, for example, by a report of the Provost Marshal General of the German Army *(Heeresfeldpolizeichef)* summarizing the partisan situation during the period from July 1942 to March 1943: "Parachutist groups no longer acted exclusively on their own but for the most part joined existing bands and carried out the missions given them (intelligence missions, sabotage against particularly important military objects, etc.) with the help of the bands. . . ."[4]

On the other hand, the policy of keeping Soviet agents away from the partisans seems to have been in effect even later. A report of Sixteenth Army of January 1943 said: "All agent groups operating in the rear of the enemy are strictly separated from the partisan movement. They are forbidden to cooperate with the bands. . . ."[5] This was even more true of the above-mentioned Special Groups of the Red Army. According to No. 9 of the *Bulletins on Partisan Warfare,* they were "independent groups

[1] OKH/GenStdH/FHO, *Nachrichten ueber den Bandenkrieg Nr. 1,* 3 May 1943, p. 3 (GMDS, H 3/738) [hereafter cited as *Nachrichten*].

[2] 339. Inf.Div., Ic, "Taetigkeitsbericht," 8 August 1942, p. 7 (GMDS, 339 ID 22441/7).

[3] 221. Sich.Div., Ic, "Betr.: 3 Funk-Agenten (Fallschirmabspringer)," 24 July 1942, p. 2 (GMDS, 221 ID 29380/9, Anlage 16).

[4] HFPCh/im OKH/Gen.z.b.V./H.Wes.Abt./GFP, "Allgemeiner Ueberblick ueber die Bandenbewegung fuer die Zeit vom 1.7.1942—31.3.1943," 10 April 1943, p. 4 (GMDS, OKW/734).

[5] AOK 16, Ic/AO, "Beurteilung der Bandenlage," 6 January 1943, p. 1 (GMDS, AOK 16, 36588/142).

which are subordinate to the Intelligence Section (2d Section) of the Red Army. They operate independently of the bands in the rear of the German front. . . ."[6]

The German reports do not indicate why the Soviets kept their intelligence operatives away from the partisans. One motive obviously was security—the necessity of protecting agents by making their presence and missions known to as few people as possible. Another motive may have arisen from a basic principle of Soviet intelligence operations to which reference has previously been made; namely, to cover a particular target by different sets of agents who work completely independent of each other. In practice, this principle of separation seems to have been violated frequently by agents who lost their bearings or otherwise got into trouble and fell back on the partisans for help.

The fact that the partisans in the early phase of the war apparently had little formal contact with Soviet Intelligence personnel does not imply that there was no cooperation between the two. The report of the Provost Marshal General on the partisan situation during the second half of 1941 indicates that the bands even at that time performed certain intelligence jobs for the Red Army. For instance, the partisans were known to have been entrusted with:

. . . destruction of telephone and radio communications trucks, passenger cars, motorcycle messengers, other motorcyclists, cyclists, messengers on horseback and on foot. Every means must be used to transmit papers taken from messengers and all other captured documents and information to the nearest staff headquarters of the Red Army or to higher partisan headquarters.

With all means and forces at our disposal, information must be gathered concerning the enemy: his activities; the continuity and location of his front-line positions; his tanks, artillery, air force, other troop units, and location of headquarters staffs. This intelligence must be forwarded to the front units of the Red Army.[7]

From 1942 on the German reports refer more frequently and more explicitly to the utilization of the partisans for Soviet Intelligence. A counterintelligence summary of Eleventh Army dated 14 March 1942 is prefaced by the statement: "The activities of Soviet Intelligence and the partisans often overlap to a considerable extent. Therefore, it is necessary to suspect espionage in connection with any partisan activity and to assume that espionage suspects are also engaged in partisan activities."[8]

A report of Second Panzer Army on the partisan situation in the

[6] *Nachrichten Nr. 9,* 11 June 1944, p. 2.
[7] HFPCh im OKH/GenStdH/GenQu/Abt.K.Verw., "Erfahrungen ueber Aufbau, Aufgaben, Auftreten und Bekaempfung der Partisanenabteilungen," 15 January 1942, p. 37 (GMDS, Wi/ID 2.717).
[8] AOK 11, AO, "Abwehrnachrichten Nr. 4," 14 March 1942, p. 1 (GMDS, AOK 11, 35774/10).

Bryansk area in April 1942 speaks of greater coordination of efforts between the bands and the Red Army, noticeable also in the field of intelligence: "In the first week of April, for example, about 750 men were filtered through the front to join the partisans. In addition, the espionage and intelligence net is being steadily widened and more elaborately organized. . . ."[9] This, according to the report, was but one aspect of Soviet attempts to step up partisan warfare as part of their over-all military effort. The greater utilization of specially trained partisans brought into the rear area by planes was also noted. These partisans not only had special sabotage missions as well as orders to reinforce local bands, but also had the task of collecting information for Soviet Intelligence and of transmitting this information immediately by radio.[10]

The growth in partisan intelligence activities coincided in time with increased Soviet air support for the partisans. In fact, airpower became a highly useful tool of partisan intelligence, just as it was a very important factor in the Soviet reorganization of the partisan movement in the beginning of 1942. One is almost forced to conclude that the increasing utilization of the partisans for Soviet intelligence purposes was not an isolated phenomenon but was rather the direct result of, and one of the motives behind, the reorganization which was designed to bring about greater effectiveness of the partisans and a closer integration of the movement into the Soviet war effort. When the Soviets ordered a further intensification of partisan warfare during the winter of 1942–43, one of their principal objectives apparently was an increased flow of intelligence for the Red Army and NKVD. An intelligence report of Second Panzer Army, stationed in the Bryansk area, commented in detail on Soviet measures undertaken during the winter of 1942–43 to step up partisan warfare and mentioned some of the specific tasks to be accomplished:

> Further measures to increase the striking power of the bands: (aa) Organization of a special intelligence service for the bands' own use. For this, Communist Party members are to be employed who must infiltrate leading positions in the OD [*Ordnungsdienst*, the German-run indigenous police force]. (bb) Closer cooperation between regular agents and bands. . . .[11]

The report of the Provost Marshal General for the period from July 1942 to March 1943 states: "The number of partisan agents has increased

---

[9] PzAOK 2, Abwehrgruppe, "Auszug aus den Berichten ueber die Partisanenlage im Gebiet zwischen Front und Brjansk vom Gen.Kdo. des XXXXVII. Pz. Korps," 26 April 1942, p. 1 (GMDS, PzAOK 2, 30233/66).

[10] HFPCh im OKH/GenStdH/GenQu/GFP, "Entwicklung der Partisanenbewegung in der Zeit vom 1.1.—30.6.1942," 31 July 1942, p. 15 (GMDS, HGr Nord 75131/113).

[11] PzAOK 2, Ic/AO III, "Abwehrblatt Nr. 1/43," 14 January 1943, p. 3 (GMDS, PzAOK 2, 75915).

parallel with the reorganization and strengthening of the bands. They form the main contingent of persons arrested on suspicion of espionage."[12]

The Panchenko band, uncovered by the Germans in early 1943 after months of investigation, furnishes a particularly striking example of partisans serving Soviet Intelligence. It was credited by the Germans with having played a highly significant role in the Soviet military intelligence network on the Bryansk and Southwest Fronts:

An investigation of partisan activities in Mikhailovka Rayon (SSE of Dmitrovsk) which was started in July 1942 led to the uncovering of the Panchenko band. Several actions to break up this band failed, and the investigation, under the direction of a chief informant and conducted on a stepped-up scale in connection with Operation "Polar Bear" in January 1943, resulted in an entirely new evaluation of this group. The analysis and comparison of the extensive results of the investigation available so far indicate that the Panchenko band must be credited with an importance which goes far beyond the previously known or recognized scope of partisan activity.[13]

Evidently the Germans recognized the real character and mission of this particular partisan band only after its detection, and the report makes it quite clear that they had never before observed partisan intelligence activities on such a scale and in such close liaison with the Red Army.

Documents dated 1944 indicate that the Soviet High Command relied increasingly on partisan intelligence. An SD report of 1 March 1944 may serve as an illustration: "The location of the partisan center of gravity has significant connections with [Soviet] operational intentions and undertakings. ... To some extent regular Soviet troops are mixed with partisan units in which cases the Soviet military leaders are utilizing the partisans' precise knowledge of the localities and the results of their intelligence work."[14]

The available materials do not present a clear picture of the channels of command and reporting between the partisans and Soviet Intelligence. Apparently, the partisans started to gather combat intelligence for the Red Army even during the first few months of the war, but there is no evidence that the Soviet leadership had, prior to the war, worked out plans and procedures for the utilization of the partisans in the field of intelligence. Regular Soviet agents were under orders to keep away from the bands, partly, it appears, because the Soviet authorities initially had little control over the bands and did not want to expose their trained intelligence personnel to unnecessary risks. These considerations lost weight

[12] HFPCh im OKH/Gen.z.b.V./H.Wes.Abt./GFP, "Allgemeiner Ueberblick ueber die Bandenbewegung fuer die Zeit vom 1.7.1942—31.3.1943," 10 April 1943, p. 6 (GMDS, OKW/734).

[13] Abwehrtrupp 107 to PzAOK 2, Ic/AO III, "Bande Pantschenko im System des Nachrichtendienstes der Brjansker-Front und der Suedwest-Front," 5 February 1943, p. 1 (GMDS, PzAOK 2, 75915).

[14] Chef Sipo. u. SD, IV D 5, "Kurzbericht ueber die Lage und Taetigkeit in den besetzten Ostgebieten," 1 March 1944, p. 2 (GMDS, EAP 99/1104).

after the Soviet authorities had established closer control over the partisan movement.

From the beginning of 1942 the partisans were drawn closer into the Soviet Intelligence network, and there are indications that by the winter of 1942–43 a formal chain of command had been worked out between the NKVD and Red Army on one side, and the partisan staffs on the other, at least for military intelligence purposes. [See Fig. 4.] Partisans were given special training in Soviet intelligence schools. The communica-

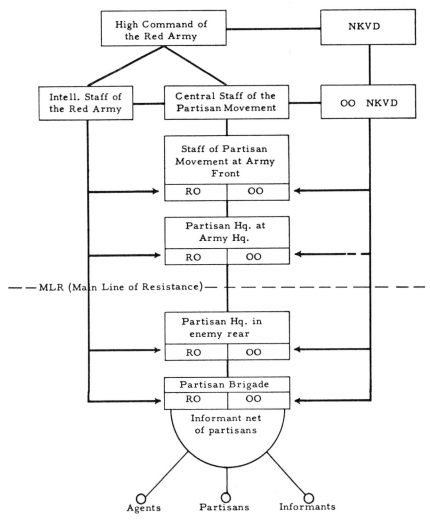

Figure 4.—Cooperation between partisans and Soviet intelligence. *Source:* OKH/-GenStdH/FHO, *Nachri·chten ueber den Bandenkrieg Nr. 1,* 3 May 1943, Anlage 6 (GMDS, H 3/738).

RO (*Razvedyvatelnyi Otdel*) = Intelligence Service of the Red Army
OO (*Osobyi Otdel*) = Intelligence Service of the NKVD

tions system of the partisans, particularly their radio transmitters, served as an important, and often the only, link between Soviet agents and the outside.

Although the German documents reveal no clear-cut division of labor in Soviet Intelligence operations behind the German lines, it appears that in the cities and larger towns the Soviets relied primarily on agents whom the Red Army and NKVD had left behind, had recruited directly, or had brought in by various means. In the countryside, on the other hand, the partisans' role in intelligence work increased in importance as the war went on, even though for special missions Soviet Intelligence continued to send regular agents into the rural areas behind the front. Some of them operated independently; others had orders to join the partisans or to fall back on them for various kinds of support. The activities of these agents and of the partisans frequently overlapped and their identities became blurred. The Soviet Intelligence network in the German rear was highly complicated, and it is not surprising, therefore, that the Germans were never fully able to understand its organization or defeat its operations.

§II. Intelligence Assignments of the Partisans

In this section the intelligence activities of the partisans will be discussed in terms of specific assignments and results. As indicated in the previous section, the partisans procured intelligence information not only for their own purposes but also for the Red Army and the NKVD. Scattered evidence of this appears in some German reports as early as 1941, but it was not until 1943 that the Germans realized the full scope of partisan intelligence activities. In September 1943, *Fremde Heere Ost* put it as follows: "As far as intelligence work is concerned, the partisan brigades and detachments have the task of conducting military espionage for the Red Army as well as extensive intelligence activities for the agencies in charge of political and economic affairs. . . ."[15]

Probably the most concise and specific statement on the partisan intelligence mission is contained in a Soviet directive entitled "Manual for the Partisan Intelligence Scout," which the Germans captured late in 1942. It sets three basic tasks for partisan intelligence activities in the rear of the enemy: (1) intelligence for the Red Army; (2) intelligence for the political agencies of the oblast; and (3) intelligence pertaining to the security and operations of the bands.[16] A fourth point, political intelli-

---

[15] *Nachrichten Nr. 4,* 10 September 1943, p. 5.
[16] PzAOK 2, Ic/AO, "Feindnachrichten Nr. 1/43, Anlage 11: 'Merkblatt des Kundschafters der Partisanen,'" 31 January 1943, p. 1 (GMDS, PzAOK 2, 37075/159).

gence, which was later added to this list in a report by *Fremde Heere Ost,* seems to be largely identical with the second point.[17] The "political" agencies of the oblast presumably included both Government and Party organs as well as the NKVD which had either been evacuated or were functioning illegally in the area under German occupation.

In terms of U.S. intelligence concepts, the first and third tasks constitute "tactical" missions; that is data which have an immediate bearing on the conduct of operations in the field: the collection of information on enemy order of battle, location of troops and installations, battle plans, morale, etc. The second and fourth tasks might be called "strategic" missions in the sense that information on the political and economic conditions of the occupied territories, the organization of the German administration, and the reaction of the local population to the occupation was essential to the Soviet Government in assessing the long-range capabilities of the Germans. It is doubtful whether a distinction between the "tactical" and the "strategic" mission would serve as a useful frame of reference since the intelligence activities of the partisans cannot always be fitted into such categories. When, for example, the partisans penetrated the *Ordnungsdienst* (OD), which was used by the Germans both as an indigenous police force and as an auxiliary in antipartisan warfare, their objectives may have been both to provide the Soviet authorities with information on the workings of that organization and to protect their own security by placing informants in the OD who would warn the bands about any moves against them.

A. PARTISAN INTELLIGENCE ACTIVITIES
FOR THE RED ARMY

It is difficult to determine with any degree of accuracy when cooperation between the partisans and the Red Army in intelligence matters began. There can be no doubt that the Red Army and the sections of the NKVD concerned with military intelligence did everything possible to obtain information on German troop dispositions and movements, operational plans, location of headquarters, staffs, airfields, and a host of other data important to the conduct of operations. While Soviet Intelligence presumably began, soon after the outbreak of war, to draw on the partisans as sources of needed information, specific intelligence assignments appear only rarely in German reports for 1941 and even 1942. First mention of such assignments was found in a report of V Corps of September 1941 which mentioned that the mission of the partisans included: "Collecting information concerning airfields, supply installations, and headquarters."[18]

[17] *Nachrichten Nr. 1,* 3 May 1943, p. 3.
[18] V. A.K., Ic, "Erfahrungen in der Partisanenbekaempfung," 2 September 1941 (GMDS, V AK 17647/22).

Captured reports of a partisan unit operating in the Smolensk area indicated that this unit had systematically performed intelligence work for the Red Army[19] between May and September 1942. What kind of information the Red Army requested from the partisans in 1941 is also evident from the summary report of the Provost Marshal General for January 1942 which has been cited above in another context: "With all available means and forces at our disposal, information must be gathered concerning the enemy: his activities, continuity and location of his front-line positions, tanks, artillery, air force, other troop units, and location of headquarters staffs. This intelligence must be forwarded to the front units of the Red Army."[20]

A much more detailed and specific list of intelligence assignments is contained in the "Manual for the Partisan Intelligence Scout." In addition to the usual targets—troops, installations, communications—partisan agents were also instructed to look for evidence of German preparations for chemical warfare and to procure, if possible, German documents of all kinds, particularly samples of identity papers. The list of assignments follows:

I. Collecting Information on the Enemy for the Red Army
Recognize the enemy by the braids on his uniform:
    White braid—infantry; red braid—artillery; green braid—mountain troops; cherry-red braid—chemical warfare troops; pink braid—armored troops; golden-yellow braid—cavalry; blue braid—medical troops; black braid—engineers; lemon-colored braid—signal troops; blue braid with airplane—air force.
    Take note of the traffic; count the tanks, light tanks, armored cars, trucks, passenger cars, motorcycles, bicycles, guns, vehicles, horseback riders, trailers, etc. Distinguish between open trucks, which appear more seldom, and those with roofs. The 7-ton truck carries 32 men; the 5-ton truck, 18 men plus arms and ammunition. Observe if the enemy soldiers carry a field-grey round container; it holds the gas mask.
    In case of troops marching through, distinguish whether they are Germans or Hungarians, Slovaks, Italians, Rumanians, and others. Note how many there are.
    Remember the markings and figures on the technical equipment of the enemy. [Tactical markings of German divisions follow. Notes A and B contain explanations of these tactical markings.]
Note C
Remember the enemy is preparing for chemical warfare against us; distinguish between tank cars and other cars moving on the railroads; observe carefully the unloading of chemical warfare materials from the cars, motor vans, etc. Note the markings on the means of transportation. A yellow ele-

---

[19] XXIII. A.K., Ic, "Taetigkeitsbericht, Anlage 25, 'Meldung Anlage 3,' " 5 June 1942, p. 2 (GMDS, XXIII AK 76156).
[20] HFPCh im OKH/GenStdH/GenQu/Abt.K.Verw., "Erfahrungen ueber Aufbau, Aufgaben, Auftreten und Bekaempfung der Partisanenabteilungen," 15 January 1942, p. 19 (GMDS, Wi/ID 2.717).

phant signifies the presence of poison gas, which is packed either in glass ampules which resemble aerial bombs or in balloons, kegs, etc.

1. Tear gas—marked by white bands or rings.
2. Vomiting gases[21]—marked by blue bands or rings.
3. Choking gases—marked by green bands or rings.
4. Blister gases—marked by yellow bands or rings.

Attempt to obtain samples of the enemy's chemical warfare materials (chemical bombs, shells, mines, bullets, gas masks, antigas paulins [protective covers], etc.).

Supplementary information about the enemy can be obtained from a large number of sources of a nonmilitary[22] nature:

1. Orders of the Day, decrees of the enemy, staff correspondence.
2. Envelopes, letters, covering letters with APO numbers.
3. Paybooks, identification disks.
4. Registration papers for heavy and light tanks, automobiles, motorcycles, etc.

Note D

Take necessary measures to note all data and make sketches, where necessary, to mark the presence of enemy bunkers, trenches and tank traps, minefields, wire entanglements, antiaircraft guns (also their number); sketch troop billets in relation to buildings and streets (how long billeted there); approach routes; locations of kitchens, rations, and supply points; repair facilities, garages for automobiles and tanks; gasoline tanks (periods of gasoline issue); horse stables and places where horses are kept at night.

Also note the location of staff sections, giving number and street as well as such data as how far these headquarters are located from the church, fire brigade tower, billets, railroad line, factory chimneys, from rivers, brooks, through highways, roads. . . . Note also the armament of troops resting in garrison.

Note E

Every day the following information must be obtained regarding rail traffic: the number of military trains passing through and in what direction; how many troops carried; how many wounded; how many officers; the number of light and heavy tanks, armored cars, guns, vehicles, cavalry, gasoline cars, large crates, etc.; places of loading and unloading; locations of depots.

Traffic on through highways (*Rollbahnen*) and roads must be observed. It must be ascertained where the enemy erects temporary landing strips, airfields, and where he conceals his planes at night; also the number of planes and their types (bombers, fighters, transport planes).

It is urgently requested that upon the completion of intelligence missions documents and charts pertaining to the enemy's location be submitted and such other materials as may contribute to the annihilation of the enemy.[23]

An interesting illustration of the type of information to be collected by the partisans is given in a list of intelligence assignments which a partisan

---

[21] The German term is *aetzend* meaning "etching," but from the context it is obvious that vomiting gases such as Adamsite are meant.

[22] Probably should read "nontactical."

[23] *Nachrichten Nr. 1,* 3 May 1943, Anlage 7. This is the same "Merkblatt des Kundschafters der Partisanen" cited at the beginning of this section. Citation from the *Nachrichten* is made because of their more convenient form.

otryad[24] was to cover during the period of one month. The targets included strength, composition, and location of German troops; security plans and measures; work routine of German garrisons; names of native policemen and other collaborators; location of staff sections, airfields; and railroad installations and their protection.[25]

The following is an example of an early intelligence report by partisans to the Red Army. Dated September 1941, it came from a partisan unit operating south of Leningrad and was addressed to Marshal Voroshilov, commander of the Northwest Front.

Intelligence Report
from the far rear territory of the enemy
Map 1:100,000
area south of the village of Lyady
3 September 1941

In the area defined by the Peschenka Sanitarium Gryasno-Domishche-Batovo, the enemy is establishing a defense position. In the village of Domishche (in the school) the staff of a larger unit has been located; it is protected by a reinforced unit equipped with heavy tanks and trucks. West of Domishche the enemy is concentrating heavy tanks and heavy artillery. In the area of Petkinaya Gora, coordinates 62, 64–80, the enemy is moving heavy artillery into position; a few planes are at the airport of Domishche; the airport is protected by antiaircraft guns. Position near Hill 184. The enemy patrols the Domishche-Lyady area daily with tanks and tank reconnaissance cars. Along the Volosovo-Gryasno road the enemy is bringing up new reserves consisting of heavy tanks, armored reconnaissance cars, and antitank guns with tractors. The vehicles are located in the cemetery of Domishche and the area mentioned above; they are well camouflaged.

Evaluation

The enemy is employing an armored division as a reserve in this area, whose task it is to strike a blow at our troops fighting in the area of Siverskaya-Vyritsa. I am asking you to order the dropping of parachutists in the area of the Budanov swamps, coordinates 58, 68, from where we shall lead them directly to the enemy. This drop area cannot be observed by the enemy. Marking: 3 campfires in one line. We expect the dropping between the 7th and 11th. I request further directives.

Commander of the Unit
5 September 1941
[signed] Kopytov[26]

Samples of intelligence procured by the partisans which would be of value both to the Red Army and the bands may be found in the following excerpts from reports of the so-called Stalin Brigade, a partisan unit which, under the command of a Lt. Col. Okhotin, operated in the Polotsk-Nevel area in the northern border region of Belorussia.

[24] A Soviet term used most frequently to designate an independent partisan unit.
[25] *Nachrichten Nr. 9*, 11 June 1944, p. 10.
[26] 8. Pz.Div., Ic, "Taetigkeitsbericht vom 23.8.41—31.12.1942," 3–5 September 1941 (GMDS, 8 PzD 24131/2, Anlage 41).

Results of Reconnaissance and Intelligence
4 September 1943

1. Village of Rybankovo. On 20 August, occupation force relieved by 100 Cossacks. Not determined how these are armed.

. . . .

4. Occupation forces at Stayki, Dukhino unchanged. Between the villages of Borovkov, Zavolchikha, Tropki, along the paths used by the partisans are German mines. Ambushes were laid along the roads. [A long list of names follows.] Approaches to the communities of Taporsky and Stayki are also mined. . . . Source: agent reports of the 2d Battalion and the scouting group.

. . . .

7. From 27 August on, daily rail traffic of 5 transport trains from Polotsk in the direction of Bygosovo carrying civilians, cattle, and wounded coming from Bryansk, Gomel, Vitebsk, and Minsk.

8. Fifty per cent of the laborers working on the Polotsk-Bygosovo rail line have been shipped to Germany.

. . . .

11. Morale of German troops and police is poor.

12. Polotsk. The guard at the airport has been strengthened. Transport planes are landing. . . .

24 August 1943

Dretun: 1 battalion of 406th Regiment for guarding railroad. Airport has up to 40 bombing planes stationed there.

Baravukha I: Staging area, up to 5,000 Germans. Youth in training. Armament: 3 AA guns, very heavy machine guns, 3 field pieces, number of machine guns and mortars not determined.

Beloye: Police school. 100 men, about 15 of them Germans, 76mm gun, 2 antitank guns, 2 80mm mortars, number of machine guns not determined.

All above-listed posts are fortified with dugouts, trenches, wire entanglements. Approaches are mined.

Altogether there are in the surrounding communities 6,367 Germans, 182 policemen, 139 Vlasovites. Armament: 4 76mm guns, 9 antitank guns, 3 AA guns, 11 8cm mortars, 26 5cm mortars, 26 heavy MG's, 40 light MG's, 49 submachine guns.

On 12 August the daily bombing and burning of villages in Rossono Rayon started. An average of up to 10 planes of the JU-88 type participated, taking off from airports at Polotsk-Dretun. At Polotsk, Idritsa, and other places occupied by the Germans, young people born in 1925 and 1926 are being called up for shipment to Germany.

> The Chief of the Intelligence Section
> Capt. Kozlovsky[27]

The most detailed examples of partisan intelligence reports are contained in the German account of the history and record of the Grishin Regiment, a unit that operated over a wide area of Army Group Center from December 1941 until 1944. The Germans were impressed with the range and

[27] PzAOK 3, Ic/AO, "Nr. 5394/42," 19 September 1943, p. 5 (GMDS, PzAOK 3, 40252/7, Anlage 33). Another sample of a tactical partisan intelligence report contains information on the location of German airfields and aircraft stationed in the Bryansk area.

caliber of information collected by the intelligence staff of this unit and forwarded to Moscow:

The S-2 reports of the battalions were collected and evaluated by the regimental staff and then forwarded to Moscow. The monthly intelligence reports to Popov, the chief of the partisan staff with the Western Front, are conspicuous for their wealth of details. Troop movements, strength of garrisons in towns and villages, staffs, security of bridges, ammunition, and ration dumps, freight traffic, harvesting, shipments of grain, recruitment and shipment of workers to Germany are reported in greatest detail. . . .[28]

Samples of these intelligence reports follow:

1. 5th Battalion, 20 September 1943

In Smolensk Oblast on the major supply route of Smolensk-Krasnoye, Smolensk-Gusino, German troops were observed retreating in the direction of Orsha. In the areas of Pochinkovo, Dukhovchina, and Yartsevo refugees consisting primarily of policemen, starostas,[29] and mayors are arriving daily. Smolensk is being evacuated. The editorial staff of the German newspaper, *Novyi Put* [New Way] has been transferred to Belostok. Harvesting and transporting of grain are being accelerated. The staff of a German army was transferred from Smolensk to Tolochin between Minsk and Orsha. Field fortifications along the Dnepr and the Sozh are being speeded up; pillboxes and trenches are under construction.

Roslavl has been evacuated; [there is] uninterrupted traffic of motor vehicles on the Roslavl-Mstislavl highway. The Germans are taking everything with them, even such trivial things as furniture or potted flowers. A large fuel dump is located in a small grove on the Mogilev 2-Shklov rail line, about 200 meters from Mogilev 2. Our air raid seriously damaged the airport in Shatalovo; 45 airplanes and all supply dumps in the vicinity have been burned out.

2. 2d Battalion, 5 September 1943

A course in espionage for boys and girls was concluded on 4 August according to natives of Mogilev.

3. Intelligence report from Mogilev, 7 September [1943]

On 25 August, 500 infantry troops occupied the camp next to the airport. The concentration camp adjoining the Dmitrov Factory contains about 500 people including 276 Jews. A small troop training area which can accommodate about 1,500 men is located behind the automobile repair shop [and there is another area] in Chapayev for about 1,000 men. The guard regiment of the "people's" army ["Volksarmee," probably refers to indigenous units] is billeted on the grounds of the artillery regiment near the Mogilev 2 railroad station. The regiment fights against the partisans. The regiment is commanded by Colonel Kononov. A pigeon station containing about 500 pigeons is located on the road to Vydritsa [?]. A vegetable storage place has been set up near the railroad station adjoining the overpass. Locomotives are being repaired in the automobile repair shop. The meat combine is functioning; the sausage department is located in the former newspaper building. Airplane parts are being manufactured in the pipe foundry. There are about 1,000 troops in Mogilev excluding those in the training areas. There are no armored units.

---

[28] *Nachrichten Nr. 7,* 8 December 1943, p. 4.
[29] Village elders.

Antiaircraft batteries are stationed on the bridges. At the present time there are about 500 motor vehicles in Mogilev.

4. 5th Battalion, 8 September 1943

Changes and transfer involving the German 4th and 9th Armies are being executed at this time. Rumors say that the greatly weakened 9th Army is being strengthened by reserves and by parts of the 4th Army. This includes Staff 675 of the 4th Army with the following officers: Major Kuehn, Captain Alzt (illegible), and 1st Lt. Broer; this staff is being transferred to the 9th Army and will remain in Krichev where the staff of the 9th Army will also be moved. The staff of the 4th Army with its commanding general, Heinrici, is still located in Shumakhi (illegible), south of Roslavl. It is strongly protected by antiaircraft batteries. A shift of the 4th Army to the Ukraine or to Italy is expected momentarily. The 9th Army will then take over the present sector of the 4th Army. Army supply commander is situated in Klimovichi, southeast of Krichev, together with Colonel Zipperman von (remainder of name illegible). Antiaircraft batteries are almost completely lacking.

A large airport serving as a base for long-range aircraft and containing a fuel supply depot is located in the village of Shumkovka near the highway. A motor pool . . . is situated in the village of Selets on the Krichev-Roslavl highway. Cars are parked along both sides of the highway under the trees throughout the entire village. There are no antiaircraft batteries. A large depot for winter supplies (skis, sleds, and clothing) is located near the Krichev 2 railroad station. . . .[30]

The Soviets, however, were apparently not satisfied with the reports of the Grishin Regiment and in particular criticized the quality of the tactical intelligence procured. This is what the German report, which was based on captured records of the band, has to say:

[The caliber of] tactical intelligence is being repeatedly criticized in the orders [coming down from Moscow]. For example, Major Lazarev is being reproached for not being able to recognize and report in time the enemy's encirclement plans. In a report of December 1942, four women scouts who had not carried out their missions are named; another report dated January 1943 names a woman scout who had been sentenced to death for repeated nonexecution of missions and other violations.[31]

[30] *Ibid.*, p. 10. The information given by the 5th Battalion on 8 September 1943 regarding changes in assignments and locations of the German Fourth and Ninth Armies is in complete disagreement with the situation pictured on German tactical maps of the period. For example, the Situation East *(Lage Ost)* map of OKH for 8 September 1943 indicates that Headquarters of Fourth Army was north, not south of Roslavl. Ninth Army Headquarters was not in Krichev but about 100 miles to the southeast; Fourth Army was never scheduled to go to Italy or the Ukraine but remained in Army Group Center throughout the war. What apparently confused the partisans in this instance was the fact that Second Panzer Army headquarters, minus its units, had indeed left the area in August 1943 for Yugoslavia and that its sector had been taken over by Ninth and Second Armies, necessitating considerable regrouping of German forces.

[31] *Ibid.*, p. 4. Another example of willful false reporting by partisan agents is to be found in a report of a German antipartisan task force in the Bryansk area which, during a big operation against the bands, captured a partisan intelligence dispatch. The agent who reported sighting only two trains at a railroad station in the area

The Grishin Regiment was badly mauled by the Germans near Mogilev in October 1943 but continued its activities into 1944. A report of *Fremde Heere Ost* of February 1944 stated that the band was assigned to reconnaissance tasks for the Red Army in the area of Army Group Center: "According to reliable sources, the 13th Regiment (Grishin), location: SW of Belynichi, received orders to conduct intelligence work for the Red Army regardless of the difficult situation. . . ."[32]

Other specific examples of extensive and apparently reliable partisan intelligence work done for the Red Army have been found in records pertaining to the Yelnya-Dorogobuzh area. Partisan records captured by the Germans and interrogations of prisoners revealed that the information forwarded by the bands was quite accurate.

As far as later developments are concerned, the materials at present available provide only a few hints. It appears that tactical intelligence work by the partisans for the Red Army assumed increasing significance and became an ever more important aspect of partisan warfare, particularly since the operations of the bands were being synchronized with those of the Red Army.

B. POLITICAL AND ECONOMIC INTELLIGENCE

In addition to military intelligence, either for themselves or the Red Army, the partisans also gathered and forwarded to Moscow information on the political, economic, and social conditions of the German-occupied territories. Specifically, the Soviet Government was interested in the following points: how the German occupation was organized, how it functioned, to what extent it had consolidated its position, reactions of the population to it, what social and economic effects the occupation had produced, and similar matters.

In the winter of 1941–42, Soviet Intelligence apparently made a large-scale effort to procure information of this type, using masses of agents, including highly trained Party members and politruks as well as women and children. According to an intelligence report of Eleventh Army, dated March 1942, their specific missions included the following: (1) What factories have been restored and are again in operation? (2) Are there Russian deserters, and, if so, where? (3) Which inhabitants have not obeyed the evacuation order? (4) Names of mayors. (5) Names of auxiliary policemen.[33]

---

was actually shot in the middle of a forest, in a hide-out from which he could not possibly have seen the trains. (Gruppe Jolasse, "Gefechtsbericht ueber Unternehmen Dreieck und Viereck vom 17.9.—2.10.1942," 19 October 1942, p. 3, GMDS, Korueck 27894/3.)

[32] OKH/GenStdH/FHO (I), "Anlagen zum Lagebericht Ost (Feindlage-Banden) Nr. 327," 5 February 1944 (GMDS, H 3/227).

[33] AOK 11, AO, "Abwehrnachrichten Nr. 4," 14 March 1942, p. 1 (GMDS, AOK 11, 35774/10).

Although the partisans were not included in the enumeration of agents contained in the report, the fact that they too were utilized in this connection may be deduced from the statement with which the Eleventh Army report begins: "Activities of Soviet Intelligence and the partisans often overlap to a considerable extent. . . ."[34]

While the reports of the field commanders do not contain specific references to political or economic targets, a very detailed listing of intelligence assignments in these fields is attached to the *Bulletin on Partisan Warfare No. 4.* This list was prepared by *Fremde Heere Ost* on the basis of captured Soviet documents. Purporting to constitute the operational intelligence directive of the Central Staff of the Partisan Movement, it contains 172 questions, grouped into 21 fields, and may be taken as a good indicator of the efforts and care with which the Soviets were trying to obtain a picture of the situation in the occupied territories. A few of the most interesting questions in the political, administrative, economic, social, and cultural spheres should be noted:

Organizational structure of the local administration.
Heads of the most important organs of the local administration.
Enterprises in operation (factories, plants, individual workshops).
Condition of public utilities.
Condition of the workers: regulation of work, working hours, wage questions, standard of living.
Forms of utilizing the land and methods of farming.
What is being taxed?
Methods of tax collection.
What kinds of goods and foodstuffs are supplied to the population?
Do grade and high schools exist in towns and in the rayon?
Medical care for the population.
What newspapers are published and what is their circulation?
Relationship of the Germans to the different religious currents. To what currents is preference being given?
How is the nationality question being solved by the Fascists in the occupied territories?
Attitude of the urban population toward the administrative measures of the occupiers (workers, "white-collar" employees, intelligentsia, and especially the specialists in science, technology, and art).
Of what elements is the police composed?[35]

Related to these were other questions designed to elicit the most detailed information on all aspects of the German occupation.

C. CONCLUDING REMARKS

The foregoing examples show that the intelligence mission of the partisans comprised very diversified tasks, ranging from simple reconnaissance

[34] *Ibid.*
[35] *Nachrichten Nr. 4,* 10 September 1943, pp. 7–10; cf. *Nachrichten Nr. 1,* "Merkblatt fuer politische Erkundung," 3 May 1943, Anlage 8 (GMDS, H 3/738), which is given in full in Appendix, Document 13.

to complicated assignments of a political nature. Unfortunately, the documents do not reveal what priorities were given to the various assignments, nor do they permit of easy deductions on this point. Nevertheless, it seems safe to assume that the intelligence and security requirements of the bands themselves had to be satisfied first, particularly during the early period of the war. Second priority probably went to the procurement of intelligence useful in Soviet military operations, while political and economic intelligence presumably occupied third place. Obviously, much depended on the current military situation and on local conditions. Thus, it seems entirely possible that under the appropriate circumstances every effort of the partisans was bent toward obtaining information for the Red Army, while at other times their intelligence work focused on political questions, especially when such information was important to Soviet psychological warfare. A closer analysis of the basis on which intelligence assignments were given to the partisans and the priorities placed upon them will be possible, if it can be done at all, only after more detailed information has been assembled on specific areas and periods.

§III. Intelligence Operations of the Partisans

To carry out the various assignments outlined in the preceding section, the partisans gradually built up an elaborate intelligence and security system. This system may be compared to a series of concentric circles. First and innermost were the guards and outposts who protected the band's hide-outs and camps.

Security measures depend on the size and strength of the detachment. They always aim at surrounding the entire encampment and are instituted on the basis of observation. The task of the detachment is to evade contact with the enemy and remain undetected. Under all circumstances, observation posts must be set up along the roads and paths on which the detachment moves towards its rest camp. This is necessary because the detachment may be pursued by enemy troops which have detected it. If the detachment should be detected, the guards must warn it by prearranged signals. The detachment selects special guards for this task. The guards may use flares, but fire only in exceptional cases, and only when they are satisfied that the detachment covered by them can safely get away without a battle.[36]

Then, there were the *Kundschafter,* or scouts, who were either members of the bands themselves or closely affiliated with them. They served, as one Soviet directive put it, as "the eyes and ears" of the commander of

---

[36] Komm.d.Sich.Tr. Sued, Ia, "Die Partisanenabteilungen und ihre Taktik," n.d. (GMDS, HGeb 39502/19).

the band[37] and collected most of the information. From the missions of the *Kundschafter,* described in detail in the previous section, it is evident that they constituted the real core of the partisan intelligence network.

Finally, the bands were screened by an outer ring of informants in cities, towns, and villages. For the most part these informants were not full-time agents and often did not know the whereabouts of the bands. They kept in contact with the partisans through liaison agents or "cut-outs" to warn the bands of German plans and moves.

It is desirable that each group have informants in the communities occupied by the enemy. Through these, essential information about the enemy and his objectives must be procured and, upon occasion, supplies replenished. For this purpose [to act as informants] people must be selected who appear least suspicious to the enemy (old men, women, adolescents, etc.), so that they are available during combat periods. Care must be taken in contacting these informants, so that they obtain no knowledge whatever about the whereabouts of the detachment.[38]

The nature of the partisan informant net is indicated by the statement of a partisan who was captured by an SS unit early in 1943:

The local partisans are brought together in intelligence detachments and are sent to visit their relatives in the vicinity in order to gather information. These relatives and friends of the partisans compose the real informant net of the bands. Banding local partisans together in a secret intelligence unit safeguards the security of the informant network. . . .[39]

Village residents who worked in towns were also used as informants:

In many cases the existence of an informant net in villages close to the partisan base could be observed. In another case, it could be ascertained that spying was done both by people who resided in the locality and by those who worked in small towns and returned to their native villages on Sundays. There they delivered their information to the bands, were interrogated more closely, and were given new assignments. This system is extremely effective and involves no risk for the enemy.[40]

The persons recruited for the partisan intelligence net were solemnly inducted by the following oath:

Pledge of Partisan Intelligence Informants

I, . . . , pledge to the Intelligence Section:

1. To report all persons and groups who engage in espionage against the Red Army and the partisan movement.

---

[37] PzAOK 2, Ic/AO, "Feindnachrichten Nr. 1/43, Anlage 11: 'Merkblatt des Kundschafters der Partisanen,'" 31 January 1943, p. 1 (GMDS, PzAOK 2, 37075/159).

[38] HFPCh im OKH/GenStdH/GenQu/Abt.K.-Verw., "Erfahrungen ueber Aufbau, Aufgaben, Auftreten und Bekaempfung der Partisanenabteilungen," 15 January 1942, p. 17 (GMDS, Wi/ID 2.717).

[39] SS Kav.Div., Ic, "Vernehmungsniederschrift aufgenommen durch Sicherheitspolizei u. SD, SK 7a, Erkundungstrupp Nakaten," 18 January 1943, p. 3 (GMDS, XLI AK 29021).

[40] *Nachrichten Nr. 1,* 3 May 1943, p. 4.

2. To report all observations of the enemy and his equipment.

3. To discharge honestly and promptly all missions given me by the officer in charge of the intelligence section.

4. Never to talk to anyone about my connections with the intelligence section.

5. To sign all reports made by me under the cover name of . . . in order to maintain complete security of information.

If I do not discharge the missions entrusted to me, I shall be shot.[41]

The German documents do not contain specific and explicit information concerning the basis on which agents were selected for partisan intelligence work. It may be assumed, however, that at least two criteria were applied: (1) The agent had to have a good knowledge of local conditions. (2) He had to have a good cover; that is to say, he had to be in a position to get around easily and as inconspicuously as possible. It was for this latter reason that the partisans relied heavily on women, children, and older people, as indicated in the quotation from the Provost Marshal General's report cited above. A number of other reports corroborate this point. In March 1942, rear area command of Fourth Army said: "They [the partisans] also possess an excellent intelligence service for which they prefer to use women and children in order to avoid suspicion."[42] A report of the 339th Security Division from the same period stated. "Small children and very old men who seem to be completely harmless persons are the best scouts. In this way they [the partisans] are always informed about impending operations and can best evade them."[43]

The 221st Security Division was informed by some partisan deserters that in one case a 14-year-old boy had thoroughly reconnoitered the situation for a band of partisans which was planning a raid on a German construction unit.[44] Praising the intelligence service of the partisans, the rear area command of Second Panzer Army reported the following concerning the categories of people employed as agents: "Their sources of information are scouts, the population which frequently sympathizes with the bands, men, women, children, or spies clothed in German army or railway uniforms. . . ."[45]

A partisan who was captured by the 83d Infantry Division in May 1942 said that his unit employed twenty women as agents.[46] Even cripples and

[41] *Nachrichten Nr. 9*, 11 June 1944, Anlage 9.

[42] Korueck 559, Ic, "Erfahrungsbericht ueber die Partisanenbekaempfung im rueckw. Armeegebiet," March 1942, p. 1 (GMDS, Korueck 29236/3).

[43] 339. Inf.Div., Ic, "Nr. 138/42 geh.," 14 February 1942, p. 1 (GMDS, Korueck 19030/3, Anlage 22).

[44] 221. Sich.Div., Ic., "Vernehmung von 2 Ueberlaeufern aus Kamenka," 15 April 1942 (GMDS, 221 ID 22639/6, Anlage 18).

[45] Korueck 532, Qu/Ia, "Richtlinien fuer die Bekaempfung der Partisanen durch die im Sicherungsdienst an Eisenbahnen und Strassen eingesetzten Truppen," 23 May 1942 (GMDS, Korueck 29239/3).

[46] 83. Inf.Div., Ic, "Feindnachrichtenblatt Nr. 17," 25 May 1942 (GMDS, 83 ID 24230/5).

other physically handicapped people were being used: "In view of the credulity of German soldiers, the Soviet partisans frequently use cripples, primarily as agents. Some cases are also known in which healthy persons camouflaged themselves by putting on bandages or inflicting loathsome wounds upon themselves."[47] A similar statement was contained in the summary report of the Provost Marshal General on the partisan situation from July 1942 to March 1943: "To an increasing degree the enemy is employing cripples, especially amputees, as agents because he figures that such persons arouse less suspicion and will not be challenged during checks. . . ."[48]

The question to what extent the partisans were actively being helped by the population in their intelligence operations is, however, not an easy one to answer. The German reports, some of which have been cited above, suggest that this help was considerable and widespread. Even in 1942 the Provost Marshal General said that, in spite of the threat of death penalties against those aiding the partisans, some persons were still willing to risk such support in different ways.[49]

On the other hand, most of the German reports for 1941 and 1942 describe the people in the occupied territories as being basically friendly to the Germans and even willing to aid them in their fight against the partisans. For example, some were willing to become informants for German intelligence units. Under the impact of later developments, which lie beyond the purview of this chapter, popular attitudes changed, but even then, sullen indifference seems to have been more common than open hostility toward the Germans. Under these circumstances and in view of the fact that intelligence work for the partisans involved great personal risks, it may be assumed that only the most active and loyal adherents of the Soviet regime volunteered for such activity, while others did so only to provide themselves with some kind of insurance against the day when the Soviets would return. From the rest of the population, the partisans could expect only passive neutrality or, at most, warnings of impending danger. A captured Soviet document, dated September 1941 and containing instructions to Soviet agents and a description of conditions likely to be encountered by them, said:

There are, however, many elements among the population who sympathize with the partisan movement and the Soviet regime. But, since they fear the consequences, they are using utmost caution in their activities. Thus, it has happened that our agents have received signals to leave a village because the

[47] AOK 11, AO, "Abwehrnachrichten Nr. 4," 14 March 1942, p. 4 (GMDS, AOK 11, 35774/10).
[48] HFPCh im OKH/Gen.z.b.V./H.Wes.Abt./GFP, "Allgemeiner Ueberblick ueber die Bandenbewegung fuer die Zeit vom 1.7.1942—31.3.1943," 10 April 1943, p. 6 (GMDS, OKW/734).
[49] HFPCh im OKH/GenStdH/GenQu/GFP, "Entwicklung der Partisanenbewegung in der Veit vom 1.1—30.6.1942," 31 July 1942, p. 23 (GMDS, H.Gr. Nord 75131/113).

Germans were in it; they were given food . . . and were advised to get out, or be captured by the Germans. . . .[50]

This description of the people's loyalty to the Soviet regime seems to have been more optimistic than the facts warranted. Nevertheless, the fact remains that partisans could count on passive, and sometimes even active, support of the people, as is borne out by the following report from the Bryansk area:

The population, under intimidation by the partisans, betrays nothing and nobody. Most of the time, it is possible to obtain information only by constant persuasion and by the assurance that we want to help. In principle, the sympathy of the people, particularly of the women, girls, and children living in villages seldom visited by Germans, lies with the partisans who even offer rewards for especially good intelligence information. . . .[51]

This situation created a problem with which the Germans attempted to deal in several ways. The author of the report just quoted, the intelligence officer of a German security division, recommended shooting all persons encountered outside their place of residence.[52] A less drastic, but widely used method was the restriction of the movements of the civilian population, particularly at night and in areas close to the front. An OKH directive of October 1941 ordered strict control of civilian road traffic.[53] Even before that, in September 1941, Ninth Army had put into effect a curfew and had set up restricted zones: "(a) Inhabitants are forbidden to leave their communities during the hours of darkness (i.e., from one hour after sunset until one hour before sunrise). (b) Along the railroad lines inhabitants are forbidden to enter a strip one kilometer wide on both sides of the embankment, except to tend their fields or to cross the area by public roads."[54]

Many other German orders also stressed the threat to security arising from the fact that civilians moved about rather freely, and urged commanders to put an end to this traffic. One of the strictest orders was issued by the rear area command of Fourth Army in October 1941: "Throughout the entire army rear area freedom of movement has been canceled. During the day all persons of military age (17 to 65), who are wandering back and forth between communities, are to be picked up and

---

[50] AOK 4, Ic, "Anlage 3 zu Feindnachrichtenblatt 18: 'Grundsaetzliche Anweisung fuer den geheimen Nachrichtendienst der Geheimen Nachrichten-Abt. des Stabes der 21. Armee vom 1.9.1941,' " n.d., p. 1 (GMDS, AOK 4, 13767/5).

[51] 339. Inf.Div., Ic, "Nr. 138/42 geh.," 14 February 1942, p. 1 (GMDS, Korueck 19030/3, Anlage 22).

[52] Ibid.

[53] ObdH/GenStdH/Aus.Abt.(Ia), "Richtlinien fuer Partisanenbekaempfung," 25 October 1941, p. 7 (GMDS, EAP 38-x/14).

[54] AOK 9, Ic/AO/O.Qu., "Partisanenbekaempfung," 2 September 1941, p. 2 (GMDS, AOK 9, 14162/7).

sent to a prison camp. At night, any civilian on the highways and in open country will be fired on. . . ."[55]

The security situation was aggravated when the German losses mounted in the winter of 1941 and many sectors of the front were thinly held, with large gaps in the line. This made infiltration and line-crossing possible on a large scale, as the rear area command of Fourth Army pointed out in February 1942:

[The Russian people] see what is happening on our side, and what they do not see or experience directly, they hear through their excellent intelligence service. Since we have no continuous forward line, traffic of every kind from the Soviet side and back again is possible, and extensive use is being made of such crossings. New partisan bands have infiltrated, Russian parachutists are being dropped and are taking over leadership. . . .[56]

Weak spots in the German front, especially the boundaries between corps or divisions, were exploited by the Soviets not only for infiltrating agents, but also as points to be attacked in attempted breakthroughs. Information about these soft spots was obtained from local elements, according to a report of Second Panzer Army:

It has become known that the Russians are making extensive use of information obtained from the local inhabitants. Repeatedly, it has been observed that the enemy is accurately informed about the soft spots in our front and frequently picks the boundaries between our corps and divisions as points of attack. The movement of the inhabitants between the fronts must, therefore, be prevented by all possible means.[57]

Apparently, the interdiction of free movement of civilians proved effective in checking Soviet intelligence activities conducted either by regular agents or partisans. In October 1942, Third Panzer Army stated: "The prohibition of civilian movements proved to be a very effective means for curbing hostile bands and enemy agents."[58]

Besides restricting civilian traffic and setting curfew hours, the Germans also instituted a strict registration of the residents of all localities in order to check on transients among whom there might be partisans and Soviet agents. Summing up the effects of civilian traffic upon the security situation and the German measures to control it, the Provost Marshal General said the following in the middle of 1942:

The appointment of reliable mayors and indigenous policemen in communities recently cleared of partisans has proved to be an effective device for preventing

[55] Korueck 559, Qu. to 137. Inf.Div., "Tagebuch Nr. 4090," 8 October 1941 (GMDS, Korueck 13512/2, Anlage 25).
[56] Korueck 559, Qu., "Lage im rueckwaertigen Armeegebiet," 1 February 1942 (GMDS, Korueck 29236/2, Anlage 75).
[57] PzAOK 2, Ic/AO, "Feindnachrichten Nr. 1/42," 2 January 1942, p. 3 (GMDS, PzAOK 2, 37075/170).
[58] PzAOK 3, Ic/AO, "Abwehrschutzmassnahmen gegenueber der Zivilbevoelkerung," 14 October 1942 (GMDS, PzAOK 3, 25784/43).

the formation of new bands in such communities and in the adjacent woods. The mayors and police, in conjunction with German troops in the vicinity and with secret field police and military police detachments, watch closely over the pacified area, paying particular attention to the registering and screening of all persons newly arrived in the area.

To combat the dangers arising from the migration of the population the secret field police is constantly conducting large-scale checks. These revealed that among the migrating crowds, which are composed of evacuees, returnees, and food hoarders, numerous partisans and enemy agents can be found.

Satisfactory results have been achieved by checking pedestrians on the streets.[59]

[59] HFPCh im OKH/GenStdH/GenQu/GFP, "Entwicklung der Partisanenbewegung in der Zeit vom 1.1.—30.6.1942," 31 July 1942, p. 39 (GMDS, H.Gr. Nord 75131/113).

CHAPTER VI

Airpower in Partisan Warfare

Gerhard L. Weinberg

Introduction

The use of airpower to organize, support, and direct a partisan movement was one of the major innovations of the war in the East. This combination of modern technology with a primitive form of warfare enabled the Soviet High Command to fashion a military and political weapon of tremendous strength from a guerrilla movement relegated by its very name to the "little war." It is the purpose of this chapter to examine the methods used and the success attained by air support, and, in order to complete the picture, to describe the German use of airpower in antipartisan warfare. A discussion of the relation of airpower to partisan warfare cannot be lifted completely out of context without causing distortions and misunderstanding; its peculiarities and significance arise from two settings: air operations over the Eastern front, and partisan and antipartisan warfare behind the German lines. Some sketch of the first and frequent references to the second, at least in general terms, will be necessary to give meaning to the events examined here.

Although the German Air Force began the war on the USSR with a numerical inferiority in planes, it had better planes and a far more experienced and efficient organization. These two factors—superior equipment and wider experience—together with the surprise attack and the rapid capture of many airfields enabled the Luftwaffe to attain air superiority in the first months of the war. From October 1941 on, however, the German Air Force was increasingly hard pressed. Lack of adequate pilot and machine replacements, continuous overworking of fighter units, the growing length of communications lines, and Soviet numerical superiority combined to effect a change. Henceforth, the Germans could attain air superiority only on one front at a time by concentrating their forces for specific operations. German strategy in 1942 placed major emphasis on attacks toward Stalingrad and the Caucasus on the southern front, thus forcing the withdrawal of planes from the central front, behind which most of the partisan centers were located. By this time and increasingly so in the next two years, the mounting strength of the Red Air Force gave the Soviets secure dominance in the air over most of the Eastern front. While German Air Force units were repeatedly withdrawn from the Eastern front to cope with threats elsewhere (the Mediterranean theater, the Allied air offensive against Germany), the Red Air Force was strengthened by British and American planes. This combination of adverse circumstances could not be offset by German efforts to increase plane production, to make greater use of obsolescent planes, and to depend increasingly on the air forces of the Axis satellites.

Certain special factors affecting the air war in the East must also be considered. German insistence on holding areas surrounded or all but surrounded by the Red Army was a burden on the German Air Force, which was forced to commit large numbers of planes in an effort to supply such garrisons. The long front line and the relatively short Soviet air flights made German fighter interception more difficult and less frequent than on other fronts. In addition, the lack of an effective warning system made it possible for the Soviets to use planes obsolete by western standards.[1]

All these factors obviously favored the Soviets and hindered the Germans. The superiority attained by Soviet Air Force operations in partisan warfare was therefore not surprising. The war in the East, however, was decided on the ground; and it was the ability of the Red Army to force the Germans into retreat which made it possible for the Red Air Force to make the contribution which is described here.

§I. The Role of Airpower in the Formation and Control of Partisan Units

In 1941 the Soviet government relied to a considerable extent on the organizers and officers flown into the partisan areas, though on a far smaller scale than later in the war. In this way failures in areas overrun by the enemy could be remedied, at least to some extent; efforts to recruit Red Army stragglers could be supported; and control over the small groups in existence could be established.

[1] For published reports on the air war in the East, see Asher Lee, *The German Air Force* (New York: Harpers, 1946).

Another point not implicit in the situation in the occupied areas in 1941 is the impact airpower had on the general attitude of the population toward the Soviet regime. The appearance of "men from Moscow" no doubt served as a reminder that the long arm of the Soviet Government still reached into places abandoned by the Red Army. In a country in which partisan warfare was organized largely from the outside (unlike Yugoslavia, for example), airpower was essential to the formation of a partisan movement, not only because many of the leaders had to be brought in by air but also because the continuing power and presence of their old regime had to be brought home to a reluctant population. [For a discussion of the attitudes of the population in 1941, see Chap. IV.]

From time to time in subsequent years, it became necessary to reorganize the partisan movement locally for one reason or another. Thus, a group of partisan units in one area might have suffered heavy losses in a major antipartisan operation or the leadership of a group of bands might have been dispersed by a smaller but more surprising German blow. At other times, the performance of the partisan groups in a given area might not have been up to Soviet expectations. In such cases airpower provided one of the few means of reviving or reorganizing the partisans in these areas. In general, these situations followed either antipartisan operations or developments within the bands; they will be discussed in these two categories.

In the larger centers of partisan activity, the Germans periodically conducted major operations against the bands. In these operations, additional German forces were transferred to the area and were employed for a short period of time in a concentric drive. Usually these operations inflicted some casualties on the partisans, who immediately dispersed into small groups which scattered over wide areas. After the German troops returned to their strongpoints or to the commands from which they had temporarily been withdrawn, the partisans would attempt to re-form their units in the same vicinity. To accomplish this, replacements had to be found, gaps in the cadres had to be filled, morale had to be bolstered, and the reorganized units had to be made combatworthy again. These were not easy tasks. The mission of the Red Air Force in all this was to fly in new leaders, additional cadres for the dispersed units, and supplies to replace what had been lost in battle.

The available evidence indicates clearly the significant role airpower played in the revival of the partisan movement in a number of areas which the Germans thought they had successfully cleared. Thus airborne cadres and reinforcements speedily reorganized the partisan movement near the Polisto Lake following a German operation in the late summer of 1942, and this process was repeated after subsequent German operations in the same area. The extensive use of airpower was instrumental in supporting the speedy revival of the partisan movement in the Bryansk area, following such German operations as "Vogelsang," "Nachbarhilfe," and "Zigeuner-baron." [See Chap. VIII, Sect. III, B, 2.] In the summer and fall of 1943, after the major German operations, "Kugelblitz" and "Maigewitter" in northern Belorussia, the Red Air Force flew in cadres and extended other support to revive the partisan movement there. Similarly, in the area east of Smolensk great efforts were made throughout the second half of 1942 and early 1943 to revitalize a partisan movement which had been over-whelmed by the German antipartisan operation, "Hannover." In this case, the attempt failed.[2]

§II. Supplies and Reinforcements

A. MILITARY SUPPLIES

1. Invasion to December 1941

Most military supplies obtained by the partisans in 1941 were from local sources such as supply dumps, material left by retreating Red Army units, and weapons abandoned in the areas of the major encirclement battles. Although some weapons were probably sent through gaps in the front, these belonged primarily to men being shipped in to join the partisan groups. A fair estimate would probably be that nine-tenths of the partisans' military supplies in 1941 were obtained from the local sources just mentioned, and that the remaining tenth was flown in.[3]

[2] See Chap. VII, Sect. V, C, D, and E.

The difference in the outcome of Soviet attempts to reorganize the partisans in areas hit by antipartisan operations lies in the nature of the German operations. In those areas (Bryansk, for instance) where German operations led chiefly to the dispersal of the partisans and where most of the people whom the Germans reported as killed were nonpartisan members of the local population, the task of reorganizing the movement was relatively simple—given time and cadre replacements. However, when the Germans made an effort to distinguish between the partisans and the population (and the only major example of this was the operation in the Smolensk area) and when, as a result, most of the actual partisans were killed or captured, the infusion of new cadres was not sufficient. In such cases only a mass infusion of men could have produced an effective fighting force, since the problem here was one of replacing rather than reviving the partisan movement. (Thus when one partisan unit in the Caucasus disintegrated, it was virtually replaced by a group originally sent in to reorganize it.) The operations in the Belorussian area mentioned above represent an intermediate stage; there the Germans had concentrated on the real partisans to a greater extent than usual, and the ultimate outcome of the efforts to revive the movement cannot be determined, since the Red Army retook the area not long after these efforts got started.

[3] The figures estimated here and on the following pages are impressions based on an examination of a mass of documents dealing with the partisan movement, rather than on a compilation of statistical data on air support operations. These estimates

Air supply operations in 1941 fall into two categories. The most important were the weapons and ammunition carried by the men flown in as partisans; frequently additional supplies for these men were dropped at the same time. In this way the men were provided not only with their immediate needs but also with something of a supply base. The second type was the supplying of weapons and ammunition both to groups which had previously been parachuted in and to other units which had been established earlier in the occupied territory. This type could be of considerable importance; a request for air supplies from a group operating south of Leningrad, for example, stresses the need for explosives, hand grenades, and other supplies. On the whole, however, it is clear from what is known about the over-all partisan conditions in 1941 that the material brought in by air, though useful, was not a significant factor in the supply picture.

2. January–June 1942

The first months of 1942 witnessed a tremendous growth in the partisan movement. It was at this time that large numbers of Red Army stragglers were mobilized into the movement and that many Red Army men were sent through the front to join the partisans. In a period of roughly six months the number of partisans in the occupied area increased from about 30,000 to about 150,000. Obviously the arming of this huge additional force presented a supply problem whose successful solution is one of the most remarkable feats of the whole movement. Although the general problem of supply is beyond the scope of this chapter, the main sources of supplies can be indicated briefly. The following estimates may be suggested tentatively to give some idea of the relative order of magnitude of the various sources. About 50–60 per cent of the additional supplies needed came from the occupied area itself. This included the weapons some of the stragglers still had as well as the small quantities captured from the Germans; most of this "local" material, however, was what the partisans literally picked up on the 1941 battlefields, especially after the snow melted in March and April. About 30 per cent of the additional supplies came from men who were sent in to join the partisan movement. Of this 30 per cent perhaps two-thirds was carried through the front—as around Vitebsk and Kirov—and one-third was flown in. The remaining 10–20 per cent of the additional supplies was delivered to the partisans by the Red Air Force. Thus, of the tremendous quantity of supplies needed for

---

have been made so as to give the reader a concrete idea of the relative significance of various sources of supply. In all cases, a margin of error must be allowed. At the same time, the actual figures are unlikely to have been vastly different. Thus, in the instance referred to, it is possible that instead of one-tenth, as little as 5 per cent or as much as 20 per cent may have been supplied by air; on the other hand, there can be no doubt that a significant quantity was dropped and that it was certainly not as large as one-quarter of the total.

the build-up of the first half of 1942, some 20 to 30 per cent was transported by air. The importance of weapons so transported was probably slightly higher than these percentage figures indicate, because the material flown in was of better quality and contained a higher proportion of automatic weapons. Nevertheless, if the estimates given above are even approximately correct, of the 150,000 partisans active by the late summer of 1942, three-quarters had weapons which came from the occupied area or had been carried through the front, while one-quarter had weapons which had been dropped to them or which they had carried when they themselves were flown in.[4]

3. Summer 1942—Summer 1944

As we have already seen, the partisan movement had attained a strength of about 150,000 men by the late summer of 1942. During the following year its total strength rose to perhaps a little over 200,000; following the German retreats of the second half of 1943 it probably decreased to slightly over 150,000, its approximate size when, at the end of June 1944, the Soviet summer offensive quickly retook practically all of the formerly occupied areas.[5] If this great number of men was to continue to have military value, it had to be provided with large quantities of military supplies: weapons, ammunition, explosives and mines.

a. Weapons and Ammunition

The great demand for supplies of weapons and ammunition during this period sprang from several causes. Many of the partisans' original weapons became unserviceable. German antipartisan operations, though generally not inflicting serious casualties on the partisans, often took a heavy toll in equipment: supply dumps were captured, and much equipment was lost as the partisans sought to avoid battle by dispersing in small groups. [On this subject, see especially Chap. VIII, Sect. III, B.] Furthermore, the local recruits frequently had no weapons at all. Also, there was a constant need to replace weapons lost or beyond repair and to replenish ammunition stocks. Finally, the tactical characteristics of partisan warfare in the second and third years of the war in the East put a premium on firepower.

[4] For air supply in the first half of 1942, see, in addition to German sources, A. Fyodorov, *Podpolnyi obkom deistvuyet* (Moscow: Voennoye Izdatelstvo Ministerstva Vooruzhnnykh Sil Soyuza SSR, 1947, Vol. I), p. 111.

[5] These figures, of course, disregard changes in the composition of the partisan movement during this period. On the whole, these changes had little effect on the supply problem; weapons were needed regardless of who was in the movement. The major change in composition—the slow replacement of Red Army stragglers by local recruits—probably involved a slight increase in supply requirements for the same number of men, because a larger proportion of Red Army stragglers had brought weapons with them and because the fire discipline of the stragglers was better than than of the local recruits.

Engagements were short, and the partisans depended on superior firepower to cover their retreat when they were unexpectedly engaged by the Germans, or to inflict heavy casualties when they ambushed the Germans. Likewise, the attacks on rail communications, whose requirements in terms of explosives and mines are discussed below, also reinforced the need for superior firepower. Since the Germans relied primarily on the so-called strongpoint system to protect their lines of communication, the partisans depended upon rapid small arms fire to tie down German strongpoint garrisons while demolition details placed their charges on the rails. All these factors led the partisans to rely heavily on automatic weapons of all sorts—machine pistols, light and heavy machine guns, antitank rifles.[6] Although the partisans had large quantities of these weapons by the summer of 1942, they constantly needed replacements and substitutions for less useful weapons.

It is clear from the available evidence that during this two-year period the Red Air Force transported a steady stream of weapons and ammunition to the partisans. The documentation covers almost all the areas of partisan activity and emphasizes repeatedly the large proportion of automatic weapons flown in.[7] During this period, weapons were sent through the front only infrequently and little serviceable equipment was left lying around in the woods. Furthermore, whatever the partisans captured from the Germans or obtained from collaborators who deserted from the Germans was likely to be of poor quality, since the German security troops had notoriously inferior equipment and were deficient in automatic weapons; the equipment of the antipartisan collaborator units was, if possible, even worse. Under these circumstances, the following estimates may not seem unreasonable. Of the weapons and ammunition acquired by the partisans during the two years after the summer of 1942, at least two-thirds was flown in.[8] As a result, by the summer of 1944 probably half the total armament of the partisans had been brought in by air or had been carried by personnel flown in.[9]

[6] To a lesser extent, the partisans used light and medium mortars.
[7] See, in addition to German sources, P. Vershigora, *Lyudi s chistoi sovestyu* (Moscow: Sovetskii Pisatel, 1951), p. 191; and V. Andreyev, *Narodnaya voina (zapiski partizana)* (Moscow: Gosudarstvennoye Izadetelstvo Khudozhestvennoi Literatury, 1952), p. 343.
[8] One of the most impressive pieces of evidence supporting the thesis that most of the weapons and ammunition were supplied by air is the collection of partisan questionnaires kept by the 281st Security Division. Partisan prisoners and deserters were asked how their unit supplies were secured; practically all of them indicated that weapons and ammunition came by air while most of the food came from the local population. The period covered was 1943–44. (GMDS, 281 ID 45072.)
[9] It should also be noted that, in this period, some of the larger partisan units were receiving artillery by air, primarily 45 mm and 76 mm guns. (H.Gr. Mitte, Ia, "Bandenlage im Grossraum Rossono," 10 June 1943, GMDS, H.Gr. Mitte 65002/22.)

b. Explosives and Mines

The summer of 1942 saw the beginning of the "war of the rails." From this time on, partisan attacks on the German-controlled railways were one of the main characteristics of partisan warfare; efforts to disrupt German traffic became the most important partisan military activity and remained so until the Germans retreated from the USSR. To a lesser extent, the partisans also mined the highways which the Germans used to supply their armies. All this activity required vast supplies of explosives and mines. Only to a small extent could these come from local supplies found or captured by the bands; and partisans who came through the front lines, if they managed to carry anything, were usually overburdened with weapons and ammunition. Probably as much as 90 per cent of the explosives and mines, therefore, had to be brought in by plane. This was especially true when the partisans were to carry out a concerted attack on the rail lines in coordination with a Red Army operation. Thus the big attacks of early August 1943 and of 19–20 June 1944 (in the former, 8,600 and in the latter, 9,600 charges were placed on the rails in the area of Army Group Center alone) could not possibly have been carried out without an advance air supply of explosives.

The virtual dependence of the partisans on air supply to carry on their military activities is evident from a number of sources. Available material on individual bands indicates how essential air supply was to their operations.[10] Several German reports on the last months of 1943 attribute a decline in partisan attacks on the railways to a shortage of explosives; this, in turn, was due to a decrease in air supply brought about by bad weather and by front line demands on the Red Air Force. The increase in the number of attacks in 1944 was attributed to an increase in air supply.

4. Special Items

In addition to the supplies already mentioned, special items of importance to the military operations of the partisans were transported by the Red Air Force. Of these the most important were radio equipment and batteries, virtually indispensable equipment for maintenance of control and coordination of activity. We have already noted that many partisan leaders who were flown into an area carried radio equipment with them; similarly the radio specialists sent in by air brought along their own. However, it was necessary to keep the partisan bands supplied with both radio equipment and batteries during the entire period of the German occupation. There is evidence that, starting early in 1942, such items were delivered periodically

---

[10] G. Linkov, *Voina v tylu vraga* (Moscow: Gosudarstvennoye Izdatelstvo Khudo-zhestvennoi Literatury, 1951), pp. 236–37; "Taetigkeits- und Erfahrungsbericht der Banditengruppe Kotschurow," 23 July—9 September 1942 (GMDS, AOK 16, 36588/68).

to the partisans by the Red Air Force. In one such shipment, of the eight or ten parachutes dropped, the Germans captured five, which contained among other things, one radio set, thirty batteries, and twenty dry cells. A Stalin order of March 1943 provided that henceforth radio equipment for the partisans was to be sent exclusively by air.

Other items dropped to the partisans were compasses and maps and, in a few instances, spare parts for tanks and sighting equipment for antitank guns. Occasionally spare parts for damaged Soviet planes and gasoline for partisan-operated trucks and tanks were parachuted in; for this latter purpose, a special type of container was devised.

B. FOOD

Securing adequate food supplies was a difficult problem for the partisans throughout the war. Normal production suffered from the war's disruptive effects; heavy German requisitions took the place of the marketing quotas which had previously been imposed by the Soviet regime; in addition, the soldiers of both armies—and after the initial fighting this meant the Germans—confiscated vast quantities of food for their own use. These conditions were typical of the whole occupied area. The partisans had special difficulties since most of them operated in the Great Russian-Belorussian area, which was normally a food-deficit area. As a consequence, hunger was one of the recurrent problems of virtually all partisan units.

In spite of these difficulties, the partisans were expected to rely on requisitions from the local population for their supplies. The food sent in by air was, on the whole, small in quantity, and in most cases was primarily for purposes of morale (for example, chocolate and vodka). In addition the occasional air supply of such food items as sugar, salt, sausages, and bacon provided a welcome supplement to the inadequate and often monotonously uniform rations of the partisans. [The folder of partisan questionnaires cited in n. 8 is also revealing on the minor role which air supply played in the over-all food supply of the partisans.]

There were, however, two types of situations in which air supply of food was provided on a large scale. The first was when special geographic factors made it impossible for the partisans to obtain food by local requisitioning. The one example of this type which we know about was the Crimea, where the partisans were in mountainous terrain, and the adjacent agricultural areas were farmed by members of a nationality group (the Crimean Tatars) strongly hostile to the Soviet regime and engaged in large-scale collaboration with the Germans. Once German operations had deprived these partisans of their initial and rather lavish supply of food, the 2,000 or so partisans who continued to operate in the Yaila Mountains were in very difficult straits. Hunger and starvation hit hard among them; and instances of cannibalism are recorded in captured Soviet documents. Since the Soviet

High Command was obviously interested in maintaining a partisan force in the Crimea, air supply of food—in addition to weapons and ammunition—was resorted to. There is evidence to show that this was continued over a period of at least two years and that the partisans were largely dependent upon these supplies.[11] The situation in the Crimea has, of course, changed since the Soviet regime chose to punish the Tatars with banishment. The fact that a partisan movement could be maintained under such adverse circumstances is, however, of great significance and shows that the large-scale use of airpower can offset some obstacles to the existence of a partisan movement.

The second type of situation involved a temporary food shortage in a major area of partisan activity. Although there is not enough information to allow generalizations, it seems likely that in any area of relatively low food production (and because of their swampy, mountainous, or heavily forested character, such areas are usually best suited for partisan warfare) there comes a time when the drain on the food supply reaches a point where it is necessary either to reduce drastically the number of partisans or to import considerable quantities of food. This process was undoubtedly hastened by the German practice of combining large-scale looting with almost all antipartisan operations, not only to obtain food for their own needs but to deprive the partisans of it. As the partisans evaded battle, the German troops and the accompanying looting teams were generally able to penetrate areas previously under partisan control and, independent of their success or failure to destroy a substantial proportion of the partisans, were able to drive off large numbers of cattle and remove or destroy great quantities of food. Early in 1943 the Germans also started to use antipartisan operations for large-scale slave-hunting with the (partly intentional) result that many peasants, whose labor in the fields might eventually have benefited the partisans, were instead carried off as slave labor to Germany. [For some sample statistics, see Chap. VIII, Sect. III, B.]

In two major areas of partisan activity the food situation deteriorated to such a low point in 1943. Even in the early part of that year, increasing amounts of food had to be flown to the partisans in the Bryansk area, and by summer large-scale air supply of food was necessary. Since the Soviets retook the area late in the summer of 1943, the long-term effectiveness of these measures cannot be determined. In the second area, around Vitebsk in northern Belorussia, the picture is somewhat clearer. After the German operations "Kugelblitz" and "Maigewitter" in the spring of 1943, a serious food shortage developed. Ponomarenko, the Chief of Staff of the Partisan Movement, visited the area to inspect the bands and, on noting the food shortage, ordered that supplies be flown in to the partisans. The Germans

---

[11] I. Kozlov, *V Krymskom podpolye: vospominaniya* (Moscow: Sovetskii Pisatel, 1947), pp. 76–77, 79.

immediately recorded a marked increase in supply flights to the partisans and believed, on the basis of "dependable information," that these flights were primarily for food deliveries. With this help some of the partisans in the area continued to maintain themselves, although the subsequent decline in the size and number of units here probably indicates that the food flown in was not sufficient to sustain the movement at its former strength. Nevertheless, the continuation of partisan activity here shows that the Red Air Force helped sustain this sector of a most important center of partisan warfare.

C. CLOTHING

In general, the partisans were expected to secure clothing in their area of operations. Air supply of clothing was usually restricted to special areas, such as the Crimea,[12] or to special items of clothing which were difficult or impossible for the partisans to obtain locally. Probably boots were the most important item of this kind. A prodigious amount of marching, frequently in the most difficult type of terrain, characterized most partisan operations, and, unfortunately for the partisans, good shoes were a consumers' item most difficult to come by in the Soviet Union. To obtain combat boots was thus an especially vexing problem. Various references indicate, however, that those directing the air supply system were aware of this deficiency, and considerable quantities of boots were apparently delivered. Another such critical item was winter clothing. The Grishin Regiment, one of the large roving bands, requested and received air shipments of clothes for the 1942–43 winter. Thus, although the partisans generally had to collect their own, occasional air shipments were no doubt a welcome and highly useful supplement.

§III. Special Aspects of Air Support

A. TACTICAL AIR SUPPORT
OF PARTISAN OPERATIONS

In a number of instances, there was sufficient direct coordination between partisan activities and Red Air Force operations that one may accurately speak of tactical air support. Two types of air operations were involved: those giving tactical air support to the partisans by attacking their enemies and those providing the partisans with additional supplies to cope with enemy operations.

Tactically, the Red Air Force could assist in several ways. Occasionally the partisans would radio requests that hostile villages or those presumed

[12] *Ibid.,* p. 79.

to contain German units be bombed. In one instance a plane attacked a German train which had been derailed by the partisans. In March 1943 a Soviet plan was afoot to destroy the Kaminsky Brigade, a collaborator organization which had administrative autonomy in several rayons south of Bryansk; this was to be accomplished by an operation in which defection within the unit, partisan attacks, and a Red Air Force raid were to be combined. The Germans uncovered the plot, and the only part of the plan effected was the air raid.[13] The towns containing the headquarters of German security units in the Bryansk area were repeatedly bombed early in 1943. And in April 1944 special Red Army commandos were dropped to reinforce partisan detachments about to launch an attack on several fortified villages (*Wehrdoerfer*). No other instances of such operations have been found. Undoubtedly there were more, although it is clear that this kind of cooperation existed only on a small scale and was of little significance to over-all partisan operations. Nevertheless, the Germans appear to have been quite concerned about the possibility of partisan ground attacks on strongpoints—especially at bridges—after the garrison had sought shelter from an air raid.

More frequently, Red Air Force planes attempted to help the partisans when a major German antipartisan operation was underway. By attacking German headquarters, supply routes, and troop columns, the planes were to relieve the pressure on the partisans or enable them to break out of encirclements. Reports on operations of this kind are available for most of the major antipartisan operations and for a few of the smaller ones. Although in one instance as many as 156 planes flew support missions in one night, none of these tactical air operations against antipartisan forces met with any degree of success. Various factors may have been responsible for this failure. In most cases, the number of planes involved was so small that results other than a partisan morale boost could hardly have been expected. When the number of missions increased, certain other factors inherent in the situation lessened the chances of success. German antipartisan operations usually consisted of concentric attacks on a large partisan-held area. Numerous small German units starting from a wide circle advanced slowly to its center, combing the countryside for partisans and hoping to force them to fight when cornered. The small groups of German soldiers moving through wooded terrain hardly offered promising targets for air attack. There may also have been technical difficulties. Although the partisans were able to communicate with the planes by radio, it is not likely that under the strained circumstances of an antipartisan operation the communication system functioned so smoothly as to allow the coordination of Red Air Force attacks with an attempted partisan breakthrough.

A somewhat different type of tactical support was the air transport of

[13] See Alexander Dallin, *The Kaminsky Brigade: 1941–1944* (Maxwell AFB, Ala.: HRRI), December 1952, Technical Research Report, No. 7, p. 33.

supplies to bands hard pressed by German operations. In such cases, the partisans frequently requested supplies by radio. In October 1943 the Grishin Regiment was in a precarious position because of major German action against it. When the regiment's requests for air supplies were not heeded, an appeal was sent directly to Stalin. "The encirclement has now been on for six days. . . . No rations, no ammunition. For ten days we have been asking our superiors for help. None has come. . . . We ask that help be sent us." Thereupon air supply was promised and the Germans noted that supplies were in fact dropped.[14] A number of similar incidents are reported from such major areas of partisan activity as the Bryansk forest and northern Belorussia. In the case of the latter, air supplies flown in during a major German operation in the Lepel area early in 1944 ran up to a hundred flights a night.

The value of such supplies in a period of crisis was undoubtedly great because of both their tactical use and their morale effect. It is unlikely, however, that they determined the outcome of the operations in which they were used. Although Grishin broke out of his encirclement, the partisans in the Lepel area suffered a serious defeat. Without detailed studies of the tactical situation in each operation, the question of the significance of air supply must be left open.

B. LIMITATIONS IMPOSED BY AIR SUPPORT

One possibility explored in the course of the research on the partisan movement has been that air support imposed certain limitations on the partisans, such as reduced mobility caused by the necessity to stay close to an airfield, the inability to use terrain unsuitable for airfields, and the necessity to detail guards to the airstrips. Although some evidence has been found to support a positive conclusion to this investigation, on the whole the findings are negative. With few exceptions, German antipartisan operations were not successful in clearing out major centers of partisan activity. Therefore, the partisans were able to reassemble in their old operational area and resume use of their old airfields.[15] Since most of the bands stayed in the same general part of the occupied area, the problem of reduced mobility arose only in exceptional cases. Thus one partisan group trying to escape from a major German operation was delayed by orders directing it to guard an airfield where planes were expected. On another occasion, one of the roving bands enlisted other detachments to help hold a large airfield on a frozen lake where supplies were to be delivered for a raid deep into German-occupied territory.[16]

There is no evidence that the terrain needed for airfields constituted a

[14] For the intercepted radio messages and other details, see GMDS, AOK 9, 52535/13.
[15] A good example of this is the airfield at Kovali, less than twenty-five miles from the headquarters of the 707th Security Division at Zhukovka.
[16] Linkov, p. 376.

374 / VI. AIRPOWER IN PARTISAN WARFARE

problem. In the winter, frozen bodies of water were available as sites. In the summer, those areas which supported extensive partisan activity always provided some dry, flat, open space for landing fields or contained open bodies of water which accommodated flying boats.

It is clear that the airfields had to be guarded, but providing guards apparently presented no great difficulty. Because the fields were usually located near the headquarters of a brigade or other partisan unit of considerable size, the task of guarding the field frequently was assigned to the headquarters detachment, which included the men guarding the unit staff. In some cases a platoon or company was assigned to guard the airfield, either permanently or on a rotating basis.[17] Drop-areas were apparently guarded in the same manner. Considering the size of the partisan groups involved, in all cases where we know that guard details were assigned, the drain on manpower was apparently insignificant.

One other aspect of limitations imposed by air support was the possibility that partisan groups might have become "spoiled" if they received supplies by air and did not have to collect them on their own. The instances of such "softness" were undoubtedly rare. One is given in the diary of a woman partisan and a second one is indicated by an order of the Kovpak Regiment cautioning its members to capture weapons and collect combat supplies by all possible means, and not to wait for supplies from Moscow.[18] Such isolated instances were of no significance for the movement as a whole.

C. GERMAN EFFORTS TO COUNTER AIR SUPPORT
1. Interception of Planes

The most obvious way to cope with air support of the partisans would have been to intercept Soviet planes. The Germans recognized the importance of airpower in building up the partisan movement only after the movement had already attained dangerous proportions. Thus it was not until 1942 and 1943 that they began to stress the need for interdicting Soviet air support. One of the most incisive reports on the need for such interference stated:

According to the observations of the 221st Security Division, the partisans receive weapons and ammunition as well as officers and commissars by planes. Recent observations have led to the conclusion that newly organized bands are led by officers and commissars brought in by plane, rather than by those recruited from the local population. Because the forces available to the security division are very weak, the bands cannot be destroyed at this time. In order to

---

[17] For examples, see, in addition to German sources, Fyodorov, p. 466; Vershigora, p. 176.
[18] HSSPF Ost, "Bericht ueber die Bekaempfung der Kolpak-Bande," 2 September 1943, p. 7 (GMDS, EAP 170-a-10/5).

decrease the strength and combatworthiness of the bands, or to prevent the formation of new ones, it is most important that the air traffic be interrupted.[19]

Occasionally Soviet planes on partisan support missions were shot down, but on the whole the Germans were unable to interdict partisan air support. The factors responsible for this were presented above in the introduction.

2. Efforts to Trap Soviet Planes

Unable to intercept partisan support planes in the air, the Germans began in the summer of 1942 to set up fake landing fields. They imitated the recognition symbols used by the partisans to communicate with Soviet planes in an effort to get the planes to land on fields under their control. Elaborate efforts were made; the directives ordering the establishment of the fake airfields generally were prefaced with remarks to the effect that such airfields had been successful elsewhere. The available evidence indicates, however, that such favorable results were rarely achieved. Only three instances of successful deception have been found. The most successful of these took place in late May 1942 in the area east of Smolensk. In a period of a few days, seven Soviet planes were captured or destroyed in this manner. In the summer of 1942 in the Bryansk area two planes were trapped. On one occasion the Germans held a partisan airfield in the northern Ukraine and took from a Soviet plane which landed on it one of their most valuable partisan prisoners, Captain Ruzanov, an adjutant of Strokach, Chief of Staff of the Ukranian Partisan Movement. The Germans had to use one of two methods in most of their efforts to trap these planes. First, they flew their own reconnaissance planes in the evenings to determine the signs being used that night by partisan groups in the area, and then transmitted this information for use at the fake airfield. Secondly, they attempted to capture a partisan airfield in the hope that Soviet planes would continue to land there.

3. Fake Drop-Areas

The complement to fake airfields were fake drop-areas. Simultaneously with the construction of such fields, the Germans also instituted the use of partisan flare and fire signs to induce Soviet planes to drop supply containers on German-held areas. In the same period during which the Germans were able to trap seven planes in the Smolensk area, they also succeeded in getting Soviet planes to drop over sixty supply containers. Similar efforts in the same area at a later date were apparently not so successful. In the Bryansk area, the Germans also had mild success.

[19] Gem.Flakabteilung 303 (v), Flakuntergruppe Gomel, Ia, "Einsatz von Nachtjae-gern," 17 June 1942, p. 1 (GMDS, 221 ID 36509/5, Anlage 316).

During the antipartisan operation "Zigeunerbaron," a German regiment obtained supplies from the Soviets four nights in a row; the fifth night bombs were dropped instead. In another operation the Germans received supply drops twice.

Like the efforts to trap planes on fake airfields, German attempts to divert supply drops to their own areas were relatively ineffective.[20] German failure to capitalize on the frequent mistakes made by the Soviets in dropping both personnel and materials was undoubtedly due to a lack of specialists and equipment rather than to an absence of promising opportunities.

4. Bombing Airfields

Since they were unable to drive the partisans permanently out of their areas of concentration, the Germans tried to interrupt their air supply system by bombing partisan airfields rather than trying to capture and hold them. A number of such bombing incidents are recorded. In one case, a small group of reconnaissance planes, which were regularly engaged in antipartisan operations, repeatedly bombed partisan airfields, once destroying two planes on the ground. In another case German bombers destroyed a partisan landing area on a frozen lake by dropping enough explosive to crack the ice.[21] Another German tactic was to drop bombs which would explode either on touching or on concussion of any kind within thirty days. Other bombing efforts were made—not always successfully, for at least one case is recorded where such bombing did not interfere with the continued use of the field by the partisans. The Germans lacked the large number of planes needed to scout the partisan airfields and to bomb them regularly. In any case, it is doubtful if the majority of these fields were rewarding targets, since they had neither permanent runways nor elaborate structures. A suggestion that the German Air Force drop defective weapons and bombs to the partisans from captured Soviet planes was never followed up.

5. The Spotting System

One basic problem of all German efforts to cope with Soviet air support was the development of an efficient spotting system. Without such a system, they were, in effect, ignorant of who or what was entering and leaving areas supposedly under German control; they also did not know the location of airfields and the volume of supplies the partisans received

---

[20] One method the Soviets used to dampen German enthusiasm for taking supply containers destined for the partisans was to parachute bombs looking like supply containers and timed to go off shortly after landing. (203. Sich. Div., Ia, "Divisionsbefehl Nr. 55," 24 August 1942, p. 3, GMDS, 203 ID 29186/2, Anlage 74.)

[21] Vershigora, pp. 202–3; S. A. Kovpak, Ot Putivlya do Karpat (Moscow: Gosudarstvennoye Izdatelstvo Detskoi Literatury Narkomprosa RSFSR, 1945), pp. 105–6.

through them. It is understandable, therefore, that the Germans made great efforts and elaborate plans for reporting planes, parachutists, flares, and fire signals. The statistical information on air support which was gathered by such sources and has been utilized in this study shows that the spotting system was obviously of some benefit. Nevertheless, perennial German complaints about units failing to carry out their spotting duties—to say nothing of the fact that partisan control over large areas prevented the Germans from covering all the occupied territory—show that the system never functioned in a really satisfactory manner.

In conclusion, one may say that German efforts to cope with partisan air support began rather late and, though not lacking in ingenuity, were never conducted on a scale commensurate with the problem. On the whole, partisan air support reached those for whom it was destined; if it did not, the fault seldom lay with the Germans.

§IV. Airpower in Antipartisan Warfare

The potential value of airpower in German antipartisan warfare was great. Its most obvious use in this connection—the interdiction of partisan air support—has already been alluded to; in addition, the possibilities for the Germans to observe and attack partisan units through airpower were almost unlimited. An occupying power with sufficient planes and an effective warning system to intercept partisan support planes would have had an easier time fighting the partisans than the Germans did. If, in addition, its air resources would permit the continuous harassing of partisan units, the very existence of bands could be made most difficult. Partisan formations are very sensitive to air attack. If this fact could become apparent even when air operations were limited drastically by the meager German resources, the real potential of airpower in antipartisan warfare must be considerable.

By the end of 1941 the German commanders in the East began to recognize that air strength would be invaluable in fighting the partisans, but the situation at the front made the assignment of planes to antipartisan warfare impossible at that time. Not until the spring of 1942 were planes systematically sent on missions against the partisans. By that time, the partisan movement had grown to such an extent that the Germans had tremendous difficulty coping with it, especially in view of their inadequate security forces. Under these circumstances, airpower in antipartisan warfare became primarily a matter of assigning planes in small groups or individually to support specific antipartisan operations, or to attack known partisan concentrations when planes were available but there were not enough security troops for offensive action. It must be kept in mind that the numerical inferiority of German planes obtained on the Eastern front during the whole period of antipartisan operations. This inferiority imposed rigid limitations on both the number and type of German planes used. Reliance was placed primarily on small reconnaissance planes, various obsolete trainer and bomber models, and medium bombers temporarily detailed to antipartisan missions.

A. RECONNAISSANCE

To understand the importance of aerial reconnaissance in antipartisan warfare, one must first examine the problems faced by the German security forces. German headquarters and support units were stationed in the larger towns and by their very presence generally acted as a deterrent to partisan activity in the vicinity. Security forces were generally located in garrisons in the smaller towns, with strongpoints in the villages and at strategic points along the main lines of communications. In the vast areas between garrisons and at any distance from the main roads and railways, especially in the occupied parts of Belorussia and the RSFSR, there were usually no German troops and few informants. In these areas the partisans organized their units and established their camps, moving up against communication lines only to carry out raids. Periodically the Germans captured prisoners and secured information from them, but it was difficult to send reconnaissance patrols into this area because of the danger of ambushes. Under these circumstances it is not surprising that, as soon as they realized the seriousness of the situation, toward the end of 1941 and at the beginning of 1942, the German commanders with responsibility for security in the rear areas demanded that the German Air Force fly reconnaissance missions. And early in 1942 when the major German antipartisan operations began, similar requests were issued. In such operations the German units, penetrating territory unknown to them and fighting an enemy who alternately evaded combat and struck from some unexpected direction, apparently felt lost. Their appeals for air support in the form of reconnaissance missions were understood and heeded: starting with an operation in the Bobruisk area in March 1942, air reconnaissance became a standard feature of major antipartisan operations.

From the very beginning German experience reports on the use of planes for reconnaissance purposes are uniformly favorable. Their concluding reports on virtually every large-scale antipartisan operation include a section in which the value of reconnaissance missions is stressed.[22] What

[22] Examples will be found in Chap. VII, Sect. III, B, 2, and V, A, 3. The Germans soon discovered, however, that, unless there had been frequent flights over a given partisan-held area, any sudden appearance of reconnaissance planes before an anti-

success these operations had was often due in large measure to this type of air support, a conclusion which is not surprising considering the ease with which the partisans collected information about the Germans, and the difficulties the Germans had securing information on the partisans.

The value of this type of air support grew as the partisans gained control of larger regions and the Germans were increasingly limited to the areas near the railway lines. German experiences in the use of airpower in reconnaissance missions are best described in a report by the security division which was responsible for security in the area from the western part of the Bryansk forests to the Dnepr.

For some time the division has had at its disposal from the Tactical Reconnaissance Group 11./12 a reconnaissance flight [3 planes] of the Focke Wulf 189[23] type for employment in antipartisan warfare. The division has had such excellent experiences with the employment of these planes that it suggests to higher headquarters that it request the permanent assignment of such reconnaissance flights to the security divisions for the following reasons:

1. Reconnaissance

Considering the large size of each security [division] area and the resulting incomplete coverage in guarding the area by strong points and informants, keeping the entire area under constant supervision (by ground troops) is impossible. Only through the continual employment of reconnaissance planes is it possible to carry out constant reconnaissance of the *whole area* and to obtain an accurate enemy situation report, especially for areas temporarily not accessible to the troops. Examples:

> Partisan airfields south of Novozybkov and Propoisk.
> Partisan camps in the forests southwest of Belinkovichi.
> The appearance of partisans south of Novozybkov.

In addition there is the factor of *speed;* reconnaissance can be initiated in a few minutes and the findings reach the troop commanders with equal speed (ground-airplane radio communications, message drops). In partisan warfare especially, because the enemy situation changes constantly, such timely and speedy reconnaissance acquires great significance. [Antipartisan] operations undertaken after time-consuming ground reconnaissance and reports by informants and other inhabitants frequently fail because the enemy situation has undergone basic changes in the meantime.[24]

Five months later the same division reported on its experiences with these reconnaissance planes in an equally enthusiastic tone. The other security

---

partisan operation was a "tip-off" for the partisans. Three methods of dealing with this problem were devised. Sometimes no planes were permitted to fly over the area until the attack had actually started. Secondly, whenever possible, reconnaissance flights were flown with such frequency over all areas that the partisans would notice no change when a major attack was about to be launched. Thirdly, reconnaissance missions were incorporated into the regular flight pattern or were sent over the area in straight flight in the hope that their real purpose would not be recognized.

[23] The Focke Wulf 189 was a twin-fuselage fighter-bomber often used as a reconnaissance plane which carried four 100-pound bombs and two machine guns, as well as cameras.

[24] 221. Sich.Div., Ic, "Einsatz bewaffneter Luftaufklaerung," 21 June 1943, p. 1 (GMDS, 221 ID 36509/5, Anlage 312).

divisions were not assigned such groups of planes because of Air Force shortages. The reports from these divisions indicate, however, that whenever reconnaissance missions were flown in their areas, the results were similarly impressive.

B. COMMUNICATION

The Germans also used airpower in antipartisan warfare to provide communication between various units as well as between headquarters and subordinate units. As German formations converged on a partisan stronghold, the problem of communication became extremely difficult, and light reconnaissance planes which could carry messages and liaison officers offered extremely valuable services. A German unit isolated in partisan-held territory could be reached by plane when radio communications failed or were jammed by the partisans.

This use of airpower was of particular value to the Germans because it eased one of the most serious operational problems they faced in combating the partisans.[See Chap. VII, Sect. III, B, 2.]

C. SUPPLY

The ability to send supplies by air to isolated garrisons and mobile striking forces could have been of great value to the Germans. Their small security forces, the difficult terrain, and the lack of roads obstructed efforts to move supplies overland. These difficulties enhanced the value of airpower, and there is no doubt that a far more effective antipartisan campaign could have been conducted if the Germans had had more planes. This shortage made it impossible for them to capitalize on the potential use of airpower and thus imposed severe limitations on their operations. Although the German Air Force apparently realized the need to provide supplies for isolated units operating in the difficult terrain at considerable distance from their base, the number of recorded successful air supply operations is very small. One German strongpoint, surrounded by hostile forces and evidently beyond the range of supply convoys from other strongpoints, was supplied with nine containers of weapons and ammunition by planes which flew three different missions. In one of the largest antipartisan operations in Belorussia, isolated German units were supplied by air with food and ammunition. No doubt there were other instances of this sort, but on the whole the German lack of planes frustrated such attempts.

D. BOMBING AND STRAFING IN
ANTIPARTISAN OPERATIONS

With the exception of reconnaissance, missions to bomb and strafe partisan installations were more frequent than any other type of air support operation.[25] Starting in the spring of 1942 with the first major antipartisan operations, German Air Force planes flew tactical support missions for practically all such operations until the summer of 1944. Although there were variations, the number of planes involved usually ranged from three to fifteen, and each plane generally flew several missions. For the most part, the reports on these missions are favorable.[26] Bombing was of particular value in those areas where the partisans had prepared heavy field fortifications which severely handicapped German security troops, often deficient in heavy weapons. Strafing proved to be especially effective against partisans attempting to escape encirclement or crossing rivers and open areas. Although the German reports do not stress the point, it is clear that air support gave a morale boost to the German troops—often over-age and otherwise second-rate units who were engaged in a type of fighting which tended to be particularly demoralizing and which frequently found them outclassed in military equipment.[27]

Conversely, the most important effect German air support had on the partisans appears to have been on their morale rather than on their material strength. The partisans were extremely sensitive to air raids, and usually attempted to move, often in panic, as soon as an attack started. Numerous reports stress that morale was badly shaken and that panic spread even when material damage was slight. One of the Soviet memoirs admits as much. The commissar of a crack partisan unit, the Kovpak Regiment, mentioned to another high-ranking partisan officer that the physical damage of air attacks on his unit had been minor, but that the effects on morale had been serious.[28] There is evidence, however, that some of the well-trained troops flown in to strengthen the partisans, as well as some of the more experienced units, were less affected by air attacks.[29]

There were certain problems in tactical air support which the Germans never solved entirely. Coordination of air action with the advance of

[25] General missions flown to harass the partisans are discussed below; only missions in direct support of specific antipartisan operations are discussed here.

[26] For examples, see Kozlov, p. 238; also this book, Chap. VII, Sect. III, B, 2 and V, A, 3.

[27] There are few useful statistics on antipartisan air missions flown by the German Air Force. The only series of figures which gives some idea of the German effort is for 1943 in the area of Army Group North, which covered the territory between the Gulf of Finland and the Velikiye Luki–Rositten Railway. No missions were flown in January, February, March, and April. Thereafter the figures are: May—9; June—38; July—4; August—55; September—71; October—610; November—251; December—82. The autumn peak is related to several major antipartisan operations conducted at that time. (HGr Nord, Ia, *Der Feldzug gegen die Sowjet-Union der Heeresgruppe Nord, Kriegsjahr 1943*, 24 December 1944, GMDS, Lib. 2441.)

[28] Vershigora, p. 448.

[29] The explanation for sensitivity of partisan units to air attacks probably lies in their basically irregular character, their lower discipline, and their limited experience with air attacks. Since the turnover in membership was rather high, these factors did not lose their importance as rapidly as they might have been expected to.

ground troops proved to be extremely difficult; occasionally German planes bombed villages occupied by their own troops or already cleared of partisans. Air-ground communication and recognition presented especially knotty problems because of the terrain and the poor equipment of the security troops. [See Chap. VII, Sect. V, A, 3.] The control of the planes by air force headquarters, which received requests for support from the German security units through various higher army headquarters, sometimes proved difficult. After considerable experience, the Germans discovered that the best way to cope with such problems was to assign small groups of planes (usually obsolescent models and liaison planes) to units with territorial security tasks. Such planes flew on the orders of these units and supported their day-to-day activities and minor operations. In large operations, special air force liasion officers were assigned to the headquarters of the German units in order to direct such other formations as had been made available for the operation. [See Chap. VII, Sect. III, B, 2.]

The potential of tactical air support for antipartisan operations is well shown by the 221st Security Division report quoted above:

During [antipartisan] operations the employment of armed reconnaissance planes offers special advantages. Enemy units which have been surrounded and are hiding in trackless swamps can be attacked with bombs and machine guns. Enemy preparations inside a pocket for mass break-outs can be discovered [so that] reserves can be moved in time to the spot selected for the break-out. Enemy units which succeed in breaking out can be pursued and scattered, and heavy casualties [can be inflicted].[30]

Only a lack of planes prevented the Germans from using airpower more extensively to support their attacks on partisan centers. It is at least possible that with substantial air support these operations would not have failed as frequently as they did.

E. BOMBING AND STRAFING PARTISAN-HELD AREAS

In addition to supporting specific antipartisan operations, German planes also raided territory on missions which were a cross between nuisance attacks and strategic bombing. All villages in partisan-controlled areas were attacked; partisan camps and installations discovered by aerial reconnaissance were bombed and strafed; and an effort was made to spread confusion and destruction in the territory controlled by the partisans. Though such attacks occurred occasionally in 1942, the main efforts were directed against certain large areas which came under partisan control in 1943 and 1944. In Belorussia particularly, there were large partisan-

[30] 221. Sich.Div., Ic, "Einsatz bewaffneter Luftaufklaerung," 21 June 1943, p. 2 (GMDS, 221 ID 36509/5, Anlage 312).

held areas which the Germans did not enter for months and sometimes years; it was on these that German air raids concentrated. Bombs were dropped by planes whose crews acquired their bombardier training in this manner. There is no doubt that these attacks took their toll on the morale of the population; their effect on the partisans is problematical. While hits were scored on some partisan encampments and in a few instances ammunition dumps were exploded, on the whole it is doubtful if these attacks had the effect the Germans imagined. Manpower was not a major partisan problem at this time, and what casualties were inflicted could always be replaced. Supplies were less plentiful, but since the dumps were usually small, little could be lost in any one attack. If the attacks had deleterious effects on partisan morale, as was the case in air attacks coincident with antipartisan operations, this type of warfare provided time to repair the damage. It appears that the partisans eventually got used to the attacks. On the other hand, it must be borne in mind that this was often the only method the Germans had of attacking partisan units in these areas and of controlling their strength and effectiveness; certainly it was more effective than no interference at all. It might be concluded that although attacks on partisan-held areas have a nuisance value and, in individual instances, will inflict serious damage, decisive results can be attained only by employing far greater forces than those which were available to the Germans. [Information on such operations will be found in Chap. VII, Sect. III, B, 2.]

F. DISTRIBUTION OF LEAFLETS

Airpower's importance in spreading written propaganda to the partisans and the population in partisan-held areas is obvious. Dropping leaflets from planes was sometimes the only way the Germans could conduct psychological warfare operations against the bands. Even in areas not under partisan control, the sparsity of German security forces often made air distribution of propaganda materials the alternative to no distribution at all. A discussion of the contents and effectiveness of such materials is outside the scope of this study, which finds of interest, however, the German opinion that because these leaflets were dropped by plane, their effectiveness was enhanced.

G. FLY-OVER EFFECT OF AIRPOWER

The material already cited on the effects of air attacks on partisan morale leads to the assumption that the fly-over effect of planes must have been considerable. It is clear that the appearance of German planes made the bands uneasy and often induced them to change their location, in the belief that a German attack was imminent. The only definite evidence on this subject, however, concerns the effect of German planes on the population, and the role they played in impressing the people with the continuing power of the Germans.

H. PARTISAN EFFORTS TO COUNTER GERMAN AIR OPERATIONS

The partisans quickly learned to camouflage their encampments so that they were difficult to identify from the air. As the bands became more accustomed to air attacks, the frequency and accuracy of their antiaircraft fire increased. Massed small-arms fire was responsible for the shooting down of several planes in 1942 and in each of the following years; in 1943 in one operation alone four planes were destroyed in this manner. Antiaircraft guns of 20 mm caliber were also used. The effectiveness of partisan fire was probably due to the fact that in most cases the Germans depended largely on slow, obsolescent planes for antipartisan operations. The poor planes plus the increasingly heavy antiaircraft fire probably forced the Germans to guard their planes more carefully than would generally be necessary in a situation where planes attack troops without air cover.[31] On the whole, however, partisan countermeasures did not impede the air invader's operations sufficiently to make German ground and air commanders deem it unprofitable.

I. THE POTENTIAL OF AIRPOWER IN ANTIPARTISAN WARFARE

It has been noted that the Germans were never able to employ airpower extensively in their fight against the partisans. It may be of value, therefore, to indicate some of its potential uses, which are not always apparent from an account of German experiences. The importance of interdicting enemy (in this case, Soviet) air support cannot be stressed too much. In the initial stages of a partisan movement, such interference strikes at the most important component of the movement—the cadres without which it would fall apart. Any substantial cut in the number of cadres would prevent the bands from expanding to the extent they did while opposing the Germans. Interdiction in the later stages would reduce the partisans to military impotence if their stores were simultaneously subjected to air attack. Furthermore, the loss of a high percentage of the planes engaged in partisan-support missions might well lead to the abandonment of such operations; the extremely low ratio of losses in World War II can undoubtedly be attributed to the willingness of the Soviet High Command to commit as many planes as it did in support of the partisans.

Once a partisan movement of some size is in existence an adequate

---

[31] It is interesting to note that in the last year of the war the partisans began the establishment of a spotter system in the large areas under their control.

number of planes can produce certain important accomplishments. The whole concept of the large roving band would then become obsolete. Such bands can operate only in areas in which the occupying power has virtually no planes, since partisan bands moving long distances must stay reasonably close together and cannot avoid crossing open territory from time to time. Under such circumstances—and even more obviously if they are forced to move through open country—these bands could be completely destroyed by strafing, by bombs, or by rockets fired from planes.

An occupying power, faced with a partisan problem and without substantial forces to pacify its rear areas can significantly reduce the partisan threat, if planes of the type used in the later stages of World War II for ground-support operations are available in numbers sufficient to keep up sustained air attacks on the partisans. If there are not enough planes to interdict air supply and to carry out continuous nuisance raids over the entire rear area, such a procedure should be applied to one sector at a time. In those few instances in which the Germans thoroughly crushed the partisan movement in one area, they found that the Soviet High Command could not revive it in spite of concentrated efforts. [E.g., see Chap. VII, Sect. V, C, D, and E.] It seems wiser, therefore, to concentrate limited air resources on one area at a time and clear it thoroughly, rather than to disperse them thinly over a vast territory with the result that the partisans are not crushed anywhere and the population, seeing the ineffectiveness of the antipartisan measures, increasingly turns to the partisans.

It is clear from the available evidence that air operations against the partisans affect their morale negatively. It must be kept in mind, however, that unless ground forces exploit this weakened situation *immediately*, partisan cadres can re-establish firm discipline and control. The only other way to take advantage of this situation is to assure the partisans by words and deeds that deserters and prisoners will be treated decently. By contrast, when the German planes turned back, it did not take long for the partisans to recall that they would almost certainly be shot if they fell into enemy hands.

It should be apparent that airpower can play a significant and even decisive role in antipartisan warfare, providing its importance is recognized early and its employment is on a scale commensurate with the dangers to be faced.

PART II
Case Studies

CHAPTER VII

The Yelnya-Dorogobuzh Area of Smolensk Oblast

Gerhard L. Weinberg

Introduction

Two reasons prompted the selection of the Yelnya-Dorogobuzh area, which lies in the west-central part of the European USSR near Smolensk, for detailed treatment. This area saw the first appearance of a large-scale partisan movement powerful enough to hold a substantial slice of territory (2,000–3,000 square miles) behind the German front, and it comprises the first, and probably the only, instance in which the Germans crushed a partisan movement of such size. A study of this area may give some insight into the factors which affected the development, organization, control, and operations of the partisan movement in the first year of the war in the East (summer of 1941 to summer of 1942). Likewise, such a study may furnish some clues as to the factors which caused the destruction of the movement—factors which were, in turn, integrally connected with the movement's nature and structure.

The German documents have provided a considerable amount of evidence on developments in this area. This material has been exploited not only to present a full picture and analysis of the partisan movement here, but also to offer possibilities for comparison with other case studies.

At the end of July 1941, German forces advancing on the central part of the Eastern front took Smolensk and entered the western part of the Yelnyra-Dorogobuzh area. The front remained fairly stationary until the beginning of October when the Germans launched a major offensive in the direction of Moscow. In the initial stages of this offensive, a large number of Soviet units were surrounded in the Yelnya-Dorogobuzh area (the so-called Vyazma pocket), and efforts were made by the Germans to round them up. While these efforts were in progress, the bulk of the German forces moved on eastward.

The turning of the tide before Moscow at the beginning of December 1941 was followed by a Soviet breakthrough. In the second half of January 1942 the spearhead of the Soviet counteroffensive reached into the Yelnya-Dorogobuzh area in an attempt to cut the Smolensk-Vyazma road and railway, the main German supply route in the area. Though supported by large-scale drops of airborne units, the Soviet effort was thwarted and parts of the spearhead were cut off from the main body of the Red Army when the Germans closed the gap in their line.

The regular and airborne units thus trapped in the area were joined by a large partisan movement which was then being formed. Because the first German efforts to clear out this area were unsuccessful, there was time for the partisan and regular units to consolidate their position. This forced the Germans to stage a major operation. In the two weeks at the end of May[1] and the beginning of June 1942, all or parts of nine German divisions mounted an attack which shattered the partisan movement in the area. The attack was then followed by extensive mopping-up operations.

From the middle of June 1942 to March 1943 the area, on the whole, was free of partisan activity. A German withdrawal in March 1943, designed to shorten the front of Army Group Center, resulted in the reoccupation of the eastern part of the area by regular Soviet forces, while the rest of the area was retaken by the Red Army in the course of the great German retreats of August and September 1943.

Partisan Warfare

Preparations for the formation of partisan units had been made by the Soviet High Command before the German forces reached the area, and the first efforts to activate partisan groups were made in August and September 1941, at a time when the front ran temporarily through the westernmost part of the area. These efforts were confined largely to bringing in groups of men through the front and by air to organize many small partisan groups which might later be of service to the Red Army. The German offensive of October burst into these beginnings, temporarily disrupted them, but at the same time unintentionally provided them with

---

[1] "To a question by the President regarding guerrilla operations, Mr. Molotov replied that the partisans were most active in the Moscow-Smolensk-Mozhaisk (Dorogobuzh) sector. They numbered 9,000 irregulars and parts of 2–3 cavalry divisions under General Belov. They were in absolute control of an egg-shaped area measuring some 60 kilometers east and west by 20–30 kilometers north and south. They were, however, less conspicuous in other areas." [Memorandum of conversation among Roosevelt, Molotov, and others on 30 May 1942, quoted by Robert E. Sherwood in *Roosevelt and Hopkins, An Intimate History* (New York: Harpers, 1948), p. 567.]

the human material out of which a large-scale partisan movement could eventually be formed. A great number of Red Army stragglers went into hiding in the area, and German efforts to round them up were largely unsuccessful. Lacking the necessary time and enthusiasm to do a thorough job of combing through the area, the German units generally brought out only those men who were willing to become prisoners of war, and many of these escaped after brief encounters with the German methods of treating prisoners. At the same time, many of the lower-level Party, State, and NKVD functionaries had also gone into hiding in the area, thus providing the nuclei for the small partisan groups which existed in the last three months of 1941.

The partisan movement grew tremendously in the two and a half months between the middle of January and the end of March 1942, expanding from small groups of five to thirty men to large and well-organized formations totaling close to 10,000 in all. How was this accomplished? The basis of expansion was provided by the large number of Red Army stragglers left behind from the 1941 battles. Most of them had settled in the villages; a few may have been marauding in small groups. These men were rapidly mobilized by organizers of two main categories: those on the spot and those brought in. The men on the spot were the Party, State, and NKVD functionaries mentioned above. Many of them already had small groups of followers, and with these to lend support to their commands, they proceeded to call up the able-bodied men—meaning generally the Red Army stragglers—for service as partisans. As their units grew in size, the organizers rose in rank and position; the original group of followers often became the first company of a battalion and, later, of a regiment. Thus a successful organizer might rise from the equivalent of a squad leader to that of a regimental commander in a few months; the rank and file, however, appear to have had few prospects for advancement beyond the position of squad leader. The organizers who were brought in, usually by air, but occasionally through the front, either joined the staffs of the growing units set up by the men on the spot, or began forming units of their own.

The available accounts of this mass mobilization indicate that primary emphasis was placed on the redrafting of Red Army stragglers. A large proportion joined without much objection, but some apparently went along only under the threat of force. Recruitment among those who had lived in the area before the war was more difficult, and except for a few people who had a stake in the Soviet system, men could be induced to join only by threats. Because the regular units which had been cut off by the Germans had suffered heavy casualties, some of the men drafted at the beginning of 1942 were enrolled as replacements for these units rather than as recruits for the partisan detachments.

What were the partisan units like? Certain characteristics are very clear. Probably about 75 per cent of their members were former Red Army men who had either evaded the German mopping-up operations of 1941 or had escaped from prisoner-of-war camps. The units were organized along military lines—the formal system of squads, platoons, companies, battalions, and regiments frequently being imposed on units with little organic cohesion. The widest variation appears to have been in the number of battalions per regiment, which ranged from three to seven. This may be the only surviving indication that the accidents of war and the qualities of the individual commander played a great role in determining the size of partisan units in the first year of the war. At one time, probably at the beginning of April, two partisan divisions, one consisting of three and the other of five regiments, were formed. However, the most important operational command appears always to have been the regiment.

As previously stated, the partisan units were recruited for the most part from Red Army stragglers. As the supply of Red Army men was exhausted, recruitment turned more to members of the local population, with special emphasis apparently being placed on re-examining those who had escaped military service for medical reasons. In view of the fact that the local population in this area is overwhelmingly of Great Russian nationality, it may be assumed that the local recruits were Great Russians. What evidence is available on the subject indicates that this was also true of the vast majority of the Red Army men. The age distribution reflected the predominance of Red Army stragglers; the heaviest concentration was in the group from eighteen to thirty. Most of the cadres seem to have been from the lower strata of the governing apparatus. The political background of the members is more difficult to ascertain. The scanty evidence indicates that the percenage of Communist Party members was slightly higher than in the Red Army after the mobilization of 1941. Training did not present much of a problem because most of the partisans had had some sort of previous military training. Ten-day courses were evidently considered sufficient to acquaint the others with the rudiments of infantry warfare.

Control within the partisan units was threefold. There were military officers at all levels, from the squad up. There were political officers, apparently from the company level up. There were Special Sections of the NKVD at the regimental level and in some cases at the battalion level. This triple control system was at times confused by the fact that many of those holding military positions were former NKVD or Party officials, while the political officers frequently were in charge of military assignments. Furthermore, there appear to have been some cases in which the positions of commander and commissar or commissar and NKVD representative were held by one person. The power held by the military and political officers over the men was very great indeed, and there are indications that at times this power was seriously abused.

The triple system of internal control mirrored the control mechanism directing the movement from the outside. The military chain of command above the regimental level is quite clear. The regimental commanders received their orders from General Belov, the Commander of the II Guard Cavalry Corps which had broken into the area in January 1942. These orders came to the regiments directly or through divisional headquarters which had probably been established to facilitate tactical direction of the lower units. Belov himself, once he was in the area, was under the command of the Soviet West Front, Marshal Zhukov's army group in the central part of the Eastern front. The external control function of the NKVD appears to have been exercised by Special Sections at each of the levels above the partisan regiment. This was also true for the commissar system, but here there was the added complication of the territorial authorities of the Communist Party. Some sort of authority was apparently exercised by the oblast committee (over and above the possibility that the Smolensk Oblast Committee may have organized one of the regiments). Although the evidence is scanty, it might be said that the Party had some external supervisory power over the partisans in matters of discipline and in seeing to it that the partisans maintained a proper level of activity; specific tactical control, however, was reserved for the military command structure.[2]

Discipline within the units was strict. The only question connected with discipline on which substantial documentation is available is the complex of factors bearing on morale. These may be separated into two main categories: the different morale levels of the components of the partisan movement and the effects of a number of specific situations and events on morale. Important differences in morale can be observed between the local recruits, the former Red Army men, and the cadres. For the most part, the local recruits were unwilling members of the partisan movement, served in it without enthusiasm, and were prone to desert when an opportunity arose. The former Red Army men were generally less inclined to object to induction; one has the impression that many of them joined from a sense of duty and without much pressure. Those who had escaped from German captivity were especially immune to ideas of desertion and often passed on this attitude to other members of the same unit. At the same time, a great many of the former Red Army men were not exuberant about their membership in the partisan movement and were detained as much by fear of their own officers as by fear of German mistreatment.

---

[2] It is possible, but unlikely, that some of the orders ascribed to General Belov in fact came from the Smolensk Oblast Committee of the Party which may also have been at Dorogobuzh for a while.

The cadres had the best morale. They largely identified themselves with the Soviet regime and, whatever their personal preference, they knew that the Germans would so identify them in any case and would exterminate them if given the chance.

Though it is not explicitly stated, it is reasonable to assume that the early successes of the partisans in this area and the great strength which they attained were important factors tending to bolster morale in the first part of 1942. But there were also important conditions which caused poor morale; among these were periodic supply difficulties, the occasional instances of abuse of power by the commissars, and the high casualty rates.

The operations of the partisans in this area were conditioned by the particular tactical situation which put them, together with regular units, in control of a substantial area. To defend this area against attack, the standard small arms equipment was not adequate. Supporting weapons— artillery and tanks—were of great importance. The partisan units were able to assemble a considerable number of guns, primarily 45 mm anti-tank guns and 76 mm guns. Tanks which had been abandoned in the area at the time of the 1941 battles were repaired and put into use with the help of spare parts and gasoline flown in by the Red Air Force. The use of these tanks in support of partisan counterattacks was reported with some surprise by the Germans.

The partisans devoted much attention to intelligence. Intelligence work was organized formally, carried out with considerable energy, and rewarded with a good deal of success. The partisans in this area apparently did not engage in political intelligence work for the Soviet government. The explanation for this presumably lies in the fact that in the large area under partisan control the whole Soviet system of administration, including the NKVD, was re-established as discussed below.

Sometimes German soldiers captured by the partisans were killed, but many were interrogated and sent to a jail at Dorogobuzh. Some of the latter were put to work at menial tasks for the partisans; others were kept in jail, and their fate is unknown; at least one German radio operator was flown out.

The partisans' military activity consisted primarily of defending the area under their control. To accomplish this, much effort was devoted to the construction of field fortifications. The small counterattacks mounted by the partisans and the skirmishes with German troops were all carried out in a manner closely resembling the operations of regular troops.

In the area under partisan control, the Soviet system was re-established. The collective farms, some of which had been broken up by the peasants, were reorganized under new managers. Local government officials were appointed and the regular rayon administration reintroduced. Those who had collaborated with the Germans were punished: some were executed, others were sentenced to jail, still others were inducted into the partisan movement. There is good evidence to indicate that on the one hand, punishment for collaborating was meted out with careful attention to evidence of collaboration, while on the other hand, the punishments inflicted on each collaborator varied widely and with perhaps intentional unpredictability.

The attitude of the population toward the Germans and the partisans is difficult to assess. The German defeats in the winter of 1941–42 undoubtedly played a most important role. Up to that time, the population, at least in its overt behavior, had been inclined to favor the Germans, although this did not deter them from helping escaped prisoners and Red Army stragglers as individuals rather than as partisans. Once the population had grasped the extent of the German defeat, their attitude underwent a marked change, which in some ways reflects on the motivation of their earlier friendly reception of the Germans. The population now adopted a more cautious attitude. As peasants, they still looked with disfavor on a regime which had brought them the collective farm system, but they began to reckon on its possible return, a possibility which turned into reality for some months in the first half of 1942. The population tended to support the partisans in areas controlled by the latter. On the whole, one has the impression that, because of bitter experiences, the population adjusted its overt behavior to the prevailing power situation.

Partisan psychological warfare consisted primarily of their very presence in the area. The available sources point to a partisan belief that their presence in large numbers and the reinstatement of the Soviet system in the area under their control were by themselves adequate proof of the power and indestructibility of the Soviet regime and sufficient inducement to the population to give needed support to the partisan forces.

The Germans, on the other hand, made a considerable effort to increase desertion from the partisan units by turning their psychological warfare operations to the differential morale situation within the units. In the spring of 1942 they began to distinguish between partisan deserters and other prisoners, promising decent treatment to the former in contrast with their previous practice of killing both. Realizing that the point of greatest vulnerability in the partisan units was the local recruit who had been forced into the partisan movement, all possible media—leaflets, posters, choruses, letters from deserters—were utilized to convince these men that their involuntary enrollment in the partisan movement would not be held against them. Knowing that past Nazi conduct made any approach to the former Red Army men especially difficult, the Germans stressed that good treatment, jobs, and land awaited those who deserted. By this time, the Germans had also come to realize that they were performing a valuable service for the Soviet High Command by executing all captured political officers. This policy was contributing noticeably to the fighting spirit of the partisan, as well as the regular army units, since the cadres, who played a very large role in maintaining morale, knew what fate they could expect at the hands of the Germans. In an attempt to cope with this problem, Hitler permitted an experimental relaxation of the order for the execution of political officers; this new policy was first applied in the German offensive to clear the partisans from the Yelnya-Dorogobuzh area. For the first time German appeals were extended to the political officers with promises that their lives would be spared. The evidence indicates that, in spite of efforts made within the partisan units to counteract this German activity, substantial numbers of partisans deserted. The deserters included representatives of all components of the partisan movement, although the local recruits furnished proportionally the largest contingent.

A most significant problem facing all partisan units was that of supply. In this area, the highly developed partisan organization included a formal structure for handling supply problems. The main source of food and clothing was the operational area itself. Munitions and weapons were collected largely from matériel abandoned in the great battles of 1941. The political authorities re-established in the area under partisan control played an important role in securing food supplies from the local population. The role of airpower in providing supplies is discussed below.

The available medical services were rather extensive. In the western part of the area, on which our information is most complete, there were at least five field hospitals. These had small permanent staffs and cared for ten to twenty-five partisans each. In addition, there were small medical details in the units, probably starting at the company level. The complete absence of complaints about medical care would seem to indicate that the provisions in this regard were adequate.

Soviet air support for the partisans in the Yelnya-Dorogobuzh area was particularly extensive. The rapid mobilization and staffing of the large partisan movement in the first months of 1942 would have been impossible without the help of officers and commissars flown in by the Red Air Force. The fact that many of the partisan groups had been organized by men brought in by air or included officers flown in to serve as members of their staff was of great importance in the control over the partisan movement. The courier service maintained between the partisans and the other side of the front also facilitated liaison and control.

Air supply operations for the partisans included constant transport of reinforcements in addition to large quantities of matériel. Ammunition, weapons, mines, and similar military supplies were flown in on a large scale and were certainly an important factor in the rapid arming of the large number of partisans mobilized with such speed in early 1942. Essential for the utilization of the abandoned tanks which the partisans put into service were the gasoline and spare parts flown in by the Red Air Force. Items of clothing, particularly boots, as well as some food, were regularly flown in. Food deliveries were apparently concentrated on such special items as sugar and, perhaps, sausage. The numerous references to the air transport of tobacco seem to indicate that the Soviet High Command recognized the importance of this supply factor to troop morale.

Other morale boosts provided by air support were the provision of medical supplies and the evacuation of the wounded. The available materials on other aspects of the role of airpower—for example, tactical support of the partisans—either do not allow generalizations or do not lend themselves to summarization. A number of interesting details have been found on the technical aspects of air support which should be of great help in preparation of a general description of Soviet methods.

Antipartisan Warfare

The presence of large partisan forces in the Yelnya-Dorogobuzh area naturally alarmed the Germans. Their first efforts to cope with the situation consisted of minor antipartisan operations, which proved to be completely inadequate and ended uniformly in failure. A more ambitious operation was planned for March 1942 but was not carried out on the scale originally intended. Actually it consisted solely of the action of one German division in opening a corridor through the partisan-controlled area. This corridor was certainly of value to the Germans, but the danger presented by the partisan movement persisted. The Germans, therefore, planned a major offensive which was launched by two corps, including all or parts of nine divisions, on 24 May 1942. With a force substantially larger than the combined regular and partisan units facing them, the Germans were able to carry out their plan of destroying the mass of the Soviet forces. Of the 15,000–20,000 regulars and partisans in the area at the start of the German attack, about 2,000 were able to break out of the encirclement and another 2,000–3,000 went into hiding individually or in small groups within the area itself. The balance of the forces were either killed or captured. The available statistics on partisan and German casualties, however, show that the fighting was severe and that the partisans made a determined effort to hold back the attacking forces.

In both the limited operation of March 1942 and the major German offensive in May, the air support given the German forces was a factor of importance. Air reconnaissance proved particularly helpful. The bombing and strafing of partisan concentrations varied considerably in effectiveness. Material damage and human casualties were apparently of significance only in cases where close tactical support of advancing German units could provide a substitute for the German deficiency in artillery. Otherwise, the material effect of bombing in particular appears to have been slight. The morale effect, on the other hand, was apparently considerable. Air attacks were greatly feared and caused confusion and even panic regardless of material damage inflicted. This is a point of sufficient importance to bear reexamination in the light of findings in other areas.

Having destroyed the partisan movement in the area, the Germans directed their efforts to preventing its revival. These included military pacification, political measures to keep the population from aiding the partisans, and preventive action against the anticipated Soviet attempt to revive the movement by air. The German efforts were successful. From the summer of 1942 to the fall of 1943, when the Germans retreated from the area for good, there was no partisan activity of consequence in the area.

Evaluation

What were the partisan accomplishments in this area and what is the explanation for the German success in preventing the rise of a new movement? The Germans considered the partisans in this area a failure since they never scored a major military victory. It is true that the partisans failed to cut the main supply route of German Army Group Center, but the large diversion of German troops in the spring of 1942 to meet the partisan threat must in itself be considered an accomplishment of military importance. The fact that, for almost two months, two German corps were occupied with the preparation and execution of an antipartisan operation is certainly remarkable; it is also unique. At no other time did the Germans employ such a force in an antipartisan operation. It is not unreasonable to suppose that had they always been able to send two corps against such concentrations, the partisan units in other areas would not have fared so well.

This last point helps explain the German success in crushing the partisan movement in this area. It might be said that the partisan success in building up such a large organization so near the front was the cause for bringing down upon themselves a German force which for once was adequate to the task. A second factor of significance is implicit in the foregoing. The partisan movement had assumed such a complete military character that it had to be dealt with in a military manner by regular troops. Thus, in this area, the distinction between the partisans and the population was sharper than usual, and the Germans kept this distinction in mind. Instead of resorting to collective punishment measures which usually affected the nonpartisans more than the partisans, the Germans consciously tried to restrict their operations to the latter. This came at a time when the population had not yet become strongly anti-German and, therefore it was relatively easy to achieve. After the offensive, adherence to this policy enabled the Germans to hold the remnants of the partisan units to tiny groups of men concerned exclusively with problems of survival. The fact that new groups of partisans flown into the area by the Red Air Force were unable to revive the movement seems to indicate that air support for the organization of a partisan movement can be successful only when potential recruits already exist in the area.

The most valuable contribution of the partisan movement in the Yelnya-Dorogobuzh area to a study of the Soviet movement as a whole is its detailed picture of that stage in the development of partisan warfare which saw the expansion of small groups to substantial units consisting largely of former Red Army men. In this area, the life of the partisan movement was cut short at just this point. But the autopsy provides us with a detailed picture of this phase and establishes many of its salient characteristics. At the same time such a study helps identify those aspects of the partisan movement which differ in the various stages and those which remain constant.

§I. The Yelnya-Dorogobuzh Area, 1941

A. THE AREA AND THE WAR IN 1941

The Yelnya-Dorogobuzh area forms the eastern part of Smolensk Oblast. It is a food-deficit area lying well north of the black-soil region. It consists to a considerable extent of woods and swamps, including also much relatively poor farm land, some wastelands, and some areas which grow hay for a small dairy industry. The main product, aside from subsistence crops, is flax, and the only industrial establishments are those for the processing of flax. The Smolensk-Sukhinichi railway, on which Yelnya lies, cuts diagonally through the area from northwest to southeast. Figure 5 gives an outline of the area. The population is overwhelmingly Great Russian (over 90 per cent) and predominantly agricultural. The impact of the war on these people in 1941 was somewhat different from that in many other parts of the USSR overrun by the Germans in that year, for this area witnessed a local Soviet victory. This difference may have had effects on the attitudes of the population considerably greater than its intrinsic significance.

In the middle of July 1941, the German armies arrived in the Smolensk area. Yelnya, a town of about 4,500 inhabitants at the headwaters of the Ugra and Desna Rivers, fifty miles southeast of Smolensk, was taken by the Germans on 20 July 1941. Then the German offensive on the central part of the front (the route to Moscow) came to a halt as the Germans transferred substantial forces southward to encircle Soviet troops in the Kiev area and as Soviet resistance in the center stiffened. In August and September there was no advance in the center; on the contrary, on 5 September 1941, Soviet counterattacks led to the recapture of Yelnya in one of the first Soviet local victories of the war.

On 2 October 1941 the Germans resumed their offensive on the central front. The Soviet lines broke almost immediately. Yelnya fell on 5 October. On 7 October the German columns which had cut through the Soviet lines north and south of Smolensk met at Vyazma, an industrial town on the road

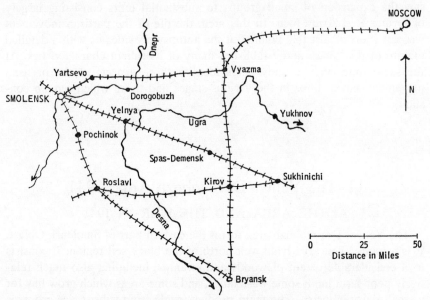

Figure 5.—The Yelnya-Dorogobuzh area of Smolensk Oblast.

to Moscow about eighty miles east of Smolensk. Trapped in the pocket (*Kessel*) were large parts of the Soviet Nineteenth and Twenty-fourth Armies. Dorogobuzh, a town of about 8,000 on the upper Dnepr, where the headquarters of the Nineteenth Army had been located, was captured on 9 October. On 13 October, the Germans claimed that the pocket had been cleared of Soviet troops, and by 2 November 1941 a firm front existed east of Vyazma. Soon thereafter, the Germans moved on toward Moscow.

Behind the German front as it existed before the offensive of 2 October, the organization of a partisan movement had been started by the Soviets as early as July and August. Furthermore, it soon became evident that the pocket created by the German offensive had not been completely cleared, as had at first been claimed by the Germans. A substantial basis for the organization of a partisan movement remained, consisting of local functionaries of the Communist Party, Red Army stragglers, escaped Soviet prisoners of war, and other elements in the local population. As the Germans marched farther east, the first stirrings of partisan warfare appeared in this area; the German retreat in December brought about a situation especially conducive to the rapid growth of a partisan movement. The first growth of partisan activity in the Yelnya-Dorogobuzh area will be described in the following section. The setting, produced by the developments just traced, can be summarized as follows: The German invaders passed around the region in a rapid movement eastward, leaving large areas which seemed pacified as the German armies continued their advances in October and November 1941.

B. PARTISAN ORGANIZATION IN THE SMOLENSK AREA BEFORE 2 OCTOBER 1941

What actually happened when the Germans arrived? A member of the Smolensk NKVD charged with checking up on the other members of his NKVD group had the following to say on this question: "Upon the arrival of the German troops they [the NKVD] fled from Smolensk. Some of the NKVD fled to the vicinity of Vyazma, others to Dorogobuzh. He was with the latter group. About 20 men stayed in the area of Dorogobuzh with the assignment of remaining behind in the territory occupied by the Germans to organize partisan detachments."[3]

The activity begun in the vicinity of Dorogobuzh and Vyazma and the probable fate of the destruction battalions will be discussed below. The point which needs to be stressed here is that the German advance led to the (apparently random) scattering over the countryside of Soviet functionaries who knew that they were supposed to organize partisan units.

At about the same time, the latter part of July 1941, large parts of the Soviet 214th Airborne Brigade were sent on foot through the front south of Smolensk (probably in the general area of Pochinok). Operating for three months as partisans in civilian clothes, the brigade received its orders by radio from the Red Army while its commander repeatedly passed through the front for personal conferences with Soviet officials.[4] In the middle of August, when the front in this sector had been stabilized, two other companies of this brigade were dropped by parachute into the Smolensk area; these troops also were to engage in partisan warfare.[5]

Once behind the German lines, what did these men do? Interrogations of several members of the 214th Airborne Brigade and of partisan units organized by them are revealing not only for the light they shed on the activities of the brigade and those conected with it, but also for an under-

[3] 221. Sich.Div., Ic, "[Meldung] an Befehlshaber Heeres-Gebiet Mitte, Ic," 14 April 1942 (GMDS, 221 ID 22639/6, Anlage 16).

[4] V. A.K., Ia/Ic, "Die Luftlandetruppen der Roten Armee, Teil I: Textheft," 23 March 1942, p. 2 (GMDS, V AK 20384/7).

[5] *Ibid.* Other units of the 214th Airborne Brigade were dropped near Pochinok in February 1942. (106. Inf.Div., Ic, "Gefangenenvernehmungen," 23 February 1942, GMDS, V AK 20384/7.)

standing of similar operations which must have escaped the attention of the Germans. The basic assignment of the men sent through the lines or dropped by parachute was the organization of partisan detachments, as the following quotations from the German report indicate:

Recruitment of additional partisans from pro-Communist elements in the population, Red Army stragglers, homeless civilians, and people working on collective farms.

Organization and strengthening of cells of additional partisan groups in as many localities as possible.

. . . .

At the moment, the assignments and activity of the partisans appear to be confined to creating an extensive organization so that, at a later time of active operations, an adequate base will be available.[6]

The more detailed comments of a partisan who had been the radio operator for one of the groups organized by the 214th Airborne Brigade show what this meant in practice:

After the destruction of the 145th and 149th Divisions in the vicinity of Roslavl, many groups of the battered units remained in the forests behind the German front. They were collected near Pochinok by a captain (Shemav) [presumably an officer of the 214th Airborne Brigade] and organized into partisan detachments.

The unit with which he is familiar consists of approximately 180–200 men; it is divided into 3 groups of about 60 men each.

The first group was sent off to be employed in the area south of the Smolensk-Dorogobuzh road. . . .

The second group, to which he himself belonged . . . was sent over the Smolensk-Dorogobuzh road to make contact with parachutists who had landed there and to organize partisan units in the Dukhovshchina area (about ten miles northeast of Smolensk). . . .

The third group went from Pochinok . . . to Velizh. . . . It is supposed to organize partisan units in the Velizh area and also to establish contact with the numerous partisans of Belorussia. . . .

Each of the above-named groups has two radio transmitters, plus a submachine gun per man, explosives, and hand grenades. Weapons and explosives are dropped by planes with which the groups are in communication. . . . The groups themselves do not go into action as complete units but have the assignment of organizing new partisan groups of five to ten men each. . . . Basically their immediate assignment is not the committing of acts of sabotage since the result would be that individual units would come to the attention of the German Army. Their assignment is rather the formation of a complete and coherent organization behind the German front. Acts of sabotage . . . are undertaken only when they can be done thoroughly and when the group can be certain of escaping capture.

. . . Dropping people by parachute serves to strengthen the leadership corps of the individual groups. . . .

[6] V. A.K., Ic, "Erfahrungen in der Partisanenbekaempfung," 2 September 1941, pp. 3–4 (GMDS, V AK 17647/22).

Until the capture of this partisan, continuous radio communication existed among the three groups and with the Soviet Army and planes.

The individual partisans usually work on collective farms in the daytime. The purpose of their work, however, is not to earn bread but to recruit and organize partisan groups and to encourage others in resistance and sabotage.

. . . .

The population support the partisans to a very large degree (*in weitestgehendem Masse*). They supply them [the partisans] with the best provisions, slaughter for them, give them white bread, hide them, and help them on their way.[7]

The material cited above shows that a partisan movement, though still in its infancy, was already in existence around Smolensk before the Germans resumed the offensive on the central front on 2 October 1941. In its first stages, this offensive succeeded in surrounding large numbers of Soviet troops in a pocket near Yelnya and Dorogobuzh between Smolensk and Vyazma. We must now turn eastward to this area and trace the developments there in October 1941.

C. THE VYAZMA POCKET, OCTOBER–NOVEMBER 1941

On 2 October, German forces broke through the Soviet lines north and south of Smolensk. The armored units which led the German pincers met near Vyazma on 7 October. Caught in the pocket were large numbers of Soviet regular units as well as a large part of the population. Some of the pocket area had been fought over in July and August. It was characterized as follows by Third Panzer Army:

> After the beginning of the advance on 2 October, the troops entered an area which had been prepared for war in quite a different manner: the population had been employed for weeks in preparing earthworks so that it had not been possible to bring in the potato harvest or to make the fall sowing; the livestock of the collective farms had been driven off almost everywhere; the harvested crops and larger buildings such as schools, meeting places, and other public buildings had been set on fire. . . .[8]

In the pocket the Soviet system now crumbled. Collective farms were broken up by the peasants, who retrieved enough stray horses from the broken Red Army units to continue their work.[9] However, the Soviet Government had made plans for the organization of partisan warfare in the area, and these must be examined.

---

[7] V. A.K., Ic, "Vernehmung des Partisanen Tokatschew Peter Iwanowitsch," 29 August 1941, pp. 2–5 (GMDS, V AK 17647/22).

[8] Pz. Gr. [PzAOK] 3, Ic/AO, "Stimmung der Bevoelkerung," 25 January 1942 (GMDS, PzAOK 3, 20839/5). This report refers specifically to the northern pincer of the German offensive, but there is no reason to believe that things were different in the area traversed by the southern pincer.

[9] XXXXVI. Pz.K, Ic, "Partisanenherrschaft im Smolensker Gebiet," 18 June 1942, p. 1 (GMDS, 23 ID 24182/16).

Some partisan detachments had been established before the German October offensive. In Vyazma the Germans found the text of the first assignments given one such partisan group. Excerpts from this order give some idea of Soviet intentions.

Secret

28 July 1941   Assignment No. 1

To: The partisan unit of Comrades S. I. Marchenkov and M. S. Vereshchagin which is active in a strength of 350 men.

The unit of Comrades Marchenkov and Vereshchagin, after the necessary or planned abandonment by parts of the Red Army of the Sychevka-Vyazma-Staroye Beshmutovo line, must remain in the rear of the Germans and establish the main strongpoint in the area of Dashkovka-Krasnoye Polyanovo-Selivanovo in order to fulfill the following tasks:

1. Destroy camps with food, gasoline, and war materials set up by the Germans in Vyazma Rayon.

2. Systematically destroy the Smolensk-Vyazma, Vyazma-Bryansk railroad lines and the main Moscow-Minsk highway in Vyazma Rayon; effect the derailment of trains and destroy the supply of war material and food.

3. Prevent the use of the Vyazma airport (Dvoyevko) No. 62 by destroying planes, gasoline, and war material.

4. Kill higher and lower level German war staffs; destroy communication cables and the officer corps; capture high German officers and hand over to units of the Red Army any documents which contain valuable information about the enemy.

5. Set up in the unit two or three diversionist groups which will perform special tasks for the commander and the commisssar.

.   .   .   .

Officer in Charge of Special Assignments of the West Front, First Lieutenant [signed] D. Selivanov

Contents noted:

Commander of the Detachment, Comrade Marchenkov
Commissar of the Detachment, Comrade M. Vereshchagin[10]

As already indicated, members of the Smolensk NKVD had fled to Vyazma and Dorogobuzh at the end of July. In October they told the population within the pocket area to await the organization of partisan detachments.[11] Some officials fled with the retreating Red Army but returned soon after. Thus, not long after the German occupation of Yelnya, a Communist Party functionary returned to organize partisan units.[12] Many Soviet officials took to the woods[13] where they could easily make contact with Red Army stragglers. A high-ranking military commander is supposed to have "stayed

[10] AOK 11, Ic/AO, "Feindnachrichtenblatt Nr. 198/42," 3 January 1942, Anlage 2 (GMDS, AOK 6, 18156/22).

[11] 221. Sich.Div., Ic, "[Meldung] an Befehlshaber Heeres-Gebiet Mitte, Ic," 14 April 1942, p. 1 (GMDS, 221 ID 22639/6, Anlage 16).

[12] 221. Sich.Div., Ic, "[Meldung] an Befehlshaber Heeres-Gebiet Mitte, Ic," 27 April 1942 (GMDS, 221 ID 22639/6, Anlage 20).

[13] XXXXVI. Pz.K., Ic, "Partisanenherrschaft im Smolensker Gebiet," 18 June 1942, p. 3 (GMDS, 23 ID 24182/16).

behind after the battle of Vyazma, concealed guns, kept up communications with Moscow, and organized the partisans in this area."[14] Although other details are not available, it is clear from the foregoing that the Soviets made an effort to organize partisan units in the pocket. The first and most obvious "customers" of this organizational activity were the Red Army stragglers from the units which had been broken up by the German advance and trapped in the pocket. But these men were at the same time the obvious quarry of the Germans who were trying to clear the pocket. These German efforts must be recorded and evaluated.

On 10 October 1941 the German Ninth Army issued an order for clearing the northern and central part of the Vyazma pocket. The 255th Infantry Division and an SS Cavalry Brigade were assigned to this job.[15] The southern part of the pocket was to be cleared by the 137th Infantry Division and later by the 8th Infantry Division under the general direction of the Commander of the Rear Area of Fourth Army.[16]

It would appear that the German clearing effort was successful in some respects and unsuccessful in others. Many prisoners were brought in and there was little or no partisan activity at first; however, when it became necessary to withdraw the German troops and send them to the front again, partisan activity increased. Thus the Commander of the Rear Area of Fourth Army wrote in a letter to the Commander of the Army Group Rear Area Center that there had been practically no partisan activity in his area. But then he continued: "Unfortunately I have had to give up the 137th Infantry Division to the front and have also lost two-thirds of the 8th Infantry Division. For the time being we work with few troops and one notices that unfortunately the partisan movement (*das Partisanentum*) is growing."[17] The 255th Infantry Division was engaged in a persistent effort to collect the remaining Red Army men. The local military government office in Vyazma reported as follows on the situation in the first half of November 1941:

No partisans or partisan activity was noticed in the area of the military government office, but in the pocket about ten miles west and southwest of Vyazma bands of Red Army men are still on the loose, often staying in dugouts. A

[14] 221. Sich.Div., Ic, "Kriegsgefangene Rotarmisten Archipow u. Smirnow," 27 May 1942, p. 2 (GMDS, 221 ID 22639/6, Anlage 63). According to the interrogee, Smirnov, this officer was a brigadier general, but this may have been the officer's rank when Smirnov was captured in May 1942. There is no other evidence of a general's being in the Yelnya-Dorogobuzh area in the initial stages of partisan organization in 1941.

[15] AOK 9, Ia/Qu 2, "Einsatz der 255. I.D. und SS-Reiterbrigade Fegelein zu Sicherungszwecken," 10 October 1941 (GMDS, Korueck 16552).

[16] Korueck 559, Qu, "Tgb. Nr. 4265 an 8. Inf.Div.," 23 October 1941 (GMDS, Korueck 13512/2).

[17] Generalleutnant von Unruh, Korueck 559, "[Brief] an General der Infanterie von Schenckendorff," 9 November 1941 (GMDS, Korueck 13512/2).

major operation was carried out against them by the 255th Infantry Division on 7 November 1941. The attention of the division was called to the fact that Russian field hospitals and villages scattered in remote areas where Red Army men have gathered will furnish the basis for the formation of partisan groups unless prompt action is taken there (*wenn dort nich zugegriffen wird*).[18]

The reports of the 255th Division list substantial numbers of prisoners picked up in the clearing operation. The report of 28 October 1941 places the number at 2,236 as of that date.[19] By 17 November an additional 1,294 prisoners had been rounded up.[20] The report containing this figure, however, also stresses that many Red Army men were still at large in the area and that minor partisan activity appeared to continue. Similarly, the 137th Division's concluding report on clearing operations states that the division brought in approximately 15,200 prisoners, but that many others still remain in the area.[21]

When the reports on clearing efforts by the Germans are compared with later reports on the activity and composition of partisan groups in the same area, one is struck by the fact that the latter stress the presence of large numbers of Red Army men from the pockets. As will be seen in subsequent sections, this is as characteristic of the Yelnya-Dorogobuzh area as it is of many other important areas of partisan activity. The explanation for this is not always explicit in the German documents. Certain important points are obvious. For one thing, the German units were usually pulled out of an area before they had a chance to finish their job. As has already been pointed out, the forces in the rear area of Fourth Army were removed, and at the beginning of December, the 255th Division was also transferred to the front. The SS Cavalry Brigade, an outfit whose excessively ruthless methods made it of dubious value in any case, was likewise given other assignments.

But this was not all. The German tactics in the 1941 campaign made an important, though unintended, contribution to the growth of the partisan movement. The Germans depended on armored pincers to cut off large parts of the Red Army which were then to be mopped up by German infantry units. This naturally led to German advances along roads, over relatively dry ground, and through areas which had to some extent been cleared of trees. The result was that surrounded Red Army men tended to be con-

---

[18] OK Vyazma (I/593), "Taetigkeitsbericht der Ortskommandantur I/593 in Wjasma fuer die Zeit vom 2.–15.11.1941," 16 November 1941, pp. 1–2 (GMDS, Korueck 17326/11).

[19] 255. Inf.Div., Ia, "An A.O.K. 9/O.Qu.," 28 October 1941, p. 2 (GMDS, 255 ID 25337/2, Anlage 389).

[20] 255. Inf.Div., Ia, "Bericht an Befh. rueckw. H.G. Mitte," 17 November 1941, p. 4 (GMDS, 255 ID 25337/3, Anlage 604).

[21] 137. Inf.Div., Ia, "Abschliessender Bericht ueber die Befriedung des Raumes Juchnow-Wjasma-Dorogobusch-Jelnja-Kirow in der Zeit vom 12.–25.10.41," 25 October 1941 (GMDS, Korueck 13512/2, Anlage 37).

centrated in areas away from roads, in swampy regions, and in dense forests. Such regions provided both the best concealment for those who wanted to hide and the most difficult access for those who wanted to clear the area. Thus, the stragglers were almost forced into the type of country ideally suited for partisan warfare—often the same places into which the Soviet functionaries who were supposed to organize partisans had fled before the German advance.[22]

The German units assigned the task of clearing these almost roadless, very swampy, and heavily forested areas had often just come from front-line fighting, were supposedly resting behind the front, and expected to be sent back to the front in the near future. It is hardly surprising that, under these conditions, the German troops exhibited little enthusiasm for the endless trudging through forests and wading through swamps or snow, such activity being necessary to round up not just those Red Army men ready to surrender voluntarily but also those trying to hide out, i.e., the potential partisans.[23] A report of the military government office in Vyazma on the second half of November 1941 is both descriptive and prophetic:

There is still no indication of the formation of partisan groups or of partisan activity in the area of the military government office. On the other hand, the pocket has not yet been completely cleared of Red Army men, who will now withdraw with the escaped prisoners of war into the remote villages and who will probably not fail to be affected by the propaganda planned by the Soviets for the winter. The major operation of the 255th Infantry Division had little success since it never reached the remote villages because of the poor, snow-covered roads; the individual units contented themselves with collecting such booty in the woods as they could use themselves.[24]

The attitude of the population was another factor which undoubtedly contributed toward the ability of large numbers of Red Army men to hide in the woods or to disappear by settling in the villages. It is difficult, if not impossible, to assess with accuracy the attitude of the population in the Yelnya-Dorogobuzh area toward the Soviet system, the Germans, and the partisan movement at this time. Although the issue cannot be dealt with here in all its ramifications, certain points can safely be made. The partisan movement as a consciously anti-German organization fighting against the occupier was not yet strong. Most of the Red Army men as well as many of the partisans who were moving about individually or in small groups

[22] This process is well explained in Korueck 559, Ic/AO, "Taetigkeitsbericht [1. September 1941—20. Oktober 1941]," 20 October 1941 (GMDS, Korueck 13512/3).

[23] A good picture of the roving stragglers is given in a report of a detachment of the secret field police which had been scouting the area southwest of Vyazma. (GFP/Gr. 570, Sonderkommando Korueck 559, "Bericht," 20 November 1941, GMDS, Korueck 13512/3.)

[24] OK Vyazma (I/593), "Taetigkeitsbericht der Ortskommandantur I/593 in Wjasma fuer die Zeit vom 16.–30.11.1941," 1 December 1941, p. 2 (GMDS, Korueck 17326/11).

were viewed by the population not as members of bands raiding the villages for supplies, but as individual persons in need of help. This was particularly true of escaped prisoners of war whose mistreatment by the Germans was widely known among the population and was an extremely important factor in keeping Red Army stragglers from turning themselves in.[25] One partisan was quoted above as saying that the population readily supported the partisans. This does not necessarily mean that the population supported the partisans as partisans. The same man also related an experience which may have been typical for persons hunted by the Germans:

> Thus this prisoner had . . . met an officer of the [German V] Corps on his way. He [the partisan] had taken along a girl on the road through the village and had told her that if a German soldier wanted to ask him for information [about himself] she was to say that she was his sister. The prisoner was stopped by the German officer, the girl gave the information, whereupon the officer went on his way.[26]

Although large elements among the local population received the Germans in a friendly manner, they were no doubt seriously influenced by the widespread wild requisitioning by German soldiers. The 255th Infantry Division was very outspoken on this subject:

> The division would like to call special attention to the great danger which the large number of [German] stragglers in all parts of the area constitutes both for the maintenance of discipline and for the pacification of the country.
> These soldiers, who have been left behind by other units to guard munitions or . . . vehicles which have gotten stuck, continuously requisition and loot in the villages in a manner which embitters the population and practically drives it into the arms of the partisans.[27]

The result of the events reported here was that, when the German units left the Yelnya-Dorogobuzh area for the front and no large units were im-

---

[25] The following report by the commander of the artillery regiment attached to the 255th Infantry Division gives some idea of the prisoner-of-war situation:

Conditions in the Transient POW Camp 231

18 November 1941

. . . .

   The prisoners of war, who number at present about 7,000, not counting the wounded, are accommodated in the shell of a factory building which gives protection only against the rain. On the other hand, the prisoners of war are exposed to the cold without any protection. The windows which are several meters high and wide are without covering. There are no doors in the building. The prisoners who are thus kept practically in the open air are freezing to death by the hundreds daily —in addition to those who die continuously because of exhaustion. . . . (Art.Regt. 255, "Zustaende im Dulag 231," 18 November 1941, GMDS, 255 ID 25337/3, Anlage 611.)

[26] V. A.K., Ic. "Vernehmung des Partisanen Tokatschew Peter Iwanowitsch," 29 August 1941, p. 5 (GMDS, V AK 17647/22).

[27] 255. Inf.Div., Ia, 13 November 1941 (GMDS, 255 ID 25337/3, Anlage 558). The whole subject of the conduct of German soldiers in the East cannot be treated in this study. A revealing presentation of the difficulties this presented for the Germans themselves may be found in Korueck 559, Ic/AO, "Manneszucht (Verbotenes Requirieren und Pluendern)," 4 September 1941 and OB AOK 4, "Sonderbefehl zur Aufrechterhaltung der Manneszucht," 11 September 1941 (GMDS, Korueck 13512/3).

mediately sent to replace them, the area harbored cadres whose mission was to organize partisans, and also contained many Red Army men separated from their units and hidden in and around the villages away from the main lines of communication. With sparks and tinder in the same area, fires could be expected.

D. THE PARTISAN MOVEMENT, OCTOBER–DECEMBER 1941

Soviet plans and preparations for the establishment of a partisan movement in the Yelnya-Dorogobuzh area before and during the German advance have already been mentioned. Evidence has also been cited showing that the German mopping-up operations in the Vyazma pocket, which includes the Yelnya-Dorogobuzh area, were not a complete success. The next point of interest is the partisan situation during the remainder of 1941. Two limits can be set to this investigation. In the first place, the deep Soviet penetrations of the German front in January 1942 touch upon the area of this case study and mark the conclusion of one phase of the partisan movement. This phase, covering the last three months of 1941, therefore requires separate treatment. In the second place, it will become apparent that only a part of the partisan potential was brought into the organization at this time and that a great many of the Red Army men not rounded up by the Germans settled down in villages or hid quietly during the winter of 1941 and were not mobilized into the partisan movement until late January, February, and March 1942. This unorganized manpower, whose continued freedom was touched on above, will be considered here only insofar as it appears to have been actively partisan as early as 1941. However, Red Army stragglers who engaged periodically in raiding for food cannot always be distinguished from those units whose purposes went beyond mere survival, to attempt conscious acts intended to hurt the German Army.

There were two main kinds of partisan activity in the Yelnya-Dorogobuzh area in 1941. The first, the most important, and the least adequately documented was the organization of partisan groups from among scattered Red Army men and members of the local population. The second was attacks on German communications, raids on villages for supplies, and ambushes on small German detachments or individual vehicles.

Some evidence on the organizational efforts was presented in the preceding subsection. It would appear that the organizers were particularly successful among the former teachers.[28] Some definite form of partisan organization existed though its exact nature is not known.[29] Judging from the partisan groups whose activities came to the attention of the Germans, it

[28] 221. Sich.Div., Ic, "[Meldung] an Befehlshaber H.Geb.Mitte, Ic," 27 April 1942 (GMDS, 221 ID 22639/6, Anlage 20).
[29] 221. Sich.Div., Ic, "Kriegsgefangene Rotarmisten Archipow u. Smirnow," 27 May 1942, p. 1 (GMDS, 221 ID 22639/6, Anlage 63).

would appear that there were fairly small groups—five to fifty men—each operating more or less independently.[30] In any case, it would appear that the destruction battalions which were supposed to be organized and might have been expected to play a major role did not, in fact, operate to any noticeable extent. The detailed reports on the area immediately following the German occupation make practically no mention of the presence of these units.[31] In 1942 these battalions do not reappear. In this area, in any case, they seem to have been a failure.

Partisan activity in the Yelnya-Dorogobuzh area increased slowly during November 1941 as the German troops failed to round up all the Red Army men, while the extermination squads of the security police (*Einsatzgruppen der Sipo und SD*) failed to apprehend all the Communists and Soviet officials, and the German troops began to withdraw from the area.[32] A German security division characterized the activity of the partisans as follows:

Partisan activity consisted exclusively of raids on villages for provisions and winter clothing and of construction of winter shelters. Planned attacks on individual vehicles of the armed forces or guards of the billets did not occur. There were few instances of sabotage—interruptions of telephone communications exclusively. On the other hand, it has been established that the partisans now attempt to terrorize all Russians who collaborate with the [German] troops, e.g., members of the indigenous auxiliary police, mayors, kolkhoz chairmen. The partisans took part in actual combat only when they were attacked and could no longer avoid it.[33]

While attacks on collaborators are confirmed elsewhere,[34] the reports of the 255th Infantry Division indicate that there were some acts of sabotage and quite a few attacks on German soldiers individually or in small groups.[35]

[30] 255. Inf.Div., Ia, "Kriegstagebuch der 255. I.D., Teil VII," 8 November—8 December 1941, *passim* (GMDS, 255 ID 25337/3).

[31] This absence of references to the destruction battalions does not appear to be due to any lack of information or understanding on the part of the Germans. The records of the rear area of Fourth Army present a picture of rather careful police work, including a special effort to turn up members of the destruction battalions, but only once, in Spas Demensk, did they find anything. (GFP/Gr. 570, Sonderkommando Korueck 559, "Taetigkeitsbericht der Gruppe G.F.P. 570 Sonderkommando Korueck 559, vom 1.11.41.—8.11.41," 8 November 1941, GMDS, Korueck 13512/3.)

[32] *Ibid.;* Generalleutnant von Unruh, Korueck 559, "[Brief] an General der Infanterie von Schenckendorff," 9 November 1941 (GMDS, Korueck 13512/2).

[33] 286. Sich.Div., Ia, "Taetigkeitsbericht fuer Monat November 1941," 4 December 1941, p. 2 (GMDS, 286 ID 16182/3, Anlage 143).

[34] Befh.rueckw.H.Geb.Mitte, Ia, "10-Tagesmeldung, Stand 31.12.41," 1 January 1942, p. 3 (GMDS, HGeb 14684/4, Anlage 280); Korueck 559, Ic/AO, "Verzeichnis ueber aufgetretene Partisanenfaelle und deren Bekaempfung (Aufgenommen in der Zeit vom 9.11.—15.11.41)," 15 November 1941 (GMDS, Korueck 13512/3).

[35] Sample reports on such small incidents may be found in 475. Inf.Regt., Ia, "[Bericht] an 255. Inf.Div., Ia," 15 November 1941 (GMDS, 255 ID 25337/3, Anlage 575) and in 255. Inf.Div., Ia, "An Befh.rueckw.H.Geb.Mitte," 17 November 1941, p. 5 (GMDS, 255 ID 25337/3, Anlage 604); see also the periodic reports of the intelligence officer of Fourth Army Rear Area during the period 19 September—29 November 1941 in GMDS, Korueck 13512/3.

At the end of the year there was apparently a decline in the little partisan activity which existed; by that time, according to the Germans, the partisans had collected enough provisions for their winter quarters, to which they retired.[36]

The view of the situation in the Yelnya-Dorogobuzh area in the last months of 1941, based on the material presented here, is of a partisan movement in its infancy. There seemed to be strange rumblings in the countryside, but there was little obvious activity of consequence to the invader. The partisans neither hindered nor even affected the continued advance of the Germans, and there is no evidence to indicate an effort to activate them at that time. However, the change of tide at the front was to be felt very quickly in even the remotest village.

§II. The Soviet Breakthrough and the Organization of a Large-Scale Partisan Movement, January–March 1942

A. THE SOVIET BREAKTHROUGH AND ITS IMPLICATIONS

The German offensive on Moscow reached its zenith on 6 December 1941. The strength of the attacking German forces had been more apparent than real. Most of the divisions were "burned out" by the rapid-pace fighting over tremendous distances without adequate reserves. The result was that, once the Soviets struck back with fresh forces, the German retreat was accelerated until it became a rout, and the German lines were frequently broken as their various armies attempted to withdraw along the main lines of communication. In January and February the German retreat and the Soviet advance began to affect the area of this case study.

In the middle of January 1942, the southern pincer of a Soviet effort to surround a large part of German Army Group Center pushed into the area south of Vyazma. Supported by large drops of airborne units,[37] the IV and V Airborne Corps, the Soviets attempted to take Vyazma, to cut the Vyazma-Smolensk road and railway, and to link up with the Soviet northern pincer which had broken through the German front west of Rzhev and was heading southward. In addition to these troops, smaller units were dropped farther west between Vyazma and Dorogobuzh; their activities

[36] Befh.rueckw.H.Geb.Mitte, Ic, "Taetigkeitsbericht Ic (Dezember 1941)," 3 January 1941, p. 1 (GMDS, HGeb 14684/4).

[37] The diary of one of the men dropped in the course of this operation is to be found in PzAOK 3, Ic, "Auszugsweise Uebersetzung aus dem Tagebuch eines Fallschirmjaegers," 19 January—25 February 1942, pp. 83 ff. (GMDS, PzAOK 3, 25784/41).

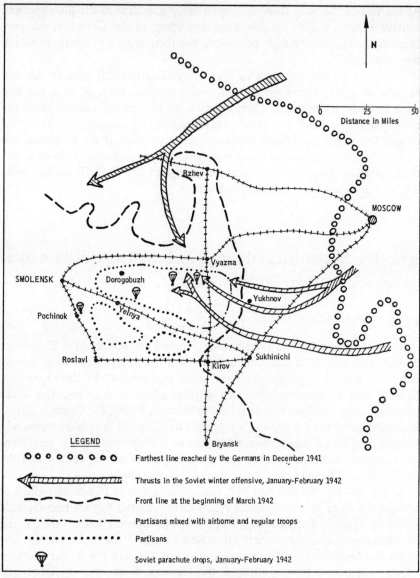

N

0   25   50
Distance in Miles

Rzhev

MOSCOW

Vyazma

SMOLENSK

Dorogobuzh

Yukhnov

Pochinok

Yelnya

Roslavl

Sukhinichi

Kirov

LEGEND

Bryansk

○○○○○○○○○ Farthest line reached by the Germans in December 1941

Thrusts in the Soviet winter offensive, January-February 1942

Front line at the beginning of March 1942

Partisans mixed with airborne and regular troops

Partisans

Soviet parachute drops, January-February 1942

Figure 6.—The front situation in the Yelnya-Dorogobuzh area, December 1941—
March 1942.

will be discussed in detail below. The Soviet thrusts are indicated in Figure 6, which may help to show, in a general way, the front situation from December 1941 to March 1942 in relation to the Yelnya-Dorogobuzh area.

In the latter part of January and during all of February the German troops fought bitterly to hold some sort of line and finally succeeded in halting the Soviet thrusts just short of their objectives. The gaps torn in the

German front by the Soviet attacks north and south of Yukhnov and between Yukhnov and Sukhinichi were closed, and those Soviet troops remaining west of the new front were cut off. These units were the Thirty-
third Army in the northeastern part of the pocket and the IV Airborne
Corps and the I Guard Cavalry Corps in the central and southern part.

The resulting tactical situation is indicated in outline on Figure 6. It
should be kept in mind, however, that except in places where a firm front is
indicated, no continuous and well-defined lines existed. In the vast area
behind the new German front which was infested with partisans, airborne
troops, and other regular Red Army troops,[38] the situation was confused,
especially to the Germans, who at first had no means of dealing with this
new pocket.[39]

The implications of these events for the attitude of the population are of
the greatest importance. The belief of the people in the superior strength
of the German Army and the imminent collapse of the Soviet government
disappeared. Whatever the wishes of the population might have been, the
expectation that the Soviet system might return sooner or later was now
abroad in the land. The Commander of the Rear Area of Fourth Army reported:

> The situation in the army rear area has undergone a basic change. The area
> might have been considered as practically pacified and free of partisans; the
> population was completely on our side—so long as we were victorious. Now the
> Russian population is no longer convinced of our strength and power. They see
> what is happening to us; and what they do not see or experience, they hear from
> the excellent Soviet net of agents.[40]

[38] After the Soviet breakthrough in January and February 1942, there were numerous units of regulars in the Yelnya-Dorogobuzh area, especially in the eastern part.
The presence of these regular units requires some clarification of the scope of this
study. As will be seen, the regular units, because of their situation behind the German
lines, tended to operate somewhat like partisans; while the partisans, who came under
the control of and frequently even joined the regular units, tended to become more
like regular troops. In this chapter, chief emphasis is given to the partisans and those
regular troops who operated most like partisans. This generally means the western
part of the pocket; in the eastern part there was a predominance of regulars, at least
at first, and a regular front soon developed. Events of general importance for an understanding of the area as a whole, or of special interest for an analysis of the partisan
movement and antipartisan warfare, will be taken up regardless of whether they concern primarily either the partisans or the regulars.
[39] The detailed accounts on which this summary of the tactical situation is based
are to be found in PzAOK 3, Ic/AO, "Feindnachrichtenblatt 'Hannover' (abgeschlossen: 18.6)," 18 June 1942 (GMDS, Korueck 27819/1); Korueck 559, Ic/AO, "Taetigkeitsbericht fuer die Zeit vom 9.2.—22.2.42," 24 February 1942 (GMDS, Korueck
29236/3, Anlage 5); 106. Inf.Div., Ic, "Gefangenenvernehmungen," 23 February 1942
(GMDS, V AK 20384/7); XXXXVI. Pz.K., Ic, "Feindnachrichtenblatt Nr. 4 (Stand
vom 10.5.1942)," 10 May 1942, p. 1 (GMDS, PzAOK 3, 25784/9, Anlage 27); V.
A.K., Ia/Ic, "Die Luftlandetruppen der Roten Armee, Teil I: Textheft," 23 March
1942, pp. 14–20 (GMDS, V AK 20384/7).
[40] Korueck 559, Qu, "Lage im rueckwaertigen Armeegebiet," 1 February 1942
(GMDS, Korueck 29236/2, Anlage 75).

And again: "The Russian population no longer believes in the strength of our armed forces. It has experienced the retreat of our troops and sees now that we are no longer masters of the situation in the rear area."[41] The effects of this were clearly stated by the same command: "In the present situation it is easier for the partisans than [it was] last summer to win adherents, to draw the hesitant over to their side, and to induce those who fear a return of the Bolsheviks to support their efforts."[42]

Although the documents are not explicit on this subject, the changed expectations of the population caused by the front situation probably had a great deal to do with Soviet success in recruiting partisans in 1942. This factor may well have been of special importance to the former Red Army men who had been in hiding through the winter. Perhaps they now began to fear a Soviet military trial for desertion if they did not answer the summons to join the partisans.

B. THE FORMATION OF A LARGE-SCALE PARTISAN MOVEMENT

In the latter part of January 1942 a headquarters was established in Dorogobuzh which directed the partisan movement in the surrounding area. At the beginning this headquarters may have been commanded by local Communist Party officials,[43] but for most of the time it was under the command of General Belov, the Commanding General of the I Guard Cavalry Corps, or an officer appointed by him.[44] Apparently on the basis of orders issued from Dorogobuzh, a great effort was made in the second half of January, in February, and in March 1942 to build up a partisan movement of great size. Although no copy of orders issued at this time has been found, there can be no question that directives went out to recruit units from among the Red Army men and the local population. The politruk of the Afanasyev Partisan Detachment said:

In February, Afanasyev, the detachment commander, presented activity and situation reports to General Belov at a conference in Dorogobuzh. He received from General Belov the order to mobilize the male population of his area and to send to Dorogobuzh those who had already served [in the Red Army], especially

---

[41] Korueck 559, Kommandant, "Bericht ueber das Partisanentum im rueckwaertigen Armeegebiet," 25 February 1942 (GMDS, Korueck 29236/2, Anlage 97).

[42] Korueck 559, Ic, "Erfahrungsbericht ueber die Partisanenbekaempfung im rueckw. Armeegebiet 559," transmitted with the intelligence activity report for 23 February—8 March 1942 (GMDS, Korueck 29236/3).

[43] XII. A.K., Ic, "Gefangenenvernehmung," 28 March 1942, p. 3 (GMDS, XII AK 21985/8, Anlage B 2).

[44] Evidence on the existence and role of the command at Dorogobuzh can be found in 221. Sich.Div., Ic, "Anlage zu Div. Befehl Ia 42/42 geh.Kdos. vom 14. April 1942; (Ic) Feindlage (Stand 14.4.42)," 14 April 1942 (GMDS, 221 ID 22639/2, Anlage 95); 221. Sich.Div., Ic, "[Meldung] an Befehlshaber Heeres-Gebiet Mitte, Ic," 13 April 1942, p. 2 (GMDS, 221 ID 22639/6, Anlage 15); 221. Sich.Div., Ic, "Vernehmung des Politruk Iwanow," 15 April 1942, p. 1 (GMDS 221 ID 22639/6, Anlage 17).

Red Army men[45] in the younger age groups. These people were to be sent there [to Dorogobuzh] with their weapons—rifles and light machine guns. From there these people were to be brought by plane to the Red Army. The airfield on which these planes land is two miles south of Dorogobuzh. Once a week a plane came and picked up 20 men. At the same time these planes bring specially trained troops, in particular those who are to occupy leading positions (commanders). Up to now [11 March 1942] no such men have joined the Afanasyev Detachment.[46]

While there is no other evidence on the subject of flying men out of this area to the Red Army, there is much very good material on the organization of partisans by parachutists, like those described in the quotation, and on the recruitment of men from among the local population and the Red Army stragglers. As will be seen, many of these were sent to Dorogobuzh for training as well as for assignment to regular units or partisan detachments.

The boost given to the organization of partisan groups by parachutists was repeatedly stressed by the Commander of the Rear Area of Fourth Army.

These militarily well-trained parts of the partisan movement are reinforced in a planned manner by parachutists who are now being dropped especially in the pacified areas, where they organize the partisan movement, give military training to the civilian population, and provide them with weapons.[47]

The partisan movement has grown tremendously in recent weeks, above all as a result of the landing of commissars and officers of the Red Army, but also because of the propaganda leaflets dropped, and not least as the result of the requisitioning of cattle, horses, and hay [by the Germans]. The commissars attempt to organize a popular mass movement (*Volksbewegung*), and it seems as if enthusiasm for entry into the partisan movement has already spread in wide circles in the country population.[48]

Even later the reports stress the same points: "In recent weeks the partisan movement attained great dimensions in the army rear area, above all because of the dropping of Soviet commissars and Red officers, because of the enemy propaganda leaflets, and not least because of a whispering and recruiting operation carried out by the enemy's intelligence network."[49]

[45] The German here reads *Kriegsgefangene*—prisoners of war—but it obviously refers to escaped prisoners of war; as in many other cases, it means those men who had actually escaped from prisoner-of-war camps as well as those Red Army men from the pockets who had escaped capture by the Germans.

[46] 221. Sich.Div., Ic, "Vernehmung des Politruk Iwanow," 15 March 1942, p. 1 (GMDS, 221 ID 22639/6, Anlage 17).

[47] Korueck 559, Ic, "Erfahrungsbericht ueber die Partisanenbekaempfung im rueckw. Armeegebiet 559," transmitted with the intelligence activity report for the period 23 February—8 March 1942 (GMDS, Korueck 29236/3).

[48] Korueck 559, Ic/AO, "Uebersicht ueber die Partisanenbewegung im rueckwaertigen Armeegebiet," 5 March 1942, p. 1 (GMDS, Korueck 29236/3).

[49] Korueck 559, Ic/AO, "Uebersicht ueber Partisanenbewegung und Bekaempfung in der Zeit vom 1.3.—15.3.42," 16 March 1942 (GMDS, Korueck 29236/2, Anlage 105); cf. Befh.rueckw. H.Geb.Mitte, Ia, "Taetigkeitsbericht fuer Monat Februar 1942," 13 March 1942, pp. 2–3 (GMDS, HGeb 24693/2, Anlage 87).

Reports on individual localities of the Yelnya-Dorogobuzh area confirm the correctness of the above descriptions. Two deserters from a partisan unit near Pavlova, south-southwest of Yelnya, stated: "The [partisan] movement was organized by Russian parachutists who first called up the Red Army stragglers in the area and later also [called up] all others capable of bearing arms."[50] A deserter from the area around Yelnya reported on two other localities near that town: "In Mutishche as well as in Fedorovka Red functionaries who parachuted and organized partisan warfare in February occupy leading positions [in the partisan detachments]."[51] A report on events in a village southwest of Dorogobuzh shows a similar picture:

This changed when Bolshevik airborne troops landed in the rear of the German army and began to re-establish the Soviet system. At first the stragglers and wounded from the battle of Vyazma who were staying in the villages were called up again, partly under coercion. Then the class of 1923 [those born in 1923] which had not been mobilized in the fall [of 1941] was called up.[52]

The following record of an organizer brought in by air is of considerable interest:

Panov was an agronomist by profession.... He had long been a Communist. When the war broke out in June 1941, he took a Russian car from Yelnya and drove with some associates to Vyazma. He did not stay there long, however, but drove to Moscow in the same car when the German troops approached. [In Moscow] he reported to the NKVD. There he received orders to keep himself ready for possible employment. Until February 1942 he stayed with his family in a small city on the Volga and was then suddenly summoned to Moscow to the NKVD. There he and other leading Communists were trained 40 to 50 days in espionage and sabotage. In the middle of March 1942 he was brought by plane with other partisan leaders to Dorogobuzh ... at the time when the Russian army of Belov had broken through there. From Dorogobuzh, Panov then received direct orders to establish partisan and sabotage groups in Yelnya Rayon. This assignment was in fact not difficult for Panov since he had lived in Yelnya Rayon since his youth and had later been a directing agronomist there. He was therefore very familiar with all local conditions. According to his own confession, Panov was successful in organizing partisan groups in several *volosts*,[53] mainly north of the Smolensk-Spas Demensk railway.[54]

[50] 221. Sich.Div., Ic, "Ueberlaeufer-Aussagen," 26 May 1942 (GMDS, 221 ID 22639/6, Anlage 57).
[51] 221. Sich.Div., Ic, "Ueberlaeufer im Jelnja-Abschnitt," 23 May 1942 (GMDS, 221 ID 22639/6, Anlage 54).
[52] XXXXVI, Pz.K., Ic, "Partisanenherrschaft im Smolensker Gebiet," 18 June 1942, p. 1 (GMDS, 23 ID 24182/16).
[53] The *volost* is an old administrative division consisting of several adjoining communes and their land.
[54] Chef Sipo u. SD, Sk, 7c, Trupp Jelnja, "Ueberholung und Ueberpruefung von verdaechtig gemeldeten Elementen in Jelnja," 5 December 1942, p. 1 (GMDS, Wi/ID 2.503, Anlage 29). Spas Demensk is on the Smolensk-Sukhinichi railway about 35 miles southeast of Yelnya.

At this time many partisan detachments were organized in accordance with orders issued by men who apparently were leaders of small partisan groups which had stayed under cover during the preceding months. Others were set up by functionaries delegated for that purpose. Some samples will illustrate this part of the organizing effort. The politruk quoted above gave the following details on the establishment of the Afanasyev detachment:

In January [1942] Afanasyev appeared as the commander of the Victory (*Pobeda*) Partisan Detachment of the Yelnya area. Ivanov [the informant] was adjutant and first politruk of this detachment.

Afanasyev is a Party member who was exempted from serving in the army as organizer of a partisan detachment. Afanasyev came from the "OO" Section[55] of the NKVD.

The two of them set up a partisan detachment in the area around Yelnya in the following manner: Red Army stragglers, who had stayed in the various villages, were examined by them and brought together in groups in the individual villages. They received a written draft call from Afanasyev, who also issued written appointments to the squad leaders. . . .[56]

A partisan who deserted to the Germans gave the following account of his mobilization from Kruglova, a collective farm northwest of Yelnya:

At the end of March 1942, 16 armed partisans from Seltso, under the command of an officer, arranged an assembly in Kruglova. The officer explained that Dorogobuzh had been taken, that Yelnya was occupied, and that soon the Red Army would also arrive here. The classes 1897–1926 [those born in the years 1897–1926] were called up. Because of fear . . . he and 20 other men reported at Glinka.[57] They were given a medical examination in Yakovlevichi.[58] Most of them were accepted and only a very small proportion released.[59]

A similar course of events was reported from Khoteyevo, a village about 12 miles southwest of Yelnya:

About five weeks ago [the last week of March 1942] 12 partisans armed with rifles and light machine guns came to the village of Khoteyevo toward evening and occupied the exits and entrances of the village. Their leader was the former village teacher from Khoteyevo, Ivan Svirkov (30 years old, married). In the beginning of January he had joined the partisans as one of the first volunteers. His assistant is Nikolai Osokin, 25–27 years old, Red Army straggler, in Khoteyevo since October 1941. Appointed by the German economic administration as agronomist for four communities in the fall of 1941, he voluntarily joined the partisans about two months ago [the end of February 1942]. The other ten partisans were supposedly Red Army stragglers.

[55] *Osobyi Otdel*, Special Section or Counterintelligence Section of the NKVD.
[56] 221. Sich.Div., Ic, "[Meldung] an Befehlshaber Heeres-Gebiet Mitte, Ic," 14 April 1942, p. 1 (GMDS, 221 ID 22639/6, Anlage 16).
[57] Glinka is a railroad station on the Smolensk-Yelnya line about 15 miles northwest of Yelnya. It was held by the partisans at this time (February–June 1942).
[58] Yakovlevichi is a village just north of Glinka.
[59] 221. Sich.Div., Ic, "Ueberlaeufer," 8 May 1942, p. 1 (GMDS, 221 ID 22639/6, Anlage 32).

V. [the informant] together with 24 other people recruited by force in Khoteyevo came to Panykova,[60] where a small partisan outpost is located. From Panykova they were taken to Vasilyeva.[61] In the same night half of the impressed recruits were sent on to Dorogobuzh. The rest of the impressed (including V.) were sent to Shcherbino[62] together with a staff. . . .

In Shcherbino they were divided [and assigned] to the various [partisan] units. . . .[63]

Another partisan deserter told of a similar incident in a village in the Shcherbino area.[64] In this case the recruits were put into the Lazo Partisan Detachment, then still in its formative stage. They were treated as prisoners at first and accepted only as full partisans after a period of time (and presumably a careful investigation).

An interesting account was given by a prisoner who, before he was taken into the partisan movement, had been working on a collective farm ten miles east of Yelnya:

About two weeks ago [middle of March 1942] the local mayor came to him and asked him to come to a building in the village. He was accompanied by an armed partisan. In the building ten men from his village, aged 16–44, collected. In the neighboring village of Novo Andreyevka they came together with 40 other men from the surrounding area. From there they went by sled to a village (Seimisha) about ten miles east of Yelnya accompanied by the mayor but not by the partisan. There they were registered by a partisan. . . . From Seimisha they were taken on foot to Dorogobuzh. . . .

In Dorogobuzh they were presented to a commission of regular officers who were wearing their insignia of rank. They were examined by a military doctor. A colonel was the highest ranking officer he saw sitting on the commission.

The medical examination resulted in his release and that of 20 others who were found unfit for military service.[65] These 21 men were sent off to their homes.[66]

Sometimes the new recruits were enrolled in partisan units stationed in the immediate surroundings of Dorogobuzh itself. "On 16 March about 30 partisans (with rifles and one light machine gun) took along three men from the village of Kulagina to Glinka. They were taken from there together with about 100 men to Dorogobuzh to the 1st Partisan Regiment

---

[60] Panykova probably refers to Pankovo, a village near Khoteyevo.

[61] Vasilyeva is a village south of Khoteyevo.

[62] Shcherbino is a village southwest of Yelnya at which a higher partisan headquarters was located.

[63] 221. Sich.Div., Ic, "[Meldung] an Befehlshaber Heeres-Gebiet Mitte, Ic," 28 April 1942, p. 1 (GMDS, 221 ID 22639/6, Anlage 22).

[64] 221. Sich.Div., Ic, "Ueberlaeuferaussagen," 7 April 1942, p. 4 (GMDS, 221 ID 22639/6, Anlage 8).

[65] The informant claimed that he had been exempted from service in the Red Army on medical grounds.

[66] 221. Sich.Div., Ic, "Gefangenenvernehmung," 29 March 1942 (GMRS, 221 ID 22639/6, Anlage 5).

which belongs to the Dedushka Division. The Division Staff is in Fedo-rovka (three miles southwest of Dorogobuzh)."[67]

Some of those recruited in the early part of 1942 were enrolled in the regular units located in the area. These units had suffered heavy casualties in the course of their offensive operations and in the German counter-attacks which had cut them off from the Red Army. They now tried to refill their ranks with new recruits from the area. Thus, one deserter from the eastern part of the Yelnya-Dorogobuzh area gave information to the Germans which they summarized as follows: "The deserter Mikhail Alexeyev, born 17 November 1919, is from Staraya Niviki and was picked up by partisans there on 2 March; in addition to him they took eight other inhabitants of Staraya Niviki. They were taken to a squadron[68] which was staying in Sapronovo and were enrolled in it. One man was shot immediately because he had made garrison caps for the Germans."[69] A prisoner told how he was drafted into the 3d Cavalry Regiment from a village about 20 miles northwest of Yelnya: "On 14 March 1942 the mayor of the collective farm . . . demanded that he and four other in-habitants of Rudlova report in Gorbovo[70] on 16 March. In Gorbovo a commissar and a doctor were present. Of the five people from Rudlova three were declared fit and two were sent home because of illness. [The three] were assigned to the 3d Cavalry Regiment."[71]

One must not assume from the foregoing that all partisans were enrolled in the movement under duress. The Germans generally liked to give this impression, and they were no doubt supported in it by the captured par-tisans, who were unlikely to confess that they had joined voluntarily.[72] It

[67] 221. Sich.Div., Ic, "Ueberlaeufer aus dem Glinka-Abschnitt," 11 May 1942, p. 1 (GMDS, 221 ID 22639/6, Anlage 38).

[68] The reference is to a part of the I Guard Cavalry Corps.

[69] 23. Inf.Div., Ic, "[Meldung] an V. A.K., Ic," 26 April 1942 (GMDS, 23 ID 24182/16).

[70] Gorbovo is a railway station on the Smolensk-Yelnya line about 20 miles north-west of Yelnya.

[71] 221. Sich.Div., Ic, "Gefangenenvernehmung," 6 May 1942 (GMDS, 221 ID 22639/6, Anlage 27).

[72] The following quotation from a German interrogation summary may be ex-amined in this connection: "Major Popenka, commander of the 1st Partisan Regi-ment, says that he had been in the Vyazma pocket and had hidden until February 1942 in a village, working as a locksmith. He was drafted by the Belov Cavalry Corps in March 1942 and entrusted with the command of the newly activated 1st Partisan Regiment." (5. Pz.Div., Ic, Gefangenen-Vernehmung," 18 June 1942, GMDS, 5 PzD 21828/2.)
It is certainly possible that Major Popenka was one of the many Soviet officers who had been in the Vyazma pocket and had disappeared is one of the villages of the area; but it is rather unlikely that Belov drafted a major who (since he had to be *drafted*) was trying to escape further service and then put him in charge of a parti-san regiment. The comment of the German interrogator that Popenka "made a very stupid impression" should perhaps be applied to the interrogator himself.

is clear, however, that a good many men joined the partisan movement voluntarily and some of them admitted as much.

The G-3 of the 64th Rifle Division, which had been smashed in the fighting around Minsk, came into the Yelnya area in December 1941 and settled in a village for the winter. The Germans reported on his interrogation as follows: "At the beginning of February 1942, on orders from Moscow, partisan groups were formed everywhere. He joined the group of Kosubsky, a former teacher. At first Zykov said he was just a Red Army straggler. But when it became known that he was a professional officer, he was appointed chief of staff of the Kosubsky detachment."[73] A man who was picked up by the Germans in Yazveno, a large village about 20 miles west of Yelnya, said that he was a tractor driver by profession and had joined the partisans voluntarily on 27 or 28 February 1942.[74] One partisan deserter claimed that he had not joined voluntarily, but that the group into which he was enrolled had been recruited on a voluntary basis.

In March 1942 a partisan group of local volunteers was set up by Mark Sinanchov in Bereskino.[75] In spite of protests, Nikonov had to join the group. It consisted of 25 men from Bereskino and was brought to Plotki, [then to] Yakovleva, and finally to Dorogobuzh by Sinanchov who was a Party member and had been a clerk in the Red Army. From there [Dorogobuzh] he [Nikonov] was given two weeks' sick leave by a medical commission.[76]

The recruiting effort described in this section was supported by Soviet appeals to the population to join and support the partisans. Sections of such appeals illustrate the kind of approach used:

To the Soviet Young Men and Women
in the Areas Occupied by the Germans

In the days of crisis in the great patriotic war in which the fate of our country is being decided, Soviet youth fight together with their fathers and brothers, set an example of the greatest patriotism, and perform marvels of courage and devotion.

Collect information concerning the strength and movements of the enemy and pass it on to the partisans and the unit of the Red Army! Support the partisans with provisions, warm clothing, and scouting activity!

Cut the telephone lines of the enemy and damage the German vehicles!

. . . .

[73] Korueck XII. A.K., Ic, "Einvernahme des Leonid Sykow," 17 December 1942, p. 1 (GMDS, XII AK 28746/9, Anlage D 8).

[74] 221. Sich.Div., Ic, "[Meldung] an Befehlshaber H.Geb.Mitte, Ic," 12 May 1942 (GMDS, 221 ID 22639/6, Anlage 39).

[75] Bereskino is a village about eight miles west of Yelnya.

[76] 221. Sich.Div., Ic, "Partisanenueberlaeufer aus der Gegend Plotki," 30 May 1942, p. 1 (GMDS, 221 ID 22639/6, Anlage 66).

The generation which is growing up is rising against the Germans. Thousands of youths are taking an active part in the fight against the Germans.

And again:

Death to the German Occupier!

The retreat of the Germans provides a welcome opportunity for a wide expansion of partisan warfare. Do not allow the Germans to settle down in the areas they have occupied. Destroy the living strength of the enemy and wreck and smash his technical [equipment].

It is necessary to destroy the German conquerors to the last man so that you may be liberated from Fascist slavery. The Red Army is beating the Germans at the front, and it is your job to hit them in the rear areas.[77]

Another leaflet reported by the Germans contained information about alleged German atrocities in the Dorogobuzh area and reported that many of the local inhabitants who had been summoned to register as prisoners of war with the Germans had instead joined the partisans.[78]

The events of January–March 1942 were summarized by the 221st Security Division in a report of 3 April 1942.

According to the information received to date, there were until the end of February a large number of villages which had not been touched by the partisans. One has the impression that, at first, weak partisan groups or nuclei of regular troops settled in the five centers named; that during the winter months they gathered Red Army stragglers, Communists, and members of the destruction battalions; and finally, reinforced and strengthened by airborne troops and supplies parachuted in, they proceeded openly to a mobilization in the Dorogo-buzh-Yelnya-Spas Demensk area.[79]

This report appears to fit the material which has been found on the Soviet effort to organize the partisan movement in the Yelnya-Dorogobuzh area on a mass basis. Parachutists, government and Party functionaries, and other local partisan leaders were able to organize substantial numbers of people into the partisan movement during the first months of 1942. Operating in an area which the Germans had not been able to clear completely of Red Army stragglers and of others actually or potentially sympathetic to the regime, the organizers enlisted recruits either as volunteers or by "tapping people on the shoulder" and reminding them of their obligations to the Soviet state. The total number recruited at this time is not known though it probably amounted to several thousand.

By the end of February 1942 the partisans and the regulars with whom they were associated controlled most of the Yelnya-Dorogobuzh area.

[77] PzAOK 4, Ic/AO, "Abwehr-Nachrichten Nr. 6," 13 March 1942, pp. 1–2 (GMDS, PzAOK 4, 22457/54).

[78] XXXXVI. Pz.K., Ic, "Partisanenherrschaft im Smolensker Gebiet," 18 June 1942, p. 4 (GMDS, 23 ID 24182/16).

[79] 221. Sich.Div., Ic, "Anlage zu Div.-Befehl Ia Nr. 243/42 geh. vom. 3.4.1942; Feindlage," 3 April 1942, p. 2 (GMDS, 221 ID 22639/2, Anlage 52).

They held Dorogobuzh and almost took Yelnya.[80] The initial German reaction to this situation will be described since it gives an interesting picture of the relative strength of partisans and Germans in this part of the rear area in the spring of 1942.

§III. The First German Efforts
to Destroy the Partisans

A. INITIAL GERMAN REACTIONS; SMALL-SCALE ANTIPARTISAN OPERATIONS; FAILURE

The war diary of the Commander of the Rear Area of Army Group Center gives a dramatic record of partisan activity in the Yelnya-Dorogobuzh area as reported to a German command.

29 Jan. 1942—Telephone call of Army Group Center, G-4, inquiring whether the Commander of the Rear Area of Army Group Center can spare any troops to combat partisans and parachutists around Yelnya. Answer is "No."

. . . .

31 Jan. 1942—In the Yelnya-Dorogobuzh area (Army Rear Area of Fourth Army and Fourth Panzer Army) the partisan movement is gaining the upper hand. Reports on ambushes and acts of violence are received almost daily; a partisan field hospital is supposed to have been set up in Yelnya.

. . . .

15 Feb. 1942—Report is received that Dorogobuzh has been evacuated in the face of superior partisan forces.[81]

. . . .

20 Feb. 1942—The G-4 of 10th Panzer Division reports. . . . The division is carrying out reconnaissance in the direction of Dorogobuzh. Results: The area east of the Dnepr is infested with well-armed partisans under unified command. The roads are heavily mined. The whole male population is being recruited and is trained in special training areas. It would appear that the partisans are constantly reinforced by airborne troops.[82]

As the situation deteriorated—from the German point of view—the first remedial efforts were made. Top priority was given to relieving the garrison at Yelnya, which was surrounded by the partisans and held only

---

[80] Befh.rueckw.H.Geb.Mitte, Ia, "10-Tagesmeldung, Stand 28.2.42," 3 March 1942, p. 2 (GMDS, HGeb 24693/2, Anlage 77); Korueck 559, Qu, "Bericht ueber die Lage in Jelnja und Umgebung," 31 March 1942 (GMDS, Korueck 29236/2, Anlage 107).

[81] A brief account of the German evacuation of Dorogobuzh in the face of superior partisan bands will be found in Bezirkslandwirt Sdf. (Z) Stratmann, "Bericht des Kreislandwirts von Dorogobusch ueber die Aufgabe der Bezirkslandwirtschaft am 15.2.1942," 23 February 1942 (GMDS, Wi/ID 2.717).

[82] Komm.Gen.d.Sich.Tr.u.Befh.i.H.Geb.Mitte, "Kriegstagebuch Nr. 2, 1.1.–30.6.42, Fuehrungsabteilung" (GMDS, HGeb 24693/1).

parts of the town. Most of the details of the German operations in the last days of February and the first weeks of March 1942 are of no interest. The following two general accounts of the events, however, throw much light on the situation at that time. The first report was prepared by the Commander of the Rear Area of Fourth Army.

Report on the Situation in Yelnya and Vicinity

Toward the end of February the situation in the Yelnya-Glinka-Baltutino area had deteriorated to such an extent—as a result of the reinforcement of the partisans, who had been fighting there for quite some time, by airborne and regular enemy troops from the Dorogobuzh area—that it seemed necessary to prevent the further advance of these enemy groups, in order to protect Smolensk.

[Fourth] Army therefore requested General von Unruh [Commander of the Rear Area of Fourth Army] to close off the area described above as soon as possible and announced that it was prepared to aid in organizing security troop units from among the service troops of units stationed in the vicinity. In spite of the very tight general situation and the lack of men fit for combat, it was possible to set up a reinforced gendarmerie company armed with mortars and heavy machine guns for an operation in this area. It was [also] possible to get the 27th Panzer Regiment, which is quartered in Pochinok, to contribute four companies of 80 men each for security tasks in the area. The airbase at Shatalovka also sent one company from the construction units with one antiaircraft gun. In the period from 28 February to 5 March 1942 this group [of security units] moved up [from Pochinok] to Baltutino; it was joined by the economic administration detachment of First Lieutenant Dr. Spann. The latter had had to evacuate Glinka and had made a fighting retreat to Strigino. The recapture of Baltutino was accomplished without heavy fighting. Only in the following days during the advance toward Glinka did serious fighting take place in which, aside from other casualties, First Lieutenant Dr. Spann lost his life. This energetic intervention of the Braukmann Group[83] succeeded in stopping the further westward advance of the enemy forces and contained them in the Yasveno-Glinka area. Combat patrols repeatedly went as far as Yelnya itself, and the Baltutino-Yelnya road was generally kept open. The partisans mixed with regular troops began the general attack on Yelnya on 13 March 1942, [which led to] the encirclement of the [German] garrison. The Commander of the Army Rear Area gave Braukmann Group orders to do everything possible to reopen the connections with Yelnya without regard to the difficult situation in Baltutino itself and in spite of the poor road conditions (the partisans were making repeated attacks with patrols on Baltutino at night and sometimes during the daytime from the northwest and north). [The orders were] to detach as many men as possible for the relief of the Yelnya garrison.

However, the patrols sent toward Yelnya were much too weak: 100 to 150 men ... to be able to make headway against the enemy who was equipped with heavy weapons. Furthermore, all the villages from Petrovo on to the east were occupied by strong enemy forces so that it seemed impossible to spend the night in houses. The heavy casualties inflicted by the enemy—a quarter of the whole combat patrol—forced the commander of the combat patrol to withdraw at night to Baltutino. . . .[84]

[83] Braukmann Group was the name of the group of security units sent to Baltutino.
[84] Korueck 559, Qu, "Bericht ueber die Lage in Jelnja und Umgebung," 31 March 1942 (GMDS, Korueck 29236/2, Anlage 107).

A report of the Commander of the Rear Area of Army Group Center records an unsuccessful attempt by his forces to retake Glinka by moving along the railway from Smolensk.

The area east of Smolensk and around Dorogobuzh is heavily infested [with partisans]. Dorogobuzh has been in enemy hands since 15 February 1942. The enemy is in control of the whole area up to the Dnepr and has already crossed the Dnepr several times with combat patrols. In the north he is moving against the arterial highway.[85]

On orders of the Commander in Chief of Army Group Center, the Bicycle Squadron 213 was sent to Glinka . . . to clear up there. It had to be withdrawn after a few days when the localities in the vicinity were occupied by partisans and encirclement was threatened.[86]

This series of small defeats emphasized to the Germans what some of them had been saying since January—that practically nothing could be done against the partisans unless larger forces were made available for antipartisan warfare. The Commander of the Rear Area of Fourth Army had pointed out this difficulty at the end of February. He not only indicated the inadequate strength of his own forces, but also recognized that inflicting heavy casualties on the partisans often had little long-range effect—a fact which the Germans appear never to have grasped fully.

Formerly, when the army area was almost pacified, I had at my disposal one and two-thirds divisions aside from the two gendarmerie detachments which were available for employment. Now, when the danger is getting greater by the day, I have only three guard battalions,[87] two gendarmerie detachments, and the service troops. . . . In spite of all preparations we suffer many disappointments because the enemy is stronger and has heavy weapons. . . .

The daily small-scale operations no longer lead to our goal. It is true that they inflict casualties on the enemy, but the enemy can always fill these gaps again. The employment of the rest of my troops—the butcher companies, parts of the prisoner-of-war guard companies, and the agricultural administration— resulted in the killing of more than 300 of the enemy last week and more than 500 the week before. These apparently relatively high casualties are nevertheless only a drop of water on a hot stone and hardly make themselves felt.[88]

A similar conclusion was reached by Fourth Panzer Army. Its counter-intelligence bulletin of 1 March 1942 states: "Combating partisan groups by quick and short employment of small units usually promises little success."[89]

[85] The reference is to the Moscow-Smolensk highway.
[86] Befh.rueckw.H.Geb.Mitte, Ia, "Taetigkeitsbericht fuer Monat Februar 1942," 13 March 1942, p. 4 (GMDS, HGeb 24693/2, Anlage 87).
[87] The reference is to *Wach-Bataillone,* units organized for guard duty and composed of very poor troops.
[88] Korueck 559, Kommandant, "Bericht ueber das Partisanentum im rueckwaertigen Armeegebiet," 25 February 1942 (GMDS, Korueck 29236/2, Anlage 97).
[89] PzAOK 4, Ic/AO, "Abwehr-Nachrichten Nr. 5," 1 March 1942, p. 2 (GMDS, PzAOK 4, 22457/54).

The obvious conclusion to be drawn from these first German efforts to deal with the partisans is that only the employment of substantial forces offered any hope of success. Such actions as setting up collection centers for information concerning partisans[90] could be of value only if the information gathered could be acted upon. This neither the Commander of the Rear Area of Fourth Army[91] nor the Commander of the Rear Area of Army Group Center[92] could do with the forces at his disposal.

B. OPERATION "MUNICH"—SUCCESS AND FAILURE

1. The Course of Operation "Munich"

The first major effort by the Germans to clear out the partisans of the Yelnya-Dorogobuzh area was started on 19 March 1942. This operation, under the code name "Munich," was part of an ambitious effort to destroy the main centers of partisan activity in the rear area of Army Group Center. After many pleas and complaints, the Commander of the Army Group Rear Area was promised more troops by the High Command of the Army and immediately began to prepare for major operations. A few words about this general effort are necessary.

At the beginning of March 1942, the serious partisan situation impelled the German High Command to take immediate steps to protect the communication lines of the German armies fighting on the central sector of the Eastern front. Orders were issued for operations against those major areas of partisan activity which appeared to be most dangerous.[93] One division (the 707th Infantry) was brought in to destroy a partisan concentration near Bobruisk in southeast Belorussia. It swept through the area in a few days, killed about 3,500 people (most of them peaceful inhabitants), and was whisked off to fight other partisan centers in the Bryansk area. The Germans soon realized that this operation ("Bamberg") was a complete failure, and the Bobruisk area continued for several

[90] Korueck 559, Ic/AO, "Errichtung von Partisanenmeldestellen im rueckw Armeegebiet des AOK 4," 10 March 1942 (GMDS, Korueck 29236/2, Anlage 103).

[91] For a report on the forces of *Korueck* 559 at this time, see Korueck 559, Qu, "Einsatzbereitschaft der dem Korueck 559 unterstellten Wach-Btle. und Feldgendarmerie-Abteilungen," 5 March 1942 (GMDS, Korueck 29236/2, Anlage 100).

[92] For a report on the forces of the *Befehlshaber des rueckwaertigen Heeres-Gebietes Mitte* at this time, see Komm.Gen.d.Sich.Tr.u.Befh.i.H.Geb.Mitte, Ia, "Antrag auf Zuweisung von Truppen zur offensiven Partisanenbekaempfung," 16 April 1942, pp. 4–7 (GMDS, HGeb 24693/3, Anlage 131).

[93] OKH/GenStdH/GenQu/OpAbt, "Nr. II 427/42 g.K.," 1 March 1942 (GMDS, HGeb 24693/2, Anlage 79); Befh.rueckw.H.Geb.Mitte, Ia, "707. I.D. und Ls.Div.," 5 March 1942 (GMDS, HGeb 24693/2, Anlage 81); Befh.rueckw.H.Geb.Mitte, Ia, "Partisanenbekaempfung," 7 March 1942 (GMDS, HGeb 24693/2, Anlage 82); Befh.rueckw.H.Geb.Mitte, Ia, 10–Tagesmeldung, Stand 9.3.1942," 10 March 1942, p. 1 (GMDS, HGeb 24693/2, Anlage 84); Befh.rueckw.H.Geb.Mitte, Ia, "Nr. 79/42 g.Kdos.," 19 March 1942 (GMDS, HGeb 24693/2, Anlage 92); H.Gr.Mitte, Ia, "Nr. 2070/42 g.Kdos.," 19 March 1942 (GMDS, HGeb 24693/2, Anlage 93).

years to be a focal point of successful partisan activity. In the typology of antipartisan warfare, the operation to clear the Bobruisk area in the spring of 1942 may serve as a model of the inhuman, stupid, and utterly futile operations which the Germans conducted at short intervals throughout the war in the Belorussian-Great Russian area.

The Yelnya-Dorogobuzh area was, as it turned out, to be handled differently. A corps group was established under the Commander of the Rear Area of Army Group Center. It was to consist of three divisions—the 221st Security and the 10th and 11th Panzer. The original plan was to drive on Yelnya from Pochinok, to relieve the German garrison at Yelnya and clear the surrounding area. Then an advance northward from Yelnya was to link up with an attack southward toward Dorogobuzh from the Smolensk-Vyazma railway. After these pincers had met, the remaining partisans in the triangle between Smolensk, Yelnya, and Dorogobuzh would, it was assumed, be easily destroyed. Because of the dangerous situation at Yelnya, all available forces were attached to the 221st Security Division, which had been assigned to reopen communications to it. Dangerous developments elsewhere forced the abandonment of the planned pincer movement, and the push on Yelnya and subsequent battles in that vicinity therefore came to be all that was carried out of Operation "Munich."[94]

Most of the tactical details of Operation "Munich" are of no special interest and will not be recounted. It seems best, however, to give a short summary (which should be read with reference to Figure 7) and to discuss in some detail the one aspect of the operation which is of general interest— the use of airpower by the Germans in support of their attack.

Because of the dangerous situation at Yelnya, task forces of the 221st Security Division were sent ahead on 25 and 26 March 1942 to relieve the German garrison. By 28 March 1942 the Pochinok-Baltutino-Yelnya road had been opened and Yelnya relieved.[95] In the following days partisan counterattacks against this road were beaten off by the Germans, but sporadic fighting on both sides of the road continued for several weeks. In the first two weeks of April the Germans attempted to clear the Yelnya environs and throughout the month of April there were skirmishes between Germans and partisans north and south of the town. Since the plan to drive north from Yelnya on Dorogobuzh had been abandoned, minor drives by the 221st Division were undertaken. At the end of April, units of the division drove north from Yelnya toward Ushakovo and northwest from Baltutino on Yasveno. These moves were

[94] Komm.Gen.d.Sich.Tr.u.Befh.i.H.Geb.Mitte, Ia, "Taetigkeitsbericht fuer Monat Maerz 1942," 13 April 1942, pp. 3–5 (GMDS, HGeb 24693/3, Anlage 126).

[95] Befh.rueckw.H.Geb.Mitte, Ia, "Unternehmen 'Muenchen,'" 28 March 1942 (GMDS, HGeb 24693/2, Anlage 102).

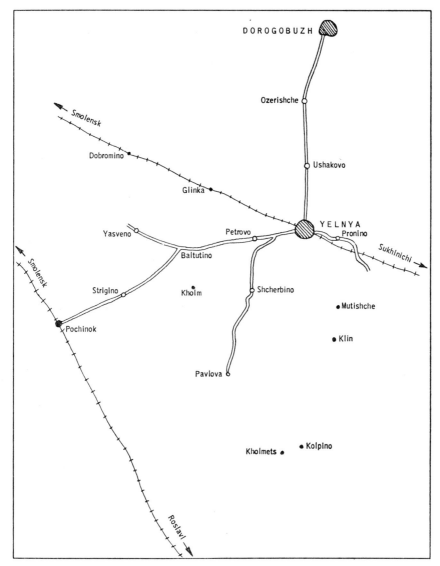

Figure 7.—The area around Yelnya.

designed to provide a springboard for the major antipartisan operation
which the Germans expected to have to conduct at a later date. Both German attacks were at least partly successful, but only after bitter fighting and
heavy casualties.[96] By this time operations were literally bogged down,

[96] Komm.Gen.d.Sich.Tr.u.Befh.i.H.Geb.Mitte, Ia, "Taetigkeitsbericht der Abt. Ia
fuer Monat April 1942," 7 May 1942 (GMDS, HGeb 24693/3, Anlage 173); 221.
Sich.Div., Ia, "Befehl fuer Unternehmen gegen Uschakowo und Jasweno," 23 April
1942 (GMDS, 221 ID 22639/2, Anlage 124); Gr. Schenckendorff, "Gruppenbefehl,"

and the 221st Division had to wait until the last part of May before undertaking further antipartisan activity.[97]

2. The Use of Airpower

In the spring of 1942 the Germans attempted the first systematic use of airpower in antipartisan warfare. On 11 March a special antipartisan squadron was established, with Bobruisk as its station. "Its assignment is antipartisan warfare, when possible in cooperation with operations of the ground forces. Since the squadron is the only one in the entire area of the army group available [for antipartisan warfare], its employment can be considered only against especially important and promising targets."[98] Procedures were established for sending requests for air support from German ground units through higher headquarters to the VIII Air Corps, which commanded the antipartisan squadron, and for sending reports on air operations back to the ground units.[99] "Munich" was one of the first operations in which planes of the antipartisan squadron participated.

Operations of German planes in support of "Munich" fell under three headings: (1) periodic attacks on partisan targets considered rewarding or of general importance, (2) support for the operation of the 221st Division to relieve Yelnya, and (3) support for the attacks of the 221st Division on Ushakovo and Yasveno.

As early as the first half of March 1942 German planes started bombing recognized centers of partisan activity. Glinka, Klin, and Mutishche were hit repeatedly at this time.[100] Verbilovo and two neighboring villages (a few miles north of Pavlova) were bombed in the middle of April "with success," according to the Germans.[101] On 24 April 1942, Pavlova, an important partisan center south of Yelnya, was bombed, again "with good results" according to the Germans.[102] The German Air Force was also called upon to help German intelligence officers keep track of partisan

27 April 1942 (GMDS, 221 ID 22639/2, Anlage 151); 221. Sich.Div. Ia, "Nr. 337/42 geheim," 30 April 1942 (GMDS, 221 ID 22639/2, Anlage 173); 221. Sich.Div., Ia, "Nr. 338/42 geheim," 1 May 1942 (GMDS, 221 ID 22639/2, Anlage 174).

[97] For the operations of the 221st Division in March and April 1942, see 221. Sich.Div., "Kriegstagebuch Nr. 4: 20. Maerz 1942–47. Juni 1942" (GMDS, 221 ID 22639/1).

[98] Befh.rueckw.H.Geb.Mitte, Ia, "Partisanenbekaempfungs-Staffel," 13 March 1942 (GMDS, HGeb 24693/2, Anlage 85).

[99] AOK 4, Ia, "Fernmuendliche Meldung an Korueck 559," 11 March 1942 (Korueck 29236/2, Anlage 104); PzAOK 4, Ic/AO (Abw. III), "Abwehr-Nachrichten Nr. 6," 13 March 1942, p. 2 (GMDS, PzAOK 4, 22457/54).

[100] Korueck 559, Ic/AO, "Uebersicht ueber Partisanenbewegung und Bekaempfung in der Zeit vom 1.3–15.3.42," 16 March 1942, p. 1 (GMDS, Korueck 29236/2. Anlage 105).

[101] Korueck 559, Ic/AO, "Auftreten von Partisanen im westl. und noerdl. Armeegebiet," 19 April 1942 (GMDS, Korueck 29236/2, Anlage 118).

[102] Ibid., 27 April 1942.

activity by conducting air reconnaissance over objectives indicated on maps transmitted to the air force.[103]

The second type of air operation in support of antipartisan warfare was connected with the German drive to relieve Yelnya. From the very beginning, air support by reconnaissance and bombing was considered essential for the success of "Munich."[104] In the crucial days at the end of March when task forces of the 221st Division were trying to open the road to Yelnya, requests for air support were sent out almost daily.

There is, unfortunately, little material which deals explicitly with the effectiveness of this German air support of antipartisan activity. However, certain tentative conclusions can be advanced. Given the weather conditions which restricted German ground forces pretty much to the few available roads, it is clear that the reconnaissance provided by the air force was of utmost importance in giving the 221st Division a better picture of the partisan situation. One must also not overlook the importance of such reconnaissance to the relatively small German forces, operating deep inside partisan-infested areas, which had to know whether and where the partisans were gathering troops for major counterattacks or flanking movements.

The effectiveness of German bombing and strafing is more difficult to analyze. Two possible results may be pointed out: actual casualties inflicted and damage to partisan morale. As for the former, the number of casualties inflicted and the damage done appear to have been rather slight and probably quite insignificant. Unless by some chance an important partisan officer was killed, the verdict—given in the first part of this section—on small antipartisan operations which inflicted casualties but did not crush the partisan bands would appear to hold. The partisans were hit at the point where they could most easily afford to be hit, with little if any effect on the general situation in the area.

One other contribution of the air force to these antipartisan operations must be mentioned. At times the isolation of German troops in the vast territories occupied but not entirely controlled made communication by plane the only means of effective coordination of operations. Thus the Commander of the Army Group Rear Area had a plane which enabled him to visit his widely scattered units and personally to supervise their operations.[105]

---

[103] Korueck 559, Ic/AO, "Partisanenauftreten im rueckw.A.Geb.559," 12 May 1942 (GMDS, Korueck 29236/2, Anlage 141).

[104] 221. Sich.Div., "Besprechungspunkte fuer die Besprechung mit Generallt. Pflugbeil, Stichwort 'Muenchen,'" 19 March 1942, p. 6 (GMDS, 221 ID 22639/2, Anlage 2). General Pflugbeil was the commander of the 221st Division.

[105] Befh.rueckw.H.Geb.Mitte, Ia, "Fernschreiben Nr. 1509 an 221. S.D.," 4 April 1942 (GMDS, 221 ID 22639/2, Anlage 58); 221. Sich.Div., Ia, "Geeignete Landungsplaetze fuer Fiesler-Storch in der Naehe des Stabsquartiers," 13 May 1942 (GMDS, 2221 ID 22639/2, Anlage 233).

Two observations should be made on the German antipartisan operations of early spring 1942 in the Yelnya-Dorogobuzh area. The ambitious plan to deal a severe blow to partisans preparatory to their final destruction failed. On the other hand the German 221st Division was able to take and hold a deep salient in territory formerly held by the partisans. The control of key positions here was valuable in subsequent fighting and enabled the Germans to collect information about the partisans and regular units which they shortly were to combat.

§IV. The Local Population Between Partisans and Germans

A. PARTISAN POLITICAL AND ADMINISTRATIVE ACTIVITY

In those parts of Smolensk Oblast which came under partisan control in 1942 the Soviet system was re-established. The organs of Soviet local government—the village soviet (*selsovet*) and the rayon administration—began to function again.[106] New local officials were appointed either by Belov or by the partisan groups in the various localities.[107] The municipal administration of Dorogobuzh was re-established.[108] An effort was made to rebuild the Komsomol in the area.[109] Furthermore, "the agricultural utilization of the area was taken in hand, the collective farms were re-established, managers were appointed, and the regular Soviet system established."[110]

The establishment of Soviet rule in partisan-controlled parts of Smolensk Oblast is described in detail in a German intelligence digest.

Furthermore, the village soviets were re-established. They were manned partly by former members and partly by people forced to do so. At the same time the mayors appointed by the German troops were shot, as were others who were

[106] 221. Sich.Div., Ic, "Beutepapiere," I May 1942 (GMDS, 221 ID 22639/6, Anlage 90); 221. Sich.Div., Ic, "Partisanen-Ueberlaeufer aus der Gegend Schtscherbino," 26 May 1942, p. 1 (GMDS, 221 ID 22639/6, Anlage 56).

[107] 23. Inf.Div., Ic, "Befehl Nr. 62," 25 May 1942 (GMDS, 23 ID 24182/16).

[108] A German list of Soviet officials reportedly in hiding after the German offensive of 24 May 1942 included a Party secretary of Dorogobuzh and his aide, a former mayor of Dorogobuzh; a commissar of the rayon military committee and his deputy; the head of the political section of the NKVD in Dorogobuzh; and the chief of the Dorogobuzh Rayon militia. (Korueck 590, Ic, "Feindnachrichten," 24 June 1942, GMDS, Korueck 27819/1.)

[109] GFP Gr. 570, "Einsatzplan der Geh.Feldpolizei Gruppe 570 fuer die Zeit vom 13.–einschl. 19.9.1942," 22 September 1942, p. 2 (GMDS, AOK 4, 24260/21).

[110] 221. Sich.Div., Ic, "Ueberlaeufer aus Raum Jerschitschi," 21 August 1942, p. 1 (GMDS, 221 ID 29380/9, Anlage 19).

known to have been in the service of the Germans. . . . Since the collective farms had been re-established in the meantime, the spring farm work was done in the collective farm manner (*kolchosweise*). . . . The household plots (*Gaerten*) were also tilled. . . .[111]

The digest then quotes from the report of one of the partisans at a meeting held under Communist Party auspices. "The partisans of our rayon have already liberated nine commune areas from the German occupiers. Now the collective farms are functioning again in this area, there are ambulances and hospitals, and the machine tractor stations [have been re-] organized."[112] The digest quotes from a letter sent to Stalin which was supposedly signed by 15,000 partisans and inhabitants of a rayon in Smolensk Oblast.

Living in an area temporarily occupied by the German barbarians, we have experienced four months of nightmare, ridicule, looting, murder, and rape at the hands of the Fascist riffraff.

It was hard to live cut off from the fatherland and to breathe the foul smell of the lying Fascist propaganda. Our hearts ached when individual traitors—traitors to the fatherland—went over to be lackeys of the Hitlerite bandits and, together with them, plundered and mistreated our people.

Now there are no more Fascist occupiers left on the soil of our rayon and a part of the neighboring rayons. Thousands of them have been destroyed; in March alone we killed 1,300 Fascist barbarians and wounded over 1,000. Simultaneously with the destruction of the Hitlerite occupiers, revenge is being taken mercilessly on the lackeys, the traitors to our fatherland.

Together with units of the Red Army, our heroic guard cavalry,[113] we are steadfastly defending our fatherland which has been liberated from the Fascists, establishing new partisan detachments in the rear of the enemy, liberating additional villages and towns from the occupier, destroying railroads and bridges, and fighting in the rear of the looting Fascist army.

In the villages and towns liberated from the German occupiers we have re-established the organs of the Soviet administration. On the collective farms we have begun the spring sowing. We know that not only weapons but also bread is needed for victory over the Hitlerite bands. . . .[114]

An account of events in the village of Preobrazhensk in the eastern part of the area illustrates these general descriptions. A certain Bolotnikov had been given a position in the forestry administration by the Germans. When the partisans and airborne troops entered the village at the end of January or the beginning of February 1942, Bolotnikov turned the seven local policemen over to the NKVD. The policemen were executed, while Bolotnikov was at first under some suspicion for his own past activities.

[111] XXXXVI. Pz.K., Ic, "Partisanenherrschaft im Smolensker Gebiet," 18 June 1942, pp. 1–2 (GMDS, 23 ID 24182/16).

[112] *Ibid.*, p. 5.

[113] The reference is to the II Guard Cavalry Corps commanded by General Belov.

[114] XXXXVI. Pz.K., Ic, "Partisanenherrschaft im Smolensker Gebiet," 18 June 1942, pp. 5–6 (GMDS, 23 ID 24182/16). Small omissions in the quotation have been filled in from *Izvestya,* 26 May 1942.

Then, however, Bolotnikov was made mayor of the village and some of the Soviet officers stayed in his house. During the period from 25 February to 24 May 1942 (probably the period when he was mayor) Bolotnikov provided supplies to the partisans and airborne troops. When the Germans attacked the area, Bolotnikov went into hiding.[115]

In the foregoing, reference is made to those who had collaborated with the Germans and were being punished by the partisans. There is some interesting material on this subject. Men who had collaborated with the Germans by serving as mayors or members of the auxiliary police (*Ordnungsdienst*) were arrested by the partisans. Several were taken to a jail in Glinka where they were interrogated.[116] From there, collaborators were taken to the prison in Dorogobuzh where they were examined further, and some of them were sentenced to prison terms. Such collaborators probably constituted a majority of the seventy Russians in the Dorogobuzh jail at the beginning of April.[117] Those collaborators not given prison sentences were either shot or made partisans. Thus a sixteen-year-old auxiliary policeman was separated from the older prisoners after his capture. "On the first day he got nothing to eat, on the second day [he was given some] bread, on the third day he was informed that he was now a partisan."[118] An interesting incident involving partisan punishment of auxiliary police who had served the Germans concerns the fate of the police of Danino, a village just south of Yelnya. The following account is based on three separate interrogations, two of former members of the Danino auxiliary police and one of another inhabitant of Danino.[119] Near the end of March 1942 the partisans attacked Danino, eventually overwhelming the local garrison which consisted only of auxiliary police. Most of its members were captured and taken away together with a few other local people, probably former Red Army men who had not joined the partisans. Of the forty or fifty persons thus arrested, six had apparently performed some police function under the Soviet regime; these men were executed

---

[115] This account is based on three interrogations grouped together in the records of the 137th Infantry Division under 137. Inf.Div., Ic, "Vernehmung des Partisanenverdaechtigen Bolotnikow Matwej," 15 September 1942 (137 ID 30245/6).

[116] 221. Sich.Div., Ic, "Vernehmungen," 31 March 1942 (GMDS, 221 ID 22639/6, Anlage 7).

[117] 221. Sich.Div., Ic, "[Meldung] an Befehlshaber H.Geb.Mitte, Ic," 27 April 1942 (GMDS, 221 ID 22639/6, Anlage 21); 221. Sich. Div., Ic, "Aussage des aus russischer Kriegsgefangenschaft entflohenen Schuetzen August Moj, 3.Zug 4./L.S.Batl.557," 27 May 1942, p. 1 (GMDS, 221 ID 22639/6, Anlage 62).

[118] 221. Sich.Div., Ic, "Aussage eines von Partisanen gefangenen und entflohenen Polizisten," 14 May 1942 (GMDS, 221 ID 22639/6, Anlage 41).

[119] 221. Sich.Div., Ic, "Ueberlaeufer suedlich Jelnja," 7 May 1942, p. 1 (GMDS, 221 ID 22639/6, Anlage 31); 221. Sich. Div., Ic, "Ueberlaeufer aus dem Suedabschnitt," 10 May 1942, p. 1 (GMDS, 221 ID 22639/6, Anlage 37); 221. Sich. Div., Ic, "Ueberlaeufer im Jelnja-Abschnitt," 23 May 1942, p. 1 (GMDS, 221 ID 22639/6, Anlage 54).

immediately. Thirty-five were taken to a neighboring village where they were interrogated by a high-ranking officer and a commissar. They were then lined up; the first nineteen were shot; the other sixteen were separated into small groups which were distributed among the partisan companies in the area. There they were kept under careful guard for a short time and later were formally enrolled in the partisan movement.

The above evidence, especially the incident concerning the Danino auxiliary police, tends to support a hypothesis on the subject of partisan treatment of collaborators, a hypothesis which requires examination in the light of additional sources. Unlike the Germans, who often relied on indiscriminate mass terror (which usually meant that most of those punished were nonpartisans while most of the partisans went unharmed, thereby putting a premium on resistance activity), the partisans, at least in areas in which they were sufficiently secure to feel they had time, tended to single out for punishment those who in fact had worked with the Germans. There is not a single report of partisan punishment of a noncollaborator for collaboration in this area. Those who had collaborated, however, were punished either by execution or by being forced into the partisan movement against their will; both types of punishment were designed to strengthen the partisan movement by putting a premium on noncollaboration. In following this course, the partisans were apparently willing to stake the chance that some of the former collaborators might later return to the Germans (which in fact some of them did) against the assumption that many would become good partisans and that the fate of those executed would serve as a deterrent to desertion.

During the period when the partisans occupied much of Smolensk Oblast, they inducted the local population into their service in two ways. In the first place, in a number of localities in the area the partisans appear to have tried to create a sort of auxiliary partisan movement in the form of a home guard (*Einwohner-Wehr*).[120] Secondly, labor battalions consisting of local inhabitants were supposedly organized for special support operations such as the building of boats on the Dnepr at Dorogobuzh.[121] The scanty character of the sources dealing with these topics suggests the necessity for examining such programs in other areas of partisan activity.

B. THE "BANDITS"

One facet of the problem of direction and control is that of the partisans who escaped from Soviet control without going over to the Germans. In an area of large-scale partisan activity, like the Yelnya-Dorogobuzh area,

[120] 221. Sich.Div., Ic, "Partisanen-Ueberlaeufer aus der Gegend Schtscherbino," 26 May 1942) GMDS, 221 ID 22639/6, Anlage 56).
[121] 221. Sich.Div., Ic, "Ueberlaeufer aus dem Glinka-Abschnitt," 11 May 1942 (GMDS, 221 ID 22639/6, Anlage 38).

partisan deserters or former Red Army men who did not want to join the partisans could hide in a village or in the woods only with the greatest difficulty. They could go to the Germans, but many either did not want to do this, or were afraid of what the Germans would do to them. From the little evidence available, it would appear that some of these men tried to get together in small groups which subsisted by requisitioning from the peasants and tried to evade contact with both the Germans and the partisans, fighting against both when necessary. These men were called "bandits" by the partisans. One partisan deserter reported: "It happens almost every day that a few [partisans] desert and flee into the woods. They are then pursued and called 'bandits' by the real partisans. Frequently there are battles between the partisans and the 'bandits.' "[122] Another partisan deserter interrogated at the same time by the Germans gave practically the same report.[123] One possible source of new members for these "bandit" groups was men who had deserted from a partisan unit, but who at the last minute became too frightened to go to the Germans. They had burned their bridges behind them but were afraid to cross the one which led to the Germans.[124] In any case, a group of documents captured from a partisan detachment which operated somewhat north of the Yelnya-Dorogobuzh area indicate that in the general region of Smolensk there were quite a number of these "bandit" groups which were not under Soviet control.

C. THE ATTITUDE OF THE LOCAL POPULATION

The effort to define precisely the attitudes of the population of the Yelnya-Dorogobuzh area toward the partisans and the Germans is hampered by a lack of specific information. No Soviet reports on this subject have been found. The Germans were only on the fringes of the area and knew little of what was going on during the period of partisan occupation. Most persons interrogated by the Germans were deserters who tended to say what they thought the interrogator wanted to hear. German preconceptions about the "racial characteristics" of the Russian people sometimes produced obvious befogging, sometimes imperceptible slanting, in their reports. It may be best to present the available bits of evidence and then advance a hypothesis which might bring these pieces together.

Some evidence on the attitude of the population has already been presented, either explicitly or implictly. The fact that so many Red Army stragglers were able to hide out and subsist in the villages during the

[122] 221. Sich.Div., Ic, "Ueberlaeufer aus dem Glinka-Abschnitt," 10 May 1942, p. 2 (GMDS, 221 ID 22639/6, Anlage 37).

[123] *Ibid.*

[124] See, for example, the report on the two other partisans who had intended to go over to the Germans with the man whose interrogation is recorded in 221. Sich. Div., Ic, "Ueberlaeufer-Aussagen," 9 June 1942 (GMDS, 221 ID 22639/6, Anlage 73).

winter would indicate a willingness on the part of the population to help these men, probably as individuals in trouble, rather than as representatives of the Soviet regime. The failure of the Germans to achieve victory in 1941 and the successes of the Red Army in the winter of 1941–42 profoundly affected popular attitudes, replacing the previous confidence in Germany victory with the expectation of the Soviet government's return to the area. [See above, Sect. II, A.] The reports on the composition and morale of the partisan movement in the area showed that the local recruits formed a relatively small proportion and that their morale tended to be poor. This may reflect a negative or at least reserved attitude of the local population toward the partisans and the Soviet regime.

The inability of the Germans to deal effectively with the partisan menace at the beginning of 1942 was believed by the Commander of Army Rear Area Center to have had repercussions on the attitude of the population. His report states: "The confidence of the population in the strength of the German Army is declining as it gets the impression that we are not subduing the partisans. It is therefore more inclined to support or even to join the partisans."[125] On the other hand, another report states: "A fact of importance to us while fighting the partisans is that the majority of the population, especially in the rural areas, is by no means inclined favorably to the partisans."[126] A later report of the Commander of Army Group Rear Area Center draws the following picture:

Attitude of the Civilian Population:
Now, as earlier, it can be stated that the population as a whole is not inclined to be hostile [to us]. The successes of the winter offensive which were announced by Stalin have not materialized, and with this the confidence of the population in the German armed forces has returned. The issuing of the agrarian order[127] and the celebration of the Easter holidays have lifted the morale of the population. Now, as earlier, large segments cooperate in antipartisan warfare. At the same time things are really hard for the peasant. The [German] armed forces take his last horse and often his last cow, while the partisans also take everything from him. Of what use is the agrarian reform to the farmer if he has no horse to help till the land?

[125] Komm.Gen.D.Sich.Tr.u.Befh.i.H.Geb.Mitte, Ia, "Antrag auf Zuweisung von Truppen zur offensiven Partisanenbekaempfung," 16 April 1942, p. 4 (GMDS, HGeb 25693/3, Anlage 131).
[126] Korueck 559, Ic, "Erfahrungsbericht ueber die Partisanenbekaempfung im rueckw. Armeegebiet 559," transmitted with the intelligence activity report for 23 February–8 March 1942, p. 2 (GMDS, Korueck 29236/3).
[127] In the middle of February 1942 the Germans issued a decree which provided for certain changes in the agrarian system. This order was designed to meet peasant objections to the collective farm system which the Germans had retained because they thought it would aid their plans of exploiting the population. The changes made were more nominal than real; private farms—the chief desire of the peasants—were not provided for in the new system, which consisted mainly of changing the name from "collective farms" to "communal farms." Though the household plots were enlarged slightly, the peasants were soon disillusioned with this "reform."

The population in the areas dominated by the partisans of course does not dare show sympathy for the Germans. It is completely terrorized by the partisans.[128]

A German intelligence digest on events in the partisan-occupied areas of Smolensk Oblast includes the following summary of popular attitudes: "The advancing German troops[129] were generally looked upon as liberators and the partisans were cursed. The ruthless conscription measures and the executions of deserters[130] were considered especially harsh. In a few localities the population aided in tracking down partisans in hiding."[131]

Though of a somewhat later date, the report of the Commander of the Rear Area of Third Panzer Army concerning popular attitudes during August 1942 is of considerable interest. By that time the Yelnya-Dorogobuzh area (the northern part of which is covered by his report) had been largely cleared of partisan groups.

The progress in the pacification of the country is mirrored in the attitudes of the population. Rumors concerning Soviet successes at the outset of the fighting around Rzhev[132] caused apprehensions, especially among those segments of the population who work for the German armed forces in administrative or other positions. . . . When the German successes in the Caucasus became known[133] and the conviction took hold that the German defensive front [134] would hold up against all attacks, the rumors died down. The situation is similar in areas in which partisans repeatedly appear. The population there is frightened and subdued. Aside from a few individual instances in which a certain segment of the population not only sympathizes with the partisans and provides them with shelter but also supports the whole Soviet system and aids the [partisans'] efforts, one must recognize that the great majority of the population is gaining confidence in the German armed forces and is willing to aid in the pacification of the occupied territories. The number of cases in which warnings (which can be followed up with good results) are given of partisans and anti-German elements is increasing. This fact rates especially high because the difficult food situation is having repercussions on the morale of the population. There is the danger that the partisan movement will show a great increase if the food supplies needed by the population are not assured.[135]

[128] Komm.Gen.d.Sich.Tr.u.Befh.i.H.Geb.Mitte, Ia, "Taetigkeitsbericht der Abt. Ia fuer Monat April 1942," 7 May 1942, pp. 2–3 (GMDS, HGeb 24693/3, Anlage 173).
[129] This refers to the German offensive against the partisans in the Yelnya-Dorogobuzh area which began on 24 May 1942.
[130] Presumably this is a reference to the fact that a large proportion of the deserters were local people who had been forcibly recruited into the partisan movement.
[131] XXXXVI. Pz.K., Ic, "Partisanenherrschaft im Smolensker Gebiet," 18 June 1942, p. 3 (GMDS, 23 ID 24182/16).
[132] In the summer of 1942, Soviet forces attacked the forces of Army Group Center in the Rzhev area.
[133] In the summer of 1942 the German offensive on the southern part of the front crossed the lower Don and advanced into the Kuban area and the northern Caucasus.
[134] The reference is presumably to the front of Army Group Center, which was exposed to continual Soviet attacks starting in late July 1942 and lacked reserves for major counterattacks.
[135] Korueck 590, Ia, "Monatsbericht, Monat August 1942," p. 1 (GMDS, Korueck 27819/2, Anlage 38).

Two partially contradictory characteristics of popular attitudes emerge from this material. There is on the one hand a distaste for the Soviet regime which persistently manifests itself in a variety of ways. There is, on the other hand, a constant tendency to adjust to the desires of the side, German or Soviet, which happens to be more powerful at any given time or appears to be winning. Large segments of the population had welcomed the Germans. When the Germans suffered setbacks in the winter, they found that "the population was completely on our side, as long as we were victorious." When the operations of May and June 1942 ended partisan control of the Yelnya-Dorogobuzh area, the Germans found the population again with them.

This apparent contradiction might be resolved by differentiating between the latent sentiments and the overt actions of the population. The predominantly rural population of this area was perhaps generally inclined to be dissatisfied with the Soviet regime. At the same time, the people tried to adjust their overt behavior to the exigencies of the moment—not unlike the shift in "convictions" of Communist Party members with each change of the Party line. To explain this tendency of the population one need not resort to those metaphysical speculations about the Slavic "soul" or the "racial characteristics" of the Russians which the Germans used to justify their policies. There may be a simpler explanation. Perhaps these people—mostly peasants eking a bare subsistence out of a poor soil—were chiefly concerned with surviving under whichever regime came out on top. (It should be borne in mind, however, that this explanation applies to approximately the first year of the war in the East. As the population became more clearly aware of the real German aims, their frustration increased, while the difficulty of adjusting to the power situation decreased. On the one hand it became clear that neither side offered what the people wanted; on the other hand, the similarity of the contending powers meant that the shifting of allegiance brought less inner conflict with latent sentiments.)

§V. The Partisan Movement, June 1942–September 1943

A. THE GERMAN OFFENSIVE

1. Plan and Practice

The rapid formation of a large partisan movement at the beginning of 1942, the failure of the first German efforts to destroy this movement, and the consequent consolidation of a large partisan-controlled area immediately to the rear of the German central front led the Germans to make plans for Operation "Hanover" to crush this threat to their forces. It was to become the largest antipartisan operation of the war in the East. The very success of the partisans for once forced the Germans to take really drastic action.

The German plan in broad outline was as follows: Under the over-all command of Fourth Army, two corps were to attack the eastern portion of the partisan-held area, one (the XLVI Panzer Corps) from the north and east, the other (the XLIII Corps) from the south and southeast. After clearing the eastern part of the area and thus opening the northern section of the Vyazma-Bryansk railway, these units were to advance westward while other units already in action there would maintain a cordon around the western part of the partisan-held area. It was hoped that in this way all Soviet units in the area would be completely destroyed.

Figure 8 may help explain the German plan. The XLVI Panzer Corps was to attack with one panzer (the 5th) and two infantry (23d and 197th)

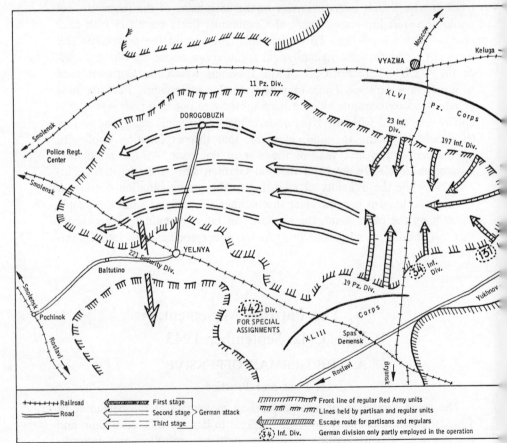

Figure 8.—The German offensive, 24 May 1942.

divisions; the XLIII Corps also was to attack with one panzer (19th) and parts of two infantry (34th and 131st) divisions; and other units (11th Panzer Division, Police Regiment Center,[136] 221st Security Division, parts of 442d Division for Special Assignments[137]) were expected to keep the Soviet units from escaping destruction. There were also plans to use a special collaborator unit to capture General Belov's staff and to give air support to the German advance.[138]

It is practically impossible to estimate the actual strength of this imposing array of German divisions. All the units were under strength and some of them were in fact only remnants of battle-worn divisions. A guess at the total number of forces engaged in the operation would range between 30,000 and 45,000. Under the circumstances then prevailing among German forces in the East, this represented a considerable effort. Interesting in comparison with the above figures is the German estimate that Soviet units in the area numbered just under 20,000.

In practice, the German operation pretty much ran according to plan. The starting date was 24 May, and by 30 May the eastern part of the area had been fairly well cleared. The German units then re-formed for the advance westward.[139] In the first two weeks of June the German units moved through the western part of the partisan-held area,[140] and in the third week of June minor operations were carried out to hunt down remnants of the Soviet units.[141] In fact, however, a substantial portion of

---

[136] A regiment consisting of men from the German uniformed police (*Ordnungspolizei*) under the command of the Higher SS and Police Commander for Army Group Area Center (*Hoeherer SS- und Polizeifuehrer Russland Mitte und Weissruthenien*).

[137] A combination of a divisional staff experienced in antipartisan warfare with a miscellaneous conglomeration of under-strength and second-rate units which was at this time charged with the security of the rear area of Fourth Army.

[138] The above summary is based on the following: H.Gr.Mitte, Ia. "Heeresgruppenbefehl fuer die Unternehmung 'Hannover,'" 10 May 1942 (GMDS, AOK 4, 24336/24, Anlage 29); AOK 4, Ia, "Befehl fuer Bereitstellung und Angriff zum Unternehmen 'Hannover,'" 10 May 1942 (GMDS, XLIII AK 31644/21, Anlage 43); XXXXVI. Pz.K., Ia, "Befehl fuer das Unternehmen 'Hannover,'" 10 May 1942 (GMDS, PzAOK 3, 25784/9, Anlage 27); 23.Inf.Div., "23. Inf.Div.im Unternehmen 'Hannover,'" Kartenanlage in "3 Jahre Einsatz der 23.Inf.-Div." (GMDS, 23 ID 77624). The role of a number of small German units in the operation has been ignored.

[139] AOK 4, Ia, "Fernschreiben an Gen.Kdo. XII. u. XXXXIII. A.K.," 30 May 1942 (GMDS, XLIII AK 31644/21, Anlage 195); AOK 4, Ia, "Bericht ueber Unternehmung 'Hannover' 1. Abschnitt, 24.5–31.5.," 1 June 1942 (GMDS, AOK 4, 24336/24, Anlage 72); Gr.Schenckendorff, Ia, "Gruppenbefehl," 2 June 1942 (GMDS, 221 ID 22639/2, Anlage 280b).

[140] 221. Sich.Div., Ia, "Nr. 462/42 geh.," 7 June 1942 (GMDS, 221 ID 22639/2, Anlage 292); AOK 4, Ia, "Nr. 1427/42 geh., Fernschreiben an XXXXIII. A.K.," 8 June 1942 (GMDS, XLIII AK 31644/22, Anlage 80); Komm.Gen.d.Sich.Tr.u.Befh. i.H.Geb.Mitte, Ia, "Korpsbefehl Nr. 106," 14 June 1942 (GMDS, 221 ID 22639/2, Anlage 349).

[141] See, for example, 5. Pz.Div., Ia, "Divisionsbefehl fuer die Bereitstellung zum

the Soviet units managed to escape southward. This escape as well as the casualties suffered by both sides in Operation "Hannover" will be discussed below.[142]

2. The Graukopf Organization
(Experimental Organization Osintorf, Experimental Organization Center)

At the end of 1941, German Armed Forces Intelligence and Counter-intelligence (*Abwehr*) initiated the formation of a special unit of Russian nationals at Osintorf, northeast of Orsha. It consisted of former prisoners of war, was commanded by an *émigré,* Colonel Sakharov, and went under a variety of names, among them *Graukopf-Verband, Versuchsverband Osintorf, Versuchsverband Mitte, Sonderverband,* and others. It will be referred to here as the Graukopf Organization. The unit was outfitted in captured Soviet uniforms and originally was supposed to engage in diversionist activities behind the Soviet lines. It was the first combat unit of Russian nationals set up by the Germans and officered by Russians. Its history is of major interest in the over-all picture of Soviet defection in World War II.[143] For the purposes of this chapter only its early use in combat can be reviewed.

At the time of its first employment, the Graukopf Organization numbered between 350 and 400 men.[144] Its basic assignment was to penetrate the partisan-held sector of the Yelnya-Dorogobuzh area and destroy General Belov and his staff.[145] The organization was to pass through the front not far from Spas Demensk, seize General Belov's headquarters, use Belov's communications center to issue orders to the Soviet units under his command, and spread propaganda among the Soviet troops.[146] Exact details of the proposed use of this organization were given orally to the XLIII Corps which commanded the attack against the southern side of

---

Unternehmen 'Junikaefer,' " 16 June 1942 (GMDS, 5 PzD 21578/4, Anlage 136); AOK 4, Ia, 'Befehl fuer die Saeuberung des rueckw. Gebietes suedlich der Rollbahn," 19 June 1942 (GMDS, LVI AK 35738/4).

[142] A brief discussion of the "Hannover" operation together with some erroneous deductions about its effects may be found in Kurt von Tippelskirch, *Geschichte des Zweiten Weltkriegs* (Bonn: Athenaeum Verlag, 1951), p. 292.

[143] Information on this organization can be found in George Fischer, *Soviet Opposition to Stalin* (Cambridge: Harvard University Press, 1952), pp. 43, 100, 210; and Peter Kleist, *Zwischen Hitler und Stalin, 1939–1945* (Bonn: Athenaeum Verlag, 1950), p. 200.

[144] Compare AOK 4, Ia, "Nr. 1163/42 gKdos., Fernschreiben an XXXXIII. A.K.," 7 May 1942 (GMDS, XLIII AK 31644/21, Anlage 13) and V.O. Abw.II z.H.Gr.Mitte, "Graukopf, 2. Bericht," 27 May 1942, p. 2 (GMDS, XLIII AK 31644/21, Anlage 170).

[145] H.Gr.Mitte, Ia, "Heeresgruppenbefehl fuer die Unternehmung 'Hannover,' " 10 May 1942, p. 3 (GMDS, AOK 4, 24336/24, Anlage 29).

[146] V.O. Abw.II z.H.Gr.Mitte, "Nr. 100a/42 gKdos, Bericht," 11 May 1942 (GMDS, AOK 4, 24336/24, Anlage 37). The contradictory nature of the last two assignments given to the organization was apparently not recognized by the Germans.

the partisan-held area.[147] Prior to the attack, German troops were to be informed of the existence of a collaborator unit wearing Russian uniforms; special symbols were used to avoid confusion on the German side.[148]

The Graukopf Organization was committed on the night before the German attack of 24 May. The Soviets, however, had learned of the plan in spite of German efforts to maintain secrecy. Two Soviet officers who deserted on 24 May told their interrogator that they knew of a "special organization which is supposed to consist of White Guardists and is to operate behind their own [Soviet] lines."[149] According to the captured intelligence officer of the 214th Airborne Brigade, the Soviets had been tipped off by a deserter from the Graukopf Organization the day before the German attack.[150]

A good picture of the experiences of the Graukopf Organization in "Hannover" is included in a top secret report containing comments of the commanding general of the XLIII Corps.

The commanding general declared in a conference on 26 May [1942] that the experimental Graukopf Organization had attained successes of great value for Operation "Hannover" in spite of failing to attain the ambitious goal [of] destroying Belov's staff.

He pointed out that even the appearance of a White Guardist detachment behind the Red lines must have caused confusion, [at first] because the Reds did not know where the organization came from and how it had passed through the front; later because telephone wires had been cut, commissars and politruks had been killed, several hundred men had been captured, and captured enemy weapons had been destroyed; [and finally] by [its] participation in several engagements with [enemy] detachments which had been quickly summoned by radio or telephone and which suffered heavy casualties, practically causing a panic.

Because the enemy did everything to get the [members of] the organization into his hands dead or alive (statement of a captured Red telephone operator who overheard the communications of [Belov's] staff to the units), he [the enemy] had to withdraw from the front, and perhaps also from his reserves, detachments which may be estimated at about 1,000 men (statements by prisoners of war and observation of the officers of the [Graukopf] Organization after conversation with the commanders of the Red detachments themselves). Thus his powers of resistance were weakened, something which apparently contributed to the capture of Platonovka (24 May) and also to a more rapid advance by the [regular] troops. In their confusion the Reds were finally shooting at each other (statements by prisoners of war). . . . Commissars and poli-

[147] AOK 4, Ia, "Befehl fuer Bereitstellung und Angriff zum Unternehmen 'Hannover,'" 10 May 1942, p. 1 (GMDS, XLIII AK 31644/21, Anlage 43).

[148] XXXXVI. Pz.K., Ic, "Feindnachrichtenblatt Nr. 5, Ergaenzung zu Feindnachrichtenblatt Nr. 4 vom 10.5.42," 12 May 1942, p. 2 (GMDS, 23 ID 24182/16); 23. Inf.Div., Ic, "Feindnachrichten," 17 May 1942 (GMDS, 23 ID 24182/16). ,

[149] XXXXIII. A.K., "Tagesuebersicht fuer den 24.5.1942," 24 May 1942, p. 2 (GMDS, XLIII AK 31644/33, Anlage 1).

[150] 131. Inf.Div., Ic, "Gefangenenvernehmung," 10 June 1942 (GMDS, 131 ID 22120/2, Anlage 142).

truks had allowed themselves to be duped and misled into giving up their weapons along with their men. . . .

One must not overlook the fact that the [Graukopf] Organization [moved] through unfamiliar territory which turned out to be heavily fortified and [also] ran into elite units. . . .

. . . Continuous contact with the enemy also led to high casualties in the [Graukopf] Organization (of 350 men only about 100 have returned so far). . .[151]

This description is supplemented by other documents which mention the employment of the Graukopf Organization. Fourth Army's report on the first stage of Operation "Hannover" stresses the confusion produced in Soviet ranks by Graukopf.[152] The organization also provided the Germans with some useful intelligence on the disposition of Soviet units.[153]

Soviet reaction to the employment of this organization was approximately as indicated in the report quoted above. Captured members of the organization were apparently not shot immediately. Thus one group of twelve was able to escape after capture.[154] A captured supply officer of the IV Airborne Corps stated that the Shabo Partisan Regiment and other units of the IV Corps had captured twenty men of the Graukopf Organization; ten of these had been flown to Moscow and the other ten had stayed with the corps staff.[155] Especially interesting is an entry for 1 June 1942 in a Russian officer's diary which was found by the Germans.

. . . It begins with 23 May. . . . In the area of our corps the presence of a diversionist group employed by the Germans was ascertained. It consisted of [former] prisoners of war who are equipped with our uniforms and weapons. The command of this group was in the hands of White Guardist émigrés—a lieutenant colonel,[156] a major,[157] and others. This group constitutes a great danger; the fight against such diversionists is very complicated and mistakes can easily be made. However, it was soon possible to scatter and partially destroy the group. As has been confirmed, the group was assigned to find Belov's staff and complete its bloody work [there]. We are still amazed by the trickery of the Germans.[158]

[151] V.O.Abw.II z.H.Gr.Mitte, "Graukopf, 2 Bericht," 27 May 1942 (GMDS, XLIII AK 31644/22, Anlage 170).

[152] AOK 4, Ia, "Bericht ueber Unternehmung 'Hannover' 1. Abschnitt 24.5.–31.5." 1 June 1942 (GMDS, AOK 4, 24336/24, Anlage 72).

[153] XXXXIII. A.K., "Tagesuebersicht vom 28.5.42," 28 May 1942 (GMDS, XLIII AK 31644/33, Anlage 25).

[154] XXXXIII. A.K., "Tagesuebersicht fuer den 31.5.42," 31 May 1942 (GMDS, XLIII AK 31644/33, Anlage 30). For a report on five members of the organization who were shot after capture, however, see 331. Inf.Div., Ic, "Im Ruecken des Feindes, Uebersetzung des erbeuteten Tagebuches des Angehoerigen der Roten Armee Jewtuschenko," 31 May 1942, p. 4 (GMDS, 331 ID 31476/11).

[155] 131. Inf.Div., Ic, "Gefangenenvernehmungen," 6 May 1942, p. 3 (GMDS, 131 ID 22120/2, Anlage 138).

[156] Probably Colonel Sakharov.

[157] Probably Major Bocharov.

[158] XXXXIII. A.K., Ic, "Auszugsweise Uebersetzung aus dem Tagebuch eines russ. Offiziers," 14 June 1942 (GMDS, XLIII AK 31644/33, Anlage 68).

The Graukopf Organization in Operation "Hannover" did not accomplish what the Germans had hoped for—the destruction of General Belov and his staff—but it was nevertheless of considerable value. German experience proved that the confusion which can be created by a unit like this—and which in fact was created—can be of great importance if immediate advantage is taken of it.[159]

3. Air Support for Operation "Hannover"

Air support was considered essential for the success of the German operation against the partisans and regulars in the Yelnya-Dorogobuzh area. Air reconnaissance was important in an attack on an area wholly under Soviet control. The fact that the German units were inadequately equipped with artillery led to the assumption that the main nests of enemy resistance could be stormed only immediately following attacks by bombers and dive bombers.[160] Air reconnaissance for the operation was conducted on a large scale before and after the attack. Long-range reconnaissance was to determine whether reinforcements were being brought to the main line of resistance at the points to be attacked. Short-range reconnaissance was to be carried out in part by a squadron of planes whose services could be requested through the air force liaison officer at Fourth Army and in part through the one reconnaissance plane placed at the disposal of the two corps conducting the operation. Identification symbols to be used by the German ground troops were specified in advance, and message drop-areas were agreed upon.[161]

These plans were apparently carried out. Although the relevant German Air Force records—if any—are not available, the report of Fourth Army on the first phase of "Hannover" indicates the usefulness of air support. "Immediately following the period of bad weather the Air Force could be employed with good results against individual, tenaciously defended localities and for battering surrounded enemy groups."[162] The same report mentions that the German Air Force dropped leaflets in an experimental attempt to induce political officers to surrender.

The only difficulty which appears to have been encountered by the Germans in providing air support for the operation consisted of inadequate marking of the advancing German front line. In spite of constant regulation

---

[159] The 5th Panzer Division employed a small group of collaborators, the von Renteln Volunteer Company, who were also dressed in Russian uniforms, in the "Hannover" operation. The unit was quite successful, to judge by the experience report prepared by the intelligence officer of the division.

[160] XXXXVI. Pz.K., Ia, "Befehl fuer das Unternehmen 'Hannover,'" 10 May 1942, p. 4 (GMDS, PzAOK 3, 25784/9, Anlage 27).

[161] AOK 4, Flivo/Ic/Ia, "Fernschreiben Nr. 1294/42 geh. an Gen.Kdo. XII., XXXXIII., XXXXVI., LVI., A.K., 1. Flg.Division," 23 May 1942 (GMDS, AOK 4, 24336/24, Anlage 46).

[162] AOK 4, Ia, "Bericht ueber Unternehmung 'Hannover' 1. Abschnitt 24.5.–31.5.," 1 June 1942, p. 2 (GMDS, AOK 4, 24336/24, Anlage 72).

of recognition symbols,[163] the Air Force complained about the failure of ground units to mark their positions with sufficient care. The complaint stressed the following: "This is especially true for rapidly advancing attack operations in which the current location of the front line is not transmitted with the required speed and accuracy to the combat formations about to take off, or where upon arrival at the target, [the location transmitted] may no longer be accurate *(ueberholt sein kann)*."[164]

B. PARTISAN REACTIONS TO THE GERMAN OFFENSIVE

1. Fight[165]

As can be seen from the above sketch of Operation "Hannover," the German advance proceeded with rapidity and largely according to plan. This does not mean, however, that the partisans and Soviet regulars did not put up a fight. In describing the action, all the German reports stress the same point: the Soviets resisted bitterly at first, but after initial resistance was broken, their units collapsed extremely rapidly. Thus the German division which attacked the sector of the Soviet front held by the Shabo Partisan Regiment reported that the regiment defended itself tenaciously in the fortified positions it had built but was unable to conduct defense in depth.[166] The same thing happened when Belov moved other units, both regular and partisan, to face the advancing Germans.[167] The 1st Partisan Regiment was similarly broken up.[168] The report of Fourth Army on the first phase of "Hannover" stresses that, while the Soviet forces resisted bitterly at a few points, in general the regular and partisan

[163] XXXXVI. Pz.K., Ia, "Befehl fuer das Unternehmen 'Hannover,'" 10 May 1942, p. 4 (GMDS, PzAOK 3, 25784/9, Anlage 27); XXXXIII. A.K., "[Funkspruch] an Flivo," 10 June 1942 (GMDS, 221 ID 22639/2, Anlage 322).

[164] Lw.Kdo.Ost, Fuehr.Abt., Ia Op., "Fernschreiben Nr. 1143/42 geh. an Bef.H.Geb.Mitte," 10 June 1942 (GMDS, 221 ID 22639/2, Anlage 344).

[165] The arbitrary division of this subsection must not be taken to mean that certain partisans or partisan units fought, others hid, and still others fled. One partisan unit might fight, then flee, try to hide, and finally be forced to fight again. Since it is neither possible nor even important to trace the day-to-day fate of each partisan unit in the area, the topical approach is probably the best way of analyzing partisan actions in the face of the German offensive.

[166] 23. Inf.Div., Ic, "Feindfeststellungen," 8 June 1942, p. 1 (GMDS, 23 ID 24182/16).

[167] *Ibid.*, pp. 2–3. Some details of Belov's troop dispositions in the face of the German advance may be found in two Soviet documents captured by the Germans, a tactical order of Belov of 1 June 1942 in XXXXIII. A.K., Ic, "Befehl vom 1.6.42," 16 June 1942 (GMDS, XLIII AK 31644/33, Anlagen 34–35) and a tactical report to Belov from the commander of the 2d Guard Cavalry Division in XXXXIII. A.K., Ic, "Tagesmeldung 1.6.42," 16 June 1942 (GMDS, XLIII AK 31644/33, Anlagen 36–37).

[168] 5. Pz.Div., Ic, "Gefangenen-Vernehmung," 18 June 1942 (GMDS, 5 PzD 21828/2).

units fell apart in a few days.[169] By the time the Germans began the second phase, the Soviet units had been greatly weakened.[170] When the German advance westward ran into the partisan regiments around Yelnya and Dorogobuzh, these also were quickly defeated.[171]

Although a considerable number of partisans fled from the area or went into hiding, there can be no doubt that heavy casualties were inflicted on the movement as a whole. German reports on partisan casualties in antipartisan operations must usually be discounted heavily; a large proportion of those killed were often innocent bystanders and sometimes even pro-German inhabitants executed in collective punishment measures. In the case of the "Hannover" operation, however, the situation was somewhat different. In this instance there was a good deal of fighting between regular German units and fairly well-defined and identified Soviet units. There appear to have been none of the indiscriminate massacres which were generally characteristic of German antipartisan operations. Therefore, the figures given by the Germans in this case may be considered as a fairly accurate reflection of the casualties actually suffered by the Soviet forces.

The German statistical reports on combined Soviet casualties—partisan and regular are not listed separately—present the following picture in summary form. The Germans claimed 5,361 prisoners[172] and deserters, a figure which may be accepted as accurate. The Germans counted 2,943 dead and estimated another 1,150.[173] This gives a total of 9,454 casualties. To this figure must be added at least 1,000 more casualties inflicted in the fighting during the period immediately prior to 24 May.[174] Thus, the grand total would be about 10,500. Adding to this the 2,000–3,000 men the Germans estimated were still hiding in the general area and the 2,000 or so others who fled by the middle of June, one comes close to the total number of partisans and regulars who had been reported in the Yelnya-Dorogobuzh area in the middle of May 1942.

These statistics must be compared with German casualties in the same operation. The Germans reported their own casualties during the main

[169] AOK 4, Ia, "Bericht ueber Unternehmen 'Hannover' 1. Abschnitt 24.5-31.5.," 1 June 1942, p. 1 (GMDS, AOK 4, 24336/24, Anlage 72); cf. PzAOK 3, "Besprechung am 28.5.42 mit O.B.Heeresgruppe Mitte bei Pz.A.O.K. 3," 28 May 1942 (GMDS, PzAOK 3, 25784/9, Anlage 41).

[170] XXXXIII. A.K., Ic, "Feindnachrichtenblatt (abgeschlossen am 1.6.42)," 1 June 1942 (GMDS, XLIII AK 31644/22, Anlage 20).

[171] See, for example, the report on the fate of the Kosubsky Regiment in Korueck XII. A.K., Ic, "Einvernahme des Leonid Sykow," 17 December 1942, pp. 1–2 (GMDS, XII AK 28746/9, Anlage D8).

[172] A small percentage of suspects were probably included among the prisoners.

[173] An "estimated" figure is given for only one corps; a figure for the other corps has been estimated by the author.

[174] Thus about 500 of the casualties inflicted by the 221st Division alone were not included in the report of the 43rd Corps since that division was subordinated to the Corps only during Operation "Hannover."

part of the operation as 468 killed and 1,524 wounded or missing.[175] To these figures must be added the 200-odd casualties suffered by the Germans in the period just before "Hannover," giving a total of about 2,200 German as compared with about 10,500 Soviet casualties.[176]

In view of the numerical inferiority of the Soviet forces and the military character of the units on both sides this may be considered a creditable, if not exactly heroic, performance on the part of the Soviet partisans and regulars. [The differing German view and the reasons for the divergence of interpretation were discussed in the evaluation of partisan accomplishments, at the end of the introduction to this chapter.]

2. Hide

Even in the early stages of Operation "Hannover" a number of the partisans and regulars attempted to hide singly or in small groups.[177] The Soviet administrative functionaries appointed during the period of partisan control attempted to disappear in the forests.[178] Some groups hid in the

[175] The number of men missing in action in this figure of 1,524 is about 200. The circumstances under which a majority (133, all from the 221st Security Division) disappeared would indicate that well over 100 of the 1,524 must be added to the 468 reported killed.

The inclusion of the wounded category in the German casualty figures, when none is given for the partisans, is not as misleading as might at first appear. Under the circumstances at the time of Operation "Hannover," the overwhelming majority of the wounded on the Soviet side either died of their wounds or were picked up by the Germans; they are thus already covered by the figures for Soviet killed or captured.

[176] In the absence of an overall report on Operation "Hannover," the foregoing statistics have been derived from reports of the two German corps which participated. (XXXXIII. A.K., Ia, "Gefangene u. Beute fuer die Zeit vom 24.5.–13.6.42," 14 June 1942, GMDS, XLIII AK 31644/22, Anlage 159; and XXXXVI. Pz.K., Ia, "Nr. 1994/42 geh. an Pz.A.O.K. 3," 20 June 1942, GMDS, PzAOK 3, 25784/9, Anlage 74.) These were supplemented by a number of other documents. (23. Inf.Div., Ic, "Feindfeststellungen," 8 June 1942, GMDS, 23 ID 24182/16; 23. Inf.Div., Ic, "Feindnachrichten," 21 June 1942, GMDS, 23 ID 24182/16; H.Gr.Mitte Ic/AO, "Flugblatteinwirkung auf Kommissare und Politruks," 22 June 1942, GMDS, OKW/637; 221. Sich.Div., Ic, "Taetigkeitsbericht des Ic vom 22.III. bis 17.VI.1942," 18 June 1942, p. 2, GMDS, 221 ID 22639/6, Anlage 114; V.O. Abw.II z.H.Gr.Mitte, "Graukopf, 2. Bericht," 27 May 1942, GMDS, XLIII AK 31644/22, Anlage 170; XXXXIII. A.K., "Tagesuebersicht fuer den 31.5.42," 31 May 1942, GMDS, XLIII AK 31644/33, Anlage 30.) The fact that the figures for the Soviet casualties (together with the figure for those in hiding and those who fled) account for the total number of partisans and regulars estimated to have been in the area would appear to confirm the accuracy not only of the statistics but also of the impression recorded above that in Operation "Hannover" the partisan casualties were really partisan casualties and not murdered civilians. In this case, also, the partisans reported killed or captured were actually killed or captured; they do not reappear a few weeks after the reported "success" of the operation. (This type of "reincarnation" is one of the most obvious clues to the identification of those antipartisan operations in which large numbers of nonpartisans were killed and reported as enemy casualties—a very common occurrence in the German effort to fight the partisans.)

[177] AOK 4, Ia, "Bericht ueber Unternehmung 'Hannover' 1.Abschnitt 24.5.—31.5.," 1 June 1942, pp. 1–2 (GMDS, AOK 4, 24336/24, Anlage 72).

[178] XXXXVI. Pz.K., Ic, "Partisanenherrschaft im Smolensker Gebiet," 18 June 1942, p. 3 (GMDS, 23 ID 24182/16).

area around Baltutino and south toward Roslavl.[179] All the German reports on the conclusion of "Hannover" agree that a substantial number, perhaps 2,000–3,000 men, remained hidden in the area.[180] Some of these men were already re-forming into small partisan bands in June,[181] but this was apparently exceptional. Practically all the groups in hiding were not combatworthly and were concerned exclusively with surviving.[182] Some of them tried to join the German-sponsored auxiliary police or attempted to fool the Germans into thinking that they were in fact such police formations.[183]

On the other hand, the partisan leaders in hiding were apparently awaiting a relaxation of German efforts so that they could start again with the formation of partisan units,[184] and to further this purpose, some of them infiltrated the administration organized by the Germans in the areas they had cleared.[185] These activities will be discussed below.

3. Flee

We have seen that most of the partisan units collapsed after a short period of resistance. Some units tried to flee southward from the very beginning.[186] Others fled repeatedly before the German advance, but were periodically forced to fight again either by the tactical situation or on General Belov's orders, and then fled again.[187]

When the German advance reached the western part of the partisan-held area, General Belov himself decided to reassemble the remnants of his forces and attempt an escape through the encircling German troops

[179] 221. Sich. Div., Ic, "Ueberlaeufer aus Raum Jerschitschi," 21 August 1942, p. 2 (GMDS, 221 ID 29380/9, Anlage 19).

[180] PzAOK 3, Ic/AO, "Feindnachrichtenblatt 'Hannover,'" 18 June 1942, pp. 3–4 (GMDS, Korueck 27819/1); XXXXVI. Pz.K., Ia, 'Nr. 1994/42 geh. an Pz.A.O.K. 3," 20 June 1942 (GMDS, PzAOK 3, 25784/9, Anlage 74); 221. Sich.Div., Ic, "Ueber-gabeverhandlung," 16 June 1942, p. 1 (GMDS, 221 ID 22639/6, Anlage 114). It is interesting to note in this connection that one of the supply officers of the partisans near Dorogobuzh took substantial food supplies into hiding with him. (Korueck 590, Ic, "Feindnachrichten," 15 August 1942, p. 3, GMDS, Korueck 27819/2, Anlage 31.)

[181] 5. Pz.Div., Ia ["Befehl"], 10 June 1942 (GMDS, 5 PzD 21578/4, Anlage 121).

[182] This is well illustrated by the description of remnants of the Kosubsky Regiment in Korueck XII. A.K., Ic, "Einvernahme des Leonid Sykow," 17 December 1942, p. 2 (GMDS, XII AK 28746/9, Anlage D8).

[183] Korueck 590, Ic, "Feindnachrichten," 16 July 1942, p. 2 (GMDS, Korueck 27819/2, Anlage 15).

[184] Korueck 590, Ic, "Feindnachrichten," 24 June 1942 (GMDS, Korueck 27819/1); Korueck 590, Ic, "Feindnachrichten," 16 July 1942, p. 3 (GMDS, Korueck 27819/2, Anlage 15).

[185] Chef Sipo u. SD, Sk 7c, Trupp Jelnja, "Ueberholung und Ueberpruefung von verdaechtig gemeldeten Elementen in Jelnja," 5 December 1942, p. 2 (GMDS, Wi/ID 2.503, Anlage 29).

[186] This appears to have been true of parts of the Kosubsky Regiment. (Korueck XII. A.K., Ic, "Einvernahme des Leonid Sykow," 17 December 1942, pp. 1–2, GMDS, XII AK 28746/9, Anlage D8.)

[187] See, for example, AOK 4, Ia, "Nr. 1427/42 geh. Fernschreiben an XXXXIII. A.K.," 8 June 1942 (GMDS, XLIII AK 31644/22, Anlage 80).

southward to the Bryansk area. Around 3 June, Belov told his regulars and partisans that they were surrounded and that they should try to join the Lazo Regiment (which was in the southern part of the Yelnya-Dorogobuzh area) and break through to the Bryansk forests where other assignments awaited them.[188] On 9 June, Belov with at least 2,000 men broke through the German lines near Berniki, crushing a battalion of the 221st Security Division holding that part of the German front along the Baltutino-Yelnya road (see Figs. 7 and 8).[189] He joined his forces to remnants of the Lazo and Kosubsky Regiments in the vicinity of Mutishche. From there Belov, Lazo, Kosubsky, Yudenkov (commissar of the Kosubsky Regiment) and other officers were flown out; most of the men moved farther south to join partisan forces in the area around Kirov and Bryansk.[190]

A number of the groups which thus escaped actually became a part of the partisan movement in the Bryansk area. Remainders of the Lazo Regiment were active there.[191] Belov himself was apparently brought back into the Bryansk area and held a position of some importance in the partisan movement west of Bryansk.[192] The fate of these partisans does not, however, fall within the scope of this chapter.

C. GERMAN EFFORTS TO PREVENT THE REVIVAL OF PARTISAN ACTIVITY

1. Military Pacification

In planning Operation "Hannover," the Germans anticipated that many partisans would attempt to hide and that considerable efforts would

[188] XXXXIII. A.K., "Tagesuebersicht fuer den 14.6.42," 14 June 1942 (GMDS, XLIII AK 31644/33, Anlage 69).

[189] AOK 4, Ia, "Nr. 1453/42 geh. an nachr. Pz.A.O.K. 3," 10 June 1942, p. 1 (GMDS, PzAOK 3, 25784/9, Anlage 50); Korueck 559, Qu, "Befehl," 10 June 1942 (GMDS, Korueck 29236/2, Anlage 158); XXXXIII. A.K., "Tagesuebersicht ueber den 10.6.42," 10 June 1942 (GMDS, XLIII AK 31644/33, Anlage 54); 23. Inf.Div., Ic, "Feindnachrichten," 21 June 1942 (GMDS, 23 ID 24182/16). For the heavy casualties suffered by the 221st Security Division at this time, see 221. Sich.Div., Ia, "Sich. Batlne 555, 557, 573," 12 June 1942, p. 2 (GMDS, XLIII AK 31644/22, Anlage 144).

[190] Korueck XII. A.K., Ic, "Einvernahme des Leonid Sykow," 17 December 1942, p. 2 (GMDS, XII AK 28746/9, Anlage D8); Korueck 559, Qu, "Tgb. 1643/42 an Fla.Abt. 721," 14 June 1942 (GMDS, Korueck 29236/2, Anlage 163); 221. Sich.Div., Ic, "Ueberlaeufer aus Raum Jerschitschi," 21 August 1942 (GMDS, 221 ID 29380/9, Anlage 19); AOK 4, Ia, "Befehl fuer die Saeuberung des rueckw. Gebietes suedlich der Rollbahn," 19 June 1942 (GMDS, LVI AK 35738/4); PzAOK 3, Ic/AO, "Feindnachrichtenblatt 'Hannover,'" 18 June 1942, p. 3 (GMDS, Korueck 27819/1).

[191] 221. Sich.Div., Ic, "Banditenlage im Raume der Sich.-Division 221," 15 September 1942. (221 ID 29380/9, Anlage 2); see also 707. Inf.Div., Ic, "Feindnachrichten fuer die Truppe Nr. 13," 19 October 1942 (GMDS, 707 ID 27797/4, Anlage 192); XII. A.K., Ic, "Feindlage-Wochenbericht fuer die Zeit vom 15.–21.11.42," 21 November 1942, p. 2 (GMDS, XII AK 28746/9, Anlage A30).

[192] 221. Sich.Div., Ic, "Beitrag zum Ia-Befehl, Feindlage," 26 October 1942, p. 1 (GMDS, 221 ID 29380/9, Anlage 4).

have to made to clear the area thoroughly.[193] This estimate proved to be correct. At the end of the operation there were many partisans and regulars (perhaps 2,000–3,000) left in the area, hiding individually or in small groups.[194] The need for persistent watchfulness and careful searching was heavily stressed by the higher German commands.[195] Therefore the continued employment of substantial forces in the area was considered necessary.[196]

Accordingly, the German commands with jurisdiction and responsibility for security in the area formulated and carried out plans for military pacification.[197] These activities, which included a small operation against a 300-man band in the western part of the area,[198] were generally successful. The reports clearly show that in the period from the middle of June to the end of September the Germans were successful in rounding up a considerable proportion of the partisans still at large and in preventing small groups from engaging in activity of any consequence.[199] As a result, one

[193] XXXXVI. Pz.K., Ic, "Feindnachrichtenblatt Nr. 4," 10 May 1942, p. 3 (GMDS, PzAOK 3, 25784/9, Anlage 27).

[194] 221. Sich.Div., Ic, "Uebergabeverhandlung," 16 June 1942, p. 1 (GMDS, 221 ID 22639/6, Anlage 114); XXXXVI. Pz.K., Ia, "Nr. 1994/42 geh. an Pz.A.O.K. 3," 20 June 1942, pp. 1–2 (GMDS, PzAOK 3, 25784/9, Anlage 74); Korueck 590, Ic, "Feindnachrichten," 16 July 1942, p. 1 (GMDS, Korueck 27819/2, Anlage 15).

[195] See, for example, PzAOK 3, Ic/AO, "Feindnachrichtenblatt 'Hannover,'" 18 June 1942, pp. 3–4 (GMDS, Korueck 27819/1).

[196] Korueck 590, Ia, "Sicherung der Roll- und Eisenbahn," 16 August 1942 (GMDS, Korueck 27819/3, Anlage 34c). Most of the German regular divisions were, of course, withdrawn after the conclusion of Operation "Hannover," but the local rear area commands did keep substantial forces. For a short time a panzer division was also sent in to help with the pacification. (PzAOK 3, Ia, "Gefechtsbericht vom 1.–30.6.42," 30 June 1942, GMDS, PzAOK 3, 25784/15; 20. Pz.Div., Ia, "Divisions-Befehl Nr. 85," 22 June 1942, GMDS, 20 PzD 24209/29.)

[197] Details may be found in the following documents: PzAOK 3, Ia, "Sicherung des rueckw. Armeegebiets," 7 June 1942 (GMDS, PzAOK 3, 25784/9, Anlage 48); Korueck 590, Ia, "Sicherung des rueckw. Armeegebiets," 16 June 1942 (GMDS, Korueck 27819/1); Korueck 590, Ia, "Befehl zur Sicherung des rueckw. Armeegebiets" [18 June 1942], p. 2 (GMDS, PzAOK 3, 25784/25); AOK 4, Ia, "Befehl fuer die Saeuberung des rueckw. Gebietes suedlich der Rollbahn," 19 June 1942 (GMDS, LVI AK 35738/4); 20. Pz.Div., Ia, "Divisions-Befehl Nr. 85," 22 June 1942 (GMDS, 20 PzD 24209/29); "Deutsche Uebersetzung des russ. Flugblattes AFP 34" [June 1942] (GMDS, 20 PzD 24209/41); Korueck 559, Qu, "Beurteilung der Versorgungslage," 30 June 1942 (GMDS, Korueck 29236/2, Anlage 181); Korueck 559, Qu, "Befehl," 2 July 1942 (GMDS, Korueck 29236/2, Anlage 183).

[198] This was Operation "Swampflower" (*Sumpfbluete*). See Korueck 590, Ia, "Sumpfbluete," 9 July 1942 (GMDS, Korueck 27819/2); Korueck 590, Ic, "Feindnachrichten," 16 July 1942, p. 1 (GMDS, Korueck 27819/2); Korueck 590, Ia, "Monatsbericht fuer Juli," 7 August 1942 (GMDS, Korueck 27819/2).

[199] XII. A.K., Ia, "Taetigkeitsbericht ueber Sicherung und Befriedung des rueckw. Korpsgebietes in der Zeit vom 15.6.—15.7.1942," 19 July 1942 (GMDS, XII AK 28746/9, Anlage A9); XII. A.K., Ic, "Taetigkeitsbericht des Korueck XII. A.K.," 10 September 1942 (GMDS, XII AK 28746/9, Anlage A14); PzAOK 3, Ic/AO (Abw.III), "Bandenwesen fuer die Zeit vom 26.4.—31.7.1942," 14 October 1942 (GMDS, PzAOK 3, 25784/43); PzAOK 3, Ic/AO, "Taetigkeitsbericht Nr. 5, 27 April —31 Juli 1942," 31 July 1942, p. 15 (GMDS, PzAOK 3, 25784/35); PzAOK 3, Ia,

of the German armies in the area could report that in the period 1 October
1942 to 18 January 1943 the army rear area was virtually free of
partisans.[200]

2. Political Pacification

Though relying primarily on the continued presence of military force
to pacify the area, the Germans realized that political measures would
be necessary to re-establish peace and quiet in the territory they had
wrested from the partisans. Their plans stressed that an important prerequisite for effective political pacification was a careful and continuing
differentiation between partisans and partisan-sympathizers on the one hand
and the rest of the population on the other. Collective punishment—an
approach popular with the Germans because of its apparent simplicity—
was to be avoided in this area. (The documents indicate that this caution
was actually heeded.) Efforts were to be made to get the population to
aid the Germans in tracking down the remaining partisans; decent treatment of the population was to serve as the incentive for such aid.[201]

To carry out these plans, the Germans tried to win over the population
by propaganda measures. These included attempts to blame the partisans
for the troubles suffered by the population and to convince the latter that
partisan activity, such as looting, hurt them but did not harm the Germans.[202]

A second aspect of German political pacification was the re-establishment of an auxiliary police organization *(Ordnungsdienst, Selbstschutz)*.[203]
An illuminating report on the formation of some local auxiliary police
units in this area reads, in part, as follows:

Vskhody Rayon Agricultural Leader   22 November 1942
Report on the Measures Taken for the Pacification and
Economic Utilization of Vskhody Rayon

"Gefechtsbericht Juli 1942," p. 6 (GMDS, PzAOK 3, 25784/15); PzAOK 3, Ic/AO
(Abw.III), "Bandenwesen fuer die Zeit vom 1.8.—30.9.1942," n.d. (GMDS, PzAOK
3, 25784/43).

[200] PzAOK 3, Ic/AO, "Taetigkeitsbericht Nr. 7 fuer die Zeit vom 1. Oktober 1942
bis 18. Januar 1943," 18 January 1943 (GMDS, PzAOK 3, 29195/30).

[201] PzAOK 3, Ic/AO, "Feindnachrichtenblatt 'Hannover,'" 18 June 1942, pp. 3–4
(GMDS, Korueck 27819/1); 221. Sich.Div., Ic, "Taetigkeitsbericht des Ic vom 22.
III. bis 17. VI. 1942," 18 June 1942, pp. 4–6 (GMDS, 221 ID 22639/6, Anlage 114).

[202] Unfortunately few details of this progaganda campaign are recorded in the available documents. (Wi Kdo f.d. Bereich PzAOK 3, "Lage und Taetigkeitsbericht fuer
die Zeit vom 23.5.—22.6.1942," 25 June 1942, GMDS, PzAOK 3, 21729/2; Korueck
590, Ia, "Sicherung des rueckw. Armeegebiets," 16 June 1942, p. 3, GMDS, Korueck
27819/1; PzAOK 3, Qu. 2, "Gedanken zur Propaganda in den besetzten russischen
Gebieten, Vorschlag eines Propagandamittels," 23 November 1942, GMDS, PzAOK 3,
27140/11.)

[203] Some material on the reorganization of an auxiliary police in this area will be
found in Korueck 559, Qu, "Beurteilung der Versorgungslage," 30 June 1942 (GMDS,
Korueck 29236/2, Anlage 181) and in Korueck 590, Ia, "Ordnungsdienst," 16 June
1942, annex (GMDS, Korueck 27819/1).

On 4 June 1942 the economic detachment gave me the assignment of agricultural reconstruction in the Vskhody-Znamenka area which had just been liberated.

. . . After a few days I settled in Vskhody. At first it was impossible to think of reconstruction work; even strong [German] units were being attacked constantly, and partisans were in localities removed from the through-roads. There was some cattle left in the immediate vicinity of Vskhody, and I decided to get it out [by organizing] armed patrols, since it would have been slaughtered by the partisans anyway. In this manner, we slowly collected about 30 cows. Then the population could get milk from us daily. Through these patrols I came to know Russians who really wanted to cooperate. Furthermore, we became well known in the countryside, and each day we received reports on partisan camps, hideouts, and attacks. In cooperation with the detail guarding the bridge,[204] the patrols covered a wider and wider area. When the local military government office moved away shortly after my arrival, I took over its duties. I designated the few Russians of good will known to me to be village mayors and armed them. They performed valuable services for us and were very useful in fighting the partisans. However, they were in constant danger of being killed, and I therefore decided to set up a self-defense organization in these localities. People who had been checked carefully were armed with weapons which had been captured or had been supplied to me. The type and number of each weapon given out was carefully registered and the name of the person to whom it was issued (*Traeger*) was recorded. The very reliable chief agronomist [of the rayon] was appointed chief of police and was given supervisory powers. This arrangement proved to be successful in practice; after partisan attacks on villages had been repulsed several times and prisoners had been taken, more and more localities expressed an interest in protecting themselves. I and my associates continuously traveled about with a truck to organize self-defense forces in individual localities or to destroy small partisan groups.

I announced everywhere that any who had weapons without my permission would be punished and that all such weapons were to be turned in. At first this surrender [of weapons] proceeded slowly; then we conducted house searches in a number of villages and when we found weapons not covered by permits, [we then] also took away the weapons of the self-defense organization. News of this measure got around quickly, and, as a result, the self-defense organization had a stake in the surrender [of unauthorized weapons] since otherwise it, too, was punished.

[The self-defense organization] was issued rifles and pistols only; all machine guns and submachine guns were withdrawn.

Those Russians who had been armed defended themselves energetically and protected their villages and thus took a large number of prisoners. Drastic action was taken against mistakes made by the self-defense organization; however, this was necessary in only a few cases.

.   .   .   .

At the end of August when a rayon military government office was established, I turned over to it the membership list of the self-defense organization, most of whom were absorbed into the auxiliary police. . . .[205]

[204] There was an important bridge over the Ugra at Vskhody.

[205] Geb.Landw. Wzschody, "Bericht ueber von mir getroffenen Massnahmen zur Befriedung und wirtschaftlichen Erschliessung des Gebietes Wzschody," 22 November 1942 (GMDS, Wi/ID 2.503, Anlage 22a).

Although the auxiliary police units, like the ones described in the foregoing account, rendered valuable services in suppressing small partisan bands which remained in the area, it was clear to the Germans that the continued presence of German troops was essential, both for the actual conduct of antipartisan operations and as a supporting force for the auxiliary police.[206]

In general, the political efforts of the Germans, combined with their military activity, appear to have been successful in restraining the local population from giving support to the partisans. It was apparently for this reason that Soviet efforts to reorganize a partisan movement in the area failed to achieve significant results. The population generally held aloof from the partisans and on occasion even helped the Germans track them down.[207]

3. Preventive Measures Against the Reintroduction of Partisans by Air

In view of the fact that the partisan movement in the Yelnya-Dorogobuzh area had initially been organized to a considerable extent through the use of airpower, it is not surprising that the Germans anticipated that Soviet efforts to re-form the partisan movement after Operation "Hannover" would include heavy emphasis on flying in new officers and reinforcements. In response to orders from Army Group Center, detailed plans were worked out to combat this anticipated Soviet effort. Air warning stations were established, and a special mobile reserve was formed to cope with air drops too large for the local units to handle.[208] Furthermore, the German Air Force was requested to have its planes watch for all signs indicating a revival of partisan activity in the area just cleared.[209] Orders to this effect were issued by the German Air Force command in the East on 1 July 1942.[210]

In the fall and winter of 1942 the Germans continued their efforts to prevent the re-establishment of a partisan movement through the use of airpower. The Germans clearly felt that, with the area well pacified,

---

[206] Korueck 590, Ia, "Monatsbericht fuer Juli," 7 August 1942 (GMDS, Korueck 27819/2).

[207] PzAOK 3, Ic/AO (Abw.III), "Bandenwesen fuer die Zeit vom 26.4.—31.7.1942," 14 October 1942 (GMDS, PzAOK 3, 25784/43); Korueck 590, Ia, "Monatsbericht Monat August 1942," 26 August 1942 (GMDS, Korueck 27819/2, Anlage 38); PzAOK 3, Ic/AO, "Bandenwesen fuer die Zeit vom 1.8.—30.9.1942," 14 October 1942 (GMDS, PzAOK 3, 25784/43). The second reference is quoted in Sect. IV, C.

[208] PzAOK 3, Ia, "Nr. 2372/42 geh. an Heeresgruppe Mitte," 20 June 1942 (GMDS, PzAOK 3, 25784/9, Anlage 75); XXXXVI. Pz.K., Ia, "Nr. 1994/42 geh. an PzAOK 3," 20 June 1942, p. 1 (GMDS, PzAOK 3, 25784/9); 20. Pz.Div., Ia, "Divisions-Befehl Nr. 85," 22 June 1942, p. 2 (GMDS, 20 PzD 24209/29). See also, PzAOK 3, Ic/AO, "Feindnachrichtenblatt 'Hannover,'" 18 June 1942, p. 3 (GMDS, Korueck 27819/1).

[209] H.Gr.Mitte, Ia, "Nr. 5130/42 geh. an Luftwaffenkommando Ost," 23 June 1942 (GMDS, PzAOK 3, 21729/2).

[210] Lw.Kdo.Ost, Fuehr.Abt., Ia Op, "Partisanenbekaempfung," 1 July 1942 (GMDS, PzAOK 3, 25784/26).

airpower offered the only avenue of approach for a revival of partisan warfare.[211] They ordered that old Soviet landing fields in the area be watched with great care for possible signs of renewed use.[212] In October, when an increase in air activity was expected, the warning system was made more extensive, and elaborate plans were made to mislead Soviet planes into dropping their supplies on German-held drop-areas or landing on German-held fields.[213] By promising rewards and threatening severe puishment,[214] efforts were also made to induce the local population to supplement the German warning system.

D. SOVIET EFFORTS TO REVIVE THE PARTISAN MOVEMENT

At the end of Operation "Hannover," 2,000–3,000 partisans and regulars were left scattered in the area, and it was to be expected that the Soviet Government would attempt to use them as the basis for a revival of partisan activity.[215] Some of the partisans appear to have gathered together almost immediately to engage in minor operations.[216] The vast majority of those who went into hiding, however, apparently were concerned exclusively with surviving. Their small groups restricted operations to gathering food for themselves and otherwise remained as inconspicuous as possible. They were not combat units and seemed to recognize this fact.[217] The officers also went into hiding, supposedly to reorganize the partisans once German pressure had eased.[218] Some of the officers apparently had been given orders to infiltrate the local administration which the Germans were expected to re-establish in the area. Thus one official of the administration in Yelnya confessed in December 1942 that he had been instructed by the NKVD section at Belov's headquarters to secure a position in the German

[211] Korueck 590, Ic, "Feindnachrichten," 15 August 1942, p. 1 (GMDS, Korueck 27819/2, Anlage 31).

[212] *Ibid.*

[213] Korueck 590, Ia, "Bekaempfung feindlicher Kampf- und Transportflugzeuge," 9 October 1942 (GMDS, Korueck 27819/3).

[214] Korueck 590, Ia, "Bekaempfung feindlicher Kampf- und Transportflugzeuge," 11 November 1942 (GMDS, Korueck 27819/3).

[215] PzAOK 3, Ic/AO, "Feindnachrichtenblatt 'Hannover,'" 18 June 1942, pp. 3–4 (GMDS, Korueck 27819/1); XXXXVI. Pz.K., Ia, "Nr. 1994/42 geh. an PzAOK 3," 20 June 1942 (GMDS, PzAOK 3, 25784/9, Anlage 74); Korueck 590, Ic, "Partisanentaetigkeit im rueckwaertigen Armeegebiet," 27 July 1942 (GMDS, Korueck 27819/2).

[216] 5. Pz. Div., Ia ["Befehl"], 10 June 1942 (GMDS, 5 PzD 21578/4, Anlage 121).

[217] 221. Sich.Div., Ic "Ueberlaeufer aus Raum Jerschitschi," 21 August 1942, p. 1 (GMDS, 221 ID 29380/9, Anlage 19); Korueck 590, Ic, "Feindnachrichten," 16 July 1942, p. 1 (GMDS, Korueck 27819/2, Anlage 15); Korueck XII. A.K., Ic, "Einvernahme des Leonid Sykow," 17 December 1942, p. 2 (GMDS, XII AK 28746/9, Anlage D8).

[218] Korueck 590, Ic, "Feindnachrichten," 24 June 1942 (GMDS, Korueck 27819/1; Korueck 590, Ic, "Feindnachrichten," 16 July 1942, p. 3 (GMDS, Korueck 27819/2, Anlage 15).

administration in Yelnya. He was to await the re-establishment of a partisan movement and then pass on to the partisans any knowledge of German troop dispositions he might have acquired. He was to secure a position which would give him access to some funds which he would use to support the partisans. Furthermore, in cooperation with another man who secured the position of agronomist of Yelnya Rayon, he was to spread Soviet propaganda among the peasants.[219]

The available German reports which describe partisan activity during the late summer and fall of 1942 show that the partisan movement remained small and ineffective in spite of Soviet efforts to revive it. These efforts consisted to a large extent of dropping small groups of partisans by air, presumably to organize new detachments.[220] The sporadic partisan activity which did result from this was apparently largely dependent upon air support, not only for officers and reinforcements but also for supplies. This is shown in a detailed survey of the partisan tactical situation for the third week of August 1942 prepared by the rear area command of Fourth Army.[221] In contrast to the period before "Hannover," the Soviet Air Force at this time apparently tightened up on the system of recognition signs which were changed periodically, perhaps to frustrate German efforts to trap the planes.[222] What partisan activity did exist, however, was evidently of little concern to the Germans. The partisans were still concerned chiefly with survival, and their operations consisted almost exclusively of trying to find places where there were no German troops so that they could collect food for themselves.[223] In August 1942 the Germans learned that seven partisans had killed two partisan leaders and had dispersed with the intention of deserting—the first instance of this kind to come to the attention of the German command in the area.[224]

Soviet attempts to revive partisan warfare in the Yelnya-Dorogobuzh

[219] Chef Sipo u. SD, Sk 7c, Trupp Jelnja, "Ueberholung und Ueberpruefung von verdaechtig gemeldeten Elementen in Jelnja," 5 December 1942, p. 2 (GMDS, Wi/ID 2.503, Anlage 29).
[220] PzAOK 3, Ic/AO (Abw.III), "Bandenwesen fuer die Zeit vom 24.4.—31.7.1942," 14 October 1942 (GMDS, PzAOK 3, 25784/43); Korueck 590, Ic, "Feindnachrichten," 15 August 1942, p. 1 (GMDS, Korueck 27819/2, Anlage 31).
[221] Korueck 559, Qu, "Sicherung des rueckw. Gebietes," 26 August 1942 (GMDS, Korueck 29236/2, Anlage 213).
[222] Korueck 590, Ic, "Feindnachrichten," 16 July 1942, p. 2 (GMDS, Korueck 27819/2, Anlage 15); XII. A.K., Ic, "Feindlage-Wochenbericht fuer die Zeit vom 8.–14.11.1942," 15 November 1942, p. 2 (GMDS, XII AK 28746/9, Anlage A 29).
[223] PzAOK 3, Ia, "Gefechtsbericht Juli 1942," p. 6 (GMDS, PzAOK 3, 25784/15); Korueck 590, Ic, "Feindnachrichten," 15 August 1942, p. 2 (GMDS, Korueck 27819/2, Anlage 31); PzAOK 3, "Bandenbekaempfung," 11 October 1942 (GMDS, PzAOK 3, 29195/9; Korueck 559, Abt. VII, K.-Verw., "Lage- und Taetigkeitsbericht fuer die Zeit vom 1.10. bis 31.10.1942," 8 November 1942, pp. 1–2 (GMDS, Korueck 29236/6).
[224] Korueck 590, Ic, "Feindnachrichten," 15 August 1942, p. 2 (GMDS, Korueck 27819/2, Anlage 31).

area and the failure of these efforts can be understood on the basis of a report of Third Panzer Army.

The Partisan Situation in the Period 1 August—30 September 1942

.   .   .   .

Compared with the areas of neighboring armies and of Army Group Rear Area [Center], partisan activity in the area under the jurisdiction of [Third Panzer] Army has been slight. In the Army Rear Area the partisans consist mainly of remnants of the units smashed in the Dorogobuzh[225] and Belyi[226] pockets. Without their leaders, these groups cannot be considered as combat units fighting the German armed forces, but rather as robber bands acting independently and attacking villages not held by the Germans to gather food. The active combat groups which appear in the Army Rear Area and also in the corps areas consist of men recently sent through the front or of parachutists.[227] These fresh units are generally well equipped with automatic rifles, submachine guns, hand grenades, and also explosives. These groups are small —10 to 20 men—and are energetically led. However, they lose their combat efficiency quickly because they are seldom supported by the population (as a result of difficulties in securing provisions) and because they are quickly tired out by constant harassment and pursuit by mobile antipartisan units.[228]

E. THE FATE OF THE PARTISAN MOVEMENT, JUNE 1942—SEPTEMBER 1943

The material presented above shows that the partisan movement did not attain significant proportions in the second half of 1942. It had been crushed by the German offensive and was effectively held down in spite of Soviet efforts to revive it. A German report asserts that from the beginning of October 1942 to the middle of January 1943 there was virtually no partisan activity in the area.[229] This is confirmed by an article which appeared in the 11 January 1943 issue of the official organ of the Smolensk Oblast Committee of the Communist Party. The accomplishments of the partisans in the oblast during the preceding three months are listed here as the blowing up of four trains, one bridge, and four kilometers of tele-

---

[225] The reference is to Operation "Hannover."

[226] The reference is to an operation conducted by the Germans shortly after "Hannover" to clear the area north of the Smolensk-Vyazma railway.

[227] Material on two such groups, including diaries of some of their members, can be found in Korueck XII. A.K., Ic, "Vernichtung der Diversantengruppe Kusjmin und der Partisanengruppe Sykow durch Jagdkdo.Hartwig XII. A.K.," 17 December 1942 (GMDS, XII AK 28746/9) and 137. Inf.Div., Ic, "Rueckwaertiges Gebiet/ Agenten und Partisanen," 25 November 1942 (GMDS, 137 ID 30345/14).

[228] PzAOK 3, Ic/AO (Abw.III), "Bandenwesen fuer die Zeit vom. 1.8—30.9.1942," 14 October 1942 (GMDS, PzAOK 3, 25784/43).

[229] PzAOK 3, Ic/AO (Abw.III), "Taetigkeitsbericht Nr. 7 fuer die Zeit vom 1. Oktober 1942 bis 18. Januar 1943," 18 January 1943 (GMDS, PzAok 3, 29195/30). See also, Wi In Mitte, I/Id, "Lagebericht Nr. 26," 4 February 1943, p. 5 (GMDS, Wi/ID 2.122); PzAOK 3, A.Wi.Fueh., "Lagebericht fuer die Zeit vom 16. Dezember bis 15. Januar 1943," n.d. (GMDS, Wi/ID 2.438).

phone lines; cutting the railway tracks three times; and killing thirteen collaborators.[230] In comparison with the rest of the occupied areas of the RSFSR and Belorussia, these partisans successes are so minute that their very recording constitutes an admission of complete failure. There is no evidence to indicate that the situation changed during February and March. In March the Germans conducted a large-scale planned retreat in which they gave up the so-called Rzhev salient. In this operation, the Germans gave up Vyazma and Rzhev. The front then ran northwestward from just west of Kirov to slightly east of Smolensk. This operation, known as "Buffalo," was designed to permit the withdrawal of German units by drastically shortening the front of Army Group Center; it was completed on 22 March 1943.[231]

Through Operation "Buffalo" the easternmost sector of the Yelnya-Dorogobuzh area was evacuated, the central part became the combat zone, and the western part fell directly behind the German front. In those sections which remained under German control, the presence and watchfulness of substantial numbers of German troops prevented partisans from forming groups or engaging in activities of note.[232]

The Soviet High Command itself realized that there was no partisan movement of consequence left in the area. This is shown by the arrangements which it made in 1943 for the disruption of the railroads supporting the German units in the Bryansk-Orel area. In the spring of 1943 the Germans began with the movement of troops into the Bryansk-Orel area for their summer offensive (Operation "Citadel"). Two rail lines were used for the German troop and supply transports: the Gomel-Bryansk line, which was double-tracked, and the Smolensk-Roslavl-Bryansk line, which was single-tracked. The Soviet command increased its attacks on these two railroads immediately, although a different method was used for each of the two lines. While the Soviet High Command relied primarily on the partisans to disrupt traffic on the Gomel-Bryansk line, the Smolensk-Roslavl-Bryansk line was attacked constantly by Russian planes.[233] In July

[230] *Rabochii Put* [The Workers' Way], No. 2 (35), 11 January 1943, p. 2.

[231] H.Gr.Mitte, Ia, "Nr. 2839/43 geh.," 22 March 1943 (GMDS, PzAOK 3, 335568/19).

[232] This is clear from the excellent records of the XII Corps which had the responsibility for security in most of the German-held part of the area. The records show that great care was exercised by the corps, but no signs of activity were noted.

[233] This and the following statements are based on Hermann Teske, *Die Silbernen Spiegel* (Heidelberg: Vowinckel, 1952), pp. 179–82, 192–97. In 1943 Teske held the position of Chief of Transportation of Army Group Center (*General des Transportwesens Mitte*) and in this position was primarily concerned with the functioning of the railway system in the area behind the central part of the Eastern front. Whatever the value of other portions of his memoirs might be, there can be no doubt that the sections on the railway situation in 1943 which are used in this study can be considered generally reliable, especially since they are obviously based to a large extent on contemporary notes and documents.

and August, at the time of both the German and the Soviet offensives, this pattern was repeated; the job of hindering the German transports on the Gomel-Bryansk line was entrusted to the partisans, on the Smolensk-Bryansk line, to the Soviet Air Force.[234] The same thing happened again in late August and September at the time of the great German retreat in this area. It seems obvious that the Soviet High Command recognized its failure to revive the partisan movement in the Yelnya-Dorogobuzh area and resorted to other forces to achieve its goals for the summer campaign.

The failure of the German summer offensive and the success of the Soviet campaign forced a major German withdrawal which began near Bryansk and continued farther north as well. During late August and in September a planned German withdrawal on that part of the front which passed through the Yelnya-Dorogobuzh area led to the Soviet reoccupation of the entire area. Smolensk itself was evacuated by the Germans on 24 September. No information has been found on the fate of the partisans in the area at the time of the German evacuation.

A unique curve of partisan activity in the Yelnya-Dorogobuzh area is discernible in the period from the first efforts to organize partisans in the summer of 1941 to the end of the German occupation. That part of the original effort which centered upon the destruction battalions was never successful. Other efforts produced only a few insignificant groups which threatened the Germans only at the time of the Soviet victories of January 1942. Thereupon the partisan movement flourished—to be crushed by one blow early in the summer. In spite of Soviet efforts to revive it, the second year of German occupation saw no significant partisan activity in the area at all.

The basis of the partisan movement had been the Red Army stragglers (organized around a nucleus of Government and Party officials, officers, and commissars brought in by plane). The Red Army stragglers had been completely absorbed in the great organizational effort of early 1942. The movement based upon their membership had been crushed before it could grow strong roots among the local population. It thus lacked the strength to capitalize on the growing tide of anti-German sentiment in the occupied area in the late summer of 1942, when this tide might have provided replacements for losses and perhaps even greater strength. A second effort, in which the local people would have been organized around the same type of nucleus as the first, proved to be impossible under the circumstances.

[234] It is of interest to note that the partisan attacks on the railway system were increased tremendously throughout the rear area of the central front during the few days at the end of July and the beginning of August; the exception was the Yelnya-Dorogobuzh area.

CHAPTER VIII

The Bryansk Area

Kurt DeWitt and Wilhelm Moll

---

§I. Summary and Conclusions

A. 1941 MILITARY EVENTS
AND INITIAL OCCUPATION

German forces first entered the Bryansk area when the Second Panzer Group—later called the Second Panzer Army—under General Heinz Guderian captured the city of Roslavl on 1 August 1941. During the following three weeks the important rail junction of Mglin and the towns of Unecha and Pochep were occupied by units of this group, which was assigned to cut off the retreat of Soviet forces concentrated around Gomel. Operations in this area, however, came to a halt about 24 August 1941 when, as a result of Hitler's decision to conquer the Ukraine before continuing the attack on Moscow, Second Panzer was shifted to the offensive against Kiev.

After Kiev fell at the end of September, the drive toward Moscow was resumed, and the new offensive began on 1 October with a powerful thrust by Second Panzer. [See Fig. 9.] Driving northeastward from the Ukraine, its armored spearheads broke through the Soviet lines and entered Orel on 3 October. While one corps pressed on toward Moscow, another wheeled around to the west and, by driving along the Bryansk-Orel highway, sealed off a large body of Soviet troops south of Bryansk. The city itself was taken on 7 October. Meanwhile, the German Second Army had started a frontal attack from the west which completed the encirclement of the Red Army forces. Two Soviet armies, the Third and the Thirteenth, were compressed into a pocket near Trubchevsk and were forced to surrender on 20 October after failing in several attempts to effect a mass break-out.

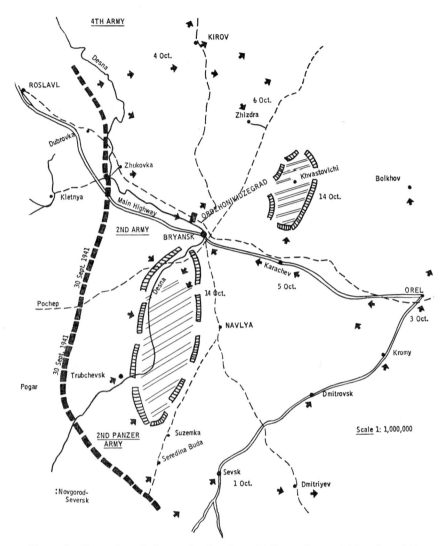

Figure 9.—Bryansk encirclement battles, from 30 September to 14 October 1941.

Simultaneously, another pocket was formed north of Bryansk by elements of Second Panzer and Second Army which, by converging from the east and west, closed a steadily tightening ring around the Soviet Fiftieth Army in the vicinity of Khvastovichi. This pocket was eliminated on 17 October and netted the Germans more than 50,000 prisoners.

With the surrender of Red Army forces in these two pockets, the military conquest of the Bryansk area was virtually complete; however, German control of the area remained tenuous and limited in scope. One reason for this was the shortage of troops available for occupying and pacifying the conquered territory. After the combat units had pushed on to the east, the responsibility for administering and securing the area was assumed by rear echelon commands. The forces at their disposal were barely sufficient to hold the major centers and protect the main lines of communication. They were wholly inadequate for occupying the more remote regions of the vast hinterland and for rounding up the thousands of Red Army soldiers who had worked their way out of the pockets or had escaped from German prisoner-of-war enclosures. These stragglers and fugitives became an important reservoir of manpower for the partisan movement.

The troops at the disposal of the Rear Area Command of Army Group Center (*Heeresgebiet*), whose jurisdiction at first was only the western sector, but later, during part of November and December, was extended all the way to Bryansk, included one security division. The sector assigned to this division far exceeded the Bryansk area. The Korueck of Second Army, which was in charge of the eastern part, had no division-size units but only guard and military police battalions. To cope with the growing security problem, particularly the threat posed by increasing partisan activity, a regiment of a regular infantry division—the 56th—was brought back from the front on 29 October. The commander of the 56th Division also exercised the functions of the Army Rear Area commander of Second Panzer Army, which had taken over the sector from Second Army.

On 10 December 1941, shortly after the beginning of the great Soviet counteroffensive, the 56th Division elements had to be pulled out because they were needed at the front. The security tasks reverted to the regional military government detachment (*Feldkommandantur*) at Bryansk, which had available only a guard battalion and a police battalion plus some military police detachments.

The defeat of the German Army before Moscow and the subsequent retreat not only drained away German manpower but also aggravated the security problem in the Bryansk area in an even more direct manner. Early in January 1942 the Red Army was able to recapture Kirov, an important rail center north of Bryansk, and to open a gap in the German front between the Fourth Army and the Second Panzer Army. Through this gap a steady stream of reinforcements, leaders, and supplies was sent to the partisan bands which had been organized south and west of Kirov behind the German lines. Although a German attempt, beginning on 15 February 1942, to retake Kirov was beaten off by the Red Army with the support of the partisans, the Germans were at least able to drive the partisans out of some of the northern towns, such as Dyatkovo and Bytosh, which they had held temporarily.[1]

[1] The above account of military events is based largely on Heinz Guderian, *Erinnerungen eines Soldaten* (Heidelberg: Kurt Vowinckel, 1951); and Kurt von

B. EARLY MANIFESTATIONS
OF PARTISAN WARFARE

German records pertaining to the Bryansk area reveal evidence of partisan activity as early as October and November 1941. The first bands were small, consisting usually of six to eight men led by a local Party or government official. Another type of band was the so-called destruction battalion, a unit organized by the NKVD in advance of the German occupation with the mission of guarding public buildings and fighting airborne troops. Many of these destruction battalions did not survive the first weeks of the war. Only one larger band was active during this period. It was composed of members of a school for partisans which apparently had been set up at or near Kletnya before the Germans occupied the area. Later it was reinforced by Red Army parachutists and stragglers. Thus the composition of this band—a mixture of local volunteers and Red Army men who had escaped from the pockets or from prisoner-of-war camps—in many respects set the pattern for the partisan units which operated in the Bryansk area early in 1942. For more than three weeks this band conducted raids on villages, killing the German-appointed mayors and requisitioning food and clothing. It also mined highways and attacked German military vehicles.

Although there is little information available on the organization of the earlier partisan bands, the German reports record many incidents of partisan activities during December 1941 and January–February 1942. As a matter of fact the partisans were able to control large sections of the area, including some of the more important rayon centers. This was possible largely because German security forces were not sufficient to occupy these towns permanently. The Germans had little difficulty in clearing the partisans away from objectives which they considered important enough to seize, but once the troops had left, the partisans would immediately return and punish those who had collaborated with the Germans or had shown hostility toward the Soviet regime. The vast forest regions of the Bryansk area facilitated the growth of the partisan movement by providing shelter from German attack and locations for camps and bases.

Despite these conditions favorable to the partisans, the Germans would probably have been able to deal effectively with the problem during the winter of 1941–42 if it had not been for their military reverses. Defeats by the Red Army not only denuded the rear areas of their already meagre security forces but also shook the confidence of the local population in eventual German victory. Furthermore, the successful Soviet counteroffensive brought the front close to partisan strongholds, thereby enabling the

---

Tippelskirch, *Geschichte des zweiten Weltkrieges* (Bonn: Athenaeum Verlag, 1951). See Fig. 9, showing the Bryansk encirclement battles; see also Fig. 10, showing the major partisan centers in the Bryansk area, i.e., the North Forest, South Forest, and the Kletnya-Mamayevka Forests.

bands to establish contact with the Red Army. As a result, the partisan movement underwent significant structural changes: it was reorganized along military lines and placed under tighter controls, both internal and external.

This was particularly evident in the northern sector, where the Soviet recapture of Kirov and the breaching of the German front made close co-operation between Red Army units and partisan groups possible. The bands which had been organized by local NKVD and Party officials were placed under direct control of a Soviet division and received reinforcements and supplies from the Red Army. In return, the partisans supplied the Red Army with food, and with manpower recruited in partisan-held territory. When the Germans attempted to retake Kirov and to close the gap between the Second Panzer and Fourth Armies, the partisans supported the Red Army not only by disrupting German communication lines in the rear but also by defending certain sectors of the front.

C. INTENSIFICATION AND GROWTH
OF THE PARTISAN MOVEMENT

The strengthening of the partisan movement in size and organization continued throughout 1942 despite German efforts to hamper its development. The standard type of partisan unit in early 1942 was the independent detachment or otryad, which increased gradually in strength until it reached from 100 to 400 men. The new recruits were Red Army stragglers, discharged or escaped prisoners of war, or members of the local population. Although the drafting of local residents on a broad scale did not start until the fall of 1942, there is some evidence, at least for the northern sector, that considerable numbers of men of military age were conscripted for the bands as early as the beginning of that year. The leadership of the earlier bands consisted of local Party or government officials, as well as Red Army officers who had either survived the encirclement battles or been sent in from the outside, usually by plane.

Transporting leaders and specialists to the partisan areas was not the only way in which Soviet air power was employed for the support of the bands. From the spring of 1942 on, the partisans received supplies of various kinds (particularly weapons, ammunition, and certain types of food) by planes which either dropped their cargoes or landed on specially prepared strips. The planes employed on these missions included small, single-engined trainers as well as American-built transport aircraft of the C-47 type.

The increase in size of the partisan bands was accompanied by a revision of their internal organization. The otryads were divided into companies and platoons similar to regular Red Army units. The introduction of a military pattern of organization was completed early in 1943 when brigades, subdivided into battalions, companies, and platoons, were established. The brigades were largely created by merging several independent detachments. The purpose of this reorganization was to ensure closer control and better coordination as well as to improve striking power. In addition, it strengthened government and Party control over the bands. Mention has already been made of Red Army control over partisan bands in the northern sector; in the south, external control was exercised through a command staff directed from Yelets, where the headquarters of the Bryansk Front and apparently also the Party Committee of Orel Oblast were located. The command staff was headed by D. V. Yemlyutin, a former NKVD official from Orel and one of the outstanding partisan commanders in the occupied area. It exercised close tactical control over as many as thirty to forty partisan detachments, and later over all brigades in the southern sector. In the western parts of the Bryansk area, i.e., in the Kletnya and Mamayevka Forests, external control was in the hands of the West Front of the Red Army. Air power helped significantly in Soviet direction of the bands by providing one of the most important links between partisan centers and Soviet headquarters in the unoccupied territory.

The strengthening and reorganization of the partisan bands enabled them to intensify and expand their activities, which were aimed, broadly speaking, first at the German military supply system and, secondly, at the whole German effort to control and exploit the occupied area. Attacks on communication lines generally took the form of blasting rail installations, mining highways, and ambushing trains and motor vehicles. Between May and October 1942 over 1,000 such assaults were reported by the Korueck of Second Panzer Army which had jurisdiction over the larger part of the Bryansk area.

Another major type of partisan activity was the effort to prevent the Germans from stabilizing their occupation regime and from utilizing local manpower and resources. To this end the bands raided villages, stole food and cattle, and meted out severe punishment to people who collaborated with the Germans or were otherwise hostile to the partisans. Special targets of partisan reprisals were the officials of the local indigenous administration and the various auxiliary police and military units that the Germans had organized. Raids on villages and requisitioning of food and manpower, on the one hand, served to meet the immediate needs of the bands, which to a large extent had to live off the land. On the other hand, they formed part of a definite pattern of psychological warfare which was designed to keep the people from supporting the Germans and to maintain their allegiance to the Soviet regime. These efforts grew more and more successful as the people recognized the unwillingness and inability of the Germans to satisfy some of their basic aspirations and needs, and as the certainty of German victory faded.

The gravity of the partisan problem was recognized by the German field commanders as early as February 1942. In their view the partisan movement constituted an immediate and ever-growing threat to the security of the German rear areas, and they demanded additional troops to deal with it. Their pleas resulted in the assignment to the Bryansk area of an additional security division—the 707th. In June 1942 the first major antipartisan operation was conducted against the bands in the northern sector; it involved one armored regiment and two infantry regiments. The operation inflicted considerable losses on the partisans and their supporters and temporarily dispersed the bands, though most of the partisans, including their leaders, managed to escape death or capture and simply moved to other areas where they reassembled for future activities. Furthermore, many of the persons whom the Germans included in their casualty figures must be classed as members of the local population rather than as active partisans. This operation, both in terms of results achieved and methods employed, established a pattern for most antipartisan operations which were to follow in 1942 and especially in 1943. It failed in its major objective, namely, the complete destruction of the partisan movement in this area.

Although, according to original German plans, rear area security measures were to be limited to major supply routes and communities, the field commanders realized soon after they occupied the area that the partisan movement could not be defeated by purely defensive strategy. However, the available troops were so scarce and so inferior in quality that the Germans had to emphasize mainly the protection of highways, railroads, and military installations. Strongpoints were established at regular intervals along the main highways and railroads, and all communities on or near supply lines were kept under strictest surveillance. Moreover, small mobile antipartisan units were organized to prevent the bands from blowing up installations and rails. On the whole, this essentially defensive system of highway and railroad security succeeded in keeping supply lines open. It failed, however, to curb the growth of the partisan movement, which flourished in the forests and swamps and which was hardly affected by these German measures.

D. THE FINAL PHASE AND
THE GERMAN RETREAT

As a result of German inability to cope effectively with the partisan menace, the bands, while not increasing in total numbers, maintained the strength they had attained in 1942.[2] Whatever losses they suffered, they

[2] In the fall of 1942 the German commander of the rear area of Second Panzer Army estimated the number of partisans in his area at from 10,000 to 15,000. In May 1943, just prior to the large antipartisan operations, his estimates of partisan strength ranged from 15,000 to 20,000, a figure probably somewhat exaggerated. According to the best sources available, partisan strength may be estimated at from 12,000 to 16,000 during the latter part of 1942 and in 1943.

made up by wholesale conscription of the local population. Internal as well as external controls assisting in centralization of command and tactical coordination were further improved. Air support of the bands also increased in scope and effectiveness.

Partisan forays on German communications assumed major proportions during March 1943 when the Red Army was attacking the southernmost part of the Bryansk area, and all partisan activities were coordinated more and more with Red Army operations. Perhaps the most spectacular success was the destruction of two important bridges; the Desna bridge near Vygonichi was wrecked during the night of 7 March and the Revna bridge near Sinezerki, on 13 March 1943. On 1 April the Second Panzer Army admitted that partisan activities had temporarily interfered with supply operations but had failed to produce the effect that the strength of the bands, their well-organized command, and good equipment had led the Germans to fear.

During the March offensive the Red Army reached the Desna River, and its spearheads established contact with partisan units near Trubchevsk, but a German counterattack foiled an attempt by combined Red Army and partisan forces to capture Orel from the rear by advancing along the Seredina Buda–Navlya railroad.

Coordination between partisan activities in the German rear and Red Army operations was particularly evident during the great battles following the last German offensive in Russia, namely the attempt to retake Kursk and to eliminate the Orel salient. This offensive, known as "Citadel," began on 5–6 July 1943 but almost immediately ran into a massive Soviet counteroffensive, which not only stopped the German attack but eventually pushed the Germans entirely out of the Bryansk area. On 22 July 1943, approximately ten days after the start of the Soviet countermove, the partisans began to attack the railroads leading to the front by a series of chain demolitions, a method in which tracks were blasted at many—sometimes several hundred—places simultaneously.

It is remarkable that this upsurge in partisan activity followed the largest antipartisan operations ever undertaken by the Germans in the Bryansk area. During May–June 1943 three operations involving two army corps (a total of ten divisions) were conducted in the northern, western, and southern sectors in order to clear out the partisans before the beginning of the German drive for Kursk.[3] Most of the troops assigned for this work came from the forces assembled for "Citadel." As in previous large-scale opera-

[3] In the largest of these operations, "Zigeunerbaron," staged in the southern sector from 16 May until 6 June 1943, six German divisions participated. At approximately the same time, from 19 May to 19 June 1943, two division-sized task forces under Army Rear Area Command 559 fought the bands in the Kletnya-Mamayevka Forests. The third operation, lasting from 21 May to 30 May 1943 and directed against the partisans in the North Forest, involved two divisions and two regimental combat teams under the direction of a corps.

466 / VIII. THE BRYANSK AREA

tions, the results were disappointing. According to their estimates, the Germans killed up to 50 per cent of the partisans, but the bands as units were not destroyed. The survivors moved into other parts of the area, where they reassembled and were brought up to strength by taking in local recruits.

German failure to destroy the partisan movement, as well as German defeats at the front, produced far-reaching effects on the attitude of the civilian population and on the morale of the thousands of indigenous collaborators. Beginning in 1942 the Germans had organized military combat units and auxiliary police formations composed of Soviet nationals who had either been recruited locally or had been drawn from the prisoner-of-war camps. By 1943 there were thirteen military battalions—the so-called *Ostbataillone*—and twelve local defense battalions in the rear area of Second Panzer Army. In addition, in the western parts of the area several thousand auxiliary police had been recruited. These collaborator units furnished approximately one half of the German security forces regularly assigned to the rear areas.

E. CONCLUSIONS

The evidence presented in this study leads to the conclusion that the partisans in the Bryansk area were unable to exert a decisive influence on the course of military operations. Their persistent attacks on German rail and road communications harassed, but failed to disrupt for any extended period of time, the movement of supplies to German troops at the front. The partisans also were unable, and in most cases unwilling, to give direct tactical support to the Red Army, except for a brief interlude in 1942 in the northern part of the area around Kirov. True, the partisans forced the Germans to adopt a static system of defense that involved giving up large areas between the communications lines and retiring into strongpoints, but this was caused by the shortage of German troops rather than by the fighting power of the partisans. When the partisans were engaged by German troops in open combat they were usually routed, and only the inadequate methods of German antipartisan warfare and the favorable terrain saved them from complete destruction.

Though the German commanders always viewed the partisan threat in the Bryansk area with particular alarm and though they devoted relatively large resources to counteracting it, they were motivated less by fear of the local bands than by realization that the Bryansk region, because of its central location and wooded terrain, consituted an almost perfect base for partisans from many parts of the occupied territories. Its thick forests provided shelter for bands that had been driven from other sectors or that had been mauled in German antipartisan operations. Here these bands could regroup, fill up their ranks, and replenish their supplies from the extensive food and ammunition dumps hidden in the woods. Here they could set up more or less permanent camps, central command posts, and training grounds. The Bryansk Forest, especially the part stretching for about fifty miles south of Bryansk, served not only as an important base for the indigenous bands but as a staging area for the so-called roving bands, which were chiefly of Ukrainian origin. Most important among them were the groups led by Kovpak and Fyodorov, which arrived in the Bryansk Forest early in 1942 and were developed during the subsequent months, under order from Moscow, into bands strong enough to make extended raids into areas of the Ukraine where little or no partisan activity had got under way before.

Though the partisans indigenous to and operating in the Bryansk area showed little effectiveness as military forces, they scored impressive successes in the field of psychological warfare. The Germans had found, upon their arrival, that large segments of the population were willing to co-operate with them or at least tacitly to accept German rule. But gradually this attitude shifted to one of indifference and finally to more or less open hostility. Part of the blame for this change must be laid to certain basic German occupation policies which completely ignored the needs and aspirations of the people and aimed at the ruthless exploitation of the area. These policies doomed all attempts by local German commanders to win the allegiance of the local population and to alleviate the hardships of the occupation regime. They also reduced all promises of reform, such as the proposed agrarian reform, to empty gestures, thereby nullifying any German propaganda and psychological warfare efforts.

On the other hand, the partisans in their propaganda cleverly exploited the failure of the Germans to live up to their promises, and their willingness to employ incredibly ruthless methods of suppressing the local population. Wholesale slaughter or evacuation of civilians from the large areas subjected to major antipartisan operations undoubtedly contributed greatly to the embitterment of the indigenous population. In contrast to the Germans, the partisans ordinarily did not use terroristic methods against the population as a whole, but primarily against those who collaborated with the Germans or were openly hostile to the bands. In this sense the partisan movement was a constant reminder to the people that Soviet power had not completely disappeared from the occupied territories. As the movement grew stronger and the possibility of German victory grew ever more remote, the people became increasingly unwilling to oppose the bands or to co-operate with the Germans. The partisans, by extending their sphere of influence, by killing German collaborators, and by successfully obstructing all German efforts to pacify the Bryansk area, paved the way for the return of the Soviet regime.

§II. Institutional Characteristics
of the Partisan Movement

Since the Bryansk area as defined in this study actually consisted of three distinct centers of partisan activity, it is difficult to present a clear outline of the organization and control of the partisan movement which is accurate for all sectors. The types of bands operating in the various sectors, the background of the leadership, and the chain of command differed substantially. The same holds true for the methods by which Soviet authorities controlled the movement from the outside. Some of the bands were organized and directed by the Red Army, others by the Party or NKVD; and there is evidence that the internal structure of the movement was influenced to a considerable extent by the external controls exercised over it.

A. ORGANIZATION

1. Types and Size of Units

It appears that the development of the partisan bands in the Bryansk area went through three stages, which will be discussed in some detail below. Though these stages did not always coincide in time in the various parts of the area, one trend is discernible everywhere. The small and independently operating bands which constituted the majority of the early partisan formations were gradually transformed, by a process of absorption or amalgamation, into larger units and brought under unified command. One difficulty in tracing this development arises from the fact that the designations of partisan units in the German reports do not follow a consistent pattern and are often contradictory. Such terms as "detachment," "group," "battalion," and "company" are used indiscriminately and frequently interchangeably.[4] Not until 1943, when the partisans in the Bryansk area were reorganized along more military lines into brigades, battalions, and companies did the terminology of the German reports become more uniform.

a. The Initial State, 1941

Information on this period is extremely scant. It appears that most of the first bands were aggregations of Red Army stragglers, trapped or cut off by the great encirclement battles near Smolensk, Vyazma, and Bryansk. A

---

[4] For example, the Rear Area Commander of Second Panzer Army gave the strength of the partisans in the forests south of Bryansk as "35–38 groups of 100 and 300 men each" (Korueck, PzAOK 2, "Taetigkeitsbericht, Oktober 1942," n.d., p. 20, GMDS, Korueck 29239/1) while Second Panzer Headquarters itself spoke of "35 detachments of 100–300 men each, which together formed Partisan Group C." (PzAOK 2, Ia, "Novembermeldung fuer die Zeit vom 27.10. bis 10.11.1942," 11 November 1942, p. 2, GMDS, PzAOK 2, 37075/90.)

partisan captured near Roslavl in August 1941 told his interrogators that remnants of two Red Army rifle divisions had been collected into three partisans groups of fifty to sixty men each which were to attack German supply routes in anticipation of a Red Army offensive.[5]

Other types of early partisan units were the so-called diversionist groups and destruction battalions, which apparently accounted for most of the activities carried out by the partisans at that time.[6]

b. The Second Stage, 1942

During the winter 1941–42 the organization and leadership of the partisans were greatly strengthened. This was most noticeable in the areas south and northwest of Bryansk, according to a report made by Field Marshal von Kluge, commander of Army Group Center, to General Halder, Chief of the Army General Staff.[7]

One of the reasons for this development undoubtedly was the military situation. Early in January, in the course of their great counteroffensive begun in December 1941, Soviet forces were able to recapture Kirov, an important rail center on the Bryansk-Vyazma line, and to breach the German line between the Fourth Army in the north and the Second Panzer Army in the south. Through this gap the Red Army, during the following months, sent a steady stream of reinforcements for the partisan bands which had been set up in the German rear in 1941. A sizable force of partisans was thus created in the area north of Bryansk.

The German 339th Infantry Division made several attempts to destroy this force and to re-establish contact with units of the Fourth Army. During the most ambitious of these attempts (the antipartisan operation "Vogelsang," undertaken in June 1942) several different types of partisan units were encountered:

(1) Partisan regiments, consisting of 1,000–1,500 men, led by Red Army officers; they were composed of Red Army stragglers and of local partisans selected after special military training. These regiments were organized and commanded like regular military formations and had the task of fighting German troops.

(2) "Pure" partisan formations, consisting of several detachments of 30–150 men, each of which operated in two groups. Their members were local residents who had received some military training but had not been accepted for service in the partisan regiments described above. While their

[5] Abw.Gr. I beim AOK 9, "Partisanenorganisation im Raume der Strasse Minsk-Moskau (Vernehmung eines gef. Partisanen)," 31 August 1941, p. 1 (GMDS, Wi/ID 2.296 b).

[6] AOK 2, Ic/AO, "Erfahrungsbericht ueber Partisanenbekaempfung fuer die Zeit vom 1. August bis 31. Oktober 1941," p. 4 (GMDS, NOKW-1836).

[7] OB, H.Gr.Mitte to Chef des GenStdH, 24 February 1942, p. 2 (GMDS, PzAOK 3, 20736/6).

chief mission was the disruption of German communications, they were sufficiently strong and well armed to be employed in military operations at the front if necessary.

(3) Self-defense units, consisting of the entire male population of the villages not occupied by the Germans. Some women and youths were included in these units.[8]

c. The Third Stage, January–July 1943

The report of the Rear Area Commander of the Second Panzer Army on the partisan situation during the period November 1942—April 1943 stated that in January 1943 a complete reorganization of the partisan movement had begun in all partisan-infested areas. "The individual groups," the report said, "were being formed into battalions and brigades and put under unified command."[9] Similar information came from the XLVII Panzer Corps which occupied the southern sector of the Bryansk area: "The partisan groups are organized into brigades and battalions. . . ."[10] A great number of individual brigades together with their subordinate units were subsequently identified by the Germans and were listed in the periodic German order-of-battle reports. These reports indicate, however, that the brigades were by no means uniform in size and internal composition. For example, in February 1943 nine brigades were identified in the South Forest. Their strength ranged from 500 to 1,500 men each, and they included from three to nine detachments which presumably were the equivalents of battalions.[11]

In April 1943, in the North Forest, the area north of the Bryansk-Roslavl railroad and east of the Desna River, the Germans reported the existence of the following three brigades: Maltsev Brigade [sometimes also referred to as a division], 7 battalions, total strength of 1,300–1,400 men; Bytosh Brigade, 3 battalions, total strength of 700 men; Orlov Brigade, 10 battalions, total strength of 1,400 men.[12] These three brigades, incidentally, apparently sprang from detachments and regiments operating in the area early in 1942.

[8] 339. Inf.Div., Ia, "Bericht ueber Unternehmen Vogelsang," 11 July 1942, pp. 8–10 (GMDS, 339 ID 44418/5).

[9] Korueck, PzAOK 2, "Halbjahresbericht November 1942—April 1943," 20 May 1943, Anlage Ia (GMDS, PzAOK 2, 37075/91).

[10] XLVII. Pz.K., Ic, "Feindnachrichtenblatt," 15 March 1943 (GMDS, XLVII AK 37241/9, Anlage 176). However, no Soviet order regarding formation of brigades is available.

[11] 442. Div. z.b.V., Ia, "Vermutliche Gruppengliederung innerhalb der Brigaden," 25 February 1943 (GMDS, PzAOK 2, 37075/90).

[12] Korueck 532, Ic, "Feindlage, Stand 26. Maerz 1943," 28 March 1943, p. 3 (GMDS, PzAOK 2, 37075/91). Cf. PzAOK 2, Ia, "Meldung ueber Bandentaetigkeit in der Zeit vom 28.2.—31.3.43, Anlage 4, 'Gliederung der Banden,'" 1 April 1943 (GMDS, PzAOK 2, 37075/91).

Lastly, in the western part of the Bryansk area in the dense Kletnya and Mamayevka Forests, four brigades divided into two regiments were reported. The regiments consisted of three battalions of three companies each. The strength of a company was 80–90 men.[13] In addition, some of the brigades had "special troops" directly attached to brigade headquarters. Thus, the Danchenkov Brigade had a supply company, a ration detachment, a demolition platoon, and a reconnaissance platoon.[14] In May 1943 the four brigades in the western part of the area were combined into two groups of 2,000 and 2,400 men respectively; one (the northern group) operated in the Kletnya Forest, and the other (the southern group), in the Mamayevka Forest.[15]

The armament of the different brigades also varied considerably. In the western area just described, each brigade was equipped with the following heavy weapons: 3 AT [antitank] 45 mm guns, 1 120 mm mortar, 1 82 mm mortar, 6–7 50 mm mortars, 8 bazookas, 8 heavy machine guns. Presumably, these weapons were handled by heavy weapons companies attached directly to regiments or battalions. In addition, each of the other companies had: 6 light machine guns, 50 submachine guns and other automatic rifles, 2 hand grenades per man and adequate supplies of ammunition. No mention is made of the number of rifles available.[16]

The three brigades of the North Forest were armed as follows in March 1943: Maltsev Brigade—3 76 mm guns, 3 AT 45 mm guns; each battalion —10–20 submachine guns, 1–2 heavy mortars, several bazookas, undisclosed number of machine guns. The Bytosh and Orlov Brigades had no heavy weapons such as artillery pieces and mortars, but each battalion was armed with several machine guns, submachine guns, and bazookas.[17]

One of the brigades in the South Forest was reported to be equipped with four light guns, four AT guns, and one heavy mortar. Each of the subordinate units also had one light mortar.[18] The problem of arms and equipment is mentioned here only to underscore a point that has already

[13] 98. Inf.Div., Ic, "Feindnachrichtenblatt ueber die Partisanengruppen des Kletnja-Waldes," 12 May 1943, p. 1 (GMDS, 98 ID 38038/10, Anlage 167).

[14] 707. Inf.Div., Ic, "Feindnachrichtenblatt Nr. 1/43, Anlage 1, 'Vermutliche Bandengliederung im Waldgebiet noerdlich der Linie O'Grad-Shukowka u. Kletnja-Bd. Geb' " [hereafter cited as 707. Inf.Div., "Feindnachrichtenblatt Nr. 1"], 21 June 1943 (GMDS, 707 ID 41762/2).

[15] 98. Inf.Div., Ic, "Feindnachrichtenblatt ueber die Partisanengruppen des Kletnja-Waldes," 12 May 1943, p. 1 (GMDS, 98 ID 38038/10, Anlage 167). See also Korueck 559, "Ic-Bericht zur Bandenlage fuer das Unternehmen Nachbarhilfe," 13 May 1943, p. 1 (GMDS, 221 ID 39509/15).

[16] Korueck 559, "Ic-Bericht zur Bandenlage fuer das Unternehmen Nachbarhilfe," 13 May 1943, p. 2 (GMDS, 221 ID 39509/15).

[17] Korueck 532, Ic, "Feindlage, Stand 26. Maerz 1943," 28 March 1943, p. 3 (GMDS, PzAOK 2, 37075/91).

[18] Auffrischungsstab 3 [XLVII Pz.K.], Ic, "Feindnachrichtenblatt," 10 May 1943, p. 4 (GMDS, XLVII AK 37241/6).

been emphasized in connection with the size and internal composition of the brigades, namely the lack of uniformity in organization and strength. Evidently, no standard table of organization and equipment had been devised for the brigades. Apparently some of the brigades which appeared in 1943 were not newly formed units but rather detachments on which the title "brigade" had been conferred in recognition of their size and accomplishments in partisan warfare. Others were evidently formed by combining a number of independent otryads. Many of the subordinate units of a brigade were designated by names rather than by numbers, one of them usually bearing the name of the brigade commander, which suggests that this was the original detachment around which the brigade had been built or out of which it had grown. Components of brigades that had suffered heavy losses as the result of German antipartisan operations sometimes joined other brigades.[19]

The designations of the bands in the German reports and in the published Soviet sources frequently vary. The Germans usually referred to the otryads and brigades by the name of their leaders, except for those that were named for important Soviet personalities or that bore patriotic titles such as *Za Rodinu* (For the Fatherland). Occasionally, the units were given numerical designations, such as 1st, 2d, 3d, 4th Kletnya Brigades.[20] On the other hand, Soviet books on partisan warfare published since the war usually refer to the otryads, at least in the earlier stage of partisan organization, by the name of the rayon or town in which they were activated and from which their members were presumably recruited. For example, the otryad that the Germans named for its commander, Duka, is identified in a Soviet source as the "otryad of Bryansk City partisans." In the same book the Romashin detachment is called the "otryad of Bryansk Rayon partisans."[21] Undoubtedly, the formation of the brigades in part represented an attempt by the Soviet authorities to infuse principles of military organization and command into the partisan movement. The great diversity in size, internal composition, and equipment of the brigades indicates, however, that this attempt was only partly successful. Despite their military titles many of the partisan formations, even during the later stage of the war, retained some of the

[19] For example, see the order-of-battle list of brigades in the South Forest in February 1943 where this was true for six of the nine brigades listed. (442. Div.z.b.V., Ia, "Vermutliche Gruppengliederung innerhalb der Brigaden," 25 February 1943, p. 1, GMDS, PzAOK 2, 37075/90.)

[20] As a result of the large-scale German antipartisan operation "Zigeunerbaron" in the southern sector in June 1943, the Romashin Brigade suffered heavy losses, and its remnants joined the Duka Brigade. (Abw. Tr. 107 beim PzAOK 2, Kdo O'Grad, "Die Bewegungen der Bandenbrigaden 'Duka,' 'Romaschin' und 'Smert nemetzkim okkupantam' waehrend und nach dem Unternehmen 'Zigeunerbaron,' " 21 June 1943, pp. 2–3, GMDS, PzAOK 2, 37075/168.) In the north, the Bytosh Brigade was almost wiped out during Operation 'Freischuetz' and taken into the newly formed Korchalov Brigade. (707. Inf.Div., "Feindnachrichtenblatt Nr. 1/43," *op. cit.*)

[21] P. Vershigora, *Lyudi s chistoi sovestyu* (Moscow: Sovetskii Pisatel, 1951).

characteristics of irregular forces. Why such great differences existed between the various bands has already been suggested above: the role played by the Red Army, Party, and NKVD in the formation and control of the bands was reflected to some extent in peculiarities of organization. Other factors influencing the character of the units have also been mentioned. They include the mission of the bands, the caliber of leadership, and the social and military background of their members. This last problem will be considered in the following paragraphs.

2. Composition of the Bands

a. Recruitment and Reinforcement

From the scanty evidence available for 1941 it appears that the bulk of the Bryansk partisans of that period consisted of Red Army officers and soldiers who had been cut off from their units during the great encirclement battle of Bryansk (1–20 October 1941). In the course of that battle the Soviet forces had been compressed into two pockets, one near Khvastovichi in the eastern part of the area, the other near Trubchevsk in the southern part. Remnants of the Soviet Fiftieth Army which had been destroyed in the Khvastovichi pocket apparently had drifted westward through the German lines, for in November 1941 the German Second Army reported that stragglers from the Fiftieth Army had joined members of a partisan school near Kletnya in the western part of the area in activities which included attacks on German transport vehicles, raids on villages, and the shooting of several mayors installed by the Wehrmacht. This partisan group was later reinforced by thirty parachutists specially trained in Moscow.[22]

As explained in the previous section, the reorganization and build-up of the partisans in the Bryansk area occurred in the winter of 1941–42, particularly in the northern part of the area, where the Red Army had actually broken through the German front, and was utilizing the gap to send through a constant stream of reinforcements to the partisans west and south of Kirov, which was held by Soviet troops. According to a report by the German 339th Division, these reinforcements amounted to 150 men in the beginning of March 1942, and to 750 men during the last days of March and the early part of April.[23] As a result, the partisan formations in this sector were apparently strongly mixed with Red Army or former Red Army personnel. In March 1942 the XXIV Corps estimated that the partisans north of Bryansk numbered 10,000 men "of whom one-third were regular troops."[24] A partisan unit of 1,500 to 2,000 near Lavshino was reported

[22] AOK 2, Ic/AO, "Erfahrungsbericht ueber Partisanenbekaempfung fuer die Zeit vom 1. August bis 31. Oktober 1941," 17 November 1941, p. 4 (GMDS, NOKW–1836).
[23] 339. Inf.Div., Ia/Ic, "Nr. 177/42.," 18 April 1942, p. 3 (GMDS, 339 ID 29087/4).
[24] XXIV. A.K., Ic, "Feindnachrichtenblatt Nr. 82," 1 April 1942, p. 2 (GMDS, XXIV AK 17416/30).

to be composed largely of Red Army men.[25] In April 1942 the 339th Division, on the basis of captured partisan documents, noted that the partisans around Bytosh, another partisan center in the north, comprised the following elements: former officers and Red Army soldiers surviving from the encirclement battles; escaped prisoners of war and stragglers; party officials and NKVD and Komsomol members; leaders and specialists sent in from army staffs (NKVD).[26]

Reports like these just cited do not indicate clearly whether the Red Army personnel with the partisan formations were still regular soldiers or had permanently joined the partisans. More light is thrown on this question by information that the Germans obtained from documents and prisoners in the course of an ambitious but largely unsuccessful operation to destroy the northern bands. In the final report on this operation, details are given on the partisan regiments which had been activated early in 1942.

Officers of the Red Army who were regarded as particularly able assumed command [of these partisan regiments]: Lt. Col. Orlov in Dyatkovo Rayon and Major Kaluga in Rognedino Rayon.

Well-tested, highly decorated officers were assigned to their staffs and as subordinate commanders. Through the front west of Kirov 400 to 500 battle-tested troops of the Red Army were sent to each of the regiments to serve as cadres and instructors.

The formations were activated from: (aa) Red Army personnel cut off during the encirclement battle. (bb) Men from the various partisan groups. (cc) Men from 18 years up who were eligible for military service; these were mobilized in the villages.

The groups listed under (bb) and (cc) above were separated and trained on special drill grounds and camps. Those that made a good showing were selected for the two partisan regiments; the others were distributed among the regular partisan groups. . . .

The Orlov and Kaluga Regiments were counted as part of the Tenth (Tula) Army and were directly subordinate to the Army High Command in Moscow or the command of General Zhukov [commander of the Western Front].[27]

In order to keep the military organization of the group intact for future joint operations with the Red Army, the Orlov Regiment was broken up into smaller units at the beginning of the German antipartisan operation mentioned above.[28] Its close ties with the Red Army were confirmed by the interrogation of a partisan captured near Dyatkovo in August 1942. In describing the partisan order of battle in this area he identified the Orlov detachment, then 700 men strong, and the "Galugo" detachment (most

[25] Kommando-Stab Brand, Ic, "Feindlage," 28 February 1942, p. 1 (GMDS, Korueck 19030/3).

[26] 339. Inf.Div., Ic, "Anlage 6 zu Nr. 177/42, 'Ergebnis der im Pesotschnja-Tal durchgefuehrten Ermittlungen,'" 12 April 1942, p. 6 (GMDS, 339 ID 27087/4).

[27] 339. Inf.Div., Ia, "Bericht ueber Unternehmen Vogelsang," 11 July 1942, pp. 9–10 (GMDS, 339 ID 44418/5).

[28] *Ibid.,* p. 10.

probably the same as the Kaluga group mentioned above) and added that these two groups were composed of Red Army men of the Sixteenth and Tenth Armies.[29] Additional information on the relative numbers of Red Army men and partisans making up the bands is found in the interrogation of another captured partisan, a former Red Army lieutenant who had been discharged from a German prisoner-of-war camp, had settled in Rognedino Rayon, and was later drafted by the partisans. He said that in May 1942 a battalion belonging to the Soviet Tenth Army came into the rayon to carry out the following tasks:

1. Drafting of all Red Army men who had remained in the area as survivors of the encirclement battles or as discharged POW's.
2. Mobilization of those men born in the years 1923 to 1925.
3. Organization of the partisans. The Red Army men and draftees were utilized, first of all, to bring the battalion's strength up to 300 men and, after that, to reinforce the partisan groups.[30]

From the foregoing it appears that, at least in the sectors close to the front, Red Army and former Red Army personnel constituted the core of the early partisan units, acting both as a stiffening force of experienced fighters and as instructors for various elements of the local population that were being recruited. A number of German reports point out that this was often forced recruitment.[31] In June 1942 a nineteen-year-old girl partisan told her German captors that she and other inhabitants of her village were taken from their homes into the woods by so-called "active partisans," soldiers who had remained behind after the encirclement battles. These formed a band of 300 men and issued arms to the civilian men drafted by them.[32] In Zhukovka Rayon, partisan formations were activated by drafting discharged or escaped prisoners of war as well as all young men who had not yet seen military service. Refusal to join was punished by death.[33]

b. Background

(1) AGE GROUPS.—Aside from the general statements, quoted above, that men between the ages of fifteen and fifty-five were drafted by the partisans, no detailed figures on the distribution of age groups within the bands are available. Some examples pieced together from various reports may prove to be interesting, but they can hardly form the basis for generaliza-

[29] Komm. rueckw. Korpsgebiet 447, Ic, "Interrogation of Nikolai Stepanowitsch Sinowkin," 1 September 1942, p. 1 (GMDS, DW-55B).

[30] 339. Inf.Div., Ic, "Interrogation of Sidor Kletschko," 5 July 1942, p. 1 (GMDS, DW-55B).

[31] Korueck PzAOK 2, Ic, "Taetigkeitsbericht," 1 May 1942, p. 1 (GMDS, Korueck 29239/1).

[32] Orts-und Bereichskommandant Chwastowitschi [Interrogation Reports], 23 June 1942, p. 1 (GMDS, 134 ID 28200/32).

[33] 707. Inf.Div., Ic, "Feindnachrichten fuer die Truppe," 30 July 1942, p. 2 (707 ID 27797/3).

tions. Interrogation of a certain B. K. Nikitin, who before his capture was a member of a partisan detachment dispersed by the Germans in June 1942, revealed that his group, apparently not a very large one, included men of the ages shown in Table 2. Some women and children were also

TABLE 2

Ages of men in B. K. Nikitin's partisan detachment

Age	Number of men	Percentage
18–20	10	21
21–25	9	19
26–30	7	16
31–35	6	14
36–40	9	16
41–50	6	14
Total	47	100

with the detachment.[34] Nikitin's diary, which was found by the Germans before he was seized, indicates that the unit he belonged to was neither particularly active nor effective.[35]

There is evidence that some of the partisans were quite young. The Molotov Brigade, a unit operating in the southern sector, was reported to include, in addition to civilians and a small number of former Red Army men, persons born in 1927 and 1928, or boys who were then (1943) fifteen and sixteen years old.[36]

(2) SOCIAL BACKGROUND.—Unfortunately, most of the German interrogation reports, while giving other personal data, do not mention the occupational background of the prisoners. Since other information on this point is also scarce, it is difficult to make a systematic analysis of the social origins of the Bryansk partisans.

Since the area is predominantly rural, many of the partisans recruited locally, especially those conscripted, must have been peasants, that is to say, members of a kolkhoz or sovkhoz. There is evidence, however, that some of the local volunteers and even more of the partisans sent in from the outside had an urban background. A report of the regional military government office at Bryansk for the last three months of 1941 stated that the partisans around Bytosh were composed primarily of workers of the glass factories at Bytosh, Dyatkovo, Ivot, and Star.[37] A captured letter indicates

[34] 134. Inf.Div., Ic, "Vernehmungsbericht des Partisanen Nikitin, Boris K," 6 August 1943, pp. 2–5 (GMDS, 134 ID 28200/32).
[35] 134. Inf.Div., Ic, "Tagebuch des Partisanen Nikitin, P.K. [sic]" [translation from Russian], 30 June 1942 (GMDS, 134 ID 28200/32).
[36] Auffrischungstab 3, "Feindnachrichtenblatt," 10 May 1943, p. 4 (GMDS, XLVII AK 23241/6).
[37] FK 184 [Activity Report for 12 October 1941 to 25 January 1942], 25 January 1942, p. 5 (GMDS, PzAOK 2, 30233/65).

that one of the earlier bands in the same general area was made up of young workers from the Stalin works at Ordzhonikidzegrad.[38] The captured diary of the "chekist" detachment which operated in this area in 1942 was composed by volunteers from an unidentified factory at or near Tula. These men had formed the unit in April 1942, over the protests of the factory manager, who did not want to lose his skilled workers. After some training on the factory grounds, the group was transported by train via Moscow to a place close to the front from which the men, with the help of local guides, infiltrated the German lines.[39] Finally, another German report on the northern partisans said that, at the end of March 1942, 150 untrained volunteers who had been sent through the lines into the partisan area were male and female factory workers from Moscow.[40]

Reports which deal with the social origin and political affiliation of the partisan leaders indicate that many of them were Red Army officers as well as Party, Komsomol, and local government officials—people who had close ties with the Soviet regime and therefore a higher stake in it than most of the rank-and-file partisans.[41]

Information on the party affiliation of the ordinary band members is difficult to find. The captured work log of the politruk of a partisan company states that only six partisans in his company (which presumably had a strength of 80–150 men) were Party members. Some others appear to have belonged to the Komsomol.[42] Seventy per cent of the men in a detachment operating near Ivot were reported to be Komsomol members.[43] That other detachments were also made up of a high proportion of Communist youths is indicated by the letter, mentioned above, from the Ordzhonikidzegrad partisans who called themselves "Komsomol partisans of Ordzhonikidzegrad."[44]

[38] [PzAOK 2, Ic, "Translation of captured letter from Komsomol partisans of Ordzhonikidzegrad to their fellow workers of the Stalin factory"] n.d. (GMDS, PzAOK 2, 30233/66, envelope in back of folder).

[39] [331. Inf.Div.] "Tagebuch der Partisanenabteilung 'Tschekist' " (translation from Russian), n.d. (GMDS, 331 ID 31476/11).

[40] 339. Inf.Div., Ic, "Nr. 177/42," 12 April 1942, p. 6 (GMDS, 339 ID 29087/4).

[41] For example, the commander of a detachment in the eastern sector was the local MTS director, the deputy commander was the former secretary of the *raikom*. (Bereichskdtr. Chwastowitschi, "Vernehmung von Partisanen der Partisanenabteilung 'Kampf fuer die Heimat,' " 2 September 1942, p. 2, GMDS, 134 ID 28200/32.) The leader of the Bryansk rayon detachment was identified, both by a captured partisan and by a Soviet journalist who wrote an account of partisan warfare after the war, as the secretary of the Bryansk (rural) *raikom*. [Orts-und Bereichskommandant Chwastowitschi, "Vernehmung des Partisanen Kokuschow," 29 June 1942, p. 1, GMDS, 134 ID 28200/32; cf. V. Andreyev, *Narodnaya voina (zapiski partizana)* (Moscow: Gosudarstvennoye Izdatelstvo Khudozhestvennoi Literatury, 1952), p. 285.]

[42] 707. Inf.Div., Ic, "Feindnachrichtenblatt fuer die Truppe Nr. 16," 10 November 1942, p. 1 (GMDS, 707 ID 27797/4).

[43] Abw. Gr. bei PzAOK 2, "Vernehmung des Sergei Michailow," 10 June 1942 (GMDS, PzAOK 2, 30233/66).

[44] [PzAOK 2, Ic, "Translation of captured letter from Komsomol partisans of Ordzhonikidzegrad to their fellow workers of the Stalin factory"] n.d. (GMDS, PzAOK 2, 30233/66, envelope in back of folder).

Lastly, a German report speaks of a special battalion for the disruption of rail communications which was "composed primarily of Party members and had been activated in Moscow early in 1942." The report said that for reasons of security it was later given the cover name, "Ground Battalion of the Air Force, No. 1124." It is doubtful that this unit was a genuine partisan band; probably it was organized as a special sabotage unit of the Red Army.[45]

B. DIRECTION AND CONTROL

1. Internal Control

The military character of the partisan movement is reflected in the command structure of individual units. Even in 1942, when most of the partisan bands were not fully organized along military lines, their command set-up corresponded to that of regular Red Army formations. It invariably consisted of a commander, a commissar, and a chief of staff, though the latter, at least in the beginning, was often called "aide to the commander" or "adjutant," a more appropriate title in units of less than battalion size.[46] The larger detachments also had other officers who commanded such subordinate units as companies and platoons. As the units grew in size and organizational complexity, the number of officers also increased. For example, the officer complement of some of the brigades in the Kletnya Forest consisted of commander, commissar, chief of staff, deputy chief of staff, two battalion commanders, three company commanders, nine platoon leaders, six politruks [commissars on company level]. Some of the platoon leaders were not commissioned officers, but sergeants.[47] Obviously, this was not the complete officer complement. Since each battalion had three companies of three platoons each, the number of company commanders should have been six and of platoon leaders eighteen.

The chain of command above brigade level will be discussed in the section dealing with external control, since even those higher command echelons that were physically located on the German side of the front were agencies of Soviet control rather than integral parts of the partisan movement.

Next in importance to the commander was the commissar, whose chief

---

[45] XXIV. A.K., Ic, "Feindnachrichtenblatt Nr. 84," 6 April 1942, p. 2 (GMDS, XXIV 17416/30).

[46] Korueck 532, Ic, "Vernehmung des Sirgej Herbatschow," 13 June 1942 (GMDS, PzAOK 2, 30233/66). German sources on internal command organization during the early period of partisan warfare are not abundant. The best account is contained in the memoirs of the partisan leader Kovpak whose band operated at the southern edge of the Bryansk area for several months in 1942. [Sidor Kovpak, *Ot Putivlya do Karpat* (Moscow: Gosudarstvennoye Izdatelstvo Detskoi Literatury, 1945).]

[47] 98. Inf.Div., "Feindnachrichtenblatt ueber die Partisanengruppen des Kletnja-Waldes," 12 May 1943, p. 1 (GMDS, 98 ID 38038/10, Anlage 167).

function was the political indoctrination of the members of the band. His position as political control officer did not, however, give him authority to override decisions of the commander or countermand his orders. The commissar nevertheless seems frequently to have played a leading role in the conduct of the bands' operations, since he usually was the deputy commander and assumed leadership if the commander was killed, captured, or reassigned. For example, the commander of the 2d Kletnya Brigade, Kaluga, was wounded in action early in January 1943 and was evacuated by air. When his plane was shot down over the German lines and Kaluga was captured, the commissar of the brigade (and thus deputy commander), Lebedev, who had immediately assumed temporary command after Kaluga's wounding, formally became the new commander. Lebedev himself was killed shortly afterwards by a mine that exploded in partisan headquarters in the Mamayevka Forest.[48] Another commander of one of the brigades in the North Forest, Korchalev, had been commissar of an otryad before he became brigade leader.[49]

As indicated in the previous section, the personality and experience of the commander and his lieutenants often had a decisive influence on the development and performance of the band. It is necessary therefore to inquire into the social and military background of the leadership corps.

It appears that many of the leaders of the early partisan bands were Red Army officers. A report of Second Panzer Army on the partisan situation in the rear area said: "[Our] informants confirm that the leadership [of the bands] generally is in the hands of officers (mostly senior staff officers) and commissars. . . ."[50]

Many of the leaders in the northern sector of the Bryansk area seem to have had a military background. The commanders of the two partisan regiments encountered by the Germans in the spring of 1942, Orlov and Kaluga, were identified in German reports as particularly able officers of the Red Army. Orlov was reportedly a lieutenant colonel and Kaluga a major. Their subordinate commanders were reported to be "well-tested, highly decorated officers."[51] The military background of Kaluga is confirmed in a captured partisan document in which the commander of the 330th Red Army Infantry Division orders certain partisan detachments

[48] 707. Inf.Div., Ic, "Abschlussbericht zu den Unternehmen Klette I & II," 10 February 1943, p. 2 (GMDS, Korueck 44404/3, Anlage 231).
[49] 707. Inf.Div., Ic, "Feindnachrichtenblatt Nr. 143," 21 June 1943, p. 4 (GMDS, 707 ID 41762/2).
[50] PzAOK 2, Qu 2, "Partisanenlage im rueckwaertigen Armeegebiet," 20 February 1942, p. 2 (GMDS, Korueck 19030/3). The commander of the partisan group which operated in the Kletnya Forest in the fall of 1941 was a senior officer who had been brought in by plane. (AOK 2, Ic/AO, "Erfahrungsbericht ueber Partisanenbekaempfung fuer die Zeit vom 1. August bis 31. Oktober 1941," 17 November 1941, p. 4, NOKW-1836.)
[51] 339. Inf.Div., Ia, "Bericht ueber Unternehmen Vogelsang," 11 July 1942, p. 8 (GMDS, 339 ID 44418/5).

to follow the orders of "First Lieutenant Galog" (presumably Kaluga) so as to effect close coordination with Red Army operations. This document is dated February 1942, five months before the German report cited above was issued; it is quite possible that Kaluga was promoted from first lieutenant to major during this interval, which was marked by violent fighting between the partisans and the Germans.[52]

Another captured document indicates that the chief of staff of an independent partisan detachment in the Ordzhonikidzegrad area was a Red Army captain who had formerly commanded a rifle regiment of the 279th Division, part of the Soviet Fiftieth Army.[53] This army was virtually destroyed in the encirclement battles of 1941, and the captain, a man by the name of Markov, probably was a straggler who had joined the partisans. His unit was apparently later absorbed by the brigade led by Orlov.[54]

Korbut, the leader of another brigade in the northern sector, apparently was a major in the Red Army. His unit, sometimes called the 3d Partisan Division, had originally been commanded by the aforementioned Kaluga, who in the fall of 1942 had assumed command of a brigade in the Kletnya Forest.[55]

Not all partisan commanders in the north, however, were military men. The organizers and leaders of detachments activated in 1941 and early 1942 around Dyatkovo and Bytosh seem to have been predominantly Communist Party, government, and NKVD officials. For example, a report of the German regional military government office at Bryansk for the last three months of 1941 stated that the head of all the partisans around Bytosh was the director of the local glass factory, and the Party secretary of the Dyatkovo *raikom* also played a leading role among the partisans there.[56] The Romashin and Duka detachments, which later became brigades and operated with considerable success south of Bryansk, also were active in the Dyatkovo region in April 1942. Both German and Soviet sources indicate that Romashin was a secretary of the Party committee of the rural Bryansk rayon.[57] Two subordinate commanders of

[52] 339. Inf.Div., Ia/Ic, "Uebersetzung von Beutepapieren aus dem Pesotschnja-Tal," 18 April 1942, Anlage 7–4 (GMDS, 339 ID 29087/4).

[53] Markov, "Bericht an den Chef der 8. Abt. des Stabes der 16. Armee-Bachtin," 13 June 1942 (GMDS, PzAOK 2, 30233/66).

[54] Korueck 532, Ic, "Feindlage, Stand 26. Maerz 1943," 28 March 1943, p. 3 (GMDS, PzAOK 2, 37075/91).

[55] *Ibid.* See also Gen.Kdo. Korps Niedersachsen [code name for LV. A.K.], Ic, "Feindlage im Raum nordwestl. Brjansk," 16 May 1943, p. 1 (GMDS, LV AK 36358/9).

[56] FK 184 [Activity report for 12 October 1941 to 25 January 1942], 25 January 1942, p. 6 (GMDS, PzAOK 2, 30233/65).

[57] Orts- und Bereichskommandant Chwastowitschi, "Vernehmung des Partisanen Pankrat Kokusehow," 29 June 1942, p. 1 (GMDS, 124 JD 28200/32). See also Andreyev, p. 285; and 134. Inf.Div., Ic, "Partisanen-Vernehmungsbericht," 2 July 1942, pp. 4–5 (GMDS, 134 ID 28200/32).

the Romashin detachment were chairmen of village soviets.[58] Duka was secretary of the Bryansk City *raikom*.[59] Both Duka and Romashin later were made Heroes of the Soviet Union.[60]

A number of partisan leaders in the northern sector, particularly in the early part of 1942, appear to have been NKVD officials or agents. A German report, which was based on captured partisan documents, states: "The supervision of the partisan leaders, who as a rule are NKVD people, is in the hands of the NKVD central office of the unoccupied territory. . . ."[61] The role of these NKVD leaders will be discussed in detail in the part of this section dealing with external controls.

The background of the partisan commanders in the southern sector is more difficult to determine. German reports giving the order of battle of the bands in this area list the names of the leaders but contain no hints on their background. The interrogation of a nurse who had spent considerable time with the Stalin Brigade in the South Forest and, after deserting to the Germans in 1943, gave them a complete order-of-battle list of the bands there, provides little information on this point. One of her statements, however, may serve as a clue.[62] She said that Koshelev, the commander of the Chapayev Brigade, enjoyed a reputation as a military expert among the partisan leaders of the south, which suggests that most of the others had little or no formal military experience. The commander of the Stalin Brigade, a Captain Zmorokov, appears to have been a Red Army officer, but the deserter referred to him rather contemptuously as a "rear echelon soldier."[63] Judging by her comments, the commissar and the chief of staff of the brigade were more forceful and competent than the commander. The commissar, who held the Order of Lenin, had organized the original detachment from which the brigade developed. The chief of staff is described as "the most capable of the leaders, a man who had escaped from many traps."[64] It is likely that these two officers played an important, if not a decisive role, in the leadership of the brigade, as may have happened in other cases when the commander of a partisan unit was overshadowed in personality and experience by one or several of his chief lieutenants. Nevertheless, there is no evidence that this occurred frequently, nor must the fact that all orders of the partisan commander were countersigned by the commissar and the chief of staff be regarded

[58] 134. Inf.Div., Ic, "Partisanen-Vernehmungsbericht," 2 July 1942, pp. 4–5 (GMDS, 134 ID 28200/32).

[59] Vershigora, p. 42.

[60] 318, Inf.Div. [code name for 18. Pz.Div.], Ic, "Feindnachrichtenblatt Nr. 5/43," 14 May 1943 (GMDS, 18 PzDiv 32207/12, Anlage 405).

[61] 339. Inf.Div., Ic, "Nr. 177/42," 12 April 1942, p. 1 (GMDS, 339 ID 29087/4).

[62] 404. Div. [code name for 4. Pz.Div.], Ic, "Vernehmungsbericht Nr. 22P," 5 June 1943, pp. 3–4 (GMDS, 4 PD 34335/16, Anlage 86). The leader of one otryad is identified as the former director of the cannery at Trubchevsk.

[63] *Ibid.*

[64] *Ibid.*

as a sign that authority within the bands was divided. Nothing found in the records pertaining to the Bryansk area indicates that the commissar, for example, had the right to override decisions of the commander or to countermand his orders.

2. External Control of Partisan Units

Although the early history of the Bryansk partisans is obscured by lack of information, there are indications that efforts were made from the very beginning to exercise some measure of control over the bands from the Soviet side of the front. In these efforts, the Communist Party, the Red Army, and the NKVD apparently all participated. The nature of the specific agencies created for control and direction of the partisans begins to become clear from the available sources only in the spring of 1942, but even after that date their exact form and composition remain beclouded by conflicting and contradictory evidence.

Moreover, there was never a single chain of command in this area, for reasons that will become apparent. The diversity of command structure above the brigade level stemmed largely from the fact that the area as defined for this study, while lying almost entirely within Orel Oblast, cut across the jurisdiction of different Soviet military headquarters. Consequently, the partisans in the various sectors of the area came under the control not of one, but of several command echelons on the Soviet side.

A. Party

There is no evidence on the nature and extent of Party control before the spring of 1942. It must be assumed that, by then, Party control concerned itself primarily with matters of discipline and organization, rather than with tactical problems. It was at this time, too, that the Party organization began to exercise some control and supervision over the bands. The available evidence, however, pertains only to the southern sector. In April or May 1942, a representative of the Orel Oblast Committee (obkom) flew to the headquarters of the partisan command in the South Forest at Smelizh, and from then on regular ties were maintained between the obkom and the bands.[65] The Smelizh command post housed the headquarters of a staff that controlled all partisan detachments in the area south of the Navlya and east of the Desna Rivers. Chief of this staff was Yemlyutin, a former official of the Orel Oblast NKVD; A. D. Bondarenko, a Komsomol organizer and rayon Party secretary, was commissar. The composition and functions of the Yemlyutin staff, which will be discussed in more detail in the paragraphs dealing with Red Army control, evidently did not become known to the Germans until the fall of 1942 when a number of its orders and documents fell into their hands.

[65] Andreyev, p. 306.

These documents reveal that the Yemlyutin staff was called the United Partisan Detachments of the Western Rayons of Orel Oblast.[66] Apparently this title had been conferred upon it during the course of a meeting of prominent partisan leaders with Stalin, K. E. Voroshilov, and P. N. Ponomarenko in Moscow in August 1942. According to a Soviet source, Yemlyutin was formally confirmed at the meeting as chief of the Partisan Detachments of the Western Rayons of Orel.[67]

At the same time, the relation of the Orel Oblast Committee to the partisans was also formalized by the appointment of A. P. Matveyev, secretary of the *obkom,* as Chief of the Orel Partisan Staff.[68] The exact functions and area of responsibility of this staff are not described in either German or Soviet sources; it appears, however, that the staff had control only over the bands under Yemlyutin's command, that is to say, over the southernmost sector of the Bryansk area. In 1942 the partisans in the northern and western sectors were already under the control of the West Front and other Red Army commands. Early in 1943, as we shall see, the Red Army took command of the southern sector as well, and the Orel Staff then became the Staff of the Partisan Movement of the Bryansk Front.[69]

b. Red Army

The reorganization and strengthening of the partisan movement in the winter of 1941–42 was to a large extent the work of the Red Army. It has been explained above that Red Army and former Red Army personnel constituted the core of the early bands and that Red Army officers were among the leaders. There is evidence, moreover, that early in 1942 contact was established between the partisans and regular Red Army commands. This can best be demonstrated by a survey of events in the northern sector.

In the course of the operations that the Germans conducted in February–April 1942 against the forces defending Kirov, they captured a number of documents that give fairly good insight into methods of co-ordination and control of the partisans by the Red Army. The partisans in this sector not only engaged in disruptive activities in the German rear but also helped to defend the southern flank of the Kirov salient.

[66] Korueck 532, Ic, "Befehl Nr. 98 der Vereinigten Partisanen-Abteilungen in den westlichen Rayons des Oreler Gebietes, 2 Oktober 1942," 19 December 1942 (GMDS, PzAOK 2, 30233/6).

[67] Vershigora, p. 42.

[68] *Ibid.*

[69] No documents pertaining to the manner and date of this change can be found. The only evidence to the effect that the two staffs were identical is a report dated August 1943 in which Matveyev is mentioned as Chief of the Partisan Movement of the Central Front, the Central Front by then having taken over the sector of the Bryansk Front. (Korueck 580, Ic, "Monatsbericht August ueber Bandentaetigkeit," 28 August 1943, p. 3, GMDS, AOK 2, 60311/21.) See also Andreyev, p. 347.

The Germans summed up the situation as follows: "The partisan movement in this area receives its instructions directly from the Red Army.... The local leadership is in the hands of a partisan main staff to which a number of other partisan staffs are subordinated. The partisan staffs in turn have one or several groups under them. Strength of these groups generally is 80–100 men...."[70] The missions of the partisan units were described as follows:

1. Extensive sabotage and interference directed against the occupying power.
2. Reconnaissance in the enemy rear.
3. Occupation and defense of as many villages as possible.
4. Recruitment of men capable of bearing arms; requisitioning of supplies in partisan-held areas.
5. Propaganda activities directed at the population and at German forces.
6. Direct support of Red Army combat operations.[71]

In addition to these functions the partisans were to supply certain products, particularly food and animal fodder, to the Red Army. The latter, in turn, supplied the partisans with arms and ammunition, chiefly from captured German stocks.[72]

The manner in which these tasks were to be accomplished is spelled out in more detail in another German report. The first of them—disruptive activities in the enemy rear—was the primary, over-all mission, which the individual partisan detachments were expected to carry out largely on their own initiative and without specific orders from above. The execution of the other missions, however, was subject to direction and control by higher headquarters. As far as missions 2–5 above were concerned, specific instructions were worked out jointly by the partisan staffs that controlled the units involved in any one operation and the headquarters of the (Soviet) Army facing the area in which the partisans were active. For support of combat operations by partisan bands and assignment of special missions, orders were issued directly by Army headquarters or by the Red Army division that had jurisdiction over the sector. The partisan staffs were required to channel to Army headquarters recruits who had been mobilized in the partisan-held areas and to forward reports on actions completed and information collected.[73]

In February and March 1942 the partisan detachments in the northern sector received tactical orders from the 330th Rifle Division, whose headquarters were at Kirov. The documents captured by the Germans include

[70] 339. Inf.Div., Ia/Ic, "Nr. 177/42," 12 April 1942, p. 1 (GMDS, 339 ID 29087/4).
[71] *Ibid.*, p. 2.
[72] *Ibid.*
[73] 339. Inf.Div., Ia/Ic, "Uebersetzung von Beutepapieren aus dem Pesotschnja-Tal," 18 April 1942, Anlage 6, pp. 4–5 (GMDS, 339 ID 29087/4).

several such directives. On 19 February 1942 the 330th Division ordered several partisan detachments to place themselves under the command of a Red Army officer so as to insure full cooperation with the Red Army.[74] On 21 February the Buchino detachment was ordered by the division to proceed to Kirov to receive a special assignment.[75]

In a German evaluation of the captured documents, the commander of this detachment, Akimochkin, was said "to possess the special confidence of the commander of the 330th Division." It seems that the divisional commander had appointed him immediately after the Buchino detachment had established contact with the Red Army, an indication that Akimochkin was considered more competent or more reliable than the original organizer and leader of the detachment.[76]

Measures like these apparently were taken because the Red Army command was dissatisfied with the degree of coordination between the various bands. According to German estimates this lack of coordination was regarded by the Soviet authorities as an impediment to activity directed against the Germans. To overcome this deficiency, more competent leaders were sent into the partisan area in order to establish a unified command and to achieve closer coordination among widely scattered partisan units as well as with the Red Army. In this fashion the Red Army command hoped to utilize the bands more effectively in support operations.[77] A number of villages in the Kirov sector were defended by mixed partisan and Red Army units. For example, the village of Malyi Zheltoushki was held by 200 Red Army troops and 40 partisans. Command here, as in the case of other combined forces, was in the hands of Red Army officers.[78] Contact between these forces and Kirov was maintained by regular daily courier service. A similar service also existed with the partisan headquarters at Bytosh and Dyatkovo.[79] As the result of energetic German efforts to reduce the enemy forces in this sector, the traffic from the partisan areas to Kirov was limited to the following categories: weekly officer courier from Kirov to Buchino, transportation of some letter mail, and infiltration of specialists, such as agents, reinforcements, and NKVD leaders.[80]

The close cooperation that existed between partisan units and the Red Army in the Kirov area is also revealed in the captured diary of one partisan detachment sent in from the outside. The author noted that on 18 May 1942 the detachment commander went to division headquarters at Kirov

[74] *Ibid.,* Anlage 7–4. This document has already been cited above, n. 52.
[75] *Ibid.,* Anlage 7–5.
[76] *Ibid.,* Anlage 8.
[77] *Ibid.*
[78] *Ibid.,* Anlage 6.
[79] *Ibid.*
[80] 339. Inf.Div., Ic, "Nr. 177/42," 12 April 1942, p. 3 (GMDS, 339 ID 29087/4).

(obviously the 330th Division) to receive instructions. The division proposed that the detachment attempt to break through the German lines. But, the author said, "we did not agree with this." Thereupon a regimental commissar appeared at the detachment command post and ordered the partisans to capture a forester station which housed a German outpost detail of forty men. This move would open the way through the front to the partisan-held territory in the German rear. The detachment set out on this mission only to discover that the outpost was located between two German-held villages from which the partisan flanks could be threatened. Thereupon the partisan commander refused to carry out this assignment too.[81] Such a refusal is an interesting commentary on early partisan–Red Army relationships, although it is doubtful if definite conclusions regarding the effectiveness of Red Army control over the partisans can be based on such incidents.

Despite local successes against the partisans in April 1942, the Germans failed to halt Red Army efforts to strengthen the partisan movement in the northern sector. Red Army stragglers, discharged or escaped prisoners of war, and the physically best-qualified elements of the local population were organized into two partisan regiments under the leadership of Red Army officers Lieutenant Colonel Orlov and Major Kaluga. Details about these units and their leaders have already been provided in the sections on internal organization and control. Important here is the relationship of these partisan regiments to the Red Army. According to German intelligence reports, "they formed part of the Tenth Army and were directly subordinate to the Red Army High Command in Moscow and Zhukov's command."[82] Information obtained later from captured partisans confirmed that the two partisan regiments in the north were controlled by the Tenth and Sixteenth Armies,[83] which were part of the West Front commanded by General G. K. Zhukov. This would explain the statement in the earlier report to the effect that the partisan units were directly subordinate to Zhukov.

The West Front apparently was also the echelon through which the Red Army exercised control over the bands in the western sector of the Bryansk area. A German report of January 1943 stated that the four brigades in the Kletnya Forest had been combined into "the Fourth Partisan Division (Tenth Army), Staff West Front."[84] The same report noted the existence of another staff, possibly of a partisan division, headed by Maltsev.[85] The

[81] 331. Inf.Div., Ic, "Anlage zum Taetigkeitsbericht, 5.2.42—28.12.42," n.d. (GMDS, 331 ID 31475/11, Anlage 63).

[82] 339. Inf.Div., Ia, "Bericht ueber Unternehmen Vogelsang," 11 July 1942, p. 9 (GMDS, 339 ID 44418/5).

[83] Kdt.rueckw.Korpsgebiet 447, Ic ["Interrogation of Nikolai Stepanowitsch Sinowkin"], 1 September 1942, p. 1 (GMDS, DW -55B). See also 339. Inf.Div., Ic, "Interrogation of Sidor Kletschko," 5 July 1942, p. 1 (GMDS, DW 55-B).

[84] Korueck 532, Ic, "Feindlage im Korueck-Gebiet," 30 January 1943, p. 1 (GMDS, PzAOK 2, 37075/90).

[85] Ibid., p. 2.

band led by Maltsev is referred to in other German reports as the "Third Partisan Division."[86] It is possible that these divisional staffs were patterned on the two partisan divisions—the 1st and the 2d—which had been formed in the Yelnya area in 1942. [See Chap. VII.] Perhaps they were organized by Soviet General P. A. Belov, the former chief of all partisan forces in the Yelnya area, who was reported to have assumed command of the partisans in the Roslavl-Bryansk-Gomel area in October 1942.[87] Belov's presence in the Bryansk area, if it occurred, seems to have been short; in any event it is not mentioned in other German reports.

Red Army control over the partisans in the eastern and southern parts of the Bryansk area was exercised first through the Bryansk Front, and from April 1943 on, through the Central Front. Both of these army groups had their headquarters at Yelets most of the time.

The bands operating in the eastern sector around Karachev were directly under the Soviet Sixty-first Army, one of the armies under the Bryansk Front. According to German reports, these bands were, however, not partisans but rather special sabotage units composed of Red Army personnel operating under control of the Intelligence Section (*Razvedotdel*) of the Sixty-first Army.[88]

Southeast of these bands, in Mikhailovka Rayon, the rayon Party secretary Panchenko commanded about 2,000 partisans, who were organized into five detachments.[89] Panchenko's command, under the title of Staff of the United Partisan Detachments of Kursk-Orel Oblasts, resembled in composition and function the Yemlyutin staff in the Southern Bryansk Forest,[90] but, in addition to regular partisan activities, it engaged in widespread espionage for the Red Army. The extent of these activities is indicated in the report that a German intelligence unit made after an exhaustive investigation; the close control of the Red Army command of the Bryansk Front is also emphasized:

It must be assumed that Panchenko's staff is under the direction of the partisan section of the Bryansk Front.
Panchenko's headquarters staff has also embarked on extensive espionage activities; in this work it is subordinate to the RO (*Razvedotdel*, Intelligence

---

[86] Korueck 532, Ic, "Feindlage, Stand 26. Maerz 1943," 28 March 1943, p. 2 (GMDS, PzAOK 2, 37075/91). See also Gen.Kdo. Korps Niedersachsen [code name for LV. A.K.], Ic, "Feindlage im Raum nordwestl. Brjansk," 16 May 1943, p. 1 (GMDS, LV AK 36358/9).

[87] 221. Sich.Div., Ia, "Vorschlag fuer ein Unternehmen gegen die Bandengruppen im Waldgebiet Mamajewka-Kletnja," 30 October 1943, p. 1 (GMDS, 221 ID 35408/2, Anlage 285).

[88] Abw. Tr. 107 bei PzAOK 2, Kdo O'Grad, "Bandenlage im Waldgebiet Karatschew," 15 June 1943 (GMDS, PzAOK 2, 37075/168).

[89] Gruppe Widder, "Aktenvermerk," 7 October 1942 (GMDS, PzAOK 2, 37075/90).

[90] Mikhailovka itself lies outside the area of this study. Panchenko's band is discussed here because its activities reached into the Bryansk area.

Section) of the Bryansk Front and presumably is also in contact with the RO of the Southwest Front. In carrying out intelligence work in the rear area the activities [of the Panchenko band] touch those of the partisan staffs at Bryansk and Lokot, the system of contact and relay points thus forming a wide perimeter around the front of the [German] Second Panzer Army between Bolkhov and Ponyry and reaching deep into the sector of the army on the right flank. . . .[91]

The role of the Bryansk Front in relation to the partisans in the southern sector is more complicated. It will be recalled that the bands there, while remaining nominally independent, were subordinated, in 1942, to an operational control staff commanded by Yemlyutin. The tight control that this staff exercised over the individual detachments is demonstrated in two captured orders. These documents show that the detachments were not only given operational orders detailing their missions but also instructions as to how and where to establish their camps and to train their members.

That Yemlyutin was in close contact by radio and airplane with the headquarters of the Bryansk Front at Yelets is evident from a number of German reports.[92] What is less clear is who were Yemlyutin's superiors at the Bryansk Front. Several German sources state flatly that Yemlyutin received his instructions from the *Osobyi Otdel* (or "OO," the NKVD Special Section) of the Bryansk Front.[93] In view of the fact that he was an NKVD official it is not unlikely that he had contact with the "OO."[94] On the other hand, a captured partisan informed the Germans that he had been assigned in April 1943 to the Partisan Staff of the Central Front (which had taken over the area of the Bryansk Front). He further stated that the function of this staff was to pass on orders from the Central Front to the partisans of the Bryansk Forest. Most of these directives were of an operational nature: orders for the demolition of certain bridges and for raids on specific villages. The partisans, on their part, radioed back to the staff requests for arms, ammunition, and explosives. The head of the staff was Commissar Epishin, and in addition to his assistant, a lieutenant, the personnel consisted of thirteen enlisted men.[95]

[91] Abw. Tr. 107 bei PzAOK 2, "Bande Pantschenko im System des Nachrichtendienstes der Brjansker-Front und der Suedwestfront," 5 February 1943, p. 1 (GMDS, PzAOK 2, 75915). The intelligence work of the partisan bands is treated in more detail in Chap. V.

[92] XXXXVII. Pz.K., Ic, "Feindnachrichtenblatt, Anlage 2: Bandenlage," 15 March 1943 (GMDS, XLVII AK 37241/9, Anlage 176). See also 404. Div. [code name for 4. Pz. Div.], Ic, "Vernehmungsbericht Nr. 22P," 5 June 1943, p. 3 (GMDS, 4 PzDiv 34335/16, Anlage 86).

[93] Auf.St. 3 [code name for XXXXVII Pz.K.] Ia, "Feindnachrichtenblatt," 10 May 1943, p. 1 (GMDS, XLVII AK 37241/6). See also PzAOK 2, Ic/AO, "Feindnachrichtenblatt Nr. 2/43," 1 March 1943, p. 4 (GMDS, PzAOK 2, 37075/159).

[94] German reports persist in referring to Yemlyutin as a lieutenant colonel; some call him an officer of the Red Army. This may be explained by the fact that Yemlyutin's rank in the NKVD probably was equivalent to that of lieutenant colonel in the Red Army.

[95] 45. Inf.Div., Ic, "Vernehmung des Nikolai Makarow," 19 July 1943, p. 1 (GMDS, 137 ID 37583/9).

Judging by this report alone, the partisan staff of the Central Front at Yelets exercised little direct control over the partisans but served mainly as a transmission point. It is probable, however, that the organization to which the captured partisan belonged was not the partisan staff itself but merely its communication center, an assumption which is supported by the fact that it was located not at Yelets, but at a small railroad station outside it.

The relationship between Yelets and the partisan command of the Bryansk Forest is somewhat clarified by a series of documents which the Germans captured in 1943. These documents also indicate that certain changes had been made in the summer of 1943 within the partisan command on the German side of the front. Yemlyutin had been succeeded by a Lieutenant Colonel Gorshkov.[96] The staff now called itself the Southern Operative Group.[97] It numbered, according to another report, 300 men, had its own "OO," signal detachment, guard company, hospital, and printing plant for the partisan newspaper *Partisanskaya Pravda*.[98] The Operative Group issued strict and detailed instructions to its subordinate units, usually on the basis of broader instructions that it received from the Soviet side. The captured documents indicate that some of the directives were issued by the Central Partisan Staff at Moscow and were signed by its chief, Ponomarenko himself.[99] Other orders to Gorshkov and the brigade commanders under him originated with Matveyev, chief of the partisan staff of the Central Front and secretary of the Orel *obkom*. In July 1943, for instance, Matveyev severely criticized the bands for prematurely breaking off an operation against German rail communications which had begun on the night of 22 June 1943. Complaining that two brigades had issued false reports about their participation or rather nonparticipation in the operation, he threatened reprisals in case of future occurrences of this kind:

I must warn all commanders and commissars of these brigades that they will be relieved of their posts and turned over to a military tribunal if they fail to carry out my orders during the operation planned for the night of 28 July.
Explain to all brigade and otryad commanders and commissars that we are

---

[96] The reasons for relieving Yemlyutin, who went to Moscow in June and did not return, are not clear. It is possible that the Soviet command wanted a man with more military experience to head the partisans, since the summer offensive was being prepared. Gorshkov's succession is confirmed by 137. Inf.Div., Ic, "Partisanen-Vernehmung," 15 June 1943 (GMDS, 137 ID 37583/9), and Korueck 532, Ic, "Feindlage im Korueckgebiet, Stand 22.3.1943," 24 June 1943, p. 2 (GMDS, PzAOK 2, 37075/91).
[97] AOK 9, Ic/AO, "Kampf-Befehl Nr. 0025 des Stabes der suedlichen operativen Gruppe," 2 August 1943 (GMDS, H 14/14). The term "operative group" denotes an echelon of the partisan chain of command which by the middle of 1943 had also been established in other areas. It had essentially the task of operational control of individual partisan bands for the purpose of insuring close tactical coordination. Cf. Chap. IX.
[98] Korueck 532, Ic, "Feindlage im Korueckgebiet. Stand 22.6.1943," 24 June 1943, p. 2 (GMDS, PzAOK 2, 37075/91).
[99] For example, Radiogram Ponomarenko to Gorshkov and all commanders of partisan brigades and detachments, n.d. [July or August 1943?] (GMDS, H 14/14).

committed to carry out sabotage against the railroads to prevent the enemy from removing equipment from our cities and from bringing up reserves to the front. We must also see to it that the population is not taken away as Fascist slave labor.

Reports concerning the start and execution of this operation must reach me on or before 29 July of this year.

[Signed] Matveyev[100]

From the documents and reports cited above, the following tentative picture of the command setup in this part of the Bryansk area emerges:

1. The individual partisan brigades were under close operational control of a command staff (located on the German side of the front) which, by the middle of 1943, was called an "operative group." It evidently corresponded to what was designated in other areas as "an operative group in the rear of the enemy."[101]

2. By the summer of 1943 the operative group which was commanded first by Yemlyutin and later by Gorshkov had become a sizable and well-equipped headquarters, in close and regular communication with its subordinate units on one side, and the headquarters of the Bryansk, later the Central Front at Yelets on the other.

3. There is no evidence that the Red Army exercised much control over the bands in the southern sector before 1943. During 1942 the Orel Partisan Staff, presumably under Party control, directed the partisans here and formed the intermediate echelon between the Yemlyutin staff and the Central Staff of the Partisan Movement in Moscow.

4. Early in 1943 the Red Army, through the Bryansk Front command at Yelets, entered the picture, and the Orel Partisan Staff was then attached to the Bryansk Front headquarters and called the Staff of the Partisan Movement of the Bryansk Front. Later, when the area was taken over by the Central Front, its title was changed accordingly.

5. The partisan section of the Red Army command at Yelets acted not only as a relay point for orders from Moscow and for reports submitted by the bands; it also exercised a considerable degree of direct supervision and control over the bands. This is indicated by the strong communication in which Matveyev reprimanded the partisan leaders for their failure to carry out assignments and threatened stern disciplinary measures in case of future noncompliance.

c. NKVD Controls

The information available on the relationship of the NKVD to the partisan movement in the Bryansk area concerns the northern sector only. On the basis of captured documents and information obtained from local

---

[100] Matveyev to Gorshkov and Savronov, 25 July 1943 (GMDS, H 14/14).

[101] See Chap. IX; also OKH/FHO, *Nachrichten ueber den Bandenkrieg Nr. 1,* 3 May 1943, Anlage 2 (GMDS, H 3/738).

residents, the Germans summarized the situation in April of 1942 with regard to organization and leadership of the partisans between Kirov and Bryansk: "The partisan movement in the area receives its instructions directly from the Red Army. The partisan leaders, generally NKVD men, are being supervised by the NKVD office in the unoccupied territory. The local leadership is in the hands of a partisan main staff to which a number of partisan staffs are subordinated. . . ."[102]

The commander of the main staff, located at Dyatkovo, was an NKVD "member" named Surozov and an engineer by profession. The commander of the Bytosh staff and the deputy commander of the Buchino staff were also identified as NKVD members.[103] This does not necessarily mean that these persons were full-time NKVD officials. More likely they were local people who had been working for the NKVD as agents or informants before the Germans invaded.[104] Apparently, the NKVD fell back on these local agents to organize and command partisan detachments early in 1942. To supervise the organizational work and check on the reliability and efficiency of the partisan commanders, the NKVD sent inspectors into the partisan area, presumably from its office at Kirov. One of these inspectors was captured by the Germans in April 1942. He had been commandant of the NKVD jails at Smolensk and Yukhnov since 1927. After being evacuated to Novo Sibirsk in July 1941, he returned to Smolensk Oblast in January 1942 and was appointed chief of the NKVD of Kuibyshev Rayon, which was then behind the German lines. His task was to organize and control the partisans there; he began on 15 March 1942.[105] When he was captured, a report intended for the NKVD at Kirov was found on his person. This report contains an evaluation of various partisan leaders and observations on the morale of the bands, gathered during the period from 22 March to 2 April 1942.[106] Judging from the report, external control over the partisans during this period was not strict, and the authority of the NKVD to give orders did not remain unchallenged. Sokolov, the NKVD deputy leader of the Buchino detachment, for example, had been relieved of his command apparently without approval by the NKVD. The NKVD inspector was even accused of being in contact with the Germans.[107] The report does not make clear to what extent he was able to reassert his authority.

As will be recalled from the documents cited in the previous section,

---

[102] 339. Inf.Div., Ia/Ic, "Nr. 177/42," 12 April 1942, p. 1 (GMDS, 339 ID 29087/4). This document is also quoted in the section on Red Army controls.

[103] *Ibid.*, Anlage 2.

[104] This is supported by the statement in a captured document that Sokolov, the aforementioned deputy commander of the Buchino staff, had been disenfranchised for a time, which would mean that he had been convicted of a crime or for political activities. Such persons were frequently recruited as NKVD informants. (*Ibid.*, Anlage 3.)

[105] *Ibid.*, Anlage 5.

[106] *Ibid.*, Anlage 3.

[107] *Ibid.*

tactical command over the partisans in this part of the Bryansk area was in the hands of the Red Army. NKVD control seems to have focused largely on security of personnel, i.e., on checking the loyalty and efficiency of the leaders and members of the bands.[108] This is also evident from the statement of a partisan deserter, who told the Germans that in April 1942 an officer in NKVD uniform appeared in his sector (the same general area to which the previous documents refer) to investigate the reliability of individual partisans. On orders of this NKVD officer, two men of the deserter's unit who had been serving in the German indigenous administration and had then been conscripted by the partisans were shot. The deserter himself was afraid that certain incriminating parts of his own past would be revealed.[109]

The work of checking on the reliability of the members of the bands was conducted not only by NKVD men sent in from the outside but also by representatives inside the bands. Reports from other areas indicate that by 1943 each brigade had a regular NKVD security section, the "OO," as part of its staff. No explicit statement confirming this arrangement for the Bryansk area can be found, but it must be assumed that the brigades there had similar agencies. Moreover, the existence of an "OO" on the staff of the operative group in the South Bryansk Forest is revealed in two German reports of June 1943.[110]

§III. Operational Characteristics of Partisan Warfare

A. DISRUPTIVE ACTIVITY IN THE GERMAN REAR

1. Partisan Objectives and Plans

The emphasis placed on the disruption of supply lines is expressed both in German and in partisan sources. In November 1942 the Germans captured several documents in the Bryansk area that reveal the great impor-

[108] One German report said, however, that in the northern sector "the NKVD attached to Army headquarters," presumably referring to the *Osobyi Otdel,* supplied the partisans with instructions on tactics and organization as well as with weapons, explosives, trained leaders, and specialists. (339. Inf.Div., Ia/Ic, "Übersetzung von Beutepapieren aus dem Pesotschnja-Tal," 18 April 1942, Anlage 6, p. 4, GMDS, 339 ID 29087/4.)

[109] Korueck 532, Ic, "Ueberlaeuferaussage," 25 June 1942 (GMDS, PzAOK 2, 30233/66).

[110] Korueck 532, Ic, "Feindlage im Korueckgebiet, Stand 22.6.1943," 24 June 1943, p. 2 (GMDS, PzAOK 2, 37075/91); 137. Inf.Div., Ic, "Partisanenvernehmung," 15 June 1943 (GMDS, 137 ID 37583/9).

tance of the disruption of communication lines in the general context of partisan objectives. The documents, which were signed by the commander, commissar, and chief of staff of the United Partisan Otryads of the Western Rayons of Orel Oblast and the top partisan command in the southern part of the Bryansk area, include a plan that lists the following basic partisan tasks:

1. Extension of the partisan movement in the occupied territory.
2. Disruption in the rear areas of the enemy.
3. Destruction of railroads, bridges, and other lines of enemy communication.
4. Destruction of the enemy's manpower and equipment.
5. Activation of operations of all partisan otryads through raids deep into the enemy's rear, through attacks on enemy garrisons in order to destroy them and to impede antipartisan activities in partisan-held rayons.
6. Organization and conduct of continuous reconnaissance and especially intelligence, through agents who are to be infiltrated into all government organs in the rear of the enemy.[111]

A second document requests certain partisan units to prepare for the winter with a view to disrupting supply lines during this period. Specifically, the order states, "1. The commanding officers of the partisan otryads must take all measures necessary to prepare for the winter, in order that they may combat the German usurpers successfully during the entire period: mainly with diversion on railroad trunk lines to interdict the scheduled transportation of troops, armaments, and technical supplies to the front."[112]

Another order, found in the captured materials mentioned above and addressed to the partisan otryads of Vygonichi Rayon, lists in detail certain special missions which are to be carried out by the otryads. The first requests the otryads to interrupt the Gomel-Bryansk railroad. It prescribes the number of men to be employed in this task (not less than 150), the type of armaments to be carried by each man, the exact location of the proposed activities (between Krasnoye and Vitovka), and the date of the operation. Moreover, the different types of disruptive activities are stated in detail, e.g., systematic derailment of trains, explosion of two bridges, propaganda among the civilian population. Furthermore, the order contains other assignments, such as the destruction of a railroad bridge, and the cutting of telephone wires. In two instances, specific target dates are mentioned, e.g., fifteen trains were to be derailed by 30 October, or a bridge was to be blown up by 20 October 1942.[113]

Additional data on Soviet disruptive activities can be found in a leaflet

---

[111] PzAOK 2, "Plan fuer die Kampfoperationen der Partisanen-Abteilungen gamaess dem Befehl des Volkskommissars fuer die Verteidigung Genosse Stalin Nr. 00/89 vom 5.9.42.," n.d. (GMDS, PzAOK 2, 30233/66).

[112] PzAOK 2, "Befehl Nr. 98 der vereinigten Partisanen-Abteilungen in den westlichen Rayons des Oreler Gebiets," 2 October 1942 (GMDS, PzAOK 2, 30233/66).

[113] PzAOK 2, "Aufgaben fuer die Partisanen-Abteilungen, Die Abt. des Rayons Wygonitschi," n.d. (GMDS, PzAOK 2, 30233/6).

which was dropped over the Bryansk area (evidently some time before 16 February 1942, because it was appended to a German report of that date). It read in part:

> The technically well-equipped German Army requires an uninterrupted and secure connection with the rear area to supply its troops with fuel, ammunition, food, and spare parts. Slight damage to a road suffices to create a traffic jam in a very short time. As a result large quantities of technical material could become an excellent target for our air force or artillery within a short time. . . .
>
> All this illustrates how important it is to cause destruction to the supply lines and routes of retreat.
>
> All highways and railroads must be destroyed. . . .[114]

A German evaluation of partisan aims also underscored the importance of attacking communication lines. In May 1942 a Korueck directive enumerated the following partisan goals:

> The *first* is disrupting supply [*lines*] for the Army. The Soviet Government knows the importance of the railroad for our supply [system] and tries to interrupt or to damage the tracks which are being used. Recently attacks on railroad bridges have increased. . . .
>
> The *second* is combating the *Ordnungsdienst* in German service and the rural population which is working for the German forces.
>
> The *third* is harassing the population through the dissemination of enemy propaganda. . . .[115]

2. General Review of Partisan Disruptive Activities

In May 1942 the Germans noted that partisan warfare in the Bryansk area was characterized "almost exclusively" by demolitions of railroads and highways and by ambushes of German forces.[116] Periodic German reports throughout the occupation indicate that this type of activity—i.e., sabotage, attacks on strongpoints, demolitions, and other mehods employed by partisan groups to destroy German lines of communication—was the major concern of the partisans in the Bryansk area. As the war progressed, the Germans carefully observed the methods employed by the partisans in pursuing their objectives. Their reports are replete with lengthy and detailed descriptions of the technical aspects of sabotage on railroads, planting of mines, and preparing of ambushes.

Because of the paucity of good highways and railroads (all the tracks had to be changed to standard gauge so as to permit the Germans to operate

[114] PzAOK 2, "Auszugsweise Uebersetzung eines russ. Flugblattes an die Bevoelkerung der besetzten Gebiete ueber Partisanentaetigkeit," n.d. (GMDS, PzAOK 2, 37075/170, Anlage 2 zu PzAOK 2, Ic/AO, "Feindnachrichten Nr. 7/42 v. 16.2").

[115] Korueck 532, Qu/Ia, "Richtlinien fuer die Bekaempfung der Partisanen durch die im Sicherungsdienst an Eisenbahnen und Strassen eingesetzten Truppen," 23 May 1942, p. 3 (GMDS, Korueck 29239/3).

[116] Korueck, PzAOK 2, Ic, "Taetigkeitsbericht," May 1942, p. 2 (GMDS, Korueck 29239/1).

their rolling stock), it was important to protect the existing lines of communication and thereby to ensure the uninterrupted flow of supplies to the troops at the front. Although the Germans succeeded, on the whole, in preventing major breakdowns, hardly a week passed that did not witness at least one demolition on the major railroads and highways crossing the Bryansk area. Moreover, there were continual attacks on railroad guards and strongpoints which made it necessary to station permanent security forces along the main lines of traffic.

A general view of the degree of partisan demolitions and attacks on railroads and highways in the Bryansk area (under Korueck jurisdiction) may be obtained from the summary report of the Korueck commander. [See Table 3.] The report states that, although the number of demolitions during the second period (i.e., November 1942 to April 1943) appears smaller than during the earlier period, partisan activities directed at railroads and highways actually increased, since the railroad from Bryansk to Dmitriyev, which was frequently interrupted, was outside the jurisdiction of the Korueck for two and one-half months. Moreover, it is pointed out that attacks during the second reporting period were more intensive, since they were carried out not only by smaller groups but also by partisan units of up to 600 men.[117]

TABLE 3

Partisan demolitions in the Bryansk area,
from the summary report of the Korueck commander

Period	Successful demolitions	Prevented demolitions	Attacks against guards
May 1942—October 1942	260	301	540
November 1942—April 1943	236	222	553
May 1942—April 1943	496	523	1,093

The figures quoted above cannot serve as a yardstick of the over-all effectiveness of partisan disruptive activities, since little information is available on the length of interruptions in the traffic caused by these demolitions. All that can be said is that, on the average, in each month approximately thirty-eight demolitions succeeded as against forty that were prevented; and that partisans made an average of eighty-four attacks against railroads or highways.[118] Only one attack during this period has been mentioned specifically as having had really damaging effects on the German supply sys-

[117] Komm.d.rueckw.Armeegeb.d.2. PzAOK, "Halbjahresbericht November 1942—April 1943," 20 May 1943, p. 2, Anlage 2a (GMDS, PzAOK 2, 37075/91).
[118] A Korueck report of March 1942, reporting on demolitions on the Bryansk-Pochep railroad, stated "Every one of these demolitions interrupts traffic for at least 12 hours." (Korueck, PzAOK 2, "Br.B.Nr. 36/42 geh.," 8 March 1942, p. 1, GMDS, Korueck 19030/3, Anlage 29.)

tem. This was the destruction of the railroad bridge over the Desna River near Vygonichi, which was blown up by partisans during the night of 7 March 1943. The attack caused a temporary interruption of one of the major supply routes serving the Second Panzer Army. For a few days all supply trains had to be re-routed via Smolensk-Roslavl. The Korueck of Second Panzer considered this a "very considerable success" by the partisans. [See n. 124.]

3. Disruptive Activities and Organization

The preoccupation with interrupting communication lines influenced the organization of the bands, and also led to increased specialization within them. This development was supported by the partisan leadership in the unoccupied areas of the USSR, which trained demolition specialists and brought them into the rear areas by air, and also supplied the bands with explosives.

The following types of units were involved in activities aimed at the destruction of the German supply system: [119]

(1) The individual partisan band, which was most commonly engaged in sabotage and demolitions. This was particularly true during the earlier period of the occupation. The bands received instructions advising them on methods for blowing up trains, planting mines, and so forth.

(2) Specialists brought in by air, who were attached to existing bands. These specialists, who had been trained in the unoccupied part of the USSR, became important in the later stages.

(3) Demolition groups or commandos, which were also brought in from the outside and which operated in conjunction with a partisan band. Frequently, the commandos would use a band's camp as a base of operations, but would carry out their missions independently of the band. Others operated completely on their own. In the Bryansk area, a unit of this type was located north of Karachev. The unit, which was composed exclusively of Red Army personnel brought in by air, engaged in intelligence as well as sabotage missions.

4. Operational Methods

The German reports contain many descriptions of partisan operations aimed at interrupting supply lines. Generally, such operations may be grouped under four main headings. The first type of operation, which may be called "covert," required a small group of partisans or demolition experts who, during the night, made their way quietly to the highway or rail-

[119] For reports illustrating these types of partisan units, see, 707. Inf.Div., Ic, "Feindnachrichten Nr. 1," 23 July 1942, p. 1 (GMDS, 707 ID 27797/3, Anlage 100); 221. Sich.Div., Ic, "Banditenlage im Raum der Sich. Division 221," 15 September 1942, pp. 4–5 (GMDS, 221 ID 29380/9, Anlage 2); Chef Sipo u. SD, Einsatzgruppe B., S.k.7c, "Bandenerkundung durch V-Mann L.," 13 September 1942 (GMDS, 221 ID 29380/9, Anlage 31).

road, where they planted mines and cut telephone wires and poles. An illustration of this type of operation is furnished by the following German report of July 1942, which mentions four partisan battalions in the Dyatkovo-Bryansk area. The partisan groups of one of the battalions were charged with the following tasks:

The groups are employed for demolitions. Each group has for this purpose 2 to 3 demolition experts who were brought in by air. Mines and explosives are also brought in by air. For the blowing up of railroads, old Russian ammunition boxes (zinc) are used.... These boxes are buried under the tracks. Through its pressure the moving train sets off the explosion. The partisans leave 2–3 scouts behind who report on the results of the demolition. Mines with electric ignition are also used. In such cases, several groups are lying in ambush to the left and right of the railroad and open fire from machine guns after the demolition. Current observations have shown that the partisans generally plant mines during the late evening hours up to 2300.[120]

In most cases, because the demolition commandos operated from the camps of the bands (which were located in the forests, far distant from the target area) the commandos were forced to make long marches to reach the railroads and highways. To facilitate these operations special staging camps (*Durchgangslager*) were established close to the communication lines, where the commandos could spend the night before carrying out their mission. Partisan hide-outs in villages were also used. A report of June 1943 from Army Group Rear Area described these methods in some detail. It stated that the demolition commando squad, composed of eight to ten men, would be taken in a horse-drawn cart from the camp to the village closest to the target area. After spending the night in the village, the group would advance on foot to the railroad. Four of the men armed with machine guns would act as guards while the others (four to six men) planted the mines.[121]

The establishment of staging camps was of considerable importance in winter when adverse weather conditions strained human and material resources. In October 1942 the Germans destroyed a staging camp situated eight kilometers from the Bryansk-Zhukovka railroad. The camp was large enough to accommodate fifty men.[122]

[120] 707. Inf.Div., Ic, "Feindnachrichten Nr. 1," 23 July 1942, p. 1 (GMDS, 707 ID 27797/3, Anlage 100).
[121] 221. Sich.Div., Ic, "Ic-Befehle und Mitteilungen Nr. 9," 22 June 1943, p. 2 (GMDS, 221 ID 36509/6, Anlage 121).
[122] 707. Inf.Div., Ic, "Lagebericht fuer Monat Oktober 1942," 27 October 1942, p. 1 (GMDS, 707 ID 27797/4); see also 707. Inf.Div., Ic, "Lagebericht fuer Monat Dezember 1942, I January 1943, p. 3 (GMDS, 707 ID 41762/1, Anlage 3) for an excellent description of partisan demolition tactics. The staging area mentioned here was located only five kilometers from the railroad. Mines were not buried under the tracks but placed before the moving train, thus making it impossible for the railroad guards to detect the explosives. For a general description of the above-mentioned activities, see 221. Sich.Div., Ia, "Banditenlage im Nord-Ost-Raum der Division," 24 September 1942, pp. 1–2 (GMDS, 221 ID 35408/1, Anlage 245).

The second type of partisan technique used in attacks against communication lines may be described as the "assault" method; this entailed large-scale attacks on German strongpoints guarding railroads and highways. During these attacks, demolition groups would blow up lines or destroy bridges.

The Germans first mentioned attacks by superior partisan forces on strongpoints in October and November 1942.[123] This "new tactic" was employed more and more as the bands grew in size and strength. Probably the most successful and spectacular attack of this kind was the above-mentioned assault on the railroad bridge over the Desna River near Vygonichi. The operation, which was carried out by the Romashin partisan band on 7 March, involved 600 men, who attacked the German forces guarding the bridge simultaneously from the east and the west. The attackers approaching from the west were beaten off; the other group, however, succeeded in blowing up the bridge.[124]

Several other frontal attacks on major supply lines should also be mentioned. Thus, on 13 March 1943 the Romashin band unsuccessfully attacked German forces at Sinezerki with a view to destroying the railroad bridge over the Revna River (on the Bryansk-Lokot railroad). Five hundred partisans of the Danchenkov band attempted an attack on the Vetma bridge (three kilometers northwest of Zhukovka) on 1 March 1943. They were driven off by the German units guarding the bridge. On 14 March 1943 the same band attacked again. This time the assault was directed at the town of Akulichi (four kilometers northeast of Kletnya) and at a railroad bridge on the Zhukovka-Kletnya line. The band succeeded in blowing up the bridge and in inflicting casualties on the Armenian battalion which was guarding the bridge (nine killed, fifteen wounded, and five missing).[125]

Another method employed in attacks on railroads was the so-called chain demolitions (*Seriensprengungen, Reihensprengungen*). These blasting attempts were carried out both with and without large-scale frontal attacks.

[123] 221. Sich.Div., Ia, "Monatsbericht fuer die Zeit vom 1.11.—30.11.1942," 5 December 1942, p. 2 (GMDS, 221 ID 35408/2, Anlage 385).

[124] Komm.d.rueckw.Armeegeb. d. 2. PzAOK, "Halbjahresbericht (November 1942—April 1943)," 20 May 1943, p. 2, Anlage 2a (GMDS, PzAOK 2, 37075/91); Auffrischungsstab 3, Ic, "Feindnachrichtenblatt," 10 May 1943, p. 5 (GMDS, XLVII AK 37241/6); Korueck 532, Ic, "Feindlage, Stand 26. Maerz 1943," 28 March 1943, p. 4 (GMDS, PzAOK 2, 37075/91); PzAOK 2, Ia, "Meldungen ueber Bandentaetigkeit in der Zeit vom 28.2—31.3.43," 1 April 1943 (GMDS, PzAOK 2, 37075/91, Anlage 1); Wi Kdo Brjansk, "Lagebericht Maerz 1943," 15 March 1943 (GMDS, Wi/ID 2.85). For an evaluation, by the Chief Transportation Officer of Army Group Center, of the effects of the destruction of the Desna bridge on German rail communications immediately preceding the German offensive of summer 1943, see Hermann Teske, *Die silbernen Spiegel* (Heidelberg: Kurt Vowinckel, 1952), pp. 181–82.

[125] Korueck 532, Ic, "Feindlage, Stand 26.Maerz 1943," 28 March 1943, pp. 2–4 (GMDS, PzAOK 2, 37075/91).

The Germans in the Army Group Rear Area first noted this "completely new tactic" in February 1943. A report commenting on it noted that, on 18 February 1943, a band of some 150 men had stealthily approached the Unecha-Krichev railroad and placed seventy-two explosive charges under the tracks. The report claimed that during this operation seventy small demolition groups had been at work simultaneously.[126] During the following month, the same unit again reported chain demolitions, which, however, were combined with attacks on German railroad guards and sabotage of telephone installations.[127]

In the Army Rear Area of Second Panzer a chain demolition, combined with a frontal attack on railroad troops, occurred as early as October 1942. The attack, directed against the Bryansk-Lgov railroad near Deryugino on 13 October 1942, was the subject of a special report, which stated that strong bands totaling 350 men attacked the security forces while special demolition commandos, operating on a stretch 2.4 kilometers long, blew 178 gaps in the line. An estimated fifty commandos carried out their operations while the German forces were pinned down by partisan fire. Interrogations of captured partisans revealed that the demolition specialists had been trained for three months in Tula and had been flown in on seven transport planes. The report pointed out that previous destructions of the railroad, effected by individual mines which were either thrown in front of moving trains or buried under the roadbed, had been repaired within a relatively short period. It warned that there were not sufficient spare tracks available to replace those damaged in mass demolitions.[128] Inasmuch as few chain demolitions were noted in further reports, it may be assumed that this type of attack on railroads played a minor role in the over-all partisan effort to interdict German supplies.[129]

---

[126] 221. Sich.Div., Ia, "Reihensprengungen an der Strecke Unetscha-Kritschew," 21 February 1943, p. 1 (GMDS, 221 ID 36509/8).

[127] 221. Sich.Div., Ic, "Bandenlage im Divisions-Bereich im Monat Maerz 1943," 4 April 1943, p. 1 (GMDS, 221 ID 36509/24, Anlage 4).

[128] PzAOK 2, Ia/Id, "Nr. 2501/42 geh.," 30 October 1942 (GMDS, XXXV AK 35113/2).

[129] Mass demolitions are again mentioned in July-August 1943. Teske, pp. 192–95, notes *Massensprengungen* beginning on 22 July. In a chart showing demolitions during July 1943 (i.e., the period of the Orel battle) two chain demolitions are mentioned on the Unecha-Bryansk railroad and on the Navlya-Bryansk railroad respectively. Further mass demolitions took place in August 1943. According to Teske, the average daily demolitions rose from 36 in July to 45 in August in the area of Army Group Center. The 211th Security Division, which controlled the western rayons of the Bryansk area, also noted mass demolitions during August 1943. While an average of 33 demolitions took place every month during the period from January to July 1943, 1,201 demolitions were recorded in August 1943 in the area under the jurisdiction of this division (from the Dnepr River in the west to the Pochep-Mglin area in the east). (22. Inf.Div., Ic, "Taetigkeitsbericht des Ic vom 1.1 bis 31.8.1943," 19 November 1943, p. 1, GMDS, 221 ID 36509/24.)

Occasionally there are references attesting to certain ingenious tricks designed to outwit German railroad security units. In September 1942, for instance, a report noted that partisans set off mock demolitions some 150 to 1,500 meters north of the Seltso-Rzhanitsa railroad to divert the attention of the German troops from the partisans' real objective, the destruction of the railroad.[130] In another situation, the partisans telephoned the garrison of a strongpoint and, pretending to speak for an encircled OD unit, appealed for help, thus attempting to induce the garrison to leave its post.[131]

A third destruction method directed at German supply lines consisted of raids by partisan units on communities situated on the main avenues of traffic. For insance, on 24 September 1942 some 600 partisans (some dressed in German uniforms and using heavy artillery) attacked and burned Ryabchichi (24 kilometers northeast of Kletnya) on the Bryansk-Roslavl highway. The population of the village and the militia were killed. A few days thereafter, on 2 October 1942, an even stronger band (1,000 men, according to prisoner-of-war interrogations) attacked Peklina on the Bryansk-Roslavl highway. Four-fifths of the houses were burned, and thirty civilians were killed. Some fifty telephone poles were blown up during this attack. The German report describing these attacks explained that they were apparently designed to provide the partisans with winter supplies.[132] The thorough destruction of telephone poles as well as the ruthless treatment of the population located in communities on the main highway seems to indicate that these attacks were also directed against supply lines.

A fourth method involved attacks against individual German vehicles and trains. Although the major objective of such attacks lay within the sphere of partisan psychological warfare, frequent raids against German transportation facilities had military and economic effects as well. Under the circumstances travel on highways and railroads became highly dangerous.

Attacks on vehicles and trains, mostly from ambush, may be regarded as one of the oldest types of partisan warfare. As early as October 1941 par-

---

[130] 707. Inf.Div., Ic, "Lagebericht fuer Monat September," 30 September 1942, p. 6 (GMDS, 707 ID 27797/4).

[131] 221. Sich.Div., Ic, Ic/Befehle und Mitteilungen Nr. 9," 22 June 1943, p. 2 (GMDS, 221 ID 36509/6, Anlage 121).

[132] Korueck, PzAOK 2, Ic, "Taetigkeitsbericht, Monat Oktober 1942," October 1942, p. 21 (GMDS, Korueck 29239/1). According to a report by a security division operating in an area northwest of the Bryansk area (Orsha-Smolensk), the partisans had received instructions to prevent the local population from carrying out railroad and highway maintenance work for the Germans. In implementing these instructions the bands had been ordered to destroy villages on major highways and railroads. (Komm.Gen.d.Sich.Tr. u.Befh.i.H.Geb.Mitte, Ia, "Auszuege aus Meldungen der 286. Sich.Div. [Gr.Geh.Feldpol. 723 v. 25.10.42]," 29 October 1942 GMDS, HGeb 31491/2, Anlage 161.) Similar orders for partisans in the Bryansk area have not been found.

tisans assaulted fourteen German trucks and cars in the Kletnya area during a three-week period.[133] Attacks from ambush increased in number and intensity during the following months. On 9 March 1942, for instance, some 500 partisans attacked a repair train near Zhurinichi (twenty kilometers east of Bryansk) after the train had run on a mine; 224 German soldiers, including 3 officers, fell victim to this assault.[134] Attacks on trains and vehicles continued throughout the occupation.[135] There are no records indicating how many soldiers and officers were killed in attacks of this kind. By making highways and rail lines unsafe for travel, except in convoy and under heavy guard, an additional obstacle was laid in the way of the smooth functioning of the supply system.

B. ANTIPARTISAN WARFARE

1. Protection of Communication Lines

The protection of major railroads, highways, and supply installations was the primary task of the German security forces in the rear areas. To accomplish it the Germans established a system of strongpoints situated at regular intervals along the main supply routes. Attacks by partisans on communication lines made it necessary to supplement with other forces the units regularly stationed in the strongpoints. In April 1942, for instance, the security troops guarding the Pochep-Vygonichi railroad were reinforced by a special railroad security platoon. This platoon was to combat partisans in the villages situated in the vicinity of the railroad.[136] Another method designed to bolster the security forces was the employment of armored trains that patrolled the railroad. Such a train was used on the Ordzhonikidzegrad-Zhukovka line in April 1942.[137]

In addition to measures aimed at strengthening the stationary railroad security forces, small rear area units (generally two to three companies) were deployed to communities or camps located near communication lines that were either controlled or threatened by the partisans.[138]

---

[133] AOK 2, Ic/AO, "Erfahrungsbericht ueber die Partisanenbekaempfung fuer die Zeit vom 1. August bis 31. Oktober 1941," 17 November 1941, p. 4 (GMDS, NOKW/1836).

[134] Wi Kdo Brjansk, Fuehrungsgr., "Lagebericht Nr. 4," 23 March 1942, p. 3 (GMDS, Wi/ID 2.474); Wi In Mitte, "Kriegstagebuch der Wirtschaftsinspektion Mitte Nr. 3, I.4.—30.6.1942," n.d., p. 68 (GMDS, Wi/ID 2.30).

[135] For a chronological account of partisan activities, especially acts of sabotage and "hit and run" attacks on lines of communication, see Kgl.ung.108.le.Div. Nr. 653.v.2.VI.43.Abt.I.b., "Zusammenfassende Lagemeldung ueber Bandentaetigkeit und besondere Ereignissen bis 31.5.43.," n.d. (GMDS, 221 ID 36509/9, Anlage 46).

[137] Korueck 532, Qu/Ia, "Br.B.Nr. 182/42 geh.," 7 April (GMDS, Korueck Korueck 29239/3, Anlage 73).

[137] Korueck 532, Qu/Ia, "Br.B.Nr. 182/42 geh.," 7 April 1942 (GMDS, Korueck 29239/3, Anlage 77).

[138] Reservepol. Batl. 82, "Gefechtsbericht zum Angriff am 31.3.42 auf Subowka," 2 April 1942 (GMDS, Korueck 29239/3, Anlage 68); Korueck, PzAOK 2, Qu/Ia,

The extent of the problem for the Germans may be judged from the fact that, during March 1942, the partisans stopped traffic on the Bryansk-Lgov railroad and prevented the Germans from operating the Bryansk-Roslavl line. The main highways (Bryansk-Roslavl, Bryansk-Karachev, Bryansk-Zhizdra) were also threatened to such a degree that traffic could be carried on only in convoys.[139] In April 1942 traffic on the Bryansk-Roslavl railroad was resumed; however, the partisans succeeded in carrying out demolitions regularly, laying from fifteen to twenty mines almost daily.[140]

There was no major antipartisan operation in the Bryansk area until the summer of 1942. Until that time, all efforts had been directed toward strengthening German units stationed on the main supply routes. The strongpoint system was improved,[141] and special mobile forces (*Bewegliche Kampfeinheiten*) were organized to conduct offensive operations against the partisans.[142] Another type of antipartisan unit was the *Jagdkommando*, which consisted of small, mobile units, designed to fight the partisan demolition groups or commandos that threatened the security of the supply lines.[143]

Another device commonly employed to protect communication lines was the special security zone, established up to fifteen kilometers in depth on both sides of the railroad. Brushwork and forests were cleared, all civilian residents registered, and movements of the people controlled day and night. Nonresident civilians were admitted in such zones only if they possessed special passes.[144]

The strongpoint system, reinforced by small mobile units operating in the vicinity of the major railroads and highways, remained in operation throughout the occupation of the Bryansk area. By the end of October 1942 the commander of the Army Rear Area reported that the main lines of communication were being kept open.[145] However, major antipartisan

---

"Bericht ueber das Unternehmen auf Lager suedostwaerts Batogowo 2.4.1942," 3 April 1942 (GMDS, Korueck 29239/3, Anlage 71); Korueck PzAOK 2, Qu/Ia, "Gefechtsbericht ueber die Unternehmung zur Freimachung des Brueckenkopfes von Sinezerki am 1. u. 2.4," 4 April 1942 (GMDS, Korueck 29239/3, Anlage 72).

[139] Korueck, PzAOK 2, Ic/AO–I/III, "Verluste im Kampf mit Partisanen im Raum um Bryansk im Monat Maerz 1942," 2 April 1942 (GMDS, Korueck 29239/3, Anlage 70).

[140] Korueck 532, Ic/AO, "Anlage zu den Verlustlisten vom 2.5.42 fuer Kriegstagebuch," 2 May 1942 (Korueck 29239/3, Anlage 114).

[141] Korueck 532, Qu/Ia, "Richtlinien fuer die Durchfuehrung der Wachaufgaben an Eisenbahnen und Strassen," 27 April 1942 (GMDS, Korueck 29239/3, Anlage 105).

[142] Korueck 532, Ia, "Bewegliche Kampfeinheiten," 16 September 1942 (GMDS, Korueck 27894/2, Anlage 19).

[143] Gruppe Gilsa, Ia, "Bandenbekaempfung durch Jagdkommandos," 21 September 1942 (GMDS, 216 ID 30186/8, Anlage 46).

[144] 221. Sich.Div., Ia, "Monatsbericht fuer die Zeit vom 1.10.—31.10.1942," 8 November 1942 (GMDS, 221 ID 35408/2, Anlage 306).

[145] Korueck 532, Ic/Ia, "Halbjahresbericht (Mai–Oktober 1942)," 11 November 1942 (GMDS, Korueck 27894/2, Anlage 124).

operations against the strongholds in the forests were considered essential by the German commanders in order to pacify the entire rear area completely and to put an end to the continual disruption of transportation facilities. Their decision was based on the conviction that an essentially defensive concept of antipartisan warfare, limited to the major railroads and highways, though helping to keep the supply lines open, would fail in the long run if the partisan movement was allowed to develop unchecked in the large forests.[146]

2. Major Antipartisan Operations

A number of major antipartisan operations were conducted in the Bryansk area, beginning in the summer of 1942; as a rule they were carefully prepared in advance and were carried out by strong forces, some of which were brought in from the outside. Generally the operations followed the same pattern. The forest areas where the partisans had their permanent camps and installations were surrounded by German troops. After the troops had closed the circle, they advanced in stages toward the center. Villages located in this encircled area were destroyed (unless they were being used as strongpoints by the Germans), and the civilian population was evacuated. When the operation was completed, small units remained in the area to prevent partisans who had not been captured or killed from organizing new bands. Lack of troops, however, prevented the Germans from controlling the forest area permanently.

The following discussion of the major antipartisan operations is organized according to the geographic areas which consistently saw a recurrence of German efforts against the partisans. The repetition of antipartisan operations in such regions as the Bryansk forests illustrates the dependence of the partisan movement on the geographic characteristics of the area. [For the major partisan areas, see Fig. 10.]

a. Northern Area

During the early part of the occupation of the Bryansk area, the wooded sections north and northwest of Bryansk were particularly endangered by partisans. The organization of bands was helped by the Red Army's counteroffensive during the winter of 1941, which had opened a gap between two German armies, enabling the partisans to receive reinforcements and supplies. By 1 April 1942 partisan strength in this area was estimated at

[146] Korueck, PzAOK 2, Qu/Ia geh., "Akten-Notiz," 7 April 1942 (GMDS, Korueck 29239/3); Korueck 532, Qu/Ia, "Betr.: Vorschlag fuer den Einsatz der 707.J.D.," 13 April 1942 (GMDS, Korueck 29239/3); Korueck 532, Qu/Ia, "Einsatzbefehl," 24 April 1942 (GMDS, Korueck 29239/3); Korueck 559, Abt. Qu., "Lage im rueckwaertigen Armeegebiet," 1 February 1942 (GMDS, Korueck 29236/2, Anlage 75); Korueck 559, Kmdt., "Bericht ueber das Partisanentum im rueckwaertigen Armeegebiet," 25 February 1942 (GMDS, Korueck 29236/2, Anlage 97); Korueck 532, Ic/Ia, "Halbjahresbericht (Mai–Oktober 1942)," 11 November 1942, p. 2 (GMDS, Korueck 27894/2, Anlage 124).

10,000 men.[147] (In all likelihood this figure was exaggerated and presumably included the civilians in villages under partisan influence.) In February 1942 German forces had come in contact with these units during an unsuccessful attempt to retake the town of Kirov. In the following months, the partisans continued their activities in and around the cities Dyatkovo, Ivot, and Star.

In May 1942 it was decided to undertake a large-scale antipartisan operation, which became known as "Vogelsang." It lasted from 5 June to

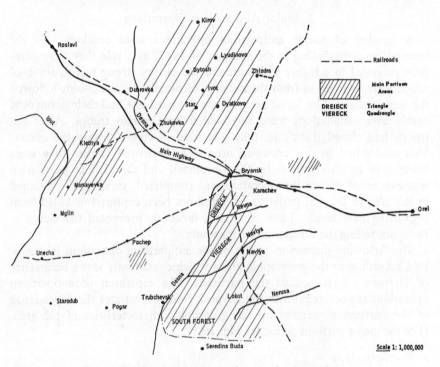

Figure 10.—Partisan concentrations in the Bryansk area.

the end of the month, and involved one armored and two infantry regiments, totaling 5,500 men. The combat strength of the partisans was estimated at between 2,400 and 2,550 men.[148] The operation proved fairly successful, at least from a short-range point of view, although a number of partisans, apparently forewarned, succeeded in escaping from encircle-

[147] XXIV Pz.K., Ic, "Feindnachrichtenblatt Nr. 82," 1 April 1942 (GMDS, XXIV AK 17416/30).

[148] Previously, the bands in this area had been estimated at from 3,000 to 5,000 men. (Korueck, PzAOK 2, Abt. Qu/Ia, "Taetigkeitsbericht," 1 April 1942, p. 69, GMDS, Korueck 29239/3.) For orders regarding "Vogelsang" see XXXXVII.Pz.K., Ia, "Korpsbefehl fuer Unternehmen 'Vogelsang,'" 29 May 1942 (GMDS, 339 ID 44418/4); 339. Inf.Div., Ia, "Div. Befehl Nr. 1 fuer das Unternehmen 'Vogelsang,'" 1 June 1942 (GMDS, 339 ID 44418/4).

ment. Final German figures on partisan casualties were as follows: 498 captured, 1,193 (counted) dead, and 1,400 (estimated) wounded. Moreover, 2,249 men in the age groups from sixteen to fifty were arrested; 12,531 persons were evacuated from the area. The booty included, among other things, 3 planes, 4 heavy guns, and 101 horses.[149]

The Germans listed their own casualties as 58 killed, 130 wounded, and 1 missing. The final report by the German unit in charge of the operation stated that the partisan organization was destroyed at a decisive moment, i.e., prior to its commitment in combat.[150]

Korueck of Second Panzer Army did not agree with this favorable account. Its activity report for June 1942 contains the following:

The success did not measure up to expectations. The partisans continued their old tactics of evading [contact], withdrawing into the forests, or moving in larger groups into the areas south and southwest of the Roslavl-Bryansk highway and into the Kletnya area. Although no attacks were noted in the pacified section, mines continued to be planted and . . . several vehicles were damaged.[151]

The interpretation given by Korueck is justified by a closer examination of the figures, which show that, although all the partisans appeared to be accounted for in the German casualty statistics, many of them in fact had moved to other areas, had fled temporarily, or had hidden on the spot. The later reappearance of these partisans suggests that a large proportion of the casualties reported by the Germans consisted in fact of nonpartisan members of the local population.

Although "Vogelsang" succeeded in providing temporary relief,[152] it did not put an end to partisan activity in the area. In July 1942 new partisan forces were reported moving in, and in August the Korueck noted that the regions to the east of Zhukovka were one of the main enemy strongholds in the entire Korueck area.[153] By October 1942 partisan strength in the area was again estimated at 2,000.[154]

Although attempts were made in the months following "Vogelsang" to keep the forest area north of Bryansk free of partisans, the bands con-

[149] 339. Inf.Div., Ia, "Unternehmen Vogelsang," 11 July 1942 (GMDS, 339 ID 44418/4).

[150] *Ibid.*, p. 25.

[151] Korueck, PzAOK 2, Ic, "Taetigkeitsbericht," June 1942, p. 6 (GMDS, Korueck 29239/1).

[152] The Germans occupied the major towns (Dyatkovo, Ivot, Star). Moreover, the number of demolitions on the main railroads declined considerably during June 1942. (Korueck, PzAOK 2, Ic, "Taetigkeitsbericht," May, June 1942, pp. 2–7, GMDS, Korueck 29239/1.)

[153] Korueck, PzAOK 2, Ic, "Taetigkeitsbericht," August 1942, p. 12 (GMDS, Korueck 29239/1).

[154] Korueck, PzAOK 2, Ic, "Taetigkeitsbericht," October 1942, p. 22 (GMDS, Korueck 29239/1); 707. Inf.Div., Ic, "Lagebericht fuer Monat Oktober 1942," 27 October 1942 (GMDS, 707 ID 27797/4, Anlage 202).

tinued to control part of this area. In May 1943, 3,000 partisans were reported here.[155] Another large-scale operation called "Freischeutz," employing two German divisions and two regimental combat teams, was undertaken between 21 and 30 May in order to destroy the partisan forces,
which included a partisan division and two brigades.

The German forces were supported by two formations of light bombers
and fighters.[156] The final report by the German corps in charge of the
operation stated that the bulk of the partisan forces had been destroyed
although individual enemy groups succeeded in escaping from encirclement.[157] The following figures indicate partisan losses: 1,459 killed, 420
captured, 6 deserted. Furthermore, 2,392 persons were evacuated. This
would account for approximately 2,000 of the 3,000 partisans, leaving only
1,000 in the area. The report stressed the fact that the nature and extent of
the terrain, the shortage of German troops, and the short period in which
the operation had to be completed prevented it from being a complete
success.

Another report on the same operation throws doubts on the effectiveness
of "Freischuetz" as well as on the accuracy of the German statistics cited
above. It pointed out that after the operation there were still 1,500 partisans in the area. Moreover, it claimed that the final figures on partisan
losses included more than 300 women and children among "captured partisans" and at least 200 to 300 such persons among "killed partisans." The
report concluded that total destruction of the bands in the northern area
was not possible during the summer.[158]

By 18 June 1943 the number of partisans in the North Forest was again
estimated at 2,000.[159]

b. Western Area (Kletnya-Mamayevka)

One of the foremost areas of partisan concentration was the forest region
around Kletnya and Mamayevka. As early as October 1941 the Germans
had battled partisan forces in this region.[160] In August 1942 strong con-

[155] 707. Inf.Div., Ic, "Feindlage. Stand 18.5.43," 18 May 1943 (GMDS, 707 ID
41762/1).
[156] LV. A.K., Ia, "Unternehmen 'Freischuetz,'" 7 June 1943 (GMDS, LV AK
36358/9, Anlage 167). German and collaborator losses were 27 killed, 84 wounded,
and 2 missing.
[157] Ibid., p. 11.
[158] Abwehrtr. Pz. 107 b. PzAOK 2, "Bericht ueber den Einsatz des Kommandos
waehrend des Unternehmens 'Freischuetz,'" 3 June 1943 (GMDS, PzAOK 2,
37075/168).
[159] Abwehrtr. Pz. 107 b. PzAOK 2, "Zusammenfassender Bericht ueber die Bandenlage noerdlich and suedlich Brjansk nach Abschluss der Unternehmen 'Freischuetz'
und 'Zigeunerbaron,'" 18 June 1943 (GMDS, PzAOK 2, 37075/168). Another
report of 24 June 1943 stated that from 1,500 to 2,000 partisans were in the area
north of the Ordzhonikidzegrad-Zhukovka railroad. (Korueck 532, Ic, "Feindlage im
Korueckgebiet, Stand: 22.6.43," June 1943, GMDS, PzAOK 2, 37075/91.)
[160] AOK 2, Ic AO, "Erfahrungsbericht ueber Partisanenbekaempfung fuer die Zeit
vom 1. August bis 31. Oktober 1941," 17 November 1941 (GMDS, NOKW 1836).

centrations of partisans estimated at approximately 4,000 men were reported in the area.[161] An operation in October 1942, directed against the partisans in the Kletnya Forest and mounted by a German force of some 1,600 men, was entirely unsuccessful. The partisans had apparently been warned of the impending operation and had succeeded in avoiding or in breaking out of encirclement. Total partisan losses numbered only 43 dead and 2 captured; 127 male civilians were evacuated.[162] Apparently the operation did not impede partisan growth, since on 30 October the partisans in the Kletnya Forest were estimated at 6,000 men. Therefore, another antipartisan operation was proposed.[163]

The second major German effort in this western forest area, "Klette II" (15 January to 9 February 1943), also failed to destroy the partisans. More than half of them (from 3,900 to 4,300 of the estimated 6,500) managed to escape from encirclement in three successful break-outs. Many more hid in the woods and were not discovered by the Germans. The final report by one of the German units participating in this operation admitted that the bands had been only dispersed.[164] Partisan losses were reported as 441 killed, 126 captured, and 178 deserted.[165] On 27 February 1943 the Korueck reported that the bands in the forests were reorganizing[166] and on 1 April 1943, the Second Panzer Army stated: "The strong band around Kletnya which was dispersed by our operation 'Klette II' has reassembled."[167] In May 1943 partisan strength in the Kletnya-Mamayevka Forests was estimated at 8,000 men, although the actual strength was probably around 6,000.[168]

[161] Korueck, PzAOK 2, Ic, "Taetigkeitsbericht," September 1942, p. 15 (GMDS, Korueck PzAOK 2, 29239/1).

[162] For reports on "Klette," see 707. Inf.Div., Ia, "Unternehmen 'Klette,' " 7 October 1942 (GMDS, 707 ID 27797/4, Anlage 180); 707. Inf.Div., Ia, "Divisionsbefehl," 20 October 1942 (GMDS, 707 ID 27797/4, Anlage 194); 707. Inf.Div., Ia, "Betr: Unternehmen 'Klette' vom 12.-25.10.1942," 23 October 1942 (GMDS, 707 ID 27797/4, Anlage 198).

[163] 221. Sich.Div., Ia, "Vorschlag fuer ein Unternehmen gegen die Banden-Gruppen im Waldgebiet Kletnja-Mamajewka-Wassiljewka (ostwaerts bezw. westlich Iput)," 30 October 1942 (GMDS, 221 ID 35408/2, Anlage 285); Korueck 532, Ia, "Vorschlag fuer das Unternehmen 'Klette II,' " 16 December 1942 (GMDS, Korueck 27894/3).

[164] 707. Inf.Div., Ic, "Abschlussbericht zu den Unternehmen 'Klette IIa vom 15.1–20.1.43,' 'Klette IIb vom 22.1–9.2.43,' " 10 February 1943 (GMDS, Korueck 44404/3, Anlage 231).

[165] Komdt.d.rueckw. Armeegeb.d. PzAOK 2, "Halbjahresbericht November 1942–April 1943," Anlage 3, p. 3 (GMDS, PzAOK 2, 37075/91).

[166] Korueck 532, Ic, "Feindlage, Stand: 26.2.1943," 27 February 1943 (GMDS, PzAOK 2, 37075/90).

[167] PzAOK 2, Ia, "Meldungen ueber Bandentaetigkeit in der Zeit vom 28.2–31.3.43," 1 April 1943 (GMDS, PzAOK 2, 37075/91, Anlage 1).

[168] GFP Gr. 729, "Taetigkeitsbericht fuer Monat Mai 1943," 25 May 1943 (GMDS, 221 ID 36509/24, Anlage 19). Other reports estimated partisan strength in the Kletnya Forest at from 3,000 to 3,500 men, and in the Mamayevka Forest at from 2,000 to 3,000 men. (707 ,Inf.Div., Ic, "Feindlage, Stand: 18.5.43.," 18 May 1943 GMDS, 707 ID 41762/1; Korueck 559, Ia, "Operationsbefehl fuer das Unternehmen 'Nachbarhilfe,' " 13 May 1943, GMDS, PzAOK 2, 37075/153.)

During May–June 1943 two German division-sized task forces under Korueck 559 were committed against the bands in the forests. The operation, which went by the code name of "Nachbarhilfe," represented the largest antipartisan effort in this forest area. It lasted from 19 May to 19 June 1943, and the final report claimed that German forces had scored a "visible success." The bands had been broken up into "small and very small bands."[169] Partisan losses were reported as 571 killed, 369 captured, and 24 deserted. Moreover, 16,900 "suspects" had been evacuated. The large booty included, among other things, one plane. The reports also stressed the large number of partisan leaders killed in this operation.

Though "Nachbarhilfe" inflicted significant losses on the partisans, in July 1943 their forces were again occupying the Mamayevka Forest.[170] They were reinforced during August by air drops. A report of 26 August stated that the Mamayevka Forest was again occupied by bands, although not in their previous strength.[171]

c. Southern Area

The wooded area to the south represented the third major partisan region in the Bryansk area. It is bordered on the west by the Desna River and on the east by the railroad from Bryansk to Lokot (to Kharkov). The northern part of the area, i.e., north of the Navlya River, saw the first of two major antipartisan operations in this area. It was called "Dreieck [Triangle] und Viereck [Quadrangle]," and it extended from 16 to 30 September 1942. The Germans reported 2,244 partisans killed and captured, but, as may have been expected, part of the enemy forces either escaped in a southerly direction over the Navlya or were flown out by Russian planes. In October 1942 some of these forces returned to their former operating area.[172] During the winter and spring of 1942–43 the bands were reorganized and strengthened. In December 1942 from 6,000 to 7,000 partisans were reported in the Navlya area.[173]

From 16 May to 6 June 1943 "Zigeunerbaron," the greatest antipartisan operation in the Bryansk area, was conducted in the southern forest sec-

[169] Korueck 559, Ia/Ic, "Abschlussmeldung ueber Unternehmen 'Nachbarhilfe,'" 19 June 1943 (GMDS, 221 SichDiv 36509/16). See also H.Gr.Mitte, Ia, "Monatliche Meldung ueber Bandenlage," 4 July 1943 (GMDS, HGr Mitte 65002/22). German losses were 66 killed, 143 wounded, and 24 missing.

[170] 221. Sich.Div., Ic, "Bandenlage im Divisions-Bereich fuer die Zeit vom 26. Juni bis 25. Juli 1943," 27 July 1943, p. 3 (GMDS, 221 ID 36509/24, Anlage 8).

[171] 221. Sich.Div., Ic, "Bandenlage im Divisions-Bereich fuer die Zeit vom 26. Juli bis 25. August 1943," 26 August 1943 (GMDS, 221 ID 36509/24, Anlage 9).

[172] Korueck 532, PzAOK 2, "Taetigkeitsbericht," September 1942 (GMDS, Korueck 29239/1).

[173] Komm.Gen.d.Sich.Tr.u.Befh.i.H.Geb.Mitte, VII/Mil., "Monatsbericht fuer Monat Dezember 1942," 9 January 1943, p. 7 (GMDS, HGeb 31491/6). See also XXXXVII. Pz.K., Ic, "Anlage 2 zum Feindnachrichtenblatt vom 15.3.1943," 15 March 1943 (GMDS, AK XLVII 37241/9, Anlage 76).

tion; it involved six German divisions (five infantry and one armored) plus supporting forces including aircraft which dropped, among other things, 840,000 surrender leaflets. The German forces inflicted considerable losses on the partisans, although, as in earlier antipartisan operations, destruction was not complete. Of 6,000 partisans in the area 1,584 were killed, 1,568 were captured, and 869 deserted; among nonpartisans 15,812 persons were evacuated. Moreover, 207 camps and 2,930 bunkers and firing posts were destroyed; the booty included 21 heavy guns and 3 tanks.[174] A comparison between the estimated number of partisans in the area before the operation (6,000) and the number after (4,000–4,500) would indicate that among the claimed casualties (3,021) must have been a large number of nonpartisans.

Reviewing the accomplishments of the major antipartisan operations in the Bryansk area during 1943 ("Zigeunerbaron," "Nachbarhilfe," and "Freischuetz"), an intelligence report stated that, although these operations had greatly weakened the bands, the complete destruction desired by the Germans had not been achieved. The reporting agency doubted whether it was possible during the summer months. Every time, the bands had dissolved into small units that dispersed and hid in the swamps, thereby avoiding contact with the German forces. As for the South Forest, the area south of the Navlya River, the report estimated that, at the time of writing, this region harbored some 4,500 partisans.[175] A report by Second Panzer Army on "Freischuetz" and "Zigeunerbaron" also warned that the command staffs of the bands had not been destroyed and that a gradual build-up of partisan strength must be expected unless the Germans undertook further operations against them.[176] Although there were several smaller antipartisan operations in the Army Rear Area during June 1943, German offensive intentions on the front deprived the Korueck of sufficient forces to continue an effective antipartisan campaign. A short time later the Bryansk area was evacuated by German troops.

3. Evaluation

An examination of the German sources on antipartisan activities in the Bryansk area shows that the Germans succeeded in preventing the partisans from crippling communication lines and halting the movement of material and men to the front. At the same time, antipartisan operations failed to destroy the movement. Despite large-scale German efforts, the strength

[174] Auffrischungsstab 3, Ia, "Tagesbefehl," 9 June 1943 (GMDS, PzAOK 2, 37075/91); H.Gr.Mitte, "Abschlussmeldung ueber das Unternehmen 'Zigeunerbaron,'" 8 June 1943 (GMDS, HGr Mitte 65002/25).

[175] Korueck 532, Ic, "Feindlage im Korueckgebiet, Stand: 22.6.43," 24 June 1943 (GMDS, PzAOK 2, 37075/91).

[176] PzAOK 2, Ia/Id, "Lage im rueckw. Armeegebiet in der Zeit vom 27.5–26.6.43," 1 July 1943 (GMDS, PzAOK 2, 37075/91).

of the partisans in this area remained relatively constant. The level of their activities directed against the German rear, as reflected in the number of demolitions and raids carried out, also showed little variation. According to German estimates, there were between 12,000 and 16,000 partisans in the area throughout 1943, even though the Germans claimed to have killed or captured about 12,000 partisans in their major antipartisan operations alone.[177] At the same time, partisan activities, as expressed in figures on demolitions and attacks on German transport, also remained more or less constant.[178] Figure 11 shows that, in general, partisan attacks on lines of communication in the Korueck area declined somewhat after a major antipartisan operation. Within a relatively short period, however, renewed increase is noticeable.

The consistent rise and fall of the curve showing successful demolitions throws an interesting light on German antipartisan efforts in the Bryansk area. The major antipartisan operations, even if successful according to the German reports, succeeded only temporarily in diminishing partisan strength. In many instances, the partisan bands were broken up or scattered, and supplies and equipment were lost. After the completion of the operation and the withdrawal of German units, the bands, which in most cases avoided annihilation, reassembled and strengthened their positions with the aid of reinforcements and supplies brought in by air.

Another result of German tactics in antipartisan operations was the

---

[177] The following estimates were reported for the Korueck area: 31 January 1943, from 10,000 to 15,000 partisans; 20 May 1943, from 15,000 to 20,000 partisans; and 18 June 1943, i.e., after the completion of two of the largest antipartisan operations, from 13,000 to 14,000 men. (PzAOK 2, Ic/AO, "Feindnachrichten Nr. 1/43," 31 January 1943, GMDS, PzAOK 2, 37075/159; Kmdt.d.rueckw.Armeegeb.d.2.Pz.AOK, "Halbjahresbericht [November 1942–April 1943]," 20 May 1943, PzAOK 2, 37075/91, Anlage 14; Abwehrtr.Pz.107 b.Pz. AOK 2, "Zusammenfassender Bericht ueber die Bandenlage noerdlich und suedlich Brjansk nach Abschluss der Unternehmen 'Freischuetz' und 'Zigeunerbaron,'" 18 June 1943, p. 3, GMDS, PzAOK 2, 37075/168.)

[178] During the six-month period from May to October 1942, 1,101 assaults were reported in the Korueck area. From November 1942–April 1943, Korueck reported 1,011 assaults. A comparable development was noted in the territory under jurisdiction of the 211th Security Division (which controlled the western rayons of the Bryansk area). Monthly "engagements" with partisans for the second half of 1942 were as follows: July, 54; August, 43; September, 58; October, 58; November, 58; December, 57. Acts of sabotage, for the same period, were: July, 57; August, 55; September, 62; October, 49; November, 57; and December, 72. (221. Sich.Div., Ic, "Monatsbericht fuer die Zeit vom 1.–31.Juli 1942," 5 August, p. 3, GMDS, 221 SichDiv 35408/1, Anlage 129; 221. Sich.Div., Ia, "Monatsbericht fuer die Zeit vom 1.8.–31.8.1942," 5 September 1942, Anlage; GMDS, 221 ID 25408/1, Anlage 218; 221. Sich.Div., Ia. "Anlage zum Monatsbericht fuer die Zeit vom 1.9.–30.9.1942," 6 October 1942, GMDS, 221 ID 35408/2, Anlage 258; 221. Sich.Div., Ia, "Anlage zum Monatsbericht fuer die Zeit vom 1.10.–31.10.1942," 6 November 1942, GMDS, 221 ID 35408/2, Anlage 306; 221. Sich.Div., Ia, "Anlage zum Monatsbericht fuer die Zeit vom 1.11. bis 30.11.1942," 5 December 1942, GMDS, 221 ID 35408/2, Anlage 384; 221. Sich.Div., Ic, "Monatsbericht fuer die Zeit vom 1.–31. Dezember 1942," 2 January 1943, p. 2. GMDS, 221 ID 29380/9, Anlage 98.)

wholesale killing of civilians who were not really partisans. While this may have increased the number of casualties which the German commanders could claim to have inflicted, it did not weaken the fighting strength of the partisan movement, but rather tended to drive the civilian population into the arms of the partisans.

The following factors were most prominently mentioned in German reports attempting to explain the failure of antipartisan operations to destroy the partisan movement:

a. Lack of Troops

Rear area commanders complained bitterly because sufficient forces were not available to engage the partisans in continuous combat. On 7 November

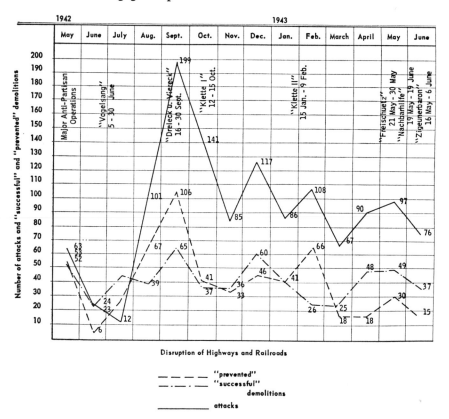

Disruption of Highways and Railroads

— — — — "prevented"
— .— .— "successful"
demolitions

———————— attacks

Figure 11.—Partisan disruptive activities. *Sources:* Korueck 532, Ic/Ia, "Halbjahresbericht (Mai–Oktober 1942)," 11 November 1942 (GMDS, Korueck 27894/2, Anlage 124); Kmdt.d.rueckw.Armeegeb.d. 2. Pz.AOK., "Halbjahresbericht (November 1942–April 1943)," 20 May 1943, Anlage 2 (GMDS, PzAOK 2, 37075/91); Korueck 532, Ia, "Strassen- und Eisenbahnsprengungen im Korueck-Gebiet, 27.4.—26.5.1943," 20 May 1943 (GMDS, PzAOK 2, 37075/91); Korueck 532, Ia, "Strassen- und Eisenbahnsprengungen im Korueck-Gebiet, 27.5—26.6.1943," 29 June 1943 (GMDS, PzAOK 2, 37075/91).

1942 the Commander of the Army Group Rear Area stated emphatically that most of his troops were tied to the lines of communication and that it was impossible to defeat the bands with his present forces.[179] At about the same time, the Commander of the Army Rear area also pointed out that necessary antipartisan operations were hardly possible with the forces under his command. Most of his men were engaged in protecting highways and railroads some 899 kilometers long.[180] The same reason was given for the resurgence of the partisan movement in areas which had been subjected to large-scale antipartisan operations. A final report covering the major part of 1943 stated that the various small and larger antipartisan operations could not arrest the general growth of partisan influence. Permanent occupation of the pacified areas was not possible because of the troop shortage.

Therefore, the partisans had the opportunity, after the termination of antipartisan operations, of reoccupying their former areas and thus making the success of these operations illusory. . . . Any removal of troops or [even] a temporary withdrawal of troops from pacified areas resulted in reoccupation by the partisans.[181]

b. Shifts of Security Forces

The rear area commanders also protested against the continuous shift of security forces under their command. The Korueck of Second Panzer Army pointed out that the constant changes in the composition of troops under his command severely limited his capacity to combat the partisans. Not a month went by without a shift of railroad security units, he said, adding that the temporary removal of an infantry division had hampered one of the larger antipartisan operations. He expressed the view that troops committed to antipartisan warfare had to know the terrain and that the constant change of units had a very negative effect on German antipartisan efforts.

Another factor mentioned in this report was the high average age of German forces employed in antipartisan warfare, which was reportedly 35 years. Insufficient training and equipment further diminished the over-all combat capabilities of these troops.[182]

[179] Komm.Gen.d.Sich.Tr.u.Befh.i.H.Geb. Mitte, Ia, "Erfassung landwirtschaftlicher Erzeugnisse," 7 November 1942 (GMDS, HGeb 31491/3, Anlage 183).
[180] Korueck 532, Ic/Ia, "Halbjahresbericht (Mai–Oktober 1942)," 11 November 1942, p. 2 (GMDS, Korueck 27894/2, Anlage 124).
[181] 221. Sich.Div., Ic, "Taetigkeitsbericht des Ic vom 1.1. bis 31.8.1943," 19 November 1943, p. 2 (GMDS, 221 ID 36509/24).
[182] Komdt.d.rueckw.Armeegeb.d. 2. Pz.AOK, "Halbjahresbericht (November 1942–April 1943)," 20 May 1943, pp. 2–4 (GMDS, PzAOK 2, 37075/91). See also Korueck 532, Ia/Ic, "Halbjahresbericht (Mai–Oktober 1942)," 11 November 1942 (GMDS, Korueck 27894/2, Anlage 124).

c. Lack of Time

Lack of time in which to complete major operations was also advanced as a reason for the inability to inflict decisive defeats on the partisans. This was mentioned in particular in a report on "Freischuetz" which was "completed" in nine days. The final report alleged that enemy breakthroughs could have been prevented had the troops been permitted to proceed at a slower pace in clearing out the encircled area.[183]

d. Antipartisan Methods

Some blame for the failure of the major antipartisan operations must be laid to the German practice of killing captured partisans and of evacuating great numbers of civilians in partisan-infested areas. Such practices undoubtedly inhibited potential defectors. This factor was recognized in a frank report by the 221st Security Division, dated 3 December 1942, which criticized the practice of refusing to treat as deserters those partisans who left their units immediately before, during, or after combat. The report also stressed that promises made to deserters should be kept under all circumstances, thereby implying, of course, that such promises had not always been kept in the past.[184]

The effects of such methods on German psychological warfare are obvious. During "Freischuetz," for instance, 500,000 surrender leaflets were dropped, and only six partisans deserted. A final report stressed the inadequacy of the leaflets: (1) they failed to recognize the psychological make-up of the bands, and (2) they could not be used as safe-conduct passes.[185] "Nachbarhilfe" netted only 24 deserters, although partisan morale was regarded as poor.[186] The importance of treating deserters fairly was also stressed in the final report of "Zigeunerbaron," which produced 869 deserters. The report lauded the effects of 840,000 surrender leaflets and stated that the rapid dissemination of written promises that not everyone in the partisan area would be killed indiscriminately stimulated desertions.[187]

---

[183] LV. A.K., Ia, "Unternehmen 'Freischuetz,'" 7 June 1943, p. 11 (GMDS, LV AK 36358/9, Anlage 167). See also Gen.Kdo. XXXXVII. Pz.K., Ia, "Erfahrungsbericht 'Zigeunerbaron,'" 2 July 1943 (GMDS, PzAOK 2, 37075/60) for similar complaints.

[184] 221. Sich.Div., Ic, "Betr.:Ueberlaeufer," 3 December 1942 (GMDS, 221 ID 29380/9, Anlage 69).

[185] LV. A.K., Ia, "Unternehmen 'Freischuetz,'" 7 June 1943, p. 11 (GMDS, LV AK 36358/9, Anlage 167).

[186] Korueck 559, Ia/Ic, "Abschlussmeldung ueber Unternehmen 'Nachbarhilfe,'" 19 June 1943 (GMDS, 221 ID 36509/16).

[187] XXXXVII. Pz.K., Ia, "Erfahrungsbericht 'Zigeunerbaron,'" 2 July 1943, p. 18 (GMDS, PzAOK 2, 37075/60).

e. Climatic Influences

Practically all reports dealing with antipartisan warfare rated the winter months as the most favorable time for antipartisan operations.[188] In November 1942 the commander of Army Group Rear Area, in a report requesting further security troops, pointed out that it was important to have troops on hand during the winter months when the swamps froze and thus permitted freer troop movements.[189] Only one report argued that the last weeks in April and the first weeks in May were the most propitious time for antipartisan operations; this report also recommended winter action, because traces could be detected more easily in the snow.[190] The fact that the largest antipartisan operations in the Bryansk area were carried out during the summer may, therefore, in part explain their inconclusive results.

C. COLLABORATION WITH THE PARTISANS

The German reports contain little information on which to base a systematic analysis of indigenous collaboration with the partisans. The following, therefore, represents an evaluation of the more typical, and in most cases sketchy, generalizations which occur frequently in German sources dealing with group behavior.

Probably the most common observation in reports describing the relations between the civilian population and the partisans is the claim that the rural population was most hostile to the partisans and, therefore, least inclined toward collaboration. As late as February 1943 German reports stressed the antipathy of the peasant class toward the partisans. One report expressed this feeling as follows: "Nowhere . . . did civilians participate in acts of sabotage or support such [acts]. The rural population as always rejects the partisans."[191] Similar statements can be found in other sources. Some of them also asserted that the rural youth was basically anti-Communist. "It can be stated, in principle, that the Russian peasant, insofar as he is free from partisan influence, subordinates himself completely to the German agencies. Also, only a very small percentage of rural youth is pro-Bolshevik."[192]

[188] Abwehrtr. Pz. 107 b. Pz.AOK. 2, "Zusammenfassender Bericht ueber die Bandenlage noerdlich und suedlich Brjansk nach Abschluss der Unternehmen 'Freischuetz' und 'Zigeunerbaron,'" 18 June 1943, p. 3 (GMDS, PzAOK 2, 37075/168); Korueck 532, Ic, "Feindlage im Korueckgebiet, Stand: 22.6.1943," 24 June 1943 (GMDS, PzAOK 2, 37075/91).
[189] Komm.Gen.d.Sich.Tr.u.Befh.i.H.Geb.Mitte, Ia, "Erfassung landwirtschaftlicher Erzeugnisse," 7 November 1942, p. 2 (GMDS, HGeb 31491/3, Anlage 183).
[190] XXXXVII. Px.K., Ia, "Erfahrungsbericht 'Zigeunerbaron,'" 2 July 1493, p. 4 (GMDS, PzAOK 2, 37075/60).
[191] Wi Kdo Brjansk, "Lagebericht Februar 1943," 15 February 1943, p. 1 (GMDS, Wi/ID 2.85).
[192] Wi In Mitte, Chefgruppe La, "Lagebericht," 30 September 1942 (GMDS, Wi/ID .59).

Despite frequent references to the antipartisan sentiments of the rural population, it should be kept in mind that the partisan movement could hardly have grown and become effective without the support of at least a considerable portion of the peasant population.

The urban population, on the other hand, was regarded by the Germans with great suspicion. Although there were occasional reports, particularly during the early stage of the occupation, which argued that a preponderance of the urban population did not sympathize with the partisans,[193] many sources claimed that there were more hostile elements here than among the rural dwellers. In December 1941 one report stated: "The cities are the cells of partisan activity, which is almost generally rejected by the country population (peasants)."[194] Significant in this connection is the fact that most of the larger cities, e.g., Bryansk, Roslavl, remained firmly in German hands throughout the occupation and that the people had few personal contacts with the partisans. On the other hand, living conditions were probably worse in the cities because of food, housing, and fuel shortages. Furthermore, some of the cities were subjected to air raids which caused much damage. During the critical months in the summer of 1943, when the Germans were gradually withdrawing from the Bryansk area, the urban population openly sided with the Soviets. Comparing them with the rural population, one report said: "The urban population . . . has always inclined toward the bands, [and] goes over to them more and more openly."[195]

As might be expected, young people who had been raised under the Bolshevik regime were more favorably inclined toward it than the older people and were looking forward to the return of the Red Army. This is indicated in the following report of September 1942: "The rumor predicting the approach of Red troops continues to be spread in Bryansk. Young people hope [that the Red Army will return]; experienced [i.e., older] people fear [that this will happen]."[196] Furthermore, among the partisans young people were considered the most enthusiastic fighters. Speaking about an antipartisan operation south of Bryansk in the fall of 1942, a reporter stated, "Noticeable was the relatively large number of young men and girls [*Flintenweiber*] who, educated completely in the Communist ideology, fought to the very end."[197]

In the spring of 1943, when more and more civilians openly sympathized

[193] Wi Kdo i.Ber.d.2.PzAOK, "Lagebericht Nr. 5," 18 April 1942, p. 2 (GMDS, Wi/ID 2.474).
[194] Gen.Kdo.XII A.K., Ic, "Taetigkeitsbericht fuer die Zeit vom 6.11 bis 5.12, 1941," 6 December 1941, pp. 1–2 (GMDS, XII AK 24630/7).
[195] Wi In Mitte, Stab Abt. I/Id, "Lagebericht Nr. 34," 1 October 1943, pp. 3–4 (GMDS, Wi/ID 2.59).
[196] Korueck 532 (PzAOK 2), Ic, "Taetigkeitsbericht," September 1942, p. 19 (GMDS, Korueck 29239/1).
[197] Gruppe Jolasse, Stab Pz.Gren.Brig. 18, "Gefechtsbericht 'Dreieck und Viereck' vom 17.9–2.10.1942," 19 October 1942, p. 46 (GMDS, Korueck 27894/3).

with the partisans, the young people were also given special mention. A report from the Army Group Rear Area, speaking about the effects of partisan propaganda, said: "The young people feel deprived of their goals in life and are, therefore, particularly susceptible to enemy propaganda. As a result [they] go over to the bands in numbers."[198]

It is regrettable that the German sources on propartisan attitudes among the civilian population do not furnish specific materials illustrating these sympathies. Undoubtedly the partisans had many followers both in rural and urban areas who furnished them with valuable information. Moreover, a considerable part of the bands was made up of local residents. It is doubtful, however, whether these local elements enthusiastically supported partisan aims. As the war progressed and as larger areas came under partisan domination, the civilian population had little choice but to collaborate with the power in control. The drafting of local residents into the bands often forced the civilians to side with the partisans, since German treatment of relatives of band members was particularly harsh. In some cases the remaining civilians, mostly old men, women, and children, followed the partisan draftees into the woods to escape German reprisals; there, though they led miserable lives in so-called civilian camps, they were useful to the partisans because they could gather berries and wood and perform other services.

[198] 221. Sich.Div., Ic, "Politische Ueberwachung der Bevoelkerung," 31 May 1943, p. 2 (GMDS, 221 ID 36509/24, Anlage 26).

CHAPTER IX

The Polotsk Lowland

Ralph Mavrogordato and Earl Ziemke

This study is an attempt to describe the history and characteristics of the partisan movement in a geographically limited area—the northeastern sector of Belorussia or, as it will be called in this chapter, the "Polotsk Lowland." In this region the partisan movement became a well-developed and militarily significant force which represented a serious danger to the German rear echelons and, at times, to the front itself. The German reports contain abundant information on the partisans here, since German observers were more concerned with the partisan problem in regions where the movement was dangerous than in those where its existence was merely a nuisance.

The partisan movement in the Polotsk Lowland was not a closely knit organization but consisted rather of several loosely connected partisan complexes. Study of an area which contained more than one partisan complex makes it possible to observe the interrelationship, or the lack of it, between different partisan complexes operating in close proximity. However, the existence of several separate partisan areas within a single region makes it more difficult to present as clear and precise a picture as might be obtained from selecting a more limited geographic area. On the other hand, the inclusion of material available on the various partisan complexes in the Polotsk Lowland makes it possible in a study of a geographically limited area to throw light on a wider variety of partisan objectives, organizations, and operations.

§I. Geographic, Economic, and Ethnographic Character of the Region

A. TOPOGRAPHY

The Polotsk Lowland is a distinct regional subdivision of the western USSR in topography as well as in locales of partisan activity in World War II. The land forms are entirely of glacial origin, exhibiting characteristics typical of terminal moraines: poor drainage; low, isolated groups of hills, seldom over one hundred feet in height; depressions, excepting those which form river beds, generally blocked by glacial debris; numerous lakes, ponds, potholes, and swamps.[1] Lakes are the distinctive topographic feature. These cover the entire region, vary greatly in size, and in some places form connecting chains. There are some exceptionally concentrated lake groups, the most significant of which lie north of Lepel and between Polotsk and Nevel.[2] Marshes, bogs, and moors are scattered throughout the region, not in extensive zones as in the Pripet Marshes of southern Belorussia but interspersed between the lakes and dry land areas. The Polotsk Lowland is drained by the western Dvina River, but the drainage pattern is complicated by the fact that the region lies astride the low drainage divide of western Russia. The Dvina, flowing in a northwesterly direction, empties into the Baltic Sea; however, the Berezina River and other tributaries of the Dnepr, which empty into the Black Sea, also flow from the area. The result is a poorly defined, sluggish system of drainage which in wet seasons, particularly during the spring thaws, produces flood conditions. At least 25–30 per cent of the land area is covered with forests, which in some cases form extensive, heavily wooded zones. There are no large unforested areas.[3]

B. MILITARY GEOGRAPHY

While the Polotsk Lowland can be classified as a plain, the patchwork of interlocking lakes, swamps, forests, and irregular hills and depressions impedes movement overland, even for short distances. Ground observation is severely restricted by the absence of commanding heights, and air observation is hampered by the prevalence of dense forests.[4] Movement of vehicles and troops across or within the region is restricted to the poorly organized rail and road networks. The road net in the entire western sec-

[1] Theodore Shabad, *Geography of the USSR, A Regional Survey* (New York: Columbia University Press, 1951), pp. 467 ff.

[2] OKH/GenStdH/Abt. IV (Mil.-Geo.), *Militaergeographische Angaben ueber das Europaeische Russland: Weissrussland, Textheft* (Berlin, 1941), p. 51 (GMDS, H 29/ID 2.30).

[3] Wi In Mitte, Statistischer Arbeitsausschuss, "Anlage Nr. 1 zu Lagebericht Nr. 32," 30 July 1943 (GMDS, Wi/ID 2.59).

[4] OKH/GenStdH/Abt. IV (Mil.-Geo.), *Militaergeographische Angaben ... Weissrussland, Textheft*, p. 51.

tion—west of Polotsk—is exceptionally poor.[5] Few of the roads, with the exception of those connecting such major cities as Polotsk, Vitebsk, Nevel, Borisov, and Orsha,[6] are passable under all weather conditions. Most of them are suitable for motor vehicle traffic only in the dry summer months, completely impassable during the spring and fall wet periods,[7] and of limited usefulness during the winter, depending on snow and other weather conditions.

Nevertheless, the Lowland is strategically located in relation to several major transportation routes. [See Fig. 12.] The southern boundary of the region extends almost to the important Warsaw-Minsk-Smolensk-Moscow railroad and highway route, which was the main line of march and chief supply route for German Army Group Center in the invasion of the Soviet Union. The Leningrad-Kiev railroad and highway pass directly through the region via Nevel, Vitebsk, and Orsha. There are also important secondary rail lines. One running northwest from Smolensk through Vitebsk and Polotsk connects with Riga and other Baltic ports. The same line branches southwestward west of Polotsk toward Vileika and thence to Warsaw, furnishing an alternative to the Warsaw-Minsk-Smolensk route.[8] During World War II the terrain plus the commanding position of the Polotsk Lowland in relation to these major lines of transportation combined to make the region a center of Soviet partisan activity.

C. ECONOMY

Although agriculture is the chief element in the economy, the region itself is not a valuable agricultural area. Dairying and flax growing are the main types of agricultural activity. Although flax is widely grown, it is of less importance here than in the western oblasts of the Russian SFSR.[9] Buckwheat is cultivated as a local food staple. Oats, and to a lesser extent rye and potatoes, are grown in the area around Vitebsk.[10] Vitebsk Oblast, which comprises the eastern half of the Polotsk Lowland, is relatively more productive than Polotsk Oblast, which forms most of the western part.

The status of agriculture seems to have been related directly to the suc-

[5] *Ibid.*

[6] Borisov and Orsha lie just outside the Polotsk Lowland on the south.

[7] The spring thaws, which last about a month, crop up in almost every discussion of the road system of European Russia. The vast majority of the roads, particularly in the Polotsk Lowland, are unpaved. In the winter the earth roadbed is frozen to a depth of several feet. In the spring the frost disappears first from the upper levels of the ground. The frozen subsoil prevents the water from the melted snow and ice from filtering downward, thereby producing several feet of extremely thin mud. Once the frost has entirely left the ground, the water sinks rapidly and the earth becomes solid again.

[8] OKH/GenStdH/Abt.IV (Mil.-Geo.), *Militaergeographische Angaben ... Weissrussland, Strassenkarte Weissrussland.*

[9] Shabad, p. 473.

[10] The type of grain produced is often taken as an index to the agricultural possibilities of a given area. The best areas produce wheat; the second-rate areas, rye; the mediocre areas, oats; and the distinctly poor areas, buckwheat, a crop of low value.

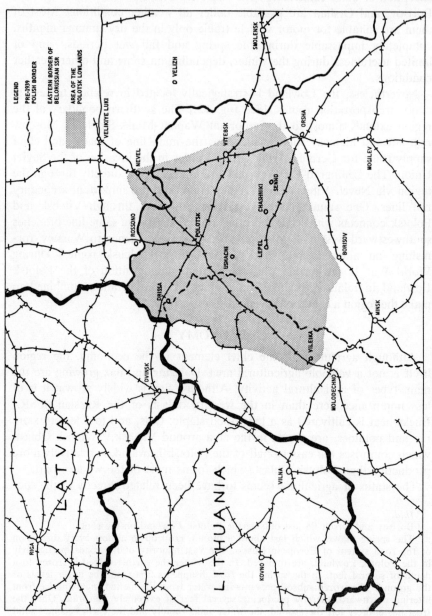

Figure 12.—The Polotsk Lowland in relation to western USSR.

cess of the partisan movement in the region, principally since conditions unfavorable for successful agricultural development seem to furnish the best milieu for successful partisan operations. Paradoxically, the partisans, aiming to deprive the enemy of the food produced in an occupied territory, operate most efficiently in areas where such production is of relatively small consequence. The figures for Vitebsk Oblast in Table 4[11] provide

TABLE 4

Land use in Vitebsk Oblast, 1943

	Square miles	Percentage of total area
Agriculturally useful area (including meadows, wooded pastures, etc.)	8,484	55.0
Forests	4,377	28.7
Mixed swamp and forest	1,154	7.4
Other areas (including wastelands of various kinds)	1,402	8.9
Total area	15,417	100.0

Source: Wi In Mitte, Statistischer Arbeitsausschuss, "Anlage Nr. 1."

part of the explanation. The proportion of land suitable for agriculture was probably considerably higher in Vitebsk Oblast than in Polotsk Oblast. It must be remembered, too, that much of the land described as suitable for farming was probably marginal or submarginal.

A further indication of a low agricultural development and thus of a favorable environment for partisan operations is the mode of settlement of the land. The average density of rural population in 1941 was sixty to eighty persons per square kilometer; however, there were several large areas of very low density. Principal among these were the lake district north of Polotsk and the forested area north of the Vitebsk-Smolensk line with average densities of less than twenty persons per square kilometer. The nature of the terrain determined the settlement of such land—generally isolated individual farmsteads, unusually small rural villages (most of them with fewer than 300 inhabitants), and relatively few rural market towns. Only the eastern half of the Polotsk Lowland had been intensively collectivized by 1941.[12]

To the degree that it is unsuitable for agriculture, climate might also be said to favor the development of partisan activity. Compared with the northern and eastern reaches of European Russia, the climate of the Polotsk Lowland is mild. Compared with the rest of Belorussia, it is cer-

[11] Wi In Mitte, Statistischer Arbeitsausschuss, "Anlage Nr. 1 . . ."
[12] OKH/GenStdH/Abt.IV (Mil.-Geo.), *Militaergeographische Angaben . . . Weissrussland Textheft,* p. 52.

tainly less mild and tends toward the severe type of continental climate. Table 5 is based on a division of Belorussia into four climatic zones. The Polotsk Lowland falls entirely within the zone designated as Northern Belorussia. For a rough comparison the average statistics of the other three zones are given.[13]

TABLE 5

Climate of Belorussia

	Northern Belorussia	Average for the remainder of Belorussia
Average yearly temperature	41°F.	44°F.
Monthly mean temperatures:		
January	18°F.	22°F.
March	27°F.	30°F.
July	63°F.	66°F.
November	30°F.	32°F.
Minimum temperature	−37°F.	−28°F.
Maximum temperature	90°F.	94°F.
Average annual rainfall	25.4 inches	21.5 inches
Average depth of winter snow cover	13.7 inches	9.4 inches
Average duration of snow cover	110 days	88 days

Source: OKH/GenStdH/Abt.IV (Mil.-Geo.), *Militaergeographische Angaben ...* *Weissrussland, Textheft,* pp. 12–15.

The major urban centers are Vitebsk (population in 1939—167,420), Polotsk (1928—25,830), Nevel (1932—12,460), and Lepel (1932—6,500).[14] Polotsk and Nevel are fairly important road and railroad junctions; aside from this, their economies are limited to processing products of the local countryside. Polotsk, a very old city, has an electric power plant, a cannery, sawmills, distilleries, and flour mills.[15] Nevel has a brick works, a milk-drying plant, and sawmills;[16] and Lepel has an electric power plant, operated on locally extracted peat, and sawmills.[17] Vitebsk, the only

[13] OKH/GenStdH/Abt.IV (Mil.-Geo.), *Militaergeographische Angaben ... Weissrussland, Textheft,* pp. 12–15.

[14] The Soviet Union did not publish complete census figures. Shabad, p. 511, gives the 1926 population of Vitebsk as 98,850, which indicates a 169 per cent increase for that city between 1926 and 1939. Since the Soviet Union in general experienced a period of rapid urbanization during the late 1920's and the 1930's, and since the process of urbanization probably went on in Polotsk, Nevel, and Lepel at about the same rate as in Vitebsk, we can estimate the populations of these cities in 1939 at 42,700, 19,900, and 10,400 respectively.

[15] OKH/GenStdH/Abt.IV (Mil.-Geo.), *Militaergeographische Angaben ... Weiss-russland, Textheft,* p. 147.

[16] OKH/GenStdH/Abt.IV (Mil.-Geo.), *Militaergeographische Angaben ... Zentral-Russland, Ortschaftsverzeichnis,* p. 48.

[17] OKH/GenStdH/Abt.IV (Mil.-Geo.), *Militaergeographische Angaben ... Weissruss-land, Textheft,* p. 136.

large metropolitan center in the area, is the second largest city in Belorussia and a significant cultural and industrial center. In addition to its position as a railroad and highway junction, its factories turn out metal goods, weapons, machinery, and tractors; and one large plant produces optical glass and lenses. It is an important center of textile and clothing production, processing cotton and wool in addition to the locally grown flax. It also has sawmills, woodworking and furniture plants, canneries, and distilleries.[18]

The cities suffered a disastrous decline in population as a result of the war. In 1943 Vitebsk had a population of 36,000, or 22 per cent of its 1939 population; the 1943 population of Polotsk was 15,046, or 58 per cent of the 1928 population and probably no more than 25 or 30 per cent of the 1939 population.[19] The populations of the other cities also declined sharply.

D. THE PEOPLE

The Polotsk Lowland consisted primarily of Vitebsk and Polotsk Oblasts. Polotsk Oblast, an area of 6,900 square miles, supported a population of 460,000; and Vitebsk Oblast with 7,600 square miles had a population of 640,000. Since the boundaries of the two oblasts did not correspond exactly with the boundaries of the Lowland, the sums of the oblast area and population figures are only a rough equivalent of its total area and population. In very general terms it can be said that the Lowland comprised about one-fifth (14,500 square miles) of the total area of Belorussia (postwar boundaries) and had about one-seventh (1,100,000) of its total population. The above population figures are estimates for 1947.[20] The full results of the 1939 census were not published for this area. We may assume that the wartime population was probably smaller than the 1947 estimate and that the prewar figure was appreciably larger.

There are no unusual ethnographic features which might have influenced the development of partisan warfare in the region. The geographic boundary of the Lowland extends farther north and east than the Belorussian linguistic boundary (as shown on recent Soviet maps), but no particular significance can be ascribed to the language differences, which in any event are slight; earlier data indicate a considerable eastward extension of the Belorussian linguistic boundary. More important, the pre-1939 Polish-

[18] *Ibid.*, p. 159. In this paragraph the present tense is used on the assumption that the general economic conditions still exist even though the information itself originated in 1941. It is likely that the trend since the end of the war has been toward restoring economic activity to the 1941 level.

[19] It is safe to assume that all the cities in the Polotsk Lowland, as well as in all of Army Group Center area, throughout the war contained about 20–30 per cent of their prewar populations. In the period of the German retreat the populations of some cities rose temporarily when evacuees from areas near the front were moved in.

[20] Shabad, p. 502.

Soviet border passed through the region on a north-south line roughly forty miles west of Polotsk and Lepel. About 25 per cent of the region, then, lies in pre-1939 Polish territory. During most of the war the partisan movement was less developed in this western segment than in the east, probably because the Soviet command believed that this un-Sovietized territory would provide a less favorable political environment for partisan operations. It is also true that the western segment was not so important strategically as the area farther east.

In terms of population statistics the region does not differ markedly from the rest of Belorussia. The most thinly settled area lies in a broad band extending northward from Borisov through Lepel and Polotsk. There the density of population is twenty persons per square kilometer or less.[21] On the other hand, the territory near Vitebsk is one of the most densely settled areas in Belorussia with a population density of eighty or more persons per square kilometer.[22] In the Vitebsk area the urban population constitutes about 25 per cent of the total, while in the western segment of the region, particularly in the pre-1939 Polish territory, the urban population barely reaches 20 per cent.[23]

The war produced some significant temporary population changes. We have already noted the depopulation of the cities, which largely resulted from the movement of city dwellers to the country where prospects for making a living were appreciably better. As a consequence, in Belorussia the wartime population was about 83 per cent rural.[24] There were also important shifts in sex and age groupings, though these shifts were typical of German-occupied territories in general and in no way were distinguishing features of this particular area. In 1943 the population consisted of 58 per cent women and 42 per cent men. Nearly 50 per cent of the male population was under sixteen years of age; only about 31 per cent of of the total male population was between the ages of sixteen and forty-five. The women comprised nearly 65 per cent of the total population in the sixteen to forty-five age bracket.[25]

[21] OKH/GenStdH/Abt.IV (Mil.-Geo.), *Militaergeographische Angaben ... Weissrussland, Textheft,* pp. 22, 53.

[22] *Ibid.,* p. 22.

[23] *Ibid.*

[24] Wi Stab Ost, Chef Gr. La, "Die Landwirtschaft in den besetzten Ostgebieten, 1942," February 1943 (Wi/ID 2.84).

[25] Wi In Mitte/Stab I/I Wiss., "Allgemeine statistiche Angaben ueber den Bereich der Wirtschaftsinspektion Mitte," 1 July 1943 (GMDS, Wi/ID 2.55).

§II. Summary of Historical Events

A. MILITARY EVENTS, 1941,
AND INITIAL OCCUPATION

The Polotsk Lowland was taken by German troops within three weeks after the outbreak of war. On 22 June 1941 Army Group Center, comprising five armies, including the Second and Third Panzer Armies, launched its attack across the 1939 German-Soviet border. The first phase of the offensive thrust the German Army beyond Smolensk, some 400 miles to the east; the mere occupation of territory was not considered as important as the destruction of the Soviet forces. Following the strategy of destroying the enemy by pincer movements, Army Group Center within ten days succeeded in creating large pockets in the Minsk-Novogrodek-Bialystok area, containing hundreds of thousands of Soviet troops.

In the judgment of the German General Staff, two rivers, the Dnepr and the Dvina, represented the easternmost line on which the Russian forces would have to make a stand to protect the industrial regions farther east. To forestall any such attempt, the two Panzer armies which spearheaded the German advance resumed their drive on 3 July 1941, even before the Minsk pocket was cleared. Mopping-up operations were left to the slower moving infantry divisions which completed the task by 11 July 1941. On 4 July the German Third Panzer Army established bridgeheads over the Dvina, west of Vitebsk. After fording the Dvina, one wing of Third Panzer Army swung north to make contact with Army Group North in the vicinity of Nevel. Advance units of the infantry divisions followed rapidly, reaching the Dvina near Polotsk by 9 July 1941. The capture of Smolensk on 16 July prevented the Red Army from forming a defensive line along the Dnepr and Dvina. Fighting in the vicinity of Polotsk had been intense for a few days, but the Soviet forces were outflanked and could not establish a line. In less than three weeks, German forces had overrun the Polotsk Lowland without, however, creating another large pocket in this area. The second encirclement battle was fought around Smolensk and was successfully concluded by the Germans as early as 5 August 1941. The further course of the German offensive, which came to a halt in December 1941 just a few miles from Moscow, has no bearing on this study.

The rapid German advance and the early occupation of the Polotsk Lowland affected significantly the development of partisan warfare in this region. In the brief interval between the start of the campaign on 22 June 1941 and the German occupation of the Polotsk Lowland, it was not possible for the Soviet authorities to carry out extensive preparations for partisan warfare, although a beginning was made. On the other hand,

their rapid advance prevented the German troops from taking full possession of the areas through which they passed and allowed Soviet officials
to continue the organization of a partisan movement behind the German
lines. No large units of the Red Army were cut off within the Polotsk
Lowland. Thus the situation differed somewhat from that in other major
centers of partisan activities such as the Bryansk Forest or the Yelnya-
Dorogobuzh region, where Red Army soldiers provided an enormous
reservoir of manpower for a potential partisan movement. Though also
present in the Polotsk Lowland, Red Army stragglers and even smaller
Red Army units were not so numerous here as in these other areas.

The German Panzer units which forged ahead of the infantry divisions
utilized only major roads and by-passed many enemy forces. Speed was
of the essence even for the infantry divisions, although large and dangerous
pockets had to be eliminated. After the front had been pushed eastward,
one or more infantry divisions were assigned for short periods to specific
areas within the Polotsk Lowland to gather Red Army stragglers and to
search for weapons and supplies left behind by the Red Army. Final
pacification was left to the second-rate troops of the security divisions.
According to the German plans, based on the assumption of a short and
decisive campaign, even the security divisions were to be concerned
primarily with the protection of the main lines of communications. Until
the end of July 1941, one security division, the 286th, was responsible
for the entire railroad and highway from Lezno to Minsk and Orsha, a
distance of almost 250 miles.

At the beginning of August 1941, the 286th Security Division was
assigned the areas along both sides of the Borisov-Orsha railroad including
Lepel, Tolochino, and Senno to the north and Mogilev to the south. The
region north of Lepel-Tolochino remained without security troops until
later in August, when the 403d Security Division moved eastward and
occupied Polotsk, Nevel, and Velizh. In addition to the security divisions,
the SS extermination commandos *(Einsatzgruppen)* entered the Polotsk
Lowland, engaging in their notorious activities of eliminating "undesirables," chiefly Jews and Communist officials. These squads may have
been successful in liquidating some of the Soviet officials who were potential organizers of a partisan movement, but a sufficient number escaped
to carry on the work.

The security divisions set up regional and local military government
offices and appointed indigenous mayors and village elders, while members
of the German economic staff set up offices to administer the economic
exploitation of the country. Most German personnel were concentrated in
larger towns, especially in Polotsk and Vitebsk,[26] from where they planned

---

[26] When the Germans moved into the two cities, they found them largely destroyed
and void of population in accordance with Stalin's scorched earth policy.

to administer the countryside. The large forests and swamps in the Polotsk Lowland were never completely occupied and provided a favorable environment for development of a partisan movement.

B. EARLY MANIFESTATIONS OF PARTISAN WARFARE

1. Initial Organization

Some attempts to set a partisan movement in motion were made in the brief period available to the Soviets before the German armies overran the Polotsk Lowland. According to Tsanava, the Soviet historian of the Belorussian partisan movement, "during the first days of the war, the Communist Party of Belorussia and its Central Committee on orders from the Central Committee of the All-Union Communist Party and Comrade Stalin began creating a Party underground and organizing a partisan movement."[27] In Directive No. 4 of the Central Committee of the Belorussian Communist Party and the People's Commissars of Belorussia, distributed widely in leaflet form, the basic assumptions for the creation of the Belorussian partisan movement are stated.

Partisan detachments will be formed in each plant, transportation enterprise, each state and collective farm; they will consist of men, women, and youth capable of fulfilling the tasks of the people's defense (partisans). The partisan detachments will be composed of volunteers—patriots of our Socialist fatherland. . . . When organizing partisan detachments, commanders and commissars will instruct the partisans in their tasks, see to it that they are speedily trained . . . and acquaint them with the simple tactical concepts of contact with the enemy. . . . To command the partisans, staffs will be formed in the executive committees and factory committees (on the oblast, rayon, and village levels).[28]

In the eastern oblasts of Belorussia, which include Vitebsk Oblast, destruction battalions, some of them composed of industrial workers and diversionist groups, were set up to remain behind the German lines.

Shmyrev, one of the important partisan commanders in the Vitebsk area and formerly the manager of a factory, organized a partisan detachment on 7 July 1941 in his home village of Pudoti near Surazh, a few days before the Germans occupied the area.[29] At the same time other detachments were probably set up in different localities within the Polotsk Lowland. While local Communist Party officials attempted to create a partisan movement in the Polotsk Lowland, both before and after the Germans occu-

[27] L. Tsanava, *Vsenarodnaya Partizanskaya Voina v Belorussii protiv Fashistskikh Zakhvatchikov* (Minsk: Gosizdat BSSR), I (1949), 44.

[28] H.Gr.Mitte, Ic/AO, "Uebersetzung der Richtlinien Nr. 4," 2 September 1941 (GMDS, PzAOK 3, 20839/5).

[29] For the history of the Shmyrev Brigade, see especially II. SS Kav.Regt., "Partisanen-Tagebuch Nr. 2," 5 July—17 August 1941 (GMDS, Waffen SS, I. and II. SS Kav.Regts. 78037/196).

pied the territory, additional leaders were sent in by air or through the front during the first few weeks of the German invasion.[30]

After they had reached their destination, these partisan leaders contacted local Communist Party officials such as secretaries, managers of kolkhozes, rayon Party secretaries, and others who had remained behind. At first, the organizers restricted their activities to remote villages where they mobilized the local manpower of military age into a militia under the command of local Communist leaders or Red Army officers.

A German infantry division assigned to comb the Polotsk-Vitebsk-Nevel area spoke of "partisan regions" as early as 20 July 1941 and reported that roads were mined daily. The division remained in this section for only a few days before moving on to Velizh-Usvyat-Nevel; in both areas the troops of the division were unable to come to grips with the partisans.[31]

The partisans, as they first appeared to the Germans, were described by a member of the Vitebsk Economic Staff on 8 August 1941. In Vitebsk Oblast, the report stated, there are numerous Red Army stragglers and followers of the Communist regime who are exerting pressure on the population. Any actions by German troops or police units, however, would be pointless, the report continued, because the partisans operate as individuals or in very small groups and could not be eliminated by regular military or police operations.[32] The partisan groups may not have been so small as the Germans thought, since they carefully avoided contact with German troops and split up into very small units whenever danger arose.

2. Popular Reactions to the Partisan Movement

There are indications that in general the indigenous population did not react favorably to the Soviet attempt to create a partisan movement. The objections, a German report commented, were based on the ruthless requisitioning by the partisans and not on any ideological considerations.[33] The people with whom the partisans came into contact during the early phases of partisan warfare consisted almost exclusively of peasants who may well have resented the interference with their agricultural activities and their normal life pattern. Since partisan activities from the very beginning were frequently followed by German reprisals, which punished the population more than they hurt the partisans, the peasants had an additional cause for antipathy toward the partisan movement. Even the

[30] One of the partisan leaders flown into the Vitebsk area was Linkov, whose memoirs were published by the Soviet Government after the war. [Grigorii Linkov, *Voina v tylu vraga* (Moscow: Gosudarstvennoye Izdatelstvo Khudozhestvennoi Literatury, 1951).]

[31] 256. Inf.Div., Ia, "Kriegstagebuch fuer die Zeit vom 1.11.1940—21.13.1941," entries for 20 and 21 July 1941 and 3 August 1941 (GMDS, 256 ID 22306).

[32] AOK 9, Iv. Wi., "Versprengte Soldaten und kommunistische Umtriebe hinter der Front," 8 August 1941 (GMDS, Wi/ID 2.296).

[33] 403. Sich.Div.,Ic, "Taetigkeitsbericht,Ic,Oktober 1941," n.d., p. 4 (GMDS, 403 ID 15701/3).

partisans confirm that the indigenous population did not, at first, receive them well. One partisan, describing his early experiences in the northern part of the Polotsk Lowland, commented in a letter written in 1942: "There were many police and other riffraff who fought side by side with the Germans [probably referring to indigenous collaborators]; the population was also against us."[34]

It is very likely that, when the Germans first passed through their region, many of the peasants were glad to be freed from Soviet rule. However, the partisan movement, activated by Communist Party officials, proved to them that they had not yet escaped Soviet control. Nevertheless, during the summer and fall of 1941 the peasants had no reason to believe that a continuation of such control was inescapable, since Soviet power appeared to be on the verge of final destruction. While the German armies were accompanied by a myth of invincibility, the partisan movement was not yet firmly established. The friendly reception which the German troops received when they first entered is confirmed by all German reports on the subject, although it is unlikely that those who did not share this feeling were very demonstrative in showing their dislike of the Germans. The favorable reaction to the Germans was soon dampened by the critical food shortage and German behavior in general. In the late fall of 1941 a German report stated that the indigenous population had become more and more disposed toward active participation in the fight against the partisans.[35] Apparently the Germans began to realize only then that antipartisan warfare could not be waged successfully without the support of the indigenous population, and noted further that increased efforts to enlist such support were not completely unsuccessful.

3. The Partisans, Fall of 1941

The number of partisans in the Polotsk Lowland in the fall of 1941 was considerable, although a precise estimate is impossible. The Germans often discredited estimates given by members of the indigenous population as greatly exaggerated, probably because they themselves were unable to come into contact with larger partisan groups, which usually split up into smaller units and avoided combat. It also seems that in 1941 the partisans were not so active as their numerical strength might have permitted. Lack

[34] PzAOK 3, Ic/AO, "Entwicklung der Bandenlage im Bereich der 3. Pz-Armee im September 1943," 2 October 1943, Anlage 3 (GMDS, PzAOK 3, 40252/7). The quotation is taken from one of 200 letters captured by the Germans when they shot down a plane carrying mail to the Soviet rear. The original letters are not available; only extracts which the Germans considered representative and significant were translated.

Linkov (p. 74) also mentions that partisans dropped by parachute in the Polotsk Lowland had to keep to the woods, not daring to enter villages or farms where they might have been betrayed.

[35] 339. Inf.Div., Abt.VII, "Lagebericht," 15 November 1941 (GMDS, 339 ID 13914/6).

of experience, difficulties with the population, low morale because of continued Soviet defeats, and a heroic feeling arising from just staying alive and eluding the Germans were some of the reasons for their relative in activity. A report for the area of the 403d Security Division for August 1941 indicates that several thousand partisans were in the area assigned to the division.

The partisan detachments consisted of former Red Army stragglers, some peasants, Komsomol members, minor government officials, and industrial workers who had been organized into destruction battalions before the Soviet armies retreated eastward. Reinforcements, especially leaders and commissars, were brought in by land and air.[36] In addition, small groups were parachuted behind the lines with specific sabotage missions,[37] becoming partisans whether their mission was accomplished or not. Other sources of manpower were found among the local men of military age and among the large number of escaped prisoners of war whose experiences in German camps were apt to make them determined resistance fighters. The partisans were organized into detachments and led by commanders and commissars, some of whom were Party or NKVD officials, while others were Red Army officers. The basic units were the otryads.[38] At this time there is no evidence of close supervision over partisan activities by external agencies or of coordination among otryads or with the Red Army.

In the summer and fall the partisans engaged in the type of activity laid out for them in general Soviet directives. The main emphasis was on the disruption of German lines of communications. Railroad tracks were dynamited, trains blown up, telegraph and telephone communications cut, roads mined, and bridges dynamited. Attacks on German troops occurred only rarely when isolated vehicles or patrols were ambushed. The partisans concentrated in the same regions which were to remain centers of partisan strength throughout the war: the areas north of Polotsk, the Rossono area, the Ushachi area between Polotsk and Lepel, the Senno-Chashniki sector southwest of Vitebsk, and, finally the triangle formed by the cities of Nevel-Velizh-Vitebsk. [See Fig. 14.] The Velizh sector became a strongpoint of the Belorussian partisan movement at a very early date. Partisans in that area were reported to be occupying the same positions and fortifications which had served the "White" (anti-Soviet) partisans of the revolutionary days.[39]

---

[36] One German report claims that the Red Army in the second half of September sent through the front groups of 100 men, each equipped to carry on partisan warfare. (403. Sich.Div., Ia, "Lagebeurteilung," 4 November 1941, p. 2, GMDS, 403 ID 15701/3.)

[37] *Ibid.*, p. 4.

[38] The otryad (detachment) was a partisan unit of varying strength, usually of company size.

[39] A German report claims that the Demidov-Surazh-Velizh region contained

The partisans' general disruptive activities in the German rear in 1941 had no serious effects on German military operations. The Germans suffered some losses and some damage to their equipment, but it amounted to very little. The political and psychological implications for the population of the Polotsk Lowland were probably much greater. It is interesting that this is also the judgment of Linkov, who writes: "From the purely military point of view this [blowing up bridges and vehicles] was insignificant, mere diversion; but its political significance was enormous."[40]

As winter approached, the sabotage activities of the partisans declined as requisitioning of food and winter clothing from the indigenous population absorbed more of their attention and effort. At the same time pressure on the population increased; cases became more frequent in which kolkhoz officials working for the Germans, mayors and village elders appointed by the Germans, and other civilians who showed inclinations to collaborate, were threatened, abducted, and even shot.

The reasons for the relative ineffectiveness of the disruptive activities of the partisans in the summer and fall of 1941 are difficult to assess, but several factors probably contributed to it: (1) The hostile attitude of the population forced the partisans to operate cautiously to avoid being betrayed. (2) The inexperienced partisans were neither well organized nor controlled by the Soviets behind the front. (3) Much time was devoted to exerting pressure on the population to convince them that the war was not yet lost and to prove to them that the partisans and not the Germans were the legitimate authority. (4) The efforts to increase the partisan movement by collecting Red Army stragglers, training recruits, and in general perfecting the internal organization distracted them from their other task of disrupting the German supply lines. (5) In all these activities the partisans were, of course, hampered by German countermeasures.

Partisan attempts to tighten their organization [reported a German security division] could be prevented. . . . Several larger concentrations could be dispersed in the regions south of Lepel [and] north of Starye Dorogi. . . . In constant pursuit the partisans were partly destroyed and partly deprived of their leaders. Therefore partisan activities were confined to the looting of villages. . . . The few attempts at sabotage were recognized in time and successfully prevented.[41]

This report overemphasizes German successes and does not take into consideration that large areas were only rarely, if ever, visited by German

___

"White" partisans until 1927 and that they did not surrender until promised safe conduct by Soviet authorities. (403. Sich.Div., Ia, "Lagebeurteilung," 4 November 1941, p. 1, GMDS, 403 ID 15701/3.)

[40] Linkov, p. 111.

[41] 339. Inf.Div., Abt. VII, "Lagebericht," 15 November 1941 (GMDS, 339 ID 13914/6).

troops. In these areas the partisans continued their operations in comparative safety, but in general German countermeasures were not entirely without effect.

4. Reorganization of the Partisan Movement

In the winter of 1941–42 important changes took place, affecting both the partisan movement and the situation on the front. Early in December 1941 the German offensive against Moscow had come to a halt a few miles short of its goal. [See Fig. 13.] A Soviet counteroffensive, as if waiting for this signal, started immediately and forced the German armies westward. Hitler insisted that the German Army hold its ground without retreating, but it proved impossible to hold back the Soviet forces along a broad front. Major towns and strategic positions were defended, but in between the Soviet Army could maneuver almost at will. A disaster for the German forces was averted either because the Red Army itself was not strong enough to exploit its breakthrough without first eliminating the German forward positions, or because its conservative military strategy and a possible over-estimation of German strength prevented such a course. Soviet troops did, however, operate far to the rear of German advance positions, and units of the Soviet Third and Fourth Assault Armies penetrated to within a few miles of Vitebsk. The region of Velizh-Usvyat was overrun by these units, and a gateway was opened up to the German rear which was to remain a weak spot throughout the war. The Vitebsk Corridor, as it came to be called, provided an easy route for the partisans in the Velizh-Vitebsk-Nevel area and farther west to receive supplies and move personnel through the front in both directions. By early spring the Soviet offensive weakened, and German forces, bolstered by reinforcements, re-established their positions and a fairly continuous front line. The Third and Fourth Assault Armies gave up the Velizh-Usvyat region and withdrew to the northeast. The Vitebsk Corridor, however, was now guarded by partisans who kept open this lifeline to the Red Army and the Soviet hinterland until the spring of 1943.

There are no indications that the partisans of the Polotsk Lowland supported the Soviet offensive to any extent; apparently they exhibited a high degree of inertia. Just what happened at this time is not clear, but the partisans seem to have adopted a policy of inaction and reorganization. The Soviet offensive had forced the Germans to dispatch more troops, even second-rate security troops, to the front, leaving only a minimum to protect the supply lines. The partisans, however, did not engage in extensive sabotage activities, and the German reports contain little information on them during the winter of 1941–42. Inertia may not have been the only reason for this inactivity. The severe winter made operations difficult. Swamps and lakes which normally protected partisans retreats were now frozen and

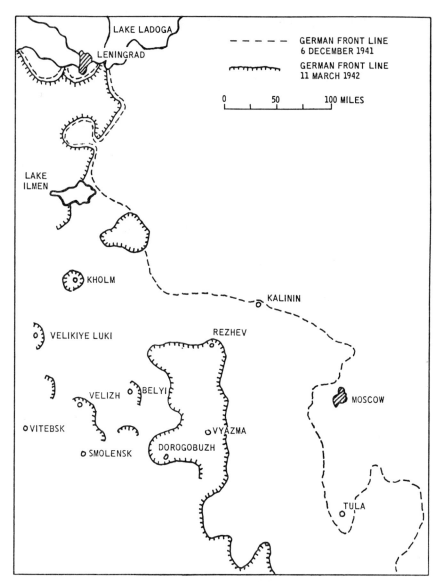

Figure 13.—The German front, 6 December 1941—11 March 1942.

could be crossed easily by German security forces, although the latter were in no position to engage in large-scale activities. The partisans probably concentrated on a process of reorganization which began in the late winter. The period of the Soviet offensive, when German security forces were even less in evidence outside major towns or strongpoints, was ideally suited to exert pressure on the indigenous population to gain new recruits and to compel cooperation, using the recent successes of the Red Army as a powerful psychological warfare weapon. In the spring of 1942 the partisans re-emerged as a stronger and more effective force. The Vitebsk Corridor enabled them to receive supplies and reinforcements not only by air, but through a direct land route to the Red Army. In March 1942 the German Third Panzer Army reported:

> There are indications that the partisan movement in the region of Velikiye Luki—Vitebsk—Rudnya—Velizh now is being organized on a large scale. The fighting strength of the partisans heretofore active is being bolstered by individual units of regular troops. Thus, the partisans receive trained leaders as well as heavy weapons, artillery, antitank guns, etc.[42]

Similar developments took place in the other areas of the Polotsk Lowland.

C. INTENSIFICATION OF PARTISAN WARFARE

1. Growth of Partisan Movement

The partisan movement continued its growth throughout 1942. After the Soviet winter offensive, the German forces had again consolidated their positions without attempting to eliminate the huge bulge in their lines west and south of Toropets. From this bulge the Soviet Third and Fourth Assault Armies threatened the German flanks throughout 1942 and the spring of 1943 until the German withdrawal movement (the so-called *Bueffelbewegung*) shortened the front. The area east of the Polotsk Lowland, however, was not important in front operations in 1942 until the start of the Soviet second winter offensive against the Velikiye Luki sector, resulting early in 1943 in the recapture of that city.

The front east of the Polotsk Lowland was weakly held by German forces of corps strength which could not form a continuous line. The Vitebsk Corridor was therefore easily kept open by the partisan detachments in the Nevel-Velizh-Vitebsk sector. The partisans here, as everywhere in the Polotsk Lowland, had perfected and tightened their organization. In some cases several loosely organized otryads were merged into one brigade. More often, one otryad expanded to become a brigade which was then subdivided into several subordinate otryads. The new brigade remained under the command of the leader of the original otryad. The brigade commanders, while independent within their own operational area, came under control of higher partisan staffs or operative groups on both sides of the front. On the Soviet side, there was the staff of the partisan movement with the Kalinin Front, headed by Belchenko, an NKVD officer, and located near Toropets; under his control the operative groups with the Third and Fourth Assault Armies functioned. Contact with the partisan brigades was main-

---

[42] PzAOK 3, Ic/AO, "Partisanenbekaempfung," 19 March 1942 (GMDS, PzAOK 3, 20839/2).

tained by radio and air, but also by direct movement through the front. The partisan brigades now executed their attacks on railroads and their other activities in close cooperation with, if not in subordination to, the Soviet Army.

The partisans in 1942 had little reason to fear the German security forces. During the first Soviet winter offensive these forces had been reduced and were never brought up to the strength necessary to curb the partisan movement. Most German observers agreed that after the partisans had become a strong force the only way to bring them under control by military action was to conduct large-scale antipartisan operations and to follow up by stationing sufficiently strong security troops throughout the area. The necessary forces for such action were never available. By force of circumstances, concentration of security forces along the main routes of communications continued even after the Germans had clearly recognized that the partisan movement could not be brought under control by such defensive tactics. German security measures, at best, prevented the partisans from completely paralyzing the railroads, but did not stop extensive attacks on roads and railroads. The limited antipartisan operations conducted in the spring and summer of 1942 by the 201st Security Division[43] merely caused the partisan brigades to seek temporary shelter elsewhere. The excellent intelligence and mobility of the partisans gave them the opportunity to shift their location or go into hiding until the German troops withdrew again. Hardest hit by these operations was the indigenous population. It seems to have been common German practice to burn down indiscriminately villages suspected of cooperating with the partisans. The Germans, however, were unable to enter many rural areas because the partisans had become a powerful force.

The growth of the partisan movement by November 1942 is well illustrated by the statistics compiled by the Economic Staff for Vitebsk, and listing the administrative subdivisions (*Amtsbezirke*) under partisan or German control.[44] [See Table 6.] In the three regions the partisans ruled in 45 per cent of the combined area including all of Osveya, Rossono, and Ushachi Rayons. In another 21.7 per cent, for all practical purposes, the partisans had control, but were not strong enough to prevent German military units from entering. The Germans controlled only 32.8 per cent. The area under German control included the cities of Vitebsk and Polotsk, the surrounding area in which more German troops were stationed, and the territory close to the railroads and major roads. It is no exaggeration to say

---

[43] The 201st Security Division became responsible for the greater part of the Polotsk Lowland west of the Nevel-Vitebsk line in the spring of 1942.

[44] Wi Kdo Vitebsk, "Monatsbericht," 23 November 1942, p. 12 (GMDS, Wi/ID 2.770). The figures indicate the number of administrative subdivisions under the various economic staffs.

that by the end of 1942 the partisans were in virtual control of the rural areas of the Polotsk Lowland.

The Vitebsk Corridor, through which contact with the Red Army was maintained, played an important part in the growth of the partisan movement in the Polotsk Lowland. Supplies and reinforcements were channeled through this lifeline; the reinforcements included a considerable number of regular Red Army soldiers who were sent to the rear to strengthen the partisan brigades. Extensive use was also made of airplanes to bring in

TABLE 6

Administrative subdivisions (*Amtsbezirke*) of the Polotsk Lowland
under partisan or German control

Economic staffs	Under German control	Under partisan control	Germans could enter only under military protection
Vitebsk	73	62	42
Polotsk	9	51	12
Lepel	26	37	17
Total	108	150	71

Source: Wi Kdo Vitebsk, "Monatsbericht," 23 November 1942, p. 12 (GMDS, Wi/ ID 2.770). The figures indicate the number of administrative subdivisions under the various economic staffs.

supplies and reinforcements. In addition to the partisan complex which guarded the Vitebsk Corridor, other centers of partisan strength appeared: the Rossono area to the north of Polotsk, including Rossono and Osveya Rayons; the Ushachi area between Polotsk and Lepel; the region of Senno-Chashniki between Vitebsk and Lepel; and the territory between Lepel and Borisov. In each of these areas the partisan brigades formed a complex, probably under unified command.[45]

The partisan brigades achieved control over large areas by exerting pressure against isolated German strongpoints; they raided the supply convoys, food and ammunition dumps, and sometimes attacked small garrisons directly. To avoid annihilation of the garrisons, the German troops were withdrawn, since reinforcements for the garrisons were not available. The administrative centers of Osveya and Rossono rayons were surrendered to the partisans by September 1942, while the rayon center of Ushachi was given up in December of that year. In addition, numerous smaller strongpoints were also left to the partisans by default.

Within the areas over which the partisans gained control they conscripted

[45] Such unified command certainly existed later in the war and probably functioned as early as 1942.

the population, partly to strengthen their own forces, but also as an additional source of manpower for the Red Army. The recruits were sent through the Vitebsk Corridor to the Soviet rear where they were trained; sometimes they returned to become partisans. Excess food supplies, cattle, and horses were also channeled through the front to the Red Army.

2. Shifting Allegiance of the Population

In view of partisan strength and relative German weakness, it is not surprising that the allegiance of the indigenous population shifted more and more to the partisans. From 1942 on the partisans represented stability, while the Germans became the disturbing element. In 1941 the Germans controlled, even if they did not occupy, the rural areas, while the partisans conducted merely hit-and-run raids. In 1942 the partisans and the political staffs attached to them controlled and administered the countryside, which German military or police units only occasionally invaded to requisition manpower and agricultural products. The partisans partly re-established Soviet administration. Communist Party officials and staffs were attached to their brigades, and under protection of the partisans the Komsomol engaged in propaganda and political work among the population. Indiscriminate looting was replaced by more orderly requisitions. The partisan relationship to the civilian population became institutionalized and assumed a definite pattern.

To what extent the population voluntarily cooperated with the partisans or to what extent they bowed to a superior force is difficult to estimate. Many people joined the German collaborator and indigenous police units which actively fought the partisans. In the spring of 1943, 26,000 collaborators, most of them recruited in prisoner-of-war camps, were fighting on the German side in the rear area of Third Panzer Army,[46] but the rate of desertion to the partisans increased tremendously as the Soviet forces pushed the German armies westward.

D. GERMAN ANTIPARTISAN OPERATIONS, 1942–43

German antipartisan operations were not conducted on a substantial scale until the late fall of 1942. Minor operations had been started by the 201st Security Division in the summer of that year, but by order of the German High Command even they had been suspended to supply additional forces for the protection of the railroad network from partisan attacks.[47] In October 1942 a whole combat division, the 12th Panzer, was assigned

[46] The Third Panzer Army assumed command over the 201st Security Division, and over almost the entire area of the Polotsk Lowland in February 1943. [No author] "Die 3. Panzerarmee in der Zeit vom 21.1.—5.3.43," n.d. (GMDS, PzAOK 3, 35568/16).
[47] Wi Kdo Witebsk, "Monatsbericht," 23 November 1942 (GMDS, Wi/ID 2.779).

to conduct antipartisan operations between Nevel and Polotsk. The result of one operation carried out by this division was that eighty partisans were killed or captured while thousands escaped. Instead of proving to the population that German forces could still cope with the partisan menace, the people were left with the impression that the German forces had been completely outwitted. Other operations in the same region proved only slightly more effective.

By late summer of 1942 the conduct of German antipartisan warfare had undergone important changes. The SS and Police assumed exclusive jurisdiction in the civilian-occupied territories, while antipartisan warfare in the military areas became the responsibility of the operations sections of the armies. Security of the rear areas was no longer considered a mere problem of logistics. This change of German attitude reflected the realization that the partisan actions had a direct impact on combat operations. The effect of this reorganization on antipartisan warfare in the Polotsk Lowland was limited because of the scarcity of German security troops, but it did result in a greater participation of SS and Police forces.

The SS and Police operations against the partisans in the Polotsk Lowland were conducted in a particularly brutal and ruthless manner. Villages in partisan-controlled areas were burned to the ground, and cruelties against women and children were commonplace. The partisans were quick to exploit the German atrocities for propaganda and psychological warfare. One of these SS operations was carried out in the fringe areas of the Rossono partisan center by SS General von Jeckeln. The region was laid waste; the civilian population was killed or evacuated, and the villages were burned down.[48]

Operation "Kottbus," executed on a larger scale, was conducted by SS General von Gottberg in May and June 1943 against the strong partisan brigades between Lepel and Borisov. Sixteen thousand troops, both German and indigenous, penetrated the partisan-held area against strong resistance after experiencing considerable difficulties. Reporting to Rosenberg on the first phase of this operation, the German Commissar General (*Generalkommissar*) for Belorussia pointed out that among the 5,000 people shot for suspicion of collaborating with the partisans, there were many women and children. He also argued that if for 4,500 enemy dead only 492 rifles were captured, the implication clearly was that the dead included many peasants who were not necessarily partisans.[49] The effect of these operations on the partisans was negligible. Within a few weeks they reappeared as strong as ever.[50] During the operation, partisan brigades to the north of the area came

[48] Wi Kdo Witebsk, "Lagebericht," 23 March 1943, p. 7 (GMDS, Wi/ID 2.439).

[49] Gen. Kom. f. Weissr., "An den Herrn Reichsminister fuer die besetzten Ostgebiete," 5 June 1943 (IMT, PS-1475).

[50] Notwithstanding the claim by von Gottberg that almost 10,000 partisans and partisan helpers were killed. (RFSS u. Chef d.Deutsch.Pol., Chef d. Bandenkampf-

to the aid of the partisans under attack. This may explain some of the difficulties which German units encountered. It also testifies to the increasing strength, fighting spirit, and coordination within the partisan movement.

The first antipartisan operations which could claim to have had a lasting effect on the partisans of the Polotsk Lowland were executed by the Third Panzer Army in the Velizh-Nevel-Vitebsk region early in 1943. The territory east of Vitebsk-Nevel at that time was again located immediately behind the front. Early in 1943 the Soviet winter offensive succeeded in recapturing Velikiye Luki. In the early spring German retrograde movements to shorten their lines had also brought the area northeast of Vitebsk closer to the front. The antipartisan operations were prompted by the desire to eliminate the threat against the German supply lines in an area so close to the front. Total partisan strength in the Velizh-Vitebsk area was estimated at about 6,000 partisans, a considerable number of whom were killed or captured during the first of these operations, "Kugelblitz."

The Third Panzer Army made an attempt not to alienate the population completely. The burning of villages was prohibited, and the final report pointed out that only those who were obviously partisans or partisan helpers had been shot.[51] Two more operations, "Donnerkeil" and "Maigewitter," followed "Kugelblitz." One result of the operations was that the partisan food supply was taken by the Germans, and a serious food shortage developed for the remaining partisans. After "Maigewitter" the Chief of the Central Staff of the Partisan Movement, Ponomarenko, visited the partisan brigades and ordered that food be sent to the partisans by air. The German antipartisan operations, the food shortage, and the westward movement of the front combined to reduce the importance of the Velizh-Vitebsk partisan complex. The partisan brigades west of the Vitebsk-Nevel line, reinforced partly by the remnants of the brigades of the Velizh-Vitebsk sector, now assumed greater importance.

E. FINAL STAGES OF PARTISAN WARFARE AND THE GERMAN RETREAT

1. The Strategic Significance of the Partisan Areas

The growth of the partisan movement in the Polotsk Lowland was favored by the existence of many lakes, swamps, and extensive forests which made it difficult for the inadequate German security forces to detect and fight the partisan brigades when they first organized and expanded during 1941 and 1942. However, the rapid growth and great strength of the partisans in 1942, and continuing into 1943, cannot be considered a local devel-

verbaende, "Sondermeldung ueber das Grossunternehmen 'Kottbus,'" 23 June 1943 (NMT, NO-2608).

[51] GFP Gr. 717, "Unternehmen 'Kugelblitz,'" 14 March 1943, p. 4 (GMDS, PzAOK 3, 35568/51).

opment caused only by favorable conditions. The partisan movement became strong as the result of a conscious effort and strategic plan in which the individual brigades and partisan complexes were assigned specific roles.

There were several instances of coordination between partisan activities and Red Army needs. Interference with the German railroad and supply system, partisan recruiting activities to obtain manpower for the Red Army, and partisan intelligence reports serve as examples of such coordination. It appears, moreover, that the entire geographic complex of the Polotsk Lowland, including the partisan brigades active there, played an important part in the strategic planning of the Red Army during the last phases of the war.

The centers of partisan strength within the Polotsk Lowland were further strengthened and equipped in 1943. The four heavily fortified centers of the partisan movement became increasingly more important. The Rossono area at the junction between Army Group North and Army Group Center was built up in the spring and early summer of 1943. Here a Soviet general, Trufanov, was reported to be organizing systematically all partisan units, which allegedly included 2,000 regular soldiers, who were equipped with heavy weapons and were well supplied by air.[52] Total partisan strength in the Rossono area was estimated at 10,000–12,000 men, organized into medium- and large-sized brigades, tightly controlled and under strict military discipline. The roads into the Rossono area were blocked and the approaches guarded by partisan detachments, while the interior was completely controlled by them.

The Ushachi area was similarly developed. It extended from Lepel to Ulla-Dokshytse and contained from 12,000 to 15,000 partisans under the leadership of the former Lepel Party secretary, Lobanok. This area had also become inaccessible to German troops, because of partisan roadblocks, minefields, and other defensive installations.[53] A third center was located between Lepel and Borisov, where heading an operative group was a Soviet colonel, Machulsky, plenipotentiary of the Staff of the Partisan Movement for Belorussia in Borisov Rayon, and secretary of the Communist Party of Minsk Oblast.

Strong partisan forces were also located in the area east of Lepel, near Kamen-Chashniki-Senno, although the region was not so well defined as the others. There the partisan brigades were under the command of General Dubrovsky, who probably also held a post in the Communist Party or NKVD. In the summer and fall of 1943 Dubrovsky attempted to consolidate and extend partisan control by systematically attacking and eliminating German strongpoints east of Lepel. An order of 5 July 1943, attributed to

[52] PzAOK 3, Ia, "Nr. 17/43," 21 April 1943 (GMDS, PzAOK 3, 35568/17).
[53] HSSPF Russl. Mitte u. Weissr., Ic, "Feindlage im Raum Lepel-Ulla-Polozk-Dokschyze," 11 April 1944, p. 1–2 (GMDS, Waffen SS, Dirlewanger 78028/15).

Stalin, instructed Dubrovsky to work out plans for the partisans to attack the town and rayon of Lepel, eliminating all German strongpoints in that area. For the attack, up to 4,000 partisans were to be used, and another 2,000 were to be kept in reserve. In addition, support by the Soviet Air Force was to be extended in the form of bombing attacks against the town of Lepel.[54] The action against Lepel did not materialize within the time limit of thirty days allegedly specified by the order. Partisan pressure in the whole area, however, increased sharply, and by the end of September the German Third Panzer Army reported that the Vitebsk-Polotsk-Senno-Lepel region was so strongly infested with partisans that it became increasingly difficult to maintain strongpoints there. Most roads were closed to German traffic; only a few major thoroughfares could be traveled under heavy military protection.[55] In August 1943 the partisans, assisted by special demolition squads of the Red Army, executed mass attacks against the major railroad lines which completely paralyzed the German rail system for several days. Heavy attacks continued throughout the fall of that year.

In October 1943 a powerful Soviet offensive started against the Vitebsk sector of the front. The commander of the Kalinin Front, General Yeremenkov, ordered his troops to annihilate the enemy and to take "the second capital of Belorussia, Vitebsk."[56] The close cooperation between the partisan brigades and the Red Army actions, as well as the specific role which the partisans played in connection with the Soviet offensive, is clearly stated in a report of the Third Panzer Army in October 1943:

The development at the front has demonstrated that the partisans and the Red Army demolition squads have been assigned the task of preparing the way for the Red Army. In the operational plans of the Red Army the two partisan areas, Senno-Lepel and Rossono, seem to serve two different objectives. In the Senno-Lepel region the partisans have recently begun to destroy all road communications. The Vitebsk-Lepel road has always been the object of strong disruptive activities by the partisans. . . . Destruction of bridges through fire and demolitions has occurred in assembly line fashion. Recently, however, the partisans have no longer restricted themselves to this highway and the roads leading to our own strongpoints, but have extended their activities to all roads leading from the front to the rear which could at any time be used by German troops; these roads have been made impassable through digging ditches, plowing up [the road surface], demolitions, mining, and roadblocks. . . . The intention is clearly to prevent German troops from withdrawing further to the rear; this is confirmed by all reports concerned with this subject. The permanent nature of these destructions and their continuation even while the German forces are disengaging themselves and withdrawing (*Absetzbewegungen*) indi-

[54] 286. Sich.Div.,Ia, "An Befh. H.Gr. Mitte, Ia," 27 July 1943 (GMDS, HGr Mitte 65002/22).
[55] PzAOK 3, Ia, Ic/AO, "Lage im rueckw. Armeegebiet Pz. AOK 3," 28 September 1943 (GMDS, HGr Mitte 65002/23).
[56] For complete text of order, see AOK 16, Ic/AO, "Feindnachrichtenblatt Nr. 71," 19 October 1943, Anlage 3 (GMDS, HGr Nord 75131/88).

cate that the Red Army . . . is not planning to continue its advance into this region, but rather intends to use the area as a buffer against which the withdrawing German armies would be pressed.

The transportation network in the Rossono area presents a remarkable contrast to this situation. Here the bridges over the Drissa and in the interior are demolished; there are roadblocks, but evidence of total destruction . . . is completely lacking. No changes in the road situation have been observed for a long time. A reconstruction of roads would not meet with any great difficulty, since the civilian population and the partisans . . . could be utilized for this purpose at short notice. . . . Statements by deserters and intelligence agents indicate that the Red Army is planning to penetrate into the Rossono area, while similar opinions have not been advanced for the Senno-Lepel region.[57]

The Soviet offensive against Vitebsk resulted in a breakthrough between Nevel and Vitebsk early in October 1943. The towns of Gorodok, Nevel, and Dretun were captured by the Russian armies and a deep salient northwest of Vitebsk was thereby created. [See Figs. 14 and 15.] Simultaneous attacks to the northeast and southwest of Vitebsk failed to gain ground, and the weak German forces were able to prevent a major breakthrough. Such

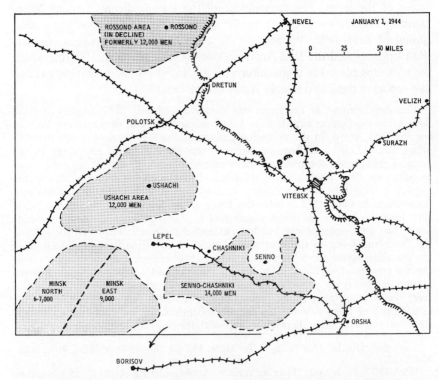

Figure 14.—Partisan concentrations and front line, 1 January 1944.

[57] PzAOK 3, Ic/AO, "Aufgaben der Banden in den Grossraeumen Senno-Lepel und Rossono," 18 October 1943 (GMDS, PzAOK 3, 49113/37).

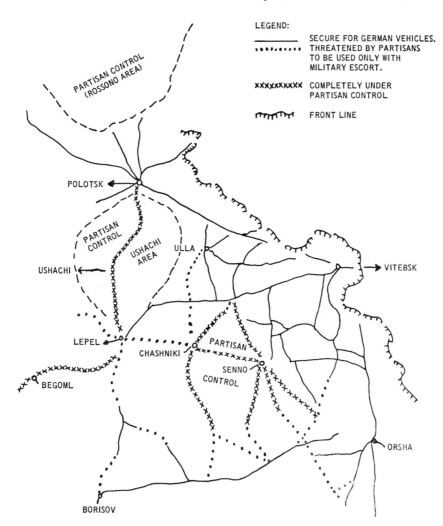

Figure 15.—Partisan control of roads, March 1944.

a breakthrough would have resulted in forcing the German Third Panzer Army into a cul-de-sac between the Red Army and the partisan areas west of Vitebsk between Polotsk and Borisov. One result of the Soviet offensive was that a major antipartisan operation against the Rossono area, personally conducted by SS General von dem Bach-Zelewski,[58] had to be called off so that the task force could reinforce the German front and prevent the Russians from expanding the Nevel salient.

[58] Von dem Bach-Zelewski was appointed by Himmler as chief of all antipartisan warfare units in June 1943. In this capacity he had sweeping powers of command in all areas designated as "Partisan Warfare Areas" in occupied Europe, whenever he chose to assume such command. (RFSS, "SS-Befehl," 21 June 1943, NMT, NO-1621.)

In the winter of 1943–44 Soviet intentions to drive the German Third Panzer Army against the partisan regions behind the front and thereby prevent its escape did not materialize, because the German forces were able to hold Vitebsk and temporarily check the Russian advance.

The Soviet breakthrough north of Vitebsk greatly reduced the strategic significance of the Rossono area. In October 1943 the more active brigades were reported to be shifting their location to the west to Dvinsk and Baranovichi. Partisans in the Rossono area at that time still numbered from 10,000 to 12,000. Those remaining considered themselves the advance guard of the Red Army. They assembled seventeen- and eighteen-year-old recruits for the Red Army; incorporation of partisan brigades into the Red Army did not occur except in isolated instances. More often partisans would act as scouts for the Red Army to guide and assist military units in the terrain with which the partisans were thoroughly familiar.[59]

The Senno-Lepel and Ushachi region was further fortified and strengthened as the Rossono area declined in importance. In Ushachi alone partisans numbered between 12,000 and 15,000. The fight for control of the roads, vital for the movement of the Third Panzer Army in case further German withdrawals should become necessary, became a tug of war between the partisans and the German security forces. The Germans and their collaborator units, after heavy fights, temporarily opened the road from Lepel to Vitebsk and established strongpoints along the way.

2. Soviet Reoccupation of the Polotsk Lowland

In the struggle over control of the region between Lepel-Vitebsk-Orsha, the Kaminsky Brigade played an important role.[60] The brigade was originally formed in Lokot, south of Bryansk, where Kaminsky headed a self-governing district set up by the Germans early in the war. As the Soviet armies reoccupied the Bryansk area, the Kaminsky Brigade, consisting of approximately 6,000 fighting men, and its following of 25,000 civilians were evacuated to resettle in Lepel and the partisan-controlled territory of Lepel-Polotsk-Vitebsk. After its relocation from Lokot by September 1943, the brigade had lost much of its effectiveness as an antipartisan unit. Difficulties with a hostile civilian population, the plotting of some officers and men with intent to desert to the partisans, a shortage of food, and the fact that the brigade and its following had been uprooted were some of the factors which contributed to its inability to gain the upper hand against the partisans in the new territory. Nevertheless, with the aid of the Kaminsky

---

[59] AOK 16, Ic/AO, "Feindnachrichtenblatt Nr. 71," 19 October 1943, p. 6 (GMDS, HGr Nord 75131/88); PzAOK 3, Ic/AO, "Feindnachrichtenblatt Nr. 12," 29 November 1943 (GMDS, HGr Nord, 75131/88).

[60] For an analysis and history of the Kaminsky Brigade, see Alexander Dallin, *The Kaminsky Brigade: 1941–1944* (Maxwell Air Force Base, Ala.: HRRI, December 1952), Technical Research Report, No. 7.

Brigade, the Germans were at least able to give battle to the partisans. The partisans, on the other hand, were diverted because they were exerting every effort to prevent Kaminsky from gaining a foothold. In this they were partly successful, since the Kaminsky forces and the attached civilian population were restricted largely to the town of Lepel and to several strongpoints along the Lepel-Vitebsk and Lepel-Senno roads. Even here they were subjected to continuous attacks.[61] For a time in November 1943 all approaches to the town of Lepel were completely cut off by partisans.[62] The civilian population attached to Kaminsky was again evacuated in early spring 1944, but the military unit continued to fight partisans in the Polotsk Lowland as part of SS antipartisan forces until the last Soviet offensive swept past Polotsk in June 1944.

Although the first Soviet attempt to take Vitebsk in the winter 1943–44 failed, a renewal of the offensive was only a matter of time. The Soviet High Command correctly anticipated German intentions of destroying the partisans in the immediate rear of the German Third Panzer Army and the German Fourth Army,[63] thereby eliminating the danger to their lines of retreat. The partisan brigades in the Ushachi area received specific instructions to hold the area against any German attempt to take it. After the Soviet winter offensive of 1943–44 had run its course, air supply of the partisans was stepped up, internal discipline was tightened, and extensive preparations for a defense of the Ushachi area were made by the partisan brigades under the leadership of Lobanok. At the same time, the Germans were preparing to execute antipartisan operations against the partisans in the Ushachi area, the area between Lepel and Senno, and the area between Lepel and Borisov. Two of these operations, "Fruehlingsfest" and "Regenschauer," were planned to attack the partisans in Ushachi in April 1944, while another large operation, "Kormoran," against the brigades between Lepel and Borisov, was to follow. Two important purposes were to be served by these operations: the German lines of retreat were to be made secure, and the partisans were to be weakened to prevent them from executing attacks against the roads and railroads. These attacks constituted a heavy drain on the already inadequate German supplies. In January 1944 partisan strength in the Ushachi area and the adjoining territory to the east was estimated at 18,000 men. They were reported to have lost almost completely the characteristics of partisans, and to resemble closely regular troops.[64]

---

[61] H.Gr. Mitte, Ia, "An OKH GenStdH/Op. Abt.," 9 November 1943, pp. 11–13 (GMDS, HGr Mitte 65002/24).

[62] PzAOK 3, Ic/AO, "Feindnachrichtenblatt Nr. 12," 29 November 1943, p. 15 (GMDS, HGr Nord 75131/88).

[63] The westward movement of the front had brought the German Fourth Army to the southern sector of the Polotsk Lowland.

[64] PzAOK 3, Ic/AO, "Entwicklung der Bandenlage im Bereich der 3. Pz-Armee im Januar 1944," 1 February 1944, p. 6 (GMDS, PzAOK 3, 62587/12).

The German forces were able to start "Fruehlingsfest" and "Regenschauer" before the Soviet offensive against Army Group Center got under way. In the middle of April strong German forces, estimated roughly at over 20,000 men, started the attack against the partisan complex in the Ushachi region.[65] Despite determined resistance, the operations succeeded in dispersing and largely annihilating the partisan brigades which had controlled the region since 1942. Soviet bomber and fighter support as well as diversionary frontal attacks against the German lines northeast of Polotsk failed to influence the outcome of the operation.[66] Partisan losses after several weeks of combat were estimated by the Germans at 7,000 dead and over 7,000 prisoners.[67]

The defeat of the partisans in the Ushachi area probably prevented an even more complete and sudden collapse of the German front after the Soviet offensive was renewed in June 1944. If the partisans had still controlled the area, the German Third Panzer Army would have found its escape route blocked. German successes against partisans of the Polotsk Lowland in the final stages of the war, however, were far from complete. The second major operation against the partisan complex between Borisov and Lepel was not started until the beginning of June and could not be completed before the Soviet offensive began later the same month. Just before this offensive got under way, partisans again carried out thousands of mass demolitions, exceeding in scope even those effected in August of 1943. Although most attacks were carried out farther west, the Vitebsk-Orsha and Polotsk-Molodechno lines also suffered heavily. At a crucial moment the German rail system was again paralyzed. In spite of the large antipartisan operations, the partisans remained a powerful force.

Within a few days after 22 June 1944, when the Soviet offensive began, the Polotsk Lowland was overrun by the Soviet armies in a drive which did not halt until it reached the Vistula a few weeks later.

The fate of the partisan brigades in the Polotsk Lowland after the Soviet offensive is not clear, since German records at that time are incomplete and concerned primarily with direct front operations. It is likely that the majority moved westward to continue harassing German communications, but the Soviet advance was so rapid that undoubtedly many partisans found themselves behind the front and were probably incorporated into the Red Army.

---

[65] Kampfgr. von Gottberg, Einsatzbefehl fuer das Unternehmen 'Fruehlingsfest,' " 11 April 1944 (GMDS, Waffen SS, Dirlewanger 78028/15). The exact number of German troops involved is not stated; they included SS and Police units, German and indigenous troops provided by Army Group North, and a substantial part of the VI Army Corps.

[66] PzAOK 3, Ic/AO, "Entwicklung der Bandenlage im Bereich der 3. Pz.-Armee waehrend des Monats Mai 1944," 27 May 1944, p. 1 (GMDS, PzAOK 3, 62587/12).

[67] Ibid., Anlage 1.

§III. Institutional Characteristics:
The Brigade

After mid-1942 the standard partisan unit in the Polotsk Lowland was the brigade. For the purposes of this discussion it is assumed that all commands above the brigade level were organs of either Communist Party or Red Army control and, therefore, should be considered separately from the direct partisan troop commands. The standard brigade staff consisted of a commander, a commissar, a deputy commander, a chief of staff, and occasionally in the larger brigades, a brigade adjutant. The composition of the staff varied from unit to unit; in some, certain staff positions were not filled. Many brigade staffs had chiefs of intelligence and special NKVD officers. Others had Army or Party instructors and inspectors. These latter were technically not members of the brigade staffs, but it can be assumed with certainty that as long as they were attached to a brigade they had an important influence on the operations of the unit.

The subdivision of the brigades was irregular. Some were divided into battalions (four or five) and then into otryads. Others were subdivided directly into otryads, of which a brigade might have as many as twenty or as few as three or four. The battalion and otryad commands ordinarily consisted of a commander, a deputy commander, and a politruk (a politruk corresponded to a commissar, but at a lower level).

A. THE BRIGADE COMMANDER

The brigade commander was probably the most important individual in the partisan movement. On the German side of the front he had no permanently assigned superior officer. Of necessity, his orders from superior authorities were most often general rather than specific, with the exact method of execution left to his discretion. The brigade itself was often the creation of the commander. With no regular supply or recruitment services, the size and operating efficiency of the brigade frequently depended on the commander's ability to organize stocks of weapons and food. The energy and ability displayed by the commander in finding recruits and integrating them into the brigade was undoubtedly important. To a certain extent, the reputation of the commander, based on his demonstrated ability to keep his men fed and armed and his skill as a tactical leader (one who achieved victories without excessive casualties), served to attract recruits and contributed to the spirit of the brigade. The commander's reputation probably also determined the amount of support the brigade received from the Soviet side. Above all, the operating efficiency of the partisan movement depended almost entirely on the individual brigade commanders. The brigade headquarters was the focal point for control of partisan operations. Orders from higher echelons could be put into effect only by the brigade commanders. Since each brigade operated as a self-contained unit, the execution of orders depended directly on the energy, skill, and daring of the individual commander to a far greater extent than in a comparable regular military unit.

It was Soviet policy to associate the fame of the brigade with the name of its commander; thus we hear of the Dubrovsky Brigade, the Okhotin Brigade, the Grishin Regiment, and others. The reasonably successful brigade commander could achieve renown and the appearance, at least, of personal prestige quite out of proportion to the significance of the unit he commanded. The brigade commander was made a romantic figure, a reincarnation of famous partisans of the Civil War and earlier periods.

The unskilled commander could virtually destroy the usefulness of his brigade. The following report by an instructor of the Vitebsk Oblast Party Committee is illustrative:

I report that on 27 August 1943, a staff conference took place in the Falalayev Brigade at which the reports of the detachment commanders, Semyonov and Dyumin, on detachment combat operations in the current month and on the execution of order 0042 were heard. At the meeting it was established that the Semyonov detachment has neither killed a single German nor blown up a single railroad during this month. Semyonov explains his inactivity by pointing to the poor equipment of his detachment and the current training of sabotage details. . . .

At this conference I sharply condemned the inactivity of the detachment. I stressed the low combat efficiency of the detachment and particularly of Detachment Commander Semyonov and Commissar Andreyev; I pointed to their inactivity and their inability to lead the soldiers and direct the whole life of the detachment toward carrying out combat assignments. I also pointed out the badly organized security system and the poor staff work.

Then, instead of condemning the inactivity of the detachment and taking the appropriate concrete action for raising the combat activity of the detachment, individual commanders, especially Sazykin and Semyonov, began to express dissatisfaction with my remarks. Semyonov voiced the reproach that while one demands everything, nobody brings help by supplying clothes, shoes, and rations.

I noted that with the exception of the commissar, Shendelev, no one condemned this attitude of covering up inactivity by pointing to material things [shortages]. As for Falalayev, at the conference a softness showed up in regard to the demands of the commanders; they were given no concrete assignments for raising combat activity. The attitude of Detachment Commander Semyonov toward the inactivity of his detachment was not condemned [by Falalayev?]. Instead of admitting his mistakes, Semyonov came forth with counterarguments and accusations against those who pointed out his shortcomings.

I am of the opinion that Semyonov is lacking leadership qualities; a self-centered commander cannot secure proper conduct of combat operations. Furthermore, Semyonov tries to keep out of operations during the execution of assignments. It is not his custom to stand alongside his men in combat. In addition, he is lax in his personal behavior and will not recognize that this damages and undermines morale. . . ."[68]

As an upshot of the unfavorable report by the instructor, Falalayev was ordered removed from the command of the brigade. (Note the rapidity of communication. The meeting was held on 27 August. The instructor communicated his impressions to the secretary of the Executive Committee of Vitebsk Oblast which was located on the Soviet side of the front, and on 28 August, Commander Falalayev was dismissed.) The following reveals that even the efforts of the Party-appointed instructors were not enough to straighten out the affairs of the brigade:

I report that on 28 August 1943, the Chief of Staff of the Partisan Movement for Belorussia, Comrade Kalinin, transmitted a radio message according to which Sazykin is confirmed in the position of brigade commander in place of Falalayev.

In my opinion, Falalayev has slipped his protégé and drinking companion, Sazykin, into this portion in order to continue to cover up his own dirty intrigues. The latter does great things, in discourse—in fact he is a real careerist. Sazykin is involved in the shootings and sordid business in the brigade. It was established that Sazykin drank *samogon* [moonshine vodka] with Falalayev and that he is considered the deputy of the brigade commander on line duty, although at the present this position does not exist. The soldiers and officers of the brigade have no respect for Sazykin because of his intrigues. Sazykin has shot many soldiers, officers, and peaceful local inhabitants.

The appointment of Sazykin to Falalayev's position was made without the knowledge of Brigade Commissar Shendelev or me. Shendelev turned over the radio message signed by you to Falalayev, who took advantage of this and apparently substituted the name of Sazykin for Sviridenko. . . . Therefore I am sending the commissar, Shendelev, to you and await your directives in this matter.[69]

The situation found in the Falalayev Brigade probably existed from time to time in many of the other brigades as well. There was a natural inertia in the partisan brigades which even energetic commanders could hardly overcome. With a poor commander such as Falalayev the whole brigade apparently sank into inactivity. Usually the units could not be given specific orders concerning how to carry out their missions, and it was even more difficult to keep a close check on the accomplishments they claimed. A partisan unit could, for example, devote an excessive amount of time to plundering and requisitioning from the peasants, or it could attack minor objectives, avoiding important targets because they were more strongly guarded or because an attack might provoke German retaliation.

[68] PzAOK 3, Ic/AO, "Nr. 5507/43," 19 September 1943 (GMDS, PzAOK 3, 40252/7, Anlagen 28, 29).

[69] PzAOK 3, Ic/AO, "Nr. 5507/43," 19 September 1943 (GMDS, PzAOK 3, 40252/7, Anlagen 28, 29).

The tendency of the partisan brigades to concentrate in large partisan-controlled areas such as Rossono and Ushachi gives evidence for a tentative conclusion that the inertia noted within individual brigades permeated the whole partisan movement. It might appear that the ability of the brigades to hold extensive territories within the German zone of occupation represented a definite achievement. On the other hand, it is well known that the large partisan areas were for the most part left to the partisans by default, since the Germans did not attempt to hold them. It follows that the brigades to some degree were taking the line of least resistance by gathering in relatively safe regions where the possibilities of immediate contact with the enemy were reduced and where they could engage in the safer pursuits of camp building, provisioning, and constructing fortifications.

B. THE OFFICERS

There were four types of partisan officers: those who achieved their rank as leaders within the movement alone; officers trained behind the Soviet lines to command partisan units; regular Soviet Army officers detached for duty with the partisans; and officers who had been cut off in the occupied territory during 1941. The last two categories made up the majority of the partisan officer personnel. While no exact statistics are available, the Germans always assumed, probably correctly, that the aim of the Soviet command was to have a large segment of the partisan officer personnel composed of regular army officers.[70] The command problems of the partisan brigades were very similar to those of regular army units; and the Soviet command, particularly in defense centers like Rossono and Ushachi, frequently tried to use partisans in place of regular units. Therefore, there was nothing remarkable about the appearance of large numbers of regular officers in the partisan brigades.

The following order illustrates in part how other individuals were selected for training as partisan officers:

To: Commander of the Partisans, Comrade Bulanov

According to the directives of the Central Staff of the Partisan Movement, the Staff of the Partisan Movement [of the Fourth Assault Army] has set up courses for company commanders for training as commanders of partisan units, staff commanders, and heads of diversionist groups. Five persons are to be selected from among those fighters who are most reliable, politically most experienced, morally most steadfast, and unreservedly devoted to the Socialist fatherland, and who have also already distinguished themselves in battle. Two are to be selected as unit commanders, two as staff commanders, and one as head of a diversionist

---

[70] Okdo. H.Gr.Mitte, Ia, "Monatliche Meldung ueber Bandenlage," 4 June 1944, p. 5 (GMDS, DW/55d Partisans) and 4 July 1943, p. 2 (GMDS, HGr Mitte 65002/22); HSSPF Russland Mitte und Weissruthenien, Ic, "Feindlage im Raum Lepel-Ulla-Polozk-Doksohyze," 11 April 1944, p. 2 (GMDS, Waffen SS, Dirlewanger 78028/15).

group. Those who have been selected for training as staff commanders must have had seven years of general education. The selected men are to be sent on 8 August 1942, to the Partisan Operative Staff with the Headquarters of the Fourth Assault Army.

3 August 1942
Commander of the Operative Group of the Partisan Movement with the
 Headquarters Fourth Assault Army
Senior Battalion Commander, Sokolov[71]

The commanders who attained their rank entirely within the partisan movement were an important group—they represented the spirit of the movement. The brigade commanders from this group were frequently publicized as heroes, while the regular army officers with the brigades remained in the background. For the most part, they came from the lower middle ranks of the Party hierarchy; some had been rayon Party secretaries. Though they ranked technically as minor officials, they were members of the Soviet elite and, therefore, persons of some importance quite apart from their rank in the partisan movement. While some of them were only figureheads and their brigades actually were run by regular army officers, others were genuinely successful as partisan leaders. One of these was Brigade Commander Lobanok, who had been a rayon Party secretary before the war. He became a brigade commissar, later commanded his own brigade, and finally, as head of an Operative Group, directed the partisan defense of the Ushachi area against the Germans. Another was Markov, before the war a deputy in the Supreme Soviet of the Belorussian SSR, who commanded the Voroshilov Brigade and directed all the partisan brigades in Vileika Oblast.

In the main, however, the average partisan had poor prospects of rising in the movement. The top command positions almost certainly went to men like those just described—men who had achieved some prominence in the Communist Party. Ordinary Party members may have had opportunities to become junior officers, but the general tendency was to install regular army officers or specially trained officers at all levels in the brigades.

C. THE COMMISSAR

The commissar system was never abolished in the partisan movement as it was in 1942 in the Red Army. A captured chief of staff of a brigade gave the following information concerning the partisan commissar system:

Relations between the commander and the commissar . . . are clearly defined. Both are equal. In military matters the commissar may not give the commander directions, and in political matters the commander [may not direct] the commissar. Both can punish for military as well as political crimes without listening

[71] H.Gr.Mitte, Ic/AO, "Erbeutete Banden-Geheimebefehle," 13 September 1942 (GMDS, HGr Nord 75131/93).

to the other's opinion. Once the commissar has given an order it cannot be revoked by the commander and vice versa. The commander and the commissar eat better.[72]

Every brigade, regiment, battalion, and otryad had a commissar or politruk. The commander and the commissar were equals with different functions. Since the partisan units exercised an unusually high degree of independence in their operations, the commissar performed an important function as a means of checking on the energy of the commander and the operating efficiency of the unit. Since partisan activity was political as well as military, the commissar probably exercised an important influence on most of the undertakings of the unit.

The commissar system seems to have been better integrated into the partisan movement than it was in the Red Army. In the Army it stood primarily for political interference in essentially military affairs. In the partisan movement there was no very clear distinction between military and political matters. As was pointed out, many of the brigade commanders were Party officials in peacetime. There was no rigid functional differentiation between the commissar and the commander and officers. In the Biryulin Brigade, for example, Commander Biryulin started his career as the commissar of the unit.[73] In the early stage of its organization, the First Belorussian Partisan Brigade had three individuals nearly equally qualified for the post of unit commissar. Two of these were assigned command duties over sections of the unit, and one eventually rose to the rank of brigade commissar. It is worth noting that in this instance the two individuals became commanders and not politruks (subordinate commissars) of the subordinate groups.[74] The commander of the Za Rodinu Otryad was a former Red Army commissar, and the brigade commissar was a secretary of the Vitebsk Oblast Party Committee.[75] Sometimes Party men preferred to command units. Lobanok, commander of the Stalin Brigade, was a former rayon Party secretary and had been the commissar of the Dubrovsky Brigade until the summer of 1943, when he formed his own brigade and assumed the post of commander. Markov, the commander of the Voroshilov Brigade, was a deputy to the Supreme Soviet of the Belorussian SSR.[76] Other Party men chose the post of commissar. When the Mstitel Otryad was organized in June 1942, the Party representative chiefly responsible for the creation of the brigade took for himself the position of commissar.[77] In the case of the Okhotin

[72] PzAOK 3, Ic, "Vernehmung des Stabschefs der Bandenbrigade Alexejew," 25 April 1944 (GMDS, PzAOK 3, 62587/13).
[73] Tsanava, I, 175.
[74] "Partisanen-Tagebuch Nr. 1," pp. 1, 3, 4; "Partisanen-Tagebuch Nr. 2," p. 15.
[75] Tsanava, I, 180.
[76] *Ibid.,* 178, 189.
[77] *Ibid.,* 180.

Brigade both the commander and the commissar were chairmen of rayon Party committees.[78]

On the whole, the commissar was not the disturbing element in the partisan movement that he was in the Red Army. There was no division between the officer and commissar groups of the sort which prevailed in the Army. Socially, politically, and professionally, partisan officers and the commissars had similar, or even identical backgrounds, and the line between the regular officer group and the commissar group was not sharply drawn. Officers sometimes shifted from one group to the other. The danger always existed that with neither being clearly subordinate to the other, friction could develop in individual instances. The evidence does not indicate that the problem reached serious proportions. It is certain that in some brigades the commissar was actually superior to the commander, simply because he held a higher rank in the Party. In other brigades, the commander by virtue of his Party status probably overshadowed the commissar; the Stalin and Voroshilov Brigades are examples.

The commissar was the watchdog of the Party. In addition the Party itself entered directly into the workings of the partisan units. Each brigade included among its personnel a number of Party members. One brigade totaling 1,113 men had 40 (3.5 per cent) Party members, 87 (7.8 per cent) Party candidates, 334 (30 per cent) Komsomol members, and 652 (58.7 per cent) without Party affiliation.[79] The low percentage of Party members and candidates was not too remarkable. It probably was about equivalent to the percentage of Party members among the entire population. Furthermore, in the last years of the war, the bands were increased by large numbers of unwilling recruits, either individuals recruited by force or opportunists whose reliability was always somewhat in question. In addition, many of the best partisans were too young for Party membership, which accounts for the higher percentage of Komsomol members. Nevertheless, the Party became a genuine force in every partisan unit. Party members were expected to form the cohesive element by furnishing leadership and examples for the non-Party personnel.

Conclusions

If the strength of the partisan movement in the Polotsk Lowland is measured by its ability to maintain itself and even expand within territory which the Germans had hoped to occupy and administer, then it was very success-

[78] *Ibid.*, 178.
[79] PzAOK 3, Ic/AO, "Drei erbeutete Berichte," 19 September 1943 (GMDS, PzAOK 3, 40252/7, Anlagen 30–33).

ful. The following factors help explain why the partisan brigades could become a powerful force in this area:

1. Favorable terrain: extensive swamps, lakes, and virgin forests.

2. Physical proximity to the Red Army during most of the war, a factor which allowed direct contact with regular military forces and supply bases.

3. Strong efforts by the Soviet command to strengthen the partisan movement here.

4. Support from the indigenous population after an initially hostile or indifferent attitude.

5. Failure of the German High Command to provide sufficient forces to act decisively against the partisans, or to follow up antipartisan operations with strong security forces stationed throughout the rural areas in order to prevent the reorganization of the partisan brigades.

The effectiveness of the partisan movement, however, cannot be evaluated exclusively on the basis of its numerical strength. It is also necessary to review its accomplishments in the light of its objectives. Apparently, the partisan movement in this area had two major goals: (1) to assist in the defeat of the German armies by disruptive activities in the German rear, by providing intelligence for the Red Army, and by diverting German troops from front operations; and (2) to reinstitute and maintain Soviet controls over the indigenous population. To these, a third objective was added during the latter part of the war: to assist the Red Army directly in military operations.

Partisan disruptive activities succeeded in causing considerable damage to German rolling stock and supplies, beginning in the summer of 1942 and increasing through the late fall of 1943. At least twice during the war, in August 1943 and again just before the Soviet summer offensive of 1944, the partisans succeeded in completely paralyzing the German rail transport system for prolonged periods. While it is impossible to judge the over-all effect of these disruptive activities on military operations, it can be said that on these two occasions at least the mobility of the German Army was seriously impeded at crucial moments. The most pervasive effect of the partisans' disruptive activities was a steady drain on German supplies, particularly rolling stock. The partisans' advantageous strategic location in relation to major railroads played an important part in these successes. Partisan intelligence was generally considered by the Germans to be excellent, and there was probably very little that the Red Army did not know about the strength and disposition of German units. The continued diversion to the partisans of men and matériel which the Red Army also needed indicates that partisan operations must have been considered important.

On the whole the partisans were unable to divert German troops from the front on a scale large enough to be effective. At peak strength they numbered between 35,000 and 40,000; yet they never tied down an equivalent number of German forces. Partisan attacks, as a rule, were executed with small forces, and regular combat was avoided whenever possible. Large-scale combat operations against the partisans were invariably instituted by the Germans who chose the time and place. Taking the calculated risk that attacks against their system of communications might be increased and that isolated strongpoints might have to be surrendered to the partisans, the Germans were always able to withdraw troops engaged in antipartisan operations and transfer them to the front when they were urgently needed. They could also schedule their antipartisan operations when the front was comparatively quiet. The drain on German front-line troops, therefore, was not excessive, particularly since many antipartisan operations were fought with police and collaborator troops, which were unsuited for front-line duty. In a way the partisan movement was directly responsible for increasing the manpower available to the Germans for military duty. The German plans for the invasion of Soviet Russia did not envisage the use of collaborator troops. The policy of tapping this source of manpower was adopted by the Germans only after experience had shown that such troops were needed to curb the partisans. In the spring of 1943 approximately 27,000 collaborators were fighting with the Germans in the Polotsk Lowland. Without the partisan movement, this source of manpower would probably have been directed as labor to German factories.

The ability of the partisans in this area to enlist the support of a substantial part of the population must be counted among their major successes. It is unlikely that either the partisan movement or the re-establishment of Soviet controls corresponded to the desires of the majority of the population, judging by the initial hostility to the partisans and the rather favorable reaction to the early German occupation. Later German policies and terror methods, coupled in rural areas with the *de facto* control exercised by the partisans, left the population with little choice but to support one side or the other. A peasant in the Ushachi or Rossono area was under direct control of the partisans; he had to do their bidding or else desert to the Germans and become a collaborator. A peasant in areas temporarily controlled by the Germans—and all rural areas fall into this category—likewise had either to collaborate with the Germans and expose himself to the partisans' wrath or else to join the partisans openly. To stand aloof and favor neither may have been the desire of many, but, by the very nature of partisan warfare in the Polotsk Lowland, such a course was virtually impossible. The partisans succeeded in frustrating any attempt the Germans may have wanted to make at introducing an agrarian reform and reinstituted Soviet policies instead. As the war progressed and the strength of the partisan movement increased in direct proportion to the decline of German military power, even the collaborator troops deserted to the partisans in great numbers and accepted the inevitable re-establishment of Soviet power.

The third objective of the partisan brigades in the Polotsk Lowland—to collaborate directly with the Red Army—failed. This failure, however, does not reflect greatly on the effectiveness of the partisans, since it certainly was not a mission for which the partisan units were created, but rather was assigned to them when their very strength seemed to make such assistance feasible. According to German records the Soviet winter offensive of 1943–44 against Vitebsk was designed to push the German armies into the solid partisan regions in the Polotsk-Lepel-Borisov area, thereby preventing their escape. The partisans were assigned only a passive role in this scheme, although their numerical strength should have enabled them to execute direct attacks against the German defense lines. The attempt failed because the Red Army could not break the German lines. Before the Soviet offensive was renewed in the summer of 1944, the German Third Panzer Army took steps to remove this danger to its retreat routes. In April 1944, at a time when the Soviet winter offensive had come to a halt and the summer offensive had not yet started, a major antipartisan operation dispersed the partisan brigades in the Ushachi area. This successful German operation frustrated possible plans for systematic, large-scale, army-partisan tactical cooperation in the 1944 summer offensive of the Red Army.

CHAPTER X

The North Caucasus

Alexander Dallin

§I. Background

A. THE AREA AND THE PROBLEM

The area considered in this chapter covers the territory south of the Rostov-Astrakhan line—the steppe, desert, and mountain regions of the North Caucasus and its northern approaches which were occupied by German Army Group "A" from July 1942 to February 1943, and the remaining Kuban (Taman) bridgehead which the Germans held until September 1943.

In several respects this area differs from other centers of partisan activity. These peculiarities may be ascribed to five major factors: (a) the nature of the terrain, (b) the ethnic composition of the area, (c) the brevity of German occupation, (d) the distinctive nature of German occupation policy, and (e) the military situation. A brief survey of these elements is essential for an understanding of the partisan movement which arose in this region.

1. Geography and Economy

a. Terrain

In landscape and terrain, the territory may conveniently be divided into three distinct types: (1) the steppe in the northern part of the area, substantially an extension of the fertile agrarian region that covers much of the Ukraine, dotted with large villages and Cossack stanitsas, and covering major parts of Krasnodar and Ordzhonikidze Krais;[1] (2) the arid and sparsely inhabited semidesert and desert areas in the northeast of this area,

---

[1] *Krai* is a Soviet administrative unit corresponding to an oblast but containing autonomous regions. In 1943, Ordzhonikidze Krai was renamed Stavropol Krai; its capital, Stavropol, was known as Voroshilovsk from 1935 to 1943. This krai must not be confused with the town of Ordzhonikidze, the capital of the North Osetin ASSR. *Stanitsa* is the term for a Cossack rural settlement.

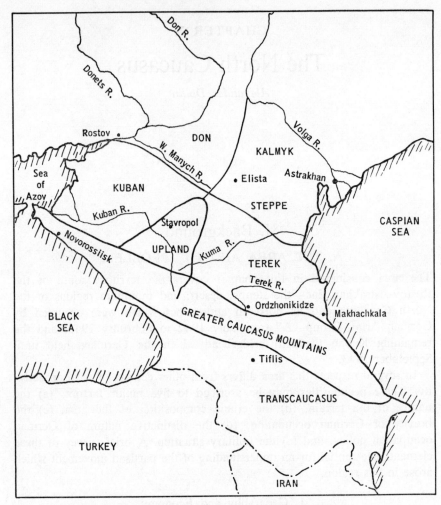

Figure 16.—Geographic regions of the Caucasus.

covering the Kalmyk ASSR and the adjacent areas;[2] and (3) the mountain ranges extending across the Caucasus from the Black Sea to the Caspian coast and including a variety of geological formations—uplands, valleys, rocky mountains, and alpine peaks.[3] [See Fig. 16.]

As one moves south toward the Kuban and Terek Rivers, the steppe

[2] On 27 December 1943 the Kalmyk ASSR was abolished for alleged "treason" during the war, but it was re-established in 1956. In this chapter, references are to administrative units in existence as of 1942–43.

[3] This division into three major regions corresponds to the classification in L. S. Berg, *Natural Regions of the USSR* (New York: Macmillan, 1960), pp. 113, 202–40, 351.

and desert gradually yield to hilly terrain with numerous rivers and ravines, in the center of which are the Stavropol uplands (over 2,000 feet high). Farther south, one encounters volcanic and partly eroded sedimentary formations; here are the mountainous forest and grazing areas as well as the mineral spas around Pyatigorsk. Next, the Greater Caucasus chain arises, a formidable barrier of glaciers and rocks—its highest peak, Mt. Elbrus, is 18,500 feet—passable only during certain months of the year.[4]

Finally, the Black Sea coast south of Anapa rises abruptly into steep lateral mountain ridges, while the estuaries and often the courses of the major rivers, such as the Kuban, form numerous swamps and lagoons, particularly prevalent along the Sea of Azov.

This rapidly varying and often difficult terrain presented special military problems to the defenders but also to the invader.[5] However, in the general spirit of optimism in 1941–42 the German High Command looked with little concern upon the terrain factors of the impending Caucasian operation. Only the high mountains—scheduled to be by-passed at both ends and penetrated only through the Georgian Military Highway, the traditional north-south passage—were considered obstacles of major proportions.[6]

For the partisans, of course, the swamps and lagoons offered good hideouts, as did the forests which cover large stretches of the uplands, especially in the western sector; finally, the mountains were bound to provide comparative safety from the Germans, albeit at the price of considerable hardship for the partisans themselves.[7] Many partisan units established themselves neither in the unprotected flatlands in the north, nor in the steep and barren ridges of the higher mountains in the south, but rather in the foothills, where they had the benefit of forests and mountains without exposing themselves to the hazards and handicaps of hunger, frost, immobility, and isolation.

[4] For a more detailed description, see Theodore Shabad, *Geography of the USSR* (New York: Columbia University Press, 1951), pp. 209–232. For a description of the mountain passes and the military problems they raise, see OKH/GenStdH/OpAbt (IIb), "Studie Kaukasus," Anlage 4, "Gelaendebeschreibung" (GMDS, H 22/364b); and OKH/GenStdH/Abt. IV (Mil.-Geo.), *Militaergeographische Angaben ueber das Europaeische Russland: Kaukasien . . . Ergaenzungsheft: Strassen und Paesse im Kaukasus-Gebirge* (Berlin, 1941) (GMDS, H 29/ID 2.26); V. N. Delone, *Vershiny zapadnogo Kavkaza* (Moscow: Gosizdat Fizkultura i sport, 1938).

[5] With regard to the Kuban area, for instance, Berlin warned in advance: "This maze of water courses and swamps and thick underbrush presents exceedingly great obstacles for military movements. In the Civil War it played its part as an area of escape and hide-out for the inferior party." (OKH/GenStdH/Abt. IV, Mil.-Geo., *Militaergeographische Angaben . . . Kaukasien: Textheft,* Berlin, 1942, p. 56, GMDS, H 29/ID 2.27.)

[6] *Ibid.,* p. 45; OKH/GenStdH/Op Abt. (IIb), "Studie Kaukasus," Nr. 1550/41 (GMDS, H22/364b).

[7] The Greater Caucasus Mountains had provided effective hiding places for outlaws, draft-dodgers, and rebels under the Soviet regime. The mountainous terrain helps explain the greater incidence of revolts in the North Caucasus.

b. Transportation

If horses in the steppe, mules in the mountains, and camels in the desert characterized the mode of transportation in vast parts of this area, railways and highways had likewise come into their own. The economic importance of the oil produced here was partly responsible for the fact that the railway system (except for the Kalmyk ASSR) was more closely knit and in better condition than it was in most parts of the USSR. The main trunk line led from Rostov to Baku over Armavir and Mineralnye Vody to the Caspian, with feeder lines to the major towns south of the line, such as Cherkessk (Batalpashinsk), Kislovodsk, and Nalchik. Of particular interest to this study are also the north-south line from Rostov to Novorossiisk, the Kuban line from Novorossiisk to Kropotkin, and the mountain line from Tuapse to Armavir.[8]

The quality of roads varied considerably. There were a few major highways of first-rate quality, but the mountain roads in particular were dirt roads at best and during the winter months could hardly be used by motorized troops and heavier weapons.[9] In terms of German supply and combat operations, the most important were those radiating from Novorossiisk; the north-south roads through Maikop, Armavir, Stavropol, and Pyatigorsk; and the highways leading to the Maikop oil fields.

c. Economy

The economy of the Caucasus reflects its geographic divisions. The chernozem soil and warm climate make the Kuban region one of the most fertile agricultural surplus areas of the Soviet Union; winter wheat, sun flowers, and maize are the main products. The lower Kuban delta and the Black Sea coast farther south enjoy a subtropical climate which permits the cultivation of rice, cotton, and tea. The extensive steppes and high plateaus are centers of animal husbandry, where sizable sheep herds are found.[10]

The most valuable resource of the Caucasus, however, is oil. The Baku fields alone accounted for about two thirds of Soviet crude oil output in 1941 (about twenty out of thirty million tons). At that time, the two major

[8] The Germans found the railway system in relatively good shape. (Wi Kdo z.b.V. 10, "Kriegstagebuch Nr. 2," p. 6, GMDS, Wi/ID 2.528.)

While there was no railway in the desert area between the Volga and Terek Rivers, mention should be made of the Kizlyar-Astrakhan line, which was built in haste in 1941 and later provided the sole railway link between the nonoccupied Caucasus and the central areas of the USSR.

[9] The Red Army found itself handicapped by the same circumstance. See Vitalii Zakrutkin, *Kavkazskiye zapiski* (Leningrad: Leningradski pisatel, 1948), pp. 123 ff. For a study of the Caucasus in earlier military operations, see W. E. D. Allen and Paul Muratoff, *Caucasian Battlefields . . . 1828–1921* (Cambridge: Cambridge University Press, 1953).

[10] See also Alexander Vaatz, *Landwirtschaft zwischen Don und Wolga* (Berlin: C. Y. Engelhard, 1942).

fields in the Northern Caucasus were the Groznyi area, stretching from Malgobek to Gudermes, and the Maikop area, extending northwest almost to the Kuban estuary; together they accounted for about 8 per cent of the Soviet oil production.[11] In view of the crucial importance of oil for the Soviet war economy, it was natural that the wells, refineries, pipelines, and special equipment of the industry became objects of particular attention for the Germans, the Soviet Army, and the partisans alike.

Moreover, the North Caucasus possesses significant deposits of manganese, tungsten, and coal—all of importance to both warring sides.[12] Heavy industry was less developed, with some chemical industry near the oil areas and extensive cement production near Novorossiisk. Finally, the electric power system harnessing the mountain rivers had been considerably expanded under the Five-Year Plans.

2. Administrative and Ethnic Divisions

The area's numerous administrative subdivisions, which lie within the Russian SFSR, reflected the complexity of the population, composed as it is of a greater variety of ethnic groups than any other European area of comparable size. Both larger units, Krasnodar and Stavropol Krais, contained "autonomous regions"—a Soviet device for the administration of small and fairly compact ethnic units forming, as it were, islands within Great Russian (or Ukrainian or Georgian) territory. Thus Krasnodar Krai included the Adygei Autonomous Region (with its capital at Maikop), and Stravropol Krai included the Cherkess (Circassian) and Karachai Autonomous Region (with Cherkessk and Mikoyan-Shakhar, respectively, as capitals). The remaining territory on the southern and eastern fringes of the area was divided into autonomous SSR's within the Russian Republic: the Kalmyk ASSR (capital: Elista); Kabardino-Balkar ASSR (capital: Nalchik); North Osetin ASSR (capital: Ordzhonikidze); Chechen-Ingush ASSR (capital: Groznyi); and Daghestan ASSR (capital: Makhach-Kala). [See Fig. 17.]

[11] OKW/Wi VIa, *Die Wehrwirtschaft des kaukasischen Raumes,* Teil I: *Darstellung* (Berlin, 1942), pp. 29–32 (GMDS, Wi/ID 2.1022); Anton Hantschel, *Baku* (Berlin: E. S. Mittler, 1942).

See also the extensive files of the *Technische Brigade Mineraloel* (TBM), a special military-economic organization established for the exploitation and custody of Soviet oil resources and industry (GMDS, Wi/ID, *passim*), and Heinrich Hassmann, *Oil in the Soviet Union* (Princeton: Princeton University Press, 1953).

The 1941 plan called for a total yearly output of 34.6 million tons, of which over 23 million were to be produced in the Azerbaidzhan SSR, i.e., the Baku and adjacent areas; 2.6 million in the Chechen-Ingush ASSR, i.e., the Groznyi area; and 2.8 million in the Krasnodar Krai, i.e., the Maikop and adjacent fields (USSR, Gosplan, *Gosudarstvennyi plan razvitiya narodnogo khozyaistva SSSR na 1941 god,* Moscow, 1941, p. 654; republished in facsimile, Ann Arbor, Mich.: Edwards Brothers, 1951).

[12] For details, see Demitri B. Shimkin, *Minerals: A Key to Soviet Power* (Cambridge: Harvard University Press, 1953), and S. S. Balzak, V. F. Feigin, and Ya. G. Vasyutin, *Economic Geography of the USSR* (New York: Macmillan, 1949).

As the administrative divisions indicate, the mountain areas and their northern approaches were inhabited largely by non-Slavic nationalities. Of the prewar territory of the USSR, these and the Crimea were the only areas of non-Slavic settlement occupied by the Germans.[13] The population north of the Kuban-Terek line, on the other hand, was about 90 per cent Slavic, with a strong Ukrainian concentration between Rostov and Krasnodar, and with Great Russians predominating in the coastal and steppe areas between Novorossiisk and Pyatigorsk. The urban population was largely Russian, with sizable Jewish and Armenian minorities.

The Kalmyks, inhabiting the desert and steppe between the Eastern

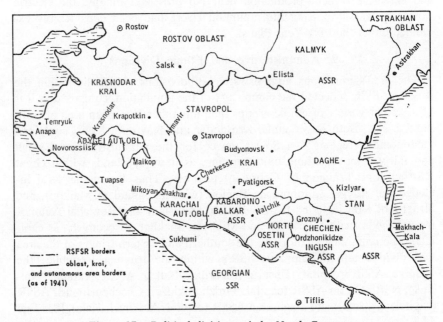

Figure 17.—Political divisions of the North Caucasus.

Manych and Volga Rivers, were a Buddhist people, engaged chiefly in animal husbandry. The other non-Slavs, known as Mountaineers (*gortsy*), included a considerable number of Moslem groups. Thus the Circassians, Adygeis, and Kabardins were largely Islamic proto-Caucasians, as were the Chechens and Ingush, living in the rich oil area around Groznyi, and the Karachai and Balkars, two small Turkic groups in the Central Caucasus. The Osetins, on the other hand, were partly Christian and probably Indo-European.

It should be borne in mind that the Caucasus was conquered by Russia

[13] In addition, the Baltic States and Moldavia, annexed by the USSR in 1940, came under German occupation.

only in the 19th century. Some of its nationalities—notably Daghestanis and Chechens—had long waged a bitter struggle against the Russians. Too small and, in some instances, too backward to aspire to political independence, the Mountaineers had nevertheless voiced insistent demands for economic and political equality and for cultural and territorial autonomy within the Russian empire. Soviet policy initially catered to these groups, giving them schools, press, alphabets, and formal self-government within the Soviet Union and fostering some feeling of ethnic distinctiveness. And yet there was evidence that the Mountaineers had not become fully adjusted to Soviet rule. The impact of communism, dialectical materialism, atheism, collectivization, industrialization, and emancipation of women on Mountaineers, Moslems, shepherds, and nomads with tribal customs and traditions of their own made the North Caucasus, in the eyes of many observers, an area of particular vulnerability in terms of Soviet controls and popular loyalty on the eve of World War II.[14] [See Table 7.]

TABLE 7

Population characteristics of the North Caucasus
(excluding the Kalmyk and Daghestan ASSR's)
according to the census of 1939

	Area (1,000 sq. km.)	Total pop. (1,000)	Urban pop. (1,000)	Rural pop. (per sq. km.)	Urban pop. (% of total)
Krasnodar Krai	81.5	3,173	765	29.5	24
Stavropol Krai	101.5	1,949	394	15.3	20
Kabardino-Balkar ASSR	12.3	359	85	22.3	24
North Osetin ASSR	6.2	329	155	28.1	47
Chechen-Ingush ASSR	15.7	697	199	31.7	29
All North Caucasus	217.2	6,507	1,598	22.6	25
All USSR				5.4	33

[14] No detailed studies of the North Caucasus exist in the English language. For historical background and general surveys, see Walter Kolarz, *Russia and Her Colonies* (New York: Praeger, 1953), Chapter VII; A. Sanders (pseud.), *Kaukasien* (Munich: Hoheneichen, 1941); Arthur Byhan, *La civilisation caucasienne* (Paris: Payot, 1936); Louis J. Luzbetak, *Marriage and the Family in Caucasia* (Vienna: St. Gabriel's Mission Press, 1951); Paul Kentmann, *Der Kaukasus* (Leipzig: Goldmann, 1943).

The Cossacks have not been listed above as they are ethnically a part of the Slavic group.

On the population of the Caucasus, see Frank Lorimer, *The Population of the Soviet Union* (Princeton, for League of Nations, 1946), pp. 138–39, 152, 158, 162, 243; Vahe A. Saragian, "The Problem of Caucasian Population Statistics Under Tsarist and Soviet Rule," *Armenian Review* (Boston), VI (1953), No. 3, pp. 107–24; M. Danko, "Les peuples du Caucase," *Voix des peuples* (Geneva), November 1942, pp. 451–64; A. Bogdanov, "Movement of Population in the Caucasus," MS (New York: Research Program on the USSR, 1952). According to the census of 1939, the area (not including the Kalmyk and Daghestan ASSR's) had the population shown in Table 7 of the text.

B. THE CAMPAIGN AND THE OBJECTIVES

In accordance with Hitler's directives, the plans of the German High Command for the war in the East included an occupation of the Caucasus. The original plans called for the North Caucasus to be conquered in the fall of 1941. But the unexpectedly strong resistance, the arrest of the German advance at Rostov, and the general failure to attain military objectives in 1941 resulted in postponing the Caucasus invasion until the spring of 1942. From a military point of view, the operation had as its goal "conquest of the Caucasus oil areas; by autumn 1942, opening of the Iranian-Iraqi border passes for further advance."[15]

Politically, this statement of the Operations Division of the General Staff pointed correctly to two major German objectives in this area: (1) the conquest of Caucasus oil, and (2) the establishment of a springboard for further operations in the Near East—a giant pincer aiming at Suez and an eastward drive to link up with the Japanese forces expected to advance through India.[16] In addition, the severance of the overland supply route from Iran was expected to help eliminate Stalin from the conflict.[17] The North Caucasus in itself was an object of lesser interest to the Reich (except for its oil resources)—a fact of substantial importance for German occupation policy there.

The launching of the 1942 summer offensive was delayed until the end of June. With the seizure of Rostov on 23 July the occupation of the Caucasus began. Army Group "A" had been established under Field Marshal List, comprising the Seventeenth Army and the First Panzer Army as well as a number of Rumanian divisions. The Red Army, pressed back along the entire front south of Kursk, evidently decided not to attempt delaying actions in the flatlands of the Kuban and North Caucasus. Instead it withdrew into the Caucasus mountains and prepared to defend such key points as Novorossiisk on the Black Sea, a gateway to western Georgia and Batum, and Ordzhonikidze, Groznyi, and Makhach-Kala in the eastern Caucasus, in order to bar the way to the major North Caucasus oil fields, the Georgian Military Highway, and the Caspian coastal road to Baku. As a result, the German advance across the North Caucasus plain and highlands was rapid to the point of making thorough occupation and combing impossible. By 6 August the Yeisk-Armavir Railroad was in German hands; two days later the first oil fields at Maikop—destroyed by the Soviets—were

[15] OKH/GenStdH/OpAbt. (IIb), "Studie Kaukasus," Nr. 1550/41 (GMDS, H 22/364b); *ibid.*, "Besprechung bei O Qu I am 24.10.41.," p. 1 (GMDS, H 22/364a).

[16] On the latter goal, see Annex V to minutes of 13 April 1942 (*Fuehrer Conferences on Matters Dealing with the German Navy, 1942*, U.S. Dept. of the Navy, Washington, D.C., 1948, p. 65).

[17] Ciano's report on his conversation with Ribbentrop, 29–30 April 1942 in *Ciano's Diplomatic Papers* (London: Odhams Press, 1948), pp. 481–84.

captured and before the end of the month the mountain passes across the Greater Caucasus had been seized. The Seventeenth Army occupied the Western sector and concentrated its forces for a drive on Novorossiisk, which fell on 10 September.

Another drive, across the mountains toward Tuapse, failed. Meanwhile, the First Panzer Army rapidly slashed south past Stavropol in the direction of Groznyi. Although Pyatigorsk was reached on 9 August, the advance stalled, in large measure because of supply and manpower difficulties; it was not until the end of the month that a new push, which led to the capture of Mozdok, was made.

With large German units committed at Stalingrad and the outlook there increasingly gloomy, Army Group "A" failed to receive the support it had expected. The "greatly distressed" Hitler blamed List for failing to attain the desired objectives and removed him from his command—almost simultaneously with the dismissal of General Halder as Chief of the General Staff. At the same time, Hitler admitted that Baku could no longer be reached in 1942. Still Makhach-Kala and Astrakhan were to be seized before winter so as to give the Reich an opportunity to exploit the North Caucasus oil.

German forces in the Caucasus were unable to make a decisive breakthrough. The attack toward Tuapse proved to be a costly failure, and the advance on Groznyi in October and November was halted east of Nalchik and Alagir. These two sectors, on which the Germans concentrated their forces for a penetration, were precisely the ones on which the Red Army had also concentrated its strength. The tactical situation remained substantially unchanged until December. Colonel General (later Field Marshal) von Kleist (commanding the First Panzer Army and later Army Group "A") and the new Chief of the General Staff, General Zeitzler, failed to obtain Hitler's consent to withdraw from the overextended Caucasus front. With the German armies at Stalingrad encircled and threatened with annihilation, the danger of having the Red Army isolate all of Army Group "A" loomed ominously.[18] Finally Hitler yielded: First Panzer Army was permitted to withdraw; Fourth Panzer Army, swinging in from the north, held open an escape gap through Rostov, while the Red Army pressed on—

[18] For brief surveys of the Caucasian campaign and German strategy there, see Kurt von Tippelskirch, *Geschichte des zweiten Weltkriegs* (Bonn: Athenaeum-Verlag, 1951), pp. 280–86; Walter Goerlitz, *Der zweite Weltkrieg, 1939–1945* (Stuttgart: Steingrueben-Verlag, 1951), I, 350–60; Helmuth Greiner, *Die oberste Wehrmachtfuehrung, 1939–1943* (Wiesbaden: Limes-Verlag, 1951), pp. 399–432; Augustin Guillaume, *La guerre germano-soviétique* (Paris: Presses Universitaires, 1948), pp. 57–58. Among the memoir literature on the campaign should be considered the account of the Belgian "Rexist" leader, Léon Degrelle, *Campagne de Russie* (Paris: Cheval Ailé, 1949), pp. 121–88; and the diary of a Luxemburg soldier with the 125th Infantry Division, Albert Borschette, *Journal russe* (Luxembourg: Ed. Paul Bruck, 1946).

both westward from the Volga to Kharkov, and northward across the Caucasus.

The German withdrawal, begun about 1 January 1943, was rather successfully completed by late February. The bulk of German forces was rescued. What remained was a bridgehead around the Kuban estuary and the Taman peninsula, which the Germans held for another eight months, thus tying down the forces of both sides. In view of the general German withdrawal in 1943, it could not be used as a springboard for further operations in the Caucasus.

A few considerations stemming from the military situation are of relevance to the fate of the partisan movement in this area.

1. The German occupation came a year after the invasion began, thus giving the Soviet authorities ample time to prepare evacuation, destruction, and partisan activities in this region.

2. The campaign for the Caucasus, important as it was for both sides, was overshadowed by the simultaneous life-and-death struggle at Stalingrad. As a result, manpower and resources committed on the German as well as on the Soviet side were smaller (and at times poorer) than might otherwise have been the case. Hence, the German forces available for antipartisan activities were numerically small and received little priority in replacements and equipment. Likewise Soviet support of their partisans in this region was a matter of relatively secondary attention, and the partisans were thus constrained to fend for themselves.

3. The partisans were assigned two major objectives: the disruption of German supplies and the defense of the mountain passes against German southward penetrations. The first did not attain the crucial significance that had been anticipated because German transportation and supply facilities proved inadequate; thus the tasks of the partisans were considerably reduced in scope and importance. The second task was a reflection of the shortage of Soviet manpower in the area; but once again German weakness frustrated any plans to attack the Caucasus mountain front in force (with one exception, which was adequately handled by the regular Red Army). The Caucasus equation thus had two factors of low valence: the German and Soviet Armies. The variable—the partisan movement—to a considerable extent was bound to become a function of the unknown: the attitude of the indigenous population.

4. The relative sparsity of German forces and the military inactivity along the higher mountain front produced a situation in which both sides held only certain tactically important sectors, mountain passes, and arteries of communications. The same was true of the vast Kalmyk desert and steppe providing the geographic gateway to the Volga estuary and the Caspian. As a result, overland contact across the front lines (more properly, in many instances, across no man's land) between Soviet and German-

held territory was intense. It permitted (a) the infiltration of units across the mountains and desert into the German-occupied area, and (b) the passage of partisan units from the Northern Caucasus into Soviet-held areas.

5. It will be meaningful to divide the brief span of German occupation into two distinct periods: the period from August 1942 to January 1943, during which the German Army was in control of the North Caucasus, seemed generally victorious, and—as will be shown below—appeared to have indigenous feeling overwhelmingly on its side; and the period from about February to September 1943, when the German-held area was reduced to a small bridgehead, with the German Army in retreat on other sectors of the front, with Soviet initiative and morale much improved, and with popular sentiment more hostile to the occupying forces.

A special case in terms of German goals, Soviet interests, brevity of occupation, ethnic and geographic features, the North Caucasus remains an important variation to consider for an understanding of alternative developments in the partisan movement.

C. SOVIET POLICY IN THE CAUCASUS, 1941–42

By the beginning of the Second World War, Soviet nationality policy had produced a situation whose effectiveness in the Caucasus the outside world had little opportunity to assess.[19] The effort to win to its side certain local elements—particularly the youth—by granting cultural and educational opportunities and thus creating a vested interest in the maintenance of the regime had presumably had some success. At the same time, the North Caucasus had traditionally been the stronghold of hostile elements; and even in the mid-thirties, revolts—though ineffectual and easily suppressed—had broken out in Daghestan and elsewhere in this area.[20] On the eve of the war, a more serious revolt had erupted in the Chechen-Ingush Republic and lasted well into the war period. Although the republic was not occupied by the Germans, a part of its area became insecure and in effect was lost to Soviet control—a fact that may well have cost the Chechens their nominal autonomy and, for a large number of them, their lives.[21]

[19] There is no adequate account of Soviet policy in this area. See Kolarz; see also A. Zagolo, "A Political History of the North Caucasus," MS (New York: Research Program on the USSR, 1952).

[20] See, for instance, Alexei Orlov, "Dagestanskoye vosstaniye," MS (New York, Research Program on the USSR, 1953).

[21] See Alexandr Avtorkhanov (Uralov), *Narodoubiistvo v. SSSR* (Munich: Svobodnyi Kavkaz, 1952). The Chechen-Ingush ASSR was liquidated on 11 February 1944 for alleged "treason." Though a large part of its population was evidently anti-Soviet, mass collaboration with the Germans was physically impossible because the bulk of the area was never German-occupied. It is true, however, that here as elsewhere in the Caucasus the Germans made a special effort to establish contact with indigenous

The Chechen area represented only the most dramatic instance of popular discontent. Soviet response to latent disloyalty consisted, typically, in a policy of both the "carrot and the whip." In addition to suppressing overt opposition, Moscow reduced the number of Chechen and other North Caucasus troops in the Red Army to a trusted minimum. The *émigré* account cited above is supported by German intelligence, which claimed that:

According to an order of the High Command of the Red Army, dated 14 April 1942, all Chechens were released from military service. The 46th Replacement Rifle Regiment on the basis of this directive separated 700 men. The reason given for the directive was the assertion that the Chechens had repeatedly been rebellious and completely unreliable and were worthless to the Red Army. Thus, for instance, in the middle of November 1941 the rebellious Chechen village of Baran in Shatoi Rayon had to be suppressed with the aid of an officer candidate school in Groznyi; the latter suffered dead and wounded in the operation. In the adjacent forests there are bands of Chechens who have, for example, raided the area of Shelberoi, burned the documents, and killed the deputy chief of the militia.[22]

Another report, perhaps exaggerated, claimed that after May 1942 the Red Army drafted no Chechens, Ingush, Kabardins, or Osetins.[23]

This policy of prophylaxis was supplemented by a new rash of "concessions," fully in line with wartime tactics adopted in the rest of the Soviet Union and high-lighted by such measures as the liberalization of religious policy, extension of national-patriotic themes, and the muting of militant Communist slogans. According to German sources, the Red Army established a special commissariat in October 1941 to counteract pro-German propaganda and sentiment in the Caucasus, in anticipation of a sudden German penetration there. When the military situation was stabilized early in 1942, this unit was allegedly dissolved. But when the German attack was resumed a half-year later, a new body was formed, with the purpose

---

leaders through agents dropped by parachute both before and after their occupation of the North Caucasus. These operations, only partially successful, did succeed in identifying some collaborators-to-be. The most notable operation was "Shamil," in which groups were parachuted at various places between Groznyi and Makhach-Kala both in August 1942 and in January 1943. (13. Pz.Div., Ic, "Unternehmen Schamil," 28 August 1942, GMDS, 13 PzD, 30301/35, Anlage 12; Abwehr-Trupp 203, "Taetigkeitsbericht, 1.10.–1.12.1942," 26 November 1942, GMDS, PzAOK 1,24906/19, Anlage 131; Dienststelle F.P. Nr. 46865, "Bericht ueber das Sonderunternehmen 'Schamil,'" 5 January 1943, pp. 1–36, GMDS, OKW/208.) See also the more detailed but not entirely reliable accounts in Forschungsdienst Ost, Ic/AO, "Politische Informationen," Heft I, no. 14 (15 August 1944), pp. 7, 29–31.

[22] Abwehrtrupp I bei AOK 11, Tgb.Nr. 936/42, "15. Ersatz-Schtz.Brig. in Gudermes —Nordkaukasus," 22 June 1942 (GMDS, 3 PzD 30938/54, Anlage 217).

[23] Abwehrtrupp 203 bei PzAOK 1, "Die Lage im Terek-Gebiet" [October 1942?], p. 2 (GMDS, OKW/690, Anlage 5376/42).

of combating German paratroop agents and propaganda drops, and of assembling intelligence data on Caucasians abroad.[24]

Likewise fearing defection to the Germans in the event of combat in the Caucasus, the Soviets late in 1941 instituted a political amnesty and in general trod a path of unusual circumspection. According to a German agent, the effect of these measures was substantial indeed.

For the time being [he reported in January 1942] the morale of military and civilian personnel in the Caucasus area is good. The political amnesty of early December 1941 in the Caucasus, which involved tens of thousands of persons, had a good effect and strengthened Soviet authority. In Georgia, Armenia, and Daghestan, Soviet officials have established new national soviets, which have proved to be useful auxiliary organs for military and communal organizations. Without the consent of these soviets no requisitions are carried out and no significant military or civilian measures executed. . . . In general, the Soviet authorities have adopted a new course in the Caucasus, hoping thereby to secure the Caucasus hinterland, which in the future would supply them with important reserves of food, matériel, and manpower.[25]

When the Germans penetrated the northern approaches of the Caucasus, the Soviet policy of concessions went even further. In the adjacent Transcaucasus, the German High Command was constrained to admit, the regime had been successful in fortifying itself by means of "far-reaching concessions made especially to Georgians and Armenians regarding the expression of national aspirations; e.g., Armenian national books and songs which had been forbidden, are now allowed."[26] The shift of the object of popular complaints from the Soviets to the German scapegoat, coupled with concessions to national and social demands, was evidently successful in the area south of the Caucasus Mountains. In the North Caucasus, however, loyalty appears to have increased little if at all.

During the sudden German advance from July to September 1942, defeatism among military and civilian personnel in the North Caucasus reached serious proportions. As in the first months of the war, disorganization was severe once contact with higher Soviet echelons was disrupted.[27] On 28 July 1942 Stalin issued the famous Order No. 227. Pointing to the retreat beyond Rostov as its specific stimulus, the severe decree

---

[24] OKW/Ausland/Abwehr, Abt. II ["V-Mann-Bericht"], 17 August 1942, p. 2 (GMDS, OKW/690, Anlage 878/42). While the German source was evidently a strongly nationalistic Georgian working out of Turkey, whose value judgments and some exaggerations are hardly to be trusted, there appears to be a factual kernel to his report.

[25] OKW/Ausland/Abwehr/Ausl., "Nr. 0223/42 geh.," 27 January 1942 (GMDS, EAP 3a-11/1).

[26] OKW/Ausland/Abwehr, Abt. II, "Mil. Att. Bukarest meldet," 31 August 1942 (GMDS, OKW/638, Anlage 4628/429).

[27] Interesting Soviet admissions on this score are recorded by Zakrutkin.

provided for the formation of "blocking units" which were to prevent the Red Army from retreating farther, and for summary court-martial of officers and men accused of cowardice or defeatism.

Commanders, commissars, and political workers of troop units who of their own free will abandon their positions can no longer be tolerated if they permit a few panic-makers to determine the situation at the front and to drag soldiers along in retreat, thus opening the front to the enemy. Panic-makers and cowards must be liquidated on the spot. . . . NOT ONE STEP IN RETREAT WITHOUT ORDERS FROM HIGHER HEADQUARTERS! Commanders, commissars, and political workers who abandon a position without an order from higher headquarters are traitors to the fatherland and must be handled accordingly.[28]

Morale was indeed at a low point if such extreme measures had to be adopted by the Soviet command. As a Soviet war correspondent admitted, "There are comrades among us who have so strongly reacted to the August [1942] retreat that they have all but lost their equilibrium. I met such people in the woods. They are undoubtedly honest and good people, but they lacked firmness of spirit, *sangfroid,* and tranquillity."[29] The situation remained serious even after the German advance was halted. A top secret order of the Eighteenth Soviet Army of 12 October 1942 accused officers and political personnel of "being excessively cowardly in the face of enemy airpower."

The commanders and political personnel often report incorrectly on the real situation and conceal inadequacies in their units. . . . On 11 October soldiers and officers strolled ten kilometers behind the front. . . . The rations in the 408th Rifle Division are poor. Soldiers do not receive enough bread, and no hot meals are issued. . . . The politruk of 4th Company, 670th Regiment is being turned over to the military tribunal for abandoning his unit. . . . The commander and commissar of 2d Battalion, 663d Regiment, Bulgakov and Bagayan, are to be turned over to the military tribunal for abandoning the line of combat without orders. The commander of 663d Regiment, Major Labayan, is relieved of his command and transferred to a punitive battalion because of cowardice and willful misrepresentation. The deputy rear area commander of 408th Rifle Division and the divisional supply officer are under arrest for fifteen days for failure to carry out orders. . . .[30]

Such a crisis in morale interacted with the low morale among large segments of the civilian population. Civilians drafted for military service

[28] USSR, Red Army, Supreme Command, "Order No. 227," 28 July 1942 (original and German translation in GMDS, OKW/690; relevant excerpts also in *Voelkischer Beobachter,* Berlin, 7 August 1942).

[29] One order read: "Prepare grenades and 'Molotov cocktails' [for a planned operation]. While the commanding officer goes to the armored units, not one man is to be allowed out of the trenches. The first man to flee is to be shot on the spot." (Zakrutkin, pp. 139, 247.)

[30] 18th Red Army, "Prikaz voiskam 18 Armii No. 00450," 12 October 1942 (original and German translation in GMDS, XXXXIX AK 32155/1, Anlage 10).

at times deserted en masse.[31] Other civilians were impressed by the hurried retreat of the armed forces. On the other hand, the Red Army distrusted the population so much that, in order to avoid all risks of "defeatist contagion," it ordered: "The Red Army is categorically forbidden to have contact with the indigenous population."[32] And when the city of Ordzhonikidze was under attack early in November, the local garrison was ordered "to turn over to the military tribunal all panic-makers, spreaders of false rumors; to shoot deserters, spies, marauders, and scoundrels on the spot."[33] Leading Soviet officials, such as M. I. Kalinin and L. P. Beria, made fiery appeals and introduced patriotic slogans,[34] but it seems most dubious that they were of substantial significance to the population. While south of the Caucasus battle line German efforts to instigate popular revolts were a failure, collaboration in the German-held areas was perhaps more extensive than elsewhere on occupied soil—so much so that after recapturing the area, the Soviet government felt constrained to liquidate several Mountaineer regions and republics. Willingness to cooperate with the Germans was undoubtedly furthered by the stringency of last-minute Soviet measures of repression and by the low state of morale of the retreating Red Army.[35]

D. GERMAN POLICY IN THE NORTH CAUCASUS

In the gamut of German policies toward the occupied USSR, the Caucasus occupied an exceptional position. Of all the areas under German control in the East, this one was to fare best. Some of the reasons may briefly be restated as follows:

(1) The primary strategic function of the Caucasus was a springboard

---

[31] See, for instance, the account of the desertion on the Georgian Military Highway of fifty Osetins drafted in July 1942 in V. A.K., Ic, "Gefangenenvernehmung," 3 November 1943 (GMDS, V AK 42202/6, Anlage 146).

[32] 810th Rifle Regt., "Combat Order No. 006," 15 August 1942, par. 11 (German translation in GMDS, 1 GebD 27920/31, Anlage 705).

[33] Ordzhonikidze garrison, "Prikaz No. 21," 5 November 1942, Zakrutkin, p. 279.

[34] Kalinin speech in USSR Embassy, London, *Soviet War News,* 26 October 1942, pp. 3–4; *Antifashistskii miting narodov Severnogo Kavkaza, Kovsem narodam* [13 August 1942] . . . (Moscow, 1942), also reported in *Soviet War News,* 3 September 1942.

[35] A subsidiary factor deserving some consideration is Allied wartime policy toward the Caucasus. While its ramifications exceed the framework of this chapter, it may not be amiss to point out that German intelligence spoke of British broadcasts (presumably from Iran) to the population of the Caucasus, promising the Transcaucasian nationalities autonomy after the war, stressing German goals of conquest, and warning against naive expectations of freedom under German rule. There is no Allied confirmation that such broadcasts were made. (See Papen's report to the German Foreign Office, OKW/Ausland Abwehr/Abwehr II, "Telegram aus Tarabaya . . . Nr. 1215," 29 August 1942, GMDS, OKW/638, Anlage 4628/42; and RMfdbO., Abt. I/5 [probably by von Mende], "Bericht ueber die Reise nach der Tuerkei vom 14. bis 29.8. 1942," 1 September 1942, p. 2, GMDS, EAP 99/37.)

for German operations in the Near and Middle East. A colonial policy was not required in this context.

(2) In the German view, the peoples of the Caucasus were non-Slavs, in large part "Aryans," who were not discriminated against on "ideological" grounds.

(3) Of all the occupied areas, the Caucasus was geographically farthest away from the Reich and not intended to become an area of German settlement.

(4) The influence of Turkey on the German Foreign Office and of Caucasian *émigré* politicians on Rosenberg helped push through more reasonable policy directives than were possible in Slavic areas.

(5) Unlike the two *Reichskommissariate* (Ostland and Ukraine), the North Caucasus never came under civilian administration; instead it was ruled by a group of military men, diplomats, and some of the more astute officials of the Rosenberg ministry who were delegated there on detached service.

(6) Not only were the agencies concerned with the occupation of the Caucasus more realistic, by and large, but the individuals sent there— partly by intent, partly by a fortuitous combination of circumstances— were among the more humane and politically wise in the Nazi system.[36]

Hitler himself paid particular attention to the Caucasus as a source of oil—a resource of crucial importance to the German war economy. His attitude toward the future status of the Caucasus, however, was less definite than toward the Great Russian and Ukrainian areas. On the one hand, he asserted, "The Caucasus plays a particularly important role in our considerations because it is the greatest source of oil. If we wish to obtain its oil, we must keep the Caucasus under strictest supervision. Otherwise, the hostility among the tribes living in this area, fraught with blood feuds, would make any worthwhile exploitation impossible."[37] At his request the military campaign was repeatedly geared to a concentration of forces against the oil fields, rather than against other targets in the Caucasus.[38]

On the other hand, he told Himmler that German interests demanded

---

[36] For a discussion of German high-level policy, see Alexander Dallin, *German Rule in Russia, 1941–1945* (London: Macmillan, 1957). On Turkish pressure, see USSR, Ministry of Foreign Affairs, Arkhivnoye Upravleniye, *Germanskaya politika v Turtsii (1941–1943 gg.)* (Moscow, 1946); Edward Vere-Hodge, *Turkish Foreign Policy* (Ambilly: University of Geneva, 1950); and an unbalanced Soviet account, I. Vasilyev, *O turetskom 'neitralitete' vo vtoroi mirovoi voine* (Moscow: Gospolitizdat, 1951).

[37] Harry Picker, ed., *Hitlers Tischgespraeche* (Bonn: Athenaeum-Verlag, 1951), pp. 80–81.

[38] Auszuege aus den Aufzeichnungen zum Kriegstagebuch des Wehrmachtfuehrungsstabes," Greiner, pp. 408–9. On the significance of the oil factor in German aspirations, see also p. 189. German planning went so far as to envisage an *Autobahn* from the Reich via Rostov to Maikop, Groznyi, and Baku. (Rosenberg to Meyer, 20 October 1941, IMT Document 1057-PS.)

the control of oil resources but not the annexation of the Caucasus;[39] he approved the propaganda directives, which were considerably more liberal than those for the rest of the East; in substance their theme was: "Under the Germans you shall live as you please."[40] At the same time, he vetoed a suggestion to include a specific reference to future independence for the Caucasus.[41] The future status was not to be prejudged.[42] What Hitler evidently had in mind was a formally independent Caucasus with a puppet regime dependent on the Reich. Inferior as this status promised to be, it foreshadowed considerably more nominal autonomy than the Fuehrer was willing to concede the "Eastern Slavs."

Such an attitude was welcome to the proponents of an anti-Russian *cordon sanitaire*—notably Rosenberg and his followers. In their view, the Caucasus was to be one link in the chain of buffers to be erected around the western and southern peripheries of Muscovy. Like Hitler, Rosenberg stressed from the outset the "extensive exploitation of the vast oil areas." More politically attuned to separatist formulas, however, Rosenberg insisted: "The securing of German military objectives and the supply of raw materials in the Caucasus must, however, be attempted—and this is the most important *future* task—not by direct military and police methods but largely by political means." The solution was to be a federation of the four Caucasus states—North Caucasus, Georgia, Armenia, Azerbaidzhan —with Germany as the "protecting power." Only military and naval bases and German security forces around the oil fields would represent direct extraterritorial participation by the Reich. As in the rest of the USSR, the Great Russians were to assume a subordinate position, with the non-Russians—in this instance, the Caucasians under Georgian leadership—in authority on the spot."[43]

[39] Himmler to Schellenberg, 14 July 1942 (GMDS, EAP 161 b-12/124).
[40] RMfdbO.I/1, "239/42" to Grosskopf (Foreign Office), 10 April 1942 (State Dept., AA 250817/18); specimens of German leaflets, April–May 1942 (GMDS, OKW/637).
[41] Wi Stab Ost [OKVR Dr. Stock], to Min. Dir. Riecke, 20 August 1942 (GMDS, Wi/ID 2.678, Anlage 4).
[42] The existence of alternatives is confirmed in Lammers' report on Hitler's directives: "If in the future bodies more or less dependent on the Reich are to be established out of the peoples of the Caucasus, the Foreign Office would have absolutely nothing to do with them. . . . If, however, independent states should be created out of the Caucasus territories, the Foreign Office could *then* establish diplomatic relations with them." (Lammers to Rosenberg, "Zustaendigkeitsabgrenzung zwischen dem Auswaertigen Amt und dem Reichsministerium fuer die besetzten Ostgebiete," 12 July 1942, GMDS, EAP 99/394.)
[43] Rosenberg, "Instruktion fuer einen Reichskommissar in Kaukasien," 7 May 1941 (IMT, 1027-PS). The territorial organization as outlined by his ministry on the eve of the invasion called for the creation of "General Commissariats" in Georgia, Azerbaidzhan, North Caucasus, Krasnodar, and Ordzhonikidze, and "Main Commissariats" [*Hauptkommissariate,* a somewhat inferior unit] for Armenia and the Kalmyk area. (18 June 1941, IMT, 1035-PS.) The pro-Georgian attitude of Rosenberg (not shared by Hitler) was fostered by the concept of a "Berlin-Tiflis Axis" spread

However far apart on other issues, the "separatist" concept of Rosenberg was in this instance echoed by the "Russland-Gremium" under Ambassador Count von der Schulenburg and others in the Foreign Office. In connection with an attempt to enroll the support of Caucasian *émigrés* on the eve of the German push into the Caucasus in late spring 1942, Schulenburg called a conference of refugee politicians in Berlin. While its ramifications and the ensuing transfer of *émigré* affairs from the Foreign Office to the Rosenberg Ministry are beyond the scope of this chapter, the attempt is significant for the outlook of that segment of the Foreign Office which—like Schulenburg or his former Counselor of the Embassy, Gustav Hilger—had maintained a generally sympathetic attitude toward the Soviet population and that which—like von Hentig and von Papen—was attuned to the enlistment of Turkish good will. Schulenburg spoke of a "separate state with its own government" in the future Caucasus; the Foreign Office, he averred, favored a system in which—not unlike Slovakia—German authority would be represented by envoys and consuls.[44]

The views of this group were summarized by a German officer commanding a collaborator unit, who was dismayed to hear such "liberationist" talk from a visiting commission including Ambassador von der Schulenburg, Counselors Herwarth and Pfleiderer, and General von Koestring—all "old Russia hands."

[According to their views] independent states must be established in the Caucasus. . . . The states would be independent to about the same extent as Slovakia. . . . The several states would be grouped together in a Caucasian Federation whose executive organ would be a Federal Council, in which a German representative would have the veto power.

The officer was startled to discover that "the Foreign Office is cleverly winning the support of the *Wehrmacht*." Finally, he added: "The worst, however, of what I experienced, was a statement by Herr von Bittenfeld [Herwarth]: some of the gentlemen in the *Ostministerium,* notably Braeutigam and Mende, have the same point of view as the Foreign Office."[45]

The political plans have been traced in some detail because they constituted the background against which actual policy decisions were made. In practice, the key to the engineering of the "propopulation" wing of the Army was Colonel Count von Stauffenberg, chief of the Organizations

---

by such Georgian advisers in Berlin as "A. Sanders" (Alexander Nikuradze) and "K. Michel" (Mikhail Akhmeteli). According to this view, the Georgians were "the Germans of the Caucasus," while the Armenians were the inferior nationality. Relatively little attention was paid to the North Caucasus in these formulations.

[44] Schulenburg, memorandum of 15 May 1942 (GMDS, AA-DW 34); and RMfdbO., "Aufzeichnung" [n.d., presumably June 1942] (GMDS, EAP 99/37).

[45] Gloger, CO Azerbaidjani Bn. 804, to Zimmermann, RMfdbO., 13 July 1942 (NMT, NG-1657). Dr. Otto Braeutigam and Professor Gerhard von Mende were high officials in the political department of the Rosenberg Ministry.

Section of the OKW and later a leader of the 1944 plot against Hitler. It was through him that some of the appointments to the Caucasus were made: General Koestring was to become Governor-General under the military occupation (thus eliminating *Reichskommissar*-designate of the Caucasus, Arno Schickedanz by a *fait accompli*), with Herwarth as his adjutant; Dr. Otto Schiller, a specialist in Soviet agriculture, was to carry out the agrarian reform; Dr. Otto Braeutigam, whose last position had been German consul general in Batum, was sent to Army Group "A" as a representative of the Rosenberg Ministry.

Whether hypocritical or not, the leitmotiv of the German attitude toward the Caucasus was to be "friendship" toward the indigenous population. Theodor Oberlaender, who commanded a unit of indigenous collaborators, stated this view in a memorandum which received wide circulation: "Without cooperation from the local population the Caucasus cannot be held—or can be held only with heavy casualties." Two themes, he argued, must dominate German policy there: self-government for the ethnic groups, and cultural and religious freedom.[46]

When Braeutigam's appointment to Army Group "A" was weighed, Stauffenberg and Altenstadt, chief of the Military Government Section of the Quartermaster General's Office, agreed that "terms like 'freedom,' 'independence,' 'cooperation' are to be used" in German appeals in the Caucasus, much unlike other occupied areas.[47] In his instructions to Braeutigam, Rosenberg in turn advised:

> The Caucasus is a region of unique ethnic multiplicity. For this reason, if for no other, the representative [of the Reich] will be expected to evince an utmost measure of sensitivity, tact, and ability to adjust. The geopolitical role of the Caucasus as a bridge to the Near East points in the same direction. This suggests the style of administration which—unlike the Ukraine, the Central, and North-ern sectors—combines greater discretion with careful observation [and] far-reaching responsible use of an indigenous population devoted to the Reich, under German supervision (*Oberaufsicht*).[48]

The Army, on its part, officially assumed an attitude which seemed to point in the same direction. In a communication, the Rumanian General Staff, which was dispatching several of its divisions to join the German Seventeenth Army, was informed:

> The German Reich considers the peoples of the Caucasus, including the Kalmyks, Kuban Cossacks, and Terek Cossacks, as well as the Don Cossacks, as

[46] Dr. Theodor Oberlaender, "Deutschland und der Kaukasus" (Chef d. Sipo u. SD, "Anlage 5 zu Meldungen aus den besetzten Ostgebieten, Nr. 13," 24 July 1942, GMDS, DW-SD 3).

[47] OKW/GenStdH/Abt. Kriegsverw., "Niederschrift ueber die Besprechung beim Leiter," 13 September 1942 (GMDS, EAP 99/471).

[48] RMfdbO., "Anweisung fuer den Bevollmaechtigten des Reichsministers fuer die besetzten Ostgebiete beim Oberkommando der Heeresgruppe A," 27 October 1942 (GMDS, EAP 99/36).

friends. The behavior of German and allied troops must correspond to this attitude. All headquarters, troops, and agencies are to be impressed with the necessity of benevolent treatment of the population. . . .[49]

Indeed, a leaflet distributed to all German troops moving into the Caucasus spoke a language unfamiliar to the soldier inured to *Untermensch* propaganda:

The troops entering the Caucasus are
(1) To treat the Caucasus population as friendly peoples, except when they show themselves to be anti-German.
(2) To lay no obstacles in the path of the aspirations of Mountaineers striving to abolish the collective farm system.
(3) To permit the reopening of places of worship of all denominations and the conduct of religious services, customs, and ceremonies.
(4) To respect private property and to pay for requisitioned goods.
(5) To win the confidence of the population by model conduct. . . .
(6) To give reasons for all harsh military measures toward the population.
(7) To respect especially the honor of the Caucasus women.[50]

Just as Field Marshal von List issued the above order, so General von Rocques, who commanded the security forces and rear area of Army Group "A," declared the "unlimited cooperation of the population" to be a major goal requiring special "psychological" treatment by all German agencies.[51]

The two armies in Army Group "A" adopted a similar approach. The posters of the Seventeenth Army read: "We bring you the right to own property, freedom from the kolkhoz system, freedom of labor, freedom to develop natural culture, and freedom of religion. . . . Thousands of volunteers, sons of the peoples of the Caucasus, are fighting on our side for the honor and liberation of the entire Caucasus."[52] Just as the above order admonished the population to fight "spies, partisans, and diversionists," so the Army admonished its own troops: "An important means of preventing personal and material support of the partisans by the population lies in the proper treatment of the population. He who plunders, steals cattle, and threatens and thrashes the population is driving it into the hands of the bands."[53]

[49] Dt. Heeresmission in Rumaenien, Begwegliche Staffel, "An den Chef des Koeniglich Rumaenischen Grossen Generalstabs, Herrn General Steflea, Operatives Memorandum Nr. 7," 5 October 1942 (GMDS, Dt.HM. Rum., 38800/2).

[50] Heeresgr. A, OB, *Befehl an alle im Kaukasus eingesetzten Truppen* [n.d., probably August 1942] (GMDS, EAP 99/37, OKW/638, Russia Misc.)

[51] Komm.Gen.d.Sich.Tr.u.Befh.i.H.Geb. A, "Monatsbericht.—Berichtszeit 1.–30.9.42," 9 October 1942 (GMDS, HGeb A 31242/2, Anlage 110).

[52] [AOK 17, OQu.,] *Vozzvaniye k grazhdanskomu naseleniyu Kavkaza* [n.d.] (GMDS, AOK 17, 51019/7).

[53] Armeegr. Ruoff [AOK 17] Ic/AO, "Besondere Anordnungen fuer Banden- und Spionagebekaempfung (11)," 5 December 1942, p. 4 (GMDS, AOK 17, 25354/38).

First Panzer Army acted in similar fashion.[54] The Foreign Office representative assigned to it could report after a few weeks that the actual situation fully confirmed the wisdom of a special German policy for the Caucasus. Considering even the narrower German goals of oil and grain, it was important to bear in mind that "to have the nationalities of the Caucasus as our friends means to achieve anything we desire." And the implications were not limited to personal behavior of German troops. The official continued: "The friendship of these peoples will be guaranteed only when they are given *complete* political independence. . . . An immediate declaration of unlimited freedom . . . seems desirable." And General Wagner, Quartermaster General of the Army, echoed these words in a report to Hitler. Among the recommended measures he listed: "Public declaration about political intentions in the Caucasus, guaranty of full political independence in close military and economic cooperation with the Greater German Reich." All authority was to remain in the hands of the Army until the occupation was over; dissenting elements, whether *Wirtschaftstab Ost,* SS, or Rosenberg's staff, were to be kept under control.[55]

While the significance of such directives and intentions must not be overrated, and while diverse elements among German and Rumanian personnel in the Caucasus failed to comply with them, the unique place which the Caucasus represented in German planning contributed to making it a special case in popular reactions and, indirectly, in the fate of the partisans there.

E. THE GERMANS AND THE INDIGENOUS POPULATION

Though only indirectly of significance for the fate of the partisan movement, the interaction of German policy and indigenous response is of significance because its result importantly determined the choice of the population between Germans and partisans.

---

[54] Abwehrtrupp 203 bei PzAOK 1, "Die Lage im Terek-Gebiet" [October 1942] (GMDS, OKW/690, Anlage 5376/42).

[55] VAA bei PzAOK 1, "Aktennotiz betr. die Auffassung zur Frage der politischen Zukunft der Kaukasusgebietes," August 1942; and OKH/GenStdH/GenQu, "Notizen fuer Fuehrer-Vortrag," September 1942 (both in GMDS, DW AA-17, 316942/48). See also Kleist's address of 15 December 1942 to the German propaganda staff for the Caucasus: "The best propaganda inward and outward is a satisfied and hopeful population who knows that it faces a better future than under the rule of the tsars and Stalin. The population must know that we are trying our best in its interest, even though we cannot give it everything it hopes for . . . and that we are of good will to help even in little things. . . . A distinction in principle cannot be made between Mountaineers, Cossacks, and Russians. We need all of them. The Russians are no exception because they are particularly valuable men. Today they are no longer in conflict with the indigenous population." ("Schlussbemerkungen des Herrn Oberbefehlshabers Generaloberst von Kleist," 15 December 1942, GMDS, EAP 99/37.)

1. Culture and Religion

Of all German moves, the reopening of Orthodox churches, Moslem mosques, and Buddhist temples appeared to evoke the least opposition. Especially in the Moslem areas, the festive celebration of holidays, apparently, was widely acclaimed. While the shortage of personnel and facilities was serious in the field of education, the reopening of local schools, with considerable emphasis on indigenous tradition, language, and symbols, received popular support.[56]

2. Economic Policy

German economic organization in this area, as elsewhere, was in the hands of an "economic inspectorate," subdivided into six "commandos."[57] German exploitation was primarily concerned with oil, coal, lumber, as well as grain and food for the Army. While considerable efforts were made to restore oil and coal mining installations, the yield was meager. The lack of fuel and electric power forced a severe curtailment of economic activity.[58]

The severe labor shortage—due in part to Soviet mobilization, evacuation, and flight—was relieved by two measures which evoked support from some strata of the population in the Caucasus. On the one hand, special rations were allocated to those working for the Germans, and on the other, no forced labor was to be recruited. Intended as a political palliative, this measure also proved to be of economic benefit on the spot.[59]

3. Agriculture

A perennial Achilles' heel of the Soviet regime and a major object of German exploitation in the East, agriculture exemplified the special solu-

[56] H.Gr. A, Ib, "Verwaltung des Kaukasus-Gebietes," 7 September 1942 (GMDS, Wi/ID 2.291); Komm.Gen.d.Sich.Tr.u.Befh.H.Geb.A, "Monatsbericht.-Berichtszeit 1.-30.9.42.," 9 October 1942 (GMDS, HGeb 31242/2, Anlage 110); Befh.H.Geb. A, Abt. VII, "Lagebericht der Abteilung VII fuer die Zeit vom 16.11. bis 15.12.1942," 28 December 1942 (GMDS, EAP 99/159); WiStab Ost, Abt. I/Id, "Monatsbericht . . . (1.12.–31.12.1942)," 16 January 1943, p. 19 (GMDS, Wi/ID 2.336); Chef Sipo u.SD, "Meldungen aus den besetzten Ostgebieten," No. 24, 9 October 1942, and No. 34, 18 December 1942, pp. 10–13 (GMDS, DW SD-6).

[57] *Wirtschafts-Inspektion Kaukasus* was divided into Wi Kdo 15 for Army Group Rear Area "A"; Wi Kdos 6 and 10 for the First Panzer Army; and Wi Kdos 5, 11, 16 for the Seventeenth Army Area (GMDS, Wi/ID 2.248, Anlage 63a).

[58] Wi Stab Ost, I/Id, "Monatsbericht . . . (1.10–31.10.1942)," pp. 11–12, and "Monatsbericht . . . (1.11.–30.11.1942)," pp. 10–11 (GMDS, Wi/ID 2.336); Wi Kdo z.b.V. 16, "KTB Nr. 1 . . . vom 17.8.1942 bis 1.2.1943, Teil 2," (GMDS, Wi/ID 2.1354); Wi Kdo z.b.V. 10, "Kriegstagebuch," September 1942, p. 7 (GMDS, Wi/ID 2.427).

[59] GFP Gr. 626, "Lage und Stimmung der Bevoelkerung in den besetzten Gebieten," 25 September 1942, p. 2 (GMDS, PzAOK 1, 24906/19). In practice, voluntary recruitment for labor in the Reich was instituted, and toward the end of the occupation some forced labor was also conscripted in violation of directives.

tion adopted for the Caucasus. As elsewhere, the agrarian reform of 15 February 1942 was to be proclaimed, abolishing the collective farms in name. But in the Caucasus, immediate distribution of cattle was envisaged, and "not agricultural communes but private farms are to be created."[60] Such a move necessarily took greater cognizance of popular opposition to collective farming than did the standard agrarian reform. General Wagner, in recommending the prompt execution of the reform, told Hitler in September 1942 that this "will be one of the most effective propaganda measures" that the Reich could employ.[61]

In practice, opposition in Germany to "full reprivatization" forced a limitation of this far-reaching program. Nevertheless, two measures were unique in the Army Group "A" area: during the first year, from 30 to 40 per cent of the land (as opposed to 10 per cent in the Ukraine) was to be transformed from collectives into agricultural cooperatives with enlarged private plots; and the mountain areas, engaged primarily in cattle-breeding, were to see a prompt transformation into individual holdings.[62] The latter compromise solution did not deprive the Reich of the grain from the richer agrarian areas of the North Caucasus, and it did permit a reform where it was least likely to obstruct German needs. Coincidentally, the privileged areas were those inhabited by the Mountaineers, while the grain areas were primarily those inhabited by Slavs: a solution entirely acceptable to the Rosenberg Ministry.

German reports are unanimous in affirming popular opposition to collective farming, regardless of the peasants' nationality. While conditions and practices varied considerably, in many instances the population promptly elected village elders on its own and began appropriating grain and livestock. The main indigenous complaints about German agricultural officials concerned arbitrary confiscations and lack of sufficiently speedy and far-reaching agrarian reorganization.[63]

While agricultural administration remained in indigenous hands to a greater extent than elsewhere under the Germans, the implementation of

[60] OKW/Wi Amt und Wi Stab Ost VO bei OKH/GenQu, "Vortragsnotiz fuer den Herrn Generalquartiermeister," 29 June 1942 (GMDS, Wi/ID 403).
[61] OKH/GenQu, "Notizen fuer Fuehrer-Vortrag," September 1942 (GMDS, DW AA-17, 316943); also VAA Lohmann's recommendations (*ibid.*, 316946/7).
[62] Wi Stab Ost, "Durchfuehrung der Agrarordnung im Gebiet des Nordkaukasus," 24 September 1942 (GMDS, Wi/ID 403); RMfdbO., "Anweisung fuer die Bevollmaechtigten fuer die besetzten Ostgebiete beim Oberkommando der Heeresgruppe A," 27 October 1942, pp. 3–4 (GMDS, EAP 99/36).
[63] Wi Kdo z.b.V. 10, Gr. La, "Aktenvermerk," 10 November 1942, p. 2 (GMDS, Wi/ID 2.528); Abwehrtrupp 203 bei PzAOK 1, "Die Lage im Terek-Gebiet" [October 1942], p. 4 (GMDS, OKW/690, Anlage 5376/42); Wi In A, Chefgr. La, "Bericht ueber die Agrarverhaeltnisse des Kuban-Gebiets Gau Krasnodar," 9 September 1942 (GMDS, EAP 99/39); Komm.Gen.d.Sich.Tr.u.Befh. H.Geb. A, Ia, "Monatsbericht.-Berichtszeit 1.–31.10.42.," 8 November 1942, p. 5 (GMDS, HGeb 31242/2, Anlage 196); PzAOK 1, AWiFue, "Aktenvermerk," 13 November 1942, p. 1 (GMDS, Wi/ID 2.248, Anlage 31); WiStab Ost, I/Id, "Monatsbericht," 20 November 1942, p. 24, and *ibid.*, 16 December 1942, p. 6 (GMDS, Wi/ID 2.336).

580 / X. THE NORTH CAUCASUS

the reform was much delayed. The proclamation did not come until December 1942, but then it was made the occasion of considerable festivities staged by Germans and collaborating officials to the sound of national singing and dancing and accompanied by considerble dining and wining.[64] In reality, the formal reform measures were "too little and too late." As a German official reflected, solemn promises did little good unless their good faith could be demonstrated to the population.[65] With the passage of time, popular disappointment in the Germans increased correspondingly.

Three facts should be borne in mind. (1) Partly by intent, partly from weakness, the Germans did not obstruct peasant initiative even before the reform was officially announced. This passive acquiescence helped forestall popular resentment. (2) The occupation was too short to permit anti-German feelings in this realm to crystallize. (3) What hostility was generated in this domain was concentrated in the northern parts of the occupied Caucasus and the towns, precisely the two areas where organized resistance was bound to be least effective; the areas where the partisans roamed were inhabited to a considerable extent by Mountaineers and other rural groups who felt less cause for active opposition to the Germans.[66]

[64] The agrarian reform was enacted in the Stavropol region, Circassia, and Karachai on 6 December; in Kabardino-Balkaria on 18 December, the day of the Moslem Bairam; and in the Krasnodar region on 20 December—a mere ten days before the German retreat began. Apparently Field Marshals von Kleist and List were sympathetic to a far-reaching reform, as was Baron von Hahn, the representative of *Wi In Kaukasus* in Nalchik. Nevertheless, the German-approved indigenous officials claim to have exerted pressure on the Germans to obtain consent to their demands. Especially in Karachai and Kabarda, the reform in substance sanctioned what the peasants had meanwhile carried out by themselves. (Wi Kdo 6, Gr. La, "Vierteljahresbericht fuer die Monate September, Oktober, November," 30 November 1942, GMDS, Wi/ID 2.170; WiStab Ost, I/Id, "Monatsbericht . . . 1.12.—31.12.1942," p. 4, GMDS, Wi/ID 2.336; 13. Pz.Div., Ic, "Propaganda in den Feind," 12 October 1942, GMDS, 13 PzD 30301/35, Anlage 10; Sonderstab Oberst Nagel, Kdr. [Wi Kdo z.b.V. 16], "Taetigkeitsbericht fuer die Zeit v. 24.11. bis 22.12.42," 22 December 1942, GMDS, Wi/ID 2.1354, Anlage 9; Schuenemann, "Auch im Kaukasus Aufloesung der Kolchosen," *Deutsche Allgemeine Zeitung*, 4 November 1942; Selim Shadov, "Natsionalnoye pravitelstvo v svobodnoi Kabardino-balkarskoi respublike v 1942 godu," MS, Russian Research Center, Harvard University.) On the festivities in Nalchik, see also Erich Kern, *Dance of Death* (New York: Scribners, 1951), pp. 124–25; Braeutigam ["Bericht"], 22 December 1942 (GMDS, EAP 99/37). On detailed texts of speeches to be delivered in Russian and German, see AOK 17, Ic/AO, "Feierliche Verkuendung der Agrar-Ordnung," 2 December 1942 (GMDS, AOK 17, 25354/38, Anlage 10).

[65] Wi Kdo z.b.V. 10, "Aktenvermerk," 10 November 1942 (GMDS, Wi/ID 2.528); PzAOK 1, AWiFue, "Aktenvermerk," 13 November 1942 (GMDS, Wi/ID, 2.248, Anlage 31). Some of the German personnel objecting to a speedy implementation insisted that the population was "too indolent," "too backward," or "too stupid" to run their own farms; others cited instances in which the peasants had actually carried out the reprivatization on their own without German assistance.

[66] Wi In Kaukasus, Der Inspekteur, "Erfahrungsbericht der Wi In Kaukasus," 8 April 1943 [hereafter cited as Wi In Kaukasus, Der Inspekteur], pp. 16–17 (GMDS, Wi/ID 2.602a); and Befh. H.Geb. A, Abt. VII, "Lagebericht," 28 December 1942 (GMDS, EAP 99/159).

4. German Propaganda

Time and again German officials complained about the inadequacy of German propaganda—both in quantity and in quality. The special Propaganda Detachment did not arrive until December 1942. On the whole, the lack of information made the population susceptible to wild rumors, some of which were attributed to Soviet counterpropaganda. Above all, retrospective summaries complained, the gap between propaganda and practice remained striking. "Decent treatment and land" were the only two tangible expressions of positive policy which were exploited in propaganda. The urban elements were most negatively affected by these shortcomings of German psychological warfare, which, however, only in a secondary manner affected the attitude of the population in the partisan areas.[67]

5. Nationality Question

In most of the occupied East, the Germans limited indigenous government to the local level; in large parts of the North Caucasus and of the Cossack area south of Rostov, however, "regional self-government" was permitted, thus giving the population a larger share of responsibility and a greater stake in the regime. Though barring the establishment of sovereign states, Hitler had agreed to the "furtherance of the national, cultural, and economic development of the Caucasus peoples."[68] Army Group "A" for its part decided that the emancipation of the Caucasus had to proceed in stages. At first, indigenous self-government was to be established in each ethnic area. After the harvest of 1942, German administration was to be replaced by this indigenous government. The final phase of "full self-government" was indefinitely postponed. In the immediate future, regional government was to be limited to the Mountaineer areas.[69]

Although German reports on national feeling are strikingly incomplete and full of stereotypes confirming the observers' preconceptions (whatever

[67] Abwehrtrupp 203 bei PzAOK 1, "Die Lage im Terek-Gebiet" [October 1942] [hereafter cited as Abwehrtrupp 203 bei PzAOK 1], pp. 2–6 (GMDS, OKW/690, Anlage 5376/42); Wi In Kaukasus, 2. Staffel, OfA, "Beitrag zum Kriegstagebuch fuer die Zeit vom 15. bis 31.12.42.," 8 February 1943, p. 2 (GMDS, Wi/ID 2.248, Anlage 65); Wi In Kaukasus, Der Inspekteur, pp. 15–17; Wi Kdo z.b.V. 10, "Kriegstagebuch Nr. 2," October 1942—May 1943, p. 4 (GMDS, Wi/ID 2.528; [Wi Kdo 6?] "Aktenvermerk: Stimmung und Haltung der russischen Bevoelkerung Pjatigorsks," 27 November 1942 (GMDS, Wi/ID 2.291); Befh.H.Geb. A, Abt. VII, "Lagebericht der Abteilung VII fuer die Zeit vom 16.11. bis 15.12.1942," 28 December 1942 (GMDS, EAP 99/159). In the last stages of the campaign the Germans also dropped their Russian-language newspaper, *Utro Kavkaza*, by plane. (Prop.Abt. K, "Taetigkeitsbericht," 16 May 1943, GMDS, OKW/734.)

[68] Der Fuehrer, WFSt/Qu (Verw.) [no title], 8 September 1942 (GMDS, DW/AA-17).

[69] H.Gr. A, Ib, "Verwaltung des Kaukasus-Gebietes," 7 September 1942 (GMDS, Wi/ID 2.291).

they might have been), some tentative conclusions seem warranted. (1) There was no evidence of friction between Russians and Ukrainians; nor did the Slavic elements who remained under the Germans show any pronounced pro-Soviet leanings.[70] (2) The non-Slavs, while not generally aspiring to separate statehood (a rather unrealistic goal in view of their small size and the concomitant difficulties of such a "solution"), appeared susceptible to indoctrination. Initially, no anti-Russian feelings existed among them—or even among prisoners selected for training as German propagandists; according to the report of a training center, "no hostility against the Russians could be found," and "no clear or conscious anti-Semitism could be noticed among the [trainees]"; "the question of the future independent statehood of the Caucasus areas was raised by none of the participants." On the other hand, attachment to local traditions, languages, and peculiarities was strong.[71] While the situation was too fluid, the reporting too spotty and biased, and the reactions too varied to oversimplify the picture, some of the nationalities—particularly the Moslem and Turkic ones—appeared to have a greater "defection potential" than others.

The Kabardins and Osetins and perhaps also the Cherkess (Circassians) —more assimilated into the Great Russian stream and containing a larger percentage of Christians—seemed least inclined to collaborate, and often assumed an attitude of "watchful waiting." Even in their areas, however, there was no difficulty in creating collaborator regimes.

The Balkars, on the other hand, were more prone to join the Germans —a conclusion borne out by the subsequent liquidation of their autonomous area by the Soviet Government. The same is true of the Chechens (of whom only a few came under German rule): the consensus was that they were "extraordinarily helpful and friendly."[72]

---

[70] Komm.Gen.d.Sich.Tr.u.Befh.i.H.iGeb. A., Ia, "Monatsbericht.-Berichtszeit 1.30.9. 1942," 9 October 1942, p. 1 (GMDS, HGeb, 31242/2); Befh.H.Geb. A., Ia, "Monatsbericht.-Berichtszeit 1.–30.11.42," 8 December 1942 (GMDS, HGeb A, 31242/2); Wi Stab Ost, Abt. I/Id, "Monatsbericht . . . (1.12.—31.12.1942)," 16 January 1943, p. 19 (GMDS, Wi/ID 2.336); Chef Sipo u. SD, "Meldungen aus den besetzten Ostgebieten Nr. 18," 23 August 1942 (GMDS, DW SD 5).

[71] VAA bei AOK 11, "Erfahrungen bei den Lehrgaengen fuer Propagandisten unter den freiwilligen Kaukasiern," Anlage to Report No. 260, 24 March 1942 (GMDS, EAP 3-a-11/1). As late as December 1942 the Military Government Section of Army Group Rear Area "A" reported: "Tensions among the various nationalities could not be noticed." (H.Geb. A., Abt. VII, "Lagebericht," 28 December 1942, p. 2, GMDS, EAP 99/159.)

[72] When, preceding the Germans' arrival, an intelligence team tried to establish anti-Soviet bands on enemy soil, it found that "indigenous bands were organized and put to work in the Balkar territory (something impossible among Kabardins and Osetins)." (Abwehr-Trupp 203, "Taetigkeitsbericht, 1.9.—1.12.1942," 26 November 1942, GMDS, PzAOK 1, 24906/19, Anlage 13.)

The foregoing paragraphs are also based on Korueck 531, Abt. Qu., "Auftreten von Banden," 10 September 1942 (GMDS, Korueck 31373/2); 13. PzDiv., Ic, "Unternehmen Schamil," 28 August 1942 (GMDS, 13 PzD 30301/35, Anlage 12); Dr. Otto

Most clear-cut perhaps was the attitude of the Karachai, which cost them, too, their autonomy after the Red Army returned. From beginning to end, German reports stressed the "friendliness" and "pro-German" behavior of these Mountaineers. A local police force was promptly established; the Karachai partisan unit, consisting mostly of high government, Party, and NKVD officials, found no popular support, On the contrary, the final report of the German field gendarmerie states that, in the destruction of the Karachai partisan unit, "the cooperation of the [indigenous] militia and the population must be stressed particularly."[73] At an early date the Germans sanctioned the formation of indigenous self-government for the entire "autonomous region"; the Seventeenth Army appears to have planned the establishment of five such "governments."[74] Justifying the national committees on the grounds of military necessity, the Quartermaster General's Office of the General Staff approved their formation in mid-November.[75] The extent to which the German military authorities were willing to go was best illustrated by the unique procedure of recognizing the claim of the Karachai Committee to former state property:

> The High Command of Army Group "A" has decreed that the former [Soviet] state property in the Karachai Autonomous Region is in trusteeship (*treuhaenderisches Eigentum*) of the Karachai nationality. Accordingly the Karachai Regional Committee has claim to the proceeds (*Ertraege*) of state enterprises, forests, etc., as directed by Army Group "A" on 8 November 1942.[76]

This policy of giving the indigenous groups at least nominal control over internal affairs and some economic functions appears to have rewarded the Germans. To the end of the occupation, there was no evidence of opposition in the Karachai area.

Such limited steps seemed adequate, at least in this first period, to satisfy

---

Braeutigam ["Bericht an RMfdbO."], 22 December 1942 (GMDS, EAP 99/37). See also Abwehrtrupp 203 bei PzAOK 1; Dulag 152, Abt. Abwehr, "Vernehmungsbericht," 19 October 1942 (GMDS, PzAOK 1, 24609/30); 13. Pz.Div.,Ic, "Propaganda in den Feind," 12 October 1942 (GMDS, 13 PzD, 30301/35, Anlage 10); Polizeifuehrer Terekgebiet, "Staroste sela Kizlyar," 6 December 1942 (GMDS, 111 ID 34428/13, Anlage 61); PzAOK 1, AWiFue, "Aktenvermerk," 13 November 1942 (GMDS, Wi/ID 2.248, Anlage 31).

[73] Feldgendarmerie-Trupp 418, "Bericht ueber die Vernichtung und Selbstaufloesung der Partisanen-Bande," 14 September 1942 (GMDS, XXXXIX AK 32155/1).

[74] [Chef Sipo und SD] Einsatzfunkstelle Woroschilowsk Nr. 2971, "Verwaltung des Kaukasusgebietes" (wire to RSHA, Kommandostab Ost), 27 September 1942 (GMDS, EAP 161-b-12/124); Wi Stab Ost, I/Id, "Monatsbericht . . . (1.12.—31.12.1942)," 16 January 1943, p. 20 (GMDS, Wi/ID 2.336). Presumably the five areas of regional self-government (in addition to the Cossacks) would have been the Karachai, Kabardino-Balkar, Osetin, Chechen-Ingush, and Cherkess (Circassians). In practice, only the first two received a form of self-government.

[75] See file in GMDS, EAP 99/471.

[76] Sonderstab Oberst Nagel [Wi Kdo z.b.V. 16], "An Verteiler," 30 November 1942 (GMDS, Wi/ID 2.1354, Anlage 8); Diary of Dr. Otto Braeutigam, entry for November–December 1942 (GMDS, EAP 99/535).

indigenous "political" aspirations. Carried out in a generally more benevolent atmosphere than prevailed in other areas of German military government and executed among groups which cherished their distinctiveness without setting a premium on political independence, the totality of German measures helped create a situation in which, as one German report put it, "the [Caucasus] population had little interest in engaging in partisan warfare against the German armed forces because a part of their old prerogatives had been restored."[77] The limits of this policy, however, will be apparent from the following section.

6. Variations in Popular Attitudes

If the initial response to the Germans varied generally between "watchful waiting" and distinct cooperation,[78] there were also inhibiting factors at work from the start. Not the least of these was a fear of the return of Soviet forces.[79] Secondly, while German Army behavior occasionally impressed the population by its contrast with the unruliness and poverty of Red Army troops,[80] the abuses perpetrated by individual members of the occupation forces, and especially by Rumanian troops, dampened what enthusiasm had initially developed.[81] Interested largely in problems within its immediate range of experience, the population rarely broke with the Soviet regime in articulately ideological terms.[82]

Deterioration of pro-German sentiments was apparent from about October on; it was manifest first in the urban areas. The stabilization of the front made German claims of rapid conquest of the Caucasus questionable—and the urban population was best informed about the military situation. Even more important were the food shortages and the concomitant drop in the standard of living (which had been generally higher than in the adjacent area to the north) as well as the resultant gap between wages and prices and the flourishing black market.[83]

[77] GFP Gr. 626, "Taetigkeitsbericht fuer Monat November 1942," 25 November 1942, p. [2] (GMDS, PzAOK 1, 28280/2, Anlage 1601).

[78] Chef Sipo u. SD, "Meldungen aus den besetzten Ostgebieten, Nr. 18," 28 August 1942, and ibid., No. 24, 9 October 1942 (GMDS, DW SD 5); 4 Geb.Div., Ic, "Taetigkeitsbericht vom 4.6.42—15.1.43," entry for 8 August 1942 (GMDS, 4 GebD, 28591/10).

[79] [Wi Kdo 6?] "Aktenvermerk: Stimmung und Haltung der russischen Bevoelkerung Pjatigorsks," 27 November 1942 (GMDS, Wi/ID 2.291).

[80] Abwehrtrupp 203 bei PzAOK 1, p. 2; GFP Gr. 626, "Taetigkeitsbericht fuer Monat September 1942," 25 September 1942, Anlage 1, p. 2 (GMDS, PzAOK 1, 24906/19, Anlage 16).

[81] Ibid.; also correspondence in GMDS, EAP 99/37; see also Harvard University Refugee Interview Protocols, series B 6, passim.

[82] See, for instance, Abwehrtrupp 203 bei PzAOK 1, p. 2.

[83] Wi Stab Ost, Abt. I/Id, "Monatsbericht" for October 1942, 20 November 1942, p. 24; ibid. for December 1942, 16 January 1943 (both in GMDS, Wi/ID 2.336); Wi Kdo 6, Gr. La, "Vierteljahresbericht fuer die Monate September, Oktober, Novem-

Though less intense and less apparent, discontent appears to have increased among the rural population, too. German failure to institute drastic change or bring about tangible improvements in many areas contributed to it, as did delays in the implementation of the agrarian reform.[84]

The German occupation of the Mountaineer areas and the Central Caucasus was not sufficiently long to permit such changes of attitude to be translated into action. In a process of mutual stimulation, however, German policy became more intransigent and popular responses more hostile as the military situation deteriorated. By December literally hundreds of civilians suspected of helping Soviet partisans and agents were being "liquidated"; SD teams were stepping up their activities; in violation of official directives, conscription for forced labor was begun.[85] On the eve of its retreat in January–February 1943 all inhibitions were swept away in the areas still occupied by the German Army; in a desperate effort to extricate manpower and matériel from the Caucasus, the Army indiscriminately requisitioned and demolished, evacuated and liquidated, leaving behind a trail of resentment. By the spring of 1943 the policy which was being pursued in the Kuban bridgehead by the remaining German forces was similar to that applied generally in the occupied regions of the USSR.

In March 1943, for instance, in retaliation for the killing of German soldiers in villages north of Novorossiisk, "all able-bodied male residents between the ages of seventeen and fifty-five are to be shot, and the remaining population is to be evacuated."[86] Similar measures were applied indiscriminately; by June almost the entire civilian population in this area had been moved out. The German V Corps, in charge of antipartisan warfare, directed: "Popular fear of harsh [German] measures must be greater than the terror of the [partisan] bands."[87] Entire zones were declared off-limits, and both German and civilian personnel were forbidden to enter them.[88]

---

ber," 30 November 1942 (GMDS, Wi/ID 2.170); GFPGr. 626, "Taetigkeitsbericht fuer Monat September 1942," 25 September 1942, Anlage 1, pp. 1–2 (GMDS, PzAOK 1, 24906/19, Anlage 16); H.Geb. A, Abt. VII, "Tagebericht der Abteilung VII fuer die Zeit vom 16.11 bis 15.12.1942," 28 December 1942, pp. 1–2 (GMDS, EAP 99/159); H.Geb. A, Ia, "Monatsbericht" for October 1942, 8 November 1942, p. 1, and *ibid.* for November 1942, 8 December 1942, pp. 1–2 (both in GMDS, HGeb 31242/2).

[84] Wi In Kaukasus, Der Inspekteur, pp. 16–17; Chef Sipo u. SD, "Meldungen aus den besetzten Ostgebieten, Nr. 34," 18 December 1942, pp. 14, 26–32 (GMDS, DW SD 5).

[85] 73. Inf.Div., Befh. des rueckw. Gebietes, "Terminmeldungen zum 5.12.43," 3 December 1942, p. 6 (GMDS, 73 ID 27963/5). See also Vladimir Petrov, *My Retreat from Russia* (New Haven: Yale University Press, 1950), pp. 130–32.

[86] Gr. Wetzel, Ia/Ic, "Bandenbekaempfung," 11 March 1943 (GMDS, V AK 41306/10, Anlage 34); Chef Sipo u.SD/EK 10a, Teilkdo Krymskaja, "An das V. A.K. Ic," 1 February 1943 (GMDS, V AK 41306/10, Anlage 17).

[87] 73. Inf.Div., Ic, "Taetigkeitsbericht," April 1943, p. 4, and *ibid.,* May 1943, p. 9 (GMDS, 73 ID 38849).

[88] Gr. Wetzel, Ia, "Fernschreiben an Kgl. rum. Kav. Korps . . . ," 17 March 1943 (GMDS, V AK 38037/4, Anlage 210).

But even these extreme measures could not compensate for the exposed position of the German bridgehead. In the end the V Corps realized its weakness:

> The Kuban bridgehead must be built up into a fortress. Every hill and every elevation must be a strong point by itself ... but if the necessary manpower is not provided, it will be merely a question of time until the defense of Novorossiisk collapses and the bridgehead's inevitable decrease in size will take place under the most difficult conditions.[89]

Several times Soviet forces attacked the bridgehead and gradually succeeded in whittling it down. It is indicative of the double weakness in the area—German jitters about agents and partisans, and the virtual nonexistence of such agents—that in August 1943 the Seventeenth Army promised a three weeks' furlough to every soldier apprehending a Soviet partisan or agent. Such a promise would have been unthinkable in Belorussia or the Bryansk forests, where it would have reduced the available German forces below any operational level; however, it reflected the determination of the German command to ferret out all "enemies."[90]

From the spring of 1943 on, what little population remained in the area of the Kuban bridgehead was overwhelmingly hostile to the Germans. All the benefits previously accumulated by a German policy aimed at the creation of popular good will were thrown to the wind in a composite of ruthlessness and defeat.

§II. The Caucasus Partisans:

Two Case Studies

The partisan units operating in the area between Rostov and the Greater Caucasus Mountains may be divided into three major types.

The Neftegorsk partisans represent a complex of several local destruction battalions operating in close conjunction with the Soviet command, withdrawing across the front line over the undefended mountain paths, and sallying forth into German-held territory for special operations. In this area the higher headquarters, evidently unique in Soviet partisan warfare, was a *kust*—literally, a "bush." The image was that of a stem, or center, controlling and directing the outlying branches.

[89] Gr. Wetzel, Ia/Ic, "Beurteilung der Lage," 8 May 1943 (GMDS, V AK 40394/3, Anlage 334).
[90] AOK 17, Ic/AO ["Nr. 1640/43 g."], 21 August 1943 (GMDS, XXXXIX AK 42047/22, Anlage 18). Evidently only limited use was made of this provision. It naturally encouraged the denunciation of innocent men in the troops' attempt to obtain furloughs.

The Yegorov complex represents a concentration of several widely scattered destruction battalions or detachments for operation in a sector to which the Soviet command attributed special importance. [For a discussion of the identity of Yegorov himself, see below, subsection A, 7.]

The Kalmyk area reveals another no man's land into which occasional groups of partisans were sent from the Soviet side. After completing specific assignments, they returned to their original bases.

The activities of the Yegorov complex and the partisan group of the Kalmyk area are described in some detail, for they present many especially interesting features.

A. THE YEGOROV COMPLEX

The origin of the partisan groups of the Yegorov complex must be traced back to the six or more battalions from whose cadres they were formed. Three of these—Anapa, Varenikovskaya, and Verkhne-Bakanskaya—were located in the area in which Yegorov's men operated; the others came from localities considerably farther north: Shcherbinovka, Kamyshevatka, and Rostov. The southward movement of the latter groups falls into the general pattern of partisan units withdrawing to the wooded and mountainous areas.

1. Shcherbinovka

The Shcherbinovka Destruction Battalion (actually of company size) was established at the end of July 1942, at the time of the new German offensive against Rostov. Its initial strength was seventy men and five women—more or less normal for a destruction unit in this area. The formation of the "battalion" was greatly assisted by the rayon NKVD. After fulfilling its functions as a destruction unit—demolishing the local electric power station, a mill, and (as a German report put it) "other objects of military importance"—the group, early in August and just ahead of the German troops, moved southward into the area of Gostagayevskaya.[91] The selection of this locale is significant: (a) the same vicinity was assigned to several other destruction units—suggesting movements on a regional level; (b) the area east and south of Gostagayevskaya was the closest forest and mountain area (the coastal region from Shcherbinovka south abounded in swamps and lagoons, but the orders deprived the partisans of the opportunity to hide there and instructed them to travel on to Gostagayevskaya, over 150 miles away); (c) in view of the uniformity of this practice, one might surmise that the Red Army command did not

[91] Einsatzkommando 10a, Br.B.Nr. 16/43, "Schtscherbinowskaja-Bande," 6 January 1943 [hereafter cited as Einsatzkommando 10a], pp. 1–2 (GMDS, V AK 41306/10, Anlage 2).

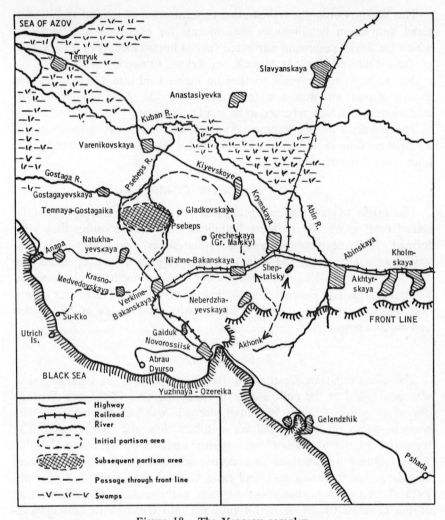

SEA OF AZOV

Temryuk

Slavyanskaya

Anastasiyevka

Kuban R.

Varenikovskaya

Kiyevskoye

Gostaga R.

Gostagayevskaya

Psebeps R.

Krymskaya

Abin R.

Temnaya-Gostagaika

Gladkovskaya

Psebeps

Natukha-yevskaya

Grecheskaya
(Gr. Mansky)

Abinskaya

Kholm-skaya

Anapa

Nizhne-Bakanskaya

Shep-talsky

Akhtyr-skaya

Krasno-Medvedovskaya

Verkhne-Bakanskaya

Neberdzha-yevskaya

FRONT LINE

Su-Kko

Utrich Is.

Gaiduk

Novorossiisk

Akhonk

Abrau Dyurso

BLACK SEA

Yuzhnaya - Ozereika

Gelendzhik

Pshada

━━┿━━┿━━	Highway
	Railroad
	River
⌐ ⌐ ⌐	Initial partisan area
▨	Subsequent partisan area
━ ━ ━	Passage through front line
—V—\(—V	Swamps

Figure 18.—The Yegorov complex.

anticipate stopping the Germans north of the Caucasus mountain area—a hypothesis that will need to be considered in another context.

Evidently the decision to move south came as something of a surprise to the destruction unit, whose supplies and food stocks had been concealed, in accordance with the general practice, in bunkers and caches near Shcherbinovka. These were abandoned in the southward move and in part were later uncovered by the Germans on the basis of leads supplied by informants and captured documents.[92]

[92] 454. Sich.Div., Ic, "Taetigkeitsbericht fuer den Monat Oktober 1942," 7 November 1942, p. 1 (GMDS, 454 ID 34026/4). Evidently some partisans in the general vicinity of Shcherbinovka remained on the spot, particularly near Alexandrovka and Yeisk. See also n. 97, below.

The unit was commanded by Mikhail Kleshnev, inspector of the Shcherbinovka *raiispolkom;*[93] the commissar was one Salsky, a Communist fanatic.[94] After some twenty-five men had been lost through desertion, sickness, or German action, the unit was organized into two platoons of twenty-one men each, and a headquarters detachment consisting of Kleshnev and his wife, the commissar, a medical officer, a nurse, two cooks, and a baker.[95]

From Gostagayevskaya, the unit moved into the adjacent wooded mountain area, where a summer camp was established. Soon after—probably still in August—a winter camp was built on the Temnaya Gostagaika River (southeast of Gostagayevskaya), where several of the other units that were to come under Yegorov's command had already arrived. When and how first contact with the neighboring groups was established and their eventual subordination to one command was effected, the Germans were unable to learn. From September on, the group was idle except for a reconnaissance platoon, whose functions, according to the Germans, included:

... the provision of food, intelligence on German and Rumanian troops, providing names of the *Buergermeister* and chiefs of [indigenous] militia installed by the German troops. In addition, it carried out an attack on a German truck, in which the German officer ... was murdered and the truck seized; twice it exploded [strips of] track of the railroad near Nizhne-Bakanskaya. Furthermore members of the band lured the *Buergermeister* of Gladkovskaya from his home and kidnapped him. . . .

That the Shcherbinovka partisans cooperated with the neighboring groups is illustrated by the fact that while this unit kidnapped the mayor, members of the Varenikovskaya group killed him. Other operations were planned jointly with the various partisan units in the area. The Shcherbinovka group had its contact men and informants in various towns in the area, where, among other things, it distributed leaflets reproduced in the unit under the direction of its energetic politruk, Dyatlenko.[96]

2. Kamyshevatka

A second unit came from Kamyshevatka, likewise over 150 miles to the north. Its history, available in less detail, appears to have paralleled that of the Shcherbinovka group, except for a greater passivity and probably greater disorganization within the unit. It also made the trek south under

---

[93] Rayon executive committee.

[94] 9. Inf.Div., Ic, "Vernehmung eines Banditen," 13 December 1942 (GMDS, 9 ID 30150/4, Anlage 145) [hereafter cited as 9. Inf.Div., Ic, "Vernehmung eines Banditen"]; and Einsatzkommando 10a, pp. 1–2.

[95] 9. Inf.Div., Ic, "Vernehmung eines Banditen."

[96] Einsatzkommando 10a, pp. 1–2. Contact men are listed in Gostagayevskaya, Krasnyi Psebeps, Greko-Maisky, Prokhladnyi, and Kurandupe.

its commander, Zavchenko, and commissar, Goncharov, and established itself in the hills southeast of Gostagayevskaya.[97]

3. Rostov

The third unit descending from the north was something of an anomaly. For reasons that are not entirely clear, this detachment from Rostov (located in the adjacent oblast to the north) joined the movement toward the mountains north of Novorossiisk, arriving near Verkhne-Bakanskaya in late August. As will be shown, it is likely that the Rostov area was attached to the North Caucasus partisan command before the Germans arrived. At

Figure 19.—The staging area of the Yegorov complex.

Verkhne-Bakanskaya, the Rostov unit divided; some of its men (at least seventeen and perhaps more) joined the local partisan unit; the remainder crossed the mountains, southeast of Novorossiisk, and established themselves at Pshada, a village southeast of Gelendzhik, located, as in the case of the Neftegorsk kust, not far from the front lines and in the sector of the Soviet Black Sea Front.

[97] Einsatzkommando 10a, "Bandenunternehmung bei Prikubanskij," 6 January 1943, p. 2 (GMDS, V AK 41306/10, Anlage 1); *ibid.*, "Schtscherbinowskaja-Bande," 6 January 1943, p. 3 (GMDS, V AK 51306/10, Anlage 2); 73. Inf.Div., Ic, "Vernehmung des Kalatschow, Eugen Wassiljewitsch," 15 January 1943, p. 3 (GMDS, V AK

The group that remained in the Verkhne-Bakanskaya area was under the command of Kuzma Andreyevich Miroshnichenko, who had been a school inspector in the area west of Rostov; the commissar, Nikolai Ivanovich Halchenko, came from the same area; both were Ukrainians. The members included two youthful radio men and a shoemaker from Azov, who had joined the unit on its way south.[98] These Rostov partisans remained rather inactive.[99]

The group that had moved south to Pshada was even more immobilized on the Soviet side of the front. The actual headquarters in command of its operations, reportedly under strong NKVD influence, was a few miles from Akhonk, in the mountains east of Novorossiisk. This location suggests that the staff came from Novorossiisk—a hypothesis reinforced by the fact that the commander at Akhonk, a certain Popov, had been secretary of the Party *raikom* of Novorossiisk. Equally important is the fact that Akhonk was closest to the gap in the German lines east of Neberdzhayevskaya, through which a considerable part of the physical contact between the Soviet side and partisans operating in the German rear was maintained. Only in December did this group cross the front line back into German-held territory to participate in partisan action.[100]

41306/10, Anlage 6) [hereafter cited as 73. Inf.Div., Ic].

It is likely that other units from the region between Rostov and Novorossiisk were also slated to proceed south toward the same area of concentration. The Temryuk partisans, commanded by two secretaries of the local Party unit and including "almost all politruks, commissars, leaders of Party offices, leaders of the NKVD, and political agencies" were organized into groups of from twelve to seventeen men. The Germans located several officers and at least one of the NKVD espionage officials from Temryuk in the Gladkovskaya area, where the Yegorov group was concentrated (see Fig. 19). At least a part of the Temryuk unit did, however, remain in the vicinity of its home base. (Abwehrtrupp 301, "Bericht ueber die Taetigkeit des Abwehrtrupps 301," 26 September 1942, GMDS, V AK 26340/9.)

Other units were established near the port of Primorsko-Akhtarskaya, at the northern end of a vast swamp area on the Sea of Azov. The German forces identified what they suspected was a sizable partisan unit here in the first days of September 1942. Evidently it consisted of local residents as well as Red Army and Red Navy personnel cut off by the speedy German advance east of this naval base. The unit— the Germans exaggeratedly feared it to be 500-men strong—heavily mined the vicinity and withdrew into the swamps. By the middle of September, German estimates of its strength had dropped to thirty-five men, of whom ten surrendered voluntarily. Some evidently moved southward, probably trying to join the Gostagayevskaya-Bakansk concentration. The Germans had little trouble with the remaining group near Primorsko-Akhtarskaya. By the end of October its members had scattered, and most of them were apprehended. (Korueck 550, "Kriegstagebuch Nr. 11," Anlagen 118, 127, 168, 203, 336, GMDS, Korueck 26772/2, 3, 4; and AOK 17, Ia," Bandenlage vom 14.8.— 15.12.42," GMDS, AOK 17, 25354/26, Anlage 9.)

[98] 9. Inf.Div., Ic, "Bandengruppen," 2 December 1942 (GMDS, 9 ID 30150/4, Anlage 140); Einsatzkommando 10a, Teilkommando Krymskaja, "Banden," 1 February 1943 (GMDS, V AK 41306/10, Anlage 17).

[99] 9. Inf.Div., Ic, "Feindl. Banden- und Agententaetigkeit," 11 November 1942, p. 2 (GMDS, 9 ID 30150/4).

[100] Einsatzkommando 10a, Teilkommando Krymskaja, "Banden," 1 February 1943, p. 3 (GMDS, V AK 41306/10, Anlage 17).

4. Bakansk

The local Verkhne-Bakanskaya partisan unit, composed of men from the rayon, remained initially in the area of its formation. Later it absorbed the Rostov group, and a part of its members withdrew southward to Pshada. About forty men remained in the area under the command of Kuzma Vorobyov, formerly chairman of the Party cell at the Verkhne-Bakanskaya cement plant; the commissar, Sergei Zadremailov, had been

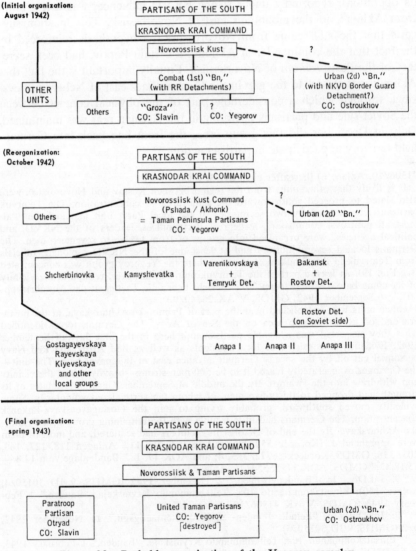

Figure 20.—Probable organization of the Yegorov complex.

secretary of the Party committee at Verkhne-Bakanskaya; other officers were Ivan Babiyev, head of the NKVD branch there, and Ivan Yurchenko, the adjutant, who had been in charge of the local army recruitment office (*voyenkomat*). There is no evidence of extensive unit activity until November.[101]

5. Varenikovskaya

The Varenikovskaya unit began in a similar manner, moving into the mountain forests east of Gostagayevskaya when the Germans approached. The uniformity of the pattern becomes strikingly apparent: the group did not seek concealment in the excellent swamps of the Kuban River close to its home town.[102]

6. Anapa

More complex, and in this region unique, was the organization of the destruction battalion in Anapa. Perhaps the larger population[103] accounted for the larger groups recruited here. Actually, three distinct units were created which, though operating jointly, were organized independently. Each of them conformed to the median size of from fifty to one hundred members. The three units jointly constituted the Anapa Destruction Battalion (as of June 1942). In August, in anticipation of the German arrival, the NKVD (through its chief for Anapa Rayon, Vladimir Bulavenko, who had the over-all responsibility for the unit, and the battalion's chief of staff, Pavel Akimovich Frolov, chief of the Anapa Party *raikom*) divided the battalion into its three constituent units—thenceforth known as Anapa I, Anapa II, and Anapa III. The three groups moved eastward toward Krymskaya—precisely into the area on which the other five partisan units were converging.[104]

Anapa I (code name "Anyuta") was commanded by Kuzma Prikhodko, a local official; Frolov became the unit's commissar. At first located east of Natukhayevskaya, where it had ample food supplies and led a "pleasant

[101] 9. Inf.Div., Ic, "Bandengruppen," 2 December 1942, p. 2 (GMDS, 9 ID 30150/4, Anlage 140); 9. Inf.Div., Ic, "Feindl. Banden- und Agententaetigkeit," 11 November 1942 (GMDS, 9 ID 30150/4, Anlage 133). Peter Ignatov, *Zapiski partizana* (Moscow: Gosizdat, 1949), in an interesting but not always reliable account of partisan warfare in this area, states that the Bakansk rayon unit was under the command of a Cossack chairman of a stanitsa soviet, "Nikolai Vasilyevich," whose last name is not given (p. 535). There is no evidence in the German files to corroborate this statement.

The unit also included several women partisans (among them the former chief of the Special Section of the Verkhne-Bakanskaya *raiispolkom*) as well as some straggler soldiers who joined the group in the woods.

[102] 73. Inf.Div., Ic.

[103] Anapa is a port on the Black Sea with a 1939 population of over 15,000.

[104] 9. Inf.Div., Ic, "Vernehmungs-Ergebnisse," 7 December 1942 (GMDS, 9 ID 30140/4, Anlage 141); 73. Inf.Div., Ic, p. 3; AOK 17, Ic/AO, "Fahndungsliste," 5 December 1942 (GMDS, AOK 17, 25354/38) [hereafter cited as AOK 17, Ic/AO, "Fahndungsliste"], pp. 3, 18 (which claims, perhaps erroneously, that Frolov had been an NKVD official).

life" (as its chief of staff later told the Germans), as the result of German combing operations the unit was forced to move northeastward in mid-September. From its new base on the Temnaya Gostagaika River, where the Shcherbinovka detachment was already established, it engaged in only two operations before November—blowing up a bridge at Anapskaya and twice laying three road mines between Natukhayevskaya and Krasnyi Psebeps, on a mountain road scarcely frequented by the Germans. Even later, when the partisan groups were spurred to greater activity, its orders were still "not to engage in combat actions."[105]

Anapa II (code name "Oryol," i.e., "eagle") was initially commanded by Bulavenko himself, the Anapa NKVD chief. Like its fellow units, it was relatively inactive; since Bulavenko appears to have maintained general supervisory powers over the three units in the first two months of the German occupation, radio contact was maintained between his headquarters and Anapa I and III.[106]

Anapa III (code name "Sokol," i.e., "falcon") was a smaller unit with headquarters near the Nizhne-Bakanskaya railroad line. It was evidently not sufficiently strong or well organized to fend for itself and received supplies from the adjacent Varenikovskaya and Shcherbinovka groups. Its commander, Mitrofan Tereshchenko, had previously been an official of the Anapa Party *raikom;* its commissar, Dmitrii Kravchenko, was reportedly a local Communist. Neither of them seems to have been an effective or popular leader. Once again, its activities until November were insignificant.[107]

As the result of their operations in November and of the heavy casualties sustained by the groups, the three Anapa partisan detachments were reunited into one Combined Anapa Group totaling twenty-seven men. Bulavenko again became commander and Frolov, commissar—the two men who had, evidently at the behest of the NKVD, organized the entire Anapa enterprise half a year earlier.[108]

7. Reorganization

There have been ample suggestions in the above material that the partisans in this area were steered from one higher headquarters; that their

[105] 9. Inf.Div. and 73. Inf.Div., Ic. After its movement out of the Natukhayevskaya area, its food caches there were betrayed to the Germans by two deserters from Anapa I.

[106] 73. Inf.Div., Ic, pp. 1, 3. Radio equipment and at least one of the Anapa radio operators were supplied by the Red Army.

The German records abound in confusions between Anapa II and III. The above statement is based on the testimony of the Anapa Chief of Staff, Yevgenii Kalachev, perhaps the most reliable of the captured partisans.

[107] *Ibid.;* 9. Inf.Div., Ic, "Vernehmungs-Ergebnisse," 7 December 1942 (GMDS, 9 ID 30140/4, Anlage 141).

[108] 73. Inf.Div., Ic.

withdrawal from their home areas and their concentration in the forests north of the Anapa-Krymskaya line were planned in advance; and that the selection and direction of the new combined group were in line with a broader Soviet policy for the use of partisans in this region. Organization and control, as usual, were in the hands of trusted Party and NKVD personnel. All the units were of urban origin, and only very few members appear to have joined "spontaneously" after the initial organization of the groups. Likewise, the number of military stragglers who joined the partisans was minimal. The degree to which the six groups displayed any operational activity varied; but, even granting their relatively small size, the zeal and effectiveness of the units compared unfavorably with that of most partisan organizations in other major areas of partisan activity.[109]

The first mention of the partisans in this area in a German report on a corps or army level relates to late September; until then their activity appears to have been scarcely noticed by the Germans.[110] In an effort to spur the units to greater action, to induce better coordination and perhaps subordination, and possibly to improve liaison with Soviet army headquarters, a new commander arrived early in October. The identity of the man, Yegorov, remains in dispute. It appears most likely that he was the Viktor Alexandrovich Yegorov described in a German document as the former NKVD representative for the Novorossiisk railroad network. This identification is plausible because (1) the entire operation (as the description of the Akhonk headquarters suggests) was organized with active NKVD support; (2) independent evidence confirms the organization of partisan units by the NKVD from among the personnel of the Novorossiisk railroad; (3) the man who led the subsequent rescue operation aimed at contacting Yegorov was one Slavin, who had been in command of the railroaders' partisan unit, "Groza."[111] Furthermore, Yegorov came to his

---

[109] It is probable that additional units from this area (from Kiyevskaya and Rayevskaya) were slated for inclusion in this group. Some small units operated in the area west and southeast of Krymskaya, along the Novorossiisk-Krasnodar railroad, especially at Taponov and Abinskaya. Some of these operations were carried out by detachments of other partisan units stationed farther away. Several of the locally recruited groups evidently dispersed and returned to their homes without effectively participating in the struggle. (See Gr. Wetzel, Ic, "Vortrag von Oblt. Dr. Roesch ueber Bandenlage," 31 December 1942, p. 1, GMDS V AK 29052/2, Anlage 62 [hereafter cited as Gr. Wetzel, Ic]; Banden-Jgd. Kdo. Lt. Nieland, "Bericht ueber die Taetigkeit des Kommandos," 2 October 1942, GMDS, 9 ID 30150/4, Anlage 115; 9. Inf.Div., Ic, "Feindliche Banden- und Agententaetigkeit," 11 November 1942, p. 2 GMDS, 9 ID 30150/4, Anlage 133.) The indigenous groups operating near Krymskaya are not to be confused with new, and more effective ones, landed from behind the Soviet lines north of Novorossiisk in December. (See Wi In Kaukasus, 2. Staffel, AO, "Beitrag zum Kriegstagebuch fuer die Zeit vom 15. bis 31.12.42," 8 February 1943, GMDS, Wi/ID 2.248.)

[110] AOK, 17, Ia, "Bandenlage voc 14.8.—15.12.42" (GMDS, AOK 17, 25354/26, Anlage 9).

[111] A German summary states that the Soviet antiaircraft organization (PVO, *Protivo-vozdushnaya oborona*) organized three partisan groups of about twenty men

command post in the hills from Su-Kko, a town on the coast north of Novorossiisk.[112]

His appearance and assumption of command appear to have caused no noticeable strife within the partisan units. The smooth acceptance of his direction strongly suggests that he carried orders from higher headquarters and that the partisan groups were directed to accept his command. Unusual in this connection and probably indicative of the degree to which he and his Soviet superiors distrusted the local partisan leadership was the fact that he became both commander and commissar of what was now known as the "United Taman Partisans" (for Taman Peninsula). As chief of staff, he selected Yevgenii Kalachev, originally chief of staff of Anapa I, a Red Army officer in the Civil War but (at least so his German interrogators believed after his subsequent capture) not politically active under the Soviets, and formerly an economist and statistician in Anapa.[113]

It is obvious that Yegorov found the units in what he considered a most unsatisfactory state. One of his first moves was to replace some of the unit commanders,[114] and generally to tighten discipline. He communicated to

each in Novorossiisk. (The use of the PVO system for the organization of partisan units is confirmed by a Soviet account for the Krasnodar area; see Ignatov, p. 12.) These were supervised "by the NKVD through a lieutenant of State Security," possibly Yegorov. The units in question withdrew into the mountains north and northeast of the city. One of them was led by Slavin. (Abwehrtrupp 301, "Taetigkeitsbericht ... in Noworossijsk," 26 September 1942, p. 3, GMDS, V AK 26349/9; and 9. Inf.Div., Ic, "Vernehmungs-Bericht," 16 September 1942, GMDS, 9 ID 30150/4, Anlage 109; Ignatov, pp. 535, 555; Ignatov, *Na Tamani* [Moscow: Vozenizdat, 1946], pp. 4–5.)

[112] 73. Inf.Div., Ic, "Vernehmung," 15 January 1943, p. 3 (GMDS, V AK 41306/10, Anlage 6). There is considerable confusion in German sources on Yegorov's name: some call him Viktor Alexandrovich and others speak of him as Alexei. Soviet accounts, doubtlessly for reasons of *konspiratsiya,* describe him as "Yegorin" without giving any details. (Ignatov, pp. 555–98; and Ignatov, *Na Tamani,* pp. 4, 61.) He was, at any rate, not identical with the Captain Yegorov who headed the Nalchik militia and organized the partisans along the Terek River. (See GFP Gr. 626 ["Memorandum"], 8 October 1942, p. 1, GMDS, 3 PzD 30938/55.)

A number of partisan units operated in the coastal area between Anapa and Novorossiisk, especially near the Su-Kko and Topolnaya gaps as well as Lake Abrau. According to German accounts, they "maintained regular contact with motor torpedo boats and gunboats, which constantly appeared along the coast, by means of light signals and perhaps by radio as well." (Gr. Wetzel, Ic.) As in Yeisk and Primorsko-Akhtarskaya, a number of regular army and especially naval troops appear to have participated. (V. AK, Ia, "Kriegstagebuch II, Heft 7," entry for 25 September 1942, GMDS, V. AK, 26340/2.) Late in October and again in November, German anti-partisan operations were carried out to wipe out these units, as well as those farther inland at Krasno-Medvedovskaya. (10. Rumaenische Inf.Div., GenSt, Buero 2, "Bericht ueber die Banditensaeuberungsaktion im Abschnitt des IR 38," 31 October 1942, GMDS, 73 ID 27963/5, Anlage 736; and Chef Sipo u. SD, "Meldungen aus den besetzten Ostgebieten," No. 29, 13 November 1942, GMDS, DW-SD 5.)

[113] 73. Inf.Div., Ic, p. 1.

[114] Thus, upon his arrival, he demoted and ousted from their positions the commander and commissar of the Varenikovskaya group, Matveyev and Tarasov. (9. Inf.Div., Ic, "Vernehmung eines Banditen.") The new commander of Varenikovskaya was Pavel Begunov.

the units a Soviet order, giving them the choice between increasing their activity or withdrawing to the Soviet side of the front (for subsequent service in the Red Army). While there were clearly elements whose enthusiasm was short of the Soviet ideal and while there were sick, wounded, and over-age partisans whose evacuation across the front lines was desirable, a major factor contributing to a lowering of morale and to the ensuing decision to move some men to the Soviet side was the critical food shortage. Some of the supply bases of the units had been abandoned near their original places of organization; other supplies had been used up; still others had been discovered and plundered by the indigenous population. Indicative of the isolation of the partisans and the neglible extent to which they found support among the rank and file of the local residents is the fact that the population provided them with virtually no food. The supply situation became so critical by late October and early November that Yegorov informed his offiers that "extensive marches" were about to begin. Those unfit to undertake them—primarily old, sick, and weak partisans[115]—were to be sent to the Soviet side of the lines.[116] About 20 October a sizable part of the Verkhne-Bakanskaya unit made an unsuccessful attempt to cross the lines and escape southward. Having failed to cross in force, the group broke up into small squads in order to cross at the gap south of Neberdzhayevskaya. The Germans calculated that of the original Verkhne-Bakanskaya group only a headquarters team of four men remained behind on occupied soil for the purpose of organizing a new partisan unit.[117] While a few men may have made the crossing successfully, the bulk evidently remained near the front zone in small and scattered groups which repeatedly tried to find the gap and in the process were slowly decimated by the Germans.[118]

Late in November another group of sixteen men started off from the Shcherbinovka and Anapa groups. Commanded by the demoted Matveyev, whom Yegorov had evidently ordered out of the area, the detachment included at least four women and one fourteen-year-old boy. Matveyev had orders to proceed across the front to the Gelendzhik area (probably to

---

[115] 9. Inf.Div., Ic, "Banden- und Spionagebekaempfung," 11 December 1942 (GMDS, 9 ID 30150/4, Anlage 148).

[116] 9. Inf.Div., Ic, "Vernehmung eines Banditen."

[117] 9. Inf.Div., Ic, "Feindl. Banden- und Agententaetigkeit," 11 November 1942 (GMDS, 9 ID 30150/4, Anlage 133). The German report states that up to that date the Verkhne-Bakanskaya group had apparently not participated in any attacks or raids on German installations or personnel but "was fully occupied by relieving the extraordinarily difficult food situation, which is due largely to the negative attitude of the population toward the bandits and the lack of food supplies." (*Ibid.*, p. 2) The movement across the front was led by one Bobrov, whom the German roster confusingly described as an "agricultural commissar" and a Party member from Verkhne-Bakanskaya. (9. Inf.Div., Ic, "Bandengruppen," 2 December 1942, p. 3, GMDS, 9 ID 30150/4, Anlage 140.)

[118] 73. Inf.Div., Befh. des rueckw. Geb., "Terminmeldungen zum 20.12.42." 20 December 1942, pp. 5–6 (GMDS, 73 ID 27963/5); Gr. Wetzel, Ic.

Pshada). But Matveyev, obviously disgusted with the treatment he had been accorded by Yegorov, deserted his team with a twenty-year-old girl who had become his mistress; she was the daughter of the German-installed mayor of Varenikovskaya, where the couple hoped to hide. The remainder of the team proceeded to cross the Verkhne-Bakanskaya-Krymskaya railroad, avoiding towns and hiding in the forests. Failing to find the gap in the front line, the group wandered around aimlessly for weeks, living mainly on corn cobs. (Since the gap was sizable and frequently traveled by partisans, their failure must have been due to lack of adequate orientation and liaison.) Early in December it split into three sections, each of which was to attempt a crossing alone. By the middle of the month, at least six members had been killed or captured by the Germans, and another two or more had deserted. For all practical purposes, the group ceased to exist.[119]

Without going into details of subsequent operations, it may suffice to state that in the following two months Yegorov dispatched additional groups across the lines every time the situation on occupied soil became difficult. These tactics, coinciding as they did with similar practices in other sectors of the front from Novorossiisk southeastward, make plausible the assumption that they stemmed from directives from higher headquarters which, sensing the futility of sacrificing the remaining partisan forces, preferred to withdraw, retrain, and reorganize them for action at a more propitious moment.

Meanwhile Yegorov reorganized his remaining force—a total of some 260 men out of an original group of about 500. Its orders were to avoid battle with the Germans and their allies and to carry out raids in small detachments. Motivated partly by the need for food, the activity was stepped up from late October on. So long as Yegorov's control was effective, the rate of desertion appears to have been low; only when groups separated did they easily succumb to the temptation of returning to a "peaceful civilian life."

8. Destruction

So long also as Yegorov's men were in control of a substantial area, crucial not so much by its size as by its proximity to several key arteries of communications, they remained a thorn in the German flesh, since supplies for forthcoming German operations southward were scheduled to be brought in by rail and truck from Krasnodar to Novorossiisk. At the same time, Yegorov's men raided the countryside. The Germans concluded that:

> The fact that they terrorize the rural population through forcible confiscation of food depresses it and makes it partially insecure. As a result of various abuses

[119] 9. Inf.Div., Ic, "Vernehmung eines Banditen"; 73. Inf.Div., Ic.

and even shootings the residents feel . . . in danger. Their attitude suffers particularly when German help is not promptly available or indigenous self-help cannot be promptly organized. . . .[120]

A first German raid on the Gladkovskaya area on 3 October led to the dispersal of the partisans, who, having been forewarned, scattered to avoid apprehension. Given the active participation of SD units in these operations, considerable severity was exerted. Yet the first German efforts were not successful in destroying the groups, which reorganized and soon renewed their "nuisance operations" against German supply roads and railroad lines.[121]

It was therefore decided to conduct a well-prepared operation against the partisans. German security police units in cooperation with the field gendarmerie were scheduled to begin their attack on 17 November. Yegorov, however, was again forewarned by his informants and observers in neighboring towns, and thus the German operation lost the crucial element of surprise even before it began. In the first two days, the Germans captured and destroyed two partisan camps which Yegorov had meanwhile abandoned by skillfully moving out of the area. In the following days a new attack was staged. Hard-pressed and numerically inferior to the attackers, the partisans broke through the sector of the encirclement held by Rumanian troops, and with some losses in manpower, supplies, and arms, moved into the area of Gornyi. (Yegorov himself led a foray into Su-Kko, where he had hidden before taking command of the unit, to replenish food stocks; later he returned to Gornyi.) Here it was decided on 24 November to send another group of men across the German lines; five of them surrendered, and the remainder evidently dispersed after failing to make it. When the Germans attacked again at the end of the month, Yegorov's men had moved out. With the antipartisan operation more and more in the hands of the SD, German tactics increased in ruthlessness and lack of discrimination. Thus on 29 November alone, the SK task force (*Einsatzkommando* 10a) killed 107 residents of Verkhne-Bakanskaya for "direct or indirect" connection with the partisans. Nevertheless, the partisans themselves escaped.[122]

Yegorov had meanwhile "streamlined" his depleted force by pooling the remnants of the three Anapa groups (as described above); the new Anapa

---

[120] Chef Sipo u. SD, "Meldungen aus den besetzten Ostgebieten," No. 29, 13 November 1942 (GMDS, DW SD 5).

[121] Gr. Wetzel, Ic; Gr. Wetzel, Ia/Ic, "Bandenbekaempfung," 5 October 1942 (GMDS, V AK 29095/2, Anlage 43).

[122] Gr. Wetzel, Ic, pp. 3–4; Chef Sipo u. SD, "Meldungen aus den besetzten Ostgebieten," No. 32, 4 December 1942 (GMDS, DW SD-5); 73. Inf.Div., Befh. des rueckw. Geb., "Terminmeldungen zum 5.12.42," 3 December 1942 (GMDS, 73 ID 27963/5); Einsatzkommando 10a, "Schtscherbinowskaja-Bande," 6 January 1943, p. 2 (GMDS, V AK 41306/10, Anlage 2).

and Varenikovskaya teams remained with the leader; the others tried to cross the front but the attempt failed. The partial German success in frustrating the effective operating ability of Yegorov was increased by severing his communications with some of the subordinate units. After losing contact with headquarters, the Shcherbinovka and Kamyshevatka groups, subordinated to one command, suffered a breakdown in discipline and morale: by mid-December only thirty-five of eighty-five men remained.[123]

A similar fate befell most of the other splinter groups. The most fanatical eighteen formed a new group under the command of Salsky, the extremist commissar of the Shcherbinovka unit, with Goncharov, commissar of the Kamyshevatka group, as commissar. Determined and well-armed, this small team was perhaps more feared by the Germans than had been the far larger and less active units whose remnants it represented. However, in a skirmish with the indigenous militia at Krasnyi Psebeps, it lost another six men. The remaining group, under Yegorov's command, tried and failed on Christmas Eve to cross the front line into Soviet-held territory, only to move north again in an attempt to cross the Kuban River. After sustaining heavy casualties, it was completely dispersed.[124]

By January 1943, just as the German troops were preparing to abandon the area, the partisans ceased to be a threat. Except for the "small but exceedingly dangerous Salsky group" the Germans had nothing to fear. Here and there partisans returned to abandoned forest camps (for instance, at Temnaya Gostagaika), but in the face of continued German antipartisan actions (involving SD detachments, part of an infantry division, Cossack troops fighting on the German side, Rumanians, and indigenous militia—

[123] Einsatzkommando 10a; 73. Inf.Div., Ic, p. 2. Eleven men from the Shcherbinovka group were sent back to their home base in December—in part, to escape German antipartisan operations, in part, to carry out sabotage assignments in an area with which they were familiar and where they had hidden food stores. This return movement in effect marked a recognition by the Soviet command of the error committed in ordering the unit south. (Einsatzkommando 10a, p. 2.) The only effective operation of the bands was the explosion of a bridge on the Verkhne-Bakanskaya–Krymskaya railroad.

[124] Einsatzkommando 10a; 73. Inf.Div., Ic; AOK 17, Ia, "Monatsmeldung ueber Bandenlage," 28 December 1942 (GMDS, AOK 17, 27760/14); Korueck 550, Ic, "Bandenmonatsmeldung," 23 January 1943, "Anlage 3 to Korueck/Ia Nr. 9/43 geh." (GMDS, Korueck 34678/2, Anlage 37). This attempt was similar to another unsuccessful operation in which about thirty-eight men under Kleshnev, former commander of the Shcherbinovka partisans, tried to cross the river at Prikubansky, but were ambushed by a German army unit.

The Germans, amply forewarned of Yegorov's coming attempt to cross the Kuban, had seized all fishing boats. Only a few partisans managed to get across the swamps and the Kuban and Abin Rivers. (See also Einsatzkommando 10a, "Bandenunternehmung bei Prikubanskij," 6 January 1943, GMDS, V AK 41306/10, Anlage 1.) At the same time, the Germans intensified combing operations north of the Kuban and as far north as Azov, Yeisk, and Anastasiyevskaya to apprehend such partisans as might attempt to return home. (*Ibid.*)

all in relatively small numbers) they were easily picked off.[125]

For the first six weeks of 1943 members of the same bands were identified by Germans on the same date in widely scattered areas. Their numbers were frantically seeking to hide, to escape German persecution, or to cross the front lines. In the overwhelming number of cases their efforts were in vain.

Noteworthy in this connection is the fact that even at this late date, when the German retreat from the Caucasus had already begun, the indigenous population occasionally helped the Germans apprehend the partisans.[126] Lack of food and the severe winter frost helped paralyze the partisans' will to resist. In one instance, the population captured two partisans who were "begging for bread and were half frozen." One of the key leaders of the entire partisan movement in this area, Commissar Frolov, was found frozen to death in mid-January.[127]

Paradoxically, just as the Yegorov partisans were exerting every effort to avoid the Germans and to stay alive, the Rostov unit, which had proceeded immediately to Pshada south of the front line and had been reinforced meanwhile with men from Gaiduk and Verkhne-Bakanskaya (to a total strength of twenty-eight men), crossed the front line from south to north between Akhonk and Neberdzhayevskaya in order to blow up bridges and rail installations between Novorossiisk and Krymskaya, and to report troop movements to the Soviet command. Raids on German vehicles proved futile although a few explosions were carried out. The group, which was to return to Pshada after completing its mission, was dispersed and in part destroyed by German forces in January.[128] Its remaining members presumably stayed in the occupied areas until the Red Army returned two weeks later.

[125] An additional unit, consisting of the destruction company formed at Gaiduk (north of Novorossiisk) had initially cooperated with the Varenikovskaya and Rostov groups. A part of its thirty-eight members returned home at an early date and abandoned the partisans. The remnant was seized or killed piecemeal. Its leader, Vladimir Chernov, second secretary of the Verkhne-Bakanskaya *raikom,* was seized late in January; its commissar was killed a few days earlier. (V. AK, Ic, "Taetigkeitsbericht, 1.1.43—30.6.43," entries for 19 and 21 January 1943, GMDS, V AK 41306/9; Einsatzkommando 10a, Teilkommando Krymskaja, "Banden," 1 February 1943, pp. 1–2, GMDS, V AK 41306/10, Anlage 17; and AOK 17, Ic/AO, "Fahndungsliste," p. 3.

[126] See, for instance, V. AK, Ic, "Taetigkeitsbericht, 1.1.43—30.6.43," entries for 21 January 1943, "Bandits caught by *Buergermeister,* auxiliary police and civilians"; and for 25 January: "Residents of Psebeps seize two partisans..." (GMDS, V AK 41306/9).

[127] V. AK, Ic, "Taetigkeitsbericht," entry for 21 January 1943 (GMDS, V AK 41306/9); 73. Inf.Div., Ic, p. 2.

[128] Einsatzkommando 10a, Teilkommando Krymskaja, "Banden," 1 February 1943 (GMDS, V AK, 41306/10, Anlage 17). The group included several men who had originally been with Yegorov but had fought their way across the lines, now returning to lead the new men. They were commanded by Vasilii Beznochenko, formerly first secretary of the Verkhne-Bakanskaya Rayon Party Committee.

Meanwhile Yegorov with his staff—a total of twelve men—returned to Su-Kko, then to the vicinity of Novorossiisk, apparently because he was well acquainted with this area. However, on the way eight of his twelve men deserted, remained behind, or died. Of the remaining four, his chief of staff Kalachev was captured on 12 January at the quarries of the "Proletarii" cement plant in the suburbs of Novorossiisk. Yegorov himself escaped. There is only one mention of Yegorov in the following weeks: a captive partisan claimed to have seen him and a few other partisans near Nizhne-Bakanskaya late in January.[129] By early February the area was under Soviet attack.

In a sense, neither German nor partisan objectives were attained. The Germans succeeded in dislodging the Yegorov bands but failed to destroy them as a unit and, in particular, failed to destroy their headquarters. Moreover, considering the small size of the partisan formation, German casualties were high. At the same time, the effectiveness of the partisans was crucially impaired by weather, terrain, German attacks, and failure to obtain significant popular support. The contribution of Yegorov's men to harassing or tying down German forces—let alone destroying their supplies and means of communication—was minor indeed. To the end, personnel was virtually limited to members of the original destruction battalions—not because the partisans wished it so but because of the reaction of the indigenous population.

A perspicacious intelligence officer of the German V Corps (which directed antipartisan warfare in this area) concluded that:

The constant skirmishes, the supply difficulties, and the winter weather make it impossible for a sizable group to operate. . . . The systematic effort to create a larger partisan organization has been crushed; further partisan operations can have only local significance. [Nevertheless] the lack of food and the weather will force the remnants of the bands to undertake more and more raids on kolkhozes, columns [of vehicles], and various strongpoints.[130]

One of the primary purposes of the Yegorov group was the interdiction of the flow of German supplies to the front through Novorossiisk.[131] In this, it failed. Nevertheless it continued to concentrate its efforts in this area. Its strategic value later led the Germans in their retreat to maintain a bridgehead north and south of the Kuban delta (Novorossiisk was the largest city); and similarly the Soviet command shifted its attention to this area in 1943 in an effort to clear the North Caucasus and prepare for a landing in the Crimea. After the winter frost and spring floods, small groups of partisans again made their appearance in the hills and forests north of Novorossiisk. The German aims to destroy the surviving nuclei had not

[129] *Ibid.;* 73. Inf.Div., Ic, p. 2. V. AK, Ic, "Taetigkeitsbericht," entries for 12 and 21 January 1943 (GMDS, V AK 41306/9).

[130] Gr. Wetzel, Ic, p. 4.

[131] 9. Inf.Div., Ic, "Banden- und Spionagebekaempfung," 11 December 1942 (GMDS, 9 ID 30150/4, Anlage 148).

been realized.[132] Yet the partisans who remained were unable to carry out any effective missions. Substantial Soviet help from the outside was still essential for the activation of units in the spring.

The subsequent history of the Yegorov band is shrouded in mysteries and contradictions. The Germans never quite found out what happened to it; the Soviet accounts are spotty and palpably untruthful. Apparently the partisan headquarters south of the lines lost contact with Yegorov early in 1943, and all efforts to locate him or even determine his fate failed. The only Soviet account dealing with Yegorov (and calling him Yegorin) frankly describes the situation as follows: "The Germans also crushed the headquarters of the Taman area partisans under Yegorin. His complex [*soyedineniye*] included the otryads[133] from Gostagayevskaya, Rayevskaya, Kiyevskaya and Varenikovskaya stanitsas, all grouped around the Anapa partisans. Contact with Yegorin ceased." The survivors had evidently split into small teams which maintained no liaison with the Soviet command. "The Headquarters of the Partisans of the South repeatedly sent its planes to Taman Peninsula [the Soviet account continues]. The fliers had the task of discovering the partisans, dropping them food and ammunition and, if possible, landing and flying out the sick and seriously wounded. But all efforts to find Yegorin's men failed."[134]

Meanwhile, by spring 1943, the command of the Partisans of the South had moved to Krasnodar, which had been reoccupied by the Red Army. It ordered the formation of a new unit to be parachuted into the area north of Novorossiisk. Consisting of 120 men, most of whom had lived there before the war, the otryad was placed under the command of Slavin, the former chief of the "Groza" unit, the detachment of Novorossiisk railroad partisans which had been all but destroyed by the Germans.[135]

---

[132] These aims were summarized in the directive issued by V Corps in January 1943: "As a result of destroying the most active bands, raiding and destroying their supply camps and bases, and constantly pursuing the remnant groups, the partisan organization in the sector [of this corps] has been so much demolished that it is unable to undertake substantial and systematic operations [and is] half-starved and weakened by the winter weather.... It is essential to track down and liquidate even the smallest partisan units so that there are no nuclei left in the spring to form new organizations." (V. AK, Ia/Ic, "Bandenbekaempfung," 17 January 1943, GMDS, V AK 41306/10, Anlage 8.)

[133] A Soviet term used generally to designate an independent partisan unit of relatively small size.

[134] Ignatov, pp. 535, 555.

[135] *Ibid.*, pp. 552, 556; and Ignatov, *Na Tamani,* p. 5. It is curious that the later of these two sources (1949) no longer gives the number or origin of these men, which are indicated in the earlier (1946) version. According to German interrogations of captured partisans, Slavin was a Jew. (9. Inf.Div., Ic, "Vernehmungsbericht," 16 September 1942, GMDS, 9 ID 30150/4, Anlage 109.) The fact that Slavin was sent in to find Yegorov supports the thesis that Yegorov, whom he knew personally, had also been an officer of the Novorossiisk Railroad NKVD. Slavin's group of 120 men consisted of four platoons and a headquarters detachment. Most of the men had not previously been partisans.

All four platoons were parachuted into the area west of Krymskaya. After about a week, they discovered some wounded men and corpses from Yegorov's units. Ignatov relates, "It was clear that the Germans had destroyed Yegorin's otryad. . . . Later it became known that Yegorin had treacherously been tricked into going to Rayevskaya ['treachery' suggests the work of an indigenous collaborator] and was handed over to the Germans."[136] According to the Soviet account, Yegorov never revealed his identity to the Germans. This seems likely, as his apprehension would surely have been widely heralded in German intelligence reports. Moreover, in June 1943 a German report spoke of the group uncovered in Novorossiisk which was providing support to "Yegorov's partisan group." The tasks of this group, seized on 11 June, were (according to German interrogation summaries):

. . . providing food and medicine for the Yegorov partisans, reporting on events in Novorossiisk, evacuating and transferring personnel who do not wish to be evacuated to the partisans; providing intelligence on the morale of the German Army and the mood of the civilian population; engaging in propaganda among the *Hiwis* [*Hilfswillige*, volunteer auxiliaries with the Germany Army]; and transferring Hiwis to the partisan group.

Commanded by "Ostroviyeshov," the Novorossiisk organization was set up to help and support the partisans north of the city.[137]

For Yegorov's ultimate fate we have only Ignatov's fantastic account, which must be rejected on several counts. According to him, Slavin had one of his officers play the role of an SS officer who inspected the Anapa jail, found Yegorov there, then staged a daredevil attack on it, freed Yegorov, and shipped him back by sea behind the Soviet lines.[138] This account is in clear contradiction to several known facts and, even if it has some real basis, is highly "romanticized."[139] Of Slavin's own unit, we are

---

[136] Ignatov, pp. 561–64.

[137] 73. Inf.Div., Ic, "Taetigkeitsbericht [for June 1943]," p. 14 (GMDS, 73 ID 38849); Kampfgr. von Buenau, Ic, "Feindnachrichtenblatt," 21 June 1943, p. 3 (GMDS, 73 ID 38849, Anlage 20).

Ostroviyeshov is identified as chief of staff of the "Second Destruction Battalion in the Enemy's Rear." It is possible that this was the Second Novorossiisk Destruction Battalion which had remained within the city, while the First (including Slavin and Yegorov) had left when the Germans approached. Moreover, given the German inexactitude in the spelling of Russian names, it is possible that "Ostroviyeshov" was in reality Alexander Ostroushko, commander of the NKVD Border Guard Detachment in Novorossiisk and later a partisan leader in the same area. (AOK 17, Ic/AO, "Fahndungsliste," pp. 17, 23.) In general, the Germans suspected the Border Guards of providing nuclei of partisan groups around Novorossiisk. (Armeegr. Ruoff, Ic/AO, "Besondere Anordnungen fuer die Partisanen- und Spionagebekaempfung [9]," 25 August 1942, p. 1, GMDS, AOK 17, 25354/38.)

[138] Ignatov, pp. 582–97.

[139] According to the earlier version, Yegorov merely "succeeded in escaping from the Anapa jail and participated in the last struggles for Taman" in September 1943. (Ignatov, *Na Tamani*, p. 61.) The later account claims that, when Yegorov was freed

told, only ten men survived.[140]

The Yegorov group thus represented an effort to impose a competent leadership on a number of destruction detachments combined under one command in what the Soviet leadership considered propitious terrain and a strategically important location. The failure of his units in 1942—in effect, their utter dissolution—reflected not so much Yegorov's lack of ability (of which there is no evidence) but rather the over-all situation in which his men, few in numbers, received little or no support from the indigenous population.

B. THE KALMYK AREA

A special situation obtained in the Kalmyk ASSR and the region south of it to the Terek River, the steppe and desert area between the Volga estuary and the Daghestan mountains near the Caspian Sea. This vast territory, economically of little value and poor in transportation, had an exceedingly fluid front line, with enormous gaps undefended by either side. For the German advance, it was a link between the Stalingrad front and the forces fighting around the oil fields of Mozdok and Groznyi; for the Soviet defense, it had some importance in preventing the enemy from reaching

---

from Anapa jail by the partisans, he was seriously ill. (Ignatov, p. 598.) According to this account, the fake SS officer, Berezhnyi, became Ignatov's friend after the war; the earlier version stated that Berezhnyi was killed in 1943. (Ignatov, *Na Tamani,* p. 61.) The whole account of Berezhnyi's exploits as an SS officer in Varenikovskaya and Anapa is strangely out of keeping with the balance of Ignatov's book. No dates or details are given, and he speaks of Yegorin, not Yegorov, although obviously the same person is meant. There are other reasons that lead to the dismissal of the Ignatov version: in every instance of successful exploits, the partisans received army and government decorations; there is no evidence of the bestowing of such honors on Yegorov's would-be liberators. Granting even that one man, Berezhnyi, knew enough German and was well enough versed in German organization to pass for an SS officer for several weeks (as Ignatov would have the reader believe), it is most unlikely that several of his men could act as rank-and-file SS men in German uniforms, mixing with German soldiers, without ever betraying themselves. The partisans' inadequate knowledge of the Germans is revealed in the account itself: Berezhnyi claimed to be one "Schwarz," allegedly an official sent by the "Gauleiter" of the Crimea to the Kuban area on an inspection. It should have been obvious to every German soldier that the "Gauleiter" (Alfred Frauenfeld) controlled only the northern approaches of the Crimea and had nothing to do with the German Army command there, let alone with the Kuban area. Even less believable is the fact that Schwarz was an SS officer. Finally, the German records nowhere mention either the Schwarz comedy or the Anapa jail break. These records include the reports of the Anapa and Varenikovksaya garrisons and Military Government Sections, and the diaries of V Corps and Seventeenth Army. It is inconceivable that none of these would have reported the facts and warned other units against a repetition of such an impersonation. (Monthly reports and special reports of OK 1/805 [Varenikovskaya] and OK 1/921 [Anapa], O Qu VII, GMDS, AOK 17, 51019/8; V. A.K., Ic, "Taetigkeitsbericht," 1 July—31 December 1943, GMDS, V AK 42202/1; AOK 17, Ic, "Eigene Nachrichtenblaetter vom 24.7.—22.10. 1943," GMDS, AOK 17, 38214/39.)

[140] Ignatov, *Na Tamani,* p. 61. The later version no longer admits the decimation of Slavin's detachment.

the Caspian Sea and advancing north along the Volga. The Soviets had hastily built a railway parallel to the Caspian shore line between Astrakhan and Kizlyar, connecting with the Transcaucasian Railway and providing the only rail link between Transcaucasia and the central parts of the USSR. The fluidity of the front line is well illustrated by the numerous deep penetrations of both sides, the Germans occasionally raiding the Astrakhan-Kizlyar line and advancing patrols to the Caspian, and Soviet cavalry advancing to the vicinity of Budyonovsk and beyond, a good one hundred miles behind the "front."

While the northern part of the Kalmyk ASSR was in the area of the German Fourth Panzer Army fighting near Stalingrad, its southern part and the adjacent area constitute an organic part of the region studied in this chapter. The partisan units operating here were under the same over-all command as those farther west. Two special factors must be borne in mind: (1) the absence of natural concealment in the desert and steppe, except in the swamps and on the islands along the Kuma and Manych Rivers, and the Manych Canal; and (2) the fact that the Kalmyk population apparently went further in collaborating with the Germans than did most other national groups.

In the few towns like Elista and Budyonovsk, units established before the Soviet withdrawal followed the same pattern as elsewhere; they included local destruction and sabotage teams as well as groups slated for regular partisan activity.[141] While the Germans suspected the existence of partisan units, during the first weeks of occupation they identified few, apprehended scarcely any, and were virtually undisturbed by them.[142] Yet these few encounters permitted the German Army authorities—short of personnel, and relying to a considerable extent on Cossack troops for anti-partisan activities—to identify some general characteristics of partisan organization in the area.

The over-all direction of partisan units lay in Astrakhan. This was a logical choice, since Astrakhan was both the nearest large city on the Soviet side of the lines, and also reputedly the headquarters of all partisan warfare in the Caucasus.[143] Most of the partisan operations appear to have

[141] In Elista the urban sabotage group, commissioned to burn down or blow up buildings occupied by the Germans, was uncovered by the Germans in November. It was headed by the German-appointed mayor and his deputy. (AOK 17, Ic/AO, "Besondere Anordnungen fuer Banden- und Spionagebekaempfung [11]," 5 December 1942, pp. 2–3, GMDS, AOK 17, 25354/38.)

[142] On 7 September, for instance, a German infantry patrol and a gendarmerie detachment sought to apprehend a group of partisans in the "impenetrable" Manych swamps near Novo-Manychevskoye, but without success. (444. Sich.Div., Ic, "Kriegstagebuch," entry for 7 September 1942, GMDS, 444 ID 30260/2.) [hereafter cited as 444. Sich.Div., Ic, "Kriegstagebuch"]

[143] On Astrakhan as the point from which partisan warfare was directed in the area between the lower Volga and the Terek Rivers, see *ibid.*, entry for 19 December;

originated there; indeed, the partisans who were left behind displayed little activity and in all probability dispersed and returned home. The main base on the Soviet side from which partisan detachments and supplies were taken across the lines was at Chernyi Rynok, a town south of the Manych Canal near the Caspian Sea and located on the new Kizlyar-Astrakhan railroad. Ammunition depots, supply dumps, and an airfield were located there, evidently with the specific task of supporting and supplying the partisans.[144]

Most partisan activities in this area consisted of raiding parties sent out from time to time from headquarters on the Soviet side of the front and returning there. Some of these groups were sent in on foot, some on horse and camel back; still others were parachuted in. One must distinguish, however, between occasional operations, primarily to gather intelligence, staged by Soviet army units in this region,[145] and the more widespread activities emanating from Astrakhan and Chernyi Rynok headquarters.

In only one known instance did the Red Army itself organize partisan units (a German impression which may be erroneous).[146] Finally, the NKVD played its part, largely perhaps by providing some leadership to the locally formed partisan groups. This is exemplified by the action on 10 September, the first encounter of some consequence, in the area between Kaya-Sulu and Terekli-Mekteb, a stretch abandoned by the Red Army but never properly occupied by the Germans. The closest German garrison (O.K. I/829 at Achikulak) dispersed the partisan band with the aid of indigenous auxiliary troops. "The band's camp was located in a hilly steppe area to which no paths led; it was well camouflaged and prepared for defense." Of the thirty or thirty-five partisans, four were killed and five surrendered; the others escaped, since the Germans decided that "they could not be pursued, because of the difficult terrain." Three factors are of interest in this operation. The commander of the unit was an NKVD officer, who was one of the four killed. The supplies captured by the Ger-

---

Wi Kdo 6, Gr. La, "Vierteljahresbericht fuer die Monate September, Oktober, November," 30 November 1942, p. 3 (GMDS, Wi/ID 2.170); HGeb A, Ia, "Monatsbericht.-Berichtszeit 1.–30.11.42," 8 December 1942, p. 3 (GMDS, HGeb 31242/2, Anlage 246).

[144] 444. Sich.Div., Ic, "Kriegstagebuch," entry for 29 December 1942. See also Sect. IV of this chapter.

[145] For instance, the Soviet 30th Cavalry Division, located east of Achikulak, used local Komsomol members to collect information on Germans and indigenous collaborators behind the German lines. (PzAOK 1, Ic, "Partisanenbewegungen ostw. Budenowsk," 7 October 1942, GMDS, 3 PzD 30938/54, Anlage 221.)

[146] The German staff of the Cossack regiment engaged in antipartisan warfare between Achikulak and Manych Canal "had the impression that Russian cavalry in spite of its relatively good equipment, artillery pieces, and heavy weapons, has no offensive intentions but has above all engaged in new recruitment for replacement of its own units and also organized partisan groups." (XXXX. Pz.K., Ia, "Kriegstagebuch Nr. 4," entry for 27 September 1942, XXXX AK 27759/1.)

mans in the abandoned camp included, besides several boxes of ammunition and hand grenades, some rifles and two Russian machine guns, and also magazines for U.S. submachine guns. Finally, the surrender of the five partisans was affected by a German trick: the German officer in charge of the operation asked the wives of local residents known to be with the partisans to go and get their husbands, promising them impunity. It was symptomatic that, despite the NKVD officer in charge, five men promptly agreed to return.[147]

October passed quietly in the area.[148] The only recorded action took place on 22 October when the Germans apprehended two partisans who had been sent to the Elista area from Astrakhan after training there.[149] From then on, units appeared on a somewhat larger scale—significant not because of their size but because of the paucity of other armed elements on either side in this sector. The ensuing skirmishes were of varying results. In the words of a German report,

> There have also been various encounters ending partly in German successes, and partly in failure for the German troops and the Cossack regiments. The partisan hide-outs are in part well concealed; they often use the swamps along the Manych and the impassable terrain. Interrogation of captives indicates that the leaders of the groups receive special training in Astrakhan and are then brought in by plane and parachute. Frequently the bands withdraw temporarily, only to make new sallies from their hide-outs.[150]

On 1 November a German-commanded Cossack cavalry squadron ran into a group of partisans trying to cross the Manych in the direction of Raguli. They were obviously informed of the tactical situation since this was a sector particularly bereft of German troops. According to German findings, this group—like the earlier ones—had been trained at a partisan school in Astrakhan and were sent in as two detachments of twenty men each (plus one female nurse). Priority for such assignments was given to former residents of the Kalmyk area, men and women alike, who, after receiving instruction in the use of weapons and explosives, were dispatched along the Manych in order to form larger contingents in the rear of the Germans and to carry out sabotage missions on designated dates.[151]

[147] Korueck 531, Qu., "Auftreten von Banden," 10 September 1942 (GMDS, Korueck 31373/2, Anlage 136).

[148] Upon taking over this area, the German security division "found no formation of bands. Reports [about partisans] were usually exaggerations of indigenous residents." In the month of October, the Soviet Air Force periodically bombed urban, transportation, and military targets in this area and perhaps dropped agents as well. (444. Sich.Div., Ic, "Kriegstagebuch," entry for 10 October 1942, p. 15.)

[149] Chef Sipo u. SD, "Meldungen aus den besetzten Ostgebieten," No. 29, 13 November 1942 (GMDS, DW SD-5).

[150] Wi Kdo 6, Gr. La, "Vierteljahresbericht fuer die Monate September, Oktober, November," 30 November 1942, p. 4 (GMDS, Wi/ID 2.170).

[151] H.Geb. A, Ia, "Monatsbericht.- Berichtszeit 1.–30.11.42," 8 December 1942, p. 5 (GMDS, HGeb 31242/2, Anlage 266). The group of forty-two had dwindled to

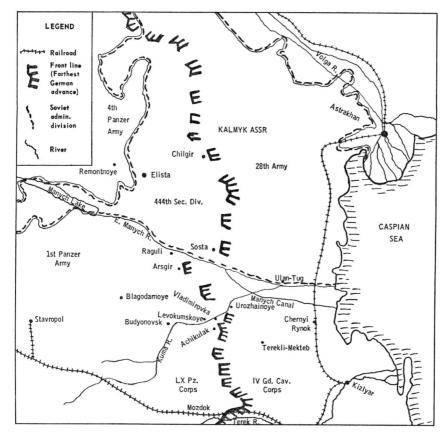

Figure 21.—The Kalmyk region, as of December 1942.

Remnants of the same groups were later located near Elista and farther east along the Manych, but their effectiveness appears to have been minor. One new form of activity listed in the German reports was the attempt of these "cavalry partisans" (as the Germans called them) to drive off the cattle with them.[152]

The operation that has perhaps the greatest interest took place late in November and in December 1942. [See Fig. 21.] It amounted to the in-

---

thirty-two at the time of this encounter, when five were killed or captured. The group had with it five camels and three horses, machine pistols, hand grenades, road mines, and pistols. One German and three Cossacks were killed during the skirmish. (H.Geb. A, Ia, "Tagesmeldung," 2 November 1942, GMDS, HGeb 31242/2, Anlage 211; and 454. Sich.Div., Ia ["Meldung"], 22 December 1942, GMDS, 454 ID 34026/3, Anlage 96.)

[152] Large cattle herds were reported at the partisan camp on an island in the Kuma swamps east of the junction of Kuma and Manych Canal. Evidently the partisans tried to drive them off in an eastward direction in November. (PzAOK 1, Ic, "Partisanenbewegungen ostw. Budenowsk," 7 October 1942, GMDS, 3 PzD 30938/54, Anlage 221; and Chef Sipo u. SD, "Meldungen aus den besetzten Ostgebieten, Nr. 30," 20 November 1942, GMDS, DW SD-5.)

filtration of hundreds of partisans—German estimates varied between 400 and 800—from Astrakhan into the Kuma-Manych sector and westward in the direction of Budyonovsk. The groups were evidently well trained, well armed, and organized in standard fashion into companies and platoons with politruks. Considering that the sole defensive force in this sector was a small number of German troops stationed at widely scattered points, plus the indigenous collaborators and parts of two Cossack collaborator units, it is hardly surprising that the partisans had no trouble entering the area and in effect roaming at will over hundreds of square miles.[153] We have both the German day-by-day account and the diary of a young partisan officer who participated in the operation after receiving special training in a partisan school in Moscow and then in Astrakhan. One gathers that the operation was not under direct Red Army control. In Astrakhan briefing sessions were held with the evacuated People's Commissariat [of the Interior?] of the Kalmyk ASSR and with the *obkom*[154] headquarters of the Komsomol. During the operation, the Germans captured a partisan officer carrying documents and a seal reading "People's Commissariat for Mobilization for Levokumskoye Rayon."[155] While the operation seems to have been timed so as to precede a limited Red Army advance in this sector, actual partisan activities were hardly in direct coordination with the Army. Operations included the posting of leaflets demanding the formation of partisan units in some villages; the killing of collaborators; and the seizure of settlements, presumably both as a symbolic measure of re-established Soviet control and a deterrent to collaboration.

Since the unit had been trained and organized outside the area, the presence of men and women unfamiliar with the Kalmyk territory was to be expected. The names of Russians and Ukrainians prevail; one woman was Polish. In view of the extensive popular acceptance of German rule, it is not surprising that the young Soviet officer from Stalingrad whose diary has been preserved adopted a hostile attitude toward the Kalmyks as such. (He speaks of an operation "against the Kalmyks," while elsewhere, referring to Great Russians, he singles out attacks against "collaborators.")

The existence of friction and disagreements among the officers of one of

[153] From Astrakhan, they proceeded to Ulan-Khol, on the Caspian, and thence inland along the Kama River, establishing camps and headquarters in the swamp area near Ulan-Tug (Farm 4, Sovkhoz 109). From there, they raided a number of villages and settlements in all directions, concentrating especially on the more densely settled area between Budyonovsk and Velichayevskoye.

[154] The oblast committee.

[155] The German record clearly contains a mistranslation. "Volkskommissar fuer die Erfassung im Rayon L." is an incongruity; it could have been either a *voyenkomat* (draft office), instituted for the purpose of recruiting replacements; or else a people's commissariat (probably the People's Commissariat for [Grain] Procurement) may have established a subordinate regional unit to carry out tasks on the German side of the front.

the partisan units involved by this operation is no less interesting. On this as well as the morale and supply aspects, some excerpts from the diary are of significance:

27 November 1942: We arrive in Ulan-Tug. Here we have already [encountered] Germans. I requisition a calf, twenty chickens, and other things. We have shot seven traitors to the fatherland, among them Ensign Filipov, Lieutenant Monakhov, and Sergeant Rybalko. Traitors! That's their way. We shall deal in like manner with anyone who raises his hand against the fatherland. I am a high officer, after all, the aide to the unit [otryad] commander and chief of reconnaissance. I shall fight to my last breath. . . .

29 November 1942: This was a bad day. We went from Farm 3 of Sovkhoz 109 to Plavensky [the German text incorrectly reads Pawlenskoje] to get water. . . . On the way back we got on top of our own mines, which we had laid ourselves (ten mines). [Two men] were killed, [two others] seriously wounded. . . . There is no bread but we have plenty of meat and *kasha.* . . .

. . . *7 December 1942:* There is disorder in our unit. Commander Vasiliyev does not at all behave the way he should. He has relieved me of my jobs as deputy commander and chief of reconnaissance and made me detachment commander. . . . It is degrading. . . . *14 December 1942:* I went to the Korova Kolkhoz to procure a horse for myself. There I joined another otryad to participate in the operation against the Kalmyks. . . . *16 December 1942:* I am back with the Vasiliyev unit. He threatened to shoot me. We are moving on. *18 December 1942:* We have reached the real Germans now. We caught the two traitors Zavorotynskis. I personally shot one of them. *20 December 1942:* The Germans have seen us. Our supplies [*Tross*] are lost. We were surrounded but fought our way out. *21 December 1942:* We are being pursued. Again skirmishes. I shot a German officer, a policeman. I took a golden ring and other items from the German. We have destroyed about fifty Germans and Cossacks. . . . *28 December 1942:* We are moving in the direction of Chernyi Rynok. *30 December 1942:* We are in Chernyi Rynok and await our superiors from Kizlyar.

The description tallies closely with the German accounts. One further point should be noted: throughout almost the entire operation the partisans were well informed about military events on other fronts (for instance, at Stalingrad)—presumably by radio—and were even able to send off letters to relatives and friends in unoccupied parts of the USSR. The effectiveness of the operation is doubtful. The Germans failed to detect the unit for over two weeks and then, hurriedly throwing in what little forces were on hand, managed to cut off and seize its supply train. But the bulk of the partisans escaped, and when Kalmyk and Cossack collaborator units raided the partisan base in the Kuma swamps on 27 December, it had already been evacuated. The most striking success of the operation was the temporary seizure of several settlements—notably, the towns of Velichayevskoye and Urozhainoye—but the partisans' failure to reach Budyonovsk, the original objective, is a measure of their inability to complete a mission.[156]

[156] 444. Sich.Div., Ic, "Kriegstagebuch," December 1942, pp. 19–22; Gr. Wetzel, Ic, "Uebersetzung aus dem Tagebuch des Iwan Kowalenko," 2 May 1943, pp. 13–15

The partisan movement in the Kalmyk area was almost entirely imported. It was properly organized only in the last months of the German
occupation, and its contribution to Soviet military operations was negligible. It acted with some slight success as "the long arm of the Soviet Government," meting out retribution to indigenous collaborators and saving
some cattle from the Germans. Given the unique opportunities offered by
the wide open and ill-defended area, the Soviet command clearly did not
make the most of the situation, largely one suspects because available
partisans were used in areas that were considered more critical. As elsewhere in the North Caucasus, however, the absence of local support was
a crucial handicap to the successful conduct of partisan warfare.[157]

§III. Organization and Control

The Soviet preparations which were made in the North Caucasus in
advance of the retreat of the Red Army generally paralleled activities in
the areas seized by the Germans in 1941. In comparison with such areas
as Western Belorussia or the Baltic States, however, there was ample time
here to plan and execute the establishment of destruction units and partisan units as well as the eastward evacuation of personnel and equipment.
Actual planning and practice seem to have been affected but little by experience on other sectors of the front in the first year of the war. With the
exception of the strategy employed (particularly, the preliminary planning
to concentrate widely dispersed destruction units in one critical area as
partisan groups) the organization and controls of the partisan movement
in the North Caucasus reveal a striking failure, or at least a time lag, in
applying the lessons which had been learned elsewhere.[158]

(GMDS, V AK 41306/10, Anlage 67). The partisan whose diary was cited above was
killed in a subsequent operation after being parachuted into the western Caucasus in
the spring of 1943. See also PzAOK 1, Ic, "Partisanenbewegungen ostw. Budenowsk,"
7 October 1942 (GMDS, 3 PzD 30438/54, Anlage 221).

[157] When the Germans abandoned the Kalmyk area, literally thousands of Kalmyks
joined them in a northwestward trek and were later reorganized into the "Kalmyk
Cavalry Corps."

In the Kalmyk area north of Army Group "A" partisan and sabotage activity was
on about a similar scale. In October the German Fourth Panzer Army apprehended
a total of sixty-two persons, largely trained in Astrakhan and sent in to carry out
demolition and mining. (PzAOK 4, Ic/AO, "3. Taetigkeitsbericht der Abt. Ic/A.O.,"
5 January 1943, GMDS, PzAOK 4, 29365/1.)

[158] The one organizational peculiarity in this area, the so-called kust, was evidently
due to the specific situation—a front line stretching across a high mountain range,
and the partisans in proximity to this front—and not to an over-all change in organizational directives. This is borne out by the fact that Soviet partisan units formed
thereafter on all sectors of occupied territory failed to espouse the kust technique
of organization.

Moreover, large parts of the North Caucasus had experienced a "dress rehearsal" in late November 1941, when the German Army seized Rostov and was poised at the gateway to the Caucasus. At that time, destruction and partisan units were readied in various towns and cities; numerous supply bases and caches were prepared; and underground Party units were organized to go into action after the Germans arrived.[159] Likewise, plants and personnel were evacuated at that time, only to be returned in February 1942 and to resume their work until the following summer.

The basic pattern of Soviet organization and activity remained unchanged. Destruction and later partisan units were formed in most localities. The major forms of relevant activity were destruction, evacuation, preparation of underground work, and the activation of the partisan movement.

As has been pointed out, many groups retreated to the Soviet side, or else dispersed. One may suggest that this process was caused not so much by German attacks as by deterioration of morale and discipline due primarily to (1) lack of food and supplies, (2) frost, (3) a sense of futility, (4) unfavorable contact with the indigenous population, and (5) friction within the unit. The relative importance of these factors varied from case to case, but in the main they mattered in the order indicated above.

The history of the Yegorov complex exemplifies the partisans' critical food and supply situation. Except for those whose sallies into German-held territory from their mountain bases were short-range and sporadic, almost all groups were poorly supplied, especially with food. The lack of rations is more frequently cited as a cause of defection to the Germans than any other single factor,[160] and the preoccupation of the bands with raiding neighboring villages was due primarily to this shortage. Also, from about October 1942 to March 1943, the winter weather imposed additional hardships on the partisans, especially those operating in the high mountains.[161] It is natural that the lack of food and the frost contributed to sickness and physical inability to carry out assignments—a fact which in turn had important repercussions on morale.

Another group of factors had more direct relevance to German policy.

[159] 1. Geb.Div., Ic, "Fernmuendliche Mitteilung [von] . . . Qu.Abt.," 27 December 1942 (GMDS, 1 GebD 27920/37, Anlage 1608); [HFP?], "Vernehmung," 10 August 1942 (GMDS, 111 ID 34428/9, Anlage 27); H.Geb. A, Ia, "Monatsbericht. Berichtszeit 1.–30.11.42." 8 December 1942, p. 6 (GMDS, HGeb 31242/2, Anlage 246); Ignatov, pp. 7–13; Ignatov, *Podpolye Krasnodara* (Moscow, 1947), pp. 6–8; Wi Stab Ost, Abt. I/Id, "Monatsbericht . . . (1.4—30.4.1942)," 18 May 1942, p. 9 (GMDS, Wi/ID 164a).
[160] 46. Inf.Div., Ic, "Vernehmung," 16 December 1942 and 46. Inf.Div., Ic, "Vernehmung," 11 December 1942 (both in GMDS, 46 ID 39033/18, Anlagen 74 and 120); Einsatzkommando 10a, "Schtscherbinowskaja-Bande," 6 January 1943 (GMDS, V AK 41306/10, Anlage 2).
[161] See Sect. II, A, of this chapter for the Yegorov unit; also XXXXIX. (Geb.) A.K., Ic, "Taetigkeitsbericht," August 1942—January 1943, p. 61 (GMDS, XXXXIX AK 32155/1); and Technische Brigade Mineraloel, Ia, "Monatsbericht der TBM. fuer die Zeit vom 1.–31.12.1942," 31 December 1942, p. 5 (GMDS, Wi/ID 2.3).

With the partisan formations generally small and ineffective, faced with hardships and with little prospect of success or reward, it was natural that many of their members should become attuned to the way the civilian population lived and the treatment accorded them by the Germans. Outstanding in this connection were three phenomena: (1) lack of popular help for the partisans; (2) occasional surprise at German treatment which was less harsh than had been expected; and (3) at times, the presence of nationality considerations which facilitated a break with the Soviet partisans. In general, a feeling of futility seems to have engulfed many of the units operating on German-occupied soil. Their small expeditions and raids seemed to have had no effect on the German military potential; their work was more and more a struggle for survival; virtually no new members were recruited among the people with whom they came in contact. There was no prospect of an early termination of the war, and most of the isolated groups had little knowledge of the titanic battle shaping up at Stalingrad, the supply difficulties, and the overextension of German lines which were already creating major problems for the German high command. In their own little sectors, they saw nothing but cause for war-weariness, even though their partisan experience had been immeasurably shorter than in other areas.

It was this general sense of indifference—rather than articulate political considerations—that contributed to defection. In one instance, a partisan sent out on a reconaissance mission learned that the occupation authorities were not shooting all Party members. In consequence this Communist overcame his fear and soon surrendered to the Germans.[162] In other cases, desertions resulted from persuasion by friends or relatives among the civilian population.

For some elements among the national minorities, German policy—or what they learned of it—seemed reassuring. As a German report put it in somewhat exaggerated but basically correct terms:

Since the Caucasian population has again been given some of its old privileges, there is no reason, or only small reasons, for it to wage partisan warfare against the Germans. The result was the frequent dissolution of these groups [composed of Mountaineers]; Communists and criminals remained, while the others returned to their places of residence. . . ."[163]

In a few instances, discipline became so lax that the partisans simply became marauders without "political orientation." In one case a group of six specialized in the seizure of horses, cows, and calves whose meat they

---

[162] 46. Inf.Div., Ic, "Vernehmung," 11 December 1942, pp. 2–3 and "Vernehmung," 4 January 1943 (both in GMDS, 46 ID 39033/18). Actually, most captured partisans were shot.

[163] GFP Gr. 626, "Taetigkeitsbericht fuer Monat November 1942," 25 November 1942, p. [2] (GMDS, PzAOK 1, 28280/2, Anlage 1601).

then sold at substantial prices.[164]

Desertions occurred primarily among the rank and file. Nevertheless, officers, including chiefs of staff and platoon commanders of the disintegrating units, often were captured by the Germans. Only the top echelons seem to have held fast: not a single commander of a larger, regular partisan unit was captured, except for the leaders of the Karachai group—all four of whom were non-Slav Mountaineers.

The above situation suggests a simple "recipe" for the classical situation that developed. The main elements were: (1) failure to receive additional food and supplies from the Soviets; (2) lack of popular support, which would have included food; and (3) general demoralization of the partisans. At that moment the Germans had only to concentrate their efforts on interrupting the partisans' supply lines and on capturing supply bases and depots; then the partisans, cut off from all sides, would surrender in considerable numbers. Indeed, the incidence of German antipartisan expeditions aimed against supplies, rather than the partisans themselves, apparently reflected German awareness of this situation.[165]

The lowering of morale left the partisan officers and the Soviet command several alternatives for revitalizing the partisan movement. (1) In some instances, as in the case of Yegorov, a new man was sent in to take command of the unit. This procedure was comparatively rare and was evidently resorted to only where such a "shot in the arm" promised to save a deteriorating situation in a militarily important area. (2) In 1943 importation of new units was stepped up. The goal was not so much to boost morale and discipline among surviving partisans as to make new manpower available; usually, the new units operated independently of the old ones. (3) Generally the partisans were given the opportunity to transfer across the lines to the regular Red Army if it was believed that their low morale was due to fear of the German environment. This in itself may be an indication of the low priority placed on the Caucasus partisan movement by the Soviet High Command. On the other hand, the assumption was certainly that the removal of men with lower morale and stamina would improve the fighting spirit of the remainder. (4) The same can be said of the systematic dispatch of sick and overage partisans across the lines. In addition, it eased the food situation and gave the units greater mobility. Finally, it created a more homogeneous group since it left men of more nearly

[164] 545. Sich.Div., Ic, "Taetigkeitsbericht fuer den Monat Dezember 1942," 8 January 1943, p. 4 (GMDS, 454 ID 34026/4).
[165] On the Yegorov and Kalmyk areas, see Sect. II. This technique was also used in the high mountains with success. As the XXXXIX Corps reported, "A general ebbing of partisan activity set in after the band lost its great supply base." (XXXXIX. [Geb.] A.K., Ic, "Taetigkeitsbericht," June 1942—January 1943, p. 60, GMDS, XXXXIX AK 32155/1.)

equal age and outlook.[166] (5) In at least one instance, the commanders of the unit hit upon a face-saving device: as snowy weather made their passage across the Greater Caucasus impossible, they asked the men to disperse and go home "over the winter months," and reassemble in the spring. . . .[167]

All these steps are in themselves a measure of the deterioration of morale in 1942. It is important to note that the situation changed in 1943: in the remaining bridgehead, popular feeling swung sharply against the Germans, and, with the Soviets again on the offensive, there is no evidence of partisan defections because of war-weariness or a sense of indifference. Presumably only the most stalwart partisans remained; they were bolstered by *Hiwis* and others who had broken decisively with the Germans, and by Soviet men and women who had received special indoctrination and training. There was physical evidence of German chaos and catastrophe. What surrenders took place at that late date were due almost exclusively to military factors. While in 1942 most captured partisans had evidently willingly given the Germans considerable information about their groups and had often even cooperated in apprehending their former comrades, in 1943 there is evidence of partisan reticence and refusal to cooperate. In both instances the variables were German policy and the tide of battle.

Another facet worthy of some attention is friction within partisan units. Evidently such occurrences were more widespread than the Germans realized. When Yegorov removed Matveyev as unit commander, the demoted official was undoubtedly resentful and eventually defected from the partisans. In the case of the young partisan whose diary has been quoted above [Sect. II, B], his demotion by the unit commander, presumably for lack of perspicacity in action, added to his previous grievances: lack of news from home, lack of a girl friend, lack of food, lack of support from the population, and lack of decorations. A boy who (according to his diary) had often weighed suicide, he nevertheless fought on relentlessly because of a righteous wrath against the Germans. It should be borne in mind that he was sent into occupied territory in March 1943—after the tide of battle had changed—that he came from Stalingrad and was much concerned about his family there, and that he had undergone intensive special training.

His case suggests a generalization applicable to many others. Grievances contributing to a deterioration of morale were ubiquitous. They did not, however, lead automatically to defection, which was restrained—in propor-

---

[166] Examples of such practices have been given above; see also Ignatov; and 46. Inf.Div., Ic, "Vernehmung," 11 December 1942, p. 3 (GMDS, 46 ID 39033/18, Anlage 59). Some "cowards" were dropped from the units even before they left their original rayon. (Ignatov, pp. 20–25.)

[167] XXXXIX. (Geb.) A.K., Ic, "Taetigkeitsbericht," June 1942—January 1943, p. 61 (GMDS, XXXXIX AK 32155/1).

tions varying from case to case—by (1) inertia, (2) fear of the Germans, (3) hatred for the Germans, (4) devotion to the Soviet cause and blind obedience to Soviet authority. In the Caucasus, the anti-German element among the indigenous population was clearly smaller than elsewhere. Hence particular importance must be attributed to the problem of leadership and submission to authority.

The evidence, spotty and incomplete though it is, strongly suggests that a breakdown of leadership usually induced a breakdown of controls. Self-control was habitually absent, and the dispersal of partisan units into small teams or the isolation of individuals from their officers and higher commanders resulted in a much higher rate of desertion. This was particularly true if such dispersal came in the wake of German attacks. There are some indications that the leadership, largely without army experience, was unable to cope with the difficult tasks facing the partisans.[168] In other cases, when put in a difficult situation, a subordinate officer "left it up to the individual men to act as they saw fit." He himself went home, and many of the men followed his example.[169] In general, as a German report pointed out at an early date:

In view of the largely positive attitude of the population of the Caucasus toward the German occupation authorities, the intelligence activities of Soviet agents meet with difficulties. The same is true of partisan activity. Thanks to the active assistance of the population, it proved possible to destroy small partisan groups while they were in process of organization or soon after, since without leadership they had no cohesion, and suffered from a lack of food.[170]

The history of one brigade represents a "classical" example illustrating almost all of the above factors. While the situation here was more clear-cut than usual, the fate of the unit differed largely in degree rather than in kind from that of its neighbors.

On 10 August 1942 a partisan unit of about 180 men was set up in Mikoyan-Shakhar, capital of the Karachai Autonomous Region [see Fig. 22]. Together with another 60 men from Dzhegutinsky, a neighboring rayon of the same region, it was to constitute the partisan battalion of the Karachai Region. Heterogeneous in national composition, the groups included

---

[168] Feldgendarmerie-Trupp 418. "Bericht ueber die Vernichtung und Selbstaufloesung der Partisanen-Bande," 14 September 1942 (GMDS, XXXXIX AK 32155/1).

[169] 46. Inf.Div., Ic, "Vernehmung," 17 December 1942 (GMDS, 46 ID 39033/18, Anlage 78); Einsatzkommando 10a, "Schtscherbinowskaja-Bande," 6 January 1943, p. 2 (GMDS, V AK 41306/10, Anlage 2).

[170] GFP Gr. 626, "Taetigkeitsbericht fuer Monat September 1942," 25 September 1942 (GMDS, PzAOK 1, 24906/19, Anlage 16).

On the other hand, there were individual instances where units continued to fight actively after the disappearance of their leaders. There are not enough details to permit inferences about the specific reasons for the maintenance of controls in this situation. See, for instance, 4. Geb.Div., Ia, "Fernspruch der Div., Eglseer [an A.K.]," 23 September 1942 (GMDS, XXXXIX AK 28576/7, Anlage 518).

sizable contingents of Russians, Karachais, and local Osetins; about 60 men came on foot; another 60 brought their horses; others came with carts and wagons. In addition to some recruited rank-and-file civilians, the battalion included considerable numbers of NKVD, militia, Party, fire fighter, law court, and bank officials. According to one source, the NKVD staff which had been evacuated from Stavropol, as well as a member of the Supreme Soviet of the USSR, joined the group. In advance of the German occupa-

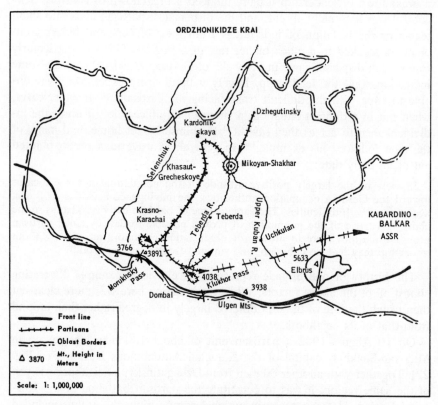

Figure 22.—The Karachai region.

tion, supplies for three months had been set aside, though no caches were established for them.[171]

The speed of the German advance prevented the effective organization of the unit. In effect, the battalion never fulfilled its tasks: to disrupt transportation behind the German lines and to terrorize indigenous collaborators. It was not merely the surprise arrival of the enemy that frustrated the plans. According to German investigations, two other crucial fac-

[171] 1. Geb.Div., Ic, "Taetigkeitsbericht Ic—Einsatz Russland, Teil IV," report for 20 August 1942 by Pz.Jg.Regt. 44 (GMDS, 1 GebD 27920/29, Anlage 445).

tors intervened. "The mixture and multiplicity of nationalists was a cause of friction which . . . led to the voluntary dissolution of the band. [Moreover] the leaders were not up to their tasks."[172]

Promptly after their formation, the units moved from Mikoyan-Shakhar southwestward into the high mountains south of Krasno-Karachai.[173] Evidently an attempt was made to cross the Greater Caucasus mountain passes to Marukhskoi Pass. When this failed, a part of the units—largely the Russians and Osetins, leaving behind the Karachai who wished to remain on their native soil—moved eastward to Klukhor Pass, which had meanwhile been occupied by the Germans, and then proceeded farther east. What caused this frantic movement and dispersal was above all (1) German ability to cut off the main arteries of communication and to seize the few possible mountain routes south, and (2) German seizure of the partisans' supplies and heavy weapons, which had evidently followed south toward Krasno-Karachai behind the bulk of the force.

Now defections in considerable numbers afflicted the partisans. The Dzhegutinsky group, which had formed a separate company, separated from the Karachai command and moved on westward by itself; small bands later reported along the upper Pshish and Kyzgych Rivers may have been the remnants of this band. The Russians evidently hid in the mountains on the right bank of the Teberda River and moved on into the Kabardino-Balkar area, but engaged in no action. Of the initial Mikoyan-Shakhar group there were soon only forty men left. The remainder—mostly on foot—returned to their own villages. Unable to settle down anywhere because of fear of detection and denunciation by the population, the remaining forty horsemen roamed the countryside in futile efforts to "take root." By early September the group had dwindled to nine Karachais and four Osetins, including the headquarters of the whole band. Further disagreements and feuds among these men led to the dissolution of even this remnant. The last four leaders were apprehended by the collaborating indigenous militia: Commander Isakov, deputy NKVD chief for the Karachai Region; Commissar Erkenov, Party secretary for the Karachai Region; Chief of Staff Akbeyev, NKVD chief for Mikoyan-Shakhar Rayon; Guide Meikulov,

[172] Feldgendarmerie-Trupp 418, "Bericht ueber die Vernichtung und Selbstaufloesung der Partisanen-Bande des Oblaskes [*sic*] Karatschaj," 14 September 1942 (GMDS, XXXXIX AK 32155/1) [hereafter cited as Feldegendarmerie-Trupp 418]; Chef Sipo u. SD, "Meldungen aus den besetzten Ostgebieten," No. 32, 4 December 1942 (GMDS, DW SD-5).
[173] See Fig. 22. The units proceeded over Kardonikskaya, Khasaut-Grecheskoye south along the Aksaut River. Strangely, they did not take advantage of the excellent routes and facilities along the Upper Teberda spa area. It is possible that regular Red Army stragglers joined the partisan bands near Krasno-Karachai, as German reconnaissance reports speak of a total of about 600 men, including army officers. (1, Geb.Div., Ic, "Taetigkeitsbericht Ic—Einsatz Russland, Teil IV," especially reports of 17, 20, 21, 23, 24, 25 August 1942, GMDS, 1 GebD 27920/29, Anlagen 411, 419, 445, 452, 454, 489, 497, 498, 511.)

teacher in Mikoyan-Shakhar. The names suggest that all four were Karachais. In the following days another fifteen partisans were captured, including the supreme judge of the Karachai region, the politruk of the Mikoyan-Shakhar fire fighters, and the commandant of the Mikoyan-Shakhar militia, who had all been platoon commanders in the partisan unit. At the same time the local Komsomol secretary, the *raikom* secretary of the Party, the editor of the Karachai Party paper, and several officials of the regional State administration were captured. After interrogation these nineteen were shot. After the middle of September, there was no partisan movement in the Karachai region.[174]

§IV. Soviet Agents and the Partisan Movement

At different periods of the German occupation, intensive use was made of agents who informed the Soviet authorities of intelligence collected behind the German lines and carried out specific sabotage missions. (1) Agents at times operated in groups tantamount to air-dropped partisans with functions identical to those of the indigenous partisans. (2) German confusion and failure to distinguish between local partisans and agents reflected the close overlapping of the two categories. (3) Teams of agents often had instructions to contact existing partisan groups.[175] (4) Organizationally, it appears, the dispatch of agents from the Soviet side was under the same command as the transfer of partisans to occupied areas; some of the same individuals were used for both types of activities at different times. (5) Finally, a definite relationship seemed to exist between the use of agents and partisans: at different times and places, the Soviet command evidently preferred one to the other. For instance, the failure of larger partisan units to survive and to carry out their missions led to a greater emphasis on the use of agents flown in during the later period of the occupation. Although the number of drops declined during the winter months, it reached its peak during the spring of 1943.

While German records fail to make distinctions between different types of airborne operations of this kind, one may surmise that organizationally there were agents dispatched directly by the NKVD, and others trained by schools closely connected with the Red Army and operating in coordination

[174] Feldgendarmerie-Trupp 418; XXXXIX. (Geb.) A.K., Ic, "Taetigkeitsbericht," June 1942—January 1943, p. 60 (GMDS, XXXXIX AK 32155/1); AOK 17, "Bandenlage vom 26.9.42," map (GMDS, AOK 17, 25354/26).

[175] 101. Jg.Div., Ic, "Vernehmung," 5 April 1943 (GMDS, 101 JgD 35517/11, Anlage 11).

with the higher headquarters responsible for the conduct of partisan warfare. In addition to this organizational dichotomy—reflected in part in the different assignments these teams received—three situations may be pointed out in which agents were dropped with particular regularity or intensity: (1) in areas where the local partisan units had been destroyed or were on the verge of destruction; (2) in sectors where agents' activity was desired in support of Soviet tactical operations, especially near the front lines; and (3) for the conduct of special reconnaissance or sabotage missions. In some instances, the agents were to return to the Soviet lines; in others, they were to join the local underground or partisans; in still others, they were to submerge after carrying out their missions and continue to operate under cover until the Red Army returned.

The NKVD operations are exemplified by the drops in the Terek area. The available evidence suggests that the NKVD operatives, like the others, were also used to support Red Army operations. In August 1942 a destruction platoon was established in Mozdok, a center of the North Caucasus oil industry, under the name of the "Terek" unit. Its tasks included, as one would expect, the destruction of railroad installations, oil tanks, and other economic units, as well as raids on German installations and small German troop units. The unit was brought into being by the local chief of the NKVD, Blizenyuk, who became its commander. Although reasonably well equipped (including four U.S. machine pistols and four British rifles, along with Soviet equipment and 20,000 rounds of ammunition), his unit of thirty-one men failed in its assignment. The speed of the German advance led to the loss of its supplies; morale appears to have been low, and many members abandoned the group. Initially, it was to have maintained contact by radio with headquarters in Groznyi, presumably the headquarters of the partisan command for the Terek area, and headquarters of the Soviet Army Group in the eastern part of the North Caucasus. But by mid-September the unit had failed to contact Groznyi, and many of its members had abandoned the group or had been captured.[176]

At this point a decision was evidently reached by the Soviet command to drop agents into the Mozdok area, then a center of bitter combat. Some agents were sent in across the lines by the NKVD in September,[177] and others were dropped by parachute. The tasks of both groups were primarily intelligence and espionage rather than sabotage.[178] One group, for instance,

[176] 111. Inf.Div., Ic, "Fuehrungsanordnung Nr. 7," 20 September 1942 (GMDS, 111 ID 34428/10, Anlage 65); GFP Gr. 626, "Taetigkeitsbericht fuer Monat November 1942," 25 November 1942, p. 2 (GMDS, PzAOK 1, 28280/2); GFP Gr. 626, "Taetigkeitsbericht fuer Monat September 1942," 25 September 1942, p. 3 (GMDS, PzAOK 1, 24906/19, Anlage 16).

[177] 3 Pz.Div., Ic, "Taetigkeitsbericht Nr. 2," 30 September 1942 (GMDS, 3 PzD 30928/49); 3 Pz.Div., Ic, "Betr.: Partisanen- und Agentenwesen," 27 September 1942 (GMDS, 3 PzD 30928/49, Anlage 3).

[178] *Ibid.;* also GFP Gr. 626, "Taetigkeitsbericht fuer Monat November 1942," 25 November 1942, pp. 1, 5 (GMDS, PzAOK 1, 28280/2).

dropped near Mozdok on 20–21 September, was charged with blowing up or burning German cars, billets, bridges, railroads; its primary assignment, however, was to collect information on German and indigenous troops, location of air force and armored units, and related data.[179] Captured agents revealed that they belonged to a group of eighteen trained in and dispatched from Groznyi. According to German intelligence, NKVD headquarters in Ordzhonikidze, Groznyi, Nalchik, and Makhach-Kala sent out such units (Nalchik was later occupied by the Germans). These agents were to gather information on strength and nationality of Axis forces; branches of service; number of armored vehicles, other vehicles, and guns; tactical insignia and symbols; headquarters, planes, ammunition, fuel and supply dumps; morale of troops and population; treatment of the population by the German authorities.[180]

The NKVD agents, so far as can be determined, were thus used to replace the partisans who had failed in this assignment. Similar instances were reported in which, in addition to agents left behind as well as those filtered through the lines, agents with radio equipment (according to the Germans, operating as a radio group, or *Funkgruppe*) were dropped by parachute. While most agents had little or no previous training, some had undergone special schooling under the NKVD in Tiflis.[181]

In addition to this hypothetical category of NKVD agents, however, the bulk of agents whose activities approximated those of regular partisans was clearly directed by a high Soviet headquarters. One report speaks of an army major, instrumental in the training and organization of such groups, who was due to "fly back to Moscow shortly."[182] The organizational connection with partisan warfare direction is strongly suggested by the following facts.

Many of the trainees later dropped on occupied soil received schooling and instructions at Astrakhan, which was also headquarters for the Partisans of the South. As a matter of fact, the school they attended was the same one which trained partisans. Another school in Kizlyar seems to have served the same dual purpose. (A third large school for partisans and agents, primarily for the western sector of the Caucasus front, was located

[179] GFP Gr. 626, "Tgb. Nr. 362/42 geh.," 25 October 1942 (GMDS, PzAOK 1, 24906/19). This document sums up the over-all situation: "In the current month partisan activity decreased, while an increase of instances of espionage was noticeable."
[180] GFP Gr. 626, "Taetigkeitsbericht fuer Monat November 1942," 25 November 1942, p. [5] (GMDS, PzAOK 1, 28280/2). See also TBM, Btl. Fachkraefte, "Vernehmung von Fallschirmspringern," 15 December 1942 (GMDS, Wi/ID 2.833a); FK 538 (V), Abt. VII, "Lagebericht fuer die Zeit vom 16.9 bis 15.10.1942," 15 October 1942 (GMDS, AOK 17, 51019/1).
[181] GFP Gr. 626, "Taetigkeitsbericht fuer Monat January 1943," 3 February 1943, p. 2 (GMDS, PzAOK 1, 28280/2).
[182] 101. Jg.Div., Ic, "Vernehmung," 5 April 1943 (GMDS, 101 JgD 35517/11).

at Sochi).[183] After the recapture of Krasnodar by the Red Army, the units moved there in February–March 1943 and were stationed at the airport of Pashkovskaya for final training and dispatch.[184]

A further connection with the partisan movement can be established because of some of the personalities involved. A partisan whose diary was quoted above and who had undergone special training in Moscow and Astrakhan was sent across the lines into the Kalmyk steppe in November 1942; in March 1943 the same man, with a group of others, was parachuted from Pashkovskaya into the area north of Novorossiisk.[185] After returning from the abortive mission into the Kalmyk steppe, he was sent to Kizlyar and assigned to the "sabotage group of Burnin." According to his diary entry of 11 February 1943, "In two days we are to fly to the Crimea to the Germans." Actually he was dispatched into German-held territory on 25 March and was dropped in the Yegorov area. The organizational connection of the partisan movement with the Crimea has been discussed above; First Lieutenant Burnin was presumably the same man who, according to other sources, had replaced Yagunov as a partisan leader in the Crimea.[186] The personnel of partisan and paratroop-agents teams was thus presumably interchangeable.

The above material suggests another deduction. In both instances the dispatch of partisans to German-occupied areas of the North Caucasus was a last-minute improvisation: the personnel were originally slated to be sent elsewhere (in one instance, to Stalingrad; in others, to the Crimea). The Caucasus front thus received relatively secondary attention. A partial reason for this may be the relatively meager results expected from using agents there.

Finally, some of the agents dispatched into occupied territory from Astrakhan or Krasnodar had specific directives to contact the surviving

[183] *Ibid.;* GFP Gr. 13, "Vernehmung des Agenten Pawel-Wassiliwitsch Karpenko," 26 June 1943 (GMDS, 50 ID 33502/3).

[184] 101. Jg.Div., Ic, "Vernehmung eines Agenten," 3 July 1943 (GMDS, 101 JgD 38434/8, Anlage 32); GFP Gr. 13, "Vernehmung des Agenten Pawel-Wassiliwitsch Karpenko," 26 June 1943 (GMDS, 50 ID 33502/3, Anlage 41); 101. JgDiv., Ic, "Vernehmung," 5 April 1943 (GMDS, 101 JgD 35517/11, Anlage 41). Another possible link may be found in the fact that men recruited for a parachute partisan unit were stationed at Akhonk, the advanced headquarters of partisans operating across the lines near Novorossiisk. On Akhonk, see above, Sect. II, A, 3.

[185] Gr. Wetzel, Ic, "Uebersetzung aus dem Tagebuch des Iwan Kowalenko," 22 May 1943, pp. 15–17 (GMDS, V AK 41306/10, Anlage 67).

[186] *Ibid.;* XXXXII. A.K., Ic, "Bericht ueber die Kaempfe in den Steinbruechen von Adshim-Uschkai," 14 November 1942, p. 2 (GMDS Befh. Krim, 29072/13). Another captured agent confirmed that he, too, after training at Pashkovskaya, had been slated for dispatch to the Crimea but was eventually parachuted into the area north of Novorossiisk. (101. Jg.Div., Ic, "Vernehmung eines am 27.4 morgens . . . gefangenen russischen Fallschirmagenten," 3 May 1943, GMDS, 101 JgD 35517/11, Anlage 1 zu "101. Jaeg. Div. Abt Ic 104/43.")

indigenous partisans. This fact was most clearly established in the spring 1943 drops into the area where the Yegorov complex had previously operated.[187] The organization and employment of the teams dropped into the occupied area seem to have conformed closely to the over-all pattern established in April 1942: the plan was to drop by parachute eleven-man teams of "diversionists" primarily into areas where the original partisan bands had been destroyed.[188] Both the composition and the armament of many teams dropped in the North Caucasus follows the pattern established in this directive. The other type of team consisted of two men. These operated specifically as demolition squads and were dropped for such tasks as blowing up a given bridge. Each man was armed with two mines, two hand grenades, and a "Finnish knife." These two-man teams were used primarily in the spring of 1943 against the Kuban bridgehead.[189]

While there may have been instances of parachute drops of such agents prior to the winter months, the available material suggests that activity was stepped up in December 1942.[190] In January individual drops were reported, for instance, to blow up the tracks of the Belorechenskaya-Armavir Railroad,[191] but the winter weather made further drops difficult. At the same time, the Soviet advance obviated the need for using parachuted agents since the Red Army expected to recapture the area momentarily. Only in late March were similar operations resumed: the weather improved, and the Germans, abandoning most of the area south of Rostov,

[187] Ignatov, p. 555; 101. Jg.Div., Ic. "Vernehmung von drei in der Nacht vom 25./26.3. in Gegend suedl. Warenikowskaja abgesetzten Banditen," 5 April 1943, p. 2 (GMDS, 101 JgD 35517/11, Anlage 42).

[188] Leiter GFP Ost, "Partisanenbanden," 18 August 1942 (GMDS, 444 ID 30260/2, Anlage 41). The directive, according to the Germans, called for the creation of eleven-man teams including a commander, a (male or female) nurse, two demolition experts, two radio men, and five reconnaissance and liaison men. It may be suggested that their activities in the Caucasus concentrated more heavily on intelligence than on sabotage.

[189] AOK 17, Ia, "Bandenlage vom 1.5.—31.5.43," 31 May 1943, p. 1 (GMDS, AOK 17, 34957/15); Gr. Wetzel, Ic, "Betr.: Fallschirmbanditen," 29 April 1943 (GMDS, V AK 41306/10). It is likely that one or two such teams were also dropped north of Stavropol on 15–16 December 1942. The Germans found only the parachutes and equipment: among other things, explosives, batteries, hard zwieback, and cans of meat. (Befh. H.Geb. A, Ia, "Monatliche Bandenmeldung," 27 December 1942, GMDS, HGeb A, 31242/2, Anlage 274); GFP Gr. 13, "Vernehmung des Agenten Pawel-Wassiliwitsch Karpenko," 26 June 1943 (GMDS, 50 ID 33502/3); 454. Sich.Div., Ic, "Taetigkeitsbericht fuer den Monat Dezember 1942," 8 January 1943, p. 3 (GMDS, 454 ID 34026/4).

[190] For instance, in the oil area near Neftegorsk, where at the same time partisan groups were likewise being filtered through the front. (TMB, Ia, "Monatsbericht der TBM. fuer die Zeit vom 1.–31.12.1942," 31 December 1942, p. 13, GMDS, Wi/ID 2.3; see also 454. Sich.Div., Ia ["Meldung"], 22 December 1942, GMDS, 454 ID 34026/3, Anlage 80.)

[191] Korueck 550, Ic, "Bandenmonatsmeldung," 23 January 1943, p. 3 (GMDS, Korueck 34678/2).

consolidated their forces in what remained of the Kuban bridgehead. The Soviet purpose was now clearly to revitalize what remained of the partisan groups which had been operating during the winter months.

Apparently sizable groups were flown into the area, because instances in which up to thirty men parachuted in were not unusual. While many eluded capture, most were young and inexperienced soldiers without extensive training and were prone to surrender or disperse. On the whole, however, they appear to have performed better than those sent in during the previous months. A lull followed the rather intense activity of March and April; greater activity was resumed again in June.

Considerable emphasis was placed on the training of radio men, some of whom had received extensive schooling in Moscow and in the Caucasus. Contact with the new Pashkovskaya headquarters was one of the things impressed most forcibly upon the personnel; a relatively complex code was used. Often women were assigned to the teams as radio operators and nurses. While a few of the parachuted agents had extensive training (for instance, nine months in the paratroop school at Sochi), most of them were regular Red Army soldiers, of whom a considerable number volunteered for this assignment. Some had made one practice jump at Pashkovskaya; some had never even flown before they were sent into action. In addition to standard rations and equipment, they also carried false German documents. The flights were usually made in U-2 training planes, from which the agents jumped at a height of 400 to 600 meters; after the jump they buried or destroyed their parachutes. Occasionally other planes were used—for instance the R-5, a one-engine reconnaissance plane, and for larger groups, usually the DC-3.[192]

[192] See the various reports cited in notes in this section. An interrogation report also speaks of about twenty "MIR's" stationed at Pashkovskaya. There was no such model. It refers either to an MBR-2, an older monoplane, or (since the report identifies it as a fighter) the MIG-1; in the latter case, it could scarcely have been used for dropping agents. (GFP Gr. 13, "Vernehmung des Agenten Pawel-Wassiliwitsch Karpenko," 26 June 1943, GMDS, 50 ID 33502/3, Anlage 41.) By June 1943, perhaps as a result of more substantial lend-lease shipments, reports spoke of Douglases, i.e., DC-3's, dropping larger teams (up to 13 men), while U-2's continued to bring in smaller units. (V. A.K., Ic, "Taetigkeitsbericht," entry for 22 June 1943, GMDS, V AK 41306/9.)

According to a captured agent, of about 180 students at the Krasnodar school, six underwent special radio training. This involved test operations between the outskirts of town and the Krasnodar headquarters; memorization of codes; camouflage of radio equipment. Radio contact was to be established at midnight the night after the jump. The equipment consisted of one U.S. radio set, three spare tubes, two bulbs, twelve batteries (including four of U.S. make), two 12-meter serials, a cable, a condenser with two fuses, a flashlight, a watch, and a keyer. All items were in a rubber wrapper. In other instances, transmitters of the "Sever" type were used. One report mentions the shortwave transmitter and receiver, "Sever-bis," with eight batteries and four elements. In one group, spare batteries were distributed to all members of the group.

Several reports stress the low morale of these teams. (The German reports, it is true, are based only on interrogations of captured agents, usually one or several of every team.) Moreover, it seems to have been generally true that the lack of effective leadership led to disorganization and a breakdown in discipline.[193] Most indicative perhaps is the diary of a young Soviet soldier who, in another area, had acted as a partisan officer after undergoing special training in Moscow and who, despite a multitude of complaints and an adolescent flair for drama, had a righteous wrath against the Germans. The following excerpt reflects both the morale of the Zazarukov group, to which he belonged, and the failure of its mission. It also indicates the subsequent attempt to return to Soviet territory.[194]

8–15 March: We were in Krasnodar. I went to the Pashkovskaya airport. I belong to the Zazarukov group. Things aren't bad. The morale state of affairs is worse.

22–24 March: I am at the airport.
25 March: We took off in a Douglas at 2400 from Pashkovskaya Airport.
26 March: At 0100 we were dropped by parachute about thirty kilometers from Novorossiisk at Khutor 74. I landed quite well except that my right leg is out of joint. We jumped from a height of 400 meters.
27 March: I am in the Varenikovskaya-Gostagayevskaya-Akkermanskaya triangle. To this extent everything is in order, except for the fact that of our eleven men only seven are here.... We sit in the forest. It is cold. But this can't be helped: we are spies, saboteurs.
28–31 March: We are being pursued. According to rumors, Kamova was caught. Popov was killed. One is supposed to have surrendered voluntarily. The scoundrel! Now only three of us are left.
1–8 April 1943: I wander from forest to forest. I observe the activities of the Germans. They are real robbers. According to rumors, they have hanged five parachutists in Varenikovskaya. They are looking for us but can't catch us. On 2 April they almost got us, but Alexander Ishchenko (born 1906) saved us. He has assumed responsibility for getting us across the front. We sit in the forest and starve, freeze, and are wet. Twice it snowed. It is horrible. We have countless lice. I don't even think of surrendering to the Germans, I'd rather shoot myself. I dream of my dear ones, and read old letters. I am in exile. I have been away from home for ten months.

A few days later he was found dead.

Under such circumstances, even the staunchest anti-German partisans were stymied. If their performance, as judged by the Germans, is any index to their effectiveness, these groups can scarcely be rated highly. Their

[193] GFP Gr. 626, "Taetigkeitsbericht fuer Monat September 1942," 25 September 1942 (GMDS, PzAOK 1, 24906/19, Anlage 16); Rumanian Army, S.S.I. [Intelligence], Unterabt. Kaukasus, "Informationsblatt," 29 April 1943 (GMDS, V AK 41306/10, Anlage 63).
[194] Gr. Wetzel, Ic, "Uebersetzung aus dem Tagebuch des Iwan Kowalenko," 2 May 1943, p. 17 (GMDS, V AK 41306/10, Anlage 67).

tasks—as elsewhere, almost identical with those of regular partisan bands—were in practice reduced to occasional mine-laying and demolition operations, and to some transmission of intelligence to the Soviets.[195]

§V. Summary and Conclusions

The partisan movement in the North Caucasus was first prepared in late 1941 when the Germans were expected to push southward beyond Rostov. At that time, the evacuation of certain industrial installations and of top personnel in government and economy was begun. In a number of localities the nuclei of destruction battalions were formed, apparently in line with the pattern generally applied throughout the Soviet areas threatened by German troops. By early 1942, however, when it became clear that the German advance had been stopped, at least temporarily, a reorganization took place. In terms of upper commands it probably conformed with the over-all pattern established in the Soviet partisan movement sometime in the first half of 1942, although it continued to treat the local units as the basis of the organization.

It appears likely that, once the Soviet Army command had decided to retreat to the Caucasus Mountains without attempting to make a stand between Rostov and the mountains, plans for the partisan movement were drawn up accordingly. Trading space for the integrity of its forces (and neglecting the deterioration of morale resulting from headlong retreat), the Red Army was to reach the mountains relatively intact and make a stand there. Orders were issued for the advance formation of partisan units in each rayon (usually on the basis of local destruction battalions established with the active participation of the NKVD). The units were instructed to assemble on the northern slopes and foothills of the Caucasus Mountains in accordance with a definite pattern of defense, in which every partisan unit would occupy, as it were, a certain sector behind the German lines. Not all units by any means succeeded in becoming cohesive groups or in moving south; moreover, urban detachments were left behind in most towns and cities, in accordance with pre-occupation directives. But in Krasnodar Krai at least, the partisans managed to reach a no man's land front area which ran close to the ridges of the Greater Causasus range. The situation in Stavropol Krai is less clear although it appears to have followed the

---

[195] According to German intelligence, the assignment of tasks to the agents and to the partisans was identical in such instances. (OKH/GenStdH/FHO, *Nachrichten ueber Bandenkrieg, Nr. 1,* 3 May 1943. p. 4, GMDS, H 3/738.)

same general pattern. Partisan activity had a dual purpose: as elsewhere, the interruption of German transportation and communication behind the front lines, and the defense of mountain sectors of the front where neither the German nor the Soviet Army had adequate forces for regular combat.

In this area the organizational peculiarity was the kust system—a series of headquarters, located just south of the mountain front on the Soviet side, which controlled several detachments, usually from the same or adjacent rayons. It was this series of kusts that constituted the link between internal and external control of partisan units. Their staffs consisted largely of the same (but perhaps higher-ranking) personnel as the senior leadership of the partisan detachments under their command. They received their orders, directly or indirectly, from the highest headquarters of partisan warfare in this region, the Partisans of the South, which included the North Caucasus, the Kalmyk ASSR, the Astrakhan area, probably Stalingrad Oblast, and perhaps the Crimea as well. As a territorial command and in subordination to Moscow headquarters, the Central Staff of the Partisans of the South operated in a manner analogous to the Central Staffs of such other regional partisan commands as Belorussia and the Ukraine.

There was strikingly little popular inclination to join the partisan units established during the weeks before and during the German occupation. Some rayon groups were never properly organized; many others seem to have dispersed before ever acting as partisan units. In an area where geographic features facilitated concealment from Soviet authorities and in a political climate which combined long-range national aspirations of the Mountaineers, special traditions of the Cossacks, and striking instances of general defeatism in 1942, anti-Soviet sentiments, both among Slavs and non-Slavs, were strong when the Germans arrived in August of that year. The immediate effect was that the budding partisan movement failed to obtain reinforcements and supplies. Most of the partisan units, which were intended to attain company strength, remained in the magnitude of from thirty to seventy-five men and consisted substantially of the nuclei and cadres selected in advance and without the projected increase in strength.

The Soviet High Command paid little attention to the North Caucasus partisans. Partly because of their weakness and failures, partly because of the shortage of Soviet personnel and supplies at the time of Stalingrad (and perhaps in preparation for defense against the expected German push into the Transcaucasus), few efforts were made to reinforce the partisans from the Soviet side. The use of airpower was also reduced to a minimum for the same reasons, and also because of geographic and climatic conditions. Moreover, many partisan detachments, clearly in accordance with orders from higher Soviet echelons, were inactive until November or December 1942 at the kusts south of the front, to which they had retreated either before or just after the Germans arrived in the North Caucasus.

They failed to take full advantage of the vast gaps in the front line, both in the West Caucasus mountains and in the Kalmyk no man's land, through which entire regiments could have infiltrated.

In the northern part of the area under discussion, particularly in the open plains but also in the Stavropol upland, virtually no partisan activity developed. In the south, i.e., along the mountains, there were five partisan centers, four of which appear to have been selected in advance by the Soviet command: (1) the wooded and hilly area north and south of the Novorossiisk-Krymskaya rail lines and highways, major arteries for German transport which the partisans were under orders to cut; (2) the oil area south of Maikop, particularly around Neftegorsk, a sector of obvious economic importance; (3) an area farther east, in a gap between two German army corps; here Soviet regular army units remained pressed against the mountains for some time and in reality became partisans until a substantial part was withdrawn southward across the mountain passes; this is the only instance of unpremeditated partisan concentration, against which the Germans were obliged to conduct two systematic antipartisan operations (Hubertus I and II); (4) the area around Nalchik and to the east of it, crucial for the defense of the approaches both to the Groznyi oil fields and to the strategic Georgian Military Highway leading into Transcaucasia; (5) the open area of the Kalmyk ASSR and the Terek area where, had the Germans advanced farther, presumably an attempt would have been made to prevent the invading forces from systematically using the transportation system along the Caspian Sea.

The actual damage the partisans inflicted on the Germans in terms of personnel and supplies was small indeed. The partisan contribution to the Soviet war effort was primarily one of nuisance value, and the tying down of relatively small German and collaborator forces.[196] There is no evidence that the partisans ever seriously impeded German combat preparations or operations; the same cannot be said of the extensive destruction carried out by the partisans *before* the Soviet retreat. The passive defense of the otherwise open mountain sectors was a success—but only because the Germans never mounted an offensive in impassable terrain at a time when climate and supply difficulties prevented such an attack. In the only sectors

[196] Soviet claims concerning the accomplishments of its partisans were fantastic and palpably wrong. According to one account, a sixty-man unit from Krasnodar (admittedly one of the best) inflicted the following destruction on the Germans between August 1942 and early February 1943: "16 locomotives blown up, 392 railroad cars with troops or supplies blown up, 41 tanks, tankettes [whippets?], and armored cars, 36 heavy weapons, over 100 small guns and mortars, 113 cars and trucks, over 100 motorcycles with trailers, 34 bridges blown up . . . over 8,000 Fascists killed or seriously wounded." (Ignatov, p. 275.) This destruction by one single unit of what would have amounted to a German division was clearly a considerable exaggeration, which contrasts strikingly with the monotonously uniform German reports from higher and lower echelons of both Seventeenth Army and First Panzer Army about the virtual ineffectiveness of the partisans.

where the Germans attempted deeper penetrations, they were met by regular Red Army troops. It appears, then, that the judgment of the Soviet command in assigning the partisans to the defense of least sensitive sectors was correct. On the other hand, the active assignment given the partisans—the disruption and destruction of German supply lines—was a complete failure. Finally, the psychological impact of the partisans on the indigenous population appears to have been negligible. At first they were widely rejected; and the increasing tide of popular sentiment against the Germans in the final period of the occupation was due not to the partisans but largely to German behavior and policy.

The initial popular proclivity for making a break with the Soviet regime (though by no means uniform or unanimous) fostered the restriction of the original partisan units to people who had a stake in the regime. Thus the detachments had strikingly high ratios of Party, NKVD, and State officials in their membership, and a disproportionately small number of rank-and-file citizens, particularly peasants.

Several major factors stand out from the available evidence as causes for the failure of the partisan movement in the North Caucasus. The first of these was the more fertile soil for anti-Soviet disaffection which this area represented, particularly the Moslem areas (as well as the Buddhist Kalmyk region). Equally important perhaps was the very fact that the German occupation lasted only a short time. As elsewhere, it took time for resentment against the new masters to crystallize; conceivably stronger anti-German movements might have arisen had the German forces remained longer. In addition, the speed of the Soviet retreat and the impression of superior German forces and techniques exerted a paralyzing effect for at least the initial weeks. The absence of stragglers from the Red Army—largely because the entire Soviet force withdrew rapidly from Rostov to the Greater Caucasus chain—made it impossible to reinforce the initial partisan cadres by army personnel. Thus the initial collapse of the destruction battalions, transformed into partisan units, came at a time when the rank and file were witnessing Soviet disorganization, retreat, and a serious drop in morale. And, once the partisans had withdrawn into the mountains, they were far removed from densely populated areas and urban centers from which replacements and support might have come, and they operated in areas inhabited only by those elements who were precisely among the most determined foes of the Soviet regime.

Finally, the German occupation here was unique in purpose, techniques, and explicit policy. In an area which remained under military control; where some of the most farsighted military commanders and best-qualified German experts on Soviet affairs were put to work; where Germany had no plans for resettlement and direct colonization or annexation; where some consideration was given to the effect of German policy on neighboring neutral Turkey; where racist dogma was not invoked against the non-Slavic population, German policy was from the outset considerably more circumspect of indigenous feelings and aspirations than elsewhere. Though abuses and variations of behavior were considerable, this policy went so far as to establish regional self-government for and by the indigenous population in Karachai, Kabardo-Balkaria, and a Cossack area south of Rostov. Likewise, the agrarian reform prepared for this area was more far-reaching than that introduced elsewhere in the German-occupied USSR. This difference in German policy—utilitarian, at times half-hearted, and often more symbolic than real—was apparently sufficient to keep certain elements of the population from joining the partisans.

The importance of this policy was brought home early in 1943 when, in their rapid retreat from the North Caucasus, the German forces adopted practices which were in all significant respects similar to the retribution and extermination methods employed farther north. At that time—with the Soviet armies again on the offensive—popular sentiment swung sharply against the Germans. But by then the partisans were of little more than local tactical value to the Red Army.

The contrast between the North Caucasus and "classical" partisan territory in Belorussia and the Western RSFSR is well illustrated by the nature of the partisans. In the Caucasus as well as in the North, the initial core of the movement came from officially organized destruction battalions. In both areas, most of them proved ineffectual and eventually disintegrated. In the Caucasus, this marked in substance the end of the movement, which never "graduated" to the next phases in which units were inflated in size and strengthened in popular prestige and support. In the north, in contrast, stragglers from the Red Army, elements brought in from the Soviet side, and finally recruits from the civilian population itself revived and reinvigorated the partisan cause. In the Caucasus, there were no stragglers to join the partisans, the Soviet side gave little support, and the indigenous population supplied even less.

The importance of the two different policies pursued by the Germans was brought home to some of the German officials themselves. It may be appropriate to conclude with a excerpt from a memorandum by Dr. Otto Braeutigam, who was representative of the Ministry for the Occupied Eastern Territories with Army Group "A" and deputy chief of the Political Division of that Ministry. After criticizing German failure to win popular support in the occupied regions and indicting German personnel for "pushing the population into the hands of the partisans," Braeutigam continued:

How easy it would have been to win [the support of] the population was illustrated in the administration of the North Caucasus territory where Army Group "A" coordinated its measures with the Ministry for the Occupied Eastern Territories. The speedier implementation of the agrarian reform, the prohibition of

632 / X. THE NORTH CAUCASUS

measures of compulsion in the recruitment of labor, and a humane treatment of the population led to a simply enthusiastic cooperation of the peoples of the North Caucasus. This resulted in the utter absence of a partisan movement, even though it is precisely the Caucasus that might have provided the best [geographic] basis for it; in thousands volunteering for the police and the army; in higher quotas of economic procurement; and in a stronger refugee movement when the German troops withdrew. . . .[197]

Discounting some exaggeration and oversimplification, the basic conclusion—the effect a different German policy had on the fate of the partisan movement—remains as a key factor in the failure of the Soviet partisans in the North Caucasus.

[197] Otto Braeutigam (RMfdbO., II Pol.), "Aufzeichnung," 27 July 1944 (GMDS, EAP 99/451).

CHAPTER XI

The Dnepr Bend Area

John A. Armstrong

§I. Geographic, Economic, and Ethnographic Character of the Region

Compared with the intense partisan activity in the northern Ukraine, Belorussia, and the Smolensk and Bryansk areas, partisan warfare in the Dnepr bend region of the southern Ukraine was insignificant. The number of active partisans totaled in all scarcely two thousand. Moreover, this comparatively small force was active only for a period of four months—from the beginning of September 1941 until the first week of January 1942–and the total achievements of the groups were of small consequence. Nevertheless, partisan development in the Dnepr bend region differs so markedly from that in the northern occupied areas that a careful examination of its nature may be expected to throw considerable light on the conditions under which it arose and the circumstances which made its large-scale development impossible.

Many of the differences between partisan development in the north and in the south derive from differing geographical features of the two regions. North of Kiev, wooded areas are numerous. To be sure, most of the region has been cleared for cultivation and consists of extensive areas of open land; in general, however, forested districts were available as partisan sanctuaries. Moreover, in large parts of this region ill-defined divides between the watersheds of the rivers form extensive swamps which greatly add to the difficulty of penetrating the forests. In the Ukraine south of Kiev, extensive forests and swamps are rare. Down to the line running from Pervomaisk to Kharkov, however, the plain is partially wooded and some wooded sections are extensive. Below this line the true steppe begins; its only forest areas are those in the immediate vicinity of watercourses which provide sufficient moisture to grow trees. The Dnepr bend region lies in the steppe zone; as a result, the possible shelter for partisan groups operating there is severely limited. Essentially the sheltered areas are confined to the extensive swamps created by the numerous subsidiary channels of the Dnepr, which, below the city of Zaporozhye, becomes a sluggish and meandering stream, and to the extensive wooded district along the middle course of the Samara, a tributary of the Dnepr which drains the area just east of Dnepropetrovsk. Each of these areas covers approximately 150 square miles, but together they comprise less than 1 per cent of the total area of the Dnepr bend region. Moreover, these two wooded areas are separated by eighty miles of open land and a still greater expanse of coverless steppe lies between them and the wooded areas to the north. [See Fig. 23.]

From the point of view of its suitability for partisan activity, the open nature of the terrain and the remoteness of the Dnepr bend region from other potential centers of partisan warfare are of most immediate interest. In order to understand the importance of the region as a center for disruptive activities, however, it is necessary to examine the economic and social context as well, for in these respects, too, the Dnepr bend presented marked contrasts to the more northerly regions which were also occupied by the Germans. From the economic standpoint, the most striking characteristic is the great importance of the industries and mines of the region. The Dnepr bend region was, next to the Donbas region, the most important industrial area of the Soviet Union which came under German control. Moreover, since the still more industrialized Donbas region to the east was almost constantly on the edge of the zone of military operations, it is no exaggeration to say that the Dnepr bend region constituted the largest single concentration of industrial enterprises in the East, which remained under firm German control for a considerable length of time.

A brief description of the economic development as it existed at the outbreak of the German-Soviet war may be useful as an aid to understanding the potential importance of the partisans in the Dnepr bend region. The region was composed of four major industrial centers. In the northern part, two cities, Dnepropetrovsk and Dneprodzerzhinsk formed a major center of heavy industry in the USSR. Dnepropetrovsk, the fourth largest city of the Ukraine, had over 500,000 inhabitants in 1939. Twenty miles north of this city is Dneprodzerzhinsk, with 147,000 inhabitants. A number of smaller industrial towns lie along both banks of the river between these major cities. The chief emphasis of this region was heavy industry—arms and munitions, steel, locomotives, chemicals.

Some fifty miles to the south, a few miles above the great westward bend of the Dnepr was the large hydroelectric development based on the Dneprostroi dam. Using power produced at this project, supplemented by steam-generated electricity produced largely in Dneprodzerzhinsk, numerous industries were developed in Zaporozhye, a city of 250,000 inhabitants. The most important industry based on the large electric supply was aluminum refining; other metallurgical and manufacturing industries had also been built up. About one hundred miles west of Zaporozhye is the city of Krivoi Rog, the center of rich hematite iron ore deposits, which in 1941 produced two-thirds of the iron (by ferrous content) extracted in the USSR. Some of the ore was refined in the mine area; more was sent to the river cities or beyond to the coal fields of the Donbas. The Krivoi Rog mines

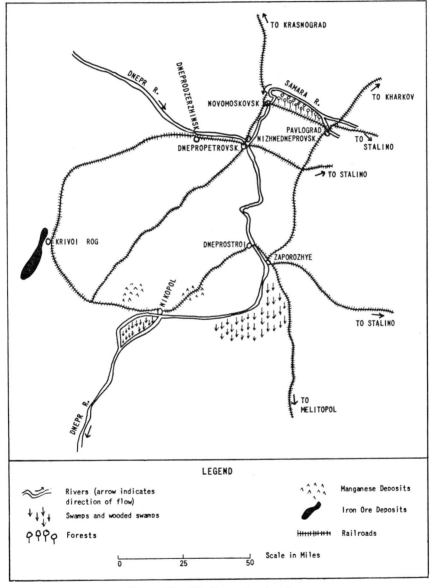

LEGEND

Rivers (arrow indicates direction of flow)		Manganese Deposits	
Swamps and wooded swamps		Iron Ore Deposits	
Forests		Railroads	

Scale in Miles
0   25   50

Figure 23.—The Dnepr bend region.

formed the basis for the iron and steel industry of the entire Ukraine.

About equidistant from Krivoi Rog and Zaporozhye, on the Dnepr south of the latter city, was a fourth center of industrial activity around Nikopol, a city of 58,000 inhabitants in 1939. The most significant resource of this center was very large deposits of manganese ore. Compared with the importance of the iron ore of Krivoi Rog these deposits were minor, for they furnished only 35 per cent of the total production of the USSR, which has additional deposits of the mineral in the Caucasus and Siberia. They constituted, however, a potentially vital source of supply for Western Europe, which has very few manganese mines. Germany was to have received nearly one-fourth of the output of the Nikopol area under the terms of the economic arrangements made in consequence of the Molotov-Ribbentrop pact of 1939.[1]

All of the industrial districts described above, with the exception of Zaporozhye and some of the suburbs of Dnepropetrovsk, lie on the western side of the Dnepr. This area, which is a flat, open, but fairly well-watered plain, is admirably suited to extensive crop cultivation and produced large crops of wheat and other grains. East of the river, the region was more predominantly agricultural and constituted one of the major wheat-growing districts of the Soviet Union. To the south it merges with the Nogai Steppe, a flat, almost completely treeless plain, which was even more renowned as a grain-producing district. At the northern edge of the eastern bank region at the opposite ends of the wooded Samara valley were two industrial centers of secondary importance, Novomoskovsk and Pavlograd. The latter city specialized in light manufactures while Novomoskovsk formed a subsidiary of the Dnepropetrovsk metallurgical center.

One of the major objectives of Soviet tactics in the summer of 1941 was to prevent these important resources from falling intact into the hands of the enemy. Consequently, great efforts were made to destroy or remove the industrial, transport, and mining facilities before the Red Army evacuated the area. Here, as elsewhere, these operations were not completely successful. This was especially true of the area west of the Dnepr, which, although it contained the greater share of the industrial and mining plants, had to be evacuated in great haste. While many machines were removed from the Zaporozhye aluminum works, the factory itself was largely intact, together with the essential electrolysis apparatus. Its future operations depended, however, on the availability of enormous quantities of electric current, which could be provided only by the Dneprostroi complex. Although the generating machinery there was not extensively damaged, the partial destruction of the dam temporarily eliminated the water power

[1] OKW/Wi Rue Amt (Wi VIa), "Orientiergung Nr. 5," 28 July 1941, p. 1 (GMDS, Wi/ID91).

necessary to operate it.[2] The metallurgical industries of the Dnepr cities were also out of operation for the time being. So, to a large extent, were the iron mines of the Krivoi Rog basin, which had been crippled by the removal of mine shaft machinery and transportation facilities.[3] On the other hand, while the eastern section of the Nikopol manganese district was similarly badly damaged, the western part was in fairly good condition, especially since the shallow depth of the pits rendered resumption of extraction operations comparatively easy even where the machinery had been destroyed or evacuated. Moreover, there were fairly large quantities of ore which had already been mined that could be concentrated in an almost unharmed plant before export to Germany.[4] The great importance of this mineral for German war industry is indicated by the German decision to divert some of the remaining machinery from Krivoi Rog to Nikopol in order to obtain a supply of manganese as soon as possible.[5]

The demographic and social characteristics of the Dnepr bend region are closely related to its economic development. Throughout the Ukraine, the city population differed in ethnic composition from that of the surrounding rural districts. While the countryside was almost entirely Ukrainian, the cities, prior to 1926, usually contained a non-Ukrainian majority composed largely of Russians and Jews. Since published data of the Soviet census of 1939 did not include information on urban ethnic composition, it is impossible to make any conclusive analysis of conditions in 1941. It seems probable, however, that the proportion of Ukrainians had increased significantly because of the influx of peasant to the cities during the period of the Five Year Plans. Since the Dnepr bend cities grew at an enormous rate between 1926 and 1939, it is very likely that their composition changed to an especially marked degree. Because of the relatively late settlement of the area (it was virtually a no man's land until the eighteenth century) and the comparatively extensive nature of grain cultivation, the population is not so dense as that of the northern Ukraine, and, although most of the villagers are certainly Ukrainian, there is probably less feeling of national distinctiveness here than in the north. Moreover, the industrialization of the region brought together in the cities persons of all the Soviet nationalities, but especially Russians, Jews, and uprooted Ukrainian peas-

[2] OKW/Wi Rue Amt (Wi VIa), "Zusammenstellung wichtiger Meldungen ueber die Ostgebiete, Nr. 12," 10 November 1941, p. 3 (GMDS, Wi/ID 191).
[3] OKW/Wi Rue Amt (Wi VIa), "Orientierung ueber die wehrwirtschaftliche Bedeutung der besetzten und im Bereich der Kampfhandlungen liegenden russischen Gebiete, Nr. 7," 22 September 1941, pp. 5–6 (GMDS, Wi/ID 86).
[4] Wi In Sued, "Kriegstagebuch Nr. 1, Schlussuebersicht ueber den Kriegseinsatz 1941," p. 5 (GMDS, Wi/ID 192).
[5] OKW/Wi Rue Amt (Wi VIa), "Orientierung ueber die wehrwirtschaftliche Bedeutung der besetzten und im Bereich der Kampfhandlungen liegenden russischen Gebiete, Nr. 7," 22 September 1941, p. 5 (GMDS, Wi/ID 86).

ants. The tempo of city growth resulted in a wholesale change in the ratio of urban-rural elements in the population as well as in the ethnic ratio, but it is questionable whether many of the newer inhabitants of the cities had become thoroughly urbanized either in their way of life or in their psychology. Nevertheless, the region presented a marked contrast to the demographically more stable areas of German occupation in the north.

Thus, at the outbreak of the war, the characteristics of the Dnepr bend region which influenced the development and course of the partisan movement were the following: (1) the open terrain and the isolation of the possible centers of partisan activity from wooded and swamp areas to the north, (2) the great importance of the industries and mines, (3) the complex and dynamic social and ethnic composition of the population.

§II. Summary of Historical Developments

In the initial German plan of operation against the Soviet Union, the campaign in the Ukraine was allotted a secondary role. Nevertheless, during the offensive in the summer of 1941, the German armies and their allies soon reached the west bank of the Dnepr along most of its course. By mid-August they had occupied the entire Dnepr bend region west of the river including all the major cities and had developed a bridgehead east of the river near Dnepropetrovsk.[6] At the Dnepr line the southern armies encountered strong Soviet opposition, and they halted temporarily while the main German effort was directed toward Moscow. However, when Hitler decided that an offensive against the Soviet armies in the Ukraine should, for the time being, take precedence over the northern advance, the drive in the south was quickly resumed.[7] Early in September the lower Dnepr, south of Nikopol, was crossed, and the Germans and their Italian, Hungarian, and Rumanian allies rapidly pushed through to the Sea of Azov.[8] Shortly afterward the advance east of the bend proper was resumed; by mid-October the entire region was in German hands, and the front line ran considerably to the east of it.[9]

The month's delay in the German advance undoubtedly facilitated Soviet efforts to create a partisan movement designed to harass the German advance and occupation, and thus to offset in some measure the defeats suffered by the evacuating Red Army. Apparently the Soviet regime was

[6] Kurt von Tippelskirch, *Geschichte des zweiten Weltkriegs* (Bonn: Athenaeum Verlag, 1951), p. 220.

[7] *Ibid.*, pp. 230–31.

[8] *Ibid.*, p. 234. The fact that the Italian, Hungarian, and Rumanian troops comprised a high proportion of the Axis forces in the initial conquest of the Dnepr bend area creates difficulties for this study, since only very scanty reports from non-German military units are available.

[9] *Ibid.*, p. 235.

especially anxious to establish partisan groups along the courses of the major rivers, where they could find shelter in marshes and woods and at the same time be in positions favorable for interrupting German lines of communication by destroying bridges.[10] This tactic was especially adapted to conditions along the Dnepr, where tangled marshes provide almost the only shelter in the region and where the breadth of the river makes interruption of communications a special danger. Consequently, it is not surprising that, even while the Red Army still occupied the bank opposite Nikopol, a group of partisans was formed in the swamp southwest of that city. The core of the band consisted of 350 men specially trained for partisan warfare in Stalino, but it was augmented by several smaller groups. Well-armed with light infantry weapons and explosives, the group entrenched itself in the heart of the swamp; it immediately began raiding the surrounding villages in order to obtain supplies and recruits.[11] The Germans soon noted the presence of partisans in the area,[12] but they appear to have been too occupied by Red Army units, which still held part of the east bank, to be able to deal with the partisans. A few weeks later an attack by an SS regiment decimated the ranks of the partisans, but the action was broken off before it could result in complete elimination of the partisan danger, probably because the regiment was needed elsewhere.[13]

On 8 October the 444th Security Division was ordered to relieve the SS formation in the Nikopol area and to clean out the partisan nest. About five battalions composed of about 2,500 men were available for this task. By 16 October these units had taken positions which encircled the partisan-infested area.[14] In the meantime, however, the partisans had been alarmed by the SS attack, and later they received specific warning of the German encirclement. About one-third of them were able to slip across the river on the night of 17–18 October; they then headed for the nearest major partisan center 150 miles to the north, the "Black Forest" southwest of Cherkassy. The remaining 350 men stayed to face the German attack which began the next day.[15] In a slow but thorough operation, the Germans closed in on the partisans during the following week, and succeeded

[10] 444. Sich.Div., Ltd. Feldpolizeidirektor, "Tagebuch Nr. 623/43," 5 November 1941, p. 3 (IMT, NOKW-1519) [hereafter cited as 444. Sich.Div., Ltd. Feldpolizeidirektor].

[11] *Ibid.*

[12] See, for example, 1. Gebirgsdivision, "Kriegstagebuch vom 16.8. bis 31.10.41," 18 September 1941 (GMDS, 1 GebDiv 15792/11), which states that "the night passed uneventfully. According to statements of the inhabitants, numerous soldiers as well as partisan bands have hidden along the Dnepr and extort food from the population during the night. On the other side of the river, occupied by the Rumanians, there is a great deal of shooting every night."

[13] 444. Sich.Div., Ltd. Feldpolizeidirektor, p. 5.

[14] 444. Sich.Div., "Bericht ueber den Einsatz der verstaerkten Sicherungsdivision 444 in der Dnjepr-Niederung in der Zeit vom 9. bis 27.10.41," pp. 1–2 (GMDS, HGeb 16407/7) [hereafter cited as 444. Sich.Div., "Einsatz in der Dnjepr-Niederung"].

[15] 444. Sich.Div., Ltd. Feldpolizeidirektor, p. 5.

in practically wiping them out. Two hundred and forty perished or were captured in the swamp itself, and one hundred were caught between Niko-pol and Krivoi Rog after they had temporarily evaded the Germans by slipping through the encircling lines in boats under cover of darkness.[16] By 26 October the Nikopol area had been pacified; the cost to the Germans for the entire operation was twenty-seven men killed, one officer and thirty-one men wounded.[17]

Although the campaign just described eliminated the partisan group west of Nikopol, there was some further partisan activity in the Dnepr swamps east of that city. During November 1941 the SD conducted several minor operations against three small groups totaling about ninety men with the result that they were completely destroyed. The records of these operations are scanty and contain little information on the background and activity of the partisans attacked; however, the information obtained was apparently accurate, since the diary of the commander was used to confirm interroga-tions of a number of prisoners. From the SD account, it appears that the groups east of Nikopol were not recruited in the Dnepr bend region; rather they were composed of Red Army men recruited in Moscow, then assigned to partisan work and given special instructions in Stalino and Chaplino.[18] The leadership was composed of Party functionaries, who were evidently also from the Moscow area. Apparently the groups were assigned to the Dnepr region strictly as a military diversionist force. When they reached the swamp area (apparently before the Red Army had finished its evacua-tion of the region: a major deficiency of the SD accounts is their omission of dates), these groups did not even have a local guide. Very little informa-tion on the composition, activities, and organization of the groups is avail-able, and there is none on the subsequent relations of the groups with the local population.[19]

While the Nikopol area was being cleared of partisans, German occupa-tion of the Pavlograd-Novomoskovsk area was just getting under way. The Red Army still held the bank opposite Dnepropetrovsk, and during this period the Soviet authorities formed a number of local defense units known as destruction battalions (istrebitelnyi batalyon). At first these formations were given only guard duties, but, when the German armies approached, their members went into the woods between Pavlograd and Novomoskovsk and began the construction of a partisan camp. At first the group num-

[16] This group is not to be confused with the earlier detachment which left for Krivoi Rog to carry on specific anti-German activity; apparently it reached its destination. The interrogations of the group which was captured, however, provide most of the information for the German reports on the campaign since most of the partisans who remained in the swamp were killed.
[17] 444. Sich.Div., "Einsatz in der Dnjepr-Niederung," pp. 7–8.
[18] The German text reads "Tschaplin," which apparently refers to Chaplino, a small town near the front area.
[19] Chef Sipo u. SD, IV A 1, "Ereignismeldung UdSSR Nr. 141," 3 December 1941, pp. 7–8 (GMDS, DW SD 43); Chef Sipo u. SD, IV A 1, "Ereignismeldung UdSSR Nr. 146," 15 December 1941, pp. 21–24 (IMT, NO-2835).

bered about 1,000, but within a few days (by early October) the leaders deliberately reduced the force to one-third of its original number by sending the less useful or reliable members to their homes. The remainder, who constituted a fairly enthusiastic "hard core," made elaborate preparations for a winter campaign of partisan activity; they secured large stores of provisions and munitions and built comfortable and well-protected quarters, in many cases utilizing dugouts which had been constructed before the war as part of an artillery range.[20]

The location of the Novomoskovsk group was ideal if one considers the availability of targets alone. [See Fig. 24.] While there were no major industries in the area—unless one includes the suburbs of Dnepropetrovsk, about twenty-five miles away across open country—there were ample opportunities for partisans to disrupt communications. Both Pavlograd and Novomoskovsk were major rail junctions. A railroad from Dnepropetrovsk follows the west bank of the Samara River to Novomoskovsk and from there branches off in two directions. The railroad to Krasnograd parallels the Samara for ten miles, while the line to Pavlograd crosses the Samara just above Novomoskovsk, and cuts across the arc of the river which encloses the forest. From Pavlograd in turn, the railroad, after crossing a tributary of the Samara, branches off in two directions. One double-tracked line proceeds in a northeasterly direction toward Kharkov, crossing the Samara River again, while a single-tracked line leads to Stalino. All of these railroads are paralleled by paved highways; in addition there is a highway from Zaporozhye to Novomoskovsk, which crosses the Samara River opposite the latter city. This transportation network offered an obvious target for sabotage and other disruptive activity, especially since its vulnerability was greatly increased by numerous bridges. The attractiveness of the target was especially great under German occupation because the routes—particularly the highway from Novomoskovsk to Pavlograd cutting across the arc of the Samara—constituted a main supply and reinforcement artery for the German forces in the Donets basin.

The partisan camp was well situated for action against German communications. It was located in the northwest corner of the forest, in its deepest part, and was partially protected against surprise attack from motorized forces by virtue of being half surrounded by the arc of the Samara, which at the same time offered no obstacle to partisan raids westward, since it is easily fordable by lightly armed troops. Pavlograd and its bridges were comparatively remote, but it was possible to interrupt the major Novomoskovsk-Pavlograd communications axis by sorties from the wood, which extends for nearly twenty miles parallel to the roads, at a distance of only five miles from them.

In view of the favorable conditions, it is a little surprising that more extensive operations were not undertaken at an earlier date by the well-

<hr>

[20] 213. Sich.Div., Ic, "Taetigkeitsbericht," May–December 1941, pp. 9–10 (GMDS, 213 ID 14424/4).

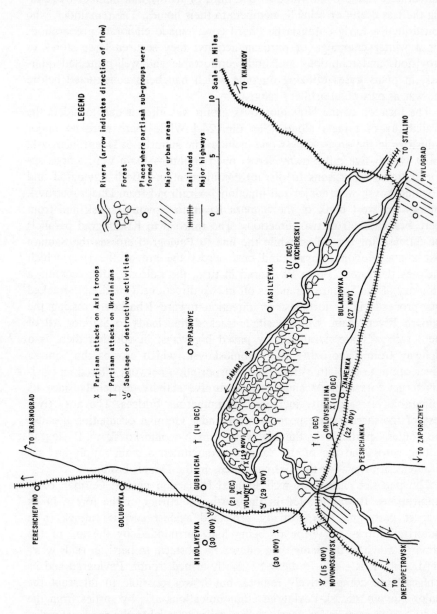

LEGEND

Rivers (arrow indicates direction of flow)

Forest

○ **Places where partisan sub-groups were formed**

Major urban areas

Railroads

Major highways

X Partisan attacks on Axis troops

† Partisan attacks on Ukrainians

⤳ Sabotage or destructive activities

Scale in Miles

0   5   10

TO KHARKOV

TO STALINO

PAVLOGRAD

TO KRASNOGRAD

PERESHCHEPINO ○

GOLUBOVKA ○

NIKOLAYEVKA ○
(30 NOV) ⤳

GUBINICHA † (14 DEC)

POPASNOYE ○

VASILYEVKA ○

X (17 DEC)
KOCHERESKII ○

(21 DEC) X
YOLNOE ○
(29 NOV) ⤳

X (19 NOV)

SAMARA R.

ORLOVSHCHINA
† (1 DEC)
X (10 DEC)

ZNAMENKA
X
(22 NOV)

BULAKHOVKA
⤳ (27 NOV)

PESHCHANKA ○

TO ZAPOROZHYE ↓

NOVOMOSKOVSK
⤳ (15 NOV)

TO DNEPROPETROVSK

Figure 24.—The Novomoskovsk-Pavlograd area.

supplied and highly organized partisans. However, from the tactical stand-point the same factors which made the partisan lair well-located for dis-ruptive activity rendered it highly susceptible to concerted attack by the Germans. It was relatively easy for the Germans to use the network of roads to assemble troops on all sides of the wooded areas within a short time. If they should be attacked by such an overwhelmingly superior en-veloping force, the partisans would be in an extremely perilous position, for the small area of their sanctuary made protracted evasion impossible. Consequently it appears likely, although there is no direct evidence on the point, that one motive of the partisans was to husband their forces until the general strategical situation made disruption of German communica-tions in the eastern Ukraine a matter of major importance to the Red Army's over-all strategy.

At any rate, activity of the Novomoskovsk partisans was much slower in developing than was that of the Nikopol band. Although the group was fully established by early October,[21] an attack on a kolkhoz near Volnoye on 2 November was apparently the first raid carried out by its partisans; the first serious threat to German communications developed in late No-vember.[22] Even then, partisan activity of only slight effectiveness was carried on by small groups under cover of night, or by persons ostensibly working for the Germans. Consequently, it may be classified as under-ground rather than partisan warfare, although the groups undertaking it were part of the main partisan force. Nevertheless, the Germans realized that a potential threat existed and proceeded to organize a campaign to eliminate it. An infantry regiment which had been assigned to security duties in the Kremenchug area was relieved of this duty and directed, by an order of 4 November, to take part in the attack on the Novomoskovsk partisans. While preparations were being made for this transfer, however, the regiment had to be diverted to the front where the situation had be-come critical.[23] By mid-November the German armies had been halted on the lower Don; it soon became apparent that the protracted battle, de-veloping into a defense against powerful Soviet counterattacks, would re-quire the use of all available forces.[24]

In spite of this disruption of the plan to attack the partisans, the

[21] One section, at least, went into the woods on 27 September. (Gruppe Geheime Feldpolizei, Dienststelle Feldpost Nr. 41308, "Taetigkeitsbericht fuer Monat Januar 1942," 25 January 1942, p. 3, GMDS, H Geb 75124/12.) It has been impossible to determine the number of this unit.

[22] *Ibid.,* p. 11. Instances were destruction of a highway bridge between Novomo-skovsk and Pavlograd during the night of 22–23 November; destruction of a railroad bridge in the same neighborhood, 29–30 November; burning of a German-occupied garage west of Novomoskovsk, 30 November.

[23] 213. Sich.Div., Ia, "Divisionsbefehl fuer den Einsatz ostw. des Dnjepr," 4 No-vember 1941, p. 1 (GMDS, 213 ID 14424/2).

[24] Befh.rueckw.H.Geb.Sued, Ia, "10-taegige Meldung," 30 November 1941 (GMDS, HGeb 30910/37).

Novomoskovsk area was transferred on 8 December to the operational area of the 444th Security Division, and the decision to undertake a campaign of annihilation against the partisans was maintained. At first only two battalions of troops, two detachments of the secret field police, and a "Cossack" auxiliary company were available; consequently, a direct attack on the wooded area was deemed inadvisable. Measures were taken to surround and seal off the forest, however, and to investigate the surrounding villages for suspicious persons.[25] Treatment of the civilian population suspected of assisting the partisans was deliberately made extremely severe; families of partisans were imprisoned and threatened with death if they failed to notify the Germans of any contacts with their relatives.[26] Probably because of a growing sense of desperation caused by the gradual encirclement carried out by the Germans and also because of a diminishing food supply, the partisans sharply increased their activity during December.[27] Among their most important attacks was a major raid carried out during the night of 10 December by some 200 men armed with numerous machine guns upon a camp of Soviet prisoners of war used by the Germans for construction work in the vicinity of Znamenka, a few miles south of the forest. The partisans fought a brief but sharp action with a detachment of German troops and succeeded in freeing (or, in some cases kidnapping) over 200 prisoners without loss to themselves. On 21 December they made a similar attack in force upon the village of Volnoye but were repelled with severe losses by a German company.[28]

On the same day, the first battalion of the 190th Infantry Regiment, which was being dispatched to Novomoskovsk as the backbone of the force designed to annihilate the partisans, arrived. After four days spent in placing the troops in position and combing the villages on the border of the forest, the real penetration of the wooded hide-out began. The whole campaign in the forest lasted only a week, being completed about 1 January. Very little resistance was offered by the partisans, who were either caught in flight or were burned to death or blown up in their underground bunkers. A much more serious danger to the German troops was the bitter cold which reached minus twenty degrees Fahrenheit and caused numerous frostbite casualties. In all, 242 partisans were killed and 160, including 95 of the prisoners of war liberated at Znamenka, were captured. Most of

[25] 444. Sich.Div., Ia, "Bericht ueber die Bekaempfung der Banditengruppen im Waldgebiet Nowo Moskowsk-Pawlograd," 22 January 1942, p. 1 (GMDS, HGeb 30910/37) [hereafter cited as 444. Sich.Div., Ia, "Bekaempfung der Banditengruppen"].

[26] 213. Sich.Div., Ia, "Kriegstagebuch Nr. 2, vom 1.1—31.3.1942," p. 2 (GMDS, 213 ID 19661/1).

[27] The German accounts are rather contradictory on this point. While p. 5 of the report cited just above (n. 26) states that the partisans were unwilling to take retaliatory measures in response to German mistreatment of their families, reports of individual attacks demonstrate that there was a sharp increase in activity.

[28] 444. Sich.Div., Ia, "Bekaempfung der Banditengruppen," p. 2.

them were shot after interrogation. Mopping-up operations continued for about two weeks, but the essential part of the campaign had required about the same length of time as had been needed for the destruction of the Nikopol band.

A few days after the destruction of the Novomoskovsk partisan group, the great winter counteroffensive of the Soviet armies in the Ukraine began. The starting point of the offensive was Izyum, about 130 miles northeast of Dnepropetrovsk. At its maximum penetration, late in February 1942, the Soviet drive had covered half this distance; consequently the front line was only thirty miles from the Samara.[29] Throughout the spring and winter the Red forces apparently endeavored to reconstitute a partisan movement, or at least to form partisan scouting bands, in the area threatened by their spearheads. To accomplish this, they parachuted in a number of individual soldiers and small parties; the Germans carefully noted all such incidents but reported no cases in which the parachutists secured local support.[30] No further partisan activity of any importance was reported from the Dnepr bend region until the beginning of the final withdrawal of the Germans from the Ukraine in 1943.[31]

[29] AOK 2, Ic, "Kartenanlagen 14–18, Feindnacher. Blaetter I.II.42—1.III.42" (GMDS, AOK 6, 1856/6).

[30] Befh.H.Geb.Sued, Ic, 7 May 1942, p. 1 (GMDS, HGeb 30910/37). See also the map of partisan activity in the area of the 444th Sich.Div. during March and April 1942, which indicates that there were only two cases of parachutists and three of isolated partisan activity in the area surrounding the Novomoskovsk forest. (Befh. rueckw.H.Geb.Sued., Ic, "Partisanenvorkommen im Heeresgebiet Sued 15.3—30.4.42," GMDS, HGeb 22571/10; and Wi Kdo Saporoshje, "Kriegstagebuch der Befehls-stelle Nowomoskowsk vom 1.7—7.9.1942," GMDS, Wi/ID 2.183, which, although it contains a detailed record of events in the area, makes no mention of partisans.)

[31] Toward the spring of 1943, after the Soviet recapture of Kharkov, this partisan activity became significant. "The partisan danger is especially great in the wooded districts south and southwest of Zaporozhye. Granaries have been set afire in a number of places, since for a long time it has been impossible, with the weak forces, to guard all economically valuable objects." (Wi Stab Ost, "Monatsbericht 1.4—30.4. 1943, Die wirtschaftliche Lage in den besetzten Ostgebieten," 17 May 1943, p. 4, GMDS, Wi/ID 357.) These activities, however, appear to have been sabotage rather than true partisan attacks. However, in the Novomoskovsk area, which was close to the front, partisans or irregular military bands reappeared and closely cooperated with the Red Army. "Monday, 15 February, I drove in the morning to Pereshchepino. ...In the meantime, however, the situation had become much more critical, for the northern part of the rayon was occupied by strong bands as well as by isolated groups of Red Army troops. ... In Bogatoye, a place a few kilometers east of Pere-shchepino, the gendarmerie and the Ukrainian *Schutzmannschaft* had exchanged heavy volleys with a big band at an early time. Moreover, the village of Berdyansk, north of Pereshchepino, was already occupied by enemy forces and a combat patrol approach-ing the place was fired upon from the houses. ...The same morning the village of Popasnoye was occupied by bands and Red Army troops. ... About 2100 the Wehr-macht and the gendarmerie forces in Pereshchepino had to evacuate the village and withdraw to Golubovka, since strong forces of regular Russian troops had occupied the places." ("Sonderbericht ueber die Februarereignisse im Gebiet Nowo-Moskowsk," n.d., signature illegible [probably the *Gebietskommissar* of Novomoskovsk], p. 2, GMDS, EAP 99/418.)

§III. Evaluation

The Dnepr bend region presented numerous and highly important targets for partisans. The presence of a large urban population might be expected to have provided numerous recruits, for the cities were the traditional strongholds of the Communist Party. An early start was made in organizing the resistance movement, and ample supplies of munitions were placed at the disposal of the partisans. In spite of all these advantages, the partisan groups achieved nothing beyond serving as a minor source of irritation and compelling the temporary diversion of a few thousand German troops. Within a few months after their formation they were completely destroyed as coherent groups; from then on the region remained one of the most peaceful districts under German control in eastern Europe.

One reason why the partisan groups failed to produce greater results was the unfavorable natural environment. Behind the northern half of the German front, almost endless swamps and forests offered facilities for protracted evasion and ample shelter in which to regain strength after temporary reverses. The small hide-outs of the Dnepr bend region, on the other hand, could be thoroughly combed by the Germans in the course of a single campaign. Moreover, the terrain in the north facilitated partisan operations by enabling soldiers of the Red Army who were cut off by the German advance to remain at liberty for long periods of time in out-of-the-way districts until they could be gathered together by partisan leaders. In the open plains of the south such troops were soon rounded up by German forces.

The base of support of the Red partisans was further restricted by the attitudes of the local population. While evidence collected for this study does not in itself form the basis for sweeping conclusions concerning popular attitudes, it is apparent that the general feeling was one of neutrality, if not active hostility, toward the Soviet regime and the partisans. The latter could secure active support only from relatives or from agents especially recruited in advance of the German occupation, while the Germans, too, could count on the support of a minority of the population. In some rural areas by late 1942, the disappointment arising from the Germans' failure to implement their promises of land reform and the resentment caused by excessive requisitions made the peasants willing to shelter the partisans. In the Dnepr bend area there was no such willingness. There was likewise no flight of men to the forests to escape intolerable conditions such as brutal recruitment as *Ostarbeiter* and wholesale reprisals against villages in partisan areas. On the contrary, in the Novomoskovsk area the German reprisal technique appears to have reached a level of severity (which could probably have been maintained for only a short time) which was just sufficient to deter the population from helping the partisans without being so excessive as to drive it into their arms. The amount of terrorism employed, combined with the obvious determination of the Germans to root out the partisan bands with overwhelming force, appear to have cut down and then to have destroyed the links between the partisans and the villages before these connections had become deeply rooted. Quite possibly lack of such connections in later periods was one factor which prevented the revival of the partisan movement in the Dnepr bend region.

Since the great bulk of the partisans were drawn from groups which were strongly attached to the Soviet system, one might think that they would have constituted an especially valuable force. Up to a point this was true; their desperate resistance and their frequently stubborn refusal to supply information to the Germans are indications of their determination. On the other hand, the fact that so many were urban men and that the remainder were drawn partly from sedentary occupations probably made them unfit for the rigors of life in the woods and unskilled in woodcraft so valuable in partisan operations. The elaborate preparation of winter quarters indicates the desire of city men for material conveniences as well as an obsession with the importance of the mere existence of the group—a "partisan band in being" concept—as opposed to a more active policy of inflicting maximum damage on the enemy before being wiped out. The bureaucratic background of some of the leaders and the overcomplexity of the organizational structure were probably additional factors favoring the persistence of this relatively passive attitude.

In comparison with partisans operating later, all groups active in 1941 were handicapped by lack of experience and training and by the relative inefficiency of the support and liaison system developed by the over-all Soviet partisan command. Time and experience remedied these defects to a considerable extent, while the breakthrough of the Soviet armies in the winter of 1941–42 brought powerful reinforcements to the partisan groups in the north. Those groups which survived the first period of trial were also greatly supported by the belief in eventual Soviet victory, a confidence which increased with the successes of the Red Army. Consequently, it is probably safe to conclude that, in spite of all the defects of the partisans themselves, they could not have been eliminated so rapidly and thoroughly had not the Germans concentrated sufficient forces against them at an early stage of their growth. That the Germans did so is probably due to the fact that the forces required were relatively small and that they could be drawn from the whole southern part of the area of Army control. In the north, where each security unit was confronted with vastly greater tasks, such concentration was more difficult; as has been shown, the military situation after the beginning of the winter made such employment of troops in the rear area difficult even in the southern region. The importance of a rapid assembling of sufficient force to "kill," not merely to "wound," the partisan band during the first stage of its development and before it achieves broad acceptance and cooperation among the surrounding population is one of the major lessons of the Dnepr bend operations.

In a broader perspective, a major value of the study of the Dnepr bend partisans is that it emphasizes the fact that, given favorable circumstances and a prompt and determined application of force, the partisan danger could be eliminated. In the general consideration of the partisan movement, especially in the northern occupied regions, the over-all picture is one of steady growth of the bands and increasing success of their activities. This picture may create the impression that there is something inherent in the eastern European scene which makes it impossible for an invader to establish secure authority. In demonstrating that this was not always the case, this study may help place the entire partisan movement in a truer light.

Reference Matter

Selected Soviet Sources
on the World War II Partisan
Movement

Introduction

A large number of documents concerning Soviet partisan activities—including numerous reports written by the partisans themselves—were captured or picked up by the Germans in their operations on the Eastern front. Many of these have been found scattered among German files captured during or at the end of World War II. Some of these are presented in this volume in English translation. The selection has been based on general importance, representative character, and special interest. Because the research work in the course of which these documents were found concentrated on the central part of the Eastern front, most of the documents deal with partisan affairs in this area, the center of partisan concentration throughout the war. If some themes recur with great frequency, this is only a reflection of partisan warfare as it really was.

In most cases, only German translations of these documents have been found. To judge by the few instances in which both Russian original and the German translation are available, the translations are fairly reliable. Nevertheless, since the originals were often wordy and complicated, the translations are frequently poor stylistically and occasionally incomprehensible. The English translations presented here have been made as literal as possible, and literary style has been sacrificed to avoid the danger of introducing additional errors.

It is the opinion of the War Documentation Project Staff that these documents are authentic. They are taken from secret German files kept by the Germans for their own guidance and reference in combat, and were not intended for propaganda or similar purposes. It seems most unlikely that the Germans would have concocted any of these documents in order to fool themselves. Furthermore, none of the documents appears to be a Soviet plant. There was no reason to let misleading general directives to partisans fall into German hands, and there does not seem to have been any effort to let the Germans "find" tactical orders designed to mislead them. As can be seen from the German sources, the partisan reports often contain exaggerations and inventions. This, however, would seem only to confirm their authenticity since the Germans were in a good position to check such facts as the number of their own trains blown up by the partisans.

The documents have been grouped in topical sections for convenient reference. Such organization must necessarily be flexible when reports touching on a variety of topics are translated in their entirety. Documents originating with the same partisan group have been kept together and put under the most appropriate section heading. Documents from two important partisan units make up separate sections.

Brief introductions to sections and to individual documents or small groups of documents have been prepared in order to help place the matrial in its context. A number of technical Russian terms have been retained: oblast for province, rayon for county, poselok for settlement, starosta for village elder, politruk for political officer, Front for army group, kolkhoz for collective farm, and sovkhoz for state farm; in addition, the term "police" as used in the Soviet documents refers to the indigenous auxiliary police, the *Ordnungsdienst* (frequently abbreviated OD) and the *Schutzmannschaften*. Annnotations are provided in footnotes to explain other technical terms and points of special significance which might otherwise not be clear. A list of sources is given at the end of the collection. From this listing, the location of the German originals in the captured files can readily be determined.

In general, commentary has been held to a minimum inasmuch as these and many other Soviet and German documents are used and analyzed at length in the War Documentation Project studies which have become chapters of this book. In this collection the general reader may obtain some insight into Soviet partisan warfare as seen primarily from the vantage point of the partisan, and the specialist will find a selection of representative source material hitherto unknown or not readily accessible.

The plan of issuing this collection originated with the War Documentation Project in the spring of 1953. Dr. Gerhard Weinberg, in close cooperation with the undersigned, acted as over-all coordinator and provided introductions to the sections. The translations were prepared by Dr. Ann Beck, Mr. Kurt DeWitt, Dr. Fritz Epstein, Mr. Ralph Mavrogordato, Dr. Wilhelm Moll, Mr. Roger Nelson, Mr. Eric Waldman, Dr. Hans Weil, Dr. Gerhard Weinberg, and Dr. Earl Ziemke. Dr. John Armstrong and Dr. Alexander Dallin reviewed the completed manuscript in an advisory capacity. Editorial and technical assistance was given by Mrs. Florence Dallin, Mrs. Jean Powell, Mrs. Nina Whiting, Mrs. Peggy Windsor, and Miss Gloria Young. Professor Philip E. Mosely, Chairman of the War Documentation Project Standing Committee, and Mr. Hans J. Epstein, War Documentation Project Officer, promoted in every possible way the preparation of this collection.

Dr. Fritz T. Epstein
Director of Research
War Documentation Project

§I. The Organization of the Partisan Movement in 1941

DOCUMENT 1

This order was apparently the basic directive for partisan warfare, implemented by orders like that reproduced as Document 2.

Workers of the World
Unite!

Copy

Top Secret [Soviet Classification]

The Central Committee of the All-Union Communist Party [TsK VKP(b)]

Nr.P34/250

18 July 1941

To: The Central Committee of the Communist Party of the Ukraine
            The Central Committee of the Communist Party of Belorussia
            The Moscow Oblast Committee of the VKP(b)
            The Kalinin Oblast Committee of the VKP(b)
            The Central Committee of the Communist Party of Estonia
            The Smolensk Oblast Committee of the VKP(b)
            The Leningrad Oblast Committee of the VKP(b)

The following order is to be made known to the Oblast Committees and Rayon Committees of the Party.

Order of the Central Committee of the Communist Party concerning combat organization in the Rear of the German Army.

In the War with Fascist Germany, which has occupied a part of the Soviet territory, combat in the rear area of the German Army acquires particular importance. Its task is to create unbearable conditions for the German invaders, to disorganize their lines of communications, supply and military units, to paralyze all their measures, to destroy the hoarders and their collaborators, to support everywhere the organization of partisan cavalry and infantry units and destruction groups; to spread the wide network of our Bolshevik organization in order to carry out all measures against the Fascist occupiers. In this battle against the Fascist invaders we still have quite a number of methods and opportunities, which have not as yet been utilized, for inflicting severe blows on the enemy. In all these activities we will receive in every town and also in every village willing support from hundreds, even thousands of our brothers and friends who find themselves under the boots of the German Fascists and who are expecting our help in the organization of the struggle against the occupiers.

To give this combat activity in the rear area of the German Army greater *élan* and fighting force it is necessary that the leaders of the republics and of the oblast and rayon organizations of the Soviet Party [*sic*] take over the organization on the spot themselves; they personally must organize the work in the rayons occupied by the Germans, create groups and units of selfless fighters who are already engaged in a battle of annihilation against the enemy's troops and in their destruction. There are still a few cases in which the leaders of the Party and Soviet organizations of the rayons threatened by the Fascists shamelessly leave their combat posts and retreat deep into the rear area to safe positions, thus becoming deserters and pitiful cowards. In the face of these shameful facts the heads of the republic and oblast organizations of the Party are not taking energetic measures. The Central Committee of the VKP(b) demands from all Party and Soviet organizations, especially from all their leaders, that they put an end to such unbearable conditions, and reminds them that the Party and the Government will not hesitate to take the most severe measures in regard to those slackers and deserters; it hopes that the Party organizations will take every step to purge these traitors from the Party organizations, and will concentrate all their efforts on destroying the enemy at the front and in the rear area, and will make every preparation for a victory against the Fascist bands.

In this connection, the Central Committee of the VKP(b) demands that the Central Committees of the Parties of the republics and the oblast and rayon committees of the occupied oblasts and rayons, and those threatened with occupation, carry out the following measures:

1. Particularly reliable, leading Party, Soviet, and Komsomol activists, and also non-Party members devoted to the Soviet regime, who are acquainted with the circumstances in the rayon to which they are to be assigned, must be selected for the organization of Communist [underground] cells and for assuming leadership in partisan activities and in the destruction campaign. The assignment of workers to certain regions must be carefully prepared and camouflaged; for this purpose each group (two to three men) must get in touch with only one person; groups to be assigned are not to come in contact with one another.

2. In those rayons which are threatened by enemy occupation the leaders of the Party organization must organize secret underground cells without delay, to which they immediately assign a number of Communists and Komsomol members.

In order to insure that partisan activities will spread widely in the rear areas of the enemy, the Party organizations must create immediately combat and paratroop units from among those who participated in the Civil War, and from among those comrades who have already distinguished themselves in destruction battalions and in units of the home guard, and also from among workers of the NKVD and NKGB. Communist and Komsomol members who are not used for work in the secret cells must also be enlisted in these groups [combat and paratroop units].

The partisan units and secret groups must be supplied with arms, ammunition, money, and valuables for this purpose; the necessary supplies have to be buried and hidden ahead of time.

Signal communications between the partisan units, the secret cells, and the Soviet-side rayons must be established; for this purpose the organization must be supplied with radio equipment; couriers, codes, etc., must be used; the distribution and preparation of leaflets, slogans, and newspapers must be accomplished on the spot.

3. The Party organizations under the personal guidance of their first secretaries must select experienced fighters; these must be comrades who are devoted to the end to the Party, and who are personally well known to the leaders of the Party organization, and are experienced in the work of organizing and providing leadership for partisan activity.

4. The Central Committees of the republic Communist parties, the oblast committees and district committees must report, through a specially designated [covert] address, to the Central Committee of the VKP(b), the names of those comrades who are selected as leaders of the partisan groups.

The Central Committee of the VKP(b) demands that the leaders of the Party organizations personally direct the struggle in the German Army's rear, that they arouse the enthusiasm of those persons who are devoted to the Soviet regime by personal examples of bravery and selflessness, so that the whole struggle will be of direct, generous and heroic assistance to the Red Army which is fighting the Fascists at the front.

The TSK of VKP(b)

> *True copy:* The head of the Special Section of the Stalingrad Oblast Committee of the VKP(b)

(Myakinin)

DOCUMENT 2

> The following set of instructions is one of the basic Soviet documents in the development of partisan warfare in World War II. Quoting Stalin's famous speech of 3 July 1941, this document lays down basic principles of partisan organization and activity and provides tactical hints for partisan operations behind the enemy lines.

"Confirmed": [for the ?] Commander of the Northwest Front
[signed] Brigadier General Sobechikov[1]
20 July 1941

Member of the War Council
[signed] Shtykov

*Instruction Concerning the Organization and Activity of
Partisan Detachments and Diversionist Groups*

General Directives

1. The partisan movement has arisen as a popular movement in the enemy's rear areas. It is called upon to play a mighty role in our patriotic war. The

---

[1] Soviet military ranks are given in U.S. equivalents throughout this appendix in accordance with the following:

Soviet rank	U.S. equivalent
Major General	Brigadier General
Lieutenant General	Major General
General	Lieutenant General
Colonel General	General

Thus, Sobechikov's rank is given in the original as Major General.

basic objectives of partisan warfare in the rear of the enemy have been clearly stated by the Chairman of the State Committee for Defense, Comrade Stalin: "Partisan units, mounted and on foot, must be formed; diversionist groups must be organized to combat the enemy troops, to foment partisan warfare everywhere, to blow up bridges and roads, damage telephone and telegraph lines, set fire to forests, stores, transports. In the occupied regions conditions must be made unbearable for the enemy and all his accomplices. They must be hounded and annihilated at every step and all their measures frustrated."[2]

2. First and foremost, partisan detachments and diversionist groups must be established in the main operating areas, that is, the areas of greatest concentration of the enemy. The partisan detachments are to be organized as combat units or diversionist groups according to their function.

3. Partisan detachments must be well armed and sufficiently strong for active operations in the enemy rear. The total strength of such a unit may amount to 75–150 men, organized into two or three companies, with the companies divided into two or three platoons.

4. The basic operating sections of the combat units will be the company and the platoon. Their basic duties—carried out as a rule at night or from ambush—are attacks on columns and concentrations of motorized infantry, on dumps and ammunition transports, on airfields, and on railroad transports.

The operations must be carried out in areas in which forests furnish cover for the units. Such an area can consist of up to two or three administrative rayons; operations are to be carried out only against the main lines of communication of the enemy. Each administrative rayon should contain at least one partisan combat unit.

5. Aside from combat units, diversionist groups of 30–50 men are to be created in each rayon. These will be organized into five to eight groups of three, five, or ten men each. The diversionist groups must be so organized that the partisans of one group do not know those of any of the other groups. The organization of these groups, above the level of the individual unit, exists only for the purpose of controlling their operations and organizing new groups.

6. The basic objectives of the diversionist groups are as follows: the destruction of telephone and telegraph lines, the burning of gasoline dumps and transports, the destruction of railroad lines, the destruction of individual trucks and small groups of vehicles and the capture of documents found on them, the burning of armored vehicles by means of incendiary bombs, the killing of enemy officers, the spreading of rumors designed to produce panic among the enemy troops (rumors concerning the appearance of Soviet tanks or airborne troops in their rear).

7. In all the areas still occupied by the Red Army, the NKVD [People's Commissariat of the Interior] and NKGB [People's Commissariat of State Security] offices are to organize destruction battalions to combat enemy airborne troops in our rear. In the event that these areas should be evacuated by

[2] For the complete text of this speech of 3 July 1941, see Joseph Stalin, *The Great Patriotic War of the Soviet Union* (New York: International Publishers, 1945), pp. 9–17.

the Red Army and occupied by the enemy, the destruction battalions must remain in the area and change over to partisan warfare.

8. The local rayon Party and Soviet offices and the representatives of the NKVD and NKGB are fully responsible for the organization of the destruction battalions and for their conversion into partisan units.

It is categorically forbidden to dissolve the destruction battalions; if they split up or retreat to our rear area, the head of the above-named offices will be brought to account before the War Tribunal.

9. The primary basis of the organization of the partisan movement must be the mass formation of combat units and diversionist groups.

Tactical Employment of Partisan Combat and Diversionist Detachments

Only bold and resolute actions of the partisan detachments will guarantee success and bring the Red Army substantial help. The strength of the partisans consists in their having the initiative and in their unexpected actions.

Bases for the actions of the partisan detachments are the ambush and sudden, short raids on the objective after which the detachment scatters into small groups and reunites at the rendezvous. Actions are undertaken only at night or before dawn when the vigilance of the enemy guards slackens. Advance on the objective takes place only at night after the objective and the approach route have been reconnoitered by daylight.

If the objective of the raid is guarded, one must remove the guard quickly and noiselessly (with ranger tactics) or go around him. The partisans ought not to return fire.

After the raid, or if it failed, the partisans escape pursuit and reunite at a previously indicated rendezvous three to five kilometers distant from the operation point.

As a rule, in escape from pursuit one must first take a false direction of march. If the enemy pursues the detachment, a small group of the boldest partisans must be assigned the task of covering the withdrawal of the main group. The covering group must pull back in a false direction. If the pursuing units are foot soldiers, one must surprise them either by using the main group for a flank attack or by proceeding to capture and destroy the objective denuded by the withdrawal of the enemy guards; thus the real mission will be fulfilled.

For their destructive actions in the rear of the enemy, the partisan detachments and diversionist groups must utilize local resources on a broad scale; for example, for the demolition of railway tracks, the rails must be loosened with the help of a wrench, which is available in every signalman's hut. For destruction of communication lines, the poles should be sawed off.

Plain bottles filled with gasoline[3] are to be used to set fire to gasoline tanks or armored cars (a bundle of rags or twigs, soaked in an inflammable fluid, is to be bound at the bottom of the bottle); the bottles are to be thrown at the fuel tanks and motor vehicles in raids on parking places of the enemy's motorized troops.

[3] Known in English as "Molotov cocktails."

Railroad trains can be halted by laying a pyre on the rails. When the train has stopped, it is to be fired on from ambush, and soldiers climbing out must be destroyed by machine gun and rifle fire as well as by hand grenades. For the fight against motorized units raids on resting places are to be carried out at night and the personnel as well as the gasoline supply destroyed.

For the fight against the enemy's air force, raids on airfields are to be undertaken and planes destroyed on the ground. Groups of three to five men are to be formed from among the good shots; they will approach the airport under cover and destroy from ambush low-flying planes landing and taking off. In addition to its tasks, the areas of activity are to be laid down for the partisan detachment. These areas must include large woods to screen secret maneuvers and hiding places.

Destruction of Traffic Routes and Means of Communication

The most substantial interference in railroad and truck transport is attained through the destruction of bridges (blowing up, undermining, burning).

For the destruction of rails, small groups (three or four men) must be assigned. Derailments must be effected simultaneously on a series of railway sections, thus rendering the repair more difficult. As derailment locations, steep downgrades are to be chosen, where the train moves at high speed and is harder to stop. The loosened rails must be removed from immediately in front of the train so that the engineer will not notice the damaged stretch. Three or four men (who sit in ambush) can do this by tying to the rails strong rope or telegraph wire which can be obtained by destroying communication lines. If the road is double track, it is sufficient to derail one track since thereby both will be blocked. Simultaneously with the destruction of the rails, communication lines running along the railroad must be destroyed by cutting the wires after sawing off the poles. The more poles downed, the harder is the repair.

A good means of interference is linking wires together. This is achieved by joining all wires on the pole by a thin, unobtrusive wire, the end of which leads down the pole and is buried.

Occupation and Destruction of Encampments

The destruction of gasoline and munitions dumps has priority at all times. Usually these dumps are located far from inhabited areas; they are carefully guarded and have good communications connections. For that reason communications with the outside must first be broken in order to occupy and destroy [the dumps].

For the occupation of encampments the following groups ... must be assigned: (a) A group for destruction of communications with the outside. (b) One or a few groups with automatic weapons and grenades to cover the section where the enemy guards are and pin them down. (c) A few groups armed with hand grenades, gasoline bottles, and rifles for the actual occupation after the destruction of the guards.

The raids are to be carried out only at night or at dawn. In ample time prior to the raid on the camp, daytime reconnaissance must secure information on the position of the posts and guard room, the telephones and signal arrangements, and the concealed approaches to the camp and the posts. It is essential for the group leaders to acquaint themselves personally with the objective of the action in daylight.

After occupation of the camp, immediate steps are to be taken for its destruction by setting fires at various places (by using gasoline bottles, effectively shooting up gasoline tanks and cisterns with inflammable missiles, and other means).

After completing the task, the detachment concentrates at the rendezvous previously set by the commander.

Ambushes and Raids in the Fight Against Living Enemy Targets

The partisan detachments have unlimited possibilities to carry out sudden short raids from ambush on living targets of the enemy. Such raids engender panic in his ranks, induce him to flight, and create confusion among his units and subdivisions whereby his further movement is held up and serious losses are inflicted on personnel and matériel.

Partisan warfare can be especially effective against troop units marching at night. In most instances, large units of the enemy carry out their marches at night, when they are less threatened by planes. Night raids from ambush are suitably carried out simultaneously by some groups (platoons) with reinforced firing capacity. Such groups can impede the advance of whole divisions and bring about disorder.

Ambushes for raids are best set along roads. The best ambush is the edge of a wood, 150–250 meters from the road, on which movement of enemy columns is expected. Ambushes against living targets should not be arranged near a road, for after the first shots the groups can be attacked by enemy columns.

The region between ambush and road should be open, so that the use of the total fire power of machine guns and rifles is assured. The fire should be directed obliquely at the road and preferably by cross fire along the road. This firing system must be sustained within each group. It is a good idea to station on the flanks of the groups, 30–40 meters from the road, two or three skilled grenade-throwers who, after rifle fire against the column has started, throw hand grenades at it.

The ambush must not be detected by the enemy's security patrols. This is achieved by the arrangement of ambushes 100–150 meters from the road and by absolute quiet within the group (at night the flank guards of the foe are sent out 50–100 meters from the road). Smoking, movements in the group, talking, etc., are categorically forbidden in ambush. The mouth must be covered with the sleeve, cap, or something of the like in case of involuntary coughing.

Firearms attacks are to be carried out only against the main forces and not against forward security units and detachments. The latter must be allowed to pass by. Ambushes in platoons must be organized in intervals of 500–700 meters and the firing attack is to begin simultaneously upon signal of the leader. The position of the leader is with the middle group or with the group which, in the direction of the enemy's advance, is closest to the enemy.

The opening of fire from the first machine gun of the leader's group can serve as the signal. In the ambush no entrenchments are to be made since these can lead to discovery.

When time permits, matériel abandoned by the enemy must be destroyed. First, the motors of the vehicles are to be ruined by rifle shots. Horses used for the horse-drawn guns must be shot. All light weapons (rifles, machine guns, munitions as well as hand grenades) must be taken along for utilization in future battles. Surplus items are to be wrecked, so that they cannot be used later.

At night it is relatively easy for partisan detachments to bring about a fight of two enemy columns against each other. To achieve this, small partisan groups between the two columns open fire simultaneously on both columns.

Operations against motorcycle riders, infantry transported on motor vehicles, or marching infantry can be especially effective. Small groups of three to five partisans, in ambush along the road at intervals of 100–150 meters, can inflict a serious defeat on the enemy, scatter his columns, and send them fleeing in panic.

For ambushes and raids against columns of motor vehicles a section of the road on a high embankment or with ditches along the road is to be selected. In all cases, the partisans must strive to erect road blocks with felled trees, destroyed bridges, abandoned vehicles set crosswise, etc. These road blocks will be useful only if in their vicinity (150–200 meters in the direction of the foe) ambushes are set up with one or two groups to shoot at the enemy troops as they crowd together.

The partisan detachments and their groups must be mobile and not detectable by the enemy. To increase mobility, detachments and groups must count only on captured vehicles and on those furnished by the population. Vehicles tie the detachment to roads and are more of a hindrance than a help. Riding horses, even when unsaddled, are a good means of locomotion; but as a rule mobility is to be assured by training in rapid marching, tactical march, and especially in night marching.

For marching movements paths in fields and woods are to be preferred. Inhabited areas must be avoided. It is better to march extra kilometers than to be discovered by the foe.

March discipline must be high. Smoking and conversation are forbidden at night.

Upon unexpected contact with the foe at night, one should not open fire but rather quickly escape from the foe and change direction several times.

On the detachment's route of march two to three men are to be left behind for 20–30 minutes, in order to learn whether or not the foe or his agents are following its trail. The latter are to be taken prisoner and executed.

For its own security the detachment or group dispatches two to three scouts during the day, 300–500 meters ahead; at night, 100–150 meters ahead. It is desirable to send the scouts on horseback; in this case they are to be 1–1½ kilometers ahead. To the rear the detachments are guarded by two scouts. In the column itself observers are assigned ahead and to the sides for reconnaissance. It is the detachment's duty to avoid unexpected contact with the enemy. If small groups of the enemy are identified, they should be allowed to pass by and the main force should be attacked from ambush. The foe is to be hit wherever he appears.

The well-prepared organization of rest periods is one of the most important considerations of the detachment in the rear of the enemy. The foe will strive to take the detachment by surprise during its rest. Therefore, the detachments must always be in permanent battle readiness. The particular diversity and tension of the work of the partisan detachments require great attention [to the problem of rest] in order to preserve the strength of the partisans.

The authority of the commander of the detachment will be firm if the partisans see in him not only a valiant, bold fighter and a good organizer of sudden raids on the enemy but also a careful, solicitous leader.

The resting place is as a rule in woods (and thickets), remote from roads and inhabited points and in the winter or at especially rainy times, in isolated buildings (woodsmen's huts, single farms). One should not stay in the same place for more than two successive days. The resting places (hideouts) must be changed daily if possible.

Immediately before arriving at the chosen resting place, the detachment (group) must take a marked change of direction in its approach route and leave behind a listening post of two or three men in an ambush to seize people who try to ferret out the detachment.

In case an alarm [is sounded] while [the unit is] at rest, a rendezvous is to be made known beforehand. The partisans rest with their weapons, the commanders among their troops. The resting place is to be guarded closely on all sides by double posts. If an inhabited region is chosen as a resting place, it must be enclosed on all sides by guards who do not let inhabitants and members of the detachment pass without special order. The troops of the detachment are to be sheltered in houses and barns in compact groups with their commanders. The commanders are not permitted to have separate quarters.

Consequently, the resting places must conform to the following requirements: (a) Create the best rest conditions; remain unnoticed by the enemy from the ground and from the air. (b) Good places for detection of unexpected raids by foot troops must exist. (c) Rapid assembling upon alarm and the existence of assembly places must be assured. (d) The distance from large roads and inhabited regions must be sufficiently great.

The partisan movement is a mass movement of the whole people. The partisan movement splinters, tires out, and weakens the forces of the enemy and brings about advantageous conditions for the Red Army's counterattack. The strength of the partisans rests in their activeness, initiative, and boldness. Basic methods of work are sudden night raids from ambushes on enemy units in the rear.

The primary sources of supply for weapons, munitions, and provisions are loot taken from the enemy. Stores which only a limited number of persons know are to be created from surpluses in various hiding places.

The partisan detachments do not wait for assignment of tasks from above; they operate independently according to the instructions of the great leader of the peoples, Comrade Stalin: "Create intolerable conditions for the enemy.... Destroy him at every step, undermine all his measures," in order to liberate our fatherland from foreign invasion.

> Head of the Administration of Political Propaganda of the Northwest Front, Brigade Commissar [signed] Ryabchi
>
> Chief of the 10th Section of the Political Administration of the Northwest Front, Captain of State Security Asmolev

DOCUMENT 3: The Partisan Oath

Every partisan had to swear a special oath upon formal entrance into the partisan movement. This oath is of considerable interest, both because of its emphasis on loyalty and discipline and because of its propagandistically patriotic tone.

I, a citizen of the Soviet Union,[4] a true son of the heroic Russian people, swear that I will not lay down my weapons until the Fascist serpent in our land has been destroyed.

I commit myself without reservation to carry out the orders of my commanders and superiors and to observe strictest military discipline. I swear to work a terrible, merciless, and unrelenting revenge upon the enemy for the burning of our cities and villages, for the murder of our children, and for the torture and atrocities committed against our people. Blood for blood! Death for death!

I swear to assist the Red Army by all possible means to destroy the Hitlerite dogs without regard for myself or my life.

I swear that I will die in frightful battle before I will surrender myself, my family, and the entire Russian people to the Fascist deceivers.

If, out of fear, weakness, or personal depravity, I should fail to uphold this oath and should betray the interests of my people, may I die a dishonorable death at the hands of my own comrades.

DOCUMENT 4

This report on the organization of partisan groups in the area of the Soviet Northwest Front is probably the earliest Soviet document on partisan warfare captured by the Germans. The only date in the document itself is 13 July 1941; on the following day the Germans took it from a Soviet courier plane which had made a forced landing. Not only the early date is of special significance but also the information provided on the organization and control of partisan groups from the Soviet side of the lines.

[4] For partisans who were members of the Belorussian or Ukrainian SSR, the appropriate name of the SSR was substituted here, and also in the following phrase, "Russian people." The oath was also used in the Belorussian (and presumably the Ukrainian) language. See WB Ostland, Ic/WPr, "Feindpropaganda," 7 November 1942 (YIVO, Occ E 3).

To: Commissar of the Army, 1st Class, General Mekhlis   *Top Secret*
Moscow, Main Administration of Political Propaganda
of the Red Army   *Copy No.* 1

*Political Report of the Administration of Political
Propaganda of the Northwest Front*

On the Organization of Partisan Units

A special section, designated as No. 10, has been established with the Administration of Political Propaganda of the Front. Its task is the direction of partisan movements in the rear of the enemy. It carries out all work regarding the organization, armament, and direction of the activities of the partisan units. The section maintains constant contact with local Party organizations and partisan units regarding the movements of the latter.

The Administration of Political Propaganda of the Front has dispatched 52 political workers of the middle and older age groups for immediate organization and direction of the partisan movement and for work in the rear of the enemy.

On 13 July 1941, 22 partisan units were set up in the operational area of the Northwest Front (Luga, Velikiye Luki, Bologoye). The leaders of these units are Communists, mainly political workers of active status in the Red Army who were selected by the Administration of Political Propaganda of the Front. The leaders of six units were political workers from local organizations or leaders of collective farms. All the leaders of partisan units have been thoroughly instructed. Every one has been given a memorandum drawn up by the Administration of Political Propaganda of the Front. It contains detailed directions for the activities of the units and their subunits.

The partisan units were organized as follows: The unit is basically composed of 50–80 men and is subdivided into 5–8 subunits. One special unit consists of 300 men. Its commander, Comrade Krasavin, is the functionary of the Party district of Ostrov; Comrade Yakushev, Captain of Frontier Troops,[5] has been named chief of staff. In addition, this unit has been given 11 leaders of intermediate command level who are used as company and platoon leaders. Six demolition instructors from the engineer corps are also attached to the unit.

The equipment of the unit consists of 300 rifles, 14 light machine guns, 4,500 bullets, 1,000 hand grenades, 300 bottles with incendiaries, 300 antitank mines, and 100 kilograms of explosives.

This unit operates in the area of Ostrov-Staraya Russa. On 12 July it assembled in the Dno area and advanced toward the rear of the enemy.

The other 21 units contain fewer men (50 or less) and have various tasks in the rear of the enemy which they perform in small groups. All these units are equipped with guns, grenades, and one or two light machine guns or automatic guns. The units operate in the following areas: Pskov-Luga, Ostrov-Staraya Russa, Opochka-Kholm.

In addition to these 22 units, mopping-up battalions have been organized in

[5] Frontier troops were part of the NKVD.

each area by organs of the People's Commissariat of Internal Affairs and the People's Commissariat of State Security. It is the task of these units to fight enemy parachutists in the rear of our troops. These units are at present carrying out their tasks and usually retreat with the Red Army or the evacuated local population when the enemy approaches. Depending upon the retreat of Red Army troops and the number of destruction units located with them, two or three of the latter are combined in one area.

The Administration of Political Propaganda of the Front has taken measures to assure that after the advance of the enemy these mopping-up units will be transformed into partisan units operating in the rear of the enemy.

By sending political workers to the partisan units and to local Party and Soviet organizations, the Administration of Political Propaganda of the Front is at present working to expand the partisan movement in the rear of the enemy.

I shall send a supplementary report on the results of partisan activities.

> Head of the Administration of Political Propaganda of the Northwest Front, Brigade Commissar [signed] Ryabchi

DOCUMENT 5

In 1941 the Soviet Government attempted to organize a partisan movement in the Ukraine as well as in Belorussia; its efforts in the former territory were never as successful as in the latter. The early organization of partisan groups in the Ukraine is well illustrated by a document, presumably dating from early September 1941,[6] reporting on partisans near Poltava. Of special interest are the details concerning partisan training and the stockpiling of supplies for the coming operations behind the German front.

Top Secret

To: Chief of the Counterespionage Division of the [People's] Commissariat of Internal Affairs, Lieutenant of State Security, Comrade Shchirbinkin, City of Poltava

Activity Report

Subject: The organization of partisan units, their composition, and the work of the sabotage battalion

In the rayon of Lubny, four partisan units and one sabotage battalion have been organized. The partisan units have been organized from among Party members on the basis of voluntary enlistment for the fight against fascism.

All the partisan units are organized in the western part of the rayon, on the right bank of the Sula River in the forests between the villages of Biyevtsy, Yankovtsy, Khaleptsy, Makovtsy, Luka and Klepchi.

The partisan units consist of 129 men, 19 of whom belong to the leadership and 110 to the rank and file. There are 81 Party members, 18 Party candidates, and 26 non-Party members. Among them are 30 workers, 37 kolkhoz members, and 59 functionaries and employees [of the state].

---

[6] The report itself refers to a previous report of 30 August; the Germans took Poltava on 18 September.

The leaders of the partisan units, whose efficiency reports were submitted to you on 30 August 1941, are comrades selected from the Party membership as morally strong and politically tested.

From the ranks of those who came to the partisan units, 25 men were rejected after examination for the following reasons: 15 men for cowardice and unreliability in their activities, 10 men for other reasons; for instance, Party member Petulko, director of the Lekhsyryo Factory said: "I say categorically, I cannot do this; I am too recent a Party member." The same thing was said by Plakida, director of the instruction division at the Institute of Pedagogy.

The sabotage battalion was formed at the beginning of combat operations and had a strength of 300 men of different age groups. During the training stage, 65 men were excluded from the battalion for various reasons. Among those excluded were 3 kulaks,[7] 1 man with a criminal record, and 61 physically unfit men.

Prior to their mobilization into the Red Army, that is up to 30 August 1941, the battalion had 235 men, including 18 men in leadership positions. After the mobilization, 202 men remained in the sabotage battalion, including 18 men in leadership positions. Among them are 69 Party members and candidates, 57 Komsomol members, and 76 non-Party members.

The sabotage battalion consists of 2 rifle companies; each company has 3 platoons.

In the period following the outset of combat operations and the organization of the sabotage battalion, alert duty was set up with the staff in the strength of a platoon. At night this guard platoon has the task of protecting the most important installations in the city. During the daytime the platoon has six hours of duty.

The parts of the sabotage battalion which are not on duty are called upon to drill every other evening for two hours from 7 to 9 P.M. In addition, tactical exercises are carried out by the whole battalion every Sunday.

Since the organization of the battalion, 48 hours of tactical training have been held, 46 hours of shooting practice, 48 hours of field service, and 10 hours of instruction in Red Army regulations—altogether 152 hours.

The following equipment is available for the sabotage battalion and the partisan unit:

7.62 mm rifles	540
carbines	431
heavy machine guns	1
light machine guns	1
foreign machine guns	3
pistols and revolvers	18
7.62 mm rifle ammunition	24,422 rounds
foreign rifle ammunition	57,756 rounds
hand grenades	90

The partisan units are fully provided with food and other material. Except for gasoline bottles, gasoline, and blankets, stores have not been collected.

Arrangements have been made to leave behind a terrorist group of seven

[7] A former peasant landowner.

men who will operate individually. Besides, we will dispatch a partisan group of seven men into enemy-occupied territory. We shall announce the composition of this group at a later date.

> Chief of the [People's] Commissariat of Internal Affairs at Lubny
> Lieutenant of State Security [signed] Kiselev

DOCUMENT 6

This remarkable biography of one of the most important central directors of the partisan forces is by his captured aide. After the war T. A. Strokach held important positions in the Ukrainian police organization.

Life History and Characterization of the Chief of the Ukrainian Staff of the Partisan Movement, Colonel General Strokach.

Timofei Amvrosiyevich Strokach was born in 1900 in Siberia (his native town or village are not known to me). He is of peasant origin. Until he was eighteen he lived in his parents' home, tilling the soil and hunting wild animals.

When he was nineteen he joined the Red Army. He participated in the Civil War and at that time attended a course for Red Commanders. From 1919 until the present he served without interruption in the Red Army. Two of his brothers fell during the Civil War. His father died in 1920; his mother, two brothers, and two sisters are still living (where they live and what they do, I do not know). During 1922 and 1923 Strokach held leading positions in the Eastern frontier troops.

St.[rokach] took part in the battles against the "Basmachestvo" [the Basmach revolt of the Moslems in Turkestan] for which he received from the Revolutionary War Council a silver watch with a special dedication. For his participation in the battles on the Chinese Eastern Railway he received from the Revolutionary War Council a pistol with a special dedication and a silver-lined holster as well as a citation as "Participant of the Battle on the Chinese Eastern Railway."

St. has been a member of the All-Union Communist Party since 1924 (I cannot give more specific dates), but St. graduated from the Central Officers School of the Frontier Troops of the GPU. He also took a special advance course for officers of the Eastern frontier troops. In 1934 or 1935 he graduated from the Military Academy with special commendation from the Central Executive Committee [of the USSR, abolished in 1936] and the Revolutionary War Council.

St. claims that he has also worked in the following capacities: commandant of the officers school of the frontier troops in Kamenets-Podolsk and Tiraspol; commander of the 24th border regiment of the NKVD; commander of a border detachment; deputy commander of frontier troops on the Western and Rumanian Frontier. After graduating from the Academy he received the rank of major; and in 1936 or 1937, the rank of colonel. In 1936 he lived in the Ukraine, where he was deputy commander of frontier troops. He was nominated as a candidate for the Supreme Soviet and subsequently elected as a deputy. He also was a delegate to the 18th Party Congress.

In 1939 St. was appointed Deputy People's Commissar of Internal Affairs of the Ukrainian SSR by the Cadre Section of the Central Committee of VKP(b) and the Central Committee of the People's Commissariat of Internal Affairs [obviously the Personnel Directorate of the NKVD is meant]. He remained in this position until August 1941 when he, like many other members of the Central Committee of the Presidium of the Ukrainian Supreme Soviet and of the NKVD, was trapped by the German forces. The only strategist of this group, St. had to get them out of the encirclement. He collected six to seven thousand officers and men from among the encircled forces, broke through the ring near Kiev and fought his way to Voronezh in the following twenty-one days. For saving these high personages from the encirclement, St. received the Order of the Red Banner. In 1939, when he was Deputy Commissar of Internal Affairs of the Ukrainian SSR he was given the rank of Major of State Security (one diamond on the collar insignia). In 1942, by decision of the Central Committee of the VKP(b) and by order of the NKVD (USSR), Strokach was relieved of his duties and placed at the disposal of the High Command. His position [in the NKVD of the Ukraine] has so far not been formally filled; provisionally it is being held by the chief of the Fourth Section of the NKVD of the Ukrainian SSR, Major (now Colonel) of Border Guards, Reshetov. Strokach now holds the position of chief of the Ukrainian Staff of the Partisan Movement [which is attached] to the Central Committee of the VKP(b) and the High Command [of the Red Army]. He is a member of the Central Committee of the VKP(b) and the KP(b)U.

In February 1942, St. was awarded the title of Commissar of State Security, third grade, corresponding to the rank of Colonel General in the People's Commissariat of Defense. Captain Rogozkin of the Grizodubov [cavalry] squadron under the Ukrainian Partisan Staff, who arrived in Bryansk Forest from Moscow by Douglas plane on 27 or 28 May 1943, stated that Strokach now had the title of Colonel General and was wearing gold epaulets with three gold stars.

Decorations and Awards Held by Strokach

Order of Lenin, two Orders of the Red Banner, one Order of the Red Star, one Order of the Red Banner of the Toilers, Twentieth-Anniversary-of-the-Red-Army medal, insignia of "Honorary Chekist," decoration for "participation in the Battles along the Chinese Eastern Railway," two insignias as a deputy of the Supreme Soviet of the USSR and of the Supreme Soviet of the Ukrainian SSR; also numerous other diplomas and valuable gifts.

Strokach's Positive and Negative Character Qualities and Special Traits

Light blond; 1.8 meters tall; well-fed; very large, round head; straight, pointed nose; very small, deep-seated grey eyes; thin blond hair, receding hair line; scar over the right eye; smooth-shaven; three gold teeth in front; large mouth, thick lips. Most of the time his glance is kindly but sometimes it becomes penetrating and his eyes narrow and take on a sly expression. When talking he always has a friendly smile. In dealing with visitors he is studiedly courteous and formal; on and off duty his manners are cultivated; in conversation he is reflective, calm, and shows evidence that he is well-read. He is very curious and inquisitive; he has great self-control, at least up to a certain point; once this limit is reached his reaction becomes unpredictable. He is frugal, has no particular hobbies, is often too trusting. Where his own interests are involved, he is inclined to cheat and to ingratiate himself with his superiors, particularly in the Central Committee and the High Command.

He can drink quantities of vodka well; drinking makes him merry and talkative. He likes company and music; but he declines to read any kind of literature, political or belles-lettres, except for newspapers and magazines. He eats plenty of anything put in front of him. He likes funny stories and jokes; in company he is gay and full of humor. When in the circle of his trusted associates and under the influence of drink he always rails against the Jews; he is angry that they are not at the front or on the collective farms. In 1942, at Stalingrad, a member of his staff, Uralovsky, a Jew, used illness as a pretext for refusing to carry out an assignment in the German rear; the next day St. dismissed [from his staff] seven Jews, giving "well-founded" reasons in each case. Generally, he dismissed many Jews, although many remained. St. has said that really all Jews should be sent away but that it would be too obvious and cause too many disagreeable consequences. He has several love affairs which he keeps secret from his subordinates as well as his family. He had a mistress, a radio operator of the staff, of whom only I knew.

The Soviet upper strata, that is government circles and high personages in Stalin's entourage, have great respect for him; his subordinates and the population in general like him, and he has few enemies, for he is fair. He is easy to influence (a number of examples could be cited). He works [every day] from 1000 to 1700 and from 1900 to 0500 hours, sleeps only 4–5 hours a day and always looks very tired. He talks in his sleep; it happens very frequently that he answers questions put to him while he is asleep. (He used to take treatments for this but no longer has time for them.) He has great work endurance and is very accurate; when something goes wrong in the course of his work, he takes it very hard and drowns his sorrow in vodka.

St. places great value on precise execution of orders. Therefore he makes great demands upon himself and his subordinates. He appraises his associates correctly. Stalin is very satisfied with his work; his aides in the Kremlin frequently telephone St. to ask how he is. Every week he receives gifts from the Kremlin.

[signed] Captain Ruzanov.

24 June 1943
Loetzen

§II. Soviet Directives to Partisans

DOCUMENTS 7–10

In July and August 1942, during the period of the great Soviet retreats on the southern part of the Eastern front, an effort was made by the Soviet High Command to increase partisan activity in the occupied areas. On 1 August 1942 the Central Staff of the Partisan

Movement issued an order (Order No. 0018) reproaching the partisans for letting so many German troop and supply transports through to the front and calling upon them to redouble their efforts. This order was widely distributed and copies of it fell into German hands at various scattered points in the occupied territories. The copy translated here (Document 8) was taken from a partisan scout near Senno in the northern part of the pre-1939 Belorussian SSR. Three documents found with it have also been transplanted. The first (Document 7) is a covering letter to Order No. 0018 which is of considerable interest since it shows the importance attached to the directive (Document 8). The other two documents (Documents 9 and 10) are orders of the Operative Group for partisan activity at the headquarters of the Fourth Assault Army, which may represent at least a part of the effort of this group to implement the directives contained in Order No. 0018.

DOCUMENT 7

Covering letter, envelope: Top Secret

To the commander of N/O [*narodnoye opolcheniye,* Home Guard] No. 29, Bulanov
[From] Operative Group of Fourth Assault Army

Covering letter, contents: USSR People's Commissariat of Defense

Top Secret
Copy No. 10

Operative Group of the Partisan Movement with the Headquarters of the Fourth Assault Army
To: The commanders and commissars of the partisan brigades; copy to Comrade Bulanov
7 August 1942, No. 29

I herewith transmit Order No. 0018 of 1 August 1942 by the Commander of the Central Staff of the Partisan Movement at the Headquarters of the Supreme Command. I propose to make the contents of the order known to all the commanders and, as far as feasible, also to all the commissars of the brigades. The units of Kirpakh and Bulanov, which operate independently, are also to be informed of this order, which is to be endorsed by personal signature. After the order has been received, all members of the units are to be made acquainted with it.

The Operative Group at the Command of the Fourth Assault Army is to be advised of the execution of the order. After thorough study of the order, it is to be returned with endorsement.

The Commander of the Operative Group of the Partisan Movement with the Headquarters of the Fourth Assault Army

Senior Battalion Commissar
[signed] Sokolov

DOCUMENT 8

Top Secret

Copy No.

Order

by the Commander of the Central Staff of the Partisan Movement
at the Headquarters of the Supreme Command

Contents: Increase of activities of the partisan troops in the rear area of the
enemy

No. 0018   1 August 1942, Moscow

The Red Army, which is heroically fighting for its fatherland, tenaciously
defends every inch of its Soviet soil and inflicts tremendous losses in men and
matériel on the enemy. The enemy who brings up reserves against us from
the areas in the distant rear and from other combat areas, continues to threaten
the vital centers of our country.

Very many new enemy divisions coming from France, Belgium, Holland,
and Germany, and equipped with artillery and tanks, continuously unload
their equipment near the front line and enter into combat with the Red Army,
after they have passed undisturbed through thousands of kilometers because
of the inactivity of individual partisan groups.

Hundreds of enemy trains and trucks continue to supply combat equipment,
food, etc., in spite of the fact that our partisan troops exist everywhere.

Those parts of the Red Army which are heroically fighting at the front
against the ever more ferocious enemy expect, within the next few days, more
help from the partisan units which operate in the enemy's army rear area. To
all commanders of the staffs of the partisan movement on the army group
staff, to the commanders of the operative groups on the staffs of the armies, to
all partisans, commanders, and commissars of the partisan units, [who should
be] overcoming all obstacles and defying death, goes the following order:

1. Fulfill our duty toward our fatherland; fulfill all the tasks which Comrade
Stalin has assigned to the partisans; increase partisan warfare in the rear area
of the German occupiers; disturb the intelligence network and supply lines
and the transportation system; destroy the headquarters and the technical equipment and spare no bullets "against the oppressors of our fatherland."

2. Strike immediately the strongest blows against the supply lines of the
enemy, and let no train with men, food, and technical supplies pass to the
front; this must be done by systematically organizing according to plans the
derailment of trains, blasts, and fires. Blows must be struck unceasingly in the
rear area of the enemy by placing our own forces at the focal points of the
roads and railroad connections.

3. It is not enough to be satisfied with blasting tracks and derailing locomotives or parts of the train; it is absolutely necessary to destroy the crew. The
locomotives especially are to be thoroughly destroyed by blasting, burning, or
setting fire to the steam boilers with armor-piercing shells and by exploding
and burning the coal tenders (Behaelter). Gasoline is to be destroyed after
shooting and killing the crew of the transports and the railroad guards.

4. The enemy's supply system is to be obstructed by destroying bridges, road
connections, railroad centers, and storage facilities of equipment, food, and
gasoline.

5. Procrastination and inactivity, still to be found in some partisan groups, must by all means cease; it is necessary to attack the enemy with the greatest possible energy. All commanders and commissars of partisan units are requested to recommend immediately for the highest state decoration and rewards any complete unit of partisans responsible for a train derailment. If such a recommendation cannot be submitted immediately, documentary evidence of the heroic deed is to be retained and the recommendation is to be made later.

This order is to be made known to all partisan units. On behalf of the Commander of the Central Staff of the Partisan Movement at the Headquarters of the Supreme Command,

(P. Ponomarenko)

Identical with the original. The Commander of the Operative Group of the Partisan Movement with the Headquarters of the Fourth Assault Army.

Senior Battalion Commissar, Sokolov

Printed in 10 copies
7 August 1942

DOCUMENT 9

To: Commander of the Partisan Group, Comrade Bulanov

According to the directives of the Central Staff of the Partisan Movement, the Staff of the Partisan Movement [of the Fourth Assault Army] has set up courses for company commanders[8] for training commanders of partisan units, staff commanders, and heads of diversionist groups.[9] Five persons are to be selected from among those fighters who are most reliable, politically most experienced, morally most steadfast and unreservedly devoted to the Socialist fatherland, and who have also already distinguished themselves in battle. Two are to be selected as unit commanders, and one as head of diversionist groups.[10] Those who have been selected for training as staff commanders must have had seven years of general education. The selected men with fighting ability are to be sent on 8 August 1942 to the Partisan Operative Group with the Headquarters of the Fourth Assault Army.

> Commander of the Operative Group of the Partisan Movement with the Headquarters of the Fourth Assault Army
> Senior Battalion Commissar, Sokolov

3 August 1942

DOCUMENT 10

To: Commander of the Partisan Group, Bulanov

I direct that the Operative Group of the partisan movement submit at once data regarding combat efficiency and number of persons, in accordance with the blank form sent out earlier. The area of operations is to be indicated.

> Commander of the Operative Group of the Partisan Movement with the Headquarters of the Fourth Assault Army
> Senior Battalion Commissar, Sokolov

4 August 1942

[8] *Kompanie-Fuehrer-Kurse.*
[9] The German text, evidently in error, reads *Divisionsgruppen.*
[10] See n. 9.

DOCUMENT 11

In the fall of 1942, during the period of the great Soviet retreats on the southern part of the Eastern front, directives were issued by the Soviet leadership to increase partisan activity in the occupied areas. One such directive is Order No. 0018 (Document 8).

A second document of this kind (Document 11) appeals to the population as a whole, especially to those who have been collaborating with the Germans, and charges the partisans with supervising the execution of this order. Several points are worthy of special note. The document itself is dated 12 August 1942 and quotes a German document dated 19 July 1942 from Novgorod-Seversk, then deep inside the occupied area. The appeal to the collaborators is particularly clever: it contrasts the Germans' proneness to punish their own collaborators with the Soviet willingness to pardon them for their past deeds.[11] It is interesting to note in the second paragraph of the order that the Ukrainian national hero Khmelnitsky is listed among the great heroes of Russian history, in whose name the people are now summoned to demonstrate their devotion.

Order

of the Commander of the Partisan Movement in the Territories
Temporarily Occupied by the Germans

The bandit, bloodsucker, and cannibal, Hitler wrote in his program: "In order to dominate the Greater German Reich and the whole world we must first destroy all Slavic peoples—[Great] Russians, Poles, Czechs, Slovaks, Ukrainians, Belorussians. To reach this goal it is necessary to lie, betray, and kill." The German Fascist band carries out this order of the crazy man. The German occupiers kill, rob, and destroy our people in the temporarily conquered areas and destroy the wonderful towns and villages of our people. It is impossible to recount all the atrocities which have been perpetrated and are still being perpetrated by the Germans. All German orders are elaborated so as to carry out the program of the crazy Fuehrer. The commandant of the town of Novgorod-Seversk, Major Palm, issued an order on 19 July 1942. I quote a few samples from it: "It is absolutely forbidden to leave the village. All people—men, women, and children—who leave the village will be shot at. The cattle can be grazed only in a radius of 100 meters around the village. Boating on the Desna is forbidden; fishing is also forbidden. Grinding in the mills is likewise forbidden. The delivery of milk, eggs, and berries is to be stopped immediately and not to be carried out."

This shows that the Germans fear the rebellious people and the attacks by the Red partisans and have therefore stopped carrying milk, eggs, and berries out of the villages. The Russian people must take advantage of this. Everywhere, in the entire occupied territory, it must rise to fight the German robbers and make it impossible for them to plunder it. Give the Germans no more provisions (bread, cattle, hay, etc.) and drive them from our land.

[11] A collection of other appeals to those collaborating with the Germans will be found in Sect. V.

Expecting that the order will not be carried out by the police and the starostas, Palm writes: "If the order is not carried out by the police and the starostas, they will be considered partisans and will be treated like partisans."

In their impotence in the face of the rebellious people and the ever-growing partisan movement in the occupied areas the Germans accuse their servants, the starostas and police, of being partisans and have them shot. This certainly will happen everywhere. Servants are used for a while and then the Germans either have them shot or send them to Germany where they perish.

In my order of January 1942, I ordered the starostas, policemen, and all others not to help the Germans. At the same time I warned everyone that whoever continued to collaborate with the Germans would be destroyed as a traitor to the great Russian people. Sufficient time has passed, and there has been the opportunity under one pretext or another to cease performing this degrading work for the Germans. In view of this, I have ordered all partisan groups to destroy or severely punish all traitors to the Russian people, as some groups have already done to a certain extent. We must unite all forces of the Russian people for this battle and for expelling the German occupier from our native Russian soil.

I order:

1. All village and city mayors, rayon and district leaders, officials of the indigenous administration, police, so-called "Cossack Volunteers,"[12] and other employees of the occupation administration to quit their work from the day this decree appears.

2. All starostas, policemen, so-called "Cossack Volunteers," and others who have erred and have turned against their people to give up the fight against the Russian, Ukrainian, and Belorussian peoples, the Red Army, and the Red partisans.

I call upon all citizens in the areas temporarily occupied by the Germans, regardless of where they might have been previously, to rise and to take up, each and everyone, the protection of the USSR as declared patriots, and to fight for the honor, freedom, and independence of the fatherland. We men and women must prove ourselves worthy of our great forefathers, A. Nevsky, D. Donskoi, K. Minin, D. Pozharsky, Suvorov, Kutuzov, B. Khmelnitsky, Belinsky, Chernyshevsky, Pushkin, T. Shevchenko, Gorky, and the heroes of the Civil War, Chapayev and Shchors.

3. In the name of the freedom and independence of Russia, I say to all who still have a feeling of proud nationalism of independent people that whoever from now on ceases to serve the Germans against his own people, regardless of what he has been up to now (starostas for the Germans, policemen, so-called "Cossack Volunteers," etc.), will be amnestied by the Red partisans, the commanders of the Red Army, the Soviet Government, and the whole Soviet people from the day this order is issued. All will forgive you because they know that many of you were prisoners and others were forced to help the Germans. Many of you were deceived and misled in various ways by the German cannibals.

4. In the interests of every farmer, worker, member of the intelligentsia, and

[12] Units of Cossacks established by the Germans to fight the partisans.

the whole country, the following is absolutely forbidden: No citizen may turn over bread, hay, potatoes, or other products to the German occupiers who have stolen everything from the people and have left the villagers to their fate, starving and without clothes.

Though organized, united, and indomitable, we let the Germans continue to rob our people and land. Instead, we must meet German pillaging with our whole strength and organization. People who do not carry out this order and who turn over bread, cattle, hay, and other products to the Germans will be severely punished by the arm of the Revolution, and all their property will be confiscated.

5. Starostas, police officials, so-called "Cossack Volunteers," and other individuals who continue to serve the Germans after the proclamation of this order will be considered traitors and arch enemies of the people of the USSR and will be mercilessly destroyed.

6. The commanders of the partisan battalions are responsible for supervising the execution of this order.

Comrades! Workers! Peasants and intelligentsia of the temporarily occupied territories! Rise together as one man for the unquestionably victorious battle against the enemy of mankind, against the bloodthirsty German Fascist bands. Take up arms and arise to defend your families, your property, your villages and towns, your native land!

Policemen, so-called "Cossack Volunteers," starostas, and others who still serve the Germans, turn your weapons against the German occupier at once. Join the ranks of the fighters against the Fascist occupier, the great family of the USSR. Join the ranks of the Red partisans who are fearless in the fight against the enemy. Together with our Red Army of the front and of the rear areas we will destroy the German occupiers and drive them from our land. Only when our land has been cleansed of the German Fascist carcass, can a peaceful and happy life be built.

Death to the German occupier! Forward, my dear comrades, under the banner of Lenin and Stalin to the complete destruction of the German Fascists in the year 1942.

> The Presidium of the Supreme Soviet of the USSR
>
> Commander of the Partisan Movement in the Territories Temporarily Occupied by the Germans [signed] Sergeyev
>
> Major General, Hero of the Soviet Union, Corps Commissar, Karpov

12 August 1942

DOCUMENT 12

The partisan movement was always linked closely to the Communist Party. The following directive,[13] ordering the Communist Party to devote its efforts to the activation of the struggle against the invader, documents this relationship.

> *Work Plan and Program of the Communist Party [VKP(b)][14] of the Rear Area 1943*

[13] Only selected passages of this lengthy document have been translated here.

[14] VKP(b), All-Union Communist Party (of Bolsheviks).

The Communist Party of the Rear Area, which corresponds to the Communist Party of the national republics, is the organized vanguard of the proletariat in areas of the USSR occupied by the Fascists; it is the highest form of its organization.

The Communist Party of the Rear Area is above all an armed, anti-Fascist organization in the rear of the enemy; it is held together by conscious, iron, proletarian discipline.

The Party makes the necessary preparations and organizes and leads a proletarian, anti-Fascist, popular resistance in the rear of the enemy; it works resolutely in building up flexible and mobile partisan shock units which prove themselves worthy of the designation of International Proletarian Avengers[15] in the fight for the victory of the Socialist fatherland of the world proletariat over fascism.

. . . .

The program of the VKP(b) serves as a basis for the activity of the Communist Party of the Rear Area. All actions of its members incompatible with this program or deviating from it constitute offenses against militant Party discipline.

After the primary mission is accomplished, which is also the only task of the Communist Party of the Rear Area, namely the expulsion of the Fascist intruders, the Communist Party (of Bolsheviks) of the Rear Area will be merged again in the ranks of the All-Union Communist Party (of Bolsheviks).

Party Members and Their Duties

1. Anyone can become a Party member who is filled with hate toward fascism and believes in the final world-wide victory of the proletariat, who acknowledges the Party program, who takes an active part in one of its organizations and is prepared to give his whole strength, and, if necessary, even his life in the great struggle against the Fascist intruders, and who also regularly pays membership dues.

2. The Party member is obligated: (a) To maintain strictest military Party discipline. (b) To participate actively in the political life of the Party, the country, and the world. (c) To put into practice the Party policy, to execute immediately all decrees, assignments, and orders of the Party organs and military leaders. (d) To explain the real situation on the anti-Fascist fronts of the World War to the non-Party masses and to restore and strengthen among them the belief in final victory of Soviet power over fascism. (e) To work incessantly to raise his level of Communist doctrine and the standard of his practical military capabilities. (f) To be as hard as granite if arrested by the Gestapo or the police, and even unto death, under no circumstances and under no threats of the hangman, to betray the Party, military, and state secrets entrusted to him by the Party and the fatherland. (g) To obey most strictly at all times all rules of underground work and never to forget that the Party fights fully encircled and must expect attacks by the enemy from all sides. (h) To be ever conscious that he works in his own land among the Soviet people and fights against the occupation bands and intruders whose expulsion is his civic duty.

3. Admission into the Party is effected only after previous acceptance by the

---

[15] *Internatsionalnyi Proletarski Mstitel*, **I.P.M.**

chief and is an individual, personal admission. Only such persons are admitted as Party members who have been examined by the chief or by the unit members and have proved on several occasions their ability in the execution of underground missions as well as their devotion to the proletarian revolution.

. . . .

5. Each Party member is an anti-Fascist fighter and has the designation of an International Proletarian Avenger.

. . . .

The Organizational Structure of the Communist Party (of Bolsheviks) of the Rear Area

8. Basic to the establishment of the Party organization of the rear area is the appointment of officials which is regulated as follows: (a) All Party officials are appointed from the top down, with the exception of the unit[16] leaders (*Nizovoi partiinyi organizator*), who are chosen by a simple majority of the unit members. ... (b) Party officials are obliged to render an account of their activity to the next higher ranking Party official at specified intervals. ... (c) Strictest Party discipline and subordination prevails under the commanding authority. ...

9. The Party is territorially constructed according to economic districts. The unit (*Nizovaya organizatsiya*) comprises a village or part of one, a section of a city, a kolkhoz or *sovkhoz,* a mine, a factory, or a similar enterprise. A Party rayon (*Rayonnaya organizatsiya*) comprises an oblast or an industrial district ("basin"). A center (*Zentrum*) comprises the area corresponding to the sector of a Front.

10. The unit is the nucleus of the Party. ...

11. A group of units (*Gruppa nizovykh organizatsii*) is led by a local Party committee (*Pervichnyi partiinyi komitet*) and constitutes a local organization (*Pervichnaya organizatsiya*), in which the number of units may not exceed 12 and the number of members may not exceed 100.

12. The rayon committee (*Rayonnyi partiinyi komitet*) is the directing organ of a rayon Party organization, directs the local organizations, and is in charge of a given territory of strategic importance.

13. The center (Central Committee of the Communist Party [of Bolsheviks] of the Rear Area) directs all rayon Party organizations in the sector of the occupied area adjoining a Front region and is therefore the highest commanding Party office of the Communist Party.

14. The liaison between the local organizations and the units is maintained directly through the office of chiefs (*Shefstvo*). ...

15. On the cell level, the lever which sets off the activity of the units is the chief (*Shef*). The chiefs are the founders and directors of units. The chiefs form the organizational basis of the Party. ...

. . . .

Activating the Underground Party Leadership and the Liaison of the Center with the Units

The liaison among Party organizations is of decisive importance in the illegal work of the Party.

[16] Commonly known in early Bolshevik terminology as the "cell."

18. The liaison of the center with the subordinate offices is maintained through continuous transmission of activity reports which must be submitted by the lower Party offices to the higher ones.

. . . .

23. The chief represents the liaison between the local organization and the units. . . .

24. The funds of the Party and of its organizations consist of the membership dues of Party members and other payments.

25. The admission fees and monthly dues of Party members are established as follows:

Admission fee	30 rubles
Monthly dues	20 rubles

26. The organization of flexible and mobile partisan detachments and diversionist groups and single acts of sabotage directed against the invading Fascist hordes represent the concrete and only goal of the Communist Party (of Bolsheviks) of the Rear Area.

27. Each unit must devote all its strength to this goal and is obligated to work ceaselessly among the non-Party toiling masses in order to mobilize them for the fight against fascism and to establish combat units of International Proletarian Avengers.

28. Only an iron, military, Party discipline, only correct and practical execution of the directives and orders of the higher Party organs and military commanders through the lower Party offices and the Party members, only the solid unity of will of the Party organizations and of the will of the whole Party, only the resolute and prompt action against all conditions which could be injurious to the great cause of the struggle of the proletariat against fascism, only the highest art of conspiracy and readiness of each Communist for self-sacrifice will result in directing the mighty stream of holy, proletarian, avenging will of the toiling masses against the Fascist bandits and into the proper and best channel, i.e., the mass rising of the proletariat against fascism.

§III. Partisan Tactics

DOCUMENT 13

Soviet Intelligence Service
List of Essential Elements of Information

Organized according to the work schedule of the Political Section with the Espionage Division of the Central Staff of the Partisan Movement

I. Administration
  1. Organizational structure of the local administration.
  2. System for selecting the organs of the local administration.
  3. Those possessing the active and passive franchise. (a) Social status. (b) Nationality. (c) Age. (d) Education. (e) Participation of women in elections and administration.

4. Dependence of the local organs of administration on the German commands.
5. Heads of the most important organs of the local administration.
6. Individual characteristic orders and instructions regarding questions of administration should be sent to the staff; if possible, the originals.

II. Administrative measures
  1. Reorganization of the population.
  2. Passport regulations.
  3. Right and time for being on the street in towns and villages.
  4. Measures taken regarding prisoners of war.
  5. The staff should be sent: (a) Specimens of passports with all entries concerning residence authorization.[17] Samples of personal identification papers and travel permits from towns to villages, from villages to towns, to another rayon, district, etc. (b) Characteristic orders and instructions regarding these questions.
  6. Existing regulations and arrangements for travel from occupied Soviet territory to Germany and back.

III. Economic situation
  1. Enterprises in operation (works, factories, individual workshops).
  2. What is being produced in the enterprises and how much?
  3. Number of workers in the enterprises.
  4. Who is in charge of the enterprises?
  5. Restoration of the evacuated enterprises.
  6. Organization of new enterprises.
  7. Situation of railway transport.

IV. Condition of public utilities
  1. Water supply.
  2. Canalization.
  3. Housing.
  4. Heat and light.
  5. Street car traffic, etc.

V. Labor conditions
  1. Forms and methods of recruiting and hiring labor.
  2. Condition of the workers. (a) Regulation of work in the enterprises. (b) Working hours. (c) Wage questions. (d) Standard of living.
  3. Situation and conditions among "white-collar" workers.
  4. Shipment of workers to Germany. (a) Methods of recruiting. (b) Reports about conditions of work and the situation of the Russian workers in Germany.
  5. What is the work output of those who have been forcibly recruited by raids and other methods for the enterprises?

VI. Agriculture in the occupied territories
  1. Forms of utilizing the land and methods of farming. (How do the Fascists deal with the kolkhozes, sovkhozes, and MTS?[18] To whom and in what manner is land being sold?)

[17] This refers to the visas which the German administration placed on the Soviet domestic passports issued to all residents.
[18] Machine-Tractor Stations.

2. Status of sowing (percentage of planted areas and quality).
3. How did the harvesting proceed?
4. Status of means of traction and agricultural equipment.
5. Measures of the Germans and the local administrative agencies to increase the yield.
6. Peasant attitudes towards the measures of the Germans and the local administrative agencies.
7. What official documents have been issued on these questions?
8. How is the agricultural administration organized?

VII. Taxation policy of the Germans in the occupied territories
   1. The kinds of taxes introduced by the German Fascists in the occupied territories (bread, other products, money).
   2. What is being taxed (livestock, dogs, houses, etc)?
   3. How high are the taxes?
   4. How are people taxed who cannot work?
   5. Is the whole population informed about tax rates?
   6. Does unified tax regulation exist for whole districts, or do individual rayons have their own rates?
   7. Are deadlines fixed for paying taxes?
   8. How does the taxation policy of the Fascists influence the standard of living of the population?
   9. What countermeasures are taken by the population against the taxation policy of the Germans?
   10. Methods of tax collection.
   11. What penalties are used by the Fascists against citizens who do not or cannot pay their taxes?
   12. Who is exempted from the tax?
   13. What orders and instructions have been issued and published regarding this question?

VIII. Supply and trade
   1. What kinds of goods and foodstuffs are supplied to the population?
   2. Supply system (cards, coupons, single rations, etc.).
   3. Organization of trade. (a) Private trade. (b) Cooperative trade, etc.
   4. Prices of foodstuffs and goods.
   5. Black market and the attitude of the local population toward it (support, hindrance).

IX. Public education
   1. Do grade schools exist in the towns and in the rayons?
   2. Do high schools exist in the towns and in the rayons?
   3. What universities have been opened and where?
   4. Composition of the student body, social, national, etc.
   5. The personnel of the educational institutions.
   6. Political attitudes of students, professors, and teachers.
   7. What fields are taught in the various educational institutions: grade schools, high schools, and universities?
   8. What text books are used and how large is the supply?
   9. Supply of teaching materials to the pupils.

10. From what funds are the schools supported?
11. Tuition in grade schools, high schools, universities.
12. Percentage of children of school age who actually attend the schools.
13. What languages are used for instruction?

X. Culture and art
1. The operation of movie theaters. (a) What films are shown? (b) What is the attendance? (c) How does the population react to Fascist films?
2. What theaters are open (playhouses, operas, etc.)?
3. Program of the theaters.
4. Composition of the theater personnel.
5. Activity in the other arts: writing, music, painting, etc.
6. Do organizations and groups of artists exist?
7. Heads of the artist organizations.
8. Condition of cultural monuments. (a) Historical. (b) Those created in the Soviet period.
9. Admission prices for theaters and movies.
10. What museums are open, and what is the condition of the museums which existed under Soviet power?
11. To what extent is the ideological and topical content of the repertoires understandable and persuasive to Soviet spectators?

XI. Press and publishing activities
1. What newspapers are published and what is their circulation?
2. Personnel of the press.
3. Editors.
4. Publication of proclamations, appeals, etc., as leaflets.
5. What periodicals exist: political, artistic, etc.?
6. Publishing activities. (a) Belles-lettres. (b) Technical literature. (c) Political literature. (d) Agricultural literature.
7. Political line of each newspaper, periodical.
8. Prices of newspapers and periodicals.

XII. Public health
1. By whom is medical care for the population paid or is it free?
2. Hospitals, ambulances, pharmacies, etc., in existence and operating.
3. Supply of medicines.
4. Number and composition of medical personnel.
5. How and by whom are health institutions financed?
6. Do private health institutions exist?
7. Condition of health of the population. (What kinds of illnesses are treated most frequently in towns, in villages, etc.?)
8. Incidence of epidemics.
9. Extent of venereal diseases and methods of fighting prostitution.

XIII. Religion
1. Where and when have churches and convents been reopened?
2. What religious currents and groupings exist? (Orthodox Church, Seventh-day Adventists, Protestants, and other sects.) Internal struggles among the various church and sectarian groups. Which ones are supported by the

occupiers? Have the occupiers succeeded in using churches as an instrument to influence the population and to propagate their policy?

3. The role of the church in propagating Fascist policy.
4. Is the attitude of all the churches hostile toward the Soviet power?
5. [missing]
6. What are the German regulations for the performance of church ceremonies by the population (baptisms, weddings, etc.)? Are citizens obliged to attend church ceremonies or is attendance voluntary?
7. Relationship of the Germans to the different religious currents. To what currents is preference being given?
8. What attitude do the Germans take toward the doctrine of the sectarians who refuse to carry weapons?
9. Compulsion exercised by the Germans to bring Soviet youth to observe church ceremonies (confession, confirmation, baptism).
10. By what funds is the church supported?
11. Is land being given to the church?
12. Does the church pay taxes?
13. What church congregations exist and how are they distributed?
14. From where and in what manner are priests secured?
15. Relation of the population to the church.
16. In what ways can adherents of the church be used for the struggle against the German occupiers?

XIV. Attitude of the Germans toward the various nationalities and activities of the nationalist organizations
1. How is the nationality question being solved by the Fascists in the occupied territories? Attitudes toward the Russians, Ukrainians, Belorussians, Tatars, etc.
2. Attitude of the Germans toward the various nationalist tendencies.
3. The aims of the Fascists in the nationality question (attempts to win people over to their side, creation of hostility among the peoples of the USSR, splitting of unity of the Soviet peoples, etc.).
4. How do the Hitlerites exploit the nationalist organizations for Fascist propaganda among the people?
5. Anti-Bolshevik agitation in the nationalist organizations.
6. Percentage of nationalists in the local administration.
7. Do the Germans promise any one nation national independence and autonomy and on what basis?
8. The suppression of national aspirations of the population in the occupied territories.

XV. Atrocities and lootings of the Fascists against Soviet citizens
1. Atrocities and use of force by the Hitlerites which are committed against the citizens of the occupied territories.
2. What strata of the population and what nationalities are especially exposed to chicanery and plunder?
3. Under what pretext do the Fascists commit atrocities and lootings?
4. Participation in the atrocities and looting by formations from the coerced states (Rumania, Hungary, Finland, Italy, etc.).

XVI. Political sentiments of the population in the temporarily occupied territories
 1. The faith of the population in the inevitable annihilation of fascism by the Red Army.
 2. Attitude of the urban population toward the administrative measures of the occupiers (workers, "white-collar" employees, intelligentsia, and especially the specialists in science, technology, and art).
 3. Attitude of the various strata of the population in the villages toward the administrative measures of the occupiers (kolkhoz peasants, individual peasants, former kulaks, etc.).
 4. Attitudes of the population in the towns and in the country toward the nationalist organizations.
 5. Attitude of the population in the towns and in the country toward the partisan movement.
 6. Activities of the Party and Komsomol organizations in the occupied territory.
 7. How is Soviet propaganda being spread among the population (propaganda by word of mouth, leaflets, etc.)?
XVII. Morale in the enemy army; political morale of the armies of the enemy (Germans, Italians, Rumanians, Hungarians, Finns, etc.)
 1. Attitude of the officers and soldiers toward carrying the war to the Soviet Union.
 2. How is the myth of the invincibility of the German Army being destroyed under the influence of the heroic resistance of the Red Army (especially the morale among the Rumanian, Hungarian, Finnish troops, etc.)?
 3. How do officers and soldiers assess the ability of the German Army to fight on two fronts? Are they informed about the preparation of a second front by England and the United States?
 4. What is the attitude toward winter warfare?
 5. What is the attitude regarding food and equipment?
 6. What effect do letters from home have on the soldiers and officers?
 7. What is the attitude of the soldiers of the occupation armies toward the looting, thefts, and chicaneries against the local population in the occupied territories?
 8. Do the soldiers believe in the victory of the German Army? Why don't they surrender?
 9. How do the soldiers and officers judge the activity of the partisans?
 10. Relationship between the Germans and the coerced armies (Rumanians, Hungarians, etc.).
XVIII. Tactics of the Fascists in the fight against the partisan movement
 1. Use of regular troops against the partisan detachments.
 2. Organization of punitive detachments and police formations and their role in the fight against the partisans.
 3. To what extent are measures (such as clearing and combing of the forests) ordered in the fight against the partisans being carried out?

4. Activity of the Gestapo; sending agents and informants into the partisan detachments.
5. Burning villages and evacuation of the population from the villages.
6. How is the security of roads and bridges organized by the Fascists, and who is used for this activity?
7. What measures are being taken by the Fascists to destroy the link between the partisans and the population?
8. Organization of punitive and police detachments from anti-Soviet elements by higher German organs for the struggle against the partisan movement.
9. Participation in the fight against the partisans on the part of coerced troops (Hungarian, Italian, Austrian, Czech, Polish, etc.); what troops show the strongest activity in the fight against partisans?
10. Sending of enemy agents into the partisan detachments and the results of the struggle against these agents.

XIX. The organization of "volunteer" units and detachments from the population of the occupied territories by the German command
1. What detachments and troop units have been organized and where are they stationed (exact number and name)?
2. From what social and national strata are these detachments and troop units organized?
3. For what purposes are these "volunteer" detachments and troop units organized?
4. By what methods are these detachments and troop units being recruited?
5. What advantages are enjoyed by the recruits of these detachments and troop units?
6. What documents are issued to each member of these detachments and troop units?
7. Combat efficiency and political attitude of these detachments and troop units.
8. What is the composition of the leadership of these detachments and troop units?
9. Organization of the detachments and troop units in the fight against partisans.
10. Measures on our part for the subversion and destruction of the "volunteer" detachments.

XX. Organization of indigenous police in the occupied territory by the German command
1. For what purpose are such police units being established?
2. Of what elements is the police composed?
3. Manner and methods of recruiting the police.
4. Rights and duties of the police.
5. Equipment, uniforms, and salary of the police.
6. Facilities and maintenance of the police.
7. What advantages do the members of the police enjoy?
8. Participation of the police in the fight against the partisans.

XXI. The enemy's measures for preparation of chemical attacks [gas warfare]
    1 What kind of chemical troops does the enemy have and where are they stationed in the occupied territory?
    2. Composition of the chemical troops and their equipment.
    3. Are these troops at full strength and ready for active chemical warfare?

DOCUMENT 14: Manual for Political Reconnaissance

I. Political measures of the German High Command in the temporarily occupied territories
    1. What measures have been taken to establish the Fascist order?
    2. Military and civilian administration agencies in the territory.
    3. Who is employed in the agencies (names and a short account of characteristics)? Their work formerly and now.
    4. From what funds is the administrative apparatus paid?
    5. How does the population react to the political measures of the Germans?
    6. What rights have been conceded to the local population?
II. Fascist propaganda among the population of the temporarily occupied territories
    1. Who is in charge of the propaganda among the population?
    2. Kinds of propaganda (gatherings, lectures, addresses, films, radio, etc.). What kind of printed matter is being distributed (newspapers, journals, proclamations)?
    3. Do clubs, village libraries, and theaters exist?
III. Economic measures of the occupation authorities
    1. What orders and regulations have been issued in the recent past?
    2. Taxation of the population in money and in kind?
    3. Organization of the economic administration.
    4. Who is in charge of industrial enterprises?
    5. Who is the owner of soil and mineral resources?
    6. How are the industrial enterprises being restored and the mineral resources exploited?
    7. Measures for the restoration of means of transportation and their use.
IV. Agriculture
    1. Orders and instructions to the kolkhozes.
    2. Status of public property (public buildings, livestock, inventory, and other agricultural implements).
    3. Measures and preparation for spring sowing. Kinds of seed, utilization of agricultural equipment and means of traction. Participation of the population in the spring sowing and their attitude toward it.
    4. Preparations for the harvest.
V. Partisan activities in the occupied territories
    1. Prospects for the development of the partisan movement during the summer.
    2. Attitude of the population toward the partisans.
    3. Support given by the population to the partisans.
    4. German measures for fighting the partisans.
VI. Atrocities of the Germans in the occupied territories
    1. Looting of the population.

2. Destruction of towns and villages.
3. Slavery and serfdom; carrying away the civilian population into captivity.
4. Destruction of the national culture of the peoples of the USSR.
5. Atrocities and rape.
6. Treatment of Soviet prisoners of war.
7. How and where does the population of the destroyed towns and villages hide?

DOCUMENT 15

From time to time the higher staffs of the partisan movement sent out inspection officers to the detachments under their command. It seems that occasionally staff officers were sent out to examine performance in a specific type of activity. The unique document translated here contains the instructions given to a Soviet officer on the Staff of the Partisan Movement at the Kalinin Front who was sent into Smolensk Oblast in the spring of 1943 to inspect the intelligence activities of the partisan brigades operating there. The detailed specifications set forth in the instructions thus indicate the concrete intelligence interests of a Soviet army group.

Certified: Deputy Chief of the Central Staff of the Partisan Movement at the Kalinin Front, Lt. Col. Shelymagin

12 April 1943 *Top Secret*

To: First Assistant to the Chief of the 1st Section of the Staff of the Partisan Movement at the Kalinin Front, Comrade Major Arkhipenko.

Intelligence Assignments

The following must be effected with respect to the partisan brigades of the Smolensk area:

1. Confer personally with the intelligence officers of the partisan brigades and detachments. Request reports about the activities of the individual brigades. Satisfy yourself that Order No. 00189 (Point 9)[19] is known. Determine whether detachments have reconnaissance groups. A list of names of deputy brigade commanders and deputy chiefs of intelligence sections will be submitted. The list must include all necessary personal data and information on positions held.

2. Satisfy yourself that an agents' net exists. Request that there be agents in all inhabited places within the operational area of the brigade. Request that data be transmitted by radio according to the following scheme: registration number, surname, first name, patronymic, age, business and residence address, category of work for which agent has been selected.

3. See to it that within the operational area of each brigade, reconnaissance groups (three to five men) are sent out at once to watch the roads, troop movements, and supply traffic. Results of such observations are to be transmitted regularly by radio, including the identification marking of motor and other vehicles and tanks.

4. Request the brigade command to obtain from prisoners the number of

[19] The text of this order has not been found. Presumably it is an order of the Soviet High Command pertaining to partisan intelligence activities.

each enemy troop unit in the brigade's operational area and paybooks of the enemy dead. The number of each new troop unit must also be procured at once.

5. Request the brigade command to ascertain within the next few days the existence of any fortifications within the brigade's area of operations. Sketches of such fortifications must be captured and the location of the guards ascertained.

6. Find out within the near future whether and where there are anti-Soviet national units,[20] staffs, and depots as well as enemy ration points.

7. Deputy brigade commanders and deputy chiefs of intelligence sections are to be instructed as to the nature and form of the reports. They are to be oriented thoroughly on all points. Reports must state by whom and where the reports were made. Abstract terms such as "strong movements" or "large concentrations" are inadmissible.

8. Deputy chiefs of intelligence sections of the brigade are to be alerted to the necessity of capturing various kinds of documents (paybooks, letters, diaries, orders, statements, anti-Soviet literature, papers of the agricultural administration, and similar materials). Such papers are to be forwarded to us immediately, stating where, when, and under what circumstances the papers were captured.

9. Inform yourself personally of how intelligence work and self-defense is organized. Instruct [the units] that intelligence activities must be carried on without interruption and that they constitute at present the major task to be perfomed by the partisans for the Red Army.

10. Attached hereto are two compilations [of intelligence information] to be verified by the brigade.

Assignment noted for compliance	Chief of the 2d Section
Major Arkhipenko	Major Garusdovich
February 1943	

§IV. Partisan Reports

One of the best sources for a study of partisan operations is the partisans' own reports. Even if they were not always accurate, they usually reflected rather clearly the type of activity in which the partisan group and its members were engaged.[21]

DOCUMENT 16

Activity Report of a "Troika" carrying on clandestine propaganda

(Secret)

On the activity of the troika in the Dedovichi Rayon area for the period November 1941 to July 1942 inclusive.

---

[20] Units composed of Soviet nationals fighting on the German side.

[21] Documents pertaining to the Grishin and Kovpak bands will be found in Sects. VII and VIII, respectively.

In July 1941 the enemy reached Dedovichi. The Red Army began its retreat. The rayon administration was evacuated to Vyazovka. The village selsoviets[22] were free to choose the date of their evacuation, depending on the military situation.

On the basis of the Stalin appeal of 3 July 1941 the Communists present in Vyazovka decided to form partisan units in Dedovichi Rayon. Several days later it became known that the first partisan unit, named after the "Leningrad Okrug Committee of the Party," was to be formed in the forests of Ponestovki. The Dedovichi destruction battalion was merged with this partisan unit.

On 27 July the partisans went to the forest, and thus began the partisan warfare in our area.

The Germans occupied Dedovichi Rayon and immediately established civilian organs of administration. The former Chairman of the Communal Affairs Branch of the rayon soviet, a shady character, Pinagin, was appointed Mayor of the rayon with headquarters in Dedovichi. Among the mayoral staff were other elements hostile to the Soviet Union. The rayon was divided into the following districts:

Yaskovo	District Elder—Saudal
Malyshev	District Elder—Kudryavtsev
Kipino	District Elder—Filipov.

Each district included three to five village soviets. The Mayor, just like the District Elders, represented authority in the district and was subordinate to the Kommandanten.[23] The kolkhozes were called villages and were governed by starostas. The starostas received orders from the Mayor at a weekly meeting. They are controlled by the District Elders.

These hostile elements have misappropriated the kolkhoz property, divided the harvest evenly among the number of persons in the village, and turned over to the Germans active workers of the kolkhoz and selsoviet, who later were shot. For instance, the kolkhoz chairman Mikhailov, from the kolkhoz "Red Star"; Grigoryev, from the kolkhoz "Komuna"; Kurov, Burov, and others. The following kolkhoz chairmen have sabotaged the orders of the Germans and have hidden grain for bread: Grigoryev, Gegorov, Sisoyev.

In the beginning the partisans did not get in touch with the local population because they feared treason. After the attacks on several German strongpoints, the partisans gradually mingled with the population and were supplied with food because of their successes. For instance, in August, Sudoma was attacked and about fifty German soldiers and officers were liquidated. Good results were also achieved with other operations. In September, Plotovets Station was attacked and many Germans perished there also. During this time the kolkhozniks often did reconnaissance for the partisans. Already in the first month of the war for the fatherland it became necessary to conduct propaganda among the population. The Brigade command had sent political workers and other Communists to the nearby villages. The partisans did not yet have propaganda material but were using for their work radio news issued by the

[22] Administrative committees for each village; village soviets. (Also used later for the district administered by such a committee.)

[23] Local German commanders; also *Ortskommandanten.*

Information Bureau—rarely newspapers and leaflets. Through this propaganda the population began again to believe in the victory of the Red Army and therefore started to support the partisans to a certain extent, for instance, [by] donating warm winter clothing. Gradually the population became convinced that the enemy will have to be defeated.

By October of this year [1941] the situation had changed so much in our favor that the formation of a troika and the re-establishment of Soviet authority could be considered and begun. What caused the change in the situation? Although the German army had occupied the whole rayon, it was not able to fortify it completely, and had only strongpoints along the railroad lines. The major part of the population remained faithful to the Soviet regime and to the Communist Party. By order of the [partisan] Brigade the troika was formed in November.

Chairman: A. G. Porudzenko, previously employed by the civil administration of Dedovichi;

For Party affairs: E. M. Petrova, previously employed by the rayon Committee of the Party;

For special tasks: V. I. Millbook, formerly with the Dedovichi police.

In addition, the following persons [were attached to the troika]:

Agronomist: P. Razuyev, previously employed by the rayon agricultural administration;

Supplies: F. S. Potatov, formerly tax inspector;

Propaganda and Labor: Redkin;

Secretary: Loseva;

Commander of the troika's partisan unit [*guard?*]*:* Dubov.

In November 1941 the troika departed to its headquarters and started its work. The work of the troika grew out of the existing situation and led to the following results:

1) The conduct of a broad propaganda program of mass indoctrination and recruitment among civilians;

2) The re-establishment of all Soviet organs [of government];

3) The re-establishment of all kolkhoz institutions dissolved by the Germans;

4) Abolition of all German measures;

5) Organized help of every kind by the population for the partisans;

6) Death to all traitors.

1. Propaganda for Mass Indoctrination and Recruitment Among the Population.

The troika began its work on 6 and 7 November with festive meetings in the kolkhozes on the occasion of the twenty-fourth anniversary of the great Socialist October Revolution. These meetings were conducted with great political exertion and with active participation by the population. In the beginning the activity of the troika consisted in conducting meetings at the different kolkhozes. There they [troika] members [reported] on the re-establishment of Soviet organs, kolkhoz institutions, the participation of all Soviet peoples in the fatherland war against the Fascists, the methods of fighting in the enemy rear area, fighting against the traitors to the fatherland, etc. A great help were the leaflets dropped from our planes, containing the report of Comrade Stalin of 6 and 7

November. The wonderful words of Stalin strengthened the population's belief in a victory of the Red Army and raised active resistance against the German occupation. The result of this work was large shipments of food supplies made by the peasants to the partisans and complete ignoring of German power by the civilians. As a result, the Germans sent armed troops into the villages for requisitioning who, on their way, were liquidated by the partisans. The Germans had heard about the existence of the troika but, because of lack of manpower, they were not able to undertake anything against it and against the partisans.

The German attack started on 1 December, with about 4,000 men supported by tanks and planes. The attack lasted over a week but achieved nothing; only the innocent civilians were victimized. In this bloody week about 30 villages were burned down and 150 civilians tortured and shot.

The success of our propaganda was made evident in this week. The population did not betray the partisans or tell about its connections with them.

After this punitive expedition the work of the troika became even more energetic.

In the New Year [1942] the fight of the partisans against the barbarians was supported with great enthusiasm by the population. All kinds of gifts and great amounts of food supplies were given to the partisans by the population; they also received letters which expressed the love of the population for the partisans, the Party, and the great Stalin.

The relations of the partisans with the population became more and more cordial. Often they sat with the peasants singing songs together. For instance:

> Hitler will be dead soon;
> Soon he will have a white coffin.
> Long will the dear little officer
> Stand on his cold little feet.[24]

In January 1942 our work began to meet difficulties. The partisan units departed to Kholm to fight there. Through informers the Germans came to know of the existence of partisan units and started to hunt the workers of the troika. They succeeded in killing the following activists:

Comrades: Vinogradov, chairman of the Yufimovo selsoviet;
　　　　　Shuyev, treasurer of the same selsoviet;
　　　　　Gegorov, chairman of the Degzho selsoviet;
　　　　　Bordanov, representative of the rayon soviet, and some other activists.

In spite of all this, in nineteen kolkhozes we conducted a festive hour on the eighteenth anniversary of Lenin's death. The work of the activists was very difficult, since they had to be prepared to be captured at any moment by the Germans. Until February [1942] we did not receive any propaganda material.

---

[24] This strange song has evidently been garbled in translation. Probably it means to suggest: (1) Hitler's white coffin is the Russian winter snow; (2) the officer (a German officer) is also about to die, i.e., "to stretch out his long cold legs" (a Russian idiom), but this is going to be a long process—also possibly a suggestion that he is left to guard the remains long after Hitler is dead; and (3) the diminutives are derisive.

In February, during the preparations for the celebration of the twenty-four year existence of the Red Army and Red Navy we received a great amount of propaganda material and our work was continued with great success.

The activity of the partisan units added to our successes.

When the difficult food situation and the heroic fight of the Leningrad population became known to the partisan units, meetings were held everywhere. At these meetings the kolkhozniks joyfully declared themselves ready to send food supplies to Leningrad. A transport of food supplies, accompanied by a letter to Stalin, increased the enthusiasm of the population for fighting the cunning enemy, and 300 kolkhozniks joined the partisan units. With tears in their eyes the population signed the letter to Stalin, a document of faith in the great Stalin, the Soviet regime, and the Party.

". . . Let dear Stalin know that we were and still are Soviet people and that no power of the enemy will be able to take away our freedom," said the sixty-year-old kolkhoznik, Comrade Teplyakov, when he signed the letter.

The carrying out of our work was attended with great difficulties, since our villages were bombed daily by German planes. During one of these attacks the village of Lamovka was destroyed. While attending a meeting three comrades —Smirnov, Vorobyov, Vakin—were killed during an attack on the Sosnitsy selsoviet.

During the celebrations of International Women's Day the activists collected money for the defense of the area. Besides this, the kolkhozniks handed in 86,500 rubles of state loan. When a radio announcement was made about a military loan [war bonds], in a few days our activists collected an amount of signatures that greatly surpassed the number of last year. For instance, the Parevichi selsoviet [gave] 8,517 rubles (4,600 rubles the previous year).

In March and April more than 70,000 kilograms of hay were put at the disposal of the 8th Guard Division. Thus the kolkhozniks showed their readiness for a united fight. Before 1 May the German planes dropped thousands of leaflets suggesting the dissolution of the kolkhozes. Because of this, activists were sent through the villages and, through their propaganda, succeeded in persuading even edinolichniks[25] to join the kolkhoz.

The delegation that went in March to the city of Lenin with presents returned on 1 May. The following [persons] were members of the delegation:

The chairman of the troika, Comrade Porudzenko;

The chairman of the selsoviet, Comrade Steskovski;

Comrade Gegorov, and the kolkhoz chairmen, Comrades Ivanov, Grigoryev, and Belyankin.

They reported on the heroic fight of the people of Leningrad at the front, the factories, and [the] dockyards, and called on the kolkhozniks to work diligently and intensively on their fields so they would be able to give more help to the partisans.

The spring sowing started, regardless of the interferences of the Germans, and was completed perfectly. Following the order of Comrade Zhdanov the

---

[25] Independent farmers, not members of a kolkhoz. The small percentage of those who had refused to join had been steadily dwindling before the war.

kolkhozniks sowed so much that it was enough fully to satisfy the needs of the population and the partisans.

Early in May began the second [German] punitive expedition against the partisan area. The Germans had thrown a whole division, with tanks, heavy artillery, and planes, into the fight. As on the first occasion, this expedition also was a failure. Because of an order by the troika, the population was evacuated to forest camps. They lived under difficult conditions and had to walk about seven kilometers to work. But the haymaking and other field work is being successfully carried on.

During this time the partisans received presents and letters in which the kolkhozniks stated their love for the fatherland and [their enthusiasm for its] defense.

Particularly characteristic in our life [here] was the cooperation between partisans and kolkhozniks. The former helped the kolkhozniks in their field work and praised them as special units and heroes of the partisans. The latter —Komsomols or non-Party comrades—worked without keeping track of working days, so quickly and joyfully that they created an even closer contact between partisans and population.

During the period from February to July, when the partisans were defending the region against the Germans, the civilians worked on fortifications—for instance, digging ditches, building tank traps, etc. Some kolkhozniks participated in reconnaissance and often even in fighting. Some of the kolkhozniks proved to be real patriots during the battle against the Germans in the rear area. For instance, the kolkhoznik Mikhail Semyonov undertook to guide the Germans from Mukharova to Gnilitsy during the December expedition. He perished, but had so guided the Germans for three days that they neither reached Gnilitsy nor caught any partisans.

In the village of Khokhlovo the spy Ivanova was bestially tortured by the Germans. When her corpse was found she was unrecognizable. Hands and feet were broken, the skin [was] torn off, a part of it hung down in shreds, and on her back alone were seventeen knife wounds. In spite of the inhuman interrogation by the sadists, the comrade revealed nothing.

Comrade Osipov, Party candidate, was captured and bestially tortured. His eyes were cut out, a hot wire pulled through his nose—but, being a proud Russian, an honest son of the Party, he did not reveal anything to the German beasts.

The kolkhoz treasurer, Yemelyanov, an invalid, during a fight in his village grabbed the rifle of a slain German and made a fighting retreat with the partisans.

The patriot Filipova Praskofia ran immediately to the partisans when German soldiers came to her village and when fourteen men quartered themselves in her house. She reported this event in the following words: "Burn my house down, don't spare it." Shortly afterwards seventy Germans were killed in the village by the partisans.

Yet many more examples of the love of the people for their country could be adduced.

During this year of battle, a body of excellent agitators has developed [and] is right now carrying vigorous Bolshevik propaganda among the working masses.

At the last meeting of the rayon ninety-two agitators were present. Along with the growth of popular political activity, the ranks of our Bolshevik Party have grown too. In nine months we lost eight Communists and accepted seventy-four new ones. Twenty-three of them joined the partisan units.

As planned, we regularly held two to three Party meetings a month. At the present time five Party organizations and four Party candidate groups exist in the partisan area. One of the Party organizations has to work all the time in the rear area of the enemy. It has achieved great success among the civilian population.

In this time the Leningrad Komsomol gained ninety-four new members. The Komsomols proved to be real helpers to all the Soviet organs. A result of the propaganda work was the re-establishment of the Party and Komsomol activities in the partisan area.

II. Re-establishment of the Organs of the Soviet Regime.[26]

Already on 8 November 1941 a secret meeting of the activists of Parevichi selsoviet was called. At this meeting Comrade Baranov was elected chairman. At the same time the political and military situation, the tasks of the troika, the selsoviets, and the kolkhozes were explained. It was ordered that the kolkhozes should be re-established in their old form and that German measures should be sabotaged at the same time. The activists' agreement to proffer all help to the partisans showed their attitude to the Party. Similar meetings were held in the following selsoviets: Bratkovo, Fedorskoye, Yufimovo, Stankov, Malyshev, and Sosnitsy.

Each activist invited to the meeting was first screened. From among sixteen selsoviets in the rayon seven were chosen. This job was very difficult and had to be performed secretly, because Fascist groups were nosing around everywhere. While the troika was engaged [on] this task we lost four selsoviet chairmen: Vinogradov, Gegorov, Shuyev, Vorobyov. After 10 May the Kipino selsoviet was also included [in our work]. Here the job had to be performed illegally since German troops were stationed nearby.

III. Re-establishment of the Dissolved Kolkhozes.

Since the kolkhozes had been dissolved in most of the selsoviets and the harvest had already been divided equally among the peasants according to the [total] number of persons, a very difficult situation presented itself to the troika. The kolkhoz cattle had been distributed among a few kolkhozniks and often the edinolichniks too had received cattle. The first task was to re-establish all the kolkhozes in their old form. All German-appointed starostas were fired and the former kolkhoz officials were called back again. The whole inventory of the kolkhoz and the herds of cattle were collected together again. The harvest was re-divided, not according to the number of persons but according to working days performed.

The elements hostile in attitude to the kolkhoz were liquidated. The further work was carried on according to the proper Party lines. By spring 1942 all

---

[26] The numbering here follows that of the original list of topics, and not that of the German translation, which is confused.

sixty kolkhozes were well prepared for the spring jobs. The preparation of the fields was excellently carried through in spite of the difficult military situation.

IV. Abolition of all German Measures.

At the first meetings the kolkhoz chairmen were forbidden to attend the weekly meetings of the District Elders and to carry out any orders given by the Germans. Most of the chairmen obeyed these orders. Those who nevertheless attended the German meetings and executed their [German] orders were severely punished or even shot.

Shot were the chairmen Kuzmin from the kolkhoz "Red Dawn" and Ivanov from the kolkhoz "Leninist Spark."[27]

Furthermore there was an attempt to persuade the officials remaining in German service to work for the troika at the same time: for instance, the District Elder of Malyshev, Comrade Kudryavtsev, who was later shot by the Germans. After his death the Germans did not appoint a new District Elder. The District Elder from Yamki was shot by the partisans and no successor was appointed either.

At the end of December 1941 the District Elder of Kipino, Filipov, was so severely wounded by the partisans that he was no longer able to work.

Our work succeeded in that no German dared any more to come to the partisan area and [German] orders were no longer carried out.

V. Medical Help.

In the beginning we had only two medical workers,[28] who practised privately. One of them was shot during the December expedition. This medical help was not sufficient for the population and the troika therefore opened a medical station, which was headed by the woman medical worker Shcherbakova.

From 23 March until now, 1,830 civilians and 162 partisans have been treated. Sixty-one partisans were hospitalized here in the medical station and nursed back to health. Recently one more medical worker was added. Medical supplies have had to be obtained under great difficulties. No epidemics occurred.

VI. Organization of Assistance to the Partisans by the Population.

The most difficult task of the troika was the procurement of food supplies and clothing for the partisans. In the beginning the kolkhozes were committed to deliver a certain amount of clothing and food supplies. When the required amount did not suffice, a voluntary relief system was brought under way. The population was so devoted to the partisans that it gave joyfully and willingly whenever there was a collection for the partisans. Besides this, the population assisted the partisans in reconnaissance activities.

VII. The Fight Against the Traitors.

The special task of the troika was the struggle against traitors and other counterrevolutionaries.

After the German occupation of the rayons many kulaks returned. They

[27] Named for a newspaper edited by Lenin.
[28] *Feldscher*—a person with medical training but not a qualified doctor.

hoped to get back their former houses and later on to possess some land. Besides this, other elements who until now had remained in hiding appeared in order to fight against the Soviet regime. These supplied the Germans with information about the partisans and about the work of the Soviet organs. They sabotaged the kolkhoz organs and looted kolkhoz property.

The task of the troika was to destroy these elements and to establish, in the enemy rear area, a basis for unhindered work in the spirit of the Soviet regime. Sixty traitors were shot, among them twenty-two kulaks. For instance, Mikhail Zhukov and his son Ivan, from Perekresnaya village of the Stankov selsoviet, completely disrupted [literally, subverted] the kolkhoz "Right Path" in the first days of the occupation. They divided the income of the kolkhoz among the population according to the number of persons, a transaction in which they were particularly interested since their family consisted of sixteen [members]. Later on, the father was appointed village chairman by the Germans and carried out their orders. When the partisans came, he pretended to be one of them but was unmasked. It was established that he was the moving spirit of the whole anti-Soviet movement, and his son was his deputy.

Still at the very beginning of 1942 it became known that the kulak M. Frolov, who had remained in hiding the whole time, had appeared in Yukhalov village of the Tipino selsoviet. He was smart enough to become, in a very short time, the village chairman of the kolkhoz "Red Dawn," and then [he] began to work against the Soviet regime. Without paying any attention to the attitude of the former kolkhozniks, he began to deliver food supplies and other things to the Germans. He also turned over Soviet activists to the Germans and reported immediately when partisans had been spotted. He also prevented the village youth from doing their military duty by joining the ranks of the partisans.

Frolov was arrested and liquidated in May.

In May 1942 a group of counterrevolutionaries, consisting of five men with their leader, Ludwig Aros, was discovered in Yelovets village. The first step in his counterrevolutionary activity was a letter he wrote to the *Ortskommandant,* in which he made it plain that he and his group [would give] complete assistance in every respect. This letter was found the next day on the body of a dead German officer.

In the fall of the same year a certain D. Gubanov from Khokhlovo village, who was not convinced that the Red Army would be victorious, delivered information to the Germans on partisans. Later on he was hired by a German headquarters as an agent. From this moment on he was a traitor. By means of deceit he turned over to the Germans for prosecution the chairman of the Degzho selsoviet, Comrade S. I. Gegorov, and the rayon representative, Yakov Bogdanov. On January 30 he was deprived of his life [*sic*] by the Germans. At the same time the secretary of the Degzho selsoviet, Alekseev, and Comrade Gegorov were shot.

At the end of December 1941 the former German teacher, Emma Funke, who was interpreter for the District Elder of Yassy, was shot for treason.

It is noteworthy that the counterrevolutionary activity developed particularly in Soshitsy selsoviet. Those engaged in this activity were mostly former kulaks who had come here from Staraya Russa. When these traitors were liquidated by us, here also the success of our activists was brought to fruition. The liquidation of these traitors and counterrevolutionary elements was carried out by order of and under the supervision of the troika.

Survey

In the past nine months the troika has achieved the following results:

The Soviet regime has been completely re-established in the territory of the eight selsoviets in Dedovichi Rayon. Normal kolkhoz life has been re-established in sixty kolkhozes. No German order is carried out any more.

As an answer to Hitler's land reform, the remaining edinolichniks in the partisan area joined the kolkhozes and a large number of kolkhozniks joined the partisan units. In the year 1942 alone 330 edinolichniks joined the kolkhozes and participated in exemplary fashion from the day of joining in the kolkhoz life. The punitive expedition and the strong pressure of the Germans did not scare the population and did not shatter their belief in our victory. In the course of this year 135 villages were burned by the Germans and 2000 families were thereby made homeless. During this time 340 civilians were shot. As an answer to these bestial acts, everyone able to carry a rifle joined the partisans. During the troika's period of duty alone, 675 people joined the partisans.

Besides the re-establishment of the Soviet regime, the troika's work was devoted to the partisan movement. In the nine-month [period] 873,000 kilograms of agricultural products, 200,000 liters of milk, and 30,000 eggs were handed over to the partisan units. These deliveries were made by the kolkhozes according to the prescriptions of Soviet law. In addition, the troika organized deliveries of clothes among the population of the partisan area. Delivered were:

> 560 short fur coats
> 700 sheepskins
> 740 pairs of felt boots
> 1000 pieces of underwear
> 2000 pairs of warm socks and gloves
> 1500 meters of material, etc.

Furthermore, the population of the partisan area made more than 2000 voluntary presents of all kinds to the partisans.

Because of the seriousness of the situation in Leningrad, the troika started a relief operation that collected more than 3000 poods[29] of food supplies in a few days. These food supplies, loaded on 200 teams, were transported by the kolkhozniks with the help of the partisans through the enemy lines.

Besides these jobs, a collection of money for the purpose of fortifying the partisan area was also taken up, which achieved the following result through willing donations: 35,000 rubles in cash and 86,600 in state loan. The number of signatures for the military loan pledged 66,000 rubles. 40,600 rubles were paid immediately.

The spring agricultural work was completely performed [to achieve] the

[29] One pood equals 36.1 pounds.

goals dictated by the military situation; 1360 hectares were sown. The seed for this had been hidden from the Germans during the winter under the most difficult conditions. In some kolkhozes the Germans succeeded in plundering or destroying the entire crop, so these kolkhozes had also to be provided with seed. The crop situation at the present time is excellent. The kolkhozniks harvest together with the partisans so that they can insure a quick harvest, and in so doing prevent the Germans from being able to requisition it themselves. With the help of the partisans, 2100 hectares of grass had already been mown by 1 August, and 1850 tons of first class hay had been stored. The hay was piled in big stacks in safe forest camps. At the same time the soil was prepared for the winter sowing. Approximately 1000 hectares were sown.

The further work of the troika has already been outlined:

I. Further identification of the population with the organs of the Soviet regime and partisan units, which has to be expressed in even greater assistance to the partisans in fighting German fascism.

II. Education of Communists and Komsomol as the elite in the battle for defense.

III. Conduct of the harvest so that not a single kilogram will fall into German hands, and so that everything shall benefit the partisans and the civilian population.

IV. Strengthening revolutionary vigilance among the activists and the population, and prevention of all treacherous attacks of the enemy. All hostile elements to be captured and liquidated.

V. Education of the population to hate everything German, because of their [the Germans'] bestial behavior.

VI. Further strengthening of the Soviet regime and the kolkhozes.

VII. Widening of our authority into the still occupied district of the rayon, and thereby the re-establishing of the former institutions.

In conclusion, it should be noted that the whole job of our partisans and of the troika was performed to re-establish Soviet authority in the area temporarily occupied by the Germans. This shows the invincibility of the Soviet policy and the blood-ties of our people to Soviet authority and the Communist Party. The Germans have not been able to succeed, and they never will succeed, in shaking the confidence of the peasants and workers of the Soviet state in the Soviet order [and] the kolkhoz way of life. The Soviet Front is so strong and has so deeply penetrated into the flesh and blood of our people [*sic*], that nobody ever will succeed in depriving the Soviet people of their historic achievements. The time is coming when no Hitlerite Pest will remain, even in the temporarily occupied sections of the Soviet Union, and afresh, as of old, the Red Flag of Soviet Power will wave unvanquished.

Our just cause is triumphant, a guarantee of which is the heroic battle of our Red Army [and] our beloved partisans, [and] the desire of the people for victory over the enemy, and finally by the appearance of the crucial fact that our holy war is led by our great Commander-in-Chief, Joseph Stalin.

Chairman of the troika of Dedovichi Rayon.
[signed] Porudzenko
Signatures of the members of the troika.
[signed] Petrova, Millbook, Tyulmanov.

[Postscript to the Troika Report, or, How Different
Things Looked to the Germans]

. . . In the partisan-infested areas the attitude still remains [a] very cowed, as, for example, east of the Dno-Dedovichi-Nasva railroad line. On the other hand, the fact that, in the evacuation of several villages twelve to fourteen kilometers southeast of Dedovichi, approximately 90 percent of the Russian population have left their villages and have entrusted themselves to the protection of the German Army, testifies to firm reliance on the latter; the remaining 10 percent, for the most part men, found, it must be admitted, the way to the other side. [The source quoted here is Wi In Nord, Id, "Monatsbericht fuer die Zeit vom 1.4.–30.4.42" (GMDS, HGeb 23107/ 17).]

DOCUMENTS 17–21

During the Soviet winter offensive, 1941–42, the Red Army drove deep salients into the rear of German Army Group Center. The northern arm of the Soviet pincers was aimed at Smolensk and Vyazma. In this area many partisan units supported the operations of the Red Army. One of these groups was the partisan detachment commanded by First Lieutenant Morogov. It operated in the area between Belyi and Smolensk from February to August 1942 and was probably mauled in the German operation in the summer of 1942 which was designed to clear this area of partisans. At that time a group of records of this band was captured.

The most interesting portions of these documents are given here. Included are two politico-military reports made jointly by the detachment commander and commissar to the section of Twenty-second Army Headquarters in charge of partisan units behind the enemy front. Also included is a roster of political meetings either of the partisan unit itself or organized by the unit for the local population.

The politico-military reports illustrate, in addition to the activities and certain organizational aspects of the unit, the control exerted by the Red Army (in this case, the staff of an infantry division) on the assignments to the partisans. References can also be found to the general attitude of the unit members and the attempt of Party and Komsomol members to fulfill their mission as leaders within the unit.

The political activities of the partisan unit in relation to the local inhabitants are well illustrated by the chronicle of political meetings held in the communities within the area of the unit. The topics of the meetings indicate the subjects of greatest concern: the orders of the People's Commissariat of Defense, a partisan proclamation, tasks of the kolkhoz peasants and other Soviet citizens in the rear of the enemy, etc.

DOCUMENT 17

To the Section of the 22d Army in charge of supervision of partisan units
Politico-military Report for March, April, and the first ten days of May 1942

1. I report that the political [and] morale disposition of the entire personnel is excellent; this is shown by a number of incidents, e.g., the partisan machine

gunner Comrade Zegolnik fired 14 belts of ammunition from his heavy machine gun during an attack upon the village of Lukino which [the Germans attacked] on 19 March 1942 in violation of an agreement[30] and thereby repulsed the attack of the Germans until he saw in front of himself dozens of dead bodies. When the Germans came close to him, he took them under direct fire and when his strength began to diminish, he still fired with his Nagan pistol at four Fascists. The Germans tried to capture Zegolnik alive. Z. did not give himself up but shot a bullet through his head, ending his life by suicide. The ranks of our best men are growing steadily: Kutayev, Gasin, Redkin, Nazarov, Shabyrin, Drozdov and others are models of discipline and organization during their combat missions, and they inspire the others.

2. The entire personnel of the unit took the oath as Red Partisans. After taking the oath, the men and officers show even better and closer unity.

3. [Communist] Party and Komsomol organizations were established within the unit (Communist Party members and candidates total five men; there are fourteen Komsomol members). They did great work in the unit and also among the population. Five conferences of Party and Komsomol members took place within the unit, and the following topics were discussed: (a) discipline, (b) care of weapons, (c) condemnation of actions of individual fighters, Communists, and Komsomol members. There were about ten general meetings[31] concerning the questions: (a) discipline within the unit, (b) care of weapons, (c) condemnation of actions of unstable comrades.

4. Orders No. 55 and 130 of the People's Commissariat of Defense were thoroughly gone over with the men and officers and were understood in their entire depth. Molotov's note, the patriotic war of the Soviet people, the morale of the German armed forces, the conduct of Comrade Litvinov at the Conference of the [Great] Powers, the proclamation of the partisans of the Kalinin Front, to which 55 men from our unit added their signatures, [were] also [discussed]. Furthermore, our unit has a radio. Five thousand leaflets were distributed among the enemy troops on the Smolensk-Belyi main supply road.

5. The unit carries on an unrelenting fight and tries to capture deserters.[32] Cases of desertion also occurred within the unit. The partisan Ivanov deserted his post and took along a light machine gun. Searches have been initiated, and the punishment of the escapee has been ordered.

6. The partisan unit carries on considerable work among the population, and in the course of March-April about 320 men were sent to the active army;[33] furthermore, six partisan groups were organized from local inhabitants for the protection of villages. Twelve meetings of kolkhoz peasants were held and the following questions discussed: (1) The international situation of the

[30] This reference to an attack which occurred in violation of an agreement (*wortbruechig vorgenommener Angriff*) presupposes an earlier truce arrangement between the Germans and the partisans.

[31] As distinct from membership meetings.

[32] Two weeks later, the unit reports killing twenty-one bandits, probably one result of this search for deserters. See Document 18.

[33] That is, to serve in the Red Army.

Soviet Union and our tasks. (2) The organization of practical assistance to the Red Army troops and to the partisan units. (3) The International Women's Day on 8 March. (4) Report about the First of May. (5) Official decree about the state loan. (6) Orders No. 55 and 130 of the People's Commissariat of Defense. (7) Proclamation of the partisans of the Kalinin Front.

The village soviets received the assistance of ten men in explaining the announced state loan. The unit paid 2,500 rubles in cash [for state bonds]. The unit accomplished a big job during the evacuation of grain from the German-occupied areas—the villages Selishche, Okolitsa, Medvedyevo, and others. Twenty-eight farms in the burned-out villages received grain from kolkhoz peasants, under our protection.

7. During its combat actions, the unit destroyed a Fascist plane Ju 88 [?] on 4 April 1942 [?]. In the neighborhood of Medvedyevo the plane caught fire and landed in the area of the village of Lukino. Furthermore, an ammunition truck was destroyed on the Smolensk-Belyi main supply road; 58 horses, 19 vehicles and sleds were destroyed at the same place. In 70 days, the unit annihilated 779 men and officers. On 19 March alone, during the fighting near Lukino, the Germans lost 403 men. In addition, 268 soldiers and officers were killed from ambush. The unit undertook 11 ambushes upon the villages of Lukino, Nefedovo, and Spiridovo, where German garrisons were stationed to guard the main supply road. The unit also made use of 6 tanks which carried guns, one of them a 122 mm gun; they opened up artillery fire on the villages of Tsytsino, Ploskaya, Yemelyanovo, Podyesenye, i.e., they created turmoil among the German occupation units there. During the same period of time, the unit had losses amounting to 20 men killed and 14 men wounded. At the moment the unit consists of 65 men. For the same period 20 men from the Zhuravlev [partisan] unit and 12 men from the local population were incorporated into the unit. Applications for acceptance in the unit are received daily from young people. On 1 May a 14-year-old boy by the name of Vasilii Malinovsky appeared at the unit [hq.] and reported that his brother Fedor had been killed and his father Joseph was wounded. "I want to take their place; it will be a great honor for me to kill the German occupiers." M[alinovsky] was accepted into the unit.

There are many like M[alinovsky] with us; for instance, [there is] Misha Borisenkov who is 14 years old and went once with a reconnaissance party. In the village of Okolitsa, the Germans caught him, [and] he was to be shot; he managed to escape and brought valuable information to the unit.

From 12 April to 12 May the unit has been protecting Medvedyevo, Berezovka, by orders of the staff of the 17th GRD.[34] On 12 May 1942 the unit will be moved from the village of Berezovka to the village of Krivets in the district of Prechistoye. A roster of the weapons will be attached to the report.

Commander of the [partisan] unit [signature]
Commissar of the unit, 1st Lt. [signature]

[34] Guard Rifle Division.

DOCUMENT 18

To the Section of the 22d Army in charge of supervision of partisan units.

Politico-Military Report

I report that the political [and] morale disposition of the personnel is excellent. This is proved by the following facts: the completion of combat missions on 26, 27, 28, and 29 May. Every day the very best people join the unit— Mutayev, Nazarov, Redkin, Gasin, Zhivoderov, and others. Discipline becomes stronger every day. The unit is quartered in the village of Marpovo [and] remains [there] because large bands showed up in the woods of Khludov on 26, 27, 28, and 29 [May];[35] the unit was forced to carry out its combat missions in strongly fortified country; two groups were entrenched in the woods, one of them 32-men strong. [This group] was annihilated from 26 to 27 May, and 11 men were captured. One heavy machine gun, 3 light machine guns, 18 rifles, 1 submachine gun, 2 pairs of binoculars, and other equipment fell into our hands as booty. This group had been hiding in the woods since 13 March because of fear of mobilization.

From 28 to 29 May, the unit moved to the Yartsevo area, to the village of Losevo, where it was discovered that a group of 37 men had lived in the woods from 14 March to 29 May [and] had become deserters, killing peaceful citizens, members of the Red Army, and members of partisan units. The group was destroyed by our unit. A heavy skirmish, lasting for two hours, had the following results: 21 bandits killed; 4 heavy machine guns, 3 light machine guns, approximately 30 rifles, 3 binoculars, and a field kitchen as booty. In addition two small groups were destroyed in the village of Demeshonki.

During the two operations on 26, 27, 28, and 29 May 1942, a total of 4 groups of bandits in the strength of 95 men were destroyed. Furthermore, our reconnaissance discovered that a staff of policemen, starostas, and bandits was located in the village of Tyukhovitsky in the strength of about 200 men. They had been disarming Red soldiers and partisans. They had received instructions from the Germans to capture Red Army officers and deliver them alive [to the Germans] and to destroy the soldiers of the Red Army as well as people trying to procure food. In the period from 26 to 30 May, 4 heavy machine guns, 1 Dekhterev heavy machine gun, 6 light machine guns, 1 German submachine gun, 68 rifles, 5 pairs of binoculars, field kitchens, and other equipment were taken as booty. The traitors to the fatherland suffered 32 men killed. Eleven men were captured alive; the remainder escaped in panic. The bandits were led into the village where they had formerly lived. Meetings took place in the villages of Losevo, Maloye Losevo, Demeshonki, Lilimovo, Pogorelitsy, Sukhovarino, Fomenki, Lvovo, Kartovo according to Comrade Stalin's Order No. 130. Furthermore, matters pertaining to protection of villages, capture of deserters, and carrying out the spring sowing were discussed. Since 15 May, the

---

[35] Apparently the bands referred to here were not partisan bands but irregular bands, composed of deserters from the Red Army and others who had reasons to be afraid of the Germans as well as the partisans or Red Army. Possibly, criminal elements had also joined these bands, which, to survive, had to fight the Germans and the partisans when attacked or pursued by either.

unit has been conducting orderly reconnaissance and has been transferring weapons from the occupied area to Red Army troops; 256 rifles, 3 heavy machine guns and [1] 122 mm [?] [gun], 3 mortars, and 1 cow were delivered to the Red Army.

Leader of the [partisan] unit, [signed] 1st Lt.
[signed] Commissar of the unit

Village of Karpovo, 1 June 1942

DOCUMENT 19

Report of the Morogov Partisan Unit Concerning Meetings, Conferences, and Discussions of the Partisans and the Local Inhabitants

(1) 1 February 1942. Meeting of the kolkhoz peasants in the village of Ploskoye. *In charge:* Commander of the Morogov Unit; Commissar [Poliyektov]. *Topic:* The task of the kolkhoz peasants in the Patriotic War; based on the report of Comrade Stalin to the plenary session of the soviet of workers' deputies in Moscow on 6 November 1941.

(2) 1 February 1942. Meeting of the partisan unit. *In charge:* Commander of the Morogov Unit; Deputy to the Commissar, Tretyakov. *Topic:* The bandit-like actions of the former officer, Ivanov. *Note:* A resolution was passed to send Ivanov to the headquarters of the 119th Rifle Division.

(3) 7 March 1942. Meeting of the women of the villages of Medvedyevo, Lukino, and Spiridovo. *In charge:* Commander of the unit; Commissar of the unit. *Topic:* The International Women's Day on 8 March and the tasks of Soviet women in the rear of the enemy.

(4) 2 May 1942. General Meeting of the partisan unit. *In charge:* Commander of the Morogov Unit; Commissar of the unit, Poliyektov. *Topic:* Comprehensive discussion of the Order of the People's Commissariat of Defense No. 130 and the proclamation of the partisans of the Kalinin Front.

(5) 2 May 1942. General meeting of the kolkhoz peasants of the village of Berezov. *In charge:* Commander of the Morogov Unit; Commissar of the unit, Poliyektov. *Topic:* Comprehensive discussion of the Order of the People's Commissariat of Defense No. 130 and the proclamation of the partisans of the Kalinin Front.

(6) 13 May 1942. General meeting of the kolkhoz peasants of the village of Lilimov, Baturino Rayon. *In charge:* Commander of the Morogov Unit; Commissar of the unit, Poliyektov. *Topic:* Comprehensive discussion of the Order of the People's Commissariat of Defense No. 130/42.

(7) 20 May 1942. General meeting of the kolkhoz peasants of the villages of Pogorelitsa and Karpovo, Baturino Rayon. *In charge:* Commander of the Morogov Unit; Commissar of the unit, Poliyektov. *Topic:* Comprehensive discussion of the Order of the People's Commissariat of Defense No. 130 and the tasks of the kolkhoz peasants in the rear of the enemy.

(8) 18 June 1942. General meeting of the kolkhoz peasants of the villages of Volno and Burkovo. *In charge:* Commander of the Morogov Unit; Commissar of the unit, Poliyektov. *Topic:* Task of the kolkhoz peasants in the rear of the enemy.

(9) 13 July 1942. General meeting of the partisans of the unit. *In charge:* Commissar of the unit, Kutayev. *Topic:* [Field] inspection of equipment and allocation of pack animals to the individual groups.

(10) 23 July 1942. Short meeting of the partisans of the unit. *In charge:* Commander of the unit, Nazarov. *Topic:* Decision on the sentences for the criminals, the former partisans, D. I. Piskunov and G. A. Kozlov. *Note:* Piskunov and Kozlov were shot as deserters in front of the assembled personnel.

(11) 20 August 1942. Conference with the lower unit commanders of the unit. *In charge:* Commissar of the unit, Kutayev. *Topic:* Tightening of discipline and guard duties of the unit.

(12) 28 August 1942. General meeting of the kolkhoz peasants of the villages of Baturino, Razdobarino, Kholm, Glinki, and Kotiki. *In charge:* Commander of the unit, Nazarov; Chief of Staff of the unit, Popov. *Topic:* Comprehensive discussion on the resolution and proclamation of the rayon committee of Baturino and the rayon executive committee addressed to the citizens of the Baturino area on the execution of the harvest campaign and the sowing of the winter grain for 1943.

(13) 29 August 1942. Swearing-in of the new numbers as "Red Partisans." [See Document 3.] *In charge:* Commissar of the unit; Commander of the unit. *Note:* Oath has been taken.

(14) 25 May 1942. General meeting of the kolkhoz peasants of the village of Sukhovarino, Baturino Rayon. *In charge:* Commander of the unit; Commissar of the unit. *Topic:* Comprehensive discussion of the Order of the People's Commissariat of Defense No. 130 and tasks of the kolkhoz peasants in the rear of the enemy.

(15) 25 June 1942. Meeting of the kolkhoz peasants of the village of Maloye-Losevo. *In charge:* Commander of the unit; Commissar of the unit. *Topic:* Comprehensive discussion of the Order No. 130/42 [concerning] the tasks of the kolkhoz peasants in the rear of the enemy.

(16) 29 May 1942. Meeting of the kolkhoz peasants of the village of Lvovo. *In charge:* Commander of the unit; Commissar of the unit. *Topic:* Comprehensive discussion of the Order of the People's Commissariat of Defense No. 130/42 [concerning] the tasks of the kolkhoz peasants in the rear of the enemy.

(17) 18 May 1942. Meeting of the kolkhoz peasants of the village of Demeshenki. *In charge:* Commander of the unit; Commissar of the unit. *Topic:* Comprehensive discussion of the Order of the People's Commissariat of Defense No. 130/42 [concerning] the tasks of the kolkhoz peasants in the rear of the enemy.

(18) 28 May 1942. Meeting of the kolkhoz peasants of the village of Gunino. *In charge:* Commander of the unit; Commissar of the unit. *Topic:* Comprehensive discussion of the Order of the People's Commissariat of Defense No. 130/42 [concerning] the tasks of the kolkhoz peasants in the rear of the enemy.

(19) 31 May 1942. Meeting of the kolkhoz peasants in the village of Pavlovshchina. *In charge:* Commander of the unit; Commissar of the unit.

Topic: Comprehensive discussion of the Order of the People's Commissariat of Defense No. 130/42 [concerning] the tasks of the kolkhoz peasants in the rear of the enemy. *Note:* According to the resolution of the kolkhoz peasants, self-protection groups will be organized from among the local inhabitants in the villages referred to in items 15 to 19.

(20) 5 August 1942. Meeting of the kolkhoz peasants of the village of Kholm in Baturino Rayon. *In charge:* Commander of the unit; Commissar of the unit. *Topic:* Comprehensive discussion of the Order of the People's Commissariat of Defense No. 130/42 [concerning] the tasks of the kolkhoz peasants in the rear of the enemy.

(21) 25 August 1942. Meeting of the kolkhoz peasants of the village of Matrenino, Matrenino Rayon. *In charge:* Commander of the unit; Commissar of the unit. *Topic:* Quickest conclusion of the harvest campaign, correct distribution of foodstuffs, and the 1943 winter sowing.

(22) 1 September 1942. Meeting of the members and candidates of the Communist Party. *In charge:* Commissar of the unit. *Topic:* Election of a Party organizer. Group leader Pankratev was elected.

(23) 1 September 1942. General meeting of the Komsomols of the unit. *Present:* Commander of the unit; Commissar of the unit. *Topic:* Intensification of the work of the unit's Komsomol organization and announcement of its September work program.

DOCUMENT 20

A large proportion of the partisans were young people, many of whom belonged to the Komsomol. The members of the Komsomol continued their organizational activities after joining a partisan group. This document, a protocol of a meeting on 27 July 1942 of the Komsomol members who belonged to the Death-to-Fascism Partisan Unit, shows the emphasis placed upon the role of Komsomol members as honor-bound to set a good example for the other partisans. The Death-to-Fascism partisan group operated in the area around Belyi, north of the Smolensk-Vyazma highway. For a report on the activity of Komsomol members of other partisan groups, see Document 21.

Protocol No. 1
of the Komsomol Meeting of 27 July 1942

Partisan Unit: Death-to-Fascism
Present: 27 men
Absent: 4 men (3 having valid excuses)
Agenda: (1) Discipline of Komsomol members during fighting and in quarters.
(2) Confirmation of the work plan. (3) Elections. (4) Miscellaneous.
It was said:

(1) Comrade Filipov spoke on the first item of the agenda. He said, "Discipline among the Komsomol members is far from satisfactory. The main reason for lack of discipline is the use of filthy [*netsenzurnykh*] words; this cursing among Komsomol members results not only in insulting each other but sometimes [is directed against] those who do not belong to the Komsomol.

"The behavior of the majority of the Komsomol members in battle is good, but there are also some (for example, Yegorov) who do not show the necessary courage."

Party Member Solovyov: "The question of discipline concerns the entire partisan unit but especially the Komsomol members. There are Komsomol members with us who should be imprisoned. One can observe cases in which Komsomol members seriously quarrel with each other and incite non-Party members to do the same."

Unit Commander Vasiliyev: "If we want to act like Komsomol members, then we must not only be an example, but we must carry the others along. This is our principal task."

(2) Confirmation of the work plan of the bureau of the Komsomol organization. The plan was accepted as a whole.

(3) Election to the bureau. Rybakov, 3; Bukatin, 15. Bukatin was elected by a majority.

(4) (a) The conduct of Komsomol Member Shulga.

Platoon Leader Brylkin: "Although Comrade Shulga is good in battle, he often likes to talk too much. He always has objections, a habit which is incompatible with his conduct as a Komsomol member. I want to cite the following example: I gave the order to bring a saddle. Shulga replied that no one had received a saddle. For this answer he was put in jail for twenty-four hours. For all this, for the remark and for the nonexecution of the order, I propose a reprimand for Comrade Shulga."

Unit Leader: "Every Komsomol member must set an example. He must always support the leader; Shulga, however, does the opposite. I second the motion of the platoon leader."

Decision: Komsomol Member Shulga is to be punished with a reprimand to be entered in his record because of his remark and the nonexecution of the order of the platoon leader, which amount to undermining the authority of his superior.

(4) (b) The conduct of Komsomol Member Novalishin.

Brylkin: "In battle Comrade Novalishin proves to be a model Komsomol member and has been proposed for a decoration by the state. As a future commander of the unit he has created complete confusion. Discipline in the unit has reached its lowest level. Comrade Novalishin has recently become a discipline problem. He went for gasoline, returned late and, in addition, drove to another village. For this, he was reprimanded by the leader of the unit."

Decision: Comrade Novalishin is to be publicly reprimanded.

Secretary of the meeting

DOCUMENT 21

The following documents were found in the Vitebsk area. They are reports to Communist Party, Komsomol, and partisan headquarters in that part of Belorussia. They were captured with other partisan reports not reproduced by the Germans, some of which are summarized in a covering note to those which were translated.[36]

[36] The covering note also explains that among the documents captured with these was a monthly report of the Falalayev Brigade which operated in the Vitebsk area and is represented by Documents 22 and 23.

To: Vitebsk Oblast Executive Committee of the Komsomol and to Comrade V. Y. Luzgin

Report on the Activity of the Komsomol Organizations of Drissa[37] Rayon for August 1943

The rayon Komsomol organization consists of 9 local sections to which 327 Komsomol members belong; in addition there are 245 unorganized youths.

Combat Activity

The best Komsomol organization in the brigade is the one in the Kirov Detachment of which Comrade Khalamenko is the commissar's deputy for Komsomol affairs.[38] In their combat activity the Komsomol members of this detachment occupy first rank. Ninety-five percent of the Komsomol members participate in the fighting. Within this detachment Komsomol and Pioneer demolition details have been formed. The best Komsomol demolition detail is that of Komsomol Member Vasilenyak which has brought about the derailment of seven enemy transport trains, two of these in August 1943. The detail of Komsomol Member Bykov brought about the derailment of two transport trains. There is competition among the Komsomol groups for the best achievement in combat.

The Komsomol members of the [Kirov] detachment addressed themselves to all the Komsomol members of the brigade concerning the activation of the struggle [and] the establishment of Komsomol demolition details consisting entirely of Komsomol members.

The appeal of the Komsomol members of the [Kirov] detachment was joyfully received by Komsomol members of the other detachments, that is; A[lex-ander] Nevsky Detachment (deputy for Komsomol affairs of the commissar is Stepan Vasilyevich Silitsky), Kutuzov Detachment (deputy for Komsomol affairs of the commissar is Vladimir Ignatovich Bykovsky).

The establishment of Pioneer demolition details has begun in these detachments; the Komsomol members are always to be found in the front ranks in these [details]. Thus the Komsomol members of the Kalinin Detachment, under the command of battalion commander Comrade Kukharenko, were the first to push forward to the embankment of the Polotsk-Drissa railroad during the execution of the combat assignment in the night of 3–4 August. The Komsomol member Nikolai Sadovsky dynamited the tracks at 10 places and [blew up] 2 telegraph poles. Sergei Moroz: 8 blastings and 3 telegraph poles; Nikolai Ushakov: 8 blastings and 1 telegraph pole. In this operation Komsomol members of other detachments also distinguished themselves—Marusya Labar: 8 blastings (KIM Detachment),[39] Brill: 10 blastings (Kutuzov Detachment), the Pioneer Tumovsky: 8 blastings (A. Nevsky Detachment), and others.

The Komsomol members of the Bezstrashnyi [Fearless] Detachment set a good example in the struggle against the Germans. All the Komsomol members

---

[37] Drissa Rayon is in the northwest corner of Belorussia close to the Latvian border.

[38] From the language used here and elsewhere in this document, it would appear that members of the Komsomol were included, generally as individuals, within the regular partisan brigades. In many detachments there was a special deputy of the commissar whose special responsibility was the supervision of Komsomol members.

[39] *Kommunisticheskii Internatsional Molodyozhi,* Communist Youth International.

know the technique of blasting excellently or at least well, and put it into practice. All Komsomol members have distinguished themselves in combat. Dmitry Stoma has brought about the derailment of 9 enemy transport trains; Ugolusk, born 1923, 7 enemy train transports and 5 Germans from an ambush; Vladimir Yelitsa, born 1923, Komsomol member since 1938, brought about the derailment of 6 enemy transport trains; Olga Ivanova, born 1924, 1 transport train, blew up 3 sections of railway track.

The training in sharpshooting is well received in the KIM Detachment (Deputy [for Komsomol Affairs] of the Commissar is Comrade Sarayeshno). Fifteen sharpshooters have been trained in this detachment. Of these the Komsomol member sharpshooter Demyan Pavlenko has 15 dead Germans to his credit and Paruchnya, 7 Germans.

The training with the sniper's rifle is coming along well in the Nevsky and Kalinin Detachments: Borisov—25 Germans; Yegor Pavlyonak—15 Germans, and so on.

The best training with weapons takes place in the Suvorov, KIM, Nevsky, and Bezstrashnyi Detachments. In these battalions instruction in the handling of explosives is also being given.

General Political Activity

The [political] work is well organized in the Bezstrashnyi (Deputy for Komsomol Affairs of the Commissar is Sakharevich) and Nevsky Detachments (Silitsky). In August 1943 the Komsomol members of the Bezstrashnyi Partisan Detachment under the leadership of Sakharevich staged two gatherings for the partisans and one for the local population. The best propaganda speaker of the Komsomol members gave several lectures and speeches for the partisans and the population. The following prepare themselves carefully for discussions and make them: Comrades Sakharevich, Silitsky, Ivan Dabnenko, Karl Ugolnya, D. Demidovich, V. Vasilenko, Alshevsky, Sarayeshno (KIM), Brill (Kutuzov).

These comrades enjoy a high standing among the partisans and population. They prepare their material in time, educate the youth by citing exemplary accomplishments of the Red Army and of their own battalions, point out the atrocities of fascism, and indoctrinate with tenacity, discipline, stamina, and a will to win.

Comrade Sakharevich and Comrade Silitsky conduct training combined with an exchange of views on the part of the agitators concerning their experiences, and they help them in the selection of material for speakers.

A front newspaper is put out regularly (3 or 4 times a month) in the Bezstrashnyi Detachment with the participation of the Komsomol members. There is a column "The Best People in Our Detachment." The work done in the publication of the front newspaper and wall newspapers in the Suvorov Detachment (Deputy for Komsomol Affairs of the Commissar is Comrade Lifovka) is also good; the publication of the front newspapers and wall newspapers in this [detachment] is directed by the Komsomol member Vailatovich.

The press of the detachment describes the life of the Komsomol members, points out the good and bad characteristics of individual comrades, and inspires them to the fulfillment of forthcoming assignments. All the Komsomol members participate in the work on the newspaper.

The Komsomol members in the Kalinin and Nevsky Detachments write leaflets and appeals and distribute them in the strongpoints. The Komsomol members of these detachments bring as much Soviet literature as possible to the population under German rule.

The work among the local young people is well organized in the Kalinin Detachment.

Thirteen new members were accepted into the Komsomol during August 1943. The Komsomol members of the KIM Detachment carry out their work among children also.

Beside the accomplishments of the organizations of the county of Drissa there are also major deficiencies:

1. The work of the detachments among the local youth is poor. In view of the fact that a large proportion of the youth is of Komsomol age, the increase in membership is extraordinarily small. There are 40 young people in Nevsky; of these 2 became new members in August. Kirov has 42 and accepted 4 in August; Lenin has 22 with no new acceptances, and so on. The Rayon Executive Committee of the Komsomol pays little attention to work among local youth.

2. The combat activity of the Komsomol members is decidedly insufficient. No Komsomol demolition details have yet been formed in the Lenin and Suvorov Detachments and others. The front newspapers are issued irregularly: in the Kirov, Nevsky, and Lenin Detachments, and in the brigade staff, only once during August. Agitational work among the masses is done, but not enough emphasis is placed on the bravery and the exemplary aggressiveness of our soldiers, officers, and partisans. Direction and exchange of experiences are lacking among the agitators.

The Rayon Executive Committee of the Komsomol (Vasilevsky) occupies itself too little with the work of the Komsomol organizations. Effective help is still given to the Komsomol organizations in a completely inadequate amount, and too little control is exercised. The Rayon Executive Committee has not yet taken the leadership in the fight of the Komsomol organization against the Germans. In August there was a meeting of the Rayon Executive Committee at which Comrade Silitsky gave a lecture on the work of indoctrination. A number of resolutions were passed, but he could not secure their execution.

There is no cooperation whatsoever with the secret agents.

Comrade Vasilevsky is more concerned with family matters than with the work of the Komsomol.

The best worker in the Rayon Executive Committee is Comrade VI. Gavrilovich. Every day he is with the Komsomol members and helps them in their work.

Every inadequacy was pointed out and practical help was given.

> The Plenipotentiary of the Vitebsk Oblast
> Executive Committee of the Komsomol
> [signed] Radanov

*The German document from which the above text was taken
contains the following additional information:*

The foregoing document was accompanied by a covering letter, dated 6
September 1943, from Poznyakov, the Plenipotentiary of the Vitebsk Oblast
Communist Party, to Luzgin, the Plenipotentiary of the Vitebsk Oblast Komsomol, criticizing the working methods and lack of zeal of the secretaries of
the Komsomol Executive Committee of Drissa Rayon. More bad than good
things could be said about them. For example, they restricted their work to the
localities in which they happened to be situated. The sabotage results were still
insufficient; many did not dare to go near the tracks because every approach
was said to be mined. The right leadership was still lacking. In the educational
work there was no mention of the heroic deeds of the Red Army and the German atrocities. A certain Rabushchenko, who had written a play on the life of
the partisans, was favorably mentioned.

Of the 1,113 members of the brigade, 40 (3.5 percent) were Party members,
87 (7.8 percent) were Party candidates, 334 (30 percent) were Komsomol
members, and 652 (58 percent) were without Party affiliation.

DOCUMENTS 22–23

There can be no doubt that in partisan warfare the role of the commander is extremely important—perhaps even more so than in regular operations. The Soviet authorities repeatedly replaced partisan commanders they thought inadequate with others considered better suited
to the task. Two documents of August 1943 show that at times this
process of replacement was not carried out as smoothly as might be
expected. They also illuminate the role played by the oblast committees of the Communist Party in the supervision of partisan detachments. Both documents are reports of the "Instructor" of the Communist Party of Vitebsk Oblast (a control officer delegated to the
brigade by the Vitebsk Oblast Committee of the Communist Party) to
the Secretary of the Vitebsk Oblast Committee of the Communist
Party.

The sequence of events reported appears to have been as follows:
At a conference of the officers of the Falalayev Partisan Brigade the
"Instructor," Shiyanov, complained about the inactivity of certain detachments of the brigade. His criticisms were apparently seconded only
by the commissar of the brigade, Shendelev. Upon receiving Shiyanov's
report on the conference, the secretary decided to replace the commander of the brigade, Falalayev, with a certain Sviridenko. Falalayev
saw the order, however, and promptly changed the name of his successor from Sviridenko to Sazykin, one of the battalion commanders
who had supported his views at the conference. The order, with the
changed name, was then apparently communicated to the Central
Staff of the Partisan Movement for Belorussia which replied by confirming the change proposed in the order. This confirmation came to
the attention of the "Instructor," who complained to the Secretary of the

Vitebsk Oblast Committee of the Communist Party about the change of name.

DOCUMENT 22

To: Secretary of the Vitebsk Oblast Committee of the Communist Party, Comrade Zhelyanin

From: Instructor of the Vitebsk Oblast Communist Party, Comrade Shiyanov

I report that on 27 August 1943 a staff conference took place in the Falalayev Brigade, at which the reports of the detachment commanders, Semyonov and Dyumin, on detachment combat operations in the current month and on the execution of order 0042 were heard. At the meeting it was established that the Semyonov Detachment has neither killed a single German nor blown up a single railroad during this month. Semyonov explains his inactivity by pointing to the poor equipment of his detachment and the current training in the details of sabotage. . . .

At this conference I sharply condemned the inactivity of the detachment. I stressed the low combat efficiency of the detachment and particularly of Detachment Commander Semyonov and Commissar Andreyev; I pointed to their inactivity and their inability to lead the soldiers and direct the whole life of the detachment toward the carrying out of combat assignments. I also pointed out the poorly organized security system and the poor staff work.

Then, instead of condemning the inactivity of the detachment and taking the appropriate concrete action for raising the combat activity of the detachment, individual commanders, especially Sazykin and Semyonov, began to express in their speeches dissatisfaction with my remarks. Semyonov voiced the reproach that while one demands everything, no one brings help by supplying clothes, shoes, and rations.

I noted that with the exception of the commissar, Shendelev, no one condemned this attitude of covering up inactivity by pointing to material things [shortages]. As for Falalayev, at the conference a softness showed up in regard to the demands put to the commanders; they were given no concrete assignments for raising combat activity. The attitude of Detachment Commander Semyonov toward the inactivity of his detachment was not condemned [by Falalayev?]. Instead of admitting his mistakes, Semyonov came forth with counterarguments and accusations against those who pointed out his shortcomings.

I am of the opinion that Semyonov is lacking in leadership qualities; a self-centered commander cannot secure the proper conduct of combat operations. Furthermore, Semyonov tries to keep out of operations during the execution of assignments. It is not his custom to stand alongside his men in combat. In addition, he is lax in his personal behavior and will not recognize that this is damaging and undermining to morale.

I request that this be noted and that Commissar Shendelev be directed to become more demanding in his requests to the commanders and to examine this whole poor state of affairs.

With greetings,
Shiyanov

DOCUMENT 23

To: Secretary of the Vitebsk Oblast Committee, Comrade Zhelyanin
From: Instructor of the Oblast Committee, Comrade Shiyanov

I report that on 28 August 1943 the Chief of Staff of the Partisan Movement for Belorussia, Comrade Kalinin, transmitted a radio message stating that Sazykin is confirmed in the position of brigade commander in place of Falalayev.

In my opinion, Falalayev has slipped his protégé and drinking-companion, Sazykin, into this position in order to continue to cover up his own dirty intrigues. The latter does great things, in discourse—in fact he is a real careerist. Sazykin is involved in the shootings and sordid business in the brigade. It was established that Sazykin drank *samogon* [moonshine vodka] with Falalayev and that he is considered the deputy of the brigade commander on line duty, although at the present time this position does not exist. The soldiers and officers of the brigade have no respect for Sazykin because of his intrigues. Sazykin has shot many soldiers, officers, and peaceful local inhabitants.

The appointment of Sazykin to Falalayev's position was made without the knowledge of Brigade Commissar Shendelev or me. Shendelev turned over the radio message signed by you to Falalayev, who took advantage of this and apparently substituted the name of Sazykin for Sviridenko. I am very indignant about this backstage maneuver of Falalayev. Therefore, I am sending the commissar, Shendelev, to you and await your directives in this matter.

With greetings,
Shiyanov

§V. Appeals to Collaborators

The appeals of the partisans to those who were collaborating with the Germans have been brought together in a special section because of the extreme importance of this subject to the partisans as well as to the Soviet Government. The collaborators aided the Germans in the administration and economic exploitation of the occupied territories. Of even greater concern to the partisans was the fact that these collaborators were a mainstay of German antipartisan warfare. They provided a large part of the troops and intelligence information used by the Germans in fighting the partisans. Their familiarity with the country, language, and people, as well as with the tactics of the partisans, made the collaborators particularly valuable allies to the Germans and especially dangerous enemies for the partisans. The efforts of the partisans to bring about defection of the collaborators are therefore quite understandable.

In general, certain themes are fairly constant in all these documents. There is an appeal to the patriotism of the collaborators.

Reference is made to the successes of the Red Army and the partisans and to the world-wide alliance to which the Soviet Union belongs, in an effort to convince the collaborators that they are on the losing side. They are reminded that even if the Germans should win, the collaborators would still suffer, a reminder for which the Germans furnished ample supporting evidence.

While the partisans threatened the collaborators with annihilation if they continued their activity, they also repeatedly assured them that if they stopped collaborating and joined the partisans, their past deeds would be forgiven both by the partisans and the Soviet Government.

DOCUMENT 24

Death to the German Occupiers!

To the Russian, Ukrainian, and Belorussian soldiers
mobilized into the German Army
What are you fighting for?

This is the second year that people are bleeding to death in the territory of the Soviet Union because of the crazy plans of Hitler, who wants to rule the world.

Millions of German soldiers were senselessly sacrificed in the course of the 13 months of war. Over mountains of dead bodies and streams of blood Hitler drives the German Army into new bloody battles.

The German soldiers and their families have already comprehended the truth that millions and more millions of Germans will never return from the battlefields to their native country. All this because of Hitler's insane plans. And now he wants to enslave a nation of 200 million as well.

Hitler attacked the Soviet Union in order to grab the raw materials of the Ukraine, Belorussia, and the Caucasus and to exploit them for the war against England and for preparation of the war against America.

The plans of Hitler fell through with a crash.

Hitler has thrown his entire manpower reserve as well as his technical skill against the Soviet Union, but he is not able to defeat the Soviet people and the Red Army. The material and moral power reserves of the USSR are inexhaustible.

While the German Army bleeds to death [in its fight] against the Soviet Union, England gathers great strength against Fascist Germany, the United States places her entire gigantic industry at the disposal of the peoples fighting Hitlerism. Only an insane man can believe that Hitler could win against this kind of world coalition.

Hitler's defeat is certain.

Mobilized soldiers, is it not a blot on your honor that you are helping to continue this criminal war? Don't you understand that you are helping the Fascists destroy innocent brothers, sisters, wives, and children of your [own] people?

Pay no attention to the voluntary police or the Fascist Army. These men are and will remain enemies of the working people. They are remnants of those who live from the labor of others. Now they have finally shown us their animal-like faces [by becoming] henchmen [of the Germans].

This is not the road for you.

Do you really want to shed your blood and sacrifice yourselves as mercenaries of fascism in [the] fight against the Soviet people, who are bravely defending the honor, freedom, and independence of their native country, their families, and their soil?

You are deceived by the lies of the Fascist propaganda.

In the end you will be unhappy if you tie yourselves irrevocably to the Hitlerites. The Ukrainians and Belorussians will be unhappy if they permit Hitlerism to rule in their country.

Fascism is slavery, corruption, poverty, hunger, and death. Everything for the fight against fascism!

Mobilized soldiers! Your brothers, your relatives, and your fighting comrades approach you. Turn your rifles against your commanders who are henchmen and the sellers of your souls.

Kill the Fascist dogs and come over individually or in groups to the partisan units. With united strength we shall liberate our native country which groans under the yoke of fascism, we shall destroy the brown plague so that it will never again soil a piece of ground.

We await you.

(This leaflet serves as a pass for individuals and for groups who come over to the Red Army or the partisan units.)

DOCUMENT 25
Death to the German Occupiers!

To the mobilized soldiers of the Ukrainian Regiment commanded by Major Weise.[40]

What are you defending?

We partisans took up arms to defend the honor, freedom, and independence of our native country—the Soviet Union! We are defending our people from destruction and slavery; we are defending our blood-soaked soil and the descendants of our fathers and children.

But what are you defending?

You are defending the life of the German henchmen who mishandled and continue to mishandle your families and your brothers' families; you are defending the interests of the German landowners who build estates on your soil while your sisters and daughters are sold into slavery. You are defending your stranglers.

The Fascists need your lives and blood, in order to fulfill their idiotic plans which consist of driving the peoples of Europe and the Soviet Union into slavery.

Down deep the German officers despise you. They regard you as traitors to [your] fatherland, [and consider you people] to whom German money

[40] Weise Regiment was a unit consisting of Ukrainians but commanded by Germans. It was employed in antipartisan warfare in the vicinity of Bryansk.

(marks) is dearer than the blood of your brothers, fathers, wives, and children.

The Fascists have one aim: War! They make money on it; you are deceived, subdued; [but you must be] unwilling to defend the interests of the enemy. The Fascists never were and never will be the friends of the Ukrainian, Belorussian, or [Great] Russian peoples.

Fascists are enemies of the working people, but you are defending them. Kill the German officers and come over to the partisan units. By doing so, you are in a position to cleanse yourselves of the infamous mark: Murderers of your own people.

Fascism will be destroyed in 1942.

(This leaflet serves as a pass for individuals or groups coming over to the Red Army or to the partisan units.)

DOCUMENT 26

Death to the German Occupiers!
To the Policemen and Mayors!
Think of your plight and return before it's too late!

Fascist Germany broke her treaty and invaded our country. Hitler had counted on defeating the USSR within a few days; however, the blitzkrieg did not succeed. Germany will be destroyed by the united forces of the USSR, England, the USA, and the other democratic countries of the world.

The manpower reserves of Germany and of her allies are dwindling. They need an armed force to safeguard their order in the occupied counties, [to carry out] the plundering of villages, and to fight our people and the partisans. For this purpose they established police units, called the *Ordnungsdienst.* Here and there traitors and egoists could be found who entered this police and took up arms against their own people and the Red Army.

We address ourselves to all policemen, mayors, and to all those who are working in the agencies of the occupying power.

Think it over! You are doing an abominable thing. You are soiling the honor and dignity of the Russian people. You are helping the enemies of our fatherland. You, former citizens of the Soviet Union, have become traitors to the land of your birth. For stooping so low and becoming enemies of your fatherland, your children, wives, and parents will curse you.

On the Kalinin and West Fronts the Red Army advances, destroys the German robbers, and drives them from Soviet soil.

For this treason to your homeland the people will judge you without mercy.

You still can save your lives and the lives of your families if you come over to us immediately.

We suggest to you, before it's too late—come over with your arms to the side of the Red Army and the partisans. Destroy the German garrisons, the means of communication and roads. Let the German trains roll down the embankments! Burn down the camps and come to us!

We guarantee life and inviolability to you and your families.

This leaflet serves as a pass to come over to the side of the Red Army and partisans. It is also permissible to come over without this paper.

DOCUMENT 27

Citizens of the Smolensk area!
Russian comrades enlisted by the enemy into the German Police!
The partisans of the Smolensk area address you.

Yesterday we received a leaflet in which traitors of the fatherland, traitors of the Russian people who became lackeys of the Germans, tried to intimidate us. We are not afraid of threats! We have helped, we are helping, and we will help the Red Army, which is not destroyed, as the Germans are proclaiming, but is inflicting ever heavier and heavier losses on the enemy. During the last three months, the Germans have lost 1,250,000 soldiers and officers, more than 4,000 planes, 3,390 tanks, and over 4,000 guns on the Soviet front.

In the fight which has lasted [now] for one year, we have destroyed in the northern part of the Smolensk area alone more than 10,000 Germans, hundreds of motor vehicles, many military trains with soldiers, officers, and supplies. The Germans in their dirty newspapers call us "forest bandits." In his correspondence, however, the enemy refers to us as a "scourge" and as a "frightening power." And herein he is right. The Germans cannot and will not be able to live wherever there are partisans! We shall annihilate them in our woods, in our villages, and wherever they appear. Every Soviet patriot from the rayons of Kaspli, Dukhovshchina, Demidov, Prechistaya, Yartsevo, Rudnya, Ponizovye and the other rayons of the Smolensk area must take revenge on the enemy for the slain fathers, husbands, and brothers, for the abused wives and sisters, for the slaughtered children, for the blood of the Russian comrades, for the fatherland!

The enemy has known how to make use of the weakness and cowardice of some Russian comrades and to hire them for his police. Others who were unwilling to join [the police were] enlisted by force and under threat of persecution of their families. But the Germans themselves despise these people and do not trust them. As reprisal for every German killed in our ambushes, the Fascists shoot dozens of policemen. Not even the Germans trust these traitors of the fatherland!

Policemen!

Against whom are you working? Against whom are you turning the weapons which the enemies of our people, the Germans, have given you? You are turning against your own people! You have raised your weapons against your brothers and sisters, the partisans!

Only by coming over to our side, only by joining in our common fight against the enemy of the Russian people, the Germans, will you cleanse yourselves of your shame and purchase your freedom from guilt.

We call upon you to enter our partisan detachments and to fight with us against the Germans. Many have already realized their guilt, have come over to us, and are fighting with us against the Germans. In one of our detachments are two platoons [composed] of former policemen. Some of them have not only atoned for their guilt, but have even been recommended for decorations by the Government for their courage in combat.

We are strong and we are numerous! We possess excellent weapons, and our determination for victory is stronger than death. We cannot be defeated. You, however, are destined for destruction. Either you will fall by the hands of the avengers of the people, who will reach you wherever you are, or you will be shot by the Germans as soon as they have no further use for you.

Come to your senses before it is too late! Think about the 150 innocent inhabitants of Kaspli, who were shot in bestial manner by the Germans in July of this year; look around and you will see dozens of villages and communities which have been burned by the Germans and hundreds of people who have been taken into slavery by them. Come to the realization that only an implacable fight against the German robbers will save you from the kind of settlement which the Germans will make with you for the help you have rendered them in their horrible crimes. By common action together with the Red Army, we shall chase the enemy from our native Russian soil.

Come to us and fight with us against the common enemy of the Russian people, the Germans. However, if you fight against us in the future as you have up to now, then a merciless judgment awaits you, if not today, then tomorrow, and if not tomorrow, then the day after tomorrow!

Mothers, wives, and sisters of the policemen!

Read this carefully and think about what is in store for your sons, husbands, and brothers if they do not come over to us but remain traitors to the fatherland. Eternal shame will come upon you and your children!

Every policeman can come over to us with this leaflet, without fear, and can enter our ranks. He will be forgiven; his life, and the well-being of his family will be secured.

Visit the camps of the partisan detachments without hesitation. This leaflet serves as a pass for a single man as well as for entire groups of policemen who come over to us.

Death to the German Occupiers!

The Commander of the Partisan Detachments of the Smolensk Area, "Batya"[41]

DOCUMENT 28

To Russians, Ukrainians, and other Soviet people deceived by the
Germans and recruited for the Fascist Army!

For two years the Red Army, the heroic partisans, and the entire Soviet people have been engaged in a life-and-death struggle against the German Fascist hordes who treacherously invaded our country, ravaged and destroyed our towns and villages, and are driving our wives, mothers, and sisters into slavery.

In the course of the patriotic war the Red Army has struck a series of devastating blows against the Germans. The Fascist Army of robbers has lost 6,400,000 soldiers and officers who were killed or captured and several thousand planes, tanks, and guns.

The Soviet partisans, the avengers of the people, have destroyed more than

[41] "Batya," a colloquial Russian term for "father," was the *nom de guerre* of Grigorii Linkov, who published his memoirs on partisan warfare after the war under the title of *Voina v tylu vraga* (Moscow: Gosudarstvennoye Izdatelstvo Khudozhestvennoi Literatury, 1951, 1959).

300,000 of Hitler's monsters; they have derailed at least 3,000 trains, destroyed more than 3,000 bridges, and have blown up and burned 300 depots of arms and munitions.

Simultaneously our mighty allies, England and America, have destroyed the German troops in Africa and, by striking destructive blows with their air force against the industrial centers of Germany and Italy, are preparing to establish the second front.

The hour is approaching when the final blow of destruction will be struck against the Fascist reptile.

And in these times, you, Russians, have agreed to serve the worst enemies of your home; you have changed into despicable servants.

Come to your senses! There is still time!

Can't you see that the Hitlerites want to use you only as cannon fodder for their own purposes?

Haven't you considered what will happen to you when the German Army has been smashed and the Hitlerites receive their well-deserved punishment for all the bestial cruelties they have committed?

You can still make up for this offense against your home [land]; you can still earn the pardon of your people.

Turn your arms against our common archenemy, against the German-Fascist monsters and their vile servants.

In this hour of the final and decisive fight against the archenemy of our people, where will you stand—you, who have been compelled or volunteered to serve the Germans?

Will you perchance defend Hitler, bearing arms against the people who have reared you?

Or will you repent, come over to the side of the Red Army, and help it to crush the enemy that much quicker?

Come over confidently, singly or in groups, to the side of the Red Army or the Soviet partisans.

Throw away your arms at once and side with the Red Army; then your lives will be guaranteed and you will have a chance to redeem yourselves in the eyes of your fatherland by relentlessly fighting against its deadly enemies. By remaining traitors you must expect an infamous death. For the penitent, pardon! For the incorrigible, death!

Political Section of the Northwest Front

This serves as a pass to the Red Army and the partisans.

DOCUMENT 29

Who is being deceived by the Traitor Vlasov?

The traitor to his country, the spy of 1936, General Vlasov, has driven you against your own people.

Before Leningrad this villain sold out an army of 50,000 men,[42] and now

---

[42] This refers to the Second Assault Army destroyed on the Volkhov front in the summer of 1942. Vlasov had taken over its command shortly before being captured by the Germans.

this scoundrel wants, with your help, to commit still another crime by inducing you to kill Russian people.

This is to the advantage of the Fascists. Their soldiers were buried before Moscow, Stalingrad, Vyazma, Rzhev, and Rostov. The rear areas are aglow with the fire of the partisan movement. The entire Soviet people have risen in defense of their fatherland. In this difficult hour in which the Germans can no more see victory than see their own ears, it was decided to exploit you; they even left you your decorations. For the Germans you are cannon fodder. The Germans themselves will hang the traitor Vlasov, but for the time being they still need him as a showpiece.

Former fighters and commanders! Think for yourselves how serious a crime it is to which you have been incited by the traitors and spies of the Vlasov type. These loathsome people are selling out [the troops at] the front; the people will never forgive them for this. Yet, for you there is still hope. One hundred and ten of your comrades from Colonel Rodionov's group, including Colonel Gavrilov, have come over to our side. They together with us will greet with a shower of bullets all those who like obedient sheep are willing to die in the interest of the German Fascists.

There can be no doubt! Victory is ours!

What are your next of kin and your relatives going to say when they find out that you are killing your own people?

Consider once more your own fate and the fate of your relatives.

Come over to our side, to the side of the united family of the people of Russia. The people will forgive your errors. They will punish you cruelly, however, if you blindly follow the corrupt half-wit Vlasov. We are ashamed of you, ashamed that you still have not recognized the truth. Desert! We await your final decision. Remember when you raise your arms against us, we too know how to shoot. Everyone who comes over to our side voluntarily will be allowed to live and will be accepted into our ranks as a true son of the fatherland. We are waiting!

Command of the Partisan Movement

Read and pass on!

DOCUMENT 30

Death to the German Occupiers!

To all so-called "Ukrainian Soldiers," "Cossacks," and "Policemen," from former soldiers (captured Red Army men) of the 221st German Division, 230th Battalion, Ukrainian Company, now "Red Partisans" [13 names follow].

Comrades! Because of existing conditions, the [pressure of] arms and treacherous fraud, the German henchmen have succeeded in getting a number of captured Red Army men and other Soviet citizens into their service. After making you their servants, the Germans have forced you to commit revolting actions in their interest. Such as fighting your own people, murdering, plundering, exploiting your people, destroying towns and villages of your native country.

Comrades! Enough of the German insolence unparalleled in history! Let us finish it. It is time to come to our senses. It is time to wake up from the devil's sleep. It is time to take revenge on the German conquerors. It is time to repay them for the murders and tortures of captured Red Army men and our citizens, for our towns and villages, and for our native country. This is the duty and sacred obligation of every fighter and citizen of the USSR. Everyone of you can do it. Always, everywhere, and at any time you can come over to us, to your own people, to the Red Army, to the Red partisans, and you yourselves can organize partisan groups.

Comrades! Follow our example. Come over to the Red partisans; destroy anyone who attempts to obstruct your decision. Perhaps the thought of coming over to the partisans provokes a fear that the partisans will take revenge on you for your service with the Germans. We know the Germans have tried by all means to convince you, as they tried to convince us, that the Red partisans and the Red Army will annihilate you as traitors to your fatherland. This is a lie. The Germans themselves haven't enough strength to fight the Red partisans and the outraged people; [therefore] they spread animosity among our people and exploit you against your [own] people. By force of weapons and ruses the Germans compel you to kill your friends and brothers in order to exploit this fight so that they may rule. The Red Army and the Red partisans understand this and take it into account. Therefore, all those who come over as friends to the partisans and to the Red Army will be received by the partisans and the Red Army with warm and brotherly greetings. The fear and worry about coming over to the Red partisans and to the Red Army is therefore unfounded. They are only trump cards in the hands of the Germans. We had the opportunity to find this out ourselves. On 23 September 1942, we 13 men left the Germans from the village of Polesye, Gomel Rayon, taking our weapons with us, and went over to the Red partisans. The partisans were very friendly in receiving us. After a friendly conversation we were told that from now on we were partisans and citizens of the USSR with full rights. When we were told that, we felt suddenly as if a different blood ran through our arteries, the clear and hot blood of a citizen of the USSR. It is impossible to describe this atmosphere, this experience of joy. We were ashamed that we had not gone over to the partisans even earlier.

Comrades! All of you must join the partisans without delay. Here are our own friends and brothers. Here are the real sons of our native country who, together with the Red Army and all the peoples of the USSR, fight against the German conquerors without regard for their own lives, but for honor, freedom, and independence of the fatherland. Only in the ranks of the Red Army or Red partisans can we take revenge upon the German cannibals for the death and torturing of our captured Red Army men, our fathers, brothers, sisters, for our destroyed towns and villages, and [only here can we] fight for the honor, freedom, and independence of our fatherland.

Death to the bandit Hitler, the organizer of the bloody world slaughter!

Long live the Red Army, our liberator!

Long live Comrade Stalin, the organizer of the annihilation of the German conquerors!

October 1942

DOCUMENT 31

Death to the German Occupiers!
To the Police!

A few days ago we still were OD men [indigenous auxiliary policemen] in Lapichi and Cherveni and served the Fascists with arms in hand and in fear of death. Hundreds of innocent citizens lost their lives through our hands. Instinctively we now ask ourselves the question: how was it possible, that we, Soviet citizens, became traitors to our fatherland, friends of the spies, Luther from Lipen, Zarin from Miradino, and of many other cannibals who drink Russian blood?

There is only one answer: The Fascists deceived us; they entangled us in their spider webs and sent us against our brothers and fathers.

After we recognized our crime against the fatherland, we decided to go over to the partisans. At first we were afraid that the partisans would shoot us, but later we decided that it is better to be shot by the partisans than to remain in the service of treason and to kill our brothers, fathers, sisters, and mothers. We came to the partisans with our weapons and said: Do with us whatever you wish. We will no longer serve the Germans. The partisans reproached us severely and said that they would give us an opportunity to make up for our guilt by fighting against the Germans.

We have taken the oath to fight to the last drop of our blood with the partisans against the German conquerors of our fatherland and for our people.

Now we are Red partisans, the people's avengers. We have found out that in other rayons of Belorussia hundreds of [former] OD men are already fighting with the partisans against our blood-enemies, the German bandits.

We are convinced of the intensity with which the population hates the OD men and we advise you with clear conscience to escape from the bloody German paws before it is too late, and to fight, weapons in hand, for your fatherland. We warn [you] however that one can come to the partisans only with an open soul; traitors and spies are quickly discovered and shot. Leave [the Germans] while it is still possible; the partisans will accept you.

The former OD men
[signatures illegible]

DOCUMENT 32

10 June 1943

Comrade Kozlov!

I believe that it is necessary to warn you that I am in possession of your letters addressed to Lieutenants Rakov and Afanasyev. Therefore, your statement "better late than never" is of no importance to us and does not impress us. These documents which I have in my hands could, if need be, be used as evidence for your own doom.

The fatherland demands from us not fancy correspondence with pretty phrases, but useful concrete work for the destruction of the enemy. In this respect we have to take chances, but you are lacking in Bolshevik power of decision. Every minute lost may cost you your life.

We specifically wish to know the following:

1. I happen to know that you have 60 men under your command. Report to me in your next letter when you, with your men and other people, can come over to us. (State exactly what road you will use and where we can meet you.)

2. Report to us the [strengths of the] following: (a) Policemen. (b) Indigenous units. (c) German units. (d) Other enemy units.

It is necessary to report exactly how many men are quartered, their location, and their armament.

3. The strength of the garrison in Propoisk and their quarters (exact location and number).

4. What is the sentiment of the population toward the partisans, especially in the leading circles? (Give 2 or 3 examples.)

5. Before coming over, you may talk about these questions to Moshei (Moshei is OD Company leader in Propoisk) if you find it necessary, because your [mutual] relation is known to us. Your decision about your wife and family is supported by us.

Comrade Kozlov this is the last letter. If necessary your document will be placed in the hands of the Gestapo.[43] Your ultimate fate will be decided there. We are speaking in simple Bolshevik words without threats. We expect your answer on 13 June 1943.

> Greetings,
> Leader of the Special Section
> [Soviet Counterintelligence Section]
> [signed] Denisov, Captain

DOCUMENT 33

Dear friend and comrade Seriozha!

By a piece of bread and by threats the German Fascists have succeeded in drawing you into their nets. With deception and threats they demand that you fight against your people and fatherland. The enemy has led you and your family onto a road from which there is no salvation. Although the Germans for the time being issue orders in our country, their cause is lost in spite of all. The course of the war, as you know, has changed considerably. The plan of the Fascist robbers has been defeated. Millions of German soldiers and officers who wanted to put you into slavery will sacrifice their lives, and their bodies will decay in the ground. We who are writing these lines were also deceived by the Germans and were on the fishhook of the cursed enemy. Now, in the hour of revenge, we are in the ranks of our comrades and are fighting, arms in hand, against the bestial Fascists.

We have derailed several troop transports with great skill. Several hundred "Fritzes" have been burned to death in shot-up trucks on the roads. This is repeated daily; you have heard it yourself.

---

[43] German translation from obviously incorrect Russian term for GFP, *Geheime Feldpolizei*, Secret Field Police. The Russians did not distinguish between the various secret police groups, but referred to all of them as Gestapo.

You, Seriozha, have a great task and you must carry out the miracle [of destruction] on the "Fritz" who sits in Propoisk. One must risk something, make a decision and display Bolshevik bravery. Many are afraid because of their past. However, through work they can make up for their guilt.

Enter the ranks of the partisans; time is running out; the hour of revenge on the Fascists is here! Close ranks against the accursed enemy!

(Give this to Grishakin.)

With friendly greetings [names follow].

[signed] Korchagin

10 June 1943

DOCUMENT 34: Letter from partisans
to the head of a labor section

To: Citizen Nikolai Kumeisha

We know that you are working as the head of the Labor Department. You are treading the path of betrayal and treason to your country, the path of fighting the Slavic people. You, a Slav, for the pittance of the Germans, are treading the path of misdeeds and crimes performed by the Germans on our soil. Each of their steps leaves the bloody imprint of those thousands of Slavic people who were tortured and murdered. Revenge and the severe retribution of the people await you in the near future. The hour of reckoning is near. The Red Army is advancing and is not far from our region. The Germans are retreating westward, but they cannot escape retribution. And what are you going to do?

You will be crushed and strangled by the people as a traitor to your country, as a participant in all the crimes and murders committed by the Germans on our soil. For you there remains only one possibility that will save your life and the life of your family. We offer you this opportunity if you [are willing to] exert all your strength in the struggle against the Germans, i.e., if you agree to work for us and to fulfill our assignments.

You must: 1) give [us] a detailed list of all the workers of the town council [*uprava*], indicating their age, nationality, domicile and attitudes; 2) give us a list of persons with whom you yourself are in contact.

Well, Nikolai. This is a very easy task, but the execution of it will guarantee your life. See here—you can either live or die at the hands of the people.

Transmit your reply and the list, and also your agreement to maintain contact with us, to the parents [presumably Kumeisha's] in the village of Podlesye.

Do it so that it will be known [only] to you and me. If you even consider betraying the bearer of this letter or even talk about it, you and your family will be liquidated by us. In order to express your consent to working with us, sign the enclosed pledge.

[Andrei]

23 November 1943   The commander of the Special Partisan Group

[Enclosure]
Pledge

I, Kumeisha, Nikolai, express my consent to execute the orders given by the commander of the partisan group. I promise to tell no one about my connection. In case of my violating this pledge I shall be executed as a traitor to my country—together with my family.

Signature

DOCUMENT 35

To the Lithuanian Soldiers!

Comrades! Soldiers! The Fascists are forcing you to guard the railroads against the partisans. The Fascists deceive you and promise you a beautiful life. In reality, however, in your fatherland they are taking away cows, horses, and grain from your fathers and brothers. They are mobilizing your brothers for the war which is being fought in their interest.

Your fathers and brothers have become aware of the swindle of the German Fascists. They enter the partisan units and fight hand in hand with the Red Army against fascism. The students of the city of Kovno [Kaunas] declared a general strike. The Fascists took gruesome revenge upon them. Ten were shot and three hundred locked in jail. However, they were liberated by the partisans. We partisans urge you to join us and turn your weapons against the German Fascists.

Strike your hated officers; disarm the Germans. Blow up the railroads and military installations. The Fascists will soon be defeated.

Partisan Detachment No. 112

[spring 1942]

§VI. Partisan Propaganda and Relations with the Local Population

DOCUMENT 36

In the spring of 1942 the head of a German military government detachment in Navlya, a town south of Bryansk, posted an appeal to the local population. The partisans therefore put up an answer which may be regarded as an excellent example of partisan psychological warfare directed at the population under German rule. It combines promises with threats, deprecates German strength, and predicts the rapid return of the Red Army.

Answer to Heinroth's Appeal

Mr. Heinroth!

It is useless to think that the appeal which is shot through with lies will help you.

Our Russian people have never been traitors and will never betray their fatherland. Our people are prepared under all circumstances to fight with deadly hatred and to protect their holy soil to the last man. In whatever manner the Fascist monsters may try to suppress the partisan movement, which has developed not only in our country but also in other countries temporarily occupied by Germany, they will not succeed.

You, Commandant, have also tried to strangle the partisan movement in our country, but none of your attempts have been successful.

Do you still remember, Mr. Heinroth, when, during the fighting at Pervomaisk, you threw away your field glasses, maps, and plans, and cried: "My legs! My legs! Save my head from the partisan bullets!" You have forgotten how we beat you at Alexeyevka, Aleshenka, Svyatoye, Kharpach, Zhuravka, Sinezverki, and Borshchevo, how we threw trains and trucks down the embankments, and how we blasted railroad bridges. We shall continue to beat you wherever you show up.

You think in vain that your planes, tanks, and *Minenwerfer*[44] will intimidate us. Your best air, tank, and *Minenwerfer* units have already been scattered by the Red Army or are stationed with frozen noses, feet, and hands somewhere in Rumania or Bulgaria; the unsuccessful, quickly trained airmen, who dropped 150 bombs on Aleshenka and with "certain" hits destroyed a grain barn and inflicted serious injuries on a spotted chicken,[45] hardly will frighten our heroic patriots.

Nothing will destroy our determination and desire to beat the occupiers who came to our country to plunder it. Hundreds of "Fritzes" and "Hanses" have already been buried in our country and still hundreds more will be killed by the partisan bullets.

Soon the hour will come when the Hitler machine will collapse under the blows of the Red Army which will destroy the German predatory army.

Comrades of the Police!
Consider who you are and with whom you associate.
Whose interests do you defend?

You are being mobilized by the Germans against your brothers, sisters, fathers, and mothers, and, against your will, you are induced to kill them.

You believe that the Germans trust you?
No, they don't trust you!

Pokrovsky, the low traitor and lackey of the Germans, who was given a house and some land in Bryansk for saving Heinroth, has also fallen into disgrace. He is no longer trusted, and he is suspected of sympathizing with the partisans; he was degraded and is held under arrest.

And who are you?
You are a blind tool in the hands of the Germans!

Don't you hear the explosions of the Red Army's bombs and shells? The Red Army is only 40 kilometers from our rayon, whose hour of liberation by the Red Army from the German blackmailers will come soon.

[44] Heavy mortars with rifled barrels.

[45] Presumably a reference to the employment of the group of bombers assigned to a Rear Area Command of Second Panzer Army for antipartisan warfare.

724 / Appendix Documents 36–38

Consider before it is too late with whom you wish to go—with us, with your Russian brothers, or with the Germans, who, in their retreat, will kill your families and will kidnap you [and send you] to Africa where you will fight side by side with others like you.

Don't believe the Germans or your leaders [when they say] that the partisans will shoot you. If you come over honestly to our side, then we will have the same goal—to destroy the German blackmailers.

Smash the Germans and come over to our side as did your comrades from Sinezverki who joined us in groups.

Thereby you will save yourself, your families, your brothers and sisters, and will atone for your sins against your fatherland.

Smash the Germans and the leaders of the militia!

Long live the partisans, the shining patriots of our country! Long live our Red Army, which shatters the Hitler bands, and its genius-commander, the great Stalin, who leads it on to victory.

Headquarters of the Armed Partisan Detachments

DOCUMENTS 37–38

When partisan detachments raided or passed through a village, they often left behind posters and leaflets for the inhabitants. Two such posters are translated here. The first was left in a village in the rayon of Gorka, southeast of Minsk; the second, in a village near Novogrodek, in Western Belorussia. Both are warnings to the local population against aiding the Germans.

DOCUMENT 37

Don't expect to receive your freedom from the German bloodhounds but rather [expect it] from your Red Army brothers. Hitler's plan has failed; soon his mind will fail also. Don't think that the Germans will be able to escape. The death of the bloodhounds will take place in our own territory. Volunteers[46] and policemen will be killed by our Red Army of workers and peasants and by the partisans. We will burn and hang, not only them, but also their parents. Do you still want to follow the Germans?

DOCUMENT 38

Do not tear down! You are being watched!
Blood for blood!

The Fascist barbarians are using every means to destroy workers and peasants. They burn the villages and execute even innocent inhabitants. The German police are the most important participant in these actions. Those who help the police and the Germans are spies, like those who carelessly talk too much about partisans and their activities. The time has come when the suffering of the partisans and of those who are in sympathy with them will come

[46] Soviet nationals who volunteered to serve in collaborator organizations fighting the partisans.

to an end. The partisans will destroy everybody who works for the police. Citizens! Belorussians! Do not doubt that the partisans know exactly who is working for the police and for the garrulous village philosophers. Nobody who attempts to engage in espionage for the Germans will escape us. The first to be destroyed will be the following:

1. Families of indigenous policemen, mayors, and starostas.
2. Spies and those who betray the partisans.

R. P. K.[47]

DOCUMENT 39

In the spring of 1943 the partisans in the area around Gomel began publishing a newspaper called *The Partisan of Gomel Oblast.* The Germans found a copy of issue No. 3, dated 22 April 1943, and excerpts translated by the Germans are given below. Beyond general attacks on German atrocities, the article contains a bitter attack on the German program of recruiting Soviet nationals for labor in Germany. Although this started out as a voluntary program, by the summer of 1942 it had become a ruthless method of forced recruitment. The German note accompanying the translation claims that the statements concerning the Gomel area are untrue; however, the same German unit—the 221st Security Division—was one of the loudest in complaining against the effects of the slave labor program on the population. The general picture painted by the newspaper is accurate though there are probably mistakes and exaggerations in some of the details.

Whoever Goes to Germany Will Perish

Soon two years will have passed since our Belorussia was enveloped by the dark night of the German occupation. By bloody terror, by mass executions and death, by fire and sword, the Germans want to introduce the Fascist system into those parts of Belorussia which they have occupied.

Hitler's men have hanged, burned, or buried alive more than 700,000 Belorussians. They have burned and destroyed our Belorussian cities of Minsk, Baranovichi, Gomel, Volkovysk, Rogachev, Grodno, Vitebsk, Zhlobin, and others.

Hundreds of schools, clubs, and other cultural buildings have been destroyed. In innumerable cases the Hitler bandits are plundering the population. Thousands of men and women are drafted by them for heavy physical labor or are sent to do forced labor in Hitler's Germany. In the town of Chechersk alone the Germans shot or hanged 450 people in one day; altogether 2,000 people have been murdered by the German hangmen there. The same is true in Korma. Thousands of people have been hanged in Gomel and in towns and rayon centers of Gomel Oblast alone.

Hundreds of villages and localities have been laid in ashes by the German occupiers.

The bandits plundered the village of Budishche in Chechersk Rayon. After

[47] Probably, Rayon Party Committee.

driving 24 inhabitants into the club, they set the building on fire. In addition they also carried out executions. This is the way the Germans ravage every rayon.

The Germans have sent thousands of people from Gomel Oblast to forced labor in Fascist slavery.

One partisan unit alone, active in Gomel Oblast, freed more than 1,000 people who were being driven to forced labor by the Germans.

The Germans are preparing lists of people from Gomel Oblast to be sent to Germany. From Korma alone about 100 men and women from this list have been sent off to Fascist forced labor.

Sons and daughters of the Belorussian people! The bestiality of the Hitler bandits has not broken your will! The Red Army is beating the Germans at the front; the partisans are beating them far behind the front.

The Red Army is not far away. The day of the great reckoning approaches. All the suffering the Germans have brought upon us will be avenged. The bestial enemy shall pay with his vile blood for all his atrocities.

Do not go to Germany, for death awaits you there. Hide in the woods; go to other villages to relatives and friends; go to the partisans. Help the partisans and the Red Army destroy the Germans on our Belorussian soil.

Comrades, men and women, partisans! Block the plans of the Hitler bandits to send people to Germany.[48]

DOCUMENTS 40–44

In their areas of operations, the partisans acted not only as a military arm of the Soviet Government but also as an agency through which the Government exercised control over the inhabitants of the enemy-occupied areas.

These documents offer information on the control of the local population by the partisans. Documents 40 and 41 are decrees of a rayon soviet re-established by the partisans behind the German lines. Documents 42 and 43 are partisan orders to the local population to cease supporting the Germans; the former document is from the Bobruisk and the latter from the Bryansk area. Both documents illustrate the unenviable position of the inhabitants in villages which were not under the firm control of either the partisans or the Germans. Whatever they did, they incurred the wrath of one or the other.

Document 44 lists the rights and duties of village commandants, who apparently were officials appointed from among the partisans in the later stages of the war to supervise the local population and secure full support from them for partisan activities. These commandants were probably appointed in areas firmly held by the partisans and operated alongside the Soviet administration re-established in the area.

[48] A short article giving a detailed account of the German atrocities in Budishche, in Chechersk Rayon, reported in shorter form above is included at this point. The date of the events is given as 11 February 1943.

DOCUMENT 40

Decree No. 1

To: the Rayon Soviet of the Workers' and Red Army Deputies of Nevel, Kalinin Oblast, 28 March 1942

In agreement with the official decree (*ukaz*) of the Supreme Soviet, dated 22 June 1941, "Concerning the State of War," the Executive Committee of the Rayon Soviet of Workers' and Red Army Deputies of Nevel and the leaders of the partisan units within the liberated areas issue the following regulation concerning traffic of persons on the streets:

1. The population is permitted on the streets only between 6 A.M. and 9 P.M. At all other times passes are required.

2. In all inhabited communities, guard units are to be organized from the local inhabitants; their duty is to stop all unknown persons and check their papers.

The chairmen of the executive committees and of the kolkhozes are held responsible for the execution of this decree.

> By order (of): Chairman of the Executive
> Committee of the Rayon Soviet
> Commander of the Partisan Unit
> Commissar of the Partisan Unit

DOCUMENT 41

Decree No. 2

To: the Rayon Soviet of the Workers' and Red Army Deputies of Nevel, Kalinin Oblast, 28 March 1942

Based on the order of the Chairman of the State Committee for Defense, Comrade Stalin (Order No. 166 on the surrender of captured material and weapons), the Executive Committee of the Nevel Rayon Soviet and the leaders of the partisan units request all inhabitants of the liberated areas to surrender the following within 24 hours from the time of this proclamation:

1. [All] available weapons and ammunition.

2. Military equipment, uniforms, and communications equipment.

3. [All] goods acquired illegally during the war and belonging to state institutions and enterprises.

4. The surrender [of the above items] must be made to the local executive committees.

Persons failing to comply with this decree will be prosecuted on the basis of wartime laws.

> Chairman of the Executive Committee
> of the Rayon Soviet
> Commander of the Partisan Unit
> Commissar of the Partisan Unit

DOCUMENT 42

Order No. 2

To: the population, workers, and employees

The great patriotic war demands that every honest citizen participate, weapons in hand, in the fight against German fascism and that in this way he help our fatherland and the Red Army which is deployed for attack.

At the front the Red Army is attacking successfully, and the end of German fascism is no longer far off.

Instead of helping the fatherland, you are helping fascism directly or indirectly. You fell trees, transport timber, and deliver wheat, hay, and other foodstuffs. In your rashness you are even going so far as to denounce those who wish to help the return of the Red Army.

I order the following:

1. The preparation[49] and transportation of timber must cease. Anyone found engaged in this work in the woods will be shot as a traitor to his fatherland.

2. Anyone who voluntarily participates in the delivery of foodstuffs or denounces the true defenders of the fatherland or their followers will also be shot.

Command of the Partisan Brigade

DOCUMENT 43

Order to the Village District of Divoka

To the peaceful population of the occupied territory from the Command of the Partisan Detachments

1. All those who volunteer for labor service in Germany will be punished by us in the most severe manner. Their entire families and [land] holdings can be destroyed.

2. We categorically forbid all deliveries of bread grain. Those who are found in the act [of making deliveries to the Germans] will be shot and their property will be confiscated. Anyone tearing down this announcement will be shot!

DOCUMENT 44

Rights and Duties of the Village Commandant

1. In accordance with military orders, the best partisans are to be appointed as village commandants.

2. The village commandant is directly subordinated to the staff of the unit and of the brigade.

3. He must prepare exact lists of the cattle, grain, and foodstuffs in the village, report means of transportation, etc.

4. He must be acquainted with the population in order to know everybody's attitude.

5. He is required to examine the inhabitants who leave the village.

[49] The Russian term probably used, *zagotovka,* comprises felling and cutting.

6. He is required to examine unknown persons entering the village.

7. The commandant must immediately pass on to the partisan unit all information which may be brought to his attention.

8. He must also transmit this information to the special section of the partisan detachment.

9. He must see to it that all orders of the [partisan] units and of the brigade are executed immediately.

10. He directs the distribution of food, etc., for the brigade and [partisan] unit.

11. He must quarter members of the [partisan] units who come into the village.

12. He is obliged to provide for the security of the village. For this purpose he must organize guard details and sentries from among the local population.

13. He must prevent plundering and excesses of the partisans in the village and report them to the leader of the unit.

14. In cases of unmilitary behavior and refusal to obey orders, he is authorized to disarm the offender and turn him over to the unit for punishment.

15. The commandant must keep records on supplies, cattle, feed, etc., issued [to the partisans], on the time of issue, and on the recipient. The recipient must sign the record. He [the commandant] must also note when the horse-team was returned.

Note: If the horse and the wagon are not returned on time, the commandant must report this to the [partisan] unit or to the brigade staff. He must never again issue anything to such persons.

DOCUMENT 45

In the summer of 1942 the Political Administration of the Northwest Front issued a leaflet addressed to the population of the occupied areas in the northwest corner of the pre-1939 USSR. This leaflet points to the action of the partisans in killing an official of the German economic administration, presumably both to encourage the local population and to impress both them and the Germans with the long and implacable arm of the Soviet government.

Death to the German Occupiers!
The End of Adolf Beck

In May 1942 the German landowner Adolf Beck[50] settled on the Gari Sovkhoz in Dno Rayon, Leningrad Oblast. Supported by the bayonets of the Hitlerite soldiers, he declared 5,700 hectares of Russian soil as his property. The population of 14 villages of the Krutets, Rovovo, and Pankratovo village soviets, including some 1,000 peasant holdings, worked for Beck from dawn till dark.

By using beastly methods ... Beck believed that he could strengthen his rule over the Dno kolkhozes [*sic*]. When the girls of the Pankratovo village

---

[50] Presumably Adolf Beck was an official of the economic administration for the occupied territories assigned to the supervision of one large state farm.

went for a walk on Sunday evening, he punished them by having them carry heavy logs. To work seven days a week for the master—this is the rule of the German, Beck. When he was drunk, he shot a group of old people, women, and children with a submachine gun.

With the aid of his Fuehrer he made plans to subjugate the peasants of the Pskov area. . . . "My property will become the center of colonization in Russia."

However, things did not work out as Beck expected. During the dark night of 28 July some local kolkhoz peasants and partisans entered Beck's home. Barns and granaries burst into flames. Shells flew in the house where Beck sat like a trapped animal anticipating death. Beck ceased to exist. . . .

The Russian people in Dno, Porkov, and in the vicinity of Pskov rejoiced. One brutal individual less. The self-confidence of the people grew. . . . The destruction of Gari is only the beginning. Beck's neighbors, the newly arrived Hitlerite landowners, the grabbers of the Iskra, Dubnyak, Dnovski Massiv, Bolyshevo, Poloneye Sovkhozes and others are still alive. . . .

Russians, destroy the properties where [the men responsible for your] evil fate are hiding. Finish off the German landowners. Don't work for them, but kill every one of them—this is the duty of every Soviet patriot. Drive the Germans from the land of the Soviets!

. . . .

Political Administration of the
Northwest Front of the Red Army

DOCUMENT 46: Soviet or Partisan Leaflet Directed at Peasants

To the Soviet Peasants of the German Occupied Territory
A Fascist Trap for the Soviet Peasants
Men and Women!

The former tsarist spy and present chief of the occupied Eastern areas, Alfred Rosenberg, has put a so-called "agrarian law" into force. The Fascists want to represent this vile decree as a great favor that they have bestowed on you. Don't believe the Fascists! They deceive you. Judge for yourselves.

Rosenberg declares that the kolkhoz will be succeeded by communal farms. In these you will have to work together and together you will bring in the harvest. Why have the Fascists introduced this regulation? To make it easier for them to rob you. As soon as the harvest is in, it will be immediately taken away from you and sent to Germany. For this reason the Hitlerites place their own administrators in charge of the communal farms. They will not only drive you on with the whip so that you will work faster, but they will also take away from you everything that you produce. The Fascists will act according to the following principle: "The work is yours, the produce ours." But that is not all. The Hitlerites say they will give you land as property. Only idiots will believe this fairy tale. In Article 6 of his "law" Rosenberg states: "Members of the communal farms who do not fulfill their duties towards the German authorities, as well as politically unreliable persons, or those who prove unable to manage their own holdings, will not be recognized in the distribution of land." The Fascists could put all Soviet peasants into this group.

Comrade peasants! The German robbers want to distribute the land of your kolkhozes not among you, but among the German landowners and holders of large estates. Minister Darré has stated: "One must deprive the Slavic peasants of their land in order to make them into dispossessed proletarians. The aim is to transfer the land to be cultivated into the hands of the German *Herrenvolk*. In the entire Eastern area, only the Germans have the right to become landowners. The land which is held by a foreign race must be made into a land of slaves."

§VII. The Grishin Regiment

The Grishin Partisan Regiment, which was first organized in 1941 and continued to operate into the summer of 1944, may not have been entirely typical of average partisan detachments; the vicissitudes of its career, however, are of the greatest interest. The documents of this regiment by themselves do not give a full record of the group's activities and problems, but they present an excellent picture of a well-established partisan band which continued to operate for several years in spite of repeated German efforts to destroy it.

The detachment developed from a nucleus of members of conspiratorial groups and escaped prisoners of war who were first organized in Smolensk Oblast in December 1941. In February 1942 a few, presumably the most reliable members of the group, were transferred to Dorogobuzh and placed under the command of S. V. Grishin. It was here that the Grishin detachment started functioning, and here also it received its official designation, "Partisan Detachment for Special Assignments No. 13." In the spring of 1942 the detachment increased greatly in numbers through the influx of additional escaped prisoners of war, deserters from indigenous German collaborator units, volunteers, and recruits from among the local population. Apparently the detachment was not equipped to handle such a large number of members, and, therefore, groups ranging from 300 to 600 men were guided through the German lines into Soviet-held territory in order to be incorporated into the regular Red Army.

In June 1942 the Grishin detachment (*otryad*) was reorganized into an independent regiment (*polk*) and was divided into three battalions. At that time the regiment consisted of about 600 members. During 1942 and 1943 the strength of the regiment varied from 400 to over 2,000 members; the latter figure was reached in September 1943 just after the Germans had attempted to annihilate the regiment through a major antipartisan operation. This campaign failed when the German military units involved were withdrawn before the operation could be brought to a successful conclusion. A short time later, however, in November 1943, the regiment suffered heavy losses and came close to complete annihilation as a result of another antipartisan operation southeast of Mogilev.

The movements of the Grishin Regiment from the spring of 1942 to the summer of 1944 covered a large area behind the central section of the German front. Starting from Dorogobuzh in the spring of 1942 the regiment first moved northwest to a region between Velizh and Demidov. The winter of 1942–43 was spent west of Smolensk and in the spring of 1943 the regiment moved south and southwest, by-passing Mogilev, where, as indicated above, it was badly decimated by a German antipartisan operation. Documents indicate that the Grishin group was again active in the summer of 1944, this time farther west on the railroad between Borisov and Orsha. The Grishin Regiment avoided open combat whenever possible unless forced by German antipartisan operations to give battle. Its activities, like those of other partisan groups, were concentrated on disrupting German supply lines by blasting railroads and setting up roadblocks, attacking and occupying villages and weakly defended German supply installations, and carrying on propaganda work among the local population. How closely its activities were coordinated and directed by the Red Army, at least during the latter stages of the war, becomes apparent from two captured orders addressed to Grishin, assigning him specific tasks in connection with forthcoming Red Army operations. The intelligence information collected by the Grishin Regiment, though often unreliable, was evaluated and forwarded to Moscow.

Weapons and ammunition were obtained partly from supplies buried by the Red Army during its initial retreat in 1941 and partly from supplies dropped by Soviet planes. In order to overcome shortages, Grishin set up his own armament repair shop. Food does not appear to have been a major problem; it was obtained by requisitioning from that part of the local population which was known to collaborate with the Germans. Obtaining food was thus combined with the terrorization and "punishment" of those persons who did not fulfill their duties in the "Patriotic War." Looting from the population at large was strictly prohibited. Whether or not individual members of the Grishin group adhered strictly to this policy would be difficult to ascertain.

The following documents include a characterization of Grishin himself (Document 47), material on the tactical operations of the regiment (Documents 48–52), intelligence reports prepared by the battalions into which the regiment was divided (Documents 53–56), disciplinary orders of the regimental or battalion staffs (Documents 57–60), an order establishing a section for agitation and propaganda within the regiment (Document 61); documents on the relations of the regiment to the operations of the Red Army (Documents 62–64); and an order concerning American planes and their crews (Document 65). Some German interrogations of former members of the regiment are given in the annex, pp. 740–44.

DOCUMENT 47: A Characterization of Grishin

Some information on Grishin, the regimental commander of the partisan group, is contained in this recommendation by the "party bureau" to the Rayon Committee of the Communist Party in Smolensk. Grishin is described as an able and resourceful leader who succeeded in inflicting severe damage on the Germans with his regiment. In addition to the personal accomplishments of Grishin, the document indicates the type of activity in which the regiment was engaged in 1942.

Translation of a Rating of Grishin made at the end of 1942

Grishin, Sergei Vladimirovich
Rank: Lieutenant
Position: Commander of the 13th Partisan Regiment
Year of Birth: 1917
National Origin: Russian
Party Membership: Communist Party Candidate
Drafted by the Military District Commissariat of Dorogobuzh

Comrade Grishin was a member of the secret partisan organization of Dorogobuzh. He participated in the liberation of Dorogobuzh.. On 9 March 1942 [the partisan commander] "Dedushka" organized a company for special assignments and appointed Grishin as its commander. G. received instructions to penetrate into the enemy rear areas. He fully justified the confidence placed in him and executed his task as well as possible. He knew how to lead his company under difficult winter conditions and during this time annihilated several armed units of Germans and police forces.

In May 1942 the Grishin Company reached Kasplya Rayon in Smolensk Oblast. In August 1942 Grishin organized a partisan regiment of 700 men and appointed suitable men to positions of leadership. The regiment was armed with captured weapons and equipment left behind and buried by the Red Army during its retreat in 1941. With his regiment, Grishin succeeded in inflicting serious losses on the enemy because of his able leadership, constant watchfulness, and necessary experience in partisan warfare. From April to November 1942 the enemy suffered the following losses in men and materials: 2,794 Germans and 225 policemen killed; 185 Germans and 18 policemen wounded; 7 Germans and 12 policemen taken prisoners; 182 vehicles destroyed and 104 damaged; the rail embankment blasted in 20 places; 27 trains derailed and 1 burned; 8 locomotives destroyed; at the same time, 11 bridges dynamited; 50 vehicles with grain and 70 cattle captured; 5 munition dumps blasted; 5 guns and 5 tractors destroyed. In September 1942 with vastly superior forces, the enemy conducted an elaborate offensive in the area held by the regiment. He succeeded in encircling the regiment, but Grishin, through his resourcefulness and tactical ability, managed to break through and inflicted considerable losses on the enemy. He led his regiment out of unfavorable terrain with negligible losses and resumed offensive operations. The party bureau requests the Rayon Committee of the Communist Party in Smolensk to recommend Grishin to the Supreme Soviet for the medal of Hero of the Soviet Union.

DOCUMENTS 48–52: Operations of the Grishin Regiment

The staff of the Grishin Regiment apparently kept files of combat reports. The Germans did not translate these in their entirety but excerpted only small portions, obviously in order to show the inhumane fighting methods of the partisans. Although it is impossible to tell whether they are representative, the excerpts are retranslated and presented here in lieu of better information on the tactics of the regiment. No dates are given, but the reports probably all refer to 1943.

DOCUMENT 48

Commissar Abakumov, Politruk Mushevich, and two partisans were killed on 14 August in the fight against the Hitlerite monsters. The death of our comrades has already been partly revenged. The enemy lost 25 dead and many wounded in front of Lokisy. Partisan vengeance will not, however, be confined to this. For each of our dead comrades hundreds of these cannibals who have been freed of their chains will be killed by partisans' hands.

DOCUMENT 49

Nine policemen were slain in battle, nine taken prisoner, of whom eight were shot and one who had deserted was allowed to live.

DOCUMENT 50

The scout leader Chubukov and the scout Pupkov stopped a naked German in the forest near the village of Usushki on 22 August and wanted to lead him to their detachment. On the way he was taken away by a captain and several men of the 14th Brigade. The captain explained that the German had escaped the day before just as he was about to be shot. I have expressed my thanks to Chubukov.

DOCUMENT 51

Several Germans who pretended to be dead were found by partisans on the battlefield. Partisan Skvortsev came across a German officer who was holding his breath and feigned death. S. decided to convince himself of his death by using his dagger. This started the "dead" man talking immediately. However, since he [Skvortsev] did not understand German, he advised the German by a deep thrust of his dagger to be silent and never to rise again.

DOCUMENT 52

Enemy losses: 13 policemen and 2 Germans burned in the stable.

DOCUMENTS 53–56: Intelligence Reports

The battalions of the Grishin Regiment seem to have issued regular intelligence reports. The intelligence information included very important, though not always accurate, tactical information as well as trivial details. These reports were collected by the regimental staff, evaluated, and forwarded to Moscow. Tactical intelligence information was repeatedly criticized for being inaccurate; in one case a female intelligence scout was ordered executed for failure to carry out her missions (Document 57).

DOCUMENT 53

2d Battalion, 5 September 1943

A course in espionage for boys and girls was concluded on 4 August according to natives of Mogilev.

DOCUMENT 54

Intelligence Report from Mogilev of 7 September [1943]

On 25 August, 500 infantry troops occupied the camp next to the airport. The concentration camp adjoining the Dmitrov Factory contains about 500 people including 276 Jews. A small troop-training area which can accommodate about 1,500 men is located behind the automobile repair shop [and there is another area] in Chapayev for about 1,000 men. The guard regiment of the "people's" army[51] is billeted on the grounds of an artillery regiment near the railroad station Mogilev 2. The regiment fights against the partisans. The regiment is commanded by Colonel Kononov.[52] A pigeon station containing about 500 pigeons is located on the road to Vydritsa [?]. A vegetable storage place has been set up near the railroad station adjoining the overpass. Locomotives are being repaired in the automobile repair shop. The meat combine is functioning; the sausage department is located in the former newspaper building. Airplane parts are being manufactured in the pipe foundry. There are about 1,000 troops in Mogilev excluding those in the training areas. There are no armored units. Antiaircraft batteries are stationed on the bridges. At the present time there are about 500 motor vehicles in Mogilev.

DOCUMENT 55

5th Battalion, 8 September 1943

Changes and transfer involving the German 4th and 9th Armies are being executed at this time. Rumors say that the greatly weakened 9th Army is being strengthened by reserves and by parts of the 4th Army. This includes [Regimental?] Headquarters 675 of the 4th Army with the following officers: Major Kuehn, Captain Alzt, [illegible], and 1st Lt. Broer; this staff is being transferred to the 9th Army and will remain in Krichev where the staff of the 9th Army will also be moved. The staff of the 4th Army with its commanding general, Heinrici, is still located in Shumakhi [illegible], south of Roslavl. It is strongly protected by antiaircraft batteries. A shift of the 4th Army to the Ukraine or to Italy is expected momentarily. The 9th Army will then take over the present sector of the 4th Army.[53] Army supply commander (ANF)[54] is stationed in

[51] In German *"Volksarmee,"* referring to indigenous collaborators.
[52] Kononov was a Cossack officer who commanded a unit of Cossacks fighting on the German side.
[53] The tactical information concerning the German Ninth and Fourth Armies does not at all agree with the German situation maps of this period. Both the Ninth and the Fourth Armies remained in the area of *Heeresgruppe Mitte.*
[54] ANF is the German abbreviation for *Armeenachschubfuehrer.*

Klimovichi, southeast of Krichev, together wtih Colonel Zippermann von [remainder of name illegible]. Antiaircraft batteries are almost completely lacking. . . . A large airport serving as a base for long-range aircraft and containing a fuel supply depot is located in the village of Shumkovka near the highway. A motor pool . . . is situated in the village of Selets on the Krichev-Roslavl highway. Cars are parked along both sides of the highway under the trees throughout the entire village. There are no antiaircraft batteries. A large depot for winter supplies (skis, sleds, and clothing) is located near the Krichev 2 railroad station. . . .

DOCUMENT 56

5th Battalion, 20 September 1943

In Smolensk Oblast on the major supply route of Smolensk-Krasnoye, Smolensk-Gusino, German troops were observed retreating in the direction of Orsha.[55] In the areas of Pochinkovo, Dukhovchina, and Yartsevo refugees consisting primarily of policemen, starostas, and mayors are arriving daily.[56] Smolensk is being evacuated.[57] The editorial staff of the German[-sponsored] newspaper *Novyi Put* [New Way] has been transferred to Belostok. Harvesting and transporting of grain are being accelerated. The staff of a German army was transferred from Smolensk to Tolochin between Minsk and Orsha. Field fortifications along the Dnepr and the Sozh are being speeded up; pillboxes and trenches are under construction.

Roslavl has been evacuated; [there is] uninterrupted traffic of motor vehicles on the Roslavl-Mstislavl highway. The Germans are taking everything with them, even such trivial things as furniture or potted flowers. A large fuel dump is located in a small grove on the Mogilev 2-Shklov rail line, about 200 meters from Mogilev 2. Our air raid seriously damaged the airport in Shatalovo; 45 airplanes and all supply dumps in the vicinity are burned out.

DOCUMENTS 57–60: Discipline

Disciplinary problems within the regiment were dealt with severely. Although the Germans did not record the author of the following orders (Documents 57–60), they were presumably issued either by the regimental commander himself or by the battalion commanders.

DOCUMENT 57

19 January 1943

For repeated failure to execute reconnaissance assignments, for violating security regulations, and for theft, the [female] scout Andrenkova is to be shot.

---

[55] A German offensive in July 1943 had broken down and at this time (September 1943) the Germans were rapidly retreating before a major Soviet offensive.

[56] As the Germans retreated, they tried to evacuate those who had collaborated with them during the occupation.

[57] Smolensk was evacuated by the Germans on 24 September 1943. The information in this report is, therefore, quite accurate.

DOCUMENT 58

11 May 1943

My persistent requests to maintain order and discipline are disregarded again and again. Lack of restraint in relations with women have been noted at different times. In seven cases this has resulted in pregnancy. These women reduce the combat readiness of their men and are a burden to the regiment in combat.

DOCUMENT 59

22 September 1943

Platoon Leader Lukanov is to be punished by ten days' arrest for extortion of vodka from natives of the village and for drinking bouts in his platoon.

DOCUMENT 60

13 October 1943

For leaving his post without orders, for cowardice, for being panicky, and for nonfulfillment of orders, Squad Leader Bacharov is to be shot.

DOCUMENT 61: Propaganda

The Grishin Regiment conducted propaganda not only among the partisans themselves but also among the civilian population. The regiment published both leaflets and a newspaper. Propaganda activities directed at the enemy concentrated on indigenous collaborators. This document as well as other information on the Grishin Regiment indicates that in 1943 numerous indigenous collaborators deserted to the regiment.

A Section for Agitation and Propaganda is to be created in order to increase agitation and propaganda activities in the regiment and among the civilian population. A section chief, two instructors, and an editor for the newspaper will be appointed. The assignments of the section for August are the following:

1. Increase of agitation in the regiment.
2. Discussions with officers and men in which the international situation, the situation at the front, and the tasks of the Red Army and the partisans in the struggle against the enemy, as well as the relations with the civilian population are to be explained.
3. Publication of leaflets for the civilian population.
4. Publication of the newspaper, *Death to Our Enemies* (one issue every five days).
5. Recreation activities for the troops.

At the same time intensive propaganda directed at the enemy is to be carried on. This type of propaganda has had considerable success among the indigenous units during the last few months.

DOCUMENTS 62–63: The Grishin Regiment and the Red Army

During the Soviet advance in the fall of 1943, between 2 October and 11 October, Grishin received an order to withdraw into Soviet-held territory leaving behind only a small unit to maintain liaison with intelligence agents and the Red Army (Document 62). He did not succeed in accomplishing this mission because a few days later his regiment was surrounded by the Germans in the vicinity of Propoisk. The spirited appeal which Grishin issued to the members of his regiment indicates how desperate their position must have been at this time (Document 63). A German report states that the Grishin Regiment was badly decimated and dispersed at the beginning of November. It was probably at this time that most of the documents translated below were captured. The Germans did not, however, annihilate the Grishin Regiment; it escaped westward.

DOCUMENT 62

The regiment has received orders to cross the front lines and to proceed to the Soviet rear area.

A reconnaissance squad under the command of Major Lazarev will remain in the present zone of operations to keep in touch with agents planted by the regiment and to relay important messages to the Red Army.

It is hereby ordered: Major Lazarev will organize this reconnaissance squad from the best scouts (male and female) of the regiment and will remain with this squad in the enemy's rear area. In the night of 2–3 October he will depart for the area around Osipovichi. Major Lazarev will receive three radio sets to keep wireless contact with the staff of the West Front.

DOCUMENT 63

11 October 1943

We are encircled. The exits from the forest are blocked. The Red Army will be here tomorrow or the day after. You can hear for yourself that the front is approaching. Today's artillery preparation tells us that the Red Army is attacking. It is our task to hold out for two or three more days; after this time contact with the Red Army will have been made. Therefore, we must hold our positions. Retreat would mean extinction. There must be no cowards or panic-raisers among us. Every honest patriot of our fatherland must shoot such people on the spot. Just a few more days, Comrades, and we will be among our own people. Hold on to your positions and thwart every attempt of the enemy to break through. We are strong and we will be victorious.

> Commander of the 13th Partisan Regiment
> [signed] Grishin
> Chief of Staff of the 13th Partisan Regiment
> [signed] Uzlov

DOCUMENT 64

In preparation for their summer offensive of June 1944 an order was sent to Grishin, presumably by the Central Staff of the Partisan Movement for Belorussia, instructing him to blast railroad tracks on the Orsha-Borisov line beginning the night of 19–20 June 1944. On 22 June 1944 the Russian summer offensive got under way. Two days earlier Army Group Center reported tremendous increases in the number of demolitions on the railroad tracks, indicating close co-ordination between partisans and the Soviet High Command. A quotation from a situation report of Army Group Center of 20 June 1944 illustrates how this order to Grishin and similar orders sent to the partisan units were executed: "The mass attacks on railroad lines ordered by the Soviet Partisan Command for 20 June 1944 in the area of Army Group Center began during the night of 19–20 June. Attacks were concentrated in the areas of Luminets, Orsha, Molodechno as well as the Mogilev-Orsha, Orsha-Borisov railroad lines. . . . The attacks on the Borisov-Orsha line, in particular, were largely forestalled. According to reports presently available approximately 9,400 blastings took place."[58] It appears likely that capture of the order to Grishin alerted the Germans in the Borisov-Orsha sector and enabled them to prevent a number of demolitions on this line.

Exploiting the lull in fighting on the Soviet German front, the enemy has increased redeployment of troops and movement of technical equipment over the railroads. In order to disrupt the enemy's transfers of troops, I hereby order you to commit all forces of your organization to the mass destruction of railroad tracks in the war against railroad tracks (*Schienenkrieg*) and to demolish 1,000 sections of track on the Orsha-Borisov line. You are to start on this operation immediately and to keep it secret. The first attack should occur during the night of 19–20 June. Continuous attempts should be made in order to halt enemy troop deployments completely. No other directives will be sent. Act independently as heretofore.

DOCUMENT 65: Grishin Regiment and the United States Air Force

In June 1944 the Germans secured the text of an order from the Belorussian Partisan Command to Grishin informing him of the possible appearance of American planes and instructing him how to deal with the crews of planes which might crash or make forced landings. Orders similar to this one were probably broadcast to other partisan groups as well. The most likely occasion for the issuance of such orders was the system of shuttle bombing inaugurated late in the war in which American planes from England flew on to the Soviet Union after dropping their bombs on targets in German-held parts of Europe.

During the next few days the American Air Force will begin its operations against troops and other enemy objects in the territories still occupied. If an airplane crashes or makes a forced landing, you are to extend every aid to the **American airmen** and to take all necessary steps to send them to Soviet territory. Every member of the American crews will have in his possession an identification [card] on which is stated in Russian: "American Air Force," as well as family and first name of the airman. The American Air Force formations will conduct the operations with four-motored Liberators, four-

---

[58] OKH/GenStdH/FHO, "Anlage zum Lagebericht Ost, Feindlage (Banden) Nr. 463," 20 June 1944 (GMDS, H 3/230).

motored Flying Fortresses, twin-motored fuselage planes of the "Gama Lightning [?]" type, and single-motored planes of the Mustang type. The insignia is a white five-pronged star in a black circle, in addition to a circle with alternating white and black strips. Every American plane which lands and every airman who comes to you is to be reported accurately.

ANNEX: German Interrogation Reports

In March and April 1943, units of the German Fourth Army conducted a major operation against the Grishin Regiment after the latter had invaded the rear areas of the Fourth Army southwest of Smolensk. During the course of this operation prisoners were taken and interrogated. Two interrogation reports of one girl and a supplementary interrogation report were found in the German Army records. The information contained in these reports is interesting but of limited reliability. The first is an army report which consolidates answers given by a peasant girl who had been working as a kitchen helper with the Grishin Regiment. The second interrogation of the same girl was conducted by the political intelligence agency of the SS (SD). The girl was not a full-fledged combat member of the group, and her knowledge of the administrative structure of the partisan group was anything but accurate. In parts of the document not translated here the girl explains that she joined the partisans primarily to improve her living conditions and not for patriotic reasons. In view of Grishin's criticism of discipline and his partisans' relations with women, it is possible that she was abandoned by the partisans on purpose (see Document 58). Other details, such as the presence of a considerable number of deserters from indigenous collaborator units and one German deserter, are confirmed by other reports. The supplementary report of an interrogation contains answers given by a deserter from the partisans. The reasons for his defection, unfortunately, are not contained in this document.

ANNEX A. Interrogation of Alexandra Ivanova

The Russian (female) Alexandra Ivanova gave the following testimony:

I went to school for seven years, and by profession I am a farmhand. In October 1942 partisans came to our village (Sinitsina). Since my living conditions were very bad, I decided to join them because they promised me good treatment and food. I was assigned to work in a battalion kitchen where I was working up to the time I was taken prisoner. Our partisan group operated in the area northwest of Smolensk, including the swamps to the southeast of Velizh, southeast of Demidovo near Akatovo, and near Kolyshki. During this time we had several fights with German troops, but we always succeeded in escaping from the Germans with minor losses. Combat actions on a larger scale were always avoided by our group. Wounded partisans were passed through the front lines. Two weeks ago we moved from the area around

Kolyshki into Krasnoye Rayon. Here we had to avoid the Germans because of lack of ammunition, and thus we reached the area of Monastyrshchina. The ammunition, requested by wireless, was dropped by airplanes (36 parachutes) during the nights of 22–23 and 23–24 March. We were also supplied with weapons and medical supplies. During the night of 23–24 March three former squad leaders who had been on leave in Moscow were parachuted in.

Organization of the Group: Partisan Group = regiment (more than 1,000 men) consisting of two battalions, each with two companies.

Regimental Commander: Col. Kochubei, 35 years old, medium height, black hair, Russian uniform without insignia of rank.[59]

Regimental Commissar: Lavrilov (?), of stocky build, dark blond.

There is a major with the staff (a deserter from an indigenous self-defense unit). Name unknown.

The partisan group is composed primarily of former prisoners of war as well as of 200 deserters from German indigenous collaborator units, 20 women, and 5 Jews.

Armament: 2–4 mortars; ? light machine guns (no heavy machine guns); ? antitank rifles; ? automatic weapons and rifles; ample ammunition.

Mission of the partisan group is raids on German units. The group has not undertaken any blastings (probably no explosives).

I know that the group had planned to move during the next few days to another region which is not known to me. We were warned of the approach of German troops, and our command therefore ordered an early change of location. This destination, too, remained unknown to me. The partisan group left its quarters on 24 March around 2000 hours. I alone was left behind because I was asleep. I tried to follow them after waking up and learned the direction of their march from local inhabitants. I was, however, unable to locate the group and was taken prisoner near Staiki on 25 March 1943.

A German soldier moves with this partisan group; he joined us after deserting near Kolyshki. We call him Fedya; his German name is not known to me. A squad of the partisan group waylaid a detail consisting of ten Russian prisoners of war and two German soldiers; one of the soldiers was killed. The ten prisoners of war are now fighting with us. The German soldier who was taken prisoner was shot with a submachine gun by Fedya, who had requested permission to do so. He is very active and known as a "brave hero." Personal description of Fedya: 19 years old, medium height, slim, dark blond; clothes: German uniform, without insignia of rank, probably a cavalry man, white fur cap with a Soviet Star.

ANNEX B. Interrogation Report on Alexandra Ivanova

Personal Details . . .

Substantive Details:

Partisans entered the village Sinitsina for the first time in October 1942. They came from the north and were reported to have been located east of

---

[59] Kochubei probably held some lower position in the regiment.

Velizh. The partisans remained in Sinitsina for one day and occupied quarters in the village houses. In this way they also came to our house. The partisans said that the front would be moved farther westward and that all young people should join them. The partisans inquired about our way of life and explained that one could live better with them. My father Joseph Ivanov, who is still living in Sinitsina, thereupon advised me to join the partisans, and he would carry on alone. So it happened that I joined. None of the other young people of the village joined. . . . Our route of march took us to Akatovo while the camp was being constructed in this forest. We then remained in the camp for about two months until January 1943. In addition to the camp, the villages of Shurovshchina and Marchenko were also used as quarters. An attack by German tanks in January 1943 resulted in a two-hour fight. The Germans burned the villages and destroyed the camp in the forest. Thereafter the partisan group moved to the area around Kolyshki. We occupied quarters in the villages of Makarenki, Saurmilits, Volki, etc. No camps were built. The quarters were changed repeatedly for reasons unknown to me, but probably because larger German units attacked us almost daily. We stayed in the region to the south of Kolyshki until about the end of February because of these attacks. We then moved to Lesno Rayon, crossing the railroad tracks and the Krasnoye-Smolensk highway. Proceeding from there we passed Monastyrshchina in the direction of Khoslevichi. . . . The partisan group spent the night of 24–25 March in the village of Gololobovka and departed while I was asleep. Next morning the owner of the house told me that the partisans had moved on to Lobanovka; I followed them and saw their tracks before Lobanovka. I followed their tracks for about 15 kilometers until I was taken prisoner in the afternoon by Ukrainians in German uniforms. I do not know the place where I was arrested. When I was with the group I worked in the kitchen. I can give no information as to the plans and activity of the partisan group.

Strength of the partisan group: More than 1,000 people; among these about 20 women; there are also 5 Jews with the group; there are no children; the ages of the group are from 18 to 40 years.

Leader of the Group: First in command is Kochubei; about 35 years old; he wears no rank insignia; is reputed to have the rank of major; Russian uniform without insignia; breeches and boots.

Second in command, the chief of staff, is called Grishin; about 30 years old; Russian uniform without insignia.

Political Commissar: Lavrilov, about 30 years old.

Irregular Aliens: One gypsy; one German soldier who was wounded when he joined the partisans; about 200 Ukrainian deserters in German uniforms including a major whose name I don't know but who is working for the staff. The German soldier is fighting with the Russians against the Germans; he does not speak Russian well. Combat operations are directed by the first in command, Kochubei.

Name of the Group: Kochubei Regiment.

Organization of the Group: The leader of the regiment and of the highest staff is Kochubei; he is always accompanied by 3 men; 1 major, name unknown, and 2 soldiers. The regiment is divided into 6 companies; each company has a commander whose names I do not know. There are no special technical companies.

Armament of the Group: Three portable antitank guns; about 10 light machine guns. More than half the members are equipped with Russian submachine guns; the remaining male members have rifles. Everybody is completely armed except the women (supplementary information: 3 or 4 mortars). Heavy and ordinary hand grenades are available in large numbers. Almost every partisan has 3 or 4 hand grenades at his disposal.

Other Equipment: There are no motor vehicles, about 50 horses, which, en route, are utilized as draft animals, and when encamped are used as riding horses by reconnaissance squads. Fifty pairs of skis were captured from the Germans during a raid in Kasplya Rayon, Smolensk area.... Ammunition was dropped by plane. At times there was adequate ammunition; at other times when the group was forced to fight, it happened that there was a shortage. There never was a complete lack of ammunition. Some of the rifles were equipped with silencers....

Acquisition of food: Food supplies were dropped by plane in insufficient quantities. Additional food supplies, including cattle, were acquired from the villages. There were no storage places for food; companies took care of their own food supplies after they were distributed. All bread was obtained from the villages.

Communication: There was a radio transmitter used to keep in contact with Moscow.... Aside from the daily reports of the Soviet High Command, I learned nothing about messages.... Airplanes dropped food, ammunition, and medical supplies on three different occasions. No soldiers were dropped. Airplanes never landed.

Activity of the Group: As soon as there were signs of danger the companies assembled. The order to fight or to retreat was given by the highest command. It was our job to destroy German transport vehicles and to dynamite trains; for this work we were organized into squads. Orders were given by Kochubei. Only one prisoner was ever taken, a German soldier who is now fighting with the partisans.

Morale: In general, morale among the partisans is good. There was always enough to eat. Food supplies were obtained, as pointed out above, by looting the villages.

After more searching questioning: I joined the partisans voluntarily, especially since I had my father's permission. Life among the partisans was really very nice except that the marches were very strenuous. I had several opportunities to leave the partisans; I remained however, as I was afraid that I would be arrested and shot by the Germans.

After more searching questioning: I do not know the destination of the partisan group. The destination of our marches was never made known.

Losses of the partisan group: Casualties among the partisan group were very slight. When they could not be treated by available doctors, the wounded were moved through the front by horse-drawn vehicles.

I am not able to give any additional information.

ANNEX C. Supplementary Interrogation Report on Yefimov

27 March 1943

Yefimov, interrogated on the above date, made the following supplementary comments: I was the chief of staff of the cavalry platoon and as such was responsible for clerical work only. Our cavalry platoon consisted of 30 men, among whom was a German soldier called Fedya. His real name is Friedrich Rosenberg or Rosenholz (?). He lived in the region near Hamburg, at Anufa (?). As far as I know, he is a deserter. He is very popular, but the group does not trust him and he is strictly guarded.

The regiment consists of about 1,000 partisans including 100 women who are used primarily as scouts. The regimental commander is Grishin, who is 30 years old, a teacher, and comes from Smolensk Oblast. I also know the leader of a detachment of 100 men, consisting of boys 16 to 17 years old; his name is Kochubei.

The names of the majors (deserters from indigenous units) mentioned in the [previous] interrogation are (1) Kukanov, (2) Rudenko, and (3) Sedel. The last two of these are taking leave in Moscow at this time. The leaders of the partisan group intended to move to the Bryansk forest. The move should not have taken place until a few days from now. However, after German planes began to appear over our villages and German troops were observed approaching, we received on 24 March 1943 the order to start the move immediately. We went south and crossed the Mstislavl-Khislavichi road but had to stop at Sozh since we were unable to cross the river. We turned back in a northerly direction and occupied the village of Kolobino and the edge of the forest to the north of it. After a skirmish developed on 25 March, we retreated to the forest where we remained until 26 March at 2000 hours. The same day our advance guards on the edge of the forest exchanged fire with German scouting units. After it was determined that the Germans were planning to encircle us, the whole regiment moved off in a body in a northwesterly direction. After several scouting missions we located a weakly guarded spot on the edge of the forest and made our way through the German positions in a northwesterly direction. At this time I found an opportunity to escape, and I voluntarily surrendered to the Rayon Military Government Office (RK, *Rayon-Komman-dantur)* at Monastyrshchina.

I know that the regiment intends to cross a bridge over the Sozh near Khislavichi which is supposed to be guarded by ten indigenous collaborators *(Ord-nungsdienst).* The destination of the regiment is still the Bryansk forest.

ANNEX D

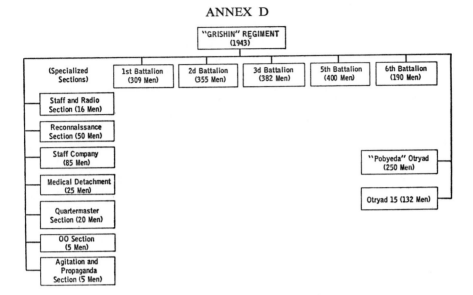

§VIII. The Kovpak Regiment

In the late fall or early winter of 1941 a small group of partisans was organized in the forests near Bryansk under the leadership of S. A. Kovpak, a Ukrainian from the Poltava area. S. V. Rudnev, the commissar of the regiment, may have been the real brains of the group. The regiment became more active in the spring of 1942, receiving reinforcements and supplies by air. In September 1942 it left the Bryansk area and spent the winter of 1942–43 in the area near Pinsk. There it carried out considerable recruiting activity, adding about 1,500 men to its former strength of about 2,000. In the spring of 1943 the regiment made a sweep through the northwestern Ukraine; in the summer it moved southward into the former Polish Ukraine, probably under orders to destroy the Boryslaw-Drohobycz oil fields. In the last stages of this movement it was repeatedly attacked and largely destroyed by German forces. A considerable number of documents of the regiment were captured at this time, and a selection of these follows.

DOCUMENT 66

Young Boy and Girl Partisans!

The whole Soviet people, our Government, and the great Stalin are watching your heroic fight with love and care. Thousands of avengers of the people who have distinguished themselves in the partisan fight against the German tyrants in the rear area have been decorated with orders and medals. Among these are 2,470 young boy and girl partisans.

Fourteen Komsomol partisans, young men and women, were awarded the distinction of Hero of the Soviet Union. The brave Komsomol partisan and Hero of the Soviet Union, Ivan Nikitin, went on 50 missions as a reconnaissance and intelligence scout and brought his battalion valuable reports. Thanks to his information 12 enemy units with about 4,000 of the occupiers were destroyed. Ivan Nikitin by himself blew up several bridges, two German motor vehicle columns, and a [German] unit, thus killing more than 350 Hitlerites.

The young Ukrainian Komsomol member, Stepan, with his battalion carried out 80 combat missions and destroyed about 1,000 Fascists. Singlehanded he destroyed 40 Hitlerites with a bayonet and hand grenades in one battle alone. The Order of Lenin decorates the chest of this partisan hero. Up to now, the Komsomol member Kuzma has killed 35 Fascists in battle. A short time ago he destroyed a German tank with an antitank grenade. During the same night he blew up a German tank squad. The young patriot was decorated with the Order of the Patriotic War.

Comrades! Members of the Komsomol! Follow the example of your heroes! Be as they are!

Comrade Stalin, the Supreme Commander and Marshal of the Soviet Union, in his order of 23 February 1943 said, "The flame of partisan warfare shall be kindled and spread; the enemy's communications shall be disintegrated by blowing up railway bridges, enemy military supply transports, weapons, and munitions being brought forward, by blowing up and burning military depots, and by raids on enemy garrisons."

Devote every effort to execute the order of the Supreme Commander, Comrade Stalin! Death to the German occupier!

Read and pass on!

Issued by the Tsk, VLKSM[60] in Moscow 1943

DOCUMENT 67: Order Issued to the Military Unit 00105

24 March 1943

On the basis of material received by headquarters of the Military Unit 00105 concerning the destructive activity of Marko Yakovlevich Savenko, Commander of the Independent Company,[61] [and on the basis of] the subsequent investigation and confrontation, it has been decided:

1. After the declaration of war Savenko evaded mobilization.

2. Very soon after the arrival of the Germans, Savenko took a position in the police; he became local commandant of the police. He was a loyal servant of the Germans and was appointed chief of the rayon police in Razvadevskoye.

3. As chief of the rayon police Savenko arranged compulsory deportation of 5,000 men to Germany for heavy labor—Communists, Komsomol members, Soviet activists, and [escaped or released former] prisoners of war. In

[60] TsK, *Tsentralnyi Komitet*, Central Committee; VLKSM, *Vsesoyuznyi Leninskii Kommunisticheskii Soyuz Molodyozhi*, All-Union Lenin League of Communist Youth, the official designation of the Komsomol.

[61] The German description of the organization of the Kovpak Regiment contains nothing about this company. Perhaps it was abolished after the incident described in this document. From the concluding sentence one could assume that it was under the direct command of regimental headquarters instead of being assigned to one of the battalions.

every village Savenko organized the village police from among the former kulaks and other persons with anti-Soviet sentiment.

4. Later Savenko was forced to flee the police in order to escape arrest [by the Germans] for crimes [he had] committed. Having fled from the police, Savenko joined the partisan movement and deceived the leaders of the underground by maintaining that the Communist Party organizations had commissioned him with the formation of partisan groups, [a deception in which] he was successful.

5. As commander of the underground partisan organization Savenko categorically forbade the shooting of Germans once the village police was disarmed. When he was battalion commander, Savenko constantly arranged drinking parties which resulted in the demoralization of the whole battalion. When intoxicated, the soldiers wanted to shoot Savenko; they killed the battalion commissar instead. Sayevich [Savenko], however, fled. After this incident the battalion moved into Belorussian territory.

6. Savenko organized a second small battalion and combined it with a battalion which had arrived from another rayon. As battalion commander and as commander of an independently operating company, Savenko proved himself a coward in a series of combat organizations; he did not have authority in the battalion, could not maintain discipline among the soldiers, etc. At that time his work was harmful to the company. On the basis of these facts, witnessed by Comrade Sevryuk, Savenko (brother), and Derenko and not denied by Savenko himself, the following order is issued:

Marko Yakovlevich Savenko, born 1907, Ukrainian, according to his testimony a member of the All-Union Communist Party (of Bolsheviks) since the year 1931, is to be executed.

This order is to be made known to all headquarters personnel and platoon leaders as well as to all men of the Independent Company.

Commissar of the Military Unit 00105
Brigadier General Rudnev

Commander of the Military Unit 00105
 Hero of the Soviet Union,
 Brigadier General Kovpak

Chief of Staff, Bazyma

DOCUMENT 68

The villages through which we are moving are inhabited chiefly by Poles; therefore one should not shoot at those inhabitants who flee. The property of peaceful inhabitants, who are not nationalistically inclined and offer no resistance, is not to be taken along. In case of encounters with [Ukrainian] nationalists, do not open fire at once.

DOCUMENT 69

To all Commanders of Battalions of the Military Unit 00117
Copy for the Commander of the 2d Rifle Battalion, Comrade Kulbak[62]

---

[62] The German heading reads: "Allen Kommandanten der Bataillone der Milit.Abt. 00117 Nur den Kommandanten d. 2. Sch.Bat., dem Genossen Kovpak." The translation given here is based on the fact that the 2d Rifle Battalion was commanded by a certain Kulbak.

If you come upon [Ukrainian] nationalists or their camps, do not touch them under any circumstances. Send negotiators and explain our policy toward nationalists through them.

Inform them that we will not touch anybody, that we will stay here only a short time and will leave the area just as we left the operational area of Captain Konta.[63]

Send Ukrainians as negotiators.

Inform the unit staff immediately of all meetings with nationalists. At the same time turn over all extra horses of the cavalry.

Chief of Staff
Major Bazyma

26 June 1943

[Note in the German:] Eight illegible signatures of commanders and commissars follow.

DOCUMENT 70

Top Secret

Along its route of march, our unit comes in contact with the Polish population in various places. The battalion commanders are fully responsible for the preparatory screening work necessary to induct honest Poles into the unit for the purpose of forming a Polish battalion.

The official induction of Poles into the unit is to be done only by the staff of the unit.

Commander of Military Unit 00117　　Commissar of Military Unit 00117
Hero of the Soviet Union,　　　　　　Brigadier General Rudnev
Brigadier General Kovpak

DOCUMENT 71: Order No. 386 of Military Unit 00117

2 July 1943

Lyubomirka

In carrying out the honorable assignment and responsibility given us by the Party and the Government, our regiment is moving about in those western areas of the USSR which are inhabited chiefly by nationalists and in which there are as yet no Soviet partisans. In these areas the inhabitants have been made to fear us by propaganda of the Germans and nationalists, who attempt to turn the feelings of the population against us.

Recently instances of looting by individual soldiers have been noticed in the regiment. After the regiment has passed through the villages, the staff receives complaints about stealing from the peaceful inhabitants. All this helps the enemy to conduct his propaganda against us—the Soviet partisans—and besmirch the honorable calling of the avengers of the people. During the night of 30 June–1 July 1943, a soldier of the artillery battery, Semyon Grigoryevich Chibisov (born 1922, Great Russian, seven years of schooling, candidate for Communist Party membership, factory worker) and Vasili Yevseyevich Alekseyev (born 1920, Great Russian, nine years of schooling, candidate for

---

[63] Presumably an officer of the Ukrainian nationalist partisans situated in an area through which the Kovpak Regiment had passed previously.

Communist Party membership) stole a bucket of lard, a bucket of honey, clothing, shoes, and other things from the home of a peaceful inhabitant in the village of Shladava. All this occurred in violation of the order of the battery commander. Neither the battery commander, the battery political commissar, nor the gun commander noticed the absence of the soldiers from the ranks; furthermore, Lieutenant Serdik, the deputy of the commander of the 5th Company, was present during the stealing, and did not stop the robbing, but rather, closed his eyes to this case of looting.

Because of this, I order:

For violation of Order No. 200, concerning robbing and looting, which besmirch the name of the avengers of the people, Semyon Grigoryevich Chibisov and Vasili Yevseyevich Alekseyev are to be shot in front of the assembled regiment. The order is to be carried out on 2 July 1943.

The commander of the artillery battery, Comrade Major Anisimov, and the commissar of the artillery battery, Nepenyashchii, are to be given reprimands. Lieutenant Serdik, the deputy of the commander of the 5th Company, is to be given a severe reprimand with . . . [64]

This order is to be read to all the assembled men.

Commissar of the Military Unit 00117
Brigadier General Rudnev

Commander of the Military Unit 00117
Hero of the Soviet Union,
Brigadier General Kovpak

Chief of Staff of the Military Unit 00117
Major Bazyma

DOCUMENT 72: Translation of a radio message
found on the body of Brigadier General Rudnev[65]

Request!

Storokachuk, Korochenko. Are here 24 hours. Situation is dangerous. German bombers are dropping bombs on us. We destroyed guns and machine guns. Fighting against us are the 4th, 13th, 12th, and 26th SS-Police Regiments; the 102d Caucasian Battalion;[66] one Belgian battalion;[67] one lieutenant colonel; Hungarians;[68] unit identification unknown. Please bomb Delyatin, Nadvorna, Kolomyja, Lvov, and the airport.[69]

1 August 1943   Rudnev[70]
1500

[64] A word or words were not legible in the Russian original.

[65] The name is written Rudnik in the German translation; clearly Rudnev is meant. The text of the report mentions that the body of the commissar of the regiment, Brigadier General Rudnev, was found after one of the engagements between the regiment and German units.

[66] Presumably refers to a Volga-Tatar battalion, which included a company of Caucasians, fighting against the regiment.

[67] Identification not clear; possibly a mistake of the German translator.

[68] Some Hungarian units had been alerted by the Germans to help prevent the regiment from crossing the Carpathian Mountains.

[69] Probably the airport of Lvov from which the German bombers were coming.

[70] See n. 65.

§IX. Partisan Diaries

During the collection of materials for a study of partisan warfare, a number of diaries of officers, political officers, and members of partisan groups were found. As a unique group of primary source materials, these diaries provide considerable insight into the operations, problems, and attitudes of partisan bands as well as matters of morale, discipline, supply, relations with the local population, personal life, control by Soviet authorities, coordination with regular units of the Red Army, and Soviet and German use of airpower in partisan warfare.

In this section one short diary and parts of another are included to illustrate other facets of partisan warfare. The first is the diary of a young member of a partisan group whose account concerns his personal life and his participation in combat activities. The second diary, that of a company politruk, also contains some interesting information on airpower in addition to some revealing material on the general types of problems facing the political officer of a small partisan unit.

DOCUMENT 73

Several documents dealing with the partisan movement north of the Smolensk-Vyazma railway are included in Section IV (Documents 17–19). In this area many partisans were dropped by parachute at the beginning of 1942 as part of the Soviet effort to encircle German Army Group Center. The following diary was kept by one such partisan from 27 January to 4 May 1942; the part prior to 15 February is translated here. It is one of the best examples of those diaries which reflect the personal habits, problems, and attitudes of the individual partisans.

Chronological Combat Diary, 1942

Vyacheslav Alexandrovich Balakin, born 1924.
My address: V. A. Balakin, Gorki, Gruzinskaya Street No. 9, Apartment 12. Maria A. Balakina (mother).

Do not forget!

Do not judge a thing by its external appearance.
The world is not as it has often been presented.
Do not forget where you belong!
"Be persistent, Cossack, one day you will be a Hetman!"
Dreams which are not tested by real experience subsequently lead to bitter disappointments.
"Haste makes waste!"

Remember!

If the bullet misses, the bayonet will come to your rescue.[71]
May the "Fritzes" die instead of us.

[71] German translator's note: "literally: The bullet is a fool, the bayonet is a hero" [a proverb originating with Suvorov].

He who desires to remain alive will not die!
Raise your head high . . . away with grief!
Always remember your slogan: Forward!!!
The longer the separation, the happier will be the reunion.

27 January. The parachutists are getting ready to jump in the rear of the enemy. At 12 o'clock at night we take off from Peremyshl. I feel fine.

28 January. At 2:15 in the morning I jump into space. One stroke. The parachute opens. I look around. Fly over forests. Land. Find skis.[72] While I am searching in vain for our men, the night passes. I search for a place to sleep in the village of Kultura.

29 January. At 4 o'clock at night Bochkarev comes to me and informs me that nine of our men have already assembled. We wonder what Lt. Pargushin plans to do. My morale is "gut."[73]

30 January. I celebrate my eighteenth birthday in the rear of the enemy. I am in Smolensk Oblast, 130 kilometers from the city of Smolensk. Morale is "gut."

31 January. Khokhlov and I were ordered to blow up a bridge. We were not successful. On the way back we stopped at the village of Versha and ate lunch. A girl attracted my attention there. She asked me to return. I promised to do so. My morale is "gut."

1 February. Sunday. It is snowing. We have no provisions left. I went with Khokhlov to the village of Olykhovka to find some food. We got a sheep and 32 kilograms of flour. The population is very friendly to us. Morale excellent.

2 February. I stroll through the village. Became acquainted with a woman (Tanya). Words were soon followed by kisses. I spent the evening with her. Felt that she was already mine but did not yet want to take her. Morale "gut."

3 February. Well, there is a new tomcat in this world!!! It was achieved at 8:10. She did not resist. Morale superb.

4 February. We prepared an ambush in the village of Bereski. We shot down three Germans in cold blood. I wounded one. One was captured alive. I captured a cigarette lighter, a gold ring, a fountain pen, two pipes, tobacco, a comb. Morale is "gut."

5 February. We again laid an ambush in Bereski. Had no success. In the evening Tanya was mine again. Morale, "gut."

6 February. She is afraid she may have a baby. So what? If she has one, she has at least a reminder of me.

7 February. Everything is quiet. Morale is "gut."

8 February. We didn't make any forays. "Tatyana" begins to bore me. She has fallen in love with me like a little girl. Today I purposely did not go to her. Morale, bad. P.S. I sit at home and am bored. Five of us live together: Khokhlov, Mironykhev, Bochkarev, Syomik.

9 February. Monday. Dreamed of Ira G. Woke up in a good mood. Drove with Syomik to Nekasterek to fetch bread—without success. We shot a traitor. Morale "gut." In the evening I went to do the same to his wife. We are sorry that she leaves three children behind. But war is war!!! Toward traitors, any

---

[72] The German translator added: "probably dropped from the plane."
[73] "Gut": good. The German translator notes that the words in quotation marks appeared in German in the captured Russian original.

humane consideration is misplaced. At 3:00 p.m. a German punitive expedition approached our village. They remained in the neighboring village of Kholmyanka and fired several shots at our village. Then they went back. Two peasants were killed.

13 February. A rumor is making the rounds that our regular troops are stationed at Yakovskaya,[74] 12 kilometers away from us. I was sent together with a soldier from the Special Group [of the Red Army][75] to find out whether the rumor was true: we did not find any troops. Tanya's love has become embarrassing to me.... I plan to start a new romance with her friend, a graduate of the 10th grade. Morale wretched.

15 February. We made an attack on the Fascist courier plane.[76] Five Germans and one of our men were killed and a rich loot was captured. Skopintsiv, who directed the operation, is a smart boy. I am thinking of joining his group. My own affairs are improving (Tanya and "F"). Spent all day long in ambush close to the village of Pelenino. Morale "gut."

DOCUMENT 74

The diary of the politruk of the reconnaissance company of a partisan detachment is interesting for the light it sheds on the political and disciplinary problems of a partisan unit. The original diary covers the period from 26 October 1942 to 6 May 1943; the section for 8 November 1942 to 30 January 1943 is given here. The company described was a part of the Alexeyev Brigade which operated in northeastern Belorussia near Vitebsk.

8 November 1942. The property stolen by the police from the kolkhoz peasants was returned to them.

15 November 1942. The cattle and property stolen from the inhabitants of the village of Ostrov by the Germans and the police were returned to the kolkhoz peasants of this village.

21 December 1942. We have received many interesting reports from the Soviet land behind the front, especially about the situation in Africa and the possibility of the start of military operations against Italy as soon as North Africa is liberated from Rommel's troops and the Mediterranean is controlled by the Allies.

25 December 1942. Today the detachment was visited by the brigade commander, who conversed for an extended period of time with the enlisted personnel as a fellow-soldier and [spoke] especially about the question of relations with the peaceful population; the reputation which the brigade had in its old combat area must be kept up. This conversation was prompted by the whole series of complaints which have reached the brigade commander about unjust actions of our partisans and illegal confiscation of property. Vaska was

[74] A town on a branch line north of the Smolensk-Vyazma railway.
[75] A ranger or commando-type unit of the Red Army.
[76] The German translator added an exclamation mark to indicate a literal translation. It probably means that the partisans attacked a courier plane which had landed in the neighborhood and got into a fight with the crew.

supposed to be shot on orders of the brigade commander for the murder of a woman, but when the entire detachment pleaded for Vaska on the grounds that he was after all only a child, the brigade commander forgave him.

26 December 1942. We went to our wounded and sent them by plane behind the Soviet front. In the beginning there were two, then three, and finally, four planes. Each made two flights and took along two wounded every time. On the return flights, they brought us ammunition.

26 December 1942. An order: In the detachment, cases of an unfriendly attitude toward the peaceful population have recently been noted. I order that the strictest measures be taken against the guilty persons upon complaints of the peaceful population concerning unjust actions of the fighters and commanders (abuses, rudeness, threats, use of arms, unlawful confiscation of property belonging to the peaceful population).

9 January 1943. Last night Mishka came from Bekhtyayev and delivered an order from the brigade commander: Everyone who married while serving with the unit will not be regarded as married and must live in separate quarters [from his wife] in the companies to which he belongs. The women of the staff are being assigned to the individual companies and their immediate transfer to these companies is demanded. This caused a great uproar which I consider justified. This order was necessary because the wife of the chief of staff of the brigade, Malvina, considered herself rather than her husband as the chief and continuously interfered in military matters. Furthermore, there are many women in the unit who literally do nothing and consider themselves only as wives of the staff members. Such conditions could not be tolerated any longer. However, it was not necessary that the dance should start this way. The most important [way] to begin would have been to ask the officers [not to permit] their wives to interfere in official business any longer. The way [in which it actually was done] makes the entire business smell like an enforced separation from a legitimate wife.

16 January 1943. Tonight the entire detachment had to assemble to listen to two orders. One of them concerned the increase of alertness and the stricter execution of guard duty; the second one, bearing the number 3/81, dealt with granting military ranks to the lower command level of our unit. The rank of staff sergeant was given to two platoon leaders; two staff sergeants were made master sergeants; all others were made sergeants or corporals. Thus since yesterday [*sic*] I am a sergeant of the Red Army, even though since 1937 I have had the rank of a technical sergeant, second class. In fact I do not care if I am now a technical sergeant or a sergeant, if only the war would end quickly. Then I would find myself a lifelong position, either as a locksmith or as a guard in my beloved North Park in Vitebsk—a good, merry, and secure life.

30 January 1943. In connection with the difficulties of the situation (frequent marches, deficiencies in food and clothing), cases of rude treatment of the population have been noted, and plunderings have occurred. I order: For permitting plunderings in the villages of Lemnitsy and Sezdrino, unlawful removal of cattle, and rough treatment of the population on 25 January 1943, the assistant leader of the supply unit [platoon], Michael Osipov, is to be punished with seven days' arrest.

§X. List of Sources

Document Number	Source
1	XXXXVIII. PzK, Ic, 6 August 1942 (GMDS, XLVIII AK 26775/13).
2	OKH/GenStdH/FHO, "Uebersetzung aus dem Russischen: Instruktion fuer die Organisation und Taetigkeit der Partisanen-Abteilungen und Diversions-Gruppen," 31 August 1941 (GMDS, HGr Sued 15417/6).
3	RFSS u.Chef d.Deutsch.Pol., *Bandenbekaempfung*, 1. Ausgabe, September 1942 (GMDS, RAM 2b).
4	OKH/GenStdH/FHO, "Ausgewertete Kurierpost eines am 14.7 notgelandeten russischen Kurierflugzeuges," 15 July 1941 (GMDS, XXVIII AK 12665).
5	HFPCh im OKH/GenStdH/GenQu/Abt.K.-Verw., "Erfahrungen ueber Aufbau, Aufgaben, Auftreten und Bekaempfung der Partisanenabteilungen," 15 January 1942, pp. 11–12 (GMDS, Wi/ID 2.717).
6	OKH/GenStdH/FHO, III, "Lebenslauf und Charakteristik des Chefs des Ukrainischen Stabes der Partisanen Bewegung General-Oberst Strokatsch," 30 July 1943 (GMDS, H 3/474).
7–10	H.Gr.Mitte, Ic/AO, "Erbeutete Banden-Geheimbefehle," 13 September 1942 (GMDS, HGr Nord 75131/93).
11	221. Sich.Div., Ic, "Partisanen-Befehl," 4 September 1942 (GMDS, 221 ID 29380/2, Anlage 115).
12	OKH/GenStdH/FHO, *Nachrichten ueber Bandenkrieg, Nr. 6* [December 1943] (GMDS, H 3/738).
13	OKH/GenStdH/FHO, *Nachrichten ueber den Bandenkrieg, Nr. 4,* 10 September 1943, pp. 7–10 (GMDS, H 3/738).
14	OKH/GenStdH/FHO, "Merkblatt ueber politische Erkundung," *Nachrichten ueber den Bandenkrieg, Nr. 1,* 3 May 1943, Anlage 8 (GMDS, H 3/738).
15	AOK 4, Ic, "Feindnachrichtenblatt Nr. 5," 4 May 1943, Anlage 3 (GMDS, AOK 4, 48448/6).
16	Korueck 584, "Rechenschaftsbericht der Troika, aufgefunden bei der Kampfgruppe Nord," 28 September 1942 (GMDS, X AK 44431/48).
17–19	XXIII. A.K., Ic, "Uebersetzung, Tagebuch der Kampfhandlungen der Partisanenabteilung des Oblt. Morogoff," September 1942 (GMDS, XXIII AK 76156, Anlage 12).
20	XXXXI. Pz.K., Ic, "Protokoll Nr. 1," February 1943 (GMDS, XLI AK 29091, Anlage 22).
21	PzAOK 3, Ic/AO, "Nr. 5394/43 geh.," 19 September 1943 (GMDS, PzAOK 3, 40252/7, Anlagen 30–33).

Document Number	Source
22–23	PzAOK 3, Ic/AO, "Nr. 5507/43 geh.," 19 September 1943 (GMDS, PzAOK 3, 40252/7, Anlagen 28–29).
24	Korueck 532, "Anlage 36," n.d. [1942?] (GMDS, Korueck 27894/2, Anlage 36).
25	Korueck 532, "Anlage 35," n.d. [1942?] (GMDS, Korueck 27894/2, Anlage 35).
26	FK 550, K.-Verw.Gruppe, "Lage- und Taetigkeitsbericht," 23 November 1942 (GMDS, 203 ID 32104).
27	XXIII. A.K., Ic, "Uebersetzung eines Flugblattes des Partisanen-fuehrers 'Batja,'" September 1942 (GMDS, XXIII AK 76156, Anlage 23).
28	X. A.K., Ic, "Uebersetzung von Feindpropaganda," 14 July 1943 (GMDS, X AK 41175/47).
29	WB Ostland, Ic/WPr., "Uebersetzung eines Feindflugblattes," 15 May 1943 (YIVO, Occ E 3).
30	221. Sich.Div., Ic, "An Prop.Abt. W. Smolensk," 9 November 1942 (GMDS, 221 ID 29380/9, Anlage 65).
31	203. Sich.Div., Abt.VII/K.-Verw., "Lagebericht fuer November 1942," 28 November 1942 (GMDS, 203 ID 32104).
32–33	OK I (V) 845, Feldgendarmeriegruppe, "B.Tgb. Nr. 1245/43," 15 June 1943 (GMDS, 221 ID 36509/9, Anlage 42).
34	Privately owned.
35	WB Ostland, Ic, "Feindpropaganda," 29 June 1942 (YIVO, Occ E 3).
36	Korueck 532, Ic, "Betr.: Ungarische Division," 25 May 1942 (GMDS, PzAOK 2, 30233/66, Anlage 1).
37	Chef Sipo und SD, Einsatzgruppe B, "Taetigkeits- und Lagebericht der Einsatzgruppe B fuer die Zeit vom 16.8–31.8.1942" (GMDS, EAP 173–g–12–10/2).
38	Geb.Kommissar Novogrodek, "Ereignisbericht ueber das Auftreten von Banden," 6 August 1942 (GMDS, EAP 99/171).
39	221. Sich.Div., Ic, "Feindpropaganda," 10 May 1943 (GMDS, 221 ID 36509/24, Anlage 36).
40–41	LIX. A.K., Ic, "Uebersetzungen," 14 April 1942 (GMDS, PzAOK 3, 20839/3).
42	FK 550, Abt. VII, "Lage- und Taetigkeitsbericht," 23 December 1942 (GMDS, 203 ID 32104).
43	HFPCh im OKH/Gen.z.b.V./H.Wes.Abt./GFP, "Allgemeiner Ueberblick ueber die Bandenbewegung fuer die Zeit vom 1.7.1942–31.3.1943," 10 April 1943, p. 3 (GMDS, OKW/734).
44	OKH/GenStdH/FHO, *Nachrichten ueber den Bandenkrieg, Nr. 9,* 11 June 1944, p. 2 (GMDS, H 3/738).
45	WiIn Nord, WiKdo Pleskau, "Kriegstagebuch Nr. 5, 1 Juli–30 September 1942," Anlage 42 (GMDS, Wi/ID.169).

Document Number	Source
46	Gr. Brandenberger, Ic, "Feindnachrichtenblatt Nr. 2," 15 October 1942 (GMDS, 8. Pz.Div., Anlage 2, 34582/44).
47–63	OKH/GenStdH/FHO, *Nachrichten ueber den Bandenkrieg, Nr. 7,* 8 December 1943 (GMDS, H 3/738).
64	Telegram from OKW/Abwehr III to OKW/WFSt, "Grosssabotageauftrag fuer Grishin," 12 June 1944 (GMDS, OKW/100).
65	Telegram from OKL/LFSt/Ic/FIO to OKW/WFSt/Ic, "Nr. 54 060/44 g," 19 June 1944 (GMDS, OKW/100).
Annex A	Korueck 559, Ic, "Vernehmung der Russin Ivanova, Alexandra," 26 March 1943 (GMDS, Korueck 44404/4).
Annex B	Chef Sipo u. SD, Einsatzgruppe B, SK 7c, "Vernehmung der Russin Ivanova, Alexandra," 29 March 1943 (GMDS, Korueck 44404/4).
Annex C	Korueck 559, Ic, "Vernehmung des russ. Ueberlaeufers Efimov," 27 March 1943 (GMDS, Korueck 44404/4).
66–72	HSSPF Ost, "Bericht ueber die Bekaempfung der Kolpak-Bande in Galizien in der Zeit vom 7.7.43 bis 20.8.43" (GMDS, EAP 170–a–10/5).
73	XXXXVI. A.K., Ic, "Tagebuch des Fallschirmjaegers Balakin," July 1942 (GMDS, XLVI AK 26080/8, Anlage 85).
74	VI. A.K., Ic, "Auszugsweise Uebersetzung, Tagebuch des politischen Leiters (Politruk) der Aufklaerer-Kompanie der Partisanen-Abteilung 'Morjak'" [May 1943] (GMDS, VI AK 44653/14).

Glossary and Key
to Abbreviations Used
in the Text

Terms are listed alphabetically; abbreviations appear alphabetically by their initial letters but are not otherwise always in exact alphabetical order. Terms including roman numerals, e.g., "Ic," are listed at the end of the Glossary; [R] at the end of a term indicates that the term is Russian.

Term	*Abbreviation*	*Translation (Remarks)*
Abschlussbericht		Final report.
Absetzbewegung		Retrograde movement, tactical withdrawal.
Abteilung Heeresversorgung	Abt.H.Vers. (Qu2)	Supply Section of the Office of the Quartermaster General /OKH.
Abteilung Kriegsverwaltung, Abt. Kriegsverw.	Abt.K.-Verw., Abt. VII	Military government section.
	Abt.Qu.	*See* Quartiermeister-Abteilung.
Abwehr		Central Intelligence Service of the German Armed Forces.
Amt VI		Foreign intelligence department of the SS in the Reich Main Security office (RSHA).
Anlage		Appendix, enclosure.
Armee-Bereich		Army area.
Armee-Korps	A.K.	Army Corps.
Armeenachschubfuehrer	ANF	Commander of Army Supply Services.
Armeeoberkommando	AOK	The headquarters of an army.
Armeewirtschaftsfuehrer	A Wi Fue	Staff officer for economic affairs at army level.

Term	Abbreviation	Translation (Remarks)
Aufklaerung		Reconnaissance.
Aussenstelle		Field office.
"Bamberg"		German antipartisan operation in the Bobruisk area, 1942.
Banden, Banditen		Partisan groups, partisans. In 1942 Hitler decided that the Soviet partisans were not partisans, but bandits. Orders were issued prohibiting the use of the word "partisan."
Bandenkampfgebiet		Partisan warfare area.
Bau-Bataillon	Bau-Btl.	Construction battalion.
Beauftragter des Reichs-fuehrers SS fuer die Bandenbekaempfung		Commissioner of the RFSS for antipartisan warfare.
Befehl		Order.
Befehlshaber	Befh., Bfh.	Military commander.
Befehlshaber des rueck-waertigen Heeres-Ge-bietes	Befh.rueckw.H. Geb.	Commander of the Army Group Rear Area (Mitte, Nord, Sued —Center, North, South).
Befriedung		Pacification.
Beutepapiere		Captured documents.
Bezirkslandwirt		District agricultural official.
Bombenfliegerschule		Training center for Air Force bomber personnel.
	BSSR	Belorussian Soviet Socialist Republic.
"Bueffelbewegung"		Large-scale German withdrawal to shorten the front of Army Group Center, February–March 1943.
"Buffalo"		*See* "Bueffelbewegung."
Chef der Bandenkampf-verbaende		Chief of antipartisan warfare units.
Chef Sipo und SD		*See* Sicherheitspolizei, Sicher-heitsdienst.
Cheka, *also* VCheka [R]		Abbreviation of the earliest Soviet secret police agency. Later OGPU, GPU, NKVD, NKGB, MVD, MGB, KGB.
Chernozem [R]		Black soil.
"Citadel"		German Army operation intended to retake Kursk, July 1943.
Council of People's Com-missars of the Soviet Union	Sovnarkom, SNK	In 1946, renamed Council of Ministers of the Soviet Union.

Term	*Abbreviation*	*Translation (Remarks)*
Diversion, diversionists		Soviet agents trained for work in espionage, sabotage, and subversion behind the enemy lines. Also used to designate special partisan groups, the "diversionist" detachments, and to refer to one phase of partisan activity.
"Donnerkeil"		Antipartisan operation in the Vitebsk area, 1942–43.
"Dreieck und Viereck"		German antipartisan operations in the Bryansk area, September 1942.
Druzhina [R]		Designation of a military-intelligence unit consisting of Soviet nationals, recruited by the SS.
Durchgangslager	Dulag	German POW transit camp.
Einsatzgruppe		Special German police and SS task forces used for execution of Jews, Communists, and "undesirable elements in the areas under military jurisdiction.
Einsatzkommando	E.K.	Section of an Einsatzgruppe.
Einwohnerwehr		Home guard; German-organized force for defense against partisans.
"Erntehilfe"		German antipartisan operation east of Vitebsk, August 1943.
Fahndungsliste		Lists of persons wanted on suspicion of espionage, sabotage, desertion, etc.
Feindlage		Enemy situation.
Feindnachrichtenblatt		Information bulletin about the enemy.
Feldkommandantur	FK	Regional military government office. *See also* Ortskommandantur.
Feldpolizeichef der Wehrmacht		Provost Marshal General of the German Armed Forces.
Feldpolizeikommissar		Commander of a secret field police (GFP) detachment.
Feldpolizei-Sekretaer		Leader of a small task force of the secret field police (GFP).
Fernschreiben	FS	Teletype message.
Filialy [R]		Branches.
Flakabteilung	Flak-Abt.	Antiaircraft artillery battalion.

Term	Abbreviation	Translation (Remarks)
Fliegerverbindungs-offizier	Flivo	Air Force liaison officer with army ground units.
Freischaerler		Freebooter; German term applied to partisans.
"Freischuetz"		German antipartisan operation in the Bryansk area, May 1943.
Fremde Heere Ost	FHO	Intelligence section of the German Army General Staff (OKH/GenStdH) concerned with information regarding the Red Army and Eastern Europe (except Poland).
Fremde Luftwaffe Ost	FLO	Intelligence section of the German Air Force General Staff concerned with information about the air forces of the USSR and other East European countries.
Front		Soviet equivalent of an army group.
"Fruehlingsfest"		German antipartisan operation in the Ushachi area, April 1944.
Fuehrerbefehl		Hitler order.
Gebietskommissariat	Geb.K.	District commissariat. Lowest level of the administration of the German-occupied areas of the USSR under civilian control (subdivision of a *Reichskommissariat*).
Gebirgs-Division	Geb.Div.	Mountain division.
Gefechtsgebiet, Gefechtszone		Combat zone.
Geheime Feldpolizei	GFP	Secret Field Police.
Geheime Feldpolizei Gruppe	GFP-Gruppe or GFP Gr.	Detachment of the secret field police.
Geheime Staatspolizei	Gestapo	Secret state police.
Generalkommissariat	GK, GenK	General Commissariat. Intermediate level of the administration of the occupied areas under civilian control (the largest territorial subdivision of a Reich Commissariat).
Generalquartiermeister	GenQu	Chief supply and administrative officer of the German Army (Quartermaster General).

Term	Abbreviation	Translation (Remarks)
Generalstab des Heeres	GenStdH	Army general staff.
German Military Documents Section	GMDS	Depository for captured German documents in the Federal Records Center, Departmental Records Branch, Alexandria, Virginia.
Glavnoye Razvedyvatelnoye Upravleniye [R]	GRU	Main Intelligence (Reconnaissance) Administration
Glavnoye Upravleniye Gosudarstvennoi Bezopasnosti [R]	GUGB	Main Administration for State Security. *See also* NKGB.
Gorkom [R]		City committee of Communist Party.
	GPURKKA, GPUKA [R]	Main Political Administration (of the Red Army).
Grenadier-Division	Gren.Div.	Name sometimes used for German infantry divisions.
"Hannover"		German antipartisan operation in the Yelnya-Dorogobuzh area, May 1942.
Hauptkampflinie	HKL	Main line of resistance.
Heeresfeldpolizeichef	HFPCh	Provost Marshal of the German Army.
Heeresgebiet	H.Geb.	Army Group Rear Area. The term *Heeresgebiet* is used to designate both the area and the command.
Heeresgruppe	H.Gr.	Army group.
Heereswirtschaftsfuehrer	He Wi Fue	Staff officer for economic matters at army group level.
Hilfswilliger	Hiwi	Indigenous collaborator attached to German military units.
Hoeherer SS- und Polizeifuehrer	HSSPF, Hoeh. SS u. Pol. Fhr.	Higher SS and Police Leader. The commander of all police forces in a particular area as direct representative of the RFSS.
Ia, Ib, etc.		*See* last page of Glossary.
Infantrie-Division	Inf.Div., ID	Infantry division.
Inostrannyi Otdel [R]	Ino	Foreign section of the GUGB of the NKVD.
International Military Tribunal (1945–46)	IMT	In Project "Alexander," used for document identification.
Istrebitelnyi Batalion [R]		Destruction battalion.
Jagdkommando		Antipartisan unit consisting of small, mobile units.

Term	Abbreviation	Translation (Remarks)
Kavallerie-Division	Kav.Div.	Cavalry division.
Khutor [R]		Small farm settlement.
"Klette"		German antipartisan operation in the Bryansk area, October–November 1942.
Kolkhoz [R]		Collective farm.
Kommandant	Kdt.	Commandant.
Kommandeur des rueckwaertigen Armeegebietes	Korueck	Commander of an army rear area, referring both to the commanding officer and to the area under his control.
Kommandierender General der Sicherungstruppen	Komm.Gen.d. Sich.Tr.	Commanding general of security troops.
Kommando-Stab	Kdo.Stab	Field headquarters.
Kommunisticheskii soyuz molodyozhi [R]	Komsomol	Communist Youth League (official designation: Vsesoyuznyi Leninski Kommunisticheski Soyuz Molodyozhi).
Kontrrevolyutsionnyi [R]	"KR"	Counterrevolutionary.
	KP(b)B (English abbreviation: CP[b]B)	Communist Party (of Bolsheviks) of Belorussia.
	KP(b)U (English abbreviation: CP[b]U)	Communist Party (of Bolsheviks) of the Ukraine.
"Kormoran"		German antipartisan operation in the Lepel-Borisov area, May–June 1944.
"Kottbus"		German antipartisan operation in the Lepel-Borisov area, May–June 1943.
Krai [R]		Soviet administrative unit corresponding to an oblast but containing autonomous regions.
Kraikom [R]		Krai committee of the Communist Party.
Kriegsstaerkenachweis	KStN	Table of organization (T/O).
Kriegstagebuch	KTB	War Journal.
"Kugelblitz"		German antipartisan operation in the Vitebsk area, February 1943.
Kust [R]		A form of partisan command, adopted primarily in the North Caucasus in 1942.

Term	Abbreviation	Translation (Remarks)
Lage		Situation (mil.).
Lagebericht		Situation report.
Landeseigene Verbaende		Indigenous troop units.
Landwirtschaftsfuehrer	La-Fue.	German agricultural official on the lowest level in the occupied USSR.
Leitender Feldpolizei- direktor		Provost Marshal.
Luftlandetruppen		Airborne troops.
Luftwaffe		Air Force.
Luftwaffenfeld-division	Lw.Feld.Div.	Infantry division made up of Air Force personnel.
Luftwaffenfuehrungsstab	OKL/FSt	Command staff of the High Command of the German Air Force.
Luftwaffen-Kommando	Lw.Kdo.	Air Service command.
"Maigewitter"		German antipartisan operation in the Vitebsk area, May 1943.
Makhorka [R]		Tobacco of an inferior grade.
Maschinenpistole		Submachine gun.
Meldung		Report.
Merkblatt	Mkbl.	Manual.
Militaerverwaltung	Mil.Verw.	Military government, military administration.
Militia [R]		Soviet uniformed police.
Minenwerfer		Heavy mortars with rifled barrels.
	MTS	Machine-Tractor Station.
"Munich," "Muenchen"		German antipartisan operation in the Yelnya area, March–April 1942.
Nachalnik tyla [R]		Commander of the Rear Area.
"Nachbarhilfe"		German antipartisan operation in the Kletnya-Mamayevka area, May–June 1943.
Narodnyi Komissariat Gosudarstvennoi Bezopasnosti [R]	NKGB	People's Commissariat of State Security. *See also* Cheka, NKVD.
Narodnyi Komissariat Oborony [R]	NKO	People's Commissariat of Defense
Narodnyi Komissariat Vnutrennykh Del [R]	NKVD	People's Commissariat of Internal Affairs.
Nebenstelle		Branch office.
Nuremberg Military Tribunal (1946–51)	NMT	In Project "Alexander," used for document identification.
Oberbefehlshaber	OB	Commander.

Term	Abbreviation	Translation (Remarks)
Oberfeldkommandantur	OFK	Superior military government office (divisional level); controlled and coordinated activities of several regional offices of military government or administered large urban areas.
Oberkommando des Heeres	OKH	High Command of the German Army.
Oberkommando der Luftwaffe	OKL	High Command of the German Air Force.
	OKL/FSt	*See* Luftwaffenfuehrungsstab.
Oberkommando der Wehrmacht	OKW	High Command of the German Armed Forces.
Oberquartiermeister	O Qu	Supply and administrative officer at army and army group level.
Obkom [R]		Oblast Party committee.
Oblast [R]		Soviet province.
Okrug [R]		Soviet district, such as Military District.
Operations Abteilung	Op.Abt.	Operations section (G-3) of OKH.
Operationsgebiet		Zone of operations (including area under military administration).
Operative Center		Highest level of partisan command in the occupied territories.
Operative Group		In connection with the Soviet partisan movement refers either to (1) a staff for the partisan movement attached to the Army or Front level; or (2) a partisan unit operating in the occupied areas.
Ordnungsdienst	OD	Indigenous auxiliary police organized throughout the German-occupied areas of the USSR.
Ordnungspolizei	Orpo	German uniformed police.
Organisationsabteilung	Org.Abt.	The organization (G-1) section of OKH.
Organization Todt	OT	German organization for the construction of roads and other public works.
Ortskommandantur	OK	German urban military government office.

Term	*Abbreviation*	*Translation (Remarks)*
Osobyi Otdel [R]	"OO"	Special section; counterintelligence section of the NKVD responsible for combating subversion, sabotage, and espionage within the Soviet armed forces. Particularly important was its task of checking the political reliability of Soviet military personnel and partisans. In 1943 the "OO" was superseded by Smersh.
Ostarbeiter		Soviet nationals recruited in the occupied territories for labor in Germany.
Ostbataillone		Military battalions with the German Army, made up of collaborators from the USSR.
Ost-Kompanie		A company of ex-Soviet nationals in German military service.
Ostland		Reich Commissariat, comprising the three former Baltic States and parts of Belorussia; one of the two major units of the German civilian administration of the occupied areas.
Osttruppen		Soviet nationals recruited for military service on the German side.
Ostverbaende		A generic term for the military units composed of Soviet nationals serving with the German Armed Forces.
Otryad [R]		In the Red Army, designation of a company-size unit; in the partisan movement, designation of the basic smaller unit, either independent or part of a larger command.
Panzer-Armeeoberkommando	PzAOK	Headquarters of a Panzer (armored) army.
Panzergruppe	Pz.Gr.	In 1941, incomplete Panzer armies.
Partizanskoye Dvizheniye Yuga [R]	PDYu	Partisan Movement of the South. Highest partisan command in the southern part of the RSFSR and the North Caucasus.

Term	Abbreviation	Translation (Remarks)
People's Commissar of Internal Affairs		*See* NKVD.
Politruk [R]		Soviet Army (and partisan) political officer at the company level.
Polk [R]		Regiment.
	PURKKA [R]	Political Administration (Red Army).
Quartiermeister- Abteilung	Abt.Qu.	Supply and administrative section.
Raiispolkom [R]		Rayon executive committee.
Raikom [R]		Rayon Party committee.
Rayon [R]		Lower Soviet administrative division.
Razvedyvatelnyi Otdel (Razvedotdel) [R]	RO	Intelligence section.
"Regenschauer"		Antipartisan operation in Belorussia in 1944
Reichsfuehrer SS	RFSS	Heinrich Himmler's title as commander of the SS.
Reichskommissariat	RK	Reich Commissariat. The two major territorial divisions of the German civilian administration of the USSR (Ukraine and Ostland).
Reichsministerium fuer die besetzten Ostgebiete	RMfdbO., Ostministerium	Reich Ministry for the Occupied Eastern Territories.
Reichssicherheits-hauptamt	RSHA	Reich Security Main Office—the central department of the security police and the SS intelligence service (SD).
Reihensprengungen		A series of demolition charges placed on railroad tracks at short intervals.
Rollbahn		Major highway used for arterial troop and supply shipments.
	RSFSR	Russian Federated Soviet Socialist Republic.
Rueckwaertiges Heeresgebiet	Rueckw.H.Geb.	*See* Heeresgebiet.
Russkaya Osvoboditelnaya Armiya [R]	ROA	Designation for the German-sponsored Vlasov formations.
Russland-Gremium		Special section in the German Foreign Office organized during World War II to study questions pertaining to the Soviet Union.
Samogon [R]		Moonshine vodka.

Term	*Abbreviation*	*Translation (Remarks)*
Schienenkrieg		"Battle of the rails." German term for the race between the partisans who destroyed the railroad tracks, and the Germans who tried to repair them.
Schutzmannschaft		Auxiliary police, usually recruited locally.
Sekretnyi sotrudnik [R]	Seksot	Secret informant.
Selbstschutz		Literally, "self-defense." Small units organized by the Germans in villages and towns which were threatened by partisan activity.
Selsoviet, selsovet [R]		Village soviet.
Sicherheitsdienst	SD	Intelligence and security service of the SS.
Sicherheitspolizei	Sipo	Security police.
Sicherungs-Bataillon	Sich.Btl.	Security battalion.
Sicherungs-Division	Sich.Div.	Security division.
Smert Shpionam [R]	Smersh	"Death to spies." *See also* "OO."
Sonderkommando		Special German police task forces in the areas of the USSR under civilian administration.
Sotni [R]		Literally, "hundreds." Units of Cossack military organization.
Sovkhoz [R]		Soviet state farm.
	Sovnarkom, SNK	*See* Council of People's Commissars of the Soviet Union.
Soyedineniye [R]		Complex.
SS- und Polizeifuehrer	SSPF	SS and police leader. Territorial subordinate of the HSSPF.
Stabschef, Chef des Stabes		Chief of staff.
Standortkommandantur		Garrison commander.
Starosta [R]		Village elder.
Stuetzpunkt		Strongpoint.
"Sumpfbluete"		German antipartisan operation in the Yelnya-Dorogobuzh area, July 1942.
	SVG	*See* Versuchsgebiet.
Svodnyi otryad [R]		Composite unit.
Taetigkeitsbericht		Activity report.
Tagebuch	Tgb.	Diary or journal.
Technische Brigade	TBM	Special German military-economic unit established for the exploitation and custody of oil resources and industry in the occupied USSR.

Term	Abbreviation	Translation (Remarks)
Troika [R]		Three-man team.
Tsentralnyi Komitet [R]	TsK	Central Committee.
	TsK VKP(b)	Central Committee of the All-Union Communist Party (of Bolsheviks).
Tsentralnyi Shtab Partizanskogo Dvizheniya [R]	TsShPD	Central Staff of the Partisan Movement. The highest level of Soviet command for the entire partisan movement, in Moscow.
	UkSSR	Ukrainian Soviet Socialist Republic.
Unternehmen (militaerishes Unternehmen)		Military operation.
VCheka [R]		*See* Cheka.
Verbindungsoffizier	V.O.	Liaison officer.
Versuchsgebiet, or Selbstverwaltungsgebiet	SVG	Experimental district.
Vertrauensmann	V-Mann	Intelligence agent, informant.
Vertreter des Auswaertiges Amtes	VAA	German Foreign Office liaison officer with an army or other agency.
	VKP(b)	All-Union Communist Party (of Bolsheviks); also Communist Party of the Soviet Union (CPSU). *See also* KP(b)B and KP(b)U.
"Vogelsang"		German antipartisan operation in the Bryansk area, June 1942.
Volksdeutscher		Racial German living outside the Reich.
Volost [R]		Old Russian administrative unit consisting of several adjoining communes.
Voyennyi Komissariat [R]	Voyenkomat	Army recruitment office.
Voyennyi Sovet [R]		Military Council, a high-level group of command and political officers at Front and other operational levels of the Red Army.
Wach-Bataillon		Guard battalion.
Waffen-SS		Military formations of the SS.
Wehrmachtsbefehlshaber	WB	Armed Forces Commander. The highest German military officer in an occupied area under civilian administration.

Term	*Abbreviation*	*Translation (Remarks)*
Wehrmacht Propaganda	WPr	Staff section for propaganda of the High Command of the German Armed Forces (OKW).
"Winterzauber"		Antipartisan operation in the northwestern part of the occupied USSR in the winter of 1942–43.
Wirtschaftseinsatz-kommando	WEK	Army economic detachments, largely for requisitioning.
Wirtschaftskommando	Wi Kdo	Regional office of the Wi Stab Ost.
Wirtschaftsstab Ost	Wi Stab Ost	Economic Staff East. Agency for the economic exploitation of the occupied territories of the Soviet Union.
Zagraditelnyi otryad [R]		Blocking detachment.
	ZAGS	Soviet vital statistics office.
"Zigeunerbaron"		German antipartisan operation in the Bryansk area, May–June 1943.
"Zitadelle"		*See* "Citadel."

ROMAN NUMERALS

Term	*Translation (Remarks)*
Ia	Staff officer for operations (U.S. equivalent: G-3).
Ib	Staff officer for supply (U.S. equivalent: G-4).
Ic	Staff officer for military intelligence (U.S. equivalent: G-2).
Ic/AO, or Ic/Abwehr	Counterintelligence officer.
IV Wi	Staff section for economics of an army, division, or regional military government office.

Selected Bibliography

I. UNPUBLISHED GERMAN DOCUMENTS

A great deal of valuable material is contained in German reports which were captured by the Allies in World War II. Many of these remain under security classification. The most extensive of these collections available to the general public was amassed for the Nuremberg trials of war criminals. Little of value on the partisan movement is contained in the published collections of evidence for these trials, but other documents obtained for the trials are available in mimeographed or photostat reproductions in various libraries in the United States and Europe. For listings of other holdings of captured German documents see the War Documentation Project Study, *Guide to Captured German Documents* (prepared by Gerhard L. Weinberg and the WDP Staff under the direction of Fritz T. Epstein) for the Air University's Human Resources Research Institute, Maxwell Air Force Base, Alabama, December 1952. The most important of these holdings, as far as reports on partisan warfare are concerned, are the following:

The Himmler File (photostats, Manuscript Division, Library of Congress, Washington, D.C., and the Hoover Library on War, Revolution, and Peace, Stanford, Calif.).

The Yiddish Scientific Institute (YIVO), "Occupation-East" collection (New York).

The Centre de Documentation Juive Contemporaine Collection (Paris).

Recently the American Historical Association has made available microfilms of very large collections of German documents.

In addition to German documents, there exist a number of small but valuable collections compiled from private sources. For the most part, these consist of manuscripts of participants composed as memoirs after the war, but the collections also contain a few contemporary documents.

The principal depositories of such materials are as follows:

Russian Research Center, Harvard University (Interview Protocols, Series B 7, and manuscripts in the same series).
Institute for the Study of the History and Institutions of the USSR, Munich.
Institut fuer Zeitgeschichte, Munich.
Research Program on the USSR, New York.
The Archive of Russian and East European History and Culture, Columbia University, New York.

II. SOVIET PUBLICATIONS

The body of material issued in the USSR on the partisan movement represents the most valuable *published* source of information on the partisans. This is quite natural, of course, since Soviet publications are able to draw on first-hand accounts by the partisans themselves. The Soviet materials must, however, be handled with great caution, since they are published in large part for propaganda purposes and frequently distort the nature of the events described. Nevertheless, judicious analysis of these works can yield much useful information, especially on the concept of the partisan movement which has been held at various times in the USSR, and the intentions which the Soviet leadership has had regarding it. Many hundreds of books and articles specifically relating to the partisan movement have been published in the USSR, and many other Soviet works contain important information about the partisans. A very considerable proportion of these works are not available outside the USSR. It has been impossible to examine even all of the works in American and West European libraries. Consequently, the following selection must be regarded as a guide to books and articles which have been found especially informative, rather than as a definitive list of the most important works on the partisan movement. The reader desiring to pursue the subject will find the more extensive listings in G. A. Kumanev, *Velikaya otechestvennaya voina Sovetskogo Soyuza (1941–1945 gg.): Bibliografiya sovetskoi istoricheskoi literatury za 1946–1959 gg.* (Moscow: Akademiya Nauk SSSR, Institut Istorii, 1960), pp. 64–76; and *Istoriya sovetskogo obshchestva v vospominaniyakh sovremmeinikov, 1917–1957: Annotirovannyi ukazatel' memuarnoi literatury* (Moscow: Izdatelstvo Moskovskogo Universiteta, 1958), pp. 279–86, very useful, although neither of these works is by any means exhaustive in its coverage. As indicated below, several more specialized Soviet accounts and non-Soviet works contain useful bibliographical information on Soviet publications.

Abramov, M. (ed.). *Bolshevistskiye gazety v tylu vraga: Sbornik materialov iz podpolnykh gazet leningradskoi oblasti v period nemetskoi okkupatsii. (The Bolshevik Newspapers in the Rear of the Enemy: A collection of Materials from the Underground Newspapers of Leningrad Oblast in the Period of German Occupation.)* Leningrad: Leningradskoye Gazetno-Zhurnalnoye Izdatelstvo, 1946. A highly useful collection of reproductions of newspapers issued by Party organizations working with the partisans.

Akademiya Nauk Belorusskoi SSR, Institut Istorii. *Iz istorii partizanskogo dvizheniya v Belorussii (1941–1944 gody): Sbornik vospominanii. (From the History of the Partisan Movement in Belorussia [1941–1944]: A Collection of Memoirs.)* Minsk: Gosudarstvennoye Izdatelstvo BSSR, 1961. A collection of short sketches of very uneven value; a few contain revelations of major importance.

Akademiya Nauk Belorusskoi SSR, Institut Istorii i Izdatelstvo "Osveta" (Bratislava [Czechoslovakia]). *Ogni partizanskoi druzhby. (Fires of Partisan Friendship.)* A series of short reminiscences by or about Czechs and Slovaks who served in the partisans in Belorussia.

Andreyev, V. *Narodnaya voina (zapiski partizana). (The People's War [Sketches of a Partisan].)* Moscow: Gosudarstvennoye Izdatelstvo Khudozhestvennoi Literatury, 1952. An extremely interesting account by a teacher of military history (and probably a prominent Party member) who became first a commissar, then a partisan leader in the Bryansk forest.

Antifashistskoye dvizheniye soprotivleniya v stranakh Yevropy v gody vtoroi mirovoi voiny. (The Anti-Fascist Resistance Movement in the Countries of Europe in the Years of the Second World War.) Moscow: Izdatelstvo Sotsialno-Ekonomicheskoi Literatury, 1962. Although this volume deals entirely with activities outside the USSR, it treats the relations between Soviet and non-Soviet Communist partisans, and is helpful in understanding the Soviet attitude toward the non-Communist resistance movements.

Arkhipova, T. I., *et al.* (eds.). *Kurskaya oblast v period velikoi otechestvennoi voiny Sovetskogo Soyuza, 1941–1945 gg.: Sbornik dokumentov i materialov. (Kurst Oblast in the Period of the Great Patriotic War of the Soviet Union, 1941–1945.)* Vol. I. Kursk: Kurskoye Knizhnoye Izdatelstvo, 1960. A collection of documents including many items on the rather insignificant partisan movement in Kursk province.

Artozeyev, G. *Partizanskaya byl. (Partisan Story.)* Moscow: Voennoye Izdatelstvo Ministerstva Oborony SSSR, 1956. A memoir of a partisan commander in the northern Ukraine during the early part of the war, especially interesting for relations with the civilian population.

Begma, Vasilii, and Luka Kyzya. *Shlyakhy neskorenykh. (The Paths of the Unsubjugated.)* Kiev: Radyanskyi Pysmennyk, 1962. One of the most important very recent memoirs, for its principal author was commander of one of the major roving bands and since the war has occupied key posts in the Communist Party apparatus in the Ukraine.

Brinskii, Anton P. *Po etu storonu fronta: Vospominaniya partizana. (On That Side of the Front: Memoir of a Partisan.)* Moscow: Voennoye Izdatelstvo Ministerstva Oborony SSSR, 1958. An important account by one of the leaders of the organizing teams sent to West Belorussia and later to the West Ukraine to revive the partisan movement.

Demyanchuk, I. L. *Partyzanska presa Ukraïny, 1941–1944 rr. (The Partisan Press of the Ukraine, 1941–1944.)* Kiev: Vydavnytstvo Kyïvskoho Derzhavnoho Universytetu, 1956. A systematic treatment with much useful information on propaganda activities.

Fyodorov, A. *Podpolnyi obkom deistvuyet (The Underground Obkom in Action.)* 2 vols. Moscow: Voennoye Izdatelstvo Ministerstva Vooruzhennykh Sil Soyuza SSR, 1947; also several other editions, including expanded versions issued by various publishing houses in 1950 and 1957. Certain significant differences exist between the various editions. An English translation (evidently based on the first edition) is available as *The Underground Committee Carries On.* Moscow: Foreign Languages Publishing House, 1952. Fyodorov's memoirs are particularly valuable because he was a high official of the Communist Party of the Ukraine, as well as one of the major partisan leaders. Although his work exaggerates the position of the Party, it provides considerable insight into reactions of apparatus officials under stress.

Glider, Mikhail. *S kinoapparatom v tylu vraga. (With a Motion Picture Camera in the Rear of the Enemy.)* Moscow: Goskinoizdat, 1947. Though not of major importance, this memoir provides some interesting sidelights on partisan propaganda in the Ukraine.

Gnyedash, T. *Volya k zhizni. (Will for Life.)* Moscow: Voennoye Izdatelstvo Ministerstva Oborony SSSR, 1960. An interesting account by a physician with Fyodorov's partisan band, particularly informative concerning operations in the West Ukraine.

Gnyedash, T. *Z partizanamy Fedorova. (With Fyodorov's Partisans.)* Kiev: Radyanskyi Pysmennyk, 1948. A much earlier version, but useful for sidelights on the postwar status of various partisan leaders.

Ignatov, P. *Zapiski partizana. (Sketches of a Partisan.)* Moscow: Izdatelstvo TsK VLKSM, Molodaya Gvardiya, 1944. A considerably expanded version in two volumes was published (same place, same publisher) in 1947. Ignatov's account is of great value for the study of the partisans in the North Caucasus area, where he was a major leader, but it is marred by exaggeration.

Institut Istorii Partii Moskovskogo Oblastnogo Komiteta i Moskovsogo Gorodskogo Komiteta KPSS. *Narodnye mstiteli. (The People's Avengers.)* Moscow: Moskovskii Rabochii, 1961. A very revealing collection of documents on the brief period of partisan operation west of Moscow in 1941–42.

Institut Istorii pri TsK KP Belorussii i Akademiya Nauk BSSR, Institut Istorii. *O partiinom podpolye v Minske v gody velikoi otechestvennoi voiny (iyun 1941—iyul 1944 gg.). (The Party Underground in Minsk in the Years of the Great Patriotic War [1941–1944].)* Minsk: Gosudarstvennoye Izdatelstvo BSSR, 1961. A brief but detailed account, useful for systematic study of partisan activities in the Minsk area.

Institut Marksizma-Leninizma. *Istoriya velikoi otechestvennoi voiny Sovetskogo Soyuza, 1941–1945. (History of the Great Patriotic War of the Soviet Union, 1941–1945.)* Ed. P. N. Pospelov et al. Vols. II-V. Moscow: Voennoye Izdatelstvo Ministerstva Oborony SSSR, 1961–1963. By far the most important Soviet work on the war period (Vol. I relates entirely to the period before Soviet entry into the war). The treatment of the partisans is more guarded than that of many of the memoirs, but is unexcelled for chronological and organizational details. The geographical and name index and the references in the footnotes increase the value of the work.

Klyatskin, S. M. "Iz istorii leningradskogo partizanskogo kraya (avgust 1941—sentyabr 1942 g.)" ("From the History of the Leningrad Partisan Region,

August 1941—September 1942"), *Voprosy Istorii,* 1958, No. 7, pp. 25–44. The best recent treatment of the Leningrad partisans under Zhdanov.

Kovpak, S. *Ot Putivlya do Karpat. (From Putivl to the Carpathians.)* Ed. E. Gerasimov. Moscow: Gosudarstvennoye Izdatelstvo Detskoi Literatury, 1945. Numerous editions exist, including one in Ukrainian, and an English translation, *Our Partisan Course.* London: Hutchinson, 1947. Kovpak is one of the most famous partisan leaders, and his account is fairly accurate as to military matters (for example, the map at the end of the volume showing his raids), though not revealing on political affairs. There are some significant differences between the earlier and later editions.

Kozlov, I. *V krymskom podpolye: Vospominaniya. (In the Crimean Underground: A Memoir.)* Moscow: Sovetskii Pisatel, 1947. A very useful account of the Crimean underground, with much incidental information concerning the partisans.

Krivitskii, A., and P. I. Krainov. *V bryanskikh lesakh. (In the Bryansk Forests.)* Moscow: Voyennoye Izdatelstvo Narodnogo Komissariata Oborony, 1943. Numerous editions, including one in Ukrainian (P. I. Krainov and I. O. Plakhtin, *Partizany bryanskikh lisiv.* [*Partisans of the Bryansk Forests.*] Kharkov: Kharkivske Knizhkovo-Zhurnalne Vydavnytstvo, 1945); and an English translation of part of the Russian original *(Tales of the Bryansk Woods.* Moscow: Foreign Languages Publishing House, 1944). Useful mainly as a presentation of the wartime Soviet line.

Kuzin, Ilya. *Zapiski partisana. (Sketches of a Partisan.)* Moscow: Izdatelstvo TsK VLKSM, 1942. English translation, *Notes of a Guerrilla Fighter.* Moscow: Foreign Languages Publishing House, 1942. Similarly useful mainly as an example of Soviet wartime treatment of the partisan story.

Linkov, G. *Voina v tylu vraga. (The War in the Rear of the Enemy.)* Moscow: Gosudarstvennoye Izdatelstvo Khudozhestvennoi Literatury, 1951, 1959. Two of several editions. Linkov was an engineer and evidently an important Party official who organized and led one of the parachutist detachments that played a major part in reactivating the partisan movement in Belorussia in 1941–42. Linkov, however, exaggerates the importance of his "Moscow" group as compared with the local Party organizations.

Lipilo, P. P. *KPB, organizator i rukovoditel partizanskogo dvizheniya v Belorussii v gody velikoi otechestvennoi voiny. (The Communist Party of Belorussia, Organizer and Director of the Partisan Movement in Belorussia in the Years of the Great Patriotic War.)* Minsk: Gosudarstvennoye Izdatelstvo BSSR, 1959. While far sketchier and less revealing than Tsanava's work, this is the only general history of the Belorussian partisans to appear in the post-Stalin era.

Liventsev, V. *Partizanskii krai. (Partisan Country.)* Ed. G. Nekhai. Leningrad: Izdatelstvo TsK VLKSM, Molodaya Gvardiya, 1951. An interesting though extremely episodic account of the partisans in southeast Belorussia.

Makedonskii, M. *Plamya nad Krymom. (Flame over the Crimea.)* Simferopol: Krymizdat, 1960. A memoir by one of the principal partisan commanders in the Crimea, unusually frank on the difficulties which his partisans faced.

Medvedev, Dmitri N. *Na beregakh yuzhnogo Buga. (On the Banks of the*

Southern Bug.) Kiev: Radyanskyi Pysmennyk, 1962. An account of an underground movement in Vinnitsa. Compiled at second hand by the author, it is perhaps mainly interesting because of the controversy it caused just before Stalin's death.

Medvedev, Dmitri N. *Silnye dukhom. (The Strong in Spirit.)* Moscow: Voennoye Izdatelstvo Voennogo Ministerstva Soyuza SSR, 1951. An earlier partial edition was entitled *Eto bylo pod Rovno (It Was at Rovno)*. Moscow: Gosudarstvennoye Izdatelstvo Detskoi Literatury, 1948. Extremely interesting for the story of the first penetration of the Soviet partisans into the northwest Ukraine, and their relations with the local population and nationalist groups.

Naumov, M. I. *Khinelskiye pokhody. (Khinel Campaigns.)* Kiev: Derzhavne Vydavnytstvo Khudozhnoï Literatury, 1960. By the commander of the roving brigade which crossed the entire central Ukrainian steppe, this memoir unfortunately stops before the unit moved out of the Khinel forest.

Nikitin, M. N. *Partizanskaya voina v leningradskoi oblasti. (The Partisan War in Leningrad Oblast.)* Moscow: Gosudarstvennoye Izdatelstvo Politicheskoi Literatury, 1943. Rather sketchy accounts by the Party secretary who directed the partisans in Leningrad Oblast.

Orlovskaya oblast v gody velikoi otechestvennoi voiny (1941–1945 gg.): Sbornik dokumentov i materialov. (Orel Oblast in the Years of the Great Patriotic War [1941–1945]: A Collection of Documents and Materials.) Orel: Orlovskoye Knizhnoye Izdatelstvo, 1960. A very important collection, including a wide variety of documents on the partisan concentration in the Bryansk forest, one of the most important in the RSFSR.

Partizanskaya borba s nemetsko-fashistskimi okkupantami na territorii Smolenshchiny, 1941–1943 gg.: Dokumenty i materialy. (The Partisan Struggle with the German-Fascist Occupiers on the Territory of the Smolensk Region, 1941–1943: Documents and Materials.) Smolensk: Smolenskoye Knizhskoye Izdatelstvo, 1962. A voluminous and revealing collection, especially important because of the rapid early development and sudden decline of the Smolensk partisan movement. The introduction contains a number of important bibliographical references.

Partizanskiye byli. (Partisan Stories.) Moscow: Voennoye Izdatelstvo Ministerstva Oborony SSSR, 1958. Some three dozen personal accounts by partisans from all parts of the occupied territories (there are also a few accounts from the Civil War period). Many are substantial in length, and contain important information; altogether this is the most important volume of collected memoirs which has appeared. It was sponsored by the "Section of Former Partisans of the Soviet Committee of Veterans of the War."

Partizany Bryanshchiny: Sbornik rasskazov byvshikh partizan. (Partisans of the Bryansk Area: A Collection of Accounts by Former Partisans.) Vol. I. Bryansk: Izdatelstvo "Bryanskii Rabochii," 1959. Similar to the preceding item, but more restricted in scope and containing fewer revelations. The book does, however, provide some interesting sidelights on major officials involved in Bryansk partisan activities. A projected second volume has evidently not appeared.

Petrov, Yu. P. "Kommunisticheskaya partiya—organizator i rukovoditel partizanskogo dvizheniya v gody velikoi otechestvennoi voiny" ("The Communist Party—Organizer and Director of the Partisan Movement in the Years of the Great Patriotic War"), *Voprosy Istorii,* 1958, No. 5, pp. 23–42. In spite of its general title and brevity, this article contains important information on the early organization and subsequent reorganization of the partisan movement and on its numerical strength.

Ponomarenko, P. (ed.). *Partizanskoye divizheniye v Velikoi Otechestvennoi Voine. (The Partisan Movement in the Great Fatherland War.)* Moscow: Gospolitizdat, 1943. Numerous editions, including English translation. While the book contains little specific information of value, the fact that it was edited by the Chief of Staff of the Partisan Movement makes it an especially interesting example of wartime treatments.

Saburov, A. N. *Za linieyu frontu (partizanski zapysy): Kniga persha, Partizanskyi krai. (Behind the Front Line [Partisan Sketches]: Book One, The Partisan Country.)* Lvov: Knyzhkovo-Zhurnalne Vydavnytstvo, 1953. By one of the most important roving band commanders, this volume is especially revealing on disputes among partisan commanders in 1941–42. Unfortunately, the projected second volume (which presumably would have dealt with Saburov's experiences in the West Ukraine) has evidently never appeared.

Shapko, Yekaterina N. *Partizanskoye Dvizheniye v Krymu v 1941–1944 gg. (The Partisan Movement in the Crimea, 1941–1944.)* Simferopol: Krymizdat, 1959. A fairly brief but systematic historical account. The book is not as frank as some of the memoirs dealing with the Crimean partisans, but is highly useful for names of major figures and for details on organization.

Sheverdalkin, P. (ed.) *Listovki partizanskoi voiny v leningradskoi oblast, 1941– 1944. (Leaflets of the Partisan War in Leningrad Oblast, 1941–1944.)* Leningrad: Leningradskoye Gazetno-Zhurnalnoye i Knizhnoye Izdatelstvo, 1945. A useful collection of propaganda material distributed by the partisans.

Shyyan, Anatolii. *Partyzanskyi krai. (Partisan County.)* Kiev: Ukraïnske Derzhavne Vydavnytstvo, 1946. An account by a prominent Ukrainian journalist who visited the partisan groups in 1943. Especially valuable on Saburov's band in the Bryansk area and on the major bands in the northwest Ukraine.

Sovetskiye partizany: Iz istorii partizanskogo dvizheniya v gody velikoi otechestvennoi voiny. (Soviet Partisans: From the History of the Partisan Movement in the Years of the Great Patriotic War.) Moscow: Gospolitizdat, 1960. Perhaps the single most valuable volume on the partisan movement, this is a collection of sixteen very substantial monographs on many aspects of the partisan movement. The treatments of relations with East European countries are especially valuable, and contain useful bibliographical references.

Sputnik partizana. (The Partisan's Traveling Companion.) Moscow: Molodaya Gvardiya, 1942. A semiofficial Soviet handbook for use by the partisans and for partisan training, published by the Komsomol press early in the war.

Strokach, Timofei. *Partyzany Ukraïny. (The Partisans of the Ukraine.)* Moscow: Ukrydav TsK KP(b)U, 1943. Strokach was a prominent NKVD official and Chief of the Ukrainian Staff of the Partisan Movement, although in this publication, issued for propaganda purposes during the war, he is identified only as a "deputy of the Supreme Soviet of the USSR."

Suprunenko, M. *Ukraina v velikoi otechestvennoi voine Sovetskogo Soyuza, 1941–1945 gg. (The Ukraine in the Great Patriotic War of the Soviet Union, 1941–1945.)* Kiev: Gosudarstvennoye Izdatelstvo Politicheskoi Literatury, 1956. While not much of this book is devoted to the partisan movement, it contains some important information, and is remarkably candid about the shortcomings of the partisan effort.

Tsanava, L. F. *Vsenarodnaya partizanskaya voina v Belorussii protiv fashist-skikh zakhvatchikov. (The People's Partisan War Against the Fascist Invaders in Belorussia.)* Minsk: Gosudarstvennoye Izdatelstvo BSSR, Vol. I (1949), Vol. II (1951). An extremely detailed account by a high NKVD official of Belorussia, since purged. It is, however, extremely distorted by an effort to enhance the role of the Party in the development of the partisan movement.

V tylu vraga: Ocherki, dnevniki, zapiski ob uchastii komsomola i molodezhi v partizanskoi borbe. (In the Rear of the Enemy: Essays, Diaries, and Sketches on the Participation of the Komsomol and Youth in the Partisan Struggle.) Introduction by P. K. Ponomarenko. Moscow: Izdatelstvo TsK VLKSM, 1943. Mainly interesting as an example of a wartime appeal to youthful patriotism.

Vaupshasov, S. *Partizanskaya khronika. (Partisan Chronicle.)* Moscow: Voennoye Izdatelstvo Ministerstva Oborony SSSR, 1959. A substantial memoir by a partisan organizer who worked under NKVD direction in Belorussia.

Vershigora, Pavlo P. *Lyudi s chistoi sovestyu. (People with a Clear Conscience.)* Moscow: Sovetskii Pisatel, 1951. One of several editions of varying length. Vershigora, a motion picture director in Kiev before the war, was an aide of Kovpak, and later commanded a roving band himself. This volume deals with the period prior to the Carpathian raid in the summer of 1943.

Vershigora, Pavlo P. *Reid na San i Vislu. (The Raid on the San and the Vistula.)* Moscow: Voennoye Izdatelstvo Ministerstva Oborony SSSR, 1960. About the author's independent operations in Volhynia and Poland; especially revealing on Soviet attitudes toward Communism in Poland.

Volonchuk, F. F. *Po tylam vraga. (At the Enemy's Rear.)* Moscow: Voennoye Izdatelstvo Ministerstva Oborony SSSR, 1961. An interesting memoir by a naval officer who led a scouting detachment into the partisan areas of the Crimea.

Yelagina, A. (ed.). *Koster na mysu. (Campfire on the Cape.)* Moscow: Molodaya Gvardiya, 1945. A series of accounts of the activities of the Taganrog underground and partisans.

III. NON-SOVIET PUBLICATIONS

In compiling this very brief list of works by German, British, American, and Soviet *émigré* authors, it has been necessary to be even more selective than in the choice of Soviet publications. There are hundreds of Western publications which touch upon the Soviet partisan movement, but they are of very unequal value. The following list is an attempt to indicate a limited number of publications which appear to have the greatest permanent value, either because they are based upon sources of unique interest or because they serve as guides to such sources. By referring to the notes and bibliographies in the works listed below, the reader will be able to locate many other significant items dealing with the Soviet partisans.

Armstrong, John A. *The Politics of Totalitarianism: The Communist Party of the Soviet Union from 1934 to the Present.* New York: Random House, 1961. Chapter XII deals with the Soviet partisans and their relations with East European Communists. Footnotes to this chapter refer to a number of important sources.

Armstrong, John A. *Ukrainian Nationalism.* 2d ed. New York: Columbia University Press, 1963. Chapter VI discusses the Ukrainian nationalist partisans and their relation to the Soviet partisans during World War II; Chapter XIII sketches the postwar development of the nationalist partisans. The bibliography lists a large number of works, including several of major importance, by Ukrainian *émigrés* concerning their contacts with Soviet partisans.

Augur (pseud.). "Die rote Partisanenbewegung," *Allgemeine Schweizerische Militaerzeitung.* CXV (June–July 1949), 441–50, 504–16. An interesting and accurate account of the organization and control of the partisan movement, tactics and missions of partisan bands, especially in the field of intelligence. Obviously based on official German sources, primarily on *Nachrichten ueber den Bandenkrieg.*

Dallin, Alexander (with the assistance of Conrad F. Latour). *The German Occupation of the USSR in World War II: A Bibliography.* Washington: Department of State, Office of Intelligence Research, External Research Paper No. 122, April 15, 1955. Contains many Soviet, *émigré,* and Western items concerning partisan activity.

Dallin, Alexander. *German Rule in Russia, 1941–1945: A Study of Occupation Policies.* London: Macmillan, 1957. New York: St. Martin's, 1957. The basic treatment of German policies in the occupied USSR. The work also contains much information on the reactions of Soviet citizens to the Germans, including extensive bibliographical references to Russian *émigré* publications.

Dallin, Alexander, and Ralph S. Mavrogordato. "Rodionov: A Case Study in Wartime Redefection," *American Slavic and East European Review,* XVIII (1959), 25–33. A study of an important counterguerrilla unit composed of former Soviet citizens which operated in the Polotsk area until its sudden redefection to the Soviet side.

Daur. "Pravda naoborot: O partizanakh v Maikope" ("The Truth in Reverse: Concerning the Partisans in Maikop"), *Svobodnyi Kavkaz* (Munich), No. 9 (12), September 1952, pp. 20–22. An interesting *émigré* account.

Dixon, C. Aubrey, and Otto Heilbrunn. *Communist Guerrilla Warfare.* London: Allen and Unwin, 1954. New York: F. A. Praeger, 1954. A general study of Soviet partisans and German antipartisan warfare in World War II. While the book contains considerable amounts of hitherto unpublished material, the picture of the partisan movement is seriously distorted by dependence on the erroneous assumption that the partisans in the Crimea, on whom the book is primarily focused, were typical of the movement as a whole. The description of antipartisan warfare is somewhat better, although—while showing a clear grasp of the principles followed by the Germans—the authors pay too little attention to the main areas of the conflict. On the whole, the military effectiveness of the partisans is overrated; their political importance is properly recognized.

European Resistance Movements, 1939–1945: First International Conference on the History of the Resistance Movements Held at Liège-Bruxelles-Breendonk, 14–17 September 1958. Oxford: Pergamon Press, 1960. Only one article is devoted to an aspect of the Soviet partisan movement—the participation of Jews. The book is extremely valuable, however, as a presentation of the attitudes of a very predominantly non-Communist group of resistance leaders; later conference proceedings (to appear) include Soviet participation.

Galai, N. "Partizanskoye Dvizheniye v SSSR v gody vtoroi mirovoi voiny" ("The Partisan Movement in the USSR in the Years of the Second World War"), *Vestnik Instituta po Izucheniyu Istorii i Kultury SSSR* (Munich), No. 4 (January–March 1953), pp. 52–66. Though inaccurate in some of its factual statements, this article is an important interpretation by a leading *émigré* student of Soviet military affairs.

Garthoff, Raymond L. *Soviet Military Doctrine.* Glencoe, Illinois: The Free Press, 1953. Chapter 23 is an account of the place occupied by guerrilla warfare in Soviet strategic thinking. Of considerable value, although certain of the concepts of partisan practice in World War II are erroneous. Bibliographical references, especially to interwar Soviet thinking on partisans, are important.

Greene, T. N. (ed.). *The Guerrilla and How to Fight Him: Selections from the* Marine Corps Gazette. New York: F. A. Praeger, 1962. Though this collection contains only one item (of secondary importance) on Soviet partisans, it is very useful for the comparative study of guerrilla movements.

Heilbrunn, Otto. *Partisan Warfare.* New York: F. A. Praeger, 1962. A theoretical discussion based on broad study. The bibliography is a useful guide to the comparative study of guerrilla operations.

Karov, D. (pseud.). *Partizanskoye Dvizheniye v SSSR v 1941–45. (The Partisan Movement in the USSR, 1941–45.)* Munich: Institute for the Study of the History and Culture of the USSR, 1954. The most substantial and systematic of studies by refugees from the USSR, this volume makes ample use of Soviet memoir material and of some German sources, evidently supplemented by the author's own experience. While much of the account and some of the conclusions are sound, parts of the book are marred by inadequate information and/or distortions that seem due to political purposes or a desire to prove preconceived ideas. Nonetheless, a decidedly useful contribution.

Koreisky, Yu., and G. Sosnovsky, "Iz ugolovnykh v partizany" ("From Criminals to Partisans"); Gromov, V., "Stalinskaya nagrada partizanam" ("Stalin's Reward to the Partisans"), *Na Rubezhe* (Paris), No. 3–4 (July–August 1952), pp. 41–43, 43–44. Somewhat sensational but interesting *émigré* articles.

Kramer, Gerhard. *Wir werden weiter marschieren.* Berlin: L. Blanvalet, 1952. A novel containing a long section on life in a German strongpoint on the Brest-Litovsk-Minsk railway. This account, although ostensibly fictitious, provides an excellent picture of the main features of defensive antipartisan warfare.

"Organizatsiya sovetskogo partizanskogo dvizheniya v Belorussii." *("Organization of the Soviet Partisan Movement in Belorussia.")* Munich, 1951. Mimeographed (99 pp.). Russian Research Center, Harvard University. A detailed account of Soviet partisan activity in Belorussia on the basis of the anonymous author's personal experiences, with some details on operation and organization but especially on supply and documentation. Reliable within the limits of the author's framework of experience and faulty recollection.

Osanka, Franklin M. (ed.). *Modern Guerrilla Warfare: Fighting Communist Guerrilla Movements, 1941–1961.* Glencoe, Illinois: The Free Press, 1962. The most comprehensive collection of articles on contemporary guerrillas, very useful for comparative investigation. While the selections on the Soviet partisans are of unequal value, the appended bibliography is a very useful guide to English-language books and articles on the subject.

Teske, Hermann. *Die silbernen Spiegel: Generalstabsdienst unter der Lupe.* Heidelberg: Kurt Vowinckel, 1952. Perhaps the most useful of published German accounts, particularly for the effect of partisan operation on the communications of the German armies on the central part of the front in 1943 and 1944.

Index

Abakumov, Commissar (Grishin Regiment), 734

Afanasyev, Commander (Victory Partisan Detachment), 417, 719

Akbeyev, Chief of Staff (Mikoyan-Shakhar deserter group), 619

Akhmeteli, Mikhail (Georgian adviser in Berlin), 574n

Akimochkin, Commander (Buchino Detachment), 485

Alekseev (secretary, Degzho selsoviet), 694

Alekseyev, Vasili (partisan, Kovpak Regiment): executed for theft, 748, 749

Alexeyev, N. (secretary, Molvotitsy Rayon), 300, 310n

Alexeyev Brigade, 148, 691, 753

Alshevsky (partisan, Bezstrashnyi Detachment), 706

Altenstadt (German officer), 575

Altz, Captain (German Fourth Army), 351, 735

Andreyev, Commissar (Vitebsk Oblast), 548, 709

Andreyev, Andrei: Politburo member, 240n, 318; mentioned in partisan propaganda as replacement for Stalin, 247, 248

Andreyev, V.: replaces Strokach, 55; memoirs of, 312

Anisimov, Major (Kovpak Regiment), 749

Anti-Fascist Committee (political and propaganda organization), 304–6

Antipartisan warfare, German: tactics, 28–31, 377–78; drain on German forces, 37, 38; objectives of, 38; Operation "Maigewitter," 174, 370, 539; Operation "Fruehlingfest," 174, 190, 545, 546; and partisan desertions, 174–75; propaganda of, 241–49; Operation "Polar Bear," 342; Operation "Hannover," 364, 438, 440, 441–44, 446–47, 448, 453, 454, 455n; Operation "Kugelblitz," 370, 539; Operation "Zigeunerbaron," 376, 509, 513; in Yelnya-Dorogobuzh area, 397–98, 422–30, 438–48; Operation "Munich," 425–30; Operation "Buffalo," 456; Operation "Citadel," 456, 465; in Bryansk area, 465–66, 501–14; Operation "Freischuetz," 472n, 506, 509, 513; Operation "Vogelsang," 504, 505; in Polotsk Lowland, 537–39; Operation "Donnerkeil," 539; and Kaminsky Brigade, 544–45; in North Caucasus, 599–600, 606–12 passim; in Dnepr bend area, 639–41, 644–65

Arkhipenko, Major (Kalinin Front): sent to Smolensk Oblast, 685–86

Armament, partisan: compared with German, 18; drain on Soviet stock, 35; supply of, 63, 158, 364–69, 396, 462; storage of, 160–61; in Bryansk area, 471

Aros, Ludwig: in counterrevolutionary activity, 694

Asmolev, Captain (State Security, Northwest Front), 662

"Ataman" leaders, 11

Bumazhov: awarded title of "Hero of the Soviet Union," 260*n*
Burchenko, D. T. (prewar Vinnitsa *obkom* secretary), 66
Burmistenko, M. A. (secretary, Communist Party Central Committee), 77
Burnin, Lieutenant: replaces Yagunov in Crimea, 623
Burov (partisan, Dedovichi Rayon), 687
Bykov (partisan, Kirov Detachment), 705
Bytosh Brigade: size of, 470; armament of, 471; in Operation "Freischuetz," 472*n*

Central Staff of Partisan Movement: radio contact of, with partisans, 19; directs Party underground, 41; disbanded in 1944, 50, 55, 111; authority of, 51, 53; command function of, 66, 108, 122–24; internal organization of, 102–3; as separate from Party, 129; and psychological warfare, 197–98; intelligence directive of, 353; mentioned, 99–100, 104, 105, 106, 108, 116, 117
Chapayev (hero of Russian Civil War), 673
Chapayev Brigade, 190, 481
Chernov, Vladimir (secretary, Verkhne-Bakanskaya *raikom*), 601*n*
Chiang Kai-shek, 245
Chibisov, Semyon: partisan shot for disorderly conduct, 748, 749
Chubukov (scout leader, Grishin Regiment), 734
Civil War, Russian (1918–20), 4, 10, 11, 12, 74, 75, 151, 180, 673
Civil War, Spanish, 11, 12, 48, 111
Collaborators, German: units of, 138, 145–47, 333; partisan recruitment of, 146–47; partisan propaganda directed towards, 146–47, 216, 227–49, 262, 283, 287; partisan treatment of, 179, 234–36, 395; partisan attacks on, 220–21; in Yelnya-Dorogobuzh area, 432–43; in Bryansk area, 463, 467; in Polotsk Lowland, 529, 555; in North Caucasus, 582–83; in Kalmyk area, 611; mentioned, *passim*
Collective farms: in propaganda, 42, 248, 255, 271–74, 282, 290–91, 293; economic importance of, 43; German treatment of, 43, 241, 246, 326–27, 579–80, 585; peasant partition of, 46, 141, 312–18, 320; in Smolensk Manifesto, 241, 246; re-establishment of, 312–18, 394, 430
Commander, partisan: represents Soviet authority, 42; qualifications of, 47–48, 52–53, 54, 94–95; and discipline, 50; in

command structure, 53, 54, 133–35, 166–67, 478–82 *passim;* and Red Army, 65, 182; function of, 94, 299; appointed by Front Staff, 123; importance of, 165–67; in Polotsk Lowland, 547–50
Commissar, partisan: in charge of propaganda, 42, 205; and Red Army, 65; appointed by NKVD and Party, 83; qualifications of, 94; function of, 94, 129–30, 167, 299, 478–82 *passim;* and influence of Communist Party, 129–30, 167–73, 393; in Polotsk Lowland, 551–53; mentioned, *passim*
Communist ideology: Stalin's revision of, 49; regarding potential satellites, 60; spread by partisans, 64, 169–70; in partisan propaganda, 66–67, 208, 247–48, 250, 252, 258, 261, 262, 264–73, 288–91, 293, 329; partisan postwar literature for indoctrination in, 70; in northern Ukraine, 85; and urban population, 142–43; and younger generation, 515–16; in North Caucasus, 569
Communist Party: underground committees of, 41; role in territorial organization of partisan movement, 77–78; as agency of control, 128–30, 393, 482–83; partisan movement tool of, 130; members in partisan bands, 145; and partisan propaganda, 199–205; and establishment of partisans in Polotsk Lowland, 527–28; mentioned, *passim. See also* Bolshevik Party
Cossack antipartisan regiment, 350, 735
Czechoslovak government: in exile, 61, 62

Dabnenko, Ivan (partisan, Bezstrashnyi Detachment), 706
Danchenkov Brigade: components of, 471; attack on Vetma bridge, 498
Darré, Minister: quoted in partisan propaganda, 731
Death To Our Enemies, 205, 737
Dedushka Division (Dorogobuzh area), 419
Demidovich, D. (partisan, Bezstrashnyi Detachment), 706
Denisov, Captain (Soviet counterintelligence), 720
Derenko (partisan, Kovpak Regiment), 747
"Destruction Battalions": size of, 79; transformed into partisan units, 79; officers of, 80; in North Caucasus, 87
Discipline, partisan: and subordination, 49; in brigade, 50, 74, 96; influence of Communist Party on, 171–72; resemblance of, to Red Army, 185; and

374; S. V. Rudnov in, 48, 745; reorganization of, 116; radio communication of, 126; propaganda section of, 205, 218n, 745–46; documents of, 745–49; mentioned, 381, 686n, 708–10

Kozlov: partisan appeal to, 719

Kozlov, G. A. (partisan): shot for desertion, 172, 702

Kramskoi (Shabo Regiment), 193

Krasavin (unit commander, Ostrov area), 663

Krasnoye Znamya, 201n

Kravchenko, Commissar Dmitrii (Anapa III), 594

Kudryavtsev (District Elder, Dedovichi Rayon), 687, 693

Kuehn, Major (German Fourth Army), 351, 735

Kukanov (German deserter), 744

Kukharenko, Commander (Kalinin Detachment), 705

Kulbak (officer, Kovpak Regiment), 747

Kumanok, P. Kh. (Sumy underground), 66

Kumeisha, Nikolai (German collaborator), 721–22

Kupala, Yanka (Belorussian poet), 215, 261, 267

Kutayev, Commissar (Morogov unit), 698, 702

Kutuzov Detachment, 705, 706

Kuzma: decorated with Order of the Patriotic War, 746

Kuzmin: shot for treason, 693

Kuznetsov, Mykola (first secretary, Central Committee of Ukrainian Komsomols), 115

Labar, Marusya (partisan, KIM Detachment), 705

Labayan, Mayor (Red Army), 570

Lammers: report of, to Rosenberg, 573

Lavrilov, Commissar (Grishin Regiment), 741, 742

Lazarev, Major (Grishin Regiment), 351, 738

Lazo Regiment (Shcherbino area), 418, 448

Lebedev, Commissar ("Galugo" Detachment), 479

Lenin, Vladimir Ilyich, 10, 49, 256, 262, 693n

"Lenin Peasant Antifascist Union," 43

Linkov, Grigorii: partisan parachutist officer, 101; memoirs of, 528n, 529n; as Batya," 715

List, Field Marshal von (German Army Group "A"), 564, 565, 576

Literaturnaya Gazeta, 68

Litvinov, Maxim: conduct at Conference of the Great Powers, 172, 698

Liventsev, Viktor: on Bobruisk area partisan movement, 314, 315n

Lobanok, Commander (Stalin Brigade), 540, 551, 552

Loseva (troika member, Dedovichi Rayon), 688

Luetzov (German hero), 217

Lukanov, Platoon Leader: disciplined for extortion, 737

Luzgin, V. Y. (Plenipotentiary, Vitebsk Oblast Komsomol), 705, 708

Machulsky, Colonel (Minsk Oblast), 132n, 540

Makhno, Nestor ("Ataman" leader), 11

Malenkov, Georgi, 129, 318

Malin, V. N. (Party Central Staff), 66

Malinovsky, Vasilii (partisan, Belyi-Smolensk area), 699

Maltsev Brigade (Bryansk area), 470, 471, 486

Malvina (partisan, Alexeyev Brigade), 148, 753

"Manual for the Partisan Intelligence Scout," 344, 346–48

Mao Tse-tung: and Chinese Communist guerrilla warfare, 12–13

Marchenkov, Commander S. I. (Vyazma area), 404

Mariyev (partisan, Bryansk area): arrested for cowardice, 186

Markov, Commander (Voroshilov Brigade), 233, 480, 551, 552

Matveyev, A. P.: Chief of Orel Staff of Partisan Movement, 131, 483; criticizes partisan operations, 489–90; demoted by Yegorov, 596n, 616; deserts, 597–98, 616

Medvedev, D. M.: biography of, 48; and NKGB, 48; publishes "On the Banks of the Southern Bug," 67–68

Meikulov (guide, Karachai command), 619–20

Mein Kampf, 251, 279n

Mekhlis, General L. Z. (head, Red Army Political Administration), 51, 82n, 258n, 663

Mende, Professor Gerhard von (official, Rosenberg Ministry), 574n

Metropolitan of Moscow, 269

Metyelev, Colonel (Ukrainian Staff), 111

"Michel, K." (*pseud. of* Mikhail Akhmeteli), 574n

Mikhailov (chairman, "Red Star" kolkhoz), 687

Zegolnik (partisan, Morogov unit), 698

Zeitzler, General (German officer): and forced labor, 246; becomes Chief of General Staff, 565

Zhdanov, Andrei: directs partisans, 47, 318; establishes prototype of partisan directing staff, 51; Leningrad partisan operation of, 51, 67, 101; and relations between Party and partisans, 67, 101, 318; feud of, with Malenkov, 318; mentioned, 106, 129, 264, 316, 690

Zhelyanin (Party secretary, Vitebsk Oblast Committee), 709, 710

Zhigunov: reports period of NKVD partisan control, 82n

Zhivoderov (partisan, Smolensk area), 700

Zhukov, Marshal (Soviet West Front), 393, 486

Zhukov, Mikhail (troika member): subverts kolkhoz "Right Path," 694

Zlenko, A. N. (member, Ukrainian staff), 66

Zmorokov, Captain (commander, Stalin Brigade), 481

Zykov: appointed chief of staff, Kosubsky Regiment, 420